D1396586

A DARTNELL HANDBOOK
on
DIRECT MAIL ADVERTISING
and
MAIL ORDER SELLING

OTHER DARTNELL HANDBOOKS

Advertising Manager's Handbook
Marketing Manager's Handbook
Office Administration Handbook
Personnel Administration Handbook
Public Relations Handbook
Sales Manager's Handbook
Sales Promotion Handbook

DARTNELL is a publisher serving the world of business with business books, business manuals, business newsletters and bulletins, training materials for business executives, managers, supervisors, salesmen, financial officials, personnel executives and office employees. In addition, Dartnell produces management and sales training films and cassettes, publishes many useful business forms, conducts scores of management seminars for business men and women and has many of its materials and films available in languages other than English. Dartnell, established in 1917, serves the world's whole business community. For details, catalogs, and product information, address: DARTNELL, 4660 N. Ravenswood Avenue, Chicago, Illinois 60640, USA—or phone (312) 561-4000.

The Dartnell

DIRECT MAIL and MAIL ORDER Handbook

by

Richard S. Hodgson

Third Edition – 1980

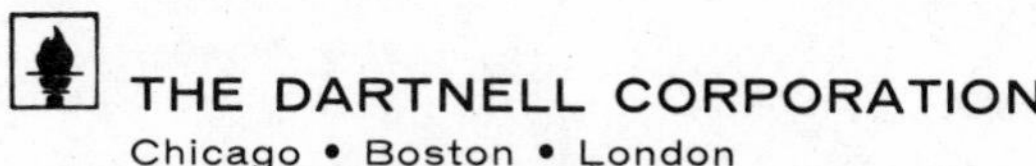

THE DARTNELL CORPORATION
Chicago • Boston • London

FIRST EDITION—1964
SECOND EDITION
1ST PRINTING—1974
2ND PRINTING—1977
THIRD EDITION—1980
2ND PRINTING—1981

Library of Congress Catalog Card
Number 73-90752

Standard Book Number 0-85013-116-2

Printed in the United States of America by
DARTNELL PRESS, CHICAGO, ILLINOIS 60640

DEDICATION

Many friends have asked how on earth I was able to find the time to put together all of the material in a Handbook such as this. The answer lies in the willingness and encouragement of a wonderful wife and four great children. Whenever Dad headed for his typewriter, it meant many sacrifices on their part and when the last word was typed, each of them justifiably shared in the satisfaction of a major project completed. Thus, the byline should include the names:

Lois Hodgson

Sue Hodgson

Steve Hodgson

Scott Hodgson

Lisa Hodgson

And to each of them this volume is dedicated with love.

Dick Hodgson

RICHARD S. HODGSON

RICHARD S. ("Dick") HODGSON got an early start in the direct mail field when he began operating his own lettershop, The Gateway Advertising Service, at the age of 14. Since that time he has worked as a printer, linotype operator, salesman, photographer, radio announcer and producer, reporter, editor, college instructor, public relations director, president of a publishing company, an advertising agency account executive, advertising and sales promotion director, creative director, corporation executive and consultant.

Today he is President of Sargeant House, a Westtown, Pennsylvania company which provides consulting services to leading direct marketing firms throughout the world. In addition, he is educational consultant to the Direct Mail/Marketing Association and conducts regular direct marketing seminars throughout the U.S. and Europe.

Before establishing his consulting business, he was Vice President of The Franklin Mint in Franklin Center, Pennsylvania. He joined The Franklin Mint as Creative Director in 1972 and later was assigned the task of organizing and launching The Franklin Mint Gallery of American Art, the success of which won for him the 1973 Marketing Communicator of the Year Award presented by Marketing Communications Executives International.

Before joining The Franklin Mint, he was Division Director of the Creative Graphics Division, R. R. Donnelley & Sons Company, Chicago—the world's largest printer. He originally joined Donnelley in 1962 as Advertising and Sales Promotion

Manager. Previously he had been President of American Marketing Services, a Boston publishing company. Prior to moving to Boston, he had been executive editor of *Advertising Requirements* and *Industrial Marketing* magazines.

In addition to the Marketing Communicator of the Year Award, he has been the recipient of numerous other honors including the Jesse H. Neale Editorial Achievement Award for outstanding business journalism; the Dartnell Gold Medal Award for excellence in business letter-writing; and Sales Promotion Executive-of-the-Year, awarded by the Chicago Chapter of the Sales Promotion Executives Association. His direct mail campaigns have won numerous awards including the Gold Mailbox of the Direct Mail/Marketing Association and the Benny Award of the Printing Industries of America.

A 25-year veteran of both active and reserve service in the U. S. Marine Corps, he served as a Marine Combat Correspondent in North China and provided on-the-spot radio and press coverage of four atomic bomb tests including the famed Operation Crossroads tests at Bikini. He presently is in the Retired Reserve with the rank of Lieutenant Colonel.

Mr. Hodgson has long been active in organizations serving the advertising and marketing fields. He served as International President of the Sales Promotion Executives Association as well as president of both the Boston and Chicago chapters, and was a member of the board of directors of both SPEA and its successor association, Marketing Communications Executives International. He has also served as president of the Mail Advertising Club of Chicago; first vice-president of the Chicago Federated Advertising Club, and first vice-president of the Chicago Business Paper Publishers Association. He also served four terms on the board of directors of the Direct Mail/Marketing Association.

In addition to hundreds of magazine articles in both consumer and business magazines, Mr. Hodgson is author of a number of books including *How to Use a Tape Recorder, Direct Mail Showmanship, How to Promote Meeting Attendance, Direct Mail in The Political Process* and *How to Work With Mailing Lists.*

A native of Breckenridge, Minnesota, he is a graduate of the North Dakota State School of Science and attended Gustavus Adolphus College, Western Michigan College and Northwestern University.

PREFACE

To preface "Dick Hodgson's book" is to try to summarize the purpose of a dictionary. Truly this compendium is a monumental work. Few people could have brought to it the expertise for selection, collation and editing that has always seemed to be a hallmark of Dick Hodgson's work.

When Dartnell had the foresight to produce the first edition of this book in 1964 there was no other collection of material on the direct mail medium that could be used as a reference book. Certainly the growth in use of direct mail advertising and the mail order method of doing business over the past decade more than justifies an update. There is much new material in this second edition, and yet the techniques and principles Dick skillfully set down some ten years ago remain the same. As mail marketers know, they work.

In reviewing the book, I'm continually amazed by its depth, common sense and straightforward narration. Most of us who have been close observers of the medium over the past several years are always fearful that some author will try to draw narrow definitions and exacting precepts. That would make a science of what is more like an art. Dick Hodgson has been wise enough to use all the qualifications that this creative, flexible method of doing business deserves.

For the student or beginner I can think of no better learning process than to browse through this book and then devoutly use it as a daily reference. If you wish to actually work in this medium or be responsible for using it effectively then you owe it to yourself to make the "Direct Mail and Mail Order Hanbook" a bible—and bibles are for reading!

For the veteran this new edition offers a rare opportunity to refresh one's memories about the advantages of this remarkable advertising medium and review the many time-honored techniques that continue to be effective. Most of us actually have to be reminded of the things we know because we sometimes forget to use them.

For those of us who continue to be fascinated by the great ranges of use and function in direct mail, this updated volume invites us to "go back to school." I hope you will share the pleasure I've had doing just that.

Robert F. DeLay
President
Direct Mail/Marketing Association

AUTHOR'S INTRODUCTION

In his Preface to the First Edition of this HANDBOOK, Pete Hoke commented: "This manual marks a milestone. It marks the beginning of a new era in which direct mail will be used as only its early promoters dreamed that it might be used . . . as a precision tool performing key functions in marketing."

I suspect that even Pete didn't realize at the time just how prophetic his words were. In the decade since the original manuscript was prepared and Pete prepared his gracious Preface, direct mail did enter into a completely new era, far exceeding in importance the dreams of its early promoters.

Three major factors are probably the most important catalysts of this change:

1. In the decade of the Sixties, the computer became the single most important tool of direct mail advertisers and changed forever many facets of the medium.
2. Vast changes took place in the postal service, the most important of which was the imposition of mandatory zip coding for third class mail.
3. Also in the decade of the Sixties, America embarked on a credit card economy and nearly everyone with a list of credit buyers discovered that his lists had great potential for mail order selling.

But even though the direct mail medium has experienced great change, most of the basic guidelines developed through years of experimentation by pioneer mailers continue to be just as viable as ever. But thanks to the reams of data which the computer has made available, we now have many more guidelines than the early direct mail practitioners were able to pinpoint. And many of the earlier guidelines have been backed up by computer analysis.

In my introduction to the First Edition, I pointed out that in preparing the manuscript for this book, I've tried to approach the assignment from the viewpoint of a reporter and editor, rather than as a direct mail practitioner. Wherever possible, I've drawn upon the knowledge of those who have had far greater experience in a particular phase of direct mail than I. This is the same approach which has been used for the revisions and additions included in this Second Edition.

So many people have contributed to the store of direct mail and mail order knowledge recorded in these pages, it is impossible to give individual credit to everyone to whom I'm indebted. Throughout the pages of the book you will find many individual credits. However, many more people added their thoughts through conversations, discussions and correspondence. I wish all of them could be singled out for the credit they deserve. But since literally hundreds of individuals have contributed in various ways, I can only express a collective "thank you" and hope each of them will find satisfaction in knowing that his wisdom as reflected in these pages is continuing to serve thousands of others who have learned or are learning to use the medium of direct mail effectively.

However, special credit must be given the Henry Hokes—the late Henry, Sr. and his son, "Pete." From the pages of their monthly magazine, *The Reporter of Direct Mail Advertising, The Magazine of Direct Marketing,* and through years of contact with this knowledgeable father-and-son team have come hundreds of ideas and thoughts which have found their way into these pages.

I'm also specially indebted to G. D. Crain, Jr., Sid Bernstein and Mike Hartenfeld of Crain Communications, Inc. for permission to include much material which previously appeared in *Advertising Age, Industrial Marketing* and *Advertising & Sales Promotion.* Along with Pete Hoke's *Direct Marketing* and its companion weekly newsletter, *The Friday Report,* these magazines should be regular "must" reading for anyone with a serious interest in direct mail and mail order advertising.

But the bulk of the credit for this HANDBOOK really belongs to one of the most unusual organizations in the world—the Direct Mail/Marketing Association.*

Over the years, it has been my pleasure to come into rather close contact with quite a number of business and professional

*Just after the Second Edition of this Handbook went to press, the Direct Mail Advertising Association changed its name to the Direct Mail/Marketing Association. Therefore, the reader will find frequent references to the older association name and its acronym, DMAA, throughout the following pages. However, regardless of whether it's DMAA or DMMA, the reference is to the same outstanding organization.

associations and, as an editor-reporter, to cover the activities of dozens more. DMMA stands unique among all of them.

Here is a common meeting ground for everyone with an interest in the use of the mails for communicating. Once caught by the DMMA spirit—and that seldom takes long—there is an open willingness to share information of all types. While sharing information is one of the chief purposes of many other groups, in none have I found such an openness as in DMMA.

It's a give-and-take proposition, with everyone contributing. One of the unique sights at any DMMA conference or meeting is to see the old pro—the mail order operator, perhaps, who may have made a fortune through his mail order activities—and the young newcomer huddled together, each seeking ideas from the other.

It is from more than two decades of attending DMMA meetings that the majority of the material in this book has come. Without such a source, writing it would have been impossible.

A special bow should be made to Bob DeLay, DMMA's president. His untiring efforts have built the Association into a potent force, with a tremendously broad program of activities and services for members. His advice and counsel have played an important role in the development of both the original HANDBOOK and this Second Edition.

Two other individuals deserve special credit—both for the tremendous amount of helpful material they made available for this HANDBOOK and their years of service to the entire direct mail fraternity. Each of them has been called "Mr. Direct Mail," and both of them richly deserve the title. They are the late Edward N. Mayer, Jr. and Robert Stone. As DMMA Education Director, Ed Mayer personally taught the fundamentals of direct mail to thousands. And through his regular columns in *Advertising Age,* Bob Stone provides a continuing post-graduate course.

And, finally, special credit must also be given Norman Guess, Dartnell Vice-President, who devoted himself to the editing of both the original manuscript and the revisions and additions for this Second Edition with a skill and dedication which were far from routine.

I would offer one caution to those who will use this HANDBOOK. Anyone who becomes deeply involved with the wonderful world of direct mail and mail order promotion and selling soon learns one vital fact: There are no real RULES for success. Some of the most startling successes have been written by those who threw caution to the wind and decided to do what "couldn't be done."

If you would seek a tight little box in which to create advertising, try some other medium. In direct mail there are few limitations except those imposed by postal regulations, personal ethics, good taste . . . and, of course, the available budget. Unlike other media of advertising, in direct mail the advertiser is the "publisher" and can pretty much establish his own boundaries.

So beware of any who would preach hard-and-fast RULES for success in direct mail and mail order. Either they are fools or simply blind to the facts.

But, on the other hand, study the techniques which have proved successful for others—not to adopt them directly to your own promotion program, but to provide direction in the wide-open spaces of direct mail creativity. This book will have served its purpose if it offers such a road map for you.

DICK HODGSON

P.S. Many of the case histories appearing in this Handbook were originally written for the first edition, which was published in 1964. In reviewing material requiring editing for the First Printing of the Third Edition in 1980, it was interesting to reflect on how little the basic principles of direct mail and mail order have changed in the past 16 years. While we now generally refer to this field as "Direct Marketing," most of today's successes follow the same general guidelines which spelled success many years ago. To be sure, the field has grown manyfold in the past two decades and the computerization of so many procedures has brought new efficiencies. And, just as in every other field, the costs of doing business have increased significantly. But today's winners are following the same general guidelines which guided so many to success in the past.

CONTENTS

Chapter 1

THE MEDIUM OF DIRECT MAIL

DIRECT MAIL is an amazing medium. It is used by more advertisers than any other advertising medium.

It is a principal form of communications for nonadvertisers.

More dollars are spent annually on direct mail than on any other form of advertising—perhaps well over $5 billion.

It produces amazing response—even from those who insist they always throw it away unopened.

It is completely flexible—bounded only by broad postal regulations, rules of decency, and whatever budget is established.

It can be used to reach just one individual or millions.

It can be made personal, even to the point of being completely confidential.

It can be almost completely controlled by the advertiser.

It can be produced in minutes when necessary and delivered with speed to whatever audience is chosen.

It can be used with equal effectiveness by the large and the small; by the experienced and the inexperienced.

YET . . .

It is the most misunderstood of all media.

It is maligned by a high percentage of its audience.

It is treated with indifference by many—even advertisers who spend millions of dollars on it annually.

It is scoffed at by other media.

It is neglected by most organized advertising groups.

It is considered unworthy of professional handling by many advertising agencies.

It is not included as a major subject in the curricula of most schools of advertising.

It is abused by legislators, the courts, and the Postal Service.

The Paradox of Direct Mail

All of these factors considered, the most amazing paradox of direct mail is that it is seldom recognized as one of the most dynamic communications and marketing tools available in our twentieth-century economy. More often than not, direct mail is treated as a necessary evil and a high percentage of users even fail to recognize they are direct mail advertisers.

One of the reasons for this paradox is that so much confusion surrounds the definition of direct mail. A wide variety of definitions have been offered, but most authorities are content to accept those which have been developed by the Direct Mail/Marketing Association.

One of the most difficult things for many advertisers to understand is the difference between direct mail and mail order. Very simply, one is a medium of advertising and communications while the other is a method of conducting a business. And then there is the even broader title, "direct advertising," which includes direct mail, but involves forms of distribution other than the mails. More recently, the term "Direct Marketing" has been added to the direct mail lexicon.

The Accepted Definitions

DMMA, in its publication, *The Story of Direct Advertising,* offers these definitions:

> *Direct Advertising* is a broad term encompassing all the diversified forms and uses of this major medium of advertising. Management's selection of a *kind* of direct advertising, like the selection of any one medium, depends upon *objective* and *result expectancy.*
>
> When an advertiser distributes his selling message in print through newspapers, magazines, car cards, and outdoor advertising, uses television or radio, he can reasonably expect that a certain percentage of this potential audience will see, read, or listen to his sales story. In such circumstances the advertiser knows from experience that it is good business judgment to send his sales message to all the readers of a magazine or newspaper, or to all viewers and listeners of a television or radio program, and pay for all—even though only some of them are prospects for his product or services.
>
> Obviously, then, if the advertiser chooses to send his sales story by mail, messenger, or salesman, he can exercise greater selection and control. Under such circumstances, by carefully qualifying his prospects, the advertiser can direct his selling message to specific individuals. This type of promotional activity, commonly called "Direct Advertising," is defined as "a vehicle for transmitting an advertiser's message in permanent written, printed, or processed form, by controlled distribution, direct to selected individuals."

Direct advertising logically divides itself into three broad classifications, determined by *what it is used for,* and *how it is delivered.*

1. *Direct Mail Advertising* includes all forms of direct advertising (except mail order) that are sent through the mails. Direct mail has been aptly called the advance agent, the missionary man, the handshake ahead of the meeting, plus the means whereby preselling and continuous contacts with customers can be economically maintained.

   Its chief functions are to arouse interest, to help customers as an aid to buying, to familiarize prospects with the name of the product, its maker, its merits, names of local distributors; also, to remove obstacles to sales, to support the sales activities of retailers, to encourage continued patronage by present and new customers as well as to resell past customers, to predispose prospects favorably so that the closely geared-in personal selling effort will produce maximum sales returns.

   Direct mail advertising is most efficient when the user appreciates its limitations as well as potentialities—and directs his mail to *prospects* instead of *suspects.* As with all advertising, *results* in the final analysis are largely determined by how many of the right kind of people see, read, and act upon it. In addition to using direct mail for its sales-building effectiveness, management finds in its diversified forms the answer to the many problems of internal and external communication.

2. *Mail Order Advertising.* This type of direct mail selling promotion includes all methods, other than personal salesmanship and space, television or radio advertising, for inducing people to send in orders by mail. Mail order promotions—whether sales letters or booklets soliciting orders for one product or a group of closely related products, or the mammoth catalogs of mail order houses embracing wide ranges of products—are designed as self-sufficient to accomplish the whole selling job without resorting to the help of salesmen and with either little or no support from other advertising media. Mail order advertising takes the place of the salesman; direct mail advertising helps him sell.

3. *Unmailed Direct Advertising.* This classification of direct advertising includes many varied forms of dealer helps such as window, counter, floor, hanging, package and counter displays, plus printed materials not sent through the mails but distributed from door to door, handed to customers in retail stores, included in packages and bundles, delivered by salesmen or messengers, or in some other manner conveyed directly to the recipient. Unmailed direct advertising is used for the same broad purposes as direct mail advertising and mail order advertising.

Direct Marketing

In changing the name of his magazine from *The Reporter of Direct Mail Advertising* to *Direct Marketing,* Pete Hoke offered this basic definition of direct marketing:

> The total of activities by which the seller, in effecting the transfer of goods and services to the buyer, directs his efforts to a qualified audience using one or more media for the purpose of soliciting a response by phone, mail or personal visit from a prospect or customer.

Milton S. Stevens of the marketing research firm bearing his name, enlisted the help of 25 experts in the direct mail field to help him come up with a definition of "Direct Mail Marketing" for a speech he delivered at the 1966 Philadelphia Direct Mail Day. Combining the responses he received, he offered this definition:

> Direct Mail Marketing is the subsequent of the larger marketing function where the initial communication is through the mail. The steps following this first message may, but need not, use the mail to affect the final action desired.

He went on to note that there may be three different actions sought:

1. The direct mail piece may ask the recipient to come to the store . . . to buy . . . to pick up a gift . . . to enter a contest. It can be simply a *traffic builder.*
2. The direct mail piece may look for a *reply,* through the mail . . . requesting additional information from a booklet . . . or a demonstration . . . or a premium. Obviously the purpose is to produce a lead for a sales call.
3. Direct mail may make a *direct sale* by getting the order for the book . . . a trial subscription to the magazine . . . a new member to the record club . . . an order from the catalog.

The Unrecognized Medium

Nearly everyone uses direct mail many times—frequently without realizing he is doing so. A classic example is a Chicago newspaper columnist who wrote a series of daily columns damning direct mail and those who use it. As is typical in such newspaper attacks on the competitive advertising medium, this columnist claimed he always threw away all the direct mail he received without even opening the envelopes.

Paradoxically, this columnist loaded his series with specific references describing mailings he had received in the past. Oddly enough, he knew a lot about their contents for a man who "never even opens the envelopes." But even more unusual was the fact that, at the very time these columns were being written, the columnist was running for an important elective position in his suburban hometown—and his main promotional method of encouraging voters to put an X beside his name was a *direct mail campaign!*

Most of the direct mail uses which touch the average citizen are less obvious than political campaigning. Graduation, wedding, and birth announcements are a form of direct mail on a highly personal level. And many average citizens make frequent use of direct mail to promote meeting attendance for their clubs, associations, churches, PTA's, and similar groups. They also frequently get involved in fund raising or membership promotions by direct mail. Such uses of the mails are just as much "direct mail" as mailings from a business trying to promote the sale of a product or service.

A Multibillion Dollar Giant

Direct mail is a giant medium. When all of its facets—including mail order promotion—are included, it represents an annual expenditure by American businesses of somewhere between 3 and 5 billion dollars. There are few businesses, organizations, or individuals who do not use the medium in one form or another.

Perhaps you have never thought of it, but you probably got your own "start" in direct mail the day you sent your quota of high school graduation announcements to your friends and relatives. You had to prepare a mailing list, address the envelopes, insert a printed message (the announcement) in the envelope, add postage, and deposit the "mailing" at the post office. This, in one of its most simple forms, is direct mail.

Your purpose may simply have been to inform your audience of the event or perhaps you were asking for action—attendance at the graduation ceremonies.

But that was *personal,* you might reply. True. But direct mail at its best is always a personal medium. While many advertisers use it in an impersonal way, its primary role among communications and advertising media is to reduce a mass message to a personal level.

Understanding Direct Mail

On the surface it might not seem the least bit important to either define direct mail or recognize its tremendous annual volume. But in failing to do so, many destroy much of the potential effectiveness of their direct mail.

If you understand you are using *direct mail,* chances are you will take better advantage of the known techniques to make the medium more effective. And if you recognize the great volume of mailed communications, you will better understand the competition you face to get attention and action.

The "junk mail" attacks of recent years have been directed

primarily at those mailing pieces prepared in ignorance by men and women who failed to understand they were using a major medium which requires skill to obtain maximum effectiveness. An interesting fact is that most people do not consider mailings they like to be direct mail at all. At a Chicago Direct Mail Day, Dr. Sidney Levy, psychological research director of Social Research, Inc., reported on motivational research studies his organization conducted to determine public reactions to direct mail. Among his findings:

> In one inquiry that we made, we asked, "What is the most famous direct mail?" Some of the respondents mentioned the Sears catalog. Others who could not think of anything were asked then about Sears' catalog, and they replied that this was *not* direct mail. When we asked them about Marshall Field's toy flyer at Christmas they also replied this was not direct mail.

Many Other Names

One reason why direct mail might be called "the unrecognized medium" is that many people do not consider the majority of direct mail pieces they receive as direct mail. This is particularly true of those who are quick to hang the "junk mail" label on the medium. Speaking at an *Advertising Age* Creative Workshop a few years ago, the author suggested:

> Go out and ask the average citizen about direct mail and you'll get an earful. And if you listen carefully, you'll learn some valuable lessons.
>
> One of the first things you'll learn is that there are a lot of honest citizens—and not just the editors of American newspapers—who are downright disgusted with direct mail. They don't like it, and they make no bones about it.
>
> But don't stop there. Get specific. Talk with these direct mail haters about the various items they receive in the mail and you'll learn a most important lesson.
>
> Ask your wife about the coupons she receives from P&G, Lever Brothers, General Mills and others. Even if she is a real screamer about all "that advertising junk" mixed in with the letters she receives from Aunt Minnie and her copy of *Glamour,* she'll tell you she loves *coupons* and will complain if the gal on the other side of the backyard fence got a coupon mailing she didn't receive.
>
> Pause a moment in church some Sunday and ask a fellow member what he thinks about the church's weekly newsletter. He'd hate to miss an issue. He loves the *newsletter,* but he hates direct mail.
>
> Ask the suburban housewife about the Sears, Wards or Penney catalog from which she orders regularly. She may be a very vocal direct mail hater, but she'll tell you she loves that *catalog!*
>
> Talk to your financial people about the annual reports they send or

receive. Vital, they'll say. They don't care much for direct mail, but they couldn't live without *annual reports.*

How about that couple next door that has such a wonderful record collection? They've joined not just one but two record-of-the-month clubs. Haven't got time for direct mail, but they eagerly await the monthly *magazine* telling about the new selections they're being offered.

Chat a bit with the most sophisticated engineer you can find. He's probably a direct mail hater from way back. But watch him eagerly gobble up the new product *announcements* he gets from manufacturers.

And don't overlook your family doctor. He really has to suffer through a pile of mail every day—and not all of it sizeable checks from his patients or their insurance companies. Says he wishes he didn't have to put up with that pile of direct mail—says it, in fact, as he jots off a note to a pharmaceutical manufacturer thanking them for the *samples* of a new drug and the *abstracts* of important medical developments.

Or visit the successful alumnus of good old Ivy University. He, too, hates direct mail. But how he loves those alumni *bulletins* that keep him posted on the Class of '03 (while they ask for a bit of a donation to build a new wing on the School of Commerce).

And how about you? Like to agree with your neighbors when they grumble about the direct mail they receive? But how quickly did you toss *letters* about this Creative Workshop in the wastebasket?

Guess you just can't blame the public for disliking direct mail. They love their coupons, catalogs, newsletters, annual reports, magazines, announcements, samples, abstracts, bulletins and letters. To them, these things aren't direct mail. Direct mail is that "other stuff"—things in which they weren't interested. So if we are to accept the public's definition of direct mail, we find it means the nonpersonal communications they receive via the mails in which they have no interest.

Personal Medium

Above all else, direct mail is a *personal* medium, even though a high percentage of advertisers choose to overlook this fact. Direct mail reaches its ultimate usefulness when the user puts it on a person-to-person basis. Top direct mail copywriters constantly emphasize the desirability of the "you" approach—talking to individuals instead of audiences.

But even if the message is an impersonal one, the recipient is likely to respond in a personal way. This, in fact, is one of the medium's biggest problems. Dr. Levy points out:

> Direct mail *is* very personal as compared to much other advertising, no matter what its specific form may be, merely because it does come in the front door into homes and presents itself to the individual. Then he has to deal with it—he has to take it into his hands and come to some decision about it—he has to react, respond to it in some way. The effect of this is to force the individual to consciously think about the issue.

Now, this has many repercussions because, for many people, decision-making is not comfortable. Having the issue thus put into their hands in this manner, they tend to be irritated . . . the individual is hostile to direct mail because he does not want his thinking process stirred up.

Having mustered up the energy for a decision, as people do with either a salesman or a piece of literature that arrives in the mail, people are often more violent in their rejection than they otherwise would be. They now *have* to do something with regard to it. They say, "I hate that stuff," and then they vigorously throw it away. It is not because the message or its form are bad but because they resent their own involvement in it and the necessity for having to decide about it.

Direct mail advertising is like any advertising in being an attempt to communicate with people, but it makes it more difficult for the audience to ignore the communication, despite the frequent throwing away. This act makes it seem as though they are ignoring it, but it is also a way in which they are dealing with it, thinking about it to some degree.

How Direct Mail Differs

The ten basic differences between direct mail and other media have been outlined by DMMA:

1. *Direct advertising can be directed to specific individuals or markets with greater control than any other medium.*

   An appeal can be directed to 100 hand-picked millionaires just as readily as to a very select professional group of 100,000 book buyers. These lists can be obtained in many cases with postage guaranteed up to 98 percent accuracy. How else, or how better could a promotion be limited, yet assure absolute coverage, than through a direct approach by mail to *present customers, or past customers, or recommended customers?*

2. *Direct advertising can be made personal to the point of being absolutely confidential.*

   Whether a letter, order blank, confidential price list, or product information—regardless of the appeal or number of people to be reached—a first-class mailing can do it. All direct mail is not of a confidential nature, but when such an approach is needed, only this medium can provide the means.

3. *Direct advertising is a single advertiser's individual message and is not in competition with other advertising and/or editorial.*

   At the moment of reception, or when a piece of direct advertising reaches the reader, it has his complete attention without any distracting elements. It will stand or fall on its appeal just as will any other advertisement—but at least it will have a better chance because there is less competition for the reader's attention.

4. *Direct advertising does not have the limitations on space and format as do other mediums of advertising.*

   Almost no limit exists as to the size, shape, style, number of colors, and all of the other elements that enter into the makeup of direct mail and printed promotion. Format ranges from the small poster stamp and miniatures to booklets, brochures, and broadsides as big as the top of a desk, to accommodate any length of message or size of illustration. The piece can be made to fit the story, and the possibilities are as boundless as the ingenuity of the designer.

5. *Direct advertising permits greater flexibility in materials and processes of production than any other medium of advertising.*

   Production of direct advertising includes every phase of reproduction known to the graphic arts—printing, lithography, photo-offset, rotogravure, steel engraving, silk screen, multigraph, mimeograph, multilith, etc. Added to these are the processes of die cutting, scoring, punching, tabbing, swatching, varnishing, laminating, mounting, all kinds of binding and folding. Because of these facilities, and because each piece is individually produced, greater latitude exists in the use of materials—all kinds of papers, inks, plastics, etc. These are the reasons why direct advertising can be custom made, can fit any pattern, can outdo any other form of advertising in physical presentation.

6. *Direct advertising provides a means for introducing novelty and realism into the interpretation of the advertiser's story.*

   Cutouts, pop-ups, odd shapes and patterns are employed to good advantage by users of direct mail. If a folder or booklet is wanted in the shape of a bottle, box, or barrel, the effect is easy to obtain. Even invisible colors and perfumed inks are used in some printed pieces for novelty and as powerful attention-getters. Odd folds and tricky pieces are used daily to sell the reader on paying more attention to a piece of literature.

7. *Direct advertising can be produced according to the needs of the advertiser's own immediate schedule.*

   For a quick promotion, or an emergency mailing to take advantage of a situation, the production of direct mail can be geared to meet the need without waiting for a publication date or for some other medium of advertising to do the job.

8. *Direct advertising can be controlled for specific jobs of research, reaching small groups, testing ideas, appeals, reactions.*

   Before the big campaigns in which other media may be employed, confidential questionnaires can be used for research—ideas, appeals, and reactions can be tested. Next to personal contact, direct mail affords the best medium for research and individual contact.

9. *Direct advertising can be dispatched for accurate and in some cases exact timing, both as to departure of the pieces as well as to their receipt.*

   Material can be mailed according to set plan. Even departure schedules are available at the post office to help achieve good timing. Dealer material can be scheduled to reach dealer counters according to plan. Sales, holiday promotions, stockholders' meetings—distributor, jobber, dealer, and consumer promotions can be timed for maximum results.

10. *Direct advertising provides more thorough means for the reader to act or buy through action devices not possible of employment by other media.*

The business reply card and envelope make it possible and easier for the recipient of direct advertising to take action. Complete order blanks and other action enclosures can also be used.

Pinpoint Medium

Ted Bihler, former DMMA chairman and business manager of *The Journal of Commerce,* calls direct mail the "pinpoint medium." He explains:

> Direct mail can do certain jobs that no other medium can do as well, just as newspapers are unchallenged for reaching the people of a given city, or the trade press is superior for bringing your sales message to those who work in a specific industry.
>
> Direct mail is the only medium which permits you to *pinpoint* your appeal to a preselected individual person.
>
> Through judicious choice of lists—compiled, purchased, or rented—direct mail offers an advertiser the unique benefits of aiming his sales talk at an individual, multiplied by the number of similar persons existing and limited only by the advertiser's own self-imposed budgetary restrictions.
>
> No other medium exists that enables you to talk to—and *only* to, if you so desire—*all* the persons of a specific income level, or *all* people who are alumni of a given educational institution, or *all* of those who work in a certain trade, or *all* individuals who live in dwellings of a selected construction cost, just to name a few of the many classifications available.
>
> In fact, if you are ready to spend the time, money, and energy necessary to do the essential research, there is *no classification* of the American populace that you cannot isolate and reach by direct mail.
>
> Direct mail is, in short, an advertising medium that permits you to talk, in exactly the terms of your own choice, to the specific individuals you desire to talk to. Thus, from the standpoint of both the *material* you include and the people you elect to address, direct mail is indeed the *pinpoint medium.*

The Changing Face of Direct Mail

There was a time, not so many years ago, when any *good* direct mail piece was sure to attract attention because it stood out from the mass of very inferior mailings in the average day's mail. But times have changed. In recent years, direct mail has reached new heights of quality—and is still climbing.

Probably the greatest impetus for quality in direct mail was the upgrading of magazine circulation appeals. One of the most important milestones was the unusual mailings developed by Les Suhler for *Look* magazine. He introduced many techniques which, after a period of ridicule from many contemporaries, were adopted rather generally. In the decade of the fifties, most

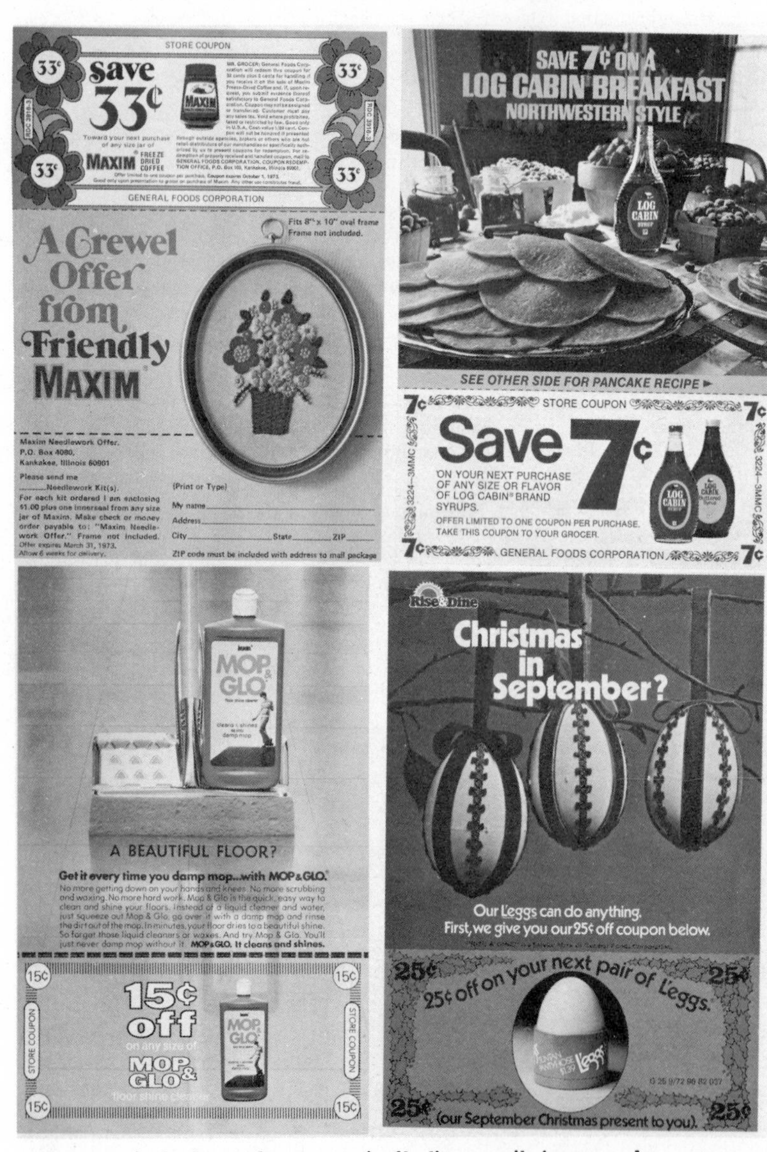

Once one of the least glamorous of all direct mail formats, the coupon now arrives with maximum use of color and illustration. These examples are of typical coupons included in cooperative mailings.

every major magazine constantly upgraded the quality of its mailings. And since these mailings had such widespread distribution, they undoubtedly influenced other direct mail advertisers to improve the quality of their own mailings.

Then, in the late 1950's, publishers suddenly discovered a previously untapped market for relatively expensive books. The lead was provided by *American Heritage,* which startled many direct mail promoters by proving it was possible to convert an audience paying $3 a year for a scholarly, paperbacked quarterly, to a new, hard-covered plush publication selling at $12 a year. Through imaginative, quality mailings, *American Heritage* converted about 85% of the old subscribers—and then used the same quality mailing techniques to sell hundreds of thousands of other buyers on the premium-priced quarterly.

Before long, other publishers were making extensive mailings to sell books in the $10 to $20 range, with great success. And as mail order sales techniques matured, the quality of the mailings was constantly upgraded. Undoubtedly these very successful book mailings have established a new basic quality level against which a large percentage of advertisers evaluate their own direct mail. The net result has been a tremendous improvement in the entire direct mail medium.

Exit the Amateurs

With these new quality standards has come another major change in the direct mail picture. Previously, many advertisers had the idea that "anyone can turn out direct mail." As a result, the majority of mailings were produced by what might best be described as "professional amateurs." Although paid to do the job, they often had very little real experience and even less knowledge of the intricacies of the medium. But since the average quality of direct mail was so low, few advertisers bothered to question the quality of their own mailings.

But as the mailings which showed up in the daily mail from publishers, and others who had discovered the worth of direct mail quality, exhibited a marked improvement, it was only natural that executives should make comparisons with the mailings their own companies were sending out. The result was increasing demand for true professionals—direct mail experts with experience to back them up.

While this transition has not yet reached all levels of direct mail, any comparison of mailings today with those used by the same companies a decade ago shows a very marked change.

UNDERSTANDING DIRECT MAIL

There have been hundreds of formulas advanced for success in direct mail, and everywhere you turn someone wants to proclaim some hard-and-fast rule about mailings. But the more you listen, the more you realize there are no shortcuts to direct mail success. For every rule that has ever been suggested, there has been another which proposes just the opposite.

A good example: A reader wrote a letter to an advertising trade magazine a few years ago asking if there were any established rules for the use of colors in direct mail. No sooner had the letter been published than the replies started pouring in, each offering what its writer was convinced was undebatable proof that certain colors pulled better response than others. Strangely enough, of over 20 replies received, *not a single one* listed the same set of "sure fire" color combinations!

Direct mail expert Leonard J. Raymond says, "The surest fact about direct mail is that you can't trust a rule or theory for longer than five minutes, and you can't apply it across the board. Someone else with a different product or service, or a different market, will find that an entirely different set of rules applies. The whole science of direct mail is one of trial and error."

Popular Misconceptions About Direct Mail

Direct mail is often misunderstood and a number of myths concerning the medium have developed over the years. Some of the most common are:

Every mailbox is flooded daily with direct mail—While the volume of direct mail has increased tremendously, the *average* American receives less than one direct mail piece per mail delivery. However, the higher the income level and the more indication an individual has given that he or she responds to mailings, the greater the number of mailings which will be received.

Most direct mail is discarded—True. But in the vast majority of cases it is discarded only *after* it has been looked at and considered by the recipient. Nobody stops to consider they are throwing away advertising when they dispose of a newspaper or magazine, but the physical action of depositing a mailing piece in a wastebasket is considered by many as evidence that direct mail is not well received.

The average citizen objects to the receipt of direct mail—This is a myth which has been advanced by newspapers who have hung the "junk mail" tag on their biggest competitor. Unfortunately, many who accept these attacks at face value fail to separate different categories of direct mail. There is "good" direct mail and "bad" direct mail, although it is unlikely everyone would ever agree to hang one label or the other on any given mailing. Some citizens do object to receiving mailings promoting products or services in which they have no immediate interest—particularly when the mailings used for such promotions are of inferior quality. But chances are these same citizens welcome announcements of special sale events from their favorite department stores, the monthly external house organ from a local automobile dealer, the weekly bulletin from their church, alumni bulletins from their college or university, the monthly announcement from a book or record club to which they have subscribed, a renewal notice from a favorite magazine, their semiannual Sears or Ward catalog, etc.

The 2% return myth—For a long time there has been general acceptance of the idea that a 2% return from any mailing is the basic standard for success. But there is no such thing as a standard return which will signal success for any mailing. In some cases, a return of one out of a thousand is considered excellent—particularly if the mailing was not intended to draw direct response. In other cases, such as a request for confirmation of mailing list information, a 90% return may be considered a failure.

In summing up an extensive study of direct mail readership, Henry Hoke, in *How to Think About Readership of Direct Mail,* makes these comments:

1. There is no such thing as a "normal" result percentage from direct mail.

2. Readership or percentage of results from any one effort may depend on a lot of other factors such as: age or reputation of company; publicity or informational background preceding request for action. In other words, the long pull.

3. Percentage of results is not always an indication of readership. Those who do not respond may do so later. They are influenced but do not act.

4. Percentage of response and readership varies with the functional purpose . . . Don't let anyone confuse you with the 2% myth. Returns depend on *purpose* and *many other factors.* Returns and readership can vary from zero to close to 100%.

Summer mailings will be a sure failure—Many direct mail advertisers have long avoided the summer months because they supposedly spell sure failure for mailings. But a lot of smart advertisers stopped to realize that if all of their competitors were avoiding summer mailings, they could command undivided attention for their own messages. As a result, most direct mail advertisers now mail the year around, keep a careful record of results, and then establish a seasonal pattern of their own if one develops. Such research has proved there is a great variance of seasonal patterns from one field to another and from one community to another.

Only short letters are read—Pure hocum! There's only one "rule"—a letter should be as long as required to provide the recipient with all of the information he will appreciate having about the product or service involved. Some of the best read direct mail letters of all time have been from seven to twelve pages long! (But don't make your letters any longer than absolutely necessary. If only one paragraph is required, don't think you have to add a lot of unnecessary verbiage just to fill out the page.)

The Big Payoff

One of the most common mistakes made by advertisers is to think of direct mail only in terms of immediate response. While this is the key to mail order success, it is not necessarily the biggest payoff for most direct mail advertisers. Like all other forms of advertising, direct mail has the ability to create lasting impressions.

Study after study has proved that direct mail is remembered long after mailings have been made. Perhaps the most important studies in this area have been conducted by Dr. Theodore H. Brown, professor of business statistics at the Harvard School of Business Administration, for Dickie-Raymond Inc. In reporting on Dr. Brown's important studies, Leonard J. Raymond commented:

> For a long time, mailers were content to count actual direct replies as their only measure of readership. A 5% return of reply cards, for example, was considered fine.
>
> But what happened to that other 95%? This altogether-too-much concentration on results, on replies, as proof of readership was shortsighted and stupid—because if we get a 5% actual return, we suspect that 95% of our mailing gets publicity and exposure value.
>
> Here was *another* great factor to be considered—the "suspected" but "unmeasured" readership of direct mail above and beyond replies received—*the effectiveness of direct mail as a pure advertising medium.*

Management Reaction to Results

Because so many advertisers think of direct mail only in terms of mail order, there is a tendency to expect immediate, tangible results —or to consider a direct mail program a "flop." Paul Bringe describes this type of management thinking, as quoted in *How to Think About Direct Mail:*

> What happens when he decides to use direct mail? He becomes result-conscious. He wants orders, and lots of them, within a week after mailing. His first mailing piece is usually a leftover catalog sheet or a few pages from his standard catalog. Copy and layout that did only a middling job when used for its original purpose, is supposed to acquire some magic power when it is put in an envelope and called direct mail.
>
> A trade book ad reprint is sent out as direct mail with an eye to the saving of plate costs, etc.; but as soon as it is called direct mail, then, by golly, it better bring in orders or he is through with it.

Fortunately, most of such misguided management thinking has been changing as more and more research has been conducted to provide clear-cut evidence of direct mail's role as an effective advertising medium—and not just a mail order medium. But there still is a tendency to expect some immediate action before a mailing can be given credit for scoring a success.

Magazine in Miniature

Because of the frequent demand for immediate results, many advertisers make the mistake of adopting mail order techniques for mailings which are primarily aimed at doing a general advertising job. Nicholas Samstag suggested looking at every unit of direct mail promotion as if it were a magazine in miniature. He called this "the editorial-advertising technique." He said:

> Just like every magazine, every mail piece should have both an *editorial* and an *advertising* content. The editorial content is the *allure* in the unit of promotion, the content which causes the recipient to want to read it whether he is a prospect or not. In short, the editorial content is that element in the copy or art or in the concept of the whole promotion piece which appeals to the human being rather than the business executive. The advertising content is, of course, the self-adulation which you, the advertiser, want to get across—or the news about your prices or the facts and figures about your giant crushing grinder machine.
>
> If your problem requires making only a simple and shallow advertising impression, you can afford to make your promotion largely editorial content, and thus tempt a large proportion of your market into reading it. But if you require a deep advertising impression, you can afford only a small editorial content, and thus, you will reach only a fraction of your possible readers. You know you are sacrificing the readership of most of your potential audience in order to make a deep impression on those who are actively and immediately in the market.

Direct Mail's Seven Characteristics

In its guide developed to acquaint advertising agency media men with the medium of direct mail, the Direct Mail Committee of the American Association of Advertising Agencies listed these seven basic characteristics of direct mail:

1. *Direct mail is selective.* The advertiser using direct mail can exercise precise control over the delivery of his message. He can direct his sales communication to the profile of such consumer characteristics as age, sex and income. This ability of direct mail to pinpoint markets in terms of scheduling and selection is especially important to the advertiser who is concerned with distribution and product availability. He can rely on direct mail to deliver his sales messages when and where he wants them delivered. A direct mail campaign can even be tailored to specific subsections of those markets. For instance, a petroleum advertiser uses lists of auto-owning residents near and around his service stations.

2. *Direct mail can be personal.* "Dear Mr. Smith," "Dear Mrs. Brown," "Dear Miss Johnson," etc.—each person gets a personal letter—directed to him or her, no one else.

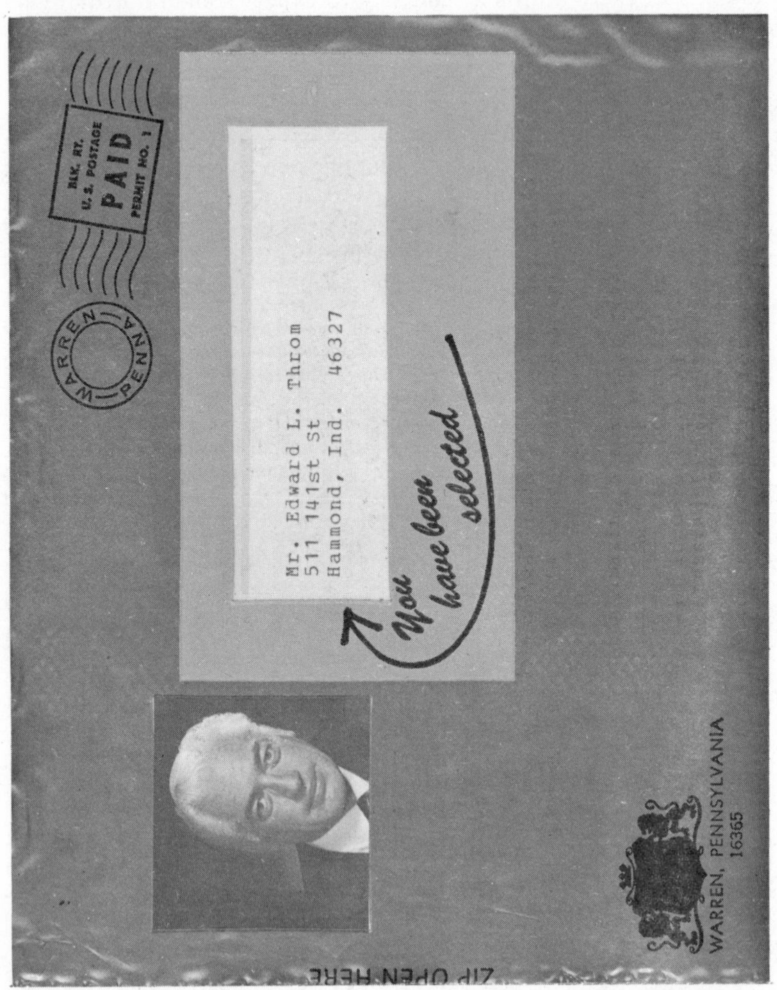

This is the envelope that bore the computer personalized letter reproduced on the opposite page. Openings in the gold-colored pliofilm envelope allow the color-picture of the NPC president and the name and address of the recipient to be seen before the mailing piece was opened. This firm believes that personal references are important to the effectiveness of direct mail, and in every mailing piece there are at least one or two uses of the recipient's name, and at least one reference to the home town to which the mail is addressed. The only other enclosure with this mailing was an order blank with illustrations and swatch samples of the slacks being offered, and an air mail, postpaid reply envelope.

SL3 03613464- MX-2

slacks headquarters for more than 9 million customers

WARREN
PENNSYLVANIA

JOHN L. BLAIR, President

Mr. Edward L. Throm
511 141st St
Hammond, Ind. 46327

Dear Mr. Throm:

I am taking it upon myself to mail 2 pairs of "Blair-Press" Permanent Press Flannel Slacks within the next few days to your 141st St address.

I'd count it a personal favor, if, when they arrive, you put a pair on and wear them around Hammond a full week absolutely free!

> These are the amazing Slacks that give you new Slacks free for any that ever lose their press -- that put an end to the expense and inconvenience of dry-cleaning and pressing forever!

You'll have a chance to prove that for yourself when your "Blair-Press" Slacks come and you put them to this test:

> Wear them hard! Toss them in your home washer. Dry them in your dryer or on a hanger. Then WEAR THEM AGAIN WITHOUT PRESSING!

You'll hardly believe your eyes, Mr. Throm! They look so perfect -- smooth, neatly pressed, sharply creased -- ready to wear anywhere with pride!

This is the miracle I want you to see for yourself -- the miracle of "Blair-Press" PERMANENT PRESS combined with a luxury Flannel of 50% Acrilan acrylic, 35% Avril rayon and 15% acetate to give you the "look" of $20 slacks for under $8 a pair!

All I need is your order form -- but I need it FAST! Our supply of these miracle "Blair-Press" PERMANENT PRESS Slacks isn't large, and in these handsome new colors and at this price, they'll go in a hurry!

To be sure of yours, better AIRMAIL your free trial order form TODAY, hadn't you?

Sincerely,

John L. Blair

President

JLB/A

Direct mail is another way of paying a personal call on a prospect. There is nothing indirect about this approach. In direct mail one can say "This is why you, Mr. Smith (not anyone else), should buy my product." You cannot say this on a mass basis in any other medium. Direct mail also offers a degree of privacy to the advertiser not available anywhere else.

3. *In direct mail there is little competition with other advertising messages.* Direct mail gets the undivided attention of the prospect. He is not distracted by adjacent advertising, competing for the client's dollar. There is no editorial content competing for attention. And the ad cannot be badly positioned in the medium used.

   (Today some direct mail users are experimenting with cooperative mailings. This involves having two or more *compatible* advertisers share mailings to prospects.)

4. *Considerable production flexibility is available in direct mail.* In other media, advertising messages have to conform to the space and time requirements of their carriers. In direct mail the advertiser can use different shapes, processes, colors, forms and sizes for his sales messages. While it is true that advertisers can design imaginative and unusual ads in other media, particularly inserts, direct mail offers the widest scope by far. For even in the case of inserts, publishers and the U. S. Postal Service impose certain requirements.

5. *Direct mail is relatively easy to change or correct.* In media where there are early closing dates and other long-term contractual requirements the advertiser can often find himself "locked in." If he wants to make a last-minute copy change in his advertising he may find it impossible in his existing media commitments. In direct mail the advertiser can make changes right up to the minute his presses start to roll.

6. *Direct mail offers sampling and unique promotion opportunities.* The direct mail advertiser can enclose samples with his letter, coupons and other forms of incentives to build store traffic or to produce sales leads. Direct mail can therefore add another *dimension* to a campaign, the third dimension of product samples and enclosures to stimulate demand and force distribution. A good example was the Schick new stainless steel blade nationwide sampling program which gave them a jump on the competition by going directly to the consumer. Direct mail can be a fast-acting medium in stimulating buying action on the part of the recipient.

7. *Direct mail is easy and economical to test and evaluate.* Direct mail is a strong testing medium that produces a measurable sample, which, when analyzed, allows you to project your findings in one or all other media.

Testing through direct mail need not be expensive. Planned correctly, it saves time and money. When handled properly, testing via direct mail yields some very valuable answers. It allows an agency to protect its client—by reducing the risk factor. When testing in small dollars provides a projectable result, this permits an advertiser to spend larger dollars in any media more profitably.

In this case, our definition of the word "profitable" is not a measure of "dollar profit" only. Many things can be tested through direct mail advertising. Each helps to control and pinpoint advertising objectives.

Following are just a few of the potential areas of mail testing:

1. Copy approaches
2. Pricing
3. Packaging
4. Determining geographic distribution areas
5. Potential market—with reference to sex, age, economics, education, etc.
6. Cost per load or order factors

In addition to mass market lists (telephone, auto registration and occupancy), there are thousands of lists available for rental which can be utilized to measure advertising effectiveness. This is done by matching profiles of a list against the client's product, service or his customers' characteristics.

By testing a portion of an available list one can accurately project the balance of the list. The number of names tested will determine the variance.

Mail testing gives quick and accurate answers. Remember: this is a highly measurable medium. It can be used as a prime advertising vehicle or . . . mail testing can help to predetermine the most profitable advertising avenue (media copy, pricing, audience selection, etc.) to follow. Properly projected, these tests will strengthen an agency's position with its clients.

The Rifle Medium

A good summary of the direct mail medium was prepared by Edwin Lex Bacon of Graybar Electric Co., in *Envelope Economies.* "Even in industrial advertising," he said, "magazines are shotguns when compared to direct mail. For intelligently planned and executed direct mail can be made to solicit only the specific companies or persons who are prospects at a particular time for the advertiser's goods or services. Direct mail is explicit. It can deliver the advertiser's message with the least amount of competition for the reader's interest. Direct mail is flexible. It will reach the reader at the time and place the advertiser selects. Space advertising must be prepared two or three months in advance for magazine publication. But a new price list has to go out to the right people in a matter of days. Direct mail does it. Direct mail is like a rifle. It doesn't delay action. It doesn't scatter your shot."

Chapter 2

HOW THE PUBLIC REACTS TO DIRECT MAIL

AT THE TIME the first edition of this handbook was written, there had been little definitive research to pin-point public attitudes toward direct mail. While the success of individual mailings left little doubt that direct mail was highly successful in reaching most every type of audience, "outsiders"—in particular, newspaper publishers—were quick to hang the "junk mail" tag on the medium and insist that it was a waste of money for advertisers, a burden on postmen's backs, an unwanted avalanche invading the privacy of homeowners' mailboxes, the major source of postal deficits and, thus, a costly burden for taxpayers.

As the junk mail attacks mounted in newspaper columns and the unsupported "evidence" was lifted from newspaper writings and used as a base for proposing increased rates for third class mail, the Direct Mail/Marketing Association decided to underwrite an independent research project to measure the real attitudes of American consumers.

The research project began early in 1963 with pilot studies. Then the A. C. Nielsen Company took over. A representative cross-section of 1,500 homes throughout the continental limits of the U.S. was drawn up and professional interviewers of the Alfred Politz Organization conducted 1,460 interviews averaging a half-hour each. In October 1964, after extensive computer analysis of the interview results, the findings were presented at a general membership meeting of DMMA and given widespread publicity.

Key Findings

In introducing the findings, Hollis V. Johnson of A. C. Nielsen pointed out that the basic objective was "to find out how people feel about direct mail, and what they say they do with it." The specific areas of inquiry were:

1. Do people like or dislike receiving direct mail?
2. Do people open and read direct mail; and if so, who opens direct mail in a household?
3. Do people act in response to direct mail?
4. How much mail does the average household receive? Among the highlights of the Nielsen findings were:

- That 85% of the people have *no* general dislike of direct mail.
- That a minimum of 75% of them open and at least glance at *all* direct mail received.
- That in three out of four homes, direct mail is opened by the *head of the house.*
- That, for most people, the problem of "cluttered mailboxes" just doesn't exist; the average home got *less than one piece* of direct mail per day during the week preceding the study.

Consumer Attitudes

The initial report also pinpointed public attitudes toward four specific types of direct mail: appeals of charity organizations and medical crusades, advertising and selling by mail, samples and coupons, and mail order catalogs. Among the key results:

- 81% of adult heads of households open and read thoroughly or glance at the charitable or medical appeals they receive, and 74% send in a contribution at one time or another in response to such appeals.
- 75% open and read thoroughly or glance at advertising and selling pieces of direct mail, and 54% purchase products advertised and sold through the mail at one time or another.
- Samples and coupons are liked by 48% and are generally disliked by only 9%.
- Three-fourths of the people open and read mail order catalogs, and two-thirds purchase from catalogs at one time or another. (Among those who actually receive catalogs in the mail—16% don't—nine of ten open and read them and eight of the ten purchase from them.)

WHAT PEOPLE SAY THEY DO WITH DIRECT MAIL

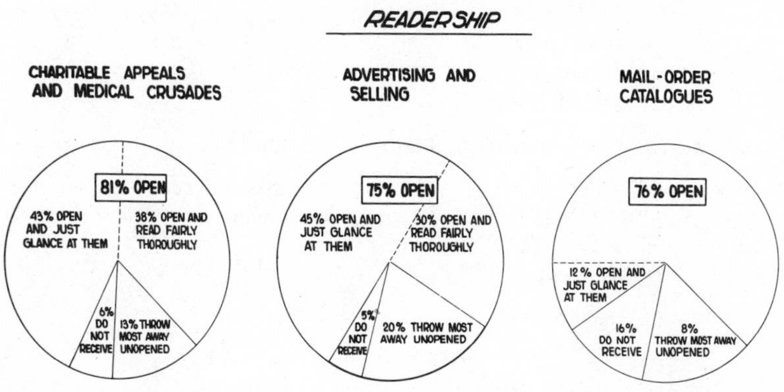

No Junk Mail

Perhaps one of the most interesting results of the study is the report by interviewers that the word "junk" wasn't even mentioned by 97% of those interviewed, even when a wide cross-section of nearly 1,500 were asked to sit down individually for about 30 minutes and discuss their feelings about direct mail. In fact, the impartial interviewers reported that the majority of people volunteered favorable descriptive terms such as "informative," "saves me money," "beneficial," "convenient," and "tells me what's new."

While the complete study findings were a book in themselves, some of the key findings should be helpful as background for anyone who wishes to visualize the atmosphere into which his direct mail pieces will be received.

Makeup of the Interview Sample	
Education of Principal Wage Earner	
Some College	22%
High School Graduate	28%
Some High School	21%
Grade School or Less	29%
Claimed Family Income	
Upper	23%
Middle	47%
Lower	30%
Marital Status	
Married	88%
Other (single, divorced, widow, etc.)	12%

Age of Respondent

Under 30 years	15%
30-39 years	24%
40-49 years	24%
50-59 years	16%
60 and over	21%

ATTITUDES TOWARD DIRECT MAIL

Enjoy All	33%
Like Some, Not All	16%
Don't Care One Way or Another	36%
Dislike	15%

Summary:

- One of 3 people enjoys receiving *all* direct mail.
- 85% of the people have *no general dislike* of direct mail.
- 15% of the people do not like to get any mail.

DIRECT MAIL VOLUME

	All Mail	*Direct Mail Only*
10 or less pieces per week	45%	83%
11-20 pieces per week	31%	13%
21 or more pieces per week	24%	4%

Summary:

- The average number of pieces of *all* mail received during the week preceding the interview was 15.3. Of this, 6.5 or *less than one piece per day* was direct mail.
- 83% of U. S. homes received less than 10 pieces of direct mail during the week preceding the interview.
- *Postal statistics indicate that there has been no appreciable change in volume of direct mail per household in the years since the Nielsen study was completed.*

WHO OPENS DIRECT MAIL?

Head of Household	75%
Each Member Opens Own	16%
Other	9%

Summary:

- Three of 4 respondents reported that direct mail is opened by the head of their household—regardless of to whom it is addressed.

- In 16% of the homes, each family member opens his own mail.
- In 9% of the homes, direct mail is opened by various combinations of family and nonfamily members.

DIRECT MAIL FUND RAISING

Attitude:

Like to Receive	21%
Varies with the Item	14%
Don't Care	31%
Dislike	28%
Do Not Receive	6%

Readership:

Open and Read Fairly Thoroughly	38%
Open and Just Glance at Them	43%
Throw Most Away Unopened	13%
Do Not Receive	6%

Action:

Contribute Frequently	16%
Contribute Occasionally	34%
Contribute Rarely	24%
Never Contribute	20%
Do Not Receive	6%

Summary:

- Two of 3 people have nothing against Direct Mail Fund Raising generally.
- Four of 5 people (81%) open and read thoroughly or glance at the Fund Raising mail they receive.
- 74% contribute to Fund Raising Appeals at least some of the time.

ADVERTISING AND SELLING BY MAIL

Attitude:

Like to Receive	22%
Varies with the Item	11%
Don't Care	34%
Dislike	28%
Do Not Receive	5%

Readership:

Open and Read Fairly Thoroughly	30%
Open and Just Glance at Them	45%

Throw Most Away Unopened	20%
Do Not Receive	5%

Action:

Purchase Frequently	7%
Purchase Occasionally	24%
Purchase Rarely	26%
Never Purchase	38%
Do Not Receive	5%

Summary:

- Two of 3 people have nothing against Direct Mail Advertising and Selling generally.
- Three of 4 (75%) open and read thoroughly or at least glance at this type of mail.
- Nearly 3 of 5 (57%) purchase products and services at least some of the time, as a result of direct mail advertising and selling efforts.

SAMPLES AND COUPONS

Attitudes:

Like to Receive	48%
Varies with the Item	4%
Don't Care	34%
Dislike	9%
Do Not Receive	5%

Action (Samples):

Usually Use	72%
Do Not Usually Use	23%
Do Not Receive	5%

Action (Coupons):

Usually Use	52%
Do Not Usually Use	43%
Do Not Receive	5%

Summary:

- Better than 4 of 5 people (86%) have nothing against Direct Mail Samples and Coupons generally.
- Samples are usually used by about 3 of 4 people.
- More than half usually use the coupons they get through the mail.

CATALOGS

Attitudes:	
Like to Receive	62%
Varies with the Item	2%
Don't Care	13%
Dislike	7%
Do Not Receive	16%
Readership:	
Open and Read Fairly Thoroughly	64%
Open and Just Glance at Them	12%
Throw Most Away Unopened	8%
Do Not Receive	16%
Action:	
Purchase Frequently	16%
Purchase Occasionally	33%
Purchase Rarely	18%
Never Purchase	17%
Do Not Receive	16%

Summary:

- Nearly 8 of 10 (77%) have nothing against catalogs generally, and 6 of 10 *like* to receive them.
- More than 3 of 4 open and read thoroughly or glance at catalogs. Thorough readership is very high (64%).
- Purchases are made at least some of the time by 67%.

Supporting Evidence

It is probably only natural to suspect that a research project sponsored and paid for by an association representing the direct mail field might not be truly objective. While DMMA made every possible effort to assure complete objectivity in the Nielsen study, suspicions concerning its validity have been expressed by those who have not seen the massive supporting evidence compiled by the researchers.

But few can suspect the objectivity of somewhat similar studies conducted by organizations in no way connected directly to direct mail production or use. Without exception, such studies have supported the basic findings of the Nielsen study. Probably the most thorough study of this kind was one conducted as part of the Southern Regional Food Marketing Project sponsored by the Agricultural Experiment stations of Kentucky, Alabama, Georgia, Mississippi, South Carolina, Texas, and Virginia.

Homemakers' Responses to Direct Advertising

The Southern Regional project involved a systematic evaluation of the attitudes expressed by more than 2,267 homemakers concerning unsolicited materials they received through the mails or which were delivered to their doorsteps. In explaining the background of the research project, its sponsors noted:[1]

> In designing the project, the aim was to cover the entire range of age, education, income, and family situation in the cities surveyed (Phenix City, Ala.; Rock Hill, S. C.; and Lexington, Ky.). Each homemaker was asked about what direct advertising material she had received, what was done with it, and whether she usually used or rejected the materials. Concern was with the kind of things she had received during a specified period of time. These were grouped under several broad categories. She was also asked to react to certain questions and to express her feeling about different methods used by advertisers. Identical schedules, interview procedures, and interpretations of information were set up for all states. Telephone and personal interviews were used and handled in such a way as to assure that there was adequate coverage of all segments of the respective markets surveyed.

Seven Types Studied

The study concentrated on seven specific types of direct advertising—local special sales advertisements, samples of products, special offer coupons or certificates, trading stamp coupons and/or trading stamps, special offer coupons in magazines, mail order catalogs and discount catalogs. The receipt and use of each of these types of advertising are shown in the table.

In commenting on these results, the authors of the report[2] stated:

> There were 1,869 white and 398 Negro homemakers in the households surveyed. Almost all had received one or more pieces of material through the mail or by doorstep delivery during the previous year. All homemakers were asked about having received seven specified kinds of direct advertising and what was done with each, i.e., frequency of use. The term "usually used" was applied to those who commonly accepted and frequently used the information or materials. Homemakers who made only occasional or infrequent use of materials were classified as "sometimes use." Both groups were considered to have a positive attitude favorable to potential sales. The recipients who "never used" the direct advertising were generally negatively inclined and/or found little merit in what they had received.

---

[1] *Homemakers' Responses to Direct Advertising* by John B. Roberts, Harold C. Young and Mildred R. Wightman. Southern Cooperative Series Bulletin 121. December 1966. Available from Agricultural Experiment Station, University of Kentucky, Lexington, Ky. 40506.
[2] Ibid.

NUMBER AND PERCENTAGE OF FAMILIES RECEIVING AND THE DISPOSITION MADE OF UNSOLICITED ADVERTISING BY MAIL OR DOORSTEP DELIVERY

	(1)	(2)	(3)	(4)	(5)	(6)
Types of Advertising Referred to	Families Reporting			What Was Done With Item By Those Receiving		
	Total No. of Respondents	Number Receiving	Percent Receiving	Usually Used	Sometimes Used	Never Used
				- - - Percent - - -		
Sample of some product	2,251	1,765	79	86	12	2
Special offer coupons, certificates, etc.	2,257	1,667	74	29	50	21
Local leaflets, flyers, advertising	2,252	1,615	72	18	60	22
Trading stamps, coupons for stamps	2,267	1,264	56	65	25	10
Mail-order catalogs	2,266	1,033	46	21	61	18
Magazine inserts, coupons, certificates	2,263	973	43	16	55	29
Discount catalogs	2,264	687	30	10	54	36

Out of the total 2,267 homemakers in the survey, 1,765 (or 79%) reported they had received some kind of sample product during the past year.

More than 70% had received both special offer coupons and local advertisements. Trading stamps reached 56% of the surveyed households, and 30% had received discount catalogs. Mail order catalogs and magazine inserts or coupons were reported by 46 and 43% of the homemakers respectively.

A review of the disposition made by the homemakers shows a wide variation in the frequency of use. For example, 86% of those receiving samples said they usually used them, 12% sometimes used samples, and 2% never did. In contrast, 10% of those who received discount catalogs were regular users, and over a third (36%) never made use of the catalogs. A further check on the percentage who almost always used the materials showed that the sample of products ranked first and trading stamp coupons ranked second. Next in order of rank were special offer coupons and discount catalogs.

It should be pointed out that the highest ranking categories all represent frequently used and repeat items and, in the case of trading stamps, a stated redemption value. Such items can be saved or held in possession of the consumers. This is also true of the special offer coupons and inserts in magazines, but the latter requires more diligence or a habit of collection. In contrast, local advertisements, and mail order and discount catalogs contain a wide choice of articles of all kinds. Many of the advertised items are semidurable goods that represent irregular purchase. Accordingly, it was not surprising to find that more than half of the respondents reported that they sometimes used this kind of material. It is important to note that, as a practical matter, few recipients of direct advertising treat everything alike and reject everything categorically. There are, however, homemakers who for various reasons do not make use of materials they receive. Among the nonusers are those in households whose demands are pretty well saturated, and there are other households whose pattern of living give a low priority to unsolicited selling efforts of all kinds.

Attitudes Toward Direct Advertising

Probably the most significant finding of the Southern study was the expression of respondents concerning their attitudes toward unsolicited advertising materials. To test the hypothesis that most homemakers object to or resent receiving mailed advertisements, literature, samples or unsolicited materials, each homemaker was asked how she felt about such materials. She was asked which of five statements most nearly described her reactions. The results:

	White	*Negro*
Very much pleased	24%	60%
Moderately pleased	45%	29%
Indifferent	24%	9%
Moderately displeased	5%	1%
Very much displeased	2%	1%

In the published report on the study,[3] the authors included the following summary:

> This study indicates that homemakers have learned to discriminate and to save or destroy various forms of unsolicited materials sent through the mails or delivered to their doorstep, with relatively little resentment. The sponsors of direct advertising are assured their material will reach the intended clientele. Beyond this point there is no control, no personal sales pressure and no inducements to the homemaker other than the persuasiveness inherent in the given piece of material. In the normal pattern of distribution, recipients of direct advertising are free to accept or reject each separate piece of information, but most do not communicate their feelings back to the senders. For the different media there is little central or systematic accounting, and not much is known about reactions and attitudes that may have developed from individual and cumulative experiences. But for many reasons direct selling has grown in importance as vendors to reach potential customers and induce sales.
>
> The hypothesis that most homemakers resent receiving unsolicited advertisements, literature, samples of products, and similar types of direct advertising was rejected in this study. About 70% of 1,850 white and 90% of 395

[3]Ibid.

Negro homemakers were either pleased or very pleased about the unsolicited materials they had received at various times in the mail or by doorstep delivery. Only 1 person in 10 was definitely displeased. Nearly three-fourths of the Negro homemakers felt people "just like to get mail even if only advertising." Slightly fewer than half (47%) of the white homemakers expressed the same view.

There were no differences between the races in their attitude toward local advertisements and the use of trading stamps, coupons, and other direct means of promotion; none of the techniques examined was widely criticized.

Attitudes of Youth

Another interesting research project is a pilot study conducted in May 1970 by Market Compilation and Research Bureau. It involved interviews with 107 students in five Southern California universities. While the questions concerning students' attitude toward mail advertising were stated in form which makes difficult correlation with other research studies, they provide evidence that even students who are often critical of anything that is identified as "The Establishment" have no strong objection to direct mail addressed to them:

"I enjoy reading it; I might even file some of what I receive away in case I need something later on."	22.1%
"I like to make my own selections in shops close to home; I never order anything through the mail."	18.3%
"I find direct mail creates more savings in the long run, better discounts and greater discretion in terms of decision making."	18.3%
"I order most of what I buy through the mail."	12.5%
"I'm so low on funds, any mail that looks like it's after a buck finds its way unopened to the waste basket."	11.5%
"I'm snowed with it. So much of it comes, I don't try to read it anymore."	11.5%
Other	5.8%

Interestingly, the average student surveyed received an average of only 6.8 pieces of direct mail per month and 75.7% of the interviewees reported they had bought things through the mail. When asked what form of advertising would most likely convince them to buy, direct mail tied for first choice with radio.

Volume of Mail

The research reports on volume of direct mail received in the average household are frequently questioned. However, postal statistics verify what the researchers have reported. Of course, there is a great deal of variance in the amount of mail received from one home to the next. In general, the more affluent, the more educated and the more active receive a considerably greater quantity of direct mail than the "average" recipient. And such individuals are the ones most likely to question the research reports.

Chapter 3

THE BASIC ELEMENTS OF DIRECT MAIL

WHILE there are certainly other factors to be considered in developing an effective direct mail program, four elements deserve special consideration. Each is discussed in greater detail in other chapters, but for a better understanding of the medium it is well to consider them from a broad point of view at this time.

Most direct mail can be broken down into four basic elements:

1. The list.
2. The offer.
3. The package (how material is presented).
4. Fulfillment.

The List

The most important essential in any direct mail or mail order program is the list of prospects to whom the mailings are sent. In *Planning and Creating Better Direct Mail,* John Yeck points out[1]:

"The list is the weakest spot in many direct mail programs because it is taken for granted. A large company may require 10 O.K.'s on the copy and art. An advertiser hovers over the printer's shoulder to see that the ink matches his sample exactly. Photos may be carefully retouched to bring out the product's name. But most people just assume that their list is in good shape. And that's dangerous. It's natural, though.

"A perfect list, like a hole in one, is just about impossible. So working on a list is frustrating. And besides, in all other forms of advertising, someone else develops the "list," or audience, for you. You buy it readymade, "as is," and use it all. They analyze it for

[1]Copyright McGraw-Hill Co.

you. They keep the addresses up-to-date; you don't have anything to say about it. So, you don't worry about it."

People on the Move

One common characteristic of just about every list is constant change. Few lists are ever up-to-date for more than a day or two. While this presents one of the toughest problems involved in direct mail, it also is an important reason why it is absolutely essential to give primary consideration to your mailing list.

An example of how the constantly moving American affects mailings is shown by some post office statistics. In just one month, the Detroit post office alone couldn't deliver 1,465,000 pieces of mail due to incorrect address. This included 385,000 first-class pieces—175,000 sent to the dead letter office and 210,000 returned to sender; 1,080,000 third-class pieces—480,000 returned and 600,000 destroyed.

McGraw-Hill circulation records show that of every 1,000 key men in industry, the following changes occur each year:

343 new faces appear to replace transfers to companies in different fields, retirements, deaths;

65 change titles due to promotions and changes within the company;

157 shift to different locations with the same or similar type of company;

Only 435 stay put in the same job, same company, same location.

Another recent study shows that the average executive on the way up will relocate nine times in the course of his career. Lew Kleid adds these statistics, which appeared in the publication, *Envelope Economies:*

The New York City Post Office received over 500,000 removal notices in one year;

Chicago had 650,000;

Philadelphia had over 300,000;

Dun & Bradstreet in the business field names 6,000 changes every day.

The 1970 census of population revealed that over 50% of all Americans five years of age or older were living in a different house from the one in which they had been living five years earlier. Of the 75 million who had moved, 47.5 million stayed in the same county, another 13.6 million stayed in the same state, while 14.1 million moved to another state. In addition, 2 million moved into the United States from abroad.

The West had the largest percentage of movers—56.6%, In the Northeast, 40% moved in the five-year period; 46% in the North Central region; and 50% in the South. But these statistics tell only part of the picture since many of the 75 million movers made more than one change during the five-year period.

What all this adds up to is that any mailing list must never be thought of as a static thing. To be of value, it must be constantly corrected. These same facts mean that when you rent, buy, or borrow a list from someone else you must make sure it has been kept up-to-date. And when you set out to develop a list for yourself, you must make sure you use the most current records and directories.

How to Start a List

There are dozens of ways to build your own mailing list. The usual starting point is your own sales records. To these you will probably want to add prospects. You will find details on the many possible list sources in other chapters of this handbook.

Many direct mail advertisers prefer to let list experts handle the entire job of compiling a mailing list, or they may prefer to buy or rent existing lists. There are thousands of different types of lists available through professional list compilers or brokers. To rent a list for one-time use usually costs between $25 and $35 per thousand names. The cost of purchasing a list outright for continuing use will depend primarily on the difficulty involved in the original compilation of the list and the number of potential purchasers who can help share the cost. Some advertisers have found it worthwhile to pay as high as $5 a name for compilation of a special list, but compilation costs are more likely to run about $50 per thousand names.

At this point a word of warning is in order. Never accept a list at face value, even from professional list suppliers or the best known names in the direct mail field. Far too many available lists have been permitted to become badly out of date or have been watered down with names of little value. The list field is a tricky business and the only way to be sure you are getting what you need is to carefully check representative cross sections of the list—and make sure the selected cross sections are of your choosing rather than those picked by the list owner.

But at the same time, don't underestimate the value of the professional in the list field. He can help you avoid many headaches in your direct mail program.

Keeping the List Alive

Once you have a list, it is important to develop a working system to keep it up-to-date. Sales records, salesmen's call reports, new editions of directories, personnel change columns in newspapers and magazines, association rosters, and other sources will provide valuable information to guide list maintenance. You'll also want to keep a close check on returned mail.

But these methods alone seldom go more than halfway in supplying the necessary information for list changes. You will probably want to send out periodic "list cleaners"—mailings asking those on your list to help you with the maintenance job by supplying up-to-date information about themselves.

Budgeting for Lists

Because of the importance of the list in the total direct mail picture, it is advisable to include a substantial amount in your annual advertising budget for list procurement and maintenance. The actual amount will have to depend upon your own individual circumstances. But if you haven't allowed at least 10% of your annual direct mail costs for the list, chances are you are missing the boat.

Some simple mathematics will show how important an adequate list budget can be. To keep it simple, suppose you make 10 mailings annually to a list of 10,000 names. Let us say the cost of the mailings is $300 per thousand, including postage. This, of course adds up to a total annual expenditure of $30,000, or $3 per name on the list.

Since there is at least 25% turnover in the average list each year, a year-old list will mean that $7,500 in mailing costs is at least partially wasted. While some of the misaddressed mailings may end up in the hands of legitimate prospects, there is certainly a loss of impact if a personal approach has been used—and remember that direct mail works best when it approaches a customer or prospect on a person-to-person basis. But at least half of this 25% will probably never reach any prospect.

So let us be conservative and think only in terms of a 12½% loss. This means $3,750 right down the drain. So, to be realistic, an expenditure of $3,750 for list maintenance can be paid for just by the loss alone. This example, of course, oversimplifies the situation. It must be remembered that the maintenance will yield "replacement names"—important prospects who would otherwise miss your direct mail story.

Names, Titles, or Companies?

One of the most frequently asked questions by direct mail beginners who are faced with the task of developing business lists is whether mailing should be addressed to an individual by name, to a position (i.e., sales manager, purchasing agent, etc.), or just to a company. The answer depends to a great extent on the nature of the material which will be mailed.

If you plan to use a person-to-person approach, it is best to use names. But, of course, names change much more frequently than titles—thus presenting a considerably more complicated job of list compilation and maintenance. The use of titles will generally see that the mailing gets to the person holding that job or an appropriate assistant. Unfortunately, however, in many cases job titles are misleading, so building a list for the average product or service involves more than just selecting a few titles and then using them in conjunction with the names and addresses of the companies you want to reach.

What this adds up to is that there is no simple answer to this question. Every direct mail advertiser should analyze the situation in terms of his own specific requirements and the types of audiences he wishes to reach with his advertising. However, the majority of advertisers have found their best lists are those complete with names of individuals and which are maintained continuously.

THE OFFER

To be effective, direct mail should seek to accomplish a specific objective. This is generally referred to as "the offer." It is the cornerstone around which direct mail copy is constructed.

While the offer frequently comes at the very end of a piece of direct mail copy, most successful copywriters spell out its details before they write a single word of copy. Failure to do so quite often results in ineffective direct mail.

Even when you do not expect the recipients of your direct mail to take any immediate action—such as sending in an order, request for literature, or asking a salesman to call—you should have a specific reason for any mailing you make. And that reason should never be kept from your audience. Perhaps you only want people on your mailing list to start thinking of how they might utilize your product. If so, tell them this is the purpose of your mailing.

The Mail Order Offer

Generally, the mechanics of the offer are of more importance in mail order than in other forms of direct mail. Since you are seeking a direct response, it is important to guide recipients to take the specific action you want—and to make it easy for them to do so.

For this reason, many mail order advertisers prepare their order forms first, and then build other elements of the direct mail package around the reply device. This not only assures coordination of all of the elements, but helps keep copy headed in a single direction.

By all means, the details of the offer should be simple and clearly understood. Many mail order amateurs have made the mistake of trying to "hide" the details of their offer in hopes of tricking some recipients into responding. The net result, however, is usually a poor response since the public is suspicious of any offer which is not crystal clear.

Preparing the Copy

Once you have your offer clearly in mind, you will want to travel a straight path in developing copy which leads the reader to the offer and then impels him into taking the action you have requested. Dozens of formulas have been developed to guide direct mail copywriters. You will find many of them discussed later in this book.

Perhaps the oldest and most frequently used formula is "AIDA" —get *attention,* arouse *interest,* stimulate *desire,* ask for *action.* This simple outline for effective direct mail copy has been used successfully since the earliest days of direct mail—and it is just as effective today as ever before. The key to success, however, is that second "A"—*ask for action.* Unfortunately, many direct mail advertisers overlook this all-important point. They write glowing copy, describing their products and services, and create a sincere desire for their wares among the recipients. And then they stop right there, without spelling out what the recipient is expected to do to fulfill this desire.

Writing Effective Direct Mail Letters

The most important element in the majority of direct mailings is the letter. To guide others in the preparation of effective direct mail, Du Pont's polychemicals department prepared a booklet, *How to Conduct a Direct Mail Campaign.* It contained these excellent tips for writing effective direct mail letters:

1. *Be friendly*—Write your letters to convey an atmosphere of warm, personal regard for the prospect. Friendliness and sincerity are attributes that are basically sound in letters as well as in conversation. Real friendliness is not possible, since it is necessary in the case of a mass audience to talk to or at the prospect instead of with him. The friendly approach is one of the greatest advantages of direct mail. Don't overlook it.

   A word of caution. Friendliness should never be allowed to border on disrespect, presumption, effusiveness, or even overenthusiasm. If your letter bears even a hint of insincerity, it may well be the last one that your prospect will read.

2. *Be clear*—Your letter is, of course, clear to you. But is it clear to the reader? Try to put yourself in his position. Remember that he does not have any background knowledge of your problem and your letter must stand unaided on its own two feet. A good rule is to use short words, reasonably short sentences, and paragraphs of six lines or less. Try reading your letters aloud. Very often, things that look perfectly logical on paper will sound absurd when read aloud.

   Another excellent precaution is to have someone else read your letter before it is printed. This gives you the benefit of a typical "first impression" to your letter and usually shows up any serious confusion or misconception caused by faulty writing.

3. *Be Anglo-Saxon*—For some reason, many of us feel we should adopt a literary style for our letters—something "better" than the words we actually use in our daily conversations. Actually, of course, the reason we use these words when we talk is because we have found from experience that they express our meaning most clearly.

   If you were to look up the words of your conversation in a dictionary, you would find that nearly all are marked "AS," meaning that they are from the Anglo-Saxon. Very few would be from Latin, Greek, French, or other sources. With a dictionary, you can actually measure naturalness. Just look up your words in a sentence, paragraph, or whole letter. If 95% are marked "AS," you are safe; if 80% or less, you are writing literary letters!

4. *Be concise*—popular opinion to the contrary, a letter does not have to be short to be concise. No letter is too long if it tells the whole story and only that. If we consider that a salesman speaks about 2,500 words in an average personal sales call, we would need a letter eight pages long to tell our complete story to one person. Yet our direct mail letter must tell the story to all the individuals on the list. It must cover all of the reasons why a prospect should do what you want him to do and answer in advance all his objections. Some of the best letters, therefore, have been more than three pages long; others have been less than a page. The moral is that the direct mail letter is supposed to sell the prospect, not just please him by being agreeably short.

THE PACKAGE

The items you use to convey your offer to your audience are called "the direct mail package." For maximum results, it is important to always think of a mailing unit as a package—with all of the elements working together, supplementing one another in achieving the results you seek.

A direct mail package can take many forms ranging from a simple self-mailer to an envelope filled with a variety of items. The possible contents of the package are almost unlimited and much in the following chapters is devoted to detailed analysis of these possibilities. To introduce the subject, however, it is well worth studying a special presentation on the subject prepared by the late William Baring-Gould, one of Time, Inc.'s direct mail experts. This presentation was a highlight of a DMMA convention in Washington, and because of its excellence it is presented here in full:

How your typist sets up a letter is important. Her object, of course, should be to make your copy look like what we hope it is—both interesting to read and easy to read.

At least nine elements or devices in a letter can affect its appearance and consequently its resultfulness:

1. *Datelines*—Many letters, for example, carry no dateline. Often there's a good reason why they don't. Maybe the letter is to be produced in quantity for use over an extended period. Yet most of us, when we write a personal letter, write the date in the upper right-hand corner of the first page.

Since all of us want our direct mail to look as personal as possible—even though it may be going to hundreds of thousands of people—let's personalize it a little if we can, at no extra cost whatsoever, by using a dateline. Maybe we can make the dateline work for us. Example: September 1976—the year in which the Warple Co. celebrates its golden anniversary as your city's favorite department store.

2. *Margins*—Keep those at top, bottom and sides as generous as you can. Frame your copy as an artist frames a picture. Remember—that white space may be too precious for words.

3. *The Salutation*—A third element that affects the appearance of a letter is the salutation.

There are four major ways of handling the salutation:

You can pay for a full fill-in: Mr. John J. Jones, 444 East 44th Street, New York, New York 10036; Dear Mr. Jones:

You can pay for a one-line fill-in, which skips the first three lines of the full fill-in and starts simply: Dear Mr. Jones:

You can save some money and start all your letters Dear Reader:

or Dear Sir: or Dear Customer: or Dear Friend: or Reverend Sir: (as was done in a letter to clergymen).

You can write a letter that starts out with a caption or headline. Maybe you will want to go right from your headline into your letter copy. Or maybe you will want to include a *Dear:*

I have never heard of a test where a full fill-in paid off in a letter calculated to get orders or inquiries (but I am sure somebody has made one). A one-line fill-in, on the other hand, sometimes justifies its extra expense. If you have a quality item which sells at a high price, it might pay you to test a one-line fill-in.

Most often, however, your choice is between a "Dear Reader" type of salutation and a headline.

A spokesman for the headline school of thought puts it this way:

> "A headline is a vital necessity for attention value. If you don't get attention you don't get readers. Newspaper editors have yet to find a better substitute for a headline. Other approaches may prove successful from time to time, but I venture the guess that they are either flashes in the pan or have not been honestly or intelligently tested by comparison. Until human habits themselves change, I'll stick along with the method that has proved so consistently successful since the day the postage stamp was first used."

The "Dear Reader" school of thought answers that by saying:

> "A headline depersonalizes a letter, and personalization is essential. Newspaper editors may not have found a better substitute for a headline, but the writer of direct mail is not writing a newspaper story. He is writing a letter. And it's plainly not true that headlines are consistently successful—many users of the mail find that they consistently get better results when they use the 'Dear Reader' salutation instead of a heading.
>
> "The best advice I can give you here is this: Try both a headline and a Dear Something salutation on each piece of copy you write. Let your common sense be the judge. If you're in real doubt, test."

4. *Paragraphing*—Some mailers like the hanging paragraph. Some like to run their copy square or flush with the left-hand margin. Others are accustomed to indenting five to ten spaces. It is largely a matter of personal preference; certainly I have never seen any tests that prove one style better than another. The one big thing to remember about paragraphing is this: Keep your paragraphs short—it makes your letter look cleaner, opener, easier to read.

Many lettermen, when they come to a particularly important paragraph in a letter, will indent the whole paragraph to the left, or indent it left and right, to set it off from the rest of the copy. We often do this with paragraphs giving prices, dates or other data involving figures.

5. *Underlining*—like indenting paragraphs, enables the mailer to put extra emphasis on key words or phrases. The more this device is used in a letter, the less effective it becomes.

6. *Asterisks*—In a long letter—a two- or three-page letter—you will probably come to a place where you want to change the mood or the subject or the tone of voice. You can signal the reader that you are going to do just that by breaking the copy at that point and inserting a few asterisks.

7. *Color*—Many mailers use a second color—red, for example—to point up headlines or subheads or key paragraphs in letters. Others hold that this tends to cheapen a letter and destroy the effect of personalization. It is a question of: Do I gain more than I lose? And it is a question every mailer has to answer for himself.

8. *Type*—Here is a tip some of you may find helpful: You probably know that typewriter type comes in a variety of sizes and styles. Pica type, for example, is bigger and more legible than Elite. If your letters are slanted to an older audience, you might find that you could increase returns by using the easier-to-read typeface, Pica.

9. *Signature*—Now we come to the signature. In a volume mailing, where the signature is reproduced by a line cut, many mailers will run that cut in black to save the cost of an extra color, say a blue that gives the impression that the letter was signed with a fountain pen. It seems to me that running the signature in black is a false economy—one that destroys any atmosphere of personalization that the rest of the letter may have built up. The cost of running the signature in blue is comparatively small—and it does a great deal to personalize a direct mail letter.

There is another advantage to running the signature in blue ink—at no extra cost you can "squiggle" important paragraphs—circle them or run hand-drawn lines down the sides. You can even misspell a word in your black plate and "correct" it on the blue plate—draw a line through it and spell it correctly. If you are using a blue plate for the signature you can also run a P.S. in facsimile handwriting.

Now a word about printing a letter on both sides of a single sheet, instead of using two sheets of paper. Of course, it costs half as much in paper to print on both sides of a single sheet—and many mailers have found that they get as good or just about as good returns when they print letters on both sides. Of course, if you have a product of high quality to sell, you should use paper of high quality and print two sheets rather than back-print one.

Letterheads

We come now to the letterhead. The first thing to remember here is that it costs no more to print a good design than it does a poor one. Simplicity of design is important in many operations—in selling a magazine of business life, *Fortune*, for example, or a newsletter service, or in fund-raising work. Particularly in writing about a charitable cause, it is a mistake to give the impression of spending too much money on printing. But a simple letterhead can still be a distinguished letterhead—striking and beautiful in its very simplicity. On the other hand, your product or company or market may require that you produce an atmosphere of richness. This gives you a chance to use engraved letterheads, expensive papers.

There are three sizes of letterheads commonly used by direct mail advertisers:

1. The first is called Monarch. It is 7½ by 11 inches. It goes in an envelope 8 by 3⅞ inches.

2. Then there's the 8½ x 11-inch sheet—the most commonly used of all. It goes in an envelope 8⅞ by 3⅞ inches—commonly called a No. 9 envelope.

3. Then there's the Baronial letterhead—a flexible size, generally square. Of course, this size calls for special envelopes.

There are also jumbo letterheads and miniature sizes. There are all kinds of trick letterheads—die-cuts, pop-ups, tip-ons, and special folds.

Here is the point to remember: If you write to the same list of people very often, it is good to vary every element in your mailing—including the size of the letterhead. If the first letter to a given group is 8½ by 11-inch in a No. 9 envelope, send the second letter Monarch. Then switch to Baronial. Then go back to your No. 9.

And this is probably as good a place as any to remind you that all direct mail letters do not have to go out on the usual piece of writing paper. We used notebook paper for a mailing to high school students.

I also recall that one of *Life Camps* most successful efforts was a piece of roofing paper that smelled powerfully of tar. Written across it was the message:

> Won't you please help us rescue one more youngster from the last of the dirty asphalt streets where he must play all summer long—unless your check arrives soon to help us send him to the green country of *Life Camps.*

The trend in direct mail today is toward using four-color letterheads—especially among magazine publishers, who like to sample the contents of a magazine on the letterhead, and often have some colorful contents to sample.

This is not to say that you cannot get some very pleasing effects using a single color on white stock or a single color on colored stocks. If your budget permits, you can also get a great deal of excitement out of two-color printing.

Envelopes

Envelopes are unhappily an often-neglected element in direct mail campaigns. We all know people who go to all sorts of trouble to dress themselves in their finest clothes, give a fresh coat of paint to the front of their house, and to put a modern look on their stores. Yet, when it comes to the envelopes in which they send their highly valuable sales messages, there seems to be a blind spot. They fail to realize that the envelope, like the suit of clothes, the fresh paint, or the store front, is the first thing seen. The envelope gives the prospect an immediate impression of our mailing—favorable or unfavorable.

Color, art, and design, the weight of the paper stock that you use—all are important in getting your envelope opened and your mail read.

So is teaser copy—although *Time* may have gone a little overboard in one instance. All the copy was on the envelope, which contained only a renewal order card.

Postage

All *Time, Money, Fortune* and *Sports Illustrated* mailings go third class, and I think you will find that most mailers are agreed that third-class postage is generally the best of them—first-class is reserved for those special classes where you want to make a prestige mailing or get increased speed of delivery. But if speed of delivery is essential to you, you might pay a little more and use airmail for its increased attention-getting values.

Should you use stamps, or postage-meter, or a printed postage permit?

Most mailers seldom use stamps—postage-meter costs less. And a printed postage permit, if it is attractively designed, is usually as good or slightly better than postage-meter. But it is well to note that postage-meter can be used to good advantage to give variety to a series of mailings to the same people.

Order Forms

Let us go on to the order form. It can make or break the sale. Here are four definite requirements for a well-executed order form.

1. The copy should be clear; the offer, if there is one, plainly stated.

2. If the name and address of the prospect are not already typed or stenciled on the form, there should be plenty of room for him to give you his name and address and any other needed information.

3. If the form is not business reply, you should make sure that the advertiser's name and address appear on the front, the back or both.

4. You should make the form look important.

A second color on the reply form adds very little to the cost and does improve returns. If you cannot run a second color, experiment with black on colored stocks.

Should all reply forms be set in type? There are very few cases where it does not pay to do so. A typeset form is easier to read, and it gives an impression of stability. If you are making a straight charge offer, your order form should have a business reply back—there is no point in enclosing a reply envelope. However, if you are making a cash offer, or a cash-charge offer, you will have to include a reply envelope.

Should it be stamped or business reply? A stamped return envelope in a sales letter will not usually increase returns. The recipient may even think that the organization is foolishly wasting its money. Exceptions: A stamped return envelope in a questionnaire mailing will usually increase your returns. A stamped return envelope in a charitable solicitation may increase your returns.

Should the business reply card or envelope use first-class or airmail postage? A few mailers have found that paying airmail reply postage increases their returns, but most mailers find that airmail reply just gets the orders back to them faster. General rule: if you have a perishable product, or a "for a limited time only" offer, it will probably pay you to use airmail reply on your business reply cards or envelopes. If you don't have such a product or offer, save your money—use first-class.

Circulars

Do circular and letter perform the same function, or do they have different jobs? Do you need both; can you leave one out—and when?

To begin at the beginning—a wise businessman knows that he cannot personally call on all his customers and prospects, so he hires salesmen. The salesmen find it impossible to make all the selling and goodwill-building calls needed, so the company writes letters. When quantity is involved, you call your letters "direct mail advertising." You still think of the letter as a substitute for a personal call. But you may be inclined to send other pieces of printed matter along with the letter.

When a salesman calls, he supplies the sell. But he often has with him some information about the product or perhaps some samples of it. So think of the letter as the salesman and the circular as his sample case.

Since the circular is the sample case, its job is not so much to sell as to provide the information the salesman needs to sell. It contains prices, specifications, pictures, background facts, case histories, and testimonials from satisfied users—all of which are ammunition for the salesman but will not make the sale without him. The circular is—or should be—too statistical, too technical, too general to stand on its own legs and convert a prospect into a customer. The circular may convince the head, but it takes the letter to reach the heart, where the sale is made. The letter, like the salesman, establishes the friendly bond, extends the hearty handshake, speaks in the cordial tone of voice.

So which is more important—the salesman or his sample case? Can you leave out the letter? Well, can you leave out the salesman?

How about leaving out the circular? Yes, you can in some cases, just as the salesman can sometimes go out without a sample case.

Here, specifically, are four cases where you can probably omit a circular:

When the product or service is well known.

When the cost is low.

When the product or service needs little explaining, no illustrating.

When a strong desire for the product already exists.

Conversely, you need a circular:

> When the product is not known, perhaps because it is a new product, perhaps because it is an old product entering a new market.
>
> When the cost is high.
>
> When it takes a lot of explaining or "has to be seen to be appreciated."

When desire has to be created or a real job of selling has to be done.

Also, when you cannot expect immediate action but want the prospect to have information about your product or service on hand.

If you decide that yours is a product or service that can be sold better with a letter and a circular than it can with a letter alone, here are a few rules for successful circulars.

1. The circular should have an impelling headline with reader benefits.
2. It should picture the product or service.
3. It should be easy to read.

   Type should be big and bold.

   Layout should lead the reader from page one to last page in logic sequence.

Special emphasis should be given to the most important paragraphs by setting them in italics or bold face or by indenting them.

4. There should be plenty of subheads.
5. You should be sure that you give all the information that is necessary for a prospect to make a decision and order the product.
6. You should make an order form part of the circular even though a separate order form is enclosed with the mailings.

FULFILLMENT

No direct mail campaign is complete until the advertiser has taken the action requested of him by those who respond to his mailings. This might seem to be so axiomatic it does not even deserve special consideration here. However, a large percentage of direct mail advertisers get so interested in the preparation of their mailings they completely overlook the fact that the real success of a campaign depends upon the fulfillment of requests and orders.

How completely neglected fulfillment can become is indicated by a study conducted by an advertising agency for Tension Envelope Corp. In its house magazine, *Envelope Economies,* Tension reported the results of this test, which involved answering every ad offering more information in three different magazines:

> This study reveals far too many firms neglect the prospect who has mailed an inquiry. Apparently neither Sales nor Advertising accepts full responsibility for turning these prospects into customers.
>
> Why does this condition exist? Apparently the inquiries are wanted. Every one of the 273 advertisements answered in this study contained an

invitation to write for more information. One out of three was couponed. Over one-third of the firms advertising in the three publications were mail order.

Yet it is evident that the mail inquiry is treated like an "orphan" by the majority of firms. Too many replies were characterized by unnecessary delays, incomplete information, lack of selling, poor coordination with local suppliers, and failure to tell how or where to buy.

One firm out of every nine completely ignored the inquiry! (Actually, the returns in this study were higher than those in many similar studies. It is not uncommon to find as many as 50% of companies contacted ignoring legitimate inquiries resulting from space advertising or publicity.) While seven out of ten answered the inquiry within two weeks, it is interesting to note that 25% of the advertisers took between two and four weeks to reply. Of the nonmail order advertisers, 75% didn't tell how or where to buy; 70% of the nonmail order firms made no followup; 14% of the mail order firms failed to enclose either an order blank or return envelope.

The firms studied in this survey spent thousands of dollars to make the first "call." How many made a return call to try to make their investment pay off? Not many. Most were content to spend their money, offer their goods or services, and then forget their investment. Only 15.2% of the nonmail order firms followed up with a second mailing. Only one out of 25 followed up more than once.

Surprisingly, the mail order firms did little better. Only 24.5% followed up with a second mailing. One out of nine followed up more than once.

While the study involved magazine ads as a starting point, personal experience has indicated that fulfillment of direct mail advertising is almost as bad.

How to Handle Inquiries

Direct mail programs which seek inquiries require an efficient program for making sure respondents get the information they ask for—and receive it promptly. As a starting point, it is worthwhile considering the eight "rules" for inquiry handling suggested by John Denler of the Allman Co., in *Industrial Marketing*:

1. Answer every inquiry.
2. Reply with a personal letter.
3. Answer each promptly.
4. Be friendly.
5. Reply fully and completely.
6. Watch spelling, punctuation, grammar, neatness.
7. Follow a workable system.
8. Start it all *today*.

Fulfillment of Mail Orders

Handling orders received through the mail is even more important than inquiry handling. In this case a customer has been created and he expects prompt and efficient service. This, however, is just the first essential.

For a mail order operation to be truly successful usually requires keeping and carefully cultivating that customer. Almost without exception, mail order operations at the best break even on the first order. But once a purchaser has made a purchase by mail, he becomes a better-than-average prospect for future business. And it is these repeat orders that yield the profit.

Chapter 4

BASIC APPLICATIONS OF DIRECT MAIL

WITHOUT QUESTION, direct mail is one of the most versatile tools available to the advertiser. It can be used to accomplish hundreds of different marketing and communications tasks. Two lists prepared by the Direct Mail/Marketing Association provide the best available guides to help the advertiser analyze how direct mail can best serve his needs.

Direct Mail Functions

The first DMMA guide is a list of the six basic functions of direct mail:

1. *Creating more effective personal sales contacts.* This includes direct mail advertising which creates a specific opportunity for salesmen to call by getting inquiries or leads for personal followup. It also means paving the way for salesmen by lessening resistance, arousing interest, educating and informing the prospect before intended sales calls, but without trying to get back an order or response from the prospect through the mail.

2. *Bringing the prospect to you.* This applies particularly to the retail field and to service businesses (like banks) which do not have sales forces. It has other applications, such as getting customers or prospects to visit new plants or special displays.

3. *Delivering background, sales, or public relations messages to customers, prospects, employees or other special groups.* This includes mailings that are designed as pure advertising. It also covers any prestige reminder or goodwill advertising, employee relations, or anything to influence selective groups along certain lines of thought or action, but without direct response being sought by mail or without any direct personal followup intended.

4. *Taking actual orders through the mail.* This function is direct mail selling or mail order selling, where every step in the sales process, from the initial contact to the final sale, is done exclusively by mail. This applies to publications, business, investment, and news services, as well as to selling merchandise by mail. It also applies to raising funds by charitable and educational organizations.

5. *Securing action from the prospect by mail.* This covers any promotion intended to secure response or action by mail, but not designed to secure an order or result in a personal contact between the prospect and the advertiser. Included in this category would be getting entries in a competition or securing requests for general information literature.
6. *Conducting research and market surveys.* This covers every phase of research, investigation, and fact-finding by mail.

49 Ways to Use Direct Mail

For many years, the basic checklist of direct mail uses has been DMMA's "49 ways" chart. While many committees have sought to expand this list, nobody has yet come up with a more efficient checklist. DMMA suggests you use this list to analyze your own direct mail program in three steps:

A. Checking the ways you are *now* using direct mail.

B. Marking the ways you are *not* now using direct mail but which could be profitable possibilities.

C. Doublechecking those direct mail applications you are now using that could be altered, improved, or increased —for greater results, effectiveness, efficiency.

In Your Own Organization

1. *Building Morale of Employees*—A bulletin or house magazine published regularly, carrying announcements of company policy, stimulating ambition, encouraging thrift, promoting safety and efficiency, will make for greater loyalty among employees.

2. *Securing Data From Employees*—Letters or questionnaires occasionally directed to employees help cement a common interest in the organization and bring back practical ideas and much useful data.

3. *Stimulating Salesmen to Greater Efforts*—Interesting sales magazines, bulletins, or letters help in unifying a scattered selling organization, in speeding up sales, and in making better salesmen—by carrying success stories and sound ideas that have made sales.

4. *Paving the Way for Salesmen*—Forceful and intelligent direct mail, persistent and continuous, will create a field of prospective buyers who are live and ready to be sold.

5. *Securing Inquiries for Salesmen*—Direct Mail can bring back actual inquiries from interested prospective customers . . . qualified prospects your men can call upon and sell.

6. *Teaching Salesmen "How to Sell"*—A sales manual, or a series of messages, will help educate and stimulate salesmen to close more and bigger sales.

7. *Selling Stockholders and Others Interested in Your Company*—Enclosures with dividend checks and in pay envelopes, and other direct messages, will sell stockholders and employees on making a greater use of company products and services, and in suggesting their use to others.

8. *Keeping Contact With Customers Between Salesmen's Calls*—Messages to customers between salesmen's visits will help secure for your firm the maximum amount of business from each customer.

9. *Further Selling Prospective Customers After a Demonstration or Salesman's Call*—Direct mail emphasizing the superiorities of your product or service will help clinch sales and make it difficult for competition to gain a foothold.

10. *Acknowledging Orders or Payments*—An interesting letter, folder, or mailing card is a simple gesture which will cement a closer friendship between you and your customers.

11. *Welcoming New Customers*—A letter welcoming new customers can go a long way toward keeping them sold on your company, products and services.

12. *Collecting Accounts*—A series of diplomatic collection letters will bring and keep accounts up-to-date, leave the recipients in a friendly frame of mind, and hold them as customers.

Building New Business

13. *Securing New Dealers*—Direct mail offers many concerns unlimited possibilities in lining up and selling new dealers.

14. *Securing Direct Orders*—Many organizations have built extremely profitable business through orders secured only with the help of direct mail. Many concerns not presently selling direct by mail can and should do so.

15. *Building Weak Territories*—Direct mail will provide intensified local sales stimulation wherever you may wish to apply it.

16. *Winning Back Inactive Customers*—A series of direct mail messages to "lost" customers often revives many of them.

17. *Developing Sales in Areas Not Covered by Salesmen*—Communities unapproachable because of distance, bad transportation schedules, or poor roads, offer the alert organization vast possibilities to increase its sales direct-by-mail.

18. *Developing Sales Among Specified Groups*—With direct mail you can direct your selling messages specifically to those you wish to sell, in the language they will understand, and in a form that will stimulate action.

19. *Following Inquiries Received From Direct Advertising or Other Forms of Advertising*—A series of messages outlining the "reasons why" your product or service should be bought, will help you cash in on inquirers whose initial interest was aroused by other media—publications, radio, television, etc.

20. *Driving Home Sales Arguments*—Several mailings, each planned to stress one or more selling points, will progressively educate your prospective customer on the many reasons why he should buy your product or service . . . and from you.

21. *Selling Other Items in Line*—Mailing pieces, package inserts or "hand-out" folders will educate your customers on products and services other than those they are buying.

22. *Getting Product Prescribed or Specified*—Professional men, such as physicians and dentists, will prescribe a product for their patients if they are correctly educated on its merits and what it will accomplish. Likewise, consumers and dealers will ask for a product by name if they are thoroughly familiar with it. Direct advertising can be profitably used for this purpose.

23. *Selling New Type of Buyer*—Perhaps there are new outlets through which your product or service might be sold. Direct mail is a powerful tool in the development of new sales channels.

Assisting Present Dealers

24. *Bringing Buyer to Showroom*—Invitations through letter or printed announcements will bring prospective customers to your showroom or factory.

25. *Helping Present Dealer Sell More*—Assisting your dealer with direct mail and "point-of-purchase" helps will sell your product or service faster, step up turnover. The right kind of dealer helps will win his hearty cooperation.

26. *Merchandising Your Plans to Dealer*—Direct mail can forcefully present and explain your merchandising plans to the dealer . . . and show him how to put your promotion ideas and material to work as sales-builders.

27. *Educating Dealers on Superiorities of Your Product or Service*—Memories are short when it comes to remembering the other fellow's product or service and its superiorities, especially

when you keep telling your dealers the benefits and advantages of your own.

28. *Educating Retail Clerks in the Selling of a Product*—Clerks are the neck of the retail selling bottle. If they believe in a company and a product their influence is a powerful aid to sales. If indifferent, they lose their sales-making effectiveness. Direct mail that is friendly, understanding, helpful, and stimulating will enlist their cooperation and up the sales curve.

29. *Securing Information From Dealers or Dealers' Clerks*—Letters, printed messages, a bulletin, or a house magazine will bring back helpful data from the individuals who actually sell your product or your service . . . information you can pass along to other dealers or sales clerks to help them sell more.

30. *Referring Inquiries From Consumer Advertising to Local Dealers*—The manufacturer can use direct mail to refer an inquirer to his local dealer for prompt attention. At the same time, the dealer can be alerted with the details of the prospect's inquiry.

The Consumer

31. *Creating a Need or a Demand for a Product*—Direct mail, consistently used, will stimulate the demand for your product or service, and will remind the customer to ask for it by name.

32. *Increasing Consumption of a Product Among Present Users*—Package inserts, booklets, etc., can be used to educate customers to the full use of the products they buy, especially new benefits and advantages.

33. *Bringing Customers Into a Store to Buy*—This applies to retailers. Personal, friendly, cordial, and interesting direct mail messages, telling about the merchandise you have, and creating the desire to own that merchandise, will bring back *past* customers, stimulate *present* patrons, and lure *new* people for you.

34. *Opening New Charge Accounts*—This also applies to retailers. There are many people in every community who pay their bills promptly and do the bulk of their buying where they have accounts. A careful compilation of such a list and a well-planned direct mail program inviting them to open charge accounts will bring new customers to your store.

35. *Capitalizing on Special Events*—Direct mail helps retailers to capitalize on such events as marriages, births, graduations, promotions, etc. Likewise, letters can be sent to select

lists featuring private sales. Other lists and format can cover general sales.

Other Uses

36. *Building Goodwill*—The possibilities of building goodwill and solidifying friendships through direct advertising are unlimited. It's the little handshake through the mail that cements business relationships and holds your customers. Certain "reminder" forms also can help build goodwill.

37. *Capitalizing on Other Advertising*—Direct advertising is the salesmate of all other media. As the "workhorse" among advertising and promotion mediums, it helps the sponsor capitalize on his investment in all visual and audio advertising—especially when initial interest can be given a lift and converted into action and sales.

38. *As a "Leader" or "Hook" in Other Forms of Advertising*—Publication space, as well as radio and television commercials, is often too limited to tell enough of the story about a product or service to make a sale. Direct mail provides the "leader" or "hook"—in the form of booklets, folders, catalogs, instruction manuals—that other mediums of advertising can feature, to stimulate action as well as to satisfy the inquirer with full story of product and service.

39. *Breaking Down Resistance to a Product or a Service*—Direct mail helps to overcome resistance in the minds of prospective customers.

40. *Stimulating Interest in Forthcoming Events*—A special "week" or "day" devoted to the greater use of a product; an anniversary, a new line launched by a dealer, special "openings," and scores of other happenings—can all be promoted by direct mail to produce sales.

41. *Distribution of Samples*—There are thousands of logical prospects who could be converted into users of your product if you proved to them its merits. Direct mail can help you do this by letting prospects convince themselves by actual test . . . provided your product lends itself to sampling by mail.

42. *Announcing a New Product, New Policy or New Addition*—There is no quicker way to make announcements to specific individuals or groups, to create interest and stimulate sales, than through the personal, action-producing medium—direct mail.

43. *Announcing a New Address or Change in Telephone Number*—When these important changes are made, a letter or printed announcement sent through the mail has a personal appeal that will register your message better than any other form of advertising.

44. *Keeping a Concern or Product "in Mind"*—Direct advertising includes many forms of "reminder" advertising—blotters, calendars, novelties. Regular mailings help keep you in the minds of customers and prospects.

45. *Research for New Ideas and Suggestions*—Direct advertising research is a powerful force in building sales. Direct mail can be used to find market facts, cut sales fumbling, chart direct, profitable trails to sales. It furnishes all the important tools for sales research, to discover what, where, how, and to whom to sell . . . and at what price.

46. *Correcting Present Mailing Lists*—Householders have an average annual change of 22% . . . merchants of 23% . . . agents of 29% . . . advertising men of 37%. Keeping a mailing list up-to-date is a most important detail. Direct mail can be employed to keep your list accurate, by occasionally asking your customer if his name and address are correct . . . or if there are others in his organization you should be reaching.

47. *Securing Names for Lists*—Direct mail can help you build mailing lists by securing names of customers and prospects from many sources—such as direct from distributors, salesmen, clerks, stockholders, employees; from people who have access to the names of individuals in specific groups; from recommendation of customers and friends; from special mail surveys, questionnaires; etc.

48. *Protecting Patents or Special Processes*—Shouting forth the ownership of such patents or processes by direct advertising can leave no question in the minds of your customers . . . present or prospective . . . as to who owns such a product or process. At the same time, it gives you greater protection from possible infringers.

49. *Raising Funds*—Direct advertising affords an effective, economical method of raising funds for worthy causes.

Chapter 5

SOME BASIC GUIDELINES FOR EFFECTIVE DIRECT MAIL

ONE OF THE MOST wonderful things about the people in direct mail is their willingness to share their experiences with others. Many of the brightest and wisest minds in the field have gone out of their way to unselfishly devote a great deal of time and effort to help others make the most effective use of the direct mail medium. Throughout this Handbook, you will find a digest of much of this shared wisdom, thanks to the willingness of so many experts to address public audiences, write informative articles, and engage in informal conversation on the subject of direct mail.

One of the problems, of course, is that this openness has made available so much excellent reference material that it is difficult to know just where to start when you're taking your first serious look at the direct mail medium. To make the task a bit easier, here's a bit of distilled wisdom from three of the most able direct mail experts plus a list of ten basic disciplines for more effective direct mail which have been constructed out of the collective advice of hundreds of others and originally presented by the author at a workshop session of the Direct Mail Advertising Association.

Seven Rules for Success

The combined wisdom of two outstanding experts—Edward N. Mayer, Jr. and Robert Stone—was originally published as a column by Bob Stone in the February 17, 1969 issue of *Advertising Age*.[1] While Bob Stone has given the title "Mr. Direct Mail" to Ed Mayer—(an honor which has the strongest endorsement of this author), Bob Stone, himself, deserves similar credit. His books, *Advertising Age* columns, articles and many speeches

[1]Copyright 1969 by *Advertising Age.* Reprinted by permission.

have imparted a great deal of helpful advice to thousands. Thus, the combination of Ed Mayer and Bob Stone makes an excellent starting point for considering how to create the most effective direct mail.

Bob Stone's Tribute to Ed Mayer

Today Ed Mayer* conducts beginner and advanced direct mail courses several times a year under the auspices of the Direct Mail/Marketing Association. These courses are open to those now actively engaged in advertising.

But his greatest joy comes from his stewardship of the Lewis Kleid Institute, a nonprofit organization devoted to teaching the basics of direct mail advertising and selling to outstanding marketing students from colleges across the nation. Selected students participate in an intensive course of study which runs several days. A number of these graduates are already actively engaged in direct mail with major companies. These students, without a question of a doubt, represent the real future of direct mail advertising and selling.

In his many years of active participation in the direct mail medium, Ed Mayer has evolved basic rules which will stand the test of time. He refers to these as "The Seven Cardinal Rules for Direct Mail Success." In this chapter I would like to review his rules as principles and point out the applications for each.

1. *What is the objective?* This is a vital principle, one so obvious that it is often overlooked. It's everyone's objective to get more inquiries or more sales, but such objectives are much too broad. Do you want more inquiries, or is your objective to get inquiries which will convert to a higher percentage of sales? Is your objective to get more sales, or is it really to get more profitable sales?

Is your objective really to get more initial sales which will convert to a higher percentage of repeat sales? Is your objective to get back investment in sales immediately, over a period of 12 months, 24 months or what? No direct mail program can be successful unless objectives are clearly defined.

2. *Address correctly to the right list.* No principle is more important than reaching the right person on the right list. What is the profile of your prospect or customer list? What lists match this profile? What is your response by Zip Code areas, by census tracts? What is the duplication of names between the rented lists you are using? What's the duplication between rented names and

*Deceased

your house list? What is the repeat business factor for each list you use? What is the bad debt factor for each list you use? Can you get better results by addressing to titles rather than individuals? Reaching the right person at the right time always has been, and always will be, a prime key to success.

3. *Write your copy to show what the product or service offered does for the reader.*

This principle relates to the importance of benefit copy, which offers benefits to the reader. It emphasizes the *you* attitude. Ed Mayer is a strong advocate of benefit copy which follows a route, starting with the most important benefit *to the reader* in the headline or first paragraph. He likewise approves of complete copywriting formulas, such as the following:

- Promise a benefit in the headline or first paragraph, your most important benefit to the reader.
- Immediately enlarge upon your most important benefit.
- Tell the reader specifically what he is going to get.
- Back up your statements with proofs and endorsements.
- Tell the reader what he might lose if he doesn't act.
- Rephrase your prominent benefits in your closing offer.
- Incite action now.

4. *Make the layout and copy fit.* What an important principle this is. Ed's referring to the importance of keeping mailings in character with the market and the offer. You use one type of direct mail to high school dropouts and quite another type to educators. Your layouts and graphics should be quite different in presenting a big ticket item in comparison to a low-cost gadget. Your copy can be more flamboyant when announcing a sale than it should be in a serious fund raising effort. Making layouts and copy fit markets and offers can make the difference between success and failure.

5. *Make it easy for the prospect to take whatever action you want him to take.* As Ed Mayer so aptly put it, "Direct mail is the action medium." Every mailing should call for an action of some type: Inquiry, purchase, referral, contribution, phone call, visit to a local dealer—an action that the mailer wants the prospect to take. You can incite action through the appeal of the offer or through the device for responding.

The appeal of the offer is of first importance. Some of the offers which overcome the barriers of human inertia and make it easy for

"The Heiress."
Here you see how useful and well-organized she is.
Soon you'll see that she's a beauty, too.
only $6.95
30 day
MONEY BACK
TRIAL OFFER
A message from Joy Hall

Dear Friend,

When I designed the Heiress (you can see only part of it above) I had three things in mind:

1. I wanted the Heiress to be the most useful accessory that any woman could own.

2. I wanted it to be beautiful, with that classic simplicity that marks so much of the best fashion design.

3. And I wanted it to sell for a stunningly low price.

Well, even my husband Murray--he's president of Ambassador Leather Goods--thinks I've succeeded. And Murray isn't a man who gives out compliments easily.

(over, please)

This classic direct mail piece is a six-page combination letter-brochure. The first page shown above does a good job of providing the basic story, complete with a photo of Joy Hall, co-owner with her husband of the successful Ambassador Leather Goods of Tempe, Arizona. Three full-size/full-color illustrations of the product in use are included inside the letter. All copy is in letter format.

the prospect to take action are free information, free trial offer, free gift for action, sweepstakes contests, money back guarantee, instalment terms.

Devices for responding are likewise an inducement to action. Direct mail, because of its very nature, is made to order for responding devices. It's easy for the prospect to respond if you give him a pre-addressed stamped reply envelope or card, or a postage free envelope or card. All other media require more effort to take action.

6. *Tell your story over again.* Ed Mayer maintains, and he's absolutely right, that most mailers don't mail often enough. In many lines of business that employ salesmen, it is found most sales are completed after the fifth call. And yet scores of people tried direct mail once, didn't get dramatic results and quit.

Consider the many successful companies which mail an informative house organ to a choice list month in and month out, and still others who mail newsletters, promotion pieces and bulletins to their lists at regular frequency every year. Then there are the astute professional mail order people who have learned you can mail the same successful piece to hot lists three and four times in a calendar year. And many of these same successful practitioners will mail to their active customers lists 12 times a year and more! Tell your story over again and again.

7. *Research your direct mail.* Ed Mayer admonishes, "Make your good packages better. Keep testing." As Ed puts it, keep trying to beat your best. Test all the time. Never stop. But make sure you test the big things, not the trivia. Test the products or services you provide, the offers you make, the copy you write, the lists you use and the timing of mailings.

Seven cardinal direct mail rules are principles to work by, live by, succeed by. The Ed Mayer principles have been the guiding light for untold numbers of today's successful practitioners. And these very same principles are nurturing the bright college students of today who will be the successful direct mail practitioners of tomorrow.

So let this be a salute to Edward N. Mayer Jr., a man who has rightly received every recognition an advertising medium can bestow, but who has to this very day always given back more than he has received. And perhaps this is the most important Ed Mayer principle of all!

Seven Deadly Direct Mail Mistakes

If Ed Mayer is "Mr. Direct Mail I" and Bob Stone is "Mr. Direct Mail II," then the title "Mr. Mail Order" must be reserved for Maxwell Sackheim. Even though he "retired" to Clearwater, Florida in 1960, Max Sackheim continues to share his immense knowledge of mail order selling techniques with others. His outstanding book, *My First Sixty Years in Advertising,*[2] is filled with excellent advice, including his "Seven Deadly Direct Mail Mistakes." This excellent set of guidelines was first published as a booklet by the Maxwell Sackheim Advertising Agency. In the introduction, Max Sackheim said:

> Most direct mail advertising calls for some sort of response. To be effective, therefore, it must be opened, read, believed and acted upon. But even if a direct reply is not desired, direct mail advertising should attract, interest and convince or it is wasted.
>
> By eliminating one or several of the Seven Deadly Direct Mail Mistakes described here, your efforts will surely improve, whether you are selling goods, services or ideas, by mail, through stores or through other channels.

Deadly Mistake No. 1—Give the Prospect a Good Reason for Not Opening Your Mailing. The surest way to ruin a mailing is to give the prospect a good reason for not even opening the envelope! This can be done in a number of ways.

One is to tell so much on the envelope that the reader "knows" he doesn't want what you're offering inside.

Still another is to be so smart, so clever, or so unbelievable as a result of whatever you print on the envelope that the recipient subconsciously says "Nuts," "Baloney" or worse, "More Junk Mail."

Rather than risk the danger of printing anything on the envelope which might give anyone a good excuse for throwing it away unopened, use a blank envelope.

Even this might be a dead give-away to some sophisticated prospects. It is better by far to use the envelope as a vehicle for carrying a message in words or pictures which might be strong enough to be used as the headline of an advertisement.

Such a headline should convey news—a promise of information—a promise of an advantage to the reader, a promise of such importance that the reader cannot afford to deny the mailing at least an opening.

If you can't say anything on the outside of the envelope that will be of genuine interest to the reader, say nothing.

2*My First Sixty Years in Advertising* by Maxwell Sackheim. Prentice-Hall, Inc., Englewood Cliffs, N. J. Copyright 1970.

Deadly Mistake No. 2—Give the Reader a Reason for Not Reading Your Mailing. Having induced the reader to open your mail, even if only by giving him no reason for not doing so, you are faced with the possibility of his discarding it unless his interest is held.

It is not enough to give him no reason for throwing your mailing away—you must definitely give him a reason for holding onto it and reading it!

You can accomplish this only by promising an adequate reward for his time and attention.

He must be promised *news* of interest to him. He must be offered a *cure* for whatever *symptom* he "suffers" from or can be "made" to suffer from!

Examine any mailing carefully. Take it out of the envelope just as any recipient would. What's the first thing you see? What's your quick impression? Is someone trying to sell you something? Is it likely to cost you money or will it do something for you? Are you being "sold" or invited to buy? What are all the enclosures about? Do they clutter the mailing up or make it look more interesting? Is the letterhead too revealing? uninteresting? too dull to invite a reading of your letter? Does the salutation promise you an adequate reward? Does the processing defeat the purpose intended? Is the offer attractive enough to deserve "top billing" or should it be "buried"?

Beware of the "so what" reaction. Indifference is normal. Only by shocking the reader, startling him, waking him up, can you gain the attention that will induce a reading of your mailing.

You know the fundamental urges which motivate people—the desire for love, beauty, wealth, leisure, approbation, health and so on. Among these you must find or create the symptom which your product or service cures. The more common the symptom, the wider your market.

If your mailing does not offer a "cure" you have given the recipient an excellent reason for not reading it.

Deadly Mistake No. 3—Make Trivial Tests. Too many direct mail people are addicted to the insidious habit of overtesting. So serious is this disease that, where it exists in its most pernicious form, the unsuspecting victim loses his ability to think for himself to judge, to make decisions, to act. His muscles of courage become atrophied and his power of discrimination calcifies. He believes the easy way out of any selling problem is to test. Why think when it is so easy to get the correct answer by mailing a couple of thousand?

But—is testing the key to personal success, or may it not, like fire, be a good thing only if there isn't too much of it?

If every test could safely be projected, much of the fallacy of testing would be eliminated. But we know how much difference there can be between the result of a test and the result of mailing.

Too many things can happen in these fast-moving times to destroy the logical or mathematical projection of a test. Within the span of a season, a month, or even a week, marked economic, competitive, or psychological changes can take place, and when they do, "blooie" go your expectations. And the element of elapsed time is only one of the dangers.

I have known of campaigns based on the result of a 200 test mailing—of weighty decisions arrived at by virtue of an infinitesimal difference in results between the use of stamps instead of metered mail, between colored envelopes and white, between No. 10 envelopes and No. 6.

One would think, after so many years of recorded experience, we would have learned that tests do not always tell the whole truth—that we will never completely formularize direct mail as long as there are changes in the weather, in world conditions, in domestic affairs, and even in local conditions from month to month and from week to week—that we will never be able to project a test with absolute assurance that the final result will be true to our original projection as long as an interval of time elapses between tests and mailings.

I am not arguing against testing, but against trivial testing. I object to tests which try to determine the best day of the week on which to mail; to tests which are intended to prove whether a price of $1.98 is better than $1.99; to tests of half a dozen or more slightly different letters; and to tests of 500, or even 1000 to determine whether a proposition or a list is worth going ahead with on a large scale.

Tests that tell you nothing or actually mislead you are worse than none.

Deadly Mistake No. 4—Make Sales, Not Customers. The difference between profit and loss in almost any business is the difference between creating a customer and merely making a sale. The one-time buyer can be a liability instead of an asset because of the selling and other costs involved in putting him on your books. A customer is someone you can afford to lose money to get. How much you can afford to lose depends on how many repeat sales you expect to make, how soon you make them, and your margin of profit on each. If you want to go broke selling direct by mail, make sales, not customers.

The best way to get new customers is to make offers your prospects can't resist. Bring them into your "store" with special sales, special bargains, special deals. Once in, they'll buy more than enough to offset the cost of getting them in. Cleverness, smart talk, wonderful logic, can only go so far. No matter how you juggle words, the order blank spells out what you are offering.

Another way to get new customers is to spend more time and thought on ex-customers. They dealt with you before and know you. If you mistreated them, confess your "crime," and beg forgiveness. If your values weren't as good as they are now, tell them why. Don't give up too easily on those names. You rent them to others—how come they can make them pay? What have you done to have driven them away from you? Find out, if you can and bring them back on your active list.

Finally, establish your acceptable percentage of returns on the basis of making customers, not sales. It's the sound way, the only way to build a successful business.

Deadly Mistake No. 5—People Won't Read Long Letters. The whole question is, what is a long letter? Any letter that is uninteresting is a long letter! Even a short letter can seem long! Indeed, a short paragraph can seem long; and a short first sentence can make the rest of the letter unnecessary if it doesn't say and mean something worthwhile to the reader.

Revising the old cliché—it isn't how you say it but what you say that makes the difference between a successful letter and a failure. The slickest writing, the finest paper, printing and art work, can't make a good idea out of a bad one or an attractive offer out of a poor one.

Give me the right merchandise, the right price, and the right audience and if I have enough to say I will make ten pages of typewritten copy pay better than one, two or three. On the contrary, with nothing much to work on, and nothing much to say, a single page might seem longer than ten pages of interesting material.

Don't be afraid to use many paragraphs, many pages, if you need lots of space in which to tell your story. It's far better to do a complete selling job on 2% than a half-selling job on 10%. If anything, most letters are too short because of the fear of making them too long.

Don't believe "people won't read long letters." People read long books, take long trips, watch long movies and plays, and read long letters provided they justify the time. They must be interesting. They must promise a profit, in entertainment, in money, in enlightenment.

Letters are long only when they seem long; when they are deadly dull, obviously selfish; when they are written to sell, not to serve.

Deadly Mistake No. 6—Let the Lists Go to the Last. Direct mail is a bull's-eye medium. Its very reason for existence rests on its ability to select the prospect or customer and aim a silver bullet with your story.

The reason many mailings fail is that they are directed to too many wrong people. Wrong people can be people who have moved, died, or who never in the world could afford or want your product.

The "right people" start with your own list—and it behooves you to keep that list clean. Whether active customers, inactives or old prospects, there is no waste quite comparable to waste on your own list. Next come the lists of mail-order buyers of related products. After that, mail-order buyers of unrelated products who have purchased through a plan similar to yours, i.e.: open account; C.O.D.; cash in advance; time payment, etc. Finally, compiled lists, preferably by logical occupations or classifications; doctors, lawyers, engineers, clergymen, automobile owners.

If you can't spend the necessary time to find the right kind of lists for you, or if you just don't trust yourself, consult a reliable list broker as you would a doctor or an attorney.

The selection of lists is so vital a part of direct mail that to give it less than the most serious thought and analysis is to commit one of the biggest Direct Mail mistakes possible! For nothing can take the place of the right marketplace!

Deadly Mistake No. 7—Forget That Your Letters Are You. Every letter you write is YOU. Every letter you send is your personality on paper. Whether you mail one or a million, each letter tells what YOU are.

When writing to a prospect, transform yourself into a prospect. Write yourself a letter. Begin where your thoughts are—on yourself, your home, your loved ones, your symptoms. Find a point of contact. Despite the many times you have been warned to think of your prospect and his problems first, and yours second, too many mailings still ooze with selfishness. Let your credo be "I want to serve you"—not "I want to sell you." Take your customers and prospects into your confidence. Make them your friends. They'll

The Inaugural Committee

has the honor to announce

the Official 1973

Presidential Inaugural Medal

and the first Official

Presidential Inaugural Plate

in the history of the

United States

An invitation has long been one of the favorite formats for mail order advertisers. *This is the cover for a 10½ by 15½ inch folder mailed by The Franklin Mint to present Official Presidential Inaugural Medals and Plates to collectors. Inside were actual size, full-color reproductions of the medals and plate.*

listen to you, will read your literature, if you make it inviting, interesting, entertaining. The moment your letters get draggy or braggy, stop. But no matter how many pages you write, if they're interesting, keep writing. You know the difference between service and self-interest. Put that into words.

If every letter you mail is YOU, it should have its face washed, hair combed, shoes shined, trousers pressed. It should command respect, earn a hearing, and deserve consideration.

You wouldn't call on a prospect dressed like a Bowery bum. Nor should you come dressed in white tie and tails. Just be yourself!

TEN DISCIPLINES FOR MORE EFFECTIVE DIRECT MAIL

The following basic guidelines were originally prepared by the author for presentation at a workshop meeting of the Direct Mail /Marketing Association. They were introduced with the following comments:

To those who have always thought of direct mail as an area ideal for unbridled creativity, the introduction of the word, "discipline," might come as somewhat of a jarring shock. However, as I analyzed how I might best address myself to the subject of getting maximum value from direct mail advertising, I became increasingly aware that not only was there no important conflict between the terms "creativity" and "discipline," but that they must really work hand-in-hand for maximum effectiveness in direct mail.

Let's stop right here, however, to understand one another on the type of discipline I'm attempting to introduce into our dialogue. I do not, for a single minute, want to imply the military discipline of conformity. Instead, the discipline of direct mail is one of providing a systems of checks and balances which prevent unbridled creativity from leading us down paths which have dead ends and thus prevent us from reaching the objectives we seek.

There are 10 essential disciplines which a direct mail creator must observe if he is to get maximum effectiveness from his mailings. Let's explore these one by one. I'm sure you will find many of them an already-established part of your everyday routines. However, even if you regularly observe all 10 of them, it might be meaningful to consider their interrelationships and applications.

Discipline No. 1

Discipline No. 1 is what I call the *"You Discipline."* We talk a great deal about a *you* orientation of letters, but this same basic philosophy can be applied to all direct mail pieces. The key question to ask yourself is "What does the recipient really want to know?" It really isn't important what *you* want to *tell* him, although I know this is a pretty hard philosophy to sell to many managements.

I'm afraid we all have a tendency to want to talk to ourselves. All too often, we imagine ourselves as a typical customer or prospect—and nothing could be further from the truth. And we have a tendency to take the easy way out—to use the language, illustrations and approaches which have proved most likely to clear through the management channels with the least discussion or argument.

This is the coward's way of producing sales promotion materials, although I must confess I am frequently tempted to be this kind of coward. But it isn't the way to produce truly effective printed pieces.

To do the most effective job, you must observe the "you discipline."

Perhaps some of you can benefit from a simple little technique I've developed for preparing copy for direct mail letters to be signed by a number of different salesmen. I'm a strong believer in the use of automatically typewritten letters, but creating copy which sounds natural when sent to a lot of different customers and prospects and signed by as many as 100 or more different salesmen is a challenging job.

My technique is to pick a list of 20 businessmen I know personally—people who represent a typical cross-section of the customers and prospects being contacted by the salesmen. Then when I start to prepare copy, I write the letter to one of the people I know personally. Next, I substitute the name of another person from my personal list and see if the copy "fits" . . . then another name, and so on. If the first approach doesn't pan out when addressed to the selected individuals, I start all over writing the letter to still another person on my list . . . trying it on other names . . . and keeping it up until I feel I have a letter which will ring true when sent to the entire list.

It's a simple technique . . . and it has proved quite successful. But there's an important caution to be observed—resist the temptation to simply edit your first copy to fit the list. It seldom works. I've had to learn the hard way that if I'm to make this system work, I must start all over each time I address myself to a new individual.

Give it a try sometime. I'm pretty sure you'll find it a help . . . and not just for direct mail letters. You'll probably find yourself preparing more effective printed promotion material of all kinds if you aim them at a known audience—but not the one you probably know best, your management.

Discipline No. 2

Let's move now from the You Discipline to Discipline No. 2—what I call the *"Package Discipline."* Don't let a single element in a "package" get out of character. This requires constant alertness, but can pay maximum dividends.

Perhaps some examples would make my suggestion more clear.

You should, for example, avoid letting some of the elements of a promotional package wait until the last minute. You may then find yourself out of time or out of budget. I can't begin to count the many fine direct mail pieces that have come limping into my office in an inappropriate mailing container and carrying a poorly addressed label. And each one has failed to achieve its intended impact because the planner stopped planning before his job was done.

But how about some other examples . . . such as those economy minded promotion men who just can't stand to dispose of old promotion material which was created to serve some long-forgotten sales emergency and now is added to mailing packages just because it's "on hand." It may impress the budget director, but detract from the selling that needs to be done.

I well remember one classic which came across my desk awhile back. One of the primary selling points was how this company had been able to hold down its prices, while competitive lines were bending under to the pressures of inflation. The only problem was that all of the prices had been blocked out—a bit too transparently—and new, higher prices imprinted.

Most cases aren't that bad . . . but never let a dust-laden inventory of anything prevent you from applying the "Package Discipline"—and asking yourself if there's any element in your kit which diminishes the total impression you're trying to create.

Discipline No. 3

Discipline Number Three is what I call the *"Audience Discipline."* This is first cousin of the "You Discipline" I mentioned earlier, but needs emphasis for I'm sure each of us can plead guilty to this promotional sin. Direct mail material should be tailored to *each* sales audience.

In a collection of home-building material I sent for recently were dozens of pieces obviously prepared for architects, builders and suppliers—and not even remotely of interest to a home buyer . . . even though all of my requests were prompted by offers of literature in consumer magazines. In fact, two firms even sent only their dealer promotion material catalogs giving me a good sales pitch on what materials to use to convince "my customers" to specify their products—and no details about the products themselves.

Admittedly, this is an extreme example. But there has been a growing tendency to try to make a single piece serve a multitude of different audiences, when many of these audiences have few common interests.

Discipline No. 4

Now, let's consider a fourth discipline—the *"Theme Discipline."* By this I mean the desirability of establishing a central theme for each promotion program—and then sticking with it.

I'm sure we've all heard the old advertising philosophy that when you are sick and tired of a promotional theme, your customers and prospects are just beginning to notice it. There's more truth than fiction in this age-old observation, and it deserves to be repeated again and again.

There's plenty of opportunity to get added mileage from your promotional dollars when you can build continuity into a program and create more solid impressions by constantly adding emphasis to a central sales theme.

Of course, there's more fun in trying something new . . . and exploring unbeaten paths. But the real challenge is to keep a good idea alive and develop new ways to tell an old story.

Discipline No. 5

Next is the *"Personality Discipline"*—making sure that every printed piece properly reflects your company's personality. Just as you can't afford to let an element of a direct mail package destroy the total effect that package is trying to create, you should constantly be on guard to make sure that each package helps establish and maintain the personality your company seeks to convey.

Have the courage to say "no" when someone insists that a sales emergency calls for a quick and cheap promotion—unless that is the image you've chosen to establish for your company. One badly done piece can completely undermine years of superb promotion effort just as an inferior product or faulty service can destroy years of confidence-building with good customers.

Discipline No. 6

This is the *"Value Analysis Discipline."* I know many of you have used this term in describing your manufacturing procedures, but it is just as important in developing effective direct mail materials.

We're constantly exposed to the printing buyer who wants to cut corners in certain areas while he devotes a major portion of his budget to his pet elements. All too often we find those who may choose top quality printing, an excellent sheet of paper and go first class 90% of the way . . . and then furnish outdated or poorly exposed color transparencies for copy. Or it may be just the other way around, with thousands of dollars and months of effort put into developing beautifully designed and written copy and then turning the whole package over to a purchasing man whose only joy in life comes from shaving a few dollars off the production bill by insisting on a less than adequate printing process or a paper stock which can't begin to provide the quality of reproduction so lovingly contemplated by the writer, designer and photographer.

Here's an area for real exercise of discipline. And it's also an area where a top-flight printing counselor should be your constant companion in every phase of planning and production. Before you spend a nickel on any element of production, be sure to carefully establish a budget level—and then adjust everything that will go into the eventual printed piece to parallel this level. Frequently it is only a simple matter of shifting a few dollars or a few hours of effort from one production area to another to achieve 100% greater effectiveness in the end result.

Discipline No. 7

The *"Follow-Through Discipline"* has been stressed time and again, but it remains the greatest wilderness in many direct mail programs.

Yet the fact remains that no promotional effort can be any better than the execution of follow-through by those who must take the next steps leading to the eventual sale. It doesn't do any good to gripe to your fellow promotion man about the failure of salesmen, distributors and dealers to execute their planned role in a coordinated marketing plan. You can have the most beautiful printed promotion material ever conceived . . . win dozens of awards for your creativity . . . draw inquiries by the thousands . . . and yet be a complete failure as a promotion expert if there's no follow-through which results in sales.

And we can't blame our supporting casts if the follow-through isn't what we planned. Chances are the fault is with our planning!

Discipline No. 8

The eighth discipline is what I call the *"Tie-In Discipline."* This calls for a constant search for opportunities to work with others who are seeking to reach the same promotional audiences with a noncompetitive sales story. Oftentimes, both your own promotion and that of a tie-in sponsor can be stronger and more productive if you pool your resources and work together.

This is particularly true within divisions of a single company. I'm constantly amazed how often promotions fail to take advantage of good will, customer loyalty and sales development created by previous efforts of others within certain companies. As a matter of fact, there are far too many who seem to feel they are failing to demonstrate their personal creative ability if they trade on the efforts of a general corporate promotion campaign when promoting a specific product or service.

Discipline No. 9

We're down now to the *"Evaluation Discipline."* I won't dwell on this except to observe that I've found plenty of evidence that many in direct mail are far too anxious to move on to the next promotion before they've done the first step in their homework—evaluating the effectiveness of the promotion they've just completed.

No direct mail program is ever complete until its effectiveness has been thoroughly evaluated—and this doesn't mean simply

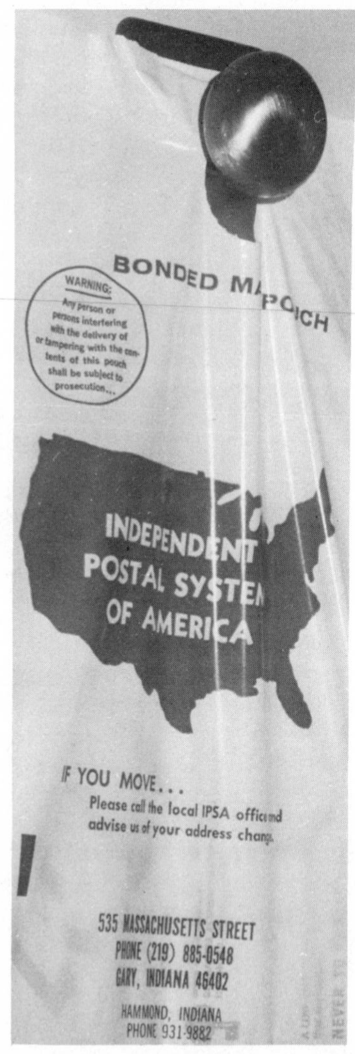

Independent Postal System of America will give U.S. Postal Service some competition.

seeking the praise of fellow promotion men. An integral part of every direct mail program should be establishing specific objectives including hard-and-fast standards denoting success or failure . . . and then including in the plan the necessary procedures to determine whether or not the objectives have been met.

My experience in direct mail leads me to add a note of caution, however. As you know, a lot of direct mail specialists pride themselves in their ability to test the comparative effectiveness of everything from whether to mail on Tuesday or Thursday to the proper angle for the placement of a postage stamp on an envelope. And, as a result, they are often so busy testing they never really get around to making the full mailing. And now that they have added computers to their collection of toys, they may even start testing the effect of mailing at 10:01 a.m. compared with 10:02!

Beware of wasting your time evaluating petty details—even if you have access to the biggest computer in the world. But also beware of living in the unreal world of imagined promotional successes when you haven't taken time to search out the degree to which you have achieved your basic objectives.

Discipline No. 10

And, finally, we come to Discipline Number Ten—the *"Plus-Value Discipline."* It's a simple point, but if I can leave you with just one worthwhile thought, I would like to encourage each of you to take a good, close look at every direct mail piece you turn out and ask yourself these questions:

- "Are there others who should receive it?"
- "Does it contain material which can be utilized in other printed pieces and promotion programs?"
- "Can it be effectively distributed again?"

While, earlier, I cautioned against trying to get too much mileage out of a single piece, there are probably far more times when direct mail people have failed to render maximum services to their companies because they didn't fully utilize a particularly effective piece.

This is the area the men are separated from the boys in direct mail. You can add "Plus-Value" to all of your efforts if you will simply take time to ask yourself now and again if you are applying equal amounts of creativity and discipline.

Chapter 6

PLANNING DIRECT MAIL CAMPAIGNS

OCCASIONALLY a single mail piece is all that is needed to accomplish a chosen marketing or communications objective. But more often, the job requires an integrated direct mail campaign—with each piece not only doing a job in itself but contributing to the total effect by laying groundwork for pieces which will follow.

Unfortunately, however, many direct mail campaigns are nothing more than a series of unrelated mailings. While each may be effective in itself, there often is a lack of coordination which will produce bonus results through a constant, carefully planned building of interest as one piece follows another.

Picking an Objective

The first step in planning a direct mail campaign is to decide on a specific objective. In the case of mail order advertisers, the primary objective is nearly always to secure direct orders. However, there may be other, intermediate objectives as well. For example, the mail order advertiser may seek to obtain names of new prospects, change the buying pattern of customers, upgrade the average order, etc.

But for other direct mail advertisers, the primary objective is seldom simply to get an order. Instead, it is generally something which will lay the groundwork for sales at a future date. One of the best guides to possible advertising objectives is a checklist, "101 Jobs Advertising Can Do," prepared by McGraw-Hill. While it was originally developed as a guide to objectives for business-paper advertising, it can be applied to direct mail as well.

1. Establish and Protect Your Company's Standing by:

   ....**Creating and retaining customers' goodwill**

   ....**Tying in with exhibits and trade shows**

   ....**Maintaining sound "public relations" policy**

   ....**Dramatizing or emphasizing the trademark**

   ....**Promoting special services**

..........Securing use of company's trade name by fabricators
..........Keeping your markets posted on new developments and future plans
..........Stimulating "word-of-mouth advertising"
..........Protecting patent rights
..........Keeping present customers sold on standing of the house
..........Establishing organization as authoritative headquarters (for engineering, etc.)
..........Discouraging substitution through product identification
..........Overcoming possible prejudices against your organization
..........Gaining goodwill of machine operators
..........Establishing the speed and scope of company's service facilities
..........Countering false or exaggerated rumors

2. Develop and Maintain Your Markets by:

..........Citing performance tests
..........Showing how to make better products
..........Cultivating future buyers
..........Educating newcomers among your prospects
..........Promoting new uses for products
.....✓...Overcoming seasonal slumps
..........Reaching all of the men who influence the buying
..........Promoting better product design
..........Teaching "value" to those who are not trained buyers
..........Offering samples for test purposes
..........Providing customers and prospects with helpful information
..........Educating your market on your product and its uses
..........Selling the services behind a product
..........Eliciting inquiries for a catalog or other literature
..........Demonstrating the laborsaving qualities of the product
..........Giving information about product advantages
..........Selling the idea of adopting a process
..........Featuring a maintenance service
..........Creating new and favorable buying habits
..........Maintaining a basic consumer educational job
..........Maintaining interest in the product after purchase
..........Establishing with the ultimate consumer a recognition of accessories or parts that are sold to manufacturers to be built into machines
..........Encouraging foresighted buying
..........Showing how to make or save money
..........Replacing foreign goods no longer imported
..........Educating consumers to more limited selections of merchandise
..........Conducting market tests
..........Protecting customers from buying old models
..........Assuring intelligent use and understanding of product
..........Securing acceptance of substitute product ingredients
..........Securing acceptance of simplified products

3. Develop and Maintain Your Distribution Outlets by:

..........Moving goods that have been sold to distributors
..........Building up dealer and agent standing with customers
..........Explaining house policies that may affect goodwill
..........Keeping present dealers sold on the standing of the house
..........Establishing jobber as source of supply
..........Attracting new distributors

..........Holding distributor loyalty
..........Helping dealers gain parts and repair business
..........Merchandising advertising and other sales helps to distributors and dealers
..........Showing buyers where stock is available
..........Helping establish new sales outlets
..........Attracting desirable dealers and agents
..........Building greater and more immediate product acceptance by jobbers, dealers, and consumers
..........Backing sales arguments with repetition

4. Increase the Effectiveness of Personal Selling by:

..........Presenting a sales story without competition controversy
..........Helping pave the way for price changes
..........Helping maintain prices to wholesale and retail outlets
..........Paving the way for effective interviews
..........Placing repetition element behind sales arguments
..........Reaching buyers with a special message
..........Reaching buyers geographically out of range
..........“Calling” more regularly
..........Preparing the way for salesmen by selling the need, type, and make
..........Confirming the salesman’s story with a printed statement
..........“Setting up” the salesman by showing his special qualifications for service to the prospects
..........Setting a sales-story pattern for salesmen exactly the way you wish it to reach your prospect
..........Attracting highest type of salesmen
..........Reaching “all” of the buying influences
..........Keeping contact with the buyer between sales calls
..........Reducing “interview time”
..........Increasing enthusiasm of the sales force
..........Getting inquiries and leads for salesmen
..........Reaching buyers who are hard to contact

5. Safeguard the Future of Your Company by:

..........Testing potential salability of new items or services
..........Opening new markets
..........Procuring new customers
..........Building up secondary items
..........Offsetting ill will of “neglected” customers
..........Maintaining the momentum built up by continuous advertising
..........Building confidence in the company’s financial structure
..........Combating illegitimate practices in an industry through cooperative advertising
..........Protecting against the price competition of unadvertised brands
..........Explaining delays in deliveries or temporary shortages
..........Informing customers why special services have been eliminated
..........Telling the user how to make products last longer
..........Forestalling the competition of new companies
..........Maintaining constant contact with customers temporarily out of the market
..........Reselling lost customers
..........Safeguarding your investment in advertising
..........Showing your confidence in the future of American industry

..........Maintaining the degree of recognition which your advertising has built
..........Preventing industry from believing that the company is slipping
..........Offering substitute products for established needs
..........Obtaining an increasing percentage of existing business

While it is important to have a single primary objective for a direct mail campaign, there is no reason why a well-planned campaign cannot also accomplish secondary objectives as well. But when secondary objectives are included, it is important to make sure they will not distract the recipient from the primary objective.

Types of Direct Mail Campaigns

Once you have selected your campaign objectives, you will generally want to settle on which of four basic types of direct mail you will need:

1. *Persuasive*—This is the type of direct mail generally used to secure immediate action such as mail orders or inquiries. In this type of direct mail, emphasis is usually placed on immediate action, and the pieces used are designed to make a direct response as easy as possible.
2. *Informative*—Most items in this category usually fall under the heading of "product literature." While some specific action may be requested, primary effort is generally directed at providing background information. Frequently, informative direct mail pieces are designed to encourage the recipient to retain them for future reference.
3. *Reminder*—While reminder direct mail may be both persuasive and informative, it generally is designed neither to produce immediate action nor to be retained for future reference. Its key purpose is usually to make the recipient stop for a minute and think about the possibility of buying the product or service being promoted.
4. *Utility*—Utility direct mail pieces often are used in conjunction with one of the three types just described. Included in this category are such items as order forms, reply cards and envelopes, samples, reference charts, folders and binders for use in filing other material, advertising specialties, etc.

Coordination With Other Media

In the majority of cases, a direct mail campaign should be coordinated with other elements of the marketing program—particularly promotion in other advertising and sales promotion media. It is the exceptional direct mail campaign which works best on an independent basis. Such exceptions are almost always those where a single direct response is required—such as a limited mail order campaign or some special function such as a survey.

Coordination, however, does not necessarily mean use of the same copy, artwork, layout, or even the same theme. It is usually a mistake to simply take a magazine or newspaper advertisement and reprint it for direct mail purposes, except where the entire purpose of the direct mail is to merchandise publication advertising.

Direct mail's usual role in a coordinated marketing program is to personalize a promotional message to specific individuals and/or specific segments of a market. Since advertising in other media involves "talking" to a mass audience, it can seldom function on a person-to-person basis. But direct mail can take a mass audience message and interpret it on a personal basis.

Budgeting for Direct Mail

Establishing the budget for a direct mail campaign or an annual program is often a difficult matter. Direct mail is the most flexible of all media, and costs are often difficult to pinpoint in advance. The most practical budgeting procedure for the majority of direct mail advertisers is the "task method." This involves deciding upon the job to be done, deciding how much money can be allocated to accomplish the job, and then developing a direct mail program to fit within the confines of this budget.

Another practical budgeting method for many direct mail advertisers is to "reroute dollars." This is a useful technique in cases where direct mail is designed to substitute for some other marketing method. For example, if a direct mail campaign can reduce the amount of time devoted to prospecting calls by salesmen, the cost of this time can be allocated to the direct mail budget. Or if direct mail can substitute for field research, the cost of such research can be considered the budget for direct mail programs designed to accomplish the same ends.

Other times, the most workable budget technique seems to be the allocation of a specific percentage of the total promotion budget for direct mail purposes. Unfortunately, there are few worthwhile guides to help establish any specific percentage. Not only will the "balance" between media vary considerably from company to company, but there is that always-present problem of no widely accepted understanding of just what mailed items should be included as "direct mail advertising."

Remington Rand's Direct Mail

How direct mail campaigns fit into the total marketing picture is well illustrated by the program of Remington Rand Division of Sperry Rand Corporation. It was described by Charles R. Pope, manager of Remington Rand's direct mail division, at a DMAA convention:

From the salesman's viewpoint, direct mail saves time, helps make friends faster, covers territory faster, and makes sales faster. From management's viewpoint, direct mail helps speed up the whole selling process, helps get more mileage out of the total advertising dollar, and helps build profits in the sales operation by cutting sales-to-expense ratios (reducing the cost per call and consequently the cost per sale).

Direct mail accomplishes these results in various ways. One of the most important at Remington Rand is the production of qualified leads for the sales force to follow up. To do this we maintain consistent monthly mailings to all major markets on most of our product lines. Such campaigns are mailed on a national scale to provide leads for about 2,000 salesmen across the country. And they produce about 100,000 leads per year. The production of qualified leads enables the salesman to better utilize his selling time by calling on executives who have expressed an interest.

This same continuous lead-producing program is frequently geared to our publication advertising. This way, our markets are exposed to double impact that paves the way for the salesman's call. Often, reprints of ads are enclosed with a mailing to help secure company name recognition and product identification. In this type of activity, the reply card is the means of inquiry.

We also use direct mail to reverse this procedure—to bring the executive to the salesman. A typical example was the campaign for our "Synchro-Matic" unit, a key punch synchronized with an accounting machine for fast production of business statistics. Here is equipment weighing over 800 pounds—a product too big to take to a prospect's office for individual demonstration, but one that lends itself well to group demonstrations.

Direct mail helped solve the problem. We were able to set up specific demonstration dates and invite selected executives to our local offices for a specific program. Here again the reply card provided an easy means for the executive to select one of five days to attend and to specify either a morning or an afternoon session. In addition, a detachable stub served as a ticket for a door prize.

But we have other programs in which we do not use reply cards to serve as leads. In paving the way for a salesman to make a product demonstration (in the prospect's office) we use a three-piece mailing campaign—each piece designed for maximum attention-getting, readership, and remembrance value. The mailings are made in rapid succession Monday, Wednesday, and Friday, in an operation controlled by the individual salesman. They build up to a request for an interview in the Friday mailing with the salesman calling Friday afternoon for his demonstration or making an appointment for a future demonstration in the prospect's office.

Such campaigns, usually with personalized letters, are set up on a national basis from the home office but with local flavoring—the letters being imprinted with the local branch logo and signed in some cases by the local branch manager, in other cases by the salesman himself, and sometimes with the additional personal touch of carrying the salesman's business card in the final letter.

We have another kind of direct mail program called a "Rap" campaign (like a rap on the door). It has been used at Remington Rand for over 50 years. It is a preestablished mail campaign initiated by the individual salesman. A Rap campaign consists of three mailing pieces, and there are a number of such campaigns set up for specific products for specific markets and in many cases special Raps to promote various applications of any given product line.

An index of Rap campaigns is available to the salesman, and from this index he selects the campaign he wants by number. Each mailing piece in a given Rap is illustrated in the index, so he can tell without further reference exactly what will be mailed. He then fills out a small triplicate form with name and address of recipient. This form is then forwarded to our mailing department where the release is automatically scheduled. The mailing department sends the salesman a copy of the form to advise him of the date of release of the first mailing piece; the second and third pieces go out at weekly intervals. The mailing department also notifies the salesman of the date of completion of the campaign. Our salesman is then ready to call on a preconditioned prospect. Prompt followup is the key to success of this procedure.

The first of the series of three mailings is usually an introductory letter—perhaps sort of a teaser. The second mailing is a little more specific—perhaps an ad reprint or a case history with a memo of transmittal—and, similarly, a third mailing builds interest up before the salesman's call. The memo of transmittal is important, as it serves to add something of a friendly informal approach, to establish Remington Rand's identity as the sender, to point up benefits, to highlight contents of the attachment, and to persuade the prospect to read it; finally, it refers him to our local office for further details. A salesman will use an average of 25 Rap campaigns a month.

Direct mail helps us in other ways, too. One way is in promoting our campaigns to our own sales organization. Preceding specific campaigns, we will often release a series of "Motivators" describing the campaign, the kind of support the salesman will receive, the purpose of the direct mail program, and how it is tied into other advertising effort from the home office. In these "Motivators," important sales angles will be emphasized by product line managers. Vocational managers issue special market sales information. New selling aids and advertising schedules are announced. Bulletins are issued to show the salesmen what's in it for them in the way of commissions and how to best utilize the material available.

And then there is the "switch"—how the salesman supports direct mail. He does this by building the mailing list. For special campaigns, our sales force will compile a special mailing list. In this way there is generated a real sense of participation and a responsibility for the success of the program. After a campaign we often send a brief questionnaire to ask for comments on how the campaign was received locally. To further stimulate interest we publicize many sales made as a result of following inquiries.

TV Guide's Direct Mail

An example of a somewhat different approach to direct mail programming is offered by *TV Guide.* This program, which has been a frequent winner of special awards, was described by Fred H. Stapleford, *TV Guide* promotion director, at a Denver seminar of the American Association of Advertising Agencies:

Our mission is to make advertisers and their agencies *TV Guide*-conscious. And do it in a hurry! We use trade and newspaper media advertising in generous measure. But we are not content to rest on those insertions. Our first use of direct mail is certainly an orthodox one: reprint mailings. We have salesmen operating out of 30 cities—some excellent, some good, some rookies. We haven't enough of them to call on each prospect every week—and we want *TV Guide* to call on you no less than once a week, sometimes oftener. The postman calls every day, so we recruit him. That's our second use of direct mail—to make sure some word about our magazine reaches each person who should have the word no less than once a week, all year 'round.

To accomplish our drop-by-drop erosion of your will to resist, we invest roughly one-third of our entire advertising promotion budget in direct mail, not counting postage. All of our direct mail is conceived and created within our own shop. Our lists and mail distribution function at three levels. National advertisers receive mail addressed by plates maintained at Radnor, Pennsylvania (*TV Guide's* headquarters). The same individual piece is usually shipped in bulk to regional offices, where it is converted for regional prospects. Conversion consists of hangers or other additives written to give a sharper focus in terms of specific area audience and statistics. Regional offices also maintain local plates for each of their editions. The same piece may be given a third conversion and mailed again, this time addressed to strictly local advertisers.

We do not, however, confine our direct mail operation to just mass production and distribution. We can and do gear specific campaigns to one category of advertiser, one agency, one specific advertiser, and, occasionally, one individual.

We deliberately seek change of pace, not only in direct mail, but in all our promotion. Sometimes we run a blitz of pieces day after day, sometimes we space a particular campaign over several weeks. We may depend on design and color, or on photo illustration, or, again, on cartoon art. Sometimes we use terse copy, on other pieces long and discursive copy. Sometimes we pitch hard-sell facts and figures, sometimes we try for the light soft-sell touch. These various changes of pace reflect the basic philosophy—planning. We produce them almost on a check-chart basis. We have even gone so far as to list all of our sales strengths, both in data and in philosophy, and require copywriters to check them off more or less in rotation as pieces or campaigns are produced. Since we have some 150 main points listed, there is little danger that the material will seem repetitious. A byproduct of change of pace is keeping copywriters and artists fresh. This happy situation reflects, in turn, in the freshness of the material they produce.

Our direct mail budget is set up on a semiannual basis. We project our basic one-a-week mailing over a 26-week period. Our maximum we arbitrarily set at three in any one week, save during a blitz. We try to make our mail reach you Tuesday through Thursday. This is because we believe that Monday is a peak load day and Friday is a catch-up day. We produce one-a-week basics in batches of six or eight (these are currently two-color french-fold pieces spotlighting individual sales characteristics). That leaves us maneuvering room to handle specials as need for them arises or to promote campaigns in selected categories.

We are under no illusions whatever that our direct mail, or any of our promotion, is a substitute for personal closing. If it succeeds in making you conscious of our existence when you begin to research a media plan, then it has done the job.

> We also use direct mail other than that for advertising promotion. Our foremost public relations mailer is called "Take One." It sells nothing but behind-the-TV-scenes anecdotes in the grin-and-bear-it style of our managing editor. We mail "Take One" to every list in the house—some 20,000 names in all.
>
> About half of our editors publish a local newsletter called "Off Camera," which focuses on area TV and advertising personalities and events. It is tailored to the specific locality covered by one edition, and must be published in that edition's office. For that reason, we let "Off Camera" come to life as each local manager believes he has staff time to devote to it. Invariably, it becomes one of our strongest soft-sell devices.
>
> Among our own employees we distribute a monthly six-page newsletter-style house organ known as "Closed Circuit." Its main purposes are to encourage a sense of unity in all *TV Guide* households (hence we mail it to the home), and to keep internal enthusiasm high.
>
> Circulation promotion direct mail centers on frequent communication with our wholesalers, using material ranging from personalized letters, to kits of material designed to stimulate special attention, to the distribution and display of issues we believe have unusual potential. Our subscription promotion effort includes regular but low-pressure direct mail.

The foregoing case histories show how important to the survival and growth of certain organizations is good planning of direct mail campaigns. If you get on the mailing list of an aggressive direct mail organization, you will be able to see some of these campaign principles at work as the various pieces of a campaign begin to come into your letterbox.

You will find it instructive to start a file of direct mail pieces coming into your home—you'll build up some fascinating examples of the good, the bad and the indifferent in this way.

Modern Approach to Direct Marketing

Lester Wunderman, the dynamic president of Wunderman, Ricotta & Kline, one of the country's most successful direct response agencies, contends that the complexity of today's marketplace calls for a more sophisticated approach to selling by mail. His thoughts, as expressed in *The Reporter of Direct Mail Advertising,*[1] provide some excellent guidelines to developing an effective campaign:

> We must know who we can sell to and why they buy or don't buy. We must stop cream skimming and make attempts to penetrate larger markets, not just the segment that is eariest to sell. We must begin to know why 97% of a list doesn't buy and 99½% of a magazine's circulation ignores us. We must plan advertising strategies that attempt to penetrate the whole market and upgrade our objectives to hit bigger market targets . . .
>
> The day of easy mail-order selling is over. The public is not so moved by our colorful mailings—or our large ads—that they will welcome our

[1]"Complexity of Marketplace Calls for Detailed Marketing Program" by Lester Wunderman. The Reporter of Direct Mail Advertising. March 1969.

messages. They are seeking a service from us which answers their needs, and unless we know who they are—what they need—and approach them in these terms, we will be squandering our advertising dollars.

Basically, a successful direct marketing campaign is one that solves the mysteries of the market place. We begin in total ignorance and have to end in wisdom. That is the total process. Before we write our first ad or mailing, we should begin to detail the things we know and don't know. We must use every tool of research to fill in as many blocks of ignorance as we can, and then vault over the others with intuition and creativity . . .

All marketing begins and continues with a problem. A problem which must be stated before it can be solved . . .

As a first, unavoidable step, you have to know exactly what your problem is. Not a general problem—but a specific one. So, define your problem, and if possible, do it in one short paragraph. If it takes two pages, you still don't know what it is.

Marketing strategy, of course, is our first basic objective. Everything which precedes leads up to it. If we clearly understand the problem, the product and the market place including competition, we can define our own marketing strategy, and at this point we are coming up to the point of creating advertising . . . We should once again be able to reduce our strategy to a short paragraph and absolutely agree on our objectives. If we do not agree on the marketing objective and strategy, then we cannot judge the value of the creative work which will soon be created. If there is tested advertising with a long history of campaign results, the problem is simple—but if you are starting from scratch or wallowing in failure or a marginal profit, it is necessary to go back and re-examine the entire process and the basis of your belief.

What are the ideas which will sell the product? An offer, a premium, a headline, an illustration, a sample? All of these might be valid selling concepts. This is the point where we are beginning to explore what may make a product or service sell. It is an investigation into a company's or product's right to exist—its salient points of salability. Do we have an introductory offer worth making? Should we offer credit, and if so, how importantly? Do we have a unique benefit to demonstrate? There are hundreds of selling concepts . . .

We are now able to build an advertising strategy. This must include gadgets, media, lists, campaign themes, campaign objectives, dates and quantities. Everything which has been considered before now becomes a planned advertising reality . . .

We now reach the point of campaign execution. Here, of course, we are dealing with actual copy, art, type, costs of printing, lists, paper, positions and rates in print media, adjacencies in radio and television—all the functions of a professional advertising group. No matter how good your planning or your strategy, it is only as good as your execution. This is no place for amateurs. In direct marketing, copy, plan, offer, art or media can make or break you . . .

Success in this increasingly competitive field requires absolute precision in execution. How do you learn to do this? There are only two ingredients—experience and creative skill . . .

> And so we come to the point where our advertising is put in front of our prospects. After all the thinking, planning, working and struggling, we are in print. At this point, we have completed that which our initiative can control . . .
>
> The most difficult of the problems that confront us in this business involves the analysis of results . . . The analysis of results is a creative process which must be kept in perspective. Facts can become a tyranny and a limitation when they are accepted at face value. It is not enough to know what failed or succeeded, we have to know why. We have to be able to see through isolated facts into patterns of opportunity.

When The Pressure Is On

Careful planning, analysis and all of the obviously important steps which should precede a direct mail campaign sometimes aren't quite as simple as we would like them to be. This is particularly true when the campaign has to start *now*. At times like these, you are forced to trade on your accumulated experience and instantly available information and plow right ahead—with fingers crossed.

Recognizing that such occasions are far too often the rule rather than the exception, Bob Stone set down some excellent basics for the hard-pressed campaign planner.[2] He noted, "If you can't test, follow the principles which work for most of the mailers most of the time. It sure beats flying blind . . . There will be variances, to be sure. But by and large, these basic principles, applied consistently, will produce better than average results:

Form of Mailing

- The letter ranks first in importance.
- The most effective mailing package consists of an outside envelope, a letter, circular, response form and business reply envelope.

Letters

- Form letters using indented paragraphs will usually outpull those in which indented paragraphs are not used.
- Underscoring pertinent phrases and sentences usually increases results slightly.
- A separate letter with a separate circular will generally do better than a combination letter and circular.
- A form letter with an effective running headline will ordinarily do as well as a filled-in letter.
- Authentic testimonials in a sales letter ordinarily increase the pull.

[2]"If You Can Test Your Market, Follow These Principles" by Bob Stone. Advertising Age. August 3, 1970.

- A two-page letter ordinarily outpulls a one-page letter.
- Computer letters ordinarily outpull printed letters, providing personalization is meaningful and the tone of the letter is low key.

Letterheads

- Specially designed letterheads, tailored to fit the sales message, will often outpull a standard letterhead.
- Two-color letterheads are usually more effective than one-color letterheads.
- Change-of-pace in letterhead appearance will increase response in a series of mailings.

Offers

- A time limit for replying usually increases response.
- The offer of a premium or special price inducement most always increases response.
- Response is increased through the use of "involvement" devices such as Yes-No tokens, stamps and sweepstakes entry forms.
- The more "generous" the offer, the higher the response is likely to be. Here is the relative rank of pull of basic offers: Free trial offer with gift for trying; straight purchase with satisfaction guaranteed; C.O.D.; cash with order.
- Installment payment terms attract more business than terms which require payment in 30 days.

Mailing Lists

- A company's house list is its best prospect list.
- A list of known mail order buyers will ordinarily outpull a compiled list.
- Telephone directories, used without discretion, usually represent the poorest mailing lists.
- A prospect list, compiled with the assistance of salesmen, often proves to be a "cream" list.
- Compiled lists of business firms, addressed to a job function, will often outpull lists with names of individuals.
- Customer lists maintained by the "recency-frequency-monetary" formula will outperform lists maintained by year of last purchase.
- The response by Zip codes reflects wide variances within each state.

Addressing

- Label addressing is most always as effective as typewritten or stencil addressing.
- Hand-written addressing, except where completely appropriate, has an adverse effect upon response.

Outside Envelopes

- Illustrated envelopes increase response if tied into the offer.
- Variety in types and sizes of envelopes pays particularly in a series of mailings.

Reply Envelopes

- A reply envelope increases cash-with-order response.
- A reply envelope increases responses to collection letters.
- An air mail reply envelope usually increases responses to "impulse" offers.

Postage

- Third class mail ordinarily pulls as well as first class mail.
- Postage meter usually pulls better than postage stamps.
- A "designed" printed permit usually does as well as a postage meter.
- Outgoing air mail postage seldom warrants the extra cost over first class.

Reply Forms

- Reply cards with "receipt stubs" will usually increase response over a card with no stub.
- "Busy" order and/or request forms which look important will usually produce more response than neat, clean looking forms.
- Postage-free business reply cards will generally bring more responses than those to which the respondent must affix postage.

Color

- Two-color letters usually outpull one-color letters.
- An order and/or reply form printed in colored ink on colored stock usually outpulls one printed on black ink on white stock.
- A two-color circular generally proves more effective than a one-color circular.

- Colored inks on an envelope corner card will generally do better than black.
- Full color is warranted in the promotion of food items, apparel, and merchandise which is faithfully depicted in full color.

Circulars

- A circular which deals specifically with the proposition presented in the letter will prove more effective than a circular of an institutional nature.
- A combination of art and photography will usually result in a better circular than one employing either art or photography alone.
- A circular usually proves ineffective in the sale of news magazines and news services.
- Deluxe, large-size, full-color circulars most always warrant the extra cost over circulars of 11 inches by 17 inches in size and under in the sale of big-ticket merchandise.

Follow-ups

- A direct sales letter that produces a satisfactory response the first time around can be expected to produce 70% or more of the original response if repeated in 60 to 90 days.
- A teaser campaign, to be effective, must consist of a series of follow-ups, released in rapid succession. The time-lag between mailings should not exceed two to three weeks.
- The ideal spacing of a year-long promotion campaign is one mailing a month.
- Best response to renewal efforts for a publication is attained *before* expiration. (If there are eight letters in a series, for example, at least six should be released before expiration.)

Best Mailing Months

- The best pulling months in order of ranks are as follows: Jan., Feb., Oct., Aug., Nov., Sept., Dec., July, April, May, March and June.

These then are the norms established over hundreds of millions of mailing pieces—the basics, the principles mass mailers live by.

But no piece on the basics should be complete without at least a brief check list for the basics of letter copy—the most important component of the typical mailing package.

Use This Letter Copy Checklist

Why not try this check list on your next piece of letter copy?

1. Does the headline or first paragraph attract immediate attention by promising the most important benefit to the reader?
2. Is interest built by immediately enlarging upon the promised benefit?
3. Is a desire to possess aroused by appealing to the emotions: Pride of possession, prestige, security, fear, enjoyment, comfort, monetary gain, affection?
4. Have you emphasized the exclusive features of your proposition in logical sequence?
5. Does the copy emphasize one big idea so strongly there can be no conflicting issue?
6. Have you used believable testimonials?
7. Have you used a guarantee of satisfaction?
8. Have you closed with a final bid for action—telling the prospect the exact unit he will receive, the price if any, how it will be sent, why he should respond now?
9. Is your letter laid out effectively so it appears easy to read?

Another of Bob Stone's columns in *Advertising Age*[3] contains a special checklist, which you may also find very helpful in planning direct mail campaigns. It's reproduced below.

For a basic checklist for direct mail advertising, see Section A of the Appendix below.

CHECKLIST FOR APPLYING THE FIVE BIG KEYS TO DIRECT MAIL SUCCESS

1. The Product Or Service You Offer

- Is it a real value for the price asked?
- How does it stack up against competition?
- Do you have exclusive features not available elsewhere?
- Does your packaging create a good first impression?
- Is the market broad enough to support a going organization?
- Is your product cost low enough to warrant a mail order markup?
- Does your product or service lend itself to repeat business?

[3]"Five Big Keys Unlocking a Direct Mail Success Formula" by Bob Stone, Advertising Age. September 11, 1967.

2. The Lists You Use

Customer List

- Is your customer list cleaned on a regular basis?
- Do you keep a second copy of your list elsewhere to avoid against loss?
- Have you developed a profile of your customer list, giving you all the pertinent demographic characteristics?
- Have you coded your customer list by recency of purchase?
- Have you worked your customer list by the classic mail order formula: Recency-frequency-monetary?
- Have you thought of what other products or services might appeal to your customer list?
- Do you mail your customer list often enough to capitalize on the investment?

Prospect Lists

- Do you freely provide facts and figures to one or more competent mailing list brokers, enabling them to unearth productive lists for you?
- Have you worked with competent list compilers in selecting names of prospects who match the profile of those on your customer list?
- Have you measured the true results of prospect lists, measuring against each list returned goods, net cash receipts per M mailed, and repeat business?
- Have you determined how often you can successfully mail to the same prospect list?

3. The Offers You Make

- Are you making the most generous offer you can within the realm of good business?
- Does your proposition lend itself to the use of any or all of these incentives for response: Free gift, sweepstakes, free trial offer, installment terms, price savings, charter offer?
- Does your proposition lend itself to the development of an "automatic" repeat business cycle?
- Does your proposition lend itself to a "get-a-friend" program?
- Have you determined the ideal introductory quantity for your proposition?

- Have you determined the ideal introductory price for your proposition?
- Have you determined the possibility of multiple sales for your proposition?

4. The Mailing Packages You Use

- Are your mailing packages in character with your products or services and the markets you are reaching?
- Have you developed the ideal format for your mailing packages, with particular emphasis on mailing envelope, letter, circular, order form and reply envelope?
- Do you work with one or more creative envelope manufacturers?
- Are your sales letters in character with your offers?
- Are your circulars graphic, descriptive and in tune with the complete mailing package?
- Does your order form contain the complete offer? Is it attractive enough to grab attention and impel action?

5. The Tests You Make

- Do you consistently test the big things: Products, lists, offers and mailing packages?
- Have you tested to determine the best times to mail your proposition?
- Have you determined the most responsive geographical areas for your proposition?
- Do you test one factor at a time against a control package to assure valid results?
- Do you use adequate test quantities?
- Do you follow your test figures through to conclusion, using net revenue per M as the key criterion?
- Do you interpret your test figures in the light of the effect upon the image and future profits of your company?

NINE KEY STEPS FOR A SUCCESSFUL DIRECT MAIL CAMPAIGN

While there are literally hundreds of factors which might be considered when developing a successful direct mail campaign—and many of them have been at least touched upon in this chapter, the nine steps listed on the facing page are probably the heart of the whole matter.

NINE STEPS TO CONSIDER IN BUILDING A SUCCESSFUL DIRECT MAIL CAMPAIGN

1. Define clearly what you're trying to say.
2. Pinpoint your audience.
3. Develop *programs* to accomplish your established goals.
4. Interpret your message in terms people understand.
5. Establish the budget you can allow to accomplish each specific goal—in terms of time, talent and dollars.
6. Work within these budget limitations to develop the best possible direct mail packages.
7. Develop individual pieces to accomplish sub-objectives—but always keep in mind the effect required from the total program.
8. Analyze your progress with each step.
9. Adjust your program as necessary to keep on the road to your specific goals.

Define Clearly What You're Trying to Say

Far too often, direct mail advertisers start out with a lack of *specific* goals for their programs—or, worse yet, no established goals other than they want more business.

It's not enough just to decree such broad objectives as "we want to attract more customers" or "we need to sell more gidgits." Nor is it enough to just add some quantitative qualifiers—"we need 500 more customers" or "we need to sell 100,000 gidgits."

The effective direct mail campaign needs very specific objectives. They may or may not be qualified by quantities—but they should be specific. In addressing a group of school administrators, the author suggested the following examples:

- During the next three years we desire to increase our enrollment from the metropolitan St. Louis area by a minimum of 10 additional students per year with special attention to boys who have an interest in science.
- We should increase gifts and pledges from 1930-1940 period graduates in non-local areas by 25% per year for four years, with an aim of gifts and pledges totalling $250,000 to be paid in full by 1980.

It was suggested that these were not necessarily good examples, but the whole point is that it's important to analyze the specific market you need to reach and what type of action you want to stimulate in that market.

An example of a program with non-quantitative objectives is one the author created for R. R. Donnelley & Sons Company. It involved sending monthly samples to a key list of high-volume prospects. Actually, the "key list" was a collection of personal lists created by individual salesmen. The salesmen selected prospects for $100,000 or more in printing sales which they felt they had at least a 50% chance of converting into customers within two years.

While the list qualifiers were quantitative, the five basic objectives of the program were not:

1. To make key prospects aware of the full range of services offered by R. R. Donnelley & Sons Company.
2. To demonstrate Donnelley's experience in every phase of the graphic arts.
3. To put Donnelley salesmen in *regular* contact with all of their key prospects even when personal sales calls were not possible or practical. (Each sample mailing was accompanied by, preceded by or followed by a personalized Autotyped letter individually signed by each salesman.)
4. To reach those who influence the selection of a printer, yet seldom come in personal contact with the Donnelley salesman calling on their company.
5. To open important doors in companies where the salesman had been permitted only lower echelon sales contacts.

At the time the author left Donnelley, this particular program had been running continuously for eight years, doing its assigned job of achieving the five specific objectives. While the results could not be measured by quantitative standards, they could be measured through serious evaluation by the salesmen and sales managers as to whether or not the program was fulfilling the five *specific* objectives established for the program.

Pinpoint Your Audience

This is an area where it is highly important to be very specific—even to the point of dividing major segments of the total audience into all possible subdivisions.

For most direct mail advertisers, there are three basic audience segments: customers, prospects and suspects. But within each of these segments there are a multitude of possible subdivisions, each of which can require special study before the most effective direct mail campaign can be developed.

Take customers, for example. There are usually happy customers and unhappy customers. There are large volume customers and small volume customers. There are those who have bought recently and those who haven't made a purchase for many months or years. There are those who buy frequently and those who have only bought once. There are those who have bought a single item and those who have bought various combinations of items. There are those who pay promptly and those who are slow to pay. There are those who are at the original address of purchase and those who have moved. Such a breakdown, of course, can go on for pages. But the point is that the more subdivisions you can isolate, the better your opportunity to do effective planning.

Where subdivisions of audience segments can be most important is when you can develop cross-relationships which help to identify the elements that can yield the greatest return per dollar of advertising cost. A careful analysis, for example, might show that you can anticipate orders at a cost of $1.00 each from customers who purchased at least twice within the past year, buying items "A" and "G" and who paid promptly on a monthly payment basis, while it will probably cost $3.00 per order from customers who have made a single purchase over a year ago, buying only a single item and paying cash.

It is, of course, easier to identify potential response patterns from customer lists than from prospects and suspects. However, analysis of what converted previous prospects and suspects to customers can be vitally important in defining your approach to these segments. Probably most important will be the list from which prospects and suspects were turned into customers. For example, a number of studies have shown that in mail order selling it is easier to obtain a customer from an outside buyer list when you use the same basic medium which originally attracted that buyer to someone else's list (i.e. if he bought from a catalog, your catalog is most likely to attract an order from him, and if he bought from a single item mailing, you'll get a higher return if you approach him with your own single item mailing).

Regardless of the details, your list is the heart of any direct mail campaign and deserves to be treated with utmost importance. Unfortunately, the average direct mail advertiser gives less *continuing* attention to his lists than they require. Too often, lists are only given real consideration—both from a time and dollar standpoint—at the beginning of a campaign when they should be an important part of campaign thinking, analysis and spending from beginning to end.

A good rule of thumb is to spend a minimum of 10% of your total budget—both in terms of time and dollars—for list analysis, development, acquisition and review.

Develop Programs to Accomplish Your Established Goals

In developing an effective direct mail campaign, it is important to put the major emphasis on programs rather than individual pieces. There is a great deal of value inherent in the parlaying effect of a continuing series of mailings—much more than many advertisers recognize.

The creative ego satisfaction involved in developing "something different" is one of the greatest culprits in the direct mail world. There may be more joy in the life of a direct mail creative man when he can always start with a fresh piece of paper, but the essence of an effective direct mail campaign is constructing programs so that each piece builds upon the impression created by those which have preceded it. At the same time, it is important to take advantage of promotional work being done through other media reaching the same audience—both your own and that of others who may be assisting you in "selling" your concept to the potential buyer.

In general, repeated messages will be more effective than a single high-impact piece. But any program may require the injection of high-impact pieces as a part of the total effort.

Any basic direct mail program will involve audiences with at least three different characteristics requiring specific approaches:

1. Break up old attitudes if they constitute a negative buying influence. Even if your prospect has never heard of you, this, in itself, can constitute a negative attitude (ie. "Can't be very important if I've never heard of them).
2. Reinforce old attitudes if they constitute a positive attitude.
3. Establish new ideas, creating new attitudes.

It is very seldom that you can integrate all three approaches at one time. Thus, each element of a direct mail campaign should concentrate on accomplishing one basic job. Most important, is determining the appropriate starting point and then deveolping a program to accomplish your ultimate objectives in a step-by-step fashion.

Even if your total budget is extremely limited, beware of trying to reach every type of customer and prospect with a something-for-everyone approach. The net result will most frequently be that you underplay your hand in reaching the best prospects and don't have the message strength to get through to the tougher prospects.

You can help your audience by presenting your story in a manner which clearly develops the benefit to be gained by accepting your offer. In most cases it is a mistake to beat around the bush, hiding your message while you try to create an atmosphere, and then bringing it out in the open after you think you've "trapped" the prospect.

You can cancel out a high percentage of the total effectiveness of a continuing direct mail program if you've played games with your audience and they've devoted time to the build up only to find you're presenting them with a proposition in which they aren't interested at that moment. Maybe they will be in the market at a later date, but chances are they will already have written you off as someone not worthy of additional consideration.

Interpret Your Message in Terms People Understand

You'll find a lot of useful information elsewhere in this volume about effective copywriting. But it is important to emphasize the importance of establishing the appropriate communications level when planning direct mail campaigns. There are really twin dangers to observe:

1. **Assuming that the majority in your audience talk and understand *your* language and thus can pick up your message if you address them as already having a certain level of basic knowledge.**
2. **Assuming that the majority in your audience are basically uninformed about your subject and talking down to them.**

Creating effective direct mail messages that avoid both of these dangers is not the easiest job in the world. It's the reason why the work of a professional direct mail copywriter is usually considerably more effective than that of an amateur—including professional advertising copywriters not truly experienced in the direct mail medium.

Too often there is a general assumption that the basic job of a direct mail program is to communicate information and then offer a means of reacting to the information provided. Unfortunately, the accumulation of information can have a boomerang effect.

A couple of examples from another medium may be useful in understanding the problems of communicating by direct mail. In one case, a special was shown on television to try to cut down on the traditional highway massacre during holiday periods. It showed the blood, gore and heartbreaks resulting from holiday highawy accidents and did its best to create an attitude of concern for highway safety. Post-show research, however, showed that those who had viewed the show were less concerned about the dangers of holiday highway traffic than non-viewers. Somehow the show had made the likelihood of a holiday accident seem less of a personal danger.

In another case, a film of race riots in a major American city was shown to audiences in the Soviet Union. Obviously, it was an attempt to create a negative image of America in the minds of Russian viewers. But what created the strongest impression was the simple fact that all of the supposedly impoverished rioters were wearing shoes!

The point of these examples is that you can't assume that your audience will react to the information you present in the way you desire unless you carefully construct your messages to not only inform but to guide your reader in coming to the conclusion you desire.

If there is any single basic guide to communicating with your direct mail audience, it is to make the job of receiving your communications as easy as possible. If the reader has to stop at any point and ask himself, "What do they mean by that?", you've created a roadblock in the path to effective communications of your message.

Establish the Budget to Accomplish Your Goals

Obviously, you must work within your allowable budget in any direct mail program. Unfortunately, however, many advertisers consider only dollars when they think about budgets. There are two other equally important factors to consider—time and talent.

Probably more direct mail pieces fail because the deadline for mailing arrived before the piece was refined than for any other single reason. One of the essential elements in laying out a direct mail campaign is to allow sufficient time not just to create the individual elements, but to add a contingent for massaging and refinement.

And don't overlook the importance of adjusting your efforts to the specific talents of those who will be available to do the job. If you have all the money in the world and can hire an expert to perform every part of the job, you've found Utopia. But that's not the case in 99.9% of all direct mail campaigns.

It's very important to recognize the limits of the people and organizations who will produce the elements in a direct mail campaign and then make plans which permit you to achieve the maximum possible within these limits.

To put this thought into perspective, consider the field of external house organs. If you have the time, talent and dollars to create and distribute a newsletter, don't try to substitute a magazine. Instead, publish the greatest possible newsletter rather than putting out an inferior magazine.

Work Within Your Budget Limitations

The example just given can be applied to all direct mail pieces. Recipients resent inferior direct mail—poorly done pieces which are probably deserving of the epithet "junk mail." They can turn off your prospect before he's "heard" a word you have to say.

The most important consideration in working within your budget limitations is to apply value analysis to every element in each piece, and each package within a campaign. This subject has been previously discussed in Chapter 5 in the section headed "Ten Disciplines for More Effective Direct Mail," but deserves special emphasis to any-but when you're *initiating* plans for your direct mail campaign.

One way to get maximum value is to take advantage of the advice available from your suppliers—not just when a job is in production but when you're *initiating* plans for your direct mail campagin.

Develop Individual Pieces

In the scope of a total direct mail campaign you'll usually want to develop individual pieces to accomplish sub-objectives. But when you do so, it is important to always keep in mind the basic overall objectives of your program.

Beware, for example, of the big, overly impressive piece interjected somewhere in a continuing program. It might do an important specific job, but could easily make all other efforts seem unimportant by comparison and thus make them considerably less effective.

On the other hand, perhaps "big" pieces are what's needed for the entire campaign. Maybe fewer mailings, with each piece designed to accomplish a higher percentage of the total job to be done.

But this leads to another caution. Don't let your presentation get in the way of the message. At one direct mail conference, a speaker claimed that at least 60% of the money spent on direct mail pieces was a waste of money. He noted that he had seldom seen a beautiful piece that said anything. He likened such pieces to an inlaid box filled with sand and went on to decry the trend toward fancier design and higher quality printing. A member of the audience had a quieting retort. "Don't do away with the beautiful boxes," he said, "just find a substitute for the sand."

Dr. Edgar B. Cale, Assistant Chancellor of Development at the University of Pittsburgh, made a comment relating to school publications which has a direct application to direct mail campaign planning. "When a publication, itself, may have long been forgotten," he said, "it may still do an important job. When you're trying to sell a customer, who knows the precise moment when his thinking turns in your direction?"

On the other hand, remember that if you turn off your audience with any single piece, you'll have a much tougher job getting them to pay attention to any pieces which follow.

Analyze Your Progress With Each Step

Once a direct mail campaign is underway, the time has begun to actively analyze your progress. It is unfortunate that a majority of advertisers frequently wait until a total program has been completed before attempting to analyze its effectiveness.

There are many methods to perform interim analysis. Sometimes it can be accomplished by seeking the comments of those who haven't actively participated in the development of the mailing pieces but understand the objectives of the program. Or you may want to do some field research among the recipients.

Regardless of the method you choose, don't settle for your own personal analysis—no matter how objective you might think you can be.

Make Adjustments as Necessary

Perhaps one of the greatest faults of many direct mail campaigns is that the planners consider the job finished when they put their initials on the original master plan. The total effectiveness of a campaign can seldom be judged before the first mailing is made. Thus, it is important to allow for adjustments any time evidence arises which can assist in restructuring program elements for maximum returns.

Another side of the coin, however, demands that you return to the established objectives and keep them fully in mind before making any change. It is not uncommon for changes to be made midway in a direct mail campaign because of some news event, advertising by competitors or an inspired whim of someone, with firm conviction that the changes will prove beneficial. But all too often, such changes fail to really prove helpful in achieving the established campaign objectives.

There are, of course, many instances when business situations call for a completely revised set of objectives. In such cases, it is seldom possible to simply adapt an ongoing direct mail campaign to do something which it never was designed to accomplish. Wisdom calls for going back to the beginning and start the campaign planning, development and execution sequence anew.

Chapter 7

MAIL ORDER

TO many people, direct mail and mail order are synonymous. While a substantial quantity of direct mail advertising is directed toward attracting return orders by mail, this is just one of the many business uses for direct mail.

Another misconception which should be dispelled is the tendency to use the term "mail order" to define a type of business. As the late Henry Hoke pointed out in "How to Think About Mail Order" (The Reporter of Direct Mail Advertising Inc., Garden City, New York): "There is no such thing as the mail order business. Mail order isn't a *business.* It is simply a method of *doing business.* If you sell jam or fish by mail, you are not in the 'mail order business.' You are in the jam business, or the fish business. If you sell subscriptions by mail, you are not in the mail order business, but in the publishing business."

On the surface, it might seem that worrying about the semantics of mail order is unimportant. Unfortunately, however, too few people have entered into mail order selling with an understanding of the fact that it is a *marketing method*—with many fine points to be mastered—and, as a result, there has been an unusually high percentage of failures among the newcomers.

The Dangers of Mail Order

Right from the beginning, it is well to consider a warning about mail order. Contrary to the high-sounding promises of some of those who want to sell you books about mail order or provide you with services to help you get started in "a mail order business," there's no easy route to success and the odds are badly stacked against the possibilities of making a fortune overnight.

A realistic view of the subject was presented by "Pete" Hoke in his foreward to Jim Howard's book on mail order *(How to Use Mail Order for Profit.* Grossett & Dunlap, New York, 1963):

Too many have the mistaken notion that mail order is something anybody "can get into," that this is the way to turn life savings into a pot of gold, that this is the perfect thing to fill idle time . . .

The reason there are so many mistaken notions about mail order is that all of us are continually exposed to it. We see hundreds of little ads in all kinds of magazines and newspapers offering all kinds of merchandise. All of us receive mail at home; catalogs full of gift items; offers of records, books, local services.

With so many advertisers offering so much, it may appear that this is the easy way to make money. You don't need a store or other expensive overhead. You need only pick out an interesting widget they are selling at the "dime store," buy a few hundred stamps at the post office, mail a letter to some names out of the phone book, then sit back and watch the orders flow onto the proverbial kitchen table. Truth is, a small number of ads or mailings ever succeed.

Nevertheless, the romantic picture of starting something with practically nothing persists. It persists partly because of the efforts of a handful of opportunists who run little ads. These ads promise the world with a fence around it. They may read: "Start your own mail order business in your home . . ." or "See how I sold $592,000 worth of precious snardies with only a few hundred dollars . . ." or "Learn the five magic formulas for mail order success which I will send you for just $5 . . ."

Can you succeed in mail order? Yes, you can if you possess an ability to study, if you are a good buyer, if you can build a large customer list. You must have all the qualities of a top retailer except a store. And don't be misled by those who show you how to develop trumped-up propositions. They *may* work for a few months, for the short term, but you can't build anything of lasting value with shoddy merchandise or shady offers.

The Mail Order Boom

Many theories have been advanced to explain the continued success of mail order selling. In the years immediately following World War II, there were scores who were convinced that the great day of mail order had passed. With nearly everyone owning an automobile, new superhighways bringing stores of all kinds within easy reach of the consumer, shopping centers offering a vast array of merchandise "just down the street," and the steady decline in rural population, it seemed only logical to these prophets-of-doom that mail order could go nowhere but down.

Yet, it not only did not head downward, it took off on its greatest boom period. Today it is stronger than ever before—and becoming a more important method of marketing with each passing day.

Why, when it seemed so logical for mail order to diminish in importance, should it skyrocket? The answer is at least three-fold:

1. The basic reasons why people buy by mail remained unchanged.
2. Retail selling became less personal with the onrush to self-service and it frequently became impossible to obtain helpful information to assist in

making a buying decision—something which can be done very effectively with mail order selling techniques.

3. The quality of mail order promotions improved tremendously, attracting the interest of sophisticated businessmen who previously had considered mail order selling beneath the dignity of their businesses. And with this interest came a willingness to at least experiment with mail order selling —often with amazing success.

Why People Buy by Mail

There are many reasons why people buy by mail—many of them based more on fiction than fact (yet very real to the mail order buyer). Among the more frequent factors:

Convenience. To a great number of people, the real charm of mail order buying is that you don't have to step outside your own door—no crowds . . . no pushing . . . no lugging home bulging shopping bags . . . no worry about finding the item you want "out of stock" and having to make a second buying trip . . . no rushing to beat the clock when you have a deadline at home or some other place . . . and many other store-shopping pressures.

Exclusiveness. One of the prime reasons for mail order's popularity is that many people feel they are obtaining something which is not available in local stores. In many cases this may be true since mail order sellers frequently concentrate on offering new and different products. More often, however, the items purchased by mail order *can* be purchased in a local store, but this fact is frequently unknown to the general public. Because of the unusual nature of many popular mail order products, they are seldom promoted by the stores which stock them and thus consumers are not aware of their availability.

Fun. To the dedicated mail order buyers—and there are lots of them—buying by mail is downright fun. They get a big kick out of thumbing through a mail order catalog, and anxiously await each mail delivery—not just to see if an income tax refund check or a letter from a favorite friend is in the postman's pouch, but so they can read through the interesting mail order offers they receive. And these same people, and many others, are like the River Bend citizens in "The Music Man," awaiting the arrival of the Wells-Fargo wagon—one of their greatest thrills comes with the arrival of a package from a mail order house. It is just like Christmas the year around. (This factor is far too frequently overlooked by many mail order sellers, yet many mail order successes have been built on this advantage alone.)

Economy. Many mail order buyers believe they can save money purchasing by mail through elimination of middlemen's profits.

While, in most cases, the costs of selling by mail balance out economies through elimination of middlemen, this belief persists.

"Personal" Contact. While the interposition of a mailman between the buyer and seller may appear to make mail order selling less personal than store buying, the increase in self-service merchandising coupled with the far-too-common indifference of today's retail sales personnel has often made mail order *seem* more personal. Many mail order firms make a special effort to develop a highly personal relationship with their customers and, as a result, often achieve a stronger person-to-person relationship than the common, cold, and impersonal local retailer.

More Adequate Buying Information. Along with the less personal retail buying relationship has come difficulty in obtaining information to assist the buyer in evaluating, comparing, and deciding upon products to purchase. In the self-service store there is often no one to which the customer can turn when a product is not self-explanatory. And even where clerks are available, more often than not they are poorly informed and/or fail to provide information a buyer seeks before making a purchase. But the successful mail order seller knows he *must* provide complete buying information if he is to make the sale and thus his copy provides the help a buyer seeks.

Lack of Embarrassment. Closely akin to the preceding point is the fact that many people hesitate to make their ignorance known. Rather than admit they do not know everything necessary to make a wise purchase (by asking questions of a retail clerk or through the possibility of selecting the wrong item from a store shelf or counter), they prefer to order by mail where they can remain a faceless buyer. In other cases, buyers prefer to order by mail so their purchases will remain a "private" matter.

Simple Credit Arrangements. In recent years, many mail order firms have developed clear-cut credit buying plans which are often far less complex than those offered—if, indeed, any plan is offered at all—by local retailers. Only in mail order, for example, do you find an opportunity to buy many desired items on the basis of small, equal payments spread over several monthly periods. Another advantage of mail order buying is that, most often, a product or service can be ordered conveniently without payment in advance.

Wide Selection. With mail order buying, the customer often has a much greater variety of choices than is conveniently available through other retail channels. This is particularly true of catalog buying.

Guaranteed Protection. Almost without exception, products sold via mail order carry a written or unwritten unconditional guarantee of satisfaction. Frequently, mail order customers are encouraged to use a product or service before making a final decision to buy. Such broad "protection" is seldom available through other buying methods, and even when it is, there is frequently a reluctance to return an item for credit for fear of having to answer too many questions about his dissatisfaction.

To these basic factors which provide the foundation for a successful mail order buyer-seller relationship can be added many other items. But probably all of them put together are less important than the single fact that lots of people *enjoy* mail order buying. The smart mail order advertiser quickly picks up this spirit and does everything possible to make his buying procedure an enjoyable process for his customers.

Improvement in Mail Order Promotions

While it is difficult to pinpoint just how and why it happened, in the decade of the 1950's there was an amazing renaissance in the quality of mail order promotions. While others may have led the way, a great deal of credit must go to the promotions for Time Inc. books, and American Heritage. Both of these publishing organizations made widespread mailings of beautiful promotion material for obviously high-quality products—frequently selling for a higher price than had previously been considered practical by experienced businessmen. The outstanding success of these promotions resulted in a rewriting of many of the accepted "rules" of mail order.

At the same time, many other mail order advertisers were upgrading their promotion material. The net result was a substantial increase in the overall quality of mail order material which was appearing in home and office mail boxes during the 1950's. And, fortunately, a high percentage of these high-quality mailings were paying off in terms of sales success.

This renaissance of quality and the resultant sales successes played a vital role in convincing sophisticated businessmen that it was not beneath their companies' and their own dignity to utilize mail order selling as one of their marketing tools. Thus, many previously reluctant businesses began venturing into the mail order field—frequently bringing to it a demand for high-quality promotion tools in keeping with the established image of their non-mail order businesses.

Once the general pattern changed in the direction of quality improvement, many established mail order firms began taking a new look at the material they had been using and decided the day had come to upgrade their own mailings. The net result is that mail order today is far difficult from what it was in years past—and the "new look" is paying off in increased acceptance by the buying public, with the increasing flow of orders giving new life to what was not too long ago considered a "doomed" method of doing business.

Three Types of Mail Order

There are three basic ways of doing business by mail order:

1. *Catalogs.* When many people think of mail order, they automatically think first of the big catalog houses such as Sears, Ward, Penney's, Spiegel, Aldens, and others. These companies, and many smaller ones, send out annual and/or seasonal catalogs from which their customers select merchandise which can be ordered by mail.

   For the most part, mail order catalogs are sent to established customers or highly qualified prospects and are expected to generate multiple orders over an extended period. Frequently, mail order catalogs are used to supplement some other business method. Retail stores, for example, may use mail order catalogs to produce orders from customers who find it difficult to make regular visits to the stores. Others use mail order catalogs to provide information about products not normally carried in stock and thus just as easy to buy by mail or phone as though a visit to the store.

2. *Coupon Advertising.* Probably the greatest number of mail order companies use advertisements in newspapers or magazines (or possibly radio, television, matchbooks or other media) to secure an initial order. Such ads may feature one or a dozen different products, but are usually distinguished by a clip-out coupon with which the prospect can order the product(s) being advertised.

   Many newspapers and magazines run special shop-by-mail sections which have proved particularly productive for coupon advertisers. While some mail order advertisers conduct the bulk of their promotion through coupon ads, the majority simply use this type of mail order advertising to either attract new customers, test the salability of new products and/or establish a stronger image in the minds of prospects and customers.

3. *Direct Mail.* The real key to successful mail order selling for the majority of companies is through the use of direct mail advertising—both to attract new customers and sell merchandise to established customers. This is the true mail order way of doing business—promoting via direct mail advertising to bring an order via mail for a product which will be shipped by mail to the customer who will pay by mail and who will then receive additional offers by direct mail, starting once again the mail order cycle.

While we shall discuss all three types of mail order in this chapter and elsewhere in this book, the greatest attention will be paid to the subject of mail order via the direct mail route.

Requirements for Mail Order Success

One of the most important keys to success in mail order is the selection of the right product or line of products. While there is probably no product which cannot be sold by mail order to at least a limited list, there are several specific requirements which will generally distinguish products which hold potential for mail order success.

A basic guide to the selection of mail order products was included in a special issue of *Envelope Economies* (Tension Envelope Corporation, Kansas City, Missouri), describing mail order marketing methods:

> The first requirement for a successful mail order item is that it have mass appeal. Obviously, the broader the market, the greater the chances for volume sales. This mass appeal does not necessarily mean that the product should be one that is needed by every man, woman, and child in the country; but, rather, one which will appeal to a broad segment of the population. For instance, many mail order offers appeal predominantly to women only or solely to men. Others appeal to only a certain group or cross section of people. This is particularly true in the field of medical mail order selling where remedies are offered for specific ailments which affect only a percentage of the population. Yet, this type of product is often highly successful as a mail order seller, because the urgency of relief creates a strong motivation for many persons so afflicted to purchase the remedy.
>
> One other characteristic that is important to a mail order item, is that it have a certain amount of "exclusiveness." It is difficult to sell by mail an item which is available in any store. Many people like to purchase for themselves, or as gifts for others, items which are somewhat exclusive or unusual, items which they are quite sure are not offered for sale by any store in their city or locality.
>
> The second requirement of a mail order item is that it contain an adequate profit. While many retail stores can successfully do business on a margin of 25% to 40%, most mail order firms would be out of business in short order if they attempted to operate on this kind of a price structure.*

*As the mail order field has expanded into more and more "high ticket" items, there are an increasing number of cases where a margin of 40% is not out of the question. This is particularly true where repeat sales can be made relatively often to an established customer list.

> Another characteristic which marks a successful mail order item is the opportunity for repeat sales. Seldom can a mail order firm build a good business selling a single item which is purchased only once. The most successful items are those which must be replaced at intervals by the users, or require a "refill" of some kind, which means repeat business. Another solution to this problem, of course, is the fact that many firms have a selection of items, and count on selling the same customers additional products or services in the future.
>
> The final requirement for a mail order item is the necessity of having a reliable source of supply. Many mail order firms have gone out of business merely because they discovered successful items, and when the orders began to pour in found they were unable to obtain a sufficient quantity of their products to fill the orders.

Desirable Product Characteristics

To these general guidelines to successful mail order operations can be added other characteristics which must be considered in the selection of products for mail order sale. Nine of these have been well outlined by Irvin Graham in his book, *How to Sell Through Mail Order* (McGraw-Hill Book Co., New York):

1. *Fulfillment of a Definite Need.* Many products are found in the "novelty" classification that are salable because they satisfy a current fad or because they are "good for a laugh." Although it is true that such items are capable of sale, their life is limited, and in a short time their appeal will be nonexistent. They do not actually cater to a basic need, nor do they offer any long-term convenience or attraction. For the moment they are popular with a fickle public, and then their salability evaporates. Therefore the advertiser contemplating the sale of such products should be conscious of what is inevitably to come and prepare to nourish his business with other items. When a product fills a need that is likely to last for some time, there is greater likelihood of having a substantial groundwork for business.
2. *Mass Appeal.* Items that are capable of sale to the great mass of people hold out maximum promise of profit. Why this is true is obvious. Any limitation of appeal that excludes any specific groups of consumers correspondingly decreases profit potentials to the extent of those groups. Although a product need not appeal to every kind of consumer to be profitable, it is evident that the larger the market the greater the profit.
3. *Selective or "Class" Appeal.* Products that are attractive to special groups of consumers are also capable of profitable sale, though to a smaller degree than items of mass appeal. One of the reasons that selective items can be promoted profitably is the fact that media with a minimum of waste circulation can usually be chosen to carry the sales message. In the case of a specialized item with definite and limited appeal such as hunting equipment, the advertiser can use *Outdoor Life, Hunting & Fishing, Fur, Fish, Game, American Rifleman,* and other "outdoor" magazines whose readers would be prospects. Also, direct mail lists highly selective in character can be purchased or compiled. Here again, because waste circulation is held to a minimum, the percentage of closures should be higher than is found in the circularization of a "general" list.

   While it is possible to advertise selective items in mass media or with general lists on a profitable basis, the chances are that the cost per order would be higher than if the message were directed only to those who are prospects. Sometimes research reveals that what was previously considered a rather small class of consumers is actually a widespread one and therefore a very profitable market. Investigation showed to one advertiser that the number of men and women who wore false dental plates was amazingly high, contrary to the commonly accepted belief that few people wore dentures. He accordingly prepared a denture adhesive for sale (through drugstores) that proved to be phenomenally profitable. Factors contributing toward its success included the fact that the product differed radically from those of competitors and that it was promoted more aggressively, particularly through the use of mail order techniques.

4. *Repeat Sale.* Here again this factor is not a *sine qua non,* but a highly desirable characteristic of a profitable item. "Repeat" buying refers to the frequency with which a prospect renews his purchase of the product. The more often he rebuys the greater the sales volume accruing. Repeat items derive their profit potentiality to a great degree from the fact that the second and succeeding sales are obtained at practically no sales cost, for the purchaser simply fills and returns the order form enclosed in the previous shipment to him. Because the profit on each of the succeeding sales is higher than that of the original (since the original order cost need not be deducted to arrive at net profit), many advertisers can afford to buy the original order at a loss; they know that succeeding sales will more than make up for the loss on the first sale. Examples of repeat items are depilatories, hair dyes, cosmetics, foods, dental-plate liners, and drugs.

   Products like self-improvement courses, pressure cookers, and vacuum cleaners are not likely to require a second purchase. If they do, the succeeding purchases are so far apart that the advantage of repeat sale is insignificant. On the other hand, these items, like many similar ones, can provide a handsome income to the advertiser even if sold only once to a fair portion of available prospects. Here, too, the reader should remember the nature of a "market." This is not a closed group of people; prospects are always coming into existence. As soon as one sale is made and the market reduced by that amount, it is likely that one, two, three, or more people have suddenly become prospects for various reasons.

   Additional points to remember when selecting a suitable product include the following:

5. *Perishability.* Will the item spoil quickly? If so, it may become valueless in transit. This is particularly true of some food products and flowers, among other items.
6. *Mailability.* The item should be conveniently mailable without danger of excessive breakage; unusually high postage or shipping costs may also affect its desirability as a salable item.
7. *Assembling.* Is the product easily assembled or compounded for packaging and mailing? If not, labor costs may make it less favorable for profit.
8. *Availability.* If the product is bought from a manufacturer, the advertiser should have definite assurance that the merchandise will continue to be available in the future to permit prompt filling of orders.
9. *Seasonability.* This characteristic tends to reduce the volume of sale. Products whose sale is restricted to certain seasons of the year (such as sun lotions, sunglasses, beachwear, or fur-lined gloves) are naturally not such great profitmakers as those capable of year-round purchase. However, this factor does not invalidate a product as a mail order item, for many are being sold profitably as part of a line of merchandise supplementing the seasonal sale of those items.

Sources for Mail Order Items

Once you understand the primary requisites for a good mail order item you still face the problem of finding something which fits these qualifications. In fact, you will need to find a continuing flow of such items if you are to perpetuate a mail order selling operation.

There are many sources to consider:

Study the mail order ads in newspapers and magazines. This should be your first step, for here you will get an idea of the types of items which make successful mail order offers. But don't be misled. Just because an item is being advertised for mail order sale does not mean it will be an automatic success—even if the advertiser is one of the most successful mail order firms. Many advertisers use mail order ads to test the sales potential of different products. So just because they are being advertised does not mean they are considered a sure winner. Nevertheless, you can get a good feel of the product possibilities by a thorough study of the ads.

Send for—and study—every mail order catalog available. Like reading the ads, you can get a feel of the product possibilities for mail order sale by analysis of mail order catalogs. Another word of warning is in order: products which prove successful for one mail order firm are not necessarily good products for another. The *established personality* of the seller can play an important role in the success of any given item. Many factors are involved, but perhaps the most important is that the company's business personality will normally attract a segment of the market with special interests. For example, an organization such as Early American Peddler of Farmingdale, New York, will obviously attract a customer list with a special interest in Early American furnishings. Thus, its catalog will concentrate on presenting items to appeal to this type of buyer. But it wouldn't be logical to conclude that a heavy weighting of a mail order program toward such items is a "natural" for a list with mixed interests. Another related factor is that many mail order firms can trade upon the previous relationships with their customers in the presentation of merchandise.

Put on your thinking cap. Many of the most successful mail order items have been developed through the ingenuity of an individual who has come up with a practical product to fill a common need—or a clever one to capture the imagination of a large buying audience.

Consider innovations. Someone else's idea may be the answer—particularly if you can think of an appealing innovation. Some of the most outstanding mail order successes, for example, have been built upon personalizing relatively common items such as shower curtains, book matches, napkins, doormats, and so forth. Often you can combine a couple of common items into something different. Or you can add a distinctive feature such as one firm did by taking a standard road atlas, adding fancy covers, and then offering it by mail order as an executive gift.

Update old items. Take a look at successful mail order items of years past by reviewing old magazines and catalogs and then consider how they might be brought up to date for the present-day market. Often you can find surplus stocks of outdated merchandise available at low cost which need only some modern thinking and promotion to become popular once again.

Search out inventions. New items are being invented every day and many of them have potential for mail order sale. You can subscribe to the "Official Gazette," weekly publication of the U.S. Patent Office, which lists all patents passed for publication. Or you can obtain "The Products List Circular," published by the Small Business Administration, which describes approximately 200 inventions in each issue. Another source for information about new inventions is the patent attorneys.

Follow trade publications. There are dozens of trade publications which regularly publish both editorial material and advertising giving *advance* information about new products hitting the market. You will find many excellent mail order product possibilities here.

Visit trade shows. Another excellent source for mail order products is trade shows. Many manufacturers time their introduction of new products to the trade show in their industry. Particularly important are the premium, gift, housewares, and toy shows. But do not overlook those not so closely associated with normal mail order products. Your next mail order idea may be awaiting you at some strictly industrial show or those aimed at tavern owners, doctors, or druggists.

Watch the news. Keeping a close watch on current events will often provide the creative man with the lead he needs to come up with a successful mail order product. One of the true geniuses of mail order, Joe Cossman, was fascinated by the Bridey Murphy craze which took the country by storm and created a special interest in hypnotism. So he combined a 12-inch recording on self-hypnosis, a book of instructions, and a "hypnotic stone"—and sold over 100,000 sets while the public interest was at its peak.

Consider new markets. One of the best avenues to mail order success is to seek new markets for an established product. For example, there are many products which have been developed for trade use which have applications either for other trades or for general consumer use. Frequently, those presently marketing such products have an interest only in serving the trade where they already have distribution and will welcome anyone who comes along and offers to cover other markets for them by mail order.

Swap products. An excellent opportunity for those already in the mail order business is to arrange to cross-promote products with others who have lists showing little duplication. Their product successes may easily sell well to your list.

Basics of Mail Order

While the selection of the right products is highly important to the success of a mail order operation, there are many other basic considerations. Earle Buckley, past chairman of the DMAA, offers these eight basic requirements for successful mail order (quoted in "How to Think About Mail Order") :

1. Have a product that is in demand by the type of people to whom the advertising is being mailed and on which there is both a low delivery cost and a high markup to allow a decent profit with what are considered good mail order returns.
2. Have the most attractive proposition possible—with regard to the product itself, the price, and the selling plan (open account, free trial, approval, cash with order, and so forth).
3. Have your advertising material so appealing at first glance (include the envelope) that those receiving it will want to read it.
4. Have the story told so truthfully, so sincerely, and so convincingly that those reading it will want to possess the product or enjoy the benefits of the service.

Administrative Management

51 MADISON AVENUE
NEW YORK, NEW YORK 10010

Saves you and your Company with this great reduced price offer!

12 months for only **$5.00**

25 WAYS TO SAVE TIME & MONEY!

How many of these 25 features could help you?

They are just a few of the hundred which have appeared in ADMINISTRATIVE MANAGEMENT recently. You'll find more, in every issue of the prestige, *"how-to"* magazine specially tailored for busy administrators.

Each month our staff of editors and well-known, authoritative contributors, *tackle, expose and explore the most important management, personnel and systems challenges facing American business today.* All of this up-to-the-minute source material in an easy-to-read, written to conserve-your-time, manner. As a subscriber you'll get clear; concise, factual help you can profit from immediately.

1. *What Middle Management Earns:* Study details in $10-20,000 range.
2. *Increasing Profits:* How leading companies do it in tight times.
3. *Security in the Office:* Planning for employee and company protection.
4. *Copying Equipment:* Annual survey of new processes and developments.
5. *Executives Develop EDP Skills:* Using computers to learn about computers.
6. *Inventory Control Problems:* Solving them with the right systems.
7. *Corporate Day Care:* Operation of daycare centers for children of working mothers.
8. *Profit Sharing:* What the government's new regulations allow.
9. *Addressing and Mailing Equipment:* Newer, automated systems.
10. *Pros and Cons of Office Service Charge-Backs:* Public utility concept to control costs.
11. *Business Letter Costs:* They're a lot higher than you think.
12. *Leasing Office Space:* Nationwide city-by-city survey.
13. *Unions:* Meeting them head on works wonders.
14. *The New Breed of Calculators:* Product details, charts, trends.
15. *Personnel Training:* The programs and equipment you need today.
16. *Fringe Benefits:* Yours and your employees. How they are changing.
17. *Alcholism and Drugs in the Office:* Rehabilitation, control and firing techniques.
18. *Converting to Landscaped Offices Saves $12,000:* Why shroud this subject in mystery.
19. *Salaries for Clerical Personnel:* Annual Survey.
20. *Microfilm-Cameras, Reader-Printers:* A super-survey of what's available.
21. *Careers:* New job horizons for administrative managers.
22. *Forms:* The latest ideas in cost-saving forms design.
23. *EDP Personnel:* Training, paying and understanding them.
24. *Absenteeism and Turnover:* How to cut these costly headaches.
25. *Responsibility/Authority:* You can't shed it.

Please turn page. . . .

THE MAGAZINE OF BUSINESS SYSTEMS, EQUIPMENT & PERSONNEL

A technique which has proved highly successful for publishers and other direct mail advertisers is a numbered list of features. This letter from Administrative Management was printed in three colors—red, orange and black.

5. Include an unqualified *guarantee* that your product or service will do all that is claimed for it.
6. Have a list that contains as nearly 100% live prospects as it is possible to find.
7. Have all mailings tested before being sent to a large list, and then, *if* sent to a large list later, properly timed so as to be received on the most favorable day.
8. Have, or build up, such a reputation for fair dealing and good value that the reader of your message will have confidence in your firm.

Building a Reputation

Of all of these points, probably the greatest emphasis should be placed on the last—building a reputation which inspires confidence. This is far more important in mail order than in most other marketing methods. Larry Chait, one of the outstanding experts in the direct mail field, has frequently emphasized that the integrity of the seller is a quality that is vital to the success of the whole mail order campaign. "While codes of ethics are part of the picture," he points out, "they cannot be the whole. Only when a company behaves with integrity over a long period of time can a corporate image grow up that is conducive to encouraging response on the part of potential customers."

The old philosophy that "the customer is *always* right" is an essential ingredient in building a desirable mail order reputation. Successful mail order marketers bend over backward to establish and maintain customer satisfaction. This extends to accepting customer complaints even when you are completely convinced there is no reason whatsoever for the complaint. Unless you are selling a big-ticket item which would involve a considerable expenditure to make adjustments without first checking out all details of a complaint, make requested adjustments cheerfully, immediately, and without question. You may lose a few dollars in a given instance, but adopting this philosophy will lead to more than ample profits in the long range to compensate for any temporary loss.

Mail Order Guarantees

An important part of establishing a successful mail order reputation is the adoption of a firm guarantee. As Larry Chait puts it: "Whoever discovered the importance of the guarantee in direct mail advertising deserves great recognition from the fraternity! Basic to many of the great direct mail successes of our times is that simple phrase which gets so many customers over the barrier: 'This product is guaranteed to be exactly as advertised and your money will be cheerfully refunded if you are dissatisfied in any way.' It is a truism that the more successful the user of direct mail, the stronger his guarantee will be stated."

Here is a representative sample of the types of guarantees offered by mail order advertisers:

> *Sears, Roebuck & Co.* We guarantee that every article in this catalog is honestly described and illustrated. We guarantee that any article purchased from us will give you the service you have the right to expect. If for any reason whatever you are not satisfied with any article purchased from us, we want you to return it to us at our expense. We will exchange it for exactly what you want, or will return your money, including any transportation charges you have paid.
>
> *Haband Co.* It is understood that if, upon receipt of ties, I find any that I don't want to wear I can return them and have my money refunded promptly and without question.
>
> *Encyclopaedia Britannica's "The Great Ideas Today."* When this outstanding volume arrives, I may examine it for 10 days at no cost or obligation. If, at the end of this time, I don't agree that this is one of the most significant works of our times, I may return it and owe nothing.
>
> *Fortune.* It is understood that I am privileged to cancel my subscription and receive a refund for the unexpired portion at any time.
>
> *Publishers Clearing House.* In addition to the publisher's own warranties, Publishers Clearing House makes you this unconditional guarantee: You may have a full cash refund—at any time, or for any reason—on the unused part of any subscription ordered through the Clearing House. This guarantee has no time limit. It is your assurance that you can order from the Clearing House with complete confidence.
>
> *The Golden Encyclopedia of Art.* Please reserve for me a first-edition copy of *The Golden Encyclopedia of Art,* to be sent to me for two weeks' free examination, without any obligation. After examining this book, I may return it—and that ends the matter—or I may keep it and remit the special first-edition price.

It is difficult to overestimate the importance of the guarantee in direct mail advertising. Here are some typical examples.

> *National Travel Club.* Naturally, you are protected by a money-back guarantee, and must be fully satisfied with the club or you may have a cash refund—at any time—on the unused part of your membership.
>
> *Ad Man's Alley.* We don't ask you to buy a pig-in-a-poke. Look over the first issue when it arrives. If you're not satisfied, mail it back. We'll refund your $100 promptly. Also, you may cancel your subscription at any other time you are not satisfied. We'll refund the remaining portion.
>
> *National Research Bureau.* Please ship—for 10 days' free inspection and use—Volume III of the *NRB Retail Advertising and Sales Promotion Manual.* I will review and use this 428-page manual. But it is to be thoroughly understood that if I am not more than pleased I may return the manual to you at the end of the 10-day inspection period—and owe you nothing.

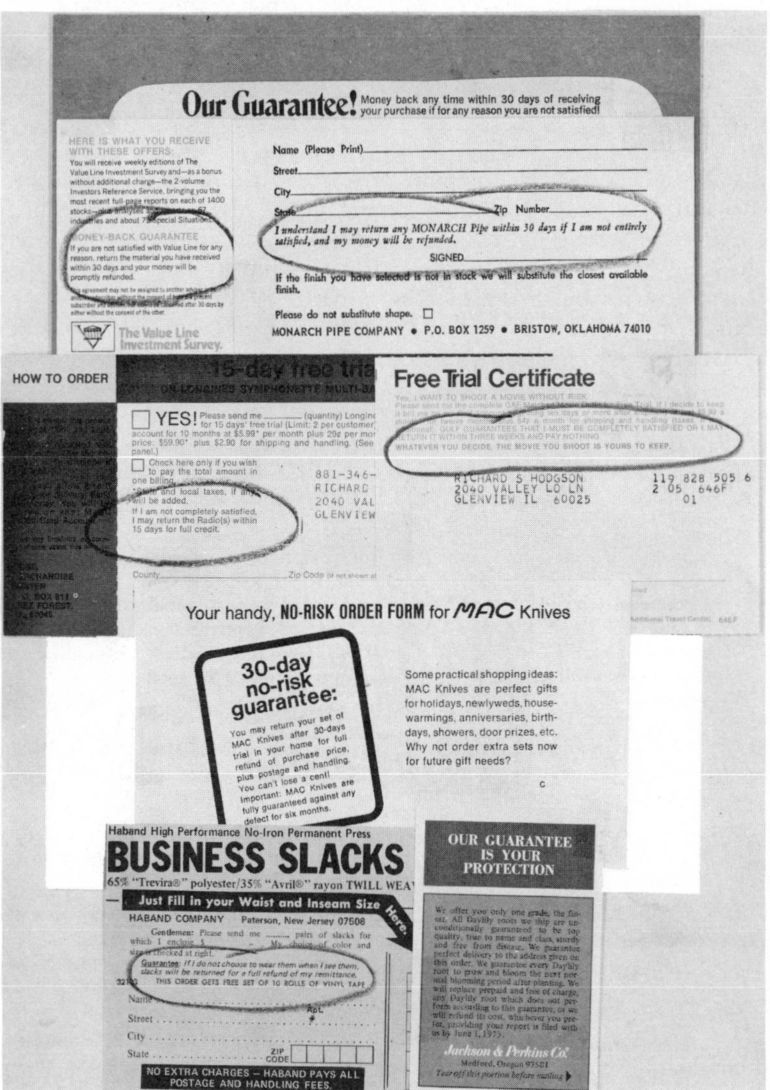

It is difficult to overestimate the importance of the guarantee in direct mail advertising. Here are some typical examples.

American Marketing Services. You don't have to send us a single penny right now. We'll gladly send you a copy of *Yankee Clipper, Volume IV,* for a 10-day free inspection. If you like it and feel it will prove valuable in illustrating your printed material and in providing useful ideas, we will bill you for the $20. If *Yankee Clipper, Volume IV,* is not suitable, just return it. There's no obligation.

Mistakes to Avoid

Credit for the development of a great many of the most successful mail order techniques must go to Maxwell Sackheim. A pioneer in selling by mail, he later headed the advertising agency bearing his name and taught many of today's mail order experts their first lesson. From his vast storehouse of experience he has outlined what he describes as "The Seven Deadly Mail Order Mistakes":

Mistake No. 1 is to offer the wrong merchandise—whether goods or services. There's an old and moth-eaten slogan that "anything that can be sold, can be sold by mail." But never in the history of commerce has a greater fallacy been advanced. One word has been omitted from the statement, without which it is meaningless. And with it, the statement is absolutely untrue. The word is *profitably.*

So the first, and most important consideration is, what are you trying to sell? Is it light in weight in proportion to its price? Except for other disadvantages, the ideal product for mail order selling would be a diamond; it is ideally light, and ideally expensive. The worst product is probably an anvil—for reverse reasons. Your mail order product must not be handicapped by excessive transportation charges in proportion to its total cost.

Is it something new—or something old with a new twist?

Is it a bargain, not necessarily price-wise but in what it does to or for the customer? In simpler words, does the advertising practically write itself because the product sells itself?

Are the price and the unit of profit high enough so that you do not have to get repeat business—or is the product one that repeats often enough so the original selling cost is not the determining factor?

Is the product simple, or is it likely to need repairs which may be difficult to obtain, and which may scare prospective buyers away?

Is it easily breakable in the mails?

Are colors and sizes involved which will cause resistance and returns?

Is there an inventory or warehouse problem?

Is there any evidence that the product is wanted by a large enough and reachable audience to make a mail order project feasible?

Is your purpose other than orders? If so, what are you trying to accomplish and what is par for your course? By what standards are you going to measure results?

If you are wrong in your selection of merchandise, all the other deadly mail order mistakes do not matter. You are licked before you start.

Mistake No. 2—is to offer merchandise at the wrong price. By wrong price, I don't mean a price that is not competitive. The lowest price never gets all the business.

What is important is your *unit price* and your *margin of profit.* If your price is too high for normal, natural, direct mail order sale, you must have compensating factors such as shipments on approval, time payments, a wide-open guarantee backed by unquestioned sponsorship, or a name like Sears, Tiffany, or Neiman-Marcus. You might even be better off trying to make the sale in two jumps, obtaining inquiries first and then following up with the big expensive pitch, or even with a salesman if possible.

The most dangerous price mistake is to have too low a unit of margin. The most inexpensive mailing costs how much? $40 per thousand? $50? Perhaps $60 if you rent a mailing list—or maybe $70 or $80 if you must use color. It may be as much as $150 or $200 per thousand, but let's start with $40 and a $2 margin of profit. In that case you would need a 2% return to break even. From a $60 mailing you would need 3%, or 4% from an $80 mailing.

Even if your tests show these results, have you allowed for a sufficient factor of safety to warrant a large mailing? It's fine if cash is not important, if you have a substantial bank account and can wait for repeat business, or if, like the magazines you can convert short-term trial orders into long-term customers. But if your budget is limited, you have no other source of revenue such as magazine publishers have, or your sales are likely to be far apart, beware of the small-unit, short-margin mail order item. Of course, you can test anything, but temper your testing with good judgment lest you run out of money before you find the right answer.

Mistake No. 3—is the wrong offer. I've mentioned wrong price, but a wrong offer can wreck the right price. For example, an open-account offer on a low-priced item might bring in a fantastic number of orders. But after you deduct bad debts, cost of collections, and bookkeeping expense you might be better off with a much smaller cash business. On the other hand, a high-priced item might demand an open-account offer, or time payments, or some other compensating inducement or incentive to buy by mail.

Mistake No. 4 is the wrong timing. It is a mistake to mail too early, but it is a calamity to mail too late. How far in advance of using-time should you mail? If your product is used in April, test in January. (Roses for planting in April are offered most successfully in January by the largest and most successful people in the business.) If purchased or used at Christmas, or as a Christmas gift, test your product as early as September—and as soon as your test results justify, shoot the works!

If you mail early, perhaps you can squeeze a profitable followup mailing in after your original mailing has gone out. One of our friends makes three Christmas gift mailings—one in September which pays, one in October which also pays, and the last one about November 10 which has paid in the past.

Regardless of the use-time, some months are poor reading months. April, May, and June are notably bad even for red-hot summer items, simply because these are poor reading months. December is bad, except for airmail gift orders. (There is considerable difference of opinion among mail order experts on the subject of "bad mailing months." Conflicting opinions are quoted elsewhere in this chapter and should be weighed carefully.)

Wrong timing also applies to customer mailings. How soon after receiving an order should you solicit another order? My answer is, often.

Mistake No. 5 is the use of wrong lists. The best lists are, of course, your own live customer names and your own inquiries. Next are lists of other people's customers who have bought related merchandise (preferably by mail); and, finally, any kind of mail order buyer. You can rent the use of many of these names, or trade the use of yours for them. (Consult a list broker for detailed information about logical lists for your use.)

Good lists are the lifeblood of the mail order business. The wrong list can sound the death knell of an otherwise good venture. Choose your lists with care, and test only to the extent that you can afford to lose.

Mistake No. 6—is the wrong format. Shall we use a Government post card? Or shall we go all out with a letter, a four-color brochure, a catalog, a beautiful order form, a big airmail outgoing envelope, a smaller airmail return envelope? Where do we begin and where do we end? In the idiom of Abraham Lincoln, a mailing, like a man's legs, should be "long enough to reach the ground." In other words, it should be adequate—not so expensive as to make the required number of responses beyond the pale of reason and experience, and not so cheap and unattractive as to get the wastebasket treatment at first glance.

Now—about copy. I always come back to the formula advanced many years ago by Walter Dill Scott of Northwestern University. He advanced the four cardinal rules of successful copy. These are still valid; at least I have never seen, heard, or read better ones despite the new jargon about motivation research, depth interviews, and the like. These four requisites are: *Attraction, Interest, Conviction,* and *Action.*

It is inconceivable that a mailing which does not attract can possibly be effective or that a mailing which falls down on any one of the other three steps can be profitable. If it does not interest after it attracts, and if it does not convince after it interests, it has lost its opportunity. And surely if it does not lead to action, if it winds up by having made only an impression, it may take years before it pays for the investment, if ever.

To induce people to drop everything in order to pay attention to you, you must shock, startle, promise a reward worthwhile, or in some other way shake them out of their complacency. You cannot expect them to read your story unless it is more important than whatever it is they are doing or thinking about at the moment. If you don't get 'em into your "store," how are you going to sell 'em?

To sustain interest, give your prospect *news!* News interests people. Are you giving your prospects all the newest news about your product, or are you taking too much for granted? Nearly all products are ordinary. There are very few new and desirable inventions or discoveries. So take ordinary items and create some news about them. As Elmer Wheeler said, "Sell the sizzle, not the steak."

Conviction depends upon believability. No matter what you say, if it isn't believed, you have lost your sale. Believability is born of sincerity. Don't underestimate the intelligence of the average reader. You know when you are stretching the truth beyond reason, and so does your prospect. Remember this: even an uneducated person's reading vocabulary is much greater than his speaking vocabulary. So don't talk down to your prospect, and don't trifle with his bump of credibility.

Finally, advertising is wasteful if it doesn't get action. One response may be worth a thousand impressions. Give the reader a chance to make a deal with you—not tomorrow or next week, but right away.

Mistake No. 7 is bad management. If you have every other qualification for success, your house of cards is bound to come down on your ears if your business is badly managed. In the mail order business practically every known business requirement must be faced. We must buy. We must sell. We must finance. We must advertise. We must fulfill. We must collect. We must control inventory. We must warehouse. Sometimes, we must even invent and manufacture.

The surest and safest way to get into the mail order business is as the byproduct of a successful, going business which now sells in other ways. If you have a business that is making money, put mail order on your payroll at so much a week or a month or a year, just as you would a new salesman who has made a reputation in some other line or with some other good company. You would give him a chance to make good even if you lost money on him for awhile.

Well, you cannot find a better potential salesman than Mr. Mail Order. He won't get drunk. He won't get sick. He won't misrepresent you. He will work 24 hours a day, seven days a week, 52 weeks a year. He will tell your story as well as you tell it. He will do a good job for you if you do a good job for him.

Mistake No. 8—is to think there are only seven! For whatever mistakes can be made in any business can also be made in the mail order business, plus quite a few that do not enter into any other form of enterprise, whether manufacturing, wholesaling, retailing, or servicing.

Mail Order Lists

When all of the facts are considered, you will find that the most important element in any mail order operation is the mailing list. It is the one basic element which, in the long run, distinguishes a successful mail order company—even more important than the products or services being offered.

For most mail order companies, the best possible list is composed of previous purchasers—particularly those who have bought a similar product from the company. One of the real mail order pros, Jim Dooley, of Atlantic Advertising Inc., points out in "How to Think About Mail Order": "A great many people who start in the mail order business do so without having a proper value of a customer list. They assume that they can make a profit from the start and fail to realize that a solid foundation of customers has to be laid first before any extensive success can be had in mail order selling." Mr. Dooley goes on to suggest that mail order sellers should start out with a building program concerned with only a break-even point in mind for several years, while they accumulate as many customers as possible.

Customer Lists

In the long run, the key to successful mail order selling will be the degree of strength in your *active customer* list—people who have bought from *you,* with satisfaction, paid their bills, and, preferably, have made additional purchases.

But you can go even further in putting your finger on key lists. By all means, those who have purchased your products by mail are far more valuable for future mail order selling than those who have responded to some other type of salesmanship. And, according to many of the experts, a mail order *credit* buyer is worth as much as four times a non-credit buyer in terms of total volume of purchases.

Still another important characteristic of the best customer list is that group of customers who have made the most recent purchases and those who have given evidence of repeat purchase patterns.

Renting Lists

Of course, if you are starting from scratch, you won't have a list of mail order customers so you will have to look elsewhere. Your best bet is to rent a list of customers from someone else who has sold a similar product or service *by mail.*

A good guide to selecting such lists was offered by the late Robert Rubin, former president of Circulation Associates Inc.[1]:

1. *The Age and Condition of the List:* If the list has been used and cleaned repeatedly, its age is not a factor. There are lists in use today that were originally compiled or acquired as much as 15 and 20 years ago, and that still have vitality.
2. *The Unit of Sale Involved in the Original Offer From Which the List Was Obtained:* A list of mail order buyers of a $5 item generally respond better than buyers of a similar item at $3 or $2 even though the values may have been comparable. Thus, a list of purchasers of one pound of candy offered at $1.25 might be less successful than a list of buyers of three pounds of the same candy at $3.
3. *The Method by Which the Names Were Originally Obtained:* Whether in response to coupon advertising in magazines and newspapers, from other direct mail advertising, through radio or TV offers, or by other methods. Most advertisers have found the direct mail buyer and the coupon clipper to be the best prospects, with the radio or TV respondent usually a distant third.
4. *The Nature of the Product Through Whose Sale the List Was Originally Compiled:* Obviously, tire buyers are better prospects for other automotive products than would be, for example, a list of buyers of airplane models.

[1]"What You Should Know About Selecting the Market," by Robert Rubin. Chapter 13 of "Mail Order Strategy" by Lewis Kleid. The Reporter of Direct Mail Advertising. Garden City, New York.

Changing Times
THE KIPLINGER MAGAZINE
Editors Park, Maryland 20782

Dear Reader:

You may wonder why I am writing you again about the continuation of your subscription to CHANGING TIMES. You may think it should be obvious to us at this point that you intend to let your subscription lapse.

> But...strange as it may seem...we have found over the years that an amazing number of CHANGING TIMES subscribers do renew after missing one or more copies.

In one month, for example, 6,414 readers renewed their subscriptions after missing from one to three issues.

I guess it's just that - as the old saying has it - "You never miss the water 'til the well runs dry."

In many cases, apparently, readers don't really feel and appreciate the advantage of having CHANGING TIMES until after their subscriptions have ended. And I'm wondering if this has also happened to you.

You may now realize that you have lost an important adviser. That's why I'm sending you another card covering the continuation of your subscription, which saves you $2 if you send your payment promptly.

But this is the last time I will be able to make you this offer on a continuation of your trial subscription. So please check the card now. Enclose it with your payment in the reply envelope. Mail it today, and we'll start CHANGING TIMES coming to you again, at once.

Sincerely,

Gordon Brant

Gordon Brant
Subscription Manager

GBB:mch

Successful direct mail advertisers continue mailing to a prospect or customer until the number of returns no longer supports the cost of a mailing. This letter from Kiplinger's Changing Times magazine is typical of the continuing efforts made by publishers to get renewals from subscribers.

And the airplane model buyers would be more likely prospects, in turn, for other "hobby" products.

5. *Other Qualifying Characteristics Such as Age and Sex of the Purchaser, Geographical Distribution, etc.:* When a broker offers you a list for rental he will, as a general rule, provide all such pertinent information on a standard card adopted and used by all reputable brokers. It is a simple matter to devise a filing system for these cards so that all of the information that is obtainable, about every list in which you might conceivably be interested, is at your instant disposal.

(There are many other sources for lists and you'll find them described in detail in Chapter 20—"Mailing Lists.")

Developing a Customer Profile

One of the first things mail order firms should do if they wish to extend their customer lists is to draw a profile of the typical customer already on their lists. An example of such a profile was provided by Elsworth S. Howell, president of Grolier Enterprises Inc.[2]:

> He lives in a city with a population of 25,000 or more. He has graduated from high school and earns over $5,000 a year. He has two or more children. He makes his living with his hands (machinist, plumber, electrician, crane operator, and so forth).
>
> In most cases, Grolier's customers are blue-collar workers who want their children to be white collar. That is why they buy encyclopedias. They like practical things. That is why they buy cookbooks, atlases, home repair guides, and informational works. They want merchandise which fulfills a home need. That is why they buy window fans, power tools, sewing machines, dinnerware, towels and sheets from Grolier's merchandise catalog.
>
> Grolier's customer profile performs two functions. It tells who the customer is and what he is like. And so Grolier knows what to offer him, and how to make the offer. It also acts as a "screen" for mailing list prospects. If prospects do not come reasonably close to the kind of people Grolier sells to, Grolier doesn't waste time and money including them on the list.

Mail Order Mathematics

Whenever mail order people gather, an eavesdropper might suspect he had encountered an assemblage of mathematicians. Figures are of utmost importance in mail order advertising and selling and it is impossible to operate a successful mail order business without spending a great deal of time keeping close tab on a variety of statistics.

While many formulas are useful, there are two basic ones:

1. Percent of Return
2. Cost per Order

[2]"House Lists . . . Your Greatest Asset," by Elsworth S. Howell. No. 3 in a series: "The Function of Mailing Lists in Direct Mail Advertising." Planned Circulation. New York.

Percent of Return

The Percent of Return formula is very simple, yet it is the basic yardstick of mail order advertising. It involves only two basic factors —the number of pieces mailed and the number of orders or inquiries received:

$$\text{Percent of Return} = \frac{\text{Number of Orders or Inquiries Received x 100}}{\text{Total Number of Pieces Mailed}}$$

For example: If you make a mailing to 100,000 prospects and receive orders from 2,000, your percent of return will be 2%.

Percent of Return is the figure you will hear quoted most often when mail order people are discussing the results of a mailing to any given list or group of lists. It has no direct relationship to the success of a mailing on a profit-or-loss basis since both the cost of the mailing and the cost of fulfilling orders of inquiries must be considered. To one mail order advertiser, a 5% return might represent an unprofitable mailing, while to the next a 1% return might represent an outstanding success profitwise.

Cost per Order

The other basic formula is used to determine the direct mail expense involved in obtaining the average order from each mailing. The factors involved are the cost of the mailing and the number of orders received:

$$\text{Cost per Order} = \frac{\text{Total Cost of Mailing}}{\text{Number of Orders Received}}$$

For example: You send out 100,000 mailing pieces at a cost of $85.00 per thousand (total: $8,500.00). You receive 2,000 individual orders. Therefore, you divide 2,000 into $8,500.00 and determine that each order has cost you $4.25.

Again, this formula has no direct relationship to the true success or failure of a mailing since a number of other factors must be considered. For example, you will have to fill the orders and ship the merchandise ordered and you will have to allow something to cover your general overhead. Then, the cost of collections and/or returns will frequently play a major role in the total profit picture in mail order.

This same basic formula, of course, can be used to compute Cost per Inquiry if you are seeking prospects rather than customers. You simply insert the number of inquiries received in place of the number of orders.

Applying Mail Order Mathematics

A study of some figures from a typical mail order program will show how these formulas are applied. The table immediately below shows the returns from a mythical mailing of an item priced at $17.50. While this table is purely fictional, it is based on actual mail order experiences. Please remember that these figures are based on earlier costs and that one must extrapolate the current costs to get some idea of today's costs and results.

For the purposes of this example, we have established the fulfillment cost of each order at $5.00 and the mailing costs at $92.00 per thousand pieces *plus* list rental charges. For easy calculating, we have rounded off all list counts to even thousands.

Records of a Typical Mail Order Program for a New Product

LISTS	Number of Pieces Mailed	List Cost	Total Mailing Cost*	Number of Orders	Per-cent of Return	Cost per Order	Income at $17.50	Fulfillment Cost at $5†	Profit or Loss
Customer List A									
Mailing No. 1	6,000	....	$ 552	450	7.5	$ 1.20	$7,875.00	$2,250	$5,073.00
Mailing No. 2	6,000	....	552	300	5.0	1.84	5,250.00	1,500	3,198.00
Mailing No. 3	6,000	....	552	168	2.8	3.29	2,940.00	840	1,548.00
Mailing No. 4	6,000	....	552	90	1.5	6.13	1,575.00	450	573.00
Mailing No. 5	6,000	....	552	60	1.0	9.20	1,050.00	300	198.00
Customer List B									
Mailing No. 1	12,000	....	1,104	264	2.2	4.19	4,620.00	1,320	2,196.00
Mailing No. 2	12,000	....	1,104	204	1.7	5.41	3,570.00	1,020	1,446.00
Mailing No. 3	12,000	....	1,104	144	1.2	7.67	2,520.00	720	696.00
Recent Inquiries									
Mailing No. 1	5,000	....	460	150	3.0	3.07	2,625.00	750	1,415.00
Mailing No. 2	5,000	....	460	90	1.8	5.11	1,575.00	450	665.00
Mailing No. 3	5,000	....	460	60	1.2	7.67	1,050.00	300	290.00
Old Inquiries									
Mailing No. 1	15,000	....	1,380	180	1.2	7.67	3,150.00	900	870.00
Mailing No. 2	15,000	....	1,380	60	.4	23.00	1,050.00	300	−630.00
Rental Lists									
List No. 1	10,000	$15/M	1,070	140	1.4	7.64	2,450.00	700	680.00
List No. 2	5,000	20/M	560	95	1.9	5.68	1,662.50	475	627.50
List No. 3	20,000	12/M	2,080	120	.6	17.33	2,100.00	600	−580.00
List No. 4	15,000	15/M	1,605	150	1.0	10.83	2,625.00	750	270.00
List No. 5	5,000	18/M	550	65	1.3	8.46	1,137.50	325	262.50
List No. 6	5,000	15/M	535	15	.3	35.67	262.50	75	−347.50
List No. 7	10,000	15/M	1,070	80	.8	13.37	1,400.00	400	− 70.00
List No. 8	10,000	15/M	1,070	55	.5	19.45	962.50	275	−382.50
List No. 9	5,000	18/M	550	65	1.3	8.46	1,137.50	325	262.50
List No. 10	20,000	15/M	2,140	200	1.0	10.70	3,500.00	1,000	360.00
List No. 11	5,000	20/M	560	75	1.5	7.47	1,312.50	375	377.50
List No. 12	10,000	18/M	1,100	70	.7	15.71	1,225.00	350	−225.00
TOTALS	231,000	....	$23,102	3,350	1.45	$6.90	$58,625.00	$16,750	$18,773.00

***Mailing costs are based on an average cost of $92 per thousand pieces *plus* list rental charges.**

†Fulfillment costs are based on an average cost of $5 per order.

NOTE: This chart was originally prepared in 1963. Since that time, inflation has boosted the cost of similar mailings to an average cost of about $200 per thousand pieces and similar lists rent for $35-45/M today.

Customer List A. A total of five separate mailings was made to 6,000 active customers—those who had made purchases from our mythical company within the past two years. These five mailings resulted in the sale of the new product to 17.8% of the active customers. The mailings were continued until the returns came close to the break-even point (which, in the case of house lists would be approximately .75%).

The total profit from the active customer group was $10,590. By dividing this profit figure by the total number of names on the list, you find that each previous customer can be considered to be worth approximately $1.75 in profits for an item of this nature (assuming, of course, that this mailing program is typical of the company's experience). This figure is important in determining how much you can afford to "pay" for a new customer.

To project this thinking, let us assume that our company will make five similar offers each year and achieves approximately the same results from each product offering. We will also make the assumption that the average customer remains active for a two-year period. Therefore, this average customer will contribute $17.50 in profits over his two-year active span. On this basis, it would be reasonable to "pay" as much as $17.50 to add a new customer to the list.

Customer List B. Three separate mailings were sent to customers who had not made recent purchases. Although this record indicates that mailings were stopped while they were still producing a profit, chances are most mail order sellers would make at least one more mailing to this list, even if a slight loss was experienced in the profit column, since this would activate a number of customers, making them stronger prospects for the next products to be promoted.

Recent Inquiries. Three mailings were also made to a list of 5,000 who had made recent inquiries. For this example, it can be assumed that these inquiries resulted from publicity and advertising directly related to the product being sold. This being the case, these mailings may not have been as profitable as this record indicates since such inquiries would have required an expenditure for the advertising and/or publicity which attracted them.

In most cases, allocating advertising and publicity costs to specific mailings is difficult. Since such names will undoubtedly be used many times in the future for other mailings—and, in all likelihood, rented at a profit to other list users—it would be improper to charge the entire cost of procurement to any single mailing. Thus, the costs are frequently allocated to general overhead, a portion of which is added to other fulfillment costs.

Many mail order operators would continue to mail to this list until the cost per order reaches the figure established as the potential value of a new customer. To continue the example we previously cited, wherein it would be possible to "pay" as much as $17.50 for a new active customer, it would thus be possible to hit a return as low as .35% and still consider the mailing worthwhile. It works out this way:

> Since we receive $17.50 from each order and the cost of fulfillment is only $5.00, each order yields a net profit of $12.50. On a .35% return basis, our recent inquiry list of 5,000 names would come through with 17 orders. That means a balance of $212.50 to cover mailing costs, which amounted to $460.00. Therefore, we have a deficit of $247.50. Divide this by the 17 orders received and you will find that each buyer represents an investment of $14.56.

Old Inquiries. Two mailings were made to an existing list of 15,000 individuals who had made previous inquiries, but had not made a mail order purchase. While the second mailing pulled only a .4% return and resulted in a loss of $630.00, it managed to convert 60 prospects to the active customer list at a cost of $10.50 each—well below the level of $17.50 we have established as the potential value of a new customer.

Rental Lists. Twelve outside lists were rented at prices ranging from $12.00 to $20.00 per thousand names. All of these lists were mail order buyers of related products. As the table indicates, there was a great variance in returns—from a high of 1.9% to a low of .3%.

Because of the additional cost of list rentals, the percentage of return must be slightly higher than that from a house list to hit the same "break-even" level with respect to addition of new customers to a list.

Under the circumstances, it is likely a mail order operator would want to make a second mailing to all lists which pulled 1% or greater if he was anxious to add as many new customers to his list as possible. And since rented lists proved so generally profitable, the operator would undoubtedly want to search out additional lists to which to make this offer. He may easily have avoided lists costing more than $20 per thousand names in his original planning, but judging from the results he obtained he now will know he can well afford to rent more expensive lists.

Many mail order people believe in applying the so-called "averaging out" principle to rented lists. This involves setting a quota for desired profit or acceptable loss and then continuing to mail to available lists until this quota is reached on a cumulative basis. To understand this theory consider another example involving just three lists and assume an established quota of merely breaking even on mailings to rented lists. To simplify things, let's consider that our mailings will cost us $100 per thousand (including list rentals) and that the product being sold will yield a net profit of $10 per sale.

> *Mailing A* goes to 10,000 and draws a return of 1.5%. Thus, we will have 150 orders and a profit of $1,500. From this we deduct mailing costs of $1,000 for a net of $500.
>
> *Mailing B* goes to another 10,000 and draws a return of 1%. Therefore, we will have 100 orders for a profit of $1,000. Mailing costs are still $1,000 so this list just breaks even. However, we still have a net profit of $500 in our cumulative total to be applied to mailings which do not necessarily break even.
>
> *Mailing C* goes to another list of 10,000 and draws but .5% return. So we have a profit on this list of $500, but we again must consider the $1,000 mailing costs and end up with a net loss of $500. At this point, however, our cumulative total is at the break-even point so we have "averaged out" to our established quota.

While this example oversimplifies the principle, it is not difficult to apply averaging out to most mail order situations. It is seldom appropriate, however, unless one of the major objectives is to obtain new customers.

Total Mailing Cost. In our example, we have established an average mailing cost of $92 per thousand pieces *plus* the cost of list rentals. While this is a simplified approach to make our example easier to analyze, it is not necessarily typical since there will be some variation in costs. For example, in using outside lists, addressing will be provided as part of the rental charge. In the case of house lists, something must be added to the mailing cost to pay for addressing charges. In addition, some list owners—particularly in the mail order field—will insist on handling all mailings sent over their lists. This may very easily result in higher processing costs than those paid to your regular mailing service.

Cost, Income and Profit. The last four vertical columns in our table tell the real story of the individual mailings. The *Cost per Order* is obtained simply by dividing the number of orders into the Total Mailing Cost. All other costs, however, are *not* involved in this figure.

Income was figured on the basis of $17.50 per order—the price of our mythical product. In actual practice, there may easily be more than one price to be considered. Many mail order operators charge more for credit orders than cash orders, or there may be a time payment plan which includes some kind of carrying charge. All such factors must be considered before a realistic income figure can be determined.

Fulfillment Cost was considered to be $5 per order. This is not necessarily a realistic figure since a great many factors must be considered in establishing an average fulfillment cost—many of them dependent upon the type of accounting system used by the mail order operator. Basically, this figure must include the cost of the product, packaging, handling, and shipping. But it is also necessary to consider such items as a portion of the general overhead, allowance for bad debts, returns, replacements of damaged shipments, and so forth.

While many experts consider it absolutely essential that the mail order selling price of any item promoted independently be a minimum of four or five times the cost of the product plus shipping costs, there is really no hard and fast rule since so many different factors are involved. Just the desirability of obtaining new customer names alone may call for a much smaller markup.

Our *profit* figures were determined by subtracting the total cost of mailing and fulfillment from the gross income. This again is oversimplifying things since many factors must be considered before a true profit figure can be computed. For example, if allowances for returns and bad debts are not included in the fulfillment cost, such items must be deducted before a realistic profit figure can be obtained. These two items in particular will be important in evaluating the true profitability of the use of rented lists. Some lists will be particularly heavy in the number of bad debts and the number who will return the product for refund or credit, while others will be particularly good from these standpoints.

To understand how much difference this will make, consider List No. 10, which brought 200 orders from a list of 20,000 for an indicated profit of $360. If this should turn out to be one of those lists which are heavy in bad debts and returns, that $360 profit could be wiped out quickly. Just 10 noncollectible accounts plus 11 returns for credit or a refund would turn what appeared to be a profit figure into a loss.

Mail Order "Packages"

While the various elements of mailing "packages" used to promote mail order sales are covered in detail in other chapters, the checklist on the next pages provides an excellent guide for basic analysis of your materials. It was designed by Old American Insurance Co. for use in improving its own mailings, but most of the points are valid for the majority of mail order advertisers.

In explaining the checklist, Joseph McGee, Old American president, noted, "According to our experience, a mailing containing envelope, letter, order form and reply envelope works best for us—hence these are the only items contained on the checklist." Mr. McGee offered these additional comments:

> *The outer envelope.* This is important because a good first impression is necessary. We don't feel it necessary that envelope and letterhead should match, but there definitely should be harmony between the two. Nor do we go for commercial color matches—we fuss around until we determine just the right shade of any color and then stick with that as our standard.
>
> *The letter.* The first 10 words of a letter are more important than the next 10,000. There's always a big temptation to hold back your "big gun" until the second or third paragraph, but it should always be first. We also like to see that our writers have formed a "bucket-brigade" through their letters—in other words, each thought or paragraph is joined with the one preceding it. Don't write like you talk—but as you would *like* to talk. Convey a feeling of friendliness. We like to use a postscript to call attention to the order form and find that the money-back guarantee is very important in establishing confidence. In our particular case, we have found the IBM Executive type and a blue ink signature work best.
>
> *The business-reply envelope.* This should be neat and attractive, and should look like a business-reply envelope if it is to be used as you want it to be by the prospect. Actually, there is more room for improvement in business-reply envelopes than in anything going through the mails today.
>
> *The order form.* Be sure the order form fits the reply envelope and be sure the reply envelope fits the sending envelope. All the key points of the offer should be included on the order form, and the form should not only look like something important but should make it easy for the prospect to say "yes." A final word—be sure the reply envelope including the order form stays glued!

EXPERIENCE OF THE MAIL ORDER EXPERTS

In the following material you will find the collected opinions, advice, and successful techniques of dozens of experienced mail order men and women. As you read through this helpful material, you will soon note that frequently two or more highly experienced mail order experts will offer directly opposite guidelines for mail order success.

This is as it should be for there is really only one basic "rule" for mail order success and that is:

There are no rules.

MAIL ORDER IMPROVEMENT CHECKLIST

This checklist was prepared by Old American Insurance Co. for use in analyzing its mail order materials.

1. OUTER ENVELOPE

Is the overall design neat and attractive?

Is the envelope related to the letterhead design-wise?

How do you rate the quality of paper stock as to color, opacity, feel?

Is the printing sharp?

Is the color of ink right?

How do you rate the positioning of elements?

Is this the best form of postage for this mailing?

Is the envelope easy to handle for inserting?

Does the window fit the order form exactly?

How do you rate the mailing piece for size?

2. LETTER

Does the lead promise a benefit?

Have you fired your biggest gun first?

Is there a BIG IDEA behind this letter?

Does the letter proceed in the logical pattern you have established for the reader?

Have you formed a "bucket-brigade" through the letter?

Have you offered proof of the pudding?

Is it clear how the reader is to order—and did you ask for the order?

Is the MONEY-BACK GUARANTEE stated clearly?

Does the letter have a conversational tone?

Does the letter have the "you" attitude?

Have you used between 70 and 80 words of one syllable for each 100 words written?

It there *anything* in the letter which may cause a legal misunderstanding?

Is the overall appearance neat and attractive?

Does the letter have a good postscript which focuses attention on the order form?

Is the letterhead related to the outer envelope design-wise?

How do you rate the quality of paper stock as to color, opacity, feel?

Is the printing sharp?

Is the ink coverage right?

How do you rate the letter for such details as proper folding arrangement, use of IBM Executive type, use of blue ink for signature?

MAIL ORDER IMPROVEMENT CHECKLIST (Cont.)

3. BUSINESS-REPLY ENVELOPE

Does the business-reply envelope *look* like a business-reply envelope?

Is it neat and attractive?

Does it conform exactly to postal regulations?

Is the printing sharp?

Are the ink colors right?

How do you rate the spacing or type elements?

Is the size adequate to carry the order form back?

Have we printed "Thank You" under the back flap?

Does the envelope flap stay closed when glued?

4. ORDER FORM

Does the order form completely summarize the proposition so that it stands alone?

Does the order form tie in with the copy in the letter?

Is all the information needed for the order handling department shown in the form?

Is the copy affirmative in nature?

Are the terms of the offer unmistakably clear?

Does a money-back guarantee (if applicable) appear on the form?

Is the design neat and attractive?

How do you rate the border design?

Is the order form "busy"?

Does the order form fit as it should if used in a window?

Is the printing sharp and clear?

How do you rate the arrangement of elements?

What may have worked well for nearly everyone selling products by mail order may *never* work for others. And what has failed for nearly everyone may be just the right technique for you.

Mail Order's Complex Techniques

Why bother to give a platform to those who suggest concrete ideas for success and those who point their fingers at specific routes to failure? The answer lies in the fact that mail order marketing is composed of complex techniques, requiring great attention to detail and constant testing. By using the guidelines offered by others you will be in a better position to recognize the areas requiring special attention.

But never say "it can't be done" until you have experimented and found out for yourself—using your own lists and selling your own products.

As you observe the frequent duplication of opinion as well as frequent differences of opinion on the following pages, it is hoped that you will feel as though you have had the opportunity to sit among the all-time greats of this business and get a good "feel" of the intricacies and complications of mail order advertising and selling.

Lew Kleid's Interviews

One of the finest studies of mail order selling and advertising methods was a series of interviews conducted by Lewis Kleid, president of Lewis Kleid Company, and originally published in *The Reporter of Direct Mail Advertising.* These were later collected into a book, *Mail Order Strategy,* which was distributed as a research report of the Direct Mail Advertising Assn. It is possible that this valuable volume is now out of print but should you want to read it, there may be a copy in your local library. The following tips have been culled from the pages of this book[3]:

Edith Walker, Direct Mail Manager, Book-of-the-Month Club:

Test Returns. I want at least 20% more orders than I actually need on a test because invariably when we follow up and use the balance of the list, it goes out in the bulk mailing and duplication and other factors cut down results two or three orders per thousand pieces mailed.

Fresh Names. As a rule, the fresher the names the better the response.

Longevity of Past Customers. We can go back as far as 15 years in soliciting our former members.

Cost per Order. The only factor to consider in mail order is the cost per order. Sometimes a lush deluxe mailing will buy orders at a lower cost than an economical budget package. In our case we have found that a handsome envelope justifies its extra expense. Ours are usually printed in four colors, using an attractive illustration and a teaser headline. Our usual mailing consists of a 6- by 9-inch envelope, letter, circular and a business reply card. They are printed on good-quality paper and in two or more colors. In the quantities that we run, the cost of extra color is not great and is justified on the basis of better appearance and more attention value.

Repeating Lists. There doesn't seem to be any problem in how many times you can use a good list.

Duplication. I am not concerned when the same person receives three or four letters from us staggered over several months. If anything, such repeti-

[3]The titles and affiliations shown for the interviewees are those at the time of Lew Kleid's interviews.

tion might be helpful. Duplicates received in the same mail, however, can cut down returns and create ill-will.

B. L. Mazel, Mail Order Consultant:

Bad Months to Mail. There is no such thing as a bad month to mail—no slump to stop activities—no holidays to be avoided. Christmas or the income tax period, Thanksgiving, Easter are all as good as any other time to mail—occasionally better. The basic factor is an analysis of what you have to sell, and a tie-in with a situation or urgency appeal.

The businessman or the investor is in business 12 months of the year and wants to make money every month. If you have something that will help him to succeed or become a better businessman, he is interested—regardless of the day of the week, the month of the year or the season.

Repeating Lists. You cannot hit a list too often. The only criterion is—will it pay out? If successive followups to the same names pull, keep at it until it ceases to pay.

Repeating Copy. It has proved profitable on many occasions to mail twice in one month to the same list using the same copy. The only change in the second letter was a memo affixed to the copy. In several instances the follow-up letter pulled better than the first letter.

Days to Mail. On the subject of the day of the week to mail or the best day to receive mail—throw all your preconceived ideas out the window. At best, the Post Office now is so unpredictable that the best-laid plans are meaningless. If the offer is sound, mail any time, every time, all the time.

Upgrading Orders. By giving the recipient an opportunity to upgrade his order it is often possible to increase dollar volume without disturbing the percentage of response. Examples of this technique in the sale of a book is to offer thumb-indexing or leather binding or copies printed on special paper—at a somewhat higher price. The strategy is simple. Just print an extra line on the order card. For example: "Just check here if you wish your copy thumb-indexed in gold at $9.95." A postscript to the letter making the deluxe offer is sometimes done—although it may not be necessary.

Letter Enclosures. Think twice before using a circular. If it seems essential, go ahead, but test it simultaneously against the same format omitting the circular. Then perhaps test it a third way without a circular but with the letter revised and expanded to incorporate the circular copy.

Leslie Davis, Special Assistant to the Publisher, "The Wall Street Journal":

Two-Side Letters. We used to put out two-page letters on two sheets. Our tests show we do better with two sides of a single sheet, save money, and actually get more orders.

Airmail Reply Request. For years we got a better return with a sticker, "Airmail Reply Requested," affixed to the message. The expense is no longer justified.

Personalization. Typing in a recipient's name originally paid. We find now that personalization no longer pays. That is on our letters. It continues worthwhile on our memo pieces.

Variation in Format. The looks of mail should be altered occasionally—and often the best thing to alter is the envelope size.

Third Class vs. First Class. Third class brings us just as many orders a thousand pieces as first class, only they come in slower.

Use of Outside Services. We think it is a good idea to retain outside talent. It has broadened our creative base and our point of view.

Duplication. Duplication is really offensive only when it is simultaneous—when two or more identical mailing pieces reach somebody in the same day's mail. It doesn't seem so objectionable when the duplicates are received at varying intervals.

If a man's name is no more than one list, he is probably a more important or more responsive prospect than the others; that is how his name got on more than one list in the first place. There must be something to the theory, because after we check lists against each other for duplication, we use the duplicates a few weeks later. Almost invariably they respond better than lists in which their names appeared.

We recover our actual cost of checking our duplicates when duplication hits 15% of total names checked. If under 15%, we still think it pays. We do not have to check all lists, by any means. We can avoid a lot of checking by scheduling lists carefully, by staggering our mailings, and by mailing different copy on lists we use at the same time and which we judge likely to duplicate each other materially.

We also check prospect lists against our subscriber names and pull them out of the prospect lists. If the percentage of such duplication is very small, we make a note of it and don't check that list against subscriber names next time. When an outside rented lists contains a heavy percentage of our subscriber names, we like it. The higher the percentage of subscriber names in a list, the better the rest of the list will usually pull for us.

John T. McKenzie, Advertising Manager, Standard & Poor's:

Letters. The copy appeal of the sales letter is the most important single factor in any mail campaign. Tests have established, time after time, that the sales letter is the most important element in the mailing "package."

Mailing Package. The ideal mail "package" is: a sales letter, circular, order form, order card, or request form and a return envelope combination.

Testing. It is rare indeed that the productiveness of a mailing list may be predicted. It is a case of test, test, and more testing.

Simplicity. It is not always the elaborate mailing piece that pays off the best. In fact, it more often works the other way. The simple piece with a good sales message very often outpulls the elaborate and more expensive mailing.

Prospect Lists. Through experience we have found that we can profitably mail to our new prospect lists for five years.

Airmail Reply. We tested airmail return cards against stamped Government return cards and found that airmail pulled better at lower cost.

Label Addressing. We checked label addressing against direct envelope addressing on 9- by 12-inch envelopes, and found to our amazement that label addressing worked well.

Paul A. Murtaugh, Advertising Manager, The Research Institute of America:

Too Much Testing. The man who becomes "test-happy" misses the BIG opportunities.

Take a Chance. Too many people in mail order selling are dangerously overtimid.

Renewals. Short-term subscriptions do not renew as well as the regular full-term subscription.

Free Samples. There is a great deal of evidence that people do not value what is sent to them free and unsolicited, no matter how good it is.

Letter Gimmicks. Too much gingerbread makes the prospect (he's getting pretty sniffy these rays) look for the fine Machiavellian hand of the tricky copywriter. I, therefore, don't use selling copy in the margins. A second color in the body copy is not common in business letters, and for that reason I usually avoid it—at least on the first page where you are dealing with snap impressions. On the following pages, I use color wherever it will add up to easier reading.

Envelope Teasers. Teasers on envelopes and headlines on the letter copy immediately flag-wave that *"this here stuff is advertising."* That is not necessarily bad if the copy is well-written—but if the envelope bears a promise which is not fulfilled in the letter copy, the teaser is likely to do more harm than good. It must be used with logic and honesty. There must be no disillusionment.

Test Variables. Mathematics simply cannot take into account the many variables of testing.

Elsworth S. Howell, The Grolier Society:

Frequency of Mailings. If you have established a friendly relationship with your customers, you just can't wear the names out. I doubt if you can ever wash out a good list by frequent mailings.

Product Testing. I cannot take any chances in waiting for a better season (to test new items) because the item might go dead by the time other mailers or retailers had given it a plug. Ours is a 12-months-a-year program. I am constantly testing.

Value of Lists. Give me a good mailing list and I will find a product for it. I've seen mediocre copy work well on a good list and good copy fall flat on a poor one. So I would rate the factors in selling by mail: (1) *The List,* (2) *The Product or Service,* and (3) *The Copy.*

Value of Company Name. Any time we use a trick company name to our customers, results drop 50% or more. I venture that a person who knows you and has done business with you is twice as responsive as an otherwise qualified mail order buyer who does not know you.

Who Should Pay Postage? House lists will produce as many replies with a plain envelope as with a business reply. More important, the percentage of cash with order is as high or higher where the customer pays his own postage on the reply envelope. On lists which we rent and where customers have not been conditioned to our methods, we find it desirable to use a standard business reply envelope.

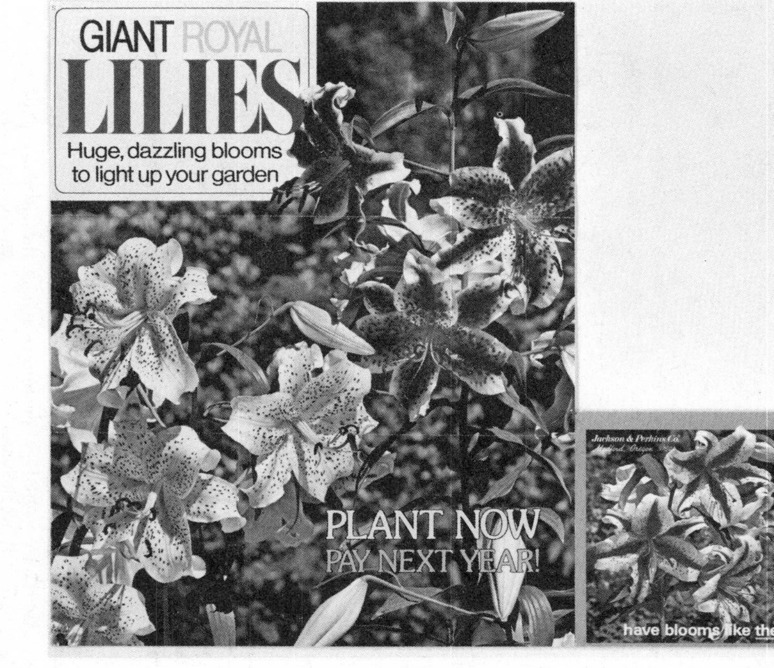

Color is used effectively by many mail order advertisers. This mailing from Jackson & Perkins Company of Medford, Oregon had both a full-color illustration on the envelope and a brilliant color cover illustration on the four-page folder enclosed.

James P. Connell, Sales Manager, The Kiplinger Agency:

Color for Letters. The cost of a second color (on letters) cannot be justified on a result basis. In any case, we prefer to maintain a business letter appearance by using only the standard one-color black multigraphed message.

Airmail. We use airmail envelopes in our renewal series for the psychological effect of not missing a single issue.

Risks. If you want to be right 95 times out of 100, you eliminate practically all risk. You eliminate the opportunity to discover new markets and new copy appeal. The idea is to average out some of the risks and mistakes with success. Most mailers do well if they are right seven times out of ten.

Expires. We never destroy an expiration name. We keep consolidating the very old ones as nixies and subscribers are removed. The oldest names work as well as any average mail order list we rent. Expires of recent years are far superior to any lists we can possibly rent.

A. P. Jurgensen, Promotion Director, Consumer Reports:

Airmail. Airmail outpulls regular business reply envelopes only in certain timely or special situations. Where there is no urgency the results may be somewhat deceptive in that the orders come in faster, but the end result is not as good as a conventional business reply.

Circulars. In every test with the exception of one, the inclusion of a circular more than paid for itself. We have a big story to tell and we need the space to tell it.

List Tests. We have made very detailed analysis of lists, hoping to find a formula for what quantity to test, but formulas in this field are like will-o'-the-wisps. Good judgment seems to be the only formula, or, to put it less euphemistically, the calculated guess.

James Dooley, President, Atlantic Advertising:

Airmail. We formerly enclosed only a business reply card. When we added an airmail reply envelope our percentage of cash-with-orders increased almost 20%. We have not tested a regular business reply envelope against the airmail reply because we feel the extra expense of airmail postage is justified since it gets the orders back to us sooner and enables us to give better service.

Number of Enclosures. The more we pack into an envelope, the more opportunity we have to get an order. The man who buys by mail welcomes and reads our various offers.

S. Arthur (Red) Dembner, Circulation Manager, "Newsweek":

Testing Letters. We test our most successful basic letter against three or four new letters every season. If one of the new letters pulls better, we switch to that copy—and if it doesn't, we keep the old copy until we find something that will work better.

Preprinted Order Forms. One of the basic ideas in direct mail is that whatever makes ordering easier helps results. We believe the fact that the recipient does not have to write out his name and address (no preaddressed order cards) makes ordering simpler. It also helps our fulfillment department because the typewriter or stencil addressing on the order cards is more legible than handwriting.

Reply Envelopes. We do not ask for a remittance with order, but we do enclose a business reply envelope along with a business reply card for those who prefer to remit. A sufficiently large percentage of respondents do send a remittance with order to justify the extra cost of enclosing the reply envelope.

Robert L. Fenton, Subscription Manager, Street & Smith Publications Inc.:

Label Addressing. When lists of comparable quality are used, labels will do about as well as any other addressing method—and labels frequently cost less.

Renewals. Subscriptions which were acquired originally by mail order methods are segregated from those acquired by field selling, since each group requires different treatment for renewal mailings.

Preaddressed Order Forms. On our magazines we have not found much difference in results between an addressed order card visible through a window envelope and a plain order card in a regular envelope. The big advantage for us is that the preaddressed order card coming back is so much easier to decipher than are handwritten order forms. Another point to remember is that order cards take less space than envelopes and are easier to ship and store.

Stacking vs. Nesting. Our tests show no appreciable advantage or disadvantage in stacking vs. nesting.

Large Lists. The larger the list, the more heterogeneous the names are.

Duplication. Gift lists may have as much as 30% duplication.

Cash vs. Credit Buyers. With magazine subscriptions those who pay cash tend to renew by cash while those who say "bill me later" tend to renew the same way.

Lawrence G. Chait, Director of List Research, Time Inc.:

Value of Lists. You may sell unattractive products to a good mailing list—but you can never sell even the best product to a bad prospect list.

Audiences. People who are doing things *today,* buying things *today,* traveling *today,* are apparently more receptive to new offers and new ideas.

Maxwell C. Ross, famous circulation expert:

False Economy. It may be false economy, even in these days of rising costs, to pinch pennies and cut corners. No economy should ever be put into effect without carefully testing what it might do to results. Our own experience has been that quality pays off. A mailing piece should have character, and if it is cheapened too much it no longer reflects the prestige and importance of the mailer.

Envelopes. A large percentage of people read all their mail, but a certain percentage won't even open the envelope if it looks like advertising. Others, in varying degrees, open the envelopes and read the contents. Since you haven't a chance unless the envelope is opened—it is vital that it be attractive and that it tempts the person to examine the contents. Teasers can help do this but are extremely dangerous. A poor teaser is worse than none at all.

The same goes for illustrations. They must be carefully planned and carefully tested. The more people you can get to open the envelope and read your letter—the more people you can sell.

Preaddressed Order Forms. We make periodic checks of the effectiveness of a preaddressed reply form visible through a window and find that it works better than a regular addressed envelope and an unaddressed order form—or a regular addressed envelope and an addressed order card.

How Weather Affects Results. Our experience shows that a mailing received during bad weather will far outpull mail received on good days. It is a good idea to study U.S. Government weather reports and try to time your mailing to reach the recipient during *bad* weather.

How News Affects Results. When the headlines (in newspapers) are extremely interesting, less attention will be paid to direct mail.

Edward N. Mayer, Jr., President, James Gray Inc.:

Perfect Mailing Package. The perfect mailing package is almost unanimously accepted today to be one that is mailed in an envelope and contains a letter, a circular, an order blank or inquiry form, and a reply envelope.

Letter Styles. Shrewd advertisers have been trying to find out for years whether a multigraphed, lithographed, or printed letter brings in the most business. The results have varied all over the lot. We have never seen any conclusive proof that one kind was better than any other.

Filled-in Letters. If you are going to have your letters filled in, be sure that you get as close to a perfect match as it is humanly possible. A sloppy, careless fill-in will always do you more harm than good.

Autotyped Letters. If you want replies to your offer, the automatic typewriter is your wonder machine.

Second Color. The use of a second color both in letters and circulars generally pays off. We don't remember more than three cases where a two-color circular didn't get more business—and at a lower cost—than a one-color job. Products that have sight appeal usually do well when the circular is printed in four colors, but two colors are about all any letter will stand.

Reply Cards. Practically always, reply cards printed on colored paper in a color of ink that is not the same as that used in either letter or circular will do a better job than two-color or single matching pieces. You will have to find out your own winning color—but contrasting color seems to be a cinch to increase your replies.

Two-Page Letters. Some find that separate sheets pay off (for two-page letters), others do not. It does seem logical, however, that if you can hold the attention of the reader down to the bottom of the first page, it won't make any difference whether he has to turn the page or pick up another one.

Separate Reply Devices. Making your order or inquiry form part of your letter, circular, or mailing piece will reduce the number of replies you receive. A separate form has increased business as little as 12% and as much as 430%.

Duplicate Order Forms. Whenever it has been tested, the enclosure of two order or inquiry forms brings in more replies than the enclosure of only one. The use of both a separate and an attached form will invariably get you more replies than either one used alone.

Folders vs. Booklets. A circular or a folder is a better enclosure for your mailing than a booklet. Booklets are in most cases not nearly as effective as the less dignified but more commercial, and thus more action-compelling, circular. There are exceptions, as usual, but by and large booklets do not pay out. Booklets seem to kill any immediacy of an offer, and results trickle in for an extremely long period of time.

Postscripts. Handwritten postscripts at the end of a sales letter increase the number of replies. There are many ways to add a really personal touch to your mailings, and practically every one of them will pay off.

Color Tests. Color tests, either of printing or paper, show one thing one week and another the following. There is no always-first color. Results vary with the weather, the news, the kind of list, and the product or service sold. The only definite knowledge we have gained about color is that in a continuing series of mailings to the same list, changing the color of paper and the color of printing will be helpful.

Maxwell Sackheim, President, Maxwell Sackheim Company Inc.:

Buying Customers. In the mail order business you should aim to *buy a customer,* not merely make a sale. The original order is important but you do not have a business unless there is some habit or repeat characteristic.

Geographic Location. The closer (geographically) the prospect is to the seller, the better the response. If you are mailing nationally, use two addresses (one for the East Coast and one for the West Coast). On the other hand, there is no disadvantage in being located in a small city as opposed to a big city.

Bill Me Later. The "bill me later" technique lends itself beautifully to automatic renewal of anything that has a repeat appeal. It is the best mail order selling device. It batters down suspicion and resistance. It immediately inspires confidence in your offer. Every device that removes resistance is bound to increase the percentage of orders. From a business point of view you must balance the increased percentage of response against credit losses. But usually the extra orders more than compensate.

Odd-figure Pricing. An odd figure gives the illusion of a price reduction or an account computed on actual costs. An even figure ($4, $8 or $10) seems contrived to make the maximum profit for the seller.

The Offer. When all is said and done, I think the *offer* is the most vital part of a mailing. A wonderful offer on ordinary merchandise is better, in my judgment, than a bad offer on good merchandise.

Henry Hoke's Roundup

One of the all-time authorities on direct mail was the late Henry Hoke, Sr., who for many years edited and published *The Reporter of Direct Mail Advertising.* In addition to regular coverage of mail order advertising in his magazine, Henry Hoke edited a special book on the subject—*How to Think About Mail Order.*

Much of the material in this book consists of the comments of mail order experts. The following tips have been extracted from the comments of these experts[4]:

Jack McDonnell, President, The Epicures' Club:

Mail Order Comes Second. Don't start a mail order or direct mail business. Start a *business* and if it happens that direct mail is the best way to run it, well and good. Too many people get the mail order bug and they decide they are going to run a mail order business. Then they hunt up the products or the idea to sell. I think it is probably the most common error that is made and probably the most expensive one that could be made.

Mail Order Economics. Buy a book on economics and determine whether the mail order or direct mail approach is the right one for your product or service. Remember, if you have something good to sell it will be copied. And your competitors will ruthlessly shoot at your most vulnerable point. If what you are selling can be better sold through stores or through agents your mail order days may be numbered.

Don't Kid Yourself. Shoot for facts—and don't kid yourself. The hardest thing in the world is to convince the guy who wants to go into the mail order business that he should not go into it.

Promote Aggressively. Go into it with both feet—*when you have got something good.* There is nothing more pitiful to watch than the person with a good idea that he does not promote aggressively.

Keys to Success. The same things make for success in mail order that make for success in other businesses. You have to have a reason for being. You have to be guided by facts. You have to plan ahead. You have to be persistent. You have to be honest.

Boyce Morgan, Boyce Morgan & Associates:

Right Product. Be sure your product is right, and that your basic proposition or offer is attractive. Then mail as regularly and consistently as you can, even though your mailings at times are small.

Seasonal Products. If you have reason to believe your product is seasonal in nature, find out what the best mailing times are *for yourself.* Even so, be in the mail as constantly as the nature of your product or service will permit.

Avoid Rigidity. Plan your mailing program well in advance, but don't let it be too rigid. Be ready to expand it or cut it back according to current returns.

---

[4]The titles and affiliations shown for each expert are those at the time of publication of *How to Think About Mail Order* (1954).

When to Change. Once you are selling successfully, don't change your formula *merely for the sake of change.* You may be tired of a sales letter, seeing it every week for six months. But your prospects have seen it only once or twice and probably won't remember it the second time. Test constantly to try to improve your mailing package, but change *only* to better the returns.

Percentage of Return. Don't take percentage returns as your standard of results, except as they are a guide to your ultimate order cost. Percentages are deceiving, because a return that is profitable for one mailer may be ruinous for another. Order costs, not percentages, should be your criterion.

Buy Orders. When you know how *much* you can pay for an order and still operate profitably, then *buy all the orders you can get* at or below that figure. That is the way to build volume and reduce the amount of fixed expenses that each order must carry.

Final Average. Play percentages, watch your overall returns, and don't be either elated or disheartened by results on individual mailings. It is your final *average* order cost at the end of a year that will determine your success or failure.

Record Keeping. Know your costs thoroughly, and keep the best records you can. The records of too many mail order businesses are very poor, and bad records are an invitation to disaster.

Mail Order Copy. Let's refuse to accept the idea that just because we must write more or less to formula to produce results, we must use the same old words and phrases over and over again.

James Mosely, Mosely Mail Order List Service:

Selecting Products. The world is full of opportunities for selling things and services by mail. My suggestion to would-be mail order sellers is to look over a great many magazines, especially of the *Popular Mechanics* type, answer lots of ads, browse around in big department stores, visit gift and toy exhibits, and so forth. Read books, such as, *The Robert Collier Letter Book,* Frank Egner's and Earle Buckley's works on mail order.

Successful Items. Successful mail order calls for selling an item that will, if possible, break even or close to it on the first sale, will get a new customer, and then will sell him other items, or repeat sales of the same item, at a good margin of profit and at low direct mail selling expense.

C. B. Mills, O. M. Scott & Sons Company:

Inquiries. We have discovered for our own purposes, that an inquiry actually instigated by some homeowner is worth 30 cold names.

Poor Direct Mail. The worst thing in mail order is the slipshod stuff which goes through the mail disguised as a selling vehicle—muddying the waters for others with a good product and a selling message well presented.

Truth in Advertising. One of the first DMAA conventions I ever attended was addressed by a man named McIntosh.[5] He made a statement I always

[5]Probably Charles H. McIntosh of Duluth, Minnesota, who was the president of DMAA in 1920.

remembered: "Nothing is worth advertising which would not sell itself if the truth about it were known."

Ed Proctor, The Guild Company:

Repeat Business. Advertising by mail is usually the most expensive way to gain new customers. Often the first sale results in a loss. However, because customers gained by mail have a tendency to be more loyal, they will, as a rule, have a greater life expectancy. Therefore, an operation should be set up so that there is an opportunity to make frequent sales to each customer. Thus, repeat business, while wiping out initial losses, can pyramid profits provided the products or services offered have broad markets and are priced right.

George Dugdale, The Drumcliff Company:

Mail Order Requirements. The mail order business needs everything that any other successful business needs, except, perhaps, an expensive, well-situated location.

Single Items. Very few can keep a mail order activity going for many years on a single item and they have to be alert to pick up good items to add to the line.

John Yeck, Yeck & Yeck:

Mail Order Copy. The most common error is to overestimate the knowledge and underestimate the intelligence of an audience.

Maxwell Ross, Old American Insurance Company:

Corporate Image. Back of every great institution there must be a great idea. So be sure that your company is founded on a great idea. What is it that sets your organization apart from all others? If you have done nothing in the way of advertising or publicity to mark it off from all of the rest of its competitors, to give it a corporate personality that is known and recognized, then you are neglecting one of the most important aids to its growth.

Lewis Kleid, Lewis Kleid Company:

Mail Order Consultants. The best bet if you haven't had a big background of experience is to buy the best talent you can afford. A mail order consultant can easily earn his fee in the mistakes he will prevent.

Chances for Success. The odds are very great against a newcomer being successful in the mail order field. For every Jack Citizen who started a "mail order business" on the kitchen table, there are countless thousands who will never make the grade. It takes more than money. It takes "original ideas," "know-how" "merchandising skill," and "fortitude."

And from Henry Hoke, himself, came this basic tip: "What is the distinguishing characteristic of a good, practical mail order proposition? The product or the service offered must be *different.* It must have some special characteristic of *uniqueness* in the product or a service which has some unique character which cannot be duplicated easily just around the corner at your favorite store."

Franklin C. Wertheim's 100 Tips

Franklin C. Wertheim has developed a reputation both as a mail order consultant and a long-time reporter of the mail order scene. In 1955, he compiled an even one hundred basic tips for mail order success. His list was published in *Advertising Requirements* under the title, "101 Tips for Direct Mail Advertising." (Tip No. 101 was a suggestion that readers of the magazine send in their own tips to the editors of the magazine.) Here are Mr. Wertheim's tips:

1. *It's the offer that counts.* All the other things add or detract, the kind of stamps, the hard sell or undersell copy, the letterhead, the reply envelope, etc. Each has its influence, but when the chips are down, *it's the offer that counts.*
2. *P. S. I love you.* After you've said and done everything in the letter that you set out to do, add a P.S. with a powerful clincher that will linger in the prospect's mind.
3. *Toss in a little something extra.* Like that proverbial thirteenth roll in the baker's dozen, something extra after you have convinced them to order makes them send in the order blank with a smile.
4. *Make it easy for the customer.* Be big-hearted and enclose a postage-paid return envelope. It is polite, and it surely ups the returns.
5. *The law of the golden bird.* Your best potential customers are the people who have already bought from you. Send them new offers at regular intervals.
6. *Don't brag.* Let the other man brag for you. Use testimonials, plenty of testimonials, stacks of testimonials. People can doubt one booster, but who can argue with a regiment?
7. *Airmail.* To people who do not get a large volume of mail, an airmail letter can be impressive. But don't use Special Delivery except under special circumstances. A Special Delivery getting to a man's house in the middle of the night or on a Sunday can well leave a bad taste when it's made for a commercial proposition.
8. *Let those tired old words rest.* Haven't met a man in a long time who was really astounded, amazed, or did it now! People are fed up with last chance! . . . once in a lifetime! . . . never again! . . . offers.
9. *Typefaces.* How about trying a sparkling new typeface on an electric typewriter?
10. *Estimating.* When estimating the cost of a mailing, have another party go over the figures. Every so often a little item like the cost of the postage is overlooked, or maybe even the cost of affixing the stamps.
11. *The "sniggllefritzz" law.* Double *g,* double *l,* double *z.* If you are not positive of the correct spelling of a prospect's name, better leave it off. He won't mind being called "Dear Sir."

12. *Use the right list.* An offer of burglar tools to bishops would most likely get as poor a response as travel folders sent to the occupant list at Leavenworth.

13. *A handwritten notation.* You can lend that needed human touch with a handwritten notation in the margin of a stiff business letter.

14. *Get down to rock bottom, broad appeals.* Most people like home-baked cake, but darn few have an overpowering interest in recipes for fried snails. Remember, despite the interest in Jaguars more people end up buying Fords.

15. *Everybody loves a bargain.* Offer one.

16. *Fire your biggest gun first.* If your headline does not get the prospect's attention, the rest of your flowing prose is going to follow the lead right into the wastebasket.

17. *The vigorish law.* If an offer is pulling even a small percentage of profit, keep it rolling. Hunt up new lists. Keep hitting the old lists from different angles. A small percent in your favor can make you a lot in the long run. (Editor's note: "Vigorish" in gambling-house parlance is the cut the house takes on every roll of the dice, usually 5%.)

18. *The over the hill to the poor house law.* If an offer is not pulling or a list does not pan out, junk it, no matter how much work and labor you have in the deal or compilation. The first loss is the best loss.

19. *Ask for the order.* It is great to be nice and chatty and friendly, but if you are trying to sell something, don't get so wrapped up in details you forget to ask for the order.

20. *Watch your calories.* If you sell by mail, a difference of one ounce to zone eight can cost as high as 26 cents. Remember, diamonds are cheaper to ship than elephants and can easily cost the same.

21. *Fill-ins.* Don't spoil a personal letter with a poorly matched fill-in. Rather, choose a different color type or even a good headline.

22. *Keep an eye on the other guy.* You may make the ruggedest rubber baby buggy bumpers of any house in the trade, but if your competitor offers him to the jobbers at $4.95 a dozen the week before your mailing at $5.95 a dozen, don't hold your breath waiting for the orders.

23. *Make that offer clear.* Sure, you wrote that copy so that any man of normal intelligence could understand it, but how about the slightly subnormals or even a very busy executive?

24. *Colored ribbons.* Colored typewriter ribbon on colored paper gives an unusual effect.

25. *Don't be a chowder head.* Listen to the old-timers. There are a thousand men of great experience eager to impart knowledge to you. You don't have to believe everything you hear, but a half-hour spent with a printer, space salesman, envelope seller, lettershop proprietor, etc., can be well worth the time and it costs you nothing.

26. *Know your postal laws and regulations.* Follow them to the letter. Your local post office may let a mailing slide by, but some n'th grade clerk in Pastafazzoola, Pennsyltucky, will pick it up and a big dated mailing can hang fire waiting for a Washington ruling.

27. *Get to know the men at your local post office.* They can save you a lot of grief and give you plenty of good advice.

28. *The crayon law.* Every inquiry rates a full and complete answer, even the famous, "I would write this letter in pen and ink, but they only allow us to have crayons in here." Who knows? It might just possibly be from a big purchasing agent on a rest cure.

29. *One picture is worth a thousand words.* Don't spare the illustrations.

30. *For guaranteed returns use a strong guarantee.* The stronger the guarantee, the stronger the returns.

31. *Use commemorative postage stamps whenever possible.* It's only a small detail, but it is surprising how many people collect them for themselves or friends or charities.

32. *You will never get rich digging the other guy's ditch.* Be the primary producer or have control over the products you sell. Do not be the lad who buys from the jobber, who buys from the agent, who gets the stuff from the importer who places his orders with the manufacturer. If anybody makes a buck in this chain, it is not going to be the joker at the end of the line.

33. *Test, test, test.* And when you are finished testing—retest!

34. *Don't grind the faces of the poor suppliers.* Sure, you must watch your costs like a hawk, but there is a big difference between getting a good, fair price and, as the Chinese put it, "Breaking the other man's rice bowl." Someday you might want a favor in a hurry and it might just be needed from a supplier you treated right—or rough.

35. *Be yourself.* Highfalutin copy and graces send your offer to that lowest of places—the wastebasket.

36. *Rome wasn't built in one mailing.* So don't expect any one offering to do the job of a steady build-up campaign.

37. *Deadbeats.* If you do hit a real deadbeat and he owes you $5 and it costs you $10 to sue him, sue him! Make life hard for him and sooner or later life becomes easier for all mailers.

38. *Keeping the paragraphs short and punchy* . . . will keep the orders many and bunchy.

39. *Don't sell buggy whips.* Even if your direct mail is prize-winning in format, it still has to offer something people go for. Sell something with a future—not a past.

40. *Fancy jobs.* For short, fancy runs where you have the time to shop around, you can get some pretty good quotes from off-shore firms. European printers are used to handling small runs in fancy formats.

41. *The way to a man's pocketbook is through his kids.* Any offer that is for the children will get a complete and sympathetic reading from parents.

42. *Put your customers to work.* Offer them premiums for securing new accounts.

43. *Mail on Monday.* Have your orders arrive toward the end of the week instead of on a Monday. Check your own mail for volume of incomings. Tuesday usually has the lowest stack of incoming, but it is hard to schedule mail to hit on a Tuesday.

44. *The only person appearing in your direct mail should be the man to whom it is directed.* Keep your own problems out of your direct mail. Nobody is worried about you, except maybe your creditors.

45. *Try addressing a piece of mail by crayon or fountain brush.* See if it doesn't get a high readership.

46. *Labels.* Okay, so your letters are neat and clean and your copy clear and sparkling. How about that tired old label on your outgoing packages? That is a part of your direct mail appearance also.

47. *Name vs. title.* A letter addressed to a title will often reach more of the men you want than a letter addressed to *an old list* by individuals' names. Men die, move, quit, resign, get fired, and change duties, but the title goes on and on.

48. *The "Gosh by Heck" law.* It is better to have your mail order literature a little on the plain-spoken, homespun, maybe even dowdy side, using square-shooting copy, than on the ultra high-gloss, sharp-worded, high-pressure, slick side.

49. *Renting lists.* If you have a good list of customers, rent it out through a reliable list broker on a one-time-use basis. Exercise never hurt a good list. In fact, it makes people more mail order conscious. The extra income is pure gravy.

50. *Go easy.* While giving your list of names plenty of exercise, do not work it to death. Once every week or two is healthy.

51. *Mail in off season.* The pull is sometimes surprising. Besides, one man's off season is another man's busy season.

52. *The "what never" law.* The customer is never wrong. You should give 100% absolute satisfaction guaranteed or money returned without question or quibble. To paraphrase Gilbert and Sullivan, "The customer is never wrong. What, never? Well, hardly ever!"

53. *Gadget letters are great attention-getters.* But don't let the gadget overshadow the offer.

54. *Give everybody time.* The photographer, printer, lettershop, copy writer will turn in a better job if not rushed.

55. *Schedule your jobs on a master time plan.* Then make sure each element meets its deadline. There is nothing more discouraging than to have a mailing almost ready to go and to then find that somebody goofed and one element, like the return envelopes, has not arrived.

56. *Try mailing from abroad.* That foreign stamp and postmark have a flavor that is hard to ignore.

57. *Don't be a pin stick of misery to your suppliers.* Everyone likes to give a nice guy a break, but the rough rider stays in the saddle only as long as he is wide awake.

58. *Get occasional competitive bids on your work even if your suppliers are reliable.* Everyone tends to stay a little more on the ball if he knows that competition is lurking quietly around the corner.

59. *Subscribe.* Take every magazine and buy every book on the subject of direct mail and mail order. Some of them are pretty miserable, but one single good idea gleaned from the whole lot will more than pay for all of them with the profits or savings from just one mailing.

60. *The bigger they come the harder they fall.* Don't copy the big boys' stuff. Just because they are big they may not be successful. Use your own ideas.

61. *Keep an idea file to help stimulate your thinking.* When anything interesting comes in, just toss it in the file for future reference. Then when that black day comes and the old brain hits a blank wall, just thumb through the file and prime the idea pump.

62. *Code every section of an offering.* Don't make the mistake of judging the pull from the overall picture. One heroic list may be carrying the ball for a lot of dodoes.

63. *Don't insult the reader's intelligence with a lot of fanciful claims.* Remember the old military maxim of giving the fellow on the other side credit for knowing as much as you do—maybe more.

64. *Keep your prices in round dollars for low-price items.* A lot of people who would not hunt up a check book, will put a loose dollar or a five spot in your return envelope. The increased orders will more than make up for the few chiselers or actual lost orders where people say they sent cash but never received the goods. Uncle Sam's mails are remarkably safe.

65. *Offer to split the loss.* An offer to split the loss does not cost you much when a man claims his cash sent to you was never acknowledged. It keeps the customers happy and keeps the few chiselers off balance. A note to the post office will alert employees to check on professional claimers.

66. *Get product insurance.* If you are selling anything that is not absolutely foolproof, product insurance is a good bet. If it is not obtainable, don't touch the item.

67. *Contract out as much work as possible.* You can probably save a dime or even a fat thousand dollars by doing addressing, folding, sealing, mailing, etc., from your own premises. Then you are no longer in the mail order business but have gone into the lettershop business. Also, a pro in any field can almost always do things faster, cheaper, and better than an amateur.

68. *In picking a trade name get one that starts with the letter "A."* This puts you near the top in trade directories. Also, some business houses pay their bills in alphabetical order.

69. *In writing copy hit them hard with that headline.* It is half the battle.

70. *Locating an address for return mail.* It is a good idea to pick a post office where they will deliver mail to you even if misaddressed, Small post offices almost always will, big post offices just will not take the trouble. Also, a smaller post office will let you skip using a box number. It looks bad and cuts down the returns.

71. *If at all possible, show the product in use.* People have lazy imaginations.

72. *Order blanks.* If you use an order blank built into a letter, you can save a piece of printing, but make sure you have a dotted line. A sketch of a pair of scissors clipping it will give the reader the impetus to action.

73. *Time payments.* A big-ticket item can be more easily sold by allowing for time payments. Check your mailing list as to income groupings.

74. *Free.* Folks, including some in Washington, are getting mighty skeptical of *free* offers that turn out to have hooks in them or conditions attached. So, if you use a *free* offer make sure it has no strings attached.

75. *Stock art.* Stock cuts, stock photography, and stock art are inexpensive and can do a mighty good job on a small budget. Use plenty of them.

76. *Fill-ins.* In using Hooven and other mechanically typed letters, insert a stop in the body copy in a logical place for once again inserting the recipient's name. At the additional cost of a penny or two, this eliminates doubt as to the individuality of the offer.

77. *The busier the man, the shorter the letter.* An opportunity seeker may have all day to consider your offer. The president of the bank may steal 15 minutes to consider 20 propositions.

78. *Make sure your phone number is on your letterhead.* There are people who will phone a thousand miles rather than hunt up a stamp.

79. *Try your next test on a four-way split.* Try the new offer against the old and each offer against itself with no change except in the coding. You may get some results that will cause you to throw away that book on statistical analysis—and drive in the future by the seat of your pants.

80. *Give a full description of your product or services.* Make it brief, but get in all the pertinent data. Just because you know all the details, do not assume that your prospect has a crystal ball in his desk drawer.

81. *Mail order propositions.* If a man comes to you with a sure-fire proposition in mail order, ask the simple question to yourself, "What does he need me for, why doesn't he swing the deal himself?"

82. *Don't cry "Wolf."* A legitimate warning of a price increase will often pay off in a quick rise in sales, but don't get the reputation of crying "Wolf" when there is no "wolf" in sight.

83. *Benefits.* Make sure that you have promised benefits and that these benefits are easily obtainable by your prospect and are inherent in your offer. Don't let him think, "This is nice but of no use to me."

84. *Handwritten address.* A handwritten address to a home will often gain attention over a typed address, particularly if personal-type stationery is used with it.

85. *In picking lists make sure you get fresh, live ones.* A lettershop recently saved a client a considerable sum by noticing that the list they were given to address from was marked, "List of Corporations in This State," and in small letters, "who have filed for dissolution during the past year."

86. *Paper stock.* An unusual paper stock or a colored stock can often add much interest to your mail. Try one of the antiques or woven papers for a change.

87. *Your type might stand a job of face-lifting.* Get hold of a good book of new typefaces. Your printer can be of great help, but watch out that he doesn't steer you back to that old, tired font that has been in the shop for 99 years.

88. *The real thing.* A swatch of material or a piece of the plastic or metal from which your product is made can give the customer the "feel" of your offer so he can judge for himself that it is worthy.

89. *Boxholder mailings.* Unless they are used for a local deal or a product of universal appeal, boxholder mailings are a waste of postage, printing, and time.

90. *Names.* If you cannot tell from the name if the party is a man, woman, or child, use the title "Mr."

91. *Services.* In using the services of experts, consultants, advisers, and advertising agencies in the direct mail field, ask the old fight manager's question, "Whom did he ever lick?" To paraphrase Goethe, "There is nothing more expensive than ignorance in action."

92. *Be the bearer of glad tidings.* Tell good news. Everybody like a happy ending. In addition to testimonials, short and heart-warming stories will produce results.

93. *Keep following up your inquiries.* An inquiry is never dead until the sender expires. At least on mass mailings, a good inquirer list will always outpull a cold list. Some of them will come to life with each sending.

94. *Carbon copies.* A carbon copy of your original letter, with a note attached saying that an answer has not as yet been received, will often stir up action.

95. *Checking readership.* In checking the readership of direct mail that does not call for immediate response, such as a house organ, try burying the attractive offer of a free gift somewhere deep down in the copy. A nice calendar or one of the company's mechanical pencils, or maybe a tour of the plant or a sample of a product will do the trick.

96. *Collecting letters.* In writing collection letters it does not hurt to give a peek at the iron fist reposing inside the velvet glove. Do this in a nice way at first—later on show the fist.

97. *Inspirational letters to salesmen.* Remember, salesmen are psychologists themselves. Make your mail concrete with facts and examples. Otherwise, the salesmen will dismiss it as "just another dose of the same old pap."

98. *Envelopes.* Brown official-type envelopes in April and die-cut front bill envelopes around the first of any month get extra readership.

99. *Trial mailings.* In sending out an expensive mailing it is a good idea to first send out an inexpensive piece under Return Requested, to clear the lists of dead wood.

100. *Do unto others as you would have others do unto you.* The Golden Rule is as true in direct mail and mail order as in every other sphere of human activity.

"Printers' Ink" Checklist

One of the best checklists for mail order was originally published by *Printers' Ink* magazine and was later reprinted in Robert Baker's book, *Help Yourself to Better Mail Order.* The checklist contains 120 basic suggestions culled from the experience of mail order advertisers, agencies and media. While many of the ideas do not have universal application, constantly reviewing the checklist will help any mail order advertiser—neophyte or pro—to avoid making costly mistakes.

Company

1. Select a brief, compact, easily remembered name.
2. Give a homey, informal touch to the company setup.
3. Use a mailing address that can handle a large mail volume (not another company's address unless you're a principal in it).

Product

4. Choose a good product of acceptable quality.
5. Select something that people need.
6. Try to select a product in considerable demand—or an unusual or unique product difficult to get elsewhere, that individual retailers can't afford to carry because of the small local demand (adding up, however, to large national demand).
7. Perhaps an item newly popular with large groups of people such as ex-GIs, Canasta players, television fans.
8. Try to tie up the source of your product to reduce competition.
9. Perhaps a product generally in short supply but available to you.
10. A product that will lead up to switching consumers to new, successor, or alternate products.
11. If supplies become low, switch products.
12. It must not be too costly to make in small quantities at first (no expensive dies).
13. Brand-new merchandise has an edge over standard catalog items.

Line

14. Develop a line; you will probably never get rich on one item.
15. Use a succession of items.
16. Promote a variety of products.
17. Sell services as well as products.

Samples

18. Offer samples if possible, particularly if the products need to be examined to be better appreciated.

19. Don't make samples superior to actual merchandise; customer will be suspicious, irritated, perhaps lost forever.

Packaging

20. Use colorful, imaginative packaging.
21. Use practical, hard-wearing, proper-size packaging.
22. Have ready supply available in proportion to product orders.

Shipping

23. Check competing transportation (mail, freight, etc.), and use cheapest.
24. Prepay postage on all paid orders.
25. Watch shipping weight so that slight excess doesn't boost shipping cost into next higher bracket.
26. Address with complete, legible information.
27. Guarantee postage so that the post office will notify the addressee.

Supplier

28. Try nearby suppliers first.
29. A reliable supplier is really the keystone of a mail order operation.
30. Will he guarantee his output for quality and volume?
31. Will he make small deliveries at first, step up production as needed?

Purchases

32. Buy at a price permitting your proper markup but keeping suppier in business.

Selling Price

33. Price should be fair.
34. Figure in prepaid postage.
35. Use round numbers—preferably one coin or one bill (not odd-cent prices) for convenience in remitting.
36. Offer money back; so figure in this cost, too.
37. Determine your break-even point accurately.

38. Figure in *all* costs: unit cost of product, itself; cost of depositing checks, wrapping, transportation, postage, damage, rejects, replacements, c.o.d. costs, refusals, bad debts, normal business overhead.
39. Get correct ratio of selling price to cost of product (generally 4 to 1).
40. Don't limit yourself to low-priced merchandise; markup is too small to be profitable.

Advertising

41. Be ready to advertise continuously, or don't even start in business.
42. Start with small space or time, perhaps classifieds.
43. If you have something real good, use large space or time.
44. Suit your advertising to the medium carrying it to appeal to its audience.
45. Base your budget and schedule on ad pull by months.
46. Don't be afraid to experiment; vary ad size or time, copy and appeal, check and double-check to find right advertising slant and selling appeals.
47. Try split-run testing if available.
48. Use special gimmicks, such as gift appeals, holidays, quantity discounts, etc.
49. Base your advertising budget on the number of inquiries needed to make the ads pay.
50. Pulling power of one ad over another may vary as much as 25 to 1.
51. Conventional selling cost by mail is 15% compared with 3 to 4% for retailers' ad budgets, but repeat orders make mail order profitable.
52. Milk a successful ad by repeating it until diminishing returns set in.
53. Get editorial mentions in shopping sections of media.

Copy

54. Use a practical, how-to approach.
55. Write tight copy.
56. White space is less important for mail order than for prestige advertising.
57. Write copy for a mass audience—write as you speak.

58. Use simple, selling copy—not stylized.
59. Prepare copy carefully to fit each medium.
60. Avoid tricky phrases; be sincere; don't exaggerate.
61. Use the *you* approach.
62. Convince the reader that you are dependable and reliable.
63. Make it easy for the prospect to act—give simple, specific directions.
64. Don't try institutional or goodwill copy, just sell.
65. Analyze readership studies to develop copy techniques.
66. Use all space effectively—sell your line in blank spaces of other products, book jackets, direction sheets, packages, boxes, wrappers, letters.
67. Use short testimonials to plug products and company.
68. Play up local or regional fame, like well-known fruit areas, Williamsburg craft shops, Southern delicacies.
69. Guarantee product and satisfaction; always offer return privilege.
70. Perhaps offer something free as a premium or bonus.
71. Key all ads to test pull.
72. Check and double-check copy for possible omissions, unclear facts, ambiguous information, confusing directions.

Art

73. Use appropriate illustration—selling pictures, not art for art's sake.
74. Be sure to include photo or clear drawing with detailed copy, particularly if product is complicated.
75. Bold headlines and other devices outpull cheesecake.

Media

76. Consult other mail order users, agencies, and media on best media for you.
77. Make sure you are in media company that is good for your product.
78. For quick pilot tests, quick return, early check on copy pull, use radio or newspapers; for the long pull, use magazines.
79. Try new media, such as television.
80. Use direct mail for followup.

81. Build a mailing list from your inquiries and customers.
82. Rent lists from reputable list houses or mail order advertisers and agencies.
83. Rent your lists to noncompeting mail order companies and direct-mail houses.
84. Keep your mailing lists restricted as much as possible to real prospects.

Agencies

85. Use an agency that is sold on mail order and really wants the account—its return will be small until its work begins to pay off for both of you.
86. Inquiries and sales will give you quick proof of the agency effectiveness.
87. Avoid agencies with clients, products, and offers too much like yours.
88. Expect to pay cash in advance and offer references—agencies are wary of mail order credit.
89. Agency commissions are generally 15% but may vary because of mail order risks.
90. Agency may net more than 4% on mail order accounts compared with 2 to 3% on other accounts.

Customer Payment

91. Ask for cash or checks, preferably not c.o.d.; but don't advertise *no* c.o.d.'s.
92. Accept checks—few bounce.
93. Obtain necessary papers to legalize checks made out to every possible variation of your company name.
94. On all c.o.d. orders ask for deposit to increase the number of paid orders.
95. Prepay postage on c.o.d. orders to avoid nondelivery, then bill for postage.
96. Avoid the phrase, *Bill Me,* in coupon or order form.

Complaints

97. Remember: The customer is always right.
98. Take care of complaints quickly, make replacement or adjustment immediately.
99. Don't be afraid to write a courteous, explanatory letter.

Refunds

100. Make immediate refunds at no cost to customer.
101. Adjust overpayments quickly.

Followup

102. Repeat business is vital to success; keep the customer sold.
103. It takes a long time to build audience confidence in buying by mail.
104. Be prompt and courteous in answering inquiries, shipping orders, explaining delays, making adjustments, refunding money.
105. Personalize all correspondence with signed letters.
106. Follow up initial sale with mailing pieces, folders, catalogs, brochures, etc.
107. At intervals mail new price lists to customers to encourage new business.
108. Ask satisfied customers to submit names of friends, neighbors, relatives, or business associates as potential customers, and offer a bonus for this.
109. Run a good piece of merchandise and work good mailing lists as long as they pay; then try them again later.
110. Be ready to answer all sorts of byproduct mail, offers, inquiries, deals, and so forth.
111. Watch out for tricky offers (worthless space or time and catalog listings, etc., in return for free products).

Keeping Records

112. Based on a keying system keep accurate records of the pull of each ad showing effectiveness of various combinations of headline, art, copy, medium, and so forth.

Catalogs

113. Mail order catalog-making is a science.
114. Offer catalogs if line is big enough, but charge small sum or restrict distribution to active customers to increase catalog value to them and save you money.

Other Means of Distribution

115. Chances are that wholesale and retail trade will gradually replace mail order volume on some items.
116. Let retailers take orders from displayed samples of items; then fill by mail.
117. If you let a retailer promote your item heavily in his market, be prepared for a drop in mail orders.
118. If you want a retailer to carry your item, do not give him concentrated mail order competition in his own market.

Miscellaneous

119. Don't be surprised if there are ups and downs depending on the seasons, days of the month, or competition from tax payments, and so forth.
120. Don't expect many returns after the first six months, but don't be surprised if orders or inquiries trickle in for years.

George Cullinan's 20 Tips

Many of the most successful mail order companies of today owe a great deal to the valuable guidance they received from the late George Cullinan. After spending 27 years with Aldens Inc., the Chicago mail order firm where he was vice-president in charge of sales, Mr. Cullinan set up shop as a mail order consultant. In addition to providing guidance to dozens of mail order firms, he was responsible for training many of today's recognized mail order experts.

Based on his personal experience, George Cullinan prepared a list of "20 Vital Questions About Direct Mail Advertising and Selling," and then set down his answers to them:

1. *Is it Better to Advertise for Inquiries or Direct Orders in Media?*
   If inquiries can be obtained for a cost not more than 50% of the cost of the selling material used to fill the inquiry and, if such inquiries are followed up properly, the percent cost to sell on results will generally be lower than that on media direct orders.

   Limitation: Inquiry advertising cannot be used repetitively in the same media without important decline in results. Direct order advertising can quite often be repeated several times with no decline in results and if there is a decline it is not as great as that in inquiries.

2. *Is It Better to Promote New Business Via Direct Orders From Media or by Mailing Catalogs to Rented Mailing Lists?*
   It depends on whether you are seeking *new dollar business* at the lowest possible selling ratio or seeking *new customers* at the lowest possible cost per new customer.

CHECKLIST OF COST FACTORS FOR MAIL ORDER OPERATIONS

Reprinted from "Help Yourself to Better Mail Order," by Robert A. Baker. Printers' Ink Publishing Company, New York.

1. Cost of product

Basic manufacturing or purchased cost of item

Shipment to your plant

Postage or shipment from your plant to customer

Wrapping materials, boxes, cartons, etc.

Allowance for losses by damage, c.o.d. refusals, replacements, complimentary gifts, etc.

Assembling labor

Packing and shipping labor

Storage costs

Bank fees for check deposits

---

2. Advertising and/or direct-mail promotion costs

Production Costs

Artwork

Photography

Retouching

Photostats

Typesetting

Reproduction proofs

Velox prints

Engravings

Electrotypes

Mats

Copy

Hand-lettering

Delivery service

Agency fees

Stock

Printing

Research

Direct Mailings

List costs

Letter, including letterhead and cost of processing

All enclosures, prorated complete production costs

Envelopes—outside and return

Addressing, folding, stuffing, etc.

Postage

Space or time

3. Overhead

Rent

Salaries (not including principals)

Utilities: light, telephone, etc.

Travel, transportation, auto, etc.

Office supplies, stationery, etc.

Research

Accounting, legal, insurance, etc.

Taxes, licenses, etc.

4. Principals' salaries and/or profits

Advertising for direct orders from media generally brings in new customers at about one-half to two-thirds the cost of new customers obtained through catalog mailings to good rented lists, but the percent cost to sell is normally higher because the average average is lower. The lower average order is caused by the fact that media ads cannot carry as many items as a catalog. The ideal situation, in which the low cost per new customer in media advertising is combined with multiple item assortments in large ads which tend to increase average order, is emerging as the newest and best way to promote new business.

3. *Which Are More Costly—Media Inquiries or Direct Mail Inquiries?*

In an advertiser's prime magazines, inquiries normally cost much less than they do by direct mail. However, the number of prime magazines for a given advertiser is generally limited, so where a large volume of inquiries is required direct mail must be used as a supplement. High direct mail costs per unit of circulation are the major reasons for the difference in cost per inquiry. Media inquiry programs are often conducted without supplementary use of direct mail, but it is rare that direct mail inquiry programs are not accompanied or preceded by some media inquiry promotion.

4. *Are Closures (New Customers) Better From Media Inquiries or From Direct Mail Inquiries?*

In almost all cases closures from media inquiries are better, approximately as much as one-third greater. This factor in favor of media must be taken into account when comparing the value of media with direct mail as an inquiry-getter, because it is the closures, not the inquiries, that are important. In other words, prime media which are better than direct mail on the "front end" of inquiry receipts, are better still because of superior closure qualities. Likewise, some marginal media, although poorer than direct mail at the inquiry stage, become better when their superior closures are considered.

5. *Which Is the Best Method of Obtaining New Mail Order Customers—Media, Direct Mail, or Catalogs—Inquiries or Direct Orders?*

None of them. The best way to get more new customers is to get more orders from old customers. A paradox? No, because it is axiomatic in mail order that a certain percentage (15% to 20%) of orders generated by mailing of selling material to old customers only, come from new customers who were given the material on a pass-along basis. This is an absolute rule. Such new customers cost nothing. They are called automatics. Most companies obtain more new customers by this means than from all direct promotional methods combined.

6. *What Is the Easiest Way to Get More Orders From Old Customers in Order to Generate More Free Automatic New Customers?*

By repeating the mailing, without change of any kind, of all material sent to old customers not less than 3 weeks nor more than 5 weeks after the original mailing. A second repeat, the same number of weeks after the first, ordinarily works profitably also.

A repeat mailing of the same material mailed an average of 30 days after the first mailing pulls two-thirds as well as the original. A second repeat mailed an average of 30 days after the first repeat pulls one-half as well as the original and 80% as well as the first repeat. At these pulls, overrun costs on the additional mailings make the repeat profitable.

MAIL ORDER LITERATURE CHECKLIST

In an article which appeared in the November 7, 1947, issue of *Printers' Ink,* Crete Dahl, of Dahl Publishing Company, suggested the use of a 12-point checklist to evaluate the completeness of mail order promotions. Each piece must contain:

1. Name of product.
2. Price.
3. Picture of product.
4. Name of firm. (When using two ads as a spread, it is well to use the firm name on both on the chance that each page may be reprinted separately.)
5. Address of firm (city and state).
6. Coupon to encourage orders.
7. On coupon, unless you encourage widespread charge sales, avoid using "Bill me." Then you'll surely get a higher percentage of orders that include checks or money orders.
8. C.O.D. orders can prove costly if they kick back. You lose the postage and c.o.d. fee, which on an order amounting to $25 or $40, may be up to $1 or more. By requesting $1 deposit with c.o.d. orders, you will increase the number of paid orders, especially if you say, "We prepay postage on all paid orders."
9. Prepare dummies carefully. Even good printers don't always follow layouts accurately. Besides—if you run up against a snag—you can decide what to do about it on the spot, thereby saving delays and author's alterations.
10. Insist on a final proof whenever possible. Curious new mistakes can creep in while old errors are being corrected. Besides, by the time a piece of copy reaches the final stage, you have a chance to get a fresh point of view. Some slight improvement may increase its pulling power. You may then catch some glaring error or oversight before it is too late.
11. Use all the space effectively. For example, the insides of book jackets are usually left blank. We use them to "sell the line" and frequently get orders from them—sometimes years later.
12. Check carefully the size of each circular that is to be inserted with bills or letters. A ¼-inch difference in width or length may make a big difference in the number of envelopes it will fit. This is an important item when envelopes are hard to get. It is surprising to see how many sizes will be delivered on orders calling definitely for No. 6's or No. 10's.

In both cases, the automatic new customers obtained from the additional orders cost nothing.

7. *Is Creativity—Copy, Headline, Layout, Art—the Most Important Element in Direct Mail, Direct Selling, or Mail Order?*

   No, not by a long shot. There are many elements far ahead of creativity in importance, such as the merchandise or service, the price or the offer, the list, the cost, etc.

   If all the elements which precede creativity are right, it is actually difficult to measure the effects of creativity at all. And if one of the four elements mentioned above is flagrantly wrong, it is a rare, if not impossible thing for creativity, however sensational, to save the day. Creativity is important but only one of eight elements affecting sales of a direct mail, direct selling, or mail order effort.

8. *Is There Any Fundamental Way to Increase Business Other Than by Adding New Customers?*

   Yes, by increasing the average annual sales of the customers you have. A company's sales volume, in simple essence, is measured by its number of customers multiplied by its annual sales.

   Then what is the best and fastest way to increase the average annual sales of customers? The best, most profitable and fastest way is by offering INSTALLMENT CREDIT.

9. *In the Eternal Quest for New Business, What Is the Value of Various Types of Customers and What Are the Criteria of Value?*

   Here are some relationships:

   A. A credit customer is four times as good as a cash customer.

   B. A customer who orders more than once in the 12-month period preceding a mailing is at least twice as good as one who ordered only once.

   C. A customer who ordered more than once in the 12-month period preceding mailing is twice as good as one who ordered more than once in the period 12 to 24 months preceding mailing but not since.

   D. A customer who ordered more than once in the 12 to 24 months preceding mailing is 50% better than one who ordered more than once in the period 24 to 36 months preceding mailing but not since.

   E. In each period sequence—12 months, 12 to 24 months, and 24 to 36 months—the customer who ordered once is only one-half as good as the customer who ordered more than once in the same period.

   F. A customer who has not ordered in 36 months is normally considered no better than an ordinary promotional name.

10. *What Is Meant by the "Plus Cost" Theory of Promotion?*

    "Plus costs" mean variable costs. In a mail order business in particular, but also true in most businesses, promotion for new business should be charged only variable, never fixed, costs. These include overrun costs on printed material or catalogs, variable (nonexecutive) salaries in operating, and variable overhead costs. In this way promotions unprofitable under average costs may become profitable by elimination of fixed charges which a company would have whether a promotion was attempted or not.

It is the true out-of-pocket cost of the promotion. Most major companies, in all lines of business, use a variation of the principle of "plus cost" or "marginal" accounting on new business promotion.

11. *From the Profit Point of View, Which Are the Most Important Selling and Marketing Elements in the Direct Selling Business?*

In the order of their importance the most important selling and marketing elements in the direct selling and mail order business are:

1. Merchandise or service and its acceptability
2. Price of the merchandise or service offered and the margin of profit at that price
3. Lists
4. Costs
5. Methods of buying—cash, credit or c.o.d.
6. Markets
7. Timing
8. Creativity

12. *When Should a Direct Mail Piece Become a Catalog?*

By Post Office Department regulation a catalog is a bound book of 24 pages or more of any standard size. Such books carry a special low postage rate but generally, because of the high minimum rate today, it is not effective as a postage saver until the catalog carries at least 48 pages.

Apart from the postage factor, however, a direct mail piece should become a catalog when the assortment of merchandise or variety of services is sufficiently broad to fill a bound book of 16 pages or more.

The major point is to get to a bound catalog as fast as possible, because the production costs, per item and per page, on a catalog compared to costs of a direct mail piece of equivalent size are much lower.

13. *Which Are More Productive, Multiple-Item or Single-Item Ads?*

In the mail order business the crowded or multiple-item ad generally pulls substantially better than the single-item, limited-item, or open ad.

14. *Does Unusually High-Quality Printing Bring Better Results Than Average-Quality Printing?*

Unusually high-quality printing quite often pulls better absolute results than average printing but very rarely in proportion to the extra cost. Average or adequate printing (as opposed to elegant printing) almost always brings more profitable results overall.

15. *How Important Is Good Customer List Maintenance?*

Good customer list maintenance is very important, in fact about as important as anything in a mail order or direct selling business. A normal list will develop from 20% to 25% errors in any given year from natural causes such as moves, deaths, filing mistakes, and so forth.

If no cleaning or maintenance is done the list is useless in 3 years from these causes alone. If the additional element of buying is added, that is, whether they are active customers or not, the uncleaned list deteriorates even faster.

16. *How Many Ways Are There to Acquire New Customers in the Direct Selling or Mail Order Business?*

There are seven standard ways:

A. Automatics—word of mouth

B. Friend promotions

C. Media advertising for inquiries

D. Media advertising for orders

E. Direct mail advertising for inquiries

F. Direct mail advertising for orders

G. Catalog mailings to rented lists

The foregoing are listed roughly in the order of cost to obtain new customers—"A" being the best or lowest cost, "B" the next best or next lowest cost, and so forth.

17. *How Do You Increase Average Order?*

The best ways to increase average order are:

A. Offering installment credit terms. This is far and away the best

B. Trading up merchandise or service offerings

C. Increasing assortments

D. *Merely raising prices*

18. *Is Charging Postage a Factor Affecting Mail Order Sales?*

Yes, charging is a factor affecting mail order sales but this does not necessarily mean it is better to absorb postage rather than charge it to the customer. Charging postage does deter sales to some degree but generally not to an important degree.

A jump from a "no charge for postage" policy to a "customer postage-pay" policy will have a noticeable but small effect on sales but an increase in postage within reason where postage has been previously charged will seldom affect sales.

19. *Does Format (Page Shape) Have Any Effect on Mail Order Sales?*

Page size or shape has little effect on mail order sales; it is the square inches per item offered that is important. A 6½ by 9½ size catalog will do neither poorer nor better than an 8½ by 11 size catalog if the square inches per item are the same, that is, if the 50% larger 8½ by 11 book carries 50% more items.

20. *What Should a Direct Selling or Mail Order Company's Markup Be?*

A company's markup (percent profit on selling price) should be sufficiently large to cover its selling, operating, and overhead costs and leave a profit, while still being competitive. Examples of markup in individual businesses which fit this definition are as follows:

A. Retail stores—general merchandise.......40%

B. Mail order companies—general merchandise.......36%

C. Mail order gift merchandise.......50% to 60%

D. Gift retail stores.......55% to 65%

E. Specialty retail stores.......45% to 50%

F. Specialty mail order companies.......45%

Louis E. Rudin's Advice:

Another outstanding mail order expert who has been willing to share his experience with others is Louis E. Rudin. Two of his many speeches to direct mail groups contain some particularly important pointers:

The Power of Disbelief[6] . . . I remember, long ago, attending a Direct Mail Day where the principal speaker was a famous pioneer in direct mail. When he came to the climax of his speech, he flashed a mailing from Banker's Life on the screen and said, "I want you to take a good look at this mailing piece. It has a stamp that must be *pasted* to the reply card, or the offer is invalidated. And just listen to this silly copy: 'This coupon is valuable. The Special Free Information Coupon above is valuable because it entitles you to complete information on the White Cross Plan.'

"Imagine, said our expert, the stupidity of this company. They are telling the reader to paste a stamp on a reply card or they won't send him information about their insurance. Do they really expect people to *beg* them to send an insurance salesman?"

At that moment, I became aware of the *Power of Disbelief.* Why? Because I didn't believe one word he said. I had the facts. He didn't. He was deciding, by the way *he* reacted, how the *world* would react. He had applied logic, and logic had told him wrong. He had hit the nail squarely on the thumb.

Banker's Life had great success with that stamp technique that year. Sensational success. More importantly, my firm (Spiegel's) also used a stamp that year—on 30 *million* pieces of mail. We tested it from Hell to Breakfast, and we had positive proof that it increased our response more than 10%. In fact, the profit on that added response was sufficient to pay for the whole mailing.

But don't assume for one moment in spite of its success that we used the stamp the next season, or the next, without testing it—or without testing about 25 different ideas against it each time.

In fact, I've used the stamp approach at other times and in other situations, and found it to have a negative effect—to reduce response to a marked degree. I've also learned that the best idea wears out after a while. So you can't rest complacently on a success, or you'll soon find yourself riding a failure to destruction.

In direct mail, there's only one thing you can be sure of: *You can't be positive.* You can only test, and test, and test again—and keep the Power of Disbelief constantly working for you. I've also learned that many of us are so busy learning the tricks of the trade that we don't learn the trade.

Sweepstakes, stamps, IBM cards, pennies in windows, gimmicks of all kinds are only the picture frame. They may enhance the picture, but it is the picture that you paint in the receiver's mind that counts. And that picture is your message, your offer.

---

[6]Address at Second Annual Direct Mail Seminar of the Southwest, Houston, March 29, 1967.

Maxwell Sroge once gave a speech in Kansas City in which he said, "I believe deeply in what I want to discuss with you today. It is a result of 200 million pieces of mail and the experience of working with clients whose total sales last year exceeded 3 billion dollars. It is simply this: 'Don't spill your guts on the outside of the envelope.' "

Mr. Sroge is emminently successful in applying *his* principle. Comes now Walter Weintz, another great direct mail pro, who says: "If you're afraid to present your proposition on the envelope, what makes you think they'll read your message after they open the envelope?"

Walter Weintz is as responsible as any man I know for the elaborate 4-color lithographed envelopes used by such mailers as Columbia Records, Time-Life, and a host of others. He is eminently successful applying *his* principle.

Is it possible for *both* principles to be right when they are so diametrically opposed to one another? I've learned that it is. It is not the principle—it is the *application* that counts. It is who is doing what to whom, and where, and when. It is the "X Factor" that determines how a mailing should be handled.

It is this "X Factor" that enables various masters to use varying principles —even opposing principles—yet still achieve the same degree of success.

Now both Mr. Sroge and Mr. Weintz are experts. And both have made public utterances on their points of view. But do you believe for one moment that they follow these public pronouncements 100% of the time? Of course not! They use their principles like road maps to show the routes they prefer to take. But they also know when to detour. So I am sure there are times when Maxwell Sroge uses 4-color super-duper, spill-your-guts, lithographed envelopes for his mailings. And when Walter Weintz hides light behind a corner card. *They know when to disbelieve themselves.*

Never Make the Same Mistake Twice[7] . . . People sometimes ask me "How can I avoid mistakes and insure success in mail order selling?" My answer is simple. Go ahead and make mistakes. *But never make the same mistake twice.*

Every day learn some new mistakes to make. You can't go forward if you don't stick your chin out. When you make mail order mistakes after you have done your best to avoid them, then go back and find out where you went wrong. Put your finger right on the reason. There is always a reason, or reasons, for mail order *mistakes.* That goes for mail order *successes* too!

You won't be able to repeat a success or avoid a failure unless you know the how and why, right down to the fourth decimal place. Avoid the mistake of believing that there is magic or mystery to either success or failure in mail order selling. The answer is always there to see—if you do not deceive yourself.

If you're looking for a magic formula, some sacred incantation that will make failures disappear or will make success certain, I have news for you. There isn't any magic wand you can wave. Success in mail order is not done with mirrors. The truth is, it requires infinite attention to detail, practice and more practice, a constant seeking after perfection to be a success at magic or mail order.

---

[7]Address before DMAA West Coast Conference, 1968.

Avoid the mistake of complacency. It is an insidious disease in mail order selling. Just because it worked once is no guarantee it will work again, or work as well the second time. Keep testing, keep checking, keep looking for a better way. Good things wear out.

Avoid the mistake of believing that some things cannot be sold by mail. Regardless of price, regardless of size, anything that can be sold *can* be sold by mail (and by *sold* I do not mean the solicitation of an inquiry; I mean the complete transaction, initiated and closed by mail). Cemetery lots, burial insurance, gravestones, homes, lots in Florida and Arizona are sold by mail. Loans are made by mail. Insurance. Movie cameras. Valuable paintings. Charity. Theater. Lobsters. There is no limit to what can be sold by mail, except the limit of the seller's creativity and the seller's knowledge of consumers and markets.

Avoid the mistake of overestimating the unity of personality. A person can be a different person in a different situation and environment. The same person can be different on different lists. Successful direct mail selling depends on creating a situation favorable to the greatest number of prospects on a list and the employment of selected stimuli to get preconceived results. Thus the readers of a serious magazine may think they subscribe because it is thorough or authoritative; whereas they subscribe because it makes them feel important—or because the magazine looks well on their desks or coffee tables—and impresses their associates.

Avoid the mistake of presupposing that goods are bought primarily on the rational base of price, quality and service rather than in terms of individual feelings, aspirations, prejudices and fears. There is always some of the personal element present even in the case of industrial buying by trained purchasing agents.

Avoid the mistake of presuming that the level of income, education and sophistication of the audience makes such difference when it comes to the use of gimmicks such as stamps or tokens or sweepstakes or computerized letters. Tests have been made showing there is no difference in response between "blue chip" audiences and the general public.

Avoid the mistake of supposing that this decision motivation is a simple thing. The reasons why people buy are as wound together as a basket of rattle snakes. Each decision is intertwined with at least a dozen others. Obviously, in creating response on a basis of factors that are inherently slippery and sometimes intangible, there is more need for any kind of information that will add some degree of definiteness. It's up to you to find out.

Avoid the mistake of thinking direct mail selling is a case of follow the leader. There is much, too much, that passes as direct mail selling, which is derivative without the copycat being aware of why it is effective—or if it really is effective—and it is almost certain that the copying is bungled with a marked reduction in response.

Avoid the mistake of hoping to create a good mail order situation without blood, sweat and tears. You cannot succeed without research and learning . . . In most instances, you cannot delegate the definition of the problem any more than you can ask a doctor for a diagnosis without telling him in detail of your symptoms. In this sense what you get out of research is proportionate to what you put into it. Problems in mail order selling occur on different levels, ranging from the most general to the most specific.

Your optimum research value will come from a definition of the problem in the most specific terms you are able to formulate.

Avoid the mistake of expecting a "free ride." The test of whether or not you have done your job is usually in your grasp, if you'll bounce your ideas against the facts of life.

Avoid the mistake of being more general than your ignorance forces you to be. Direct mail selling entails the highest form of analytical thinking and imagination and creativity and analysis in depth to answer the question "Will this produce maximum measurable results or will some other way be better?"

Avoid the mistake of thinking that advertising is merely selling in print. A salesman who knows his business adapts his arguments to the individual buyer. He fishes for reactions. He is aggressive with some, speaks softly to others. He can anticipate objections and meet them head-on, or he can meet them as they come. He can push the hesitant, wheedle the egotist, or play a whole symphony of cajolery as the occasion demands.

By contrast, in direct mail selling it is crucial that the selling argument be so well devised and disciplined that it will have the greatest possible impact on the greatest number and produce profitable action the very first time.

Your success in selling by mail depends on how well you cut through psychological, semantic and analytical barriers. You must find out what people really want and how to persuade them that your product or service best fulfills their needs. And further, you must learn the technique of having them order that product or service immediately.

In the final analysis, there isn't any insoluble mystery to mail order selling or becoming a mail order magician. Mail order selling is a business based on an orderly and logical analysis of the marketing judgments—and the proper presentation of the proposition as dictated by that analysis.

In Summary

When you boil down all of the ideas and helpful tips, you will find there are only two basic essentials for mail order success:

1. Apply some common sense . . .
2. . . . and support it with meticulous attention to each and every detail.

Chapter 8

INDUSTRIAL DIRECT MAIL

WHEN many people think of mail advertising, they automatically divide it into just two categories—mail order advertising for consumer goods and direct mail advertising for industrial products and services. While this is a highly inaccurate viewpoint, it does indicate the importance of direct mail to the industrial advertiser.

Firms which sell their wares to other businesses are major users of just about every possible type of direct mail—including, in fact, mail order. But while direct mail is highly important in industrial marketing, many companies are not even aware that they are major users of *direct mail.*

Most manufacturers, for example, regularly prepare product specification sheets, which are mailed to customers and prospects. Such a marketing procedure is so routine that many industrial manufacturers never stop to realize that it constitutes direct mail advertising. Instead of making every effort to get maximum sales results from such literature, these companies simply have an engineer put together the details required and then count on the printer to try to make the printed piece look as attractive as possible. Nowhere along the line is more than passing thought given to developing special lists for the distribution of the literature—of having an experienced direct mail copywriter translate the engineer's language into the recipient's language—of developing the best possible mailing package, including a letter to explain why the literature will be of special interest to the recipient—of utilizing the opportunity to seek out inquiries which will aid the salesmen—or even of planning followup mailings to capitalize on sparks of interest which the literature strikes when it comes into the hands of interested prospects who do not take immediate buying action.

Many other mailings, too, fail to be recognized for what they are—*direct mail advertising!* To many industrial companies, price lists, letters to prospects and customers, external house organs, special reports, marketing surveys, announcements of new sales offices, reorder suggestions, merchandising of business paper advertising, sales force communications, and other basic types of direct mail are considered something so routine they require no special attention or skills.

This paradox is probably the greatest problem in industrial direct mail, for too many industrial companies, not recognizing that most of their outgoing mail represents direct mail advertising, fail to apply many of the fundamentals which could help make their mailings more effective. Too often the material is prepared without the benefit of skilled direct mail counseling which not only would make it produce better results but would also help make it far less costly.

The Field of Industrial Marketing

There are four basic divisions of industry, each with its own marketing techniques:

1. *Manufacturers of heavy machinery, equipment, and mechanical systems.* In this field, it is most common for products to be sold directly to other manufacturers through company sales engineers. Selling is most frequently on a long-range basis, sometimes with as long as 10 years between the initial sales contact and the actual purchase and installation. Units of sale are usually in the multithousand-dollar bracket.
2. *Manufacturers of secondary components.* These are the "parts" which go into the manufacture of a finished product. Selling in this field is done both by company sales forces and through industrial distributors, supply houses, manufacturers' agents, and other types of middlemen. Marketing not only involves gaining original acceptance but keeping a line of components "sold." Once a secondary component has been "approved," chances are it will represent large-scale purchases over an extended period.
3. *Suppliers of raw materials.* Marketing of raw materials is quite similar to the marketing of manufactured secondary components. The basic difference is that there are seldom major "product differences" between what is offered by one supplier and what is offered by his competitors. Thus, effective marketing depends heavily on intangibles such as the "image" of the company, goodwill created by salesmen, etc.
4. *Manufacturers of maintenance, building, production, and nonmanufacturing supplies used in the conduct of a business.* Most frequently such supplies are sold primarily through local and regional distribution organizations, which vary from industry to industry. In the petroleum industry, for example, the oilfield supply company is a primary marketer of such products. When volume is large and repeat sales frequent and/or when customers and prospects are closely grouped geographically, a manufacturer may choose to maintain his own sales organization.

Volume of Industrial Direct Mail

Just how much money industrial advertisers spend annually on direct mail is almost impossible to determine. The primary difficulty is in determining just what items should be considered direct mail. The best guide, however, is offered by *Industrial Marketing's* annual study of industrial advertising budgets. IM's 1961 study, for example, showed that the typical manufacturer devoted just over 10% of its advertising budget to direct mail, another 16.8% to catalogs plus 3.8% for dealer and distributor helps (which usually include considerable direct mail), and 6.2% for "production." In addition, the study included a "non-media" category which accounted for another 5% of the advertising budget, and many of the items reported in this category would normally be considered direct mail—annual reports, external house organs, price lists, etc.

But this represents only part of the picture. At the same time, *Industrial Marketing* asked survey respondents about their sales promotion budgets and found that many industrial companies have set up separate budgets for sales promotion. Included in these budgets are numerous direct mail items. Other studies have shown that some companies do not include many direct mail items in either their advertising or sales promotion budgets. Thus, the total expenditure is certainly much higher than would be indicated by the "direct mail" listing in the advertising budget.

Industrial Direct Mail Uses

A very comprehensive study of industrial direct mail was conducted by Arthur Tofte of Allis-Chalmers for the National Industrial Advertisers Association (now the Association of Industrial Advertisers) in 1953. Among the findings of the Tofte study was that industrial advertisers use direct mail for a great variety of marketing purposes. The most frequent uses:

Building institutional prestige for the company name
Covering the market quickly on new products
Making advance calls for salesmen
As sales aids to dealers
As substitute salesman
To substitute for business paper or other advertising
To follow up salesmen's calls
Testing new product acceptance
Keeping the sales force informed of internal development
To merchandise business publication advertising
To supply technical information for reference use
To distribute price lists and catalogs to direct buyers

To build attendance at exhibits
To secure market information

Of these, by far the most frequently mentioned objective was to build institutional prestige for the company name. Over 60% of the respondents included this objective on their lists of direct mail uses. Next in line were to cover a market quickly on a new product, which was listed by 51%, and to make advance calls for salesmen, listed by 45%.

Importance of the Salesman

While there is a limited amount of mail order selling in the industrial field—primarily in the case of manufacturers of maintenance, building, production, and non-manufacturing supplies used in the conduct of a business, most of the sales are made by salesmen or sales engineers. Thus, most industrial direct mail is primarily designed to do two things:

1. Uncover prospects for sales followthrough.
2. Assist the salesman by providing information to the prospect which will help speed up the sales process.

Just how effective direct mail can be in assisting the salesman was shown in a survey by the Sales and Marketing Executives, International, which showed that cold calls yield an average of eight orders per 100 calls, but when direct mail is used to lay the groundwork for the salesmen's calls, the conversion ratio steps up to 38 orders per 100 calls. Dickie-Raymond, in *How to Get More for Your Direct Mail Dollar,* reports that a firm with a national sales force of 300 men analyzed several thousand sales calls and discovered that the average value in dollars of merchandise sold through cold calls was $24.50, while calls which followed up leads generated by direct mail showed a dollar value of $51.

The average cost of an industrial salesman's call is probably in the neighborhood of $35-50, but can run to $100 or more. Obviously, anything which can be done to reduce the number of calls required to complete a sale—and in industrial marketing dozens of sales calls may be required before any business results—is highly important.

According to an SMEI survey:

2% of sales are made on "first" sales call
3% of sales are made on "second" sales call
3½% of sales are made on "third" sales call
10% of sales are made on "fourth" sales call
81% of sales are made on subsequent sales calls

Advertising and the Salesman

Noted industrial adman Howard G. Sawyer says, "Salesmen should be expected to do what they can do best, and advertising should be expected to do what it can do best. What salesmen can do best is, first, to keep customers happy—through attention, service, friendship; and second, when time permits, to create new customers, using their special talents to promote the virtues of the product, make a specific proposal, counter resistance, negotiate, press for the order.

"What is it that advertising can do best? Sometimes it's to broadcast information—over more ground and faster than salesmen can do it. Sometimes it's to widen the market by revealing new areas or new uses. Sometimes it's to attract leads. Sometimes it's to influence other parties who have an indirect 'say' in a purchasing decision—architects or banks or dealers or the customers of the prospect. And sometimes it's to sell the company that's in back of the product."

THE BIGGEST MISTAKE OF INDUSTRIAL DIRECT MAIL ADVERTISING

Probably the greatest mistake made by industrial advertisers is the tendency to forget that their customers and prospects are *people*. Instead, they tend to think of them only as engineers, purchasing agents, production supervisors, etc., and to feel that a prospect's having a functional role in industry somehow eliminates the need for approaching him as a person with emotions.

"We've got a nuts-and-bolts story, so why get fancy?" they ask. The answer is *competition*. For whether industrial advertisers face up to the fact or not, the same man who buys a new car for his family, a new power tool for his home workshop, a dozen golf balls, or a carton of cigarettes is also the primary prospect for industrial products. He is exposed to thousands of advertising messages every week—all demanding his consideration, whether they be for industrial products his company will use or for consumer products he will use in his home. Only a small percentage of all of these messages will "get through" and a plain, unadorned, poorly conceived nuts-and-bolts story is likely to get lost in the shuffle.

Direct mail consultant Paul Bringe, in *Direct Mail Briefs*, reports the following details on the amount of mail received by the manager of purchasing of one department of a major electrical manufacturer:

He purchases something like 40 million dollars worth of materials a year. He and his staff of seven buyers receive about 1,000 pieces of mail a day. About two-thirds is promotional mail; the rest is business correspondence. As the top purchasing man, he gets a healthy share—but his secretary weeds out 90%, of which about half is routed to the buyers. The rest is ashcanned. He periodically reviews her discards and they've never had an argument.

What gets by the secretary to him besides what he has asked her to send in? Almost everything which is personalized with his name, i.e., on a letter. Sensibly used gimmicks and novelties make the grade. Colorful brochures (he calls them "picture books") are looked at.

But, because he averages three to four phone calls an hour, at least one meeting a day, and he and the buyers see an average of 210 vendors from Monday noon to Thursday night (Monday morning and Friday are reserved for administrative work and paperwork), *all promotional mail is taken home for reading.*

What does he look for in direct mail? Facts, not claims. Long-range information affecting markets in which he is interested. New products or applications. Unique mailings are good.

Compensating Factors

Of course, most industrial companies can't afford the large advertising budgets of consumer product companies, but they have at least two important factors working in their favor:

1. *The audiences for industrial advertising are generally smaller and more easily pinpointed.* Thus, the creative industrial direct mail advertiser can work within well-defined boundaries—something which the consumer advertiser frequently lacks. A pinpointed audience enables the direct mail advertiser to use the medium to its fullest potential by being able to personalize many of his mailings.
2. *Competition is less keen.* Much industrial advertising is downright dull. While there has been a marked trend away from the old nuts-and-bolts school, the doctrine of exciting advertising has not yet penetrated the entire industrial advertising universe. Thus, where the consumer advertiser must compete against many direct competitors who are doing an outstanding job, the typical industrial advertiser's *primary* competition is with the promotion material of other small-budget companies, many of which have yet to apply their talents and dollars to doing a creative job.

This second point, however, must be approached with caution. Many industrial admen make the mistake of looking at their direct business competitors as the only source of advertising competition. It cannot be overemphasized that the audience of industrial advertisers is composed of the same people who read consumer direct mail, and that the relatively high creative standards of such consumer advertising sets the pace against which the industrial adman must match his own efforts.

The Functional Fallacy

Nicholas Samstag called the nuts-and-bolts approach "The Functional Fallacy." *"It lies,"* he said, *"in thinking of the audience as a group of human business machines, men interested only in hard, cold, logical reasons for buying your product. 'Put the facts before them,' say the advertisers who are deceived by The Functional Fallacy, 'and watch them buy.' Only they don't buy. Often they don't even read your ads or mail pieces. They just pass over them or throw them away. Advertisers who suffer from The Functional Fallacy write some of the finest, most costly UNREAD advertising and promotion."*

Mr. Samstag also put his finger on one of the most important reasons so much nuts-and-bolts direct mail is found in the industrial field: *"Engineers, designers, and plant managers honestly believe that the ads that are packed with facts and figures must be the best kind because they are themselves so fascinated to see their own achievements in print."* And Mr. Samstag also offered a suggested alternate approach: *"Try not to advertise to the industrial buyer as a businessman, but simply as a man—a various, unpredictable, warmhearted, stubborn-headed, intelligent, fickle, but well-intentioned human being. Try to give him a breather from his world of facts while, of course, slipping in the commercial as deftly as you can."*

Importance of Buyers' Emotions

The fact that buyers' emotions plan an important role in industrial purchases was clearly shown in a study sponsored by *Steel* magazine. It commissioned Dr. F. Robert Shoaf, motivation research consultant, to determine the extent psychological factors extend into the industrial buyer's business life. After interviewing 137 managers functionally engaged in administration, production, engineering, and purchasing within the vast metalworking industry, Dr. Shoaf came to the conclusion that the industrial buyer is more human than most industrial advertisers are inclined to realize. "It's fact, not fancy," he reported, "that the large majority of buying decisions are made on an emotional basis. Evidence of this is found in the resistance offered by the *conservative* who fights change for the sake of tradition, as well as for the *overcautious* who hesitates to make decisions for fear of erring. When resistance to purchase is based on emotion, logical arguments and presentations are ineffective.

"The conservative is a follower by nature. He keeps his eye on his competition, and is more likely to take action if he is certain his competition has already purchased. He hesitates to take the first step, but he will follow. You can score with this type by showing him that he is *not* keeping up with competition.

"Whenever the overcautious manager involves himself in a decision, he feels he is taking a risk. He does not want to be a guinea pig. He needs guarantees of good faith. Marketing promotion should emphasize satisfied and enthusiastic users of your products."

When Products Are Alike

One of the key points of Dr. Shoaf's study was that "to the extent that products and services become more objectively alike, the buyer's final decision is based more and more upon subjective emotional factors." He explained:

> Anyone familiar with industry knows that there are considerably fewer differences between similar types of industrial products than industrial advertising would have you believe. Industry is simply too competitive for one product to be exclusively superior for long. Let's take a realistic look at the factors my respondents felt were just as important as price:
>
> Good delivery is one of the most important. It is the most frequently mentioned service "must." Late delivery is a broken promise. It indicates lack of proper coordination and organizational effort. It is a lack of sincere interest. It is also injurious to the pride of the buyer—to his status—reflecting upon his own abilities.
>
> Second only to delivery is the desire for product services. Dozens of testimonials from the interview data reveal that surprisingly few manufacturers make sincere and consistent attempts at service "followthrough" once the product is sold.
>
> There is no denying the importance of the corporate image. People feel safer in dealing with a company they know. But while the corporate image is important, it does not mesmerize. Corporate image is important to the extent that it serves as a reminder when the buyer is seeking suppliers, but it does not necessarily stimulate him to action.
>
> Now, a quick word about the size of the company and its influence on the buyer as a status symbol. The buyer enjoys identification with the prestige and authority-image of the industry giants. The corporate image of size can represent safety or status, or both. On the other hand, the large companies sometimes appear unapproachable, standoffish. Small vendors seem warm and friendly by comparison, more apt to give personal service and attention. In the final analysis, the buyer makes his selection of large or small on the basis of his own personal value judgments.

FUNDAMENTAL PRINCIPLES OF INDUSTRIAL DIRECT MAIL

In his *Handbook of Industrial Direct Mail Advertising* (issued by the Association of Industrial Advertisers), Edward N. Mayer, Jr., says that maximum effectiveness of industrial direct mail depends upon six proved principles:

1. *There must be a need for the product or service being advertised.* However, it is quite possible to create a need by emphasizing a want, or an unfulfilled wish of the people you are trying to sell. But keep in mind that you can't sell electric blankets to people in the tropics; nor can you sell bottling machinery to a plant that manufactures canned goods exclusively.

2. *There must be a need for the product or service being advertised at the particular time it is being advertised.* Although there is very little seasonal appeal in the sale of most industrial products, it must be quite obvious that, even though you make the best snow-removal equipment available, you are not going to be able to arouse much interest for this equipment in the purchasing agent of a plant in Dallas, Texas, during the summer's hottest spell.

3. *The proposition you are making must be attractive to the potential buyer.* Even though your bottling machine or snow-removal equipment is the very best available, unless you can find reasons—solid reasons—why your proposition is a fair and attractive one, and your prospect should buy your product rather than your competitor's—you will be wasting your direct mail advertising, and to some degree your salesman's efforts.

4. *The advertising must be prepared from the reader's viewpoint.* The fact that you have a product or service to sell, from which you are going to derive a profit, isn't interesting to your best prospect. However, the fact that he can either reduce his costs or make a greater profit through its usage is interesting to him. You must think of any direct mail advertising you do in the industrial marketing field in terms of how it can talk the reader's language—how it can present your sales story, whatever it may be, in a way that will appeal to the prospect and make him realize that he is the one who will benefit from following your suggestions.

5. *Direct mail advertising, to be effective, must be sent to good prospects.*

6. *The reputation of the advertiser must be good or at least not open to question among the people being solicited.* If there is anything in the history of your company which is detrimental, it will be extremely wise to straighten out your reputation and your market acceptance in the field, if your advertising is to be successful.

Seven Cardinal Rules

To these fundamental principles, Mr. Mayer has added "seven cardinal rules" for industrial direct mail success.

1. *Know exactly what you want your mailing to do for you.* Do you want an order—an inquiry—a chance to have a salesman call? Are you trying to open a new territory, introduce a new product, or announce a new use for an old one? Or do you want to do a goodwill or institutional job?

2. *Write your copy so that the recipient will know what your product will do for him!* Have you appealed to his selfish instincts or have you used all of your space talking about yourself, your president, and your beautiful new factory? Have you made your copy human and easy to read? Have you given all the information your prospect needs to take the action you desire?

3. *Make the layout and format of your mailing tie in with your overall plan and objective.* Many a potential success has turned into a dismal failure because someone forgot that appearance is an important part of the selling impression.
4. *Address each mailing piece (correctly) to an individual or company who can buy the product or service you have to sell.* The list is the absolute foundation of successful direct mail.
5. *Make it easy for your prospect to send you an inquiry.* Have you included a reply card or return envelope? If you are not looking for direct business, have you listed the places where your product is available?
6. *Tell your story over again.* Very few salesmen make a sale on their first call. It isn't reasonable to expect a single mailing to produce a large return.
7. *Research every mailing you make.* Never take anything for granted in industrial direct mail advertising. Don't even trust your own experience. You cannot rest on your knowledge. Times and results change. What worked last year may not work today.

The Seven Deadly Sins

The "Copy Chasers," who write a monthly column for *Industrial Marketing,* list the "seven deadly sins of industrial advertising." Their list, along with Ed Mayer's "seven cardinal rules," provides a good guide to use in checking any industrial direct mail program:

1. *The sin of being a braggart.* A lot of industrial advertising is like the blowhard—the man who interminably insists that he is better than the next guy. Claiming superiority, in itself, is not necessarily wrong—unless little or nothing is done to substantiate the claim in a friendly, persuasive, and convincing manner.
2. *The sin of talking to yourself*—instead of thinking of the other fellow. The most creative industrial advertising is that which directs its remarks to the interests of the readers—not the company doing the talking.
3. *The sin of preaching.* Faced with white paper to fill, some advertisers get a compulsion to lecture. Looking down upon the reader from the high altitude of their superiority, they *tell* the reader—rather than *invite* him—to do what they want him to do.
4. *The sin of being noisy.* Everybody hates the bugler, but a good many advertisers believe they have to make a big noise in order to get readers to stand at attention. If you have something interesting to say about a subject of interest to readers, there is no need to set your hair on fire in order to catch their eye.
5. *The sin of being messy.* Nobody likes the man who is messy, dirty, or inconsiderate. A lot of advertising, unfortunately, can be so described.
6. *The sin of trying to be cute.* Don't be smart-aleck in industrial advertising. Deliver your story in as straightforward a manner as possible—and you'll get more applause from your audience than if you put on an act.
7. *The sin of being dull.* Of all the deadly sins of industrial advertising, the worst by far is being dull. Almost all an advertising man is expected to do is to enliven the sales message with a crisp presentation of visual elements and some fast-moving copy.

Getting Readership

Roy O. Eastman, who conducts continuing studies of business magazine readership, reports that his research clearly indicates that most industrial advertising is not read accidentally, but on purpose. Jack Spurr's research studies for McGraw-Hill have shown that advertising, particularly in industry, is most effective when the prospect recognizes he *is* a prospect for a given product or service.

Many industrial direct mail advertisers make the mistake of thinking they must devote most of their effort to trying to convince a recipient of a mailing he should be a prospect for what is being advertised, rather than recognizing their mail is likely to receive the greatest attention from those who already have an established interest in the type of product or service involved. To be sure, there is often a definite need for direct mail which can move a recipient from a state of disinterest into the category of a real prospect, but too often industrial direct mail tries to do both jobs at the same time—moving a recipient into the prospect category and trying to sell the man who has already become a prospect. For maximum readership from any one of these groups, direct mail should have a singleness of purpose.

THE IMPORTANCE OF INQUIRIES

Inquiries are the lifeblood of the majority of industrial marketing programs. Without inquiries, the industrial salesman must spend the greatest percentage of his time "smokestacking" —calling from plant to plant on suspected prospects, trying to find out just who might be interested in his company's products or services. And when he does uncover a good prospect company, he goes through the whole process over again—trying to discover the persons within the prospect company who are the real buying influences. *Sales & Marketing Management* has estimated that probably 64% of salesmen's calls are made on the *wrong* person —and with the average call costing approximately $90, a lot of marketing dollars go down the drain.

Unfortunately, many industrial advertisers look at these basic facts and immediately decide the answer is to get "lots of inquiries." This, in itself, is an easy job. Just offer a free sample of most anything and you will get a bushelful of inquiries. But unqualified inquiries are little better than "smokestacking" and sometimes even worse, for they may come from the collector who loves to send in for anything that is offered "for free" and the followup sales call may lead straight to the door of a grammar-school student who found a business reply card in a post office wastebasket.

The real answer, of course, is to seek out *qualified* inquiries—a job which, more often than not, requires at least two steps. The first step is to ask for an expression of interest—and, at this point, it may be logical to try to get just as many inquiries as possible. A certain number of these initial inquiries may easily turn out to be logical prospects—often individuals salesmen have been trying to get in to see without success for a long time. But the majority will require additional qualification. This can be accomplished by asking the original inquirer to provide details which will clearly classify his degree of interest.

The Role of Direct Mail

Direct mail advertising offers a number of advantages both in acquiring the initial inquiry and in following it up for qualification purposes. Because the advertiser can develop his own initial list for the offer which produces the inquiries, it is possible to do a certain amount of advance screening. If very special attention is given to the initial list building, any inquiry resulting from a mailing may automatically qualify itself.

Another major advantage of direct mail in producing inquiries is that an "action package" can be used. A business reply card or an inquiry form and reply envelope are a logical part of the mailing.

For fulfillment of the initial inquiry and to obtain information for qualification, direct mail is usually the only logical and economical medium available. (This subject and methods for handling inquiries will be found discussed in detail in Chapter 49—"Inquiry Handling.")

Hooks for Inquiries

In the AIA *Industrial Direct Mail Handbook,* Ed Mayer lists seven basic hooks to draw inquiries:

1. *Offer additional information in booklets.* There are a great many "tricks" that can be and have been used to get requests for booklets but no one has ever combined the top ideas in five simple rules any better than Victor Schwab, president of Schwab & Beatty:

   a. *Title*—Give your booklet a title which makes it clear that it contains information which, although tied up with your product, is also useful and helpful in itself.

b. *Author*—Have it written, if at all possible, by an authority on the subject whose name is well and favorably known.

c. *Description*—Describe your booklet thoroughly and persuasively, pointing out the immediate practical value of the information on certain specific pages. Make the reader really want it!

d. *Display*—Picture it prominently. Play up your offer to send it—in your headline, or in conspicuous subheads. Make it an important unit in your advertisements.

e. *Quick Mention*—Refer to your booklet quickly in the body of your copy. Then your prospect knows, without reading too far, that he may readily send for further information about your product, without obligating himself.

2. *Guarantee that a salesman will not call on the prospect unless requested.* When you are offering booklets or just plain "additional information"—guarantee that a salesman will not call on the prospect unless asked to do so. Many an inquiry has died aborning because of the fear that a salesman would arrive with the "additional information." Thousands of people are afraid of salesmen, and will refuse to answer your mailing if they think a salesman will be knocking at their door. State definitely in your closing that no salesman will call, and then to be doubly sure put the same words on your reply form. Keep in mind, too, that although you promise there will be no salesman involved in the initial contact, you can use your salesmen for whatever further followup you plan.

3. *Close in a manner that will get action.* When you write your copy, spend as much time as you need to write an attention-getting headline or opening paragraph. Explain your offer fully; back up your selling points with testimonials from satisfied users; use every single stratagem you can find that will make your prospect read all of your copy—but be sure you close in a manner that will get action. Remember the words *Free, Now, New, How,* and others like them belong in your closing just as much as they do in your headline or opening paragraph.

4. *Find a good hook in the price and time angles.* A special price reduction, a warning that the price is going up after a certain date, a combination offer at a lower price, are only a few of the ideas that can go into your hook. Whatever price angle you use, be sure it appears on your reply form prominently displayed. The time limitation appeal, either standing on its own feet or in combination

with a price reduction or coming increase, probably has closed more sales than any other single factor.

5. *Free trial offers:* Second only to price and time as successful appeals for getting immediate action are free trial offers.
6. *Offer a premium.* Several advertisers have helped their selling program by offering some kind of premium to their prospects which had nothing whatever to do with the product or service being sold. A baseball schedule in the spring, football schedule in the fall, a booklet showing how each state voted in past elections, just before a presidential campaign, and dozens of other items that were entirely extraneous, have been excellent "door openers" for salesmen.
7. *Enclose separate reply forms in your mailings.* Tests prove that a separate reply form (usually printed on a different color paper) will bring in more inquiries than one which is part of the folder, broadside, or letter. It will pay dividends to include at least one separate and extra copy of your action form in every mailing you make.

Be Honest About Inquiries

Whatever you do, be completely honest—both to yourself and to the people who must follow up—in evaluating inquiries. Certainly every inquiry deserves some type of followup. But beware of sending a batch of unqualified inquiries to distributors or salesmen, for it takes only a couple of calls on unqualified inquirers for salesmen, who are usually suspicious of *any* inquiry to begin with, to quickly write off the potential of all future inquiries—regardless of how well qualified they may be.

In the following pages of this chapter, you will find many specific examples of successful industrial direct mail programs. In almost every case, they have one thing in common—they were designed to produce good, usable inquiries for sales follow-through.

THE GENERAL ELECTRIC STORY

Perhaps the largest industrial direct mail program in the world is that of General Electric Co. Just its apparatus sales department alone conducts as many as 200 direct mail campaigns in a single year.* The key element in GE's apparatus sales direct

*Since this case history was originally written, General Electric has made a number of changes in its methods of handling inquiries. However, the "General Electric Method" is still considered a basic model for developing effectve inquiry handling programs.

mail is a monstrous handbook—a looseleaf system with 8,800 pages covering 200 product lines for electric utility, industrial, transportation, community, and defense markets. The customer list represents more than 30,000 major purchasers who need detailed information. Each gets individual handbooks made up of various portions of the 8,800-page "monster." The material these major purchasers receive is kept up to date on a weekly basis. Every Monday morning about 75% of these customers receive one or more new or revised pages for the handbook, and during the average year almost 60% of the book will change. This requires selective distribution of more than 14 million pages of buying data. The mailing lists themselves will require from 300 to 400 changes each week.

Obviously, electronic equipment is required to handle this giant mailing job. GE has constructed a special collator, operated by punched cards which select appropriate material from 60 separate feeding stations along the 60-foot-long horseshoe-shaped collator. This "Rube Goldberg" machine not only selectively gathers a complete mailing each three seconds, but also picks up the mailing address from the punched card and automatically calculates the amount of postage required.

In addition to the 30,000 major purchasers, GE maintains lists of about 120,000 directly handled customers and prospects, who receive approximately 1½ million direct mailings per year. Highly selective tabulator cards are used for this list.

The Salesman's Role

GE's most common mailing technique is to prepare a package consisting of a brochure with a personalized tip-on or letter. These are normally shipped in bulk to sales offices, where individual salesmen receive all pieces addressed to their customers. They then screen, sign, and mail them. Because of a close salesman-customer relationship, GE seldom asks for any response to its mailings. When replies are requested, however, the returns average about 8%, and responses of 30 to 50% are not unusual.

While the letter-brochure mailing is most common, GE also uses nearly every possible direct mail format, including many showmanship and spectacular mailings. (Several examples of these are included in Chapters 31 and 32—"Showmanship Formats" and "Direct Mail Spectaculars.") External house organs are also used extensively, such as the *General Electric Defense Quarterly,* which goes to 20,000 selected government, industry, finance, educational, and publishing leaders concerned with national security. This particular house organ has won a number of honors and GE claims it "probably delivers greater impact per dollar on its audience than any other promotional medium used, either industrial or consumer."

Selling Distributors

GE's mailing program pays special attention to the company's distributors. For example, there is a pocket-size magazine called *Tips,* mailed eight times a year to a list of 6,000 distributor salesmen. It contains new product information, "how-to-sell" articles, and news of promotional and incentive campaigns. Each distributor salesman also gets a "Master Salesman Clincher Letter" every two weeks, calling attention to some specific product or feature and urging improved sales performance so the recipient can qualify for the exclusive Master Salesman's Club.

GE also supplies material for distributors to use in direct mail programs aimed at *their* customers. Special incentive programs, which are especially popular with GE, are heavily promoted by direct mail.

Sales Force Communications

Another major use of direct mail by GE is for communications with the thousand-plus apparatus salesmen. Since these men sell the products of some 50 autonomous operating departments of GE, they must constantly be kept informed, educated, and oriented on their product lines, prices, new developments, sales advice, competitive activity, etc. Because each GE department must compete to a certain extent for a share of the salesmen's time, the internal direct mail programs are often as extensive and creative as those sent to customers and distributors. The typical GE salesman receives an average of four GE direct mail pieces *every working day.*

In addition to material coming from headquarters offices, regional sales promotion operations in 17 key locations throughout the country turn out special direct mail pieces and campaigns tailored to specific local conditions.

DIRECT MAIL AS "LITERATURE"

It isn't only the industrial advertiser who fails to understand that much of what he puts into the mails is direct mail advertising. Recipients, too, often refuse to consider much of the material they receive through the mails as "advertising" at all. Hayden Ricker, of Hayden Ricker Associates, Tampa, Florida was quoted by Henry Hoke in *How to Think About Industrial Direct Mail,* as follows:

> When the occasion permits, I have asked many men what material received through the mail they have kept in file. Never did find one who didn't have some—anywhere from a single file folder to a filing cabinet full.
>
> But ask any one of them about the material he has saved, then listen carefully to what he calls it. Ninety-nine times out of 100, the stuff he has in file he will call *"literature"*—not advertising matter. He seems to make an unconscious but definite distinction between the two. It seems a lot of businessmen who are not direct mail-minded, vaguely think of "advertising" as a means of "making things seem what they ain't." But the mailing piece with information which interests him—Presto!—it loses its "advertising" stigma and becomes a useful piece of "literature" to be carefully read—and frequently saved.

Far from being a handicap to industrial advertisers, however, this line of differentiation can be a most valuable marketing aid. The impact of many industrial direct mail messages can be strengthened when material is so carefully designed that it is recognized as *literature* worth saving for future reference.

How Several Companies Contribute Longevity to Their Mailings

One feature of industrial direct mail not usually shared by consumer direct mail is its longevity. Industrial recipients make a regular practice of filing much of the direct mail material they receive. An NIAA study some years ago found that over 50% of industrial buyers contacted had literature in their files that they had saved for more than five years.

Many industrial advertisers build continuing direct mail programs around the idea of recipients establishing and maintaining a file. Sloves Mechanical Binding, for example, mails prospects a handsome 6- by 6- by 4-inch desk-top file box with a hinged cover. Then color post cards with illustrations showing unusual and effective presentations Sloves has developed for its customers are mailed at regular intervals. Each card has detailed copy on the mailing side and is slipped into a die-cut address slip, which contains a reminder that the card should be placed in the Sloves file box. When the file is sent to new names being added to Sloves' promotion list, it contains previously issued idea cards plus miniature samples of various types of binding produced by the company.

Hopper Paper Co., like many industrial advertisers, provided prospects on its mailing lists a file-size portfolio in which to keep all mailings in a series promoting Sunray printing papers. To its portfolio, however, Hopper added an interesting feature. Nine miniatures of the pieces to be included in the direct mail series were tipped inside the back cover of the portfolio. Copy explained: *"Periodically, color guide sheets, featuring all of Hopper's beautiful pastel shades, will be sent to you. As these practical guide sheets arrive, tuck them into the pocket of this kit until the series has been completed."* The miniatures built advance interest in the mailings and clearly indicated just what material should be inserted in the portfolio.

Another variation of this technique was used by U. S. Steel, which sent a filing sleeve with large, bold numerals (1 through 12) clearly visible inside the sleeve. The numerals matched tabs on various mailings, which were to be inserted in the sleeve to complete a basic reference file. Obviously, the file was incomplete until all the numerals had been covered by tabs.

Industry Service Campaigns

Many industrial direct mail campaigns draw bonus attention because they concentrate on "service-to-industry" materials. LeTourneau-Westinghouse, for example, developed two posters which won wide acclaim in the construction industry. One was "The Flagman's Code," which showed eight basic signaling techniques used by flagmen on construction sites. This poster was so popular that many contractors and state highway departments used it to establish a standard code for their flagmen. Another poster featured a set of basic hand signals which could be used to communicate information to operators of earthmoving machinery. Until the LeTourneau-Westinghouse poster came along, each foreman and often each driver had a code all his own.

One of the most unusual services offered by an industrial advertiser is *The Alpha Weathervane,* a monthly bulletin for customers published by Alpha Portland Cement Co., of Easton, Pennsylvania. Utilizing the services of Weather Trends, Inc., private meteorologists specializing in long-range forecasting, Alpha prepares a detailed bulletin with considerably more weather information than is available from the U. S. Weather Bureau. Using the Alpha information, cement users can plan their work to take advantage of or adjust to existing conditions.

Inland Steel Co. makes a weekly post card mailing with a digest of the previous week's business conditions. Material includes such items as bank clearings, bituminous coal output, business failures, steel production, wholesale food and price indexes, etc.

Industry Handbooks

One of the most effective direct mail tools used by industrial manufacturers is the industry handbook. Hundreds of such institutional promotion pieces are produced each year. They range from simple pocket folders to elaborate hard-bound books. According to Raymond P. Wiggers, writing in *Advertising Requirements,* an industry handbook is "an analytical textbook (preferably pocket-size for easy carrying and simplified use) which applies the experience and 'knowhow' of your company to the specific problems of the industry which you serve. It is an elementary book which establishes your company as an 'authority' by breaking down and simplifying great problems into well-organized and surprisingly small problems—which, as such, find simple solutions. It is the one true diplomatic approach to the industrial 'expert' who, when personally confronted by the sales engineer, refuses to listen to viewpoints other than his own. It is probably the best way in which you can put your own words into the 'difficult' prospect's mouth."

A typical example is the *Bulk Material Handbook,* published by The Frank G. Hough Co. This 60-page, pocket-size guide offers a series of tables providing basic weight and physical property information on all bulk materials, specific cost factor formulas for determining actual operations, and other formulas by which the cost of operating equipment can be figured. Hough uses its handbook in five ways:

1. To obtain qualified inquiries from publication ads
2. As the key offer to draw initial inquiries from its direct mail program
3. To obtain extensive publicity
4. As a trade-show giveaway
5. As a working tool for distributor salesmen

Other Types of Books for Industrial Buyers

An annual promotion which made friends for many years was a *Graphic Arts Progress* yearbook, published annually by Fraser Paper, Ltd. The series of plastic-bound volumes contained reprints and digests of outstanding articles about developments in the printing industry. Each year, Fraser asked editors of graphic arts publications to submit their best articles for consideration. These were then reviewed by a panel of industry leaders and the best material was selected for the yearbooks.

The Instrumentation Division of Ampex Corporation took advantage of a major speech delivered by its marketing manager to the U. S. Navy Bureau of Ships to produce an institutional book. Utilizing both the text and slides developed for the speech, Ampex produced a book, *The Tape Recorder as an Instrumentation Device*. Both paper and cloth versions were issued.

Kaiser Aluminum & Chemical Sales, Inc., publishes a series of technical books to furnish industry with useful information about aluminum. A typical example is an elaborate 234-page manual on aluminum foil. The extensive illustrated hard-cover book covers aluminum foil in modern industry applications, designing for aluminum foil, properties and availability of aluminum foil, production of foil, laminating foil, extrusion coating, printing, forming, fastening, and other subjects.

Since 1934, International Paper Company has been issuing a handbook for printers, estimators, and advertising production managers called *The Pocket Pal*. This handbook is described as "a condensation of the important phases of the graphic arts, covering the subjects adequately as a practical and educational aid." Included is a brief history of paper and printing, a description of the basic printing processes, printers' measurements, proofreaders' marks, and other reference material.

Kimberly-Clark Corporation publishes similar material in more lavish format. Utilizing the services of top graphic arts designers, this paper manufacturer regularly brings out special 8½- by 11-inch booklets, running from 24 to 48 pages, on subjects such as "How to Prepare Artwork for Letterpress and Lithography" and "Fundamentals of Printing."

But probably the best-known series of industry handbooks comes from another paper company—S. D. Warren Co. For many years, Warren issued an extensive series of aids for all who bought or produced printing. One series, entitled "How to Plan Printing to Promote Business," included nine titles:

1. Business, Its Nature and Its Functions
2. Management, Its Functions and Responsibilities
3. Management and Its Corporate Society
4. Printing, the Essential Aid to Management
5. Printing—Its Forms and Designations
6. Printing—Types and Typography
7. Printing—The Processes of Reproduction
8. Printing—Papers and Their Uses
9. Mailing—Lists and Regulations

Institutional Booklets

Du Pont reprinted a series of essays from a company publication prepared for stockholders in booklet form for direct mail use. The series, entitled *The Economic Adventures of George Small,* explained Du Pont's business philosophy, emphasizing the idea that big and small businesses can exist side by side profitably, and that the giant corporations are not the ogres they have been painted by some.

Koppers Co. produces a *Directory of Plastic Packaging Suppliers,* which it mails to customers of its customers. The 90-page booklet lists companies that buy polystyrene and polyethylene plastics from Koppers for conversion into packages. Companies are listed alphabetically by state, with a description of the kind of packages each produces.

Wesson Co., Detroit maker of carbide tools, produced a well-rounded promotion program based on service to its customers and prospects. Taking a humorously negative approach, Wesson first distributed posters featuring tips from "Careless Carlos." The "tips" told how to get the *least* out of carbides. Typical tips: "To adjust the tool, pound the tip. Tapping the tool gently to bring it up to the work is sissy stuff. Be a man! Besides, you can always borrow another hammer if you break one." Or, "Always run the toughest carbide jobs on your oldest machines. There's no sense in messing up nice new machines with the 'toughies.'" The posters were combined into booklet form and have also been adapted for editorial use as a monthly cartoon feature in *Carbide Engineering.*

Monsanto's Plastics Division helped its customers, who bought Monsanto plastics for use in plastic pipe, overcome some of the difficulties which developed in the early days of plastic pipe merchandising. To "clear the air" after some early plastic pipe had developed "bugs" and brought an unwarranted rash of bad publicity for the entire industry, Monsanto produced a dispassionate booklet which explained the true facts. It gave a brief history of plastic pipe, listed the various kinds available, clearly explained the advantages and disadvantages, drew objective comparisons between plastic and other types of pipe, gave comparative costs, outlined market potentials, and included a section on the future of plastic pipe.

Standard Pressed Steel Co. turned out a 16-page booklet on "reliability" as a public service to industry. The booklet pointed out how—and why—production errors become increasingly more costly in a technical age of faster speeds, higher temperatures, and greater forces. The only mention of Standard Pressed

Steel was an inside back cover listing of its products, but the psychological result was to connect the company with the subject—reliability.

External House Organs

A promotion tool of special importance in industrial direct mail for corporate-image-building purposes is the external house organ, which may take any form from a single-page newsletter to a slick magazine. Typical of the thousands of externals produced by industrial manufacturers:

Vectors, published quarterly by Hughes Aircraft Co. Technical articles discuss electronics and its application to products manufactured by Hughes.

Phoenix Flame, published by Phoenix Metal Cap Co. for packaging people and users of packaging products. This is one of the most famous company publications in existence and combines general interest prose and illustrations with a section illustrating new applications of Phoenix products.

Studio Light, published by Eastman Kodak Co., for professional portrait photographers. Success stories and examples of outstanding work by professional photographers are featured along with ideas for promoting sales.

Electronics Age, published quarterly by Radio Corporation of America. Articles discuss RCA developments, industry progress in electronics, and the significance of such progress.

The Cyanamid Magazine, published quarterly by American Cyanamid Co. Features include articles about the company's plants and products and case histories of product applications.

Grits & Grinds, published monthly by Norton Co. to promote better use of its abrasive products.

Distributor House Organs

A number of industrial manufacturers make external house organs available for mailing to their distributors' own lists. Standard Pressed Steel, for example, has a program which supplies individualized four-page house organs for each distributor. The inside spread is common to all the bi-monthly house organs, but each distributor gets tailored copy on the front and back pages, and is even permitted to choose his own title for the publication. Distributors pay $100 per thousand for the publication services, including preparation of the copy for the first and fourth pages. A publishing service, Distributor Publications of Stamford, Connecticut, handles the entire project for Standard Pressed Steel. The service's writers interview each distributor twice a year to obtain editorial material. Frequently a distributor chooses to advertise noncompetitive products in "his" space.

Sports Publications

Industrial direct mail often trades on the fact that most men are interested in sports. For example, The Falk Corporation of Milwaukee sends prospects for its machinery *Falk Engineered Sport Facts* nine times a year. The four-page bulletin illustrates and discusses technical facts about popular sports, such as a graph chart delineating the height at which a pitcher needs to throw a ball to register a strike against batters ranging in height from 5 feet 4 inches to 6 feet 4 inches. Since Falk's key prospects are engineering-minded, an engineer's approach to athletics wins special attention. Only a single half page in each issue of the bulletin is devoted to an article with selling and technical copy about Falk's machines.

FUNCTIONAL USES OF INDUSTRIAL DIRECT MAIL

Direct mail has a wide variety of functional uses for industrial advertisers. In fact, almost all of the 49 basic uses of direct mail described in Chapter 4 have an application in industrial fields. However, most of the basic uses can be divided into five categories:

1. Corporate Image Promotion
2. Product and Services Promotion
3. Sales Force Support
4. Chain-of-Distribution Communications
5. Solving Special Problems

Admittedly, there is often much overlapping among these categories and there are other incidental uses which do not clearly fit within any of these basic categories.

Corporate Image Promotion

Most of the uses of direct mail as literature just discussed fall within the category of corporate image promotion. The importance of this advertising objective was pointed out in a slidefilm presentation produced by *Newsweek* magazine:

> Ask the next person you meet for a quick definition of what advertising does (or is intended to do) and chances are he'll reply, "Sell something." And he'd be absolutely right. Nearly every advertisement has that quality

in common—they all are selling *something*. But it isn't always a product or service which is being sold. In many cases, an advertisement may have as its primary objective the selling of the corporation that makes the product.

Today corporate image advertising—sometimes called institutional, public relations or leadership advertising—is giving management one of its keenest tools for solving many of the problems that confront it. Because of various forces at work today, management must move in a dozen directions at once. Move to reduce costs; move to raise money for the introduction of new products; move to meet competition; move to hold or attract good personnel; move to merge or divest—to cite just a few. Advertising can help with all of these, if put to work on the entire corporate front.

To survive in today's economy, let alone grow and prosper, the successful corporation must do more than advertise its wares. It must develop and cultivate more than *customers*—it must get its story across to stockholders, employees, the trade, financial community, the communities surrounding its offices and plants—and the government.

Product and Services Promotion

The vast majority of industrial direct mail uses fall within the category of promoting products and services. This frequently involves a two-way promotion job—selling those who make the decisions about types of products to be used and then selling those who make the final buying decision and place the orders.

One of the big problems facing industrial direct mail advertisers is determining whether promotional material should be sent to the purchasing agent, the specifying influences within a prospect company, or to both. While the ideal solution for most industrial advertisers would probably be to prepare separate mailings for each group, with copy tailored to their specific interests and needs, this often turns out to be beyond the limitations of the budget.

A number of different approaches are used to meet this problem. Walter Kidde & Co., for example, sends its direct mail, advertising fire detecting and extinguishing equipment, to selective lists of people who initiate or specify such purchases, and then depends upon publicity and business publication advertising to reach purchasing agents.

In industries where catalog files are made available to all purchasing agents, advertisers frequently depend upon their advertising in these giant reference books to tell a detailed story to purchasing agents and then concentrate their direct mail on specifying influences—including special mailings of their catalog-type ads originally prepared for the catalog files.

Objectives of Product Advertising

Direct mail to promote products and services can have a variety of objectives. A survey of product advertising objectives of 863 industrial advertisers, conducted by McGraw-Hill Research, revealed 71 different types, which were in 16 different categories:

1. *To give product characteristics* (reported used by 31.4% of the respondents)
   Product quality
   Product durability
   Product dependability
   Special or exclusive features (design)
   Product performance
   Product superiority (general)
   Engineering specifications and technical data
   Product availability
   Case histories
   Safety features
   Modern design
   Promote companion item
2. *To obtain inquiries and sales leads* (23.1%)
   Get inquiries
   Get sales leads
   Get direct sales
   Get inquiries for distributors
3. *To maintain or establish product recognition* (20.7%)
   Get brand acceptance/recognition
   Maintain established recognition
4. *To aid salesmen and distributors* (13%)
   Pave way for salesmen/distributors
   Reach top management
   Reach buying influences inaccessible to salesmen
   Reach technical and engineering personnel
   Renew contacts with old or neglected customers
   Presell consumers and distributors
   Aid distributors
   Announcements
5. *To publicize company services connected with product* (13%)
   Advantage of wide range of product line
   General services ("total facilities")
   Design and engineering services
   Promote catalog and literature
   Distribution and delivery (including branches)

Other services
Jobber services

6. *To create desire to try out product* (10.7%)
7. *To introduce a new product* (10.6%)
8. *To show cost-cutting advantages of product* (9.4%)
   Product cuts cost
   Time and labor savings
   Extra value though high cost
9. *To create direct demand for product* (9.4%)
   Create demand
   Create preference for product
10. *To show product applications* (8.7%)
    Product applications and function
    How to maintain product
    Tie-in with automation
11. *To address distributors* (8%)
    Get distributor to push product
    To interest distributors
    Tell dealers about product features
    Inform parts dealers
    Dealer profit and pricing policy
    Merchandise consumer advertising
    To keep distributor goodwill
12. *To get new markets and territories* (8%)
    Stimulate new markets
    New territories
    Hold replacement markets
    Hold present markets
    Inform small or remote markets
    Stabilize market for future
    Expand market for packaged units
13. *To show product advantage/benefit* (7.5%)
    General
    Product efficiency
    Versatility
    Easy to use
    Plant modernization
14. *To address original equipment market* (2.7%)
    Get designers to specify product in original equipment
    Create original equipment manufacturer demand/recognition
    Interest designers
15. *To aid in a competitive situation* (2.7%)
    Comparison with competitor's product

Increase share of the market

16. *To support trade papers* (.5%)
    To support trade paper advertising
    Tie-in with articles

Industrial Mail Order

While the majority of industrial firms seldom seek direct orders for their products through the mails, there are a number of outstanding examples of effective industrial mail order selling. A frequently told "classic" is the experience of the Milwaukee Dustless Brush Company, which suddenly decided to eliminate its sales force of 125 men after 40 years of conventional industrial marketing. In their place, the company turned to mail order selling backed by trade publication advertising. Selling cost per unit was reduced about 30%, and within five years, sales were 400% greater than when salesmen were used.

Like most industrial sellers-by-mail, Milwaukee Dustless Brush does not depend primarily upon immediate response to its mailings for the bulk of its business. While it mails to a well-cultivated customer list monthly, many of the customers carry the company's literature in their files and order by purchase order when their needs arise.

One important use for industrial mail order, even by companies which do not regularly use it as a basic selling method, is to determine the degree of interest in new products. A number of important industrial manufacturers got their start before they had an opportunity to develop distribution organizations by mail order selling.

The Frank G. Hough Co. even sells tractors by mail order. One year it spent $20,000 on a mail campaign which produced $300,000 worth of sales for tractors costing between $4,000 and $11,500 each. A single mailing to 15,000 firms in industrial and construction fields on another occasion brought Hough 1,012 replies and sold 23 tractors totaling $140,000.

How Kaiser Sells Two Groups

An important influence in marketing industrial products is often the production worker. Although seldom contacted by a salesman and only infrequently a reader of trade paper advertising, this man frequently expresses opinions. And these opinions may be the deciding factor in the marketing process. Kaiser Aluminum & Chemical Corporation recognized this problem in the sale of its aluminum stock for manufacturing parts on automatic screw machines and turned to a nine-piece direct mail program to solve it.

Three of Kaiser's direct mail pieces were sent to white-collar industrial specifiers and buyers—two attractive booklets (explaining how aluminum can give a company a competitive advantage) plus a followup letter, mailed at two-day intervals. The remaining six pieces were addressed to machine operators and shop foremen and included a guide to feeds and speeds, a quantity/weight calculator, and an operator's manual, interspersed with promotional pieces talking up the advantages of aluminum. Separate pieces were purposely developed for the white-collar and blue-collar audiences, so Kaiser could talk to each group in its own language.

A Kennametal Campaign Which Changed Tradition

When a new product comes along, or even when there is a need to broaden the market for an older product, the first step is often to change an industry's traditional methods of operation. This is a marketing problem which is often solved with direct mail. Kennametal Inc., of Latrobe, Pennsylvania, won AIA's top award for an outstanding campaign which helped change the traditional metalworking industry practice of trying to get maximum life from every carbide insert used in cutting tools. Kennametal used the theme that companies were wasting dollars in potential machine output just to save pennies in tool life.

The campaign started with an article in *American Machinist* about a Chicago manufacturer who had issued orders that no tool was to be allowed to last more than 30 minutes. This company had discovered that what counted was getting the most from machines and men—not from tools. Kennametal business publication ads followed a similar theme: "Don't Waste Dollars in Machine Output to Save Pennies in Tool Life." Reprints of the *American Machinist* article and Kennametal ads were mailed to 23,000 tool engineers, shop superintendents, and similar buying and specifying factors.

In addition, the company prepared an educational booklet titled *There's Profit in Retiring a Tradition, which* was used in many ways in the promotion campaign. One of the most effective uses of the booklet was to put the story across to a group not regularly contacted by either the company's salesmen or routine promotion—top metalworking management. Because operating personnel in many plants were blocking the basic new dollar-saving concept, primarily because of the natural human dislike of change, it was felt necessary to dramatize the story to top management. The booklets sent to management men were accompanied by individually typed letters and a special card containing a real silver dollar and penny to dramatize the "Don't Waste Dollars to Save Pennies" theme.

The campaign was heavily merchandised to the company's 100 salesmen. Each received a portfolio containing samples of all promotion material, including publicity releases. The day before the portfolio was mailed, each salesman was sent a letter completely explaining not only the program, but also the role the salesman was expected to play to tie in with the campaign. Salesmen were required to make periodic reports, which were used to provide case history information for a regular series of *Sidelight Bulletins.* The entire campaign was also merchandised to editors of all metalworking publications and resulted in a number of publication-originated articles on the subject.

How Torrington Dramatized an Important Industry Role

Another time when direct mail can play a vital promotional role is when a company wants to clearly nail down its role as a primary supplier of products to a specific industry. For example, The Torrington Company had long played a key role in the development of the automobile industry. For an extended period of time, it had been an almost exclusive supplier of certain components, but gradually more and more competition developed and Torrington felt it was important to clearly establish its history as the leader in these now-competitive areas.

The technique used by Torrington was a continuing direct mail series featuring brochures containing original 10- by 12-inch full-color prints of historical automobiles. Lesser known vintage cars were chosen, but in each case there was a definite relationship between the car illustrated in the print and an important technological advance in which Torrington had played a leading part. The mailing list was composed of a well-defined group of about 650 key engineers, purchasing agents, and other executives in the automobile industry. Not only did the direct mail campaign make its key point, that Torrington was a "partner in progress" with automobile manufacturers, but also hundreds of the prints found an honored spot as wall decorations in the offices and homes of recipients, giving Torrington continued recognition between mailings.

Product Sampling

Direct mail sampling can be a highly effective technique in selling to industrial markets. J. R. Hess, direct mail manager for Ketchum, MacLeod & Grove, Pittsburgh advertising agency serving primarily industrial accounts, has written in *Industrial Marketing,* "If you find it hard to ignore a sample that comes through the mails, you're normal. Almost everyone responds to the curiosity appeal of a bag, a box, a package, or a bulky envelope. Expert salesmen long have known the value of getting the prospective buyer to touch, feel, hold, or try the products they're selling. With the product in his hands, the prospect gives it his undivided attention."

G. W. Donaldson, Union Bag-Camp Paper Corporation advertising manager, told a DMAA audience, "Samples are particularly effective in mailings relating to 'dull' products."

With small products, direct mail sampling is relatively simple. But when it comes to bulky items, a great deal of ingenuity is required. One of the most successful developers of ingenious sampling techniques is Robert G. Hill, former advertising manager of United States Steel's Columbia-Geneva division in San Francisco. Mr. Hill constantly sought out small items which can be constructed of different types of steel and uses them to make specific sales points related to more bulky applications of his company's products. Typical Columbia-Geneva mailings:

- A set of lacing pins for sewing up fowl
- An eyelet which assists fishermen in attaching a leader to a fly line
- A pocket-size circular wire saw with rings at the ends ("Grasp rings, pull taut, saw")
- A key ring made from Tiger Brand wire rope (with a steel tag stamped with an identification number and instructions to return the keys to Columbia-Geneva if found)
- "Try-to-take-apart" puzzles made of steel wire

Earrings, Paperweights, and Metal Letters

Pemco Corp., Baltimore maker of ceramic glaze stains, effectively merchandised new colors through a unique direct mail sampling method. When a new gray stain was introduced, Pemco sent customers and prospects earrings utilizing the latest addition to its color line. The following year, when a new brown stain was added to the line, ceramic makers received an unusual mailing piece showing a portion of a man's arm. A piece of suiting fabric was glued in place to make the coat sleeve realistic and a ceramic cuff link, featuring the new brown stain, was attached in place on the shirt cuff. Its mate was put on the other side of the folder.

Sparton Corp. used an unusual sampling program to promote its boxcar loading system, which features a distinctive aluminum crossmember:

> First it enclosed a plain sheet of aluminum foil in an envelope normally used to mail the company's newsletter, *Progress Report.* A day later, pros-

pects and customers received a letter with a small piece of foil attached, explaining that the "teaser" aluminum mailing had been sent as a reminder of the availability of the aluminum crossmembers.

A third mailing featured a roll of Reynolds Wrap, with a label attached containing copy about Sparton's use of aluminum.

This was followed by an instruction manual stapled to a sales message printed on aluminum foil.

The fifth and final mailing was a small cross section of a Sparton aluminum crossmember suitable for use as a paperweight.

A method of sampling which has found wide popularity among industrial advertisers who produce appropriate products is to print direct mail letters on an actual sample of the product. Just as Sparton printed one of its messages on aluminum foil, aluminum companies regularly use aluminum foil for direct mail purposes.

National Vulcanized Fibre Co. of Wilmington, Delaware, printed a letter on a laminated plastic it manufactures. It was used to merchandise an article reprinted from a plastics industry business publication describing the many different uses for laminated plastics.

Companies which produce cloth products, likewise, often utilize samples of their materials for a direct mail printing surface. One of the most interesting was a two-page letter from Rubber Fabrics Co. headed, "Your brassiere designer will love the 'feel' of the OTHER SIDE of this letter . . ." The message went on to read: ". . . because, as you can see, it comes to you on an actual sample of a new 'non-skid' fabric that will enable you to produce bras . . ." etc. Other examples include letters etched into copper, silk-screened on glass, and even one from a manufacturer of shingles burned into a product sample.

How B. Heller & Co. Got Samples for Testing

For some industrial products, one of the most effective marketing techniques is to obtain samples of materials or components presently being used by prospects so they can be analyzed before a "replacement" is designed and/or recommended. B. Heller & Co., of Chicago, wanted to convince sausage makers that its sausage flour would hold more meat juices and moisture than competitive brands. To conduct comparison tests, however, required use of heavy machinery and special temperatures. So Heller sent a miniature drum to 2,200 packers, along with a letter asking the packer to fill the drum with the binder he was using and send it back to Heller for impartial testing. The letter made a "bet" that Heller's Bull Meat Brand Binder would win out in the comparison test. If Heller lost the "bet," it promised to send the packer a certificate good for $100 worth of Heller products. The prospect still "won" even if Heller's brand tested best. In this case the packer got a working sample of the Heller binder along with graphs from the machines which made the tests.

Building Interest in a Catalog

The primary promotion tool for many industrial products is the company catalog. It not only is a basic direct mail tool in itself, but it also is often the focal point of a continuing direct mail program. While most companies make automatic distribution of catalogs to customer lists, there is generally more selectivity when it comes to making distribution to prospects.

Thermo Electric Mfg. Co., for example, wanted widespread distribution of a new catalog showing industrial thermocouples, but felt it important to make sure prospects had an interest in receiving copies. A newsletter describing the catalog was mailed to 13,642 prospects. Rather than using lots of copy to describe the catalog's contents, Thermo reproduced the entire 12-page catalog in miniature—reduced from 8½ by 11 inches to 2¼ by 2⅞ inches. The miniature was then slipped into a slot cut into the newsletter. The mailing drew catalog requests from 3,800—a 28 percent return. Interestingly enough, Thermo actually received several requests for quotation directly from the miniature, even though the type when reduced was probably no larger than 2 points. An important "extra" for the original mailing was that it built an advance interest in the receipt of the catalog.

Once a catalog is in the hands of customers and prospects, direct mail is frequently called upon to keep the catalog remembered. Many industrial advertisers have continuing programs of mailings designed primarily to stimulate catalog use.

Another important use for direct mail in conjunction with catalogs is to get catalog holders to make changes. New pages and sections are usually distributed by direct mail, but it takes special efforts to get many recipients to go to the trouble of replacing outdated material with the replacements.

The Isaacs Co., Cincinnati manufacturers' agent, uses a "lucky numbers" contest to increase the odds of having customers make catalog changes. Each of Isaacs' comprehensive catalogs is individually registered in the name of the person to whom it is given and a serial number is assigned. Whenever a set of catalog revision sheets is mailed, a lucky number is drawn from among the catalog numbers. Covering letters sent with the revision sheets list the lucky number. Most recipients are curious enough to check the inside front cover of their original catalog, where the serial numbers are imprinted. And once the catalog is in hand, the company figures it is more likely revisions will be made.

Still another problem is to get recipients to study an industrial catalog. Too often, catalogs are simply "filed for future reference," without so much as a glance through the pages. The Deming Company, an Ohio pump manufacturer, devised an effective method to encourage catalog readership. It mailed a 19-question quiz, offering prizes for all completed quiz forms with correct answers. Some questions were easy, but others could be answered only by referring to a new Deming catalog.

Another industrial manufacturer sprinkles cartoons throughout his catalog, with cover copy encouraging recipients to browse through the pages for a bit of industry-related humor.

Personalized Promotion

Because lists of prime prospects for many industrial products or services are often quite small, most successful industrial advertisers take advantage of the opportunity to personalize mailings. Manpower, Inc., which supplies temporary help and business services, developed a highly personalized approach to a list of companies with multiple branches which were already using Manpower services in one or more of the branches. A preprinted cover, titled *A Special Report,* was prepared, with space allowed for imprinting the names of individual companies to which the promotion would go. Inside the folder were four loose single pages, also preprinted formats, with space for imprinting both the names of the individual companies to which the reports were sent plus individualized information showing type of work done for the company, a list of cities in which Manpower was already serving the company, reasons for using Manpower services, and a list of the full range of services available. Manpower's *Special Reports* were so successful that the idea was adapted to mailings aimed at industry groups as well as individual companies.

North Shore Nameplate, Inc., developed a highly unique method of personalizing mailings. It used four-page folders, inside which it attached tearsheets of the recipients' own business paper ads. The front page of the folder showed North Shore's president clipping an ad out of a magazine. Copy read: "When I read about your product, I started to wonder if . . ." It continues inside the folder: ". . . you can reduce costs with our Therma-Cal color anodized and etched aluminum foil nameplates." All ads selected for the mailing program showed a product with a riveted metal nameplate, a decal, or a printed label, which indicated the advertiser was a logical prospect for North Shore's services.

INDUSTRIAL DIRECT MAIL FOR SALES FORCE SUPPORT

Because the salesman plays such a vital role in industrial marketing, many direct mail programs are designed to directly *support* the activities of the salesman, rather than just to create a better climate for his selling activities and furnish random leads for his followthrough. And, at the same time, direct mail is used to *sell* the salesman on utilizing the support the regular direct mail program is giving him.

Howard Swink, whose Marion, Ohio, agency handles many important industrial direct mail accounts, has said:

> Our current thinking on industrial direct mail is based on two basic ideas:
>
> 1. That it must interest the prospect in the product.
> 2. That it must *sell* the salesman who is selling the product.
>
> By this we mean two things: (a) The salesman must be convinced that direct mail is an effective tool to help him sell, and (b) the direct mail piece must present the salesman in a favorable light to the prospect, paving the way for his call.
>
> During an industrial direct mail campaign which depends on the cooperation of the sales force, direct mail should also be used to:
>
> 1. Keep the salesman informed about, and sold on, the selling plan itself. He must understand completely just *what* he is to do, and *when* he is to do it.
> 2. Induce salesmen to follow up inquiry leads immediately; an abnormal lag between the time of inquiry and the followup call usually results in a "hot" prospect turning cold.
> 3. Stimulate salesmen to report on the results of all sales calls.

Providing Answers to "What's New?"

When a company has widespread sales coverage which reaches the majority of customers and prospects on a regular basis, direct mail may draw few formal inquiries, since those interested will probably just await the next call by the salesman and request the information or literature offered in the mailing. But direct mail is nevertheless important in that it stimulates sales-oriented conversation between the salesman and his prospects.

In fact, in industries where sales calls must be made frequently, direct mail can play an important secondary role. It is inevitable that the customer usually wants to know "what's new." And unfortunately, all too often, the salesman has no ready answer. But the salesman who is supported by a continuing direct mail education and information program has a steady stream of "what's new" answers—particularly if this factor is taken into consideration in the planning of a direct mail program.

When Oxford Paper Company planned its award-winning North Star spectacular direct mail program (described in Chapter 32, it took special notice of the fact that most paper merchant salesmen must make frequent calls on the same buyer. And in the paper industry, as in so many other industries, new developments do not come along very rapidly. By using a spectacular direct mail technique, with mailings on a regular basis, the salesman was provided with plenty of "what's new" answers with built-in mutual interest. Of special importance to Oxford was the fact that the paper merchants who handle its lines also handle paper manufactured by many other companies. So having the salesman-customer conversation centered on Oxford added up to an increased percentage of the salesman's time during each sales contact being directed at Oxford's products.

How Ozalid Helps Salesmen Sell a Large Line

One major marketing problem for many industrial advertisers is that they offer so many different items their salesmen cannot possibly cover all of them on regular sales calls. The Ozalid Div. of General Aniline & Film Corporation, facing this problem, turned to a monthly mailing program aimed at selling additional items to customers being contacted regularly by salesmen. Each of the mailings talked about a specialty or accessory product the salesman might not have yet tried to sell his customers. An enclosed reply card gave the customer an opportunity to request information on any Ozalid product.

The results were excellent. One mailing, with a 15% response, turned up 1,388 prospects who thought they had an application for a new sensitized paper which had not yet even been described by the salesmen calling on them. Three months after the mailing, sales for the particular product had increased 24%. Another mailing turned up 491 prospects for a portable tracing unit and produced a 400% increase in sales of that product.

Remington Rand Plan for Encouraging Salesmen to Approach New Markets

When new market applications for a product are uncovered, there is always a problem in getting already-busy salesmen to take advantage of the new opportunities. This usually requires cultivating a whole new set of prospects and calls for a lot of difficult spadework, usually with unknown potential for commissions.

Remington Rand faced this problem when it found its Flexoprint machine had a natural application in setting up and maintaining voter lists. While a handful of successful applications had been reported, Remington Rand decided to use a test market approach before trying to get its entire sales force to go to work on this new sales opportunity. It chose New York State and mailed a letter with an enclosed reply card to each secretary of state and election commissioner in all counties in New York. A case history report was offered. The mailing drew better than a 3.5% response and a special sales effort was made on followup calls.

When the unusually excellent results had been carefully analyzed, Remington Rand expanded the program on a nationwide basis. Salesmen were convinced that they should put real effort behind the program by being given detailed information on the results of the New York market test and the selling techniques which turned out to be most successful in converting inquiries to sales. A national mailing produced better than 4% inquiries, and sales conversions were excellent, thanks to the advance work done to convince the sales force of the opportunities and techniques for successful conversion of inquiries to sales.

Dramatizing the Salesman

Many industrial direct mail campaigns make a very special effort to feature individual salesmen. Ohio Seamless Tube, for example, mailed authentic-looking "Wanted" posters to 5,000 customers and prospects. The posters featured the salesman calling on each customer. Typical "post-office bulletin board" style was followed with front and side view "mug shots" of the salesmen, fingerprints, description, accomplices, record, and even a "reward." The posters were headed: "This Man is WANTED by the F. B. I." F. B. I. was defined as meaning "Fraternity of Better Industries." Copy stuck to a light touch, such as the warning note: "This man is armed (with plenty of experience and ability). Lacks fear of any problem involving steel tubing." The reward: "Help with design, cost, production, and price problems."

Malcolm W. Black & Co., New York manufacturers' agent, regularly sends giant post card mailings, frequently featuring pictures of salesmen with headings such as "It'll Pay You to Know This *Black* Sheep." Another industrial advertiser spots illustrations of salesmen throughout its selling literature and changes the illustrations during the press run so that recipients receive copies with pictures of "their" salesmen only.

Introducing New Salesmen

Because of the importance of the almost personal salesman-customer relationship in most industrial selling, one of the toughest promotion problems comes when a new salesman must be introduced. Most companies want to try to establish a new personal relationship as quickly as possible. This problem was "brainstormed" by a group of Milwaukee industrial admen. Among the 129 possible solutions developed in the session were the following:

- Have the salesman write a personal card or letter.
- Send a series of picture post cards signed by the salesman to each prospect for several days preceding the initial sales call. They could come from points en route from the home office to the city where the prospect is located, and each could carry a "report" on progress of the trip with a promise such as "I'll see you Wednesday."
- Send one cuff link and tell the prospect the new salesman will be around in a few days to deliver the mate.
- Send a deck of cards with all the aces missing and have the salesman deliver the aces on his first call.
- Send a series of mailings on problems the salesman has solved.
- Have the salesman's wife write a letter introducing her husband (and include a photograph of the wife, if she is photogenic).
- Send a news clipping containing a picture of the salesman.
- Run a classified ad in the local newspaper telling about the salesman, and then send a copy of the paper (with the ad circled) to each prospect in advance of the salesman's first call.
- Send a plastic record with a message from the new salesman.
- Have the salesman's name or photo worked into an ad reprint.
- Send each prospect a list of books and ask him to check the one he wants free—then have the salesman deliver it on his first call.

Goddard & Goddard's Successful Introduction Plan

One company which used an effective direct mail program to introduce a new sales representative was Goddard & Goddard, which was faced by a serious time problem in introducing a new representative in the highly important and competitive New York

City area. Once the former representative, who had built up a wide following during the 30 years he had represented the company, let it be known he would be leaving, competitors were quick to stalk Goddard & Goddard's customers in the territory. Since there were 1,500 customers and prospects to be covered, it would obviously be a considerable period before the new representative could completely "make the rounds."

Goddard & Goddard decided on an eight-week mailing program, with one mailing per week to the entire list. The first piece was an announcement from the former representative saying "good-by" to his customers and telling of the change. The second mailing was a letter headlined, "Hello—I'm looking forward to seeing you soon." It featured a photo of the new sales representative, with hand extended, ready to shake hands. The letter told of the new man's background. To maintain continuity in the campaign, this photo was repeated on each mailing.

The third mailing was another letter and a condensed catalog; then another letter and a bulletin on a special line that needed a special push in the area. The fifth mailing included a handy calculator which could be used by the recipients. The sixth mailing was another letter with a reply card offering to have the new salesman call personally or to have the company's big catalog sent. This drew a return of 10%, the majority of the cards asking the representative to make a personal call. The seventh mailing was another letter-bulletin combination; and finally, mailing number eight again featured a large reproduction of the salesman's photo as the frontispiece of a letter. So successful was the campaign that the new representative was able to show a 50% sales increase during his first year in the territory.

Keeping Salesmen Remembered Between Calls

Another industrial marketing problem which can be solved by an effective direct mail program is "filling in" during periods between salesmen's calls. This is particularly important in fields where repeat orders are frequent—and particularly where it is common to place orders by phone or purchase order whenever the need for a product arises.

Where a personal salesman-customer relationship has been cultivated, direct mail is frequently on a personal basis, with special mailing pieces which are either signed by the salesman or in some way feature him as an individual. One industrial manufacturer, for example, has a regular program through which salesmen can make a monthly mailing to prospects' homes with samples of consumer products produced by the company. Another company makes effective use of picture post cards which are preprinted and preaddressed, but signed and mailed by salesmen at whatever point they may be on certain days of each month.

United States Plywood Corp., for one example, regularly uses post cards to "cover" for salesmen who, for one reason or another, have to miss regular sales calls. If a salesman becomes ill and is removed from circulation for a while, customers receive personally signed post cards informing them of what has happened to the salesman and what steps have been taken to serve the customers during the salesman's absence. At vacation time, customers receive similar cards.

Symons Clamp & Manufacturing Co. Sales Call Followups

Industrial salesmen often use special direct mail pieces to capitalize on interests aroused during sales calls. Symons Clamp & Manufacturing Co., for example, supplies salesmen with a series of four followup mailings. Each features teaser copy plus a place for the salesman to insert his business card, which carries his picture. Four mailings are used:

1. The first piece is mailed a day or two after the salesman's first visit and thanks the prospect for his courtesies.
2. The second piece, mailed a week later, suggests the prospect see Symons' concrete foundation forms in use, by visiting a nearby construction site, which is mentioned in a space provided inside the folder.
3. A third mailing suggests the prospect give the salesman a call.
4. The fourth piece is sent just before the salesman plans another sales call and suggests "problems" the prospect may want to discuss with the salesman.

Boosting Telephone Orders

Many industrial advertisers, particularly distributors supplying component parts and materials, depend primarily on telephone orders. While salesmen may make contacts with the phone buyers, direct mail is called upon to keep the company and its phone number constantly in mind.

Edgcomb Steel Co. of Philadelphia regularly sends its telephone buyers folders showing pictures of all the company's inside salesmen. Beside each picture in a folder is the salesman's name, the kind of products he handles, and his telephone extension number. These folders, which are distributed annually, are often kept for quick reference when phone orders are to be made.

Another concern, Industrial Bearing Co. of Baltimore, puts the emphasis on its telephone number. Jumbo post cards are mailed monthly, and sales directly traceable to just one mailing, costing $267, amounted to $40,000.

The Rolled Steel Story

Rolled Steel Products Corporation of Chicago parlayed a $1,300 investment into a $7,000,000 annual volume in just eight years through a combination of direct mail promotion and telephone orders. Rolled Steel uses seven basic types of direct mail in contacting its customers and prospects:

1. Flyers of from one to eight pages, sent out almost daily to list steel carried in inventory. These are sent to various combinations of the 22,000 names on the company's customer list, which is indexed so that mailings can be pinpointed to the specific needs of buyers. The company estimates that there are more than 1,000 different list combinations available for these mailings.
2. Jumbo post cards carrying shorter listings of available steels.
3. Periodic letters to prospects to acquaint them with Rolled Steel's operations. Recipients are encouraged to fill in reply cards so that their names can be placed on the permanent mailing list.
4. Prospective customers also are frequently sent survey forms on which they can indicate what types of steel they normally use.
5. Letters sent by individual salesmen to their lists of phone customers. Because almost all contact is by telephone, these letters carry a picture of the salesman so that the buyer will have a chance to "meet" the man from whom he buys.
6. Reprints of newspaper and magazine articles of interest to steel buyers.
7. A more formal brochure describing the company's background and operations.

Every Rolled Steel mailing urges the recipient to call the company collect to place orders or to obtain information. Through this direct mail-telephone order combination, which involves an average of 60,000 mailing pieces a month and over $6,000 monthly in telephone bills, the company has sold orders ranging from a $7.50 order for 100 pounds of steel to an order for 3,000 tons at a total of $450,000.

CHAIN-OF-DISTRIBUTION COMMUNICATIONS

In industrial direct mail, various types of "middlemen" can enter into the picture. Not only do distributors and agents often play an important role in a successful industrial direct mail program, but other manufacturers and customers' customers also get involved. For example, when Murray Mfg. Corp. decided to offer a lifetime guarantee for its circuit breakers, it took advantage of the chance to promote its product at four different levels:

1. To the distributor
2. Through the distributor to electrical contractors
3. Through the electrical contractors to building contractors
4. Through the building contractors to the homeowner

Distributors were furnished a variety of sales promotion materials, including envelope-stuffer folders and other direct mail pieces, and similar pieces were made available to electrical and building contractors.

Industrial distributors play an important role in industrial direct mail. According to a study by *Industrial Distribution,* 74% of America's industrial distributors consider direct mail the most effective form of advertising they can use (and another 12% were undecided as to which medium was most effective for them). This same survey showed that one-quarter of the industrial distributors make weekly mailings to their customers and prospects, another 16% mail every other week; and another 31% mail at least monthly.

A very important function of industrial direct mail is to tell a prospect where he can obtain a product he has seen advertised in other media. Unlike most *consumer* products, the purchasing source of many *industrial* products is not obvious—particularly when a specific brand is desired. So many manufacturers make it a standard practice to merchandise their business paper advertising through direct mail with accompanying letters designed primarily to identify the local sales outlet. Industrial distributors, too, make mailings on their own which feature reprints of ads originally run by the manufacturers they represent, but with copy added, saying, in effect, "You've heard about this product. If it interests you, we're the firm from which you can buy it."

Promoting Through "Outsiders"

The aid of other manufacturers is often recruited in promoting industrial products. Du Pont, for example, wanted to promote the use of its Super Cordura sewing thread to 500 major manufacturers of feed and fertilizer for use in closing their product bags. Eleven manufacturers of multiwall bags supplied the entire market. Since these 11 bag manufacturers were the recognized "authorities" on all matters relating to the use of the bags, Du Pont arranged for each bag manufacturer to send direct mail pieces promoting Super Cordura thread to every feed and fertilizer customer.

Du Pont has also used direct mail to sell through the buyers of its customers' customers. A Canadian division makes four-times-a-year mailings to hardware dealers and to paint stores across Canada to promote nylon bristles in paint brushes. While Du Pont does not make paint brushes, it does supply the nylon to the manufacturers who do. The hardware and paint dealer campaign is used to build a demand for the brushes made by Du Pont's customers.

The campaign uses an interesting soft-sell technique. Each mailing features cartoon illustrations showing "Mr. Nutley, the Screwy Customer," making impossible requests of the dealer. Typical: "I want a piece of glass but I don't know the size because I can't read a rule." Dealers are encouraged to send in actual "screwy" requests they have encountered, and are paid $5 for each situation used in the continuing, highly successful campaign.

A Monsanto "Use-the-User" Campaign

Monsanto used an unusual combination of business publication advertising and direct mail in a roundabout promotion to paper companies for its Mersize, used to size paper. Promotion was directed not only to the paper converters who were the basic customers of the paper manufacturers (who were Monsanto's direct customers), but to those who bought from the paper converters, as well. The basic promotion problem involved was that Monsanto already had pretty much saturated its market. To get additional business for Mersize, it had to create more demand for the papers in which Mersize was used.

The first step was to create new ways in which liquid-resistant papers could be used. Monsanto's agency, Gardner Advertising, conducted an "idea contest" among some 200 of its personnel. The resulting ideas were then screened carefully and 18 promotable applications were retained. A team of top industrial designers and creative artists then went to work to turn the ideas into usable designs, which were illustrated and described in an 11- by 15-inch brochure. The same basic ideas were adapted to a series of 12 different publication advertisements.

Then the entire campaign was beamed at the two important secondary audiences: (1) paper converters, to interest them in making and selling the new paper products, and (2) businesses which could use the products, to induce them to turn to the paper converters as a source. Monsanto's own customers—the paper mills—were encouraged to cooperate in the program.

How Pittsburgh Corning Sold the Specifiers

When Pittsburgh Corning Corp. developed a new line of sculptured glass modules (glass blocks with built-in design), one of its basic promotion jobs was to open the eyes of architects to the potential of the new line. A series of six direct mail pieces was designed with special emphasis on handsome appearance and dignified copy, to establish an essential quality of *involvement* between the architect and the sculptured glass modules.

The first mailing was an adaptation of material originally prepared for a sales meeting—sketches showing the salesmen how the new blocks could be used effectively. Pittsburgh Corning discovered that architects were "borrowing" these sketches from the salesmen for their own use, so a brochure was prepared featuring reproductions of the sketches on a translucent stock—a medium with which architects work daily.

The second mailing was embossed to give a three-dimensional effect, which dramatized the sculptured effect of the blocks. Four additional mailings featured outstanding photographs reproduced by sheet-fed gravure to create the proper mood of texture, light, and shade.

Slant/Fin Campaign for Cultivating New Outlets

Another common marketing problem for industrial advertisers is to line up new distribution outlets. A particularly successful campaign for this purpose was developed by Slant/Fin Radiator Corp. The company mailed a series of 11 testimonial letters from wholesalers already handling Slant/Fin's line. Each of the letters was mailed over a present wholesaler's name and covered an important point such as:

How Slant/Fin delivers worthwhile profits

How Slant/Fin protects the wholesaler's territory

How Slant/Fin sells in a competitive market

The mailings to a list of 1,600 wholesaler prospects produced 180 leads which were converted into 49 active accounts (plus many more which were expected to become active in the future). First-year business directly traceable to the direct mail program was valued at more than $250,000.

An interesting aspect of the program was a followup in which Slant/Fin thanked cooperating wholesalers who participated in the testimonial program, making a special mailing utilizing the artwork from the original wholesaler pieces (each featured a picture of the wholesaler giving the testimonial) to contractors in the wholesaler's territory.

How Universal Form Clamp Sold Distributors on Direct Mail

Universal Form Clamp Co. used a simple, yet effective, technique to convince distributors that they should sign up for a company-sponsored direct mail program. Instead of offering the program to distributors in the traditional merchandising brochure, Universal just mailed samples of the series—complete with each distributor's imprint—to the distributors. There was no accompanying letter or any information covering how the cards were to be used or to offer additional cards. The distributors quickly took action—*asking* for the "missing details" and *demanding* additional cards they could send to their mailing lists.

The mailing pieces, themselves, were extremely simple. On the face of each of the post-card mailers was a simple word or phrase associated with a common sign—*For Rent, Reserved, Welcome, Information, For Sale, Do Not Disturb,* etc. On the mailing side of the post cards, quick, to-the-point messages tied in with the sign copy on the face. For example, on the "Reserved" card, copy read: "Reserved . . . a copy of Universal Form Clamp Company's catalog No. 759 containing 54 pages of concrete forming products is reserved for you. Phone or write for your copy now!"

Stran-Steel's List-Improvement Program

Lists can be just as important in distributor direct mail programs as for company programs. Stran-Steel Corp. which makes prefabricated metal buildings for industrial use, found that many of its dealers were dissatisfied with a company-originated direct mail program for which the dealers furnished the mailing lists and paid part of the cost. Primarily, the dealers were grumbling about the low return on the mailings—an average of about 1%. The corporation found that it was not primarily the mailings, but the lists, which were at fault. So when it came time to produce the next dealer direct mail campaign, Stran-Steel concentrated attention on the development of better mailing lists.

The first step was to analyze inquiries which the company had received as a result of business publication advertising. These were divided by four-digit Standard Industrial Classification

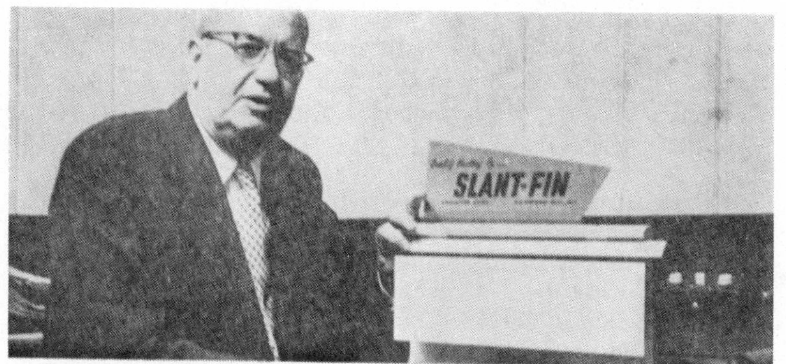

HOMEOWNERS LIKE IT, CONTRACTORS LIKE IT, I LIKE IT...
AND I KNOW YOU - AS A WHOLESALER - WILL, TOO!

It's really easy for me to list seven important reasons why Slant/Fin Baseboard is bound to make as big a hit with you as a wholesaler as it has with me:

1) Slant/Fin's price is competitive, consistent with the quality of the product.
2) It's sold through legitimate wholesalers only.
3) Each unit is packaged separately and assembled within the carton, for ease of handling.
4) Contractors like the way it installs--with a complete range of sizes available to eliminate costly cutting on-the-job.
5) Its fin-design eliminates noise and contractor call-backs.
6) The design is low, attractive and inconspicuous.
7) Homeowners like the way it looks and operates.

Now, how many other products that you stock can lay claim to such an impressive roster of selling benefits? Add to this the support Slant/Fin gives wholesalers, and you've got a mighty powerful argument for getting the full story on Slant/Fin Baseboard soon!

That's why I've sent you this letter-- to encourage you to get the straight facts on all seven points I've listed above-- absolutely without obligation.

Slant/Fin will be delighted to give them to you. Just mail them the enclosed card today.

Cordially,

Raymond C. Green, Jr.

Raymond C. Green & Co.

RAYMOND C. GREEN & COMPANY PLUMBING AND HEATING SUPPLIES
700 SUMMIT AVENUE • JENKINTOWN, PENNSYLVANIA • TUrner 4-2770 • WAverly 4-2720

This letter was one of a series of 11 testimonial letters mailed out by wholesalers for Slant/Fin Radiator Corporation.

categories. The number of inquiries in each category was compared with the total number of well-rated companies in that classification. SIC classifications which represented the highest percentage of inquiries compared to the total number of prospects were then selected for the new mailing program.

Dealers were offered series of four mailings each for six different market categories composed of the SIC classifications indicating the greatest interest in Stran-Steel buildings. Each mailing featured a letter, a reprint of a magazine advertisement, and a reply card. This time Stran-Steel provided the mailing lists. The new mailing program attracted 168 cooperating dealers, contrasted with 109 using the previous program. But more important, with the list research conducted for them, the total number of names increased from 60,000 to 168,000. And returns, too, increased greatly—from 1% to 4.4%.

USING INDUSTRIAL DIRECT MAIL TO SOLVE SPECIAL PROBLEMS

Industrial direct mail comes into its finest hour when called upon to solve special marketing problems. Although it would take a whole series of books to even start to describe all of the thousands of special industrial marketing problems which have a logical solution via a direct mail program, the following examples will indicate many of the possibilities.

How Celanese Located New Markets

One important use for industrial direct mail is to find and develop new markets. Celanese Corporation of America, for example, marketed a flame-retardant plasticizer originally sold only for flameproofing doll wigs. While the company was sure the product had additional applications, its product development department had not found time to conduct the necessary research to determine just what markets represented the best potential. So a direct mail letter, with a reprint of a business publication ad listing the properties of the product, was sent to the company's basic mailing list. An enclosed reply form offered literature and evaluation samples.

Ninety days after samples and literature had been sent to all who requested them, another letter was mailed, asking for results of sample evaluations. A followup letter was mailed within 30 days to all who did not respond to the original request for sample evaluation results.

Result: 73% of those who received samples gave their evaluations, and this information uncovered several new markets, including major opportunities in the paint and varnish and expanded plastics fields.

Another direct mail program was then directed to these two new markets. The net result was a 100% increase in volume for the product within two years, and just one of the first accounts more than paid for the entire direct mail program. The company definitely credits 109 initial purchases to this direct mail program.

Taking Advantage of Special Opportunities

While most industrial sales involve long periods of sales conditioning, negotiations, and other marketing procedures, there are many occasions when the cycle of selling can be stepped up. For example, a strike of elevator operators in downtown Chicago presented a timely promotion opportunity for a manufacturer of automatic elevators.

This manufacturer quickly made a special mailing to the managers of all buildings where elevators had been affected by the operators' strike, stressing the advantages of self-operated elevators. This direct mail program quickly brought back "hot" leads which led to a number of immediate sales and to a 600% increase in sales within a year.

Getting Prospects to Contact Dealers

Peerless Photo Products, Inc., used a four-letter campaign designed to get prospects to contact distributors. The sequence of the letters was particularly important:

> The reply card with the first letter requested a free ten-day trial of Peerless' Dri-Stat photocopy equipment. Since distributors know that getting a machine in a plant or office for a trial practically amounts to an order, they were quick to take action on all replies they received.
>
> The second letter offered a demonstration.
>
> The third letter offered additional information.
>
> The fourth letter offered a free booklet.

While distributors are often indifferent about handling inquiries which do not clearly indicate an immediate order possibility, they were preconditioned to followups on the Peerless mailings because the first letter used a technique which, while not producing a particularly high percentage of returns, produced a high rate of conversions. Once a pattern of inquiry followups was established, momentum took over. The campaign resulted in between 5% and 10% returns, and dealers reported that they converted at least 25% of the inquiries into orders.

How American Brass Kept Production Facilities Busy

Many industrial companies make effective use of direct mail to keep specific production facilities operating at capacity. The American Brass Co., for example, faced the possibility of downtime on some costly production equipment in its Fabricated Metal Goods Division, which produces small metal parts for the original equipment market. So a special mailing was made to a list of 46,000 prospects, inviting them to send a sample part—or a drawing of a part—for the company to quote on.

While the mailing drew only 650 requests, this response represented a potential of many millions of pieces which the production equipment could turn out. Just one request alone included a part which American Brass could redesign and provide at half its original cost. The prospect agreed to pay a tooling charge of $1,200, and ordered an initial test run of 10,000 parts. The test was successful and resulted in subsequent orders in lots of one million with yearly consumption estimated at 50 million pieces, billing at $55,000. The cost of the original mailing was less than $3,500.

American Welding's Plan for Meeting Changing Market Conditions

In industry it is not unusual for a manufacturer to find that technological progress suddenly causes one or more of its best markets to "dry up." When this happens, direct mail often can be called upon to locate new markets which represent sales opportunities for the products no longer being sold.

American Welding, for example, found the market for its principal product—welded components for military jet aircraft—disappearing as the U. S. rapidly advanced into the Space Age. The company's first step in locating new outlets for its products was to analyze past and present customers to see what markets with major potential might have been overlooked.

All customers were divided by four-digit Standard Industrial Classifications. Then the total number of customers in each of the 99 SIC classifications which covered the company's past and current markets was compared with the total number of manufacturers in the category. For example, in SIC 3522—"farm machinery, except tractors"—American Welding found they had sold only three of 423 manufacturer prospects.

Still further analysis by SIC classifications was made of "turndowns"—requests for quotations on component parts which previously had to be turned down for one reason or another. (See SIC two-digit list at the end of the chapter.)

With this information carefully analyzed, direct mail programs were designed to do a vertical job of promotion to each of the SIC markets considered to represent major potential. Mailing pieces feature actual product examples which had been developed for companies within each SIC-classified industry chosen for direct mail promotion. All of the mailings asked for the opportunity to quote on specific component needs.

This approach represented a major change from American Welding's previous advertising, which generally took a broad-scale approach and was designed to interest industry in general, rather than any specific market. Similar changes were applied to the company's business paper advertising. Both the direct mail program and space advertising pulled a substantially increased number of inquiries.

How United Carbon Products Reached a Small, Well-Defined Market

Direct mail is a particularly important medium for industrial manufacturers aiming at relatively small, well-defined markets. When United Carbon Products Co. decided to move into the rapidly developing semiconductor market to sell its graphite production tools, it soon discovered that a list of 500 names pretty well covered all primary prospects—approximately 10 key contacts in each of the 25 biggest semiconductor manufacturers and another 250 miscellaneous contacts. A direct mail program was planned to accomplish four basic objectives:

1. To get across to all qualified prospects a long and complicated story on what the company thought it could provide in better "purity" and "machining excellence"—something that would be difficult to do in the limited copy space of publication ads
2. To sell in depth to each primary buying influence, to the point where he would be forced to think of United Carbon Products whenever the need for graphite arose
3. To build the company's stature as compared to the low-priced, low-quality "alley shops," by spelling out the big differences in quality, service, and guarantees
4. To gain access and recognition for United Carbon Products representatives in their efforts to give technical assistance

To accomplish these objectives, the company used a 12-week mailing program, consisting of six mailings at biweekly intervals. Each mailing consisted of a letter with an attached letter gadget, with copy concentrating on a single major selling point; a reprint of a publication ad; and an unusual reply device. Instead of enclosing business reply cards, the company used preprinted Western Union collect telegram forms, addressed to the company's technical director to give the form added importance. The message read: *"Like to see you concerning our graphite problems. Let me know when you're coming."*

In addition, United Carbon Products was the first supplier to distribute a catalog devoted to semiconductor graphites. An interesting aspect of the program was that, as new prospect names were added to the mailing list, they were started with the beginning of the direct mail series so they would receive the full sales story just as had the original prospects. Within 18 months, United was able to register as the major graphite supplier to the semiconductor industry and could refer back to a stack of Western Union telegrams from top people in most of the largest semiconductor plants in the United States. United's annual sales volume in this market area increased from a starting point of $150,000 to over the $1-million mark in less than three years.

An Allis-Chalmers Mail Campaign for Overcoming Price Competition

In many markets, industrial manufacturers are plagued by "low bid" competition. For example, Allis-Chalmers encountered increasing difficulty in selling pumps to the municipal waterworks market, where it became more and more common for the orders to go to the lowest bidders on specified pump installations. Allis-Chalmers decided to counter the trend with a three-pronged advertising campaign:

1. To convince customers that price is not the *only* important criterion for granting a pump order
2. To demonstrate the importance of experience, on-time delivery, and dependable service
3. To get its own sales force to spend more time on this high-potential product and market

Three ads in a humorous vein appeared in publications aimed at waterworks, and then Allis-Chalmers turned to an equally humorous four-piece direct mail campaign.

The first mailing was an eight-page folder featuring reprints of the publication ads. This was followed by a folder entitled: "Wanted: Guinea Pigs. No 'experience clause' necessary." The cleverly illustrated piece showed the danger of installing low-priced pumps which had not yet been thoroughly tested.

The third mailing included both sheet music and a recording of an original ballad, "Promises." The lyrics ran:

You promised that day in December
That I'd get my pumps in the Fall.
That was three years ago last December.
I should not have believed you at all.

Chorus

Oh, you menaced my job and my future
Made a dope out of me and my kind
For the promise you made in December
Was a cad's way a contract to bind.

The final mailing was a four-page folder. The cover showed a waterworks commissioner with his head just barely out of a sea of water and the caption, "I screamed for pump *service* and they send me a salesman!" Copy emphasized Allis-Chalmers' ability to provide trained servicemen quickly when needed. When the folder was opened, a die-cut snorkel tube popped up from the center fold. To underscore the theme, Allis-Chalmers offered a free snorkel when the enclosed reply card was returned.

The humorous approach made its point and the company's pump sales showed a 13% immediate increase, followed by another 21% increase in the first three months of the following year.

How Armour Chemicals Used Direct Mail to Keep Goodwill During Periods of Shortage

There are times when an industrial advertiser finds himself face to face with an honest case of having more business than he can handle. This often presents the dual problem of maintaining interest of prospects even though they cannot be supplied with the product immediately and of not offending present customers who are "standing in line" awaiting delayed deliveries. Armour Chemicals faced this problem during a period when lingering wartime price controls and other factors seriously limited its production of fatty acids. A combination space advertising and direct mail program provided the solution. Knowing that someday it would again come face to face with a highly competitive market situation. Armour developed a program of six helpful technical publications of special interest to industries which could utilize fatty acids. These publications were offered through a regular business publication advertising program.

But to avoid offending customers whose orders were already

backlogged or had been turned down, Armour made an advance mailing to its customer list, offering to send each of the technical publications just as soon as they were published and before being offered in space advertising. This mailing drew replies from 1,189 key buyers in 609 firms—representing both present customers and many who had not been in contact with Armour for several years. When the ads appeared, they drew 15,028 requests for the technical booklets and charts.

The literature was mailed with a letter containing an invitation to write Armour's Technical Service Department for additional information on fatty acids. Armour then carefully screened all of the inquiries and sent Reply-O-Letters to all legitimate prospects, offering additional information and samples and asking for information on fatty acid use and applications. A followup letter was mailed to all who failed to reply to the first letter.

While the campaign was still running, the fatty acid shortage suddenly disappeared. Armour promptly made a mailing to the prospect list which had been developed through the requests for technical literature, announcing the availability of the product. Orders immediately poured in and Armour added more new customers than in any previous year in its history. Of the new customers, over 65% were traced *directly* to the technical literature program.

Dennison's Plan for Driving a Wedge Into Markets in Which Competitors Were Firmly Established

Any time an industrial manufacturer decides to go after sales in a previously undeveloped market, he is likely to find that competitors have spent many years building effective sales contacts and that special promotion programs are required to command a share of attention. Such a problem faced Dennison Manufacturing Co. when a new law required garment makers to identify the contents of their fabrics. Dennison already had a machine which was ideal for adding variable information to identification tags and labels, but had few sales contacts in the garment industry. Competitors, on the other hand, had long been selling this market other products and thus were in a position to move quickly to take advantage of the newly developed need for imprinting machines.

To locate prospects, Dennison offered a book, *How to Cut Costs and Increase Profits Through Textile Fiber Labeling,* in business publication ads and in a series of three mailings to a large list of suspected prospects. This offer drew immediate response, since the subject was of "hot" interest. Included were 600 excellent prospects for Dennison's machine.

The next step was to send a series of six attention-getting mailings to this list of prospects. The first four mailings were colorful folders, each featuring a cartoon "monster"—the monsters being problems caused by the new labeling act (i.e., Multiple Tag Monster, Hand Stamping Monster, etc.).

Each of the folders had a built-in reply card plus sample imprinted string tags hanging from a hole punched in the folder. The fifth mailing was a two-page automatically typewritten letter offering a demonstration of Dennison's imprinting machine. Enclosed was a 9- by 12-inch poster featuring the four cartoon monsters which had appeared in the previous mailings. All prospects who did not respond to the first letter were sent a carbon copy followup, with a brief memo attached. The campaign did its job, and Dennison was quickly a factor in the new market.

How Ansul Chemical Got Salesmen to Push Neglected Products

A common problem for many industrial manufacturers—particularly those with extensive lines—is getting salesmen to devote a reasonable amount of effort to every product. Often, salesmen tend to neglect items which do not fit into their basic selling pattern. When such problems exist, manufacturers frequently turn to a direct mail program which either encourages customers to lead salesmen into conversation about the product needing additional attention or to draw specific inquiries which the salesman must follow up.

Ansul Chemical Co., for one example, introduced a new line of fire extinguishers, with features which differed from the basic line the company's salesmen were used to handling. As a result, the salesmen continued to concentrate most of their sales effort on the more familiar line, and thus sales for the new line were disappointing.

With the salesmen's cooperation, Ansul compiled a list of 1,200 customers and prospects for the new line and launched a showmanship direct mail program. The first mailing featured five giant playing cards—the ace of clubs, the five of spades, the five of clubs, the six of spades, and the seven of spades. Copy explained that poker experts warn against trying to draw to such a hand, and then launched into a quick message warning against gambling with fire. The mailing also mentioned that the Ansul salesman would have an important announcement soon. A second mailing was along the same lines as the first.

The "important announcement" came in the third mailing,

again a set of giant cards. The announcement was a choice of three special "deals" which involved a premium offer tied in with purchases of the new fire extinguisher line. A fourth mailing recapped the offer—again using a set of giant cards plus a paperback book, "Poker According to Maverick." The poker theme was carried through right up to the salesman's call. Those who inquired about the new line received a real deck of cards.

Not only did the campaign succeed in immediately boosting sales of the new line, but it also built an enthusiasm within the sales force which resulted in continuing full-line selling, rather than just concentrating on the older, more familiar products.

Chapter 9

RETAIL DIRECT MAIL

THE direct mail advertising used by retail business is something of a blend between the mail order style and that used for non-mail order product promotion. While, in the majority of cases, the basic aim is not to get recipients to send orders through the mails, many of the basics of mail order advertising still apply. Most retail direct mail attempts to secure buying action for specific products within a short period of time. But it has a corollary aim—building store traffic, which the advertiser hopes will result in the sale of non-advertised products. And, like mail order, one of the key elements in successful retail direct mail is an up-to-date list of known buyers —in this case, the store's active customers.

But to think of retail direct mail mainly in terms of product promotion is a mistake, for the medium is used by progressive retailers to achieve a wide variety of objectives—ranging from opening new charge accounts to educating employees. Yet while direct mail has so many potential uses for retailers, its application is still far from reaching a level of maturity. In his authoritative book, *Successful Direct Mail Advertising and Selling,* Robert Stone observes, "Retail direct mail has yet to reach its golden era. For its use in relation to the potential has been infinitesimal."

Not the Dollars but How They Are Used

The National Retail Merchants Association made an extensive survey of department stores' direct mail advertising and reported:

> Direct mail is a selling tool that fits naturally into the hand of the department store. The store's roster of customers is a ready-made mailing list; its position in the community gives its mailing pieces a prestige that those from other sellers do not enjoy; its standing with its resources puts

> many forms of outside help at its disposal. Yet, with all these advantages, the department store's performance in the field of direct mail rarely evokes shouts of approval from its customers, its resources, or its management. Experts in direct mail say that the trouble is not in the amount of money the stores spend (one dollar on direct mail for each 14 or 15 spent on newspaper advertising), but in the poor use to which they put their direct mail dollars. Individual stores demonstrate by their superlative results how much direct mail can accomplish when it is well used; so do individual resources whose packaged campaigns are adapted to department store use.
>
> Many a sacred cow, however, would have to be dispensed with before the ideas of these successful users of direct mail could be applied in the typical department store. And many a misunderstanding about direct mail's function would have to be cleared up not just in the sales promotion director's office, but also among buyers and merchandise managers and other members of the store's management team.

The basic problem for most retailers when it comes to direct mail is that there are few *completely* "ready-made" advertising packages available for their use. Thus it is much easier to spend promotion dollars in newspapers, radio or television, where the publisher or broadcaster is willing and able to do most of the thinking and planning for the retailer. Even in cases where a manufacturer or publisher of syndicated formats offers imprinted and ready-to-mail material, there is still the problem of developing or selecting a mailing list.

Retailer Resistance to Direct Mail

This has been a major problem for manufacturers who develop direct mail programs for retailer use. Many excellent dealer direct mail programs, which have produced outstanding results where applied, have fallen by the wayside because of the difficulty in getting sufficient retailers to agree to participate. Even in cases where the manufacturer has offered to handle everything—including development of a suitable mailing list—the percentage of participation often falls far short of what it should be because of the reluctance of retailers to use the medium. There are a number of reasons for this retailer resistance:

1. Most retailers are busy people, directly involved in everything from buying to selling, delivering, servicing, accounting, and store maintenance. Each of these functions—and the dozens of others demanded of every retailer—requires thought, effort, and expenditures. As a result, retailers resist anything which requires them to move in a new direction.
2. Many times a retailer has experienced disappointing results in the past through an ill-conceived and poorly executed direct mail program and has closed his mind to any future use of the medium, even when well-planned, professional direct mail programs are offered. "I've tried direct mail," he reports, "and it won't work for me."

3. Many retailers have a strong resentment toward mail order sellers and carry over this resentment to the basic medium of mail order advertisers. This is particularly true in smaller cities and towns where local merchants often feel they have a franchise on the purchasing of the products they sell by all who reside in their trade area. They frown upon anyone who "violates" this imagined franchise.
4. Even though he may "hate" mail order, the retailer often thinks of direct mail only in mail order terms. He feels he must get mail order results before a direct mail program can be considered successful. Thus, he fails to consider the plus values obtainable through increased store traffic, image-building, and other relatively intangible benefits he usually obtains with his advertising in a direct mail program.
5. The primary advertising counselor for most small and medium-size retailers is the space salesman for the local newspaper. He naturally frowns upon any medium which competes for the retailer's advertising dollar (and, of course, his commissions) and usually feels quite strongly that his own medium offers any retailer the maximum return for each advertising dollar he can spend. Because he calls upon the retailer so frequently, his voice carries a lot of weight when any advertising program is discussed.
6. The retailer is particularly susceptible to the "junk mail" myth. Because he, himself, is often deluged with piles of direct mail from his suppliers—particularly if his store carries a wide variety of lines—he quickly nods his head in assent when he hears tales of the flood of mail reaching everyone these days . . . and how most of it goes in the wastebasket unread.

Media Selection Checklist

A checklist of general factors which govern retailers' choice of media was spelled out in the Charles M. Edwards, Jr.-Russell A. Brown textbook. *Retail Advertising & Sales Promotion*[1]:

1. *Clientele sought by store.* Prospect, customer; charge or credit purchaser; a store-wide buyer or a patron of only one or few departments.
2. *Type of store.* Specialty shop, department store, chain store; large or small store; drugstore, grocery store, and so on; nonpromotional, semipromotional, or promotional store.
3. *Trading area of store.* Where does the store's business come from? The whereabouts of the customer in relation to the trading area of the store and the circulations of different media.
4. *Location of the store.* Urban, suburban, or rural; central or distant location; principal or secondary shopping district; shopping center.
5. *The message to be sent.* Private, personal, or "to-whom-it-concerns"; of limited or general interest; promotional or institutional; and so on.
6. *The means of communication available and their appropriateness.* The types and numbers of media at the disposal of the advertiser, and their acceptance among customers.

[1]Copyright Prentice-Hall, Inc.

7. *The cost of available media.* Absolute and relative cost of advertising in different media; the more selective a medium is, the higher is its cost. (Person-to-person versus station-to-station telephone calls, for example.)
8. *The money the advertiser has to spend.* Money available for advertising purposes; the amount that the merchant has and can afford to spend sets very definite limits to his expenditures.
9. *The competition to be met.* The experience of others provides many valuable lessons: the advertiser may learn what to do and what not to do by observing competitors' experiences with different media; he may wish to offset their endeavors and to outdo them.

To this list should be added at least two important items which were not mentioned in the Edwards-Brown checklist:

10. *Promotional materials available.* Most retailers are offered a wide variety of promotional aids by the manufacturers whose products they sell or by their trade associations and commercial syndicators of promotional services. The availability of these aids—and frequently cooperative promotional allowances offered if they are used—can play a vital role in the selection of any medium.
11. *Personnel and/or services available.* To do the best possible advertising job requires the aid of experts. The skills available to the retailer—either from his own personnel or from outside services available to him—can be a major determining factor in media selection.

Readership of Retail Direct Mail

At a DMMA convention, Harry Deines, of J. Walter Thompson Co., reported the results of a six-year study of readership which gives good evidence of direct mail's ability to serve retailers. He detailed the findings from five surveys made two weeks after the mailing pieces involved had been received.

1. On a series of automotive mailings, the recall of individual pieces ran from a low of 45% to a high of 70%. Among those who recalled the mailing, the recall of the dealer whose name was imprinted ran 58% to 70%.
2. In an association mailing there was a recall of 67%, with 20% having read thoroughly and 70% having read some.
3. In the case of a post card mailing for an oil company, there was an 81% recall on a single piece and a 67% recall on the dealer's name.
4. In a paint mailing, the recall was 34%.
5. In a kitchen equipment mailing, there was a 66% recall of the piece and a 40% recall of the dealer's name.
6. We also found that people keep direct mail advertising around the home for quite a while—contrary to the popular impression that most advertising mail hits the wastebasket immediately. For example, in a recent mailing, we found that two weeks after it was received, 38% of the receivers still had the mailing piece in the home when interviewers called.

7. We were interested in finding out differences in recall of direct mail by women as compared to men. We found that women do indeed read direct mail and that their readership is influenced to some extent by the kind of piece was recalled by 27% of the men, but by 47% of the women. In the case of an automobile, we found the advertising recalled by 60% of the men and 65% of the women.

Other Readership Evidence

Two other research projects add still further evidence of the value of direct mail for retail promotion. One study, conducted by Daniel Starch & Staff for a chain of department stores, involved over 2,000 personal interviews during a period of two weeks after the mailing of a circular in eight selected cities. The interviewing was done inside the stores after customers had made their purchases. It was discovered that one of every four customers reported receiving the circular—and of these, 60% interviewed during the first week after mailing said their visit to the store was a direct result of reading the circular; 42% made a similar report during the second week. Even more impressive was the fact that 17% of total cash purchases in the stores during the first week were made by circular-receiving customers; 11% during the second week. The average sale to circular customers was $5.99, as compared with only $4.72 for noncircular customers.

Other Starch findings showed circular customers didn't always buy an item they specifically came in to buy and that circulars pulled for a considerable period, with 20% of the circular customers reporting purchases as a result of reading circulars sent over a month earlier. Contrary to the general impression consumers do not like to receive direct mail, a total of 78% of those who did not receive the circulars expressed a desire to receive them in the future.

In commenting on the survey, Dr. Starch confirmed that the results of this study were typical of hundreds of similar surveys his organization has conducted.

Esso Research

Another research report of special interest was made by William Farley, Esso's director of sales promotion, at a DMMA convention. He described a survey involving 1,670 interviews in 12 cities to determine reader reaction to Esso mailings imprinted with the names of local dealers. The interviews were made between 10 and 20 days after receipt of mailings. Interviews were at mail delivery time in order to reach the person who normally received the family mail. There was an average recall factor of 57.8% even though some of those interviewed may not have been the ones receiving the mailings or the ones to whom the mailings were addressed. (It should be noted that Esso discovered the majority of wives regularly open direct mail addressed to their husbands—and 75% of those interviewed were women.) Of those remembering the piece, 83.7% remembered the products advertised and 79.8% correctly identified the brand by name. (All product identity features were obscured in the samples shown during the survey.) The most important finding from a retailer's standpoint, however, was that 64.8% of those who saw the mailing piece were able to correctly name the dealer whose imprint was on it, and an even greater percentage (70.2%) were able to give the station location.

This Esso survey provides some concrete evidence of direct mail's ability to create a favorable image for a retailer. Mr. Farley reported: "More than half of the people who hadn't seen any of the direct mail had no opinion whatsoever about their neighborhood Esso dealer. Seeing one single piece made a difference and the figures began to swing from 'no impression' to 'favorable impression.' Those who saw two or more pieces gave the dealer an overwhelmingly favorable rating with 77.8% supporting him. Only 16.2% still had not made up their minds at this point."

ADVANTAGES OF DIRECT MAIL

From these typical surveys, there's good evidence to support the fact direct mail is much more than a mail order medium for retailers. It can perform the same role as any advertising medium, yet it has some very definite advantages:

Highly Selective

Through direct mail, the retailer can single out logical prospects for specific merchandise and pinpoint his message to them. By proper choice of the list, he can eliminate much of the waste coverage of mass print and broadcast media.

Flexible

The retailer can add or subtract names as he desires. He can mail to one customer or one million. He can aim at men, women, or children; bargain hunters or quality seekers; the customers of a single department or the entire store. He can also spread his promotion over any time period he chooses and thus control traffic in his store.

Privacy

In many retail situations, privacy is of utmost importance. By use of direct mail, an advertiser can control the audience of his promotion and thus keep competitors in the dark, preventing them from immediate countering with an offer of similar merchandise at lower prices. Direct mail's privacy also makes possible special offerings to select groups, without creating ill will among other prospects and customers.

Business Identity

Because almost complete creative freedom is offered by direct mail, a retailer can build a very special identity into every mailing. While it is possible to gain this advantage to a certain extent through the creative approach to space and time advertising, these media, by their very nature, impose severe limitations.

Wide Variety of Formats

The creative freedom of direct mail affords the retailer the opportunity to keep his expenditures within whatever bounds he chooses. He can mail imprinted post cards or elaborate brochures; simple black-and-white pieces or lavish color broadsides. He can include swatches or complete samples. He can tailor each mailing to the problem at hand and choose the printing process suitable for the story being told.

Avoids Competition for Attention

When a direct mail piece is in the prospect's hands, it usually has undivided attention for the moment. Contrast this with the giant Thursday food pages in a metropolitan daily, where you may find dozens of different stores offering nearly the same merchandise on successive pages. Very seldom will a single day's mail contain mailings for identical types of merchandise from two or more different retailers.

Almost Certain to Be Encountered

Since very few people ever discard any piece of mail without at least scanning its contents, a retailer's ad is certain of being "encountered" by the vast majority of prospects. With space advertising, the retailer has the dual handicap of originally reaching only a portion of prospects and then possibly being missed because a page wasn't turned. Broadcast advertising can, of course, be completely unencountered when a radio or TV set isn't on or the dial is at a different spot.

Gets Into the Home

When direct mail is addressed to homes, it is almost certain to be read in the homes. Likewise, direct mail can be directed to offices or other points where buying decisions are likely to be made.

Special Attention to Customers

Since present customers almost always represent the best source for future business, they require special treatment. Direct mail provides the opportunity to address special messages to this important audience.

Personal

Because direct mail can be addressed to individuals rather than an audience, it provides special promotional opportunities. One of the most universal of all human desires is for recognition. Through direct mail—and letters in particular—a retailer can appeal directly to known individuals with messages directed to their specific interests. Noted retail advertising consultant Carrie Mills Rowland points out in *Advertising in Modern Retailing* (copyright Harper & Row, 1954):

> The personal appeal of direct mail is important from a psychological point of view. The woman receiving the announcement of a sale through the mail is far more flattered than if she had read about it in the paper; she feels that she is a member of a specially chosen group whom the retailer considers important enough to notify. It flatters her; it is an answer to her snob instincts. This is particularly true if the mailing piece is sent to a group of people who do not ordinarily receive much mail; the receipt of a letter or card is an important event in such a person's life.

Results May Be Traced

Because the specific audience of any direct mail promotion can be pinpointed, it is possible to make a thorough analysis of results. Many times, retailers use direct mail tests to determine the best possible promotional approach for other media.

Lasting Power

Direct mail has special advantages in working over an extended period. According to the advertising director of the Zale Jewelry chain, the average mailer has a life span of about three weeks. Howard S. Mark, advertising manager of The Robert Simpson Co. Ltd., of Toronto, adds that "direct mail is the only method by which you may hope to have the prospect or customer retain your message for future reference." Even a short "lasting period" can be important, such as the cases where additional members of the family need to be exposed. While a wife may dog-ear a page in a newspaper to show her husband when he comes home in the evening, she is much more likely to save a direct mail piece for him to look over.

Mass of Information

Direct mail makes possible relatively economical distribution of a mass of information. Multiple pages or special sections in newspapers can be very costly, particularly for the small or medium-size retailer with a geographically limited market. But complete catalogs or flyers can be distributed by mail for little more postage than is required for a simple mailer.

Complete Coverage

When absolute saturation coverage is required, direct mail is frequently the only medium available. The district office for a major variety store chain in New England, for example, finds that by using 25 newspapers, only a maximum of 89% of the Boston metropolitan area's families can be covered. "With direct mail," the chain's ad director reports, "we can cover all the homes in each neighborhood 100%. Not only do these mailers have lasting value—they're seldom destroyed—but in addition we're assured that each home gets our advertising."

Use of Color

Many products require realistic color production for successful promotion. While rotogravure sections of Sunday newspapers offer quality color reproduction, the cost is usually far beyond the budgetary limitations of the average retailer. But with direct mail—particularly through the use of preprinted materials supplied by manufacturers—realistic color illustrations can be used by the majority of retailers.

Makes Retailers "Equals"

Through direct mail, the smaller store has an opportunity to compete successfully with the giant retailers whose promotion budgets may run into the hundreds of thousands of dollars annually. By building his own identity into a mailing piece, the smaller retailer can make his voice heard over the multimedia shouting of the bigger stores. And on the other side of the coin, direct mail gives the bigger store the chance to compete with the personal relationship which usually is more common between the smaller retailer and his customers. Through the use of letters, even the largest store can develop a personal bond with its customers.

DISADVANTAGES OF DIRECT MAIL FOR RETAILERS

While the advantages of direct mail for the retailer listed above have been described in as positive a way as possible, the medium is not without its disadvantages.

Cost

One of the major items discouraging more extensive use of direct mail in retailing is the cost factor. Although a retailer may pretty much write his own ticket on how much he wants to spend for any mailing, even the most simple of mailings may cost more than he cares to spend. Retailers frequently fail to recognize the true cost per *reader* when evaluating newspaper versus direct mail advertising. While it usually costs more to reach each subscriber of a newspaper by direct mail than to place a similar message in the advertising columns of the newspaper, this method of cost evaluation completely overlooks such factors as the readership which can be expected for any newspaper advertisement, "waste circulation" of the paper, competition for attention, etc.

Time Required

As mentioned previously in this chapter, many retailers just don't want to take the time required to develop a direct mail program. Since they can advertise in space and time media with practically no effort if they so desire, they often use such advertising in preference to direct mail without even a second thought about the relative effectiveness of different advertising media.

Deterioration of Mailing Lists

No mailing list remains up to date for more than a few days, at best. Even an active customer list soon deteriorates. The average rate of address change is 15 to 30% annually, depending upon geographical location and the nature of a store's clientele. In addition, a retail store has a constantly changing audience of customers as once active buyers become inactive. James Rotto, of The Hecht Co., a major Washington, D. C., department store, once estimated that "out of every hundred customers who stop buying at any certain store:

1 is either dead or unaccounted for;

5 are influenced by friends to buy elsewhere;

3 move to parts unknown;

9 buy elsewhere because of price inducements;

14 have unadjusted grievances and take their business elsewhere;

68 drift away because of the store's indifference toward them."

Unless a continuous maintenance effort has been made, a retailer's mailing list has to be thoroughly up-dated before a direct mail program can be economical and effective. It is, of course, possible to rent outside lists, but the majority of effective retail programs start with the use of a list of active customers.

Too Selective for Some Stores

Since most direct mail draws much of its effectiveness from being addressed to a specific audience, many stores feel it is impractical for them since their growth depends on constantly advertising to large masses.

Objectionable to Some

Some retailers hesitate to use direct mail for fear of offending customers or prospects who feel advertising does not deserve a place in their mailboxes. This is most apt to be a retarding factor in cities where local newspapers have campaigned viciously against so-called "junk mail." Some retailers also worry about the accuracy of their mailing lists and fear they may offend customers whose names have been spelled wrong.

Need for Special Skills

By far the most valid objection of retailers to the use of direct mail is that it requires special skills to be effective. However, there are direct mail service organizations which can handle all details for the retailer and many syndicated and manufacturer-sponsored direct mail programs are available for most retail businesses.

In the long run, the advantages of direct mail far outweigh the disadvantages for any retailer.

RETAIL JOBS DIRECT MAIL CAN DO

A comprehensive guide to the jobs direct mail can do for retailers was prepared by Howard Emerson for *Electrical Merchandising Week*[2]. While his guide was directed at appliance-TV-housewares dealerships, it applies equally well to many other types of retailers.

Basic traffic building is a fundamental project for your direct mail. You can reach your customers and prospects with product and price offers through direct mail either as a supplement to your advertising in other media or as your sole sales building effort in market areas where other media are not practical for your operation.

Selectivity of the group that will receive your mailing is the big advantage direct mail offers you for this basic traffic building job. Your market may make it practical to mail to your whole list, but should you wish you can pick the recipients by various purchases, neighborhoods, etc.

Announcing promotions is the second basic job for your direct mail advertising. Whereas the job above was to build traffic for a specific product or group of products with availability and price the incentive, this project is to create interest in a specific event. You may feature products and price as the features of the event, but the direct mail effort is designed primarily to ballyhoo the event itself—"February Clearance Days," "Anniversary Celebration," "Warehouse Sale," etc., in which all products in your store are being pushed.

Direct mail's advantage here is the "personal" quality that can make the announcement an invitation rather than just an advertisement.

Maintaining personal contact with your customers can be done only through direct mail, personal call or the telephone. All other media carry your message to the customers of other dealers as well.

Direct mail offers you the chance to cue your message to a particular type of customer. Building and keeping your "image" is a necessary job for all your advertising, and direct mail can play an important role in the work.

Direct mail's flexibility of format, selectivity in mailing, and personal approach can bring you "face to face" with your customers and prospects to re-emphasize the image they expect you to have, and which they respond to. As a discounter, you recognize the recipient as "one who appreciates advance notice of a bargain"; as a caterer to the country club set you hold your image with an offer "for the discriminating, the select few," etc.

You can balance your market through careful use of direct mail advertising more effectively than through any other medium. For most dealers that has become a crucial job because of the steady shift in population.

The selectivity that direct mail offers you can concentrate your printed sales efforts in neighborhoods or communities where your records show you are not getting your share of the volume of traffic.

Specific market groups can be reached by either "addressee" or "occupant" direct mailings to promote: (1) your store as having specific features of

[2]"How to Advertise by Direct Mail" by Howard Emerson. Electrical Merchandising Week. January 6, 1964.

interest to the group; or, (2) a special group of your products because of their interest to this market grouping.

Direct mail's advantage to you for this pin-point promotion is illustrated by special mailings on large freezers to rural box holders.

Charge account solicitation, particularly when made through special offers, is another way for you to consider profitable use of direct mail. Pre-selecting neighborhoods, using lists of known good credit risks, and other controls can step up response and direct your appeal to minimum risk families.

For maintaining charge accounts and for keep-up contact with charge customers to sell more merchandise, direct mail becomes the foundation of a whole merchandising program.

Personalized promotions—direct to one person, one family, or to a limited group with a common interest is another use of direct mail that can be profitable to you in many market areas.

Best known are personal letters or other mailings to customers or prospects on their birthdays, to newlyweds, to new parents, new graduates, etc.

Changes in your policies, etc., offer you another excuse to use direct mail profitably. When you change the hours your store is open, when you increase your service facilities, when you add new brands or new types of products, when you open a new department or special display, personalized direct mail can be an important part of your advertising program.

Your competitors' customers are fair bait for your direct mail advertising and you should keep in mind ways to reach them through this medium. You start with this problem in most markets: people reasonably satisfied with your competitors' prices and policies may not be interested enough in a change to pay sufficient attention to your advertising to note the small differences that give your store the advantage. Then turn to direct mail as a supplement to the ads.

Secondary tasks for direct mail in your overall advertising program are almost too long to be covered here. Some, however, you should not overlook as you study ways to make this growing medium more profitable to you:

- Follow up on prospects who visit your store and do not buy is a use of direct mail dating back to the early days of this business. Today it is used too little at a time when it is difficult to get a salesman to follow up in person. You know your market. You know whether the prospects who "walk" from your store would ever consider coming back. If most of your "walks" are through indecision you are missing the profit boat by not following up.
- Thanks to new customers for trading with you and to old customers for coming back, is another vital job for direct mail. To both groups it indicates that you consider the purchase as part of a long range relationship.
- Handling complaints is a direct mail or telephone job so obvious that it needs no explanation. However, later in the HANDBOOK, we'll discuss how you can use direct mail to turn the complaints into sales building contacts.
- Direct selling—using direct mail to ask for the order to come to you by mail—is the foundation for a multi-billion dollar industry but it holds little value in most appliance-TV-housewares dealers' advertising program.

SIX BASIC TYPES OF RETAIL DIRECT MAIL

While there are hundreds of different varieties of direct mail used for retail promotion, six basic types account for the majority of today's volume:

Statement Stuffers

Probably the most universally used form of retail direct mail is the enclosure sent along with the monthly statement to charge customers. The majority of these "stuffers" are supplied to retailers either without cost or for a very minimal charge by manufacturers. They range all the way from simple black-and-white imprinted sheets just the size of a statement envelope to elaborate full-color folders. Often these enclosures have a coupon for use in ordering featured products by mail. But, like other retail direct mail, they are primarily designed to build store traffic. A number of department stores prepare their own statement enclosures, frequently featuring a variety of products. There are three basic types of store-prepared enclosures:

1. *Single sheets,* ranging from pieces just the size of the folded statement to elaborate broadsides folded to fit the mailing envelope.
2. *Packets of uniform-size slips,* each featuring a separate product or group of products. Jordan Marsh Co., Boston, regularly inserts a miniature envelope-size portfolio containing about a dozen individual sheets describing special products with its monthly statements.
3. *Small envelope-size booklets* which are really miniature catalogs. Chicago's Marshall Field & Co., for example, includes a little 3¼- by 5½-inch booklet with each monthly statement. It illustrates and describes about 50 items and includes a page which can be torn out and used as a mail order form.

Weight of the stuffers constitutes a major problem for many retailers. The custom of enclosing customers' sales checks with statements, which started during World War II, has now become quite commonplace and has reduced the number of enclosures which many retailers can use and still stay within weight limitations. Many times, the selection of manufacturer-supplied enclosures is decided primarily on a weight basis.

The use of statement enclosures is usually scheduled many months in advance, with store-prepared material always given preference over that supplied by manufacturers. However, when a newly developed store enclosure forces replacement of supplied material, the manufacturer's enclosure may be rescheduled or used as a package enclosure instead.

Dealer-Identified Direct Mail

Frequently, the only direct mail used by a retailer is that supplied by the manufacturers whose products he sells. In most fields, a retailer has a wide variety of direct mail programs from which he can choose. Because there are so many special factors to be considered in the development of successful dealer-identified direct mail programs, the entire following chapter is devoted to this subject.

Catalogs and Flyers

The use of multiple-page direct mail units is common among many retail businesses. There are two basic types: (1) seasonal catalogs and (2) flyers advertising special sales. Department stores are the most frequent users of catalogs, including both the seasonal variety and those grouping special types of products. For example, department stores often prepare catalogs for January White Sales, Easter, Mother's Day, Father's Day, Graduation, Back-to-School, and Christmas plus special catalogs covering such related item categories as housewares, furniture, and fashions.

Flyers, which usually take the form of multiproduct promotions printed on newsprint stock, are most frequently used by discount houses and more specialized retailers including hardware, auto supply, variety, and garden supply stores. Frequently these flyers are used to promote special sale events.

Special Letters

The letter represents direct mail at its finest and retailers are among the foremost users of direct mail letters—even though many of them fail to recognize that their letters are, in fact, a form of direct mail advertising. Retailers use special letters for announcements, invitations, maintaining contact with customers, securing new customers, reactivating old customers, collecting overdue accounts, building goodwill, and dozens of other purposes. Some of the letters are individually typewritten; others are printed, mimeographed, or multigraphed.

Syndicated Programs

For most every retail business, someone has developed a packaged direct mail program, which is usually offered on an exclusive basis in each area. Since the syndicated packages for specialized businesses are widely promoted directly to those in each field, we will not try to describe them here. There are, in addition, a large number of syndicated services which are applicable to most any type of retailer. These are described in Chapter 16.

Group Direct Mail

With the growth of shopping centers, a new type of retail direct mail has become increasingly common—cooperative direct mailings. These take many forms and usually involve participation by a number of merchants who have a common location. In reality, these cooperative advertising ventures are an extension of the "Shopper" or "Daily Reminder" throwaways which became popular in the depression days of the 1930's, and still continue to exist in many areas. The distinguishing feature of the "Shopper" is that it usually contains nothing but advertising and is distributed without charge to all families in a given area. Many "Shoppers" are commercial publishing enterprises, but others are a cooperative venture of a group of merchants—frequently those located in a common shopping center. While these publications usually are in a newspaper format, they are essentially a form of direct mail advertising.

One of the more unusual cooperative direct mail programs was developed by a group of Main Street merchants in Englewood, New Jersey, who faced increasing competition from newly developed outlying shopping centers. These 27 stores, plus a local bank, banded together to form the "Guild of Englewood Merchants" and began an extensive promotion program designed to keep customers from neglecting the downtown area for the new shopping centers. After establishing some basic customer-oriented policies, the merchants pooled their charge account names. From these names, a basic list of over 5,000 families was compiled and each was sent a GEM Charge Card, extending credit privileges at all 27 stores. Along with the card went a folder containing a booklet describing the GEM plan plus individual slips describing each of the stores, the national brands they handled, and any special services they rendered. In addition, a regular direct mail program promotes the merchants to 51,000 families in the Englewood trading area. Catalogs and special tabloids are used regularly to promote such special events as Easter, Back-to-School, Christmas, Fall Fashions, Home Furnishings, Clearance Sales, "Carnival of Values," etc.

OBJECTIVES FOR RETAIL DIRECT MAIL

While certainly the main objective of retail direct mail is to build increased business, there are a variety of more specific objectives. No list could possibly be complete, but the following 30 ways probably represent the most common objectives:

1. Promotion of special events
2. Promotion of special products
3. Promotion of special departments
4. Revive inactive accounts
5. Secure new charge accounts
6. Build store traffic
7. Increase buying by customers
8. Collect overdue accounts
9. Build goodwill
10. Welcome newcomers
11. Secure orders by mail for the store's merchandise
12. Secure orders by mail for merchandise not carried in stock
13. Establish a local point-of-contact for national promotions
14. Fill in missing spots in coverage of other advertising
15. Test customers' reactions
16. Dispose of limited inventories
17. Learn of grievances and prejudices
18. Solicit new ideas and suggestions
19. Personnel relations
20. Maintain continuing contact with customers and prospects
21. Get customers to help recruit new customers
22. Solve special sales problems
23. Seasonal promotions
24. Reach special audiences
25. Keep customers happy
26. Build a favorable image
27. Enlist support of other merchants
28. Clerk-to-customer contact
29. Promote new store openings
30. Get customers to bring friends with them

Promotion of Special Events

One of the most common retail uses of direct mail is to promote a special sale. In particular, direct mail is very often used to give regular customers advance notice of a major sales event. But there is also a wide variety of other special events which can best be promoted by direct mail. H. E. Brown & Co., a Long Island ladies' specialty shop, sends invitations to a pre-Christmas "for men only" Stag Night promotion. The mailings are sent to women customers but include invitations and admission tickets for the men plus a size chart which wives can fill in and give to their husbands. Many retailers also use direct mail to send out invitations to open house affairs, demonstrations, special showings, etc.

Promotion of Special Products

Many times a retailer wishes to feature a special product with limited appeal. In such cases, mass advertising seldom can do an economical promotion job. The answer is a direct mailing to the specific audience most interested in the product. Other times special products require a more adequate description than is afforded by most advertising media, and direct mail permits the use of special reproduction processes or the inclusion of samples or swatches. Wolf Brothers, Tampa clothing store, had a line of quality garments to promote. To adequately describe these garments required realistic reproduction of the fabrics. The answer: Wolf Brothers mailed 25,000 packets to its list. Each packet contained 15 cards describing the individual garments being promoted. And tipped to each card was a swatch of the fabrics involved. The result was a 40% increase in sales.

Promotion of Special Departments

Like special products, entire departments of a retail store may require promotion to select audiences—and sometimes to mass audiences as well. Very frequently, retailers turn to direct mail for such promotions. For example, Tepper's, Plainfield, New Jersey, depended almost entirely on direct mail to launch a new University Shop. The store first compiled a list of 2,000 students planning to go to college and then maintained contact with the students through mailings both to their home and school addresses. A more unusual direct mail campaign promoting a new gift shop was staged by Mattison's Federated Department Store of Tomahawk, Wisconsin. The store distributed more than 5,000 picture post cards showing its unique Cellar Shop, located in a converted bank vault. The cards were sent to motels and resorts in the Tomahawk vacation region for distribution to their guests, who, in turn, used them for mailing messages to friends at home.

Revive Inactive Accounts

A whole book could be compiled of success stories of retailers who have turned to direct mail letters to bring lost customers back into the fold. One of the most successful approaches is an automatically typewritten letter, but printed mailing pieces have also worked well for some stores. Lytton's, a Chicago clothing store, used a unique letter containing a single penny. Mailed to 30,000 inactive accounts, the letter began: "A penny for your thoughts," and went on to request frank comments on why the recipients hadn't been buying. While only 100 complaints resulted, the letter brought 13,000 renewed accounts representing $441,000 in sales. An Indianapolis department store mailed letters to 4,000 accounts which had not made purchases for six months or more and just 60 days later had rung up sales from these accounts totaling $50,200—at a promotional cost of well under 1%. Interestingly enough, approximately 20% of the accounts took time to reply to the letter and a check revealed that only one out of every 1,000 inactive accounts was dissatisfied in any way. The rest had just "drifted away."

In his manual, "How Direct Mail Solves Management Problems," Henry Hoke described a highly effective letter used by Willoughby Camera Stores for contacting inactive accounts:

> Because we here at Willoughby's are human beings, too, we are just as curious about things as is the next man.
>
> Our curiosity has been aroused any number of times about this, that, and the other thing.
>
> Today, however, the Willoughby curiosity is focused upon one person—You!
>
> In making our periodic check-up of our records, we find that it has been a good long while since you used your Willoughby Charge Account. And we are curious as to the reason why.
>
> Can it be because our service has displeased you? Or something happened not to your liking? Mistakes and misunderstandings will occur, even to the best of us.
>
> We'd like to know why you haven't used your Charge Account, and we have provided space for your story right across the way.
>
> Your reply will help us correct any mishaps, and enable us to serve our customers even better. Anything you tell us will certainly be appreciated.
>
> Won't you let us hear from you at your earliest convenience? The enclosed envelope needs no postage.
>
> Sincerely, WILLOUGHBY'S

Another inactive account renewal technique was practiced by Capper & Capper, Chicago men's store, and produced outstanding results. The store president sent a personal letter to the inactive customer, enclosing a swatch of Swiss handkerchief fabric. In the letter he offered the handkerchiefs at a special price as an inducement for the customer to reactivate his account.

Secure New Charge Customers

A personalized or semipersonalized direct mail approach is often the most efficient method for a store to add new charge customers to its lists. Frequently, mailings are made to all newcomers to a store's trading area. Kennedy's, a New England chain, sends newcomers a temporary credit card along with an invitation to visit one of its stores to sign up for a regular credit account. Another chain, Noah's Ark Auto Accessories Inc., with headquarters in Rochester, New York, uses a direct mail premium offer to build its credit accounts. It makes six credit account mailings a year to 70,000 names in addition to six general catalog mailings of 850,000 each. The first of the six credit account mailings includes a credit card plus an offer of some housewares item as a premium with the first purchase of $10 or more. Other mailings also make premium offers plus special sale offers available on budget terms. A typical mailing offering an ice bucket premium drew a 3.7% response with total sales of over $60,000. The average sale resulting from the promotion was $28.71.

A major southwestern specialty store reports it opens 54% of its new charge accounts each year through direct mail invitations. These new customers represent an annual volume of more than a million dollars. Another store added over 6,000 new accounts in four months with a mailing of 40,000 letters.

A particularly successful new account solicitation won a 1960 DMAA Award for Maskill Hardware of Royal Oak, Michigan. Maskill used a series of six unique die-cut letters. Both the letters and the double window mailing envelopes were die-cut so the name imprinted on an enclosed credit card application and an illustration of the store's sign showed through the openings. The letters, which were budgeted at $2,000, drew 258 charge account requests, 231 of which were accepted. Since the average Maskill charge customer purchases $2,000 worth of merchandising during the life of his account, and a 10% profit figure can reasonably be projected, the campaign represented $46,200 in added profits for the store.

Build Store Traffic

While most retail direct mail has building store traffic as one of its aims, many campaigns are planned to accomplish this purpose alone. Often a novelty approach is used. For example, Crest Drug Store of Linden, New Jersey, placed a large aerial photo of its basic trading area in its window and then sent a mailing inviting customers and prospects to come and "see what your house looks like from a mile up in the air."

A premium approach was used by a New York restaurant, The Lobster, to build traffic during the day. The restaurant mailed letters to 3,000 prospects and 2,000 charge account customers—businessmen located in the area. The letters offered a unique ashtray decorated with a flaming red lobster to those who came for lunch during the usually less-busy daylight hours. The prospect letter drew a return of better than 3% while the customer letter pulled 7.5%. Since most of the businessmen brought guests, traffic was substantially increased.

In an article in *Stores,* Philip I. Ross notes: "One interesting application of direct mail to a particular store problem is its growing use to encourage downtown shopping. There are several ways in which, by reaching suburban areas or thriving neighborhoods within the city, such promotion successfully . . . swells store traffic. The downtown store enjoys an advantage important to many shoppers. That is its quality of bigness, drama, and excitement. A natural tie-in that makes the most of this aura of the dramatic is the frequent staging of shows and exhibitions of fashions, model rooms and kitchens, do-it-yourself tools and supplies, merchandise from foreign shores, pets, flowers and garden equipment, and so on. A natural promotion method which can greatly increase attendance and store traffic at such events is the invitation delivered by mail. Then, whether the invitation itself is a simple or an elaborate one, the three words, 'you are invited,' seem to work miracles. And, of course, area and income-wise, the guest list is handpicked."

Increase Buying by Customers

Even regular customers can be spurred into increased activity through direct mail promotion. The Government Employees' Mart discount chain, for example, spends most of its advertising budget on a monthly house organ which is sent to those who have paid the $3 enrollment fee required for purchasing in the store. Each issue of the *G.E.M. Journal* runs 24 to 40 pages or more and contains news of G.E.M. activities plus plugs for various "headliner" items available. The store's advertising agency reports, "Although G.E.M. has the same prices day in and day out, people apparently can't break the habit of rushing out to buy as soon as the ads come in." Statistics show the Monday after the *Journal* is mailed is regularly the biggest sales day.

Collect Overdue Accounts

Direct mail has traditionally been the vehicle used to collect overdue accounts. Most every store with any volume of credit business has a regular series of credit collection letters which are used to spur customers who are slow to clear up their balances. You'll find a wide variety of examples in Frailey's *Handbook of Business Letters.*

Experience of many retailers has indicated the use of automatically typewritten letters speeds up the collection process considerably and the added expense per letter is usually offset by the fewer mailings required.

Build Goodwill

Many retailers have special letter programs designed primarily to build and maintain goodwill of customers. The Addis Co., Syracuse, New York, department store, has one of the most extensive and successful goodwill direct mail programs. Among the techniques it uses are welcoming messages for both new credit accounts and customers who become active after a period of inactivity; reminder cards sent to husbands a week before their wives' birthdays; birthday messages to children of customers; congratulatory messages on customers' wedding anniversaries; and thank-you notes to customers who pay their bills regularly.

Willoughby Camera Stores of New York sends a personal, friendly letter thanking each customer making an initial camera purchase. This is followed by another letter asking if the customer is fully satisfied with his purchase and later still another letter offering free photographic information on any problem the customer might have.

A more unusual type of goodwill direct mail is used to build advance interest in a new store. When Eagle Food Shopping Centers built a new store in Glenview, Illinois, for example, a series of self-mailers were sent to local residents with periodic "progress reports." The mailings were part of an elaborate community relations program. In addition to building goodwill, the mailings were used to solicit applications for employment in the new supermarket.

Banks serve their own and community goodwill with letters congratulating newly elected service organization leaders.

Welcome Newcomers

Direct mail is frequently used by retailers to welcome newcomers to their communities and to introduce these prime prospects to the services they offer. Most often, these letters include offers of special gifts or discounts to encourage an initial visit to the stores. In addition to individual retailers' efforts, many communities have cooperative welcoming programs to do by mail what a Welcome Wagon service does on a personal visit basis. Housewarmers of North Scituate, Massachusetts, for example, sends each newcomer a 24-page get-acquainted booklet describing North Scituate and participating merchants' stores and services. Enclosed in the mailing is a set of certificates offering gifts or discounts at participating stores. There are two advantages to this plan over in-person visitations: (1) the mailings are about half as costly as a visitation service and (2) the mailings will not intrude on the newcomer, who is frequently busy getting settled when a caller arrives. Returns of the Housewarmers gift certificates run as high as 66%.

Secure Orders by Mail for the Store's Merchandise

While most retail direct mail is not aimed at mail order response, this is an added "bonus" for many mailings. In addition, many retailers use direct mail to draw mail orders from outside their regular trade area. This is particularly true of Christmas catalogs sent out by such stores as Chicago's Marshall Field & Co. and Dallas' Neiman-Marcus.

Reporting on the increasing amount of mail order selling by retail stores, Philip I. Ross says:

> Today, more and more stores consider the mail a mass advertising medium and use it that way—not forgetting its additional advantage of customer selection. We find executives concentrating on large lists whose only criteria are that they represent families of better-than-average income. With these lists as a base, stores are reaching out to new areas. They are building a steady volume of mail order sales.
>
> Take urban residents of high average income. Despite relative proximity to the store, these people readily lend themselves to many types of mail order sales. Downtown shopping in crowded stores by public transportation is tiresome and time-consuming. Above-average-income groups have funds and have the habit of thinking ahead. They welcome the opportunity to buy by mail, particularly to stock up on such items as white goods, toiletries, household items and supplies, gifts. They respond well to fur storage, rug

and furniture cleaning, and similar offers. The selectivity of direct mail makes it possible to reach these groups without waste coverage.

There is a group being sold by mail today which represents an unusually rich and fruitful market. Its members are residents of the new suburban developments and new medium-priced home developments which are springing up like mushrooms on the outskirts of most urban centers. So much is known about these young couples with children . . . it is easy to match merchandising to buying needs. In fact, these groups "need" almost everything. Rich in small fry, but short of time and help, these mothers find shopping by mail a happy expedient.

Secure Orders by Mail for Merchandise Not Carried in Stock

A relatively recent development in retail direct mail is the use of store customer lists to promote the sale of items not normally featured in the store. Magazine publishers are major users of this technique. Subscriptions are usually handled as a regular credit purchase, although the mailings are generally prepared by the publishers. This technique is not limited by any means to magazine subscriptions, however. A number of companies offer syndicated mailing programs promoting big-ticket merchandise such as movie cameras, power tools, dinnerware and silverware, etc. Mailings are sent to a store's list and orders are returned to the store, but the merchandise is usually drop-shipped by either the manufacturer or the syndicator.

Establish a Local Point-of-Contact for National Promotions

Retailers can benefit directly from national promotion of products they handle by using tie-in mailings sent to their lists. Many manufacturers offer their dealers complete mailing packages which they can use to establish such tie-ins. Several of these are described in Chapter 10.

Fill in Missing Spots in Coverage of Other Advertising

No matter how extensive an advertising job any store does, mass media may fail to cover the store's entire trading area. In such cases it is common to mail reprints of newspaper ads to homes in the "missed" areas.

Test Customers' Reaction

Both retailers and manufacturers of products they sell often use direct mail to get customers' reactions to the products and suggestions for improvements. The Huffman Manufacturing Co., for example, sends an annual questionnaire to a selected group of buyers of its power lawnmowers. Huffman regularly receives a response of about 60%, with much valuable information to help it improve both the product and its promotion. Stores considering the addition of a new department or line also use the questionnaire technique to get a sampling of potential response.

Disposal of Limited Inventories

All too often, a retailer will find himself "stuck" with limited inventories of a particular product or line. Frequently, the inventory isn't large enough to warrant mass advertising so the retailer turns to direct mail aimed at a select list of those most likely to be interested in the product. One men's clothing store, for example, found itself considerably overstocked on size 42 suits. It checked its records and came up with a list of customers who had purchased size 42 clothing previously, then mailed a letter explaining the situation and offering special discounts. The store not only moved the entire inventory but had to quickly restock the size to serve all who responded to the mailing.

Learn of Grievances and Prejudices

When sales fall off in a department or for some line of products, many retailers turn to direct mail to find out if customers' grievances or prejudices are responsible. In such cases, direct mail is often used not only to determine the cause of the sales slump, but also to help rectify the situation if complaints are uncovered.

Solicit New Ideas and Suggestions

Just as direct mail is used to find out things which are wrong, many retailers send letters asking their customers to suggest new ways in which the store can be of service to them. Not only will such requests bring back a lot of useful information, but they can serve as a major goodwill builder. Most customers feel flattered when asked for their advice and develop a strong personal bond with any retailer who gives them an opportunity to "participate" in his business.

Personnel Relations

As a retail operation grows in size, there is sure to be less and less personal contact between management and employees. To restore a personal relationship, many retailers regularly use direct mail letters sent to employees' homes. At least one retail chain has a special personnel relations man, a psychologist whose only job is to prepare regular letters to be sent by executives to employees. Many other retailers use direct mail regularly to distribute all types of employee publications.

Maintain Continuing Contact With Customers and Prospects

A number of retailers use direct mail to maintain a nonselling contact with customers and prospects. Some use an external house organ, either custom-designed or one of the many syndicated varieties available. Many stores make regular use of the publications prepared for them by manufacturers or their associations. Others use some type of novelty mailing, such as the "Let's Have Better Mottoes Association" mailings syndicated by John Yeck of Dayton, Ohio. Another technique is to use newsletters telling about community events of special interest or offering such information as household tips. Although some of these mailings may include advertising promoting special products or services, their primary purpose is to maintain a continuing contact.

Get Customers to Help Recruit New Customers

A number of retailers have successfully adopted a technique often used by mail order advertisers, who ask their customers to recommend friends to whom promotional material can be sent. Frequently a premium of some kind is offered as a "thank you" for such help. One midwestern store developed a unique promotion by offering trading stamps to each customer who recruited a new credit customer. The trading stamps given as a new-customer premium duplicated the quantity received by the new customer for all credit purchases recorded during a three-month period.

Solve Special Sales Problems

A typical example of how retailers can use direct mail to solve a special sales problem is the dealer promotion staged by Dodge when a prolonged work stoppage interrupted the introduction of its cars. As soon as inventories had been built up after the stoppage, Dodge reintroduced the line with two special dealer mailings. The first was a poster-size piece featuring an invitation to try a new Dodge. The second was a magazine-format mailing called "Pace—the magazine for Americans on the go." Included with the "Pace" mailing were two separate enclosures. One featured self-liquidating premiums available through a visit to the Dodge dealer's showroom. The second explained the then-new automobile price-sticker legislation in a way designed to establish a feeling of confidence in Dodge dealerships as reputable places to trade. The mailings created results which rivaled a regular new car introduction and built showroom traffic which quickly made up for the inactive period.

Henry Hoke provides another interesting case history:

> Hotel Pierre in New York had opened a new dining room which was not showing a profit even though the hotel was full for luncheon every day. The promotion manager discovered that 82% of the patrons were women and only 18% were men. Here was a slow turnover because the women ate sparingly, drank little, and lingered long. A mailing list was secured of 800 top executives in the neighborhood. Another secondary list was built of sales executives within a four-mile radius. It was arranged to reserve a number of tables for men in the predominantly female atmosphere. Automatically typed letters on engraved stationery, signed with pen and ink, were sent to the neighborhood business executives, telling about the special tables for men. A second letter, offering Pierre's facilities for special events, was sent to sales executives in the larger area. How did the plan work? In three months' time the patronage in the Pierre Grill had changed from 82% women and 18% men to a surprising reversal of 55% men and 45% women. Two letters a year since the first experiment have maintained the same proportion. The profit/loss picture changed also.

Seasonal Promotions

Many retail businesses are faced with seasonal sales problems which can be solved with special direct mail promotions. Heating dealers, for example, have a major seasonal slump during warmer months and seek service and installation business to take up the slack. An outstanding example of how direct mail can play a major role is the mailing made one summer by Sappio Heating & Cooling Co. of Wichita, Kansas. Sappio mailed 3,000 post cards to prospective customers selected at random from the local telephone directory. The offer was for a $6 furnace tuneup, with a premium of a free Fram filter. Sappio received a return of 1,021, representing a gross income of $5,421.72 after the 68-cent cost of each filter premium was deducted. Total cost of the mailing was $186. But this success story had still more results—the sale of 21 replacement furnaces, 16 central air-conditioning plants, and many air-conditioning service calls as a result of contacts made during the servicing of the 1,021 furnaces.

Reach Special Audiences

Direct mail can assist retailers by reaching many different kinds of special audiences. Darling's Flower Shop of Los Angeles, for example, recognized that secretaries usually place flower orders for their businessmen bosses. So they initiated the "Because I Am a

Girl" club. Membership cards were sent to a list of secretaries. Because she is a girl, the card explained, she is entitled by birth to a variety of special considerations. The membership cards were followed by a series of clever, lighthearted letters and "Moody Cards" she could display to signal her various moods. The cards carried such slogans as "I would just like to be left alone" . . . "I'm PLEASED with myself!" . . . "I'm not my usual charming self today" . . . "Somehow I can't seem to get going." Each had a humorous illustration. The idea quickly caught on and the list was expanded from its original 1,000 to 2,500—entirely as a result of secretaries' suggestions of new names. And the secretaries also responded with a substantial increase in orders for flowers.

Another example is the "Memo Set" promotion of Houston retailer Harry Battelstein. Over 10,000 career girls receive a "Monthly Memo" newsletter giving news of fashion trends, new products, and tips on everything from hemlines to heel heights. Coupled with other special promotions aimed at this group, the newsletter has resulted in a substantial increase in business.

Keep Customers Happy

There are times when it is just as important to maintain the interest of a customer in a product he has already purchased as to attempt to sell him something new. Charlex Realty Corporation of Newark, New Jersey, representing a number of Florida real estate developments, was plagued by an increased number of cancellations from customers who had already begun buying Florida homesites. To stem the rising cancellation trend, Charlex mailed a series of four special items: (1) a phonograph record featuring a short talk on "Florida, Your Wisest Investment" on one side and an original recording, "Follow the Sun to Sunny, Sunny Florida," on the other; (2) an album of 15 photographs showing various scenes of the community in which the customer had purchased his homesite; (3) a kit containing magazine and newspaper articles about Florida; and (4) two decks of special playing cards. As a result of this direct mail campaign, the cancellation rate dropped from an alarming 10% down to a modest 3%.

Build a Favorable Image

Just as many industrial advertisers devote major sums to promotion designed to build a favorable corporate image, many retailers have this as an objective for their direct mail. An independent Glendale, California, supermarket, Country Squire, overcame the handicap of a difficult location by consistent image-building promotion, primarily direct mail. All of the store's promotion concentrated on clearly establishing a "country squire" personality for the store. Mailing pieces, which are sent weekly, use distinctive typography and layout to look as unlike the typical supermarket price-laden flyer as possible, even though the store stresses a "low prices every day" theme. Coupons and premium offers are used frequently in the mailings, each of which is built around a unique idea or a timely promotion theme. A typical mailing featured a drawing of a folding ruler and asked, "How do you measure a market?" and then went on to answer by outlining service, quality, location, selection, prices plus conveniences and complete food service. Special features of the store, such as its free coffee counter, are often featured. The success of the mailing program is measured by coupon returns, which run as high as 75%.

LaJoy, a Chinese restaurant in Milwaukee, used another image-building approach. It produced a series of six jumbo post card mailings, each featuring a full-color reproduction of Chinese *objets d'art* in a famous local collection. The historical figurines created an atmosphere of both high quality and oriental charm.

Enlist Support of Other Merchants

Direct mail also has an important role in enlisting support of fellow merchants for a variety of purposes. A Joplin, Missouri, realtor, Rolla Stevens, sends picture post cards of commercial properties he has for sale to realtors in nearby cities, along with stamps with which to mail them. He urges his fellow realtors to jot a note on each of the cards and mail them to local prospects. The realtors also get detailed property listings so they will have sales ammunition if they do arouse the interest of a local prospect.

Clerk-to-Customer Contact

One of the best ways to develop a close relationship with customers is through a person-to-person direct mail program. Many stores urge sales personnel to maintain their own "private" mailing lists of special customers and then provide special mailing pieces to which the clerk can add a personal note or his or her signature. Special pre-sale announcements are frequently handled on this basis. Here is retail direct mail at its maximum effectiveness.

Promote New Store Openings

Promotion of a new store doesn't have to wait until the doors open. When building or remodeling starts, there is likely to be a natural curiosity among those who observe the work in progress. Many retailers have taken advantage of this curiosity to lay the groundwork for the business which will be needed when the opening becomes an actuality. Letters, newsletters and picture reports sent to those in the marketing area receive an unusually high readership because of their "news" value.

When opening day arrives, a carefully planned direct mail program can produce a substantial sales volume. The Fisher-Fazio food store chain in Ohio, for example, gets excellent results from a series of six consecutive circular mailings. The first sets the pace by telling prospective customers exactly and clearly what the store will offer.

In opening a new store in an Akron suburb, Fisher-Fazio distributed 70,000 circulars with consecutive numbers. During the grand opening, a list of "lucky number winners" was posted in the meat department—at the rear of the new store. The circular also offered a number of grand opening specials and a description of what was different about the store—an in-store bakery, a sit-down restaurant, sausage shoppe and a carryout delicatessen. Key store personnel were also featured. And to start a program of buying continuity, the back page was devoted to a continuity premium program featuring monogrammed glassware.

Subsequent circular mailings keep working to get grand opening buyers to return and to attract other new customers.

Establish Regular Shopping Habits

To get customers in the habit of buying regularly at a particular retail outlet, direct mail has frequently been used to send dated coupons, entitling the recipient to a premium, discount or free merchandise—usually redeemable at one-week intervals. McDonald's, for example, has made effective use of dated coupons for free hamburgers and other food items. In one case, a 6½ by 7½ inch piece with four detachable coupons, each good for a one-week period, was inserted into a non-competitive circular for Kroger food stores. The first coupon was for a free McDonald's hamburger, the second for a free hot apple pie, the third for a cheeseburger and the fourth for a fish sandwich. Out of 242,602 inserts mailed, 73,577 were redeemed for a return of 30.3%. Additional sales with the redeemed coupons amounted to $38,996, but probably the most beneficial result was creating a pattern of weekly trips to McDonald's.

Bring a Friend With You

One particularly effective way to increase the number of customers for a store is to encourage established customers to bring a friend when they come in for a special occasion. Myer's Metered Gas Service in Manheim, Pa. used a simple direct mail promotion so successful that a mailing of only 3,000 attracted 1,500 people to a three-day event and brought over $21,000 in immediate sales.

Myer's mailed a 5 by 9 inch circular with two enclosed door prize cards. Copy read:

> Dear Customer:
>
> For some time we have wanted to do more than just say "thank you" for the business you have given us. So we are offering to you plenty of food in Smorgasbord Style. Special appliances purchases have been made. Deep price cuts have been taken throughout the store. Frankly, we are real excited over this unusual event.
>
> We will be looking forward to meeting your family on one of these special days.

Copy on the two enclosed door prize tickets read:

> This Ticket Entitles Your Family to a FREE SMORGASBORD and SPECIAL PRICES on every appliance in the store.
>
> The other ticket is for the friend or neighbor who comes with you.
>
> If your friend or neighbor makes a purchase in excess of $100, you will receive a bonus of 2,000 S & H Green Stamps.
>
> Bring this ticket with you to register for door prize drawing.
>
> Door prizes will include a 10 Cu. Ft. Whirlpool Freezer, Caloric Cub, Camping Store, and Sunbeam Percolator.
>
> Remember the dates: Sept. 17, 18, 19—9 to 9.

The 1,500 who responded enjoyed the smorgasbord at a cost to Myer's of 36 cents per head—a small price to pay to attract hundreds of friends of customers to a store event.

RETAIL MAILING LISTS

While the subject of mailing lists is discussed in detail in Chapter 20, there is a number of distinctive features of retail lists which deserve special consideration. There are two basic types of lists used by retailers:

1. Customer lists
2. Prospect lists

Each type has many variations and may be subdivided in dozens of different ways. Like mail order, it is important to identify as many different segments of the lists as possible so direct mail may be pinpointed to the most logical targets.

Customer Lists

The primary mailing list for the majority of stores is their credit customers. But even this group is best subdivided. First of all, active customers should be keyed separately from inactives. Secondly, a store may wish to key its list according to buying activity in different departments. If possible, it is also helpful to identify lists by marital status and members of the family. Thus, it is possible to make special mailings to families with children or eliminate women's fashion mailings from those portions of the list representing single men, etc. Other possible classifications include anticipated buying habits, section of residence, age, home ownership, etc.

Another method of classifying lists is according to purchasing power. One store with more than a quarter-million charge accounts has the following lists:

Platinum List

3,000 specially identified customers with very high income.

Gold List

10,000 customers whose purchases indicate they buy in relatively high brackets.

Fashion List

25,000 customers known to be interested in fashion and who have made purchases in the moderate to high brackets.

Home List

25,000 customers with purchases indicating an interest in fashions and home furnishings.

Shoe List

15,000 customers whose shoe purchases have been recorded by style preference and size.

This same store has dozens of other separate lists identified by type of work, family status, etc.

Special Lists

Other good sources for special lists include registrations of women and girls who have attended fashion shows; businesswomen who come to events staged for them; homemakers who attend lectures and demonstrations; customers who attend sewing classes; men who use special "stag" shopping sections at Christmastime. One store has even gone to a great deal of effort to develop a list of proud grandparents and makes special mailings promoting unusual gifts for children.

A particularly useful list can be developed by recording purchasers of maternity garments. And, of course, whenever a wedding gown is fitted there's a golden opportunity to start a chain of direct mail contact with a prospective buyer of potentially long standing.

While most stores have up-to-date lists of their credit customers, many overlook the gold mine represented by customers who always pay with cash. Building such lists requires special attention, but a careful watch of delivery slips, alteration tickets, and other records will yield many names. Some stores give special incentives to clerks who obtain full mailing list information from cash buyers. Sometimes, cash customers are only added to mailing lists when their purchases exceed established minimum limits.

Geographical Lists

If the customer list is relatively large, it is important to maintain it separately for credit and direct mail purposes. Since charge account lists are almost always kept in alphabetical order, they are not suitable for many mailings where it is necessary for names to be arranged in geographical order.

Geographical lists will save much time in zoning mailings and eliminate need for the large amount of space required for sorting mailings addressed alphabetically into geographical postal groups. The geographical list also permits special mailings for stores which have branches and permits selection of areas by social and economic characteristics.

Whenever two or more different lists are maintained, it is important to have a clearly established method for making sure corrections become effective on all lists. It is a good idea to have one person or one department responsible for handling *all* address changes reported. The information is then routed to everyone concerned.

Quality, Not Quantity

One of the major mistakes made by retailers is to concentrate on numbers in the development of both customer and prospect lists. The general theory is "the more people reached with direct mail, the greater the results which can be expected." Unfortunately, this theory is full of holes. As in any business, there are good customers and poor customers; good prospects and poor prospects. If budget isn't a consideration, it is probably smart to try to reach as many people as possible—*if this doesn't mean cutting down on the number of mailings which can be made and/or reducing the quality of the mailings.*

But it is the exceptional retailer who does not have to worry about how much money he is going to spend on his advertising. So it becomes important to either develop lists which are very carefully coded or to eliminate all but the good prospects and customers. The usual formula for determining which are the best customers is RFMR—Recency/Frequency/Monetary Ratio. This is the basic formula used by leading mail order firms in controlling their lists and it has long been practiced by retailers with successful direct mail programs.

In this formula, Recency involves eliminating customers who have not purchased recently. Frequency involves eliminating customers who have not purchased with any regularity. Monetary Ratio, of course, refers to the dollar volume of customers' purchases. You'll find a more detailed explanation of the RFMR formula in Chapter 22—"Mailing List Maintenance."

One direct mail service firm which makes extensive use of the RFMR formula in serving its customers is Advertisers Addressing System of St. Louis. How the technique pays off was explained by Jerome Osherow, Advertisers Addressing president, in *The Reporter of Direct Mail Advertising:*

> Recently we had occasion to completely revamp the customer list of a large retail furniture store here in St. Louis. The number of names on the list totaled 140,000 but the quality of the list had deteriorated to the point where mailing results were only marginal. It took four months of effort and a clerical bill of approximately $14,000 to bring this list into shape. When finished, the list had shrunk to 70,000 names and the mailings to this reduced list were just as effective as the mailings to the larger one. Savings: 70,000 pieces of mail at an average cost of $60 per thousand, or $4,200, *saved every mailing* plus tremendous savings in mailing list maintenance costs, storage space, etc.

Circles of Convenience

In developing good prospect lists, one of the best procedures is what is called "circles of convenience." It involves marking the location of a store on a map and then drawing a series of concentric circles around the location at regular intervals. The location of customers—particularly new customers—is then marked within the circles. A pattern of customers quickly develops. Prospect lists are then built by adding names of noncustomers who live within the circles with the greatest concentration of prospects.

In telling how his company uses this method to serve retailers, Jerome Osherow notes: "One thing unusual about the 'circle of convenience' is that often it isn't circular. It can actually be odd-shape, long and narrow, or even a cloverleaf design. The principle, however, is the same, for the 'circle of convenience' is a method to outline *what your customers have decided* is their area of convenience. In many lines of business, such as banks, savings and loan associations, and shopping centers, every survey points to one key reason why shoppers shop where they shop—the answer is always the same—convenience. Obviously, in most cases convenience decreases with distance. In our use we define the 'circle of convenience' as the smallest area which will encompass 50% of the store's present customers."

Mr. Osherow tells how this method served a St. Louis neighborhood bank, which had been mailing to a list totaling over 40,000 names. After analyzing first the bank's customers and then giving special attention to new accounts opened within the preceding year, a pattern of logical prospects could be charted on a map, which featured concentric circles covering the entire area to which mailings had previously been sent. "In areas closest to the bank," Mr. Osherow explains, "the percentage of new customers obtained per thousand pieces mailed was as much as eight times higher than the percentage obtained in the outermost ring. The percentage of new accounts obtained correlated almost perfectly with the density of present customers in these same areas. For example, in the six-block radius surrounding the bank, almost 35% of the residents were already bank customers. In the furthermost area the percentage had dropped to 4%. By merely looking at the map, one could see that results on a percentage basis could be improved almost 350% by merely eliminating the areas farthest from the bank which totaled slightly over 50% of the total prospect list."

In his *Reporter of Direct Mail* article, Mr. Osherow offered this step-by-step outline of the method for applying the circles of convenience technique:

> *Step One:* Put the names and addresses of your customers—or perhaps only new customers—on 3- by 5-inch cards.
>
> *Step Two:* Zone the 3 by 5 cards if your community has postal zones.
>
> *Step Three:* Put the cards into alphabetical order by street and then by numerical order.

Step Four: Use an enlargement of your city map for the areas closest to you. On this enlargement, stick pins to locate your customers' addresses. If the map gets too crowded with pins, start using different colored pins to indicate 10 or 100 regular pins, etc.

Step Five: After you have the area pinned, make a rough tracing of your "cream" areas. Likewise, you may indicate on the map those areas from which you draw very little business.

Step Six: After you have the areas, make up a set of 3 by 5 cards for all of the streets in those areas which you want to cover and list the starting number of the street and the end number. Your mailing list should then be arranged in street order, and you will use only streets in the area which you have proved to be most profitable for you.

Central Location Stores

While the circles of convenience technique is an excellent method for charting prospects for neighborhood businesses, it seldom can be applied directly to large, centrally located stores which draw their trade from a wide area. In such cases, it is common to break a trading area into census tracts. It will generally develop that certain areas represent much greater concentrations of customers than others. Chances are that the bulk of customers will come from areas of common characteristics such as convenience of transportation, income level, home ownership level, average number of children per family, educational background, racial background and, in some cases, average age level. Charting such factors can be difficult and costly. Many times, however, the cost and trouble of making such studies will more than be offset by savings in advertising costs and by increases in business resulting from a more accurately pinpointed direct mail program.

In many communities, direct mail service organizations have already carefully charted socioeconomics characteristics of all census tracts and have ready-to-use mailing lists coded with this information.

A more detailed discussion of methods for building, renting, and maintaining mailing lists is featured in Chapter 20—"Mailing Lists" and Chapter 22—"Mailing List Maintenance."

RECOMMENDATIONS FOR RETAIL DIRECT MAIL

Based on the results of its study of department store direct mail, the National Retail Merchants Association offers these five basic recommendations for effective retail promotion by mail:

1. *Avoid confusing direct mail with mail order.* Direct mail is not exclusively a device for getting mail orders; it can bring traffic, too.

2. *Understand direct mail's function.* Mail is at its best when the recipient feels that he has been selected to receive a special message geared to his personal interests. The mailing list may be large or small, but the mailing piece should make each individual feel that there is a specific reason for sending it to him.
3. *Time carefully; plan ahead.* When there is too great an interval between planning date and mailing date, the effectiveness of the mailing is reduced, and the complexity of the merchandising job is increased. Last-minute postponements tie up merchandise brought into stock to back up mailings.
4. *Be discriminating in accepting help from resources.* Individual resources offer varying amounts of help in direct mail, and prepare mailing pieces with varying degrees of skill. To accept mailings that do not reflect the store's personality and merchandising policies is to weaken the appeal of the store's entire direct mail effort.
5. *Keep an eye on costs.* Costs can be kept down by reducing waste circulation in direct mail and also by using equipment designed for direct mail needs. Sharing the credit department's mailing equipment and stuffing statements with poorly chosen mailing pieces often prove to be expensive economies.

99 DIRECT MAIL IDEAS FOR RETAILERS

A handly little booklet prepared by AM Corporation, "101 Ideas for Retail Store Direct Mail Advertising," serves as a starter for this collection of 99 direct mail ideas which may provide a starting point for the retailer looking for a special way to boost business. To selected items from AM's list, we've added a number of capsule case histories selected from various publications which serve the advertising and retail fields. Special credit must go to *The Reporter of Direct Mail Advertising,* the magazine of Direct Marketing, and particularly to Murray Raphel, whose regular column, "Ideas for Retailers," in that publication regularly offers outstanding help to retailers seeking direct mail advice.

1. Make a mailing to all the women's clubs in your trading area. Offer all who will serve as extra salespeople, 5% of their sales for their club's treasury.
2. When on a buying trip, mail back cards telling your customers what you have bought, why you bought it and when it will be available in your store.
3. Include an interesting recipe with each mailing to women.
4. Send a personal letter to any customer after he registers any complaint or asks for an adjustment.
5. For a brand new promotion, send your customers a blank post card. The one who can write "Smith sells Brown's shoes" (store name and brand name) the most times wins a prize.
6. Mail proof sheets of newspaper ads a day in advance of their appearance.

7. Related selling can also be done by mail. When a customer buys a dress, follow up with letters or flyers on hats, shoes, hose, etc.
8. Ask your customers by letter what merchandise they would like to see on sale. Enclose prepaid return cards.
9. Advertise a clearance sale listing the items alphabetically instead of by departments.
10. Mail a neighborhood or city road map and a letter to families outside your trading area instructing them how to get to your store. Include reasons why they should buy at your store.
11. Mail a weekly newsletter giving your customers market news, fashion productions, etc.
12. For something different, try a letter in crayon script—vary the colors.
13. To advertise small items, try mailing a miniature letter or announcement.
14. Mail letters in boxes instead of envelopes.
15. Put package inserts clipped to a prepaid reply envelope into packages as a second reminder of related merchandise.
16. Advertise a "Money Back" sale. Give the amount of each purchase back to the customer in stage money. Hold a periodic auction in which selected items go to the highest bidder—paid for with stage money.
17. Print play pennies, nickels, dimes to be sent to children on your list. They are to be saved and redeemed for special merchandise at your store. This promotion might also include a bank imprinted with the store name.
18. Write a "letter-from-a-daughter-to-her-mother" or a "letter-from-a-son-to-his-father" and mail periodically.
19. When you sell out of a hot sale item, mail "Rain Checks" to your customers and announce the date when a new shipment will arrive.
20. To improve your public relations send a letter or series of letters to your complete occupant list giving every one on it the complete history of your store (taxes paid, total employees, total payroll, etc.).
21. Mail your list cardboard nickels that can be exchanged in your store for real nickels for use in parking meters.
22. "A-Shirt-Off-Your-Back-Sale." Instead of taking your markdown on a clearance of men's shirts, advertise them at half price on a trade-in for an old one, preferably the one they're wearing.
23. Offer by mail to sell for $1 a size 46-long suit to the first man it will fit.
24. Reserve a special group of merchandise for a "Teacher's Sale" held between 3:30 and 5:30. Reach them in advance by letter.
25. To bring in complete families for such items as shoes, offer the first pair at 5% discount, the 2nd at 10%, the third at 15%, the 4th at 20%, etc.
26. In the fall or winter advertise a "Black Goods" sale instead of a "White Goods" sale.
27. Prepare a circular on cold weather merchandise. Have it addressed and sealed. But hold it until the first big snow—then mail.
28. Establish and advertise a camera workshop and offer your store, after hours, for a meeting place.
29. "Name-Your-Own-Price-Sale." Hold an auction on a selected group of merchandise. Customers bid for individual items by sealed envelopes to be returned by mail within a certain time period. Items go to the highest bidder.

30. For your next hosiery mailing, advertise three stockings for slightly more than the price of a pair. The third to be enclosed in a small envelope. Use this slogan: "Wear the Pair—Carry the Spare."

31. If you sell hosiery, try mailing one of an inexpensive pair to a carefully selected list. Offer its mate at a low price if called for at the store. Each stocking and its mate should bear corresponding numbers.

32. Instruct your hosiery department to keep a duplicate sales slip showing size, color, stock number and name and address of every purchaser. At regular intervals mail the sales slip to the customer with a reminder of your specials.

33. Mail bus and train schedules to your customers outside your trading area.

34. Advertise that any customer making a purchase when a covered alarm clock rings will be refunded full purchase price.

35. For a clearance, list merchandise in the form of a dinner menu.

36. For a mailing to teachers, list merchandise in the form of a report card. The grades are prices.

37. For a Saturday or school holiday promotion, mail imprinted balloons to children on your list. Announce that all balloons presented at a certain counter in your store will be inflated with gas, free. You will find that this promotion will give you a surprise plus. Many floating balloons will be lost in other stores. Consequently, your store name will be displayed prominently on the ceilings of your competitors.

38. For a special promotion, mail out tokens announcing the event. Have a mystery lady or man tour the streets asking for them. All those who can present the tokens receive a prize.

39. Establish and publicize periodically to your teen-age list a "gadgeteria," a special display of fad items.

40. For a public relations plus, mail all your customers a checklist of things to do before leaving for a vacation.

41. Mail card games to children on your list during the summer season.

42. A "key to fashion" promotion. Mail numbered cardboard keys to your customers. Use some of the numbers in a window display. Those who hold the corresponding number on a key win prizes.

43. Take candid camera shots of shoppers in your trading area. Use several in circulars. Give a prize to all who identify them.

44. A private one-cent sale. Mail an announcement and a token Penny to the people on your customer list. When they purchase an item from a selected list, they get an extra one free for the token.

45. Have postcards prepared in advance and ask children to sign them with their own names and send them to the mothers.

46. To build a good list of children's names, after a purchase offer to give to any child accompanied by an adult, one shiny new penny for every letter in his name.

47. Mail, regularly, a list of gift suggestions for every occasion. Birthdays, weddings, births, anniversaries, etc. Every family usually has one of these coming up in the near future.

48. Keep a check on ethnic group holidays. Direct letters to those groups in their own language.

49. When building or remodeling, send your customers periodic progress pictures with reminders of what the end result will mean to them in the way of bargains, selections, etc.

50. If you have complete information on your customers, invite those whose birthday falls on your store's birthday to a party at your store held the night before your anniversary.

51. For an anniversary promotion, try a letter or flyer in the style prevalent the year your store was opened.

52. To celebrate an anniversary, mail pieces of your birthday cake to your customers in small boxes. Small cakes with candles or legends can be delivered by messenger to city officials and other prominent people.

53. For an anniversary promotion, announce that all coins minted in the year of your store's opening and used to pay for merchandise during the sale, will be considered at double their value.

54. For Father's Day and to build your mailing list, have a "Hall of Fame" registration. Children to register their fathers. An initialed handkerchief and certificate to be mailed to every father registered.

55. Offer prizes for merchandise bought at your store many years ago and still in good condition. Make a window display.

56. Mail special cross-word puzzles to your customers. Offer prizes for correct solutions. Clues to solutions can be scattered around the store.

57. Unite with merchants in your area to have the police lift parking limits for non-residents on special days. Then mail "guest tags" to prospects in the trading area outside the city limits.

58. Advertise the many other kinds of businesses that are near your store. Mail out a diagram.

59. To get your customers shopping early for Christmas, mail them a card good for coffee or tea and a sandwich at your store or at a nearby lunch counter.

60. Send businessmen a list of gift suggestions for secretaries, newsboys, postmen, porters, janitors, etc.

61. In your October and/or November bills, enclose a slip "Give this to him (her)" with spaces for sizes and colors of everything a woman or man wears.

62. Mail out invitations to a Christmas preview of your merchandise. Event to be held after hours. No sales, but orders taken.

63. Mail a questionnaire to your customers sometime before Christmas asking them their preference in gifts and for size, style, etc., information. Tell husbands or wives of returnees by mail or phone that you have such information to help their gift buying.

64. Ask your customer to help you, and like as not he'll give you more business. He's flattered by your asking his advice, and his helping you provides him with greater involvement with your establishment.

65. One way to beat costs is for several local mailers to use the same envelope for their individual promotions. Particularly effective for shopping center neighbors.

66. A western laundry hit upon the idea of an "Executive Club" which supplies freshly laundered shirts once a week to business executives. The laundry furnishes the shirts and utilizes down time to handle this plus business. The "club" angle is thought to account for a substantial portion of the idea's success.

67. An appliance firm mails out perforated referral cards to customers, who automatically become members of it's "Twenty-One Club." The customer sends in the name of a prospect and puts his own name on the stub. Each week, drawings are made for 21 prizes. All stubs remain in the prize barrel so the more referrals, the greater the chance "club" members have of winning prizes.

68. High school students are provided with a purchase log by a New England stationer. Each purchase of school supplies is entered into the log and when the total hits $10, the student receives a discount certificate worth $1.00 on future purchases.

69. A Maine hotel sealed messages in antique bottles and sent them to prospects.

70. A midwestern furniture store staged a red, white and blue sale for customers. Each received three color-coded tickets—a white one which entitled the customer to a welcoming gift as soon as she came into the store; the blue one good for a 10% discount on anything except fair-trade merchandise, and the red ticket offering an appreciation gift if she made purchases of $50 or more.

71. A January mailing by a garden supply dealer offering an off-season lawnmower tune-up for just $4.95 plus parts kept his mechanics busy until the usual greenup rush started.

72. A southern bank had a local photographer take pictures of all Little League teams in its area then offered prints free to parents who called at the bank.

73. A California auto dealer mails simple black and white newsletters to prospects in his area offering free tickets to professional baseball games, record albums and recipes for those who come in. Also included are money-saving coupons promoting service department specials, with time limits to prompt quick action.

74. A New England office supply dealer collates statement stuffers provided by his suppliers and then sends them along with an informal newsletter which discusses the merits of the various items promoted in the stuffers plus other new merchandise he stocks.

75. A men's shop wanting to close out its inventory of men's sports jackets kept them listed at the regular price but mailed out a memorandum to store customers telling them that if they purchased a sports jacket at the regular price, the store would give them a pair of slacks, two pairs of socks and a tie, all free of charge. Recipients were told to bring the memo with them since there would be no public announcement, window signs or in-store offers.

76. Believing that cash customers are all too often forgotten, a furniture store sends a personal thank you note at the end of the month to all who have purchased for cash.

77. A service station operator sends *hand-written* notes to customers at regular intervals reminding them when their cars are due for servicing.

78. An eastern drug store installed a large doctor's and dentist's directory over its prescription counter and then mailed color picture postcards showing the directory to each doctor and dentist listed. They were asked to report any changes in their address or phone number so the directory could be kept up to date.

79. A small contractor toured his area and noted the address of every family that had a boat standing unprotected in the yard. He then mailed a letter to those addresses promoting a garage that could be built to accommodate the boat.

80. Bonwit Teller sent cosmetics customers a mailing welcoming them as charter members of the "Helena Rubenstein Herbessence Beauty Bank" at Bonwit's. Enclosed was a "passbook" in which Herbessence beauty product purchases could be recorded. The letter explained, "Every time you buy a Helena Rubenstein Herbessence preparation at Bonwit's, the resident Beauty Consultant in our cosmetics department will record your purchase in your Bank Book. After 13 weeks you may choose any Herbessence products you want in the amount equivalent to an average week's purchase." As a starting bonus, each "bank book" had a complimentary $10 "purchase" recorded.

81. Gordon's of Atlantic City mailed a monthly statement with a zero dollar balance to inactive charge accounts and enclosed a reproduction of a Confederate dollar. Copy imprinted on the invoice read: "When's the last time you received a statement saying you had a dollar *coming* to you? Here's one. All you have to do is bring the enclosed Confederate dollar bill to the store when you re-open your charge and we'll swap it for a *real* dollar credit toward your next charge purchase."

82. Another effective promotion for Gordon's was a post-Easter mailing with a list of specials enclosed within a plastic Easter egg bank. The egg was mailed in a cloth bag with an address tag reading "Look What The Easter Bunny Left For You At Gordon's."

83. Myers Brothers in Springfield, Ill. utilizes its left over statement stuffers by enclosing them in a special portfolio and having clerks hand them out to customers along with their receipted bills. The attractive portfolio is imprinted: "We loved having you today! We are happy to be of service . . . please do come back soon."

84. A new drug store that was having trouble getting local doctors to use its facilities for prescription business sent each doctor a letter along with a copy of its entire prescription price schedule. A repeat mailing also included the price schedule. The excellent results were attributed to the belief that doctors are intensely interested in seeing that their patients pay fair prices for prescriptions.

85. A boat dealer made a special mailing to registered boat owners explaining the Federal Highway Revenue Act of 1956 as it relates to boatmen. He explained that the Act authorized the refund of part of the Federal tax paid on gasoline used for non-highway vehicle purchases and offered to

provide boatmen with IRS forms needed to claim refunds if they stopped by his store.

86. A restaurant cooperated with local merchants by mailing tickets worth a dime to customers of the stores. Shoppers were invited to use the tickets for a cup of coffee at the restaurant when they came shopping.
87. Instead of mailing Christmas Club checks, a southern bank invited club members to the bank for a special Christmas Club Coffee.
88. A paint and wall paper dealer mailed out 1,000 wooden handles to prospective customers. The handles, a letter explained, were one half of an efficient pot scraper, and the recipient could pick up the scraper half of the tool by stopping by the store.
89. A southern druggist rents a helicopter for an hour, hovers over many locations and shoots aerial photos of residential sections. The resulting photos are sent free of charge to homeowners along with a letter explaining they are gifts from the pharmacy.
90. Clyde Campbell's university shops in Texas mail a summer letter to all fraternity members at the University of Texas—signed by a fraternity member who works in the shops.
91. Campbell's also mails a "College Tips" booklet suggesting apparel for all occasions to all in-coming freshmen. This is followed by a catalog mailing just before school starts.
92. A Buffalo furniture store offers brides-to-be a free personalized Pennsylvania Dutch wedding certificate. Names for the mailing are culled from engagement announcement in local area newspapers.
93. A supermarket mails a weekly shopping list mailing to regular customers. It notes specials which are being featured in the store's newspaper ads and also urges the customers to utilize cents-off coupons featured in newspapers and magazines that week.
94. A New York furniture store added a feature to its Christmas catalog in the form of a bingo game. The numbers were "called" during the store's radio commercials and those bringing a card with a winning column to the store were entitled to special prizes.
95. An Illinois appliance dealer holds a semi-annual combination sale and "clinic." Admission is by ticket only—sent to a customer list. To supplement special prices, the dealer arranges for representatives from his suppliers to be present to answer technical questions.
96. Gelula Jewelers in Atlantic City give away free high school charms to area high school graduates. When they come in, they fill out a form stating what they would like as graduation gifts. Gelula follows this with a direct mail piece to parents telling them what their children have listed as gift choices.
97. A miniature school composition book is used as a format for a back-to-school mailer by a retailer on Long Island.
98. Bateman's of Lexington, Ky. conducted a "Balloon Sale" with savings from 10 to 100%. Percentage discounts were placed inside balloons, which were then inflated and hung from the store ceiling. After a purchase, the customer pricked a balloon and received the discount listed on the slip inside.
99. Baum's in Jacksonville, Fla. promoted slow-moving summer merchandise at cut prices by promoting a "Lemon Day." Served free lemonade all day.

Chapter 10

DEALER-IDENTIFIED DIRECT MAIL

A SUBSTANTIAL portion of today's direct mail volume consists of what is commonly called dealer-identified material. While created and produced by national manufacturers, the mailings bear the imprint of local dealers who handle the manufacturers' products and are usually sent over lists supplied or specified by the dealer. Dealer-identified direct mail ranges from simple envelope stuffers, such as those you find each month accompanying your statements from local stores, to elaborate external house organs, such as *Ford Times*. In between is just about every known direct mail format.

Dealer-identified direct mail is most commonly used in franchised operations or where "big ticket" products are involved. For example, almost every major gasoline refiner makes available direct mail programs for use by local stations and much of the direct mail produced by the automobile manufacturers carries a dealer imprint. Manufacturers of major household appliances have long made available direct mail materials for use by retailers handling their products, as have furniture makers, building supply producers, and garden supply manufacturers.

Role of Dealer-Identified Direct Mail

There are three basic roles for dealer-identified direct mail programs:

1. To provide useful promotion programs in the absence of adequate promotion knowledge on the part of dealers.
2. To coordinate local level promotion with a national advertising program.
3. To provide dealers with promotional material of a higher quality than would be possible if they had to handle the entire promotion program at a local level.

The degree of promotion ability of retailers varies greatly. However, except for giant retail operations with well-staffed advertising departments, odds are that the manufacturer and his advertising agency are much more capable of developing successful direct mail than is the local dealer, even though he has a more intimate knowledge of his customers, prospects, and local conditions. In discussing a promotion program for independent gasoline dealers in *Advertising Requirements,* Thea Flaum observed:

> The man who runs the service station on the corner stands with one foot in auto mechanics and the other in business management. With one hand he pumps gasoline; with the other he counts weekly receipts for what is often a very profitable business. In theory, he is an independent businessman; in fact, he is very closely tied to the fortunes of his franchising oil company. He is both employer and employee, doing white-collar executive duties in a pair of greasy coveralls.

At least to a certain degree, much the same observation can be made of most dealers in most fields.

But no matter how expert a dealer or his staff may be, he cannot offer one promotion essential which many manufacturers find of extreme importance—complete coordination of local promotion with the basic plan developed for national advertising. Since the real payoff for any promotion program must come on the local level, many manufacturers devote a major portion of their promotional dollars to develop carefully coordinated material designed to build a sales-producing path from national advertising, through the consumer, to the sales counter of the local dealer.

But the major value of dealer-identified direct mail, as far as most dealers are concerned, is that it offers promotion pieces of much higher quality than local budgets will normally allow. Few dealers can afford to spend the thousands of dollars required for topflight copywriting, art direction, photography, and illustrations, plus multicolor printing to produce material equal to that featured in most dealer-identified direct mail.

REQUIREMENTS FOR SUCCESSFUL PROGRAMS

To be successful, a dealer-identified direct mail program must meet the majority of the following requirements:

1. The manufacturer's products should constitute a major portion of the retailer's sales or be the type of merchandise which has wide appeal to the majority of a retailer's customers with a better-than-average profit margin. The most successful programs, of course, are those which promote the dealer's main line.

2. The total sales volume which can be expected from the promotion should be high—either in initial sales or through volume achieved by repeat sales over a period of time.
3. The program should be flexible enough to accomplish the manufacturer's objectives yet give each dealer an opportunity to tailor it to fit the personality of his store. This may involve the development of a series of alternate programs or allowing sufficient space on promotion pieces so the dealer can add additional promotional material of his choice.
4. The manufacturer, his distributors, and the dealer should share the cost of the program. Experience has proved dealers give the greatest attention to programs to which they are required to contribute financially. Programs which are offered without charge are usually unsuccessful unless the manufacturer handles all facets of the promotion, including development of the list and the complete mailing.
5. The program, in most cases, should have as its aim not only the sale of the specific merchandise being promoted, but also the development of store traffic and continuing business for the dealer.
6. Sufficient time should be allowed in setting up the program to enable the dealer to plan *all* of his participation in the promotion in advance. This involves not only working the direct mail into his overall promotion schedule, but also developing advertising in other media, stocking additional merchandise required, developing in-store tie-in material, etc. Except where a dealer has no promotion program other than that provided by a single manufacturer, it may require as long as six months to properly set up an effective dealer-identified direct mail promotion.
7. Plan in advance for complete followthrough. Few nationally organized dealer promotion programs ever proceed completely according to the original plan. It is important for representatives of the manufacturer to follow through on all phases of a promotion to make sure no hitches have developed.
8. Make sure everyone who serves as a contact between the manufacturer and the dealer is fully indoctrinated and completely sold on the program. These contact men can make or break a dealer-identified promotion program. Just getting the dealer to agree to participate in the mailings is seldom enough. He must also be briefed on all phases of the promotion, assisted in setting up display materials, aided in briefing store personnel on the product and, most important of all, *kept* sold on the program.
9. Any effective dealer-identified direct mail program should not be considered something unto itself. Adequate steps are required to assure feedback of reaction, results, problems, and other information which will aid in planning future programs. A faulty dealer-identified program not only is a failure in its own right, but creates a dealer attitude which makes it extremely difficult to "sell" future programs.

Objections of Dealers

The most common complaint of dealers is that too much dealer-identified direct mail is "all manufacturer." And, in too many cases, this complaint is completely justified. Many campaigns look like just what they are—direct mail adaptations of magazine ads originally prepared for national promotion purposes.

In evaluating one of its dealer-identified direct mail programs, Richfield Oil Corp. discovered dealers not only complained because the direct mail was "all Richfield" but that it failed to take into consideration the fact that seasonal appeals vary greatly from one area to another and no direct mail program could possibly be successful unless timing is adjusted to local conditions. In addition, most of the Richfield dealers wanted to have their own say about which products and services should receive prime emphasis and they wanted to talk about themselves and their stations. (For details on the unique method Richfield developed to solve this problem, see page 297.

Fear of Duplication

Another major fear of retailers is that there will be embarrassing duplication with promotions of their competitors. A customer who has charge accounts in a number of stores may find himself confronted with identical twins—or, worse yet, triplets or quadruplets—in the form of the same mailings arriving in the same mail from different stores. This fear is, in many cases, highly justified. The author, for example, received five identical multipage Christmas catalogs for a line of radio and television sets in the same mail, each carrying the imprint of a different store. This problem becomes particularly acute when there has been some attempt to personalize the mailings for the individual retailers, such as is the case when covering letters on store letterheads are used.

To overcome this objection, manufacturers use a number of different techniques. The most simple is to schedule mailings so that not more than one is sent into any geographical area each week. A more complicated method is to develop a number of different versions of the mailing piece and allow only one retailer in any area to mail each of the versions. Sure-Fit, a slipcover manufacturer, developed an interesting technique. It prepared four-color folders showing room settings, with the slipcovered furniture in solid colors. Each retailer was allowed to prepare his own copy and to select the patterns to be featured. The patterns were then surprinted in black over the solid color illustrations of the furniture at the same time the copy was added.

Suggestions for Dealers

Philip S. Nelson, sales promotion specialist for Hotpoint, offered these suggestions for dealers who are considering manufacturer-oriented promotions in an *Advertising Requirements* article:

Don't assume that all factory promotions are whipped up in the ivory towers by ex-college boys who never sold retail. They're not. They're developed by a team of experienced managers and specialists well qualified to provide you with programs and materials that can help you sell more goods.

On the other hand, don't assume that factory promotions "as is" can give you exactly what you want in your market. They can't.

The above "don'ts" suggest the positive action that can be taken by retailers in conducting a manufacturer's retail promotion.

1. Do something that will personalize the promotion to your store, your town. Factory promotions aren't panaceas. As is, they can't possibly deliver the results they would if you added your own individual spark. Customers get tired of being wooed impersonally. They want individual attention.
2. Give the factory representative the necessary time and attention to tell you how the promotion works and how it can help you sell more goods.
3. Give the promotion your full support. You'll have to settle for less than good results if you don't enthusiastically back the program for all it's worth, and you will be wasting your time and money if you don't give it your best effort.
4. Get factory help if you need it while the promotion is in progress.
5. Report the results of the promotion to the factory representative so that he can help determine its value to you—and use it as a guide in helping you conduct even more successful future promotions.
6. Keep in mind the value and purpose of factory promotions. Remember, factory promotions are well thought out by a team of marketing and merchandising specialists and as such have more research, time, effort, and product appeal built into them than most retailers could possibly come up with.
7. Finally, adopt an open mind toward factory promotions. Evaluate each one individually but take the time to review it carefully because, for every factory promotion that won't lend itself to your operation, there is probably another that will.

Mechanics of Dealer-Identified Direct Mail

In *Successful Direct Mail Advertising and Selling,* Robert Stone offers this checklist to be followed in setting up and executing a dealer-identified direct mail program:

1. *Establish objective and theme:* There must be a major objective to be accomplished and a basic theme in the campaign to attain the objective. This is the research phase. Establish what you want to accomplish: introduction of a new model, increased seasonal business, demonstrations, companion sales of items—whatever it may be. And develop a central theme which will give the campaign continuity. Stay on the track.
2. *Develop appropriate pieces:* Your objective and theme will dictate formats and number of pieces for the campaign. Write the pieces from the dealer's standpoint. Make them local in flavor. Play up the imprints. Remember—dealer identity is of first importance.

3. *Set up mechanics for handling all details for the dealer:* The program won't sell, it won't go over, unless you handle the details. The details include printing, imprinting, and mailing operations, *plus* maintaining mailing lists.
4. *Establish a sensible cost-sharing structure:* Resist the urge to give the campaign away, even if you can afford it. Keep the cost to the dealer as low as possible, but recover a good portion of your cost. If your program is right, the dealer should be expected to pay for the preparation and maintenance of mailing lists, for postage, and for imprinting costs.
5. *Assemble proof of value, if possible:* This can be done in several ways. You may set up a pilot operation, mail the series, and have readership and identity surveys conducted. If you have conducted previous dealer campaigns, you can gather testimonials to prove their value. Or you can gather general statistics about the success of other dealer-identified direct mail programs.
6. *Sell the program through your sales organization:* All the successful dealer direct mail programs are sold through the sales organization. There are too many details involved to do it by mail. And in order to do a good sales job through the sales organization you have to (a) first sell the sales organization on the program's value and (b) provide the sales organization with a kit that will include samples, complete details, and the necessary forms for getting the program underway.[1]

BASIC TYPES OF DEALER-IDENTIFIED DIRECT MAIL

There are three basic types of dealer-identified direct mail, each with many variations:

1. Individual direct mail pieces
2. Complete direct mail campaign
3. A continuous direct mail program

At one time, individual pieces were the most common type of dealer-identified direct mail. In recent years, however, it has become more common to offer either multi-piece campaigns or a continuous month-in, month-out direct mail program. Today, even when individual pieces are offered, most manufacturers suggest they be integrated into a continuing program.

Individual Pieces

The most common type of non-campaign material offered dealers is the envelope stuffer. These stuffers are frequently designed for a multitude of uses, although most frequently the dealer encloses them with monthly statements to charge-account customers. They are also used as package enclosures and to accompany letters prepared by the dealer.

[1]Copyright Prentice-Hall, Inc.

A typical manufacturer's comment about statement stuffers: "One of the biggest problems is the battle within the store for space. The more aggressive merchandise manager or buyer gets the mailing enclosure for his department. To get our material scheduled for use at the proper time, we often have to get on a waiting list months in advance."

Some dealers develop a continuing direct mail program around the stuffers provided by the manufacturers they serve. A Boston art supply store, for example, prepares a monthly newsletter to accompany a variety of stuffers. One or two paragraphs in the newsletter are devoted to the products promoted by each of the stuffers.

Minneapolis-Honeywell Regulator Co., recognizing that heating dealers handling its products also handle a wide variety of other products, offers a mixture of different types of mailing pieces which can be developed into a continuing direct mail campaign on their own or integrated with material supplied by other manufacturers. A typical Honeywell program offered nine different stuffers, five giant post card self-mailers, two folders, and an eight-page booklet. All of the pieces were described in a 22-page manual telling dealers how to develop an effective, business-building direct mail program. The manual urged dealers to take advantage of the direct mail materials offered by all of their suppliers. "Write your manufacturers for a complete list of material available," the manual urged. "Then plan to use it consistently. You've got to get it off the shelves and into the hands of your prospects if you expect it to work for you."

Individual dealer-identified pieces are also developed to accomplish specific objectives. An oil company, for example, asked each of its dealers for a list of 50 prospects and then sent personalized letters over the signature of the company president to each name to "introduce" the prospect to the dealer. Other single mailing pieces include those prepared for seasonal promotions, new product and new dealer announcements, special selling events, etc.

Complete Campaigns

By far the most common type of dealer-identified direct mail is the multi-mailing campaign. Usually, the minimum number of mailings is three, and four- to six-piece campaigns are most common.

A major supplier of dealer-identified campaigns is Eastman Kodak Co., which has campaign packages for camera dealers, audiovisual dealers, and professional photographers—in addition to its own extensive direct mail program. A typical Kodak program is offered camera dealers. The dealer has a choice of three different plans through which he can sponsor annual mailing programs of five pieces. Under the first plan, Kodak delivers imprinted mailers to the dealers who mail them over their own lists. The charge is $1 per hundred mailers. A second plan involves Kodak handling the mailing at a cost of $3.90 per hundred to lists supplied by dealers. At the same cost, Kodak offers a third plan which includes complete preparation of the mailing list for the dealer. Most dealers prefer the third plan. Mailings are seasonal in nature and range from jumbo post cards to a colorful Christmas catalog.

The best known dealer-identified direct mail campaigns are those offered by automobile manufacturers. A wide variety of techniques is used. The majority of automobile mailings is handled by the manufacturer, using automobile registration lists covering each dealer's area. In addition, however, most manufacturers supply dealers with a variety of imprinted direct mail materials which can be sent to lists handpicked by the individual dealers. A typical Oldsmobile new model introduction kit, for example, includes preannouncement and followup post cards, self-mailers promoting the most popular model, jumbo post cards showing new body styles and color choices, post card mailers plugging an Oldsmobile television spectacular plus miniature and jumbo catalogs describing the complete line.

Devoe & Raynolds Campaign

Many dealer-identified campaigns represent complete promotions in themselves. Devoe & Raynolds Co., for example, offered paint dealers a three-mailing package built around special premium offers. Each of the three mailings, which tied in directly with Devoe's national advertising, sought to establish the dealer as the place where amateur painters could get valuable advice, information, and assistance on all matters relating to painting. The premiums—a painter's dropcloth, an angular sash tool, and a paint roller and tray set—were sold to the dealers at well below their regular costs and offered, through the mailings, to homeowners at attractive prices. A merchandising portfolio carried by Devoe salesmen summed up the cost picture for the dealers:

> The premiums included in this campaign are first-quality merchandise such as you normally carry in stock, and are offered to you at prices well below regular dealer costs. Now you can offer your customers a real bargain and at the same time realize a handsome profit on each premium transaction. You can order each of the premiums in quantities up to 50% of the number of names on the mailing list. This enables you to make your program self-liquidating. For example, if you supply your own list for a minimum order

of 250 pieces of each of three mailings, you are offered this campaign at a cooperative price of $67.20. Should you want the maximum number (125) of each of the three premiums, you are able to buy them at the special offer rate and save $67.50 (under the usual dealer prices).

Not only was the dealer able to recoup his entire campaign costs through special discounts on the premiums—all merchandise he regularly carried anyway—but he also made a slight profit when the customer accepted the premium. For example, the dropcloth was offered at a special price of 99 cents with the purchase of a gallon of paint. The dealer's regular wholesale price was 83 cents, but he was able to obtain the cloths for just 69 cents along with the mailing program.

Lees Carpeting

Another example of a complete campaign was developed by Lees to promote its carpeting. The campaign started with a gadget letter featuring a mirror as the "picture of a person who wants to make her home as pretty as a picture." The letter, signed by the manager of a store's rug department or an individual salesman, was sent with a filled-in reply card to a handpicked list of prospects. The mailing offered a booklet on home decorating.

When the requested booklets were mailed, they included a card to be presented to the person signing the original letter. The cards invited recipients to accept the store's "personal sample service" and have carpet samples delivered to them.

Two followup mailings were included in the program. A reminder letter was mailed to all who did not request the booklet within two weeks. There also was a post card with a postage-stamp picture of the salesman attached for use in following up those who requested the decorating booklet. Final step in the campaign was a followup telephone call from the salesman.

An important part of this successful direct mail program was a companion campaign of gadget letters mailed to salesmen at their homes. These mailings explained the plan in detail and told what was expected of individual salesmen. In just one store alone, the campaign produced 100 leads which resulted in 10 immediate sales totaling over $4,000 plus 15 "hot" prospects from whom definite sales were expected within a few months.

Continuous Programs

Oil companies are perhaps the most consistent users of continuous dealer-identified direct mail programs. And in this industry, the leader is Esso, which has won awards annually for the effective direct mail programs developed for its dealers. A typical annual Esso dealer program involves a series of 10 mailing pieces. Most of them feature inexpensive dimensional objects which are used to establish a theme with impact. The 10-month program costs the dealer about $50 per one hundred names and is mailed to either dealer- or company-supplied lists. Esso uses a "Gift of the Month" theme for the program and clearly identifies each mailing with this title. So successful has the program been that few dealers ever think of discontinuing their participation and Esso regularly receives many requests from motorists asking that their names be added to the list.

Most other oil companies also offer their dealers complete direct mail programs, some embarrassingly similar to the highly successful Esso program. Others are quite different. Penzoil Company of California urges oil dealers handling its products to use regular post card mailings, preferably on a monthly basis. It offers both custom-designed cards and full-color picture post cards. Its dealers in 11 western states alone mail over 20 million of these cards every year.

Another type of continuous dealer-identified program is offered druggists by Abbott Laboratories. Abbott has two comprehensive dealer aids services—"Reliable Prescriptions" and "Prescription Specialists." Druggists subscribing to these services get over 200 needed aids—most of which carry no identification for Abbott—free or at less than cost. The aids range from prescription labels, delivery envelopes, and imprinted parcel post labels to signs, business stationery, and book matches. Druggist-identified direct mail plays an important role in each of the twin aid programs. Not only are monthly mailings made for the druggists, but they are also supplied special mailing materials such as cards to welcome new arrivals to their communities and to congratulate new parents; "get well" cards to send customers; newspaper ad reprints and special mailing pieces to be sent to doctors and dentists.

An interesting feature of the Abbott dealer aids programs is that twin services are offered so that more than one druggist in a given trading area can participate without duplication. Nearly 15,000 pharmacies subscribe to the services, which have been in existence since 1927.

External House Organs

Of growing importance in the dealer-identified direct mail field are manufacturer-sponsored external house organs. Almost every automobile manufacturer, for example, offers its dealers a colorful magazine which it can send monthly to customers and prospects. Most famous of these is *Ford Times,* a colorful pocket-size magazine mailed monthly to more than 1½ million motorists.

Chevrolet, too, has a slick external house organ in its dealer-identified direct mail program. Called *Friends,* it is used by more than 90% of all Chevrolet dealers to reach nearly 1½ million buyers of Chevrolet cars and trucks monthly. Chevrolet explains the magazine's role this way:

> The magazine is intended to build and maintain goodwill for Chevrolet dealers, their products and their services and to retain the loyalty of Chevrolet owners. To build and maintain this goodwill and loyalty, more than 1,400,000 copies of the magazine are mailed each month to buyers of new Chevrolet cars and trucks. The names of these owners are kept on the individual dealer's *Friends* magazine list for a period of two years.
>
> Research has shown us that, at the end of the two-year period, these same customers are good prospects for a repeat sale. At that time, Chevrolet direct mail goes to work with sales messages that hit home. *Friends,* however, has an important job during that period of time when a customer is not in the active new-car market. The magazine has the multiple responsibility of thanking the customer for his business, informing and reminding him of his dealer's products and services, and putting him in the mood for future trading with his dealer.

Other major publishers of dealer-identified house organs are building supply manufacturers, oil companies, insurance companies, farm machinery makers, phonograph record producers, and many industrial companies. In addition, some associations and hundreds of commercial publishers make syndicated house organs available for dealer use.

Johnson Motors' "Water Ways"

Another type of house organ was offered by Johnson Motors to its outboard motor dealers. Called *Water Ways,* Johnson's dealer-identified house organ is custom made for each dealer. While editorial material is standard, a dealer can select 13 non-Johnson ads for each issue in addition to two Johnson ads which appear on the inside front and back covers. The dealers select the ads they want from a master catalog in which Johnson has gathered representative ads from every type of manufacturer supplying marine dealers—everything from big outboard cruisers and houseboats to small dinghies and floating flashlights. In addition, a dealer can prepare his own ad for half of the back cover.

Special Techniques

In addition to the more common types of dealer-identified direct mail, there are many special techniques adopted by manufacturers to serve the individual requirements of dealers in a given field.

Pet Milk Co., for example, offered grocers partially completed mimeograph stencils on which they can type in their own "specials-of-the-week" listings and prices. While a space is always included to advertise Pet Milk, the only other copy is an attention-getting illustration and headline. Suggestions for full-page layouts are sent along with the stencils, which are used by about 2,000 small grocers.

One of the most unusual techniques was adopted by Richfield Oil Corp. when it found that less than 10% of its 4,500 gasoline dealers were ordering conventional direct mail campaigns and even fewer were actually using them. Flexibility was the main aim of the new program, which included mailing cards and handbills. While basic formats were established, dealers had complete choice of copy. Nineteen 5- by 7-inch card designs and 16 handbill formats were offered. In addition, Richfield furnished dealers with a 28-page copy book, each page printed on gummed stock and containing 10 to 20 blocks of copy. All the dealer had to do was cut out the blocks of copy which served his needs and desires and then paste them in position on his choice of the basic formats.

A basic program for Richfield dealers included six cards and two handbills. In conjunction with the new program, Richfield came up with an interesting method for list building. Dealers were furnished a special "Guest Book" in which customers and prospects could be registered. It was particularly useful during special promotional events. If the dealer expected to be too busy to register his guests, Richfield assigned a junior salesman for a day or two to handle the task.

Industrial Programs

While most of the dealer-identified direct mail programs discussed above have been from retail fields, many industrial companies also provide such programs for their dealers and distributors. Most frequently these programs are technical or semitechnical in nature and aimed at specific industries and job interests. Unlike the majority of retail programs, industrial dealer-identified material is usually supplied without charge to the dealer or distributor. An *Industrial Marketing* survey of 30 industrial companies offering dealer-identified direct mail programs turned up only one company which regularly charges its distributors for mailing materials, although some charged for imprinting. While mailing material is offered without charge, most companies keep a checkrein on the quantity supplied. One company, for example, reported it limited its distributors to material valued at a maximum of 2% of the distributor's annual purchases from the company.

In the majority of cases, mailing of industrial dealer-identified material is handled by the individual dealers and distributors, although there is a trend toward greater centralized mailing. The majority of dealers and distributors in the industrial field are very secretive about their mailing lists and seldom make them available to the manufacturers they represent. Thus, when a manufacturer wants to handle the mailing, he usually must develop the lists himself.

A variety of techniques is used to make sure materials actually get mailed. One company, for example, requires its distributors to insert a special address in its file of address plates. Only when one piece is received at this address is the dealer's quantity of the following mailing piece shipped to him. Other companies require regular reports from field representatives on inventories of direct mail material on hand in dealers' and distributors' stockrooms.

COOPERATIVE ADVERTISING PLANS

Many companies have specific cooperative advertising plans for handling costs of all dealer-identified advertising. While the majority of such plans usually originate with newspaper advertising, many also include direct mail. According to a study by the National Retail Merchants Association, two of every five department stores report at least half of their direct mail costs are paid by the manufacturers whose lines they handle. A comprehensive study by Harvey R. Cook for *Printers' Ink,* covering home appliance and equipment manufacturers, indicated that about half of the companies with cooperative advertising plans included direct mail in addition to other media. Methods for handling direct mail varied considerably, however:

> While 12 of the 25 companies include direct mail and other literature in their cooperative advertising plans, participation methods vary. Two companies permit costs of addressing and postage as well as the literature itself to be charged to cooperative funds. Another company has a price list which specifies items chargeable at 50% or 100%. All cost sharing applies only to literature prepared by the national advertiser since it is generally agreed that locally prepared materials are not acceptable.

A few companies refer to literature only to explain that the factory already has shared by absorbing part of the cost before announcing its availability at less than actual cost. Frequently, the dealer's price is the rerun cost.

One company explains: "A nominal charge will be made for printed sales aids, such as envelope stuffers, brochures, and catalogs. This charge is not subject to rebate against the distributor's cooperative reserve account. Prices for such are based on a small percentage of actual costs, constituting our share of the expense."

Methods for Compensation

There are three basic methods of compensating the dealers and distributors for cooperative advertising:

1. *Fixed dollars per unit*—Under this method, the dealer or distributor is allowed a specified amount of cooperative advertising money for each unit of the product purchased.
2. *Lump sum*—Some manufacturers allocate a specific amount of money for all cooperative advertising. This budgeted amount is then divided on proportionately equal terms between all dealers and/or distributors wishing to participate in a cooperative advertising program.
3. *Percentage of price*—The most commonly used method, however, is where cooperative advertising funds are established on the basis of a percentage of either the factory price or the suggested retail selling price. Allocations frequently run between 1% and 5% of the price.

In most cases, regardless of the basis of compensation used, no cooperative payments are made until tangible evidence of advertising has been presented by the dealer or distributor to be compensated. In the case of direct mail, intent may become more important than evidence of accomplished advertising since most programs involve ordering mailing materials from the manufacturer. Cooperative allowances may be drawn upon when direct mail materials are ordered for use, rather than the dealer paying the manufacturer for his mailing pieces and then asking for a portion of the money to be returned when he presents evidence that the materials have actually been mailed.

In most cooperative advertising programs, the usual split of costs is on a 50-50 basis. In most cases, this means the manufacturer pays 50% of the cost, while the dealer pays the remaining 50%. In other cases, however, the manufacturer pays 25% and the distributor pays 25%, while the dealer is still responsible for half of the cost. Another common plan is a three-way split with manufacturer, distributor, and dealer each paying one-third of the cost.

Splitting Direct Mail Cost

When it comes to cooperative direct mail programs, the cost-accounting frequently becomes more complicated. Unlike newspaper, broadcast, outdoor, or transportation advertising, where a single bill is presented from the medium involved for all of the advertising costs, direct mail advertising frequently involves a number of separate bills. For example, there are the original cost of the mailing pieces, imprinting with the dealers' names, inserting, addressing, and postage. Each of these may be billed separately.

To simplify the procedure, many manufacturers permit cooperative advertising allowances to cover only one phase of a direct mail program. A common procedure is for the manufacturer to figure that mailing materials represent one-half of the cost of a direct mail program (usually including imprinting) and that handling, addressing, and postage represent the second half. Thus, cooperative advertising programs involving a 50-50 split, translated into direct mail expenditures, mean that the manufacturer supplies the materials and collects for them from the cooperative advertising funds, while the dealer pays all other costs out of his own pocket.

This procedure, of course, has many variations. In a number of cases, all direct mail materials are given a price and then may be purchased as needed with cooperative advertising funds. Where the manfacturer handles all facets of a mailing program, prices of direct mail materials usually include lists, addressing, handling, and postage.

Controlling Dealer Advertising

Just having a cooperative advertising program is no assurance that dealers and distributors will do a good job of advertising. Harvey Cook's study for *Printers' Ink* included research on the extent to which dealers used the cooperative advertising moneys allocated for them. Of the 25 manufacturers involved, only three reported that all of their dealers used all of the funds allocated for them, while seven reported that less than 25% of the dealers took full advantage of these cooperative advertising funds. Eleven of the manufacturers reported that half of their dealers used full allowances, seven said that 75% of their dealers took full advantage of the funds, and the other five estimated that 25% used their complete allowances.

But getting dealers to use available funds is only part of the job of controlling cooperative programs. In the case of direct mail, there is always the problem that dealers will order plenty of mailing materials and then just let them gather dust on their shelves. Since a time limit is commonly placed on cooperative advertising funds, it is not uncommon for a dealer to suddenly find himself nearing the deadline with no plans for utilizing the remainder of his cooperative allowance. In such a case, it is a simple matter just to order a quantity of direct mail materials to use up the remaining funds, with no specific plans for the utilization of these materials. Thus, many companies include some kind of specific control to make sure their materials actually get into the mails. One method is to issue a memorandum invoice for all direct mail material supplied to a dealer. It can be canceled with cooperative advertising funds, but only after evidence of mailing has been received. Other companies depend upon their field representatives to maintain personal control.

Robinson-Patman Act

In developing any kind of dealer-identified direct mail program, it is important to remember restrictions imposed by the Robinson-Patman Act, which *prohibits any payment to a customer, in consideration for any services, unless such payment is available on proportionally equal terms to all other customers competing in the distribution of such products.* The act also specifies it is *unlawful for a seller to furnish services and facilities to one purchaser that are not accorded to all purchasers on proportionally equal terms.* The term "proportionally equal" is often confusing. In the Beckman-Engle-Buzzell textbook on *Wholesaling,* this explanation is given[2]:

> The term "proportionally equal" has generally been interpreted by the courts as meaning a uniform allowance of a specified percentage of purchases or a stated amount per physical unit to all customers who are willing to perform a service and to let all customers know of such payments in order to give them the opportunity to take advantage of them by showing to the seller that they are willing and able to furnish the same services and facilities as those furnished by the favored customers.

Role of the Distributor

In a number of industries, the distributor plays a vital role in the development and handling of dealer-identified direct mail programs. This is particularly true where almost all contact with the retailer is through the distributor salesman. For the manufacturer, this presents a special problem. This was clearly defined in the *Wholesaling* textbook:

> When a wholesaler handles a wide variety of products, there is an obvious need to be selective in cooperating with suppliers. A number of criteria may be used in choosing the lines to which emphasis is to be given. One factor is *sales volume,* which is determined through a quantitative analysis of sales. A second criterion is the *profitability* of the line to the wholesaler. The supplier's *distribution policies* may be taken into account,

[2]Theodore N. Beckman, Nathaniel H. Engle, Robert D. Buzzell, *Wholesaling.* Third edition, copyright 1959, The Ronald Press Company.

preference being given to those who sell only to wholesalers. On the basis of these and other considerations, the wholesaler may select a limited number of "key lines" and give them full support. Promotional efforts by other suppliers may be given a complete "cold shoulder" or treated with relative indifference.

Some of the more aggressive wholesalers actually take the initiative in coordinating their sales and advertising efforts with those of their suppliers. An outstanding example is McKesson & Robbins Inc., a nationwide chain of drug wholesale houses. This firm organizes its efforts around a "weekly sales calendar" consisting of promotional plans, week by week, for a six-month period. The company may approach certain suppliers with a proposed campaign, offering its own cooperation in exchange for consumer advertising support by the manufacturer.

Distributors often take the responsibility for conducting cooperative advertising programs for the dealers they serve. This is particularly true in the case of distributors sponsoring "voluntary chains" such as those made up of independent grocers. Central buying offices, too, often serve the retailers they represent in preparing or coordinating various types of direct mail. A common type of direct mail prepared by these central buying offices is the Christmas catalog used by many of the small and medium-size department stores.

Insert-Mailers

Because of the increasing costs of postage, many national manufacturers have given increased attention to utilizing a combination of newspaper inserts in major markets, with the same piece converted for direct mail use in other markets. The most common format is the gravure-printed newspaper tabloid. The uses for such a piece and how it is integrated into a total merchandising program was described in a booklet prepared by the author for dealers handling GTE-Sylvania television and stereo sets:[3]

Remember the old riddle: What's black and white and "red" all over?

Answer: A Newspaper.

But it ain't necessarily so.

It has been estimated that the average American is exposed to not less than 1,500 promotional messages every waking day of his life—some, of course, are never seen or heard, others fail to communicate . . . and only a scant handful succeed in both capturing attention and delivering a message.

It's easy to test for yourself. Pick up any newspaper you're ready to discard. Go back through it and count every ad you read and make a separate count of every ad you didn't read. Unless you're the world's champion reader of newspaper ads, chances are your list of "didn't read" is many lines longer than the ones you did read.

[3]"The Fine Art of Wooing Customers to Your Store" by Richard S. Hodgson. GTE-Sylvania, Batavia, N. Y. 1971.

This doesn't mean that newspaper advertising is of small value. Far from it. If you look at the list of ads you read, chances are you'll find the majority of them were for products and services you are currently thinking about buying. (Or ones you've just bought. Funny thing. A lot of people spend more time reading ads about the kind of product they just bought. Guess they just want to assure themselves they made the right buying decision.)

But what can you do to increase the odds of gaining attention and delivering your message to potential buyers . . . and possibly interest those who haven't yet realized they should be in the market for what you're trying to sell? One of today's best answers is the colorful pre-printed insert/mailer.

What Is It?

Although it may come in any number of different styles and sizes, the most common insert/mailer is a multiple-page tabloid. A typical size is eight pages, each approximately 11 by 13 inches. Such pieces are generally printed by manufacturers in large quantities, then imprinted with dealers' names and addresses plus the masthead of the newspaper into which it will be inserted or a mailing indicia if it is to be used as direct mail advertising.

The Economics

Because the manufacturer pays the basic costs for art, copy, typesetting, plates and other preliminary costs and then takes advantage of the economics of long printing runs, the cost per insert/mailer for each dealer represents one of the best buys available in retail advertising today. And since newspapers charge less per page for inserting furnished material than they do for their regular newspaper pages, the total cost is a real bargain.

But Does It Work?

Since pre-printed newspaper inserts are no longer anything new, you might suspect they get about the same attention as a regular newspaper ad. Not so, however. Old hat or not, the insert continues to work some powerful magic when it comes to attracting readers' attention and delivering a message.

Eastman Kodak, for example, inserted a tabloid in newspapers throughout the country. A research study in three major markets showed that not only did 61% of the people surveyed remember seeing the tabloid but 30% said the tabloid had actually influenced their Christmas gift buying plans. Even more dramatic is the case of a manufacturer of appliances who used an insert. Research showed that 83% of the subscribers of the newspapers containing the insert remembered seeing it and 77% of those who considered themselves prospects for the product advertised reported reading it. Even 57% of those who didn't consider themselves in the market for the products said they read one or more pages of the insert.

Whenever other research projects are conducted, the results are pretty much the same. Among the most consistent users of insert/mailers are automobile manufacturers and year after year they report outstanding readership of this type of advertising. A Chrysler insert, for example, attracted 75% of all men and 76% of all women readers of newspapers in which it was included. Another insert by Pontiac drew the attention of 79% of all readers and 68% of those interviewed said they wished other advertisers would present their products in a similar fashion.

How About Direct Mail?

A pre-printed insert/mailer also makes an excellent direct mail piece. While postage rates have been increasing, it may turn out that the added cost for this selective type of distribution pays for itself in reaching your best potential customers. With direct mail, you have an opportunity to select the specific market segment or individuals most valuable to you. And in most cases, you'll find your insert/mailer gets greater attention when it is delivered by mail. Postage statistics show that the typical home receives an average of only one piece of advertising mail per day. Thus, it will be pretty hard to overlook your colorful message when it arrives. And readership studies show that advertising mail is read and acted upon.

Mailing Lists

There are lots of sources for effective mailing lists. For a starter, try your own customer lists. Next best are the neighbors of your customers. Chances are a local mailing service can provide a complete list to meet your needs.

To make the entire mailing procedure as simple as possible, most manufacturers arrange with a national mailing service to handle the entire job for their dealers. All the dealer has to do is specify the street boundaries and/or zip codes and an insert/mailer with his imprint and mailing indicia is sent to every home in the area chosen.

Circles of Convenience

If you want to make your list selection most effective, try a simple technique which has worked effectively for other retailers. It's called the "Circles of Convenience" technique. Just get a large-scale map of your marketing area and mark on it the homes of your most recent customers. Chances are you'll find the majority tend to live in certain areas and not in a concentric circle around your store. Convenience and habit in shopping seems to draw the majority of people in a certain direction. You'll find your best prospects for additional business are located in the other homes within those areas where your present customers live. Thus, you'll get maximum results from direct mail advertising sent into those select areas rather than by mailing to everyone in an entire area within so many miles of your store.

The Unbroken Chain

Manufacturers spend thousands of dollars each month in national media to arouse the interest of Americans in their products. Unfortunately, it is seldom possible to tell every reader and viewer of those ads that your store is the place to go to buy such products. But you can take advantage of the millions of dollars which have been invested in national advertising by using local advertising directed to your own prospects and prominently displaying your name and address as the place to buy. The insert/mailer is the logical first step.

Most manufacturers' insert/mailers are closely related to their national advertising programs. But with one major difference—the emphasis is placed on your store as the local source from which to buy. By seeing that imprinted insert/mailers get into the hands of your potential customers you can parlay the manufacturers' national advertising investment into dollars in your own cash registers.

The Next Link

The insert/mailer can be the "big gun" in your store's advertising but it can do only part of the job of drawing customers into your store and focusing their attention on specific merchandise. It simply continues the job the manufacturer began for you with magazine and television advertising.

The next link in the chain toward making a sale is to make sure your store is identified as the one which distributed the insert/mailer. That's why manufacturers make available colorful window posters and other display material which is directly related to the design of their insert/mailers. The passerby seeing such material will be reminded your's is the place that has something special to offer.

Keep 'Em Coming

And once you've drawn them inside your door, don't miss the opportunity to concentrate their attention on featured merchandise. By utilizing coordinated display material you can capitalize on the interest you originally generated through the insert/mailer. This can prove particularly helpful when sales personnel are busy or in the case of the timid buyer who "just wants to browse."

And Keep Reminding Them

Every buyer has his own pace. While an insert/mailer can stimulate more than the average amount of interest, it frequently takes repeated reminders to get maximum effect. That's the role of regular newspaper ads and radio and television commercials. By utilizing the same themes originally featured in the insert/mailer, you can build repeated impact which will eventually move slower buyers in your direction.

One Last Thought

Don't overlook the value of an insert/mailer as an in-store merchandising tool. Just seeing it around may remind a prospect of a planned purchase he thought about when he first saw the piece. And placing it in the hands of one that is about to get away may again set in motion the whole chain of events that leads to an eventual sale.

Chapter 11

PROMOTING SERVICES BY DIRECT MAIL

PROMOTING intangible services by mail, while using basically the same techniques used for other types of direct mail, requires many special approaches. There are, in fact, special techniques which are used in mail promotion of every type of service. Since it would be impossible to cover all of the different services which use direct mail, we have selected four representative types of service to indicate the approaches used:

- *Insurance*—representing the promotion of services to large audiences on a nationwide or regional basis.
- *Banking*—representing the promotion of services to large audiences on a local basis.
- *Real Estate*—representing the promotion of services primarily to very select audiences.
- *Advertising Agencies*—representing promotion of services to businessmen.

PROMOTING INSURANCE BY MAIL

There are few businesses which make such extensive use of direct mail in all of its many forms as do the insurance companies. In fact, many insurance companies devote the major share of their advertising budgets to the preparation of direct mail materials—both for company mailings and for use by local agents.

And not only do the insurance companies conduct mammoth direct mail campaigns, but local agents often develop their own personal campaigns either exclusive of or to supplement materials supplied by the companies they represent.

Standard Technique

While every possible format is used to promote insurance, one basic approach has become almost universal. It is the lead-getting mailing based on the offer of some premium. Few prospects for insurance have not received dozens of such mailings. At one time, it was almost standard to offer an imprinted pocket memo book, but today every conceivable type of premium is offered—ranging from reference booklets and road atlases to ballpoint pens, trays of cheese, toys for children, housewares, and even tickets to the opera.

Actually, there are two basic types of premium mailings. The first, which usually offers a general interest gift, is used primarily for lists of people almost certain to be logical prospects. The second, which concentrates on a premium of specific interest, is used to weed prospects from lists of unknown potential. The second type of premium mailing is most frequently used for specialized types of insurance. For example, a company or agent wishing to promote homeowners' policies might offer a booklet which will help the prospect evaluate his home insurance program or if the aim is to sell special travel policies to executives, the offer might be for an atlas of principal city streets.

In most cases, the objective is to bring about a person-to-person contact between the insurance agent and a prospect. Thus, the premium is usually distributed in person. However, the technique has been so widely used that many people refuse to respond—just because they do not want to see another insurance agent. So several companies make a specific point of the fact that "no salesman will call" and use the premium to initiate a recognition of the company so followup mailings will receive special attention.

Huge Volume

The usual format of this "standard technique" is simply a letter and reply card. Many of the major insurance companies prefer the Reply-O-Letter type of format, which consists of a letterhead with a pocket at the top and a die-cut opening so a reply card inserted in the pocket will appear in the normal address position on the letter and also show through a window in the mailing envelope. Millions of these letters are mailed annually. The New York Life Insurance Co., for example, supplies its agents with more than seven million Reply-O-Letters annually. And this is just a part of the company's direct mail program. Another million other direct mail pieces are also prepared for agent use.

Charles R. Corcoran, vice president of The Equitable Life Assurance Society of the United States, reports that his company mails some 18 million sales letters in a typical year—plus between two and three million additional direct mail pieces.

With such a huge volume of insurance mailings made annually, one might suspect returns would be at the low end of the scale. But prospects do respond—often in almost astonishing numbers. The Mutual Life Insurance Company of New York, for example, reports a response of 15 to 20% is not at all unusual for its premium-offering letters.

Higher Sales Through Direct Mail

Henry Hoke reported a case history, in "How to Think About Readership of Direct Mail," which clearly shows the value of direct mail promotion to an insurance company:

> The New England Mutual Life Insurance Co. has a continuing program of direct mail effort. First, there is a constant prodding of the underwriters in the field to sell them the idea of using the shortest distance between two strangers; that is, the mail. And second, the streamlined series of 27 letters which are at the salesmen's disposal to help them sell more life insurance. On the average, the individual agents furnish about 25 names a week, typed on cards. The letters are mailed from the home office. In one year, New England Mutual mailed 163,000 letters for their agents and received 15,704 replies. The average percentage of return on the entire program was 9.2%. One letter pulled as high as 19.7%. The lowest percentage on any one letter was 5.6%. But much more important than the percentage of response, are the figures on the effectiveness of the letters in terms of business written. Every dollar put into direct mail by the company and/or the agents returned $27 in commissions to the agents. The most significant statistical figure is that the average size policy sold as the result of a direct mail lead amounted to $7,710 contrasted with the average for the company on all business amounting to $5,716. That is, where the prospect was "softened" in advance by direct mail, the average sale was $2,000 higher than was the case where no direct mail was used.

Mailings Procedures

The mechanics of handling lead-producing programs in the insurance field varies considerably from company to company. In some cases the local agent pretty much controls everything except the original preparation of material, while in other cases the company tries to leave as little as possible to men on the local level. The Provident Mutual Life Insurance Co., for example, has a basic seven-step procedure which involves only two functions on the part of the salesman—to provide names to whom mailings are sent and to follow up inquiries which result from the mailings. The program's seven steps are:

1. Each local agent furnishes the home office a list of prospects.
2. Lists are coded, entered in a ledger, and then forwarded to a lettershop for processing.
3. The lettershop is allowed three days to prepare personalized letters and envelopes, which are then returned to the home office for checking.
4. Reply cards to accompany each letter are coded to identify the agent submitting the name. Then the home office places the letters into the mail.
5. Replies are returned to the home office, where they are checked against the lists submitted by agents. Gift items are immediately personalized.
6. Within a maximum of four days, the gift is sent to the agent for delivery. Lead cards containing all information furnished by the prospect are typed in triplicate. The agent receives the original copy. A second copy goes to the general agent and the third is filed at the home office.
7. Each day, the home office compares all life insurance application cards received from agents with the file of lead cards to determine which sales can be traced to the direct mail program.

Agent-Controlled Programs

Liberty Mutual Insurance Co. developed a program which represents a middle ground between the type of program used by Provident Mutual and programs which involve simply providing the agent with direct mail materials which he uses in programs handled entirely at the local level. Liberty's program had ten basic steps:

1. Each salesman prepares a mailing list of 1,000 names—his "prospect bank."
2. Lists are sent to the home office on a special form provided by the company.
3. Names are forwarded to a lettershop which prepares address plates.
4. Five basic mailing pieces are used in the campaign, so the lettershop addresses five sets of envelopes, inserts the letters and matching reply cards, affixes postage, and then ships the entire lot of 5,000 pieces to the salesman, ready for local mailing.
5. The lettershop also runs the address list on expiration cards, which are sent to the salesman to serve as his permanent record, and as the basis of a cold prospecting list once the mailing series is completed.
6. Each Monday, for five weeks, the salesman releases one of the mailings. As reply cards are returned to the salesman's office, he culls his list by removing and setting aside the remaining mailing pieces for all prospects replying—so they won't receive additional mailings before the salesman has a chance to make his call.
7. While the mailing program is in progress, each salesman keeps a record of returns from each mailing. (Each of the five reply cards has readily identifiable art to identify the letter with which it was mailed.)
8. At the end of the mailing series, and after all prospects who returned cards had been contacted, the salesman submits a record of results, using a special form which quickly shows immediate results of the campaign.

9. Once inquiries have been followed up, salesmen start contacting other names in their individual "prospect banks," all of whom have been preconditioned by the mailing series, but didn't send in a reply card.
10. After 100 such cold calls have been made, a second report form is submitted to the home office to aid in evaluating the total effect of the mailing program.

After an initial test of the mailing program, Liberty informed its salesmen: "Although replies for any given mailing will vary according to local conditions, from a list of 1,000 carefully picked names, checked for accuracy, the series should bring in 150 to 200 inquiries, possibly more. By following up prospects who did not send back reply cards, an equal number of good prospects should come to light."

Locally Developed Programs

A typical example of how local agents use materials supplied by their companies in developing their own direct mail programs was explained by Alfred H. Lies, Jr., of the New York Life Insurance Co., in *The Reporter of Direct Mail Advertising:*

> Agent Y, a consistent user of direct mail, takes the company's tips to heart: he selects his prospects and mails consistently.
>
> Agent Y carefully prepares a select list of prospects. With the help of his wife or secretary he screens his hometown newspaper for such possible insurance sales items as recent promotions, new owners, births, and the opening of new businesses or professional establishments in the area.
>
> After gathering perhaps 100 of these qualified prospects in a specific category, he selects an appropriate direct mail letter offering a specific appeal aimed at each prospect's possible insurance need. For example, he selects a letter which mentions a plan that will guarantee funds for the future college education of a new-born child and sends it to new parents, or a mortgage cancellation plan letter for the new homeowners in town.
>
> Next he spaces his mailings, perhaps sending out 25 a week to certain geographical areas. Upon receiving the replies, he phones for appointments making sure to schedule them so as not to conflict with his other sales calls. And, as a usual practice, he also calls on nonrepliers. He knows that because a person does not reply, doesn't necessarily mean a complete rejection of his appeal. It could be he didn't get the letter, misplaced the reply card, or forgot to mail it, etc. Experience tells him that a lot of extra business is received through contacting nonrepliers. He repeats the above process consistently. It's a regular prospecting method that he follows throughout the entire year.
>
> Finally, at the end of the year he prepares for himself a balance sheet showing the total and type of letters he mailed for the year, how many replies he received, the interviews he obtained, total number of sales and his total commissions, and he balances the total commission figure against his total mailing costs to determine the return on his investment for the year.

On the average, a consistent user of direct mail can probably figure that at least 25% of his total sales volume for the year can be directly attributed to his use of direct mail.

Noncompany Programs

Some agents—particularly those who represent more than one insurance company—feel quite strongly that company-prepared direct mail programs are far less satisfactory than those prepared at the local level and tailored to the individual agent's personality. One local insurance agency executive, Edward Lagron, explained it this way in a *The Reporter of Direct Mail Advertising* article:

> The material we were getting (for free) from the companies might win first award as beautifully designed mailing pieces, but they did not have what the agent needed. In the first place, they were too "nicey-nice"—they didn't talk like we talked—there was far too much copy and no appetite appeal. They were much too formal and as cold as a hot water bottle on a winter morning. They played up the company and bragged about it like the only rooster in the henhouse, but the average customer doesn't give a "tinker's darn" about the company. It is the agent that he has to know and trust. It became quite obvious to us that these direct mail pieces had been designed by some advertising genius on Madison Avenue, and in order to get his layout and copy "O.K.'d" by his client, he had lavishly fed his client's ego with a lot of incongruous four-syllable superlatives. Once we found out what was derailing our train, it was but a simple matter to put enough ballast on the roadbed, so that it would carry our fast, streamlined sales message.
>
> We made up some form letters in which we used most of the companies' enclosures—but our letters were very informal, very short, and interposed generously with slang. Our nonprofessional, amateurish letters might have caused intellectual advertising giants in their "ivory towers" to tear their hair and scream to the high heavens, "You can't do that—it's terrible!"
>
> The strange thing about it—the prospects apparently were as dumb as we were; they read and they bought.

Abbott P. Smith, in "How to Sell Intangibles,"[1] points out that there is a logical difference between the kind of direct mail sent out from a home office and that sent out from a local office over a salesman's own signature. The latter, he suggests, should be "simple, informal, friendly, and somewhat personal. Try to develop a personality for your business and the way you handle it. If you use repeated mailings, develop both a format and a style that will identify your letters. Build a theme for your business." Mr. Smith's "Golden Rule of Pre-Approach":

> *"Talk or write to others the way you would like them to talk or write to you under the same circumstances."*

[1]Copyright Prentice-Hall, Inc.

Many local insurance salesmen use highly effective showmanship mailings to supplement the materials supplied by their companies. One salesman makes particularly effective use of newspaper clippings which have only a remote relationship to those to whom he mails them. He has a clipping service send him stories of home fires throughout his state. He then mails them to prospects for fire insurance with his business card and the simple little note: "This could happen to you." This technique has been so successful he has sold over 75% of the homeowners in his town of 15,000 some fire insurance.

Equitable Life provides its agents with a special folder for use in mailings to new homeowners. The salesman takes a picture of the new home and then inserts it in the special card before mailing. Other companies supply their agents with special mailing pieces designed to be used for forwarding newspaper clippings about the recipient.

Prospecting, Not Selling

All of these approaches to insurance direct mail have one important factor in common—they are designed not to *sell* insurance but to uncover good prospects at a time when they can be sold by an insurance salesman. With the exception of companies who depend primarily on mail order for the bulk of their sales, most insurance direct mail does little to try to get a prospect to make up his mind on the basis of material included in the mailing. All they hope to do is to open the prospect's mind and to get him to take some sort of action to let a salesman know that his mind has at least been opened a crack and thus may be more responsive than had he been contacted without some sort of conditioning.

Sales authority Abbott P. Smith makes these comments about preapproach mailing pieces:

> Many companies provide their salesmen with direct mail from their home office that introduces the subject and, in most cases, "threatens" the prospect with a visitation from a salesman. Many such letters are sent with no thought of getting a response. The purpose of such letters, therefore, is to prepare the ground, to plant the seed of an idea, and to break the ice for the salesman. But unless the salesman calls *within a reasonable time* after such pieces are received they are of very little benefit to him. Much of this mail goes to waste not only because the salesman does not follow the material up at all, but because he does not follow it up well.

PROMOTING BANKING AND FINANCIAL SERVICES

There was a day—not too long ago—when many bankers considered it beneath their dignity to engage in any form of advertising—particularly direct mail. Some condescended to run highly institutional ads in local newspapers, usually featuring the bank clock or the official seal, but out-and-out promotion of banking services was strictly frowned upon.

Today, however, there has been a drastic about-face. The 13,000-plus commercial banks in the United States not only spend upward of $200 million annually for advertising (compared with less than $20 million in 1946), but regularly come up with some of the most unusual and elaborate promotion schemes witnessed at the local level. More than anything else, the amazing growth of savings and loan associations has probably been responsible for shaking the formerly stodgy banker out of his complacency. During the decade of the 1950's, for example, savings and loan associations boosted their percentage of the aggregate United States savings from only 10% to 25%. And, at the same time, other competitors for the savings of the American public —including mutual funds, credit unions, and life insurance—also made inroads on the banks.

Savings and loan associations, from their very beginning, made effective use of advertising, including many different forms of direct mail, and pointed the way for advertising-inexperienced bankers.

Volume of Direct Mail

Since a majority of bankers do not include the cost of many types of mailings they use regularly in their advertising budgets, it is difficult to determine just how extensive banking direct mail has become. Most published statistics indicate approximately 25% of the total annual advertising expenditure of banks is allocated for direct mail. But a very high percentage of the nation's banks do not include statement stuffers, annual reports to stockholders, market research and public relations mailings, personalized letter programs, and other basic direct mail items in their ad budgets. If all of these items were considered, it is likely the total annual direct mail expenditure by banks would exceed $100 million.

One of the most extensive users of direct mail is the nation's largest bank, California's Bank of America. While it reports an annual advertising expenditure of $5 million, it doesn't include a single penny for direct mail in its media breakdown.

Role of Direct Mail

Banking, by its very nature, is a highly personalized business. Thus, it is only natural direct mail should represent the primary advertising medium for bankers. C. Arthur Hemminger of St. Louis' First National Bank, in a Direct Mail Day speech, explained:

> To provide the amount of manpower necessary to maintain constant personal contact with every customer and prospect is obviously impossible. Therefore, the banks must depend on the mails to introduce new services to present customers, to seek new customers, to establish and maintain institutional character, to explain changes in services and policies, and to carry on 1,001 other necessary communication chores that cannot possibly be done on a person-to-person basis.
>
> A high percentage of our present customers, as well as the noncustomers who make up our market, do not use the services we have to offer for the good and sufficient reason that they don't understand the nature of these services or their potential benefits. Thus, direct mail that does not attempt to argue with the prospect but performs a service for him instead is likely to hit the mark.

Typical Bank Mailings

Mr. Hemminger went on to outline some of the many service copy mailings used by his bank. They ranged from a "1003 Household Hints" booklet to very factual material on government securities, foreign exchange rates, and regulations governing the use of commercial banks as depositaries for withheld taxes. One of the First National's more popular direct mail items is a series, "Banking for Busy Women," an informative publication with but a small amount of sell included. Other bank mailings include:

- "Why Making Out Your Own Deposit Ticket Makes Good Sense"—a completely informational piece which helps tellers deal with people who insist on having their tickets made out for them.
- "How to Balance Your Checking Account"—a helpful guide aimed at reducing the always-serious overdraft problem.
- "Why Service Charges?" helps save a lot of time that otherwise might be spent in arguments.
- Institutional mailings, such as baseball and opera schedules, forms for recording essential facts about your estate and personal documents, and city maps for newcomers.

The First National even used an extensive direct mail program to substitute for the flamboyant and expensive open houses, parties, and clambakes usually associated with a centennial celebration. To mark its 100th anniversary in 1956, the bank prepared an 84-page booklet telling the history of St. Louis and another booklet describing "The New First," which called attention to the bank's newly remodeled quarters. Other direct mail uses include market research, list cleaning, reactivation of dormant accounts, getting reactions to new services, welcoming newcomers, getting satisfied customers to recommend prospects, merchandising space advertising, and statement enclosures.

Themes for Promotion

According to a survey by the American Bankers Assn., savings accounts represent the most common theme for bank promotion, with regular checking accounts a close second. Of 3,043 banks reporting, the following themes were most common (figures in parentheses represent the number of banks reporting plans to give first, second, or third emphasis to each theme): Savings (2,467), regular checking (2,216), auto loans (1,345), personal loans (503), bank-by-mail (463), institutional (427), special checking (344), repair loans (311), farm production loans (304), drive-in banking (278), mortgage loans (246), safe deposit (243), trust service (163), business loans (120), farm equipment loans (109), free parking (97), home appliance loans (92), educational (72), night depository (62), life insurance loans (35), and correspondent banking (14).

Statement Stuffers

Few banks today overlook the opportunity to sell additional services to their checking account customers. Nearly every monthly bank statement is accompanied by at least one slip or folder promoting some bank service. While many banks prepare their own stuffers, the majority take advantage of a wide variety of syndicated services available. In addition, many banks imprint promotional messages on their statement envelopes and sometimes even on the backs of the statements themselves.

One type of statement stuffer which seems to be peculiar to banks is the enclosure of special letters with statements on a regular or frequent basis. Others include house organs, newsletters, monthly calendars, and even novelties.

A 12-month analysis of statement stuffers from one bank showed these enclosures:

- An announcement of a new automated accounting procedure
- A letter urging the purchase of government savings bonds
- A folder promoting a new automatic savings plan
- A folder listing checking account services

- Four quarterly calendars with tear-off reply cards offering information on various special services
- A promotion for the Care food crusade
- A blotter with a message promoting a daily radio show sponsored by the bank
- A broadside promoting the full range of services offered
- A sight draft to be used to transfer a savings account from some other institution to the bank. A tear-off stub described how to transfer such savings accounts.

Other Bank Direct Mail

While statement stuffers represent the most universal form of direct mail used by banks, every other format sooner or later finds its way into banking promotions. Some of the mailings used by banks include:

Federal Reserve Bank of Philadelphia developed a color cartoon booklet, "Interested in Interest Rates?" to meet requests of schoolteachers and others seeking readable, teachable explanations of the monetary system.

Mechanics Bank of Richmond, California, mailed 10,000 pillboxes in large envelopes to homes in its banking area. Each box had a prescription label reading, "Rx for Budget Troubles. Open pill and read remedy, then get your free ballpoint pen at the Mechanics Bank." A red capsule inside the pillbox contained a strip of paper headed, "Just What the Doctor Ordered!" It "directed" the reader to open an account at the bank.

Citizens State Bank of Lincoln, Nebraska, circulates a monthly eight-page magazine, "The Northeast Citizen," among 7,200 families living around the bank. Contents include stories about bank services and personnel, community news and features.

City National Bank of Council Bluffs, Iowa, mailed a brochure to report on a series of personnel promotions. Included were informal photographs and brief biographies of new officers and directors.

Manufacturers Hanover Trust Co. of New York uses many direct mail pieces to promote its international services, including a "World Time Chart" published twice a year to show differences in time between New York and important cities throughout the world; a booklet showing all holidays observed in the United States and possessions; and a foreign exchange folder, which lists values of more than one hundred foreign currencies.

First National Bank in Dallas regularly circulates news of interest to stockholders, using a "Stockholders News Release" format.

The Bank of Montreal prepared a clever little folder with a teaser message on the front cover reading, "Bet you *never* expected . . . " The sentence was completed inside the folder: ". . . a *sample* from the Bank of Montreal." And there was a real sample—a Canadian penny!

Peoples Bank & Trust Co. of Dayton, Ohio, mailed an empty box with a label reading, "Warning, Contains Troposphere: Within this box is a cross section of the new front door at Peoples Bank. (See inside lid for diagram.)" The message inside the box lid explained: "This box was filled with AIR, carefully chosen from a supply of air to be used in Peoples' new AIR DOOR. (A gently flowing curtain of air keeps the weather out; lets you know how welcome you are.) Come in and 'see' the new door at noon on Friday, November 22, or during banking hours any time. Now *nothing* stands in the way of doing all your banking at Peoples."

The Syracuse Savings Bank of Syracuse, New York, mails a carton of 25 matchbooks to new parents. Each book, in the appropriate pink or blue color, is imprinted either "It's a Boy!" or "It's a Girl!" Inside the flap of the matchbook is a list of bank services. And accompanying the matches is a certificate entitling the new arrival to a brand-new savings account with $1 already credited. This promotion regularly pulls at least one new savings account for each five mailings.

First National Bank of Lebanon, Pennsylvania, mailed out 11,000 four-page, french-fold invitations to its centennial open house celebration plus 500 personal invitations to stockholders, special depositors, correspondent bank personnel, and other VIP's and attracted well over 14,000 visitors. While no special new business solicitations were made during the open house, a special premium offer attracted 492 new accounts with a dollar volume of $192,819.

The New England Trust Company of Boston sends monthly letters to all people using any service or receiving income from trusts under the bank's management. Also in the list are persons of "third-party influence" such as lawyers, accountants, life underwriters, etc.

Citizens Bank & Trust Company of Park Ridge, Illinois, mailed "Mr. Burglar" decals to safe deposit box renters. The decal advises burglars not to bother breaking into the premises, but, rather, if he is looking for valuables, to call at the bank's safe deposit vault.

Savings & Loan Associations

Direct mail used by savings and loan associations pretty much parallels that of banks—with one major exception. Many savings and loan associations place the bulk of their direct mail budget into a regular house organ, which may range in format from an envelope-size folder to a glossy, multipage magazine. Since many of the associations concentrate on building a strong sense of participation on the part of customers, a house organ is a logical approach. But house organs are by no means the only type of direct mail used by savings and loan associations, for from their very beginning they have been extensive users of all forms of advertising.

In its "Advertising Handbook," the National Savings and Loan League points out two basic roles for its member associations' advertising:

> Its ultimate aim should be to bring people into your place of business, now or when they need or want your services. We are retailers of financial services. We have many different services to offer. Some people may be interested in one service, some in another. To a certain extent, we are like retailers of merchandise. If you study department store or specialty store advertising, you will find one thing generally true about it. Such advertising is designed to bring people into the store to see the merchandise. And our advertising should be designed for the same purpose.
>
> There is another thing advertising should *do* and that is to keep customers sold. Notice, if you will, national advertising of automobiles. Is it intended solely to try to get new buyers? Yes, of course, to a certain extent, but it also helps to keep present owners sold on the make of car they drive. Savings and loan advertising may invite new business but it should also help to keep present customers *sold.* Finally, savings and loan advertising needs to inform. It should inform the public of what you are, what you do, why your services are important to the welfare of your community and the people in it.

Pamphlet Checklist

The League's handbook devotes special attention to the variety of pamphlets which are used by savings and loan associations both as direct mail pieces and lobby material. Included in this checklist of suggested material:

The Basic List

Latest financial statement in folder or booklet form

Pamphlet describing savings services

Pamphlet outlining mortgage lending services

Folder or booklet answering questions about account insurance

Folders, pamphlets, or cards describing other standard services of the particular association: Christmas or other savings club accounts, payment of utility bills, money orders, travelers' checks, U. S. Savings Bonds, safe deposit facilities.

Optional Messages

Pamphlet describing mail savings system

Folder on investment accounts (dividends or interest paid by mail)

Pamphlet discussing accounts for children

Folder or booklet on property improvement loans

Brochure discussing renting versus homeowning

Direct Mail Results

In "How to Think About Readership of Direct Mail," Henry Hoke described the excellent results the Ninth Federal Savings & Loan Association of New York City obtains through its consistent direct mail program:

> An economical monthly blotter mailed or distributed to business executives in the trading area resulted in the opening of 501 new traceable accounts with initial deposits of $492,526. Statistics revealed that during a 4½-year period, promotion costs of obtaining new accounts by this method were 56 cents per $100 deposited.
>
> When the Ninth Federal opened a special branch opposite the United Nations, practically all of the promotion was concentrated in direct mail to business firms and individuals in the United Nations area: 1,483 accounts were opened (directly traceable to direct mail) for initial deposits of $574,603. The cost of the entire promotion campaign was $9,238.46. Thus, each dollar spent in promoting the new branch produced $62.19 in savings.
>
> Savings accounts for corporations have been promoted through letters to 1,110 Manhattan accountants. One year, three mailings to this list produced 82 new accounts with initial balances of $301,830.32. The cost, including postage, was under $300. The following year, four mailings produced 75 accounts with initial deposits of $235,346.65. The next year, three mailings brought 77 corporation accounts with $328,448.07 initial deposits. One single letter brought in 58 new accounts and $308,273.99 initial deposits.

PROMOTING REAL ESTATE BY MAIL

Realtors have long made extensive use of direct mail both to sell property and to solicit offerings for sale. Probably no single business makes such extensive use of pinpointed mailings, although many successful realtors also make mass mailings. Comments of three leading realtors, from "How Realtors Sell by Mail,"[2] give a good picture of the use of direct mail in this field:

---

[2]Courtesy of the National Institute of Real Estate Brokers.

John C. Tysen, president, Previews Inc., New York: "Direct mail takes your message direct to your prospect. Real estate brokers operate a local business. They deal with comparatively few prospects and have a comparatively small amount of money to spend on promotion. Hence, the medium which can take a message direct to a prospect should be both economical and effective for brokers."

L. A. Morris, former president, The Keyes Company, Miami: "Classified advertising is a must for any real estate office; but in classified advertising you pay to reach thousands who are not remotely interested in what you have to offer. The Keyes Company has more real estate signs than any other firm in the South; yet a prospect must see one of these signs before the company receives value, and the value varies with the prospect's interest in the particular property. Only mail gives you a *selected* coverage of *actual* prospects who can buy *exactly* what you have to sell. Mail offers you the greatest opportunity to reach logical buyers in the shortest time at the least cost."

John J. Herd, executive vice-president, Albert M. Greenfield & Co. Inc., Philadelphia: "While our surveys show that our cost per inquiry from newspaper advertising is somewhat less than from direct mail, inquiries resulting from direct mail have a far greater sales potential in our larger real estate transactions. We study each property to determine whether a direct mail approach is desirable to reach the prospective buyers most likely to be interested in it. The elaborateness and extent of the mailings are in ratio to the value of the property. In many cases, the cost of these mailings is borne by the seller or lessor of the property. Our mailing program has many indirect results. Sometimes a prospect who does not like the property offered in the mailing becomes interested in other listings. The mailings also have a tremendous public relations impact in paving the way for our salesmen. The prospect who didn't respond directly usually recalls having seen the mailing piece when contacted personally."

Variety of Formats

Realtors use a variety of formats in their direct mail advertising. Personalized letters are particularly effective, but programs also call for everything from simple post card mailings to elaborate, colorful brochures.

Since selling real estate is usually a highly personal business, letters are used extensively. Many realtors pay special attention to goodwill letters, which are much talked about but seldom used by most other businesses. One company makes systematic use of the following goodwill letters:

- Congratulations to about-to-be-wed couples and those with new children (offering help with their home plans).
- Letters of welcome to new arrivals in the city.
- Goodwill messages on special days—not only the traditional holidays but events of special local significance.

- Congratulatory letters when local residents win special honors or are elected to office in local clubs.
- Birthday and anniversary congratulations.
- Special letters commenting on events of concern to property owners (such as new taxes, various types of construction, etc.).
- Sympathy letters in case of misfortune.
- Get-well letters.
- Letters to buyers wishing them and their families happiness in their new homes.
- Similar letters to sellers.
- Letters to prospects who buy elsewhere—thanking them for giving the realtor a chance to be of service.
- Letters thanking a prospect for time given a salesman—usually with some additional reasons he might be interested in a piece of property he has looked at or suggesting other properties to be considered.
- Annual letters thanking customers for their business.
- Letters to arrive on the day a buyer or tenant moves in—offering to be of special service.
- Followup letters on anniversaries of a move-in.
- Letters to introduce newcomers to their neighbors.
- Letters to firms which have scored business successes.
- Letters thanking anyone who has referred any sort of business to the realtor.
- Letters to junior executives who have moved away from the city (on the theory they are likely to live in neighborhoods of other frequently moved executives, who may ask them for advice when being transferred to the area where the junior executive formerly lived).
- Letters keeping sellers posted on progress being made in the sale of their property.

Selling Through Neighbors

One direct mail technique which has worked very well for many realtors is encouraging homeowners to "pick" their new neighbors. Owners of nearby property are sent letters or folders telling about the property available and suggesting that perhaps they may have friends or relatives who have wanted to move into the neighborhood. Such announcements are frequently sent in advance of any advertising.

In addition, many realtors have special cards they send to all neighbors "introducing" purchasers of homes and, of course, letting the neighbors know they have been successful in representing the former owners.

While most realtors use this technique primarily for individual homes, others have found it highly successful in the sale of business and industrial property as well.

Following Up Ads

An almost universal use of direct mail is to follow up for-sale-by-owner classified ads. Many realtors make an initial contact by telephone and then make followup mailings which include detailed information on the services a skilled realtor can provide.

Realtors also use direct mail to follow up their own ads. Often, ads are reprinted on post cards for mailing to lists of known prospects. Other times the ad is supplemented with additional information and illustrations.

Continuing Campaigns

While most realtors use continuing direct mail campaigns primarily for the sale of business and industrial property, some have found the same techniques can be very successful in residential areas where there is a high rate of annual turnover. John B. Swift, Brooklyn realtor, sends out 10,000 pieces of direct mail monthly to owners of homes within an eight-square-mile area around his headquarters. Since the area has a 12% annual turnover rate, the list represents an average annual potential of 1,200 homes to be sold. Through the direct mail promotion, the Swift organization draws over 10% of the available sales in spite of healthy competition from over sixty other realtors.

A number of realtors issue catalogs of available property on a monthly or quarterly basis. In some cases, it is used only for known prospects and to acquaint other realtors with the listings, but frequently it is sent to all homeowners in a given area on the theory they not only may be interested in moving themselves but will show it to friends or relatives who might be interested in moving. Such catalogs are often used for general distribution in small homes developments which have been occupied for three or more years, during which families are likely to have increased in size or have increased in spending power. Catalogs are also a primary direct mail tool of realtors handling resort area properties. Frank W. Prouth of Portland, Maine, for example, mails a quarterly catalog to 1,000 out-of-state prospects and reports resulting sales of over 36% of properties listed.

A variation on the catalog is a regular newsletter-format mailing, frequently with a reply card on which more detailed information can be requested.

Selling Industrial Property

Realtors handling any volume of business or industrial properties must maintain up-to-date lists of prospects and keep them posted on availabilities. Since, in most areas, there is no publication which covers such prospects without a great deal of "waste circulation," direct mail is used almost exclusively for promotion. In addition, most prospect lists contain many names from nonlocal areas. Brown & Brown of Elizabeth, New Jersey, for example, keeps an active prospect list of 5,000 for each of its industrial mailings. Out of each thousand pieces mailed, Brown & Brown averages four bona fide inquiries which result in two sales.

It is not unusual for realtors to send mailings as frequently as once a week to prospects for industrial and business properties. Because of the large unit of sale, mailings are often made for each individual piece of property, although it is more common to combine several listings.

Interestingly enough, million-dollar sales are often accomplished almost on a mail order basis. Of course, there are many complicated details which have to be worked out in any real estate transaction, but it is not uncommon to bring the buyer and seller together on a firm basis solely on the basis of direct mail promotion.

Prestige Brochures

As the unit of sale increases, so does the quality and thoroughness of the promotion material. An interesting example is the attractive booklet Mar Monte Corporation used to promote a California ranch which was taken in trade on an office building. To sell the ranch, Mar Monte had an Oakland advertising agency, Kennedy-Hannaford Inc., produce a two-color, 28-page miniature booklet, featuring outstanding photos giving a scenic view of the ranch plus professionally written copy.

The 5½-inch-square booklet was mailed to a specially compiled list of members of local country clubs, hunt clubs, horsemen's associations, United States and Canadian horse show exhibitors, land developers, and real estate firms throughout the country which cater to blue chip clients. The mailing drew immediate phone calls from all parts of the country, and within 90 days the ranch was sold for $250,000 to some wealthy horse owners from the Midwest.

Prestige brochures are also commonly used in promoting residential developments, particularly those where homes appeal primarily to families in the higher income brackets. The Valhalla real estate development in Seattle, for example, mailed 6,000 copies of a handsome three-color brochure featuring elaborate artwork to a selected list of individuals with incomes of $16,000 or more. In many cases, elaborate brochures are used primarily to answer inquiries generated by an announcement mailing or to follow up qualified prospects who have inspected homes during open-house events.

Residential Checklist

In "How Realtors Sell by Mail," the National Institute of Real Estate Brokers suggests that brochures on residential property should include at least the following 50 features:

1. Listing office
2. Listing salesman
3. Construction
4. Facing of lot
5. Size of lot
6. Zoning
7. Age of house
8. Roof (guarantee, if any)
9. Type of floors
10. Type of windows
11. Description of furniture (if furnished)
12. Size and shape of living room
13. Size and shape of dining room
14. Size and shape of kitchen
15. Description of den or sunroom
16. Number and sizes of bedrooms
17. Number of baths; describe
18. Number and sizes of porches
19. Size of garage (other uses)
20. Carport
21. Basement
22. Utility room
23. Laundry
24. Servants' quarters
25. Type of water heater
26. Type of heat and air conditioning
27. Range
28. Refrigerator
29. Awnings
30. Sprinklers
31. Taxes—city
32. Taxes—county
33. Price
34. Cash wanted; terms available
35. Mortgages—present and available
36. Interest on mortgage
37. Amount of payments
38. Secondary financing available
39. Owner's name
40. Owner's phone
41. Owner's address
42. Owner's availability
43. Easiest way to see the property
44. Type of neighborhood
45. Shopping facilities
46. Bus or other transportation
47. Parks and playgrounds
48. Schools
49. Churches
50. And at least five special features or amenities that should make someone want to buy the property

HOW ADVERTISING AGENCIES PROMOTE THEMSELVES

Perhaps the most amazing paradox of modern-day advertising is the fact that advertising agencies, like the proverbial shoemaker whose children had no shoes, devote but scant attention to advertising their own services. One advertising trade magazine, tongue in cheek perhaps, even goes so far as to suggest that every advertising agency should hire another agency to handle this much neglected task.

When they finally get around to it, the majority of agencies turn to direct mail for self-promotion. Two techniques are most common: (1) external publications and (2) showmanship campaigns designed to display the agency's creative ability.

External Publications

The majority of advertising agencies using an external publication employ the newsletter format or envelope-size booklets. Probably the best-known agency newsletter is "Grey Matter," which has been published regularly for over 25 years by Grey Advertising Agency of New York. Actually, Grey publishes two regular "Grey Matter" newsletters—a national advertisers' edition sent monthly to 8,000 executives, and a retail edition which goes semimonthly to 12,000 merchandising and advertising managers in department stores and supermarkets. While in newsletter format, contents are usually in essay style and frequently each four-page issue is limited to discussion of a single subject.

Vic Maitland & Associates of Pittsburgh uses the envelope-size booklet format—a monthly eight-pager called "Tremendous Trifles." The format consists of an anecdote occupying the first two pages, followed by six pages of supporting copy of general interest material. Three thousand copies are distributed to top executives and those responsible for advertising, promotion, public relations, and marketing. An interesting feature of each issue is a die-cut triangle at the center of the front cover's right-hand side which permits the issue identification to show through from the first inside page.

A less elaborate monthly booklet external, "Take Five," is issued by Keller-Crescent Co. of Evansville, Indiana. It uses a standard self-mailer cover and contains eight pages of typewritten copy and illustrations. Contents include short notes on current events, humorous items, interesting quotations, quick biographies of agency personnel, plus a brief back page case history of an interesting advertising project for an agency client.

Showmanship Mailings

Some of the most ingenious showmanship direct mail has resulted from advertising agency self-promotion efforts. One of the most successful was a series of 14 mailings from Ross Roy Inc. of Detroit, which was directly credited with annual billings in excess of $500,000. The first mailing consisted of a wooden spice rack, a bottle of spices, and a letter. It was followed by 11 additional bottles of spices, each accompanied by a miniature letter. Each of the spice bottles had a catchy label such as "Publicity Pepper," "Open Sesame Marketing," "Savory Merchandising," and "Perfect Thyme-ing." The final two mailings were a set of noncommercial labels for the spice bottles (to cover the promotional labels originally on the bottles), then a spice cookbook.

Ralph Bing Advertising Co. of Cleveland bought 1,000 Army gas masks in a local surplus store and mailed them with copy tied in with a "Business Stink?" theme. Another trip to the surplus store netted a supply of periscopes and a copy tie-in of "How Business Is Looking Up for You."

Harold M. Norman Advertising, Green Lane, Pennsylvania, sent out a wren-size birdhouse, with this copy attached to the roof:

> With winter here, can spring be far behind? And with spring, welcome new friends, new hopes, new ideas! If you feel that a new advertising approach, or a fresh promotional outlook might help your business, we'd like to talk with you. Like the cheerful friend who will soon be moving into this little dwelling, we'd like to be the new friend who moves into your promotional plans. We might be able to "hatch" an idea or two.

American Mail Advertising Inc. of Boston sent a series of nine colorful letters from post offices in Maine with foreign names—Norway, Paris, Denmark, China, etc. Each letter featured the theme, "No Oceans to Cross" to find needed advertising services. Burroughs Direct Mail Advertising of Los Angeles made its prospects honorary executive vice presidents and mailed identification cards, followed by progress reports, dividend checks, and annual reports on a regular basis.

Ken Nelson Advertising of Minneapolis frequently mails colorful illustrated cards with famous quotations. Printed on high-quality cover stock, the cards are suitable for framing. Another Minneapolis agency, the local office of Batten, Barton, Durstine & Osborn, once mailed a large card containing 23 tipped-on postage stamps from various foreign countries to dramatize its experience in handling foreign advertising.

Carter Advertising Agency, Kansas City, Missouri, used a showmanship teaser campaign to build advance interest in a brochure describing the agency's services. The first mailing featured a solid oak picture frame with openings for three pictures. Only one opening was filled. Two subsequent mailings brought the pictures for the other openings. The identity of the sender wasn't revealed until the agency brochure arrived as the fourth mailing.

Another effective teaser campaign was used by Grubb & Peterson of Champaign, Illinois, which sent a series of five teaser post cards with cartoon illustrations of beavers and slogans built around the agency's initials—"Going Places," "Genuinely Prolific," "Group Participation," "Geographically Perfect." The fifth card offered a clue to the sender's identity. Then, the following day, in walked an agency executive bearing a 16-page brochure with a story built around a "Busy as Beavers" theme. A sixth card was mailed following the executive's in-person visit.

But probably the most ingenious of all agency promotions was one dreamed up by Creative Promotions of New York, which had hatboxes delivered to prospective clients. When the lid was removed, a helium-filled balloon, labeled "This is a trial balloon," floated upward pulling with it a cardboard arm and hand holding the advertising message.

Other Techniques

Not all agency promotion, of course, is based on these two most popular techniques. Every conceivable format has been used ranging from reprints of publication ads to regular letter mailings. Robert Aitchison of The Fensholt Co., Chicago, in *Industrial Marketing,* suggests the following direct mail program for agencies:

> Issue a direct mail piece once a month. Some mailings could consist of reprints of outstanding jobs, along with a brief covering letter. Another possibility is a series of well-designed post cards, giving brief messages about the work you have done for your various clients, possibly in the "problem, solution, and results" style. (Later, such a series could be reprinted as a booklet.) Reprints of magazine articles by members of your agency also make good direct mail pieces.

One agency which does a particularly effective self-promotion job is Marsteller Inc. It frequently prepares attractive booklets covering such subjects as its personnel, media policies, facilities, etc. It also makes extensive use of reprints of articles bylined by agency personnel. In addition, Marsteller prepares special pinpointed direct mail campaigns such as a series of 12 attractive folders answering questions concerning its qualifications in handling agricultural accounts. The folders were mailed twice a week for six consecutive weeks to 850 agricultural marketing organizations. The campaign drew immediate-potential inquiries from over 20 prime prospects for the agency's services plus requests for additional information from 62 individual companies.

Chapter 12

MERCHANDISING BY DIRECT MAIL

PROBABLY no marketing term is subject to so many different definitions as merchandising. To some it means advertising in all its forms. To others it is a synonym for sales promotion. Its most common meaning, however, and the one used here, is:

> *Increasing the effectiveness of advertising (1) by translating it into terms of advantages for dealers, retailers, salesmen, etc.; and (2) by projecting the advertiser's message beyond the audience of the media in which it originally appeared.*

The importance of merchandising is widely accepted, although far too frequently neglected. Milton M. Rockmore, president of The Rockmore Company, once noted in *Tide:*

> Every advertiser realizes that no advertising campaign is complete until it has been merchandised. If he wants to leave no stone unturned in the quest for sales he must consider the merchandising of advertising an integral part of the selling process. To achieve this, many companies use not only the merchandising services made available by media but maintain their own merchandising departments to demonstrate constantly to the dealer how hard their advertising is working for him.

Mr. Rockmore expanded on this theme in a speech before the Atlanta Advertising Institute:

> Building an effective merchandising program is not easy . . . it's a constant and never-ceasing job. Merchandising is a fan-out process. It's a job of communications. We must translate the story in terms of interest and advantages to the particular group we address it to. If we attempt to tell the salesmen of our own organization what we are doing with their advertising, we must interpret it in terms of their interest. People in the distribution chain will get behind the promotion of the advertising campaign in direct relationship to the amount of effort they think is being put behind it. In other words, they will react to excitement, to an air of movement, to an air of mobility, to enthusiasm and to the effort they are made to feel is being expended. In the job of making the advertising appropriation do more and look bigger to the trade, we know of no more effective means of accomplishing this than through merchandising the advertising.

Dozens of studies have been conducted on the effectiveness of merchandising. All of them have concluded that merchandising increases the total value of advertising at least double or triple. A study by *Sales Management,* for example, showed it is possible to "buy advertising for 47 cents on the dollar" when it is supported with adequate merchandising.

And not only does merchandising play a vital role in an effective advertising program, but it is highly essential in converting a publicity program to promotional advantage.

Role of Direct Mail

In the majority of effective merchandising programs, direct mail plays the key role. It is used not only to extend the value and impact of advertising in other media, but also to add another dimension to a direct mail program itself.

Many advertisers think of merchandising only as a method for keeping their distribution organization abreast of advertising programs. This, however, represents only one of several audiences which can be reached effectively through merchandising.

By all means, any middlemen involved in the distribution of a product should be contacted regularly through direct mail merchandising. Whenever possible, it is a good idea to merchandising advertising not only to executives of distributor organizations, manufacturers' agents, wholesalers, jobbers, supply houses, and other representatives, but to *all* of their salesmen individually. A company's own sales force, of course, should be constantly educated and kept informed through merchandising.

All retail outlets are also logical merchandising audiences. Many companies attempt to reach retailers primarily through middlemen such as jobbers and wholesalers. Often complete merchandising programs are supplied to these company representatives for mailing to the merchants they supply.

Merchandising Internally

One of the most frequently overlooked audiences for merchandising is a company's own executives and employees. "Merchandising upward" to reach management can be particularly important for the success of many advertising programs and is determined by the degree of management support they receive.

Employees, too, form a logical merchandising audience. Many companies have found that merchandising to the employee organization helps build a better understanding of a company's role in the marketplace and a sense of pride in association with their employer. This can lead to greater efficiency, fewer grievances, and less job turnover.

Financial Audiences

Many advertisers make it a special point to include the financial community in their merchandising programs. By keeping investors, bankers, investment counselors, and others informed, a company can expect better recognition not only in the handling of its securities but often in the financing of purchases of its products.

Extermital Chemicals, for example, merchandises its literature covering termite control to bankers and savings and loan associations, which are frequently called upon for information on this subject from homeowners. Many farm equipment manufacturers pay special attention to merchandising aimed at financial institutions in farm areas to build a favorable climate for loans used to purchase their equipment.

Stockholders, of course, have a special interest in a company's advertising and deserve special merchandising consideration. A number of companies make it a regular practice to send reprints of all major published articles describing the company, its products, and its personnel to stockholders. Some even issue a monthly or quarterly digest magazine which includes both article reprints and typical examples of the company's advertising.

Merchandising to Thought Leaders

Many thought-leader groups play an important role in advancing a company's reputation and that of its products and services. Judicious merchandising of advertising and publicity to thought leaders in an industry, market, community, association, educational institution, government, etc., can be highly worthwhile.

Newspaper and magazine editors also represent a highly important merchandising audience. While they are most frequently reached through press releases, merchandising of advertising and publicity in other publications can help keep them informed about new developments.

Special Audiences

One important role of merchandising by direct mail is to reach audiences who would not otherwise be exposed to a company's advertising messages. Any mass media advertising campaign, no matter how extensive, is certain to miss a portion of the audience for which the advertising is intended. And when advertising is placed primarily in specialized publications, there is almost always an audience of important prospects who do not receive the message unless it is supplemented with specific merchandising service information.

Many times a specific advertisement or series will have special interest for audiences related to those covered by the media list chosen. To reach them adequately through additional publications, however, might require too great an expenditure. In such cases, direct mail merchandising can be the answer.

Merchandising is particularly important in achieving full coverage of key customers and prospects. Frequently a basic advertising program is designed to reach everyone in a given market and then is supplemented with direct mail merchandising to *make sure* the key portion of this market is exposed to the message. Since the average company usually finds that approximately 20% of its market actually represents 80% of the buying potential, it is highly important to make special efforts to get a promotional story into the hands of this key 20%.

Merchandising to Others

The five basic audience groups listed above do not necessarily represent every possible merchandising target. The requirements will vary considerably from company to company and industry to industry.

Many advertisers, for example, make a special effort to merchandise their stories to their plant communities. Neighbors are always interested in a company, its products, and its accomplishments and a merchandising program can help cement friendly relations.

Another important merchandising audience for many companies is composed of the suppliers upon whom it must depend for its continued operation. And some companies have found it worthwhile to even include competitors as a merchandising audience.

MERCHANDISING OBJECTIVES

Merchandising direct mail differs from most other types of direct mail in that it cannot function independently. The first essential of a good merchandising program, therefore, is a good advertisement, promotion piece, or publicity article—or a complete campaign to be merchandised. Seldom can a merchandising campaign be successful if the material to be merchandised is not of good quality.

Unfortunately, many advertisers look upon merchandising primarily as a way to try to correct faults in inferior promotions —and some have even simulated merchandising campaigns to try to make up for the fact there was no advertising to begin with or to make up for lost time when a competitor has beat them to the punch with a new promotion.

While these are without question the objectives of many merchandising campaigns, they certainly should come last in any list of merchandising objectives. Actually, there are hundreds of possible objectives for merchandising by direct mail. Most of them, however, will fall within 16 basic categories.

1. *Reference Form*—Much advertising and publicity originally appear in highly transient form. This is particularly true of radio and television commercials, motion picture advertising, business films, and other audio-visual formats. There is little opportunity to give such promotion thorough study or to pass it along to others who are concerned. To a certain extent this is true of outdoor advertising, point-of-purchase displays, transportation advertising, and even newspapers—which are often read and discarded at a point far removed from the point of future reference or more thorough study.

To extend the value and impact of such promotions, the messages are often translated into a format which permits additional study and reference and then merchandised by direct mail to appropriate audiences.

2. *To Enable Filing*—Many times, advertisements can achieve the greatest results when they are filed for future reference. While this is most frequently the case with salesmen and sales outlets, it can apply to customers and prospects as well. Since it is difficult to get people to tear pages from magazines or newspapers and file them on any systematic basis—and such material seldom makes "good filing material"—"merchandising for filing" is a logical answer.

When filing is desired, it is important to clearly establish the physical nature of the file and, if possible, to provide the basic "file" required. Such "files" may range from a simple filing folder to ring binders, filing sleeves, or special file boxes. It certainly is not necessary to use the original promotion format for filing purposes, but once a basic format for filing has been established, all material intended for the file should be tailored to this format. It is also important to keep reminding recipients of such merchandising that the material is designed for the basic file and to include easy-to-follow instructions for filing. Periodic indexes can be very useful. When they are sent, it is a good idea to include a reply card on which recipients can request items "missing" from their files.

3. *Amplify or Interpret*—One of the most common objectives of direct mail merchandising programs is to expand upon an advertising or publicity message. For example, a magazine advertisement seldom can tell the full story of a product or service or interpret it in terms all audiences can relate to their specific interest. Through merchandising, however, the basic advertisement can be extended through interpretative material, additional illustrations, documentation, comments on the copy, etc.

The most common theme, of course, is "what this promotion story means to *you.*" In merchandising to a distribution organization, this theme often becomes, "How this promotion can be applied to make more sales for you."

In some cases, the most important thing to be interpreted is the language of the original promotion piece. While this is obviously the situation in merchandising material to foreign language audiences, engineering talk may easily be a foreign language to a sales force or an executive audience.

4. *Reaching Supplemental Audiences*—Few advertising or publicity messages can be expected to reach any more than a portion of the audience which should have a special interest in that message. This is particularly true of business paper or newspaper advertising, but even ads in magazines like *Time* or *Readers' Digest* cannot possibly reach all prospects for any product or service. Even if the publication itself reaches the majority of prospects, a high percentage of the recipients will not even notice your advertising or publicity message. Readership research reports indicate an average of less than 20% of the readers of a magazine note an individual ad; and it is important to remember that these research studies usually include only those who have spent some time reading the issue being researched and do not include any who have not had the time to "get at" that issue.

Often an advertiser wants to extend his message to audiences which would not normally be expected to be exposed to the media in which the ad originally appeared. For example, an advertiser might find it necessary to concentrate his basic advertising in publications aimed at engineers. Yet, in many cases, the buying of his product will also involve approvals by top management and purchasing agents, who do not normally see the engineering magazines. In addition, these publications may easily not reach those in the distribution chain who will become involved in the eventual sale. The answer, of course, is to merchandise the engineer-slanted advertisements to these important supplemental audiences.

5. *Tailor to a Specific Market*—Most companies find it economically impossible to tailor their advertising to the specific interests of all potential markets for a product or service. In most cases, there are varying interests because of geographical location, industry practices, competitive situations, and other factors. Often, the answer is to run a basic advertisement in horizontal publications covering many different segments of the market

and then merchandising the basic advertisement with supplemental copy designed to appeal to each segment of the market.

One very important division of a market can be customers vs. prospects. For example, to sell a new model to a customer already using the product concerned may easily require special copy dramatizing reasons for making a change. If the market is composed primarily of prospects who have yet to purchase any model of the product, it is only logical for the basic copy to concentrate on arousing initial interest or selling against competitive products.

6. *Add Emphasis*—Repetition can become the key factor in driving home a promotional message. Repeat advertisements in the same publications in which they originally appeared are highly effective, but even greater emphasis can be obtained when the message is separated from the competition of many similar messages and merchandised by direct mail to customers and prospects. Additional emphasis can also be obtained by changing the original form of the ad. For example, it can be printed on a better grade of paper, enlarged or reduced, have color added, points of special interest to each merchandising audience can be underscored, etc.
7. *Combine Material*—Frequently, the real effect of a promotion program comes only when efforts in many different media are combined for impact. Direct mail merchandising is often used to link all of the elements together. Complete merchandising kits are often mailed to the distribution organization, usually with samples or preprints of all of the individual elements in the program. In such kits it is important to explain not only the role of each element, but how all of the elements fit together to provide promotion impact.

Other formats are also used to present a combined promotion story. Anheuser-Busch, for example, used a unique format to present its newspaper, radio, television, magazine, and outdoor campaigns when it began its famed "Where there's life, there's Bud" promotion program. The brewer's salesmen and distributors received a phonograph record featuring the musical theme used for radio and television commercials in a colorful record jacket featuring an illustration used for newspaper, magazine, and outdoor advertising.

8. *Link Ads Together*—Just as promotion efforts from different media are brought together for merchandising impact, individual publication ads are frequently combined to tell a complete story. Many advertisers purposely plan campaigns of related advertisements so they can be linked together in merchandising a complete story. A single case history of product use seldom delivers broad impact to a wide audience of prospects with different characteristics. By linking together an entire series of case histories, however, an advertiser can create an impression of having a product or service with widespread application and acceptance.
9. *Provide Response Mechanisms*—One of the handicaps of many forms of advertising is that special effort is required on the part of interested

readers. Often interested prospects put off action and just never get around to it. Direct mail merchandising can "save the day" in such situations by retelling the original advertising story and at the same time enclosing a handy business reply card which will bring more information or a call from a salesman—or can even serve as a mail order form.

10. *Personalize*—Mass advertising, by its very nature, is impersonal communication. Direct mail merchandising provides an opportunity to convert messages for the masses into personal messages for selected customers and prospects.

11. *Advertising Insurance*—Most companies have a list of key customers and prospects. But no matter how extensive a media schedule may be, there is almost sure to be a sizable portion of this key-customer-and-prospect audience which will "miss" any particular advertising message. Direct mail merchandising to this key list provides advertising insurance.

12. *Add Drama*—New impact can be given to almost any advertisement through the flexibility allowed in direct mail merchandising. Special effects not practical in the original use can be added. The most common method for adding drama is to attach some dimensional object to a reprint. The fact the "original" is known to have appeared in a different form achieves impact in itself. Reilly Electrotype, for example, used pages in advertising trade publications with a black-and-white illustration showing a pair of dice with pennies for the "spots." For merchandising purposes, the ad was reprinted on glossy cover stock and then seven shiny new pennies were glued atop the original black-and-white illustration.

13. *Bring up to Date*—In some fast-moving businesses, it takes merchandising to keep important audiences up to date on developments. Sometimes an advertisement is outdated before it gets into print. This may not be of major importance to the broad audience to which it is aimed, but can be highly important to special audiences such as company salesmen, key buyers, and others.

In some cases, an advertisement can be given additional impact by merchandising which features an updating theme. One advertiser, for example, was promoting the number of outlets for his product. After his ad had been prepared for a list of trade magazines, two important new outlets were added. The entire theme received additional impact when the advertiser merchandised the original ad with an accompanying note explaining how the story had become outdated even before the ad appeared.

14. *Correct Faults*—While, as mentioned previously, correcting faults in advertising programs should not be the primary aim of a direct mail merchandising program, it is an immediately available tool when emergencies arise. One company, for example, prepared an insert for a business publication and then, at the last minute, discovered it did not meet postal regulations for second-class mailings. Rather than scrap the expensive inserts, the advertiser chose to run a conventional ad in the magazine describing the "banned" insert and then arranged with the publication to have the inserts addressed for third-class mailing to the entire circulation list.

More common, however, is the use of direct mail merchandising to correct typographical errors, misleading statements, or to explain other faults in the original advertising.

15. *Make Up for Lost Time*—When competitors have beat an advertiser to the punch on some new development, direct mail merchandising can be used to regain the lead. Flexibility in timing gives a definite advantage to direct mail. It isn't only action by competitors which can make this merchandising objective important, however. Changing market conditions can also be a factor. One advertiser, for example, was engaged in a long-range program to create demand for a line of air conditioners when a sudden, unseasonal heat wave hit choice market areas. To get dealers to stock up quickly, a special direct mail merchandising program was quickly instituted.

16. *Substitute for a "Missing" Advertising Program*—One of the most unusual direct mail campaigns of recent years was a simulated merchandising program used by A. H. Rice Co., Pittsfield, Massachusetts, industrial thread manufacturer. Even though the budget did not allow for an extensive publication advertising program, the company created the impression of being a large-scale advertiser by including simulated full-page magazine reprints with its "Needle Talk" newsletter mailed monthly to 2,500 carefully selected key prospects. Actually, the impressive A. H. Rice "ads" made only one appearance—as enclosures with the newsletters.

While this is a unique example, direct mail merchandising is often called into play to plug some gap in an advertising program. Sometimes it is to make up for an ad which missed the edition for which it was intended or to fill in important market segments which were overlooked in media planning.

FORMATS FOR DIRECT MAIL MERCHANDISING

Direct mail merchandising utilizes a wide variety of formats, but those most commonly used fall within 17 basic categories:

1. *Reprints and Preprints*—The basic element in merchandising advertising or publicity which has appeared in print is the reprint or preprint. Most publications offer a variety of reprint services at low cost. McGraw-Hill business publications, for example, offer four basic types of reprints—just the ad itself; ad reprints backed with the publication's cover; 8½- by 11-inch folders with the magazine cover and the ad reprinted inside; 4¼- by 5½-inch folders, which feature a miniature reproduction of the magazine's cover on the outside of the french-fold piece, a 15-line special message on the first inside fold, and the ad reprint on the fully opened 8½- by 11-inch piece.

2. *Letters*—Many types of letters are used in merchandising programs. To be most effective, a reprint or preprint should always be accompanied by a letter telling why the advertisement has special meaning for the merchandising audience. Often, advertisers arrange for the editor or publisher of the publication involved to write the letter which accompanies the reprint.

When case history advertising is used, the letters are sometimes written by an executive of the company or the individual featured in the ad. In addition, letters are often used independently of reprints to announce or describe forthcoming promotion programs.

3. *Blowups*—When advertisements have potential as window or store displays, they are often enlarged for mailing purposes. Advertisers using small space often use the blowup technique in merchandising programs to give greater impact to their ads. Another effective use of blowups is to merchandise television advertising. A scene from a television commercial can be enlarged and used as the key element in the merchandising program.

4. *Miniatures*—Miniatures of ads are often used as statement stuffers made available to local outlets. This permits dealers to tie in directly with national advertising programs. Other advertisers prepare miniatures of their ads—particularly those of an institutional nature—for enclosures in all correspondence and packages. One advertiser makes interesting use of miniatures by supplying company salesmen with new business cards each month. A miniature reproduction of a current ad is reprinted on the backs of the cards. Another company reproduces ad miniatures on monthly appointment calendars which are distributed by salesmen. Two other common formats for miniatures are picture post cards and blotters.

5. *Complete Copies*—Many advertisers, particularly when their merchandising lists are small, arrange to have complete copies of publications mailed. Front cover stickers, bookmarks, or covering letters direct attention to the advertisement or publicity being merchandised. Perhaps the ultimate in this technique was a program of The Electric Storage Battery Company, which crammed the home mailboxes of its sales force with more than 30 pounds of business publications within a 10-day period. Each of the magazines carried a cover sticker calling attention to a company advertisement plus a letter from a top executive of the publication explaining why his magazine was chosen as a medium to reach important customers and prospects.

6. *Booklet Conversions*—Reprinting an advertisement for merchandising does not necessarily mean using it just as it appeared in a publication. Often, a more effective technique is to use the same basic copy and illustrations and adapt them to a different format such as a booklet, folder, or broadside. Many times the conversions can be accomplished by cutting advertising plates into sections and rearranging them for the new format. Knox Reeves Advertising Inc., for example, ran a three-page ad in *Advertising Age,* with each page divided into four equal sections. For merchandising purposes, each of the 12 sections became a complete page in a booklet. See the next three pages.

7. *Campaign Portfolios*—Complete advertising campaigns are often brought together for merchandising purposes. A series of case-history ads, for example, can become a valuable merchandising booklet. Many companies issue monthly, quarterly, or annual portfolios displaying their full advertising programs both as merchandising mailings and for use by salesmen.

8. *Advertising-Publicity Combinations*—Advertising and published publicity items can be combined effectively for merchandising purposes. Worthington Corporation frequently plans direct mail programs which involve the

After 24 years of helping to move . . .

. . . cereals, mixes, flours, and refrigerated foods . . .

. . . candy and . . .

. . . beer and fishing equipment . . .

Knox Reeves created an excellent series of advertisements in Advertising Age *and then converted them into a booklet. Note cover at the end of series.*

. . . all kinds of industrial goods . . .

. . . public relations ideas . . .

. . . fresh produce and canned goods . . .

. . . art courses . . .

. . . and toiletries, it <u>had</u> to happen!

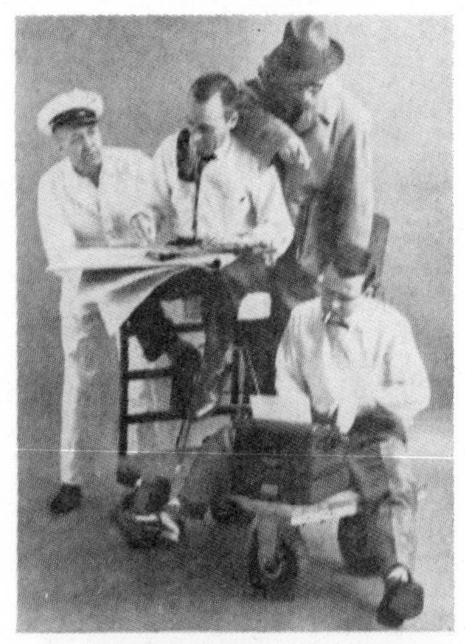

We at KNOX REEVES have moved OURSELVES!

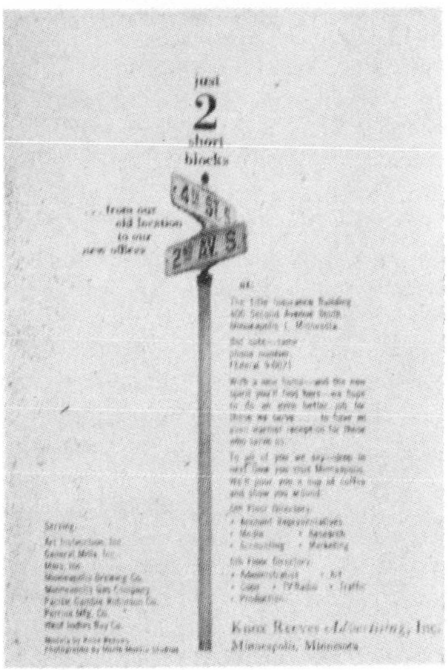

combination of specially placed technical articles, related advertisements, and additional product specification material. Most frequently, advertising and publicity are combined for merchandising new products.

9. *Behind-the-Scenes Reports*—One way to attract special attention for an advertisement is to prepare behind-the-scenes reports which give a merchandising audience a feeling of being "in" on the development of an advertisement or campaign. This is a particularly effective technique for merchandising radio or television advertising where there are no "reprints" as such to distribute. However, the technique is also used for publication advertising. Consolidated Water Power & Paper Co., for example, sends out folders showing how photographs are staged for its magazine ads. Hoffman Electronics Corporation prepared a 24-page booklet entitled, "Why We Do It the Way We Do." It not only included the purpose, philosophy and methods of the company's advertising, but included detailed information on copy, layout, typography, and special techniques for point-of-sale, radio and television advertising.
10. *Reprints in Permanent Form*—Advertisements of special merit are sometimes adapted for permanent display by laminating, framing, or mounting on easel-backed display boards. Many publishers make such conversions available at low cost. One interesting variation of this technique is to provide a special frame into which reprints can be inserted as they are received. One company, for example, sent out miniature outdoor signboard frames with an opening just the size of picture post cards. Then as new 24-sheet posters were issued, they were reproduced on picture post cards and mailed to dealers, who inserted them into the miniature signboards for cash register displays.
11. *House Organs and Bulletins*—Publications for employees, salesmen, and the distribution force are logical media for effective merchandising. While the most frequent technique is simply to reprint magazine or newspaper ads in such publications, a number of companies make it a regular practice to add merchandising copy. H. K. Porter Co., for example, published a regular series of articles in its house organ. Each article described a publication chosen for the company's advertising with special emphasis on reasons why its editorial content, audience, and special features made it a logical medium for telling Porter's advertising story.
12. *Tip-Ons*—One way to add impact to merchandising mailings is to tip a dimensional object to reprints. A number of companies tip samples of products, labels, packages, fabric swatches, or other items atop printed illustrations on reprints. Others convert black-and-white illustrations to full-color through the use of tip-ons.
13. *Contests*—Merchandising often takes the form of interest-stimulating contests. One company sends its salesmen monthly quiz sheets. To answer the questions and compete for a prize, the salesmen must study the company's advertising. Another company makes sure its direct mail is thoroughly studied by distributor personnel by having an executive call selected salesmen at home each weekend. There is no advance warning for the salesmen, although they know a certain number, selected at random, will be called each week. If the salesman can answer questions about the direct mail material, he receives a valuable merchandise prize. An industrial distributor includes a series of prize-winning numbers in his merchandising mailings. If they correspond with numbers listed on the divider pages for each section of a basic catalog issued to the customer, prizes are awarded.

14. *Showmanship Mailings*—Every conceivable type of showmanship technique is used for merchandising by direct mail. Often, an advertisement is reprinted on some unusual surface such as a napkin, coaster, towel, washcloth, metal, plastics, sandpaper, etc. Ads are sometimes mounted and then cut into jigsaw puzzles. Another popular device is to laminate an advertisement reprint and then press a recording on the surface so the ad can be "played" on a home phonograph. Frequently, the recording will include radio spots or the sound track from television commercials. Reynolds Metals Co. used another showmanship format—a deck of playing cards—to merchandise the scope of its promotion efforts to its distribution organization. Each of the cards carried an illustration and descriptive copy telling about a different promotional aid.
15. *Calendars*—Another popular merchandising format is to reprint advertisements—or at least illustrations originally used in ads—on wall or desk calendars. Many companies use the 12-month variety, while others issue monthly or quarterly calendars featuring current advertising.
16. *Regular Publications*—Many advertisers have developed special publications whose primary role is to merchandise their advertising. Most frequently these publications are aimed at the company's salesmen or distribution organization. Some advertisers, however, use such publications to reach broader lists. Harris-Intertype Corporation, for example, mails a monthly four-page newsletter to a large promotional list. Called "What's Going on at Harris-Intertype," the center spread features a reprint of a current ad appearing in graphic arts trade publications, while the front and back pages contain informal copy giving additional details on product applications featured in the ad plus items about other developments in the graphic arts industry.
17. *Telegram-Plus*—A merchandising technique of growing popularity is Western Union's "Telegram-Plus" service, which provides for delivery of reprints, product samples, or other material at a specified time along with a telegram containing merchandising information. The advantage of this service is that delivery can be made at a specified time throughout the country.

MEDIA-SUPPLIED MERCHANDISING

An important advance in advertising since World War II has been the extensive development of merchandising services made available by the various media. These services range all the way from market surveys to contacting retail outlets and, of course, merchandising by direct mail.

Magazines of all types have been particularly active in the development of increasing varieties of merchandising services. In fact, it is not at all uncommon for placement of advertising, in final analysis, to go to the magazines offering the most extensive supplementary merchandising programs. Many magazines have entire departments whose sole function is to handle merchandising projects for advertisers.

Basically, there are two types of direct mail merchandising offered by media: (1) standard programs and (2) custom-designed direct mail pieces and programs.

Standard Merchandising Services

In addition to a variety of reprint formats, most publishers are ready to provide the majority of the following direct mail services:

- *Marked copies*—A reasonable quantity of issues of publications with special page markers and/or cover stickers identifying the page on which an ad appears.
- *Letters*—Automatically typewritten or processed letters from the publisher or editor of the publication mailed to lists supplied by the advertiser.
- *Mailing Lists*—Most business publications and many other media will provide special mailing lists for merchandising purposes or assist an advertiser in developing special lists.
- *Stickers and Hang Tags*—Many publications furnish "as advertised in" stickers or hang tags which can be affixed to reprints, sales literature, or the product itself. If stickers or tags are not available, most publishers will gladly furnish special artwork or plates for use in preparation of such items.
- *Circulation Information*—To assist an advertiser in pinpointing the audiences reached by his advertising in specific geographical or market areas, most media will furnish circulation or audience breakdowns which can prove helpful in merchandising programs directed at the distribution organization.
- *Merchandising Post Cards*—Many publications offer post cards featuring a reproduction of an issue's front cover for use in mailing merchandising messages. Radio and television stations, likewise, often provide picture post cards of personalities for similar merchandising purposes.
- *Value of Advertising Literature*—Any reputable medium is more than happy to supply special literature describing its audience and what advertising it carries can be expected to accomplish. Many media also make available material to "sell" the role of advertising in general.

All of these standard services, and many others offered by individual media, are usually supplied at low cost and, in some cases, are made available without charge.

Custom Merchandising

It would be impossible to catalog all of the varieties of direct mail merchandising prepared by media to serve the specific needs of individual advertisers. Consumer magazines, in particular, have created many outstanding direct mail merchandising pieces and campaigns for their advertisers.

Redbook magazine has been one of the leaders in this field. Some of the hundreds of mailings it has created include:

- An imprinted kite sent to retailers handling Her Majesty children's petticoats to tie in with the company's *Redbook* ad which included copy, reading, "If strings were attached to Her Majesty's petticoats, they'd fly like kites."
- Top prospects for Bobbi Home Permanents were sent a reusable picture frame with an autographed photo of a model appearing in a Bobbi *Redbook* ad.
- A pair of drama-mask cuff links were used to merchandise an Ipana campaign. The tragedy mask link had "I still get tooth decay" engraved on the back, and was sent as a teaser to prospects along with a message saying a sales representative would deliver the missing link. When the Ipana man arrived, he brought with him the comedy mask link, which was engraved, "I use Ipana, as advertised in *Redbook.*"
- For Taylor Wines, *Redbook* sent a giant-size mailer with a real Taylor Champagne label tipped to an illustration of a bottle. For another Taylor campaign, *Redbook* created a four-piece campaign, with each mailing resembling a giant playing card. Each of the aces carried a reprint of a Taylor ad.
- Other *Redbook* showmanship mailers have featured neckties, mobiles, trivets, imprinted shopping bags, transparency viewers, butterflies, and a paperweight in the shape of a good-enough-to-eat cupcake.

MERCHANDISING PUBLICITY

While techniques used for merchandising publicity follow the same basic patterns of those used for merchandising advertising, there are some notable differences. In merchandising news stories, feature articles, or other types of publicity, it is highly important to give emphasis to the fact that the material has appeared in print. One of the greatest assets of publicity is that the item carries the endorsement of a publication. Even articles bylined by someone from your company gain credulity in reprint form for they carry an implied "stamp of approval" from a magazine or newspaper. The more respected the publication, the more important this implied endorsement of what is said.

Many publications offer special reprint facilities. In the case of magazines, it is often possible to have reprints prepared using either the cover from the issue in which the item appeared or special covers prepared for reprint purposes. Usually the cost of reprints from publications is considerably less than to handle the job yourself. In all cases, however, it is important to obtain specific permission for reprinting any editorial material.

Merchandising programs do not necessarily require the use of publicity which originates with the company doing the merchandising. In fact, some of the most effective merchandising can be done with magazine and newspaper material which does not even mention your company. For example, many companies watch for published material which has special reference value for their customers, distributors, or salesmen, and then arrange for reprints which are mailed to these lists. One Southwestern photoengraver, for example, regularly mails reprints of helpful material appearing in graphic arts publications to its customers as a goodwill gesture. Accompanying merchandising messages carry the theme that this company is always interested in doing "something special" to assist its customers.

Publicity Merchandising Programs

A good example of how a well-developed merchandising program can extend the value of a publicity program was explained in *Advertising Requirements* by Morris B. Rotman, president of Harshe-Rotman Inc., Chicago public relations agency serving Bausch & Lomb Optical Co. of Rochester, New York:

1. Bulletins are sent to salesmen alerting them to major publicity achievements. Where possible, these bulletins are sent in advance of the "break," so maximum use can be made of this publicity by the salesman. The bulletins not only advise the salesman of the publicity, but give him tips about the best way to utilize it in his selling.
2. *Focus,* published twice a year, is an external with a circulation of 70,000 mailed spring and fall to high school science educators and people working in science in colleges and industry.
3. Merchandising brochures are sent to optometrists, ophthalmologists, and opticians with reprints of publicity "breaks."
4. *Balco News,* the firm's internal house organ, reports regularly on the activities of the public relations program.
5. *Today,* external house organ with a circulation of 40,000, principally among the nation's optometrists, ophthalmologists and opticians, features related publicity achievements from time to time.
6. Special letters to the ophthalmic professions and Bausch & Lomb customers call attention to forthcoming publicity activities in their areas.
7. Bausch & Lomb district offices send cards to their customers alerting them to forthcoming television shows in their localities which are to deal with eyewear. Local impact is thus achieved at the time of the event, in addition to which the professionals themselves often do much on their own to stimulate patients to watch the shows.

Other Publicity Merchandising Techniques

While the Bausch & Lomb publicity merchandising program is probably as complete as any which has been developed, there are additional techniques which should also be considered. One of the most common is to prepare broadsides containing a montage of publicity items to dramatize the fact that a company, its products, and/or its personnel are "in the news." The value of such broadsides was outlined by Morris Rotman in another article, which was published in *Industrial Marketing:*

> These are some of the things a planograph can be made to say, and do:
>
> - Here is the way your manufacturer, through its publicity program, is helping to precondition your market, making your selling job easier.
> - Here is proof of the demand that is being built up for the product.
> - Here is unbiased, disinterested proof that the product is big enough and important enough to make news. This isn't us, the manufacturer, talking about ourselves. It's editors and commentators who are doing the talking . . . and they only talk about what the vast majority of their readers or listeners are interested in.

In addition to broadsides (or planographs as Mr. Rotman calls them), publicity programs are often merchandised with special booklets containing reprints of publicity in print. The Martin-Senour Co., for example, supplies its sales representatives with a 12-page booklet of publicity reprints which can be used to merchandise the company's reputation to dealers.

Other companies make up simulated newspapers or magazines containing representative reprints of publicity items. An even more common technique is to merchandise the original press release even before any publicity appears in print.

Chapter 13

BUSINESS AND PROFESSIONAL DIRECT MAIL

THERE are three important types of direct mail which are extremely difficult to fit into a specific category. Each involves a specific marketing task:

1. Promoting products to those in the distribution chain—including dealers, distributors, jobbers, wholesalers, manufacturers' agents, each of whom plays a functional role in marketing.
2. Promoting products and services to those who specify their use to the eventual buyer. Perhaps most important in this category—at least from a direct mail standpoint—are doctors, but the same type of promotion is also used to influence other specifiers such as architects, consulting engineers, etc.
3. Selling nonindustrial products and services used in a nonpersonal way by business and professional men.

While each of these categories has many distinctive characteristics, there are at least two general features which each of these three types of direct mail has in common. First of all, each of the audiences is composed of people with special backgrounds and usually with a higher-than-average education or training. This frequently results in a more sophisticated direct mail approach. Second, the products and services involved are not primarily designed to satisfy personal needs and desires but to serve members of the direct mail audiences in successfully conducting their businesses and professions.

Interestingly enough, in each of these three categories, direct mail is the *primary* advertising medium—and, for many advertisers, the only type of advertising used.

DIRECT MAIL FOR THE DISTRIBUTION CHAIN

In most cases, the company using direct mail to communicate with elements in its distribution chains has an important "built-in" advantage. Except where the objective is to induce new dealers or middlemen to take on a product or line, there is an already established personal contact. Thus, direct mail can be used to its fullest as a *personal* medium. This is particularly true in mailings to middlemen and franchised dealers.

Unfortunately, however, this often leads to the mistaken assumption that anything mailed to this audience will receive immediate and full attention, and advertisers frequently use a completely impersonal approach instead of capitalizing on the established relationship as an aid in the development of more effective communications.

While the individuals and firms which represent a company in marketing its products are certainly much closer to the manufacturer than the eventual consumer, they are most frequently independent businessmen whose first consideration is their own welfare and not that of the companies they represent. While every effort should be made to convey a feeling of mutual dependence, it is important that any direct mail addressed to this audience must recognize the basic independence which does exist.

Intense Competition

In most fields, the majority of audiences in the distribution chain handle the products of many different suppliers. And the farther along the chain you move, the greater the number of products involved. The manufacturer of each of these products, of course, desires maximum attention for his direct mail messages. Thus, the competition for attention is often very great.

But it is not just the direct mail from a dealer's or distributor's merchandise suppliers which creates competition. Just like all businessmen, these dealers and distributors are on the receiving end of direct mail promotions for hundreds of different types of products and services ranging from trucks and materials-handling equipment to reference books and office supplies.

Multiplied Audiences

In communicating with larger dealers and distributors, it is often important to reach not only the owners or key executives but all of the salesmen or clerks. This is particularly true when new products are being introduced or new selling techniques are required. Many progressive manufacturers make it a point to build and maintain home-address lists of all individuals involved in selling their products and develop special direct mail programs to keep this important audience fully informed.

It is also important to reach *all* elements in the distribution chain. Where several echelons of middlemen are involved, there is often a tendency to concentrate only on the top and bottom levels and to neglect those in between. Many times, a company feels best distribution relationships are maintained when promotion material moves through the "chain of command." Unfortunately, even though such a procedure has many advantages, it seldom works out in practice. Few distributors, for example, are promotion-oriented—particularly insofar as promotions of individual products or companies are concerned. When given the responsibility of acting in the role of a forwarding agent for direct mail material aimed at dealers, they frequently consider this job an imposition and fail to fulfill their role. As a result, most manufacturers make all mailings directly to the intended audiences. In such cases, however, it is important to keep any "bypassed" middlemen fully informed so they can tie in appropriate sales action and followthrough.

Another frequently made mistake is to use the same promotion material for all levels in the distribution chain. In most fields, different promotional approaches are required for each level of distribution. While the same basic printed material may be appropriate, it is often important to accompany it with different merchandising letters for all except the primary audience for which it was intended.

Reuse Requirements

A great deal of the material used in mailings to the distribution chain has more than passing value. Quite frequently it is utilized for display purposes, filed for future reference, or used by salesmen in their daily sales efforts. It is important to consider these extensions of promotional value in preparing any direct mail for dealers or distributors.

Theo. Hamm Brewing Co., for example, once made a statistic-laden mailing to its distributor salesmen showing how Hamm's beer had made a spectacular sales rise from a position of "just another regional brand" to one of the best sellers nationally. The company soon discovered the majority of the salesmen were carrying the piece with them and using it constantly, with the net result that most copies were soon tattered and torn. As a result, when a revised version of the mailing was prepared, the folder was printed on Texoprint, a plastic-impregnated paper which has special wearing qualities and can even be washed.

When material is likely to be filed, it is important to tailor it to fit the type of file most commonly used. In many cases, three-ring punching is desirable. When the material is likely to be displayed, it is usually wise to mail it unfolded or at least with a minimum number of folds.

Regular Publications

Many manufacturers issue regular publications for their dealers and distributors. Some are simple bulletins, while other companies create lavish magazines. Some of the finest company publications in existence are created for franchised dealers and agents. Nearly every oil company and automobile manufacturer, for example, produces a regular magazine for its dealers. These publications serve a variety of purposes including introduction of new products, merchandising advertising and sales promotion programs, sales training, progress reports, and so forth.

Like other types of direct mail, it is often essential to prepare separate publications for different levels of distribution. The farther down the chain you move, the greater the importance in shifting from primarily company-oriented editorial material to material aimed at the recipients' interests.

While many manufacturers circulate their regular house organs to distributors and dealers, these publications seldom substitute for the kind which are specially prepared for use along the distribution chain.

Incentive Programs

One of the most universal uses for direct mail is to conduct special incentive programs. Not only are such programs usually announced through special mailings, but their success often depends on regular direct mail communications both with those participating in the programs and their supervisors. R. C. Ausbeck, vice president of The E. F. MacDonald Co., the nation's biggest sales incentive organization, offers these tips in *Industrial Marketing* for such mailings:

> In order to maintain initial excitement throughout an incentive program, it is necessary to conduct a well-designed followup mailing campaign. Most successful campaign managers send out a followup mailing to every

campaign participant at least once every two weeks. These mailings, directed to the participants' homes (and often addressed to both the participant and his wife) are designed to accomplish several things:

- Offer selling hints or suggestions that will improve the salesman's performance.
- Keep each participant posted on the progress of the campaign, and how well he is doing.
- Make specific "spurt" offers for a limited period of time.
- Compliment the leaders in the campaign, and encourage the others.
- Show the wife what she can do to help her husband increase his winnings.
- Remind the participant of the rewards that can be his for putting forth extra effort.

Sometimes these mailings are simple messages on a company letterhead. In more elaborate campaigns, special mailing pieces are designed and printed—not infrequently in full color.

In addition, most incentive organizations offer a number of pretested, printed followup mail campaigns which can be adapted easily to a sponsor's particular needs. Incentive companies also maintain creative staffs to produce custom campaigns to a client's exact specifications.

Sales Training by Mail

Another important use for direct mail in the distribution chain is for training purposes. Many manufacturers offer what amount to correspondence courses for those who represent them. Depending upon the circumstances involved, the training program may vary from elaborate training manuals and lesson materials to a simple program such as one by Leonard Refineries of Alma, Michigan. Leonard mailed a daily post card to its 250 service stations. Each card offered a single suggestion for improving the business of the stations. Every effort was made to tie in with special events and seasonal situations. The "lessons" were short and to the point.

Other companies use direct mail to provide dealers and distributors with all of the tools necessary to conduct regular sales training sessions for their salesmen and clerks. A typical sales training package might include a lesson plan, suggested answers to anticipated questions, pass-out material for all who participate in the training, wall posters and charts, and possibly audio-visual aids.

Coordinating a Special Sales Program

Direct mail is often the most effective way to coordinate special marketing programs. In fact, when close timing is important it may easily be the only method which can be used.

Typical of direct mail's use as a special program coordinator is the experience of the Insulite Division of Minnesota & Ontario Paper Co. To level out a seasonal sales pattern and increase insulation sales in the summer, Insulite developed an intensive short-term promotion designed to jar dealers out of established seasonal buying and selling habits and to enthuse company and wholesaler salesmen. Special display materials were prepared to promote insulation for "air-conditioned comfort" in the summer. The following promotion schedule was followed:

1st day—teaser mailing to salesmen

4th day—detailed bulletin mailed to salesmen

5th day—complete promotion kits mailed to salesmen

10th day—teaser mailing to wholesalers

12th day—personal letter mailed to wholesalers

14th day—ads broke in lumber dealer trade publications

17th day—promotion mailing to all lumber dealers

30th day—followup letter mailed to salesmen

40th day—letter mailed to salesmen not active on program

In addition, wholesalers were encouraged to send out special mailings to their dealer prospects and customers. Insulite supplied complete mailings including promotional folders and personal letters reproduced on wholesalers' letterheads. Eighty-three wholesalers cooperated in this supplemental direct mail program. When the program was completed, Insulite's record showed a 178% sales increase over a similar period the preceding year.

Knipco Campaign

One of the most unusual—and successful—special sales programs was developed by Yeck & Yeck, Dayton, Ohio, advertising agency, for Knipco, a manufacturer of portable heaters. In 1957, Knipco developed a portable circulating hot air heater which could sell for less than $100 retail—a "natural" for farmers in northern states. But the winter selling season was close at hand and to capitalize on the new product, Knipco had to line up dealers and convince them to stock the heaters—and do it within just a few short weeks.

Knipco's answer to the problem was to provide salesmen with the necessary selling tools—and then work on the salesmen's wives with a clever direct mail program. The lure for the wives came with the first mailing—30 honest-to-goodness Knipco checks for $5 each. The only catch was that they were still unsigned. An attached letter explained that the signatures were easy to get—at the rate of one for each new Knipco dealer her husband signed. Letters of encouragement followed, reaching the wives at weekly intervals. With prodding by the wives, distributor salesmen signed up over 1,000 dealers within six weeks and had a minimum of three Knipco heaters on each of the dealers' shelves.

Other Direct Mail Uses

John Yeck, the man who created the highly successful Knipco campaign, described another effective direct mail program within a distribution chain (from *The Reporter of Direct Mail Advertising*):

> We have just finished scheduling, by mail, visits of company salesmen to over 150 hardware wholesalers across the country. We used mail because, in the past, the company salesmen have not been able to get in to see, in many cases, the president of the wholesale house. They were stopped at the buyer's desk. Because mail can go in where salesmen cannot, and because a letter from the president of a company can ask for appointments that a salesman cannot, we were able to set up a series of conferences with the buyers, sales managers and presidents of most of the wholesalers. Over 85% answered this letter to set up a conference.

In many cases, direct mail can substitute completely for salesmen. Henry Hoke told about the experience of Childers Manufacturing Co. of Houston, which sells corrugated metal roofing to dealers by mail:

> In a 41-month period Childers made 35 mailings to 15,000 prospective dealers. The 35 calls by mail were made at a cost of 7 cents per call, or $2.45 for the 35 calls to each dealer. That added up to 525,000 pieces of mail at a cost of $36,750. These mailings produced $4,435,000 worth of roofing orders. Out of the original list of 15,000 dealers, the Childers Company now has 3,500 regular customers. Childers has not dropped the other 11,500 which have not yet bought, because it is adding approximately 250 new customers per year.

These are just a few of the hundreds of different ways manufacturers use direct mail in communicating with dealers and distributors. Every conceivable format is used for mailings to the distributor chain. Many additional examples are described in Chapters 26 through 39 covering different types of direct mail formats. In particular, you will find many specific examples in Chapter 31 ("Showmanship Formats") and Chapter 32 ("Direct Mail Spectaculars"). Additional examples will be found in Chapter 12 ("Merchandising by Direct Mail").

DIRECT MAIL FOR SPECIFIERS

Reaching—and selling—those who hold a sword of Damocles over a product or service is of utmost importance in a number of fields, where a professional consultant usually makes the final decision as to what the buyer will purchase. Nowhere is this more true than in the ethical drug field, where a doctor prescribes the product which will be purchased by his patient. However, there are many other fields where a "specifier" plays a vital role.

For example, an architect frequently prescribes which of many different types of building products should be used. Consulting engineers play a similar role. Business consultants of all kinds are of special importance in the marketing of many products and services.

In some cases, there is a variation in the role of the specifier. A good example is the buying of advertising space or time. Here, the advertising agency is usually both the specifier and the actual buyer. However, the client must make the final decision and pay the bills. In promoting to this market, it is often the practice to treat both the advertising agency and the client as specifiers and buyers at the same time. Just who plays the key role in making the final decision depends upon each individual client-agency relationship.

The Basic Difference

There is one basic difference between the direct mail used to reach specifying influences and that directed to the actual buyer. Instead of directly trying to sell the product or service involved, direct mail for specifiers attempts to provide complete factual information so the specifier will be armed with the necessary ammunition not only to make decisions himself but to justify and support those decisions to those for whom the decisions are made.

Much of the direct mail material prepared for specifiers is designed for permanent filing. In most fields, a decision to recommend or specify a particular product or service is not likely to be an immediate one. Thus, direct mail advertisers try to provide the type of materials specifiers will keep on hand for the day when it becomes necessary to consider the use of the type of product or service involved.

Such reference material is usually supplemented with what might best be called "reminder direct mail." These mailings are primarily intended to remind the specifier to consider a product or service when the opportunity to specify it arises. Frequently they feature case histories which may suggest new applications for a product or service.

Showmanship and spectacular mailings are probably used more frequently for specifier audiences than any other. Often they have little purpose other than to say "don't forget me."

Medical Direct Mail

It is highly unlikely anyone receives more direct mail than the American physician. A continuing study by Clark-O'Neill, a medical mailing service firm, shows that a typical general practitioner receives about 2,000 direct mail pieces a year—or over 6 promotional mailings per mail delivery day. This flood of mail has long been the subject of constant conversation and even of Congressional investigations. Many studies—particularly by medical magazines which look upon direct mail advertising as their major competition—have indicated that the average doctor receives so much mail he just does not pay any attention to most of it. But hundreds of advertisers to the medical profession continue to devote the biggest portion of their advertising budgets to direct mail—and for good reason. Contrary to what many supposedly thorough research projects have indicated, the doctors do pay attention to the direct mail they receive and prove it by taking tangible action. Few markets can be counted on to respond in such large numbers to direct mail as do the nation's doctors.

Perhaps the best evidence that direct mail does get through to doctors was a survey on direct mail readership by Medical Advertising Service of New York. It was conducted by direct mail and drew a response of 47.6%—obvious evidence of doctors reading and acting upon direct mail! Clark-O'Neill, in *The Clark-O'Neill Indicia,* reports another case history to establish the amazing reception doctors give to direct mail:

> One of our largest pharmaceutical houses had the excellent idea of contributing monthly to the mail of some 150,000 physicians a series of interesting mailing pieces, each of which, in addition to specific product information, contained illustrative material which it was hoped the physician might want to retain.
>
> The mailing pieces almost immediately attracted the favorable attention of the doctors. A decision was made to supply on request a binder in which the monthly mailing pieces could be preserved. This offer was made to all 150,000 physicians. It was repeated three times only, and the offer batted .773—116,000 doctors said in effect, "Yes! I want to save your monthly mailing pieces. Please send me a binder."

Handling of Mail

Daniel Starch & Staff has done considerable research on the advertising effectiveness of direct mail sent to doctors. Peter Toso, projects director, reported these findings at a DMMA meeting:

> Better than eight out of ten doctors have someone who can intercept mail. This may be a nurse, a receptionist, or a secretary. Yet (1) better than half the doctors report they open all the mail which reaches their office themselves. (2) An additional 20% have an assistant sort their mail for them but the doctor still sees all the mail.
>
> This means that approximately 70-75% of the doctors actually handle the mail.
>
> On the readership of specific mailing pieces themselves, we found from three successive studies that:
>
> 1. The average self-mailer made a memorable impression on approximately 40% of the doctors and some part was read by 30% of the doctors.
> 2. The average envelope-type mailing was remembered by 45% of the doctors and some part of the mailing was read by 35% of the doctors.
> 3. The average sample mailing was remembered by approximately 60% of the doctors and some part was read by 50% of the doctors.
>
> We have found appreciable differences in the readership of individual mailing pieces ranging from a piece which was remembered by 80% of the doctors (and this was not a sample) to a piece which was only remembered by 20% of the doctors.

The Abbott Story

Few will question the fact that Abbott Laboratories of North Chicago, Illinois, was an early pace setter in pharmaceutical direct mail. Under direction of former vice president Charles Downs, Abbott pioneered many direct mail techniques now widely used both throughout the pharmaceutical industry and by direct mail advertisers generally. Abbott consistently won top awards for its direct mail advertising and was quick to give the medium a great deal of credit for the company's outstanding growth record.

Because Abbott's direct mail program was so successful in reaching an important audience of "specifiers," it deserves special study. A general picture of the company's basic direct mail program was included in the entry which won DMMA honors as the best direct mail program of 1959:

> The ethical pharmaceutical market is like no other. Our actual customers are the pharmacies and hospitals, together with the lay public who ultimately buy and consume our drugs. Yet, paradoxically, our advertising effort is aimed at neither of these groups. Instead, we direct it to a group of men who do not buy or sell our product, and often, indeed, need not even personally administer it. Yet Abbott's success or failure hinges upon their

attitude toward our products and our firm. These men, of course, are the physicians who prescribe our ethical drugs. Thus, our direct mail objective can be easily defined: to influence the prescribing habits of physicians on the behalf of Abbott wherever appropriate.

To fulfill this objective, we seek to make Abbott direct mail build good-will—to make it useful to the physicians as well as to ourselves. We look for distinctive and attractive visual formats. And where our product story requires extensive copy, we try to make our text as down to earth and informative as possible.

During the past 12 months we mailed well over 100 original pieces (not counting *Abbott Topics,* our magazine for doctors). Clearly, then, we also have to consider not only the individual effect of each mailing, but the over-all impression our total campaign is striving for. Whatever freshness, imagination, and excellence we are able to display through the year's campaign, may induce the doctor to identify those same desirable characteristics with everything Abbott does.

The mailings were directed to the following groups of physicians, in whole or in part: General Practitioners, 92,000; Specialists, 87,000; Residents and Internes, 33,000.

Obviously it is not possible to trace direct sales to our physician campaign. But we do have a yardstick of relative effectiveness. This yardstick is the number of returns on sample offers. We made 25 mailings during the year in which a reply card was enclosed offering a small sample of the product. Our returns ranged from 8% to more than 25%, with an average of 15.8%. Considering that the typical general practitioner receives approximately 5,000 mailings each year (90% of which are of a medical promotional nature), we feel that this response suggests more than satisfactory effectiveness for the Abbott direct mail campaign.

Abbott's "Abbott Topics" Magazine

Like most other major pharmaceutical manufacturers, Abbott publishes a regular external house organ called *Abbott Topics*. Abbott, in fact, was one of the pioneers in the external company publication field. In the early 1930's Abbott launched *Abbott Digest,* closely patterned after *Reader's Digest,* even to a minimum use of illustrations. After a couple of years of nearly nonexistent response, the publication was discontinued. But Abbott's willingness to experiment with direct mail formats brought about a more lavish magazine, *What's New,* which was almost an exact opposite of the unsuccessful *Digest.* Started in 1935 as an experimental quarterly, the new magazine was an immediate success and with its second issue in January 1936 became a monthly. Although today it has been reduced to a four-times-a-year schedule and has been renamed *Abbott Topics,* it continues as an important part of Abbott's direct mail program. Probably no other magazine—commercial or private—has won so many top awards. Abbott describes the magazine's function this way:

Abbott Topics, Abbott's medical magazine, is mailed four times a year to some 250,000 readers, including doctors, internes, medical students and hospital personnel. Its objective: to gain physician goodwill.

Clearly we cannot consider such an objective simply in terms of what *Abbott Topics* is to do for Abbott. We must also consider what *Abbott Topics* is expected to do for the reader. Our success with the latter in large measure governs our success with the former.

Abbott Topics serves the doctor as an educational device. It augments his regular medical journals with material he cannot easily find. It supplies him with sociomedical studies, clinical surveys, brief summaries and abstracts from a wide span of U. S. and foreign journals, full-color physiological drawings and photos, special art features, etc. Many of the subjects are also made available to him in reprint form.

Moreover, by making much use of fine art and modern graphic design, *Abbott Topics* pays an implicit compliment to the tastes of the medical profession for which it is prepared.

Abbott Topics can be regarded as a selling instrument for Abbott, but chiefly in the broad, corporate sense. Its status with readers indeed seems greatest when it is free from editorial commercialism. Hence all promotional references to Abbott products are restricted to three pages of advertising.

As the voice of Abbott, *Abbott Topics* can be a positive force in molding the physician's opinion of Abbott. The implications of having the physician think and speak well of Abbott, and engender the same attitude among his fellow MD's, among the druggists, and even the public, are incalculable. In effect, we are striving to make the physician a low-pressure salesman for Abbott.

Abbott Topics is institutional in its nature. Directly traceable sales are not expected of it. But the heavy and consistent correspondence it generates is good evidence that it is effective. During 1959, for example, we received some 27,928 requests for summaries and abstracts that appeared in the magazine. Similarly we received some 8,288 requests for reprints of cover illustrations. We mailed 52,450 samples in response to six offers during the year. Finally, a steady flow of mail has been drawn from readers commenting on various art and medical features in *Abbott Topics.*

Concrete Evidence of Direct Mail Effectiveness

To Abbott also must go credit for one of the most thorough tests of direct mail's effectiveness as a promotional tool. In a 1954 speech, Abbott's Charles Downs described a controlled experiment:

Let's call the product involved Prescription Product No. 1984. It is a good product and has very substantial prescription sales possibilities. It's therapeutically up to date, not outmoded by some new medical development or discovery. No. 1984 is not exclusive or semiexclusive with Abbott, there being 52 competitive products of like or similar composition in a market dominated by the products of three of our competitors.

At the time our experiment started, we weren't doing well with No. 1984. The product had been introduced two or three years before and had been the object of a fair amount of advertising and sales effort. But after an initial, fairly substantial flurry of sales, it slowly began to die. Our salesmen became discouraged with No. 1984 and stopped promoting it on their calls to physicians. Advertising support for the product declined.

Then we finally launched our experiment. Four relatively small areas of the country were chosen. During the first four weeks of the experiment, Abbott sent every physician in the test areas two very simple and inexpensive mailings featuring Product No. 1984. Since then, one mailing a week on the product has been sent to those doctors right down to the present time. A good many of these mailings were government postal cards. Others were small, inexpensively printed folders. An occasional letter has been used. And, at regular intervals, samples of the product, accompanied by some piece of printed advertising matter, have been sent. Our salesmen were not informed of this test campaign.

The combined average monthly sales of No. 1984 in the four test areas before the start of our experiment amounted to just $693.82. At the end of only three months, the average monthly sales had moved upward to $1,938.70, an increase of 179.4%. In six months, the rate of sale was averaging $2,536.60, or a 265.5% increase. At 18 months, 24 months, and 30 months, sales in the test areas swept on upward. At the end of 36 months, the combined average monthly sale of No. 1984 was at a rate of $5,727.05 a month, an increase of 725.4% over the $693.82 average rate at the time the test was launched. Sales of the product in the rest of the country have continued to decline.

DIRECT MAIL FOR NONINDUSTRIAL PRODUCTS

The promoting of nonindustrial products sold to business and professional men often parallels direct mail techniques described in Chapter 8 ("Industrial Direct Mail"). However, many products are less technical in nature and have wide application horizontally across the general spectrum of industries. As a result, there is generally a blending of industrial and consumer promotion techniques.

Often, the basic type of direct mail advertising used to promote these nonindustrial products sold to business and professional men depends primarily on the method of distribution. When a product is available through some type of store, it is common to use many of the same promotion techniques used for retail advertising. A typical example is the sale of office supplies, which are usually purchased through office supply stores of one type or another.

But when the normal method of selling is through individual salesmen—either a manufacturer's own salesmen or those from some type of distribution organization—it is more common to use industrial promotion techniques.

The NCR Story

An outstanding example of this second type of promotion is provided by the National Cash Register Company,* an organization which credits direct mail with playing a vital role in its success. John H. Patterson, the company's founder, is credited with developing many of the direct mail methods widely used today. The role of NCR's direct mail as described by advertising manager George W. Head: "We don't sell *machines* by direct mail, but we do sell *ideas,* and thus pave the way for the sale of machines by our salesmen."

NCR organizes its direct mail campaigns by lines of business and by business situations. Each of its campaigns consists of five or six pieces mailed at weekly intervals. Just for its cash register line alone, the company has 60 different campaigns—plus separate campaigns for accounting machines, adding machines and other products. George Head describes the NCR direct mail program this way:

> Let us assume our salesman wishes to interest a food store owner in changing from a clerk-service operation to self-service operation. There is a direct mail campaign consisting of several pieces designed to convince him he should consider making the change. Suppose he wants to convince another store owner of the danger of handwritten figures. There is a direct mail campaign to point out those weaknesses. He may want to convince another merchant he is losing money through the errors of mental addition. There is a campaign for that. If he wants to convince another he could increase sales-per-salesperson if he had daily records of the sales of each, there is a campaign to sell that idea. And so on, to meet every possible situation.
>
> Having these campaigns arranged scientifically not only eliminates guesswork, it also saves a vast amount of time for the salesman. Furthermore, it encourages him to use more direct mail because we make it so easy for him. It is well known that the best way to get a man to do a thing the *right* way is to make it *easier* for him to do it right than to do it wrong. (NCR provides salesmen with a booklet which comprehensively indexes all available direct mail campaigns for quick reference.) From all this, better selections of mailings result. All these factors contribute to making more sales with less time and effort, thus shortening the path to orders and lowering the cost of personal selling.
>
> Direct mail is coordinated with our selling plan. These direct mail campaigns are among the first steps whereby we arouse interest and prove the need for our products. Sometimes a salesman mails them *before* he calls on the prospect. Sometimes he leaves them after he has made the first call on the prospect. But in any event he follows up mailings with personal calls. And, in keeping with our selling plan, he makes calls between mailings whenever possible.
>
> As a result of combining direct mail material with personal calls, the point is finally reached where the salesman gets permission to survey the prospect's present system and to recommend a better one. When that time comes, the salesman is ready to demonstrate a system. He then has sales material to help him supplement his machine demonstrations, to visualize

*now NCR Corp.

the results the prospect can obtain. And this sales material—these systems booklets—fulfill the promises made in the direct mail that we can show him a better system for his business.

Another way we coordinate direct mail with our selling plan is to re-print, each month, the various ads that we run in publications. We supply these ad reprints to our selling organization for direct mail purposes. The salesman can (if he wishes) include these reprints with his direct mail campaigns. We carry this coordination a step further. These reprints of publication ads which are used for direct mail are also made into large window posters for our branch offices. Thus we tell a consistent story. We tell it by direct mail. We tell it in publication advertising, which we reprint for direct mail use. And we blow up these ads for window display purposes.

There is an old saying used by our cash register salesmen in addressing prospects: "Do you *guess* or do you *know* if you are losing money through hidden channels?" And this theme is a basic part of our direct mail copy. We seek to remove the guesswork for the merchant, and by systematized control over our own usage of direct mail we remove the guesswork from our use of it.

Chapter 14

FUND RAISING BY DIRECT MAIL

WHILE it would be impossible to accurately compute the total annual contributions to recognized nonprofit organizations in the United States—including charities, churches, schools, and health organizations—reliable estimates place the figure considerably above the $17-billion mark. And, of this total, more than half is probably raised by application of direct mail techniques to fund raising.

While it has long been common for national charitable organizations to use the mails for the bulk of their fund solicitations, more and more local and regional charities are turning to direct mail as a prime tool in their fund drives. Some still use the mails primarily to pave the way for door-to-door solicitation, but many have found it increasingly difficult to get volunteers to ring doorbells and now concentrate on mail appeals for their working capital.

Originally, many charities held the belief that the cost of mail solicitation ate up too large a portion of their revenues. But the rising cost of organizing and operating door-to-door campaigns, coupled with the perfection of direct mail fund-raising techniques, has led an increasing number to take the mailbox route. Many organizations are still holdouts, primarily because the professionals in charge have come up through the personal solicitation way of conducting fund drives and feel strongly that the success of their operation depends upon actively involving large numbers of people in fund raising.

Laws and Regulations

Because of highly-publicized abuses of fund raising for questionable—and even non-existent—causes, there have been increasing governmental controls. The majority of these controls have been on a state and local level.

Over half of the states and most principal cities in the U.S. have specific laws and regulations concerning charitable solicitation—in addition to more general laws concerning fraud.

Most states have followed the lead of New York, but there are many variations and, thus, it is important to check carefully the laws and regulations on the books of the specific area where fund raising is to take place.

Among the features which appear in many of the fund-raising laws and regulations are:

- Required registration of fund-raising organizations.
- A limit on the amount of net proceeds which can be allowed as a fee and expenses for a professional solicitor. (In New York, for example, a maximum of 15% of the gross raised is allowed as fee and expenses to the professional fund raiser.)
- Written consent for use of names to be solicited.
- Fund-raising contracts with professional organizations.
- Issuance of an annual report.
- Prohibitions against telephone solicitation.

Advantages of Mail Solicitations

There are at least 20 advantages to the use of direct mail for fund raising:

1. More complete control—Because fewer middlemen become involved, the organization conducting a fund drive through the mails has more complete control. In a personal-contact program, a great deal hinges on the ability and dedication of various levels of group leaders. If one of these becomes sick, overburdened with other activities, or disenchanted with the job, or if he misinterprets instructions, a major portion of the fund drive can become bogged down.

2. Wider coverage—The universe available for solicitation is considerably expanded when mail solicitations are used. Just about every corner of the world can be reached through the mails, while a personal contact program depends upon the availability of volunteers and an opportunity to sell them on helping.

3. Fewer blind spots—Many fund drives are less successful than they deserve to be because various circumstances result in temporary failures in certain areas. Unfortunately, it is often too late to institute remedial measures when these blind spots are uncovered. Since mail returns present a day-by-day record of results, it is possible to take quick action to plug any holes.

4. Less costly—Comparative costs of different methods of fund raising are often difficult to pin down. However, the bulk of evidence available indicates direct mail can be the least costly of all techniques if properly planned and executed.

5. Better cost control—One of the major advantages of direct mail is that actual costs can be carefully pinpointed and determined in advance. Other types of fund raising often involve many initially hidden costs such as extensive telephone charges, luncheons, transportation, etc. In one area, for example, just the cost of a special luncheon to build enthusiasm among United Fund volunteers exceeded the entire cost of a direct mail program in a nearby town which raised the same amount of money without personal solicitation.

6. Built-in records—Another advantage of direct mail is that it provides its own records of contributions. Quite often, flaps on return envelopes are designed so they can be filled in by the donor and then removed by the charity for record purposes. Other times, address plates are coded to become the primary record. But even when special records are necessary, there is usually less effort involved than when it is necessary to work with often inadequate (and often unreadable) reports from personal contact volunteers.

7. Takes less time of staff—Because fewer people are involved, a direct mail fund-raising program requires less time of the paid staff of a charity. It is also usually far less time-consuming to organize a complete direct mail program than to go through the annual task of lining up volunteer organizations, briefing them, and directing their day-by-day activities.

8. Outside services available—While there are professional fund-raising organizations which can take over the task of conducting any type of drive, such services are generally found only in major metropolitan areas. Direct mail service organizations, on the other hand, are available most everywhere. There are experienced and skillful professionals available to handle entire fund-raising operations or any phase of them.

9. Better chance to tell full story—While personal contact programs do present the opportunity to provide immediate answers to questions of prospective donors, chances of any volunteer being able to answer every question accurately are very slight. And even though volunteers can be supplied with informational publications to hand out to those who are contacted, there is seldom a chance of getting this material read while the volunteer stands, hat in hand, in the doorway. Fund-raising mailings, however, can include everything necessary to tell a full story, just the way those who know the story best prefer to have it told.

10. Capitalize on current events—An opportunity to tie in with important news developments can be a major plus value in many fund drives. But to do so usually requires fast action. Since it is possible to broadcast an appeal by mail in a very short time, fund raisers frequently trade on a fast-breaking news story with direct mail solicitations. One Red Cross chapter, for example, has a series of "disaster letters" ready for immediate use and maintains up-to-date lists of donors who have responded to previous appeals for special funds required when a major disaster struck. When a flood, hurricane, tornado, fire, or some other major disaster strikes, this chapter quickly adds the details to the basic letters already prepared, has envelopes addressed immediately from the always-ready lists, and can have its appeal in the hands of those most likely to help while the news is "still hot." Such a mailing supplements appeals made in newspapers and over radio and television, and has the added advantages of personal appeal with an enclosed reply device.

11. Testing is possible—By applying mail order procedures, fund-raising organizations can thoroughly test different approaches and then concentrate on those which are most productive. Because personal contact methods vary so greatly depending upon the individuals involved, it is extremely difficult to conduct thorough testing.

12. More flexible—Direct mail, of course, offers maximum flexibility. Timing, copy approach, format, and other factors can be varied to meet changing conditions and different audiences. It is often possible to make desirable changes almost instantly, while other fund-raising approaches usually require a lengthy lead time for any type of change.

13. Tailored appeals—A direct mail program can be carefully tailored to any number of different audiences. For example, it might be desirable to ask for different amounts of money from different groups. Many times, special appeals are required for maximum results from audiences with different racial, religious, geographical, or income backgrounds. With other major fund-raising methods, it is often necessary to use a single approach.

A classic example of the tailoring of a direct mail fund-raising appeal to a special audience dates back to 1927, when Lehigh University wanted to build a new electrical and mechanical laboratory. Rather than make a general appeal for funds, the university decided to try to induce a single man to put up the needed million dollars. A prestige booklet, telling of the need and the benefits, was sent with a letter to 500 carefully selected names of wealthy alumni and friends. Within two weeks, James Ward Packard mailed Lehigh University a check for $1,000,000!

14. Special treatment—Another element of direct mail's flexibility which can be most useful in fund raising is the ability to give special treatment to special individuals and groups. For example, many successful fund raisers use a completely different approach when appealing to previous donors than they use for their general appeal. In such cases, it is often important to make it obvious that the previous donor is being recognized as a close friend—someone special.

15. Continuing program—Another mail order technique which has special application in fund raising is the upgrading of donors. Many groups have found it worthwhile to promote their appeal to the break-even point to get an initial donation, since once a prospect becomes "sold" on the cause, he or she becomes a continuing supporter. Through regular direct mail contacts, these donors can be encouraged to give increasing amounts.

16. Followthrough—In personal contact programs, it is often difficult to get volunteers to make more than an initial call on each prospect. If this call is not productive, the solicitation most frequently ends right there. In a well-organized direct mail program, however, it is possible to "keep calling" until the donation has been obtained or at least until the law of diminishing returns sets in. In fact, most successful direct mail fund-raising programs do not stop the moment a donation has been obtained. Donors are immediately thanked and regularly informed on how their donations have been used, with the net result that future donations are easier to obtain. Such programs often lead to additional donations without a direct appeal.

17. Privacy—Perhaps direct mail's most important advantage in fund-raising programs is the privacy it affords the donor. Many people do not like to let others know how much they contribute to various causes, and thus respond more readily to an appeal which assures them of the greatest possible privacy. Nelson R. Kraemer, director of Christmas Seal sales for the National Tuberculosis Assn., explains, in an article which appeared in *Envelope Economies,* a publication of Tension Envelope Corporation:

> Man's place of residence has always been the focal point of the Christmas Seal sale. No canvasser stands on the doorstep, for the mailman delivers the Christmas Seal letter with its bright Christmas Seals and the accompanying message. Here, within the privacy of his own home, a man makes the decision as to whether or not he will support the campaign. If he cares to do so, the return envelope is convenient for his contribution. If he rejects this appeal, no great effort is needed to drop the mailing piece in the wastebasket. Even if it does end up in the wastebasket, the recipient often reads the enclosed educational message.

18. Personal approach—Direct mail affords a charitable organization an opportunity to make a personal appeal to donors. On the surface it might seem that the personal contact method offers the ultimate in a personal approach. However, since the person making the contact is usually a "middleman," often many steps removed from the basic organization, a direct personal relationship between the charity making the appeal and the donor is often lacking. Particularly through the use of automatically typewritten letters, it is possible to put a fund drive on a highly personal basis.

19. No "not at homes"—Many times it is difficult for volunteers to reach the person who must make the decision about a donation. But direct mail can be counted upon to reach the vast majority of prospective donors.

20. Does the complete job—The right direct mail "package" can do a complete fund-raising job in a single effort. It can inform, generate interest, ask for the donation, and provide the means for conveying it to the fund-raising organization.

Charity Giving Motivations

In his excellent book, "Handbook of Consumer Motivations,"† Dr. Ernest Dichter provides some observations on motivations behind giving to charity which are worth examining when preparing fund raising direct mail:

> When we give we play God. We feel very uppity; we are very arrogant. In one way or another, instead of feeling humility and being grateful for being given the chance to pay back our debt to humanity, the true factor that is involved is that one is capable of giving money. But there is an even more serious side—by not giving money one can play God just as well. I could give to you, you keep on begging me, keep on asking me, but I just won't. A charity organization would do well, therefore, to pay as much attention to people after they have given money as they do before.

†Handbook of Consumer Motivations by Ernest Dichter. McGraw-Hill Book Co., New York. 1964.

Giving and not giving are somehow related to attitudes that originate in our childhood days. In some peculiar way it has something to do with the relationship between children and parents. In certain areas a child can give or not give, and in giving or not giving he can, at will, maintain power over the parents. Toilet training is such a phenomenon and so is the brushing of the teeth. If the child gives up in the field of toilet training and presents himself as trained and clean, he has lost a very important instrument of his power.

In charity appeals, instead of showing needy families or needy people, it would be much better to play up to this god-like feeling and use a poster showing all the wonderful givers and telling how wonderful they feel because they have given.

A second reason for people giving or not giving is a fear of their own emotionality. A great many people do not give because they are afraid of seeing themselves as softhearted. We are trained from our first year in kindergarten to be competitive rather than to be cooperative. We are ashamed and embarrassed of calling an emotion by its true name in everyday life. When we are being asked by a charity drive to give, we are being asked to change from the everyday life experience of competition to something which is very unrealistic. It becomes a Sunday kind of giving rather than a normal everyday human experience. This may indicate from a practical viewpoint that it would be better to be brutal with people when asking them for money rather than appealing to their sentimentality. Demands for charity might be made more effectively by using the everyday language of competition.

A third reason that people do not give is because they don't know how; they are embarrassed. People often do not know how much to give. They don't know whether to give anonymously, how large to sign their name, or whether to feel elated or to feel shy about it. If they give too much, they feel like suckers; if they don't give enough, they feel like heels.

A fourth reason concerns again the parent-child relationship involved in giving. We never give readily, or as readily from the psychological viewpoint, to an anonymous person or a nonentity. It may be much easier to give to a community mother or a father symbol, to give to some real individual rather than an anonymous organization. It may be practical, therefore, to send fatherly or motherly types of people out when collecting funds rather than young people.

A fifth reason for giving or not giving concerns a fact that giving buys power. Charity workers often complain that "The moment someone has given us five bucks he thinks he has a right to criticize everything we do." This is, however, exactly why many people do give. It buys them the right to be critical. The real reason is that the giver wants to participate in the cause that he is giving to. If you do not permit him to participate in a positive way, he can participate negatively by nagging, by asking, "What are you really going to do with all that money?"

Psychological Factors

In other writings on the psychological factors involved in fund raising, Dr. Dichter has listed nine important points:

1. *Fear of Surrendering Power* . . . Like most other motivations, this is related to childhood attitudes. Consenting or not consenting repeats early training patterns. For instance, when a child accepts new training, it surrenders a bargaining point—gives up the pleasure of being cajoled. The fund raiser should understand the reluctance of people to commit themselves. If the child gives in to win applause and to please the parent, so can the contributor be made to feel that it is more pleasant and satisfying to give than it is to be obdurate.
2. *Fear of Being Forgotten* . . . "All they want is my money and then they forget about me" is a widespread complaint. The Institute for Motivational Research, Inc. in studies conducted for the Community Chest and similar organizations found it valuable to spend almost as much time and effort on people after they had given than before, to avoid this feeling of neglect. A suggestion that the giver might like to assist in future solicitations may also help offset this objection. Usually the prospect has no desire whatever to canvass, but he is flattered if he is asked. Follow-up letters of thanks, and published lists of donors which include the giver's name are powerful weapons to aid future drives.
3. *Fear of Embarrassment* . . . Ironically, many people are afraid of feeling ashamed if they do give. They don't want to be thought of as soft touches and they don't want to get on every charity's list. Pictures of needy sufferers are likely to repulse them and they are wary of displaying sentiment. Sound, hard-headed reasons for contributing are most effective answers to this attitude. We are almost always more inclined to invest money in a successful person than in an apparent failure. In public relations campaigns for fund raising, therefore, it might be well to consider the possibility of labeling contributions as a worthwhile investment.
4. *Bandwagon Psychology* . . . In giving, as in politics, everybody wants to be on the majority side. Statistical surveys have disclosed that an appeal to citizens to vote, based on the fact that many people ignore their democratic privilege, will keep more from the polls than it will send to them. Similarly, if a citizen is told that most people are cruelly negligent of the ill and impoverished, he will feel less concern about ignoring them himself. "Join with the majority of your neighbors, who are contributing to this worthy cause," is far more effective.
5. *Ignorance of How to Give* . . . Many people hesitate because they don't know how much to give, how many drives to aid, whether they should give anonymously. At a deeper level they are concerned whether they should feel casual about giving, proud or humble. Discreet information about the mechanics of donating can help.
6. *Who Benefits?* . . . Many people seem to be disturbed about the vagueness of many fund drives. To all visible evidence, the money simply goes to an organizational name. Givers wonder if all the money is used to help the cause that is involved. They want to know how much goes to the organization and what salaries its officers get. These mildly disturbing questions grow from a more deeply-rooted concern of the potential contributor: Will it benefit *me*?
7. *Giving is a Means of Gaining Control Over Others* . . . Again, as motivational researchers and being realistic, we have found that contributors often feel that the recipients of their gifts are obligated to them. Their money has bought them control and it has brought them the symbol of money—security and power.

8. *The Recipient* . . . To understand the psychology of giving also relates to the recipient. Of course, many factors which are of great importance to understanding the psychology of giving are anchored in the recipient. Institutions are more or less anonymous. We prefer, however, to give to a personal recipient.
9. *We Unconsciously Give to a Parental Figure* . . . Because of the childhood relationship giving represents, we are actually unconsciously *giving* to mother or father—or withholding from them. Our experience has shown, therefore, that a parental approach on the part of the fund raiser—whether it be an individual or an institution—is more effective than an approach based on equality between giver and recipient.

Creating a Donor Profile

For maximum effectiveness in raising funds by direct mail, it is extremely important to have a clear profile of the audience to whom the appeal is being made. In some cases, of course, the profile is the *start* of a fund-raising program—alumni of a college, members of a church, etc. But when an on-going direct mail fund-raising program is based on continued solicitation of a less immediately identifiable audience, every possible effort should be made to draw up a profile of that audience.

Ralph W. Sanders, Executive Vice President of World Neighbors, writing in the September/October 1969 issue of *Fund Raising Management* presented an example of two typical donor profiles for a mythical "Christian Bible College":

Average Donor

The average donor to Christian Bible College is a married woman around 45 years of age who has been contributing for about five years. Her interests at the college are: first, campus development; second, financial aid to needy students; and third, preparing students for Christian service. She reads about six books a year and three religious magazines. She receives both the bimonthly college newsletters and the quarterly President's letters. She reads the newsletters "thoroughly" and "skims" the President's letters. She has three children—one of whom is still at home. She lives in a community of about 50,000. Annual family income is $8,000. She may have a will but it doesn't include charitable bequests. She has a little stock. Last year she contributed to eight charitable organizations including possibly one other Christian college. She prefers to give cash once or twice a year. She attended at least three years of college—and probably completed a bachelor's degree. She is a church member—and probably a Baptist.

Super Donor

The super donor to Christian Bible College is still most likely to be a married woman, but the proportion of men is moving up. Age is older—61 instead of 45. Has been contributing longer—14 to 16 years instead of five. Interests at the college are: first, financial aid to needy students; second, preparing students for Christian service; third, improving faculty and staff; and fourth, building the endowment fund. Reads fewer books and magazines but reads all college newsletters and letters "thoroughly." Children are older and away from home. Lives in a community of 15,000 instead of 50,000. Average income is around $17,000 instead of $8,000. Has one gift annuity and owns stocks, bonds and some mutual funds. Contributed to around 20 other charities including three other Christian colleges. Unlikely to have more than one year of college—probably didn't attend at all. Is a church member—generally either a Baptist or Presbyterian.

Profile Differences

In his article, Ralph Sanders noted that the importance of differences in profiles for such groups as small donors, large donors, super donors, inactive donors and other special groups boils down to three key factors: 1) It helps you define your average donor; 2) It points up the differences between the small and large and super and inactive donors; and, 3) It makes possible preparing a plan of action based on sound marketing and communications principles.

In his hypothetical profiles, Mr. Sanders noted the following significant differences which could affect the fund-raising appeal and follow-through:

1. Age—super is an older group—16 years older.
2. Interests—these are different.
3. Community size—super lives in a small town.
4. Income—this difference is expected, but still affects the size of gift you ask for in your appeals.
5. Wills—small donors need to be convinced of the importance of making a will; super already has—needs more information about simplicity of including additional charitable bequests. Super is also in a better position to give stock if the advantages are pointed out.
6. Education—super has little college education while average donor is probably a graduate.

Getting Profile Information

For his own organization, Mr. Sanders mailed a four-page survey form, simple enough to be completed by the average person in five minutes. This was accompanied by a cover letter from World Neighbors' president explaining the need for the survey and asking for previous donors' help—and stressing that their replies would be anonymous. A postage-paid business reply envelope was also enclosed. It drew a 40% response giving the following information about donors:

1. Sex
2. Age

3. Marital status
4. Length of time they've been contributing to program
5. How they learned of World Neighbors
6. What interests them most about the program
7. How many books and magazines they read last year
8. How they read our materials—letters, newsletters, reports
9. Children
10. Community size
11. Annual family income
12. Do they have a will
13. Does it include charitable bequests
14. Own a gift annuity
15. Own stocks or bonds
16. Education
17. Church members
18. Denomination
19. Civic clubs
20. Other charitable interests.

Mr. Sanders noted that there's one other question he feels strongly should be included on a questionnaire—and that it "just might be the most important of all." It's simply this: "Is there a job which we're not presently doing that you think we should be?"

He commented: "You'll learn a great deal. Some of the answers you get in the form of constructive criticism are most valuable. Sometimes they're deserved. Sometimes they're new and good ideas. And sometimes a donor suggests you should do something you are already doing—but you must not have made this clear to him through your communications program. This 'feedback' is really invaluable and because the questionnaire is anonymous a good friend may tell you something he'd never dream of writing in a letter or saying in a conversation."

Use of a Donor Profile

In concluding his article, Ralph Sanders suggested a donor profile should help do six specific things:

1. *Know your people better.* In drawing up the profile, you'll get a new and better knowledge of your average donor and how you got him!
2. *Understand what they like about you.* This is valuable for it will help you understand why you appeal to them better than another, similar

group. Work to find ways to communicate this "uniqueness" that makes your program different.

3. *Discover what they don't like, too.* After learning what your donors would like to see you improve, your management should take a long look at the constructive criticism. Perhaps some of these are valid and should be changed. If the valid objections are not changed your organization is in trouble—and the sooner everyone recognizes it the better.
4. *Find new donors.* This is a bonus of the profile. What better way to find new donors than to seek out people who already "fit the mold" of your existing donors. For instance, if your donors are middle aged, married women from small towns, a fund raising push to metropolitan Rotary and Kiwanis clubs is unlikely to be your "market." Better to try for women's club programs in small towns.
5. *Set your fund raising goals.* A profile also will help you set your priorities in your fund raising and planned giving programs. If, for instance, your super and large donors indicate they have substantial stock investments, a program might be devised to point up the advantage of giving appreciated stock. The profile will be especially helpful in establishing planned giving priorities since it will give your development officer an indication of which areas offer the most immediate potential.
6. *Build your communications plan.* From the results, you'll also know which things it is about your organization that interest your donors. This gives your publication editor and appeal letter writers goals at which to shoot when planning issues and letters.

Fund-Raising Programs

There are essentially four basic types of direct mail programs used for fund raising. The first is the complete program, which involves no other type of fund raising. Appeals are sent through the mails to all prospects, and donations are returned by mail.

Second, direct mail can be used to supplement other types of fund raising. The basic program, for example, may involve extensive personal contact, with direct mail used to cover areas where volunteers are not available or where it is otherwise impractical to make personal contacts. Or it may be necessary to use direct mail appeals to follow through in those cases where personal contacts were not accomplished.

Many organizations use a third type of fund-raising direct mail—the advance mail contact. In such programs, mailings are used to inform prospective donors about the cause and to build an interest in advance of personal contacts.

The fourth basic type of fund-raising direct mail is for supplementary appeals. The most common application is to upgrade previous donors to a higher level. In other cases, mail solicitations are made to cover special emergencies or are supplementary appeals directed at audiences with special interests.

Mail Order Techniques

Fund raising by mail requires application of most of the basic mail order techniques described in Chapter 7. Many fund raisers make the mistake of believing that, because they represent a nonprofit organization, they have little in common with profitmaking commercial enterprises. The truth of the matter is, however, that raising funds represents one of the most difficult of all selling jobs. Not only must fund-raising mailings compete with the usually more elaborate commercial mailings for initial attention, but they must also compete for donations with thousands of other appeals from equally worthy causes. By applying proved mail order techniques, with certain refinements developed by successful fund raisers who have had years of experience in mail appeals, it is possible to overcome the dual handicaps of competition for attention and competition for donation dollars.

Basic Mail Order Format

One of the first lessons the fund raiser can learn from the mail order field is that the basic working format is the five-piece mailing so successful for selling by mail—mailing envelope, letter, enclosure with more detailed information, order form (in this case, a pledge form or other device on which the donor identifies himself and his donation), and reply envelope.

Actually, most fund raisers combine some of the elements. Most common is the combination reply-envelope/pledge-form. Frequently, return envelopes are already imprinted with the prospective donors' names and used with window mailing envelopes. Thus, all the donor needs do is to enclose his check or cash and place the return envelope in the mail. For certain appeals, however, it is important to give the donor an opportunity to furnish special information. For example, many groups give the donor an opportunity to specify for what purpose his money is to be spent. Others find that by describing what different amounts will accomplish, the average donation will be increased. Frequently, the reply envelope will have an imprinted flap such as one used by Grand Street Settlement of New York:

Here is my gift of:

- ☐ $15 to send a child to camp for one week.
- ☐ $30 to provide a two weeks' vacation.
- ☐ $45 to give a convalescent child three weeks at camp.
- ☐ $90 to give three children a two weeks' vacation.

Keep Them Giving

According to one of the country's top experts on fund raising, William E. Sheppard, Alumni Director for Haverford College, fund raising boils down to just two things: (1) get more people to make first-time contributions and (2) get those who have made one or more contributions to contribute again.

Writing in *Fund Raising Management* (May/June 1970), Bill Sheppard reported on a 1969 survey conducted by The Fund Raising Institute for which he edits the FRI Newsletter. In that survey, fund raisers were asked, "What do you do which you feel is especially effective in encouraging your first-time contributors to become second-time contributors?" The answers:

1. Acknowledge promptly.
2. Thank properly.
3. Increase the donor's knowledge about the institution.
4. Give something.
5. Publicize him.
6. Ask him to give again.

In commenting on these important techniques, Mr. Sheppard made these observations:

Acknowledge Promptly

When a person makes a gift, he or she wants to be sure it reaches the place where it is supposed to go. Thus, when a receipt is mailed out on the same day the check arrives at the institution, not only will the donor have the satisfaction of knowing the gift has been delivered but the impression of the institution is improved because the donor sees it as one which goes crisply and effectively about its business.

Thank Properly

Relatively few fund raisers believe a receipt is sufficient expression of appreciation. The personal letter gets the nod for doing the most effective job. Many institutions make a point of having the President send a letter to all *first-time* contributors. Others have the personal letter go to those who *increase* over the year before, or go over a set amount.

Increase Donor's Knowledge

The more a contributor knows about an organization and understands what its accomplishments and goals are, the more likely he is to give again. With good reason contributors are placed on the mailing lists to receive magazines, newsletters, annual reports, the case statement, reprints of articles in newspapers and magazines, etc. Chances are the new contributor has a lot to learn.

Give Something

In addition to a warm expression of appreciation, many institutions also give a donor something. What this something is varies greatly. It may be a football schedule, a calendar, a decal or a certificate of appreciation or membership. It may be something more valuable than these, such as an appointment book, a tie tac, or an etching of Old Main. A gift in return for a gift makes an impression. Depending on the kind of gift it is, it might even make a *lasting* impression as the contributor continues to wear his tie tac, as he continues to enjoy his etching of Old Main.

Publicize the Donor

Year after year, many colleges and universities laboriously prepare lists of donors for the year, then have them printed. Some are in separate reports, booklets, folders; some are incorporated with a magazine or an overall report. Most of the institutions which prepare annual giving honor rolls swear by them. In addition to giving publicity to those who give, a published donor list does, of course, give publicity to those who don't give. A name not on an honor roll can be a glaring omission, and there's no doubt that many gifts come in from people who do not want to suffer from this form of reverse publicity. Some institutions cash in on this by sending a "proof" of the year's honor roll with a note pointing out that there's still time for the recipient to get his/her name added before final printing. (Mr. Sheppard's personal comments are that he doubts this effort is worth the money. "There are so many ways to get a donor to keep on giving," he says, " and most of them take far less out of an annual giving office than this.")

Ask Him/Her to Give Again

No fund-seeking organization worth its salt will fail to ask a former contributor to give again. But many fail to ask enough. Far too often, those who have proven their interest are mailed to but once and then are left to sit while the annual giving team hustles all over the place in pursuit of strangers who might be persuaded to make a first-time gift. The famed Menninger Foundation gets better than a 75% renewal from former contributors. To do this, however, five mailings or more are employed—and each, including the fifth, pays its way. Incidentally, a Menninger test revealed that the renewal rate for the first time givers ran approximately 48%, but for those giving twice or oftener the rate rose to 85%. The moral from this, of course, is that the first givers need special attention . . . and that this extra effort is likely to be well worthwhile.

Followup Mailings

Most successful direct mail fund-raising programs include a carefully organized followup phase. Typical is the one used to follow up on Christmas Seal mailings. Nelson Kraemer described it in *Envelope Economies:*

> Every effort is made to concentrate our efforts in the traditional campaign period, Thanksgiving to Christmas. When the volume of mail hits a peak in December, a reminder card is sent out. This card carries a facsimile of the Christmas Seal and a health education message. This card goes out to all unresponsive names. At the end of December another followup card is mailed to the unresponsive names. This message is slanted at the many people who overlooked making a remittance during the Christmas rush. In January, a brief letter is sent to unresponsive contributor names. The copy in this letter emphasizes the need for funds to carry on program activities.

Copy for such followup mailings must be prepared carefully so as not to offend any who have already made contributions. Father Flanagan's Boys Town, which also mails sheets of Christmas seals, uses an attractive illustrated post card which says:

> Thank you . . . if you have already mailed your Christmas donation for Boys' Town Seals. If not—won't you, please? It will help so much. With sincere thanks and best wishes for a most happy Holiday Season . . .

Personalized Letters

There has been increasing use of computer and automatically typewritten letters for fund raising. With such letters, of course, it is possible to make a highly personal appeal and results often more than offset the higher cost. Such letters are particularly worthwhile for mailings to previous donors.

In preparing personalized letters, it is very important to use a person-to-person approach. Fill-ins, such as the amount donated the previous year or the number of consecutive years a contribution has been received, are frequently included. Many fund raisers feel quite strongly that it is a mistake to make any en-

Stamps, key tags and name labels have been successful in raising funds for deserving organizations. Among those illustrated are examples from Disabled American Veterans, National Foundation for Asthmatic Children, Boys Town, National Society for Crippled Children and Adults, St. Anthony's Guild and Amvets.

closures with personalized letters, including even reply envelopes. Experience on this matter, however, varies greatly, so it is an item which should be thoroughly tested.

Another caution which must be observed is the importance of preparing new copy constantly. Nothing can destroy the effectiveness of a personalized letter program so quickly as to send an identical duplicate letter to a donor. On the other hand, carbon copy followups are very effective. In such cases, a carbon of the original letter is made during the initial typing and then held for a given period. If a donation is not forthcoming during that period, the carbon copy is sent, usually with a short personalized note attached suggesting the original may have gone astray or that action may have been unavoidably delayed.

Stamps and Seals

Some of the most successful fund-raising appeals have been built around the use of sheets of stamps or seals. Most everyone is acquainted with the Christmas Seals, which have been used by the National Tuberculosis Association since 1907, and the Easter Seals, sent annually by the National Society for Crippled Children & Adults. While recipients are no longer asked to "buy" the stamps, they do psychologically suggest a minimum donation of one cent per stamp. In addition, the stamps are often used by the recipients on their personal mail, thus helping promote the cause through implied endorsement.

Many other organizations have found somewhat similar stamps highly effective. In addition to the Boys Town Seals previously mentioned, the National Wildlife Federation has built a major program around its beautiful wildlife stamps, plus the profitable sale of albums into which the stamps can go.

Religious organizations frequently make effective use of seals in fund-raising mailings. Some simply imprint Biblical quotations, while others prepare seals with a special meaning. St. Anthony's Guild, for example, mails booklets of St. Anthony's Guide Seals, which many of the Roman Catholic faith attach to their letters. Copy on the booklets explains: "It is a triumph of the spirit of romance to give our letters to St. Anthony's care. It is a gesture that points upward to that light-hearted sunny faith of ours, which teaches the communion of saints."

Handicraft Items

Other organizations have built continuing fund-raising appeals around useful or ornamental items, frequently produced by the people benefited by donations. Perhaps the best-known user of this technique is the Disabled American Veterans organization, which sends out miniature license plate key tags to motorists. Another example is the extensive use of personalized address labels in the fund-raising program of the National Foundation for Asthmatic Children. The Epilepsy Foundation frequently mails sheets of different types of household labels.

Unordered Merchandise

Many organizations have adopted the questionable technique of mailing out unordered merchandise with the theme that the recipient buying it will be helping support the sender's cause through profits which are made. While the procedure is legal, it frequently develops a great deal of ill will and is considered highly unethical by most charitable organizations and direct mail groups.

The most frequently used items are neckties and greeting cards, although hundreds of different items ranging from dolls and toys to books, statues, and imprinted book plates have been used. While it is usually suggested the recipient simply return the merchandise if he or she does not feel it represents a good value, the trouble involved often causes the recipient to develop a strong distaste for the sender's organization.

At one time, it was a common practice to ask recipients to return such items as Christmas Seals if they did not want to buy them, but most organizations now urge recipients to use the stamps, seals, and other inexpensive items included with mailings regardless of whether or not they make a donation—thus removing any "unordered merchandise" stigma from such mailings. The National Wildlife Federation, for example, includes this paragraph in letters accompanying sheets of its Christmas wildlife stamps:

> The stamps, as always, will add an extra touch of beauty to your cards and gifts. Please accept them and use them. A contribution is always welcome and helpful in our wildlife programs, but please do not feel you are under any obligation.

Catalogs

A popular substitute for the unordered merchandise device is the mailing of catalogs listing various items which can be purchased through a charitable organization. In many cases, such mailings are standard mail order operations except for the added appeal that profits will go to a worthy cause. Other times, special items tailored to the cause making the mailing are featured. Probably the most common type of catalog fund raising is the sale of magazine subscriptions by organizations supporting educational institutions. Other groups offer special lists of books on subjects related to their cause. Another catalog technique is to offer handicraft items produced by those helped through an organization's rehabilitation activities.

Use of Gadgets

It would be impossible to list all of the many gadget approaches which have been applied to raising funds by mail without devoting an entire book to the subject. They have included enclosing dollars or pennies with letters, tip-ons of plastic letter gadgets and specially stamped medals, mailings from foreign countries—and many of the other showmanship direct mail techniques described in Chapter 31.

There is one basic danger inherent in the use of gadgets in fund raising that is seldom an important factor in commercial mailings. Recipients may easily feel the cost of gadgets represents an unwise investment of an organization's funds. Many groups purposely try to develop inexpensive-appearing formats to imply that only a small portion of the funds raised go into promotion. Many even avoid the use of business-reply envelopes and instead imprint a message in a box designated for the application of a postage stamp: "Your stamp here will help."

Publications

Another popular fund-raising-by-mail technique is the use of special publications. Just about every possible publication format has been adapted to fund-raising use. Some of the publications are devoted entirely to contents directly related to fund raising, while others contain a variety of editorial material. One popular technique is to prepare an annual report, which is sent to previous donors along with a message requesting continuing support. Another frequently used approach is to send an educational booklet—such as a guide to better health. The same caution which must be considered when using gadget mailings applies to publications. If a publication is too elaborate or in any way seems a waste of money, it is likely to suggest an unwise use of funds. Some organizations overcome such objections by arranging to have publications donated or by setting up a special fund, which is handled separately from regular donations, for use in financing publications.

A four-point guide to an effective fund-raising publication program is offered in Harold P. Levy's book, *Public Relations for Social Agencies* (copyright by Harper & Row, 1956):

1. *Produce with a purpose*—Decide first on the specific audience or audiences you are trying to reach. For the most part, you have a different message for staff members than potential contributors, for teenagers than opinion leaders—or at least you may wish to say it differently. This is not to suggest overmeticulous screening of every production piece; many obviously are appropriate for wide readerships. It is important, however, to give thoughtful consideration to the best possible communications medium for the ends you wish to accomplish.
2. *Start with a good script*—An informational piece is only as good as the story it tells. Attractive artwork and printing add eye appeal but they will not cover up a weak or confused message. Obviously, it is not possible to strive for sparkling prose in every piece of copy that comes through an office typewriter. That would be wasteful of time, manpower, and money. But clarity, readability, and accuracy should be standard hallmarks. It is unfortunate that many agencies and organizations do not place a high enough premium on the written word. Too many executives work on the theory that "anyone" can handle a writing assignment.
3. *Dress up your production pieces*—Eye appeal can make the difference between a successful production piece and one that gains only indifferent readership, between a brochure you want to read *now* and one you can easily lay aside. This is not a plea for big production budgets. They help, but you can do a great deal without them.
4. *Plan distribution carefully*—This is the logical conclusion to any production effort. Yet it is a rule surprisingly often neglected, and we sometimes end up with supplies of carefully developed informational pieces and no clear idea what to do with them. The time to start thinking about distribution is during the planning and production stages.

In addition to publications originating with a fund-raising organization, it is often wise to seek out opportunities to use reprints from recognized publications. Frequently, "an outsider" can be more convincing in describing the worthiness of a cause than can obviously prejudiced material prepared by those directly related to the organization making the appeal.

Special Copy Appeals

Writing copy for fund-raising mailings requires application of the basic techniques used for other types of direct mail. These are covered in detail in Chapters 24 and 25. However, there are some important considerations which apply specifically to fund-raising copy. In their book, *Tested Methods of Raising Money,* Margaret Fellows and S. Koenig point out:

> A sales letter offers the reader something tangible for his money. Even if it breaks all the "rules" of good letter writing as you have learned them, some people will respond to it by buying the product offered. For there is usually a market somewhere for every commodity, be it grass seed, lumber or shingles for a house, and, therefore, there is a "return" that the reader will get when he responds to a sales letter. But in writing to ask for aid

> in creating a new chair of psychiatry in a university or in providing care for children, you are facing a different problem.
>
> You are offering something that man believes he can live without. You are competing with offers of necessities and luxuries and substituting for these products a feeling of satisfaction and happiness in helping the underdog. Although we all know that "man cannot live by bread alone," we must get the other fellow to realize it, too, and to act on that belief. To do this, we must find out what our selling point is and how we can present it so that it arouses desire.
>
> Instead of getting a vacuum cleaner for their checks, Mrs. Jones and Mr. White get a very real sense of satisfaction, a deep inner reward that makes them really happy . . . a different kind of happiness than they could get in acquiring a material possession. It is a glow they feel in their souls, and if you want to check on it more closely, analyze your own feelings when you have given something to someone who couldn't get it for himself.
>
> Every person at some time in his life experiences this feeling, for the instinct to give of oneself, one's time and money, is present to some degree in all persons and needs only to be stirred to become active. Obviously it is to this instinct, this emotion of kindliness and willingness to help others, that you must appeal if you are to touch your prospect's pocketbook. And if you are to touch his pocketbook, you must first touch his heart.
>
> . . . We know that man's heart is easier to reach than his head; that his dreams and hopes are very much like our own. Our job is to appeal to his highest and most human qualities, to recount a human situation in simple terms, so that he can feel "there but for the grace of God go I," or my son or my daughter. And we know that he will feel this, for it would be a response common to all people.
>
> Select then that part of your work which has the most human appeal and which will, therefore, create in your prospect's heart a desire to contribute. Best calculated to do this is an appeal to love, pity, patriotism, security, pride, duty, responsibility, self-interest, and self-preservation. These are the springboards of all human action.

According to David Church, there is an eight-step procedure to put across your fund-raising message:

1. State the problem.
2. Tell what is being done about the problem.
3. State what needs to be done.
4. State what your institution proposes to do about the problem.
5. Explain how your institution is able to do this.
6. Show that your institution has wide spread support.
7. State what it will cost to do what your institution wants to do.
8. State what you want contributors to do and when.

List Building

Most of the list-building techniques described in Chapter 20 can be used by fund-raising organizations. Exchanges, for example, can be particularly important for many groups. The willingness to exchange lists varies from field to field, but if you can find a group which has made a similar appeal, it is well worth any amount of effort to try to arrange a direct exchange of lists of donors. Those who have supported one health foundation, for example, are prime prospects for support of another health foundation. As in all exchanges, it is important to avoid a conflict in mailing dates. At the

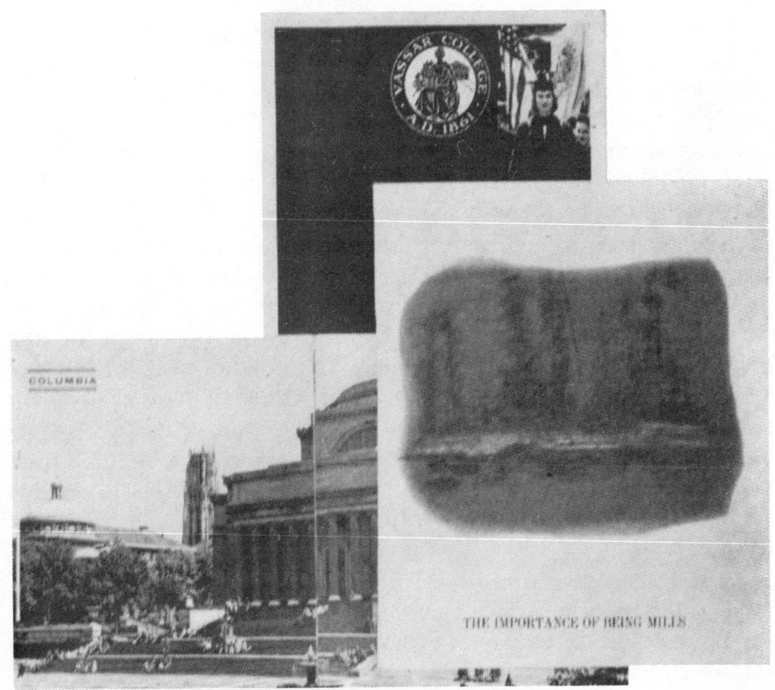

A montage of modern, attractive booklets that Mills College, Columbia University and Vassar College use to raise funds.

very least, a month should separate mailings of similar appeals to the same list.

Mailing list compilers and brokers can be of invaluable assistance to any fund-raising organization. Many of these service organizations have a long history of service to fund raisers and can be called upon not only to provide lists but to offer expert guidance in all phases of raising funds by mail.

Using Mail Order Techniques

Perhaps the most innovative organization in the direct mail fund raising field is American Fund Raising Services of Waltham, Mass. Francis S. ("Andy") Andrews, AFRS founder, found that the techniques he used successfully in building a mail order business had a direct application in fund raising. When the computer became a factor in fund raising, he was ready to apply these techniques on a major scale for a variety of religious, medical, charitable and educational institutions.

In describing his system, Andy Andrews recalls: "What started as bits and pieces of personalization and letter techniques emerged finally as a comprehensive fund raising system which has achieved very great successes for many fund raisers. The system seems deceptively simple. The basics are right out of mail order practice, but were unknown to fund raisers in the 1940's and early 1950's when we were perfecting the techniques.

"Simply stated, one prospects from either mail order lists or socio-economic lists, screening large masses for names of donors. This process is conducted at a profit if necessary, but ideally at break-even, thus utilizing the principle of averaging out or maximizing the number of donors rather than profit. This follows mail order practice of buying a new customer at a loss if necessary in order to obtain certain repeat business in the future."

By maintaining careful records which showed the "value" of a donor over an extended period of years, AFRS was able to provide cautious Boards of Directors with clear-cut evidence that it was to their organizations' benefit to "invest" in donor development.

In a manual prepared by AFRS to explain its direct mail fund raising techniques, AFRS provides both helpful ideas for fund raisers and specific examples of how the techniques it has developed can produce outstanding results:

> Solicitation mailings are the major source of funds for more than 10,000 statewide and national organizations. In addition, another 150,000 local groups solicit funds by mail.
>
> In an attempt to reach the hearts (and pocketbooks) of responsive readers, these educational, religious, health, cultural, political, and medical organizations are engaged in a tightly fought, highly competitive battle for the attention of their prospects.
>
> At the same time, both the services and the operating costs of most organizations continue to increase. This is the dilemma of today's fund raiser: as competition in the mail grows more intense, he must seek new techniques and methods to keep the net income from mailings high enough to meet the increased demands of an organization's services in the face of rising costs.

Many organizations "try" direct mail, often with pitifully poor results. Subsequently, the conclusion is drawn that direct mail "doesn't work." In fact, however, professionally prepared and executed mail campaigns can effect substantial increases in contributions and participation, year in and year out.

The Business Analogy

A close analogy can be made between raising funds by mail and running a business. In both cases, a given product or service is offered to a particular market; an investment is made to solicit support from that market; a certain level of success is experienced; the cost of realizing that success is deducted, and the organization ends up with either a net income to sustain its operations or a loss.

Successful fund raising by mail, like the successful operation of a business, requires that decisions be made on the basis of logical thought, sound information, and realism.

The staffs and supporters of health, cultural, and religious and educational institutions are often made up of deeply interested and enthusiastic people. However, this type of dedication often obscures reality when it comes to making decisions about fund raising programs. Sometimes, due only to inexperience, personal opinion becomes a substitute for logic, and enthusiasm a substitute for know-how.

Successful fund raisers always adopt a businesslike approach to fund raising. Program decisions are made not by hunch, but on the basis of facts gained from previous programs. With the objective approach, realistic appraisal replaces wishful thinking, emotional attitudes give way to proven procedures, and the professional use of probability theory supersedes guesswork.

Eight Steps in Successful Direct Mail Fund Raising

Successful fund raising programs are a result of the following series of events:

1. A person responds to an appeal for funds by mail.
2. The new contributor is thanked by mail.
3. The new contributor is involved with the institution through cultivation mailings.
4. The contributor responds to a renewal appeal. (This is the critical first year renewal.)
5. The contributor responds to the next renewal appeal. (A habit of giving has been established)
6. The contributor is upgraded in level of giving.
7. The contributor responds to a capital gift appeal.
8. The contributor becomes a deferred-giving or bequest prospect.

Personalization

As the passing parade of mail appeals grows larger, the effectiveness of truly personal letters, versus ordinary printed letters, becomes more apparent.

Different mailing formats will draw a higher or lower response. The more personal the approach, for example, the higher the response—and, of course, normally the higher the unit mailing cost. However, as the "universe" of prospects for all fund raisers is limited, they should use the most effective mailing format available to them if they are to achieve maximum return and income—even though the unit cost may be higher.

Carefully controlled tests, in fact, have proven that top quality, personalized letters actually cost less for a fund raiser to use than the most inexpensively printed mailings.

Through the use of this personal approach, dramatic increases have been made in the percentage of return, often lowering the fund raising cost-per-dollar to levels competitive with the low costs of some of the volunteer, "no-cost" door-to-door solicitations.

Cost, as always, is measured by the percentage of a contributor's dollar which goes for the cost of the mailings. Percentage measuring sticks are essential because overall costs increase as fund raising income spirals. Yet, the costs of fund raising are the pennies finally deducted from each dollar collected—and not the costs of the mailing itself.

Case in point: A major institution tested personal versus printed letters. At that time, the personal letter cost 60% more to mail than the printed letter, but the personal approach upped the percentage of return by 400% . . . increased the average contribution by 23% . . . and doubled the already substantial net income.

Recognizing the Relationship of the Contributor

One of the unique advantages of the personal letter is that the relationship of a contributor and his degree of support to an organization can be recognized in the letter copy itself, thus establishing a closer, more effective rapport, which in turn increases response. Of equal importance, a relationship with a prospect can be established by incorporating information obtained from a list source. For example, "as a resident of.................. ." This also increases response.

Suggested Amount Techniques

A number of years ago, a well-known charity invariably used this line in its annual fund raising letter: "Won't you contribute $1.00 to this worthy cause?"

Observing that most contributors did as they were asked to do, it occurred to AFRS that they might contribute another amount if the required amount was within reason. AFRS suggested substituting $2.00 for the $1.00.

The client's reaction: "People expect to give $1.00 to this organization . . . they always have given $1.00 . . . they will never give $2.00."

When the test was made, 80% of the contributions (and the percentage of return remained the same) were for $2.00. Thus, by the changing of a single word, the charity almost doubled its income.

As the result of many years of testing, the AFRS "suggested amount" rule has evolved: "Contributors tend to give suggested amounts if the suggested amount is reasonable." This simple rule is the foundation of many substantial increases in returns from fund appeals.

In one fund raising test, an amount of $15.00 was suggested as a first gift. This suggested amount was based on the average gift from other first-time donors.

The result: 50% gave exactly $15.00. 25% responded to the "or more" suggestion and gave in excess of $15.00. 25% gave less. The average contribution from more than 2,000 new contributors was within a few pennies of $15.00.

Upgrading Technique

The "Upgrading Technique" is an extension of the "Suggested Amount Technique."

In the case of former contributors, their level of support is a matter of record. Therefore, it is possible in a personal letter to say "your contribution last year of $100 is the kind of loyal support we depend on." Immediately, the letter is removed from the form letter class. The contributor knows that *you* know how much he gave previously—that *you* must have checked his record.

Once this rapport has been established with contributors, it is almost impossible for the contributor to ignore a renewal appeal by reasoning that you don't know what he gave and won't miss his support. The contributor also thinks twice before giving a lesser amount than the previous year.

Conversely, when asked in the proper way to increase a contribution from the previous base, a predictable percentage of contributors will do so—providing the new requested amount is reasonable.

A $25 contributor will upgrade to $35.00 or $50.00 because this increase is reasonable for an appeal. However, to ask a $5.00 contributor to become a $100 donor is violating the rule of asking for a reasonable amount.

The above statements are based, of course, on averages, and do not apply to specific individuals whose personal capacity to contribute may be known to be higher.

By careful application of upgrading, income from former contributors can be substantially increased. However, such upgrading must be a carefully considered process, and professional counsel is almost essential. A mechanical application of the upgrading rule can anger and alienate former contributors. Only those thoroughly familiar with the use of this most valuable upgrading technique can create an increase in income of up to 50% in a single year from renewed members.

Increasing the Renewal Rate

There is no deadlier down pull on the annual renewal percentage than the printed form letter. Most organizations take their donors for granted. They court them eagerly until they finally become contributors. Then the organization treats these new friends impersonally, failing to acknowledge and take advantage of the new relationship.

It would be ideal if every renewal letter could be individually dictated and typed by a secretary. Since this is impossible, the next best thing is the mass produced personalized letter. Using the personal approach and utilizing the upgrading strategy, we have yet to see a case where the degree of support did not take a dramatic rise.

In the case of one client, for example, these strategies increased the renewal rate by twenty percentage points (40% to 60%) with personalized appeals. Moreover, the personal letter approach resulted in a 44% increase in income from past members. 50% of all members responding to the personal appeal upped their contribution, from the previous year, as against less than 3% of those who answered a printed letter.

Investment Principle of Fund Raising

The prime source of income is, of course, the current contributor list. However, because of normal attrition among this group, it is obvious that "new blood" must be added to the active contributor list each year in order to maintain at least the status quo.

The cost of securing new contributors is relatively high, as compared to the cost of renewing an active contributor. And, as mentioned earlier, the limited size of the "universe" of prospects may dictate a larger unit investment per mailing in order to produce maximum response and apply the maximum "pulling power" to each name available.

More experienced fund raisers are willing to invest an amount of money in a new contributor equal to, or greater than, the first year's level of support. This investment principle is based on mail order practice such as that which governs subscription promotions for magazines. A mail order practitioner will pay more for a first order than he gets for it because subsequent sales to the same individual produce an unusually low sales cost and a high profit.

AFRS, in the development of its fund raising methods, translated mail order methods into fund raising practice since the two operations are identical.

The value of a new contributor is not measured by the contribution received in the first year, but by the expected "lifetime" support.

AFRS has been able to predict the lifetime value of a new contributor through statistical techniques and using certain assumptions. Recently, in order to test our assumptions, we did a study for one of our clients in which the giving habits of a group of new contributors were traced over a 5 year period.

The results more than confirmed our beliefs about the lifetime value of a new contributor. We found that one group of 3,396 new contributors, acquired at a breakeven cost of $40,000, had contributed a total of $445,150, through renewed and upgrading gifts, in just 5 years.

With contributions totaling $130 per contributor, on the average, for the first five years only, we realized that we had vastly underestimated the "lifetime value" of a small contributor, and worried unnecessarily about the cost of acquiring the first year contribution.

The importance of investment in future income cannot be emphasized enough. An organization's need is to replace renewal attrition and to increase its number of members. To do this, it must be prepared to invest in the acquisition of as many new contributors as possible. Although new contributors may be acquired at break-even cost, or even at a slight loss, it should be remembered that a long-term gain in income will result through their renewed and upgraded gifts, all at considerable profit.

Averaging Out Principle

A corollary of the Investment Principle is the averaging out principle. Once the cost of new member acquisition mailings is determined and the amount of average gift is assumed or provided through past experience, a break-even analysis can be made. If an institution invests $1.00 in order to gain $1.00 from a new contributor, then it has not initially increased net funds and is operating on a break-even basis. However, renewal income from this same break-even group will be highly profitable during the second and subsequent years as the investment theory has indicated.

Now, let us assume that the break-even percentage for a particular mailing is 2%, i.e. 2% of the total mailing is returned with an average gift of sufficient amount to just pay for the cost of the total mailing.

The averaging out theory states that as long as a 2% response rate is maintained on the entire new acquisition mailing, even though some given list does not meet the 2% criteria, a maximum number of new members will be acquired.

For example, consider response rates from the following lists all mailed in equal quantity:

List A returns	1.8%
List B returns	2.0%
List C returns	2.9%
List D returns	1.3%

Although List A and D are below the break-even point, List C's return is sufficiently large enough to carry them so that the average for all lists is still 2.0, thus maximizing the number of new contributors acquired.

Revolving Budget Concept for New Contributor Acquisition Programs

An organization that relies upon voluntary public support must accomplish three basic objectives if it wishes to grow and obtain maximum funds from the public. First, it must strive to renew 100% support of its past contributors. Although this is impossible due to normal attrition within a given contributor group, an institution must direct its efforts to renew as high a percentage as possible.

Secondly, this same group of contributors must be motivated to increase its support through larger gifts. And third, an institution must bring "new blood" into its contributor group in order to replace normal attrition within this group and further, to add new contributors for subsequent renewal income.

The Revolving Budget approach can be effectively employed to maximize the number of new contributors that can be acquired in a given period of time. To illustrate this concept let us assume the following situation: an institution's campaign is not restricted to a specific season of the year, like Christmas time, but rather it has the opportunity to solicit funds during other periods of the year; its fiscal year begins in January at which time a specific sum of money, $25,000, is earmarked for new contributor acquisition programs: the institution mails to 100,000 prospects and obtains a 2.5% response with an average gift of $10.

We are now ready to illustrate the mathematical effects of a fixed budget versus a revolving budget with two hypothetical institutions.

At year end, institution A with a fixed budget will show these results on its books:

Quantity Mailed	100,000
Percent Response	2.5%
Number of New Contributors	2,500
Average Gift	$10
Income	$25,000
Cost	$25,000
Net Income	0

Institution A has gained enough income to offset its original investment. More important, it can renew 2,500 new contributors during subsequent years at a highly profitable level.

Institution B employs a revolving budget for new acquisition purposes, which essentially means that it "turns over" its original investment money as many times as possible within a given year. Let us assume it can do this four times a year. Its books would appear as follows at year end:

Quantity Mailed	400,000
Percent Response	2.5%
Number of New Contributors	10,000
Average Gift	$10
Income	$100,000
Cost	$100,000
Net Income	0

Net income is identical for both institutions. However, Institution B has obtained 7,500 *more new contributors* than A and has also significantly multiplied its potential for renewal income in subsequent years. Further, this growth has been funded from a $25,000 investment which was used not once, but four times.

The Membership Approach

In many fund-raising situations, the strongest direct mail approach is to seek "members" rather than just "donors." One of the nation's most successful experts in the membership approach to fund raising is Dick Trenbeth of Chicago. While he was with the Art Institute of Chicago, he prepared an excellent summary of this fund-raising technique. It was featured in the June, 1967 issue of *The Reporter of Direct Mail Advertising.*

The membership approach is not only ideally suited to an art museum but can also be tailored to advance the work and financing of many other types of gift-supported organizations as well. In fact, I firmly believe that the building of a strong membership group and program can be the strongest single force in developing any organization willing to look at the potential realistically and then invest in it on a professional marketing level.

What do I mean by marketing? I mean that instead of appealing to the potential donor on the basis of a generalized service that helps others, the organization works to relate its services specifically to the *wants and needs of the potential donors.* This concept of the membership approach emphasizes benefits and privileges going out from the organization to many different types of people who may never have known that this particular organization could possibly help them personally. If the element of "support" is mentioned in the first approach, it is done quite casually, almost as an afterthought. This type of marketing involves a careful analysis of what the organization is doing or could do to attract new people.

We occasionally find it all to easy to rationalize that everyone should support us. But, how do we attract and hold the interest of everyone? Obviously we can't and don't.

Most people have a real *psychological need* of "belonging" to an organization and actually welcome the opportunity to pay dues. Hausknecht's study* indicates that this happens frequently in early middle age, presumably after the children have left home and, incidentally, when there is usually more disposable, discretionary income. These same people tend to view worthy and honorable organizations with a kind of awe. It continues to amaze me how few organizations comprehend the prestige and power they command when they go into the market place with the right kind of invitation to membership, offering distinctive privileges and such simple devices as an attractive membership card or certificate, perhaps leading eventually to getting their names on a plaque.

People tend to join organizations which offer them *specific benefits* which relate to their personal needs. These benefits may be simply a dramatized sense of helping or the offer of dependable information on a subject of present or potential interest. There may be just the promise of a few occasions each year when some sort of outing or social event is planned for the membership. But they can also include such tangible benefits as book premiums, art reproductions, regular periodicals, discounts, certificates, lapel buttons, or low-cost charter flights or tours.

Many people are genuinely lonely and *welcome the opportunity to receive regular mail,* even if it's just from an organization that counts them as part of its family . . .

*The Joiners by Murray Hausknecht. The Bedminister Press. 1962.

Some people join organizations in the *hope of acquiring knowledge or culture* that can help them solve personal problems or bring them social prestige. The key word here is "hope."

Some people have *strong emotional attachments* to organizations to which they can belong and get to know the directing officials.

The costs of a membership operation are far outweighed by substantial advantages to the organization. Let's look at some of them:

Membership provides a way of sifting out from our large and varied population a *group of friends* who have already expressed an interest in our work to the extent of parting with their money at least once. This first glimmer of interest can and must be fanned and cultivated into regular, enthusiastic support. Because it is constantly cleaned by renewal and changes of address, the membership roll becomes an invaluable mailing list for more ambitious opportunities for philanthropy or just for regular low-pressure gift solicitation in addition to dues.

Membership dues provide a fairly *predictable source of annual income* to finance future sales efforts and cultivation.

Membership enlists thousands of goodwill ambassadors whose *word-of-mouth salesmanship* can often be more effective than the organization's best mailings. Usually this advantage is justification enough for an extensive and fairly expensive program of information and cultivation to its membership. One Chicago organization owes its continuing existence to one large bequest which resulted from a member telling a wealthy woman about the agency and its work.

Membership offers an *acceptable reason for soliciting contributions* from "the family" several times a year. This can be especially important to organizations which have traditionally limited their solicitation to one focal date, usually on or around a holiday.

The membership concept greatly increases the market potential for prospecting because it can be *aimed at other than known contributors.* It can be tailored to appeal to such special interest groups as magazine subscribers, purchasers of books, mail order buyers, club members, and so on, as well as to specific age groups.

Membership provides an invaluable means of *breaking down communications barriers* as members get to know staff or board members and feel free or even obligated to air their complaints and offer suggestions for improvement.

Membership provides a way of *bestowing a permanent honor on regular donors* of substantial amounts.

The Professional Approach

A professional fund-raising organization has one major advantage over an internal organization—the ability to take a completely objective approach to the job to be done. As Andi Emerson, president of Emerson-Weeks, Inc., expressed it in a DMMA presentation, "Those who are successful have a straight-forward, business-like approach. They do not *substitute* heart for logic, enthusiasm for knowhow. They do not permit poorly-thought out, poorly-executed campaigns simply because the people involved mean well."

Miss Emerson lists nine rules used by professionals for successful fund raising through the mail:

1. The first cardinal rule for fund raising is to accept the basic fact that you are SELLING something that people will, or will not, BUY. You may be "selling" pity, or memories, or conscience salving. You may even be selling fun, or products, or services with charitable overtones—but you are a salesman. You must interest someone else in your idea, or need, so much that they will send you *their* money for ***your*** idea.
2. The second rule is to sell a specific. Please, don't try to sell the general concept of "goodness" alone! People may give money, on a personal basis, to a highly-trusted individual or group—but mass solicitation should be done for a particular person, a particular thing, a particular gap that needs to be filled. Allow the person who sends money to you to feel that he or she "bought" a chair for a hospital, crutches for a special child, a month's worth of education for a prospective seminarian, five new books for a library. It is very unfair to ask large numbers of people to hand over hard-earned money with no sure knowledge of how it will be used.
3. The third rule is to be gracious enough to explain just who you are, how long you've been in operation, and which people, if any, sponsor your activities. It pays to give a very brief outline of what you've done with money you raised in the past, and to tell why you came into being. It is virtually unbelievable how many organizations assume that everyone knows everything about them. In light of the continuing barrage of unfavorable publicity against unscrupulous charity drives, it is unbelievably bad business not to separate yourself from the masses—if you *are* honest.
4. Fourth, give something in return for a donation. Book markers, imprinted book plates, a framable certificate, mention in a publication. If the gift is large enough, send out a plaque, or put the donor's name on your letterhead. Religious fund raisers have a greater variety of things they can do or send than most, but everyone can at least send a printed "Thank you for your donation" card—and it's astonishing how few when the would-be donor sits down to fill out the slip and finds it in-of a donation—but rather about the sort of legitimate "thank you" a legitimate donor should receive . . . particularly if you want another donation.

5. Fifth, remember you are asking for money because you NEED it. Let the *obvious* quality of your mailing piece be consistent with the amount of individual donation you seek. Don't send an elaborate four-color process mailing, on coated stock with multi-die windows—to ask for $2.00. But don't send a mimeo'd "note" asking for hundreds of dollars to build a new laboratory for a university. Let common sense, not pride or haste, be the determining factor. This does not mean that inexpensive-looking mailings are "cheap." There is just no excuse for illegible printing, shoddy envelopes or cheap paper. Remember, you are writing to a human being who deserves the courtesy of receiving a decent looking package asking him to part with his money. One other thing on the subject of physical appearance. Using two colors in your letter can often be an aid to understanding the printed piece, and a blue signature looks more personal.
6. The sixth rule is to make it easy for the recipient to send back a donation. Be *sure* to include a reply envelope—and test whether asking for postage, sending a postage-free envelope, or affixing a stamp helps your returns the most. Make your donation slip easy to fill out, and don't forget to restate what their money will do, right on the slip! Too often an entire mailing effort will be vitally damaged right at the "point of sale" when the would-be donor sits down to fill out the slip and finds it inconvenient, inconsistent, inaccurate or just plain not "needful" enough. Tell him again just what you want him to give, why, how and where to send it, and what he will get in return.
7. Seventh, enclose an "extra" gift slip to be given to a friend who would *surely* like to send a donation, too. This can not only increase the number of donations received, but will also tend to strengthen the believability of the entire piece. Obviously, if you feel your cause is important enough for the recipient to tell a friend about it, then it *must* be really vital.
8. The eighth rule is to choose your lists wisely. Your own previous donors lists pay best, donors to other causes come in second, and compiled lists rank third. There are so many variations on these basics alone that the best possible advice is to consult a reputable list broker and "professional" mailers among your acquaintances. Your friends can give you much valuable advice, but the broker is likely to be the most specifically helpful.
9. The ninth, and last rule, is to write a letter to an individual, and then mass produce it for your mailings. While this sounds easy it actually is very complicated to do. The best and most simple procedure is to actually mentally choose a person you know, who knows *nothing* about your organization. Then sit down and tell him or her, in a letter, exactly why his donation is so important. Let the "human being" who is YOU write to the "human being" who is going to receive the letter. It is a terrible insult (and doesn't raise money) to use a "computer-to-computer" style.

Some Effective Techniques

One of the most outstanding direct mail fund raising campaigns of all time was the program developed by Morrie Dees which raised over $10,000,000 to support the presidential election of George McGovern in 1972. Like many successful fund raising programs, it started with a list of known supporters — 100,000 voters who had provided financial support to the McGovern organization during the primaries. The program really began two weeks before the 1972 elections. Tom Collins, the direct mail professional who prepared copy for the fund raising program, explains:

Senator McGovern had decided late in 1970 to announce his candidacy by sending out a letter. I believe Thomas Jefferson was the first one to do that, one of the few who ever did. And Senator McGovern planned to send a letter to 250,000 people. Starting early permitted McGovern to build slowly a substantial donor list as well as patiently build a grass roots organization in state after state. A variety of different direct mail techniques were used throughout the pre-convention period, but most of them had one thing in common — letters from four to eight pages in length. Tom Collins has strong feelings about the value of long letters:

> There was a good deal of controversy behind the scenes over the length of the letter when the first one went out. I understand that many people on the Senator's staff were horrified at the idea of sending out such a long letter. There is a common notion that nobody will read long copy. When asked if there were any objections from recipients about the use of long letters, Mr. Collins noted:
>
> **Any mailing you do will draw some criticism and complaints telling you that you are doing it all wrong. We got some letters from people telling us that nobody reads long copy, but in the final tally, we raised about $4,000,000 by convention time. So I have learned not to listen.**

One of the most interesting techniques used was to recontact the first 15,000 contributors and ask for their continued support — $10 each month until convention time. The mailing was accompanied by a coupon book just like those used for installment loans, with a different coupon for each month. This mailing attracted 2,000 regular donors — a response of over 13%.

New donors were also sought with news tie-ins. For example, after the Americans for Democratic Action endorsed Senator McGovern at its national convention, a fund raising letter was immediately prepared and was in the mails to ADA members five days later.

The friend-get-a-friend technique borrowed from mail order also played a role in pre-convention fund raising. An initial 17,000 names were acquired through recommendations of contributors and a mailing to this list generated approximately $20,000. Based on this success, a concentrated friend-get-a-friend program was developed.

Some of the effective techniques utilized included:

- Computer forms were ordered within 48 hours after the McGovern nomination and each pre-convention donor received a personalized letter enlisting financial support. Mailed early in August, it produced a 25% response with an average contribution of slightly more than $40, for a total of $1.1 million.
- A general mailing shown on the facing page which went to outside lists was also made in early August. It followed the pre-convention strategy of long, detailed copy and invited participation in a "Million-Member Club" announced in Senator McGovern's acceptance speech (probably the first time in history that a mailing ever received such a strong advance build-up).
- As contributions came in, contributors received "Welcome to the Club" packages including a Million-Member Club card and button plus a personalized computer letter asking them to pass out contribution envelopes and secure pledges from five friends. The letter told these first-time contributors: "After you have completed this important campaign assignment, we would like to send you a Certificate of Appreciation signed by Senator McGovern. It will be an attractive 9″ x 12″ document printed on heavy parchment paper, suitable for framing—a treasured souvenir of one of your services in this historic campaign." At the bottom of the letter was a personalized "Campaign Assignment Report Form" which could be signed and then mailed to notify "Club Headquarters" that the "Member" had completed distribution envelopes. A reply envelope was also enclosed for use in returning the report form. This friend-get-a-friend technique generated $500,000 in contributions from friends.
- Not willing to let any mailing opportunity pass without utilizing the opportunity for additional fund raising, each certificate sent out was accompanied by a letter and five more friend-get-a-friend envelopes.
- The second general mailing in early September came over the signature of Senator Edward Kennedy both to introduce a change of pace and to attract those potential contributors who might respond more readily to an appeal from a well-known supporter rather than from the candidate himself or his official organization.
- The next two general mailings came from Senator McGovern but, although similar in content, utilized different formats to generate continuing interest. The Million-Member Club appeal remained constant through the Kennedy letter and both of the McGovern letter mailings.
- While every effort was being made to solicit new contributors, previous donors were being asked to help finance specific campaigns activities. The first mailing explained: "Working with professionals, our staff has developed a complete folder with the story of our McGovern-Shriver campaign, the Million-Member Club appeal, and a built-in business reply envelope for mailing back a contribution. This folder is designed to be inserted in Sunday newspapers . . ." At the top of the computer letter was a personalized reply form giving donors the opportunity to individually finance the cost of 1,000 to 10,000 newspaper inserts at $11.25 per thousand.
- The next donor mailing had a similar appeal, but a different format. It included a personalized computer letter asking for support in buying space for a newspaper ad; a preprint of the ad; a computer-personalized contribution form, and a business reply envelope. One unique copy approach used on the business reply form was that suggested contribution amounts were not in numeric progression.

- Donors received news-oriented *Mailgrams* as the campaign progressed and it was considered too late to make continued mailings. Typical copy: "Tide turning. Boston rally drew enthusiastic response from record crowd of 100,000. To win we must reach people who don't attend rallies. Paid television is key. Deeply appreciate past generosity. You made possible nationwide TV address on Vietnam Peace Plan. Major impact expected. But we must not stop there. Urgently need funds for next TV talk. Only with your help can I be heard. Please rush $50, $100, or whatever you can by October 17 . . ."
- Probably the most unusual appeal, however, was a unique four-check mailing. A computer letter with four attached checks was sent to contributors who had supported McGovern during the pre-convention period. The basic concept was that these key supporters would provide substantial financial support during the presidential campaign period and the burden could be eased if the support was spaced over a four-month period. Thus, the checks were dated August 1, September 1, October 1 and November 1. A postscript to the letter offered a special incentive:

  In appreciation of your past help we would like to send you a souvenir of those unforgettable days when the odds against us seemed hopeless and only your steadfast support kept the campaign going. It is a sterling silver lapel pin that says "F.M.B.M."—standing for For McGovern Before Miami. This mailing pulled 25% from the pre-convention donor list of 100,000 and grossed approximately $1,000,000.

Improving Fund Raising Mail

Another ten tips for effective fund raising by direct mail were presented at the 1970 National Conference on Christian Philanthropy by Jerald E. Huntsinger, president of Huntsinger and Associates, a consulting firm in fund raising:

1. *Create a letter that looks like a letter . . .* not an advertising brochure, or an announcement. Keep the layout simple and easy to read.
2. *Write long letters.* Don't be fooled by people who say, "Since everybody is so busy, let's keep our letters short, so we will get high readership." You are not after readership—you are after response. Do you understand the difference? The shorter the letter, the higher the readership, but for fund raising, the lower the response. Your letter must be long enough so that by the time the person finishes reading the letter, he is ready to sign the contribution card. If he finishes without being convinced, then you may have had readership—but not response. Don't be afraid of two-, three-, or six-page letters.
3. *But make sure your long letter is readable.* To do this, forget all the rules of grammar you were taught in school. Use run-on sentences, begin paragraphs with And, So, Then, and other connectives. Dangle participles, split infinitives every chance you get. Write just like you talk—except don't try to be clever or humorous. Use lots of I, Me, Mine, Your, Yours. Forget the old fear that "I" is egotistical. "I" is communication—and we are concerned with communications, not rules. Work from the emotional to the logical. You won't get there the other way around. Never moralize —it blocks communication. Watch your analogies—every analogy, carried to its logical conclusion, becomes ridiculous.
4. *Use human interest stories to illustrate your letters.* Begin practically every letter with a story. Talk about people, not programs. Bring everything down to the ultimate level—how does the program affect real, living people?

5. *Connected with this, use photography, not art to illustrate your mailing.* Art is weak because art is recessive, a caricature of life. Art is not real living, but an interpretation. Photography is real.

6. *Don't buck the fund-raising season.* The season follows commercial mail rather closely, with some variations. The day after Labor Day signals the opening. The first balmy day in spring brings it to an end. Following is a chart based on returns over a three-year period for six national fund raising organizations which follow a monthly mailing program. Note the variation between November, the month of the highest return, with 100%, and May, the lowest with 45%.

January	92%
February	90%
March	80%
April	60%
May	45%
June	48%
July	61%
August	63%
September	85%
October	90%
November	100%
December	89%

7. *Write to your people more often.* This is related to the fund-raising season because you must communicate when you are most apt to receive a response. The old idea of the "once a year" appeal is definitely out—unless you want to lose touch with your mailing list. Remember, your supporters don't think about you as often as you think about them. Keep them aware of your needs.

8. *But always have an "excuse" for each letter.* Never send out a general appeal. Create each mailing package around a central project or theme. People seldom react negatively to appeals if you have a clear-cut reason for writing.

9. *Tell the person exactly what you want him to do.* Don't assume that he will read between the lines. And don't over-estimate his intelligence. Give clear directions. Explain how to fill out any coupons or cards that are enclosed. If you want a pledge, say so. If you want a check now, say so. If you want him to put your organization in his will—tell him exactly how to do it.

10. *Then make it easy for the person to reply.* Plan your reply devices—reply card, reply envelope, coupon—in a way that is simple and obvious. Make sure the reply card fits the envelope, and the envelope is large enough to take a check.

Forget The Rules

The ten tips by Mr. Huntsinger provide a logical opportunity to emphasize the *only* rule for effective direct mail . . . and that is that there are no rules. Professionals like Jerald Huntsinger can give you the benefit of their experience and what they've observed that works best for their particular institutions or clients. But to believe for a minute that any one of Mr. Huntsinger's tips will work to your benefit without actually testing its effectiveness in a live direct mail test against *your* list with *your* appeal is pure folly.

For example, his statement that "Most successful direct mail campaigns are based on lengthy letters" should be taken to mean just one thing—that *his* successful campaigns have been based on lengthy letters. Many other professionals will tell you just the opposite—that *their* most successful direct mail campaigns have been based on short letters.

In particular, beware of someone else's time schedule for direct mail effectiveness. There are many cases where May is the very best month for response and November the poorest month.

On the other hand, don't ignore suggestions from any direct mail professional—even if you have already tested and determined that some particular suggestion he or she makes is completely contrary to your own experience. Look upon the other suggestions as possible avenues to improve your results and when you have the opportunity, give them a test.

And even after you have tested, don't permit yourself the luxury of thinking you have written a rule book for all of your future mailings. Keep your eyes and ears open. When you learn of someone else's success with a technique that runs contrary to your experience, it may be time to test again. But, above all, don't get so busy testing you fail to devote your *basic* effort to producing effective mailings. Pin down direct mail's most successful people and you'll find that the vast majority of them create their mailings primarily on the basis of an intuitive sense of what's needed to communicate with the audience and convince a substantial percentage of them to take the action desired. They've listened to the "experts," read the books, conducted testing whenever possible. They may even have preached a set of "rules" for the guidance of others. But when it comes time to produce the mailing, they just dig in and let their "educated" intuition take over.

Chapter 15

SAMPLING & COUPONING

DIRECT MAIL is the ideal medium for controlled distribution of samples and coupons. While the cost-per-household reached is often considerably greater than the use of newspapers and magazines, the high degree of selectivity inherent in direct mail quickly offsets this seeming negative.

The Nielsen Consumer Attitude Study detailed in Chapter 2 provides clear evidence that the American public looks with special favor upon coupons and samples received in the mail. And, as that study showed, a high percentage of recipients use the samples they receive in the mail and redeem the coupons they receive.

In actual practice, the redemption rate of coupons distributed by direct mail considerably exceeds those of other media. Statistics developed by the A. C. Nielsen Company, which provides a national coupon clearing house service, show the following average rates of redemption of coupons:

Direct Mail	10.5%
Free Standing Insert	5%
Magazines	2.5 to 4.8%
Newspapers	2.9 to 3.3%

Major Advantages

Direct mail couponing is an especially effective marketing action medium for two basic reasons:[1]

1. Coupons delivered at home carry the special offer—the inducement—the money part—to the consumer in advance of purchase. Psychologically, coupons are money which can purchase goods at the housewife's very next visit to the store, the most compelling motive for action there can be.

[1]Descriptions from a special report prepared by O. E. McIntyre, Inc.

2. Mail coupons can reach the largest total market without wasteful audience duplication and with the greatest accuracy of market selection. Further, unlike coupons in other media, mail coupons cannot just be overlooked; they must either be used or consciously not used. In most formats, mail coupons do not need to be cut out or detached from other matter. For all these reasons mail coupons can generate more total action than other forms of couponing.

The advantage of direct mail couponing was underscored by A. C. Nielsen, Jr., president of A. C. Nielsen Co.:[2] "It seems fairly clear that the easier it is for the housewife to acquire the coupons, the more likely she is to redeem them. Direct mail brings the coupon into her hands with no effort at all. Other methods of distribution require effort on her part to cut them out."

Advantages to Participants

Each couponing program usually involves three basic participants—the manufacturer, the retailer and the consumer. The advantages which each of these participants gains from a couponing program were described by Reed Bartlett, probably the nation's foremost authority on couponing:[3]

Manufacturers

Couponing allows the manufacturer to limit his promotion effort to one special offer per family as compared to a price pack, where regular users can load up on their favorite product at a reduced price. It reaches out to potential new users of new or improved products. To put it briefly, it offers the manufacturer both flexibility and selectivity.

Consumers

While couponing saves the consumer money, it does not put on buying pressure at an inconvenient time. Coupons are—or should be—always good. But it does introduce the consumer to a new and improved product by offering an incentive to buy at a reduced cost, thus helping to find the product that is best for individual requirements. It also drives the manufacturer to continually seek to improve his product for it is a recognized fact that couponing is most effective when the product is superior in some important way to its competition.

---

[2]"Measuring Coupon Redemptions," *Printer's Ink*, July 31, 1964.

[3]From a speech at the 1964 annual conference of the Sales Promotion Executives Assn. by Reed Bartlett, Manager, Field Advertising, Procter & Gamble Co.

Retailers

The major advantage here is the opportunity it provides a retailer to move extra merchandise at regular resale prices, and at regular profit. In effect, it provides the opportunity for him to offer a sale at no cost to himself. Couponing builds added store traffic, and often will further increase a store's total volume through the sale of related items. And, with all these, there is no extra inventory, no extra warehousing, no extra deliveries to the store, no extra backroom storage, no extra shelf-stocking, no extra price markings, no fuss, no bother—until the coupon (and the merchandise) appears at the checkstand.

Disadvantages of Couponing

Reed Bartlett also has offered the benefit of his extensive couponing experience in outlining some of the disadvantages of this merchandising method:[4]

> "For manufacturers, couponing represents a sizable investment. This can be a disadvantage if much of it is wasted through mishandling. Such malpractices as misredemption (the acceptance of another product than the one which was to be sold for the coupon), theft, counterfeiting, etc. can waste the investment. It is also difficult to pinpoint the exact liability of a coupon campaign since there are so many factors affecting redemption. By liability, I mean the amount of money needed by a company to reimburse the trade for the total number of coupons redeemed. This liability has, on occasion, presented serious problems for some companies when the number of redeemed coupons greatly exceeded expectations.
>
> And couponing is certainly not profitable to the manufacturer whose product is inferior. The quickest way to kill a poor product is to coupon it. Virtually overnight, the bulk of the potential users have an opportunity to compare it with the brands they have been using and to judge it critically. If a product is standing still in the market, couponing will help to destroy it through prompting comparison with superior products available to the consumer.

The retailer claims such disadvantages in the coupon as:

- Time-consuming and troublesome at the checkstand
- Time-consuming and troublesome to sort, count and handle
- Cost of handling is greater than the handling fee
- Coupons tie up the retailer's money

What they are really saying is that couponing, like any other form of good sales promotion, requires some extra effort to be effective. Coupons—because of the 5 cents handling fee—really should be more attractive to retailers than many other promotional devices.

---

[4]Ibid.

ADVANTAGES & DISADVANTAGES OF DIRECT MAIL COUPONING

From a study prepared by the Sales Promotion Committee of the Association of National Advertisers, Inc.

Advantages of Direct Mail Couponing

1. Maximum coverage is possible
2. Good rate of redemption
3. Good selectivity of recipients
4. Maximum flexibility
5. Geographical areas can be reached exactly
6. Timing can be controlled
7. Can be effective in persuading retailers to distribute the product
8. Sometimes a sample of the product can be enclosed at little or no extra postage cost
9. Has consumer acceptance
10. Great impact on consumers, trade and sales force
11. Redemption rates relatively predictable from experience
12. Can be researched effectively
13. No special pack is necessary
14. If punched card coupons are used, counterfeiting is more difficult; also permits detailed analyses by area, differences in offers, etc.

Disadvantages of Direct Mail Couponing

1. High cost of distribution (can be lessened by cooperative couponing but possibly with less selectivity)
2. Considerable lead time is necessary
3. Mailing list may become out-dated unless checked continuously
4. Mailing houses may need careful supervision
5. Possibility of theft of coupons
6. May require advertising support in other media and at point of purchase
7. Coupons delivered in quantity to large apartment buildings may be collected, by children, janitors, garbage collectors, etc., and sold at cut rates to unscrupulous dealers
8. Undeliverable mail is often a problem

Let's look at the 5 cents handling fee this way. If coupons were baked beans, every retailer in the grocery business would be happy over a 5 cents mark-up on them. The reason should be obvious: 5 cents on a 5 cents coupon amounts to a 100% mark-up! Five cents on a 10 cents coupon equals a 50% mark-up. It so happens that coupons average out at a little under 7 cents each. This is the amount to be deducted from the regular price of the product. So 5 cents on 7 cents equals a whopping 71.4%. That's not a bad mark-up in any economic climate! But that's only half the story. Just consider these facts. With coupons, the retailer doesn't have to:

- Buy them
- Receive them at a warehouse
- Take them into inventory
- Store them at a warehouse
- Deliver them to a store
- Hold them in a back room
- Open cases
- Price-mark them
- Cart them to the shelves
- Put them on the shelves
- Give up display space to merchandise them.

Growing Need for Couponing

The most popular area for couponing by direct mail is grocery and related products. The change in retailing shows both the desirability of couponing and the decreasing problem of doing it effectively.

Back in 1939, a grocery product manufacturer wanting to expose his product to 70% of the country's food buyers needed distribution in 112,000 stores. By 1960, the number of stores required for the same 70% exposure had been reduced to only 39,500 stores and that figure has undoubtedly shrunk in the years since that time.

At the same time, there has been a proliferation of products handled by today's large food store. According to the Super Market Institute, the average supermarket stocks some 8,000 items, up from 1,500 at the end of World War II. And manufacturers of food and household items introduce an unprecedented 500 new items each year.[5]

Under such demanding conditions, it is not surprising that as many as 2,000 products are the subject of direct mail couponing annually. The effectiveness of couponing is easily documented by

[5]"Coupons Carve Out a Bigger Role as Sales Aid for New Products," *The Wall Street Journal*, Feb. 17, 1964.

actual case histories. One classic example occurred in 1962 when Colgate-Palmolive unveiled its new Ajax all-purpose cleaner. Facing tough competition from already established cleaners such as Lestoil, Handy Andy and Mr. Clean, Colgate made national distribution of coupons offering discounts off the regular price. The couponing was backed by heavy ad spending and moved Ajax from introduction to the top spot in all-purpose cleaner sales in just nine months.

Woman's Day Survey

A 1971 survey conducted by *Woman's Day* magazine, which interviewed 500 women in five major cities, showed 48% said they preferred the cents-off coupon over other forms of money-saving offers. The study showed that 41% of the women felt the major reason coupons were made available to them was to encourage trial of new products.

The average number of coupons each woman collected per week was 5.2 and the women redeemed an average of nearly seven out of ten of the coupons collected.

In the interviews, *Woman's Day* found that the higher the value, the greater the redemption rate. Where redemptions fall off is when the shopper has difficulty in obtaining the coupon, cutting them out or sending them in.

Woman's Day also interviewed store managers and reported that while 75% were generally favorable toward coupons, there were negative comments about the work, confusion and time involved in handling the coupons. The managers often considered the 3 cents-per-coupon rebate as less than their handling costs.

Some of the problems with coupon programs reflected at the store level involved failure of manufacturers to give sufficient advance notice of coupon promotions.

Why Coupon?

The five prime motivations for direct mail couponing were defined in a presentation by Paul Sampson, a former board chairman of the Direct Mail/Marketing Association:

1. To improve competitive penetration in a market.
2. To move out-of-balance inventories.
3. To stimulate product demand at the retail level as a means of obtaining retailer agreements to stock a product.
4. To accelerate the introduction and widespread use of a new product.
5. To obtain new users for an old product.

In commenting on the fourth and fifth motivations, Mr. Sampson noted: "In these last two applications we are dealing with a most fundamental reason for using coupons—to stimulate trial usage of a product so that the product 'can sell itself'."

Tips for Couponing

There have been many guidelines for effective couponing prepared by various companies which offer couponing services. A typical guide developed from a question-and-answer session between editors of *Advertising & Sales Promotion* and William Greenfield, president of Federal Distributing Corporation.[6]

> "*When should couponing be used?* Couponing is most effective when used for repeat-purchase products that are new or newly improved and which are being promoted by advertising. As for the timing of the coupon distribution, the brand should be on the store shelves by the time the coupon is offered.
>
> *What types of users find couponing most effective?* The chief users of coupons happen to be manufacturers of soap and other cleaning products. Couponing is effective for a broad range of package products and other consumer goods, however. Any consumer product that has a market can be successfully couponed.
>
> *How can couponing be made more effective?* Couponers can select their audience to concentrate where there is high redemption. The choice of the right target groups can make a dramatic difference in redemption rates, a difference that could turn an otherwise unsuccessful campaign into a successful one.
>
> *Who, then, are the high redeemers of coupons?* Generally, middle and high income groups redeem coupons much more readily than do low-income groups. In addition, the high redeemer is likely to live in an urban community, have a larger family and have a higher level of education than the non-redeemer. Middle-aged women seem to redeem more than women in other age groups.
>
> *How long does redemption take?* It generally takes at least four to six weeks before chain store redemption can be accurately determined.
>
> *In direct mail, is it preferable to use "Occupant" addressing or addressing to individual?* The cost of "Occupant" addressing is lower than addressing to individuals. This is particularly true today when each household is more mobile than in the past. An "Occupant" mailing will reach every household in the building regardless of the occupancy turnover. In addition, there will be no forwarding of coupons to markets not included in this campaign. [*Author's note: It should be noted that the spokesman being quoted represents a company specializing in "Occupant" addressing. Addressing by name is considered preferable by many advertisers, even when lists used have been compiled from such inclusive sources as telephone households, automobile ownership, etc. To determine the most desirable addressing method for any given couponing program, it is important to compare the desirability of reaching every inhabited dwelling in a given area with more selective distri-*

[6] "What You Should Know About Couponing," *Advertising & Sales Promotion*, Oct. 1964.

DO's & DON'Ts OF DIRECT MAIL COUPONING

Prepared by the Sales Promotion Committee of the Association of National Advertisers, Inc.

1. If you are distributing dollar-bill-size coupons for several brands in one mailing, don't print the coupons in perforated strip form. This practice encourages misredemption for cash.
2. Be selective. Restrict your coupon distribution to the most promising areas and prospects.
3. Don't include too many different brands in one mailing; keep the value of your coupons at reasonable levels. The higher the total value of the coupons, the greater the temptation to misredeem for cash.
4. Be sure your mailing lists are up to date. Ask for a guarantee by the mailing house that undeliverable "nixies" will not exceed a specified percentage. Even though it costs more, you may want to specify "Return Requested" to get an accurate count on "nixies" and to remove undeliverable coupons from circulation and possible misredemption.
5. Guard against theft of coupons at all points in the distribution system.
6. Allow enough lead time.
7. Ask the mailing house to hold up distribution in areas where adequate product distribution (at least 40% or 50%) has been delayed.

bution possible through the use of specialized lists. The total cost per coupon redeemed is often lower when more selective lists are used. It should also be noted that there is little forwarding of coupons "to markets not included in this campaign" when Occupant lists are used, since the vast majority of such mailings are made by bulk third class mail and there is no automatic forwarding of such mail.]

What are some of the advantages and disadvantages of package couponing? Package couponing is the lowest in cost of all the techniques. The chief disadvantage here, however, is that the customer must first buy the product to earn a lower price for a repeat purchase. The saving is deferred and hence not very appealing for a non-user of the product. On the other hand, a coupon for an unpopular product can be packed with a popular product to circumvent this problem.

Can couponing assist in marketing research? Very definitely. Users can test specific consumer groups with numbered coupons.

What additional tips would you give to users of couponing? I would like to suggest three more checkpoints for coupon users:

1. Dealers should be reimbursed without delay.
2. Dealers should be alerted about the promotion and be informed thoroughly about the specifics of reimbursement. Missionary men should be used to secure the cooperation of the trade-in coupon campaigns.
3. Wholesalers and jobbers should be given advance notice of the campaign in time to order sufficient stock.

COOPERATIVE MAILINGS

While co-op mailings are utilized for a variety of promotion purposes, they are most commonly used for distribution of coupons. There are three basic types of direct mail co-ops in wide-spread use:

1. *General national co-ops.* The main packager of such mailings is the Reuben H. Donnelley Corp.
2. *Special interest co-ops.* This type, which consists of collated promotion pieces from a group of individual advertisers interested in a specialized audience, has been growing rapidly. Typical examples of the specialized audiences: teenagers, college students, school teachers, upper income families at new addresses, new brides, new mothers, mothers-to-be, professional groups, airplane owners, etc.
3. *Publication co-ops.* These differ from the first two categories in that the promotional messages are printed and bound together like a magazine, rather than being individual promotion pieces collated together and inserted into a common envelope. While the majority of publication co-ops include at least a modest amount of editorial material, there are a number which consist entirely of promotion material. One type which has been growing in popularity in the business and professional field is a booklet containing pages of perforated business reply cards. The majority of publication co-ops are designed for special interest groups, but there are a number which are designed for general national distribution. In some cases, publication co-ops are included as one of the inserts in an envelope with individual promotion pieces from individual advertisers.

Fundamentals of Co-ops

In discussing the effectiveness of cooperative direct mail, Paul Sampson notes two fundamentals which should be noted by advertisers:

1. *A direct mail co-op is primarily an action vehicle and secondarily a channel for advertising.* A co-op is usually not used to do a pure advertising job. It is primarily a channel for getting action and the key to getting action is a certificate (or coupon) representing a price-reduction value, a sweepstake, a contest, or a traffic-building response incentive of some type.
2. *A direct mail co-op is semi-private. Do not use it where complete privacy of communication is desirable.* There are countless mail communications

situations where the use of a co-op would be inappropriate. All personalized letter promotions would come under this heading; fund raising, prestige communications, communications highlighting and dramatizing a major user benefit, and a number of others, should not be in a co-op. Also, mail-marketing programs that call for pin-point list selectivity do not fit a co-op. A co-op does lack the "me-to-you" sense of personal communication.

Growth of Co-ops

While increased postage rates have tended to reduce the frequency and size of some co-op mailings, the overall population growth and the number of specialized audience co-ops have resulted in a continuing increase in the total number of co-op mailing packages entering the mail stream each year. In addition, there is a growing number of co-op promotion "mailings" being distributed by independent home delivery services.

In commenting on the growth of co-op direct mail in the mid-sixties, Wilson B. Prophet, Jr. noted:[7]

> "In 1965 there were at least 12 national co-op campaigns with more than 200 million co-op packages, and the total number of inserts included some 700 million cents-off coupons, proof of purchase offers, and other packaged goods promotions, and about 400 million mail order offers. This represented an increase of 33% over 1964.
>
> "And as the quantity of co-op promotions has increased, their frequency has also increased to the point where there is one scheduled almost every month. This means that today an advertiser need not organize his own co-op or wait for another advertiser to do so; he is almost sure to find a promotion already scheduled to fit his marketing plans. Further, with quantity and frequency increased, it has become possible for mailing houses to lower the cost of participation to the point where it is now within the price range of advertisers with limited budgets . . .
>
> "As a general rule, a co-op package is mailed to the top 60% of the households in all major metropolitan markets, in order to have the broadest possible coverage among the consumers with the highest spending power. Each participant, however, is free to limit his participation to a region of the country, to individual states, or to specific post offices or—in many instances—census tracts within the markets, all depending on his own patterns of distribution or his sales needs. This gives him more flexibility in areas covered than he could get from regional magazines or even newspapers. Conversely, he can participate, if his requirements and budget call for it, in the entire nationwide mailing."

Inserts in Co-ops

The items included in co-op mailings cover a wide spectrum. One of the most imaginative co-op packages is also typical of general

7"Is Cooperative Mail for You?" by Wilson B. Prophet, Jr., *Advertising & Sales Promotion*, 1966.

audience mailing. It was mailed in May 1965 by O. E. McIntyre, Inc., a time when the public was showing a high degree of personal interest in zip codes and the post office was urging advertisers to help in promoting the use of zip codes.

A clever, imaginative co-op insert highlighting the zip code and emphasizing to the receiver his own zip code.

The outer envelope is shown in the illustration above. The large zip code number appearing in a window at the left of the envelope was imprinted on the perforated stub of an introductory subscription promotion by the late *Look* magazine. The stub was gummed on the reverse side. That copy read: "On the reverse side your own official United States Post Office Department Zip Code number. Compliments of *Look* magazine." On the numbered face of the stub, copy stated: "To further cooperate with the U.S. Post Office, *Look* provides you with this handy Zip Code reminder. Tear it off and affix it by means of the gummed back to your calendar, desk pad or mailbox as a constant reminder to use your Zip Code in the reply address on all letters and parcels." Simple—but a certain attention-getter.

The stub was attached to a check-size business reply card with the personalized address label on its face. Between the stub and the reply card was another check-size unit with a brief selling message for Look.

Other inserts in that co-op package included:

- A United Film Club, Inc. promotional envelope which doubled as a selling device and a mailer for a roll of film. It was typical of the copy-laden promotional envelopes used by mail order film services and included a 20 cent bonus coupon to be applied to the first order.
- A card with a perforated store coupon offering a 20 cent savings on Sucaryl Liquid or Sucaryl Tablets.

- Two three-fold pieces with perforated store coupons—one offering 15 cents off on any size of Arrid spray deodorant and the other worth 8 cents off on a 9 oz. can of Awake frozen concentrate for imitation orange juice.
- A two-fold piece with a 7 cent store coupon good on any size of Peter Pan peanut butter.
- A combination letter-ad-coupon for Gala paper towels. The 12 by 8¾ inch piece folded down to the standard 6 by 3 inch size for all enclosures in this mailing (3½ by 7 inches is frequently the maximum for co-ops). The inside spread had a four-color ad looking very much like a magazine spread in miniature. The one-page letter was a quick introduction to the then-new product and had the 7 cent store coupon at the bottom.

Teenage Co-ops

One form of specialized co-op mailing which has been highly successful is the mailing to teenagers. Generally, oversize packages are used and contain a wide variety of promotion materials ranging from coupons and samples to both promotion and institutional advertising brochures. A package put together by Teen Mail, Inc. included the following elements:

- A 9 by 12 inch mailing envelope featuring a "Spring Fling Sweepstakes." Prizes included a car, wardrobes, TV sets, jewelry, etc. Recipients simply copied an imprinted number from the face of the envelope on a coupon which was to be cut from the back of the envelope. They were asked to list offers from the mailing to which they had responded, but there was no requirement that such information be provided.
- A 50% discount offer on a subscription to *Ingenue* magazine on a 5 by 15 inches, two-color card folded to 5 by 8 inches. The lower portion of the card was a perforated business reply card.
- A three-fold 14 by 7¾ inch card folded to 5 by 7¾ inches, printed in process color, offering nine free records for joining the Columbia Record Club. The piece showed illustrations of 92 different record albums and had a perforated business reply card on the back cover.
- A full-color, four-page brochure from Singer. The front 8½ by 11 inch cover contained two coupons offering three pairs of fishnet stockings for only $1.00 when redeemed at a local Singer Center. The center spread featured eight different Singer products ranging from sewing machines to typewriters and portable record-players. The back cover featured a cut-out coupon which could be exchanged at a Singer Center for a special brochure describing Hawaiian fashions.
- A two-color 8½ by 14 inch piece from Happiness Tours which folded to 8½ by 4 inches. It encouraged teenagers to "start your own Go-Go Group and choose from nine fun-filled tours." A tear-off coupon offered free brochures on the nine featured tours—with a stated limit of five brochures per request.
- A two-color 14½ by 7 inch piece from Sudden Beauty Facial which folded to 7 by 7 inches. It contained a perforated coupon offering a regular 59 cent size of Sudden Beauty Facial if mailed with a quarter taped to the

coupon. The brochure had less than 100 words of copy, including those on the mail-in coupon.

- An 8½ by 11 inch piece folded to 8½ by 5¾ inches promoting Mini-Mist shampoo and offering a 35 cent refund for return of a clip-out coupon and a label. The outside of the piece was two-color, while the inside spread featuring the refund coupon was in full process color.
- A 7¼ by 12 inch envelope and folded flap piece promoting applications for American Airlines Youth Plan. The airmail business reply envelope called for enclosure of $3.00 for a Youth Card and had ample space for name, address and identification information.
- A 7¼ by 9 inch two-color piece which folded to 7¼ by 4½ inches and promoted Mitchum anti-perspirants. Half of the inside spread was devoted to a coupon promoting a trial package of Mitchum plus a booklet, "Understanding Perspiration." The offer required taping 25 cents to the coupon.
- An 8 by 13 inch piece which folded to 4 by 10½ inches, printed in black and red and offering: "Start your own collection of lovely Dior Lipsticks for a dollar (regular $5.00 value)." The piece included three identical coupons with the suggestion that the recipient "share this fabulous offer with your two best friends."
- An unfolded 5 by 5¼ inch slip with a teaser message on one side and a simple two-color message on the reverse. It offered 2 by 3 feet blowups of photos for $4.50—simple message and small coupon.
- An 11½ by 5 inch piece folded to 5¾ by 5 inches with two separate mail order offers to different firms at the same address. One offer showed 24 black-and-white posters offered at $1.00 each (National Graphics Co.). The other offered three $2.00 guides to summer employment (National Employment Service Institute). Both had unperforated coupons.
- A 6 by 3½ inch airmail business reply envelope with a full flap promoting memberships in the American Cultural Society at $5.00. Only membership advantages offered were savings of "25-60% on any book." Copy stated: "On your first 2 books you will save your membership fee."
- An 11 by 21 inch poster-calendar folded to 11 by 8½ inches. The lower 4 inches of the three-color calendar contained two perforated coupons offering "a full-size $1.00 cake of Neutrogena Soap, a purse size of Neutrogena Body Oil, and Smile Lip Gloss . . . plus 2 or more sunny complexion surprises" for $1.00 to cover cost of handling. One coupon was labeled "for yourself;" the other "for a friend." The back of the folded calendar contained detailed copy on Neutrogena skin care products.

Other Co-op Enclosures

These are but a few of the more-or-less standard enclosures used in co-op mailing packages. Among other techniques commonly used:

- *The Book-of-the-Month Club* has used an 8-page 3½ by 7 inch mini-catalog, with the back cover a perforated business reply card order form. This format permitted full-color display of 41 different books offered as bonuses for a trial membership.

- *Union Carbide* included five sandwich-size Glad Bags nested in a folder which also incorporated two 6 cent store coupons.
- *Nescafé* combined a 10 cent store coupon with a mail-back offer of three nylon stockings (pair n spare) for 50 cents and a Nescafé label.
- *Post Cereals* offered a $1.00 cash offer for those who returned a coupon plus seven proofs of purchase from packages of advertised cereals. This technique is sometimes used primarily to offset misredemption.
- *Howard Johnson's* used a coupon promoting a new Florida vacation area, including a $10 certificate to be presented at the desk, entitling the recipient to three days and two nights for one couple and two children at Howard Johnson's Seafaring Resort Lodge for just $10 (excepting a two-month top-season period and with advance reservations).

Postcard Mailers

In recent years, one of the most popular forms of cooperative mailings has consisted of a collection of Business Reply Cards, each offering a different product or service. They have proved especially effective for inquiries and catalog requests.

There are two basic forms of postcard mailers. One consists of a bound booklet with as many as three perforated cards per page. The other form consists of an envelope or plastic bag with a series of loose postcards. Generally the loose cards pull greater response than the booklet format. However, the cost per card for this type of cooperative is usually greater than that charged for cards in booklets.

While the advertiser usually furnishes printed pieces for insertion in most cooperative mailings, the publishers of postcard mailers provide the paper and printing as part of their service.

In many cases it is possible to participate in a postcard cooperative on a per-inquiry basis, although published rates are generally based on cost-per-thousand or a fixed fee for the entire circulation.

SAMPLING BY MAIL

While couponing is primarily a vehicle for multiple purchase consumer products, sampling by direct mail is used in one form or another by just about every type of advertiser—ranging from food products to industrial manufacturers to real estate to automobile manufacturers. Probably more ingenuity has been demonstrated in direct mail sampling than in any other form of advertising.

The simple little card shown on the following page is the heart of most consumer direct mail sampling programs. It permits the advertiser to deliver packaged samples in bulk into the postal stream, with

THE GILLETTE COMPANY
SAFETY RAZOR DIVISION
1000 DONNELLEY DRIVE
ELM CITY, NORTH CAROLINA 27822

THIS ADDRESS CARD WAS PREPARED FOR USE IN DELIVERING THE ACCOMPANYING POSTAGE PAID SAMPLE.

RESIDENT
2040 VALLEY LO ST
GLENVIEW IL 60025

OPEN BY ADULT ONLY

(TRAC II™ 2.5 OZ. SAMPLE RAZOR IN SEALED METAL CONTAINER)

The Gillette Company sampled one of their new products utilizing this address card.

addressed slips of paper used to control the distribution of those samples. The mail carrier simply matches up the addressed slip with one of his supply of unaddressed packages and delivers the two elements to the chosen recipients.

One of the interesting facts of life in sampling is that techniques are constantly changing. At any given point in time, there may be several dozen different techniques in popular use and a couple of years later only a handful remain with dozens of new methods in operation. Through all the changes, however, the tried and proved technique of sampling by direct mail remains the one sure constant.

To get a feel of sampling at one given point in time, the following article digested from *Advertising Age*[8] indicates the variety of sample distribution techniques which must be considered. A year or two later, a similar news article could be written but chances are the majority of names and distribution techniques would be different.

> Sampling programs—whether targeted, random or partially random—appear to be flourishing, along with couponing, in today's tough marketing mix.
>
> These collateral efforts—the time-honored sampling and couponing techniques, plus their computerized advanced systems—are attracting new interest among marketing men because of recent moves by large companies to carve out chunks of the business for themselves.
>
> The latest company to enter the sampling field is American Can Co., now moving into mail order cosmetics sales through an affiliation with International Beauty Club, which offers magazine readers around $20 worth of cosmetics products for $5.95.

[8]"There's Money To Be Made By Giving The Stuff Away" by Fred Danzig, *Advertising Age*, September 20, 1971.

Earlier, Gillette Co. moved into sampling with its purchase of the far-flung Welcome Wagon International organization. And Ted Bates & Co., it became known, bought into Manufacturer's Assortment Inc., producer of Value Package program. This program involves the sale of 19 products (worth more than $18 at retail) for $3.95. Customers are sought via color pages in *Parade* every few months.

While Value Package appears to have established itself as one method of targeted sampling, competing systems, by and large, also seem to be flourishing.

Random samplings, usually the "Occupant" mass mailing, door-drop or handout, are still the favored approach and the largest operation in this field is Reuben H. Donnelley Corp. Pre-screened sampling is exemplified by Compusamp Inc. and Donnelley's Sample Probe. Compusamp has handled major programs for such companies as Lever and Lorillard and recently scored a coup by adding Lever's rival, Colgate-Palmolive, for a $3,000,000 household product-toiletries sampling push later in the year.

Compusamp and Sample Probe first question prospects so that breakouts can be developed for brand switching campaigns. That is, Brand X users become desirable sample targets for Brand Y's competing product. Sample Probe phones ahead and develops a profile of the future brand recipient. While the Compusamp and Sample Probe approaches are deemed sophisticated and effective methods, they are not for the shoestring budget.

The partially selective programs are those conducted by such companies as Gift Pax Inc., which tries to screen the recipient at the time the sample is given out. Gift Pax goes to expectant mothers, servicemen and college students. The Welcome Wagon operation goes after new family move-ins.

Another phase of the door-drop sample combines with the selective program and uses milkmen to deliver samples. Indications are that this approach falters when the milkman is asked to go beyond mere delivery and collect information.

Milkmen too often are up and out too early to see their customers and, when they do, have little time to pursue questionnaires.

Another pre-screening technique that is selective, or extra-selective, is exemplified by the experimental programs initiated by the major trading stamp companies, E. F. MacDonald Stamp Co. and Sperry & Hutchinson Co. MacDonald is using Plaidland redemption centers in the New York area to distribute American Brands cigarets to customers who are smokers and who fill out a questionnaire. The S&H Green Stamp test, in Atlanta and Minneapolis, is similar. In order to qualify for samples, however, one must first visit the redemption center, which makes this approach extra-selective.

Random samplings also involve coupon mailings. Coupon mailings, simple in concept, are nevertheless not always regarded as a low-cost marketing tool. Along with misredemptions and the cost of mailing, production and fulfillment are factors that run up costs.

Handouts, of course, are always popular. The pretty girl handing out a sample was used in supermarkets by General Foods for its Maxwell House instant iced coffee powder. Cigaret companies also are occasional handout samplers, but the practice has its drawbacks. Lever Bros. made note of what could be called "Sample Skirmishes of 1969" in its annual report. "In the laundry detergent field," said Lever, "housewives received so many free samples of new laundry brands that the effect on purchase was the same as if every homemaker in the U.S. had stopped doing laundry for nearly three weeks. Similarly, enough free toothpaste samples were distributed to cover the entire nation's toothbrushing needs for a full week."

Samples, whether distributed free or sold at low, low prices, inevitably get linked with couponing, either through follow-up mailings or as package (or envelope) stuffers.

It is axiomatic that the more selective the sampling, the higher the cost, but random samplings can also prove to be costly. Nevertheless, sampling is continually going on because there is always (a) a new product someone wants to put into the customer's hands and (b) a company has a brand with a small market share in a product category that has a massive dollar total.

"I'd say that as more and more companies get into sampling and start using the refined couponing techniques," said an industry source, "the more attention they'll start to pay to what their payout ratios should be, who is making the follow-up purchases and just what it is that the promotion is supposed to do."

Effective Sampling

Techniques for effective sampling were presented by John Luick, who has had extensive experience in this area both from the client and advertising agency side.[9] He describes consumer sampling as meaning the actual delivery of a free sample to the consumer. The sample may be delivered to the home by a crew or through the mail, or it may be handed out in the street or in a store. This kind of *actual* sampling can be highly effective for a product which is demonstrably superior to its competition. It gives a product its best chance to prove itself, its best opportunity to win consumer trial and, hopefully, long-term loyalty.

However, he continues, sampling is also expensive. Even so, depending on product cost, method of delivery, geographic or socioeconomic selectivity, a national sampling can vary dramatically in costlines. Some samplings may cost $1,000,000 or $2,000,000. Some have cost as little as $12,000. Delivery by crew alone can cost between 13 cents and 15 cents per sample or $4,000,000 to "drop" on 30,000,000 homes. This kind of expense is completely beyond the reach of most manufacturers. Only a few giant marketers can accept this burden of cost, but they do so for several time-tested reasons:

First, sampling accelerates volume rapidly. With sampling, peak volume levels can be reached in perhaps four to six months after introduction. This

[9]"Sampling as a Sales Promotion Tool" by John Luick, *Advertising & Sales Promotion,* June 1964.

fast rise in volume is meaningful not only in immediate revenue, but also because it gives the new product the jump on competition.

Second, sampling can actually build a higher level of total volume for a brand. Sampling will reach potential customers who would not normally try a new entry. This, then, is sampling's big advantage over couponing. Couponing attracts the likeliest prospects for a new brand. Sampling induces trial by fringe and even remote prospects. It can intrude on a buying pattern or habit.

Third, although sampling aims primarily at inducing consumer trial, it is not without great prestige with retailers. Grocers and druggists know the power of sampling to sell goods. Thus, it becomes a powerful lever in promoting wide and fast distribution. The well-advertised, well-sampled and improved new product will not be refused good shelf space. In fact, the product will probably earn strong in-store display support. While the relationship of advertising to sampling in timing, weight, media selection and sales effort can vary substantially by product type, there is one cardinal rule which applies to any sampling: sufficient advertising must run before the sample drop to establish the value of the sample. Only sound judgment in each case can determine just how much advertising is sufficient for this purpose.

What kinds of products qualify for broad-scale sampling? Mr. Luick comments: "Not a lipstick or perfume, because color and scent are remarkably personal. Not a loaf of bread, because the profit margin is too narrow to offer a reasonable return on the expense. Not a home permanent because the frequency of purchase is too slow. Not health foods because they are bought because of an 'idea,' even if they taste bad."

Interestingly, though, all of the "unlikely products" for sampling singled out by Mr. Luick have been effectively sampled, but not through simple sampling techniques. However, with a little ingenuity, even the most "unlikely" product can be put into the hands of prospective customers. Mr. Luick summarizes the likely candidates for routine sampling as: The broader a product's use, the higher its profit margin, the more rapid its purchase rate, the better a candidate for sampling it is. Toothpaste is likely, dental floss unlikely.

Sample Size

In commenting on the question of sample size and its relation to consumer usage patterns, Mr. Luick comments that one small and broadside sample of a delightful new powdered drink might be enough to start a purchasing stampede. A larger sample of a laundry additive might be needed because only after several washings would a difference be demonstrated. Then, too, if experience and practicality so indicate, a large-size sample might be sent to heavy users of a product type in an effort to gain important volume from a relatively smaller number of customers.

Among other considerations, Mr. Luick adds, perishability is a factor in food products; breakage in bottled products; toxicity in drug products. There is also the problem of package design and protection of sample against damage before final delivery. Other variables are weather and distance between sample calls. These and other factors affect not only the feasibility of sampling in the first place, but the method of sampling as well. It behooves the sampler to try, as far as possible, to design the sample package as much like the actual retail package as possible. A miniature of the real tube would be most effective for tooth paste, for example. This presents an opportunity to establish package recognition at a most favorable time.

Sampling by Mail

Wilson B. Prophet, Jr. has prepared a number of good guides to sampling by mail, which have been published in various publications. Typical of his comments: "An old adage has it that if you have something good, all you need do to prove it is to put a sample of it in the customer's hand; once there, chances are that enough of the triers will start buying it to give you a substantial share of the market. This in a nutshell is the principle of sampling. And although several methods are available for putting your sample in the consumer's hand, mail has certain decided advantages over the others. Only mail can bring the product to millions of people simultaneously, only mail can reach suburbs, small towns and rural areas as easily as densely populated areas, only mail can be closely timed so as to tie in with print and broadcast advertising, only mail can make full use of sophisticated selectivity techniques. And with mail, delivery to the addressee is virtually assured, with no slippage."

Mr. Prophet prepared the following checklist to help marketers decide whether sampling by mail is right for their circumstances:

1. *Is the product really new?* Mail sampling should only be used if your product is new, if it is an established brand with a noticeable improvement in the product, or if the packaging represents a new and unfamiliar improvement (for example, if you have replaced a standard glass bottle with a light, unbreakable plastic one). In each of these cases, a sample will prove the virtues of the product more effectively than any amount of advertising copy. On the other hand, sampling has been used on occasion to increase the market share of an established product or to "clobber" the competition—but, before considering such a move, be sure you can afford a certain amount of waste and possible bad feeling. In the first place, a number of the samples are sure to be sent to people who already use the product, and in the second place, local dealers and distributors are likely to resent the temporary loss of sales occasioned by the availability of free samples. Obviously, these problems do not arise in the case of a new product.

2. *Is the product readily adaptable to mail distribution?* If the product is light in weight, compact in size, and forms an easily handled package, there should be no problem in mailing it. If it is heavy, bulky or odd-shaped, however, mailing costs can soar. Postal regulations and all state and federal laws should be carefully checked before mailing. The Post Office, for instance, will not accept easily breakable packages or products of any potentially injurious materials, and some regulations go into details that can only be characterized as odd. One rule, for instance, prohibits the mailing of all poisonous insects or animals—with the exception of scorpions. State and federal laws may also raise problems, especially if your product is a proprietary drug. Laws on drug mailings differ widely from state to state, and some states actually outlaw the mailing of any drugs. In order to avoid trouble, a mailer should check out all aspects of his sampling with his legal staff as well as his mailing house. The latter firm's broad experience with postal procedures and the legal aspects of mailing can be invaluable and can often prevent headaches.
3. *How closely can selectivity pinpoint your customers?* Few products find a potential customer in every household, and even the most universally used products are bought in larger quantities by some families than by others. Since sampling is a costly procedure, it is desirable to restrict distribution to the families most likely to become regular volume customers. Mail is the best medium for this, and an up-to-date mailing house is able to make practical use of the socio-economic findings of the U.S. Census Bureau and select those individual families that come closest to matching the characteristics of your ideal customer profile.
4. *Will your product fit in a cooperative mailing?* One excellent means of cutting distribution costs is the use of a cooperative mailing. In this case, of course, the sampler has less control over the selectivity of the mailing list than if he mails alone, and his package must be small and flat enough to fit into the typical co-op envelope. Cost savings, however, can far offset these disadvantages.
5. *Should a coupon be included?* When sampling by mail, be sure you consider the relative merits of including a coupon with the sample. Many marketers have found that this encourages the recipient to take the next logical step after trying the sample—buying the product, and so establishing a buying habit.

Undelivered Samples

One question which always enters a discussion of sampling is what happens to those which aren't delivered. One of the author's first direct mail experiences was operating a local door-to-door distribution service while a schoolboy in the depression days of the thirties. At that time, local sample delivery was fairly common and one of the major methods of compensation for the crew of fellow schoolboys was the "extra" samples after saturation coverage had been completed. I'm not sure if my family ever used up the hundreds of full-size packages of a popular, packaged pudding which we inherited as part of the compensation for a sampling job.

A more current report on the fate of undelivered samples was included in the *Mail Marketing Newsletter*:[10]

> Advertisers who use mail sampling, one of the most effective means of introducing new products, should be aware that postal regulations permit undeliverable samples of "valuable merchandise" to be auctioned off as dead parcel post. Of course, if the sample is marked "return requested," nixies must be returned to the mailer.
>
> McIntyre investigated this practice recently on behalf of a client who had received word from the successful bidder that 20,000 of their samples had been purchased at auction at the New York Post Office. The client's concern, of course, was that the dumping of these samples on the retail market at distress prices could do some damage to sales through regular retail channels.
>
> Postal regulations specify that undeliverable samples of food products may be donated to local charities, or destroyed. They may not be sold. Undeliverable samples of drugs must be destroyed. Undeliverable samples of cosmetics may be sold, except for lipsticks, which must be destroyed. We don't know why lipsticks are singled out for special treatment. Undeliverable samples of any other items may be donated to local charities, or auctioned.
>
> Only the samples are sold, so if the mailing contains a coupon as well as a sample, the nixies must be opened, and coupons destroyed according to postal regulations covering the disposition of undeliverable coupons before the samples can be sold.
>
> Auctions are conducted three times a year at thirteen regional dead parcel post centers. As a practical matter, it is unlikely that postmasters of small post offices, who receive few nixies because of the size of their office, will elect to forward nixies to the regional dead parcel post center. Only the largest post offices can accumulate sufficient undeliverable samples to make auctioning practical.
>
> At least one individual is known to make a practice of bidding on merchandise samples. When successful, he immediately contacts the advertiser in an attempt to ransom the merchandise. While an annoyance, the practice of selling undeliverable nixies is not a major reason against mail sampling. On a recent nationwide sampling mailing, the number of samples which appeared in post office auctions amounted to only one per thousand samples mailed.

Typical Consumer Sampling

While there is no universal consumer sample package, the most common is an addressed delivery card plus a box containing a trial size sample of the product in a miniature of its retail container, an advertising brochure and a cents-off coupon for a follow-up purchase.

Another common sampling by mail package is shown on the following page. This mailing by Bristol-Myers launched Softique Beauty Bath Oil. The one-color (pink) envelope stated simply, "Free gift of beauty and valuable coupon for you." It was mailed

[10] "Undelivered Samples," *Mail Marketing Newsletter*, O.E. McIntyre Inc., New York, August 1964.

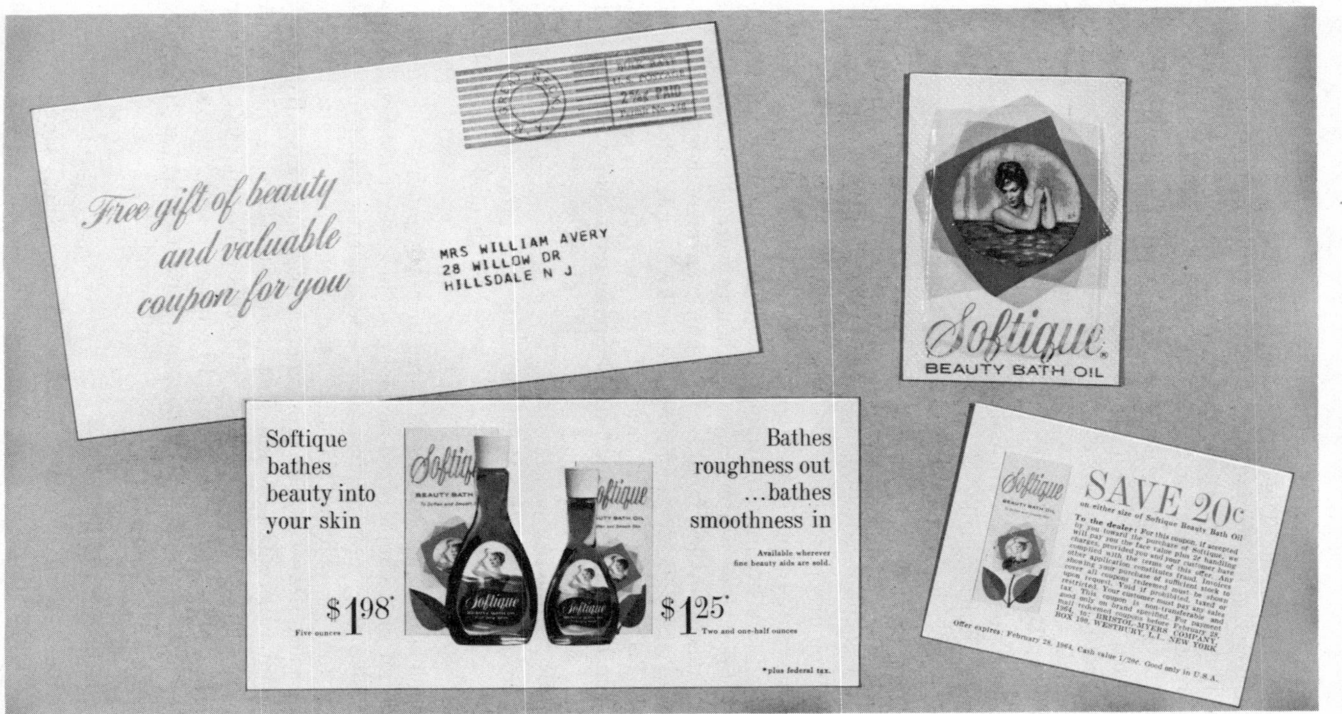

Bristol-Myers helped launch Softique Beauty Bath Oil with the above. It was mailed to selected individuals in key market areas.

to selected individuals in key market areas. Enclosed was a 6- by 5½-inch four color folder folded to 6 by 3 inches; a 2⅛- by 3⅛-inch plastic pouch containing an actual sample of the bath oil, with a full-color illustration duplicating the elements and colors used for the regular retail package, and a 3¼- by 2½-inch coupon offering 20 cents off on a purchase of the product at a retail outlet. Softique, it is reported, became the No. 1 bath oil four months after this sample mailing into test market areas.

Foremost Dairies' Milkman

To introduce its new formula instant, low-fat dry milk, Milkman, Foremost Dairies mailed a relatively large sample package— 2¾- by 3⅛ by 7½ inches. Inside was a paper and foil tetrahedron-shaped sample pack of Milkman, sufficient to make one quart. An accompanying four-color brochure stressed the product's advantages and provided simple instructions for use. A tear-off coupon offered 10 cents off on first purchase.

Because large families are the big consumers of milk, list selection was used to concentrate on families with children, in the middle income ranges. Families in apartment houses were eliminated because of the much smaller families found in apartment houses and because of the difficulty in fitting the bulky sample into small mail boxes. Because the actual taste of the product was such a vital factor in building acceptance, the sampling technique was a natural.

Multiple Products

Seven different Bristol-Myers products were promoted in a single sample mailing. The 2¼- by 2½- by 4½-inch mailing carton was labeled "Free Gifts Inside."

Contents included samples of three then-new products: Ban spray deodorant in a sample-sized aerosol container; Fact toothpaste in a travel-size tube, and Resolve, an antacid analgesic tablet, in sample size carton. In addition, six different coupons were inserted in the sample pack. Two coupons promoted sampled products—Ban spray deodorant (10 cents off) and Fact toothpaste (8 cents off). Other products couponed were Softique (15 cents off), children's Bufferin (10 cents off), Score hair cream (10 cents off), and Score spray deodorant (15 cents off). The coupons were nested in a four-color circular which displayed the three sample products.

Thunderbird Sampling

Obviously Ford Motor Company can't send actual samples of its luxury Thunderbirds to prospective buyers, but it did come up with a unique sampling technique that went a long way beyond the auto industry's usual sampling technique of offering local test drives. To expose its 1972 Thunderbirds to prospective buyers, Ford mailed personalized letters to 600,000 high income individuals in 10 major cities offering rental through Hertz at the same cost as a Galaxie 500. A gold "Thunderbird Executive Rental Card" was enclosed with the letter. The recipient simply signed the card's back to validate the offer. The personalized letter signed by Douglas T. McClure, Ford Division Merchandising Manager, read:

> A new 1972 Thunderbird is waiting for you!
>
> When business or pleasure takes you to Los Angeles, San Francisco, Miami, Boston, Washington, D.C., Chicago, Dallas/ Ft. Worth, Philadelphia, Cleveland, or Detroit ... simply stop by the metropolitan airport office of Hertz Rent A Car and present the enclosed Executive Rental Card.
>
> This card allows you to rent a '72 Thunderbird for the same price you'd pay for one of our Ford Galaxie 500's. We want you to experience the fine luxury and quality we've designed into this new car; its new roominess ... its elegantly tailored interior ... its plush, new ride that's made smoother by a longer wheelbase and a new rear suspension system ... Michelin tires that give extra long life. (The list goes on and on.)
>
> Some other good things about this offer: (1) you can use any credit card honored by Hertz, (2) this offer applies to normal Hertz discounts, and (3) you can use this plan as often as you want until January 31, 1972.
>
> So before your next trip, call Hertz Central Reservation Service at 1-800-654-3131, identify yourself as an Executive Rental Card holder and ask them to reserve your new Bird. We'll pay the difference in rates ... you enjoy the difference in driving. Have a good trip!

Hal Leonard Music Record

Thin simple records have become relatively common as a sampling method for mail order firms selling record collections, but a more unique application of this sampling technique was used by Hal Leonard Music, Inc., the Winona, Minn. publishers of marching band music for high schools and colleges. The mailing package was a 16-page 7½- by 7¼-inch plastic ring-bound booklet, with an Evatone record bound in. The booklet introduced 12 new marching band arrangements created by Bill Moffit, marching band director at

Michigan State. While sample cornet scores were shown for several of the new arrangements, that kind of sampling is hardly adequate to convey the big sound of selections which include a full score with 100 parts. Therefore, Hal Leonard included a stereo preview record with full band recordings of seven of the selections. That way, band director recipients got a real sample of what was available to them.

The above booklet, together with an Evatone stereo record, proved to be most effective.

The effectiveness of the booklet, as reported by Rapp, Collins, Stone & Adler, the agency which created the mailing, was amazing—sales ten times higher than the previous year.

Medical Sampling

There probably is no field where sampling is more common than providing doctors with new products turned out by pharmaceutical manufacturers. Literally hundreds of different samples are distributed annually to doctors either through the mail or personal delivery by detail men. To try to simplify this procedure and reduce costs, Clark-O'Neill Service Company developed a technique called "single source sampling." Each month, Clark-O'Neill sends a mailing to approximately 170,000 physicians and osteopaths in office-based practice. The mailing consists of an outer envelope, a multi-product brochure listing free samples and services available to physicians, and two postage-paid business reply cards on which the physician writes the numbers of those products and services for which he wishes to see samples. Participating manufacturers pay nothing to list their samples in the brochure but pay $1.30 for each address label resulting from a specific sample request from a physician.

A somewhat unique sampling technique was used by Pelam Inc., a Chicago firm which provides a computerized laboratory service for physicians. One of the features of the Pelam service is a computer print-out providing a detailed medical history and analysis created from a simple checklist questionnaire booklet filled out by a patient. To sample this print-out analysis, Pelam sent physicians a sample of the medical history and health questionnaire used by the service. An accompanying letter suggested that the doctor have his office assistant complete the questionnaire and return it for processing so a sample of the Pelam print-out could be sent to the doctor.

Industrial Sampling

Sampling of new products and examples of materials and services in use are a relatively standard promotion technique in the industrial field. Probably no industry depends so heavily on product sampling as manufacturers of printing papers. Every major firm in the field regularly mails both printed and unprinted samples of their papers to buyers and specifiers. Printers also lean heavily on sample distribution to demonstrate their skills. An example of one such program developed by the author is described in Chapter 6. An illustration of one of the sample mailings is shown on page 428.

Is Sampling Effective?

Several examples have already been given to show market gains accomplished through sampling. In addition, surveys have shown that sampling is one of the quickest routes to produce awareness. For example, one major telephone survey of households in a test market showed 72% of those contacted recalled having received the sample and an amazing 95% knew of the new product even though advertising in other media had been under way only two weeks. Obviously, the sample mailing played a major role in developing such awareness.

Another research project conducted by a fragrance manufacturer which had distributed foil-pack samples of perfume to teenage girls via a co-op mailing included both pre-mailing and post-mailing surveys. In the pre-mailing survey, 35% made favorable references to the brand name, while the post-mailing surveys drew 54% to 75% favorable references to the three brands sampled. Before the mailing, 11% reported they used the manufacturer's brands "regularly." After the sampling, 42% reported using them "regularly." In addition, from 70% to 81%, depending on the brand sampled, stated they intended to purchase the brand again.

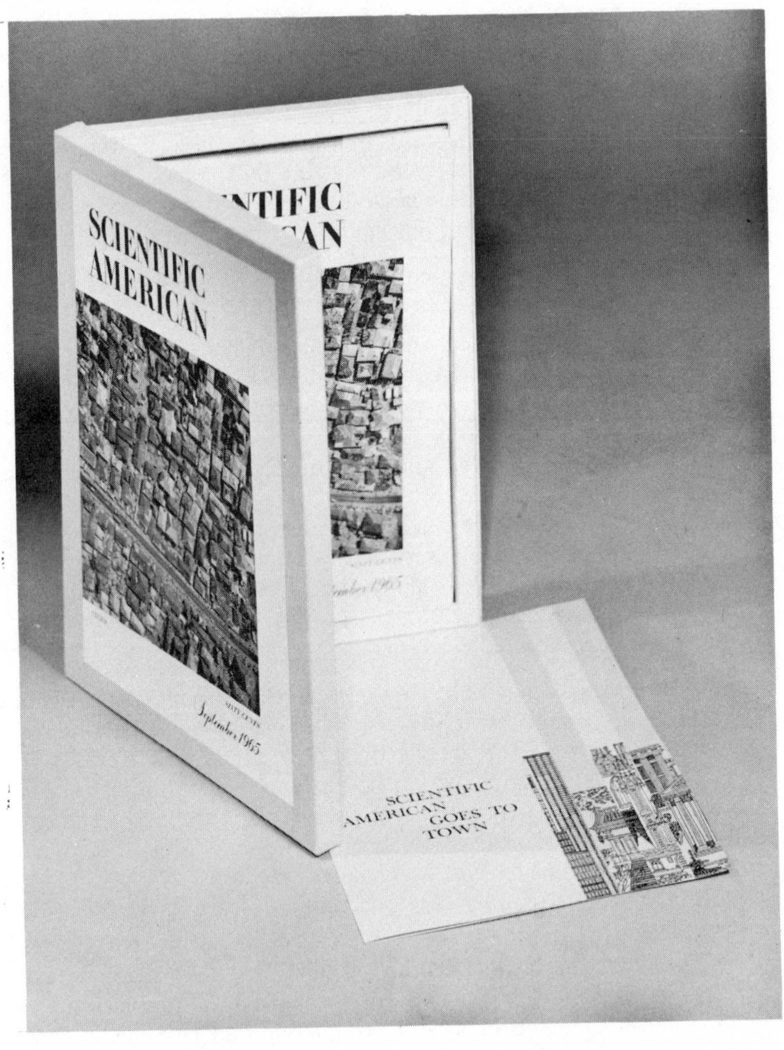

One example of the continuing flow of samples which R. R. Donnelley & Sons Company sent to a select list of primary prospects over a number of years. This mailing featured a special issue of Scientific American in a protective box designed for retention on a library shelf. The enclosed folder explained the printing services Donnelley performed for Scientific American.

TYPICAL CO-OP PROMOTION PACKAGES

From a list prepared by Uni-Mailer, 11 Beach Street, New York, N. Y. 10013

Market	Method of Distribution	Quantity	Frequency
Electrical Engineers	Postcard mailing	40,000	Monthly
Purchasing Agents of Large Corporations	Postcard mailing	65,000	5 times
High School Seniors	Publication	810,000	2 times
Doctors and Dentists Who Buy by Mail	Envelope mailing	60,000	8 times
Pharmaceutical Mail Order Buyers	Package insert	175,000	Continual
Youth Mail Order Buyers	Package insert	500,000	Continual
Business Mail Order Buyers	Envelope mailing	100,000	Monthly
Hospital Administrators	Postcard mailing	12,000	4 times
Dentists	Postcard mailing	85,000	4 times
Shirtboards		40,000,000	Continual
Servicemen	Package insert	500,000	Continual
Consumers	Envelope mailing	1,525,000	4 times
Design Engineers	Postcard mailing	105,000	3 times
Home Arts, Mail Order Buyers	Envelope mailing	200,000	4 times
Craftsmen, Mail Order Buyers	Envelope mailing	200,000	4 times
College & University Business	Postcard mailer	27,150	3 times
School Buyers	Postcard mailer	44,000	3 times
School and University Buyers	Postcard mailing	40,000	4 times
Church Buyers	Postcard mailer	50,000	2 times
Film Buyers	Envelope mailing	4,000,000	2 times
Households with Children (Suburban)	Hand distributed	2,000,000	2 times
Consumers	Poly bag with inserts	2,500,000	Continual
Librarians in Public Libraries	Envelope mailing	6,000	2 times
Librarians in Public Schools	Envelope mailing	8,000	2 times
Sports and Racing Car Accessories Mail Order	Package insert	250,000	Continual
Mothers-to-be	Hand distributed	35,000	Monthly
People Who Do Puzzles	Mailing insert	50,000	Monthly
Senior Citizens	Envelope mailing	239,000	3 times
General Consumer	Newspaper insert with envelope	2,000,000	Monthly
Direct Marketers	Postcard mailer	50,000	2 times

TYPICAL CO-OP PROMOTION PACKAGES

From a list prepared by Uni-Mailer, 11 Beach Street, New York, N. Y. 10013

Market	Method of Distribution	Quantity	Frequency
Industrial Firms	Postcard mailing	60,000	5 times
General Consumer	Newspaper preprint w/business reply cards	2,000,000	Monthly
Hospital Administrators	Postcard mailing	12,000	4 times
Metalworking Management	Postcard mailer	91,000	4 times
Metalworking and Tool Management	Postcard mailing	80,000	Monthly
General Mail Order	Package insert	150,000	Continual
Teachers at Home	Postcard mailing	1,650,000	3 times
Insurance Agents	Envelope mailing	12,000	3 times
New Jersey Industrial Companies	Postcard mailing	26,000	4 times
Scientific Researchers	Envelope mailing	100,000	Monthly
Geriatric Newspaper Readers	Preprint, reply card	5,000,000	1 time
Business Mail Order Buyers	Mail insert	170,000	6 times
Business Opportunity Seekers	Envelope mailing	500,000	7 times
R/D Engineers and Scientists	Postcard mailing	64,000	4 times
College Librarians	Envelope mailing	3,000	2 times
Restaurant Operators	Postcard mailer	60,000	2 times
Hotel Operators	Postcard mailer	34,000	2 times
Restaurant and Hotel Operators	Postcard mailer	78,000	2 times
Secondary School Administrators	Postcard mailer	51,137	2 times

Chapter 16

SYNDICATED MAILINGS

ONE of the most spectacular developments in direct mail and mail order during the mid-twentieth century has been the growth of so-called "syndicated mailings." Millions of dollars worth of merchandise are being sold annually through a tripartite combination involving a manufacturer, a packager of promotion programs and a selling organization which opens its mailing lists to the packaged promotions selling the products of the manufacturer.

While the history of this development is one of the most interesting in the entire merchandising field (and shortly we will devote several pages to the reprinting of this important story as told by one of the men most deeply involved in its development), the present state of the art can be credited directly to one individual—Albert E. Sloan. And just as that one man is the cornerstone upon which a multi-million dollar merchandising field has been built, one particular program can be credited for a major revolution in selling by mail.

This program was capsulized in a portrait of Al Sloan:[1] "The client was Bell & Howell and the campaign was a direct mail classic. Everyone was aware in those days [1959] that it was senseless to try to sell high-ticket merchandise through the mails. Bell & Howell, however, had these matched home movie outfits, selling at from $150 to $250. A Sloan-created mailing campaign reached over 50-million homes in two-and-a-half years; 270,000 persons bought a total of $50 million of camera equipment."

Finding a Market

What Al Sloan did was to create hard-selling mailing pieces featuring Bell & Howell camera outfits and then arrange to have com-

[1]"Action People," *Marketing/Communications*, May 1968.

panies with large mailing lists send the pieces to their customers—book publishers, mail order houses, auto accessory suppliers, department stores, record clubs—and most important, credit card companies.

The proliferation of merchandise mailings today sent out by most every oil company to its credit card holders; the merchandise mailings made by American Express, Diners Club and Carte Blanche, and hundreds of other high-ticket offers really originated with Al Sloan's Bell & Howell success story.

A detailed report on this epic in merchandising was published in *The Reporter of Direct Mail Advertising:*[2]

> The impact of the Sloan-Ashland camera package on the consumer mail order field cannot be minimized. Regarded with suspicion by some and pooh-poohed as impractical by others, the package offer successfully sold millions of dollars in camera equipment.
>
> Of what is a Sloan movie outfit comprised? Inside the package was an 8mm. projector, a 400-foot take-up reel, an 8mm. electric-eye camera, a 30- by 40-inch floor model tripod glass-beaded screen, a light bar with two 375-watt flood lamps, a top grain leather carrying case, a 3-month subscription to Home Movies magazine, a Woody Woodpecker cartoon, and a Castle film catalog. As free gifts for examining the merchandise, Sloan-Ashland offered one roll each of Eastman Kodachrome color film and Eastman Tri-X black and white film.
>
> "This offer," Sloan explained, "actually carried three premiums in it. The consumer keeps both rolls of film whether or not he decides to keep the movie outfit. This was our way of saying 'for your trouble, keep this free gift.' It forced the doubters to place an order."
>
> The third premium was the real clincher, and without question was one of the main reasons the response was so great.
>
> "Oddly, it was not visible until the purchase was made! It was sort of a stock dividend on an investment," he said. "As a special inducement, we offered a two-year supply of film free-of-charge to the purchaser. This meant all the black-and-white film they wanted for the next two years."
>
> There was some masterful psychology involved in the Woody Woodpecker cartoon, which apparently would serve no useful purpose other than for the children of the house. Sloan wanted to assure each purchaser that (1) he had made a good buy, (2) he could operate the projector with ease. Knowing the human mind, Sloan knew that the buyer of the movie outfit wanted to use it at once, but couldn't until his first films were taken and developed. Thus the cartoon provided the buyer with a film which he could use at once to instill confidence in his own ability to run a projector!
>
> On the statistical side, Sloan estimates that returns from a mailing will run from 4/10th% to sometimes as high as 4%, depending upon the lists

---

[2] "Why Do People Buy By Mail?" *The Reporter of Direct Mail Advertising,* March 1964. (Now called "Direct Advertising")

used, nature of the product, timing, packaging, etc. Furthermore, within the first two weeks of any mailing, 50% of the total return will be in, and at the end of four weeks, 99% of the orders will have arrived. By the 45th day, or approximately six weeks after any mailing, a rather extensive analysis can be made of consumer reaction.

"Adventures in Merchandising"

The Sloan package for Bell & Howell was the subject of an extensive study conducted by A. C. Nielsen Co. and detailed in a 51-page report titled "Adventures in Merchandising." The summation of that report is a good foundation for syndicated programs:

> *The Sloan-Ashland offer dramatically shows that the ultimate winner in the merchandising field will be the restless experimenters, thinkers, creative promoters, who try various and different promotional programs and make a continuous, concerted, overt effort to drive consumers into their commercial arms.*

The Nielsen report included an interesting profile of the buyers of the Bell & Howell camera packages:

1. An astounding 92% of the purchasers were men.
2. 25% of the purchasers were in the 35-44 year old age bracket. The age brackets of 18-24 and 45-54 tied for second with 18%.
3. 49% of the users had at least high school diplomas.
4. 50% of the purchasers were in the $5,000-$6,999 income group. The second highest grouping at 21% were in the $7,000-$9,999 income group.
5. 89% were family men.
6. 76% lived in houses, as compared to apartment dwellers.
7. Buyers included 55% who bought without shopping around; 45% visited one or more retail outlets to compare; 62% made their last photo equipment purchase in a specialty store.
8. Surprisingly, 37% of the buyers had never before purchased anything by mail.
9. Key reasons for buying were (1) the outfit represented a "good value," (2) it outpromoted and outsold the local dealers.
10. 100% of the respondents thought the Sloan offer was "believable"; 61% had the feeling of low price; 41% liked the idea of a complete outfit; 20% were sold on the Bell & Howell reputation.

Al Sloan cited three reasons for the success of the program: (1) You can't fool the customers; (2) For a "special" to be successful it must be outstanding; and (3) now more about your business than anyone else and work harder at it than anyone else.

Sloan Up-to-Date

Later operating as Whitney-Forbes, Inc., Al Sloan continued to create successful syndicated direct mail packages. Typical is his strikingly beautiful package for Voumard watches. Some of the elements are shown in the illustrations on pages 435-436. The package consists of the following elements:

Mailing Envelope

A 6- by 9-inch single window envelope (for addressed order card). The back of the envelope has a full-color bleed photograph of an ancient timepiece and the heading "Master crafted in Switzerland—an unprecedented offer . . . a wonderful opportunity."

Letter

A plain black-and-white miniature four-page letter with the mailer's letterhead. Typical copy:

Dear Credit Card Customer:

You are invited to wear, and you have the opportunity to own a luxurious timepiece created by one of Switzerland's most esteemed watchmakers.

Since 1848 the Voumard watchmakers in Neuchatel, Switzerland have produced masterpieces of precision timekeeping. At the modern factory-laboratory, old world techniques and Swiss pride-of-craftsmanship combine today's computer sciences to produce their famed jeweled movements and award-winning designs.

The man's calendar watch is the proud descendant of the original Calendar Clock invented in 1713 by the Earl of Orrery, valued at $25,000 and now a museum treasure at the Adler Planetarium in Chicago. But, unlike that original timepiece, today's Voumard calendar watch is made of the most modern materials...

It is not surprising that these timepieces are most accurate and reliable. Voumard is the designer of the Isatome, that astounding electronic timer chosen by the French Government for its space and missile program.

The Isatome was awarded an unprecedented two First Prizes at the Neuchatel Observatory Concours in 1962, plus First Prize in 1963, 1965, 1966, 1967 and 1968, for its exceptional timekeeping precision. The Isatome was selected for exhibit in the Montreal Expo as an outstanding example of Swiss precision and is used throughout the watch industry to check the operation of fine watches.

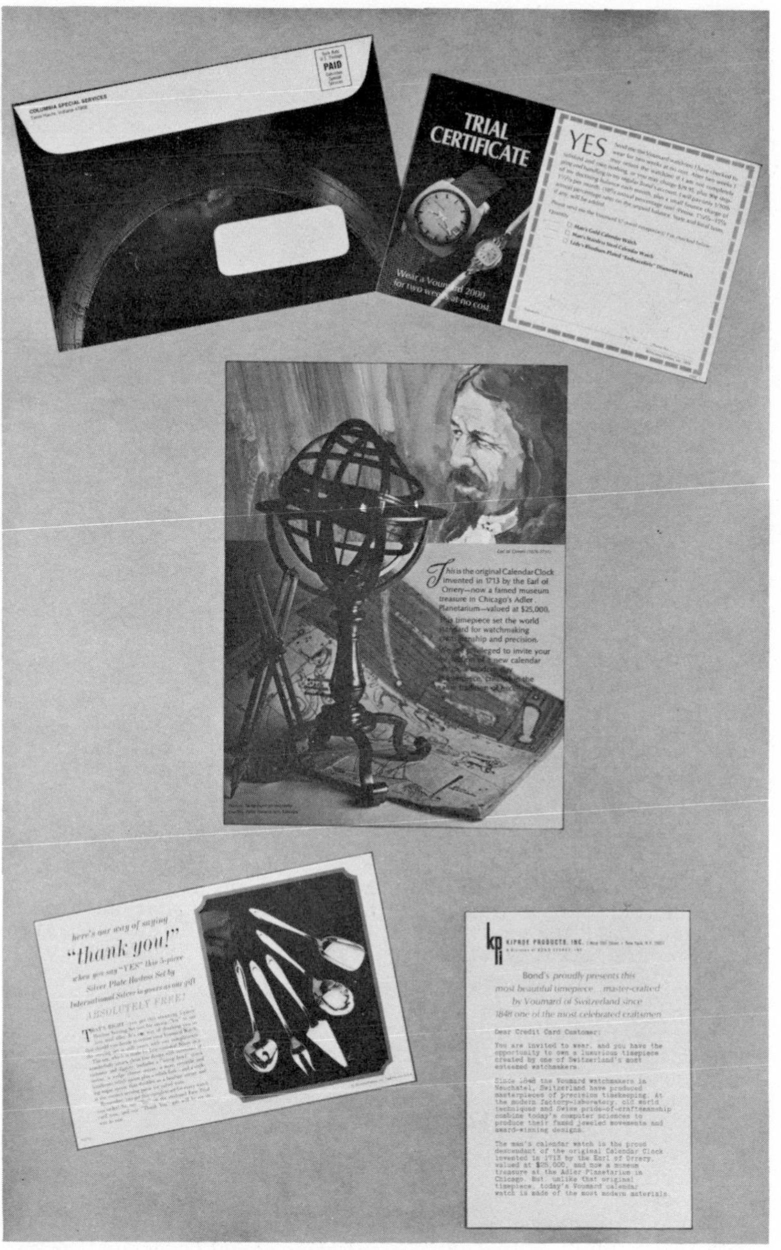

Shown here are the successful elements of an Al Sloan—created mailing for Voumard watches.

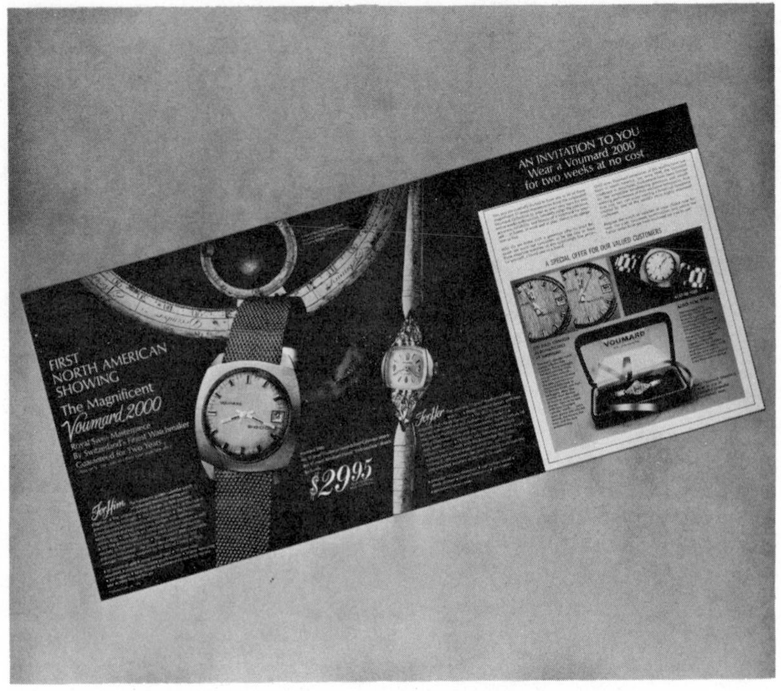

Still another part of the Voumard watch program, inviting the customer to wear it free for two weeks.

That is why Voumard can say with pride -- every Voumard 2000 is guaranteed unconditionally on all movement parts for two years. (Many other fine watches are guaranteed for only one year.) Each timepiece is engraved with its own registered identification number. This valuable number ensures your full protection for the duration of the guarantee. See the clearly stated guarantee in the brochure...

Even if you made a special trip to Europe, you couldn't get this watch at this low price, or even close to it. Order the watch today -- wear and enjoy it. Check the "YES" box on the trial acceptance certificate we have enclosed for you, and return it today while the supply of Voumard 2000 timepieces is still available.

Brochure

The front cover of the 8½- by 11-inch six-page brochure features a bleed full-color photo of the original Calendar Clock invented in 1713 by the Earl of Orrery. Two pages of the inside spread show oversize photos of both the men's and women's

Voumard watches, while the third page has actual-size photos and gives specific details. It is headed: "An invitation to you: Wear a Voumard 2000 for two weeks at no cost." The fifth page gives the credentials of Voumard of Switzerland, while the back cover tells about Voumard craftsmen and spells out the two-year guarantee. An interesting note at the bottom of the page: "The timepieces shown inside this brochure have never before been seen in North America. This is their premiere showing."

Bonus Slip

An 8½- by 5½-inch slip offers a five-piece silver plate hostess set by International Silver as a "gift" for agreeing to make the two-week trial. A full-color photo shows the set.

Order Form

The order form is also 8½ by 5½ inches and contains a stub with full-color illustrations of both the men's and women's Voumard watches. The remainder of the card has a business reply reverse. Copy on the order side reads:

YES

Send me the Voumard watch(es) I have checked to wear for two weeks at no cost. After two weeks I may return the watch(es) if I am not completely satisfied and owe nothing, or you may charge $29.95, plus 90 cents shipping and handling to my regular ______________ account.

Additional copy gives finance terms.

Polaroid Syndication Package

One of the more unique syndicated packages was developed for Polaroid Corp. by Rapp, Collins, Stone & Adler. It contained the following elements:

Mailing Envelope

A simple two-window 6- by 9-inch envelope with a regular window for address from the order card and a smaller window for a simple black-and-white picture of a Polaroid color film pack imprinted "Reserved for You." Envelope copy read: "Take your picture in color using this Polaroid color film pack. See it in 60 seconds. Use the free trial certificate enclosed."

Letter

The letter was heavy with headlines and illustrations along with the letterhead of the mailing organization. The headings in enlarged red and black typewriter type read:

WITHIN THE NEXT FEW DAYS, WITHOUT COST OR OBLIGATION, WE WILL SEND YOU A COMPLETE POLAROID AUTOMATIC COLOR PACK CAMERA OUTFIT TO USE FOR 2 WEEKS ABSOLUTELY FREE...when you place your Color Film Pack Token in the "Yes" slot on the enclosed Certificate. (Imagine your taking a color picture of your husband, wife, baby or best friend and seeing it seconds later!)

The remainder of the 8- by 9-inch four-page letter was hard sell for the offer, with alternate paragraphs in black and red. The back page was a display panel with typewriter type and illustration emphasizing an additional bonus offer—a 5- by 7-inch color enlargement of the favorite picture taken during the trial period.

Brochure

The most unique element in the package was the brochure which simulated a Polaroid camera. It was actually a die-cut open end envelope with a visible tab reading "pull straight out" —just like the tab on a Polaroid film pack. What you pulled out of the picture envelope was a die-cut brochure with a white-on-black cover reading: "If you have never had the fun of seeing your pictures as you take them ..." When you opened out the panel, the message continued: "we would like you to try the Polaroid Color Pack Camera Model 225 for the next 2 weeks absolutely free without any cost or obligation to you." The facing page had a candid full-color picture of a young girl. You next opened the brochure up and down and saw a selection of typical family pictures taken with a Polaroid color camera. Fully opening the brochure to the left revealed a full view of the entire camera kit, with copy explaining all details. The back "cover" of the tricky brochure detailed both the free pack of color film and bonus offer of a color 5- by 7-inch enlargement.

Order Card

The 8¼- by 5½-inch two-color order card had a tear-off stub. Copy was headed: "Polaroid Camera Outfit Trial Certificate. This certificate is good for 2 weeks FREE use of (1)

An impressive syndicated package prepared by Rapp, Collins, Stone and Adler for Polaroid Corporation.

Polaroid Automatic Color Pack Camera Outfit . . . without cost or obligation. Including 1 pack of Polaroid color film." There was a "Yes" box to check, which confirmed an order for the outfit on a $10 per month basis. A second box offered savings if the entire $99.95 was charged to the recipient's account at one time (eliminating shipping and handling charges of $2.50). Copy explained that the complete outfit included a Polaroid Automatic Color Pack Camera Model 225 with detachable cover, pocket album, flashgun, certificate for free 5- by 7-inch color enlargement, 12 flash bulbs, cold clip, instruction book, carrying case with adjustable strap and pack of color film. While the card had a business reply back, an airmail business reply envelope was also included in the mailing package.

Credit Card Explosion

The tremendous growth of syndicated mail order offers has a direct link to the big expansion in use of credit cards throughout America. Today, there are few mail order buyers without either a bank card, one of the major commercial credit cards or one or more oil company credit cards. It has been estimated that at least 50 million of these credit cards are in use today.

The correlation between credit cards and syndicated mailings was described by Bob Stone at an advanced seminar on direct mail at New York University:

> "The credit card explosion has opened the door for the sale of billions of dollars of merchandise direct to the consumer. Without the credit card, without installment selling made possible by the credit card, the thought of selling items in the $69.95 range, $99.95, $149.95 and over would be out of the question.
>
> "With the availability of installment credit it's almost as easy to get an order for a $99.95 Polaroid Camera outfit, for example, as it is to get an order for a $9.95 camera—cash on the barrel head.
>
> "Practically concurrent with the growth of installment credit has been the increased use of syndicated mailing pieces. A syndicated mailing piece may be simply defined as a complete mailing package, printed and ready to be mailed under the names of marketers having existing lists of mail order buyers.
>
> "There are two major advantages to both the syndicator and the user of the syndicated piece:

Advantages for the syndicator:

1. He will sell more units of merchandise, books, or whatever he is offering per thousand letters mailed—because a customer list will always, with the very rarest of exceptions, pull more orders per thousand than a "cold" list.

2. The syndicator is in the position of having millions of pieces being mailed on his behalf without any investment in selling expense and without any investment in accounts receivable.

Advantages to the user of the syndicated piece:

1. Without any investment in art and layout or creative, he can test minimum quantities of beautiful four-color mailing packages at the same cost as if he were mailing hundreds of thousands.

2. He can greatly increase his sales volume and profits by offering a wide variety of products and services to his existing customer list."

Guide to Syndicated Mail Order Marketing

An effective guide to syndicated mailings has been prepared by Alan Drey Company, Inc., Chicago list broker:

> *Your Customer List* ... According to a classic mail order belief, your customer list is probably the *best* list you'll ever find. Built over a period of time, it is proven evidence that you've found an active marketplace for your products or services. But how about going a step further? You can turn your customer list into a gold mine of "ready-made" prospects for hundreds of other products you've never before marketed. Or could never afford to market on your own.
>
> *Syndication Defined* ... A *Syndicating firm* invests its own money in the development of a complete mailing package that is printed and ready to be mailed. This package is "sold" to one or more list owners who have substantial lists of customers—preferably mail order buyers. The list owner then mails the package *under his own name,* with imprints on the letter, envelope and order card. All kinds of merchandise can be offered through syndicated mailings ... from pots and pans to books, records, vacuum cleaners, and pool tables. Naturally, there are some important, profit-rooted advantages for both the syndicator and the user of the syndicated mailing piece.
>
> *How Syndication Helps the Syndicator* ... Because a customer list will *most always* pull more orders when it's mailed under the list owner's name, the syndicator stands to sell more units of merchandise. And there are generally fewer orders rejected for credit reasons, since the list owner should have a credit-checked list. The syndicating firm is also having

millions of pieces mailed on its behalf, often without any investment in mailing expense or without any investment in accounts receivable. In other words, the syndicator's role is to select merchandise with good sales potential, and to absorb the cost of creating a sales package that will sell it most effectively. Naturally, he's gambling that some list owners will test it and that the mailings will work. The syndicator must naturally be familiar with the mail order field. Most syndicators are like wholesalers ... who work with both merchandise manufacturers and list owners. Some manufacturers have even set up their own departments or divisions for syndication.

How Syndication Helps the List Owner ... Without any investment in art, separations, or creative costs, the list owner can test small quantities of beautiful full-color mailing packages *at virtually the same cost per piece as if he were mailing hundreds of thousands.* In other words, these completely finished pieces are offered to the list owner at a fraction of what it would cost to prepare them on his own. Fact is, most list owners probably could not afford the cost of developing these packages for one-shot promotions. Through syndicated packages, the list owner can greatly increase his sales volume and profits, by offering a wide variety of worthwhile products and services. In addition, each offer gives him a chance to activate his list and keep customers buying from him over a longer period of time.

No Problems in Handling Merchandise ... Most syndicators can arrange to drop-ship merchandise for the list owner at a nominal charge. Of course, most merchandise is offered on a free trial basis, so some units may be returned to the list owner. However, in most cases, the syndicator can make provisions with the manufacturer to take these back for "refurbishing" at roughly 10% of the retail cost.

Success-Proven Syndicated Mailers

With customer lists offering an outstanding opportunity for success, it's no wonder that many companies are flourishing under syndicated marketing programs. Let's look at a few examples:

- Catalog and encyclopedia houses were among the first to generate a tremendous amount of sales volume and revenue through these individual mailings. Their lists turned out to be a ready-made market for books, housewares, tools, furniture and so on.
- And with the credit card explosion blasting a whole new way for customers to charge purchases, credit card lists are among the most successfully used for syndicated mail order marketing. Credit card organizations like Diners Club, American Express and Carte Blanche have already moved millions of dollars of merchandise to their customers at a profit to themselves, the manufacturer, and the syndicator. Aside from their regular income, they enjoy a nice extra source of revenue by syndicated offerings to their members as frequently as once a month.
- Oil companies—with their multi-million name credit card lists—are also among the most successful to enjoy syndicated product offers. Their original purpose was not the profit to be gained from sales, but rather the goodwill and credit card activity which they felt such a program would develop. The additional profit also adds up quite nicely for most of them.

- And soon we may see the day when back credit card lists will be used full-swing in merchandise mailings. We may even see syndication programs erupting in the retail store field, where little has been done in the area of one-shot mail order promotions.

Profit Set-Ups

There are many ways a syndicator and mailing list owner can work to split the mailing cost profits. These are some of the most popular methods being used throughout the country today:

1. The syndicator absorbs all preparation costs, but the list owner pays the mailing cost. He is provided with a brochure (generally in four-color printing) at quantity-run prices. In most cases, the syndicator also supplies him with artwork and suggested copy for a letter, envelope, and order card. Naturally, the list owner makes a profit on each unit of merchandise sold.
2. The syndicator pays preparation costs *plus* the cost of the test mailing. On this basis, the syndicator usually keeps all the income from the test until he recovers his initial investment, then he gives the list owner a percentage of sales.
3. The syndicator not only pays for preparation costs and the test mailing—but the full mailing as well. The list owner gets a flat fee from each unit of merchandise sold.

Some syndicators are even willing to accept payment from the list owner as the list owner is paid for the merchandise. So that if the customer's payments are drawn out over a 6 month period, the syndicator would accept re-payment at 1/6th a month for 6 months.

How to Get Started

If you've never tried a syndicated mailing before, there are a few important things you should know about how to get started. *First* of all, your customer list should be over 50,000 names to be appealing to most syndicators. *Secondly,* if you have a large cash list you must be able and willing to extend credit for monthly payments. *Thirdly,* you should have a pretty good profile of your customers so that you can slant your offers to their known interest. This helps you select products that will most likely work for you on a syndicated basis, and produce the best response. For example, if you basically have a "female" list, you would probably want to offer a woman-oriented item such as cookware. It's generally best to start off with products in the $29.95 selling bracket . . . and try higher prices later. *Finally,* you should be prepared to test a variety of different products. Not all syndicated products work on all lists. So you don't want to decide on whether or not syndicated mailings will work for you on the basis of a *single* test. Plan to test at least three or four different items.

An Important History

While this Handbook was never intended as a history of direct mail and mail order, the history of syndicated mailings serves a special function. It shows the progression of a merchandising technique from a simple beginning, through a trial-and-error development cycle, into a highly-sophisticated marketing program which has provided the extra margin enabling a large number of companies to survive.

Fortunately, an insider's view of this marketing revolution was prepared by one of the men most responsible for both its early development and continuing growth. Aaron Adler was the creative man to whom Al Sloan turned for the development of his first successful syndicated mailing packages. And even today, as a consultant of Stone & Adler, Inc., one of the country's leading direct response agencies, he continues to play a major role in the development of new syndicated packages.

His views of syndicated mailings were published in *Direct Marketing*[3] and this digested version of that article can serve as a primer on how a given form of direct mail promotion can be adapted to the changing needs of marketers as various influences affect their businesses.

When enterprising Chicagoan "Ham" Ross first got the idea of offering a packaged newspaper promotion to credit furniture and jewelry stores he had no idea how far that concept would go or how it would change over the years.

Ross's first "account opener" promotions created in about 1946 were designed to reach lower income people and stimulate new credit accounts by offering such items as highly decorated lamps, "gossip" benches, 122-piece dinnerware sets, 72-piece tableware sets, or 32-piece power tool outfits at prices usually ranging from $19.95 to $39.95.

The artwork used tended to exaggerate the qualities of the merchandise and the appearance of all the materials was designed to give a bargain sale tone to the entire promotion.

Being the kind of man who was willing to take major risks (a hallmark of most syndicators), Mr. Ross would offer the merchandise to the stores on a guaranteed sale basis, agree to pay for the advertising, take back all unsold merchandise and give the store usually 20% of the retail price on each item sold. On this basis he signed up a major outlet in each city so that frequently, on a given Sunday,

[3]"Syndicators Eye Retailers, Banks as Next Boom Market" by Aaron Adler. *Direct Marketing*. September 1969.

he had full-color ads running in as many as 300 comic sections around the country—all paid for by him!

Each Sunday that he ran, Mr. Ross was really the "man in the middle" standing between his suppliers and the retail stores betting that his knowledge of merchandise and advertising would produce the kind of sales that would more than repay his tremendous investment.

Others Enter Field . . . The success of the "Ham" Ross operation soon brought others into the field among them Fairbanks-Ward and Retailers Marketing Guild both of Chicago and both organizations are still in operation today.

Interestingly enough, one manufacturer was farsighted enough to become his own syndicator way back then—Club Aluminum, manufacturer of cookware. They initiated their own program developing promotions and materials for department, jewelry and furniture stores and sold them directly as they still do today.

Another unusual syndicator of the day was Hyland Electric, a Chicago electrical wholesaler who developed promotions utilizing merchandise of manufacturers whose products they wholesaled. For a while this operation was successful enough that manufacturers received permission from Hyland to sell these promotions to other distributors in markets not covered by Hyland. But unlike the Club Aluminum effort, this activity didn't continue for very long.

Basic Procedures . . . By this time the syndicator had developed a method of working with those of his customers who used his materials in the mail which was to become the basic procedure for most syndicators. This method filled a need by making it possible for the mailer to test a promotion with a minimum exposure. The syndicator invested his own money in the development of the mailing material and offered finished pieces at a fraction of what it would cost the mailer to prepare on his own. So that the mailer could test a proven piece for about $1,000.00 against having to prepare his own piece for anywhere from $7,500.00 to $15,000.00—and at the same time take advantage of the syndicator's experience and creativity.

The manufacturer's risk was limited to a small quantity of merchandise which usually was a stock item and the mailer's risk was confined to the cost of preparing a letter, order card and envelope and making the mailing. The merchandise belonged to the manufacturer until it was sold. And should it be returned, the syndicator made provisions for the manufacturer to refurbish it and put it back in stock, usually for about 10% of the retail price paid by the mailer.

And the syndicator bet his knowledge of merchandise and the mailer's list against the cost of his promotion that it would succeed and that his margin—the difference between the manufacturer's selling price and his selling price to the mailer—would provide a satisfactory profit. A somewhat less risky procedure than the original Hamilton Ross operation.

Enter Al Sloan ... For a number of years syndicators confined themselves to this same type of operation and creative approach. Among them was Al Sloan, head of the Albert E. Sloan operation. Sloan had developed a format which offered a better than usual quality of presentation and which has proven successful. But after a series of reverses he took stock of the situation and decided that the future of the industry lay—not with the retailer—but with those people who had large lists of credit-checked names. A decision which would considerably enlarge the market for direct mail merchandise.

About 1950 he sold a test to Spiegel's mail order house and then forged ahead rapidly enlarging his activity among such others as Alden's and the direct selling companies such as the encyclopedia houses.

Because of Mr. Sloan's insistence on fine quality literature his concept was readily accepted by these new prospects many of whom had begun to realize that the large lists they had could be put to use to produce additional profits—in many cases profits that would eventually far exceed the profit produced by the original sale under which the name was secured.

The catalog houses discovered that the sales volume and revenue produced by these one-shot mailings was in addition to catalog-generated sales. The encyclopedia houses and others found their judgment vindicated as their lists turned out to be a ready market for tools, dinnerware, towels, and other merchandise.

Manufacturers Show Interest ... Where the first selling "wave" was directed to credit furniture and jewelry stores and the second to mail order and direct selling organizations, the third "wave" which accomplished another major breakthrough occurred in 1959 and concerned itself with the merchandise itself.

The then sales manager of Bell & Howell, Max Sroge called on Al Sloan to discuss the possibility of promoting a movie camera outfit by mail. Max, because of his then lack of knowledge of the industry didn't realize that selling a $150.00 item was practically unheard of in the mail order industry. Most merchandise was offered at $29.95, $39.95 and $49.95. Almost none went over $50.00 ... the insurmountable barrier—or so everyone believed. Al Sloan knew this but was enough of a gambler to be willing to chance it.

The circular was developed and presented to prospects with great trepidation but a few such as Fingerhut Mfg. Co., Americana-Interstate, Alden's and Encyclopaedia Brittanica agreed to test it. To everyone's amazement the mailing pulled an unprecedented 1 to 2% of sales or as much as $3,000 per thousand pieces.

New Prospects ... With the actual merchandise cost running about $1,900.00 and the mailing cost about $80.00 (this was in the day of 2.5 cent bulk-third-class postage) the mailer was grossing as much as $1,020.00 per thousand profit. Not only did the unprecedented success of this mailing open the direct mail field to the sale of high-priced merchandise, but it brought in many new mailing prospects—people who never before thought of using one-shot merchandise promotions or who had previously confined themselves to their own product mailings.

A typical example of the latter is the Fingerhut Mfg. Co., of Minneapolis. For a number of years Fingerhut had been selling automobile seat covers by mail with varying degrees of success. Upon seeing a Sloan-Ashland advertisement in the *Reporter of Direct Mail Advertising* on the Bell & Howell promotion, Fingerhut called and, in talking to salesman Al Brandies, "thought" he would like to try 2,000 circulars. With the success of this test and subsequent mailings, it became obvious that the profit made in seat covers was secondary to the profit which could accrue on subsequent mailings to seat cover buyers. Taking off from there, Fingerhut today is by all accounts the largest seller of mail order merchandise outside of the major catalog operations and does a volume reported to be in the $100,000,000 range.

Flood Gates Open ... With the flood gates open to the sale of higher ticket merchandise (a necessity as mailing costs mounted) and the entry of a number of the top national brand names, the syndicator found his field of activity expanding and with it the number of syndicators in the field. Others who entered in the course of the next several years included people like Rozay-Marcus, and Brown & Gravenson, Robbins Products, Sun Gold Industries. (Sun Gold was not a true syndicator in that they did not basically develop the promotions for the direct mail seller of merchandise. But their offers were used for such purposes.)

And to the list of manufacturers who had permitted the use of their merchandise in this field was now added such well-known brands as Shetland Floor Care & Appliances, Revere Cookware, South Bend Fishing Tackle, Stetson and Syracuse China and others.

Side by side with the syndicators of "hard" goods is a group of book syndicators, made up in the main of book publishers who syndicate their books, usually to encyclopedia houses and others with lists of people who have purchased books ranging from the Encyclopaedia Brittanica to Dr. Suess children's books. Among these publishers are Children's Press with their perennially successful Young Peoples Science Encyclopedia and other sets: Career Institute, a division of Americana-Interstate with its long, successful, two-volume Practical English; Meredith Publishing, publishers of Better Homes and Gardens and a large library of cook books and others in the "home service" category; Hammond and Rand McNally with their wide variety of road and geographic atlases; J. Ferguson publishers of Bibles; and Replogle with its mailings on world globes.

Credit Card Wave ... About 1955 saw the start of a selling "wave" which has continued, with variations, to the present day and which again expanded the market for mail order merchandise both in size and in the quality of merchandise which could be offered: the use of credit card mailing lists. By this time, Diners Club, American Express and Carte Blanche lists have developed to respectable sizes—and it occurred to some bright merchandiser that here, again, was an untapped source of revenue; that in addition to its regular source of income, the credit card organization could enjoy additional volume by selling merchandise to its members.

Like most such ventures there must have been a great deal of concern as to how the retail establishments would react to such sales—but, just as obviously, the venture was so logical that it just had to be tried.

However, here a new element was added to the syndicator's method of operation. Where previously, his entire gamble (and a considerable one it could be—$10,000.00 or more) was in the cost of preparing the printed material which he then sold to the mailer—now he was asked to pay for the entire cost of the test—mailing material as well as mailing. On such a basis he would keep all the income on the test until he recovered his initial investment and then give the credit card organization a percentage of the retail price. If the test proved successful, the credit card organization would take over the expense of the large-scale follow up mailings on the usual basis.

Enter The Oilmen ... Only the typical syndicator's conviction that these lists offered an outstanding opportunity for success and his conviction that he could select merchandise which would sell, led syndicators into accepting this offer and, as subsequent events have proved, they were right.

The opportunity to charge the purchase to their credit card and return it if they didn't like it proved most popular and made these lists among the most successful ever used up to this time. Over the past 15 years, credit card organizations have moved millions of dollars of merchandise to their customers at a profit to themselves, the merchandise supplier and the syndicator. And, over all these years the number of retail establishment complaints have obviously been sufficiently minimal so as to constitute no serious hazard.

All of this however, was a prelude to the next great direct mail merchandise explosion, which interestingly enough is one of the few not initiated by the syndicator—but soon taken over by him—the oil company credit card merchandise mailings.

In 1957 the Pure Oil Company put out a little-noticed flyer offering their credit card customers a Wearever electric percolator and suddenly they found themselves so flooded with orders they couldn't meet the demand.

Shell's Motives ... Whether it was the problems created by this overwhelming demand or something else, Pure's activity in this area soon ceased.

But in 1962, the Shell Oil Company, with its advertising agency Ogilvy and Mather, decided to test the sale of merchandise to its credit card list. According to informed sources, unlike all such previous activity in other fields, Shell's purpose was not the profit to be gained from such sales, but rather the station traffic, goodwill and credit card activity which they felt such a program could engender.

In cooperating with Dick Benson, their direct mail consultant, and Len Shepard of Mark-James, syndicators, the agency and Shell developed and tested a Ram Power Saw at $19.95. In order for the credit card customer to buy the saw, he had to take the card into his Shell station and have it validated. The purpose of this, of course, was to step up station traffic. Even with this handicap, the results were far beyond the expectations of everyone. Further tests on other merchandise were conducted and the results of the test were evaluated by Shell not merely on the basis of sales and profits on the merchandise itself—but on the basis of consumer reaction in terms of increased purchases of gas, oil, and TBA.

Syndicators Move In ... With the beginning of the program, syndicators immediately saw an area for their talents, particularly so because on investigation they discovered that most oil companies had no budget for such activity nor any desire to set one up. So here again, they saw an opportunity to utilize the Diner's technique—only more so. Some not only offered to pay for the tests, but they would also pay for the full mailings as well and give the oil company a percentage of the sales.

Others offered to pay for the entire mailings and give the oil company the full markup once they recovered their promotional costs, and they would receive a nominal commission on each sale.

Still others like Ed Rubin of Tyler-Shaw locate merchandise on the basis of their knowledge of the oil company's requirements and offer it to people like Shell in the conviction that this is the most logical method of operation for an oil company interested in giving its customers the best value.

In many cases, syndicators were willing to accept payment from the oil company as the oil company was paid. So that, if the customer's payments for the merchandise were spread over a six month period, the syndicator would accept repayment at 1/6th a month for six months. In such a case, the oil company had no "front end" expenditure of any kind for mailing materials, the mailing or even for the merchandise. All they had to do was supply the labels and collect (which they were doing anyway) and all income above that was essentially profit.

Everyone Joins ... The proposals were so enticing that one oil company after another accepted and within the last few years practically every major oil company either has a full-scale merchandise program or has tried merchandise sales at one time or other.

One of the reasons why syndicators took part in this activity was the fact that oil company lists were pulling two, three and even four times as much as regular mail order lists. Most oil companies were not concerned merely with profit, but more with developing better customer relations. Thus, they were willing to work on a smaller margin which boosted returns.

Where the usual mail order lists would pull 1% to 1.5% on say a $29.95 cookware outfit, an oil company list would pull 2% to 3%. And on certain items pulls were even higher. Rumor has it that a Gulf Oil mailing on a Ross 3-band radio at $29.95 created by Douglas Dunhill has pulled as high as 5%!

With the advent of the oil company, new syndicators entered the field. Some, like Douglas Dunhill were not really syndicators in that all their promotions were developed for one client: Gulf Oil. Others were like the Peter King Company, a division of King Korn Stamp Co., whose promotions were developed for a limited group of oil companies such as Sinclair and Texaco. For practical purposes, most syndicators soon found they could work with only a small number of major oil companies because most major companies did not care to see their promotions used by their competition, as well as the fact that often a major oil company would take the entire output on a particular product.

One of the earliest to enter the field were people like Promotion Programmers, Inc., whose activity up to this point had been primarily with Mobil and American Oil; others now active are Whitney-Forbes, S & H, Top Value, and the John Plain Company, a Chicago wholesale mail order catalog house formerly selling only to retail outlets.

Syndicators Differ ... With the increasing clamour to discontinue gas station games, people like the Glendenning Organization, the Plaza Group and Creative Merchandising have been seeking to establish themselves in the credit card merchandise area with varying degrees of success.

Along with the usual type of syndicator, there has grown up a number of others whose operation is different from that of the type of syndicator we have been talking about up to now.

Mark-James, Chicago-based syndicator was the first and is probably the only one who acts as a manufacturer's representative in that they represent a factory (some of their clients are Polaroid and 3 M) with the factory either furnishing or paying for the development of the basic mailing material. Mark-James supplies material for printing and their customers have to print and pay for their own material. Mark-James operates on a commission paid by the manufacturer. Also unusual is that they sell to many syndicators who develop their own mailing materials.

Another is Marketing Associates in St. Louis who, over the past years, has created a special niche for themselves in developing multi-mailers (an idea originally developed by Mark-James). A multi-mailer is an accordion fold circular of five or six items each on an 8½- by 11-inch panel and usually all are available at the same price, around $45.00, which are mailed to finance company lists of active and inactive customers over the letterhead of another company.

Marketing Associates goes further than most syndicators in that they also handle the shipment of merchandise and in certain cases will arrange credit facilities for the mailer. From this activity, they have spread out to where they are now preparing mailings for organizations with large cash lists who wish to get into mail order credit.

Bell & Howell First . . . In addition to syndicators who have traditionally been third parties, some manufacturers themselves are discovering that they can take over the syndication function.

Bell & Howell, of course, was the first to come to this conclusion with the launching of Robert-Maxwell. Albeit the company was originally created to sell merchandise on its own. Today its function is to sell Bell & Howell promotions to the mail order industry. Others who seem interested in going direct are Soundesign, Inc., marketers of Realtone Radios, West Bend Cookware, who have done so for many years. General Electric has made some tentative approaches in this area, as have a number of others.

All of which brings up the question of the "wave of the future" for syndicators. What next big area will they discover. Up to now their function has been to introduce both the national manufacturer and the potential mailer to the benefits of selling merchandise by mail. In the course of this activity they have helped broaden the market and helped it to achieve a degree of acceptance that would have been hard to visualize as little as 15 years ago. They have learned to take advantage of the tremendous credit card explosion and the desire of most companies to achieve greater utilization of their customer list.

So, judging by history, we can expect the syndicator to continue to bet his knowledge, his experience and his money on the expansion of mail order selling of merchandise into new, uncharted areas to the ultimate benefit of the entire mail order industry.

Continuing Growth

As Aaron Adler predicted, syndication has continued to grow and many new approaches are constantly being introduced. Today, the majority of mail order firms are involved in syndication. In addition, this form of marketing has created new profit centers for banks, oil companies, publishers and many others.

One of the most popular uses of syndicated pieces today is as a ride-along with other mailings which bear the entire cost of postage. For example, package inserts are used by the majority of mail order companies. Syndicated pieces are also common as "stuffers" with bills, statements, order acknowledgements and similar mail.

Chapter 17

OTHER DIRECT MAIL USES

WHILE the preceding chapters have covered the major uses of direct mail advertising, there are many other activities that make effective use of the medium. While it would be impossible to cover every possible direct mail application, the following case histories will indicate how the medium can be useful in almost every situation where communications are required.

Clubs, Associations, and Professional Groups

Bulking large in the total volume of direct mail is the steady flow of communications to members of clubs, associations, and other groups. There are few organized groups which do not use direct mail as the primary method of communicating with members.

Probably the most common type of direct mail used by such groups is the newsletter. In recent years, the newsletter has frequently replaced newspapers and magazines in many member communications programs. It is also used to handle the transmittal of special messages such as details of conventions and special meetings.

When the Direct Mail/Marketing Association held its annual convention in Chicago in 1962, newsletters provided an excellent vehicle to build interest and promote attendance. A particular advantage was that the newsletter format permitted including last-minute details, whereas a more formal piece would likely have required greater lead time.

Local clubs also make frequent use of the newsletter format to keep members posted on activities. Nearly every chapter of the Marketing Communications Executives, International, for example, publishes a monthly newsletter for its members and the national organization has found the newsletter to be the easiest communications format to handle on a continuing basis.

Convention Promotion

Mailings to promote annual conventions of national, regional, and state groups often bring forth highly creative efforts. For example, when the National Business Publications held its spring meeting in Phoenix, Arizona, members were deluged with promotional mailings with a western flavor—many used as enclosures with regularly scheduled mailings.

In addition to specially prepared pieces, NBP arranged to obtain various pieces of Arizona tourist literature which heightened interest in the meeting location. The original pieces included such items as a folder with line drawings and descriptions of various types of palmtrees, a folder identifying the varieties of cactus, a guide to the meaning of designs found on Indian crafts, and a piece which outlined the history of cattle branding plus illustrations of the more famous Arizona brands.

Still another approach was two series of post cards. One series featured the same cartoon drawing of an Indian sending smoke signals, with a different message printed on the puffs of smoke for each mailing. The other series carried an illustration of a branding iron with an RX brand plus the standard headline, "Prescription for *Brand*-New Know-How." This series also carried copy describing program highlights—one feature per card.

Montreal Convention Success

A particularly outstanding convention promotion drew 1,250 admen to Montreal for the 1959 DMMA Convention. The handiwork of Douglas B. Mahoney, advertising manager of Frank W. Horner Ltd., the convention promotion featured nine mailings, the majority of which utilized a single, versatile piece of "theme" art:

1. The first mailing was a picture post card of the Queen Elizabeth Hotel, the convention headquarters.
2. This was followed by another picture post card featuring The Mont Gabriel Club in the Laurentian Mountains, which was to be the setting for a Dior fashion show for members' wives.
3. A unique newsletter was mailing number three. It had two "front pages"—one in English and a duplicate in French (printed upside-down on what would normally be the back page). The inside spread was in English and presented general details of the convention program.

4. A First Day Cover highlighted the fourth mailing, taking advantage of the newly issued St. Lawrence Seaway stamp. A newsletter was enclosed.
5. The fifth mailing was a special convention issue of *Provincial's Paper,* the external house organ of Provincial Paper Ltd. The colorful magazine featured direct mail subjects plus information on the convention.
6. Mailing No. Six was another newsletter plus a special flyer describing the program for wives.
7. The next mailing went to all convention registrants and DMMA members who had made hotel room reservations. It included a variety of items designed to keep convention interest at a high level, such as:

A letter outlining a special pre-registration system to eliminate delays at the convention hotels.

A hotel pre-registration form.

A special lapel button to be worn while traveling to the convention so fellow conventioneers could recognize one another.

Special luggage tags.

A 32-page visitors' guide to Montreal.

A map of Montreal.

A "How to Enter Canada" guide with information about customs regulations, admission requirements, currency exchange, and so forth.

8. Another newsletter mailing brought last-minute details.
9. A personalized first-class mailing to all members who had not registered for the convention a month before its start.

In addition to this scheduled promotion program, a number of interested organizations sent DMMA members special mailings—Trans-Canada Airlines (two special mailings), Canadian National Railways, The Alpine Inn resort, and so forth. Supporting publicity and "plugs" for the convention in regular DMMA member mailings rounded out the effective convention promotion program.

There are many lessons to be learned from this highly successful direct mail program, many of which apply not only to convention promotion but to other direct mail advertising as well. The author made these comments in a review article:

Develop a central theme and stick to it, making sure your "package" is one which can be merchandised with enthusiasm.

When possible, prepare a versatile piece of high-quality art and then avoid the temptation to try something different. Instead, build impact by repeat use.

Start your promotion early—you don't have to wait until all the program details have been worked out.

Line up support from outside organizations—particularly those who will benefit from success of your promotion.

Trade upon "romantic" aspects.

Build a strong, well-researched mailing list and concentrate your efforts on the best prospects.

Be sure to bring wives into the act.

Don't forget the followthrough. In this case, it was recognized that advance registration and/or hotel reservations did not necessarily mean actual attendance—particularly when the reservations had been made well in advance. The special efforts to "convert" these "probables" into actual attendees resulted in a very low percentage of cancellations.

Don't stop just because success appears assured. That final DMMA convention mailing undoubtedly brought in at least another 100 registrants.

Make sure your product lives up to the advance promotion. This lays the groundwork for success in the future.

Educational Institutions

Other major users of direct mail are the nation's schools. Colleges and universities, in particular, depend upon the medium to serve many purposes. But secondary schools and even kindergarten and nursery schools are frequent users of direct mail to communicate with parents and to promote special events.

But while many schools make highly effective use of direct mail, the majority of educational institutions has yet to utilize the medium in a professional way. Those schools which regularly make mailings to parents and other interested individuals have found that many problems can be solved—particularly those which result from misunderstandings and misinformation.

The most professional job of direct mail in the educational field comes from college and university fund-raisers. Several effective college fund-raising mailings call on alumni to underwrite a better teaching staff or for money for buildings.

College Catalogs

Probably the most neglected type of direct mail utilized by schools is the college catalog. While many schools have devoted considerable attention in recent years to the upgrading of catalogs, the majority still has failed to recognize that the catalog must speak the recipient's language if it is to communicate effectively.

An example of how a college catalog can do a more effective communications job is shown by some of the techniques utilized by the North Dakota State School of Science. Since this school is a combination junior college-trade school-business school, there was a problem of combining three different curriculums in a single catalog without causing confusion. This was handled by printing details of each of the school's divisions on a different color of paper. General details were presented in an introductory section printed on white paper and then three sections of photographs were included to break up the grayness of the text matter.

Two other unusual techniques were included in this catalog. One was a selection of comments on the school reprinted from widely recognized publications—to assure parents that the school had an established reputation. Then a single page was printed on card stock to draw special attention. This card contained answers to the questions most frequently asked by parents and prospective students. While the same information had always been included in the catalog, searching for it often proved difficult or discouraging and resulted in added correspondence. By putting it on the quickly found card, the catalog became a more valuable communications vehicle.

Churches

Closely related to schools in use of direct mail are churches. While still used regularly by a small minority of the nation's churches, the medium has proved highly successful when used by progressive churchmen.

Many churches, for example, have been surprised to find how useful direct mail can be in securing (and collecting) annual pledges from members. Traditionally, the every-member canvass has been on a personal contact basis for many churches. But the application of direct mail technique (usually supplementing rather than replacing personal contact) has often brought increased financial support.

A more frequent application of direct mail is the mailing of a weekly or monthly bulletin. The Glenview (Illinois) Community

Church, for example, makes weekly mailings of "The Broadcaster," a four-page bulletin in a combination newspaper-newsletter format. It includes such items as messages from the ministers; schedule of events; reports on activities of various church groups; details on Sunday School and youth programs; births, deaths, and illnesses.

Government

Probably the biggest direct mail user of all is the United States Government . . . and the biggest direct mailing each year is made by the Internal Revenue Service. Actually, all levels of government make use of direct mail techniques.

Many local governments make annual reports to local citizens through direct mail. State governments use direct mail to handle distribution of license applications, digests of new laws and regulations, travel promotion, and so forth.

Nearly every branch of the Federal Government uses large quantities of direct mail to perform a variety of communications tasks. As a matter of fact, the U.S. Government Printing Office is even in the mail order business and makes regular mailings to a large list offering a current selection of Government publications. Typical of the items promoted is the official list of "The Top 25" publications, as represented by actual purchases. A list of "Top 25" publications included:

"Food, The Yearbook of Agriculture"—$2.25

"Family Fare"—a cooking reference book—35 cents

"Nutritive Value of Foods"—20 cents

"Wood Handbook"—$2.25

"Removing Stains from Fabrics, Home Methods"—15 cents

"Starting and Managing a Small Business of Your Own"—25 cents

"Manual on Uniform Traffic Control Devices for Streets and Highways"—$2.00

"Our Flag"—25 cents

"Your Social Security"—10 cents

"Infant Care"—a 106-page book on child care, which has been revised 10 times since it first appeared in 1914 and is by all odds the most popular Government publication ever issued—15 cents

"How to Get and Hold the Right Job"—10 cents

"Guide to Subversive Organizations and Publications"—70 cents

"Effective Revenue Writing I & II"—$1.70

Market Research

One of the easiest and most economical ways to conduct market research is through the use of questionnaires and mail surveys. A guide to effective research-by-mail techniques is presented in detail in Chapter 36, "Surveys and Questionnaires."

A typical example of a research mailing was a letter and questionnaire which was mailed by Matson Navigation Co. to search out information which would indicate preferences for Pacific Ocean vacations and possible advertising approaches to appeal to logical prospects.

The questionnaire contained four pages of questions. There were just 17 questions, all of which could be answered simply by checking appropriate boxes.

Another typical research mailing is shown on page 461. Unlike the Matson questionnaire, which could be completed just by reading the questions and quickly checking an answer, this study of the lithographic industry required considerable effort by respondents. The questionnaire was mailed by National Mar-

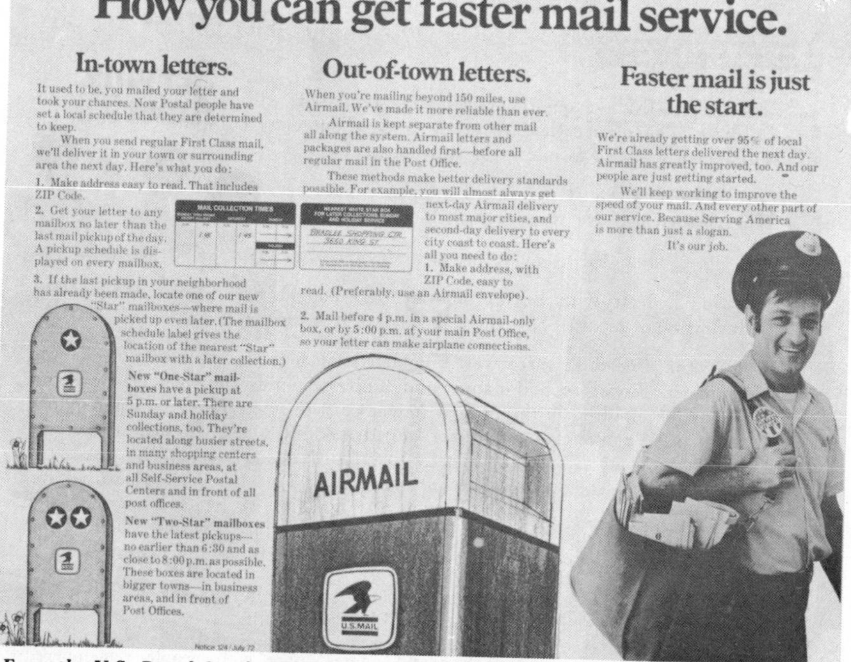

Even the U.S. Postal Service is a direct mail advertiser. This is the inside spread of a self-mailer widely distributed by USPS.

ket Analysis Inc., and contained 11 questions calling for detailed answers.

While no direct premium was offered those returning completed questionnaires, an interesting form of "compensation" was included. A letter accompanied the questionnaire which explained:

> While we are fully aware of the pressures of your daily schedule, we, nonetheless, believe that the findings of this study will prove of significant value particularly to your segment of the lithographic industry. Needless to say, we cannot compensate you commensurately for your assistance in our endeavors. We are, however, prepared to make a direct contribution to your favorite charity in at least partial recognition of your kind cooperation. A list of charities may be found at the end of the questionnaire.

Crayola's Surveys

An interesting application of direct mail to obtain marketing information was developed by Alan Holt of Binney & Smith Inc., the makers of Crayola crayons. ("How to Do Market Research for Nothing" in *Advertising Requirements.* December 1956). He created questionnaires to be included in mailings of a free book, "Creative Crafts with Crayola Crayons," offered to mothers. Al Holt explained the program:

> A series of five questionnaires were prepared, with appropriate covering letters. The plan called for sending them out one at a time, with enough time lag between to allow for shifting gears.
>
> In Survey No. 1 we asked women what they thought about washable crayons, which we were considering adding to the line.
>
> No. 2 attempted to determine attitudes toward crayons—likes and dislikes.
>
> No. 3 dealt with buying habits: who bought the crayons for Junior; during what months, how many packages at a time, etc.
>
> By the time these three were completed we had accumulated quite a pile of paper. Since we had names and addresses, plus the number, age, and sex of the children in the family, it was easy to select fairly typical buying-families. We wrote to a number of these families asking them to become members of our "Consumer Panel." Eventually about 400 families across the country were set up on Addressograph plates. This list was to be used for pretesting new products, confirming the validity of general surveys, and so on. These people gave us permission to send them sample merchandise, with the understanding they would furnish reports on the material.
>
> Survey No. 4 asked the ladies about finger-painting; we hoped to introduce a new set in a highly competitive price range.
>
> No. 5 was concerned with brand names—how well people remembered the names of our non-Crayola products, as compared to names of competitive products.

National Market Analysis Incorporated
Gateway Center
Pittsburgh 22, Pennsylvania
[illegible]

Dr. John A. Bekker, Director
Market Research and Development

November 3

American Mail Advertising, Inc.
610 Newbury St.
Boston 15, Mass.

Gentlemen:

We need your assistance to accomplish an important task.

We are presently engaged in a study of the graphic arts industry as a preliminary step toward future research programs. It is by learning the current thinking of you, the men in the trade, that future research efforts can be successfully directed to the real problems that are confronting the industry today.

While we are fully aware of the pressures of your daily schedule, we, nonetheless, believe that the findings of this study will prove of significant value particularly to your segment of the lithographic industry. Needless to say, we cannot compensate you commensurately for your assistance in our endeavors. We are, however, prepared to make a direct contribution to your favored charity in at least partial recognition of your kind cooperation. A list of charities may be found at the end of the questionnaire.

Upon completion of the various phases of this study, an industry-wide announcement is anticipated.

Sincerely,

First Class
[illegible: Permit No.] 4787
Pittsburgh, Pa.

BUSINESS REPLY MAIL
[illegible]

VIA AIR MAIL

POSTAGE WILL BE PAID BY—
NATIONAL MARKET ANALYSIS, INCORPORATED
GATEWAY CENTER
PITTSBURGH 22,
PENNSYLVANIA

Attn: Dr. John A. Bekker, Director

QUESTIONNAIRE

This survey is to be used for research purposes only. All replies will be treated in a strictly confidential manner.

What types of offset plates do you use, by percentage?

a. Grained Aluminum .... ______ %
b. Grained Zinc .... ______ %
c. Presensitized Aluminum .... ______ %
d. Wipe-on Aluminum .... ______ %
e. Wipe-on Zinc .... ______ %
f. Other types (specify) .... ______ %
g. Wipe-on/Wipe-off .... ______ %
100 %

2. Do you have your plates regrained? .... Zinc: YES ______ NO ______
Aluminum: YES ______ NO ______

3. Do you do your own graining? YES ______ NO ______

4. Do you operate your own platemaking department?
If "yes", approximately what percentage of your plates do you prepare yourself ______ %

5. What, in your opinion, are the advantages and disadvantages of the following plates?

Type of Plate	Advantages	Disadvantages
a. Grained Aluminum		
b. Grained Zinc		
c. Presensitized Aluminum		
d. Wipe-on Aluminum		
e. Wipe-on Zinc		
f. Other types (specify) (e.g., Wipe-on/Wipe-off, etc.)		

6. What types of offset printing do you do? (Please list in order of importance: 1, 2, 3, etc.)

Type of Offset Printing	Order of Importance
a. Periodicals, magazines, house organs, etc.	______
b. Catalogs, inserts, annual reports, etc.	______
c. Direct mail, point-of-sale literature, calendars	______
d. Packaging, labels, etc.	______
e. Letterheads, business forms, etc.	______
f. Banners, sign and poster material, etc.	______
g. Others (please specify):............................	______

7. Number of offset presses operated? (Please list by size and color capacity.)

Sizes	Colors				
	1	2	3	4	5 or more
Up to 17½ x 22½					
17½ x 22½ to 22 x 34					
22 x 34 to 35 x 45					
35 x 45 to 52 x 76					

8. What is your approximate annual gross dollar volume from offset printing?

a. up to $100,000 ______
b. 100,000 to 500,000 ______
c. 500,000 to 1 million ______
d. over 1 million ______

9. What is your approximate annual expenditure on offset plates? $................

10. Please indicate in order of importance the factors determining your choice of plates:

a. Quality of Reproduction ______
b. Original Plate Cost ______
c. Convenience in Using ______
d. General Dependability ______
e. Platemaking Cost ______

11. In your daily contacts with the lithographic trade, you have no doubt encountered much of the thinking and many of the difficulties that confront the industry today.

In the space below, we would welcome your comments and suggestions pertaining to the lithographic industry. In particular, we would like to hear your comments concerning lithographic plates—what the trends have been, what the demands of the future will be, etc.

• • •

NAME OF COMPANY ______
ADDRESS ______
CITY ______ STATE ______ FIRM ESTABLISHED ______ (year)

In future months, we anticipate having pertinent industry information for distribution to lithographers. Who in your plant should receive such information?

NAME ______ POSITION ______

This questionnaire completed by: ______
Name (not required—please give, if possible)
______
Position

• • •

Please send my contribution to the following charity:

American Cancer Society........ ☐
American Heart Association...... ☐
Muscular Dystrophy............ ☐
Ass'n. for Retarded Children...... ☐
Soc. for Crippled Children & Adults. ☐
National Foundation .... ☐
National Tuberculosis Association.. ☐
United Cerebral Palsy Association.. ☐
Others ....
.... ☐

Please return in the attached self-addressed envelope. NO POSTAGE REQUIRED.

This four-page questionnaire seeks technical data on the lithographic industry

Industrial Development

Direct mail is frequently the main promotion tool of groups which promote industrial development. While "spot" mailings are most frequently used—often fancy, highly detailed brochures, a number of groups conduct a continuing direct mail program.

An example of the "spot" type of promotion is a fact folder developed by the Weber County (Utah) Industrial Bureau. The folder, sent to 1,000 American manufacturers considered to be logical prospects for plants and distribution facilities in the Ogden, Utah, area, contained information on location, growth potential, transportation facilities, population, taxes, vocational training, utilities, services, resources, climate, agriculture, wage rates, and so forth. In addition to the original list, copies were sent to companies identified by news reports as getting ready for expansion of manufacturing or distribution facilities.

A particularly outstanding continuing industrial development program is the "Operation Bootstrap" program of the Economic Development Administration of Puerto Rico. How this group uses direct mail was described by E. T. Ellenis of the administration's office of public relations in "How to Sell an Island to U.S. Industry." *(Industrial Marketing.)*

> The industrial promotion unit spends $50,000 a year in direct mail (also reprints). The program is geared to reach 24,000 selected U. S. manufacturers who get three to six separate pieces a year.
>
> Mrs. Shanley limits the list to companies that have a minimum capital worth of $250,000 and employ at least 50 persons.
>
> Promotional services is currently getting a 2 percent return on its mailings, which is regarded as high in view of the product it is merchandising. Keep in mind that Puerto Rican plant sites often mean multimillion-dollar investments (Union Carbide, for instance, invested $28.5 million).
>
> EDA divides its mailings into two broad categories—general mailings which go to the entire list three times a year, and quarterly custom-made mailings sent to specific industries within the 24,000 company list.
>
> General mailings take the form of briskly written industrial newsletters in the clipped but fact-crammed Kiplinger letter style. Single-spaced, multilithed, they run from three to five pages in length and are bound with an attractive one-inch green border with the Commonwealth seal attached. They are 8½ by 11 inches in size. Problems as well as advantages are cited and interpreted for manufacturers.
>
> Frequently general mailings consist of reprints of special reports on Puerto Rico. For example, promotional services sent the 24,000 companies on its list reprints of a quarterly report published by the Government Development Bank for Puerto Rico which was full of financial and statistical information. This reprint, 8 by 11 inches, was printed on white paper, slick, and also featured new industrial developments in the island.

Occasionally, promotional services sends reprints of trend-tracing articles placed by industrial publicity to its general list; also three-page statistical surveys (one compared economic and social indexes for Puerto Rico fiscal 1955 with fiscal 1956) prepared by industrial economics.

Quarterly mailings to individual industries within the general list run about the same length as general mailings. Content-wise, however, they are more specific and provide details on opportunities and new developments. These are also multilithed, single-spaced on white paper.

One quarterly mailing to the apparel industry, titled "Current Appraisal of the Apparel Industry in Puerto Rico," outlined productivity, freight rates, and figures on profits. Similar four-page appraisals are going to metal, plastics, electronics companies within the general list.

All EDA mailings, whether general, quarterly, reprints, or statistical surveys, are accompanied by cover letters and reply cards. Cover letters are hand-signed in the name of the U. S. Director of Industrial Development, Gaspar Roca, Jr. The 3½- by 5½-inch reply cards come in individual self-addressed postage paid envelopes and invite manufacturers to ask for "facts" or a visit from an Industrial Representative.

All such letters are reproduced on automatic typewriters.

Also, hewing close to the culture-business theme of "Commonwealth" ads, promotional services often includes a tourist brochure which is sent in with its regularly scheduled mailings.

The tourist brochure folded is 9 by 4 inches, when opened 9 by 8 inches, and contains many "Commonwealth" ads and copy plus pictures of white beaches and modern hotels. Ten pages in length, it includes these headlines: "Sun and Sport—All Year Round," "The Land of Perpetual Spring," and others intended to give manufacturers the itch to get on the plane.

EDA's single most valuable promotional tool is "Facts for the Manufacturer." The 72-page brochure contains two maps, two pages of charts, 26 tables, 53 photographs, and 10 appendixes. The 10½- by 8½-inch "Facts" emphasizes taxes and other Bootstrap incentives (help in training workers, technical aid, bank loans, low-cost factory space). Unprecedented in area development promotion is the brochure's comprehensive discussion of Puerto Rico's drawbacks for some industries.

Printed on slick paper, "Facts" also cites markets and transportation, factory buildings, services (industrial, business and public), water power, living conditions, law and other background information.

Public Relations

Direct mail plays a highly important role in the majority of public relations programs. A vast amount of detail on public relations mailings is included in a companion handbook, *The Dartnell Public Relations Handbook*. In addition, you will find examples of the use of direct mail for public relations purposes in many other chapters in this HANDBOOK, including Chapter 33, "House Organs, Newsletters, and Bulletins"; and Chapter 37, "Other Formats."

Political Mailings

Even the Congressman who damns "junk mail" on the House floor is a direct mail advertiser himself when election time rolls around—and likely utilizes his free mailing permit to make regular mailings to constituents between elections. In 1962, alone, members of the House and Senate spent $4.9 million of the taxpayers' money on "free" mailings to their constituents.

Nearly every candidate for public office finds that direct mail is one of the most economical and efficient ways to present his story to voters. Techniques utilized cover almost the entire direct mail firmament—from post cards to comic books; from letters to fancy broadsides and brochures.

DMMA Guidebook

To assist candidates in more effective use of the direct mail medium, the Direct Mail/Marketing Association prepared a special guidebook.[1] It provides an effective outline to the use of the medium for political purposes:

> The Post Office Department can be your best vote getter . . . IF you consider direct mail as more than a letter or a folder stuffed into an envelope and mailed out to names on a list.
>
> Direct mail is, in fact, one of the most versatile and productive of modern mass communications media.
>
> Use it right, and it can do almost any job from building your public image as the outstanding candidate for the office you seek, to getting out a better than average vote for you on Election Day.
>
> Let's look at just a few of the functions it has successfully—and consistently—performed for candidates who have come to know and respect its capabilities at both local and national levels:
>
> *1. It Can Raise Money*
>
> In November, 1963, the Goldwater for President Committee launched a campaign to get supporters and contributions. In a single week, at a cost of less than 10% of total receipts, it had received 30,000 contributions from 30 states in amounts ranging from $2 to $100.
>
> *2. It Can Measure Public Opinion*
>
> Mailing professionally prepared questionnaires to professionally selected lists is recognized as a fast, reliable way to take the public pulse. Sometimes one mailing can do two jobs, as in the 1952 fund-raising efforts conducted by Walter Weintz for Citizens for Eisenhower-Nixon. Ten letters, each stressing a different campaign issue, were sent to ten groups of 10,000 people. *The letter that discussed the Korean War pulled the biggest response, and raised the most dollars*—thus giving an indication of the importance of the Korean situation to voters.

---

[1] "How to Win Your Election with Direct Mail" by Robert B. Hanford, Jr., Copyright 1964. Direct Mail Advertising Assn., New York.

GEORGE LILLY
CHAIRMAN
CAMPAIGN COMMITTEE

HARRIET F. BRADLEY
CAMPAIGN COMMITTEE
FOR DRANESVILLE SUPERVISOR

Dear Fellow Dranesville Citizen:

There is an opportunity this fall to continue the record of solid, intelligent representation from which we have all benefited. But to do so, your help is needed now.

As you probably realize, Harriet Bradley will be running for re-election to the Fairfax Board of County Supervisors on November 7th. The success of her campaign will depend upon our ability to publicize her record, to prepare literature, to get the word out concerning the good work Mrs. Bradley has done for us all.

This, of course, takes dollars...and we earnestly hope you will support these efforts with your "pocketbook participation" now. Candidates for office must look for financial support to many small contributors or a few large ones. We prefer to follow the first course.

It would be a serious mistake to assume that everyone knows Harriet Bradley's record. The story of her whole-hearted dedication to the needs of Dranesville and Fairfax County during the past four years is worth telling over and over. Voters must be informed of the fact that she has given us full time, non-partisan representation...that she has responded to the responsibilities of her office with intelligence, integrity and common sense judgment.

If you feel as we do, come along and help us assure that her record of accomplishment will continue.

Any amount you wish to give will be greatly appreciated and carefully spent. Please use the enclosed envelope to send your contribution today.

Sincerely,

George Lilly

George Lilly

GL:bbh
Enclosure

P.O. BOX 447 • McLEAN, VIRGINIA 22101

This letter, pretty standard for a local campaign, was mailed to 7000 residents at a cost of $700 and raised over $4000.

3. It Can Mold Public Opinion

A worthy example—a winner in DMMA's 1963 Direct Mail Leaders Contest—is that of an unknown group of candidates who, with an incredibly low starting budget of $3,000, used the mails extensively to seize victory from an entrenched Benton Harbor (Michigan) political machine. The initial mailing of 5,500 was sent first class with this instruction printed on the envelope—"Return to Sender if Undeliverable as Addressed—Do Not Forward." This assured a clean list of registered voters and the candidates were able to use third class rates for subsequent mailings at considerable saving in postage.

A simple booklet, inexpensive but attractive, was mailed to a selective list of farmers and home owners to acquaint them with an intolerable tax situation. It turned out to be a sensation. With property owners really aroused, it was decided that the time was ripe for a mail financial solicitation. The results were rewarding, both in terms of contributions and number of votes represented. Just before Election Day 2,500 vinyl records were mailed to professional, executive, and middle income voters at a cost of about 7 cents each. The tremendous interest it created made this mailing more than worth the cost.

This classic campaign, principally direct mail, ended a 60-year reign of the opposition party by a 2-to-1 vote for the insurgent group. It illustrates succinctly the ability of well-conceived direct mail to mold public opinion.

4. It Can Enlist Volunteer Workers

In 1963, John J. Lee, Jr., an able lawyer but politically unknown, decided to run for Councilman from the 5th Ward of Yonkers, N. Y. Because of limited time before the primary, Lee and his supporters decided that direct mail was the fastest and surest way to make him known to the voters and to build a working organization. One of his mailings bore down heavily on the need for volunteers. The response was overwhelming. Within two weeks, the candidate had at work a volunteer organization which surprised even the political professionals. This organization and subsequent mailings were responsible for Lee not only defeating his Primary opponent handily, but for a win over a popular opposition candidate by the heaviest vote ever turned out in an off-year city election.

5. It Can Get Out The Vote

Examples in this area are legion, but one of the most outstanding was the New Hampshire Primary election victory in March, 1964 of Henry Cabot Lodge, the man who was on the other side of the world in Viet Nam and not even an announced candidate. Early in the campaign 96,000 letters were mailed by a group of men and women who strongly believed that he was the logical man to be the Republican Party's standard bearer for President. *For the first time in political direct mail history, cards were enclosed asking the recipient to pledge his vote* for Lodge. More than 9,000 were returned. From these pledges, 6,000 persons in areas that needed more work were sent a personal letter asking that they get friends to sign pledge cards. Result: Mr. Lodge not only had the nucleus for his statewide organization (plus 1,800 volunteer workers), but the basis for his unexpected victory. Paul Grindle, one of the men who directed the Lodge campaign, gives full credit to direct mail for this spectacular write-in effort.

The Seven Deadly Sins of Political Mailings

In spite of the recognized capabilities of direct mail, many political mailings continue to ride the rut of mediocrity. John Kraft, noted New York opinion researcher, puts it this way:

"Political direct mail is almost always visually bad, verbally unconvincing, amateurish, and unimaginative. As a result it is seldom as effective as it should be. The need for professionalism is urgent, for where professionalism exists, direct mail has proved its power as a communications medium."

Specifically, here are the seven most common mistakes—the Seven Deadly Sins—committed by political mailers. Avoid these, and the effectiveness of your mailings will improve measurably.

1. The Sin of Sheer Self-Seeking

Too many political mailings are simply "Vote For Me" appeals. A statement that "Such-and-such a town needs John Doe" may be true, but it is scarcely a compelling argument to a voter. It is simply a political billboard condensed to fit a mailing envelope.

Remember that you're probably mailing to the voter at his home. Chances are he'll have time to read your message, and that an effective mailing piece can arouse his curiosity about you. Here's your opportunity to gain his confidence by telling him what you stand for (or against) . . . about what you've done (or can do) for him. *Give him the who, what, and why of your case—especially why your election is important to him. (Note that we did not say, "why his vote is important to you.")*

Even if it's only a letter, remember you've got a full page. So marshall your arguments, present them clearly, sell yourself to him, and ask him for his support on the basis of his interests.

2. The Sin of Insincerity

Like most abstract qualities, "insincerity" is hard to pin down. It shows not only in *what* you say in your letter, folder or booklet, but in *the way* you say it. It shows in exaggerated overstatement. It also shows in deliberate and transparent understatements (e.g., "I realize that I am not worthy of this high office") that represent modesty at its falsest.

Remember that a mailing piece is not a speech. It is a person-to-person communication from you to one reader—one voter. It is likely to be read—and re-read—and saved clear up to Election Day. Talk to this one other person as you might talk to him if he had invited you into his home. Don't talk over his head. Don't talk down to him. Talk with him about those things that are of interest to him.

An excellent example of a letter that achieved this person-to-person empathy is one sent out in 1960 by a political novice named Paul Young, then running for the office of Selectman in the town of Braintree, Mass. His letter started like this:

"Even my wife was skeptical when I first told her I'd agreed to run for Selectman. But when she heard my reasoning, she did a complete turn-about.

"Do you know what I told her? I just said, 'Ella, I'm sick of seeing professional politicians running for office and then doing an amateurish job when elected. It's about time somebody who might be an amateur at politics, but a professional at administration, got in and gave it a try.' "

Nothing fancy here. No big words. Not even big issues. Just a straightforward and immensely human person-to-person communication.

P.S. Paul Young, an independent, scored a major upset by winning all seven precincts of his ward.

Clearly, the Paul Young approach is not appropriate for every candidate, nor every elective office. It is, however, a fine example of how to strike *the shining and convincing note of sincerity* in political direct mail.

PAUL H. YOUNG
40 WILDWOOD AVENUE
BRAINTREE 85, MASSACHUSETTS

Dear Friend:

Even my wife was skeptical when I first told her I'd agreed to run for Selectman. But when she heard my reasoning, she did a complete turn-about.

Do you know what I told her? I just said: "Ella, I'm sick of seeing professional politicians running for office and then doing an amateurish job when elected. It's about time someone who might be an amateur at politics but a professional at administration got in and gave it a try."

This business of picking a Selectman is mighty important to you. Under our system of town government, the three-man board either is responsible for or can get action on almost every dealing you may have with the town (with the major exception of tax assessment).

In other words, they can have a great deal to say about how you and your family will live during the next few years. Just as one example, they can rule for or against allowing certain types of businesses to locate in your neighborhood.

Now, I don't expect you to make a definite decision this minute about how you'll vote on election day. But you owe it to yourself to keep informed and alert. Listen to what every candidate has to say, then choose according to the best dictates of your conscience.

As for myself, these are my major qualifications:

> B. S. degree in civil engineering...Manager of Industrial Products Operations and Assistant Plant Manager of Armstrong Cork Company...town meeting member...veteran...Chairman, Braintree Industrial & Business Development Commission...Chairman, Braintree Municipal Golf Course Operating Committee...Member, past president, and past district governor of Braintree Lions Club... Vice president, Old Colony Council, Boy Scouts of America... Member, United Fund Standing Committee...Chairman, Building and Finance Committee of South Congregational Church.

You can see that my experience has been in doing...not running for office. I can only make one promise: To do the best job I know how for you...regardless of who you are or who you know.

If you will forgive an amateurish campaign, you may gain a truly qualified Selectman. Thank you for your consideration.

Sincerely,

Paul H. Young

This introductory letter was the key element in Paul Young's successful attempt to become a Selectman.

3. The Sin of Shoddiness

Of all the sins in the book, this is the one most frequently committed in political direct-mail. It means, bluntly, buying your art and production *on price alone,* ignoring the visual impression your mailing piece makes on the reader. This is bad for two reasons:

First, shoddiness reflects not only on the taste, but on the ability of the candidate.

Second, it carries the subtle but unmistakable suggestion that maybe you don't really think the voter is worth anything better.

The surest way to eliminate shoddiness in your mailings is to get a professional in your organization who knows art, layout, typography, and printing to ride herd on the creation and production of your direct mail materials. This can be a volunteer worker, a local art studio, a free lance artist, or an advertising or public relations firm. *The point is—get competent help.* It does not have to be expensive to be good. Remember Benton Harbor, cited earlier.

Shoddiness can also be eliminated by *budgeting a little more for your production.* Spread over the total mailing list the increased cost will probably be only a fraction of a cent per addressee. But the result will be direct mail material that does credit to your candidacy, reflects respect for the intelligence of the voter you are trying to influence—and helps win your election.

4. The Sin of Non-Selectivity

Many candidates still "scattergun" their mail messages, using the same copy appeals for all groups, instead of emphasizing specific issues or campaign themes to specific groups of voters.

Direct mail is the most selective of all mass media. Indeed, its selectivity makes it superior to radio, TV, or newspapers for some candidates and some campaigns. Where radio or TV coverage might be too broad, direct mail can be pinpointed to selected areas of a state, or town—or even a ward or precinct. And it can let you talk about specific issues to people you know in advance will be most interested in those issues.

If, for example, increased police protection is needed in one area of a city, your mail message to voters in that area can take this subject as a primary theme. Perhaps, in another area the problem is road improvements or street maintenance. Fine! Your mailings to voters in this area can emphasize your stand on this local problem.

The possibilities are as wide as your imagination for using direct mail's unique selectivity to appeal to the individual interests of individual voters.

5. The Sin of Single-Shot Mailing

Virtually the only time a voter hears from a candidate is when the candidate wants something—his vote. Often he only hears from him once during an entire campaign.

Part of direct mail's power lies in its ability to establish a close, almost personal relationship between sender and recipient. Establishing this priceless relationship takes time—and more than a single mailing.

The solution is to schedule several mailings during the campaign, timing the last one to arrive as close as possible to Election Day.

Once you have won, establish continuity in your direct mail by sending periodic reports or "newsletters" that let your constituents know you haven't forgotten them, that you still value their confidence and support. In sum: sell yourself *before* the election—then use direct mail to keep yourself sold *between* elections.

6. The Sin of Non-Personalization

Secret of direct mail's tremendous readership-generating power lies in the universal appeal of—and human desire for—"getting a letter."

You can heighten this appeal by *personalizing* your mailings wherever possible . . . by using the voter's name in the salutation of a letter, for example . . . by adding a hand-written signature to a "form" letter . . . by attaching a covering note to a printed leaflet or booklet. There are a score of techniques that will suggest to the recipient that he is more than "just another name" on a mailing list.

In local campaigns, where mailings are likely to be measured in the hundreds rather than in the thousands, it is a relatively simple matter to add hand-written postscripts to letters, or hand-written notes to folders and brochures.

Even in mass mailings, there are methods for reproducing the look of hand-typed letters, and pen-written notes that, for pennies more than ordinary, non-personalized mail, will endow your message with infinitely more warmth, immediacy, and importance.

7. The Sin of Not Planning

All too often, political direct mail is treated as an afterthought. Newspaper ads, press conferences, TV and radio appearances are usually scheduled and rehearsed well in advance. All this is to the good. But mailings for the same candidate frequently look as if they had been prepared in haste and produced in panic.

For maximum effectiveness, direct mail should be made a full-fledged member of the campaign communication team from the very beginning, and its use coordinated with communications in other media. *This means preparing and dispatching your mailings so that their arrival and their message coincide with—and, indeed, reinforce—the impact of a newspaper advertisement, a campaign speech, or an important press conference.*

Planning includes deciding in advance what your direct mail will say, how it will look, to whom it will be sent, and when (or how frequently) mailings will be made.

It also includes planning for the unexpected—that is, for those new opportunities for effective mail appeals that inevitably develop in any campaign. Obviously, it is impossible to prepare for every contingency, but even a little advance preparation (of lists, suppliers, copy themes and mail formats) can avoid a lot of panic-button pushing when such emergencies arise.

One solution: have on hand, ready for use, a letter (or letter copy) that answers every possible issue and/or accusation that might be raised during a campaign. You may never have to use it, but, if the need arises, you can be in the mails within hours with an answer that can prove devastating.

Mailing Lists and How to Get Them

Good mailing lists are essential in all direct mail. In political direct mail, they are vital. *Few campaign treasuries can afford the luxury of mailing material to the wrong people.* Fortunately, getting mailing lists is less complex than it may seem.

Frequently lists can be compiled from your local telephone directory. In fact, in most cities, the telephone company publishes a directory listing telephone subscribers by street address rather than by name—thus making it a simple matter to prepare mailing lists by wards and precincts, or by the socio-economic characteristics of neighborhoods.

Other usual sources include:

Voter registrations

Property tax rolls

Automobile registrations

Business and city directories

Membership rosters of local clubs and business organizations.

On a larger scale, list "brokers" are a good source of names—and a good source for information about where to get names.

Once you have assembled the basic source documents (directories, rosters, etc.), *take time to transfer the names you want into usable form* by setting up card files (3 by 5 inches is the most common format). Once on cards, it is far easier to break your list down by geographic areas, socio-economic groupings, ethnic groupings, etc., depending on the approaches you will use in your direct mail efforts.

How to Raise Funds From Scratch

All political campaigns need money, and the bigger the campaign, the more money needed. Used properly, direct mail can raise it, fast and economically.

There are however a few ground rules in the game of fund-raising by mail, starting with how you handle your all-important lists.

First step is to divide your lists into groups according to anticipated size of contribution. Those names that represent really substantial contributors—say over $50—should receive in-person attention. Mail, where used, should be by typed (not form) letter.

The moderate size contributors (the $10, to $50, variety) can be solicited by form letter, but since you are seeking the biggest contribution possible from each person you solicit, *the more "personal" your mailing looks—and sounds—the better your returns will be.*

That leaves the balance—the vast majority of your list who are in the $1 to $10 contributor group. Obviously, personalized letters are impractical for people in this category, but there are still techniques that will make them want to give something.

1. *Give a reason for contributing.* Sure, you need the money, but what the donor wants to know is why his contribution is important. This should be an appeal primarily to emotion.

2. *Suggest specific amounts*—but leave an "open end" that puts no limit on the amount he may give. Don't, for example, say "Send your contribution to us today." Instead, say "Send $2 . . . $5 . . . $10 . . . as much as your personal desire for better government tells you to give."

3. *Give them a means of responding* by enclosing a reply envelope (either stamped, or Business Reply Mail). The former is slightly more expensive, but will provide greater returns. Ideally, the reply envelope should provide a means for identifying the donor, by including his name on the flap, or by providing space for him to write in his name.

4. *Give them your thanks.* Acknowledge every contribution, no matter how small it is. A form acknowledgement is acceptable, but it should be hand-signed—preferably by the candidate himself. This is an excellent image builder.

5. Finally, be sure to *record the name of every contributor* in a special list showing the date and size of his contribution. Even if the amount is small, his name represents a person who has signified his support of you and your campaign objectives in the most tangible of ways—in terms of hard cash. Moreover, in most states you will need such a record to report your campaign expenditures to the proper governmental authority.

Your best source of information regarding *both* direct mail formats and direct mail production is an advertising agency or a direct mail professional (perhaps a local newspaper with a job printing shop or a lettershop). The latter are experienced producers. Many are staffed and equipped to provide a complete direct mail service—from the assembly to mailing lists, to their maintenance; from copy and art services, to the actual production and mailing operations. *Made part of your "team" early in your campaign, they can become invaluable members every step of the way—from initial planning, to ultimate victory.*

In spite of our obvious and pardonable bias in favor of direct mail as a political communications medium, we would be the first to admit that it is not a "super medium" that can replace all the other forms of communication between candidate and voter.

A letter, for instance, will never beat a TV appearance, or a personal handshake in communicating a candidate's personality.

A single newspaper advertisement will inevitably reach more people at less cost-per-person than direct mail.

But the fact remains that selective, personal direct mail—when planned right, produced right—can be a powerful plus for you, the candidate, in your campaign.

It can pay off for you both before and after Election Day.

It can build support for you in terms of funds, as well as votes.

It can create a personal rapport between you and the voters that is far more lasting than a speech or a campaign button.

Use direct mail right—use it to the full limit of its remarkable potential—and then your mailmen become your couriers in bringing in winning votes.

Four Stages in Molding Public Opinion

As I. Lynn Mueller explains,[2] "The whole purpose of the political campaign is to mold public opinion so as to develop a high level of positive name and image identification for your candidate.

"In molding public opinion one must understand the decision-making process that every human goes through when forming an opinion. There are four steps to this decision-making process.

1. The first step is *awareness*—getting the voter's attention.
2. The second step is *understanding*—beginning to understand who the candidate is or what office he presently holds.
3. The third step is *activation*—motivating the voter to actively support a candidate.
4. The fourth step is *involvement*—either working for candidate or definitely deciding to vote for him.

"The goal of every campaign should be for each voter to pass through these four steps at an early stage. The campaign should then reinforce the voter's belief that he is supporting the right candidate.

"In moving through each of these stages, it must be understood that *no stage* can be avoided in molding public opinion. Direct mail can serve as the vehicle for a campaign to move the voter smoothly through one or all of these stages."

Preparing Effective Political Mailings

One of the nation's leading experts on preparing effective political direct mail is Guy L. Yolton. He has developed a particularly useful guide which provides a fundamental understanding of the techniques for political mailings:[3]

> The campaign manager planning to launch a promotion effort for his candidate cannot possibly overlook the effectiveness of direct mail. While it is, perhaps, not as personal as door-to-door calls, or telephone contacts, it is the most efficient way to personally reach a substantial number of voters and/or contributors to the candidate's campaign.
>
> In many respects, of course, the development of a direct mail program in politics is not greatly different than the direct mail effort conducted for a commercial enterprise. The rules for good copy, the use of attractive graphics, the intelligent selection of appropriate lists, the mechanics and the costs are essentially the same. The main differences are in the subtle consideration

[2]"Political Direct Mail Can Be Useful Candidate Tool" by I. Lynn Mueller, vice president, Robert-Lynn Associates, Ltd. *Direct Marketing*, February 1971.

[3]"Guidelines for Creating Effective Political Direct Mail" by Guy L. Yolton. *The Reporter of Direct Mail Advertising*, March 1968.

that you are selling *a man* and not a product. And this is where direct mail is particularly suited to doing an effective job.

That's where the question, "How professional should political direct mail be?" comes into the picture. And the answer is probably "not too.'"

There is a need for a certain friendly ingenuousness in political direct mail. Too often the mailing pieces of candidates project an image of being too slick, too calculated, too well-arranged, maybe even to well written. I suspect that part of this is due to the fact that the preparers of candidate direct mail are too frequently far removed from the candidate.

At the beginning of the campaign, the people charged with the responsibility of developing campaign literature should have ready access to the candidate himself. Sit down with him and discuss the issues. Know what his responses will be to the subjects that are uppermost in the voters' minds. Record his words and phrasings on tape if that's possible, because you should, in the preparation of written material, be able to capture the style and flavor of his language . . . particularly if there will be radio and television appearances included in his campaign.

Mailer Must Reflect Candidate's Image

The job of political direct mail is to project the image of one man, and do it in a highly convincing and persuasive manner. Bear in mind, though, that's not a particularly unique characteristic of political direct mail. It's one that's used successfully by the largest mailers in the country. A mailing piece for American Heritage always sounds like American Heritage; a piece for TIME sounds like TIME; and a piece for Haband Ties is always, by George, a piece for Haband Ties. Each of these giant mailers have to live and identify with their mailing pieces . . . and so it must be with your candidate. In other words, the direct mail should sound like the candidate . . . in his best and most lucid moments.

Now, to the actual strategy of the direct mail campaign itself. It will be conducted on two levels: the fund raising effort and the "get out the vote" effort. It's dangerous to try and do the two jobs together. There is an odd conflict between getting votes and getting money. Do not let one get in the way of the other.

The fund raising effort should be started early and it should be concentrated on your friends. Here is where personal appeals to a close-in list of supporters or suspected supporters can be most effective.

Since you will be mailing to friends, the strategy for building a fund raising piece ought to be something along the line, "of course, you believe in our platform and our candidate and therefore we are calling on you for special support." The letter doesn't have to disguise its fund raising purpose. It needs simply to state the nature of the job ahead, the opportunities for the candidate to win, the benefits that you accrue to the contributor if this happens, and a straight-out appeal for funds. There is no need in this kind of approach to go after votes. You can *believe* that those who will contribute to your candidate will vote for him. To make an even indirect inference otherwise, is the antithesis of the strategy in this kind of direct mail.

You Must Use A Letter Format

In soliciting funds by direct mail one decision that does not have to be made is the format that it should take. It *has* to be a letter. If the letter can go out over the signature of a prominent member of the community so much the better. It should never go out over the candidate's signature, for in these days of questioning political campaign funds, this kind of a mistake might be fatal. By all means check out the legal requirements in recording such funds, and let your letterhead and/or your committee listings reflect this legitimacy. There could be an appropriate enclosure with the letter: a mimeographed rundown of the candidate's record; a newspaper article reprint; or something similar that reinforces the message of the letter, printed in an obviously inexpensive way, since ostensibly, you're appealing for campaign funds that *later on* will enable you to produce campaign literature of a more "professional" nature.

Now we come to *"voter"* direct mail and this is constructed in almost the opposite way from the fund raising effort, with the main message directed to all the fine things that can be said about the candidate—his record, his qualifications, his education, his family, his clubs, his community service, etc., etc. There are an infinite variety of formats that can be used—brochures, folders, letters, broadsides, simulated newspaper formats, and many others that can employ pictures, questions and answers, interviews, thumbnail histories, and, by all means, testimonials and endorsements. In the preparation of this material, some professional help should be sought . . . but the kind of professional help that can be budget conscious, for in politics an apparent prudence in the expenditure of funds is essential.

For the voter type of mailing a number of good suggestions were offered by Robert Buehler, Public Affairs Officer for NAM at a seminar of Republican campaign workers back in 1966. Mr. Buehler suggested that three types of mailings would be effective—a kick-off letter, then a brochure, and a last-minute tabloid. If the budget permitted, these could be supplemented with endorsement letters and newsletters. In all of this, Mr. Buehler emphasized name identification as most important. The name of your candidate should appear on every page—several times per page if that seems appropriate.

At that same seminar, this writer offered some ideas on the construction of the political circular—an essential vote-seeking piece. Circulars should have a beginning and ending so that they can be read through from front to back if the reader wishes. But they also should be constructed for the spot reader, so that if he focuses on any place in the circular he can find reasons for supporting that particular candidate in the election. Pictures are most important . . . and it's worth striving for informal, real-life shots of your candidate—not those frozen, dead-pan family line-ups. Every picture should have a short caption of some kind. And the patriotic temptation to design circulars in red-white-and-blue should be resisted, primarily because halftone illustrations are going to have to use the color blue . . . which means the candidate and his family are going to come out looking blue . . . a very depressing and unnatural color.

Can you raise funds as part of the vote-getting direct mail effort? Possibly so, but it's a tricky thing to do, especially when using a broad list of voters of unknown commitment. If the mailing's main purpose is to influence votes, any fund raising effort should be relegated to a secondary position . . . not referred to at all perhaps, except by the inclusion of a simple wallet-style envelope enabling the recipient to send a contribution if he so desires.

History of Republican Direct Mail

In a speech at the 1972 DMMA Annual Conference in Chicago, veteran direct mail expert Walter Weintz presented an interesting history of how the national Republican party learned the effectiveness of direct mail:

> To the best of my knowledge, the Republicans started using direct mail on a scientific, mass basis back in 1950. At that time, Senator Robert Taft was running for his life for re-election.
>
> The big unions had announced that they had earmarked a war chest of several million dollars for a campaign in Ohio to defeat Taft, because he was co-author of the Taft-Hartley Act, which gives the Federal Government the power to halt strikes that hurt the national interest. Senator Taft was a friend of Dewitt Wallace, the head of the *Reader's Digest,* and of Al Cole, who was then the Digest's General Manager.
>
> They volunteered my services (I was then Circulation Director of the Digest) to do a direct mail campaign to help get Senator Taft re-elected.
>
> Senator Taft was convinced that he should take his stand on the Taft-Hartley Law, and, of course, we tried to talk him out of that, because we knew that blue collar workers would be against him on the basis of the Taft-Hartley Act.
>
> Fortunately, in direct mail you are able to test almost anything, including political appeals. We mailed out, as I recall, a half-dozen different letters, each one putting forward a different central idea on why the recipient of the letter should support Senator Taft.
>
> Since we needed some way to measure the effect of our different appeals, in each mailing we included a contribution card, keyed to the letter it went with.
>
> Thus, we were able to count returns from each letter and tell which pulled the best.
>
> We sent out about 20,000 copies of each letter. I was astounded when the letter which was built around a positive presentation of the Taft-Hartley Act was far and away the most successful.
>
> We subsequently mailed hundreds of thousands of Taft-Hartley letters into the blue collar worker sections of the industrial cities of Ohio: Cincinnati, Cleveland, Akron, and so on. The blue collar workers responded by voting overwhelmingly for Taft against the urging and advice and the three million dollar campaign fund of their union leaders.
>
> In addition, much to our surprise, we received a substantial number of small contributions, which helped us finance the direct mail campaign.
>
> In 1952 I went to work for the Citizens for Eisenhower-Nixon. We decided that the experience we had had on the Taft campaign gave us a beautiful model for doing direct mail on behalf of Eisenhower and Nixon.

We could test different copy appeals by mailing a series of letters, each built around a different appeal. We would ask for money, to check the effectiveness of the different appeals and to check the overall effectiveness of our campaign. We would then mail millions of letters, and the mailing would be at least partially self-financing, because it would pull for contributions.

The letters, besides raising money, would reach millions of people with strong arguments in favor of Eisenhower and Nixon. Most importantly, we would then have hundreds of thousands of small contributors who had "bet on a horse"—giving small sums ranging from a dollar up to $25.00 or so to support Eisenhower's campaign.

We reasoned that anyone who contributed money would be much more likely to go out and vote for our candidate on election day.

At the start of Eisenhower's campaign, he didn't have a clear-cut political theme, and he was burdened with all kinds of conflicting advice from well-meaning self-appointed experts. The businessmen who could get his ear told him he should concentrate on economic issues, such as the high cost of living or high taxes.

The politicians who surrounded him implored him not to say anything, it being their philosophy that campaigns are won by not taking a stand on anything. They suggested our theme should simply be, "It's time for a change."

Others were incensed over the deep freeze and fur coat scandals which had plagued the latter years of the Truman Administration. They suggested that a simple, dignified phrase like, "Throw the rascals out" would hit home. And, of course, the war in Korea was much on everybody's mind.

Mr. Cole asked me to write ten letters, each based on a different copy appeal. We sent out 10,000 of each of these letters, and in each case we said, "If you would like to see Eisenhower elected President, please send back the enclosed contribution card, together with your contribution and your name and address."

The cards were keyed, and so we were able to count results.

90% The Same

Nine out of the ten letters pulled almost exactly the same. The tenth letter, which talked about Korea, and the seeming never-ending war in which America had gotten embroiled, pulled about 2½ times as well as any of the other letters.

It was a striking, clear-cut proof that the war in Korea outweighed every other political appeal Eisenhower could make.

The results were so striking that we put together a report, and Walter Williams, Chairman of the Citizens for Eisenhower-Nixon, got on a plane and hurried out West, where Eisenhower was campaigning, and showed him these results. A few days later Eisenhower made his famous "I shall go to Korea" speech, and suddenly his campaign was off and running.

I can't say that it was the direct mail results alone which convinced him that Korea was the important issue, but Walter Williams told me that it was decisive in helping him make up his mind.

We mailed out some 20 million letters based on the Korean issue. And the interesting thing is that, in addition to getting 20 million messages out to voters, we were able to get some 300,000 voters to send us a contribution. These were 300,000 voters that we could pretty well count on.

The contributions were small. They averaged only $5 or so. But the million and a half dollars that they represented easily paid the cost of our 20 million campaign. Thus, we had harnessed a powerful self-financing political force.

That isn't the end of the story, however. Because in 1972, we were still getting contributions from those original 1952 contributors!

The names of our 1952 Citizens for Eisenhower-Nixon contributors were put in a "bank" for future use. In 1956, when Eisenhower and Nixon ran again, we wrote to these same people and asked for additional contributions, and they gave generously.

The contributions were small, and the contributors were certainly not "fat cats." On the contrary, they reminded me of the slogan which is posted in the children's zoo at the Bronx, over the guinea pig colony, "We are small, but we are many."

Together, these small contributors represented a very important part of the Republican fund raising in 1956.

Again in 1960, Spencer Olin, who was then the Finance Chairman of the Republican Party, turned to direct mail to solve his Party's financial problems. In the spring of 1960, the Republican Party was almost literally broke.

Mr. Olin asked me to "put out a letter and raise a million dollars." We mailed approximately a million letters, and we cleared the million dollars that Mr. Olin asked for. We were able to do this because we had amassed a list of dependable contributors to whom we could turn in our hour of need.

Continuing Use of Political Direct Mail

During the same period described by Walter Weintz, the national Democratic organization was also actively using direct mail. At one point, it was reported that John F. Kennedy had "the world's largest lettershop." Whether true or not, the late President and many other Democrat candidates learned how to use direct mail most effectively.

When the national campaigns of 1972 got underway, direct mail had become a well established campaigning tool and were used in a major way by both the Republican and Democratic organizations. And on the local level, direct mail had clearly established itself as a highly effective communications device for the majority of candidates.

Chapter 18

THE COMPUTER AND DIRECT MAIL

DURING the 1960's, a major revolution changed forever the world of direct mail and mail order. When the first edition of this HANDBOOK was written, the computer was something of a novelty among direct mail advertisers. While the big list houses had introduced early generation computers into their operations and innovative advertisers had tapped their company computers for list maintenance help, pre-computer direct mail techniques were still the order of the day.

While *Business Management* noted in 1963[1] that "by 1970, computers will be as common to American businesses as television sets are to American homes," *Business Week* reported in 1965,[2] "Strictly marketing uses of EDP, going beyond inventory management, are still uncommon in U.S. business."

But those who thought the computer would always be too expensive a tool to have any major impact on direct mail and mail order failed to anticipate how quickly the computer way of life would take hold in the U.S.

One of the early computer direct mail pioneers, Murray Miller of Office Electronics, described the early days of computerized direct mail:[3]

> "Two years ago [1962] our first computer was installed. Now some five hundred direct mail computer programs later, I am convinced that the potential of the computer has not been tapped by the mail order industry.

---

[1]"What You Must Know About Choosing A Computer," *Business Management*, November 1963.

[2]"Computers Begin to Solve The Marketing Puzzle," *Business Week*, April 17, 1965.

[3]"Mail Order and the Computer," by Murray Miller, *The Reporter of Direct Mail Advertising*, October 1964.

"Prior to our computer installation, we suffered from "Systems Lag," a condition which developed when existing systems could not satisfactorily accommodate increased volume. This "lag" resulted in attendant problems such as slow order processing, delayed billing schedules, pressures from advertising and financial staffs for timely reports. We, of course, focused our computer system on these critical problem areas.

"In retrospect, we suffered in two particular areas during our computer infancy stage. First, our newly hired programming staff, although technically competent, was critically handicapped in its efforts due to lack of understanding of direct mail techniques; and our management team, knowledgeable in mail order, had little or no ability in appraising programming results. Progress was slow until communications between the two groups were established.

"Secondly, when management became aware of the effectiveness of the computer system reports, the demand to generate more extensive reports became excessive. Reams of analysis were spewed forth from the computer printer too comprehensive to be digested before the follow-up report was produced. The economics of maintaining a computer installation curbed this appetite for excess reports.

"Within a two-year period, the computer systems attained a high degree of efficiency in handling routine order processing, billing and statistical data. Impressed with these benefits, we considered broadening the scope of our current applications to include direct mail forwarding, market evaluations and credit checking devices.

"The first challenge came when we were asked to develop a forecasting program by The Robert Maxwell Company, Division of Bell & Howell. Together we created a computer analysis which allows a direct mail marketer concerned with continuation or repeat sales to determine the profitability of mailing to a large list after only a few months' experience with a segment of the list.

"The computer system translates performance of mailings to all lists into comparable percentages and analyzes such factors as sales, returns, dropouts, delinquents, aging of receivables and net books sold. Standards for these factors have been developed from past experience with the same mailing program. The standards are compared to actual performance of each list and used to project probable final results of each mailing. Translation of performance into percentage figures also permits simple conversion to calculations on a per thousand pieces mailed basis.

"In a few hours our computer classifies and compares these figures as often as every two weeks, enabling the Robert Maxwell Company personnel to review simply, quickly and often the actual projected performance of many different mailings.

"The Robert Maxwell Model Program took 400 man hours to program."

When this article appeared back in 1964, the procedures described by Murray Miller were looked upon with awe by the majority of direct mail users. But within just a few years, they had become so commonplace they seemed elementary. How quickly the computer became essential in modern marketing was underscored in a 1971 *Business Week* special section:[4]

> Where computers have really paid off in the commercial world is in the countless functional and operational jobs of keeping track of fine details in production, orders, and payments. Here the computer itself has become a production machine. Huge data centers ... are set up more according to the rules of industrial engineering than to those of office routine.
>
> In the past few years, virtually all the obvious jobs have been computerized. With some 70,000 computers already at work in the U.S., the question in most applications is no longer whether to use a computer, but what sort of system to use ...
>
> There is an article of faith, enshrined in the national mythology, that the computer has all but depersonalized modern commerce. According to this creed, everything is now done by the numbers, and the individual no longer counts. Ironically, marketing men are beginning to find that just the opposite is true.
>
> Both industrial and consumer markets these days are splintering into more and more segments, each with its own highly individual requirements. And the computer is emerging as the only tool with which industry can achieve the flexibility and efficiency it needs to respond to the increasingly diverse demands of the marketplace. "Without computers, you just couldn't do it economically," says Robert D. Buzzell, a professor at the Harvard Business School.
>
> Most consumer-goods marketers have reached the "first plateau" in their use of computers. "In retailing," says Irving Solomon, vice-president of the information systems department of the National Retail Merchants Assn., "we have pretty well computerized our accounting and inventory control. Now we are moving onto the second plateau, which means we will have far more analysis of sales and trends" ...
>
> Some retailers are computerizing their charge customers to establish individual buying profiles. "Say you have 500,000 charge customers," says Paul Dowd, president of Long Island's Gertz department stores, a division of Allied Stores Corp. "Your computer can easily come up with 75,000 names of women who previously bought higher-priced dresses, shoes, or other special items. These specially selected names then can become a direct-mail target when a new shipment of high-priced dresses or shoes comes in."
>
> In its direct mail approach, Gertz could further individualize its promotion by sending computer-written letters. Basically, these are form letters with blank spaces for the recipient's college, his birthday, or other personal data available from professional listmakers. At *Playboy* magazine, a normal direct mail response averages 1.7%. But response to the magazine's use of computer letters, prepared by Standard Register Co., has run as high as a 9.9% return. The cost of new orders meanwhile was cut in half ...
>
> One reason computerized marketing has not gone further, says Joel Jensen, senior staff consultant with Arthur D. Little, Inc., is that "the typical marketing manager is not a technical guy." Jensen is quick to add,

[4]"Business Takes a Second Look at Computers," *Business Week*, June 5, 1971.

however, that this need not be a long-standing obstacle, since it reflects only an attitude and lack of knowledge. And both can be changed. "What we need," Jensen feels, "are some outstanding success stories to motivate marketing managers. The art of using computers to stimulate sales is so new and difficult that these success stories are few and far between."

"There is also a need," adds Douglas Brown, another ADL senior staff consultant, "for every company to integrate its data-gathering and to realize that data captured by computers very frequently interconnect with marketing functions and can serve other purposes." "Thus," he says, "credit cards are basically a billing mechanism. But they have an ancillary use in terms of data capture for marketing."

Above all, marketing managers must come to recognize the limits of computers. "A computer can never really replace a good salesman," stresses Lawrence J. Israel, a partner in the architectural firm of Copeland, Novak & Israel, which specializes in store design. "There is an excitement in one-on-one-selling that you can never get with computers. They can only supplement and reinforce the salesman. Once this is recognized, computers will come much closer to filling their rightful role in marketing."

The Natural Team

What the editors of *Business Week* and the marketing experts they chose to quote failed to recognize is that while the traditional marketing man was slow to join forces with the computer, the direct mail marketer was busy putting this electronic marvel to work in an amazing number of different ways.

Joel Jensen, who decried a lack of computer marketing success stories, apparently was not aware of how thoroughly the computer was already being applied to mail marketing. Throughout the direct mail fraternity, successful use of computers to solve almost every marketing problem is already an old tale.

The market segmentation which *Business Week* cited as a new development is actually a very old principle of direct mail marketing. And the introduction of computers into direct mail marketing was a natural evolution.

Five Basic Uses

While computers have an amazing variety of applications in direct mail and mail order, the most common applications fall into five basic categories:

1. Program planning
2. List development, maintenance and production
3. Computer letters and special formats
4. Order and inquiry processing
5. Marketing analysis

While many direct mail advertisers do not utilize computers for applications in each of these five categories, it is rather uncommon not to involve computers in some way for the majority of mailings.

Program Planning

The computer has an increasing role in helping advertisers plan more effective direct mail programs. As increased amounts of data are added to computer files, advertisers not only have the opportunity to more scientifically pin-point their audiences, but frequently speed up the entire concept-to-mailing sequence and introduce economies as well.

In mail order, it has become common to include a host of response and lack-of-response detail to each name or group of names on customer lists and thus make list selection for a given offer a more scientific process than ever before.

When a profit-volume analysis, for example, indicates the need of a 1% return on a planned mailing, the computer can search out past response levels for similar promotions and quickly indicate those list segments which are likely to produce the desired 1% level of returns. Most often buyers' names are segmented by initial entry—the specific mailing or other promotion to which they first responded—and then maintained on the basis of response to subsequent offers. With such detail in the computer files, the same volume of returns can frequently be achieved for one-half or less than mailing costs using pre-computer techniques of list selection.

Computer Marketing at Pfizer

An example of computer use in direct mail planning at a non-mail order firm was highlighted in a series, "The Computer in Marketing," appearing in *Sales Management:*[5]

> "Thanks to the computer, direct mail at Chas. Pfizer & Co. has become the third hand of the company's sales representatives, or detail men, as they are known in the drug industry. A computerized profile of physicians tailors direct mail promotions to the individual doctor's needs and interests and, equally important, eliminates the names of those who abhor in-the-mail huckstering. This is good economics for us, says sales operations manager Daniel F. Maloney, because we get a better return on our direct mail dollar and we build physician goodwill, which is a strong sales asset in the prescription drug field. One reason why goodwill looms so high is that the typical doctor gets about 4,000 pieces of mail a year or ten times the national average.

[5]"The Computer in Marketing—Mail Marketing," *Sales Management*, August 15, 1968. (Now *Sales & Marketing Management*).

"Any time Pfizer moves into a new product area, the profile provides an effective launching pad. Maloney explains: Our monthly analysis may show that detail men called on 55,000 general practitioners who have a geriatric practice. We don't have a product for the elderly at present but if we ever do, we'll be all set to hit the market on target.

"The starting point in Pfizer's physician profile is the American Medical Assn.'s magnetic tape listing which provides a weekly-updated roster of the country's 300,000 doctors, complete with their addresses and specialties. To obtain the additional information it needs to define markets precisely, Pfizer uses a specially-designed punched card call report, on which detail men punch perforated slots to indicate such things as a doctor's type of practice and whether he is a light, moderate, or heavy prescriber of certain drugs.

"Flexibility is the profile's biggest asset," Maloney says. Depending on the marketing man's creative ability to develop mailing pieces, we can find almost any market target he wants. We can juggle the data around so that whatever the marketing criteria, we can mail accordingly.

"The profile plays an important part in each of the six-to-eight-week promotion cycles that Pfizer mounts throughout the year. Near the close of each period, the computer scans its files to see which doctors who should have been contacted by detail men were missed and which ones were seen but not filled in on the promoted product. Then, direct mail is fired off accordingly."

Computer Lists

Probably the most common use of computers in direct mail is for list development, maintenance and production. While the big list houses and a substantial number of mail order firms and publishers had converted their lists to computers early in the Sixties, the advent of mandatory zip coding in 1967 caused a major trend toward almost universal computerization for larger lists. When the Post Office Department first announced that all third class mail would have to be sorted by zip code, it was estimated that fewer than 10% of all lists were on computers. While no authoritative statistics have been published, it has been estimated that at least 90% of all large mailing lists were computerized by 1970 and a high percentage of firms with smaller lists had at least some degree of computerization for their lists.

While it is frequently less costly to use traditional addressing systems, the greater flexibility, accuracy and speed that a computer list offers frequently more than offsets the added cost of computerization.

Advantages of Computerization

Some of the advantages of converting a list to computers were outlined by Hal Murray of Market Development Corp. in a 1968 presentation:[6]

[6]Speech at a "How to Think About Computer Marketing" seminar sponsored by Omega Press, Glen Ellyn, Illinois, May 27, 1968.

"There are some good reasons to go to a computer, particularly in direct mail. For example, if your file is really in bad shape; if it is full of duplicates, bad addresses, incomplete addresses; if you can't separate your buyers from your prospects or inquiries; if you can't make corrections at a reasonable cost, you need help.

"The computer may or may not be the answer. For example, you can convert your problems directly to a computer and you are really not better off than you were in the first place; but the conversion, itself, may be the best chance you will ever get to correct your errors of the past. This fact alone could certainly be one of the prime influences on your decision to go to a computer.

"It is not very often in life you get a chance to rectify all your errors in one operation. Maybe your file doesn't have enough information to be useful to you or to others, and here the computer can certainly answer the problem. The computer can virtually free you from the traditional space limitations of address plates or stencils or even punch cards.

"Let's take punch cards for example. If your list is on punch cards and you have one card per name and address and you have a list of half a million names, you would have to store and process 250 boxes of cards each time you run your list.

"If your list is on a computer, on magnetic tape, you could have the same data on five or six reels of magnetic tape.

"If you want to add a little information, say ten characters of purchase data or demographic information, instead of 250 boxes of punched cards you now have 500 boxes. The rigidity of the punch cards in other manual operations becomes a very difficult factor to deal with.

"If your list is on magnetic tape and you want to add these ten characters to every name and address, you add about 520 feet of magnetic tape, about a fourth of a reel. So if you need more data, magnetic tape will give you all the opportunity you need to place this data at your disposal. You can have information such as titles, recency, frequency of purchase, amount of purchase, number of purchases, demographics, billing information inventory and statistical data.

"You can add demographic factors by zip code, census tract of any other source you might have. You can then select names by income, education, sex, age, population density, home ownership, telephone or automobile ownership, dog ownership, just about any factor you can think of can be added to your magnetic tape file with very little sacrifice of space or time.

"This additional demographic information and other data hasn't changed the names and addresses on your file; it has simply made them more usable and profitable. This could be one of the best and most important uses of a computer that you could find.

"You may have all the data that you need on your list but if you can't get at it in time to fill your needs or requests of others, it doesn't help you. If you can't find it, it doesn't help you or anybody else. The computer might be the answer to this problem. If you can afford the price, the system is available to get your job done on time in any quantity."

Computer Disadvantages

While developments in the world of computers constantly make their use for direct mail lists easier and less costly, there are a variety of situations which call for caution before following the majority into computerization of lists. For example:

- *Your list is too small.* While there is no magic rule-of-thumb for the list size which makes computerization practical, the computer is generally more advantageous for larger lists—particularly when your list is already in some other form which can generate the addresses you need.
- *The list is mailed infrequently.* Even medium-size lists may not call for conversion to computer if they are used only a couple of times a year.
- *List changes are minimal.* If you have a list which remains relatively stable and is already in a form for economically producing addresses, the computer is probably unnecessary, particularly when name and address changes are not being fed into a computer file for some reason other than mailing list use.
- *Quick access needed.* While computers can turn out thousands of addresses at amazing speeds, getting the first name onto a label is frequently a frustrating, time-consuming process. Therefore, if you are faced with the problem of getting a mailing addressed at the spur of a moment, one of the traditional addressing systems may prove more practical.
- *Generate addresses directly on mailing pieces.* A major disadvantage of computers for many mailers is the necessity to generate addresses on an intermediate medium for some mailings. Most often, computer-printed addresses are generated on labels for adhesive-affixing or heat transfer. Both methods are below the quality standards demanded for top-quality mailings. While computer-compatible envelopes, invoices, order forms and other formats are available, they are frequently costly both in themselves and in the added time required for processing.
- *Little need for selectivity and testing.* One of the major advantages of having lists on a computer is the high degree of selectivity possible. Another is the simplicity with which testing can be accomplished. When neither of these requirements is present it may be more economical to utilize a traditional addressing technique.
- *Your computer is "the property" of the accountants.* In many companies, the computer was originally installed to handle bookkeeping details and installed as part of the accounting department. All too often, such circumstances work to the disadvantage of those who wish to use the equipment to generate a mailing list. Not only is list information frequently stored in a way which makes list generation difficult, but accounting assignments get top priority and others have to sit and wait to get their jobs run off.
- *Computer people don't understand direct mail.* Directly related to the previous disadvantage is another problem that is common when computers are in the hands of nondirect mail people—they just don't understand the requirements of mailers. Those whose experience in programming and operating computers is related to other disciplines frequently

try to apply the requirements of those other disciplines to list generation—often with disastrous results. Just the problem of developing a common language is often reason enough to stick to some other system for your mailing lists.

- *No other use for a computer.* As a general rule, efficient use of computers for mailing lists demands that the computer also be used to serve other needs of an organization. Even when an outside computer is utilized, the cost of developing the necessary software is seldom justified if it is to be used for just a single purpose.
- *Nonrepetitive programs.* The most economical application of a computer for direct mail lists comes when a computer program can be used frequently with few or no changes. If a new program must be written for each use, chances are another addressing method will be far less costly.

While these negative considerations must be taken into account when analyzing whether or not a list should be computerized, they should not be allowed to go unchallenged. Often what may appear to be an overriding disadvantage can turn out to be something which *proper* computerization can handle with added benefits to the mailer.

In the long run, the advantages of computerized lists generally outweigh the disadvantages. In most cases, the question is simply a matter of *when.* Fortunately, there is a lot of sources for help in making this decision.

Sources for Help

When the time comes to analyze how and when you might best put your mailing lists on a computer, you will find six basic sources of help:

- Suppliers
- Service Bureaus
- List Management Services
- Consultants
- Seminars
- Other Uses

Suppliers

There is probably no other field where so much direct assistance is furnished the customer as the computer field. The big manufacturers, such as IBM, have developed highly advanced customer assistance and training programs—not just for those who are getting their feet wet in the world of computers, but for on-going programs tailored to all levels of sophistication.

Likewise, the software suppliers also have highly developed customer assistance programs. Obviously, the odds are that any supplier-furnished assistance is likely to be heavily weighted to sell what they have to offer. But such programs frequently are the best starting point and deserve special consideration.

Service Bureaus

Because the initial investment in computers is frequently costly and it is difficult to find skilled personnel, many direct mail users start out by letting a computer service bureau handle their requirements.

In his presentation at the Omega Press seminar[7], Hal Murray noted: "With a service bureau, the operating costs are still fairly high, but your front end investment is low and your risk factor is quite low. Another good thing about service bureaus is that in most cases the programs, the system, and the documentation eventually become your property and at some point in time you will find a conversion to a computer much easier having gone through the operation with a service bureau."

List Management Services

In a way, list management services are similar to service bureaus, with the essential difference being that list managers usually have a series of set computer programs which are applied directly or adapted to the handling of a number of different customers' lists. While this usually means less flexibility, major cost savings can be gained.

If you plan to make your list available for outside rental, a list management firm may be able to handle the job in such a way that your computer conversion and maintenance costs are covered by rental income.

Consultants

While suppliers in the computer area frequently provide personnel to work as consultants with a potential customer, many direct mail users have found it advantageous to turn to independent consultants in assist in the task of converting lists to the computer.

A few years ago, most of these consultants were highly computer-oriented and often spoke a language which was difficult for the average layman to understand. But as an increasing number of lists were converted to computers, an important by-product was the availability of consultants who were both direct mail-oriented and computer-oriented, and who could more easily communicate in a language other than "computerese."

---

[7]Ibid.

Before making a commitment to any consultant, it is important to carefully check his references. A good consultant can be invaluable but a consultant who hasn't had successful experience in handling problems similar to the ones you need solved can not only be money down the drain but can foul up your list in a way which may take years to undo.

Seminars

For those who want to sit back and consider all alternatives before devoting serious attention to the possibility of computerizing their lists, there are a variety of seminars offered annually which can prove most helpful. Probably your best bet is one of the computer seminars sponsored by such organizations as the Direct Mail/Marketing Association or the American Management Association. Or if one of these association seminars doesn't fit your timetable, there are frequent seminars staged by commercial organizations.

Another possibility is to secure tape recordings of list seminars. However, the real benefit of a seminar is frequently getting answers to your specific questions—something unlikely with a tape or printed seminar transcript.

Other Users

One of the unique things about computers is that a high percentage of businessmen enjoy sharing their experiences with them. Even direct competitors spend hours discussing the joys and horrors of their computer experiences.

Mini-seminars at direct mail meetings are frequently devoted to the subject of computerization of lists and offer a good opportunity to explore answers to your requirements.

And since many firms welcome an opportunity to share their computer with other users and thereby offset some of their investment and operating costs, there is usually someone close by to whom you can turn for your initial discussions.

Computer Lists at GE

Sales Management's series on "The Computer in Marketing"[8] included a profile on how General Electric uses the computer to keep tab on its universe of potential customers:

[8]Same as #5.

"General Electric uses the computer to integrate direct mail promotions sent to industrial prospects within its over-all market planning. A computerized market data bank, maintained by the corporate industrial marketing research department (IMRD), delineates the total universe of GE's existing and potential sales. Some 17,000 plants and other places of business are coded several ways, enabling GE's industrial product groups or sales organizations 'to pull out the particular points-of-sale they want to contact in a mailing,' says William F. Williams, IMRD's systems research consultant.

"GE tabs all business establishments in customer industries, whether or not they currently buy from the company. Coded inputs include financial background from Standard & Poor's corporate file, reports from field salesmen, and government data which, while eschewing names of individual establishments, is used to compute sales totals of customer industries. Besides names and addresses, the data bank lists a company's total employment and employment at each location, the name of the executive in charge, volume bought from GE, and the potential business it represents. Also, a coded list of commodity groups is built in to identify what GE sells to whom.

"Williams' department doesn't generate any direct mail. That's done by the industrial divisions, about half of whom use the bank. 'We just suggest ways it can be used,' he explains. Some 60 retrieval programs are available to help divisions pick out market profiles. Typical tasks are selecting establishments in particular Standard Industrial Classification categories or identifying high-potential plants that haven't been visited during the last two months. Because the establishments are zip coded, mailings may be sorted according to GE's sales territories.

"As far as direct mail is concerned, Williams summarizes: 'We're not interested in building a mailing list per se; that's not the ultimate way to go. The ultimate way is the total market plan for generating total potential billings. Direct mail figures in when the bank selects the points-of-sale you want to contact.' "

Computer Letters

Perhaps the third most important application of computers for direct mail is in the production of computer letters and other direct mail formats. The importance of computer letters was described for international direct mail users at a Computer Letter Workshop in Switzerland by Bob Hanau of Reuben H. Donnelley Corporation:[9]

Computer letters are an exciting new tool for direct mail advertising. In a period of less than five years their acceptance and effectiveness have been outstanding. Like any other method of direct marketing communication, computer letters are not the sole answer to every problem, but this technique is a valued addition to the direct mail idea library.

Computer letters are personalized messages prepared on a computer and a high speed printer. For production use, the paper input is usually fan folded, control punched forms consisting of two side by side letters that are prepared

[9]"Development & Marketing of Computer Letters" by Robert C. Hanau, Manager, Resources Development, Marketing Division, The Reuben H. Donnelley Corporation. Presentation at Computer Letter Workshop, Hostellerie Rigi, Switzerland, January 13, 1971.

on business form printing presses. After computer printing, the continuous forms are bursted, slit, trimmed, folded, and processed as ordinary correspondence. The effectiveness of this form stems from the computer's ability to personalize the letter by including the person's name, address or other personal data in the heading and in portions of the body of the letter. Through special computer programming, the proper hardware configuration to utilize it, and upper/lower case type on the printer, the finished computer letter has the appearance of a personally typed communication.

Basic Types of Computer Letters

There are two basic types of computer letters—(1), the fully typed, or "full-out" and, (2) the "fill-in" letter. Fully typed letters are prepared completely on the computer's high speed printer, except for the letterhead and the signature. The date line, salutation, titles and the entire body of the letter is printed out by the high speed printer.

Fill-in type letters differ in that portions of the letter text are preprinted. Only the personal sections, which can be words, phrases, sentences, or even paragraphs are filled in by the computer printer. Because most of the letter is pre-printed, the forms can be run on the computer much faster and at a much lower cost than a fully typed letter.

As a general rule, a computer letter direct mail campaign of less than 50 thousand letters can be more economically prepared as fully typed. For this size run, it is often more advantageous to use blank continuous paper stock, process the letter on the computer, cut and trim them to sheet size and then print the letterhead and signature on a small sheet fed offset press. Another alternative, if several small campaigns with different copy are going to be used over a period of time, is to have continuous letterheads printed that can be used for printing full-out computer letters by merely changing the copy. A further variation on this technique for several small campaigns could call for using different signatures or titles with the same letterhead at a small up-charge during the forms run.

When larger quantities are involved, it is generally less expensive for the overall job to use a fill-in type letter. The higher cost of the forms preparation is more than offset by the shorter computer time.

We seen then, that computer letters depend upon:

—Specially prepared continuous forms

—A computer oriented data base with accessible detailed information for personalization

—A computer configuration suitable for a high speed quality throughput

—The mechanical ability to finish processing the letter by means of slitting, bursting, trimming, folding, etc.

Computer Letter Evolution

The personal approach has been a basic principle in direct mail advertising for years. The most personal form of direct mail contact is a regular typed business letter from a selling or soliciting organization to a potential customer. Millions of such communications are prepared throughout the commercial world every week.

Various studies by office management consultants have indicated that a dictated and manually typed letter can cost $3.00 to $3.50 each. When greater exposure is required in an effort to produce sales leads, orders or other type responses, the extension of the person to person letter becomes a direct mail campaign. Decades ago, techniques were developed to implement this type of advertising and achieve some degree of personalization by means of a preprinted letter with a typed fill-in for name, address and salutation, usually mailed in a window envelope. The quality of this type of effort varied with the means of preparing the text of the letters. The body of the letter usually did not resemble the typed fill-in portion and much of the upgraded promotional effect was lost. An improvement on this idea was the preparation of ribbon Graphotype letters. In this process, hard type was set for a grooved cylinder press, popularly known as a Multigraph machine. Thousands of impressions could be run off on letterheads through a wide cotton ribbon simulating a typewritten appearance on the copy. The typewriter fill-in, using a machine ribbon, therefore had approximately the same appearance as the body of the letter. This method greatly reduced the expense of individually typed letters, but would not permit any variation in the test. Costs for this type of medium were in the 5 cents to 10 cents range with a number of quality variations depending on the degree of control exercised.

The next development in personalized mass communication occurred during the late 1950's with the advent of automatic typewriters. These machines, typified by the Autotypist, Dura, Robo-Type, etc., are the real forerunners of computer letters as we know them today. The usual installation involves a master electric typewriter, cable connected to a control unit, which runs a bank of similar slave machines.

The typewriters are operated by means of a perforated paper tape (later models use magnetic tape control) and utilize continuous fan-folded letterheads. An operator merely types in the individual name and address and any other variable information on each letter. When this entry is completed, the typewriter automatically types the text, following the prepared spacing, capitalization, etc. Such typewriters can utilize various fonts based upon the particular make and model of the unit and the resultant letter is indistinguishable from an individually prepared letter.

A later outgrowth of the automatic typewriter for repetitive, non-manual typing is the IBM MTST, which utilizes basically the same principle, on an individual basis and a magnetic memory for text. The cost of automatic typed letters was generally in the 15 cents to 30 cents range.

The Computer's Importance to Direct Mail

During the early 1960's, with the advent of second generation computers, such as the IBM 1401 series, most of the larger direct mail companies in the United States converted their lists to magnetic tape. The development of this hardware, and its use in the direct mail industry, is probably the most significant event in the growth of targeted direct marketing.

The ability to store, update and retrieve information completely changed the character of many direct mail efforts. At that time, some simple computer letter campaigns were based on the retrieval of various information—essentially name and address—creating a letter printed in upper case characters only. These early efforts made no attempt to simulate formal correspondence.

However, the personalized nature of communications was far more interesting than a standard direct mail piece.

About 1965, as an outgrowth of computer composition and type-setting applications, IBM introduced an upper-lower case print chain for its 600LPM 1403 printer and the Universal Character Set hardware option in the Central Processor. These features permitted the computer to print either capitals or small letters based upon programmed instructions. This development was the real start of computer letter production and the hottest thing in direct mail since the introduction in the United States of the postage paid Business Reply Mail.

Refining Computer Letters

These early upper/lower case computer letters were relatively unsophisticated, and considerable trial and error in the development of copywriting and data processing techniques ensued. Most direct mail companies experimented with producing computer letters of one sort or another for their clients.

Over the next few years, many service bureaus that were not even aware of direct mail as a vital advertising media, got into the computer letter business. This is understandable, as any idle computer time that could be turned into revenue producing hours, reduced their costs and increased profit potential.

In most cases, they were dependent upon brokered tape lists or clients' mailing lists for their addressing and personalization. Many hours of midnight programming and de-bugging occurred as a service bureau programmer tried to learn the direct mail business the hard way. During this era, many computer letters just "sprinkled" the addressee's name throughout the copy, usually at the end of a paragraph or line—often to the point of being ridiculously repetitive.

The inclusion of more personalized and upgraded copy was the next logical step. By 1967, the primary use of more sophisticated computer letters appeared to be in charity solicitations and fund raising efforts where the most personal approach historically produced the best results.

For example, with new programming techniques, it became relatively simple to: refer to the date and amount of a previous contribution, to personalize the results of the last campaign in terms of neighborhood activities engaged in by the particular charity, and to point out any local efforts by a national organization planned for the following year.

At the same time, more direct mail campaign applications in the mail order field rapidly developed by referring to past activity in terms of purchases and keying current offers to the same type of merchandise.

In effect, more information stored in the computer record was utilized to qualify a prospect. Then, a personal appeal for action, based upon known information that had individual appeal, usually resulted in improved response through the appearance of personal correspondence.

From this point forward, computer letter techniques became limited only by the imagination and creativity of the copywriters, the idea men and the computer specialists. In the past several years, computer letters have been combined with order cards, perforated coupons, carbon copies, and a thousand and one "gimmicks" that creative direct mail people enjoy devising.

We have referred to commercial costs for the forerunners of computer letters, and therefore, it is appropriate to tie in the costs for computer letters. Recognizing the fact that computer applications can be extremely sophisticated or relatively simple; the cost can range from as little as 2 cents each for a predominantly preprinted communication and as low as 5 cents for a minimal fully typed letter in large quantities.

As a general rule, the selling price of the letter is determined by the amount of computer time required to produce it, barring the use of extremely expensive paper or complicated art work. An average preprinted, 2-up letter with name, address, salutation and three or four fill-ins, in large quantities, would be less than 10 cents each, ready to mail.

Computer Letter Uses

Computer letter applications are virtually unlimited. Any direct mail advertising campaign or solicitation by individual companies, hospitals, schools, churches, petroleum companies, auto manufacturers, consumer good producers, industrial marketers and retailers are all excellent prospects. It is merely a decision of the advertising or marketing manager to establish a budget that makes computer letters economically successful.

Generally speaking, the more the campaign is oriented to a personal appeal, as opposed to a mass market, the easier the higher cost of a computer letter direct mail advertising campaign can be justified. It is not reasonable to expect a canned goods manufacturer, producing a 15 cent can of soup, generally sold through a supermarket, to go to the expense of a computer letter when a cents off coupon and a brochure would be a more practical form of consumer advertising.

On the other hand, a high ticket item, keyed to a known mail order buyer, based upon a past successful transaction, easily could support the extra cost of a computer letter campaign by achieving better response.

Not every computer letter is going to be successful; just as no one can guarantee 100% success of any type of advertising campaign. The basic tenet of the offer's appeal and a qualified prospect will tell the final story. All of the factors being equal, a well conceived computer letter will generally out-draw a nonpersonalized direct mail effort.

The development of a successful computer letter campaign involves many parties. It is truly a cooperative effort on the part of a team involving artists, copywriters, EDP systems men and programmers, forms printers, the computer production center, envelope designers and manufacturers and bindery operations.

Basic Consideration for Computer Letters

The basic consideration that must be made is whether the letter will be "full-out" or "fill-in." The second step is determining the size, recognizing that from an economic standpoint, most computer letters are printed 2-up or side by side to increase computer efficiency and reduce forms cost.

At this point, the real coordination begins between copy preparation and the programming aspects of the computer production. The computer programmer can do virtually anything that the copywriter can conceive. Suffice to say at the moment, he is technically correct, but the more complicated the computer program is, the more expensive the job will be. Usually a good team effort will produce a creative piece at a reasonable cost.

In a preprinted letter, the personalized items should be entered realistically and conversationally, with enough impact to be recognizable by the reader, but still be unobtrusive.

The number of characters per line are limited by the form size. Since computer spacing print is based on 10 characters to an inch horizontally, and 6 lines to the inch vertically, an EDP print layout form is an excellent medium for making the initial rough copy. A standard Pica typewriter utilizes the same spacing and is often used to prepare a semi-finished copy.

At this point, when the copy format and fill-in lines have been determined, the test is keypunched and prepared for computer entry to produce finished copy for the printer. In the meantime, artwork can be developed for the letterhead using up to four colors, one of which normally is used for the signature.

Ordering Continuous Forms

Since computer letters are usually one-ply control punched forms, more care is required in the layout and the printing than with traditional business forms. This states the obvious, but for good reason: the quality of the printing and the print-out on the computer letter can spell the difference between the success and failure of a program in which the forms are a small portion of the total cost.

Here are some guidelines to follow in working with forms suppliers for preprinted letters:

Letterhead—The letterhead can be a company's regular stationery design or a special letterhead for a particular promotion or campaign. The latter, particularly, offers possibilities for three or four color printing as well as process printing. The cost of process printing on a normal business form is sometimes considered prohibitive.

In computer letter applications, however, the cost becomes less significant if the appearance of the letter will enhance the rate of response. On "fully typed" letters, the forms printer prints on the letterhead and the signature. This simplifies the design job but emphasizes the need to consider something extra in the way of heading design suggestions.

Address, Date, Body, and Salutation—The most important consideration in these areas on a "fill-in" computer letter is to have the printed parts of the letter match as closely as possible the personalized data printed out by the computer. This requires care and close cooperation between the forms salesman and the data processing department manager or service bureau in charge of the high speed printer.

Each type of printer produces different results, has different settings, and different operators working under different conditions. These are all factors in producing a satisfactory computer letter and the customer and printer should both be aware of them. The following procedures should produce the desired results:

1. Since the printout of the high speed printer cannot be type set, the computer must furnish "copy" for the constant information that will be printed on the form. This copy is actual printout from the computer, spaced exactly as it will be on the finished product. The plant will "shoot" this copy and also use it to match the density and appearance of the printing.

The customer should do the following preparation of copy for the forms printer:

a. Print the copy the plant is to shoot on the same paper as will be used for the actual order.

b. Record the printer setting so that it can be used as a guide when the actual order is run.

c. Use the same type of ribbon as will be used in the actual run. The customer should understand that ribbon-life will have a bearing on the match of the computer printing to the form printing. Ribbon-life should be shortened to about 50% of its normal life and the printout samples should be run at that point in a ribbon's life. The customer may want to test the variance in results from ribbon wear by running a sample printout on blank forms. Computer centers who have been involved in this activity will have a better appreciation of this problem. In either case, a proper test is necessary—it could mean the success or failure of a job.

d. A minimum of 6 sample printouts should be furnished to the plant.

2. Prepare a layout chart using all standard layout practices. It is important to identify where the plant is to position the printout copy furnished by the customer since this must line up exactly with the information to be entered from the high speed printer later. Exact and complete strike lines must also be furnished.

3. If possible, don't mix preprinting with printout from the high speed printer on the same line. If you do, the difference between the two is more apparent to the eye. Rather than mixing the two types of printing, enter the entire line from the high speed printer.

4. Some letters contain information which is underscored for emphasis. Be sure such information appears only in the preprinted portion of a letter. Unlike a typewriter, the high speed printer cannot print a line and then go back and underline it.

5. Many computer letters are mailed in a window envelope. Be sure that the position of the address on the form matches the window.

6. Be sure to consider the final size of the letter to be mailed. Because of the personalization aspect, most customers do not want perforated edges on their letters. Margins can be trimmed but the top and bottom of the letter must be chopped off on a bracket trimmer to eliminate the perfed edge. This reduces the length of the form.

7. Letters can be designed one, two, or three-wide for better efficiency on the computer. Be sure that there are enough print positions available from the high speed printer to cover the width of your design. For example, on a 132 position printer only 13.2 inches can be printed.

Forms Specifications

Computer letter forms requirements vary widely according to the specific requirements of a customer. Specifications available from most forms printers will generally cover all requirements. The most common specifications required for computer letters follow.

Form Size

Form length—most popular is 11 inch—run on a 22 inch cylinder—Some printers have 18 inch to 28 inch or other diameter which will handle different lengths on a 2, 3, or 4 deep run. Excess paper costs and trim cuts may be required for uneven multiples of cylinder diameters.

Form width—will vary from 9½ inches for letters run 1-up on the printer to over 16 inches for letters to be run more than 1-up. The width of most forms after they have been trimmed will vary from approximately 7 inches to 8½ inches.

Paper Types

The recommended papers to use for computer letters are:

1. 20 lb. Bond White
2. 24 lb. Bond White (Preferred)
3. 20 lb. Globe White
4. 24 lb. Globe White
5. 24 lb. Offset White

Ink Colors

Most printers have standard ink colors which can often be used. However, due to the promotional nature of this product, the customer will often require a special or commercial ink match. Samples of what is desired should be submitted and proofs pulled.

Number of Colors

Most computer letters utilize 3 or 4 ink colors. Most often 1 or 2 colors will be printed on the face and 1 or 2 on the back. If more than 4 ink colors are required on 11 inch length forms, the choice of printer may be more limited. In the U.S. there are some 8 color forms presses.

Perforations

Interior perforations, for coupons, etc., are often necessary. The interior perforations available on most litho presses are generally satisfactory for this requirement.

Composition

In addition to the typed or computer filled-in material, most of the composition is promotional in nature and generally supplied by the customer's art or promotional departments. In some cases process printing is required. Consult the technical section of the forms producers.

Additional details on computer formats are included on page 502 and in Chapter 27.

Other Computer Uses

Program planning, lists and computer letters are by no means the only direct mail applications of the computer. Other applications fall under the general heading of "Management Information Services," a term frequently used to describe broad-scale business use of computers. The scope of such applications was described in detail by Michael J. Fields of Information Services Incorporated:[10]

> "Basic information sources are inquiries and sales leads. An inquiry, for example, could lead to a quotation, which in turn is a sales order, lost business, no bid situation or is turned over for budgetary analysis. Product inquiries could also take a variety of forms, deriving from space ads, editorial matter, direct mail or trade shows.
>
> "Likewise, sales leads come from external sources such as trade publications, trade directories or list brokers. Or they could originate internally: from field call reports, marketing reports and sales force reports. These are the basic sources of all marketing information, regardless of what they lead to. They can be qualified, and qualitative judgment can be applied.
>
> "On a quantified basis, this information can be sorted, sifted and put into a computer—where it becomes the source for the creation of a data base. By applying various types of criteria from the output, various types of marketing reports can be generated. For example, how is the company performing relative to competition? (Whom are we getting business from, whom are we losing it to, why, where is it shifting, etc.)
>
> "In the area of applications, the same information pertains. Likewise for customers this year, who shows the most gain, where is the business coming from, where is it leading to in terms of territory or product, what is the effect of promotion on the type and number of leads, how are our ads doing, whom are we losing business to, how effective is our sales coverage, how realistic are our quotas and our forecasts? And so on.
>
> "Inquiry qualification is of equal importance to marketing managers. It can cost just as much to chase a bad lead as a good one, and the total cost of the product reflects at least in part the effectiveness of the method by which a company decides its marketing priorities. The reports on which those priorities are based can come from samples, catalogs, booklets, questionnaires, labels and letters. This might lead to a very effective lead development system—premiums, catalogs, samples, letters and labels are various by-products."

Lead Development and Follow-up

How a computerized management information system lends itself to a lead development and follow-up communications system for industrial marketing was also described by Mr. Fields:

[10]"New Image for Computers in Direct Marketing" by Michael J. Fields, *Direct Marketing*, June 1970

"Input includes general customer and sales information, inquiries, sales leads, normal maintenance, or further qualification information from various responses. All this information is keystroked, formatted and sorted, processed through input, and becomes a part of the system's updated data base.

"Additional information could come from the outside in the form of purchased data base input, the old data base master merged in with the new in the update process, etc. The marketer is now in the position, regardless of what he wants to do, of having access to all the types of report he might need—from one place.

"Let's suppose that what the marketer wants at this point is an inquiry qualification system. He takes the tape output—or the computer does—and it is sorted by qualification code, and then by qualification record. It is interpreted, and various types of communications are generated: these can be a series of letters, for example, or labels, samples, catalogs, booklets or questionnaires. This gives the user the basis for qualifying his marketing information as a part of the very process of incorporating it into his data base.

"Sales lead information is processed and normally two follow-ups are generated. Reports are recorded on the results of the first follow-up; if the lead has potential it is followed further; if not, it becomes inactive and is returned to the data base for computerized follow-up #2. If there is a potential for a sale, the salesman enters it in his "tickler" file.

"In turn, if there is no immediate sale it goes into the salesman's suspense file for further follow-up on subsequent appropriate dates. The second part of the sales form then reports back on whether there has been a sale: if not, the lead is maintained in the inactive part of the data base; if there is a sale, it is maintained instead by the salesman in his own customer file.

"Another important aspect of this system is shown in the manner in which it takes old data—the old cumulative report information in this example—and processes it, updating it with new cumulative report information.

"As status reports come due periodically, it is possible to generate various types of marketing reports. For example, the user can ask for reports on sales leads not followed up within 30 days; now the advertising manager, the marketing manager or the promotion manager has an effective tool for determining whether the optimum use is being derived by the field force from information they have spent time and money to develop. Similarly, the system lets the user know when call-backs are due.

"An equally important series in the general marketing reports is in the form of a breakout showing sales lead follow-ups, product acceptance or promotion evaluation by competition, or by application, or by customer, territory, product promotion or media (specific ads). On an even more sophisticated plane, [the system] can show the effectiveness of these various efforts on the basis of product response patterns; it can tell the user, for example, how often the lead makes this type of inquiry, why, what he inquires after, his degree of interest in a specific product, etc: It can also analyze responses by the size of the order telling the user whether he is hitting the right market, whether he should be concentrating on small orders in a broad-base business as opposed to a more restrictive type of market situation.

"The sales manager can derive over-all reports on the productivity of products, salesmen and areas. He can measure penetration of markets, or the extent of follow-up to the introduction of new products. He can decide whether the product should be redesigned—or if the advertising program should be redirected."

The Computer and Mail Order

In mail order marketing, the computer has taken over hundreds of functions which formerly were handled by handwork or less sophisticated equipment. One of the pioneers in extensive computerization of its mail order operations was Figi's Inc., a Wisconsin cheese company. Joseph E. Fouts, Figi's data processing manager, describes how the computer serves the company's needs:[11]

"We do payrolls, checks, bank reconciliations, 941's, W-2's in a couple of hours. We also do accounts receivable, inventory, mailing list analysis by zip code, and by the mailing list code on the order form.

"We can print address labels, one-up, two-up, four-up, or five-up: We do zip coding with the computer. We print shipping labels. We load trucks. We calculate cubic feet. We do gift forecasting. We also do service bureau work for other companies.

"The first Monday after mailing, we pick up our mail at the Post Office at about 7:15 a.m., and weigh it to know how many orders we have. The mail is brought down to the plant, slit on a letter opener, and sorted six ways.

"The girls open the letter and clip the check to it. (A lot of companies remove the check immediately—we do not.) They sort the mail into various categories; rush order, Christmas order, foreign order, charge order, special dated order, or inquiry. After this, the mail is picked up by girls that we call 'recorders.'

"These girls assign an order number to that particular order then take off the check, and do a fast edit to be sure the order was intended for our company and if the dollar amount looks reasonable. In 1968, we had girls checking each order quite thoroughly. We took that job away from them and gave it to the computer. We've more than doubled the speed of our recorders. They now record approximately 90 orders an hour against 44 previously.

"Next we go to the keypunch department. The first thing we keypunch is the acknowledgement to the buyer, with the mailing list code and order number. From this point on, we're a little bit different from other companies who mail back to the buyer.

"We are also mailing to gift recipients—so we keypunch a greeting to each individual. We will keypunch four different greetings, if the customer has indicated such. We also keypunch each name and address the buyer wants a gift sent to. While doing this we pick up the quantity, the gift, the gift number, and the date it is to be shipped.

11"Cheese Manufacturer Molds Computer Mail Order Complex" by Joseph E. Fouts, *Direct Marketing*, November 1970.

"From here the information goes onto computer card to tape, with the computer checking city and state. If the keypunch operator has typed the city wrong, the computer will look up the zip code provided the zip code was given. If the zip code was given, it will plug in the correct spelling of that particular city.

"Also, while it is checking the zip code, if the zip code was not given and the city was given correctly, it will assign the zip code. As the order goes through, we check the dollar amount of every gift, and all the extensions of every order. We also assign a truck route to each gift.

"We send trucks all over the United States. Every truck will carry approximately 7,000 packages. We load a truck in Marshfield, drive it out to San Francisco, and the gifts we mail from there bear the San Francisco postmark. We bring in the meter heads from various cities.

"The computer will also calculate the cubic footage of each particular gift and all the gifts going on to that particular truck. When a truck has 1500 cubic feet, the computer will throw a flag up and say, 'The truck is loaded, what do I do now?' Then we will either have an alternate route for remaining packages or send another truck to that city. Along the same lines, when it is checking gifts, the computer will throw a flag and say: 'Sorry, we don't have this gift. 'This is a particular gift you drop shift from another area. Watch out for this one.'

"The computer also flags membership gifts. We want to catch these because they are written in long hand to give a personal touch. Also, when all the packages are going out, we are taking inventory, and when we start to run low on a particular gift, the computer will throw a flag. It will give us a count of how many have been sold, and what our estimates and our forecasts are for that particular gift.

"For every order that is keypunched, we print out what we call an 'edit list,' which is an exact copy of a shipping label, except it is printed on stock form green bar paper. These edit lists are given to girls who actually sit down and hand check that order back against the edit list to see if everything is correct. The errors they find are marked in red, the errors are corrected in the keypunch department, and they again go back to the computer for correction. Our percentage of accuracy in our order processing is about 99.6%

"Labels are printed from the computer after they have been checked. We print labels daily that have special shipping dates on them. We take the labels to a postage meter machine, and the computer has told us that gift number one takes $1.05 postage, and that it is for zone 3 out of San Francisco. We put $1,05 on each shipping label for gift #1 to zone 3. From there, everything goes to the shipping department, the shipping label is put onto the package, out it goes into a truck and it's on its way."

TYPICAL MARKETING INFORMATION INCLUDED IN COMPUTER DATA FILES

Prepared by Michael J. Fields of Information Services Incorporated

- Sex
- First Name & Initial
- Last Name
- Suffix
- Title
- Company Name
- Company Prefix
- Dept., Division, Maildrop
- Street Address
- City or Town
- State or County
- Zip Code
- Sales Territory
- Product
- Application
- Inquiry Source
- Follow Up
- Follow On
- Position (Job Function)
- Date of Original Entry
- Market
- Sales Literature
- Customer/Prospect/User
- Date of Qualification
- SIC Number
- List
- Quotation
- Quotation Disposition
- Dollar Amount
- Units
- Model/Part Number
- Credit
- Competitor

Ink Jet Imaging

The computer is the key element in the latest form of personalization of direct mail pieces—ink jet imaging. At this writing there are two basic systems in use—Mead Dijit and Laser Printing with IBM's 3800. These highly flexible systems make it possible to have personalizations in a wide variety of different typefaces of varying sizes and weights—something which wasn't possible with regular computer printing.

In many cases, the use of dramatic personalization made possible by ink jet imaging has resulted in substantial increases in response. One catalog, for example, which used Mead Dijit personalization on the cover, pulled twice the number of orders in a test against a "normal" catalog with simple computer letter personalization.

Because the technology in this field is evolving so rapidly, it is recommended that an advertiser survey currently available services before planning an ink jet personalization program. One good source of information is to review the advertisements in a current issue of *Direct Marketing* magazine.

Chapter 19

STANDARDS FOR COMPUTERIZED MAILING LISTS

AS computers began to dominate the direct mail list field, the Direct Mail/Marketing Association recognized the need for developing a set of standards for the industry. A committee under the chairmanship of Allen M. Greer of McGraw-Hill Publications Company spent many months on the project and its work resulted in a set of detailed guidelines which were released in 1970.

As the computerization of mailing lists continued to grow and new computer technology entered the picture, a DMMA committee composed of Arthur Blumenfield of Blumenfield Marketing, Robert K. Sher of Marketing Electronics Corporation and John E. McNichols of The Alan Drey Company—all leading authorities in list computerization—prepared a revised set of standards, which were issued in 1977.

These Standards for Computerized Mailing Lists are widely accepted as the basic guidelines for all direct mail users and are presented here through the permission of DMMA.

Introduction

The computer has been recognized as a valuable tool in the development and maintenance of direct mail lists. It has also been recognized that if the computer is to continue to play a vital role in our business, certain standards for uniformity in editing and formating are necessary to enable us to perform such functions as matching (merging) and purging and computer letters, or to use whatever technology will be developed in the future. This represents an attempt to update standards that could apply to computerized mailing lists and which were originally promulgated in 1971. In addition to editing standards, recommendations also appear relating to the lengths of records and match code extractions. It is felt that if these areas can be standardized, we can better promote exchange of computerized lists with a minimum of special programming and clerical intervention to make records compatible.

Even though the report of the Privacy Protection Study Commission will not be issued until the summer of 1977, we anticipate that the owners of mailing lists should be prepared to eliminate certain names and addresses. Therefore, anything that will facilitate this enforced elimination will be valuable to **all** mailers.

Standard editing means simply preparing input of names and addresses in a consistent manner so that extractions and comparisons can be made using similar information. Bear in mind that the computer has no way of interpreting information that appears on your files. If it reads the word "Box," it accepts it as simply that. It does not interpret this to mean the same as "Post Office Box" such as the human mind might do when reading. Therefore, the input must be consistent to be properly identified. Once there is this consistency, match codes can be developed using like information and duplicates can be located. A side benefit of standardization is improved deliverability. It is our objective to provide you with sufficient standards to promote uniformity in comparing computerized mailing lists.

While we are hopeful the industry will subscribe to these standards, this is not an attempt to dictate methods of maintaining computer lists. We recognize there will be exceptions and not all users will find all of these rules fit their specific needs. When such exceptions are necessary, it is important here, too, you be consistent and properly document any exceptions to your editing standards. **The key to good computer procedure is documentation.** As long as a list is properly documented, the exceptions can be handled with a minimum amount of difficulty.

We have included in this report a section dealing with computer list security. It is our intention here to recommend methods of insuring against illegal duplication and sale of lists being maintained on magnetic tape or disk. Naturally, we are very concerned with this problem as an objective of this report is to provide a system which will encourage greater exchange of lists. List owners must feel that their lists are secure if we are to better promote such exchange.

DMMA instituted Mail Preference Service several years ago. It is a voluntary program which enables consumers who wish to receive less mail advertising to have their names removed from as many mailing lists as possible. MPS also has an Add-On feature for those consumers who wish to have their names added to particular types of mailing lists, such as hobbies, gardening, etc. All owners and users of mailing lists are encouraged to participate in this national program as an effective means of satisfying the consumer's desire to receive mail advertising which is meaningful to him/her and the need of direct response advertisers to target to the proper audience.

DMMA welcomes your comments regarding the contents of this report as we are most anxious to make this study as useful to the direct marketing industry as possible.

List Security

We suggest the implementation of the following rules to counter improper or illegal use of mailing lists on magnetic tape.

Detection

There is only one way to detect the fact your list has been used for an unauthorized mailing—"seeding" (another term is "salting") the list. This is simply to plant unique versions of names of real people throughout the list so these people will receive any unauthorized mailing and report it to you.

Seeding a list should be standard everytime the list is duplicated. It should be routine **whether the list is let out of your hands or not.**

Many firms use a system of seeding lists which calls for a variety of spellings of a name to identify the use. The real name may be "John J. Jones" but is seeded in the list as "Jahn J. Jones." Another method of seeding is the placing of identifying numerics directly after the surname or in the street address. For example: Thomas Lincoln Taft **101** or 230 Main St., Apt. **101.**

Seeding should be done as part of the duplicating process. While duplicating a house list for outside use, a simple program (which can be easily changed for each job) can be put on the computer at the same time. When the ZIP Code of the seed name is reached, it is inserted in the list.

This "seeding while duplicating" procedure has certain advantages over names that are permanently seeded in a list. If you are sample selecting on an nth name, ZIP Code, or alpha character basis, there is a random chance the seeded names will be by-passed.

The list of seeded names and the procedure should have management control. Whatever the procedure, the cards or program should be in the possession of the data center manager. It should be his **personal** responsibility to process the seeding program.

Discouraging Theft

In most cases the list thief acts on the opportunity rather than creating it. He may misunderstand the methods of detection or he prefers not to think about it. There is every possibility he can be discouraged if reminded about a few things. Here are four steps we can take to discourage list theft.

(1) Every reel of magnetic tape should have a small (1½″ x 1¼″) bright red sticker, which reads:

> **CAUTION**
>
> The names on this reel have been seeded to detect unlawful duplication and sale of this list.

(2) Each computer center should brief the entire staff on the value of lists, the practice of seeding, and the care and handling of lists. In other words, the computer center should be **security conscious.**

(3) Each computer center should institute control procedures as outlined below for the prevention of "accidental misuse." These procedures should be compatible with the facilities at the same time they prevent free and easy access to tapes.

(4) Each computer center that has instituted proper security measures should publicize them to put list owners more at ease and encourage the exchange of lists.

Some few list owners require a signature on a "warranty" type of form. This is a good practice, but a better method might be a voluntary statement from the computer center of the security procedures followed. Such a statement should outline the procedure for receipt, storage during inactive periods, and access to the tapes, as well as a general concern with security and the prompt return of tapes.

Accidental Misuse or Loss

The accidental violation of list security is the result of careless work. We will deal here with some means various list handlers use to prevent it.

Shipper:

1. **Every reel going out of the center should have a permanent label on it with the name and address of the center on it and an identification number.**
2. **In addition, every reel going out of the center should have a semi-permanent label on it identifying the job, the date of production, an order number and a sequence number.**
   Any time you send a reel of tape out of your office, it should be tagged with labels (pressure sensitive are most convenient) which have the following information:
   a. The name of your company.

b. The address to which the tape is to be returned.

c. The identification of the file that is on the tape (in terms that the recipient will understand, not in terms of your internal list codes).

d. The quantity of names on the file, or the approximate quantity.

e. The track and density that the tape was written in.

f. The record and block size.

Many companies find it advisable to put an additional label with their name and address on the back of the reel so the recipient will know whose reel he has even if the front label is inadvertently removed.

3. Strictly maintain a log sheet of all outgoing reels. Record all of the data on the reel plus date shipped, destination, the carrier and shipping number.

4. Always send the tapes via a method which can be traced—registered mail or air carrier. Insure each reel.

With these simple rules you can control your outgoing lists. Here is what you can do as the receiver of lists on tape.

Receiver:

1. All incoming tapes are funneled unwrapped to one person (tape librarian) who maintains a log of all incoming tapes.

2. The reel should be tagged with your identifying information. If you have a system of internal job numbers, you should label the reel accordingly.

3. The reels should be kept in a central location. There is no need for a tape to ever be in anyone's office. If a tape is not to be used for some time, it should be stored in a secure location that is under lock and key.

4. Always return the tapes promptly to the shipper. Two weeks after the completion of a job is reasonable time to keep a tape as back up for any errors.

5. Tapes to be returned should be logged out on the same sheet that was used to record receipt. Record the date, carrier, etc., and send it via a method that can be traced.

With these simple rules you can save yourself from misplaced tapes, processing errors, and the costs of replacing lost reels. You can save the shipper the expense of correspondence or calls after errant tapes and many more headaches.

We believe that the accidental violation of list security is one of the main reasons list owners are reluctant to let their lists out on magnetic tape. The nine rules outlined above go a long way to avoiding mistakes. Unlabeled and uncontrolled tapes are like the beans in the apothecary jar—after awhile they all look the same, and that's when you stop counting them.

FIELD SIZE

Field size or space allocated for the various parts of the name and address data may vary, depending upon the needs and desires of the list owner. In most instances, list rental is a secondary use of a given list, the primary use being customer record keeping.

This is not an attempt to dictate what the field size should be, nor its relative position in a tape record. The list owner is the best judge of his particular needs for his primary use; however, adequate documentation and definition of field size is quite necessary if the list is to be used by someone else.

There are a number of factors to consider when determining field size, and the emphasis placed upon each of these should depend upon the list owner. Specifically we should resolve these questions:

1. **How much information should be carried in the name and address for effective selling?**
   - **a Should we carry prefix titles such as MR, MRS, MISS and the host of military and other titles?**
   - **b. Should we carry suffix titles indicating professional status? (MD, DDS, etc.)**
   - **c. Do we want to carry first name and middle initial as well as the surname, or should we arbitrarily drop first names and carry only the initials?**
   - **d. Should we abbreviate city names? Will PHILADELPHIA PA 19124 or PHIL PA 19124 affect the use of the list?**
   - **e. Do we need building, industrial park, or company name in the address beyond what is required for adequate mail delivery?**
2. **Before going further in establishing field sizes, it is best to research our present lists to find out exactly what elements of the name and address we presently have, taking into consideration future requirements.**

Research of what we have should clearly indicate what we should provide for in establishing field size. It might be quite desirable to provide for suffix titles of respect if the information is available. Additional research into the number of characters in first name, surname, prefix and suffix titles, house numbers, street names and city names can be most useful.

Once we have determined what name and address data we want to carry, there are a couple of choices as to how it can be accommodated on magnetic tape.

Fixed Field

Each component is carried in a predetermined field and cannot exceed in length the number of characters or tape positions allotted. For example, four positions might be alloted to prefix title, eight to first name and fourteen to surname. Data could not exceed these alloted positions.

Variable Field

Data are carried one field after another and a unique, defined character is used to separate and identify each of the components. The total field must be fixed, but the elements within it are in free form. This can be illustrated by example:

@MR#JOHN JONES?1234 MAIN ST)
CRANBURY NJ 08512

Which technique to use is a matter of judgment, but most list owners use a combination of fixed and variable fields, in that each line (name, street, city, state and ZIP Code) is fixed in length but the information within it is variable. Some use the predefined characters to separate components and others, through disciplined input, build into their computer program the logic needed to separate the components.

If practical, you should consider keeping your data in fixed field format. Because this type of arrangement makes it very easy for both you and outside users to pick up, manipulate, and utilize your files, it is most often advantageous. Today's computers generally operate so fast that the extra few instructions needed to put together the separated fields so they appear properly on the label or letter are rarely noticed. However, many of the common usages to which name and address files are put are made much easier.

For example, duplicate identification, computer letters, and sorting of a file into alphabetical order all require the computer to be able to locate quickly and accurately the person's surname. If this is in a separate field, these applications are made much simpler.

The use of variable length record layouts with fields separated by special characters may help to squeeze more data onto a reel of tape, but the special programming required every time you or another user has to pull apart the record generally outweighs the advantages. In addition, the availability of higher density tape drives now make this technique relatively unnecessary.

3. What effect will field size have on computer processing costs? Theoretically speaking, the larger the field size and the more

data carried the higher the data processing costs will be because of greater tape usage and machine time. The size of the list is important in these cost considerations since a slight savings per name processed can multiply out to a significant dollar figure. However, the cost of the time required to unscramble or decode data must also be considered.

Carefully weigh the cost factors as they relate to field size, but keep them in their proper perspective.

4. **Input preparation via keypunching, scanner typing or any other means translates to direct costs. Here, as in data processing costs, we should evaluate the effect of carrying greater or less information in the name and address field.**

   Generally speaking, the fewer keystrokes needed to prepare input, the lower the cost, but again cost estimates should be developed for different amounts of data commensurate with volume and the results evaluated.

5. **Most computer printers have the ability to print a maximum line length of 132 characters; therefore, to maximize output printing speed, name and address labels are usually printed in sets from west to east (left to right). Using this technique, labels can be produced as 3, 4 or 5 across, and the label affixing equipment in use today can adequately accept and affix to envelopes or other material labels so printed.**

By making the name and address fields a length that will permit the maximum number of sets to be printed from west to east, we can optimize computer printing costs.

For example, if we used 30 characters for each line in the name and address set, the maximum number of sets (west to east) would be four (132 divided by 30 = 4, plus spacing between). If 23 characters are used for each line in the name and address set, the maximum number of sets would be five (132 divided by 23 = 5, plus spacing between).

The exact spacing requirements for the different types of label affixing equipment should be determined from the manufacturers, but usually two spaces between each set should be adequate. Using this standard, maximum field sizes for 3, 4 and 5 up labels would be as follows:

3 up	41 characters
4 up	30 characters
5 up	23 characters

Field sizes most common in the industry today were determined during the research done in preparation of this study. While not all-inclusive, it does offer a guide.

Address Component	Number of Characters Minimum	Maximum	Most Used
Name	20	30	23
Auxiliary Address Data	20	30	20 or 30*
Local Address (Street)	20	30	23
City, State and ZIP Code	20	30	23

*All fields were carried at either 20 or 30 characters.

Summary

Determination of field sizes should not be treated lightly, and all considerations should be properly evaluated and placed in their proper perspective. There is no substitute for careful thoughtful research.

Once again we would like to stress the importance of properly documenting whatever field size you determine best serves your needs.

MATCH CODE

Just as the human mind has the capacity to recognize like and unlike conditions, the computer can be programmed to recognize such conditions. By comparing various characters of a name and address record the computer can determine if they are alike and, therefore, are duplicates or if they are unlike and not duplicates. Comparing every character of the name and address to locate duplication is expensive in terms of computer time and is usually unnecessary to determine if records are alike. An extraction of key elements or characters from the file is sufficient to make comparisons for duplication or identification purposes. This abbreviated code is generally referred to as a match code.

There is no universal agreement between users of match codes as to which are the most significant characters to extract from a name and address. Lists differ in size and composition and individual needs also vary. With a customer list used for billing or fulfilling service, the match code may need to be "tight" for more positive identification. If a match code technique is used to compare lists for the purpose of purging duplicates for promotional mailing, the code might be "loose," to locate and eliminate a greater percentage of **possible** duplicates.

The one thing that must be kept in mind regarding match codes is that they depend upon consistency in order to operate. They expect to find the same characters in the same places in multiple versions of the same name and address. This means that if you have two different lists which were put together from different sources and using different editing rules, it is quite possible to generate different match codes for the same name and address.

The more sophisticated duplicate identification schemes all involve heavy use of standardizing routines which look for various versions of specific words in the addresses and convert them to one standard version. (For example, the routine would convert FIRST AVE., 1st Ave, 1 AVE, etc. to 1 AVE.) Once the standardization was done, the machine could then proceed with the extraction of the match code.

To further illustrate: extracting the first, third, and fourth letters from the surnames JOHNSON and JOHNSTON would yield the same code, JHN. If, in addition, we had extracted the sixth character, two different codes would result—JHNO for JOHNSON and JHNT for JOHNSTON—and the fact that these are not duplicates would have been recognized by the computer.

Regardless of how strong the match code, there will always be records that coincidentally have the same match code but are not duplicates. For example, a father and son with same given name living at the same address. As long as we recognize this possibility we can clerically assign an additional character to the match code, called a "tie-breaker," which would indicate these are legitimate duplicates.

To employ a match code successfully there are a couple of basic but important facts that should be recognized. They are:

(1) Input of name and address data must be disciplined so a consistent match code can be generated. If MC GRATH is sometimes input as MC GRATH (with a space) and other times as MCGRATH (without a space), the code extracted from this surname will not be consistent.

(2) The extraction code you use should be tested against a significant portion of your list to determine if it meets your requirements. If a percentage of unlocated duplication exists, is it acceptable?

The fields from which characters are extracted in most of today's match codes are as follows:

1. ZIP Code—As most mailers' files are in ZIP Code sequence, this provides a natural subdivision for customers.
2. Surname.
3. First Initial of Given Name—This overcomes the problem of sometimes having the full name and other times only the first initial.
4. House Number—As most addresses contain this, it further

isolates the customer. If the address is a BOX, that number frequently is used in place of the house number.

5. Street Name—Directionals (N. E. S. W) and compass points (NE, NW, SE, SW) are usually not included in an extraction from street name, but they can be if your needs require it. Filler or dummy codes are commonly used when there is no street name in the address.
6. Check Digit—This is usually one character and is developed by a mathematical calculation to determine if the match code was input or internally generated correctly.

The specific characters actually extracted for match codes vary according to the needs of the list owner. To illustrate, here are two examples:

(A)	Number of Characters
ZIP Code	5
Surname (1st, 2nd, and 4th characters)	3
First Initial	1
Street Number (3 low order digits)	3
Street Name (1st and 2nd characters)	2
Check Digit (number of characters in surname following extraction)	1

Example: **C**HARLES J **WI**N**T**ER
12351 PROSPECT RD
CLEVELAND OH **44136**

Code: **44136 WIT C 351 PR 2**

(B)	
ZIP Code	5
Surname (1st, 3rd and 4th characters)	3
First Initial	1
Street Number (3 high order digits)	3
Street Name (1st and 3rd characters)	2
Check Digit (internal formula)	1

Example: **C**HARLES J **W**I**NT**ER
12351 **P**R**O**SPECT RD
CLEVELAND OH **44136**

Code: **44136 WNT C 123 PO 4**

The Postal Service, in its program to speed mail handling through the use of optical character readers, is experimenting with an extraction code that would enable it to mechanically sort mail into carrier route sequence. Their initial technique will be to extract specific characters from house number, street name, city, state and/or ZIP Code, and imprint the code in phosphorescent ink on the back of the envelope. This type of extraction code will permit mechanical sorting and greatly improve mail handling by the Postal Service.

It can be seen that match codes and USPS extraction codes are quite similar in principle, the only difference being what characters are extracted. As long as computerized name and address data are disciplined according to some type of fixed rules, a match or extraction code of almost any structure can be developed through computer programming at reasonable expense.

The match code you employ should be constructed on the basis of your own particular requirements. How strong or weak a code you use or what segments of the mailing address you select should depend on your list maintenance and marketing plans.

PREFIX AND SUFFIX TITLES

Exhibits B and C at the end of this report list some of the common prefix and suffix titles, and we recommend one of the two options, but be certain you **document** which option you exercise.

1. Carry the prefix or suffix in the name field, but separate from the name with a non-print designator.

Source	Edit
CAPT J A SMITH	CAPT?JA SMITH
ENSIGN JAMES JONES, JR	ENS?JAMES JONES?JR

2. Carry the prefix and suffix in separate fields.

Source	Edit
CAPT J A SMITH	**CAPT** JA SMITH
ENSIGN JAMES JONES, JR	**ENS** JAMES JONES **JR**

Sex

Introduction of a code to identify sex is highly desirable; however, it need be used only when the list is mixed.

A suggested code is:

M Male
F Female
U Undetermined
B Business

Numeric codes could be used if desired, but be certain you **document** what code structure you use.

RECOMMENDED EDITING RULES

The material presented here has been developed after a complete review and analysis of editing rules submitted by various members of the direct mail industry. It represents what is felt to be a logical manner of carrying name and address data, as well as the easiest to input.

No attempt has been made to develop keying symbols for various components since varying input means may be used. In addition, some concerns may find it more advantageous to themselves to separate and identify components via computer programs.

A. Individual Name

1. Given name(s) and surname

a. Carry given name followed by a space, then surname.

Source	Edit
JOHN SMITH	JOHN SMITH

b. If two given names, carry first name and convert second name to an initial. Space between each segment.

Source	Edit
JOHN ALBERT SMITH	JOHN A SMITH

c. If three given names, drop third name, carry first name and convert second name to an initial. Space between each segment.

Source	Edit
JOHN ALBERT GEORGE SMITH	JOHN A SMITH

2. Given name(s), initials and surname

a. Carry given name, space, initial, space, then surname.

Source	Edit
JOHN A SMITH	JOHN A SMITH

b. If given name followed by two initials then surname, drop the second initial and carry given name, space, first initial, space, then surname.

Source	Edit
JOHN A G SMITH	JOHN A SMITH

c. If one initial preceding given name, carry as shown with one space between first initial and given name.

Source	Edit
J ALBERT SMITH	J ALBERT SMITH

d. If one initial preceding two given names, drop second given name but carry first initial.

Source	Edit
J ALBERT GEORGE SMITH	J ALBERT SMITH

e. If two initials preceding one given name, drop second initial and carry given name.

Source	Edit
J A GEORGE SMITH	J GEORGE SMITH

3. **Initial(s) and surname only**

a. Carry one initial followed by a space, then surname.

Source	Edit
J SMITH	J SMITH

b. Carry two initials, with no space between, space then surname.

Source	Edit
J A SMITH	JA SMITH

c. If three initials, drop third initial and carry first two initials, with no space between, space, then surname.

Source	Edit
J A G SMITH	JA SMITH

4. **Surname only**

Carry Ms. or Mr. depending upon the nature of the list or source involved. If Mrs. is used, carry as given. How the prefix is to be carried is a matter of individual judgment, but the consistent means of identifying should be documented. A suggested way would be to precede Mr., Miss, Ms. or Mrs. with a non-print symbol.

Source	Edit
JONES	?MS JONES or ?MR JONES
MRS JONES	?MRS JONES

5. **Compound Surnames**

Compound surnames are difficult to handle and we have, therefore, recommended a number of options. Any one of these options may serve to identify a compound surname but **be certain you document** which option you exercise, and only apply one form of the option to a list.

a. **Designators**—place non-print designator between the compound parts of the surname.

Source	Edit
R MC CARTHY	R MC?CARTHY
S VAN DER LEE	S VAN?DER?LEE

b. **Close up**—carry with no space between the compound parts of the surname.

Source	Edit
R MC CARTHY	R MCCARTHY
S VAN DER LEE	S VANDERLEE

c. **Separate Field**—establish two separate fields for surname, one for the first portion and one for the second part.

Source	Edit
A G MC CARTHY	AG **MC CARTHY**
S VAN DER LEE	S **VAN DERLEE**

Exception: Names with a prefix of Saint or ST will be abbreviated to ST and carried with non-print designator between the prefix and the main part.

Source	Edit
JOHN SAINT JOHN	JOHN ST?JOHN
JOHN ST JOHN	JOHN ST?JOHN

6. **Two word surnames**

Carry both names. If the source has a hyphen indicated, retain the hyphen. Do not add a hyphen if not present; however, you may add a non-print designator to identify that this is a two-word surname.

Source	Edit
JUAN LOPEZ-GARCIA	JUAN LOPEZ-GARCIA
JUAN RIVERA ROSARIO	JUAN RIVERA?ROSARIO

7. **Prefix title**

If prefix titles are carried, they should be identified in the record and conform to the abbreviation table.

8. **Suffix titles (status)**

1. If suffix titles are carried, they should be identified in the record and conform to the abbreviation table.
2. Occupational titles, if carried, should be identified as to record location. Abbreviations would depend upon the list compiler.

B. **Street Address (Local)**

1. **House Numbers**

a. **General**

1. Do not spell out house numbers, always use numeric form.

Source	Edit
TEN MAIN ST	10 MAIN ST

2. House number (if present) will be the first data field on the street line.

Source	Edit
10 MAIN ST	10 MAIN ST
MAIN ST 10	10 MAIN ST

b. Compound, All Numeric

Join both parts with a hyphen.

Source	Edit
14 10 MAIN ST	14-10 MAIN ST

c. Compound, Numeric and Alpha

1. Single alpha preceding the number— if not a directional (N, E, S, W), carry after the numeric portion with no space between.

Source	Edit
A 52 MAIN ST	52A MAIN ST

2. Single alpha following the number—if not a directional (N, E, S, W), carry as is with no space between.

Source	Edit
61 B MAIN ST	61B MAIN ST

3. If directional (N, E, S, W) preceding house number, move to position preceding street name.

Source	Edit
N 110 MAIN ST	110 N MAIN ST

4. If directional (N, E, S, W) following house number, leave a space between it and house number.

Source	Edit
110E MAIN ST	110 E MAIN ST
115 W MAIN ST	115 W MAIN ST

d. Multiple house numbers

Use only the first one.

Source	Edit
12, 14 MAIN ST	12 MAIN ST

e. House number with fraction following

Eliminate fraction at input.

Source	Edit
125½ MAIN ST	125 MAIN ST

2. Directionals

a. Prefix

Abbreviate directional words as follows, unless the

word is a street name. Separate from street name with one space.

North — N
East — E
South — S
West — W
Northeast—NE
Southeast — SE
Northwest — NW
Southwest — SW
Bay — BAY
Vista — VISTA

Note: Input abbreviated directionals in same relative position as received.

Source	Edit
150 NOTH MAIN ST	150 N MAIN ST
150 NORTH ST	150 NORTH ST

b. Suffix

Abbreviate same as prefix directionals. Carry one space after street designator.

Source	Edit
150 MAIN ST NW	150 MAIN ST NW

c. With single character street names

1. Prefix directionals should be abbreviated and separated from street name with a space.

Source	Edit
126 NORTH A ST	126 N A ST

2. Suffix directional (compass point), carry one space after street designator and abbreviate.

Source	Edit
130 A ST NORTHWEST	130 A ST NW

3. Street Names

a. Compound proper surnames

Carry as one word, i.e.: leave no space or apostrophe between prefix and main part (see two alpha words).

Source	Edit
720 O'BRIEN AVE	720 OBRIEN AVE

b. State, city or country name

Spell out completely only when you can positively identify the state, city or country.

Source	Edit
83 TENN AVE	83 TENNESSEE AVE
504 BALT BLVD	504 BALTIMORE BLVD
61 ENG RD	61 ENGLAND RD

c. **Numeric street**

1. Carry in numeric form, never alpha.

Source	Edit
27 FIFTH ST	27 5TH ST

2. Add suffix designator, with no space between, i.e.: ST, ND, RD, TH.

Source	Edit
281 34 ST	281 34TH ST
73 42 ND ST	73 42ND ST

d. **One alpha word**

Never abbreviate one word street names.

Source	Edit
910 GEN'L ST	910 GENERAL ST

e. **Two alpha words** (not an intersection)

1. Only the following prefix designators should be abbreviated:

Fort FT	Point PT
Mount MT	Saint ST

Source	Edit
29 FORT JAMES RD	29 FT JAMES RD
301 MOUNTAIN SLOPE ST	301 MOUNTAIN SLOPE ST

2. Second word should not be abbreviated except for those listed in 5a.

Source	Edit
809 BIG MOUNTAIN RD	809 BIG MOUNTAIN RD
710 WINDY POINT BLVD	710 WINDY PT BLVD

f. **Individual personal names** (memorial)

1. Spell out completely if known.

Source	Edit
285 JOHN F KENNEDY BLVD	285 JOHN F KENNEDY BLVD
285 JFK BLVD	285 JOHN F KENNEDY BLVD

2. If title and surname, abbreviate title according to standard abbreviations.

Source	Edit
11 GENERAL GRANT AVE	11 GEN GRANT AVE

g. **Intersections**

Separate the two street names with an ampersand with no space between.

Source	Edit
HERBERT & LEIGHTON STS	HERBERT&LEIGHTON ST

1. Two alpha street names—carry lowest alpha sequence first.

Source	Edit
LEEDS & HILL ST	HILL&LEEDS ST

2. Two numeric street names—carry lowest number first.

Source	Edit
48TH AND 3RD	3RD&48TH

3. Alpha and numeric—carry numeric street name first.

Source	Edit
MAIN & 5TH ST	5TH&MAIN ST

h. Single alpha letter street names

If street designator precedes a single character street name, reverse the order.

Source	Edit
21 AVE A	21 A AVE

i. Street names with designator preceding

Carry as given, except abbreviate designator.

Source	Edit
645 AVE OF THE AMERICAS	645 AVE OF THE AMERICAS

j. Prepositions

Drop all prepositions and connecting words not part of street name or number, such as: a, an, and, at, by, for, in, into, near, of, on, or, the, to, via, with, #.

Source	Edit
99 SOUTH ON SMITH ST	99 S SMITH ST

k. Fractions or units of measure

If the street name, do not abbreviate to numeric form.

Source	Edit
66 1 MILE RD	66 ONE MILE RD
66½ MILE RD	66 ONE HALF MILE RD

4. Street Designators

Should be abbreviated.

Source	Edit
10 HILL ROAD	10 HILL RD

5. Other local addresses

a. The following **abbreviations** will be used:

Address Contains	Edit as
BOX #, BOX, PO BOX, LOCK BOX, DRAWER, MAIN BOX, AVENUE BOX, ANNEX BOX, LOCAL BOX, BOX DRAWER, PO DRAWER, LD	BOX

RT, RTE, STAR ROUTE, OLD ROUTE, MOUNTED ROUTE, RD, NEW ROUTE, STATE ROUTE, ROUTE,	RT
RURAL ROUTE, RR	RR
RURAL FREE DELIVERY, RURAL DELIVERY, RD, DROP FREE, RURAL DELIVER	RFD
GENERAL DELIVERY	GEN DEL

b. **Combined addresses**

Only the most significant address should be carried and in the following order of preference. Note: Box number should always appear first and cannot be carried with a house number and street name.

(1) Box Number
(2) Street Address
(3) Route Number

Source	Edit
18 HILL RD BOX 15	BOX 15
ROUTE 22 BOX 801	BOX 801 RT 22
ROUTE 15 18 JONES AVE	18 JONES AVE
18 SMITH ST BOX 35 RT 6	BOX 35 RT 6

C. Auxiliary address information

This would be apartment, room number, building name, care of, non-street name locations such as: industrial park, rear of, near, etc. These data should be identified as to tape record location. It should be carried after the street name, but a designator (/) should precede it. The same editing rules that apply to street address should be applied to this auxiliary information.

D. City, State, ZIP Code

1. **City name**

   May be either spelled out completely or abbreviated according to Postal Service standards.

2. **State abbreviation**

   Use 2 character standard Postal Service abbreviation.

3. **ZIP Code**

   Use standard 5 character. If you operate in Canada, allow for 6 character Postal Codes.

4. **Punctuation and format**

   a. None should be used between city and state.
   b. Line format should be: City (space) State (2 spaces) ZIP Code.

STANDARD ABBREVIATIONS

An attempt has been made to list tables of standard abbreviations for street designations, common prefix and suffix titles. Occupational titles are excluded since they are beyond the scope of this study.

(EXHIBIT A) **Street Designation Abbreviations**

Designation	Abbreviation	Designation	Abbreviation
Alley	ALY	Junction	JCT
Arcade	ARC	Landing	LDG
Avenue	AVE	Lane	LN
Beach	BCH	Loop	LP
Boulevard	BLVD	Manor	MNR
Bypass	BYP	Park	PK
Causeway	CSWY	Parkway	PKY
Center	CTR	Pike	PKE
Circle	CIR	Place	PL
Concourse	CONCRSE	Plaza	PLZ
Court	CT	Ridge	RDG
Crescent	CRES	Road	RD
Dale	DLE	Route	RT
Drive	DR	Square	SQ
Expressway	EXPY	Street	ST
Extension	EXT	Terrace	TER
Freeway	FRWY	Turnpike	TPK
Grove	GR	Trail	TRL
Heights	HTS	Viaduct	VIA
Highway	HWY	Vista	VIS
Hill	HL	Way	WAY

(EXHIBIT B) **Prefix Title Abbreviations**

Title	Abbreviation
Adjutant	ADJ
Adjutant General	ADJ-GEN
Admiral	ADM
Airman	AMN
Airman 1st, 2nd, 3rd Class	A1C, A2C, A3C
Ambassador	AMB
Archbishop	ABP
Attorney General	AT-GEN
Bishop	BP
Brigadier General	B-GEN
Brother	BRO
Cadet	CDT
Captain	CAPT
Cardinal	CARD
Chaplain	CHAP
Chief Petty Officer	CPO
Chief Warrant Officer	CWO
Colonel	COL
Commandant	COMDT
Commander	CDR
Congressman	CONGRSMAN
Corporal	CPL
Doctor	DR
Duchess	DCHSS
Ensign	ENS
Father	FR
First Lieutenant	1LT
First Sergeant	1SGT
Fleet Lieutenant	FLT-LT
General	GEN
Governor	GOV
Group Captain	GP-CAPT
Honorable	HON
Judge	JDG
Lieutenant	LT
Lieutenant Colonel	LT-COL
Lieutenant Commander	LT-CDR
Lieutenant General	LT-GEN
Lieutenant Governor	LT-GOV
Lieutenant Junior Grade	LT-JG

(EXHIBIT B) **Prefix Title Abbreviations** (cont.)

Title	**Abbreviation**
Lieutenant Major	LT-MAJ
Major	MAJ
Major General	MAJ-GEN
Master	MSTR
Master Sergeant	MSGT
Mayor	MAYOR
Midshipman	MIDN
Miss	MISS
Mister	MR
Monsieur	M
Monsignor	MSGR
Most Reverend	MOST-REV
Mother	MTHR
Mrs	MRS
Petty Officer	PO
Private	PVT
Private First Class	PFC
Professor	PROF
Rabbi	RABBI
Rear Admiral	RADM
Reverend	REV
Reverend Mother	REV-MTHR
Reverend Mother Superior	REV-MTHR-SUP
Right Reverend	RT-REV
Seaman	SN
Seaman First Class	S1C
Seaman Second Class	S2C
Senator	SEN
Sergeant	SGT
Sergeant Major	SGM
Sister	SR
Specialist First Class	SP1
Specialist Fourth Class	SP4
Specialist Second Class	SP2
Specialist Third Class	SP3
Staff Sergeant	SSGT
Technical Sergeant	TSGT
Very Reverend	VY-REV
Vice Admiral	VADM
Warrant Officer	WO

(EXHIBIT C) Popular Suffix Title Abbreviations

Note: A complete compilation of abbreviations may be found in "Acronyms and Initialisms Dictionary," 5th Edition, published by Gale Research Company, Book Tower, Detroit, Mich.

Title	Abbreviation
Bachelor of Arts	BA
Bachelor of Science	BS
Certified Life Underwriter	CLU
Certified Public Accountant	CPA
Doctor of Dental Surgery	DDS
Doctor of Medicine	MD
Doctor of Philosophy	PHD
Fourth	IV
Junior	JR
Master of Arts	MA
Master of Science	MS
Retired	RET
Second	II
Senior	SR
Third	III
United States Air Force	USAF
United States Air Force Academy	USAFA
United States Army	USA
United States Coast Guard	USCG
United States Coast Guard Academy	USCGA
United States Marine Corps	USMC
United States Military Academy	USMA
United States Naval Academy	USNA
United States Navy	USN

See also ADDRESS ABBREVIATIONS, Publication 59 January 1976, United States Postal Service, Washington, D.C. 20260. This Publication should be available from your local postmaster.

GLOSSARY

Some of the terminology used in this presentation might be misleading, therefore, the items used are defined as follows:

DESIGNATOR	A symbol or character used to identify a particular piece of information or data.
NON-PRINT DESIGNATOR	A symbol of character that does not normally print on a computer system printer. The specific symbols vary from manufacturer to manufacturer, and even within a given manufacturer's system. Some common non-print symbols may be: ? () # ! □.
STREET DESIGNATOR	A word used to further identify a street name, such as Street, Avenue, Road, Place, etc.
PREFIX DIRECTIONAL	A word preceding street name that is used to identify the street by direction, i.e.: North, East, South, or West or combinations of these.
SUFFIX DIRECTIONAL	A word following street name that is used to identify the street by direction. Also known as compass point (NE, NW, SE, SW or N, E, S, W).
FIELD	A set of one or more characters; a unit of information.
COMPOUND SURNAME	A surname that is divided into two or more parts, but each part is not in itself a separate word.
TWO WORD SURNAME	A surname that is divided into two or more parts, but each part is a separate word.
PREFIX TITLE	A title of respect, military rank or professional status that precedes a person's name.
SUFFIX TITLE	An indicator of professional or other status that is placed after a person's name.

LIST OWNERS CHECK LIST FOR COMPUTER STANDARDS

The following check list is designed to help list owners identify the extent to which they comply to the DM/MA Standards for Computerized Lists.

I. Do you comply to the editing standards recommended for (check those rules you follow)?

A. Individual Name
- ☐ 1. Given name and surname
- ☐ 2. Given name, initials and surname
- ☐ 3. Initial and surname only
- ☐ 4. Surname only
- ☐ 5. Compound surnames
- ☐ 6. Two word surnames
- ☐ 7. Prefix title
- ☐ 8. Suffix title (status)

B. Street Address (local)

1. House Numbers
- ☐ a. General
- ☐ b. Compound, all numeric
- ☐ c. Compound, numeric and alpha
- ☐ d. Multiple house numbers
- ☐ e. House number with fraction following

2. Directionals
- ☐ a. Prefix
- ☐ b. Suffix
- ☐ c. With single character street names

3. Street names
- ☐ a. Compound proper surnames
- ☐ b. Numeric street
- ☐ c. One alpha word
- ☐ d. Two alpha words
- ☐ e. Individual personal names (memorial)
- ☐ f. Intersections
- ☐ g. Single alpha letter street names
- ☐ h. Street names with designator preceding
- ☐ i. Prepositions
- ☐ j. Fractions or units of measure

4. Street designators

C. City, State, Zip Code

II. Do you feel that the editing used in your list *substantially complies* to the Standards?

☐ **YES** ☐ **NO**

III. Is documentation available for all exceptions to the DM/MA Standards?

☐ **YES** ☐ **NO**

Chapter 20

MAILING LISTS

IN preceding chapters, the importance of mailing lists has been emphasized often. This is only logical since your lists are one of the most vital elements—in many cases *the* most vital element—in your direct mail program.

Unfortunately, however, lists are frequently given only secondary attention by many direct mail advertisers. An exception is the mail order field, where any successful advertiser quickly recognizes that the quality of his mailing lists can spell either life or death for his business. In fact, the factor which often distinguishes the successful mail order adman is his intimate knowledge of mailing lists.

To advertisers in other fields, mailing lists usually represent a departure from the nature of the rest of their business activities. As a result, lists frequently receive a back seat treatment—something to be given consideration only after creative effort has been expended on planning, designing, copy, formats, production and other activities.

Yet for real success in most any direct mail program, the same degree of creativity must be applied to the development, improvement and maintenance of mailing lists as is expended on any other element in the program. Just approaching the subject of lists in a mechanical way is seldom adequate.

Adapt Ideas From Other Fields

One of the best starting points for applying a creative approach to your mailing list is to consider the techniques used by direct mail advertisers in other fields. Most any kind of business, for example, can adapt mailing list techniques which have been developed by mail order advertisers.

Consider one of the cardinal rules of mail order list building—that those who have previously bought *by mail* represent much stronger prospects than any general list. And, even more important, those who have previously bought by mail *from you* represent your very best prospects for the sale of additional items. These basic precepts can easily be adapted by list builders in non-mail order fields. An industrial company might do well to concentrate on building a list of prospects who are known to make purchases through the same type of distribution channels he uses. And a retail store might easily decide to concentrate the greatest amount of direct mail advertising effort on its present customers, rather than diluting the available budget by also trying to reach too many who are still just prospects.

Even the mail order field can apply techniques which have worked successfully for industrial and retail advertisers. In Chapter 9 ("Retail Direct Mail") we discussed the highly effective "Circles of Convenience" list technique developed by Jerome B. Osherow. Here's a basic concept which has potential for adaptation by direct mail advertisers in every field.

The important point is to constantly search out new ideas and reconsider old ideas which can help make your lists more effective.

Rules of Thumb

While there are no hard-and-fast rules which can be applied to every mailing list, there is a number of "rules of thumb" which are well to keep in mind. It may turn out that they don't necessarily apply to your own list situation, but they should at least be considered.

The average list will change at least 25% each year. In Chapter 3 ("The Basic Elements of Direct Mail") we cited a number of statistics involving the movement of people from one place to another. They all add up to the fact that no mailing list ever is a static thing. Some lists will involve over 50% change each year (some, such as a list of high school seniors, will have almost 100% change, of course) and few will have less than 10% change.

A minimum of 10% of your direct mail budget should be allocated to list development and maintenance. This, of course, will vary depending upon the nature of your business and the total amount you are spending on direct mail. But there are very few direct mail advertisers who can afford to devote less than 10% of not only the actual dollars spent but also their time and creative effort to their lists.

Unless you have full-time list experts on your own staff, you will benefit from the utilization of outside consultants and service organizations. Even if you are convinced you have the finest mailing list ever developed, it is to your advantage to seek confirmation of your opinions from those who have made it their business to study and understand lists.

Responsibility for a mailing list should be delegated to a single individual. Nothing can ruin a mailing list faster than to allow control to be spread through too many hands. Usually, the best procedure is to spell out specific procedures for list handling and then place responsibility for seeing that these procedures are followed in the hands of a single person.

Don't take any list at face value—even your own. There is no such thing as a perfect list and the sooner you start approaching all lists with caution, the better off you will be. Mail order advertisers quickly learn that some of the poorest lists available are ones which have been developed by people and firms which have won wide recognition as top "mailing list experts." This is not to say that all lists are bad, nor that the majority of the recognized list experts have poor lists. But it always pays to do a thorough analysis of every list you plan to use—and that includes your own, which should be put to close scrutiny regularly.

Every list should be checked and cleaned not less than twice a year. While list maintenance should be a continuing process, a thorough review and updating should be done at least once every six months.

Use mechanical or computer addressing if you intend to make six or more mailings to your list. This is just a broad rule of thumb based on comparative costs of hand vs. mechanical or computer addressing. Many other factors will enter into the situation—the frequency of your mailings, the percentage of name changes, the quality of address you need, and so forth.

Take your mailing list seriously. This isn't a rule of thumb—it is a hard-and-fast rule.

SOURCES FOR MAILING LISTS

There are thousands of different sources from which you may obtain names and addresses for your mailing list. However, most of them fit within the 66 basic mailing list sources listed on page 533.

Sales Records

The primary list source for the majority of direct mail advertisers will be their own sales records. A check of purchase orders usually reveals a lot of important list information—companies, addresses, those who submit the order, those who approve the purchase, those to whom material has been shipped, size of order, frequency of purchase, type of merchandise ordered, and so forth.

Credit Records

Sometimes an even more basic list source is the company's credit records. Even if this source is not used as the list-building starting point, it is well to check credit records to eliminate undesirable names from your list. It makes little sense to promote your products or services to those who have established a bad credit record.

In the mail order field, people who have gone to the trouble to establish a credit rating with a company represent a particularly important mailing list. Many companies report that annual purchases from credit buyers are 2½ to 4 times larger than from cash buyers.

You may easily find it worthwhile to maintain a separate file of bad credit risks so such names can be quickly checked whenever new names are being added to your mailing list.

Shipping Records

Another internal list source is shipping records.

For many types of business, these records constitute a primary source for new names to be added to an already established list. In the mail order field, for example, the people to whom gift orders are shipped often represent extremely valuable prospects for future business.

In the retail field, shipping records are a highly valuable source of names for promoting the establishment of charge accounts. Some stores make it a regular practice to check every cash order against credit records to spot names for addition to promotion lists.

In the industrial field, shipping records sometimes constitute the only way to obtain names of customers from dealers, distributors, and other representatives.

General Correspondence

A regular check of all company correspondence will reveal many good names for most mailing lists. The first step, of course, is to re-

66 BASIC MAILING LIST SOURCES

Internal

1. Sales Records
2. Credit Records
3. Shipping Records
4. General Correspondence
5. Telephone Inquiries
6. Specific Requests
7. Salesmen's Call Reports
8. Sales Force Recommendations
9. Technical & Service Force Recommendations
10. Employee & Stockholder Recommendations
11. Guest Books
12. Dealer & Distributor Lists

Solicitations

13. Advertising Inquiries
14. Lead-Producing Publicity
15. Bingo Cards
16. Trade Show Registrants
17. Customer Recommendations
18. Contest Entries
19. Premium Offers
20. Sample Offers
21. Personal Contact
22. Western Union Survey Service
23. Special Direct Mail
24. Office Managers
25. Merchandise Stuffers
26. Product Registrations

Directories

27. Telephone Directories
28. "Yellow Pages"
29. Criss-Cross Directories
30. Community Directories
31. Business Directories
32. Industrial Directories
33. Chamber of Commerce Directories
34. Horizontal Directories
35. Million Dollar Directory
36. Credit Rating Books
37. Thomas Register
38. MacRae's Blue Book
39. Standard Advertising Register
40. Poor's Register
41. Who's Who
42. Social Registers
43. Association Membership Rosters

Compiled Lists

44. Labor Organizations
45. Religious Organizations
46. School Lists
47. Convention Registration Lists
48. Cultural Interests
49. Birth Lists
50. Alumni Lists
51. Voter Registration Lists
52. Contributors
53. Mail Order Buyers
54. Expires
55. Inquiry Lists
56. Automobile Lists
57. Home Owner Lists

Other

58. Trade & Consumer Publications
59. Federal Government Sources
60. Other Government Sources
61. Clipping Services
62. Local Post Offices
63. Business Services and Construction Reports
64. List Exchanges
65. List Compilers
66. List Brokers

view all inquiries which are received for information about your products and services. But other types of correspondence will also reveal good mailing list names, e.g., it is often well to review the correspondence files of your research, engineering, and purchasing departments.

Telephone Inquiries

An often overlooked source for mailing list material comes from telephone inquiries. Many companies make it a regular practice to require everyone handling such inquiries—particularly salesmen and clerks—to record all names and addresses along with basic information about the nature of the phone call. These records are then routed to the sales or advertising department for review and possible addition to the mailing list.

Specific Requests

An obvious source for new mailing list names is from those who make specific requests for literature, product information, price quotations, etc. Few direct mail advertisers can afford to neglect such important list potential.

Salesmen's Call Reports

If your salesmen are required to complete call reports, it is well to include space on the report forms in which the salesman can enter mailing list information. But even if such specific information is not included on the report forms, a check of call reports against the existing mailing list will generally turn up valuable new names.

Sales Force Recommendations

In many fields, the basic source for mailing list names is the sales force. The effectiveness of this list-building technique frequently depends upon how thoroughly salesmen are briefed on their responsibilities in list compilation. To obtain a good working list through sales force recommendations, it is well to explain very specifically just what type of names are wanted, how they are to be submitted, and what supporting material (such as product interests, buying and specifying responsibilities, and so forth) is desirable.

In most types of sales organizations, salesmen have a tendency to be somewhat lax in attention to detail. Therefore, it is well to develop some type of review procedure for all names and addresses submitted. It is also well to have some kind of program to remind salesmen of their responsibility in providing a continuing flow of new names for the list. Among the techniques which have been used successfully:

- One company makes it a regular practice to pay every salesman a cash amount for each name submitted. Minimum quotas are established and sales managers are directed to make sure each salesman meets his monthly mailing list quota.
- Another company which uses the mailing list quota system offers special bonuses for each salesman who beats his quota
- A somewhat similar technique is the use of trading stamps. A number of companies have adopted this method and send a certain number of trading stamps to the salesman (or, sometimes, his wife) for each name submitted. Frequently these are the same types of trading stamps (i.e., S&H Green Stamps, Plaid Stamps, Top Value Stamps, etc.) which are obtained from local stores, so the salesman can add his mailing list stamps to others he receives to obtain selected gifts. In other cases, companies develop their own stamp programs.
- List-building contests have also proved successful for a number of direct mail advertisers. Prizes go to those with the most accurate lists, those who have added the most names during a given period, those who beat specified quotas by the greatest percentage, and so forth.
- Mailing list bulletins are often used successfully as a method of impressing upon the sales force the necessity for continuing list-building and list-maintenance activity. One advertiser, who publishes a monthly list bulletin, includes a case history in each issue telling the story of some sale that was lost because a prospect was not on the mailing list . . . or how a sale was made as a result of direct mail promotion.

Technical and Service Force Recommendations

Even if the sales force represents the primary source for new mailing list names, do not overlook your technical and service personnel. They make regular contacts that can be converted into names for your list and often represent a better source for list-maintenance information than do salesmen.

Employee and Stockholder Recommendations

Many direct mail advertisers overlook an excellent source for mailing list names—their employees and stockholders. While such sources seldom can be the primary points of origination of a mailing list, the obvious interest of such individuals in the business welfare of a company makes it folly to overlook them.

Guest Books

Visitors to an office, plant, or store—particularly during special events such as tours, open houses, and so forth—are another excellent source for mailing lists. However, far less than one in a hundred direct mail advertisers have any established program for capitalizing on this list-building method. In many cases, such names represent a particularly potent list since a visit establishes a more personal relationship with the prospect.

One field where guest-book names have proved particularly valuable is in fund raising. Charitable institutions, schools, religious shrines, and other similar groups make it a point not only to get names and addresses of every visitor, but capitalize upon the situation by making immediate followup mailings.

Dealer and Distributor Lists

Many direct mail advertisers have dealers and distributors who maintain mailing lists which include names which should be on the advertisers' own promotion lists. Getting such names, however, often proves difficult. Some manufacturers include a provision for obtaining mailing lists as a part of their basic contract with dealers and distributors. But such an arrangement does not always produce the lists desired.

For many companies, the most successful approach to this problem is a strong promotional program which requires dealer-distributor cooperation for list development. If the dealers and distributors can be brought to recognize the benefits they will gain by participation, they usually are willing to cooperate.

In addition, many of the list-building techniques suggested for working with your own sales force can be applied to the program of getting lists from dealers and distributors.

Advertising Inquiries

For a large number of direct mail advertisers, the primary list-building system is to conduct a media advertising program which solicits inquiries. This is particularly effective in the mail order and industrial fields. In most cases, advertisers try to build some kind of qualification system in inquiry solicitation programs. There are four basic list qualifying methods:

1. *Make 'em pay*—Some advertisers require a modest payment for whatever they are offering to draw inquiries. The basic idea is that only those with a specific interest will respond. This technique is most often used by mail order advertisers who are soliciting requests for a comprehensive catalog. Unless experience has indicated that a high percentage of inquiries come from non-prospects, this qualification method should be approached with caution for it will not only eliminate most non-prospects but is likely to reduce returns from legitimate prospects who don't want to go to the bother of preparing a cash-accompanied request.

2. *Build qualifiers into the ads*—You can build qualifiers into your publication or broadcast ads. One of the most common techniques is to offer some piece of literature which will be of interest only to certain types of companies or individuals. Another technique is to request specific qualifying information such as requiring replies on a company letterhead or asking the respondent to list his position, types of products manufactured, possible applications of your product, and so forth. This approach is usually only partially successful since many respondents do not bother to follow your instructions, yet all inquiries should be serviced. Thus, it is often necessary to use this qualification method in conjunction with another qualifying technique.
3. *Delayed response*—This qualification technique involves sending only a "teaser" in response to the inquiry and then requesting some qualifying information before forwarding the "whole package." It is important to always send everything you have offered in your advertisement or make it highly simple for the respondent to furnish the qualifying information you request. The most frequently used approach is to inform the respondent that the information he seeks is available in a number of different forms and, in order to best serve his personal requirements, you would like to have the information which will enable you to select the items which best fit his needs.
4. *Followup by salesmen*—The most commonly used qualification system—except in mail order and fund raising—is to have salesmen handle the qualifying through personal contact. This technique has a number of drawbacks. First, salesmen dislike unqualified inquiries since they frequently involve a disproportionate amount of contact time for the direct sales which result. As a result, it is not uncommon for the average sales force to treat such inquiries as highly unimportant and spend very little time on qualifying. Second, many respondents will resent an uninvited sales call when they are expecting a reply by mail.

Several specific examples of inquiry qualification systems are described in Chapter 49—"Inquiry Handling."

Lead-Producing Publicity

Many direct mail lists are developed through responses to published publicity items. Business publications and shopper's guide sections of newspapers and consumer magazines provide particularly good opportunities to obtain publicity which will result in list-building inquiries.

"Bingo" Cards

The term "bingo card" is used to describe the business reply cards which some magazines include in their regular issues. Readers use these cards to request literature which has been described in the magazines. Normally, this is a free service of the publisher. The reader simply circles key numbers on the card. The publisher then takes these requests and sends them to the advertiser involved, who, in turn, sends the requested literature directly to those requesting it.

Like advertising leads, inquiries coming via bingo cards should be qualified before being added to a list for future mailings. It is probably even more important to qualify bingo-card leads since the number of respondents per publication is usually much higher (often by a ratio as high as 100 to 1) and thus more likely to include a greater percentage of curiosity seekers. The fact that it is so easy to request literature encourages responses from those who have no real interest but just think what you have "might prove to be interesting."

But even though there usually is a high percentage of remote prospects in any list coming via bingo-card response, it would be a serious mistake to treat all responses lightly. It is not unusual for readers of publications offering a reader-reply service to use it as their primary method of obtaining literature to serve immediate and future buying requirements. Many multithousand-dollar sales have developed as a result of a bingo-card inquiry.

Closely related to bingo cards is a new type of publication which is growing in popularity—a collection of individual business reply cards bound together and sent without charge to a list of individuals with a common set of interests. Unlike bingo cards, the reply card publications sell the individual reply units as advertising.

The advantages of the reply card publications are that the replies come directly to the advertiser and because each must be filled in individually there is more self-screening by respondents. Another advantage is that the advertiser prepares the specific message designed to attract the kind of respondents he seeks.

Trade Show Registrants

Trade show exhibits present an outstanding opportunity to obtain qualified names for a mailing list. There is a growing tendency to avoid passing out literature at an exhibit and offer instead to have any desired literature mailed to the prospect's home or office. General Electric, for example, has used a "Bulletin Bar" in its exhibits. Here a pretty blonde "bartender" helps visitors review available literature and then fill in order forms for the items they want. The bulletins are then mailed to the visitors.

Another effective technique was used by a metal goods manufacturer which displayed samples of all available literature. Below each sample was a pad of identifying tags. Visitors went around the exhibit and tore off tags identifying the pieces of literature they wanted. These were then presented to an attendant who attached them to either a business card or a filled-in address form. Others have applied this technique to displays of products, instead of literature.

Another imaginative technique was used by an exhibitor who had a tape recorder at his booth. Visitors simply picked up a phonelike microphone and gave their names and addresses and "told" what information they would like to have sent following the show.

Probably the most frequently used list-building technique at trade shows is the contest. Visitors are required to fill in their names and addresses on slips which are used for prize drawings. In order to qualify such names for subsequent mailings, many exhibitors make a special post-exhibit mailing telling everyone who entered where the prizes have gone. Sometimes a "consolation prize" is offered if the recipient of the mailing sends back a reply card giving information necessary for list qualification.

Customer Recommendations

A favorite list-building technique of mail order advertisers is to ask present customers to recommend friends and relatives who might be interested in the products the advertiser offers. This technique has proved surprisingly effective for other types of direct mail advertisers.

Some companies make special mailings just to obtain customer-recommended names. Frequently some reward is offered for all names sent in, while others predicate a reward on whether or not the recommended name is converted into a customer.

A number of mail order advertisers include an area on their order blanks where buyers can fill in recommended list names. Others will include business reply cards in their catalogs for this purpose. And still others will enclose pass-along literature in product packages so buyers can pass it out to interested parties, who, in turn, fill in the forms and return them to get on the mailing list.

Contest Entries

Those who enter contests represent excellent mailing list potential. All such names should, of course, be screened both to eliminate duplications (it is surprising how many people will submit duplicate entries in a contest—often using names of other members of their family or variations of their own names) and to eliminate obvious non-prospects.

Premium Offers

Like contests, premium offers provide an excellent list-building opportunity. Since premiums are normally offered to those who have already made a purchase, the list is already partially screened. It is important to recognize, however, that the person sending in for the premium may very easily be someone other than the one who purchased the product.

Sample Offers

Everyone likes to get something for nothing, so requests for samples may or may not represent good list potential. This will be primarily dependent upon the type of sample you are offering. Tell the world you are offering free candy bars to everyone who writes in and you will undoubtedly get millions of requests. But the buying power of some of the respondents will be highly questionable.

Actually, the words "free sample" have an amazing pulling power. An analysis of "bingo-card" requests by one business paper publisher indicated that offering a free sample drew an average of over three times as many requests as items where only literature was offered. In many cases, the samples involved were worth less than a cent each, yet the "free sample" offer worked its 3-to-1 magic.

All you have to do is to watch people at a show or fair to quickly recognize the fact that sample interest is a highly inadequate method of screening names for mailing list potential. There are just too many sample collectors—people who will pick up anything that is free, regardless of whether or not it has any possible value to them—to utilize a list of sample recipients as a mailing list without additional screening.

Personal Contact

Sometimes the best way to build a mailing list is to go out and "ring doorbells." Many of the best lists have been developed by hiring someone to go directly to "suspects" and ask them pointblank the questions you need answered before their names are added to the list. Often, it is not necessary to contact the "suspect" directly, but obtain the needed information through personal contact with a second party.

One of the most frequently told stories about mailing list development is the supposedly true case of the manufacturer of foundation garments who wanted to build a list of fat women whose husbands had incomes of $10,000 or more a year. The first step was to select neighborhoods where the average income was at the $10,000-plus level. Then "spotters" were hired to wait at corners in the neighborhood and watch for fat women to get off busses or out of taxicabs. The spotters would follow the women to see which building they entered. If it was a private home and there did not appear to be any type of social event in progress, the spotter would simply jot down the address for later checking against address records. If the fat lady walked into an apartment building, the spotter would ask the doorman, "Wasn't that Mrs. Jones who just went by?" The doorman would usually answer, "No, that was Mrs. So-and-so," and the spotter would jot down the woman's name and the building address. Supposedly this technique resulted in a mailing list so successful that it brought in orders for more foundation garments than the factory could produce—and at a cost of less than $1 per name!

Whether this story is true or not—and you will hear it at least once at any direct mail convention—it illustrates the degree of imagination which may be required to develop the list you need. Professional list builders insist they can develop a list to fit any need—even left-handed drummers between the ages of 55 and 60, who have Irish mothers and German fathers, drive 1970 Ford station wagons, smoke pipes, and live in split-level houses with aluminum combination windows. But the more complicated the list specifications become, the greater the cost per name.

Survey Services

Western Union offers a special service which has proved to be a valuable assist to list builders. It is most often used to either verify list information or to obtain names of individuals to supplement company information already available. The list compiler simply provides Western Union with a list of companies to be contacted and a set of questions to be asked. Then the nearest Western Union operator calls the company involved, asks the questions, compiles the information desired, and forwards it to the compiler.

Interestingly, few companies refuse to provide the information needed for list compilation. For some reason, nearly everyone assumes a Western Union operator has a special right to request such information.

Western Union Survey Service is frequently used in conjunction with other list-building techniques. For example, when Oxford Paper Company wanted to develop a list of approximately 3,000 of the largest buyers of fine printing papers, they started by developing a list of the companies which used the largest quantities of paper. Once this basic list had been compiled, letters were mailed to the companies asking for the names of the individuals who had primary responsibility for the specifying and buying of printing papers. This method yielded over 80% of the necessary individual names. Then the remaining company names were turned over to Western Union for Survey Service contact. This method brought the completion rate to 98%. The remaining 2% of the names were obtained by making personal phone calls.

In addition to Western Union, there are many other organizations which can conduct survey operations—by phone, mail or in person—to obtain list information. Use of such outside services is often more successful than performing the operation yourself both because trained professionals are used and a higher percentage of people will generally give the necessary information when the identity of the mailer is unknown. (Nearly everyone, it seems, loves a mystery.)

Special Direct Mail

Direct mail, itself, can be used to both build and maintain mailing lists. Starting with a broad list of names, many companies send out special mailings offering to send literature, publications, samples, and so forth, to those who express an interest. This is essentially the same technique previously described as "advertising inquiries," but has the additional advantage of being able to pinpoint initial recipients to a much closer degree than is possible through the use of other media.

A frequently used technique is to send a typical direct mail piece and include an offer to send future mailings of this nature to all who request them. In cases where the literature cost is considered too high to warrant mailing complete units to broad lists, it is often helpful to include some kind of representative sample with list-building mailings. One company, for example, prepared a miniature of its catalog and tipped it to letters offering copies of the full-size book.

Office Managers

A highly effective technique for building and maintaining business lists is to enlist the aid of office managers. Of all the people in a business organization, the office manager is usually best informed about specific interests of individuals *and* has the greatest interest in seeing that mail is routed to the proper parties. Therefore, he or she usually looks upon a request for mailing list information as an aid in conducting a more efficient business operation. A specific case history of list maintenance via office managers is described in Chapter 22—"Mailing List Maintenance."

Another excellent source for list aid within most companies is the secretary to the president, who has proved to take a special interest in helping advertisers direct their mailings to the right individuals.

Merchandise Stuffers

One way manufacturers who have no direct contact with buyers obtain names for promotion of related items is to enclose business reply cards with merchandise, suggesting that the buyers send them in to receive information about other products, uses of the products they have purchased, service information, and so forth.

For example, O. M. Scott & Sons Co. frequently includes offers to send its external house organ, *Lawn Care,* in packages of grass seed and other products.

Product Registrations

A similar way to obtain names of buyers for promotion purposes is to include a registration card with your products. This technique is most frequently used by appliance manufacturers offering warranties. Buyers are required to establish the date of their purchase by sending in a registration card. These cards generally request information other than simply the purchase date and name and address of the buyer. Considerable market research information can be obtained through product registration cards.

DIRECTORIES

One of the major sources for mailing lists are directories of all kinds. In our list of 66 basic mailing list sources, we have included the types of directories most frequently used by direct mail advertisers plus a few specific directories which are considered vital list sources by large numbers of advertisers. In any given field, some other directory may be the basic list reference and a list (Section F of Appendix) describes over 1,000 of the principal business directories.

In using directories for mailing list compilation, it is important to remember that no directory is ever completely up to date. It takes a long time to edit and publish any major directory, and during this time span many names and addresses change. Then the majority of directories are not revised for another year—and sometimes not more often than once every five years—so there is further chance for the material to grow stale.

Nevertheless, well-edited directories represent one of the best *starting points* for list compilation. Often, businesses will provide directory publishers with information they will not make available in answer to routine requests for mailing list help. So as long as you are willing to add your own effort to supplement the information you find in directories, you can consider this an important list-source area.

Telephone Directories

Of all directories published, telephone directories are the most frequently used for mailing lists of all kinds. A number of mailing list compilers subscribe to every available telephone directory and draw from them not only consumer names but classified lists of businesses and institutions of all kinds.

For local merchants, a phone directory represents a primary list source. In many communities it is possible to obtain not only the regular alphabetical directories but also monthly reports on new listings and changes. These changes are often looked upon as a particularly good list since they usually represent families who have recently moved—and a move usually means increased spending for household items.

"Yellow Pages"

The classified telephone directories—commonly called the "Yellow Pages"—are an excellent source for business and professional lists. As mentioned previously, there are compilation firms which regularly create nationwide business lists from their libraries of classified telephone directories.

Criss-Cross Directories

In many communities, the telephone company publishes a secondary directory which lists telephone subscribers by streets and house numbers rather than alphabetically. This directory proves particularly helpful to retailers who have a limited trade area or any advertiser who wishes to restrict his mailings to areas with specific characteristics. In major cities, criss-cross directories are usually revised on a monthly schedule.

Community Directories

While the telephone directory has replaced the once highly popular city directory in many areas, there are still many communities which have all-resident, all-family, or other listings. While such directories are often more all-inclusive than telephone directories, they vary greatly in quality and many suffer from a lack of day-to-day changes which are automatically reported to telephone companies.

Business Directories

No matter what line of business represents prospects for your products or services, chances are someone publishes a directory to cover the field. You'll find the principal business directories listed in Section F of the Appendix.

Industrial Directories

Many states and metropolitan areas publish comprehensive directories listing all manufacturers. In some cases these directories also list all business firms in a given area—or at least those which serve the manufacturers and other businesses.

Chamber of Commerce Directories

Still another source for business directories are local, area, or state chambers of commerce. These are not available from every chamber of commerce, but have been compiled by a considerable number.

Horizontal Directories

While there are many vertical directories (those which cover a specific type of business or a specific geographical area), the most commonly used directories for mailing list compilation are those which are more horizontal in nature. While our next several sources listings cover the most frequently used horizontal directories, there are dozens of others which may prove more useful in a given mailing list compilation. The major advantage of horizontal directories is the automatic elimination of duplicates—a problem which frequently plagues users of a number of overlapping vertical directories.

Million-Dollar Directory

Dun & Bradstreet's "Million Dollar Directory" is probably the most popular single source for building business mailing lists. It contains over 22,000 United States businesses which have an indicated worth of a million dollars or more. The directory has four basic sections:

1. Businesses listed alphabetically
2. Businesses listed geographically
3. Businesses listed by Standard Industrial Classifications
4. Names of top management personnel listed alphabetically

Typical "Million Dollar Directory" listings give the company name, address, S.I.C. code, line of business, annual sales volume, number of employees, names and titles of key executives, and other details.

In addition to the Directory itself, Dun & Bradstreet offers a number of related services. For example, you can obtain all listings or selected sections on punch cards, 3- by 5-inch cards, mailing labels, or magnetic tapes. Dun & Bradstreet has added a companion directory to the above entitled *The Middle Market Directory* and it has similar services for these listings.

Credit Rating Books

Credit rating firms such as Dun & Bradstreet issue regular volumes which provide credit ratings of business firms. While most of these directories do not list street addresses or provide names of individuals, they are frequently useful for mailing list compilation in conjunction with other reference material. Most frequently they are used for cross-checking lists obtained from other sources to eliminate names of companies or individuals who have poor credit ratings.

Thomas Register

"Thomas Register of American Manufacturers" lists more than 75,000 manufacturers alphabetically, including rating by capital assets. There are also classified lists by products and industries. This directory is often used as the primary business list source by compilers who want to include both large and small firms on their lists.

MacRae's Blue Book

Approximately 60,000 manufacturers and industrial firms in the U.S. are listed alphabetically and by products in this directory, which also includes the financial ratings for each firm.

Standard Directory of Advertisers

This directory lists all national advertisers and includes company name, address, products advertised, media used; and key management, sales and advertising personnel. It also shows advertising agencies handling accounts. Two editions are available—one listing companies by product categories; the other listing companies geographically. The same publisher also publishes an agency list, which carries details on approximately 4,000 leading U.S. advertising agencies.

Poor's Register

"Poor's Register of Corporations, Directors and Executives" provides an alphabetical listing of over 34,000 leading industrial corporations, together with the names of their key executives and directors. Corporations are listed by S.I.C. categories. There are also separate sections listing the individual executives and directors alphabetically, including home addresses. A separate obituary section often proves helpful in list maintenance.

Who's Who

There is a variety of who's who publications which are useful in list building. In addition to horizontal who's who directories covering the U.S. and specific geographical areas, separate who's who directories have been published to cover a number of industries and professional fields.

Social Registers

Many communities have published social registers which include names and addresses—and often additional biographical information—of leading citizens.

Association Membership Rosters

Another often excellent source for business lists are the rosters published by associations and other business groups. While many of these rosters do not contain the names of all the possible business or individuals in the fields involved, this factor often works to the advantage of the list compiler since it can provide a worthwhile screening. Many associations make it a policy to forbid membership to companies or individuals with poor credit ratings, questionable business ethics, and so forth. On the other hand, many of these rosters are far from comprehensive and represent only those firms or individuals who have a need for some special association service.

COMPILED LISTS

There are many sources from which lists can be compiled—directories being the most common, but by no means the only source. Only the more common sources are included in the basic list.

Labor Organizations

One way to pinpoint a list of people with common occupations is to use a list compiled from members of labor organizations.

Religious Organizations

While the availability of church and synagogue membership lists varies, this is a frequently used source for fund-raising membership lists. To obtain the use of such lists, direct mail advertisers often work some kind of contribution arrangement with their sources.

School Lists

Many advertisers pay special attention to lists of both students and teachers. Particularly in demand for special promotions are lists of students about to graduate. Many schools make such lists available without charge and several list compilers offer lists to cover all schools in a given area.

Convention Registration Lists

Groups sponsoring conventions often make it a regular practice to publish lists of all registrants. These are not only used for special promotions during the conventions, but also are frequently used both for pre-convention and post-convention mailings. Such lists are frequently available only to members of the sponsor group and/or exhibitors at trade shows held in conjunction with the conventions.

Just as association membership lists are often considered choice sources for the development of mailing lists, those who attend conventions are also often considered to represent a particularly good audience for direct mail of many types.

Cultural Interests

Many direct mail advertisers have a special interest in lists of those who purchase theater, concert, or opera tickets; patrons of art galleries and museums; subscribers to literary and other cultural magazines; purchasers of records, music, and musical instruments;

book buyers; and similar groups. Such lists obviously have a high potential for those who are promoting similar products, services or events and are often considered to have better-than-average potential for many other products and services promoted through direct mail.

Birth Lists

Birth lists are followed with special interest by many direct mail advertisers. New parents have been found to be highly responsive to many direct mail promotions. While makers of such items as baby foods, diaper services, and photographs are obvious users of such lists, many other direct mail advertisers consider new parents logical prospects. For example, one firm which compiles a national birth list reports that the majority of users of this list want to promote products and services far removed from the babies' needs. For example, companies which market through door-to-door sales have found new mothers and fathers particularly receptive to offers which promise them a source of additional income. Another frequent user of such lists are correspondent schools.

Birth lists are compiled in a number of different ways. Birth registration records are often available. In many communities, newspapers regularly publish lists of all new parents. In other cases, hospitals make available such information. Most direct mail advertisers, however, turn to the professionals who compile such lists and then rent or sell them to interested users.

Alumni Lists

Another excellent source for lists with high potential are alumni groups—particularly those associated with colleges and universities. Some lists are available broken down not only by school and year graduated but also by degrees awarded and other more specialized information. The availability of such lists varies greatly so it is well to check with a list compiler or broker before making plans to use any specific list.

Voter Registration Lists

Local lists are often compiled from the official voter registration lists. Obtaining such lists for direct mail use varies from simple to highly complicated. As one list expert puts it, "Occasionally they're free; sometimes there's a regular charge, and frequently you have to know someone."

Contributors

Those who have contributed to one cause or another often represent good potential for other mailers. They are, of course, particularly valuable names for those seeking a contribution for a similar cause. Most often they are obtained on an exchange basis, although many lists of this nature are available for rental and a number of list brokers specialize in making arrangements for use of such lists. Unfortunately, many contributors' lists are badly out of date and/or compiled with little attention to accuracy.

Mail Order Buyers

The best list for anyone seeking to sell a product by mail order is a list of known mail order *buyers*. Successful mail order advertisers recognize that any group of people contains only a certain percentage who can be described as "mail oriented"—those who readily respond to offers to purchase products or services by mail.

The very best list, of course, is one composed of those who have previously bought a similar product from you *by mail.* Next best is probably a list of those who have bought an unrelated product from you by mail. The reason why such lists are particularly important is that these buyers have already been convinced that you represent a reliable—and desirable—source (unless, of course, you have failed to serve them satisfactorily in the past).

In "Successful Direct Mail Advertising and Selling," mail order expert Bob Stone comments[1]:

> At National Research Bureau, we consider our customer list the most valuable asset we have. No list we buy or rent comes close to it in pull. For instance, when we launched *Sparks,* a service for small businesses, outside lists averaged a little less than 4% on a $1 offer. Our customer list pulled 14%!
>
> Why the tremendous pulling power of a customer list? There are two reasons: (1) everyone on the list has previously bought by mail; (2) every customer receiving the mail knows the firm as a result of previous purchase. Point two makes the difference. When you use an outside list of known mail order buyers, the list qualifies on the basis of mail-buying habits. When you use your own customer list you have mail-buying habits *plus* familiarity with your organization too. It's an unbeatable combination.

To supplement your own mail order customer lists, the next best source is those who have purchased similar products from others *by mail.* While many mail order companies will not rent their customer lists for use in promoting products competitive

[1]Copyright Prentice-Hall, Inc.

with their own, it is frequently possible to arrange an exchange of customer lists.

Don't underestimate the importance of "mail oriented" prospects. Many a great mail order idea has fallen flat because the promoter was unable to find enough available lists of mail order buyers within the fields of interest in the product or service he was offering. It is not uncommon to find that lists of mail order buyers will pull 10, 20, or 30 times the number of orders as can be obtained through lists of people with basically the same characteristics but who have not necessarily identified themselves as being "mail oriented." An additional advantage is that most mail order buyer lists have been screened for deadbeats and slow payers.

Expires

Many companies who solicit business by mail order may not rent their active customer lists but will offer lists of previous buyers. These lists are usually classified by year of last purchase and often by other characteristics such as amount of purchases. This is particularly true in the subscription field, where lists of active subscribers are often unavailable while lists of those who have let subscriptions expire are readily available.

In using lists of expires it is important to recognize two points: (1) such lists are often poorly maintained and may easily contain a high percentage of "nixies" (undeliverable mail); and (2) if you are trying to sell by mail order, make sure that the expires list contains a high percentage of names which were originally obtained through mail order selling.

Inquiry Lists

Another type of compiled list which is available from many direct mail advertisers—particularly those who sell by mail order—is the inquiry list. Such lists consist of those who have made inquiries —usually by mail—about a specific product or service. Such lists may or may not include inquirers who have been converted to customers.

Such lists are of questionable value for most direct mail advertisers, although there are times when inquiry lists represent the only compiled list readily available to cover some specific interest area.

Automobile Lists

The basic list source for many direct mail advertisers is automobile and truck registrations. Nationwide, state, and local vehicle registration lists are available and can be broken down in a variety of ways including by make and model of vehicle, multiple vehicle ownership, and so forth.

Manufacturers of automobiles, automotive accessories, and supplies such as gas and oil are obvious users of such lists. But vehicle registration lists are also used by direct mail advertisers in many other fields. It has generally been found that ownership of certain makes and models of automobiles is compatible with other specific interests.

Frequently, direct mail advertisers will combine vehicle registration information with other factors to isolate a particular prospect audience. For example, an advertiser might select a group of census tracts where the average income level is high. And then to further refine the list and eliminate names of individuals with low incomes who may live within these areas, the advertiser may select only families with newer models of more expensive automobiles or just families owning two or more automobiles. While this doesn't necessarily yield a 100% accurate rate, it usually produces a very high percentage of names which meet the established qualifications.

While it is possible in certain areas to obtain vehicle registration lists directly from government sources, the more common practice is to deal through compilers who have converted the registration records to coded mailing lists for rental purposes.

Homeowner Lists

Along with automobile registration lists, homeowner lists are favorites of direct mail advertisers in many fields. One problem that frequently arises in the use of such lists is that the registered owner of a given home is not necessarily the resident of that home. Therefore, such lists should be approached with caution unless your primary purpose is to reach people who own homes—regardless of whether or not they actually reside in the area you have selected for promotion.

OTHER DIRECT MAIL LIST SOURCES

Even though we have already discussed 57 different list sources, there are still at least nine other sources for mailing lists—including the three most important of all which we have left for last.

Trade and Consumer Publications

Many publications make their subscription lists or other specially compiled lists available for rental. In many cases, however, use is limited to advertisers. Generally, it can be assumed that publication lists are as up to date as any lists available.

Quite frequently subscription lists are used for direct mail which directly ties in with space advertising. Such a technique, for example, makes sampling possible and gives the advertiser an opportunity to use more copy than is practical or economical in space advertising.

Federal Government Sources

While the Federal Government is not in the direct-mail-list-compiling business, it still represents an excellent source for many kinds of lists. For example, hundreds of business and institutional directories are published by government agencies and are available at low cost from the Superintendent of Documents, Washington, D.C. 20402. You can obtain a catalog of all available government publications but the best starting point is your nearest field office of the Department of Commerce.

Other Government Sources

State and local governments are also good list sources for many direct mail advertisers. Among the lists which can frequently be obtained are taxpayers, voting lists, birth names, marriage license applicants, automobile and truck registration lists, boat registrations, hunting and fishing licenses, and so forth. The availability of any particular kind of list varies from place to place so no general "rules" can be offered. In most cases, local lettershops have a working knowedge of just what types of lists are available and can arrange to get them for you.

Local Post Offices

While postmasters are not list compilers, they can assist you with information which makes it possible to mail to certain areas without lists. For example, you can mail to all rural route boxholders without addressing by name or address. Postmasters will provide information as to how many boxholders are on each of the rural routes they supervise and all you need to do is to prepare bundles of mailing pieces for each route you wish to cover and request full boxholder distribution.

Business Services and Construction Reports

Many direct mail advertisers make regular use of special services which provide information useful for compilation of mailing lists. For example, you can subscribe to reports which list all new construction in a given area. Other services cover personnel changes, major business activity, and so forth.

List Exchanges

We have already mentioned several cases where lists are available on an exchange basis. A direct exchange on a name-for-a-name basis is often the working arrangement between mail order companies. Similar arrangements are made in other direct mail areas. List brokers frequently handle exchange arrangements and maintain the necessary records.

While a name-for-name exchange sounds quite simple on the surface, it is not an arrangement to enter without a thorough consideration of all the facts. All lists, even though they represent mail order buyers for similar products, do not necessarily balance out one another. It is not uncommon for some mail order companies to hold back their best buyers when making an exchange and offer only lists with limited potential.

It is also important to make sure that *the offers* which will be made balance out one another. Some mail order advertisers will use exchange lists to offer free samples, catalogs, or low-priced come-ons. Since such offers usually bring a particularly heavy response, they can quickly skim the cream off competitors' lists and convert the names of respondents to the mailer's own list, eliminating the need for further exchanges. There is nothing wrong with this procedure *if both parties* to the exchange are making similar offers. But if one party makes a cream-skimming offer while the other makes a direct full-price offer, the exchange quickly becomes inequitable.

List Compilers

In many cases there is no good reason why you should compile your own lists for there are many specialists ready and able to do the job for you. In fact, a list compiler quite probably has already compiled the list you need and will either rent or sell it to you for less than it will cost you to compile it.

Many list compilers have extensive catalogs of pre-compiled lists. A representative sample of the kind of lists you can obtain starts at the bottom. Most pre-compiled lists are available at between $25 and $50 per thousand names, although some of the more-difficult-to-compile lists or those with limited markets will cost as much as $100 per thousand names.

List compilers use many sources, including most of those we have listed. Some list compilers specialize in compiling a specific kind of list such as industrial lists, birth lists, retail merchants, automobile registration lists, and so forth. Others are in business to compile every possible kind of mailing list for which there is a market. You will generally find that a vertical specialist will provide the best list if you have a vertical need.

TYPICAL COMPILED MAILING LISTS

There is almost no limitation to the types of people you can reach through compiled mailing lists. The following examples show the quantity and titles of typical lists among the thousands offered by a single list compiler.

4,782	Abattoirs and Slaughterhouses
109	Abdominal Belt Manufacturers
1,441	Accordion Players (Professional)
48,622	Accountants (CPA)
9,404	Advertising Agencies
21	Agar Manufacturers
55,822	Aircraft Owners (Private)
150,090	Aircraft Pilots (Commercial)
721	Alcoholism Clinics
101	Animals (Stuffed) Manufacturers
32	Anvil Manufacturers
652	Archaeologists
30	Aspirin Manufacturers
253,114	Attorneys
19,100	Bakers
70,108	Barbershops
507	Bargain Basements in Department Stores
806	Basket Makers
559	Baths, Turkish
132,023	Beauty Salons
62	Beeswax Manufacturers and Distributors
40	Bellfounders
10	Best-dressed Ladies
132	Better Business Bureaus
34	Bird Cage Manufacturers
606	Blacksmiths
3,586	Blood Banks (in hospitals)
2,500,000	Blue-Collar Workers
15,375	Boards of Education
1,912,301	Boat Owners
7,399	Bowling Alleys
490	Brassiere Manufacturers

TYPICAL COMPILED MAILING LISTS (cont.)

5,900	Brown (firms trading under the name of)
74,567	Builders and General Contractors
67	Bulldozer Manufacturers
1,933	Business Brokers
2,500,000	Businesses, One-man
532	Button Manufacturers
186	Calico Printers
811	Camera Clubs
170	Candlemakers
83,737	Carpenters and Builders
278	Cartoonists
13	Cascara Sagrada Manufacturers
376	Cathedrals
17,820	Churches, Catholic
107	Catsup Manufacturers
3,000	Celebrities
9,524	Cemeteries
3,821	Chambers of Commerce
13,539	Charitable Organizations
1,310	Cheese Factories
23	Chess and Chessboard Manufacturers
4,000	Chinese Laundries
54	Chintz Manufacturers
23,482	Cigar and Tobacco Stores
74	Circuses
262,211	Clergymen
300,000	Clubs and Associations
388	Coffin and Casket Manufacturers
9,935	College Coaches
444,000	College Professors and Instructors
9,000	Country Stores
199	Crow Bar Manufacturers
1,823	Daily Newspapers
97	Dams
29	Date Packers
10,971	Day Nurseries
16,878	Decorators (Interior)
13	Degasser Manufacturers
10,000	Delicatessen Stores
136	Demolishers (factory)
103,424	Dentists
11,580	Department Stores
522	Diamond Cutters
92	Diaper Manufacturers
269	Dietitians' Schools
35	Dining Car Supervisors
38	Dishcloth Manufacturers
212	Divers (Water—Professional
279,774	Doctors
18	Dog Biscuit Manufacturers
11,212	Dog Breeders and Kennels
217	Doll Manufacturers
41	Door Bell Manufacturers
4,932	Doughnut Bakers
14,566	Drive-in Restaurants
48,869	Drugstores
56,102	Drycleaners
104	Dumbwaiter Manufacturers
5,536	Ear, Nose and Throat Specialists
25	Eau de Cologne Manufacturers
13,000	Economists
35,000	Editors
714	Efficiency Engineers
3,151	Electric Light and Power Companies
74,899	Elementary Schools
781,000	Elementary Schoolteachers
1,512	Elks Lodges
1,823	Embroiderers
259	Emerald Dealers
23,189	Engineers, Aeronautical
292,517	Factories
8,090	Farmers' Co-operatives
23,928	Finance Companies
18,881	Fire Brigades (Volunteer)
4,789	Firearms Dealers

TYPICAL COMPILED MAILING LISTS (cont.)

489	Fishing Clubs
25,234	Florists
89	Fox Hunt Clubs
1,402	Fruit Canners
25,054	Funeral Directors
35,219	Furniture Dealers
5,542	Garbage Collecting Firms
43	Geiger Counter Manufacturers
8,500	Geophysicists
26,134	Gift Shops
8,532	Golf Clubs
27,904	Grain Dealers
31,885	Greenhouses and Nurserymen
220,000	Grocers
170	Guided Missile Contractors
77	Harbor Masters
28,297	Hardware Retailers
95	Harrow Manufacturers
4,181	Health Officers
922	Helicopter Owners
31,254	High Schools
485,000	High-School Teachers
151	Hinge Manufacturers
8	Hobby Horse Manufacturers
4,348	Hobby Shops
16,010	Home Builders
3,726	Home Demonstration Agents
6,500,000	Home Owners (in rural and small towns)
1,067	Horse Breeders
24	Horse Blanket Manufacturers
7,318	Hospitals
6,458	Hotel and Motel Managers
16,142	Hotels
76	Hurricane Warning Stations
4	Hypnotism Schools
44	Ice-making Machinery Manufacturers
13,708	Implement Dealers
111,522	Insurance Brokers
16,878	Interior Decorators
11,278	Investment Analysts
102	Ironing Board Manufacturers
18	Jet Plane Manufacturers
31,069	Jewelers (Retail)
16	Jigsaw Puzzle Manufacturers
8,919	Judges
9,212	Junk Dealers
356	Keg and Barrel Manufacturers
10,971	Kindergartens (Private)
24	Kite Manufacturers
5,724	Kiwanis Clubs
20,000	Labor Unions
188	Lathe Manufacturers
24,807	Librarians
34,234	Liquor Stores
1,453	Livery Stables
4,955	Logging Camps and Loggers
22,004	Lumber Retailers
22,736	Machine Shops
2,734	Magazines (Business & Trade)
675	Mail Order Houses
4,806	Management Consultants
292,517	Manufacturers
53	Marquee Manufacturers
3,000	Marriage Counselors
3,281	Mayors
210	Midwives
2,563	Monasteries and Convents
48,828	Motels and Tourist Courts
70	Muff Manufacturers
8,046	Movie Theaters (Indoor)
839	Museums
4,200	National Associations
12	Naval Yards

TYPICAL COMPILED MAILING LISTS (cont.)

4,894 Newsdealers, Retail
79,749 Nurses

25 Oar Manufacturers
52 Onion Ring Manufacturers
295 Opera (Metropolitan) Boxholders
6,453 Outboard Motor Dealers

17,881 Paint Manufacturers
35,942 Paint Dealers
256 Pajama Manufacturers
51,653 Parent-Teacher Associations
8,167 Patent Attorneys
17,722 Pediatricians
135 Pencil Manufacturers
5,000 Pharmacists (Hospital)
13,006 Photographers (Commercial)
14,176 Pizzerias
46,063 Plumbers
24,052 Post Offices
25,191 Printers
19,472 Psychiatrists
78,000 Purchasing Agents
186 Putty Manufacturers

6,000 Quarries & Pits
18 Quebracho Extract Manufacturers

95 Racetracks
283,996 Radio Amateurs
5,059 Radio Broadcasting Stations
441 Railroads
101,000 Real Estate Agents and Dealers
2,340 Reducing Salons
229 Rehabilitation Centers
198,517 Restaurants

70,000 Sales Executives
54 Sardine Canners
6,090 Savings and Loan Associations
150,000 Schools and Colleges
858 Secondhand Booksellers
26,347 Shoe Retailers
10,633 Shopping Centers
588 Silk Mills
511 Ski Clubs
350,000 Sportsmen
17,100 Stamp Collectors
8,055 Stationers
725 Steel Plants
8,273 Stenographers (Court)
355 Stockyards
83 Straw Hat Manufacturers
1,067 Stud Farm Managers

2,579 Tailors (Ladies')
61,572 Taverns
11,204 Taxicab Companies
820 Television Stations
2,578 Tennis Clubs
40,017 Tire Dealers
5 Titanium Producers
214 Toll Bridges and Highways
10,042 Tourist Agents
1,649 Toy Manufacturers
41,152 Truckers

127 Umbrella Manufacturers
3 Umpires' Schools
7,127 University Deans
18,200 Upholsterers

10,342 Vermin Exterminators
110 Vest Manufacturers
2,900 Violinists (Professional)

7,534 Weekly Newspapers
96 Whiskey Distilleries
16 Wind Tunnels
370 Worm Farms

674 X-ray Laboratories and Technicians
18 Xylol Manufacturers and Distributors
17 Xylophone Manufacturers

1,280 Yacht Clubs
9,972 Yacht Owners
9 Yohimbine Hydrochloride Manufacturers
10 Yo-Yo Manufacturers

122 Zipper Manufacturers
163 Zoological Parks
24 Zwieback Manufacturers

An indication of how important it is to use current lists can be seen by some of the changes in the list quantities shown above. The catalog of the same compiler ten years earlier compared with the 1972 edition used in compiling the above examples showed such changes as:

Aircraft Pilots (Commercial) from 44,200 to 150,090
Barbershops from 24,472 to 70,108
Boards of Education from 9,691 to 15,375
Brassiere Manufacturers from 279 to 490
Cartoonists from 402 to 278
Charitable Organizations from 7,700 to 13,539
Cheese Factories from 2,669 to 1,310
Chintz Manufacturers from 25 to 54
Circuses from 14 to 74
College Professors from 105,000 to 444,000
Crowbar Manufacturers from 45 to 199
Day Nurseries from 3,499 to 10,971
Diamond Cutters from 285 to 522
Dining Car Supervisors from 56 to 35
Professional Water Divers from 55 to 212
Doll Manufacturers from 170 to 217
Doughnut Bakers from 2,786 to 4,932
Economists from 7,570 to 13,000
Finance Companies from 10,724 to 23,928
Garbage Collecting Firms from 2,765 to 5,542
Geiger Counter Manufacturers from 23 to 43
Gift Shops from 17,600 to 26,134
Harbor Masters from 122 to 77
Horse Blanket Manufacturers from 35 to 24
Hotels from 30,725 to 16,142
Implement Dealers from 22,176 to 13,708
Interior Decorators from 11,925 to 16,878
Investment Analysts from 6,150 to 11,278
Private Kindergartens from 3,499 to 10,971
Logging Camps and Loggers from 9,800 to 4,955
Management Consultants from 820 to 4,806
Marriage Counselors from 463 to 3,000
Oar Manufacturers from 16 to 25
Onion Ring Manufacturers from 100 to 52
Commercial Photographers from 6,817 to 13,006
Pizzerias from 1,800 to 14,176
Psychiatrists from 11,364 to 18,472
Railroads from 566 to 441
Secondhand Booksellers from 317 to 858
Shopping Centers from 3,974 to 10,633
Stationers from 14,200 to 8,055
Steel Plants from 377 to 725
Straw Hat Manufacturers from 165 to 83
Taverns from 31,600 to 61,572
Tire Dealers from 126,800 to 40,017
Tourist Agents from 4,848 to 10,042
Toy Manufacturers from 2,012 to 1,649
University Deans from 2,028 to 7,127
Wind Tunnels from 8 to 16
Worm Farms from 1,188 to 370

The advantage of using a list compiler's service rather than doing the job yourself—in addition to the fact you will probably save money in the process—is that experienced compilers are well acquainted with the limitations of various sources and have developed techniques for interfiling names from various sources to make their lists as accurate and complete as possible.

There is a great variety of sources for compiled lists. Most every large lettershop, for example, offers a list compilation service. (If you want information about lists available through lettershops in any community, we suggest you contact the Mail Advertising Service Association, 425 13th St. N.W., Washington, D.C. 20004.) For compiled lists which are national in scope, two good starting points in locating what you need are the "Direct Mail Directory" section found in every issue of *Direct Marketing* (224 Seventh St., Garden City, N.Y. 11530) and the Mailing List Compilers Section of *Direct Mail List Rates & Data* published by Standard Rate & Data Service, Inc., 5201 Old Orchard Road, Skokie, IL 60077.

Occupant Lists

One type of compiled list requires special discussion. This is the so-called occupant list. These are lists of just addresses, no names. They are often used when saturation mailings are desired and the direct mail message is not of a personal nature. They have the advantage of being delivered to whomever lives at a given address, with no problem of non-deliveries if someone has moved. The cost of such lists, of course, is far less than for lists with names.

Analyzing Mass Lists

A guide to assist direct mail advertisers in analyzing mass mailing lists has been prepared by R. L. Polk & Co.:

> The most important elements affecting success with mail are the *offer,* the *mailing piece* and the *list.* While you may have only one basic proposition for the consumer, there are many ways of offering it. And there are an endless number of mailing pieces with which to present the offer. But there are only a *few* mass lists to which it can be sent.
>
> Finding the *best* offer and mailing piece can only be accomplished by properly testing several approaches. And improvements can be made *only* through testing.
>
> Finding the best mass list can, to a very large degree, be determined from a careful analysis of the nature of available lists and how they relate to your requirements. Learning to use any list with maximum effectiveness also involves a good deal of testing.
>
> Fortunately, direct mail is more susceptible to scientific testing than any other advertising medium because conditions can be controlled quite precisely.
>
> The most important factors to consider about a list are *coverage, deliverability,* and *selectivity.* And price too, of course, in terms of value delivered.
>
> A. *Coverage*
>
> 1. *Who?*
>
> Whom does the list cover—and fail to cover? For example, lists compiled from telephone directories do not include phone owners with unlisted numbers or, of course, non-phone owning households. The

auto list excludes owners who register their cars at their business and all non-car owners.

2. *Where?*

Is coverage available in all post offices in the United States? Some of them?

3. *How Many?*

There are about 60,000,000 households in the United States. How many does a given list cover?

4. *How Many Twice?*

How much duplication is there within a list?

B. *Deliverability*

Deliverability depends upon the accuracy of the *source,* the length of *time since the list was compiled,* the accuracy of *"atlasing"* and the *mode of addressing.*

1. *Accuracy of Source*

Obviously, a list is only as accurate as its source. The sources vary. Minor inaccuracies don't necessarily affect deliverability or effectiveness.

2. *Length of Time Since the List was Compiled*

The mobility rate of households in this country is about 20% per year. It is highest among low income and young families. *No list* is absolutely current. Each national list is really a mixture of lists compiled at different times. The phone list is compiled from more than 5,000 directories which are issued throughout the year. The auto list is compiled from registration data available throughout the year from the 50 states and Washington, D. C. Therefore, the length of time since compilation of a given block of names and addresses varies *within* every list. It might be three months in one city and eleven months in another.

3. *Accuracy of Atlasing*

Every third class mailing piece must have a correct post office address and ZIP number. There are some 34,000 post offices in the U.S. but there are more than 120,000 communities. Community names won't do for third class mail. Atlasing refers to the business of getting the right post office or branch name on each address, the correct ZIP number and the correct street spelling along with proper directionals (NW, South, etc.). Doing the job properly is a daily and endless task.

4. *Mode of Addressing*

In post offices having foot carrier delivery service, it is permissible to address mail "occupant" or "resident." As long as the dwelling unit is occupied, the mail will be delivered. Since the "mobility" of dwellings is nowhere near as great as the mobility of families and since the post office is not obliged to forward third class mail, "resident" addressing will get better *delivery* than name addressing. In multiple dwelling units, apartment numbers must appear to ensure deliverability.

C. *Selectivity*

There are three methods available to rationally prune coverage: deletions based on the inherent selectivity of the list used; exclusions based on geographical segments; and selectivity on a household-by-household basis.

1. *Inherent Selectivity*

This is in the *nature* of the list. The phone list has inherent selectivity because it selects only listed phone owners. The auto list has it too. The "occupant" list does *not* have it since it covers all households.

2. *Geographical Selectivity*

Geographic eliminations can be made by county, post office and postal zone from all mass lists. These selections are very gross indeed from a socio-economic standpoint since units of this size invariably include a cross section of demographic groups. Some lists offer smaller geographic selection units, such as census tracts, which are rated socio-economically from time to time and are good selection units—but with very definite limitations.

3. *Household-by-Household Selectivity*

This is based on some fact known about each household on a list such as sex, number of persons in the household, year model of car owned, etc. If the factor known is *relevant to your interests,* it is by far the best selection technique. These kinds of factors possess some relevance in nearly all cases and in many cases they can be of very great importance. The latter are not always obvious before a test discloses them.

FACTORS IDENTIFIABLE IN A MASS LIST

While the R. L. Polk auto registration list is primarily a list of automobile owners, there are a number of other selectivity factors built into the list. Such multiple factors are typical of those found in major mass mailing lists.

1. Current market value of cars owned
2. Number of cars owned
3. Make of newest car
4. Series of newest car
5. Price class of newest car
6. Year model of newest car
7. Body style of newest car
8. Number of doors in newest car
9. Number of cylinders in newest car
10. Make of other car

11. Series of other car
12. Price class of other car
13. Year model of other car
14. Body style of other car
15. Number of doors in other car
16. Number of cylinders in other car
17. Sex of head of household
18. Type of dwelling unit
19. Proximity to known customer
20. Degree of metropolitanization
21. Geographic region
22. Census tract characteristics
    A. Median income
    B. Median years of school completed
    C. Percent homeowners
    D. Percent non-whites
    E. Percent "young families"
    F. Percent with children under 6
    G. Percent of dwelling units built between 1960 & 1970
    H. Growth index
    I. Percent in large apartments

List Brokers

One of the most important specialists in the direct mail field is the list broker. A competent specialist in mailing lists, the list broker can save you time, work ... and frequently money. Whether you are a list owner or a list user, you will find it profitable to work with a list broker. A DMMA Research Report[2] explains:

> List brokers can be defined as independent agents whose primary function is to arrange rental and addressing transactions between list users and list owners. Brokers represent the list owners, and the commission that they receive from them for their services usually is 20% of the amount the mailer pays. The commission is deducted by the broker before payment is forwarded to the list owner.
>
> Here it should be pointed out that often there is an overlapping of activity in the list business. Some brokers not only arrange for the rental of lists that are owned by other companies, but they also either do compilation work or buy outright certain lists which they can make available for rental.

[2]"How to Work With Mailing List Brokers," by members of the National Council of Mailing List Brokers. A DMMA Research Report. 1959. Direct Mail/Marketing Assn.

Although this may seem confusing, in the course of working with list organizations you are likely to find that each has its own particular specialty. And very often you may decide that it is wise to deal with certain organizations for specific types of lists.

It is the list broker's job to keep abreast of all developments in the list field. Most brokers have an experienced staff which is always searching for "new" lists, more detailed information about known lists, ideas which will help mailers use their lists more profitably, and anything else which will help improve the effectiveness of direct mail.

A list broker can help direct mail advertisers in many ways other than just helping to arrange list rentals. He is a particularly good source for information on list maintenance; keeping direct mail records; testing; and he often provides valuable counsel on copy, art, mailing methods, and so forth.

Functions of List Brokers

The DMMA Research Report lists the following services performed by list brokers:

Finds New Lists—The broker is constantly seeking new lists and selecting for your consideration ones which will be of particular interest. In fact, brokers spend a great deal of their time encouraging list owners to enter the list rental field.

Acts as Clearance House for Data—The broker saves you valuable time because you can go to one source for a considerable amount of information, rather than to many sources which may or may not be readily available.

Screens Information—The broker carefully screens the list information provided by the list owner. Where possible he or one of his representatives personally verifies the information provided by the list owner. In addition, brokers in the National Council of Mailing List Brokers have available to them a wealth of information resulting from the combined efforts of the members.

Reports on Performance—The broker knows the past history of many lists and usually knows the performance of ones which have previously been used by other mailers.

Advises on Testing—The broker's knowledge of the makeup of a list is often valuable in determining what will constitute a representative cross section of the list. Obviously, an error in selecting a cross section will invalidate the results of the test and possibly eliminate from your schedule a group of names that could be responsive.

Checks Instructions—When you place an order with a list owner through a broker, he and his staff doublecheck the accuracy and completeness of your instructions, thus often avoiding unnecessary misunderstandings and loss of time.

Clears Offer—The broker clears for you in advance the mailing you wish to make. He supplies the list owner either with a sample of your piece or a description of it, and by getting prior approval minimizes the chance of any later disappointments.

Checks Mechanics—The broker clears with the list owner the particular type of envelope, order card, or other material which is to be addressed.

Clears Mailing Date—When contacting the list owner, the broker checks on the mailing date which you have requested and asks that it be held open as a protected time for you.

Works Out Timing—The broker arranges either for material to be addressed or labels to be sent to you at a specified time, thus enabling you to maintain your schedule of inserting and mailing.

Working With Brokers

An up-dated DMMA publication[3] provides a guide to most effective mailer-broker list owner relations:

WORKING WITH BROKERS

How to Get the Most Out of Your Lists Brokers—Whether you are a list owner or a mailer, your dealings with the list broker will be most efficient and profitable if you have confidence in him and treat him as a trusted aide.

Mutual confidence is essential if broker-client relations are to yield maximum results.

MAILER-BROKER RELATIONS

Give Background—Discuss frankly and fully your aims and purposes as well as any past mailing experience you may have had. In that way the broker will have the clearest possible picture of your operation and be able to help you avoid many pitfalls.

Outline Goals—Discuss your goals and amibitions with your broker so he may have a full understanding of the complexity and magnitude of the job he is sharing with you.

Policies—Formulate policies based on fairness and equity so when dealing with brokers, you may minimize or completely eliminate friction. Although you will find a broker may at times call you on the phone to discuss various newly released lists he most often will mail data cards to you.

On occasion if you are working with several brokers, three or four cards covering the same lists will arrive in the same mail. You should have a policy which will enable you to decide on which presentation you will consider.

[3]"How to Work With A List Broker," Direct Mail/Marketing Assn., 6 East 43rd St., New York, N.Y. 10017.

Have Confidence—It will come to the point where you have such confidence in your brokers that you will use them as sounding boards for your mailing ideas. Since they are specialists in direct marketing techniques, use their knowledge and experience to assist you in selling your product or services. This knowledge is given, "freely" to you.

Request Newest Information—In the planning stages of your campaign, request up-to-date information on the lists you are using from your broker. At that time, request new recommendations for your current offer.

This will save much time in going through your out-of-date data cards and in fighting the losing battle of daily filing data cards.

Keep Brokers Posted—Keep your broker posted on your mailing schedules so he may properly time his efforts in your behalf. He will appreciate this consideration, and you will benefit.

State Objections—The broker's primary concern is rendering efficient service to you, but he is not a mind reader. If you object to anything he does, state your objections fully and promptly. Each broker wants and tries to keep you as a client, but misunderstandings do develop. And they can hurt you as well as the broker unless they are resolved without delay.

Consider Priority—Generally it is accepted practice that if you test a list through one broker, you should continue using it through him so long as you are satisfied with the service he renders.

LIST OWNER-BROKER RELATIONS

Get List Maintenance Advice—Consult with the list broker when deciding how to maintain your list so you may set it up the most practical, economical and rentable way.

Discuss Rates—Discuss with your broker the price you will charge for rentals and decide on a price schedule that will bring you the greatest volume of profitable business.

Supply Accurate Data—Be sure the list information you furnish is accurate.

If the addresses in a list have not been corrected within a reasonable period of time, tell the broker.

If a list contains a percentage of names of people who bought on open account and failed to pay, give this information to the broker.

If you represent your list as made up entirely of buyers, be sure it does not include any inquiry or prospect names.

If you have bought out a competitor and have included some of his names in your customer list, be sure to state this fact.

Aside from obvious aspects of misrepresentation, you will be the one who suffers when you mislead a broker.

Address on Schedule—Establish a reputation for addressing on time as promised. If you accept orders and fail to fulfill them on schedule, brokers become aware of this and find they cannot conscientiously suggest your list to potential users. If, for some reason, you forsee a delay, advise the broker immediately so he can advise the mailer.

Furnish Latest Counts—Keep the broker posted on current list counts, rates, changes in the sources of the names and the like. When the composition of a list changes, it may very well become more interesting to a user who had previously felt that it was not suitable for his purpose. In addition, when current information is offered to a potential user through the broker, it is more likely to develop activity than is an out-dated description.

Choose Brokers Wisely—Consider carefully whether to make your list available to a number of list brokers or just to one broker. There are many things to be said in favor of working with several brokers. And at times there are also good reasons for working exclusively with one broker. While the decision is yours, you should keep in mind this fact—brokers are people and each one has his own particular personality, following and sphere of influence. Therefore, as a list owner, you will be well advised not to narrow the field unless your facilities for addressing are so limited the orders one broker can develop for you will be more than sufficient to take up all available addressing time.

Protect Brokers—It takes a lot of time and effort on the part of a broker to interest a mailer in testing your list. Therefore, continuation runs should be scheduled through the original broker so long as he continues to render satisfactory service to his client. The broker is a member of your sales force, and he can only continue to do an effective job so long as you protect him on the accounts he develops for you.

WHAT YOU SHOULD KNOW ABOUT LISTS

How to Locate Lists—Well qualified and up-to-date mailing lists are the lifeblood of any direct mail business. Without them there can be no profitable business. The importance of selecting and using the best available lists is therefore obvious. For no matter how potent and effective the selling effort, no matter how well the promotion is timed, it's all to no avail if the lists are so poorly selected that the mailing fails to reach eligible prospects. Throughout the history of direct mail the problem facing mailers has been the location and selection of lists of people who are ready, willing and able to buy specific products or services. In most organizations large or small, the job of gathering information and making selections is directed by an executive who must shoulder many other responsibilities. Usually he and his staff are limited in the amount of time they can spend on list matters.

Few large companies have separate departments staffed by list specialists, whose job it is to assemble all of the list data submitted to them, to appraise it and keep it filed for ready reference and use. *The Mailing List Brokers Professional Association* has prepared this booklet with two main purposes. One is to help mailers in organizations of all sizes determine how brokers can render the most efficient, effective service to them. The other is to help list owners determine how the services of list brokers can help them build extra profits.

Specialists—The essence of direct mail is its selectivity. Where a magazine advertisement can be selective only in a broad sense, depending on such factors as the publication in which it appears and the headline which is designed to catch the prospect's eye, direct mail can be selective to a much higher degree. It is possible for brokers to secure lists of almost every type of person, but the main function of a broker is to make recommendations of markets which in his experience are most appropriate. The broker usually has a wider experience of which types of lists do best for each type of product or service than any single mailer has.

Where to Start—There is no one best way to begin learning about list procurement, selection, maintenance or rental. There are two principal alternatives—either you can do your own research job or you can call in one or more brokers. If you decide that your first move will be to get as well acquainted with the subject as possible, you can refer to the books available in the library and select those which contain specific information about the use and renting of mailing lists. Or you can start from scratch with the brokers, if you cannot spare the time to do any of your preliminary research. And as you work with them, you will find you can add rapidly to your store of knowledge on the subject of mailing lists.

Commissions—List brokers are specialists whose primary function is to find a direct mail market for a product or service and to arrange a transaction between list users and list owners. The knowledge and experience of a list broker costs the mailer nothing. He is paid by the list owner for whom he is acting as a sales representative. The standard commission he receives for his services is 20% of the rental amount the mailer pays. This commission is deducted by the broker before payment is forwarded to the list owner.

One-Time Rentals—Most lists available through brokers are "rented" rather than sold. When a rental transaction is arranged, it is with the understanding that names will be used for one specified mailing and for no other purpose. If a mailer wants to make additional uses of the same names he must arrange for it in advance. Frequently the list owner will allow a reduction in rate for double or triple uses.

Classifications—Most lists fall into the following classifications:

Customer lists are just what the term implies. A list of customers can be graded in various ways, such as media used to secure them, age of list, percentage of repeat sales, amount of money paid, method of list maintenance, etc. Customers, of course, include active subscribers to publication and services.

Inactive Customers or expires are best kept by years.

Inquiries are also best kept by years.

Prospects are compiled names, secured from directories, friends' recommendations, trade show attendance, newspaper clippings, etc.

In the case of magazines as well as clubs offering books, records and a variety of other items the active names are called *subscribers* and they are not grouped by years, since in these cases there is continuing activity. The inactive names which such companies maintain are called *expires* or *former subscribers,* and they are usually grouped by years. Inquiry lists are made up of names of people who have actually asked for information about specific products or services. They are usually grouped accordingly to the dates they inquired.

Prospect lists are names of people likely to be interested in certain types of offers. The value of such lists relies largely upon the extent of the care, discretion and accuracy with which the selection of names is made.

Compiled lists are in many respects similar to prospect lists. Many of them are culled from directories. Some are taken from membership lists, association rosters, trade show attendance records, salesmen's reports, newspaper clippings and a variety of other sources, in each case they offer the compiler an opportunity to select names on the basis of some particular interest, background, physical or intellectual standard. Descriptions of these lists also include the dates of the source material.

Assembling List Information—Whether you want to locate lists to mail your offer to or you are a list owner interested in renting your list, it is essential that your list brokers have specific information which clearly defines the lists concerned.

BROKERS SERVICES

Whether you are a list owner or a mailer, your dealings with the list broker will be most efficient and profitable if you have confidence in him and treat him as a trusted aide.

How Brokers Work With List Users—The broker performs a vital function in locating lists for the mailer. Through knowledge and experience, the list broker helps you select the markets you desire and can suggest peripheral fields that will prove lucrative. In performing this service, he does a great deal of work which would be costly, time consuming and tedious for the mailer. Were the mailer to try to do the job himself, he would get involved in a lot of extra work ... phone calls and other contacts with various list owners. Even then he would not be able to cover more than a fraction of the ground that is explored by brokers. Nor would he be in a position to make the performance studies which are so necessary a part of list selection work.

VITAL SERVICES PERFORMED BY THE BROKER

Finds New Lists—The broker is constantly seeking new lists and selecting for your consideration lists which will be of particular interest. In fact, brokers spend a great deal of their time encouraging list owners to enter the list rental field.

Verifies Information—The broker carefully verifies the list information provided by the list owner. In addition, brokers in the MLBPA have available to them a wealth of information resulting from their combined efforts. The MLBPA will be discussed in more detail later on.

Reports on Performance—The broker is qualified to check past performances of many lists.

Checks Instructions—When you place an order with a list owner through a broker, he and his staff double check the accuracy and completeness of your instructions, thus often avoiding unnecessary misunderstandings and loss of time.

Clears Offer—The broker will clear in advance the mailing you wish to make. A sample of the literature to be mailed or a description of the offer will be sent for clearance. The broker can also advise the list owner on the best rental rate to produce the greatest profit. A too high rate will discourage rentals. A too low rate might make rental unprofitable.

Checks Mechanics—The broker clears with the list owner the particular type of envelope, order card or other material which is to be addressed.

Clears Mailing Date—When contacting the list owner, the broker checks on the mailing date which you have requested and asks that it be held open as a protected time for you.

Works Out Timing—The broker arranges for material to be sent to you at a specified time, enabling you to maintain your schedule.

Delivery Date—The broker checks the date when the list user would like his material returned to his letter shop and follows up to insure meeting the mail date.

How Brokers Work With List Owners—When you work through a broker, you are dealing with a specialist who is in close touch with national list users and is well acquainted with their needs. While you must concentrate on your business and have little time to devote to your list matters, the broker and his experienced staff will spend all of their time performing services for you whether you are a list user or a list owner.

Maintenance—The broker can give advice on the most practical method of maintaining your list.

Payment—A broker usually accepts only those mailers who have established proper credit references. If there is any doubt, the list owner makes the final decision. When the broker collects payment, he promptly sends a check to the list owner.

MOST IMPORTANT THINGS TO KNOW ABOUT LISTS

NAME

1. All of the names by which lists can be identified (including any trade styles that are used for advertising purposes).

2. The name of the list owner.

TYPE

Whether the list is:

1. A customer or subscriber list
2. An inquiry or expire list
3. A prospect list
4. A compiled list
5. A combination of any of the first four

To locate a mailing list broker, check the Mailing List Brokers Section of *Direct Mail List Rates & Data* published by Standard Rate & Data Service, Inc., 5201 Old Orchard Road, Skokie, IL 60077.

How to Rent Lists

It is important to remember that all lists are rented for one-time use only. If a direct mail advertiser wishes to make a second mailing to a list, he must again pay the established rental fee. While the amount charged for rental of lists varies greatly, the average list of active buyers rents for between $35 and $45 per thousand names. Lists of prospects, expires, or other less active names average between $25 and $35 per thousand. Prices include addressing, but any other mailing costs are additional. Most list owners will provide a magnetic tape for computer addressing* or labels to attach to your mailings. A number of list owners, however, insist on handling the complete mailing themselves. In such cases, you must send all material to the list owner's mailing service and pay inserting and mailing costs in addition to the rental fee. When preparing material for mailing by a list owner, make sure that your printed indicia are correct.

The mail order list expert, Lewis Kleid *(The Reporter of Direct Mail Advertising*, February 1963), offers the following suggestions:

> *Identification*—Indicate exactly which names you want (buyers, inquiries, prospects, etc.) and which years are to be used.
>
> *Test Sample*—Indicate specific areas if geographical, years if chronological, and sections if alphabetical.
>
> *Addressing Position*—If the address must appear precisely on the order card or envelope, find out if it can be done. If samples are not ready, give precise measurements or make up "dummies" for each list owner.
>
> *Omissions*—If you wish to omit names used previously, specify this in your instructions.
>
> *Mail Date*—This should be realistic, based upon your ability to deliver material to be addressed, the ability of the printers to supply the material to the lettershop, and for your lettershop to mail. The dates should not be vague as, for example, "will mail on receipt."
>
> *Confirmation*—Before you ship material to be addressed, request confirmation of all details pertaining to the order: price, latest quantities available, and shipping point for addressing.
>
> *How Shipment Is to Be Returned*—If you say "Rush," the list owner may return addressed material by airmail or railway express, both of which are costly. If time is abundant, specify "Ship Cheapest Way."

*Between the first and second printings of this edition of the Direct Mail & Mail Order Handbook a substantial change occurred in the handling of rental lists. At the time of the first printing, only a small handful of list owners made their lists available on magnetic tape. Within a period of just a couple of years, however, the offering of list rentals on magnetic tape became commonplace and at this time approximately 85% of all rented names are provided on magnetic tape.

Packing—Instruct the list owners to return the addressed material (a) in the original cartons, (b) in the same order as list is maintained, (c) do not crush or squeeze material, (d) face material all in one direction, (e) identify each carton and package in the shipment with the name of the list, quantity, and key numbers.

TYPICAL LIST DATA CARD

Gifts—ABCD INCORPORATED	#999999 April 1970
BUYERS: 25,000 1970 $25.00 M	SEX: Mostly Women
These are buyers who have bought a wide range of various gift items.	ARRANGEMENT: Zip Code Sequence
Unit of Sale: $1.00 to $25.00	ADDRESSING: Cheshire Tape 4-UP
Source: 100% Direct Mail	ABCD Incorporated
Please send sample mail piece for approval.	1111 Abby Lane
Not available to competitive gift offers.	North Hollywood, Calif. 90000
List is kept clean monthly.	213/000-1111
EVERY MANS LIST CO., INC.	Mr. Lane
111 Every Mans Street Every Man U.S.A. 00001	GIFTS 222/231-1111

LIST TESTING

While the subject of direct mail testing is covered in detail in Chapter 48—"Testing & Projecting," an understanding of proper use of lists in direct mail would not be complete without special mention of list testing.

One of the major advantages of the direct mail medium is that it isn't necessary to take a big gamble on an expensive promotion without first testing the elements involved in that promotion. And the lists to be used certainly should be tested before the full mailing is made. This is particularly important when you plan to use rented lists. But it is also frequently desirable when you have large lists of your own.

Selections for List Testing

An excellent guide on how to specify selections for list testing has been prepared by one of the industry's leading authorities, Angelo Venezian:[4]

4"How to Specify Selections for List Testing" by Angelo Venezian. DM/MA Direct Mail Manual. Direct Mail/Marketing Assn., 6 East 43rd St., NYC 10017.

SUGGESTED FORMAT FOR A LIST ORDER FORM

EVERY MANS LIST CO., INC.
111 EVERY MANS STREET
EVERY MAN U.S.A. 00001

LIST RENTAL INSTRUCTIONS

DATE OUR # MAILER'S #

LIST

OWNER:

cc:

Offer

Please address the following:

Cheshire Tape
______ 4 up ______
______ 1 up ______
Other

RETURN TO:

VIA Parcel Post/Spec. Delivery

Wanted by
MAILER:

IMPORTANT INSTRUCTIONS TO LIST OWNER:

1. Keep a record of names addressed
2. U.S.A. Names only: Unless otherwise specified omit Canadian, Foreign and transient names
3. Mark each box or carton with name of List, Key number and mailer's offer.

THIS IS A CONTINUATION
Please omit names previously addressed ________________

THIS IS A TEST
Please address from 5 different parts of the list

GUARANTEE:
In accepting the use of these names unless otherwise specified in writing mailer agrees that they are to be used for one mailing only in connection with the offer indicated and that no part of the list will be used more than once without the list owner's written consent and the payment of an additional fee.

BILLING:
Please send statement of charges to Every Mans List Co., Inc. as soon as the job has been completed. Indicate our number, the exact quantity addressed and date shipped. Resale No.

& NAME OF LIST QUANTITY PRICE PER M KEY

List must be delivered in zip code sequence

THANK YOU

PAYMENT:
The mailer will be billed by us as special agents of the list owner. Upon receipt of payment, our check will be forwarded immediately less the standard 20% commission upon rental addressing only.

Through the years—as I have sat on both sides of the desk as a list user and as a list counselor—it has become painfully apparent that the control of list testing is one of the most important functions in any direct mail program.

For your decisions to be soundly based on future usage, you must be sure that the test selection is truly representative of the list as a whole—or at least that portion you plan to use. Otherwise, you will be in no better position *after* the test than you were *before* the test.

A test selection must be representative and the names involved should be fresh. Repeated exposure of names in static test selections tends to destroy their representativeness. This is true, even though the original selection might have formed a good cross-section.

So let's take a look at some of the ways in which test selections can be prepared:

A. N'TH NAME SELECTION

This involves the selection of names in accordance with a set numerical pattern—i.e., every 10th name, every 15th name, and so on. This procedure is followed through the entire file.

Although this method provides a truly representative sampling of the list, it is not possible (unless the file remains completely static) to ensure that names previously used in a test can be skipped in a subsequent mailing.

But if the skipping of names in future mailings is not a factor, the N'th name procedure is an excellent one.

B. NON-REPETITIVE, NON-DUPLICATING N'TH NAME SELECTIONS

The capability of list owners or managers to supply N'th name test selections that can be identified and omitted on continuation mailings is your best assurance that your test is being made properly.

Testing a list on computer, compared with a list maintained on plates, provides a greater opportunity for a true representative sampling of a file. But even computerized lists can be difficult to work with if the proper computer (software) programs required to address the file are not available and used. So not *all* computerized lists provide the sophisticated test pattern procedures to give Non-Repetitive, Non-Duplicating N'th Name Testing.

To accomplish this kind of selection requires software programs and test codes on the tape record as well as the recording of *all* tests conducted on the list. Under this procedure any changes (additions and deletions) to the file do not affect the list owner/manager's ability to supply Non-Repetitive, Non-Duplicating N'th Name Selections.

C. NON-REPETITIVE N'TH NAME SELECTION

This is the same procedure as above except that different test selections for each mailer are not called for.

This method does specifically provide a recording or flagging procedure so that names tested can be skipped in follow-up mailings.

D. ZIP CODE CROSS SECTION SELECTION

This method calls for a certain number of consecutive names selected by ZIP codes. Selection is made on the basis of the 1st, 2nd, 3rd, 4th, or 5th digits or combinations of them.

This sampling method is not quite as representative of the entire list, but it does provide an opportunity within certain limitations to skip names in future mailings.

E. GEOGRAPHICAL SELECTION

This is similar to the ZIP code selecting method, but is based on a quantity selection of names by city, county, or state. Again, the selection may not be truly representative of the list, but it provides the opportunity to skip tested areas in subsequent mailings.

F. FIRST COME BASIS

This method takes a given number of names in consecutive order from a specific point or points in the file. It is not likely to be representative of the list, but again it enables you to skip tested groups later.

POTENTIAL PITFALLS

As you go about the business of specifying test selections, here are some potential pitfalls:

1. If the list owner or broker says "Random selection provided," ask for an explanation.
2. Similarly, if the list owner or broker specifies "Scientific Cross Section" or "Cross Section Selection Available," ask for clarification. The time spent in getting a proper definition will be time well spent.
3. Test selections should be made from the entire list only, if the list will eventually be used in its entirety. If only parts of a list will be used, test selections should be made on those parts.
4. Try to get a written record of the method used on your test, including how the test selection was made, even though you have given written specifications when you placed the order. Remember—you have a sizable investment in list usage. So be doubly certain your tests are properly conducted, so future expenditures are based on sound conclusions.

BREAKDOWN

1. The number of names of each type that are available and whether or not selections can be made
2. The percentage of names of the following types and whether or not selections can be made
   a. Men's Names
   b. Women's Names
   c. Home addresses or business addresses with names of individuals
   d. Home addresses or business addresses without names of individuals

RATE

The rate per thousand for rental including addressing charges

AGE OF LIST

The years during which purchases, inquiries or compilations were made

PRODUCT OR SERVICE

What specific items or services were purchased

UNIT OF SALE

The amount of the average purchase

HOW SOLD

The basis on which purchases were made

1. Cash with order
2. Open account
3. C.O.D.
4. Credit

SOURCE OR MEDIA USED

Percentage of names derived from:

1. Direct Mail
2. Publication advertising
   a. Newspapers
   b. Magazines (State Types)
3. Directories, Rosters, etc.
4. Field Selling
5. Revolving charge or installment sales
6. Radio & TV

ALPHABETICAL BREAKDOWN OF U.S. POPULATION

The following breakdown shows the frequency with which surnames appear alphabetically in the files of the Social Security Administration. Major mailers indicate that their own lists have a similar breakdown.

Letter	%	Letter	%
A	3.03	N	1.55
B	9.30	O	1.32
C	7.66	P	4.62
D	4.04	Q	.10
E	1.64	R	5.53
F	3.36	S	9.62
G	4.85	T	3.21
H	8.48	U	.07
I	.17	V	.60
J	4.75	W	8.67
K	2.59	X	.00
L	3.62	Y	.59
M	10.51	Z	.12

Chapter 21

MAILING LIST CONTROLS

SINCE the majority of mailing lists are maintained on computer tapes or cards, much greater control of lists is possible than in days when less advanced systems were required. Four areas, in particular, deserve special consideration: (1) duplicate elimination, (2) match coding, (3) quality control and (4) list protection.

Merge & Purge

For many years, the problem of name duplication when multiple lists were used for a mailing was one of the major headaches for mailers. Not only were duplicate mailings costly, but they constituted a prime target for direct mail's critics. In addition, anyone receiving two, three or more identical mailing pieces in the same mail delivery or within days of one another had good reason to suspect the efficiency of the mailer and much of the personal element was destroyed.

The usual "solution" to this problem was simply to enclose a little slip with the mailing trying to convince the recipient that it was in his best interests to send duplicate pieces because comparing lists for duplications was more costly than simply mailing duplicates.

Fortunately, as the Computer Age made its presence felt in direct mail, a number of foresighted list experts went to work to develop efficient techniques to utilize the computer to eliminate or at least reduce duplication. While these leaders—Alan Drey Company, Inc., Lewis Kleid, Inc. and Names Unlimited—adopted different names for their systems, the general term "merge and purge" is accepted for the procedure. Today, a large variety of merge and purge systems are available from many service organizations and a number of larger mailers have developed special systems of their own.

The Basic Procedures

In a speech at a DMMA conference,[1] Robert Stone offered a composite of the procedures for eliminating duplication:

1. You rent your lists through the brokers involved in the usual way. (Almost all lists which are on magnetic tape or punch cards are suitable.)
2. The tapes or punch cards provided for rented lists, as well as the tapes or punch cards for the mailer's customer and/or prospect list, are sent to the service organization designated.
3. The service organization puts the tapes through a computerized matching process which compares the names of each list with *every* name on *every* other list ... including the mailer's customer list.
4. The net result is that the mailer receives one set of labels with no duplication whatever between the rented lists (no matter how many may be involved) and the customer lists.
5. In addition, the mailer receives a second non-duplicating set of labels that represents names of known mail order buyers, which appear two or more times on the multiplicity of rented lists.
6. Tight security is offered for all plans, giving list owners the protection they need and want.

Potential Savings by Eliminating Duplicate Mailings*

MAILING QUANTITIES

Percent of Duplication	1,000	2,500	—In Thousands— 5,000	10,000	25,000	50,000
10%	$10	$ 25	$ 50	$100	$ 250	$ 500
15	15	37.5	75	150	375	750
20	20	50	100	200	500	1,000
25	25	62.5	125	250	625	1,250
30	30	75	150	300	750	1,500
35	35	87.5	175	350	875	1,750
40	40	100	200	400	1,000	2,000
45	45	112.5	225	450	1,125	2,250
50	50	125	250	500	1,250	2,500

*Based on a mailing package cost of $100 per thousand. As mailing costs rise, savings rise dramatically.

The savings which are possible by eliminating duplicate mailings are indicated in the chart above. The chart on the following page shows an actual example of the application of a merge and purge program involving 23 lists.

[1] "Farewell to Mailing List Duplication." A speech by Robert Stone, President of Stone & Adler. DMMA Annual Conference. Chicago, November 1968.

MERGE AND PURGE PROGRAM

List No.	Total Input	Exclusive List	Multi-Buyer	Total Output	Percent of Duplication
1.	48,000	47,641	30	47,671	1%
2.	27,646	21,232	811	22,043	18
3.	24,837	20,016	833	20,849	17
4.	43,899	33,461	1,288	34,749	19
5.	25,220	18,647	614	19,261	22
6.	12,595	11,410	206	11,616	12
7.	100,220	73,445	2,700	76,145	25
8.	58,006	43,188	1,859	45,047	23
9.	24,527	20,435	598	21,033	13
10.	63,000	53,595	1,228	54,823	15
11.	25,230	18,281	968	19,249	24
12.	23,750	19,611	524	20,135	12
13.	25,272	18,158	1,319	19,477	21
14.	64,460	47,904	1,812	49,716	24
15.	47,480	42,621	600	43,221	10
16.	70,590	63,567	721	64,288	9
17.	16,700	15,432	203	15,635	6
18.	72,000	54,720	2,251	56,971	19
19.	6,000	4,544	197	4,741	49
20.	239,430	202,885	4,537	207,422	13
21.	58,682	50,035	1,077	51,112	10
22.	51,150	31,374	1,886	33,260	40
23.	32,800	24,393	1,149	25,542	22
GRAND TOTALS	1,161,494	936,595	27,411	964,006	16.5%

The total number of rented names processed (Total Input) was 1,161,494 names. There were 936,595 names, in total, on the Exclusive Lists (names which appear on the original source list, but not on any other lists). There was a total of 27,411 multi-buyer names (names which appeared on two or more lists). The rented lists were also matched against the mailer's customer list of 1,441,000 names with the result that a total of 146,522 house names were suppressed. The net result was that 964,006 nonduplicating names were used.

NOTE: Percent of duplication for each list reflects duplication against all other rented lists as well as the house list of the mailer.

Source: System Dupli-Match (Alan Drey Company, Inc.)

In his speech, Bob Stone also listed seven key advantages for the use of merge and purge:

1. Effect a better "image" in the market place.
2. Increase overall response per thousand mailed.
3. Save money by eliminating the cost of duplicate mailings.
4. For those who use sweepstakes—a reduction in the "no" responses from those who receive duplicate mailings.
5. Complete elimination of "prospect" mailings to present buyers.
6. The opportunity for follow-up mailings to the best prospects—those whose names appear on two or more direct response lists.
7. The opportunity to remove all known bad-debt names from rented lists —matching such names against the house list of known deadbeats.

Merge & Purge Problems

Utilizing computerized duplicate elimination systems is not without its problems. List broker Florence Wolf makes these four basic observations.[2]

1. Tape matching is *not* a cure-all for everybody's duplication problem. But it *is* the best answer anybody's come up with yet for the right situation.
2. For the mailer who can utilize it, tape matching really does deliver the savings in cost and the increases in returns its proponents claim. The catch: not every mailer *can* utilize it.
3. There has been a tendency, understandable but unfortunate, to ignore or play down the problems inherent in the tape matching technique. These problems are just as real as the benefits.
4. Despite the complications, tape matching is undoubtedly here to stay. If you mail in substantial volume to rented lists, then you owe it to your budget to take a serious look at its mechanics and its arithmetic. They *may* be in your favor.

Merge & Purge Examples

There are plenty of examples of effective use of merge and purge systems. Some typical case histories were reported by Alan Drey Company, Inc.:[3]

Children's Books—A leading publisher of children's books eliminated 19.5% duplicates from lists used in a single mailing. This publisher also utilized a merged list for testing purposes—using a cross-section of more than 15 merged lists, rather than trying to test each list individually.

Catalog Mailer—More than 25% duplicates were eliminated from one large mailing. The mailer not only saved on mailing costs but increased

[2]"The Computer's Role in Eliminating Duplications" by Florence R. Wolf. Florence Wolf Inc. Chicago.

[3]"Eliminating Duplicate Names." Report No. 3 prepared by Alan Drey Company, Inc., Chicago. Examples given utilized Drey's System Dupli-Match service for merge and purge.

the validity and results of a sweepstakes effort. With duplicates eliminated, each prospect only gets one chance to enter. This can mean a substantial saving in terms of handling and processing negative responses.

Consumer Magazine—A fast-growing consumer magazine was able to reduce its cost-per-order by a whopping 52.7%. Seventeen mail order lists were processed with a total of 1,451,410 names plus 500,000 subscribers (to be eliminated from rented lists.) A total duplication of 20.8% was discovered. This represented a total savings of $44,643 for the magazine. And a selected group of non-responding multi-buyers received a second mailing.

Insurance Company—A leading insurance company was able to eliminate 27% duplicates from a single mailing. And, while processing their own customer names and rented lists, an in-depth analysis by Zip Codes and census tracts was conducted. The client got a better geographic profile of its customers ... and they got a report showing total mailing penetration by Zip Code areas.

Duplicates for List Building

While merge and purge systems are primarily used to eliminate duplicates when mailing to multiple lists, a similar system can also be used to compile special lists for mailing purposes. A hypothetical example was created by Doctors George Benson and Charman L. Jain of St. John's University:[4]

The rationale for the selection of duplicates is illustrated by the use of three lists being considered by a manufacturer of expensive boat accessories:

List	*Name*
A	Boat owners
B	Public opinion pace setters (influentials)
C	Credit card holders

The advertiser considers his prime prospects to be boat owners (List A) who are also influential (List B) credit card holders (List C). The advertiser is very anxious to bring his products to the attention of the influentials (also known as the early adopters) since they exert the most word-of-mouth influence on potential buyers based on their personal experience with the product.

The influentials are known to have wide personal contacts, are socially active, and frequently have above average income and education. The enthusiastic adoption of a product by the early adopters would constitute a significant marketing accomplishment that would favorably affect the product through the balance of its life cycle.

[4]"Matching Direct Mail Lists for Duplicate Name Selection" by Dr. George Benson and Dr. Charman L. Jain. *Direct Marketing*. March 1971.

Credit card owners have above average willingness to spend, and therefore are also of obvious interest to this particular manufacturer.

No single list satisfies the complete description of the prime prospect described by this example. Names duplicated on Lists A & B or A & C would satisfy the bulk of the advertiser's requirements by identifying those who are spenders or influence spenders superimposed upon an interest in boats as evidenced by boat ownership. However, only those names that are duplicated on all the lists (in this instance) would provide the advertiser with all the sought for characteristics.

Since a single list may not provide adequate name coverage of any one characteristic, the advertiser may first find it expedient to combine a number of lists pertaining to the same characteristic and to eliminate the duplicate names before proceeding further. The process of eliminating duplicates from similar lists and selecting the duplicates from between the complementary lists is diagrammed in the illustration on page 584.

Match Coding

A key to many duplication elimination systems is match coding or extraction coding. A description of this technique was given in *Direct Marketing.*[5]

Under match-coding, specific characters of the listing are selected for comparison. A typical sequence would be the ZIP, the first, third, and fourth characters of the last name and the first four characters of the street address. Here is a sample:

John Q. Public
16 Broadway
Anywhere, USA 11530

This results in: 11530 PBL 16 BR

Once a match code has been generated for each individual on the list, the list can be sorted into match code sequence for maintenance and dupe stripping. To identify a dupe with match coding, one would compare an individual's match code with the one immediately following, and if they match character for character, one can reasonably assume that a dupe has been uncovered.

Since it is immediately obvious that misspellings can lead to different match codes for the same individual and that with the large number of names being handled today, a short match code leads to a large number of errors, variations in the basic match coding concept are being developed and used.

---

[5] "Duplicate Names on Lists Cause Wasted Dollars." *Direct Marketing.* March 1970.

Elimination of Duplicate Listings Between Similar Lists and Selection of Duplicate Listings Between Dissimilar Lists

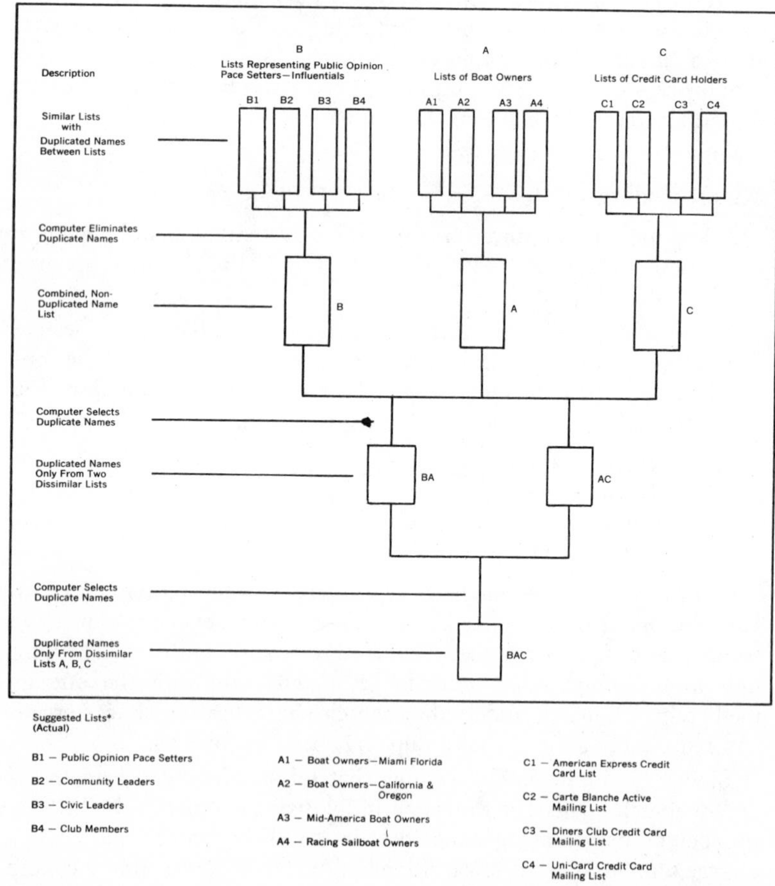

Suggested Lists*
(Actual)

B1 – Public Opinion Pace Setters
B2 – Community Leaders
B3 – Civic Leaders
B4 – Club Members

A1 – Boat Owners—Miami Florida
A2 – Boat Owners—California & Oregon
A3 – Mid-America Boat Owners
A4 – Racing Sailboat Owners

C1 – American Express Credit Card List
C2 – Carte Blanche Active Mailing List
C3 – Diners Club Credit Card Mailing List
C4 – Uni-Card Credit Card Mailing List

*Source of Suggested Lists: Direct Mail List—Rates and Data 7-2-69. Standard Rate and Data Service Inc.

Recognizing the shortcomings of match coding, another approach to the problem of duplicate identification has been designed which appears to have considerable merit. This new technique, called mathematical equivalent analysis overcomes the deficiencies associated with match coding. Simply stated, the system breaks the name and address into its various components and then statistically analyzes each component in order to determine if there are enough equal factors to identify a dupe. It does not treat specific characters as does match coding, but works with the entire name and address.

The system identifies duplicates even if the names are misspelled or misinformatted, or even if variations exist in the address. A transposed or truncated numerical address is easily handled, and variations in the street address such as Mount Carmel Ave. and Mt. Carmel Ave. are accurately identified as the same street.

The program is not restricted to names of individuals but also identifies dupes on industrial lists. Examples of dupes that have been found by mathematical equivalent analysis are shown in the reproduction of the printout sheet shown on page 604.

Reader's Digest System

One of the most highly refined match coding systems has been developed by The Reader's Digest. It was described in detail in a special manual:[6]

I—INTRODUCTION

WHAT IS THE MATCH CODE?

The Match Code is a condensation of a name and address. It is generated by a computer program that extracts parts of the name and address that are most likely to be unique to the individual subscriber and at the same time most likely to be repeated by him in any communication with us. As each individual is entered on our Master File of subscribers, he is given a Match Code based on the name and address on his order form.

The Digest Match Code is 24 positions in length. If a Match Code is too short there is a risk that there will be many identical codes in file for different people. If a Match Code is too long its contents are subject to greater inaccuracy and variability. Longer codes cost more to process than shorter codes. The 24-character code used by the Digest answers the basic requirements of uniqueness, accuracy, and economy.

WHY IS A MATCH CODE SYSTEM NEEDED?

There are two main uses for Match Code at The Reader's Digest:

1. To identify subscriber records in the computer Master File.
2. To sequence records in the computer Master File.

---

[6]"An Introduction to The Reader's Digest Match Code and Matching Routines." The Reader's Digest. Pleasantville, N. Y. June 1967.

The Match Code Identifies the Subscriber

There are actually two codes the Digest uses to identify a subscriber. One is the Match Code and the other is a 10-digit Account Number.

All subscribers have, in addition to Match Code, a unique 10-digit account number assigned to them. Normally in all our correspondence with a subscriber we highlight his number and encourage him to use it when writing to us. By entering this short number into our computers, we can look up the subscriber's Match Code from a cross-reference file maintained on magnetic tape.

HOWEVER, because our subscriber list is so large, we receive a considerable volume of mail without an account number. Also, all new subscriptions must be processed without benefit of an account number. The Match Code System allows us to keypunch the member's full name and address and have the computer extract his Match Code. Thus we have a way of entering subscriber activity into the computer without having to rely on an account number to identify the individual. More important, there is no need to maintain any manual files of names and addresses to be used in looking up a person's computer identification.

Some of our customers have many "aliases." The following names may all belong to the same person or may represent four different people.

Mrs. Joseph Jones, Jr.
Mrs. J. W. Jones, Jr.
Mrs. Mathilda Jones
M. Jones

In addition to dealing with aliases we must take into consideration the variations subscribers may provide in their mailing address. The following may be the same or different locations.

Armonk Road
333 Armonk Road
Rural Route 4

These variations can create problems in matching because the Match Code extracted for each variation may be different from the one put on the Subscriber's Master Record initially.

The set of instructions used by the computer for internal matching of accounts is a very important part of the Match Code System. These match code rules allow automatic matching of accounts where a subsequent match code for a given subscriber is not the same as the one on the Master File. Matching concepts will be dealt with later on in this book.

The Match Code Determines the Sequence of Records in the Master File

The Master File at The Reader's Digest is the major source from which mailings are made to subscribers. In initially setting up this file it was determined that it would be most economical to maintain it in good mailing sequence so that a minimum of sorting would have to be done after accounts are selected for mailing.

Post Office regulations stipulate that our high volume mailings must be "presorted" so that all pieces bearing the same ZIP Code are banded together. By using Match Code to sequence the Master File we achieve this optimum sequence for mailing since State and ZIP Code constitute the first six positions of Match Code.

The remaining eighteen positions of Match Code consist of extracted portions of name and address. Surname information is placed before address information for two reasons. First, it offers the best file sequence for internal matching routines in the computer since a subscriber always gives his Surname but does not always give a complete address. Filing by Surname within ZIP Code means that there is a better chance to find a subscriber if he varies his address. The second reason for placing Surname before address information is that it provides a good file sequence for listing in cases where the Master File must be printed.

II—DESCRIPTION OF MATCH CODE

THE VICINITY CODE (V CODE) CLASSIFIES ADDRESSES

Although the length of the Match Code is fixed at 24 positions, the content and format vary according to the type of address a subscriber gives.

The V Code classifies subscribers by type of address, placing addresses specifically into one of four classes—1, 2, 3, or 4. Using V Code to identify the general category of address—such as House #, Box #, and so on—serves three main purposes:

1. The V Code is the key which tells the computer how the extracted parts of the address should be arranged within the Match Code.
2. The V Code is actually contained within the Match Code. Its placement there assures that, while all identical Surnames within a ZIP Code are filed together, they are arranged so that those with one type of address information are filed together.
3. The V Code plays an important part in the computer matching routines which vary according to the type of address.

The kinds of addresses within each V Code are:

V Code 1 Used for addresses containing a house number and street name, even if additional information is given.

V Code 2 Used for any address not described under V Code 1, 3, or 4. This includes a street name with no house number, or with a box number, an apartment number, or General Delivery. Military addresses usually fall into this category.

V Code 3 Used for addresses containing a rural route, star route, RFD, etc., with or without a number. If a house number and street name are also given, they take precedence and the address is V Code 1.

V Code 4 Used for all addresses showing name, town, and state only. Addresses that include c/o an individual, c/o PO Box, Superintendent of Schools, or PO Box without a number, are also considered V Code 4 when no other information is given.

FORMAT OF MATCH CODE

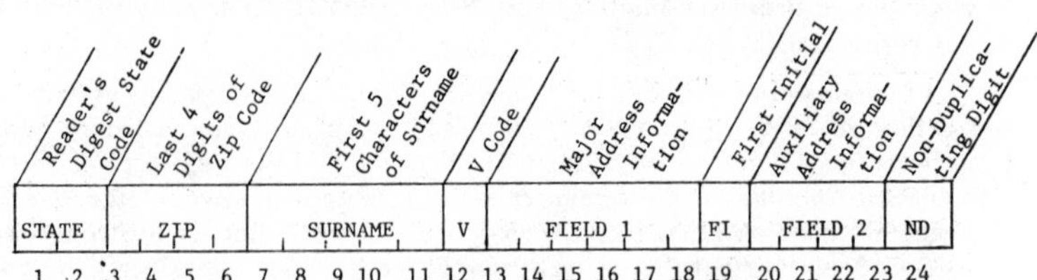

The following is a general description of the contents of Match Code:

Pos. 1-2: *State Code.* Each state has been assigned a unique numeric code to accommodate Reader's Digest mailing needs.

3-6: *Last four digits of ZIP Code.* Looked up internally by having the computer match the alphabetic city name against a Post Office Deck.

7-11: *First five characters of subscriber's Surname* or Company Name.

12: *Vicinity Code (V Code).* This digit codes the address into one of four types:

1 = Address has Street Name and House #.

2 = Any address not described under 1, 3, and 4. Includes: Box #, General Delivery, Military Address, Building Names.

3 = Rural Route, Star Route with or without a number.

4 = Addresses with name, town, and state only. Also used if only information is c/o individual, box.

13-18: Alphabetic or numeric data extracted from *major portion (Field 1) of address.* E.g. if Vicinity Code = 1, then position 13 contains 1st letter of street name and positions 14-18 contains House #; if Vicinity Code = 3, then positions 13-18 contain Route information.

19: *First letter of first name.* Blank, if none given.

20-23: *Auxiliary (Field 2) information* if given—e.g. Apartment #. Otherwise contents vary depending upon the Vicinity Code. E.g. on code 1, 1st four letters of street name; on code 2, 3, and 4, middle initial if given.

24: *Non-duplicating digit (N.D. digit)*—usually zero. However, if there are two or more accounts in file with match codes that are identical in the first 23 positions, then this position contains a unique digit to number the accounts: 1, 2, and so on.

III—ADDRESS EDITING AND KEYPUNCHING

How does the computer know which format of Match Code to extract? How does it know where specific information is located in the name and address? New orders entering the file for the first time, and correspondence where no Account Number is given, must be prepared manually for keypunching by Match Code Editors using specific editing and coding rules.

Editing reduces data to fit limited space; *coding* is interpreting information and using special symbols to indicate specific action to be taken by the computer. Editing and coding clarify work for the Keypunch operator. Just as variations in name and address can change Match Code, variations in editing, coding, or keypunching will change Match Code. Therefore accuracy and consistency in this pre-computer work is critical to the success of any Match Code System.

COMPONENTS OF A NAME AND ADDRESS

A name and address generally has the following components:

1. Name of Person or Company. May or may not contain Title or Initials.
2. Major Address Information—usually present.
3. Auxiliary Address Information—sometimes present.
4. City Name—always present.
5. State Name—always present.
6. ZIP Code—usually provided by subscriber. If not, the last 2 digits (Zone) are looked up manually if the member lives in a Zoned City.

The first 3 components above are the ones of concern to the Match Code Editor. The last 3 are visually edited by a keypunch operator as she types:

City Name The Keypunch operator types until 13 positions are punched.

State The Keypunch operator supplies, from memory, the standard 2-character abbreviation for the state. E.g. Maryland = MD

ZIP Code The Keypunch operator types the last 2 digits if any.

EDITING THE NAME AND ADDRESS

The term "field" will be used often in the discussions that follow. A field is a fixed number of characters assigned for specific information. For example, the name is keypunched into the name field.

Name This field may contain a maximum of *23 characters* including Title, spaces, and symbols.

Major Address This field may contain a maximum of *18 characters* including spaces and symbols. The data is extracted into Field 1 of Match Code.

Auxiliary This field may contain a maximum of *13 characters* including spaces and symbols. The data is extracted into Field 2 of Match Code.

Whenever a field exceeds maximum limitations, data of the least importance is eliminated or cut down by the editor. Those portions of the name and address which will become part of the Match Code are never eliminated or cut down.

GENERAL RULES CONCERNING FIELDS

Field 1 must contain the most important part of the address; Field 2 contains the Auxiliary information or least important part of the address.

Example Using Maximum Size Fields

	1	2	3	4	5	6	7	8	9	10	11	12	13	14	15	16	17	18	19	20	21	22	23
Name	B	I	S	H	O	P		F	R	A	N	K	L	I	N		F		J	O	N	E	S
Field 1	1	4	8	0		C	L	E	V	E	L	A	N	D		A	V	E					
Field 2	M	A	Y	F	A	I	R		C	O	U	R	T										

The following list which is memorized by Match Code Editors shows *the order of importance* for different kinds of address information.

House number with street name

Rural Route # or Route designation

Box #

Apartment #

Room #

Building # or Name

Institutional Name

Street name with no number

General address designations such as General Delivery, Suburbs, etc.

Field 1 and 2 must be indicated on addresses which contain two or more parts.

Field 1 is indicated by an encircled (1)

Field 2 is indicated by an encircled (2)

When an address contains three or more parts, the additional part(s) are fitted into the latter half of either Field 1 or 2, if space permits. Otherwise, the parts are omitted. When printing name and address on documents to be mailed, the computer prints Field 1 information before Field 2 information.

V CODE EDITING

The editor determines the V Code based on the name and address and edits it to the right of the name. Since V Code 1 is the most common, it is not edited. However, the Keypunch operator does punch "1" into the V Code field of the input card.

SPECIAL SYMBOLS

As seen in the preceding examples, addresses must sometimes be coded with special symbols to help the computer routines determine what information to put into the Match Code.

The symbols act as keys which may indicate a title omission, or instructions to omit a section of address data and continue searching for other data, or to stop and extract the data into the area specified for the particular V Code. The following symbols are either edited or supplied by the Keypunch operator as indicated below:

Δ *or* Λ *(Space)* — In Name Field: If in first position it indicates omission of title. Also used to extend short names to five Surname positions—e.g. Bill Cox ⎵ Λ Jr. Sometimes used for clarification—e.g. St. Λ James.

In Address Field: used only for clarification.

/ *(Slash)* Used exclusively in the Name Field to indicate the start of the Surname (or the proper name of an institution). The / is not usually edited, but keypunched automatically by the Keypunch operator preceding the Surname. Editing is required for clarification only.

- *(Hyphen)* In Name Field: used between pairs of names in place of "and" or "&." E.g. Betty and George Cory is edited as Betty-George Cory.

In Address Field:

1. Between a number and an alphabetic, the hyphen causes the computer to pick up the number and omit the alphabetic information. E.g. 222-E Main St. The E (for East) is not picked up for Match Code.

2. Between two numerics, or two alphas, the hyphen prevents a break in the series of consecutive characters. Both characters will be selected for Match Code. E.g. 18-48 Bay St. The Match Code will contain B18 Δ 48 in Field 1.

3. Before a word, the hyphen indicates that data (the characters between the hyphen and the next blank) following is not to be used in the Match Code. E.g. -Room 48. Only 48 is picked up for Match Code.

⌒ *(Loop or Curved Line)* Used to join data together. E.g. 88 St. James St. is edited at 88 St $\widehat{x}$ James St. If St. James appears in the Name Field, there is no joining.

& *(Ampersand)* Edited before a fraction in the address field. E.g. 183½ Main St. is edited as 183-&½ Main St. The fraction is not picked up for Match Code.

IV—MATCHING ROUTES

Previous sections have dealt primarily with a description of Match Code and the input processing techniques used to derive the appropriate code for a given name and address.

The sections that follow highlight the concepts and rules involved in matching. The term "transaction" will be used frequently in these discussions. A transaction is any activity entered into the computer to be applied against a Master File. For example, a Payment to be applied against a subscriber's record is entered on a Payment transaction; a New Order is entered on a New Order transaction.

Since the Match Code identifies a subscriber on the Master File and also sequences the Master File, it follows that to access a subscriber's record we must:

1. Sequence the transactions by Match Code.
2. Have a set of computer routines to perform the match.

The matching of a transaction to the Master File can be either (1) to apply an activity to an existing record (e.g. on Payments) or (2) to insert a new subscriber in his proper location (e.g. on New Orders). This processing is done in a computer run called the File Maintenance Run.

VARIATIONS IN ADDRESS

The most desirable matching condition is where the transaction carries a Match Code that is identical to the one on the Master File. Then there is no question that this is the same person being matched. However, we know addresses can vary for the same person. For example, FRANK C. AYRES in NORTIN, KANSAS may write with any one of the following addresses:

V Code 1:	33 Orchard St
2:	Orchard St
3:	Rural Route 1
4:	No Address Information given

Variations in address may also occur if handwriting is unclear. In these cases the Editor's or Keypunch operator's interpretation will decide how the address is entered.

Any one of these variations may appear on either the Master File or Transaction—thus giving rise to 16 V Code possibilities for Matching:

Master File V Code	Transaction V Code
1	1
1	2
1	3
1	4
2	1
2	2
2	3
2	4
3	1
3	2
3	3
3	4
4	1
4	2
4	3
4	4

VARIATIONS IN NAME

Although a Name variation does not affect the assignment of V Code, the first initial and sometimes middle initial are part of Match Code, and therefore part of the matching routines. It will be seen, too, that the routines sometimes go outside of Match Code and use information stored as part of the printable name and address, to determine a match. The title is frequently used in this way. We must therefore take into consideration that FRANK C. AYRES of the previous example can also appear on mail as the following.

Title on Mail Can be:	*Name on Mail Can be:*
MrMrs *or* Mr *or* Mrs *or* Other Man's Title	Frank C Ayres
MrMrs *or* Mr *or* Mrs *or* Other Man's Title	Frank Ayres
MrMrs *or* Mr *or* Mrs *or* Other Man's Title *or* No Title	F C Ayres
MrMrs *or* Mr *or* Mrs *or* Other Man's Title *or* No Title	F Ayres
Mrs *or* Woman's Title *or* No Title	Betty R Ayres
Mrs *or* Woman's Title *or* No Title	Betty Ayres
Mrs *or* Woman's Title *or* No Title	B R Ayres
Mrs *or* Woman's Title *or* No Title	B Ayres

NOTE: In keypunching, the title MR is always assumed on a man's name or an Initial only if no title is given by the subscriber.

As in address variations, differences in name can also occur because of unclear handwriting.

CATEGORIES OF MATCHES

When matching a transaction against the Master File, the matching routines classify the match into one of four categories.

1. *Exact Match* — The Match Codes on the transaction and Master File are identical.
2. *Inexact Match* — The Match Codes are not identical but enough elements of the name and address are alike to call this a good match.
3. *Non-Match* — Not enough elements are alike to call this a match.
4. *Overmatch* — The transaction matches more than one account on the Master File in the first 23 positions. Only the N. D. digit does not match—the transaction having zero and the Master Files having 1, 2, etc. (See examples on following page.)

HOW THE CATEGORIES OF MATCHES AFFECT SPECIFIC TYPES OF TRANSACTIONS

1. *Non-Order Transactions*—e.g. Payments, Changes of Address, etc.
   - A. *Exact or Inexact Match:* The transaction is processed against the Master File record.
   - B. *Overmatch:* The transaction is written for manual review with the matching Master Files. An Adjuster determines the correct account for application of the transaction and re-enters the transaction with the appropriate Account Number.
   - C. *Non-Match:* The transaction is written for manual review with up to two Surname matches—i.e. two adjacent Master File accounts with the same first 11 positions of Match Code. There is a good chance that on manual review the Adjuster will actually find the match in one of the two Master Files. (For more on this see Supplementary Rules at end of this section.)

Examples

	Transaction	*Master File*	
	Mr John Doe	J Doe	
	2505-N Estelle	2505 Estelle	
	Wichita Kansas	Wichita Kansas	*EXACT MATCH*
MC:	SSZZZZDOE□□1E2505□JESTEO	SSZZZZDOE□□1E2505□JESTEO	
	Mr Robert Carr	Mrs Beatrice Carr	
	75-S Terrace	75-S Terrace	
	Fargo N Dakota	Fargo N Dakota	*INEXACT MATCH*
MC:	SSZZZZCARR□1T75□□□RTERRO	SSZZZZCARR□1T75□□□BTERRO	
	Mr Charles Hiers	A R Hiers	
	R2	R2	
	Moultrie Ga	Moultrie Ga	*NON-MATCH*
MC:	SSZZZZHIERS3R2□□□□C□□□□□O	SSZZZZHIERS3R2□□□□ARIIIO	
	Mr Floyd Nicholson	Mrs F G Nichols	
	338-W Lincoln St	338-W Lincoln Way	
	Norton Kansas	Norton Kansas	*OVERMATCH*
MC:	SSZZZZNICHO1L338□□FLINCO	SSZZZZNICHO1L338□□FLINC1	
		Mrs Frank Nichol	
		338 Lincoln Park	
		Norton Kansas	
		SSZZZZNICHO1L338□□FLINC2	

NOTE: SSZZZZ in the **first six** positions of the **Match Codes above represent** State and ZIP Code.

2. *New Order Transactions*

   A. *Exact, Inexact, or Overmatch in Book Club only:* The Order transaction and the matching Master File item(s) are written out by the computer for manual review. This may be a duplicate new order, or an actual new order for a different person. An Adjustor will take appropriate action.

   B. *Exact, Inexact, or Overmatch in Other Products:* Same as for Non-Order transactions.

   C. *Non-Match:* A Master File record is set up and inserted into the File based on the information in the order transaction. (Note: A non-match results on a New Order when the Master File Match Code being tested is higher in value than the Match Code on the transaction.)

3. *Forced Inserts*—these transactions are like New Orders, but are forced into the Master File regardless of matching condition. N. D. digits may be affected as follows:

   A. *Exact Match:* The transaction is forced into the Master File following the original account in File. The N. D. digit on the original account with the same Match Code is changed from zero to 1. The N. D. digit on the account forced in is assigned a 2.

   B. *Overmatch:* The transaction is forced into the Master File following the last Master File account with the same first 23 positions of Match Code. The N. D. Digit on the Forced Insert is assigned the next consecutive number—e.g. if N. D. 1 is already on file, then N. D. 2 is assigned.

   C. *Inexact or Non-Match:* The transaction is forced into the Master File. N. D. digits are not affected.

WHAT THE COMPUTER TESTS IN THE MATCHING ROUTINES

The logic behind the matching routines can be framed as a question:

Considering the variations in name and address, is there enough like information that we can be reasonably sure that this is the same account?

The routines test in two main areas:

A. *Components of the Match Code Itself*

Because the Match Code categorizes information and contains the most significant parts of the name and address, the computer relies almost completely on the Match Code to determine the category of match. Certainly if there is an exact match, the matching routines need not go outside of the Match Code for testing purposes. Also, in some inexact matches only Match Code is tested—as in the following example:

Master File

Mrs J Doe
1 St NW
Moultrie Ga

MC: SSZZZZDOE□□*21*□□□□□*J*□□□□0

Transaction
Mrs J C Doe
520 1 St NW
Moultrie Ga
SSZZZZDOE□□11520□□*J1*□□□0

By cross-matching Field 1 against Field 2 (1 St against 1 St) on V Code 2 *vs* V Code 1, and determining that the first initials are equal, this was considered a good match.

B. *Titles from Name Field*

In cases where a match cannot be determined from Match Code alone—i.e. where not enough elements match to be sure this is a match, then the routines test the titles in the name fields of the transaction and Master File. For example:

Master File
Mr Robert Carr
75-S Terrace
Moultrie Ga
MC: SSZZZZCARR□1T75□□□*R*TERRO

Transaction
Mrs Beatrice Carr
75-S Terrace
Moultrie Ga
SSZZZZCARR□1T75□□□*B*TERRO

Only the first initials of Match Code do not agree. By examining the Match Code only, the routines cannot tell whether this may be a husband-wife situation or just two different people. Thus titles become important when first initials are not the same.

MATCHING RULES

The charts on the pages following outline the matching rules for each of the 16 V-Code possibilities. The statements below contain basic information concerning the rules and an understanding will be helpful before looking at the rules themselves.

1. The first 11 positions of Match Code (State, ZIP, Surname) must be exactly the same on transaction and Master File for a match to be made.
2. When Match Code fields of unequal lengths are compared (e.g. Field 1 against Field 2), the number of characters compared equals the size of the smaller field.
3. When two fields are compared they are not considered "truly" equal or unequal unless information of the same type is being compared. For example, on the following comparisons of Field 2:

MIII	: MIII	is *truly equal* because both have data of the same type.
MIII	: RIII	is *truly unequal* because both have data of the same type.

MIII : MAIN		is *not truly unequal* because a Middle Initial is being tested against other information.
MIII : □□□□		is *not truly unequal* because a Middle Initial is being tested against blanks.
PARK : MAIN		is *truly unequal* because both have data of the same type, i.e., Auxiliary information.
OAK□ : 3B□□		is *not truly unequal* if one has Auxiliary information and the other does not.

4. A transaction is matched against every Master File with the same first 11 positions until a match is found or until Match Code of the Master File becomes greater than the Match Code of the transaction. Then—

   —If an Order or Forced Insert transaction is being processed, it is inserted into the Master File.

   —If a Non-Order transaction is being processed, it is written out as a "Can't Find" or Non-Match.

   (See previous section on How the Categories of Matches Affect Specific Types of Transactions.)

5. Whenever a path leads to MATCH this is an Exact or Overmatch if the first 23 positions agree and an Inexact Match if the first 23 positions do not agree.

SUPPLEMENTARY RULES

As of this writing, The Reader's Digest is planning to add supplementary rules to its matching routines. Analysis has shown that additional matches can be made internally in the computer where there are now non-matches. The Supplementary rules are extensions of the existing rules and work with the following areas.

1. *Transaction and Master File Contents*

   Assuming the transaction matches more than one account, or the validity of a match is in question, the transaction and Master File contents can sometimes be the deciding factor on whether to make a match. E.g. if a member returns a particular product, a Return transaction is entered into the computer for that product. The matching routines will determine whether the Master File(s) in question show the product as actually shipped.

   If the product was not shipped, it is unlikely that the transaction and Master Files in question are a good match. If it was shipped, and there are no other possibilities for match, then it is likely that this is a good match.

2. *Name Field*

   It is often found that the full name fields (23 characters) or a considerable portion of the name field is the same on transaction and Master File. However, elements of the address are not enough alike for the computer to make a match under existing rules. In the future, some transactions which now result as non-matches will be subject to Name

Field tests and if they pass, they will be considered an inexact match. For example, the following could become a match in the future:

Mr Kenneth N Kingford	Mr Kenneth N Kingford
10 Winsor Dr	70 Winsor Dr
Wichita Kansas	Wichita Kansas

3. *Spelling Variations*

Often a match is not made because of minor spelling variations in the name. For example:

Mr Donald V Bigg*e*rs	Mr Donald V Bigg*a*rs
163 Knoll Dr	163 Knoll Dr
Norton Kansas	Norton Kansas

In this case the first five letters of Surname in the Match Code are different. In the future such spelling variations will be handled by the matching routines and matches made accordingly.

List Quality Control

Freeman F. Gosden Jr., then President of Market Compilation and Research Bureau, compiled an extensive list of checkpoints which a mailer should observe to maintain a quality control system for lists he rents or has compiled:[7]

1. Make sure each list is checked by someone who knows what to check for, i.e. what was ordered. This includes all details.

Many times we have filled orders to exact specifications only to find the customer made a mistake in ordering. It is better to catch the error at this point and pay for another set of labels to revised specifications than to actually mail and incur many more times the cost in postage and materials.

2. Make sure that someone physically checks the order with a singular basic frame of reference. If the checker was spending his own money for the mailing, does this list look like what he would order and would accept? Further, does this list reach the market sought and will the mail be deliverable by the Post Office?

3. Have your checker sign off and date his control quality effort. If responsibility is documented, better checking always results.

4. Check factors, not pages. There is no need to Q.C. every page.

For most elements of an order, a quick glance will answer as to whether that portion of the order is correct.

5. Don't be a nit-picker. The direct mail business is a business of percents. Remember, you can spend more time checking for a few errors than you will save by eliminating them.

The Specifics: What can go wrong with a job is perhaps an endless combination of possibilities. MCRB's average order has fourteen major factors or variables that could be produced incorrectly.

---

[7]"List Quality Control Basic to Improving Mail Response" by Freeman F. Gosden, Jr. *Direct Marketing.* January 1972.

Fortunately, few do occur and with an established quality control system these are eliminated or corrected before the list is shipped to the user.

Let's look at some of the areas that a good quality control specialist must examine:

Zip Code and Sequence. Make sure all of your labels in the order are in zip code sequence if a 3rd class mailing. This check also indicates if the order is complete.

Beginning and Ending Zip Codes. It is not difficult to imagine part of a label run being separated and not included in a shipment. A check of beginning, continuing, and ending zip codes against the order will assure that all the pieces have been delivered.

Duplication. Check for address duplication and name duplication. Most mailers do not want more than one piece of mail to a household.

Verify ordered select factors. Make sure the job has been selected properly and that factors such as sex (i.e. are male first names appearing in a female name only order), geographic area, titles, business address vs home address, etc., are correct.

Code Line. Check to see if it is printed or not printed as order specifies.

Output Format. Verify that labels are 4 up, 2 up, E-W or N-S as order requires, or labels are gummed or heat transfer as required.

Neatness and Alignment. Sometimes computers print garbled, repeat a certain portion, skip a character, print out of line. These become quite obvious in a quality control check.

"N"th name panels sometimes require extra computer selection passes. Make sure that the separate "n"th selections are not duplicate selections.

Pandering Complaints and other deletes and changes. Perhaps your label run will be made between list cleaning cycles. If so additional deletes may be necessary by hand. Quality control must keep a permanent delete record for each of your files.

Salutation Codes. Without proper guidance, the computer may do anything. "Mrs. John Jones" is fine. But be sure to check for "Mr. Jane Jones."

Quantity. This can best be verified by mailing house machine counts. However, a count after the fact or mail drop may be too late. List compilers and renters have no desire to short change a customer. But some of the inadvertent things that can happen between list production and post office include multiple boxes of labels being partially lost or misplaced, incorrect shipping labels, part of a run not being packed (or repacked).

The best check to insure correct quantity quickly is to see if the beginning and ending zip codes are on hand. On multiple boxed sets of lists ordered, the entire sequence can be quickly checked by examining each box and making sure there is a zip code continuity.

A good mailing operation can tell by "eyeballing" the size of the label run and estimate total quantity of labels in the order. If he has too many labels and not enough packages or vice versa, he should notify the list user.

A word about computer counts. Any good computer label printing system will include in its programming a procedure where total labels run are tabulated.

In our case, Market Compilation and Research Bureau deducts the number of labels quality controlled out for reasons cited above from this computer total and invoices accordingly.

A comment about overages is appropriate, too. Most list owners deliver a few hundred (or in large orders a few thousand) extra names. This amount is usually invoiced and the overage used in the assembly and mailing process to compensate for spoilage.

The aforementioned Quality Control checks might seem, at first glance, to represent a tedious process. Mailers would do well to follow all of them and others that may be peculiar to their list orders.

We would suspect that in the not too distant future mailing houses will offer a comprehensive quality control option to their customers. For a small flat fee or cost per thousand, mailing houses should be able to perform this task provided they are supplied with the proper Q.C. procedures and check list from the mailer.

Computer Letters: The basic procedures for quality control cited earlier and those items we have just discussed to specifically check for on label orders will both apply to computer letter orders. Perhaps computer letters represent an even more critical area because of the increased cost to a package and the increased importance of a quality appearance of personalized letters.

As a volume computer letter printer, MCRB has computer letter quality control check points: prior to continuous forms printing; select and print tape dump; initial computer fill-in printing; and at run completion.

There is a question relating to what point mailers can perform their own computer letter quality control check. The earlier the better.

If the list owner or compiler is also producing the letters, he will perform his own checks as the job progresses. The earliest the check the mailer may perform is at the letter shop.

If the letter is to be produced by a service bureau, the tape received by the bureau can be double checked by the service bureau before they print the letters. Tape Quality Control procedures discussed later will apply.

Specifically, here are some additional points to add to your check list when computer letters are involved.

Proper forms printing. Check to see that the continuous forms are preprinted in the proper color and all elements are proper and located correctly.

Make sure the address on the top of the letter will show through the specified window envelope properly. If the firm computer printing the letter does not also order envelopes, make sure he is supplied with several samples at the time of order, or at least properly constructed dummies.

Insure that the name and address field be post office deliverable from the standpoint of letter side slippage behind the envelope window.

Four line name/address records. Lists may contain four line addresses as well as three line. Make sure you check the fourth line and are certain they, too, will show through the window properly.

Preprint computer type match. Does the "fill in" copy match the "preprint" copy in density.

Position. Sometimes continuous forms are printed slightly off line vertically. It is best to check the top "fill in" and bottom "fill in" to make sure they are in line with pre-print copy.

Bursting and Trimming. If letters are to be shipped to an assembly point different than that of the computer printing operation, they should be mailed flat and untrimmed. The reason for this is that bruised corners caused by shipment can be trimmed off, leaving a flat clean letter.

The proper method for deleting unacceptable letters is again the felt pen. Cross out name and address area.

These will be pulled out during the assembly process after the final trim and before insertion.

Obviously, to properly quality control magnetic tape, it must be converted to printed matter so it can be analyzed. At MCRB we have developed a special program that dumps or prints out 28 computer pages representing names throughout the tape produced.

This is our quality control printout. The computer determines by itself what "n"th name sample is necessary to yield about 28 pages worth of records that represent the file from beginning to end. On a 10,000 record order that is an "n"th of 8 of 93 and yield about 672 records and on a million name order that would be an "n"th of 8 of 11,904 and yield about 672 records.

This dump is in data sequence on file and does not look like neat, clean records on labels. In fact, to the computer laymen it looks like garbage. A trained computer person should check these dumps for the same factors as described earlier in this article for printed record quality control.

In addition, the tape quality control should check:

1) Track: Seven or nine

2) Density: 556,800 or 1600 BPI

3) Blocksize: That it matches data record format

On the receipt or production of any tape, several basic factors should be quality controlled:

1) Check for header labels on start of tape to properly identify the tape. Information in a header label usually includes: 1) tape number, 2) DSNAME, which is the tape identifier, and 3) configuration of tape (i.e. system used to create tape, blocking, etc.)

2) System used to create tape. This is usually OS or DOS for IBM equipment.

For others, it is necessary to know the kind of equipment used. The need to know this data can be best expressed by stating that the same equipment is necessary to read a tape as produce that tape and if compatible systems are not available additional conversion work must first be done.

3) Physical labels on reel (external labels) must match the internal labels on tape described above. That includes the DSNAME, tape number, block count or record count, which is the total number of records on that reel.

Be sure not to confuse total records with total names. Often a name/address sequence will take more space than the capacity of one record, so it becomes an "overflow" records, which would be counted as two records although only one name/address.

To complicate this record counting is the important concept of "readable" records. A good tape quality control program will provide, naturally, the number of records read.

However, if this total is considerably short of the expected yield, you have an indication of a large amount of records that the computer could not read.

It is necessary to know how many reels to the order, for example reel 2 of 3 reels. MCRB uses a system that prints the DSNAME and tape number at the top of each page of a tape dump.

At this point, it should be pointed out that anyone requesting magnetic tape, or anyone shipping magnetic tape, should always ask for 3 items to precede or accompany a tape delivery: Printed layout or format of tape; A dump of 100 or so records (this is to insure that the actual tape matches the printed layout or format—you'd be surprised how often they do not match); A sample piece of tape (for the same reasons as cited in #2 above).

MCRB's policy of "n"th name on the entire order is more valid than a short dump of first few records. If a tape is satisfactory at the beginning, this is no guarantee it will always be. The whole tape should be examined.

The important point is to make sure the 3 items above match. If not, it is mandatory to check out with the source developing the tape.

Again, as a warning when two or more tapes are being produced make sure they are non-duplicating.

In conclusion, quality control is a mutual responsibility. Mailers have an obligation to pass on failures they uncover to the source. Likewise, the source, whether it be list owner, compiler or service bureau, has a responsibility to future mailers to correct the deficiency and prevent its reoccurrence.

Multi Buyers

When merge and purge of mailing lists first began, the initial use was to eliminate duplicate names to reduce mailing costs and the irritation caused by the receipt of more than one copy of the same mailing. But as the new process developed, greater emphasis has been placed on seeking out buyers whose names appear on more than one list of mail order buyers and concentrating promotion effort on these names alone.

For example, one catalog firm rents approximately 85 lists of people who have bought from other catalogs. A merge-purge program then identifies those whose names appear more than once in the collection of lists. These buyers, it is assumed, are truly oriented to buying from catalogs. If a name appears on four or more lists, this firm sends that name a total of three promotional mailings. If the name is on three or more lists, it is sent two promotional mailings. And if the name appears on two or more lists, it is sent just one promotional mailing. If the name shows up just once, it is considered of marginal value and will be mailed a catalog only if it meets other specified criteria.

Zip Code Deciling

One of the other criteria which is used by an increasing number of major direct marketing firms is Zip Code Deciling. This is a technique of identifying zip codes which are most productive. By comparing total sales to each zip code area, a direct marketer is able to rank geographical areas on the basis of their historic productivity.

After zip codes are given a relative ranking from one to ten on a productivity basis, mailings of outside lists can be concentrated in those areas which have the greatest potential. The general rule is that the greatest potential for additional business is not in areas which haven't previously been productive, but in obtaining new buyers in those areas which have produced well in the past.

In the example given above, for example, names which have appeared on only one outside list, while generally not utilized, will be considered if they live in zip code areas which have traditionally been above average in productivity.

It should be noted that this technique generally is useful only when large quantities are being mailed. Generally, mailers have not found it practical to use only zip code sectional centers (three digits) but if the Zip Code Deciling technique is used, smaller five digit areas must be used. Obviously, a large number of names are required before true comparisons of five digit zip codes can be made.

Mailing List Security

While the computer has made life easier for direct mail advertisers in many ways, it has created at least one major problem. A list on magnetic tape is a lot easier to steal than a ton of metal plates.

Chapter 19—"Standards for Computerized Mailing Lists"—provides a valuable guide to assist you in protecting your computerized lists. Another set of checkpoints has been offered by Lewis Rashmir:[8]

[8]"Sixteen Ways to Prevent The Theft of Mailing Lists" by Lewis Rashmir, President, Market Compilation and Research Bureau. Direct Marketing. March 1970.

1. Prevent entry of unauthorized people into data processing area. Use badges and sign-in book.

2. Have all employees sign a bonding application and a statement acknowledging all data as company property.

3. Programmers may not use machine alone in middle of the night without an operator being present as well.

4. All tapes must be controlled by *permanent* tape markings, tape numbers, and identification content labels.

5. Tapes should be stored in an identified location in cabinets that can be locked.

6. Tapes and disks cannot come into or out of the plant without shipping/receiving document.

7. Put fictitious names in the file. Bury some permanently, assign others specifically to each job. Let everyone know that this has been done.

8. Rigorously check in all mail from fictitious names and reconcile all mail from uncertain sources.

9. Have *general* management demonstrate that their normal interest in good business practices does not stop at the computer room door. Visit, question, control!

10. Have all jobs require a work order with understandable description of the work to be done.

11. Make unannounced visits, day and night, and see what is actually being run in the plant. Check work order against what is on the machine.

12. Account for all computer usage so that there is no "free" time for unauthorized use.

13. Keep special security files under lock and key with the shift supervisor personally signing out for this data.

14. Stop doing business with the cheats, crooks and mail order "con" men, who will lead your employees into temptation once they get to know them.

15. Publicize the data thieves and their receivers so they cannot steal again from another firm.

16. Insist that all applicable trade associations establish codes of ethics and identify the violators of such codes.

Chapter 22

MAILING LIST MAINTENANCE

EVEN before the average mailing list can be compiled, it begins going out of date. Few people who have not worked closely with mailing lists are aware how mobile is our American society. As we've previously indicated, the average list will change approximately 25% a year—and that figure is on the conservative side.

But no matter what percentage of change you experience on your list, it will require a well-planned and closely-followed system of maintenance. The specific plan you develop will depend upon the type of names on your list and the type of material mailed to these names.

RFMR List Control Method

In many fields, particularly those which sell by mail order, the basic list control device is the Recency, Frequency, Monetary Ratio (RFMR).

Jerome B. Osherow of Advertisers Addressing System, St. Louis, explains RFMR this way[1]:

> In the case of a men's clothing store, for example, the more often Sam Jones walks in (or phones) for neckties, shirts, suits, etc., the better customer he's likely to be. This is *frequency*.
>
> If Sam Jones came in yesterday to buy a new hat and walked out satisfied . . . chances are everything is all right between him and the retailer. The customer-supplier bond is strong. The last purchase established his *recency*.
>
> Sam isn't like Tom Brown who works in an office across the street. Tom dashes in about six times a year to pick up a couple pairs of socks or some handkerchiefs each time. Dollarwise Tom spends about $25 a year. Sam, who buys his suits, hats, shirts and many other items, spends over $500 annually with this retailer. This is the *monetary* factor.

[1]"How to Clean a Mailing List," by Jerome B. Osherow, *The Reporter of Direct Mail Advertising*, Oct. 1960.

Putting RFMR to Work

Just which factors you will select to establish a RFMR control system for your own list will depend upon your own individual circumstances. The late mail order expert, George J. Cullinan, discussing the original development of the RFMR method by the big mail order houses, noted[2]:

> A customer category which ordered within the last six months before mailing (recency) and sent two or more orders during that period (frequency) for a combined total of over $20 (monetary) was just about the cream of the list. Contrarily, a customer category which had ordered in the six to twelve month period before mailing and sent only one order for a total of less than $2 was probably the poorest segment of the list.
>
> The superiority of the first group mentioned over the second could be as high as 10 to 1. In between, there were as many as 50 categories of varying qualities all of whose repeat business could be reduced to a percent cost to sell which could be judged as profitable or unprofitable and thus mailed or not mailed as desired. If a company had established its break-even profit point on selling ratio beforehand, based on markup and operating costs, it tended to mail all categories whose selling ratio was lower than break-even and not mail to those whose selling ratio was higher than break-even . . . This circulation control method enabled mail order companies to reduce their mailings by from 40% to 55% without loss of profitable business.

In this same report, George Cullinan explained that the big mail order houses determined that the recency, frequency, and monetary factors controlled 90% of the reasons why customers repeat at a certain sales volume. Of these factors, frequency accounted for 50%; recency, 35%; and monetary, 15%.

Applying RFMR to Retail Direct Mail

In his discussion of mailing lists, Jerry Osherow presented this example:

> A small paint manufacturer had built up his "customer" list to 16,000 names over the years, but the list was encumbered with names of firms which had bought a few gallons as long as five years before and had never purchased since.
>
> We analyzed the list on an RFMR basis, using a point system. For recency, a customer who purchased within the past year was given 5 points for recency. If his last purchase was two years ago, he would get 3 points, then 2 points, 1 point, and 0 if he hadn't made a purchase in more than four years.
>
> Frequency was similarly handled and a point was awarded for each $100 of sales to establish the monetary value. The point value for each customer

[2]"A Modern Look at the Recency, Frequency, Monetary Method of Controlling Circulation," by George J. Cullinan. Research Report No. 62, published by Lewis Kleid, Inc., New York.

was calculated and all customers with less than 18 points were eliminated from the list. Customers ranging in value from 19-50 points were set up as a "regular" customer list and customers with point values of above 50 were segregated into a "prime" list. The total count shrank to 6,200 names.

Other List Control Systems

While the RFMR method, or some variation, is the most commonly used technique for the control of mailing lists in many fields, there are just as many list situations where past buying habits have little, if any, bearing on the direct mail promotion job to be done. This is particularly true in the industrial field, where the majority of direct mail programs are designed to do a continuing promotion job on customers and prospects alike.

But even if there is no buying pattern to provide list controls, some type of control system is still desirable to prevent a mailing list from getting out of hand. One of the biggest problems faced by many direct mail advertisers is that names become "locked into" a mailing list and remain there long after they have outlived their promotional usefulness.

Name Sponsor System

One of the most adaptable systems to prevent "locked in" names and assure regular list cleaning is to require some individual to "sponsor" every name added to the mailing list. These sponsors are then assigned the responsibility of reviewing all of "their names" periodically—often with the requirement that whenever a name isn't reapproved at each review period, it automatically comes off the mailing list.

One company which uses the sponsor system requires review of every name on its extensive mailing list each year. In this case, the sponsors are district or product sales managers. To reduce the burden of list review, the list is divided into ten alphabetical segments and one segment is selected each month for review. The names are run off on 3- by 5-inch cards which have preprinted instructions requiring only an appropriate checkmark and initials by the sponsor to complete. The following instructions are issued to the sales manager-sponsors:

1. The sales manager will sort his set of list cards and route them to his salesmen for review.
2. The salesman will check the cards to determine whether the name should continue to be included on the promotional mailing list. The criterion for deciding a name should be included on the mailing list is:
   (a) The *company* represents either a customer or legitimate prospect for the advertiser's services. (No company should be considered a

legitimate prospect unless the salesman assigned the account has made a personal sales call within the past six months and/or plans to make such a call within the next six months.)

(b) The *individual person(s)* purchases the type of products sold by the advertiser or has a *direct* influence on the selection of a source of supply . . .

(c) . . . or the individual's stature is such that he can be considered an important "influence" in the business world.

3. The salesman will also check the name and address on each card to determine if it contains any recognizable inaccuracies.

4. After completing the review procedures listed above, the salesman will check one of the three items printed on the list card:

   (a) If the name and address are accurate and should remain on the list, he will check "RETAIN ON LIST."

   (b) If the name is not considered suitable for retention on the mailing list, the salesman will check "REMOVE FROM LIST."

   (c) If there are inaccuracies in the name and/or address, *but a corrected version should remain on the list,* the salesman will check "MAKE CHANGES INDICATED." He will then fill out an "Advertising Mailing List" form giving the full name and address as it should appear on the mailing list, and staple the form to the original mailing list card. (The reason for a separate form for this material is that it is sent to another department of the company to have a new addressing plate prepared.)

5. The salesman will then sign and date each card and return it to his sales manager for approval.

6. The above review will be supplemented by a consideration of the following factors:

   (a) Does the total list include the names of all known customers or legitimate prospects (within the alphabetical category being reviewed) on whom the salesman has made sales calls within the past six months and/or plans to make such calls within the next six months?

   (b) Are there any primary buyers within the *companies* included on the cards he has received who are not now included (as *individuals*) on the list?

   (c) Are there any management personnel not now on the cards he has received who exert *direct* influence on the selection of a source of supply by the individuals included on the list?

7. If this additional review produces names which are considered suitable for the advertiser's promotional mailings, an individual "Advertising Mailing List" form should be filled out *for each new name.* These forms should then be routed to the sales manager for his approval.

8. When he receives list cards and Advertising Mailing List forms from his salesmen, the sales manager should indicate his approval in the space provided on the list card or by adding his signature at the bottom of the form.

9. The sales manager will forward all approved cards and forms to the Advertising Department as promptly as possible. Any cards not returned

within 10 days will be assumed to be unapproved for retention on the mailing list and those plates will be immediately removed from the list.

The reason this company insists on sales manager sponsorship rather than sponsorship by individual salesmen who must initiate and review all names is that the sales managers' positions remain constant (even if the individual filling the position changes). On the other hand, there is much more change among salesmen, with accounts frequently shifting from one individual to another as salesmen move.

While this detailed sponsorship procedure was developed to fit a particular company's operations, it can easily be adapted to meet the needs of many other direct mail advertisers. To be effective, however, it is necessary that sponsors have a full understanding of their responsibilities for the list-maintenance procedures and their review activities are continually supervised.

Day-by-Day List Control

While periodic reviews are highly important in maintaining an up-to-date mailing list, they are seldom adequate in themselves unless the list is used only infrequently. Most mailing lists, however, require day-by-day attention.

Any effective list maintenance system should have an established procedure for handling changes on a regular basis. The source of these changes will depend upon the nature of your business, but the following sources should be considered:

Nixies . . . Mail returned by the post office as undeliverable as addressed.

Salesmen's Call Reports . . . Most companies require salesmen to include mailing list change information in their regular call reports.

Customer Notifications . . . Many customers will take it upon themselves to notify an advertiser when they have changes of address. Often, however, these notifications will not come directly to the department responsible for maintenance of the mailing list, so some procedure should be established to assure that this information is automatically passed along.

News Items . . . Assigning someone to review appropriate news items in local newspapers, trade magazines, association bulletins, etc., will often yield much list information.

Directories . . . In a number of fields there are directories which provide weekly or monthly revisions. In some areas it is possible to obtain revised telephone directories monthly (usually the crisscross variety which carry listings by street address). If your list is large enough or limited to a specified area, it may prove worthwhile to compare the old with the new directories to spot changes.

Government Records . . . Local government bodies are a valuable source of list change information—birth and death records, marriage licenses, etc.

List Cleaners

The most frequently used list-cleaning device is the most simple of all—asking the recipients to help. Some mailers ask for change-of-address information with every mailing they send out, while others include list cleaners less frequently. Still others make separate mailings to get the information necessary to bring their lists up to date.

Probably the most effective list-cleaning technique for business lists is one developed by Francis S. Andrews of American Mail Advertising and used for a variety of clients. It involves sending all names for a company to the office manager of that company and asking him to make desirable corrections.

Included in this mailing is a small packet with a picture of a caveman cutting an address on a stone plate (see illustration next page). The heading reads: "We Suspect Our Mailing List Is Out of Date." A flap inside the packet holds 3- by 5-inch cards. Copy explains:

> The names and addresses shown on the enclosed cards are those carried on our current mailing list. Will you please make any necessary corrections and additions and return the cards to us in the enclosed reply envelope? Your cooperation is appreciated.

Most of the cards contain addresses but some blank 3- by 5-inch cards are always included so the office manager can suggest additional names. An autotyped letter accompanies the card-filled packets. A typical letter prepared by American Mail Advertising for an Oxford Paper Company list-cleaning mailing read:

> As a key administrative officer, you undoubtedly see dozens of mailing pieces arriving at your company addressed to the wrong individual.

This touch of humor developed by American Mail Advertising gets good results.

Because more than one-third of executive lists change each year—3 percent per month—we know that there are probably errors in our own mailing list. Will you help us bring your company listings up to date?

The cards enclosed in the "caveman" folder were addressed from the plates in our mailing list file. We would appreciate it if you would check these names and indicate the people in your organization who should receive information about Oxford's line of fine printing papers.

We particularly desire the names of individuals who actually specify and purchase printing papers. If our listing for your company is correct, just put "OK" on the cards. If we have missed the mark, please cross out the incorrect listing and give us the correct name. Blank cards are enclosed for additional listings.

When corrected, please return all cards in the envelope provided. No postage is necessary. We appreciate your help, and we will be glad to reciprocate at any time.

This mailing for Oxford drew an 87% response—an amazingly high return, of course, for any mailing. But the same basic mailing package has done even better—a 98% return when originally used to clean a Monsanto Chemical Company list. It has been used for many other direct mail advertisers and consistently does the job for which it was intended.

The secret of success in this list-cleaning technique is the involvement of a third party. The sending of requests to the office manager was most logical, since he is generally the person responsible for administration of files, routing of mail, etc. Thus, he generally appreciates the efforts of a direct mail advertiser who offers to reduce headaches caused by improperly addressed mail. The light touch provided by the caveman packet makes the correction of a mailing list something less than an earth-shaking event, yet is unusual enough to quickly dramatize the importance of the request.

American Cyanamid List Cleaner

The light touch was also applied to a successful three-unit list cleaning campaign used by the Metals Chemicals Section of American Cyanamid Company to update a list which was known to have the right companies, but not necessarily the right individuals. So before beginning a new direct mail campaign, the company contacted all 1,862 names on the special list, asking for address changes, whether or not recipients *wanted* to get Cyanamid's mailings, and requesting the names of others in the recipient's company who would be interested in Cyanamid's direct mail. The three mailings included:

1. A 4- by 10-inch studio-type card with a cover illustration of two sailors obviously "under the influence"—one listing badly and the other trying to hold him up. The headline read: "We need an assist . . . in checking our list!" Copy inside the card was in an informal style and explained that Cyanamid wanted to be sure they were reaching the right person with information which would help him on his technical questions . . . but, on the other hand, they didn't want to be pestering him with useless literature. There were boxes to be checked to provide the needed data.
2. Six weeks later all who had not replied to the first mailing received a second studio-type card with a picture of a bound-and-gagged executive at his desk and the headline: "Why don't you write?" Inside copy was similar to that in the first mailing, but started off with a reference to the previous mailing. Cyanamid added: "If you've been 'tied up,' we can understand the delay."
3. After another six weeks, all who had not yet responded received a third mailing—a letter with a sharpened pencil attached. Copy emphasized Cyanamid's reputation for "furnishing the right tool for a job"—thus the lead pencil to simplify the job of checking the boxes.

This three-part mailing series drew an 81% response, including 488 new names for the special list.

Doane Agricultural Service List Cleaner

One direct mail advertiser using an enclosure with regular mailings to get list change information is Doane Agricultural Service, which sells a $17.50-a-year publication, *The Doane Digest,* to people with a big interest in farming or ranching.

Mailings are sent to a compiled prospect list of more than a half-million names and Doane feels it desirable to weed out non-farmers and marginal farmers. So a reply card is enclosed with at least one mailing a year. Copy says:

> "If you aren't ordering now, would you like to remain on the Digest's prospect mailing list?"

There's space for comments and a note suggests:

> "If you wish to make a correction, please note it above in the 'Comments' section."

The success of this list-cleaning technique was explained by William Patrick of Doane at a Direct Mail Day conference in Chicago:

1. Most people asking to be removed from the list gave a valid reason. A lot of them have sold their farmland to take a job in town but still live on a rural route.

2. The cards uncover a large number of duplications between prospects and subscribers. For example, the farm name may appear on a prospect list and an individual's name on his subscription card. We feel that any time such duplications can be eliminated, the subscriber looks more kindly to us and printing expenses can be reduced at the same time.
3. A certain amount of goodwill is developed for direct mail advertising. Given a chance to remove himself from a mailing list, a postal patron can't very well say he's receiving "unwanted mail."
4. Despite some misgiving when the first tests were made, it has been established to our satisfaction that such a card does not cut down on response to the subscription offer being advertised.
5. And most important, we have saved $2.88 for every dollar invested in this program. That's based on the cost of mailing for three years to a prospect who "doesn't want to get our mail."

Link-Belt's Corner-Card List Cleaner

To keep its external house organ headed toward a receptive audience, Link-Belt Company regularly uses a corner card in the address area to solicit list change information. Attention-getting illustrations direct attention to a checklist with copy such as:

If you are in error, please indicate correction required and return the address impression in stamped envelope. Thank you.

☐ Please correct name, address or zip code number as indicated.

☐ Addressee no longer here. Please remove name.

☐ Not interested. Please remove name.

Tests by Link-Belt have indicated that use of the check-off boxes increases return of list corrections.

Post Office Services

The U.S. Postal Service offers two special services which are helpful in keeping a list up to date. If you print "Address Correction Requested" on your third- and fourth-class mailings, local postmasters will return the original piece with the new address of the addressee, if known, or if there is no new address, the reason for nondelivery. The return name and address of the mailer must appear in the upper left corner of the address side, with "Address Correction Requested" printed below it.

The basic charge for this service is 25 cents per piece. For additional details concerning this service, it is suggested you contact your local postmaster or review the details as outlined in *The Mailer's Guide to Postal Regulations* published by Lyle Stuart, Inc., Secaucus, N.J. This was compiled by Metro Information Services and the price of the 1975 edition is $45.00.

Unfortunately, you can't always depend on this service. Some postmasters and carriers will follow the Postal Manual to the letter, but many provide only hit-or-miss return service. Nevertheless, it usually pays to make "Address Correction Requested" mailings periodically to pick up list change information you might otherwise miss.

Post Office List Correction Service

Another special list-cleaning service is offered by the post office. You can submit your list on cards to each post office, where any known inaccuracies will be corrected. The rate is 10 cents for each card you send, with a minimum $1 charge. You must print one name to a card (about the size of a post card) and have your name in the upper left-hand corner.

The cards will be distributed to the appropriate mail carriers, who will check the names and addresses. While the carrier will seldom be able to vouch for titles or correct spelling of individual names, you will learn all addresses to which mail can no longer be delivered. When known, new addresses will be added. Generally, you will not be able to learn of any changes in personnel within a company.

This method of list correction by the post office will usually bring more accuracy than "Address Correction Requested." However, you are still at the mercy of individual carriers—many of whom do not treat this service with respect in spite of constant reminders from postmasters and the U.S. Postal Service.

You can also get your lists zip coded by the post office—a service which is provided without charge.

First-Class Followups

Many mailers use first-class mailings to follow up all "Moved—left no address" returns that result from "Address Correction Requested" mailings. Since first-class mail must be returned to you if it is undeliverable, you will quickly learn that many forwarding addresses are available, even when the carrier may have claimed they aren't.

There are two ways to handle such followup mailings: You can enclose a reply card in the first-class letter asking the recipient to send you his new address. Or, if the first-class letter is not returned, you can then write to the postmaster concerned, explaining that you have received a "no forwarding address" response to a "Address Correction Requested" mailing, yet did not receive a return on the first-class letter. A request for an explanation of the discrepancy will usually bring forth the forwarding address you seek (and often better service on future "Address Correction Requested" mailings).

In cases where the regular first-class followup does not yield a list change you particularly want, you can send a certified letter with return receipt requested. You will want to request restricted delivery service in order to get delivery only to the person you seek to reach. Your receipt will include the information as to where the letter was delivered, if you request it. The cost is quite high, but if you place a high value on your list names, it may be well worth the effort. If even certified mail does not reach the individual, you can be pretty sure the post office cannot help you locate him.

Other List Cleaning Services

Many of the list building techniques included in Chapter 20: "Mailing Lists," can be applied to the job of keeping your list clean. For example, you can use the Western Union Survey Service, compare new directories with previous editions, buy newly compiled lists to check against your own, rent lists from other companies or from list brokers, and so forth.

You do not necessarily have to handle list maintenance yourself. In fact, the majority of direct mail advertisers have the job done more efficiently and more economically by utilizing the services of a lettershop with experience in list maintenance.

LIST MAINTENANCE

American Marketing Services Inc.		List:
Plate Now Reads		Name Change
		Address Change
		New Listing
Plate Should Read		Change Notch Code Volume Returned
		Remove From List
		Bad Credit Risk

Ordered by:________________ Date:________________

List Maintenance by:________________ Date:________________

Form used by American Marketing Services for list maintenance.

Chapter 23

U.S. POSTAL SERVICE

NO medium of advertising is so dependent upon a government agency as is direct mail. The U.S. Postal Service plays a vital role in direct mail advertising—not only as the organization which makes possible delivery to the chosen audience, but also as the primary body regulating what can be sent.

Fortunately for the direct mail advertiser, the U.S. Postal Service allows wide latitude in the character and content of direct mail and offers many special services to aid the direct mail advertiser. Nevertheless, there are many important rules and regulations which must be observed.

Since not only postal rates, but the rules and regulations as well, are constantly changing, the bulk of the information about these subjects has been included as an appendix to this book, where it can be revised more often than if it were to be published in this chapter. Even so, a word of warning must be given:

> *Postal rates and regulations are changed frequently. So depend upon your local postmaster for up-to-date information and always verify published material—even that distributed by the U.S. Postal Service itself—to provide current information on postal rates and regulations.*

Like any direct mail "rule," there are exceptions to this warning. Many of those who specialize in direct mail make it a policy to keep fully informed on all developments on the postal front and may easily be better informed on certain rates and regulations than even some postmasters. But the average direct mail advertiser will do well to keep this warning in mind.

Interpretation by Local Postmasters

Considerable latitude is given local postmasters in interpreting some postal regulations. Thus, what may be allowed at one post office may be forbidden at another. In cases where you feel your local postmaster is incorrect in his interpretation of a postal regulation, it may be desirable to request a clarification from regional postal authorities or the Postal Service in Washington, D. C. In many cases, direct mail advertisers utilize the services of the direct mail trade associations to which they belong in obtaining clarification—and, in some instances, changes in postal regulations.

In general, postal authorities take the attitude that they are "in business" to serve the users of the mails, and thus often make decisions based on what they consider the *intent* of postal regulations to be, rather than simply following the words used in the Postal Service Manual. In recent years, there has been a general tendency to be more lenient in interpretation of regulations, and late revisions of the Postal Service Manual have eliminated some of the strict language used in earlier editions.

In dealing with local postmasters and employees of local post offices, it is important to remember that they have the power to make the handling of your direct mail easy or difficult. Therefore, it is to the advantage of every direct mail advertiser to obtain and keep the goodwill of everyone connected with the post offices at which mailings will be made. Continually seek their advice and assistance to help you in your direct mail programs. It pays!

Visit Your Post Office

It is strange how few people—except nursery school and kindergarten classes—ever take the time to make a tour of a post office. This is an opportunity no direct mail advertiser should miss. A thorough understanding of how your mail is handled is essential if you want continuing direct mail success. There is no better way to get a full picture than to take time to visit the post offices which handle your mailings.

It would be well not to limit your post office visitation program to just one post office. There are differences in post offices and the ways in which they handle mail. By all means, grab any opportunity to visit a large post office, such as the giant main post office in Chicago. There, for example, you can see the complicated procedures for handling parcel post, which will quickly convince the average mailer that his packaging methods are inadequate. And don't overlook the smaller post offices, particularly if a lot of your direct mail will be handled there.

Many post offices offer special instruction on various phases of mail preparation and handling. You'll have to check with your local postmaster to find out what types of programs are available for you, but don't overlook any opportunity to participate in whatever programs are offered.

Classes of Mail

While detailed information on each of the classes of mail used by direct mail advertisers is contained in Appendix H: *Postal Rates & Regulations*—the following summary will provide a basic understanding of how each class affects the direct mail advertiser:

First Class Mail

Contrary to popular belief, a considerable volume of direct mail advertising is sent by first-class mail. First class includes personalized letters, post cards—both Government postal cards and private mailing cards—business reply cards, letters in business reply envelopes and airmail.

Some of the advantages of first-class mail include:

- Priority attention, thus speedier delivery
- Few restrictions on contents
- It may be deposited in any letterbox, post office, or substation
- It will be returned if undeliverable—except post cards
- It will be forwarded without additional charge if addressee has left forwarding address

Post Cards

While rectangular cards of any size over the minimum can be mailed at the regular first-class rates, a card no larger than 4¼ by 6 inches can be mailed for less than the minimum first-class rate. (Minimum size for all mail is 3½ x 5 inches.)

All of the back and the left half of the front of post cards may contain messages. Paper stock must be at least .007 of an inch thick, but no heavier than .0095 of an inch. The stock must be either white or of a light tint. If heavier stock or a darker color is used, the full first-class rate must be paid.

Business Reply Mail

An important postal service for direct mail advertisers is business reply mail. This permits responses to be returned to the mailer without the respondent having to pay the postage. For information about business reply card and envelope formats, see Chapter 38: "Order Forms and Reply Cards" and Chapter 39: "Envelopes."

Second-Class Mail

Few direct mail advertisers have an opportunity to mail under second-class rates. The major exception is that certain institutions and societies can obtain second-class mailing permits for *regularly published* periodicals or newspapers of various types.

Controlled Circulation Publications

In a very limited number of cases, direct mail advertising can qualify for mailing as a controlled circulation publication. To qualify, however, a publication cannot be owned and controlled by individuals or business concerns and conducted as an auxiliary to advance their own business.

Third-Class Mail

The vast bulk of direct mail advertising is sent as third-class mail. Within this broad category, however, are many subclassifications which are highly important to direct mail advertisers. Among these are:

Single Piece Mailings. If a mailing consists of quantities of less than 200 pieces or 50 pounds in weight, it is considered a "single piece" mailing.

Bulk Mailings. When a mailing consists of 200 or more identical pieces and/or 50 or more pounds in weight, a special bulk rate is offered. The mailer, however, is required to obtain a permit, pay a bulk fee and perform a number of special services to qualify for third-class postage rates, including separate bundling of pieces where 10 or more pieces are going to any one city or state, proper facing of mail, and other requirements.

Bound Books and Catalogs. Books and catalogs having 24 or more pages (of which at least 22 are printed) qualify for a special pound rate when mailed in quantities of 200 or more and/or with a total weight of 50 pounds or more.

Non-Profit Organizations. A special bulk third-class rate is offered to non-profit organizations which qualify.

Fourth-Class Mail

When direct mail pieces weigh 16 ounces or more, they are mailed by fourth-class mail. In certain cases, payment of both third- and fourth-class postage is required. Included within fourth-class mail are two special categories of interest to direct mail advertisers:

Special Fourth-Class Rate. Certain books, films, printed music, tests, recordings, and scripts qualify for a special rate of postage which is not related to parcel post zone rates.

Catalogs. Catalogs weighing more than 16 ounces, but not more than 10 pounds, qualify for lower fourth-class rates. Obtain detailed information from your postmaster.

20 TIPS FOR BETTER, MORE ECONOMICAL POSTAL SERVICE

1. KEEP IN TOUCH WITH YOUR POSTMASTER. He is in a position to provide invaluable assistance in many ways. So get to know your local postmaster and his staff and take advantage of the many special services he offers to direct mail advertisers.

2. LET THE POST OFFICE HELP CLEAN YOUR LIST. There's a special list-cleaning service available through local post offices. (For details, see Chapter 22.) Take advantage of this opportunity to get help on keeping your lists up to date.

3. ZIP CODE YOUR MAIL. To get faster delivery, be sure to include zip codes for all cities.

4. USE ADDRESS CORRECTION REQUESTED SERVICE. For third-class mail, take frequent advantage of the Address Correction Requested Service. (For details, see Chapter 22: *Mailing List Maintenance.*) And, if practical, send an occasional direct mail piece by first-class mail to get automatic forwarding or return service as an aid in helping keep your lists current.

5. GIVE THE POST OFFICE ADVANCE WARNING. When you have a big mailing scheduled, be sure to alert the post office at which it will be mailed so it will be prepared to handle the mailing. The postmaster may be able to suggest an acceptable alternate mailing date which will work to mutual advantage.

6. CHECK UNUSUAL MAILINGS WITH POST OFFICE. If there is anything out of the ordinary about a mailing you are planning, be sure to check with your local post office before you put it into production. You may end up saving hundreds of dollars and plenty of time and headaches.

7. KEEP A FILE OF UP-TO-DATE TRAIN AND PLANE SCHEDULES. If you use first-class mail, it will pay to keep up-to-date schedules of all trains and planes which carry mail so you can time your mailings to get fastest service.

8. MAIL EARLY. Mail early in the day, and frequently, to avoid the last-minute pile-up of mail. You'll not only get better service, but you'll earn the appreciation of local postal officials and employees if you will schedule your mailing.

9. TAKE ADVANTAGE OF CATALOG RATES. There's a chance to save postage dollars if you can take advantage of the special third- and fourth-class rates for catalogs.

10. BEWARE CLOSE WEIGHTS. When the weight of your mailing piece is approaching the maximum limit for any step in the scale of postage rates, *be careful!* An extra fraction of an ounce may end up costing you a lot of extra postage money. One mistake frequently made is to weigh an unprinted dummy, forgetting that the ink, staples, glue, stamps, meter tapes, and other items to be added may throw the weight over the planned maximum. At times it may be important to trim just a sliver off the edges of a piece or to shift to a paper stock of just slightly less weight (and remember that designated weights of paper are only approximate—one 50-pound stock may weigh more than another which seems to have the same characteristics). You'll also want to watch humidity. It's amazing how much water paper can absorb—and water can weigh a lot.

20 TIPS FOR BETTER, MORE ECONOMICAL POSTAL SERVICE (Continued)

11. AVOID LARGE ENVELOPES. Where possible, avoid large envelopes. Not only do they add to postage costs, but there is a possibility of delay in handling "flats." If you use large envelopes for first-class mail, they should bear prominent "First Class Mail" legends on the front *and* reverse and should be white or light colored. A green diamond border, while not officially authorized by the Postal Service, has come to mean first-class mail to most postal clerks.

12. USE METERED MAIL. If you want fast service, use metered mail rather than postage stamps. This eliminates the need for post office canceling.

13. RECLAIM UNUSED METERED POSTAGE. Don't destroy spoiled envelopes and tapes with metered postage. You can redeem them at the post office for 90 percent of their face value.

14. UNDERSTAND "IDENTICAL." The post office doesn't really mean identical when regulations speak of identical direct mail pieces. The post office is talking about only three things—size, weight and number of enclosures. So you can qualify for third-class mailing rates even if you have a dozen or more different pieces to mail *if* they are of identical size and weight. This is particularly important in mailings where there are simple changes in copy, such as a changing list of dealers or distributors.

15. BEWARE COINS IN RETURNED MAIL. There's a law against destroying coins, so if you have a direct mail piece using a coin as a gimmick, be prepared to open every returned piece and remove the coin before destroying.

16. INSPECT MAILROOM EQUIPMENT REGULARLY. While every piece of equipment used to handle direct mail should be kept in tiptop shape, you'll want to pay special attention to your postal scales. Even a minor deviation can cause major headaches when compounded for all pieces of a mailing.

17. AVOID SPECIAL DELIVERY ON PARCEL POST. Don't spend unnecessary money for special delivery fees on parcel post when what you really should use is the lower cost "Special Handling." On the other hand, if you *really* want special delivery, don't pay additional for special handling—you automatically get that when you pay the special delivery fee.

18. DON'T OPEN RETURNS TO BE FORWARDED. If returns from your direct mail advertising are to be passed along by mail to some other point for handling, don't open the envelopes. You'll be able to reship unopened envelopes by third- or fourth-class mail, but must pay first-class rates if they've been opened.

19. ASK POST OFFICE FOR BANDS AND TAGS. You can get sack labels and labeled adhesive bands for separating mail from your post office without charge. You can also obtain free airmail, first-class, and special delivery labels . . . plus a number of valuable publications containing regulations and instructions for the handling of mail.

20. KEEP POSTED ON FORTHCOMING DEVELOPMENTS. Since postal rates and regulations are subject to change, it will pay you to keep abreast of the latest and *forthcoming* developments. By having a full understanding of new regulations planned or adopted for activation at a specific future date, you can often save money and headaches on your direct mail. One of the best sources for such information is the trade associations serving direct mail advertisers.

Chapter 24

DIRECT MAIL COPY

IN no medium of advertising does copy play a more important role than in direct mail. While it is dangerous to underestimate the role of the copywriter in any medium, it is downright disastrous to do anything less than place direct mail copywriting in the hands of the finest possible talent you can obtain and afford.

Unfortunately, all too often a direct mail advertiser plays the role of an amateur in a professional league and decides that anyone can write a good letter if he tries (particularly himself). As a result, much otherwise excellent direct mail comes a cropper because the copy fails to carry the heavy load required of it.

A frequent mistake is to think that any good writer can turn out result-producing direct mail copy. In too few cases, however, does this prove to be the case. Talent developed and matured in writing copy for publication advertising or other media is not necessarily in tune with the requirements of direct mail.

Seek an Expert

The best advice on copy which can be given any direct mail advertisers is to seek an experienced *direct mail* copy expert. Then work with him, or have him work with your copywriters, in developing the best techniques to meet the specific communications problems involved. With such guidance, the odds are that you or your copywriting personnel will learn many of the techniques which lead to success and eventually others will be turning to you for direct mail copy help.

In the absence of in-person help from an expert, you can turn to some of the helpful books on direct mail copywriting which are available by the score. You will find some of the best listed in Appendix C, "Direct Mail Bibliography."

Because there are so many detailed and helpful volumes available on the subject of direct mail copy, it is our primary purpose in this chapter to provide some basic guidelines for successful copywriting. This material is presented primarily to assist the direct mail advertiser in evaluating copy, rather than to try to teach writing techniques.

What Makes a Direct Mail Copywriter Different?

In his contribution to "The Copywriter's Guide,"[1] Robert D. Chase describes some of the ways in which a direct mail copywriter must be different:

> The direct mail copywriter must learn to like people—all kinds of people. He must learn to understand them, to be amused by them, to sympathize with them. He must know what motivates them; what they want to be, do, and own. He must learn to think like the common man, to talk like him, and to write the way he talks.
>
> Also, the direct mail copywriter must know business inside out. He must understand its functions and their relation to one another. He must be intrigued with manufacturing processes, know how products are distributed, the methods and problems of wholesaler and retailer. He must have an instinct for selling, must know intimately its techniques and problems. Above all, he must know the buyer, what he needs and wants.
>
> By then he is ready to learn his craft, the techniques of writing on a personal level about any product he may be called on to handle.
>
> Besides studying certain good books dealing with the techniques of writing for direct mail, the would-be copywriter should be a voracious reader over a broad landscape. He should keep thoroughly posted on current events, take a good horizontal business paper, and read extensively such masters of clear, simple English as Stevenson, Kipling, Lincoln, Conrad, Hemingway. And for depth of thought and grade of phrase, Shakespeare and the Bible.
>
> Above all, he should write incessantly, applying the techniques of direct mail advertising he has studied. If possible, he should write under the watchful eye of a copy chief who himself is a master of direct mail copy. If such is hard to find, let him learn by studying the work of others. He

[1]"The Copywriter's Guide," edited by Elbrun Rochford French. Copyright by Harper & Brothers, 1959, New York.

should write to manufacturers for information about their products. Clip coupons. Get on mailing lists. Read all of the direct mail he receives. He will quickly distinguish the good from the bad. Let him study the good. Imitate it.

In that way, like many another direct mail advertising copywriter today, he will learn his craft and be proud of his achievement.

Formula vs. Philosophy

There are two basic approaches to writing direct mail copy—to follow a set formula (and there are dozens of formulas in active use) or to work with a basic philosophy in mind. To many there may be little difference between having a well-ordered formula and a less formal philosophy as a guide. But in practice there is a vital difference.

And just as there are two approaches to writing direct mail copy, there are two approaches to evaluating copy. You can establish a checklist of points against which you judge copy . . . or you can depend primarily on the "feel" of the copy as you read it. Probably the best technique is to combine these two approaches—if the copy just does not seem to do the job, then turn to one of the basic formulas and use it as a checklist to see where the copy has failed to hit the mark.

If you find you can work best by using a formula, heed these words of warning from one of the top mail order experts, Boyce Morgan of Kiplinger[2]:

> *Let's refuse to accept the idea that just because we must write more or less to formula to produce results, we must use the same old words and phrases over and over again.*

The Case Against Formulas

One of the more outspoken objectors to the use of formulas for direct mail copywriting is Mort Weiner, a New York promotion consultant. Says Mort in the article, "How to Create Good Direct Mail in 0 Easy Steps" *(The Reporter of Direct Mail Advertising.* May 1960):

> There are at least three things wrong with checklists and checklist-thinking:
>
> 1. *They're of little help to professionals, but tend to turn amateurs into "experts."* Writing letters on the basis of a checklist or a set of do-it-

[2]Quoted in "How to Think About Mail Order," by Henry Hoke. *The Reporter of Direct Mail Advertising.* Garden City New York.

yourself devices is something like learning art by the "circle method"—one for the head, two for the body, and so on. It will work if all you want to do is draw recognizable figures, but it certainly is no substitute for a grasp of anatomy and composition, or for talent. Yet, among non-playing quarterbacks, checklists spawn the illusion that creating a good letter is an open-and-shut quasi-science, and that the chief equipment required is a complete set of do's and don'ts. Any uninhibited professional who believes that the accepted way is not always the best way is sure to find himself regularly being waved to a halt by a checklist in the wrong hands.

2. *They tend to substitute mechanical techniques for substance. Almost by definition they oversimplify.*

   A point very seldom neglected by checklist-compilers is the "you attitude." Like the Golden Rule, this is beyond criticism. In practice, however, *you* is less a three-letter word than a selling philosophy, and simply listing a "you approach" among the points on a list is a glib answer to a deep-seated problem. All too often the result of this kind of thinking is that *you's* are scattered profusely through the copy, while the story and its presentation remain basically *we.*

   Another favorite point is the use of "connectors"—conjunctions or phrases at the beginning of sentences or paragraphs to carry the reader along. Actually, of course, if a letter isn't basically well-organized, connectors won't make it seem so—and if it is, inserting them for their own sake is very likely to just add verbiage.

   The popular emphasis on the *externals* of direct mail—the type of postage used, the color of the reply card, etc.—is an only too natural outgrowth of this type of thinking. Probably 85% of the effectiveness of a mailing stems from a carefully chosen list and a skillfully presented message, but you won't always get that impression from a checklist.

3. *They make no allowance for such vital intangibles as brilliant timing, a flash of insight, or an unexpected departure from the routine—the stuff of which outstanding direct mail is made.*

   In the words of Charles L. Whittier, formerly vice president of Young and Rubicam, some years ago: "The beginning of greatness is to be different . . . the successful production of great advertising is . . . a constant struggle to avoid the usual." It seems plain that proceeding from a formula when preparing direct mail, rather than from a basic *idea,* is a good way to remain solidly earth-bound. Real creativity demands a certain amount of emotional involvement—and is anything more antithetical to this than a strictly mechanical approach?

Direct Mail Copy Formulas

There are probably more direct mail experts who disagree with Mort Weiner's central point than supporters, for direct mail formulas and checklists have been markedly accepted practice for many years. There are literally dozens of different formulas and checklists used regularly by direct mail copywriters to guide them in creating their sales stories. And many of the pro-formula copywriters are widely hailed for the consistent excellence of their copy.

While there is a great deal of similarity among most all of the direct mail formulas, some work better for a given individual than others. Chances are, however, that any copywriter will adopt a single formula and then utilize it regularly—either consciously or subconsciously.

Just which formula and/or checklist will work best for you will require a bit of experimenting on your part. Here are some of the more popular formulas and checklists in use today:

AIDA Formula

By far the most popular, and probably the oldest, direct mail copy formula is one of the most simple of all—the AIDA Formula:

A—Get Attention

I—Arouse Interest

D—Stimulate Desire

A—Ask for Action

Basically, this formula (and most of the others like it) is used to guide the development of a letter or other type of direct mail copy. Following the AIDA plan, you first concentrate on getting the attention of your reader. Once you have achieved this first objective, you concentrate on arousing his interest in your offer or the subject of your promotion message. Once you have aroused his interest, you then seek to stimulate a desire on the reader's part to have that which you are advertising. And then you ask for action—and it is amazing how often direct mail copywriters will overlook this final point.

Robert Collier Formula

Similar to the AIDA Formula is one developed by one of the greatest direct mail copy experts of all times, the late Robert Collier. He insisted the proper order for sales copy is:

Attention

Interest

Description

Persuasion

Proof

Close

Earle Buckley's Formula

Earle A. Buckley's formula for successful direct mail letters is[3]:

Interest
Desire
Conviction
Action

"You must arouse interest," he says, "or the reader won't even finish the letter. You must create a desire for whatever you're selling, or obviously you can't hope ultimately to consummate a sale. You must make your reasons for buying convincing, or the prospect won't feel it is to his advantage to buy. And you must lead him into some kind of action, otherwise his enthusiasm will cool off before you have a chance to 'cash in.'"

Victor Schwab's AAPPA Formula

Another closely allied formula has been offered by agency man Victor O. Schwab:

A—Get Attention
A—Show People an Advantage
P—Prove It
P—Persuade People to Grasp This Advantage
A—Ask for Action

The Four P's

Another popular formula is generally credited to Henry Hoke, Sr., and consists of the four P's:

Picture
Promise
Prove
Push

Frank Egner's Nine Points

One of the all-time direct mail copy greats, Frank Egner, provided a nine-point formula:

3"How to Write Better Business Letters," by Earle A. Buckley. McGraw-Hill Book Co. New York, New York.

1. The headline (or first paragraph) to get attention and arouse desire.
2. The inspirational lead-in.
3. A clear definition of the product.
4. Tell a success story about product use.
5. Include testimonials and endorsements.
6. List special features.
7. A definite statement of value to the prospect.
8. Specific urgent action copy.
9. A postscript.

Ed Mayer's 10 Rules

Edward N. Mayer, Jr., offers more of a list of rules than a formula[4]:

1. Make every letter sell.
2. Know your subject thoroughly.
3. Make your letters clear.
4. Make your letters concise, but tell the whole story.
5. Know what you want—and ask for it.
6. Use simple language and short words to tell your story.
7. Make your letters friendly.
8. Make your copy sincere.
9. Make your copy tactful.
10. Always put a hook in your copy.

Elmer Wheeler's Five Points

While Elmer Wheeler's much-publicized five points for successful salesmanship were originally directed toward personal contact selling, they are often applied equally well to direct mail copy ("Word Magic," copyright Prentice-Hall Inc., New York, New York):

1. Don't sell the steak—*sell the sizzle.*
2. Don't write—*telegraph* (find the sizzle in what you're trying to get across and then express the sizzle in a telegraphic statement).
3. *"Say It With Flowers"* (after you've found your sizzle and expressed it telegraphically, fortify your words).
4. Don't ask if—*ask which!* (Always frame your words so that you give the other person a choice between something and something else—never between something and nothing).

[4]"How to Make More Money With Your Direct Mail," by Edward N. Mayer, Jr. Third Edition. National Foremen's Institute. New London, Connecticut. 1960.

5. *Watch your bark!* (The *way* you say a thing may be as important as *what* you say).

John Yeck's Eight Fundamentals

One of our favorite direct mail experts, John Yeck, lists eight fundamentals for successful direct mail copywriting:

1. Put yourself in the other fellow's shoes.
2. Be friendly.
3. Shoot for the bull's-eye (to take the reader from where he is to where you want him to be).
4. Keep your letters clear and easy to read.
5. Make them interesting and keep them moving.
6. Be believable.
7. B.U.—be yourself.
8. Write, write, write—carefully.

Clyde Bedell's Guideposts

Long recognized as one of the nation's top advertising copy experts, Clyde Bedell suggests seven guideposts for sales letters:

1. Always say quickly the *best* thing you can say.
2. Follow a route. Have a planned road map of your work to guide you.
3. Be lucid, be clear. Reader must get the story quickly.
4. Be believed. Do not raise doubts.
5. Be complete. Do not dangle customers.
6. Sell—sell—*SELL* every word of the way.
7. Print it as clearly as you think it.

Bob Stone's Formula

Robert Stone uses this copy formula:

1. Promise a benefit in your headline or first paragraph—*your most important benefit.*
2. Immediately enlarge upon your most important benefit.
3. Tell the reader *specifically* what he is going to get.
4. Back up your statements with *proof* and *endorsements.*
5. Tell the reader what he might lose if he doesn't act.
6. Rephrase your prominent benefits in your closing offer.
7. Incite action—*now.*

Lynn Sumner's Ten Commandments

G. Lynn Sumner prepared a list of "Ten Commandments of Letter Writing" which provide a useful checklist for direct mail copywriters:

1. Learn all about your proposition before you write anything about it.
2. Organize your material. Get it down in order, from the viewpoint of the buyer's interest—not yours.
3. Decide to whom you are writing. Remember, it is a person, not a circulation or a list. You are writing a letter, not a speech.
4. When you are ready to write, keep it simple. That does not mean writing down to anybody. Avoid high-flown phrases.
5. Use meaningful words and phrases—words that stir the emotions, make the mouth water, make the heart beat faster.
6. Don't try to be funny. To try and fail is tragic. Few people can write humorous copy, few products lend themselves to it. Remember, the most serious of all operations is separating a man from his money.
7. Make your copy specific—names, places, what happens to whom.
8. Write to inspire confidence. Prove your points.
9. Make your copy long enough to tell your story—and quit. No copy is too long if it holds the reader's interest. One sentence can be too long if it doesn't.
10. Give your reader something to do and make it easy for him to do it. Tell him where to get what you have to sell, how much it costs—and why he should do it now. You've written the copy—cash in on it!

Bus Reed's Three B's

A handy little formula was created by the late Orville ("Bus") Reed, whose direct mail copy has spelled success for dozens of leading advertisers:

Benefits—tell the reader right off how your service or product will benefit him.

Believability—back up your statement of benefits with believable evidence.

Bounce—Webster defines it as "enthusiasm, vivacity, spirit, verve." Keep your copy moving. Keep the prospect interested. Transfer your enthusiasm for the benefit to the prospect.

Howard Dana Shaw's 14 Points

A longer, but also valuable checklist, was created some years ago by Howard Dana Shaw in "How to Get Ready to Write a Letter." *(The Reporter of Direct Mail Advertising)*:

1. *The goal*—What is the aim of your letter?
2. *Who*—Define your market or audience.
3. *Characteristics*—What kind of people and what's on their minds?
4. *Benefits*—What will your product do for the buyer?
5. *Objections*—Why the reader won't do what you want him to.
6. *Build confidence*—What can you say to gain the reader's confidence?
7. *Opening*—Some letter men claim it's 90% of the letter.
8. *Hurry-up*—Offer premiums, set deadlines, mention price increases, limited quantities, and so forth.
9. *Tone and attitude*—Decide on the general slant and tone of voice.
10. *Dramatization*—Comparisons, graphic ways, gadgets, and illustrations.
11. *Sales points*—Things to stress.
12. *Phrases*—Colorful terms, good sentences from previous letters.
13. *What was wrong with other letters on the same subject?*
14. *How to make the price seem low*—Contrast with competing prices, break down into weekly or daily figures, and so forth.

As you will quickly note, this is a checklist of things to do to prepare yourself to write copy rather than a guide to follow when you get into the writing itself or in analyzing already written copy. Actually, your preplanning of copy may be the most opportune time to utilize formulas and checklists.

Fact Analysis Checklist

Henry Hoke, Sr., placed much emphasis on the value of proper preparation before you start putting words down on paper. In his valuable booklet, "How to Think About Direct Mail," he stressed the value of making a detailed fact analysis of your business.

"This is one of the most important things you can possibly learn about direct mail," he said. "It is the one thing so often neglected by the pencil pushers. It is practically impossible to write direct mail copy without a fact analysis . . . unless you have been in a particular business for long years and know all the facts through intimate contact with them."

He went on to list seven basic steps in a fact analysis:

1. *The Company.* List every pertinent fact about it. Its history. Its management. Its reputation. Its standing in the community or the nation.

2. *The Product or Service.* Define the product or service. Get all the definitions you can from dictionaries, etc. Get all historical background. How the product originated. How it was developed. Make a complete catalog of everything pertaining to the product or service.

3. *The Market.* Here your knowledge of people will help. But you should catalog all the possible uses of the product or service. All the kinds of people, starting with the most important (in terms of use) and winding up with the least desirable.

4. *Your Method of Distribution and Selling.* Put down all the facts concerning past distribution methods, present distribution methods, and future possibilities.

5. *The Presentation of the Sales Message.* You should have a complete file of all former advertising. You should make a complete analysis of how your product or service has been presented to the public or a segment of it.

6. *The Media.* Make a catalog listing of all the forms of advertising which have been used to put your product or service across. It would be helpful if you could separate the amounts of money.

7. *The Sales Objective.* That is, analyze just what the sales possibilities are. In other words, your potential market. In analyzing this, you can determine the extent to which direct mail can be used, the length of the program, budget, and so forth.

Four Little Words

One of the best pieces of advice ever offered direct mail copywriters was the theme of a speech Max Ross used to deliver at advertising meetings. His theme: "Four little words form the key to writing direct mail copy that sells."

KEEP YOUR COPY MOVING!

"Writing good copy," he explained, "is like running a 440-yard dash in a track meet. If you don't start fast enough, you are left behind. If you don't keep up the pace on the backstretch, you will fall back with the pack. And if you don't have a finishing spurt left, you will surely lose the race."

In this same speech, Max Ross offered 20 concrete suggestions for direct mail copywriting:

1. Show your prospect how what you have to sell will bring him pleasure, or save him money, or increase his knowledge, or better his living standard—or any dozens of things he wants.

2. It will help you in making notes to study your own company's past literature—the direct mail pieces, the trade paper clippings, pamphlets, advertisements. Also study competitors' material that may have been accumulated by your company.

   Sift out the unnecessary items. Arrange the points in order of their importance. Then—and only then—are you ready to chart the most direct, efficient route to your prospect's pocketbook. This enables you to concentrate your full energies on one idea, then the next, in proper sequence.

   Copy is likely to gallop off into forty different directions at once unless the writer follows a route. The best way to devise a satisfactory route is to get your selling points down on paper.

3. If you think that setting down your work plan is too difficult, simply try writing the close of your letter first—before you write anything else. That will help determine exactly the purpose of the letter.

4. Don't begin writing unless you are in the right frame of mind for it! Don't start writing copy at 10:00 if you are to attend a meeting at 10:30. Don't face a stream of office traffic. Don't sit by a window that will attract your gaze. In other words, eliminate as many distracting factors as you possibly can.

5. Not only is it necessary to start writing copy with an uncluttered mind, it is also important to start with an uncluttered desk. Clear your desk before you begin to write—except for all notes, papers, and other material that you will refer to as you are doing the job. But don't clean up your desk again until the job is done—even if it means leaving your desk cluttered overnight.

6. If your thinking mechanism stalls when you first sit down to the typewriter, go ahead and start writing part of the letter. Begin in the middle if you have to—but begin!

7. Try phrasing your lead at least six different ways on the first sheet of paper you put into the typewriter. Then detach yourself from the project at hand for a moment. Pick out the lead that you think will best attract and hold attention. Keep in mind a principle from advertising consultant Richard Manville: "Advertisements that attempt to give people what

they want outpull advertisements which present those things which people do not want as much—or do not want at all."

8. When you have trouble getting a lead that satisfies you, look two or three paragraphs down from the top of your letter. The lead you want may be there.

   You will find many instances where your copy can be improved by cutting away the top paragraphs. But it works the other way too! There will also be instances where the addition of a paragraph above the copy you have already written will make a better letter.

9. It will pay you to keep thinking of leads all the time—while you are reading the newspaper, when you are listening to the radio, while you are studying magazines or books. Dramatize your lead in copy if you can.

10. Many direct mail leaders keep a "starter" file. Clip out or jot down sentences or phrases that catch your eye, that may apply to your product. Either keep them in a file folder or have your secretary paste them on loose-leaf sheets that can be found in a notebook.

11. Tell your prospect exactly what your proposition is—and what you want him to do—right at the very beginning of your letter! But be sure to conduct your own tests to see if this idea works for you.

12. Once your lead is written, and you progress to the body of the letter, please remember to *keep your copy moving!* One way to do this is to say what you have to say in an interesting way.

    Writing in an interesting manner is one of the most difficult of all copywriting tricks to learn. I say learn because I don't think it can be taught. You have to want to learn—and you have to do this job yourself.

13. Read good books by authors who have a definite style. If fiction, study the style, not the plot. If non-fiction, read only the paragraphs that attract you. Then go back to observe how what you missed could have been said in a more interesting way.

14. Subscribe to magazines that seem to have a style of their own—magazines like *Newsweek, Reader's Digest, Time. Time* is a particularly good one to study. Read good columnists whose stock in trade is telling things in an interesting way.

15. Make a conscious effort to make your daily conversation more stimulating. It will help your copywriting.

16. Another way to keep your copy moving through the body of the letter is the use of "connectors." Connectors are transitional sentences or phrases that either end one paragraph or begin the next.

    They are simply little devices that give copy swing-movement. Here are a few examples:

    - But that's not all.
    - Now—here is the most important part.
    - And in addition . . .
    - Better yet . . .
    - You will see for yourself why . . .

COPYWRITING CHECKLIST

Max Ross suggests the following steps to use when writing direct mail copy:

BEFORE YOU START TO WRITE:

List on paper the points that will interest your prospect most.

Decide which ones are most important.

Sift out the unnecessary items.

Prepare yourself mentally.

LEAD WITH YOUR BEST FOOT FORWARD:

Phrase your first words several different ways and pick out the one best suited to the task.

Keep trying to improve your lead.

AS YOUR STORY UNFOLDS:

Keep your copy moving.

Say it in an interesting way.

Use connectors.

Study to improve your style.

DON'T HESITATE TO ASK FOR THE ORDER!

MAKE YOUR LETTERS LOOK ATTRACTIVE.

- So that is why . . .
- More important than that . . .
- What is more . . .
- But there is just one thing.
- Make up your mind now to . . .
- Take advantage of this opportunity to . . .
- Now—for a limited time only—
- Here is your chance to . . .
- So mail your order today—while the special offer is still in effect.

See how these words swing evenly to the next thought. They avoid abrupt pauses. Naturally, there are dozens more. If you will go on from there and compile your own list, I am sure that you can cut your copywriting time by as much as one-third!

17. Don't leave it up to the reader to decide what you want him to do. If you want him to put his name on the order form and mail it in the reply envelope that you are providing, tell him so. Make it so plain, so easy, that he cannot possibly misunderstand!

    Further than that, tell your reader what he will lose if he doesn't act at once. If your price is going up, if there are only a few articles left, if he must mail his order by a certain date, tell him. Be specific! If you can offer him something extra for acting promptly, do so. Everyone likes to get something for nothing. That's only human nature—working on your side.

    But in any event, don't hesitate to ask for the order!

18. Never run your paragraphs too long, or too solid. Use punctuation to break up the copy. Use underlining and indentations wisely. Make your copy inviting!

19. Write your letter on a typewriter if it is at all possible. Then rewrite it—and rewrite it—and rewrite it. They say de Maupassant recopied everything he wrote 100 times. That's out of the question, of course. But do as Robert Stone suggests—recopy your work at least three times.

    This will help you achieve that goal of *keep your copy moving!* Every time you rewrite your copy you subconsciously challenge what you have already written. You can't help but improve it. This is your opportunity to cut out phrasing that can be read more than one way, that may automatically slow down your reader, or stop him altogether. And once he stops, you have usually lost him.

    Perhaps even more important than that, you have a chance to apply increased emphasis where it is needed—to point up certain statements—to play down others.

    By writing and rewriting, you will develop a better style. You will find that you unconsciously begin to:

    a. Use the present tense when possible.

    b. Use the active voice instead of the passive.

    c. Use periodic sentences instead of loose, except occasionally in the case of writing leads.

    d. Use short, simple sentence construction.

    e. Use connectors that keep your copy moving.

20. Use these suggestions as a guide, as a working manual. Follow this step-by-step outline (see box on preceding page) as much as you can. Take your time. Don't hurry. See if some of these suggestions don't make your copywriting job a little bit easier.

25 Ways to Improve Copy

A few years back, Charlie Morris and Sam E. Gold developed a list of ways to improve direct mail copy. Among their key points were the following:

1. *Believe that your readers are interested in what you are writing about.*

2. *Make an outline.* Determine your theme. Develop your appeal. Write along correct psychological lines. The first step, getting attention, is the result of provocative headlines, illustrations with stop-power, or engaging opening paragraphs.

   The second step is INTEREST, cultivated in your *attention* quality at the outset. It develops your appeal, and the exploitation of your readers' viewpoints.

   CONVICTION, third step in psychological sequence, is determined by sincerity of your approach, believability of your conclusions, selection of facts you use to prove your statements, and reasonableness of documentary evidence of claims you make.

   Finally, ACTION, the direct request for your reader to do something—send check to, with specific instructions, and so forth.

3. *Write copy as if you're writing a personal letter.* Be clear, be simple, be friendly! Copy so written is less likely to be dull, dry, and pompous. It's more likely to be sincere, down-to-earth, convincing. Readers will recognize friendliness in your tone and your words. Pocketbooks will open more easily. Good advertising copy today is warmer, more friendly than ever before. You can't go wrong by following the trend.

4. *Be a word miser!* Throw out the expendables; throw out jawbreaking words. Use direct statements, active verbs. See how many times you can strike out the word "the" the first time you reread your copy. Don't begin paragraphs with "the." and don't begin headings or titles with "the." Search for better words—something more dynamic, more vivid; action words. That vital position—first word of paragraph—rates better treatment than inactive word "the" . . . Be a word miser. Use short words, Anglo-Saxon words everyone understands. Master phrasemaker, Winston Churchill, puts it, "Old, simple words are best." Bruce Barton tells his copywriters, "Say it simply; say it in one-syllable words." Use short sentences.

   Whatever readers' "lifting" capacity, they get more ideas, more information, more inspiration when ideas-per-sentence rate is low. Short sentences decrease the mental horsepower needed to raise ideas from printed pages into readers' minds.

   Professor Rudolph Flesch and old friend Henry Hoke pitch for sentences that contain no more than 150 syllables. Paul Bringe suggests limiting sentences to 20 words. In Point 17, "Keep Ideas per Sentence Low," pace and rhythm show they, too, have places in determining sentence length. Rule of short sentences is a good one to follow when in doubt.

   Direct statements move readers' minds more quickly in a straight line than do indirect statements. Advantage of direct over indirect broadens when ideas are complex.

   Habit of trying first for subject-predicate-object should be as automatic as turning on the ignition switch of your motor car before you press the starter button.

I love Paul Bringe's recommendations for writers of direct mail copy:

a. Use short words. Doubt words with two or more syllables unless they are combinations of easy words.

b. Use picture words rather than abstract words.

c. Keep words in active tense.

d. Keep sentence length under 20 words.

e. Talk your readers' lingo.

William Cullen Bryant, when he was editor of the old *New York Evening Post,* is responsible for these suggestions to you writers:

> "Never use long words when short ones will do. Call a spade by its name, not a well-known instrument of manual labor. Let a home be a home and not a residence. Speak of a place, not a locality. When a short word will do, you always lose by a long one."

5. *Write 25 headlines.* Writing headlines for letters or advertising copy is like salesmen making calls. Make enough and you're sure to hit the jackpot with a stopper-of-stoppers. Good headlines represent letters or advertisements half written. This advice applies to the writing of opening paragraphs of letters you want to begin "Dear Friend." Successful copywriters place emphasis on the importance of the "first five words" in letters. But you can't place too much emphasis on the proper building of the entire first paragraph of copy, however long it is.

6. *Concentrate on main themes.* Letters and advertising copy should concentrate on one main theme to assure unity of impression and fullest impact. Concentration like this does not necessarily mean using a single appeal. It means all appeals integrated should support and develop the fundamental theme.

7. *Inject interesting personalities—when you have them to write about.* People are interested in other people. The more interesting the people, the more interested other people are in reading about them. Cash in on available personalities.

8. *Base copy on news—when you can.* When you can release real news you enjoy a royal road to your readers' interests.

9. *Eliminate "introductory" words.* Words used to begin sentences are, as often as not, "say nothing" words in the particular context. Norman Shidle, writing in *Clear Writing for Easy Reading,* puts it: "Some writers wind up at the beginning of every sentence like a baseball pitcher with no one on base. Instead, they should assume that somebody is always on third—and may steal home."

10. *Eliminate qualifying sentences.* Addiction to qualifying and subordinate clauses is a specific case of writing in too many ideas per sentence.

    Qualifying clauses should be used only when necessary. They need extra words; adjectives pile up and phrases multiply—needlessly. When the ideas are in subordinate clauses, they are better expressed in separate sentences.

11. *Try writing in the plural number.* You could do worse than make it a rule to write in the plural number. You'll find "plurals" help eliminate unnecessary "articles" to speed both writing and reading. An example:

"A good headline represents a letter or an advertisement half written." Blue-penciled, the sentence reads: "Good headlines represent letters or advertisements half written." Tempo of edited sentence is quicker. Opening word of the sentence is powerful, good-sounding. Four syllables are eliminated.

12. *Be specific.* Watch images appear as you read this copy: "Ruddy, juicy, tempting fruit, sun-ripened on the vines to delicious perfection. Made into Campbell's Tomato Soup the very day it is plucked. Each tomato washed five times in clear, pure running water. All skins, seeds and core fiber strained out from this smooth, rich puree. Golden butter, fresh from the country, blended in. The favorite soup of millions—and no wonder." That's specific copy! Clear, crisp, vivid. Mouth-watering!

    Now read this generalization of the same subject: "Soup made of the highest grade ingredients obtainable by our own exclusive processes. Employment of only the most skillful operatives on each task insures that the final product shall be the best the market affords. It is accepted universally as the acme of quality."

    What did it say?

    Specific words are necessary for exactness. *Economical* is less specific than *moneysaving* or *timesaving*. Lights *glare, gleam, glitter, glow*. Which is the right word for the purpose? *Go* is less specific than *walk, run, ride*. *Say* is less specific than *tell, state, declare, inform*. Seasoned copywriters won't say *apt* when they mean *likely, liable* or *prone*. They won't write *tint* when they mean *hue* or *tone*.

13. *Be grammatical! Take pains with word structures.* "This is one of the most important books that *has* been published on the subject of . . ." should read, "This is one of the most important books that *have* been published . . ." *Have* is required because *that* refers to *books*.

    Here's another example of words out of place: "This new encyclopedia will contain much brand-new coverage of *such* important and timely subjects *as* . . ." Grammatical improvement would have the sentence reading: "This new encyclopedia will contain much brand-new coverage of important and timely subjects *like* . . ."

    As a rule, don't separate verbs from subjects. Don't write, "He bitterly regretted." Make it, "He regretted bitterly."

    "To thoroughly appreciate its value you not only need to ride in it but to drive it yourself" needs correcting to read: "To appreciate its value thoroughly, you need not only to ride in it but also to drive it yourself."

14. *Don't use fatal words.* When you get to the end of your letters *ask for the order*. Don't "feel"; don't "trust"; don't "hope"; don't "beg." Don't say "if," say "when." Write: "Use the envelope I have enclosed. Your check will come directly to my desk so I may acknowledge your gift immediately." Write: "Write your check now. Send it along today." Ask—don't beg!

15. *Try writing between hyphens (-) and dashes(—).* Hyphenated expressions are effective devices to draw easily understood word pictures by condensing longer word forms.

Asides and qualifications bracketed between dashes—two hyphens on your typewriter—are effective means of emphasis. Ideal between-dashes language could be omitted from your writing without altering meaning. Too-little-used hyphens (-) can increase readability. Unusual phrases can be turned colorfully and understandably.

16. *Draw word pictures with analogies, similes, and metaphors.* Creative writing is full of comparisons—analogies, similes, and metaphors. Picture after picture unfolds, not statement after statement. Direct mail copy needs the help of symbols—drawn by analogies, similes, and metaphors—that have common meanings for readers. Image-making is a deliberate and calculated skill, suggesting much while saying little with the aid of:

    Analogies showing or implying points of similarity.

    Similes illustrating with direct comparisons—something to something else.

    Metaphors implying likeness—creating resemblances between unlike things.

    A manufacturer of paper used for milk bottles, in a letter paints this believable word picture, suggesting much, saying little. "Water from nearby artesian wells is chemically treated and filtered until pure beyond belief. It is far purer than standards set by the State for drinking water. It is clearer even than crystal."

    Smoothly integrated, these devices can add plus-values to your writing. Interest can be increased, flavor can be improved, and continuity can be rhythmic and lifting.

    Clumsily handled "figures of writing" can hurt more than help. Be sure humorous touches, vivid metaphors, and apt similes are smoothly integrated into the unity, emphasis, coherence pattern of your writing.

17. *Keep ideas-per-sentence low.* Too many ideas-per-sentence give readers mental indigestion. When sentences have too many ideas, it is quite possible readers will not pick up any of them.

    Periods as punctuation marks go far to assist readers.

    Here is writing with swing, with rhythm, with change of pace—all the elements of easy reading:

    "To People We Like"

    By Frances Lester Warner

    "The people we like! May their conversation never grow less. May their tires never flatten. May their boats never leak, their clocks never stop, their pipes never freeze, their fishing lines never part cable. May their moving vans never turn turtle. May their hydroplanes never collide.

    "May their dreams never dwindle, their loves never cease, their plastering never come down. May they be visited this day with the shrewd suspicion that we wish them well."

    Sentences are short, but vary in length at the right time. Some sentences have only one idea. In others a period pops up just in time. One more idea would have been too many.

    Limiting the number of ideas per sentence becomes more important as ideas become more complex.

18. *Sum up your sales story somewhere.* When your copy is short and simple, a single telling of your story is sufficient. But when situations demand longer, more complete copy, injecting summaries of the important elements of your proposition is vital. Favorite summing-up device of successful writers is a slogan.

19. *Don't overwrite.* A home economist from a state university was giving a cooking demonstration before a group of farm women. "Take an egg," she explained, "and carefully perforate the basal end. Duplicate the process in the apex. Then, applying the lips to one of the apertures by forcibly exhaling the breath, discharge the shell of its contents." Eighty-five-year-old Aunt Cassie turned to a neighbor, "Beats all how different these newfangled ways is. When I was a gal we just poked a hole in each end and blowed!" Think of this story when you get the urge to spread out needlessly. *Poke a hole in each end and blow.*

20. *Try a P.S.* Successful mail order advertisers use postscripts in almost all their letters. Suggest you try the P.S. in some of your letters. Tie in the P.S. with the main theme of your story. Here's an example from a recent TB and Health letter that was built around the Mobile Chest X-ray Service: P.S. Last year 17,117 neighbors—a record number—visited the mobile X-ray unit. Among them were 112 men and women who, like John Focaro, suffered unaware. Most of these neighbors now enjoy competent care and are on the road to recovery, thanks to this work of your committee."

21. *Change emphasis.* Ever reversed lack-luster sentences without changing an essential word? Get the habit. You will like the results. Choose high-impact words and ideas in your lead-offs and put crackers on your whips for closers . . . Remember, good last lines are scarcely less important than good leads. This technique of successful writers is called "emphasis by position." It's a "must" rereading chore.

22. *Watch your rewriting.* Nearly all first drafts are verbose, awkward, and disconnected. Ideas gap in some places, overflow in others. Sentences and paragraphs are muddy. First drafts are like slowly emerging shapes of statues from blocks of stone. Rough shapes are plain. But final chiseling and smoothing remain. Aesop Glim, writing in *Printers' Ink,* warns writers against "polishing" in the rewriting procedure. He quips, "Polishing is good—for pots and pans, and shoes and precious stones. It's bad for copy." Be careful not to kill copy's character or unity nor its warmth and vitality. "Don't make it a piece of self-conscious literature. Don't patch."

23. *Try reading your copy aloud.* Read your copy aloud. There is no surer way to discover how readers will read it. There is no surer way to spotlight awkward phrasing, unclear passages, cumbersome and cloudy paragraphs that need slicing into sentences, and punctuational stumbling blocks.

24. *Watch your word sounds.* Avoid unfavorable sound associations, when meanings can be expressed in another way. Watch for groups of words containing harsh sounds. Harsh sounds can sometimes emphasize ideas by slowing down reading. Words giving impressions of lightness, speed, or delicacy would ripple along without interruptions of awkward sounds. Read poetry to watch "rippling" words at work. A sense of rhythm promises to be your reward.

25. *Write "good graphics" into your copy.* Your ideas will be better received when presentation of your material conforms as nearly as possible to "graphics" of reproduction.

Here is a list of suggestions for better "graphics." The more of these that writers can "design" into their copy, the better the chances of getting emphasis in proper places:

Attractive, distinctive-looking letterhead.

Good-quality stationery (paper).

Sharp, clear, crisp typing.

Perfectly positioned body of letter. More white space at bottom than top. Approximately even spacing on each side.

Short letters double-spaced. Long letters single-spaced.

Two pages for a letter, rather than crowd one page.

Special details, points of emphasis indented and underscored.

Extra important points emphasized with color.

Paul Bringe's Advice

To better understand some of the points made by Charlie Morris and Sam Gold, it is helpful to study a speech delivered by copywriter Paul Bringe some years ago at a DMMA convention. Paul offered this advice:

> Good writing requires a knowledge of the abilities and limitations of your reader. We cannot talk with people successfully until we know a lot about them. You won't be able to get into the mind of another with little black marks on a piece of paper until you know which door to his mind is open and how wide open it is. Or, if the door is closed, you must know how to unlatch it. There is a door waiting for you in the mind of every reader and if you know your reader, it will swing open for you.
>
> *Test It.* I suggest testing everything you write for readability. This is not difficult nor time-consuming. After you do it a dozen or two dozen times, you will estimate reading level without testing. There are many different formulas for measuring readability, but the most popular, and certainly easiest to use, is the Rudy Flesch formula.
>
> The Flesch formula, and most other formulas, are based on two facts which have been demonstrated over and over.
>
> 1. The longer the sentence, the less the reader will get out of it.
> 2. The more short words, the more the reader will get out of it.
>
> Now this sounds very simple, and if we follow it to its logical conclusion we would write nothing but one-syllable words and three- or four-word sentences. Surely, then, everyone would understand—and so they would, but few would read.
>
> The Flesch formula is based on the *average* length of sentences and the *average* length of words. Some sentences must be long and some words must be long, but if they are varied with short sentences and short words, the overall readability will be good. Writing at the correct level of readability

for your audience will not in itself insure a successful piece of copy—but at least you will know you are not throwing roadblocks in your reader's path.

Verb-Adjective Ratio. The next thing to watch for is the verb-adjective ratio. Verbs are the motion words of communication—they carry the reader along, they paint pictures of action in which the reader can see himself as an actor. Verbs bring movement, excitement and flow and lead the reader quickly to the conclusion you want him to reach.

Writing you cannot put aside until you have finished has a high verb-adjective ratio, about three verbs to each adjective. This ratio follows reading difficulty. Too many adjectives force the reader to stop and reconstruct his mental picture—each additional adjective adds more qualification to your statement, adds another fact the reader must carry in his mind to arrive at complete understanding. Comic-book copy uses almost no adjectives; theses written for college degrees run as high as two qualifying adjectives for every verb.

Try to keep all action words in the present. Try to keep your story happening today, not yesterday or tomorrow. No one ever lived yesterday or will live tomorrow. All men have always lived today—the future and the past are artificial concepts we build in our minds—that takes effort and imagination. Anything you do to lessen the effort required of your reader will make your copy more successful. It takes far less effort to think about what is happening now than to reconstruct what happened yesterday or will happen tomorrow. Do not give your reader any unnecessary mental tasks—do as much thinking for him as possible and he will reward you with closer attention.

Stick to Anglo-Saxon. Have you ever had to use the word "belch" in a letter? Some people think it is an inelegant word. Suppose you were told not to use it but still had to express the action. What could you use? There is only one word and that is "eruct." Did you know there is such a word as "eruct"? And can the word ever mean "belch" to you—or could it mean "belch" to anyone else if you use the word? This is an unusual example to point up the importance of using Anglo-Saxon words whenever possible in your writing.

More Americans know more Anglo-Saxon words and use them in their normal speech than will ever know Latin root words. Anglo-Saxon words are generally short—and given a choice, we will choose a short word before a long one. They are forceful, they are direct, they are action words. They express your thoughts fast and without confusion.

Here are some common Anglo-Saxon expressions: "Stop, thief!" "Ready, aim, fire!" "Who goes there?" "Get ready, get set, go!" "I love you." "You are fired!" "Be still!" Try expressing any of these with Latin root words and you will throw away the power. When we want words of command, words to start or stop action, we use Anglo-Saxon words. And when we want to release energy, we swear, also in Anglo-Saxon.

You won't have to look up all the words you use to determine their origins. If you have a choice of words, the shorter word will usually be Anglo-Saxon, the shorter word will be more concrete and the shorter word will be easier to understand.

Don't Be Trapped. Some of us try to avoid repeating a word too often for fear of boring the reader. So we hunt for synonyms to give variety and change of pace. But we are likely to fall into a trap in our search for synonyms. There is no word in English that has the same meaning as another word. If it ever happens, one of the words will die quickly. Each word in the language has its own special meaning or it would not exist.

When you use a synonym instead of your original word, you move away from the first meaning you planted in your reader's mind. You are asking your reader to change his thought, the thought you have just given him. That is mental work for the reader. He doesn't like it and it won't do you any good. I would rather take the risk of boring the reader by repeating words and thoughts, than of losing him by quick change of mental direction. Putting it in a few words—be careful when you use synonyms.

The best way to become a good direct mail copywriter is to practice writing about other people's products or service when you don't have to do it. When you get a poor letter, try rewriting it your way. It can be a lot of fun. Sometimes you will have difficulty improving the original. But every bit of rewriting you do will strengthen your ability to write clearly, concisely, and with a readable style.

Writing Isn't Talking

Frequently, you hear the advice that advertising copy should be written as a person would talk. What is meant is that the *tone* of the copy should be conversational. If you have ever read an unedited transcript of a speech or discussion, you will quickly recognize that it is impossible to write good copy as you would speak.

Ed Kennedy, copy chief for an upstate New York advertising agency, notes these important differences in "Writing Isn't Talking" (*Industrial Marketing.* February 1959):

> In the first place, the advertisement has room for only a fraction of a speech. A man talks at the rate of about 150 words a minute.
>
> The advertisement cannot inflect its voice, cannot gesture, cannot roll its eyes, cannot burst into tears. The tricks that speakers use to sway an audience are not transferable to the printed page.
>
> The salesman's pitch to his prospects depends upon give and take between *two* speakers. When the salesman makes a claim to which the prospect raises an objection, the salesman has the opportunity to answer the objection. But the advertisement cannot talk back. When it makes a claim to which 99 out of 100 readers say "Phooey!" then "Phooey!" is the last word.

So don't make the mistake of trying to write as you would speak to an individual—or deliver a speech to an audience. You just can't get the same effect when your words are delivered in printed form.

Long vs. Short Copy

At most any direct mail copy clinic, someone will sooner or later bring up the question: "How long should a good direct mail letter be?" And the answer which the experts shoot back is that there is no rule except that a good letter will be one long enough to cover the subject yet short enough so the reader's attention and interest will not be lost.

Perhaps a classic example to prove that the length of letters depends upon the story to be told was an *11-page letter* which won a DMMA award some years ago. The single letter was mailed to 500 prospects by M. B. Ver Standig, of Washington, D. C., to sell a special research service. It pulled 161 replies in the first 45 days, with a trickle still following after results had been calculated. The letter mailing cost about $200 and brought in more than $9,000 in immediate business.

On the other hand, there is the owner of a Michigan fishing camp who sent a post card mailing to his "regulars." It had just two words—"They're biting!"—and it drew a 100% response.

ANALYZING DIRECT MAIL COPY

Thus far, most of our discussion in this chapter has been directed primarily to the writing of direct mail copy. While an understanding of copywriting techniques is helpful in analyzing and editing copy, there are additional checklists which can prove particularly helpful in this chore.

Max Ross' Checklist

One of the most helpful direct mail copy analysis tools available is a checklist developed by Maxwell C. Ross. While the guide was developed primarily as a tool for analyzing letters, most of its points apply equally as well to other types of direct mail copy. The 20-point checklist is shown on next page.

In discussing the usefulness of the checklist, Max Ross explained the three ways the guide has been used:

1. It helps us check a brand-new piece of copy quickly and easily.

2. It gives us a chance to measure older pieces of copy as they come up for reorder. (This is important because there can be as many as 200 or 300 active letters in use at one time.)
3. It helps us fight inertia—the ever-present habit of leaving things as they are just because it's too much trouble to change.

The checklist is divided into two parts—copy technique and copy editing. Max Ross explains each of the points this way:

1. *Does the lead sentence get in step with your reader at once?* You do this by talking in terms of things that interest your reader—not in vague generalities or of things *you* want. You put yourself in his place! I can't think of a better way to say it than this—get in step with your reader.
2. *Is your lead sentence more than two lines long?* In our case, we hope not. Experience has shown that our best letters have one- or two-line leads. But if it takes three lines or four lines or even more to get in step with your reader, use them.
3. *Do your opening paragraphs promise a benefit to the reader?* Lead with your best foot forward—*your most important benefit.* If you have trouble with your opening paragraph, try writing your lead at least six *different* ways. Then—when you get *six* down on paper you are quite likely to have at least one pretty good lead somewhere among them.
4. *Have you fired your biggest gun first?* Sometimes it's easy to get confused in trying to pick out the most important sales point to feature in your lead. But here is one way to tell.

   Years ago Richard Manville developed a technique that has been of great help. When you are pondering over leads, ask yourself this test question: "Does the reader want more *x* or more *y*?"

   Let me give you an example of how this works. Take two headlines, "How to avoid these mistakes in planning your house" and "How to plan your house to suit yourself." Ask yourself the test question, "Which do people want the most?" It becomes obvious, then, that more people want to plan their house to suit themselves rather than simply avoid mistakes. In this case, the one headline was 16% better than the other.

   Take another pair, "Don't swelter this summer" and "Now every home can afford summer cooling." Well, by applying the test question, you already know the answer, but do you know by how much? The second ad, which promised summer cooling, was 300% better.

   Or these two, "Your pair of Ben Hogan golf shoes will outwear any other brand" as opposed to "Cut three strokes off your score by wearing Ben Hogan golf shoes." Any real dyed-in-the-wool golfer will buy a new pair of shoes every summer if it will lower his score.

   So tell your reader how what you have to sell will bring him pleasure . . . or save him money . . . or increase his knowledge . . . or better his standard of living (or for that matter, any one of a score of things he wants) and you will have him on your side.

CHECKLIST FOR BETTER DIRECT MAIL COPY

Prepared by Maxwell C. Ross

COPY TECHNIQUE

1. Does the lead sentence get in step with your reader at once?
2. Is your lead sentence more than two lines long?
3. Do your opening paragraphs promise a benefit to the reader?
4. Have you fired your biggest gun first?
5. Is there a *big idea* behind your letter?
6. Are your thoughts arranged in logical order?
7. Is what you say believable?
8. Is it clear how the reader is to order—and did you ask for the order?
9. Does the copy tie in with the order form—and have you directed attention to the order form in the letter?

COPY EDITING

10. Does the letter have "you" attitude all the way through?
11. Does the letter have a conversational tone?
12. Have you formed a "bucket-brigade" through your copy?
13. Does the letter score between 70 and 80 words of one syllable for every 100 words you write?
14. Are there any sentences which begin with an article—*a, an,* or *the*—where you might have avoided it?
15. Are there any places where you have strung together too many prepositional phrases?
16. Have you kept out "wandering" verbs?
17. Have you used action verbs instead of noun construction?
18. Are there any "thats" you do not need?
19. How does the copy rate on such letter craftsmanship points as (a) using active voice instead of passive, (b) periodic sentences instead of loose, (c) too many participles, (d) splitting infinitives, (e) repeating your company name too many times?
20. Does your letter look the way you want it to? (a) placement of page, (b) no paragraphs over six lines, (c) indentation and numbered paragraphs, (d) underscoring and capitalization used sparingly, (e) punctuation for reading ease.

5. *Is there a big idea behind your letter?* You may wonder what the difference is between firing your biggest gun and this *big idea.* In one case, for example, the big gun may be the introductory offer on an insurance policy, but the big idea behind the letter is that here is a company which makes insurance available to the older people of our country. The *big idea* is important. My guess is that the *lack* of a big idea is why letters fail.

6. *Are your thoughts arranged in logical order?* In other words, have you got the cart before the horse? It is a fundamental copywriting truth that your reader anticipates what you are going to say. So it may help to think of your reader as a passenger in a motorcycle sidecar—and you are the driver.

   You can take him straight to his destination—surely and swiftly and smoothly. Or you can dawdle along the way, over side roads, bumps and curves, sometimes making such sharp turns that he may go shooting off down the road without you. Unless you follow a charted course and make his ride as pleasant as possible, too often he will say, "I'm tired. Let me off." This is another good reason for having a checklist to follow.

7. *Is what you say believable?* Here is a chance to offer proof and use testimonials to back up what you have said in your letter. Also, in our case we triple-check to make sure the reader doesn't misunderstand. (Notice I didn't say "true" instead of "believable." What you say may be true, but not necessarily believable.)

8. *Is it clear how the reader is to order—and did you ask for the order?* This is especially important in the insurance industry where filling out an application can sometimes be complicated. You would be surprised how easy it is to write a letter without asking for the order!

9. *Does the copy tie in with the order form—and have you directed attention to the order form in the letter?* This latter point is particularly important, we think. So we call our reader's attention to the next important step in the transaction by saying something like this: "As you look at the enclosed order form, you will notice that . . ." Do something to get the reader's attention to the order form, because this is a *key step.*

   Now we come to an extremely important part of writing copy—*copy editing.* I don't mean editing by someone else. I mean the editing you can do yourself. Let's look at the checklist points.

10. *Does the letter have the "you" attitude all the way through?* You can tell easier than you think. All you have to do is put yourself in the other fellow's place. As the little poem goes, "When you sell John Jones what John Jones buys, you must see John Jones through John Jones' eyes."

11. *Does the letter have a conversational tone?* I'm not going to tell you that you should write as you talk, because your letter might sound pretty weird if you did. Ed Mayer says, "Write with the ease with which you talk." Or—to put it another way—write as you would talk if you could edit what you are going to say. And that is what you have a chance to do here.

12. *Have you formed a "bucket brigade" through your copy?* This will take a little explaining. If you study the works of master letter-writers, you will notice that all their letters have *swing* and *movement*—a joining together of paragraphs through the use of connecting links.

Some of these connecting links are little sentences like, "But that is not all" . . . "So that is why" . . . "Now—here is the next step" . . . "But there is one thing more."

You can find literally dozens of ways to join your thoughts like this —in short, to take your reader by the hand and lead him through your copy—and to avoid what I call "island paragraphs" that stand all alone and are usually just as dull as they look to the reader.

In fact, the next time you run across one of those deadly dull letters, see if it isn't because it lacks this bucket-brigade technique.

13. *Does the letter score between 70 and 80 words of one syllable for every 100 words you write?* This is one of the most important check points to follow in writing effective copy. It is not that people don't understand the meaning of words—they just cannot cope with the way they are used. Their vocabularies are adequate, but their patience isn't.

14. *Are there any sentences which begin with an article (*a, an *or* the) *where you might have avoided it?* This is another one of our own ground rules. And we don't always follow it to the letter. But we like to try— because we think sentences which begin with those words are frequently robbed of their strength.

15. *Are there any places where you have strung together too many prepositional phrases?* This is an important check point because it is so hard to catch when you write your first draft. Now is a good place to catch them—for overusing prepositional phrases is another strength-robber.

16. *Have you kept out "wandering" verbs?* You can often make sentences easier to read by rearranging them so that verbs are *closer* to their subjects. When you let verbs wander too far away from their subjects, you make it more difficult for your reader.

17. *Have you used action verbs instead of noun construction?* You gain interest when you do this. Instead of saying, "This letter is of vital concern to . . ." say, "This letter vitally concerns . . ."

18. *Are there any "thats" you don't need?* Using too many "thats" is another strength-robber. Eliminate as many as you can, but be careful. Read your copy aloud to make sure you have not trimmed out so many that your copy will slow down the reader.

19. *How does the copy rate on such letter-craftsmanship points as (a) using active voice instead of passive, (b) periodic sentences instead of loose, (c) too many participles, (d) splitting infinitives, (e) repeating your company name too many times?* If you are going to split infinitives; if you are going to use the passive voice; if you are going to do these other things, don't do them too often. Moderation in copy is a great virtue.

20. *Does your letter look the way you want it to?*

    Your letter should assume the same proportions as the sheet upon which it is placed.

    It should not be crowded.

    The paragraph should be short—not over six lines at the most. (Not a hard-and-fast rule.)

    Appearance can be helped by indenting and sometimes numbering indented points or paragraphs.

Use underscoring and capitalization sparingly, thereby reserving emphasis for spots where needed.

Use punctuation (dots and dashes) to increase reading ease.

Other Checklists

To Max Ross' checklist can be added a number of additional points as was demonstrated by Bus Reed, who wrote to three other direct mail copy experts when he was preparing material for a class offered by the Direct Mail Club of Detroit. Bus not only got Max Ross' list, but others from Ferd Nauheim of Kalb, Voorhis & Company, and Paul Bringe—certainly two of the nation's best direct mail copy experts. Here, along with Bus Reed's own list, are the others[5]:

Bus Reed's Ten Commandments of Direct Mail

1. Be clear.
2. Be convincing.
3. Be interesting.
4. Convert features into customer benefits.
5. Answer the prospect's subconscious question: "What's in this for me?"
6. Use adjectives sparingly.
7. Use active verbs.
8. Never make a claim without offering proof you can deliver.
9. Give your copy rhythm.
10. In place of hard sell or soft sell, use sensible sell.

Paul Bringe's Ten Commandments of Direct Mail

1. Select the right list for your product or service. Without it you have nothing.
2. In all your writing talk to one person only. Never address a letter "To our Customers," or "To our Suppliers." Direct mail is always from one person to another.
3. Offer your most important benefit immediately. Recognize that your reader is selfish even as you and I.
4. Resist the temptation to display your learning. Discard all "elegant" English. Use the plain word whenever possible—and it is possible most of the time.

[5]Quoted in "Reed-able Copy," a monthly clinic conducted by Orville Reed. *The Reporter of Direct Mail Advertising*. March 1961.

5. Your writing friends are verbs and nouns—your enemies adjectives. Every unnecessary adjective eliminated increases your chance for success.
6. Don't overestimate the knowledge of your reader, but never underestimate his intelligence. He will act if you give him **all** the facts.
7. Don't talk about yourself and your product. Do talk about your reader and his problems—a letter is interesting to him if it is about him.
8. Give your reader a *reason* to believe what you say. Even the truth is unbelievable if you don't make it logical.
9. If you don't believe what you are writing—stop writing. There are no wealthy confidence men.
10. Ask for the order—again, and again.

Ferd Nauheim's Ten Commandments of Direct Mail

1. What is the precise thing I want the mailing to do?
2. What kind of people am I writing to?
3. Now that I can visualize them, what is there in my proposition that will be most appealing to them?
4. Have I discarded the thought of what is most important to me in favor of what is most important to them?
5. Taking all of my first four thoughts together, can I create an opening sentence that will make the reader want to read more?
6. Am I able to explain my proposition with unquestionable clarity?
7. Can I make it compelling without resorting to exaggeration, or even true statements that sound unbelievable?
8. What can I say to support my claims?
9. What is the easiest way for my prospects to take the action I want to take?
10. Can I give any honest reasons why they will benefit by taking immediate action?

Earle Buckley's Letter Checklist

Earle A. Buckley provides a helpful checklist for analyzing letters in his book, *How to Write Better Business Letters* (McGraw-

Hill Book Co. New York, New York. 1957):

Read it aloud and see how it sounds. That is a mighty good test and one that will uncover many weak spots.

How does it *look* when set up on your letterhead all ready to go? Impressive? Interesting? Attractive? Important? Personal?

Is it addressed to the *right person?* Writing to the purchasing agent, when the plant superintendent is really the man, will keep returns down to a minimum.

Are you using an up-to-date list? Are you reasonably sure that the names on it are those of people who *need* and should want what you have to offer and can *afford* to buy?

Is it going out at the *right time*?

The opening paragraph—does it act like a stop signal? Is it interest-creating? Does it make you want to read more?

Is your proposition a good one? Would *you* be interested in it if you were "on the other side of the fence"?

Have you told about it convincingly? Has your story "believability"? Does it sound sincere? Have you given the prospect a motive for doing what you want him to do?

Did you make the right kind of bid for action? Did you give a *reason* for acting? Have you made it easy and convenient for the prospect or customer to reply?

Have you followed a letter formula (interest, desire, conviction, action—or whatever other formula you have chosen) and adhered to its requirements?

If you are using enclosures of any kind, are they being put into the envelopes in such a way that they are sure to come out with the letter?

Finally, have you given your letter to someone else to read in order to get an outside slant on your efforts?

The Mead Checklist

Still another good checklist for analyzing direct mail letters (and much of it applies to other types of direct mail copy) is one prepared by Mead Papers Inc. It includes a scoring system which may prove helpful.

1. *If the appearance of the envelope is in its favor*............ *3 points*
   Create a good impression on your prospect even before he reads your letter. Check the appearance of the envelope, and its appropriateness to the job at hand. Make certain there's nothing to detract from the effect

you are trying to create, nothing that would enable your prospect to arrive at a negative decision before even looking inside.

2. *If the appearance of the letterhead will help the sale*..........4 points
Here, too, appearance is important. Your letterhead should give the right impression of the kind and character of your business. It should not, of course, be so cluttered that it steals attention from the letter itself. Needless to say, the paper on which it is printed is highly important. Use a standard watermarked bond of dignity and character.

3. *If the opening sentence arouses immediate interest*..........12 points
If you don't arouse interest at the very beginning, the chances of having your letter read through to the end are slim. So be sure to lead off with something of interest to your reader. Don't confuse interest with curiosity. The interest should in some way be related to the sales story that follows for you to qualify for the twelve points.

4. *If the second and subsequent paragraphs create desire by discussing benefits to the prospect*..........12 points
Your letter should not only describe your offer, it should also tell your prospects what the acceptance of your offer will do for them—how it will save them time or money, give them useful knowledge, add to their comfort. For example, don't just say that your book on tax laws was written by a well-known expert. Point out to your prospects how the purchase of this book will prevent them from making costly mistakes. Description of a product or service does not necessarily create desire.

5. *If the reasons for buying are convincing and the letter has believability*..........12 points
Certainly, everything is lost if your letter lacks conviction and believability. You may have an excellent product or service, sold at a very reasonable price, but if your letter contains statements that your prospects simply cannot accept, you will not be doing justice to your offer. Test the sales story out on yourself. Would the arguments you have used sell you? Would you buy on the basis of what you read in the sales letter?

6. *If your proposition is a good one*..........10 points
You must build your sales proposition on a firm foundation. Your sales story must offer something the prospect can use, at a fair price and one that he can afford. Again, the best way to test this is to try it out on yourself.

7. *If each paragraph leads you on to the next, and the next, giving the letter continuity*..........3 points
The paragraphs and sections of your letter must hang together to make a complete unit. Every part must develop out of the preceding one, and lead into what follows. A letter that consists merely of a number of completely separate paragraphs will sound jerky, will fail to hold the reader's attention. Make your letter smooth reading.

8. *If you have written in the language of the average prospect*..........3 points
By writing in the language of the average prospect, we mean tying in with any known peculiarities of speech common to that classification. To illustrate, you would talk in one vein to housewives, in an entirely different way to farmers, in another way to mechanics, in still another way to bank presidents or executives. If there is no so-called language for your prospect, score the points anyway.

9. *If you have used an appropriate emotional appeal: love, duty, pride, gain, self-indulgence, or fear*......6 *points*

   Your sales letter should present your proposition in logical and reasonable terms, so that your prospects can understand it clearly. But reason alone is not strong enough argument. If possible, appeal to your prospect's emotions. Make his mouth water. Tempt him through the use of working words and descriptive phrases. Make him want, and be eager to have, what your product will do for him.

10. *If you have given the prospect sufficient information to enable him to make a decision*......5 *points*

    Make your story complete. Give your prospect all the information he needs to decide whether or not he should buy or be interested in your product or service. If you don't take the trouble to complete your sales story, he certainly will not do it for you.

11. *If you have used good testimonials*......5 *points*

    While still one of the most powerful selling tools, appropriate testimonials are not always available. Don't feel that you must include testimonials merely for the sake of having them. If you can get endorsements from people who are in a position to lend prestige to your offer, use them. Otherwise, you are better off without testimonials, in which case you can still score the five points.

12. *If your letter contains a guarantee of satisfaction*......8 *points*

    If your letter is soliciting a direct order, it should by all means contain a guarantee of satisfaction. This will make your offer more convincing, and demonstrate that you are acting in good faith. If the purpose of your letter is to draw inquiries, the guarantee is not always necessary. Thus, if your letter contains a guarantee, or if one isn't appropriate, allow yourself the eight points.

13. *If you have asked for some definite action*......4 *points*

    Don't leave your reader up in the air after finishing your letter. Ask him to take a definite step—send in an order form, request further information, send for a sample. This will keep your offer *alive*, and place you in better position to take appropriate followup steps.

14. *If you have made it easy for the prospect to act*......4 *points*

    Include the means for taking action in your mailing piece. If you want your readers to send in orders, provide an easy-to-use order form plus a postage-free reply envelope. If you want them to request further information, provide a postage-free reply card. When you force your prospects to write letters, and then address and stamp envelopes, you are increasing the odds against returns.

15. *If you have given a good reason or inducement to act now*......4 *points*

    The time element will work against you unless you urge your readers to act *without delay*. When your prospects put off acting on your offer, there is always the possibility that they will forget your proposition entirely.

16. *If you have read the letter aloud, given it to someone else for criticism, or slept on it*......3 *points*

    Here are three habits well worth cultivating. Each enables you to view your letters as a typical prospect, not as the author. The brief time required for these steps often points out omissions that slip by during the original preparation. If you adopted any one of them on the particular letter being evaluated, you are entitled to the three points.

17. *If you are enclosing a folder, circular, or other sales literature with the letter*.......... *2 points*

With letters that are soliciting direct orders, some form of supporting sales literature is almost invariably needed. This gives you a chance to go into impressive detail in describing your offer. On some types of inquiry letters the enclosure may not be needed, and if that is the case you can still give yourself the two points.

Cross-out, Write-in Test

Another excellent test for copy has been suggested by Ernest S. Green of Johns-Manville Sales Corporation (*Industrial Marketing*. August 1959). "I recommend," he says, "that you test your copy with the 'cross-out, write-in test.' It is simple. It is quick. It isn't patented. You can perform it without the assistance or even the knowledge of any person other than yourself. Just take your copy, cross out your company's name and write in your competitor's."

This simple test can be highly effective. And, all too often, you will find that your copy could indeed apply to your competitor's direct mail just as well.

Mr. Green has some good suggestions to follow when your copy does not meet the simple test he has suggested. "Check your sales points. Find something you can say that your competitor can't say. If your product is used by Alaska Tech, say so. If your product is used by Hawaii Tech, say so. These progressive schools couldn't very well use a competitor's system if they have your system, could they?

"Suppose, however, your files are fresh out of fresh case histories. I suggest reaching for a telephone instead of a thesaurus. Talk to sales. Talk to research. Talk to that dealer you met in Atlantic City. Keep talking until somebody says something that makes you proud of your product, something that your competitor's legal department wouldn't possibly let it say.

"When you hear that happy something, write it down, just the way it was told to you. Use it in your copy and you'll pass the 'cross-out, write-in test' with ease and honors."

INDUSTRIAL DIRECT MAIL COPY

Writing industrial direct mail copy is not too different from preparing a message for consumer audiences. After all, the industrial buyer is *also* a buyer of consumer products. But the products and services involved often call for special copy angles.

What the Reader Wants to Know

James B. Stone of Technical Marketing Associates offers this six-point guide to preparing industrial copy in "The Reader: What He Wants to Know." (*Industrial Marketing*):

1. What Are You Selling? Recently, industrial advertising, especially in the electronics field, has become obsessed with illustrations of rockets, missiles, and jet aircraft roaring high above the earth's surface. Obviously, the advertiser isn't selling guided missiles. But what is he selling?

   After patiently wading through three paragraphs on the speed and destructive power of the Eagle IV, you discover the product—a "turboencabulator" that helps to control the fuel intake. That's fine, but the emphasis is in the wrong place. If you're selling turboencabulators, tell your potential buyer as soon as possible.

2. What Are the Specifications? Delete that flowery paragraph on how your research and development department sweated for eight years to develop the turboencabulator. Give your reader the product's performance specifications—clearly and concisely.

   When you harangue the reader with the troubles you've had in making the product, you do nothing but make him realize that directly or indirectly he is going to be paying plenty for your engineering *faux pas* if he buys the unit. I repeat—give the specifications clearly and concisely.

3. What Are the Features? Again, clearly, simply, and concisely tell your reader what your product will do that others will not. Briefcase histories are always good back-up for your selling message. But keep them straightforward and simple. No superlatives—the "professional" prospect, as a matter of principle, won't believe them.

4. How About Services? Promptness of delivery is a very important selling point. If the reader is working on a crash program, he may buy your product simply because he can get it next week rather than next month.

   Let him know if you can promise early delivery. Also, if you can offer good service on repair or replacement of the item, you are definitely one up on your slower competitors.

5. How Much Does It Cost? Unfortunately, not all prospects are in the position to buy a product on a cost-plus basis. Some are still obliged to work on strict development or production budgets, and costs count heavily in their decision to buy your product or a competitor's. Therefore, to save time-wasting inquiries and fruitless followup by your salesmen, the price of the item should be given in the ad.

   If you feel that the price might look enormous in print, you might compare it to the six-figure price recently listed in an ad for a transport plane by a leading aircraft manufacturer.

6. Where to Get More Information? Make it as easy as possible for the reader to get your sales literature or to place an order. Give him

full company name, complete address, telephone number, and perhaps the name of an inside salesman or order-taker.

Emotional Factors

All too often, industrial copywriters look at their task as strictly a nuts-and-bolts affair, forgetting that the industrial buyer must be approached as a human being. Howard G. Sawyer of Marsteller, Inc., in commenting on a study of what motivates industrial buyers,[6] outlined seven emotional factors which are highly important in preparing industrial advertising copy:

1. *Habit, complacency, inertia.* These are personal matters—nothing to do with the man's function but characteristic of the man who, as a manager, has responsibility.

   What do we do about them in advertising? The answer is clear: substitute, for an emotional block, an emotional incentive, in the form of something capitalizing upon one of the favorable emotional factors.

2. *Fear of decision.* What can we do about this in advertising?

   Pump up the prospect's personal tires by suggesting how smart he will be to buy your product. While you can't come right out and say that his choice of your product will guarantee a promotion, you can feed his ego by using words that suggest it will be to his personal advantage to make the decision your way. It is to your advantage to cultivate his spirit of enterprise.

3. *Security—the very natural desire to make a safe decision, the tendency to do nothing rather than take a chance that might snap back and hit you in the face.* When, for example, a man considers the question of a company's reliability in delivering on time, he will think less of the consequences to his company if the supplier falls down on delivery than of the consequences to himself—the likelihood of squawks from his own customers or getting hell from his superiors.

   What can we do about this in advertising? The answer I get out of this *Steel* study is to include, in your advertising message, if appropriate, assurances that delivery and service and availability are reliable (provided, of course, that it is true). You might win a customer on that point alone.

4. *Laziness.* Everybody wants to make his own job easy, and this will affect decisions he makes for his company. New associations sometimes bring problems: new contact men—an unknown quantity; new methods of handling, all the way down to billing procedures; new instructions for operating personnel—and perhaps their resentment over the unavoidable fact that their routine has been altered.

   What can we do about this in advertising? Well, demonstrate that the personal difficulties he would run up against if he switched to your product would be minimal—or less than he is experiencing now with his present source of supply. Show him that other people in his firm will be pleased with his decision—their jobs will be easier or more

[6]A study conducted for *Steel* magazine by Dr. F. Robert Shoaf. Additional details in Chapter 6, "Industrial Direct Mail."

resultful or more profitable, so he will be appreciated or rewarded for his action.

Those are some of the unfavorable factors. Here are some of the factors which are favorable and might be capitalized upon:

5. *The gambling instinct, the desire to be a hero, the ambition to get ahead in the business, that wonderful instinct to want to do a good job.* What can we do about this in advertising? Obviously, tell the buyer how he will benefit, as an individual, because he bought your product. Not just that his firm will make more money, but that he can get credit for it. Not just that his company's product will be improved, but that he can get personal satisfaction from it.

6. *Fear of being left behind.* Most of us are followers—we ride trends. What can we do about this in advertising? The answer to this is: give examples of how other companies are increasingly taking advantage of what your product offers. Use case histories, testimonials, statistics on trends.

7. *Status.* A man feels prouder of himself and his company if he buys from firms which are well respected and with which other respected companies do business.

   This calls for advertising that gives the prospect an idea of whom you do business with, manifestations of your leadership in your field, your achievements in fields related to the public welfare such as the conquest of space or medicine or better living conditions. It exalts him a little to be associated with such a supplier.

   But there is another aspect to status which is also important—and also emotional: Be sure to address the reader as a management man, not as an apprentice searching for knowledge. There is a little bit of "manager" in all of us, you must respect that fact. Industrial buyers want to be *addressed* as managers.

Objectives of Industrial Copy

Another common fault of industrial direct mail copywriters is that they too often fail to zero in on concrete, specific objectives. About as far as some copywriters go is to think in terms of writing copy for direct mail which will draw inquiries, build prestige for the company, or pave the way for salesmen.

While such objectives are, of course, important, they are too broad to be used as the real cornerstone for effective copywriting. A possible alternate approach was suggested by Carl Connable, an industrial advertising agency man, in "Setting Ad Objectives With the Reader in Mind." (*Industrial Marketing.*) "Such statements," he commented, "permit misunderstandings as to what is intended and inconsistencies of approach in the advertisements.

"These troubles can be avoided by listing the objectives in terms of *readers'* interests—by stating the things that you want the reader to *know,* or to *feel,* or to *do,* as a result of reading your ads. This method pinpoints the objectives in terms that are clear to everyone, and enables ad creators to work with the confidence that they're headed in the right direction. The result is more effective advertising, more efficiently produced."

Mr. Connable prepared a list of 38 specific objectives for industrial advertising:

Things for the reader to know:

What your product is, and what it does.

What your product looks like.

The *name* of your product.

That your company is the maker of that brand of product.

Exclusive or outstanding advantages that are inherent in your product.

Specific ways in which he will benefit by using your product.

How other companies are using your product to advantage.

That the product is used by well-known companies.

Why he can depend on your product for economy, efficiency, long life.

That it's more economical to buy your product than to make such an item for himself.

That you have a broad line of products, or a wide range of types and sizes.

That new items, or new lines, are now available.

That you make other products for related (or unrelated) uses.

Where he can buy your product.

Prices.

Specifications.

Why, in spite of price competition, your product is the best buy.

That your company is first and foremost in its field.

About special services that you provide.

If you're advertising to dealers or distributors, you may also want the reader to know:

The real and salable benefits that your product offers.

Ideas, new applications, new or exclusive features that will help him sell your product.

About market studies, sales figures and other facts that show a preference or worthwhile potential for your product.

How other distributors are making money handling your product.

That your product is widely and effectively advertised to customers and prospects in his territory.

About sales aids that are available, and how he can benefit by using them.

About special promotions, contests, special deals.

About new policies as to pricing, delivery, field service.

That distributorships are available.

Things for the reader to feel:

That your company image is one of dignity, integrity, and conservative dependability.

That your company is alert, progressive, youthful, and vigorous.

That your company is a "human," friendly outfit that he will find pleasant to deal with.

That your product is the Rolls Royce of its field—or the Plymouth—or the Jeep.

Things for the reader to do:

Write for literature, whether or not he is a prospective purchaser or a buying influence.

Write for literature only if he is a likely prospect.

Contact your nearest dealer or representative.

Ask for a demonstration.

Ask for a specific proposal or quotation.

Send for a sample.

Killing a Sales Message

Looking at industrial copywriting from the reverse point of view, Carl Connable, in another *Industrial Marketing* article, "How to Stifle Your Sales Message," offered these 12 tips on "how to go wrong":

1. Assume that the would-be reader knows as much as *you* do about your product. Mention new or advantageous features, if you must, but don't give details. In particular, don't point out that they're new, or how they make the product of value to him. That way, he'll be disinterested, or frustrated, and in either case unimpressed.
2. As an alternative, *talk down* to the reader. Assume that he knows nothing about your type of product or its uses. Thus, if you're selling burglar alarms, tell him first that burglary is a bad thing and it should be stopped. This will practically guarantee that he'll never get to your sales story.
3. Present things from *your* viewpoint—or your president's. Proud of your product? Say so! Think the reader would be a fool not to buy it? Imply that—strongly. Been in business umpteen years? Play it up, *big*. If you can be pompous about this, so much the better. There's nothing like a dazzling expanse of stuffed shirt to blind a reader.
4. Wherever possible, use the technical jargon of your specialized branch of your trade or industry. Where your plant has its own private names for things, use those names. And by all means, abbreviate freely. That way, most of the readers will be uncertain of what you mean—especially upper-level executives, who may have to approve the purchase.

5. Equally effective: Be verbose and scholarly in your writing. Never use (that is, avoid utilizing) a short word when a polysyllabic equivalent can be selected. Never consent to widely comprehensible terminology when esoteric phraseology is at your command. Abandon brevity in favor of circumlocutory sonorosity; and foresake all semblance of "shop talk" for pedantic exhibitionism such as that which you are now (we hope) perusing. That way, if you don't confuse or discourage the reader, you'll put him to sleep.
6. Be vague. Say that your product is bigger, or stronger, or more precise. But don't say why, and never indicate what you're comparing it to. Say it will save the user money—but don't say how much, or in what way. Avoid specific statements of all kinds. Otherwise, the reader might learn something of interest.
7. If you *must* include clear statements of significant facts, present them in random order. If you *organize* them, giving them proper sequence and the right relative emphasis, people will grasp what you're saying. Furthermore, when your material is well organized, you'll see gaps in your story that you'll want to fill in, to make it clearer and more complete. Better skip this entirely if you hope to succeed in stifling the sales message.
8. Use cliches, especially in headlines—and in illustrations too. You know: "SAVE TIME!"—with a picture of a watch being cut in two by a knife or scissors. (Ancient Romans probably featured a sundial for this.) "CUT PRODUCTION COSTS!"—with the bill-cutting picture. And for a *real* yawn-inducer, don't overlook "TOMORROW'S GIZMOS TODAY!"
9. *Use human-interest* pictures—a scantily-clad cutie, a baby, a charging bull—the more unrelated to the product, the better. Most readers will never get beyond such an interesting obstacle; and think how you'll brighten their day.
10. Conceal the identity of what you're selling. And when you can't avoid referring to it, make the reader guess its kind or purpose. For example, if the product is a milling machine, people won't know whether it's for cutting metal or making flour, unless you tell them. And "gages" might be for measuring pressure, size, or inches of rainfall. Play it cozy and people will never know—or care.
11. Make claims for your product that are *unbelievable,* even though they are strictly true. Some products offer advantages beyond the experience or imagination of prospective users. If that's the case with *your* product, state your claim as boldly as possible, and forget about offering proof. Only the idly curious will read further if it appears to be a fake.
12. Make it physically hard to read. Use long lines of small type—preferably printed in reverse, or on bright red or dark blue, or running across an illustration. Print heads and subheads in pale yellow or silver. Jumble it up with lots of tiny pictures. And crowd it all together as tightly as possible, so as not to waste any white space. That will eliminate response from "curiosity seekers"—and from most of your prospects as well.

There are other methods, including those for special purposes such as giving misinformation, being downright offensive, and conveying a feeling of low quality. However, the above pointers should give you adequate help in stifling your sales messages. Follow them carefully and we will guarantee that not a single one of your ads or promotion pieces will lead to a single sale.

Seven Deadly Sins

Probably the best guide to evaluating industrial advertising was a list of "Seven Deadly Sins" prepared by the anonymous "Copy Chasers," who write a monthly column for *Industrial Marketing.* This checklist can apply equally well to other types of advertising.

1. *The sin of being a braggart.* A lot of industrial advertising is like the blow-hard—the man who interminably insists that he's better than the next guy. Claiming superiority, in itself, is not necessarily wrong—unless little or nothing is done to substantiate the claim in a friendly, persuasive, and convincing manner.
2. *The sin of talking to yourself* instead of thinking of the other fellow. The most creative industrial advertising is that which directs its remarks to the interests of the readers—not the company doing the talking.
3. *The sin of preaching.* Faced with white paper to fill, some advertisers get a compulsion to lecture. Looking down upon the reader from the high altitude of their superiority, they tell the reader—rather than invite him—to do what they want him to do.
4. *The sin of being noisy.* Everybody hates the bugler, but a good many advertisers believe they have to make a big noise in order to get readers to stand at attention. If you have something interesting to say about a subject of interest to readers, there's no need to set your hair on fire in order to catch their eye.
5. *The sin of being messy.* Nobody likes the man who is messy, dirty, or inconsiderate. A lot of advertising, unfortunately, can be so described.
6. *The sin of trying to be cute.* Don't be a smart-aleck in industrial advertising. Deliver your story in as straightforward a manner as possible—you'll get more applause from your audience than if you put on an act.
7. *The sin of being dull.* Of all the deadly sins of industrial advertising, the worst by far is being dull. About all an advertising man is expected to do is enliven the sales message with a crisp presentation of visual elements and some fast-moving copy.

Andrews' 6-Point Writing Formula

In a five-part "Encyclopedia of Marketing" series in *Industrial Marketing,* Arnold Andrews set forth a set of six basic guidepoints for writers of industrial advertising copy:

1. Read over your basic material carefully several times. Study your pictures for additional information about the job. Be sure you understand clearly all the subject material. Then write a "working" headline. (Don't waste time on it; you'll write the real headline later.)

   Pull out all the usable material from your job story or other source material, develop it item-by-item, and have it typed "rough." Never mind the sequence. Just get all the pertinent facts available on a worksheet with no confusing excess material.

   Write your basic material out as simply and clearly as possible without worrying much about phrasing or sequence. Lift sections bodily from

INDUSTRIAL COPYWRITER'S CHECKLIST

1. Check the following basics:
   English . . . Spelling . . .
   Punctuation . . . Capitalization . . .
2. In testimonials or case histories, check *spelling of names* and initials against the original report.
3. Look for repetition of words or thoughts: Eliminate advertising jabberwocky—make copy read simply, straightforward, convincingly, real. Eliminate excess words—especially "a" and "the." Leave no word that does not build up the story. *Analyze each word and its meaningfulness separately.*
4. Check all words over two syllables . . . Is there another shorter word that says what you have to say? *Better two short words than one long one.* Avoid any "cute" or tricky phrases.
5. Check to see that thoughts are in *logical sequence* . . . sales arguments in most effective order. See that specifications are clearly defined, easy to follow.
6. Does copy flow through smoothly? Do you switch from one idea to another and then go back? Are your transitions "jumpy?"
7. Have you crowded too many thoughts, too many individual subjects into a single, long sentence? Are paragraphs too long?
8. Have you given adequate proof for sales argument? Remember, the reader does not believe advertising copywriters. Try to give reasonable proof of every possible claim.
9. Are heads and subheads right for headlines used? Do captions explain or supplement illustrations? Avoid "label" heads, subheads, captions. Even in specification panels, sell it—don't just label it.
10. Are your picture captions pertinent—do they describe the action or conditions shown in the photo?
11. Are all statements true—based on today's information?
12. Is copy tailored to the market? Read again carefully, studying every point, every claim, every word, every illustration, to be sure each and every one fits *this* particular buyer.
13. Will copy fit? Are captions matched in length for same number of lines in corresponding spaces? Eliminate widows in typed copy—*now*—not after type is set, when corrections may double type cost.
14. Don't forget your "action" appeal—closing paragraph should urge reader to see his local distributor *now,* or write for bulletin *today,* etc. You want him to do something—tell him the *next* logical step toward a sale. Remember you're selling a "look-see" not a "cash-on-the-line delivery-tomorrow" deal.
15. Have you covered trademark name protection correctly? Is signature copy correct and included? Will headline break properly for layout?
16. Read entire ad *aloud* for overall sense, for sound, for sales punch. Would you say it that way to the buyer across his desk? Does your copy "talk"? If it doesn't, rewrite it.
17. Also, remember when writing export ads or adaptations, metrics are used. Check as to whether both metrics and English figures are to be used, and their order of appearance.

Reprinted from "A Basic Guide to Writing Industrial Ad Copy," by Arnold Andrews. *Industrial Marketing.* December 1960.

source material if they are pertinent to your subject. Circle and number approximate sequence for the typist if that will save time. Be sure figures and facts are correct. Then work on another assignment.

2. With all facts typed out on your worksheet under a working head, sort them into groups in proper thought sequence for your ad. Start eliminating excess words. If you see some easy corrections in English or sentence structure that will help, put these in, but don't get involved in "writing" the story till you get your material retyped in the order you want to use. Also sort out and segregate your caption information at this stage. Have the usable material retyped. Then temporarily forget it and work on another ad.

3. Now *write* your copy from your edited and boiled-down source material. Keep your thoughts clear and factual. Keep your sentences short and simple. Use common words that make clear, concrete pictures. Before the retype on the above, pick out your pictures and write your captions. Then have all this rough draft material retyped, while you work on something else.

4. When your third rough draft comes back, reread and edit. Reread your source material and mentally reanalyze your sales story to be sure you've drafted a complete and logical presentation of your case. Write your subheads or paragraph leads. Write as many good headlines as you can dream up. Select the best one and have everything typed over again.

5. Reread the revised copy carefully and start to "polish." Measure words, phrases, sentences, double meanings. Study to see if you have fast, clear reading and logical sequence of thought. Analyze the necessity for each word and phrase. If it doesn't contribute to the thought, take it out. Eliminate the typical "ad-dy" copy. Check for unbelievable and worn-out superlatives. Check tailoring to your market. Check your close. Look for and eliminate trite, oratorical phrasing. Go back to original source material and read it completely, rechecking all figures used to be sure that they are accurate. Have it all retyped. Meanwhile, work on another ad.

6. When you get the fifth cleaned-up copy, read it aloud, *talking* it to an imaginary prospect across your desk. See if it sounds clear, simple, forceful. See if it *talks*. If you wouldn't *say* it that way, change it.

   Be sure your close tells the reader *what you want him to do* in a logical way. Remember he's not going to take a few thousand dollars in his hot little hand and rush to the nearest store to buy whatever you're selling. Check for signature, address, trademark registration, model number, accuracy of specifications used, ad number.

   Check for reasonable length of copy for layout purposes. See that copy lengths are matched where matched copy is needed in layout. Also mark words to be emphasized in headline. Check paragraphs and captions to see they open with reader interest. Check to see that what you are discussing is clear at the beginning of each sentence, so that the reader does not have to read through to get your idea, then reread to get your point. Then have it retyped so that the copy chief gets clean, well-typed material for editing. Neither you, nor he, can work copy intelligently when it is messed up with write-in corrections.

   Read the finished copy once more to be sure it's right—the very best you can do. Then submit it.

Reviewing Copy

In the same series of articles, Mr. Andrews points out that "copy should never be a 'one-man' job. Exchanging copy for review, suggestions and editing between writers is always a good idea." In analyzing others' copy, he suggests that attention be primarily directed toward:

1. Easy, fast readership.
2. Accuracy of information.
3. Elimination of repetitive wording.
4. Use of factual rather than generalized claims.
5. Development of specific owner-benefits resulting from mechanical features.
6. Followthrough of headline theme in copy and captions.
7. Caption copy pertinent to conditions, action, or application in photo.
8. Logical close to direct reader *action* toward next step leading to a sale.

What Not to Do

To these eight guidelines for editing others' copy, Mr. Andrews adds three types of changes to avoid:

1. Change copy to *your* wording without contributing to clearer, faster reading, understanding, and remembering.
2. Add unnecessary wordage, phrases, or copy length, without contributing to fast reading and sales action.
3. Dilute impact of important sales points by adding unimportant sales points to produce a *longer* list of sales arguments.

"Try to read as a prospect," he suggests. "Try to measure the ability of the headline to invite prospect readership. Try to measure the success of the sales presentation in bringing the prospect into contact with the salesman when he is ready to buy.

"Remember that there are three types of prospects:

1. The prospect who knows he is in the market—needs equipment of your type in order to expand production or else to replace obsolete or worn-out equipment. Here we are selling against present-day competition on new equipment.
2. Prospects who think they might be able to increase profits by adding to their current plant.
3. Prospects who feel they are currently not in the market. But they are reading to keep up to date on improved equipment against possible future expansion or replacement problems. Here we are trying to convert an indirect interest to a purchase interest by calling attention to economy and production advantages we have to offer over the partially inefficient equipment now owned by the prospect, even though the equipment may still be in good-as-new operating condition.

"The copy you are editing (or writing)," he adds, "may be directed to any one of the above audiences, or may deal with any combination of competitive problems from new or owned equipment."

Technical Writing

Much industrial direct mail involves technical writing. To obtain such copy frequently means turning to those with a technical rather than a writing background. And this often spells trouble.

When engineers write to other enginers, you *may* be on safe ground. But when highly technical minds are given the assignment of putting their knowledge in written form to communicate with a less technically minded audience, a good direct mail copy editor is almost a must.

An excellent guide to help technical writers understand the problems involved in preparation of copy was presented in a booklet prepared by Minneapolis-Honeywell Regulator Co. to guide its own personnel. The booklet, written by E. A. Murphy and John Stahr, included "Ten Commandments for Technical Writers." While these ten points were originally intended to cover the preparation of publicity articles, the same basic points can be just as easily applied to the writing of technical copy for direct mail.

1. *Thou shalt exercise thy judgment as to whether a story is worth writing at all.*

   Keep in mind what makes a story worth writing. Will it *help* the reader to cut costs, increase production, improve quality, conserve man-hours, or do a better job in any way?

2. *Thou shalt know what thou art writing about.*

   You can't be an expert in everything, but make sure that you understand your subject before you start to write. *Don't ever* let yourself be trapped into having to say, "Well, I didn't understand it either, but that's what the man said."

3. *Thou shalt think before thou writest.*

   When you find yourself having trouble putting something into words, stop trying to *write* and start trying to *think*. Once you really know what you want to say, you won't have any trouble finding the right words.

4. *Thou shalt know thy readers and write for them.*

   Use the language of the industry for which you're writing, but don't assume that *all* your readers are intimately familiar with all the engineering details of their industry. When in doubt, lean toward the assumption that your reader is chairman of the board rather than chief engineer.

5. *Thou shalt not substitute adjectives for facts.*

   The *facts* about a new process, application, or control system should be such that the reader will recognize that it is "revolutionary" or "sensational." One adjective can weaken a good noun; two can badly damage it; three can destroy it.

6. *Thou shalt be accurate, exact, and thorough.*

   No explanation needed.

7. *Thou shalt not show off thy technical vocabulary.*

   Many executives who are influential in the purchasing of your company's products have long since forgotten their calculus and chemical formulas. Exotic or new-fangled technical terms and mathematics may just exasperate them. The men you want to reach are more likely to turn the page than reach for a technical dictionary.

8. *Thou shalt not leave any unanswered questions in thy reader's mind.*

   After you've written your article, read it over, paragraph by paragraph. As you read each paragraph, make sure that any question it may raise in the reader's mind is answered right away.

9. *Thou shalt edit thine own copy as mercilessly as if it were somebody else's.*

   After you've finished writing your article, edit it surgically. Carve out all the dead wood, the parasitic words or phrases that aren't doing any work. Any phrase or sentence that you felt was especially clever when you wrote it should be regarded with particular suspicion.

10. *Thou shalt not turn essayist when thou art a reporter.*

    Resist the temptation to write an introductory treatise on the broad economic or sociological aspects of an installation or application. Be matter-of-fact and brief if you *have* to explain *why* something is significant.

TEN COMMANDMENTS FOR TECHNICAL WRITERS

By E. A. Murphy and John Stahr

I. Thou shalt exercise thy judgment as to whether a story is worth writing at all.

II. Thou shalt know what thou art writing about.

III. Thou shalt think before thou writest.

IV. Thou shalt know thy readers and write for them.

V. Thou shalt *NOT* substitute adjectives for facts.

VI. Thou shalt be accurate, exact, and thorough.

VII. Thou shalt *NOT* show off thy technical vocabulary.

VIII. Thou shalt *NOT* leave any unanswered questions in thy reader's mind.

IX. Thou shalt edit thine own copy as mercilessly as if it were somebody else's.

X. Thou shalt *NOT* turn essayist when thou art a reporter.

Chapter 25

WRITING DIRECT MAIL LETTERS

WHILE we have just covered the subject of direct mail copywriting in considerable detail, there is another type of copywriting which deserves special consideration—the writing of business letters.

In almost every direct mail operation, there is a tremendous amount of individual letterwriting to be done—in addition to writing copy for those direct mail letters which will go to an audience rather than to an individual.

We have previously mentioned the wealth of good books available on the subject of copywriting—and there are even more good volumes on the subject of business letterwriting.

Dartnell published two books, in particular, which should be used side by side with this HANDBOOK—*The Business Letter Deskbook,** by Leslie L. Lewis and *The Sales Promotion Handbook,* by Ovid Riso. While it would be too space-consuming to try to cover all of the helpful material in these books within this HANDBOOK, we have selected some particularly useful reference guides:

CHECKLIST OF GENERAL PRINCIPLES FOR WRITING BETTER BUSINESS LETTERS

1. Before starting to write or dictate, have you thought through—
   a. What the letter is to accomplish?
   b. Who will read it?
   c. What will first catch his interest?
   d. What will hold his continuing interest?
   e. What, if any, action you want taken?
   f. How you will try to get such action?
2. Is your salutation appropriately familiar or formal, as the case may call for?
3. Does your first paragraph summarize the purpose of the letter, just as a newspaper item gives the essence of the story in the lead paragraph?
4. Is the letter courteous, friendly, and considerate, to build and hold goodwill?

*Now out of print.

5. Does the letter reflect your personality favorably?
6. Does it read easily—short sentences and short paragraphs?
7. Is it as short as you can make it yet cover all the essentials?
8. Are all facts accurate and verifiable?
9. Do you use the most natural words without straining for effect?
10. Do you write from a "you" rather than a "we" or "I" point of view?
11. Do you employ emphasis—underlining, asterisks, capitals—where appropriate and useful to bring out important points that might otherwise be overlooked?
12. Do you ask questions to stimulate the reader's thinking, where appropriate?
13. Have you confined the letter to one subject, to avoid confusion or the danger of the reader's overlooking a second subject?
14. Is your language conversational rather than stilted?
15. Have you considered the time element—will the letter be received at an appropriate or convenient time for proper attention?

SEVENTEEN SUGGESTIONS FOR WRITING ADJUSTMENT LETTERS

1. Answer promptly. Don't let him nurse that grievance.
2. If you can't give a full reply at once, better send an interim acknowledgment to keep the customer happy.
3. Thank him for calling the matter to your attention.
4. Sympathize with his point of view even though he may be wrong.
5. Don't ever tell him he's wrong; if you must say "no," say "yes—but . . ."
6. If you are wrong, admit it, but don't overdo the apologies. A dignified word of regret is more convincing than a wail.
7. If the adjustment will be in his favor, tell him so promptly.
8. If you can't make a favorable adjustment, try to find something you CAN do to make him happier.
9. Never, never, never argue or lose your temper. "Win an argument and lose a customer."
10. If he's wrong, start by saying that you see why he feels as he does, "but . . ."
11. Be friendly but not flippant; a complaining customer is in no mood to take kidding.
12. Avoid short, snappy adjustment letters. A longer letter, even if he is in the wrong, shows that at least you take his complaint seriously.
13. Don't say it will never happen again; it may. But say that every effort will be made to prevent its happening again.

14. If possible, the letter of adjustment should be signed by the person to whom the complaint was addressed, even if someone else has written the adjustment letter.
15. Don't put the blame on any person or department; if your company is at fault, say "we."
16. If you MUST use a form letter (it's much better not to!) be sure it doesn't say "such a complaint is rare," since the fact that you use a form to reply shows that it's NOT rare.
17. Keep in mind the Proverb, "A soft answer turneth away wrath: but grievous words stir up anger" (Proverbs 15:1).

ABOVE ALL, REMEMBER THAT A COMPLAINING CUSTOMER IS MORE INTERESTED IN ADJUSTMENT THAN IN EXCUSES OR EXPLANATIONS.

A DOZEN DO'S AND A DOZEN DON'TS REGARDING CREDIT AND COLLECTION LETTERS

DO—

1. Make collection letters friendly and fair but firm.
2. Visualize the person to whom you are writing. What appeals is he most likely to respond to?
3. Use individually typed letters if possible; if this cannot be done, personalize the letters with at least one well-matched name fill-in.
4. Be persistent; you are entitled to the money he owes.
5. Always give him an out in the first letter: "Is there some reason why you have not met this obligation?"
6. Emphasize the "you" rather than the "we"—"your credit standing," "your good reputation," rather than "we want," "we need."
7. Make it easy for him to comply—self-addressed reply envelope, blank check, perhaps even a tiny ballpoint pen.
8. Remember that while you want the money, you also want to keep the customer's goodwill, if possible.
9. Write your "last resort" letters more in sorrow than in anger.
10. Offer help if possible—extended small payments or whatever else may be appropriate.
11. Distinguish as far as possible between customers who are temporarily hard up and those who are "deadbeats," in framing your letters.
12. Remember always that every collection letter is an action letter, so close with an action-motivating closing.

DON'T—

1. DON'T use the same collection letters for all types of customers if you can possibly use individualized letters.
2. DON'T let collection letters sound cantankerous or crabby.

3. DON'T risk using humor in your collection letters unless you know your customer well; most folks don't find being in debt funny. Also, if you kid them, they will probably pay more serious creditors first.
4. DON'T let a collection letter sound as though all you are interested in is getting the money and couldn't care less whether the customer ever buys again or not—at least, until you reach the "last resort" stage.
5. DON'T use argumentative or belligerent phrases that will get the debtor's back up; if you do, he will probably stall that much longer.
6. DON'T write "we need the money" or imply that you or your company is in financial trouble; this has proved to be the weakest type of appeal and often backfires.
7. DON'T apologize for writing; the creditor-debtor relationship gives you every right to ask for your money.
8. DON'T let a single payment period pass without notifying the customer that another payment is due.
9. DON'T imply that you think the customer is deliberately stalling; give him the benefit of the doubt.
10. DON'T overlook the fact that a collection letter is a sales letter: You are selling him the idea of paying NOW.
11. DON'T forget that libel laws apply to collection letters; word your letters so there can be no kickbacks, and always send them by first-class mail.
12. DON'T ever use a threat to sue unless you mean to back it up. When the time comes for drastic action, give fair warning and then ACT.

CHECKLIST FOR FORM LETTERS

1. Have you analyzed your correspondence to determine whether you can profit by using more form letters?
2. Are all your form letters designed so that typists can make typed fill-ins easily?
3. Is the form letter easily understood on the first reading?
4. Does it serve its purpose as well as if it were individually dictated?
5. If a window envelope is used, is there a mark to show the typist where to begin the address so that it will show in the window?
6. Is the letter easily identified, as by a number or initials printed in one of the corners?

CHECKLIST FOR GUIDE LETTERS

1. Have you analyzed your correspondence to find out whether you can use more guide letters?
2. Are your guide letters easy to read and easy to understand, reflecting the virtues of good plain letters?

3. Does each typist have a collection of guide letters with complete instructions on how to set up each letter, including instructions on making copies and preparing enclosures?
4. When a letter is answered with a guide letter, is the number of the reply letter noted on the inquiry to take the place of a file copy?
5. Do you follow a systematic plan for keeping guide letters active and for progressively improving them?
6. Do you periodically check your guide letters and revise them as necessary?

TEN TIPS FOR BETTER ORDER-ACKNOWLEDGMENT LETTERS

1. Acknowledge orders the day received.
2. Express thanks for the business.
3. If first order, also express welcome.
4. If additional information is needed to fill order, make it easy for customer to provide it.
5. Tell when and how order will be shipped.
6. If back-ordering is necessary, sell customer on necessity of waiting.
7. If substitution is necessary *sell* customer on accepting substitution.
8. If order is to be referred to dealer, send a copy of acknowledgment letter to dealer.
9. Confirm buyer's good judgment in buying from your company.
10. Enclose sales-promotion literature and encourage future orders, where appropriate.

TESTS FOR A SALES LETTER

By CAMERON MCPHERSON

How do the letters sent out over the signature of your company rate as media for promoting sales and goodwill? Just as every member of a business organization is ex officio a member of the sales promotion department, so every letter, regardless of its purpose, should aim to create acceptance for the policies and products of the company.

1. *Are Your Letters Neatly Typed and Easy to Read?* Is the letter set up with wide margins? or is it crowded up on the letterhead with too much white space at bottom? Is the type clean, sharp, and in good alignment? Are the paragraphs short? Remember that first impressions are lasting.
2. *Do Your Replies Cover All the Points Raised?* It is a good idea to mark or number all the references in a letter which require answering, so that in your hurry to get through your dictation none will be overlooked. Nothing is more disastrous to goodwill than the careless handling of requests for specific information.

3. *Are Your Letters Free from Vague Terms?* Study Emerson and Theodore Roosevelt and note their simplicity of thought and directness of statement. Note that they use short, concise sentences. They use a new sentence to express each new thought, and don't try to crowd three or four ideas into one sentence. What you are saying may be very clear *in your own mind,* but will the recipient see the same picture?

4. *Do Your Letters Come to the Point Quickly?* The opening and reading of mail is making more and more demands on your customer's time. He is in an impatient mood when he reaches your letter. So come to the point quickly. Keep on the main track. Don't take your customer on needless side excursions. Say what you have to say, in a friendly, good-humored way, and sit down.

5. *Are Your Letters Free from Hackneyed Phrases?* Are you still "begging to advise," "wishing to state," and "hoping to hear" in your letters? You don't *talk* that way, so why write that way? Endeavor to be yourself in your letters and studiously avoid these threadbare and moss-covered mean-nothings which mar so many business letters. They waste your time, the time of the person who has to transcribe your letters, and the time of the customer.

6. *Are Your Letters Cheery or Coldly Commercial?* In your desire to be concise be careful not to give a "curt" tone to your letter. No matter what your position may be, whether you are the general manager of the business or only one of many stenographers, you are here to serve.

7. *Have Superlatives Been Toned Down?* Are you working "best" and "very" overtime? Are you using such expressions as "made from the very best materials obtainable" instead of stating specifically the materials used? Are you using adjectives that have lost their effectiveness?

8. *Do Your Letters Anticipate Further Questions?* A really good correspondent puts himself in the place of the man with whom he is corresponding. He not only gives the information for which the man asks, but any other information which he thinks the man needs to reach a decision.

9. *Do You Appeal to the Recipient's Self-Interest?* There is always a temptation to talk about what we are doing, what we hope to do, and what we have done. We think everyone is interested in our problems, our troubles, our distractions. Forget yourself. Think about the man to whom you are writing. He is not interested in you.

10. *Do Your Letters Create Confidence and Ring True?* It is a real knack to be able to make the recipient feel that here is a man who is telling him unvarnished facts, and not painting a beautiful picture of something that does not exist. To do this, be careful not to overemphasize; impress without seeking to impress.

11. *Do Your Letters Ask for Specific Action?* We write business letters to get business. Sometimes we write them to get orders; sometimes we write them to get information; sometimes we write them to give information; but always to build our business. We can get more business if we close every letter with a specific request for action. If you want an order ask for it. If you want a reply ask for it.

GENERAL LETTERS

✓ Before you start to dictate, do you underscore points in the letter you are answering to make sure you will not overlook any?

✓ Do you strike at the heart of the proposition; or do you hem and haw, and beg to state, before you really get going?

✓ Do you write differently than you talk? Are your letters natural and easy, or are they stilted and dull?

✓ Is your tone simple and frank, or do you talk AT people? It's much better to talk WITH them.

✓ When there is an objection to be overcome, do you use the "yes-but" technique, or do you contradict?

✓ Does your letter reflect self-esteem or does it sound apologetic and weak?

✓ Are you considerate of the other fellow's point of view?

✓ Is your letter honest or do you say you are "surprised" and "dumbfounded" and "amazed" when you really are not?

✓ Do you try to be pompous by using big words that few people understand, including perhaps yourself?

✓ Are your sentences short and your paragraphs brief? Avoid getting the "and" habit.

✓ How about the dead phrases—the "beg to advise," the "wish to state," the "instants," and the "ultimos"? Beware of cluttering your letters up with deadwood.

✓ Are there enough "for instances" in your 100 percent letter to make it interesting and convincing?

✓ Do you anticipate the reader's "so what" attitude with which he reads every letter—yours included?

✓ How about the sequence of your points? Are they orderly and logical or do they hop-skip around?

✓ After you have secured interest and conviction, do you follow through with a request for action?

✓ Does your letter make it easy for the man to do what you want him to do?

✓ How does the letter look? Is it neatly typed on good stationery, or is it just another "one of those things"?

✓ Above all, is it the kind of letter you would like to have somebody write you, were you on the receiving end of the line?

LETTERS TO THE TRADE

✓ Does your letter put the dealer right up front in the picture, and do it quickly?

✓ Does the cash register begin to jingle before he has finished two paragraphs?

✓ Is the letter written in the dealer's language? Does it show sympathy for his problems?

✓ Dealers are hard to keep hitched—is the tempo of the letter fast enough to hold interest?

✓ Dealers are skeptical of what sellers tell them—do you use concrete cases to prove your points?

✓ Does your letter talk profits, and profits, and then more profits? And do you prove it to him?

✓ Do you show him exactly how he can make a certain profit by doing a certain thing?

✓ Do you talk about profits in amounts rather than in percentages which are hard to visualize?

✓ Does your letter sell the sizzle, rather than the steak?

✓ Can a busy dealer read your letter and get its message in 3 minutes? Four minutes is probably more time than he will give it.

✓ Is your proposition supported with dramatic enclosures based on the "What One Dealer Did" principle?

✓ Do you ask for action without pussyfooting?

✓ And do you make it just as easy as possible for the lazy dealer to say "Yes"?

Letter Appraisal Form

This appraisal form is intended to assist you in revising your own letters or in indicating to others the specific weaknesses of the letters that are submitted.

Before appraising a letter, be sure to determine its exact purpose. What message is it expected to convey? What response is desired from the addressee?

Place a check mark in the colmun "Yes" or "No" opposite each question which applies to the letter you are appraising.

IS THE LETTER:	Yes	No
1. COMPLETE		
a. Does it give, in the most effective order, all information necessary to accomplish its purpose?	......	......
b. Does it answer fully all the questions, asked or implied, in the incoming letter?	......	......
2. CONCISE		
a. Does the letter include *only* the essential facts?	......	......
b. Are the ideas expressed in the fewest words consistent with clearness, completeness, and courtesy; have irrelevant details and unnecessary repetition been eliminated?	......	......
3. CLEAR		
a. Is the language adapted to the vocabulary of the addressee?	......	......
b. Do the words exactly express the thought?	......	......
c. Is the sentence structure clear?	......	......
d. Are the paragraphs logical thought units, arranged to promote easy reading?	......	......
4. CORRECT		
a. Is the accuracy of all factual information beyond question?	......	......
b. Are all statements in strict conformity with policies?	......	......
c. Is the letter free from: (1) Grammatical errors, (2) spelling errors, (3) misleading punctuation?	......	......
5. APPROPRIATE IN TONE		
a. Is the tone calculated to bring about the desired response?	......	......
b. Is the tone calculated to build or protect good will?	......	......
c. Does the entire letter evidence a desire to cooperate fully?	......	......
d. Is it free from antagonistic words or phrases?	......	......
6. NEAT AND WELL SET UP Will a favorable first impression be created by: (1) Freedom from strike-overs and obvious erasures; (2) even typing; (3) position of letter on the page?		

To what extent is the letter likely to accomplish its purpose, obtain the desired response, and build good will? In other words, how do you rate its *general effectiveness?* Underline the word which best expresses your rating:

A. OUTSTANDING B. GOOD C. PASSABLE D. UNSATISFACTORY

IN RATING ANOTHER'S LETTER:

If the letter is "unsatisfactory," be sure to indicate the specific weaknesses which necessitate revision. Similarly, if the letter is only "passable," indicate clearly the weaknesses to which attention should be given in future letters.

What It Costs to Write a Business Letter

Based on a 1-page, 200-word letter. From a Dartnell survey.

Cost Factor	*Average Cost*	*Your Cost*	*Ways to cut cost factor*
DICTATOR'S TIME Based on a salary of $250 a week. Dictate 15 letters a day at an average of 7 minutes for each letter.	$0.72		Shorter letters, let assistants write standard replies, increase use of dictating equipment, use telephone, consider form letters.
SECRETARIAL COST Based on a salary of $125 a week and an average of 15 letters a day at 18 minutes per letter (including dictation).	0.94		Where possible use stenographic or typing department, use advanced transcribing equipment, use automatic typing where possible, develop efficient style manual and foster training programs.
NONPRODUCTIVE LABOR Time consumed by both dictator and secretary in waiting, illness, vacations, etc. 15 percent of the labor costs.	0.25		Develop stenographic pool concept, use form letters when possible, use outside service organizations when needed, enforce telephone call control at dictating time.
FIXED CHARGES Overhead, depreciation, rent, light, interest, taxes, pensions, and other costs. 50 percent of labor cost.	0.83		Review use of all available space, investigate equipment developments that control the need for more employees, study office efficiency and layout programs.
MATERIALS COST Stationery, carbon paper or copy machine sheets, typewriter ribbons, pencils, other types of supplies.	0.10		Check out savings from using the better quality ribbons, carbon, etc.; consider in-plant printing of letterheads and envelopes, have control program for waste.
MAILING COST First class postage (8 cents) plus 20 percent airmail, gathering, sealing, stamping, sorting, delivery to post office.	0.20		Plan mailing schedules to keep airmail at a minimum, use high-speed metering and mail systems to cut labor costs.
FILING COST Clerk's time (salary), cost of equipment, cost of supplies, etc.	0.16		Centralize filing department if possible, investigate new filing systems and methods, develop retention programs that save space.
TOTAL COST	$3.20		YOUR COST

Uses for Letters in Building Business

SUPPLIER RELATIONS

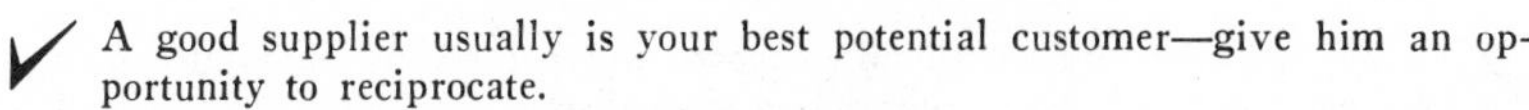

- A good supplier usually is your best potential customer—give him an opportunity to reciprocate.

- Your suppliers have friends. Many of them need your products and would buy them from you if urged by your supplier.

- Do you periodically "sell" your suppliers on your square deal buying policy, so that they will value your business all the more and serve you all the better?

- Treat your suppliers, in your letters, as you would like to have them treat you if your positions were reversed.

- Some day there will be a merchandise shortage when it will pay to be on your suppliers' blue list—the time to get on it is NOW.

CUSTOMER RELATIONS

- A satisfied customer is your best advertisement—a 100% letter will keep him a booster for you.

- When you get a new customer make a fuss over him—a 100% letter will make him feel he has found a friend.

- Your front yard is full of uncovered opportunities for getting more business—100% letters will find them for you.

- Everyone has a different idea about your company and your policies—good letters will correct any misconceptions.

- Some customers and prospective customers cannot be sold economically by salesmen—give letters that job.

- Keep feeding your customers new ideas for using your product or service so that they will be able and glad to buy.

- It costs money for a salesman to sell a buyer who never heard of you before—letters will break down that resistance.

- Eighty percent of your customers buy only 30% of their requirements from you—go after the other 70% with 100% letters.

- ✓ Your present customers have friends—the right kind of letters will get their names so you can sell them too.
- ✓ The best salesmen and the best territories get sinking spells—100% letters will pick them up.
- ✓ Your customers are continually exposed to your competitor's sales lures—use more letters between your salesmen's calls.
- ✓ A sale is not completed until the product moves out of your dealer's store—letters to his customers may help.
- ✓ When a customer pays his account promptly write him a letter—give him a reputation for being prompt pay and he'll try to live up to it.

DIRECT SELLING LETTERS

- ✓ Does the opening paragraph touch a "live" nerve?
- ✓ Will it shock the casual reader out of his indifference?
- ✓ Is there a quick appeal to the reader's self-interest?
- ✓ After awakening interest, does the letter proceed quickly to create desire?
- ✓ Is the selling strategy simple—does it concentrate on *one* dominant buying motive?
- ✓ Or, is its effectiveness dulled by attempting to cover too many buying reasons?
- ✓ Is there sufficient proof to build up confidence in the proposition?
- ✓ Does the letter show a keen understanding of the buyer's problem?
- ✓ Has an overuse of superlatives given the letter a boastful or bragging tone?
- ✓ Does it sound honest, or has a touch of "hokum" crept in to hurt it?
- ✓ Have you painted the lily? Understatement is usually more effective than overstatement.
- ✓ How about the price? If it might seem high, have you handled it as a matter of values?
- ✓ Is the offer clear-cut and straightforward? Assume the buyer is honest until he is proved otherwise.

✓ Finally, does it tell the reader exactly what you wish him to do?

✓ And does it make it easy for him to order?

TEN PRINCIPLES OF CLEAR WRITING

Keep Sentences Short. For easy reading, sentences should vary in structure and length but, on the average, should be short.

Prefer the Simple to the Complex. Many complex terms are unnecessary. When there is a simpler way of saying a thing, use it. Avoid complex sentences.

Develop Your Vocabulary. Don't let preference for short words limit your vocabulary. Intelligence and vocabulary size are closely linked; you need long words to think with.

Avoid Unneeded Words. Nothing weakens writing so much as extra words. Be critical of your own writing and make every word carry its weight.

Put Action Into Your Verbs. The heaviness of much business writing results from overworking the passive verbs. Prose can usually be kept impersonal and remain in the active tenses.

Use Terms Your Reader Can Picture. Abstract terms make writing dull and foggy. Choose short, concrete words that the reader can visualize.

Tie In With Your Reader's Experience. The reader will not get your new idea unless you link it with some old idea he already has.

Write the Way You Talk. Well, anyway, as much that way as you can. A conversational tone is one of the best avenues to good writing. Avoid stuffy business jargon. In letters, use "we" and "you" freely.

Make Full Use of Variety. Use as many different arrangements of words and sentences as you can think up, but be sure your meaning is clear.

Write to Express, Not to Impress. Present your ideas simply and directly. The writer who makes the best impression is the one who can express complex ideas simply. "Big men use little words; little men use big words."

(From *How to Take the Fog Out of Writing,* by Robert Gunning)

Chapter 26

LETTER FORMATS

WHILE thousands of different formats can be used to carry a direct mail message, the oldest format of all—the letter—still remains the most popular. Letters rank second only to the spoken word as the most effective means of communication.

This is not to imply, however, that all direct mail letters are effective. There are good and bad letters just as there are good and bad examples of all types of direct mail. Nevertheless, there are fewer chances of going wrong with direct mail letters than with any other format—assuming, of course, the copy is "right."

The Personal Approach

Direct mail at its best is a person-to-person communications medium. Since the letter is well established as a primary means of personal communications, it can be used to help bring a personal touch to direct mail advertising. In the majority of cases, the most successful direct mail "package" consists of a letter enclosed in an envelope, with descriptive literature and a means of reply. The letter's role in such cases is usually twofold:

1. To put the promotional message on a more personal basis, often explaining why the descriptive literature and the proposition it contains should be of individual interest to the recipient.
2. To make clear just what action is desired.

Because the letter is basically a means of person-to-person communications, many advertisers make the mistake of thinking they can trick the recipient into believing he is being approached as an individual rather than as a member of a large audience. There may have been a day long ago when direct mail audiences were naive enough to succumb to such trickery, but today, as one direct mail expert puts it, "there is no longer any person, not even the farthest-removed hick in the sticks, who cannot readily identify a form letter."

Yet, there are still many opportunities to use a letter to achieve an element of personalization which will help boost readership of a direct mail piece. One of the most common techniques is to explain in the letter why the individual, as a member of a particular direct mail audience, is believed to have a special interest in what is being promoted.

Newsweek Letters

An example of how a letter can be used to explain why a mailing is being sent, and in so doing help make the reader feel he is being approached as a member of a select rather than a mass audience, is a technique used by S. Arthur Dembner of *Newsweek* magazine. For over a decade, "Red" Dembner has used this opening for a three-page letter:

```
Dear Reader:

If the list upon which I found your name is any indi-
cation, this is not the first--nor will it be the last
--subscription letter you receive.  Quite frankly,
your education and income set you apart from the gen-
eral population and make you a highly rated prospect
for everything from magazines to mutual funds.
```

Another *Newsweek* letter uses a teaser technique *(see illustration, page 686)*. The first page printed in black on blue has a one-liner above the first fold:

```
Don't bother turning this page unless...
```

This continues on the middle fold of the first page:

```
you want to know...

-- WHERE - 250 miles from Boston - a 10-year-old girl
   works 10 hours a day for $3...

-- HOW Ulster children have been permanently brutal-
   ized by the violence they see and imitate...

-- WHY some New York hotel owners actually prefer
   welfare tenants to regular paying guests...
```

That's all for page one. The second, third and fourth pages of the letter are in a more conventional format, using both black and blue typewriter type on a normal white background. Page two begins:

```
Dear Reader:

You turned the page because you have more curiosity
than most people.  You're interested in knowing the
story behind the headline...the item that gets buried
on the last page of the newspaper or -- more -- likely
-- doesn't run at all.

That's why you'll enjoy Newsweek's special kind of
news coverage.
```

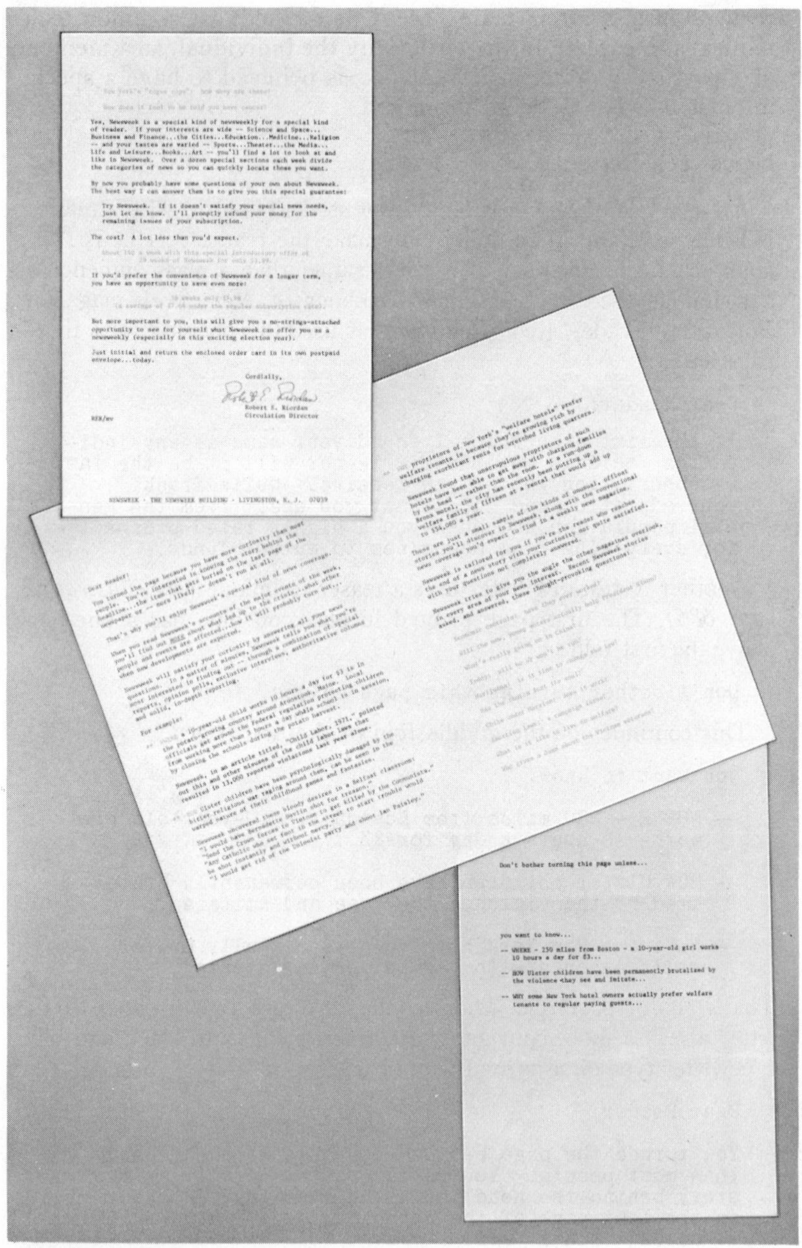

Don't bother turning this page unless...

you want to know...

-- WHERE - 250 miles from Boston - a 10-year-old girl works 10 hours a day for $3...

-- HOW Ulster children have been permanently brutalized by the violence they see and imitate...

-- WHY some New York hotel owners actually prefer welfare tenants to regular paying guests...

Dear Reader:

You turned the page because you have more curiosity than most people. You're interested in knowing the story behind the headline...the item that gets buried on the last page of the newspaper or -- more likely -- doesn't run at all.

That's why you'll enjoy Newsweek's special kind of news coverage.

When you read Newsweek's accounts of the major events of the week, you'll find out MORE about what led up to the crisis...what other people and events are affected...how it will probably turn out... when new developments are expected.

Newsweek will satisfy your curiosity by answering all your news questions. In a matter of minutes, Newsweek tells you what you're most interested in finding out -- through a combination of special reports, opinion polls, exclusive interviews, authoritative columns and solid, in-depth reporting.

For example:

-- WHERE a 10-year-old child works 10 hours a day for $3 is in the potato-growing country around Aroostook, Maine. Local officials get around the Federal regulation protecting children from working more than 3 hours a day while school is in session, by closing the schools during the potato harvest.

Newsweek, in an article titled, "Child Labor, 1971," pointed out this and other misuses of the child labor laws that resulted in 13,000 reported violations last year alone.

-- HOW Ulster children have been psychologically damaged by the bitter religious war raging around them, can be seen in the warped nature of their childhood games and fantasies.

Newsweek uncovered these bloody desires in a Belfast classroom: "I would have Bernadette Devlin shot for treason." "Send the Crown forces to Vietnam to get killed by the Communists." "Any Catholic who set foot in the street to start trouble would be shot instantly and without mercy." "I would get rid of the Unionist party and shoot Ian Paisley."

-- WHY proprietors of New York's "welfare hotels" prefer welfare tenants is because they're growing rich by charging exorbitant rents for wretched living quarters.

Newsweek found that unscrupulous proprietors of such hotels have been able to get away with charging families by the head -- rather than the room. At a run-down Bronx motel, the city has recently been putting up a welfare family of fifteen at a rental that would add up to $54,080 a year.

These are just a small sample of the kinds of unusual, offbeat stories you'll discover in Newsweek, along with the conventional news coverage you'd expect to find in a weekly news magazine.

Newsweek is tailored for you if you're the reader who reaches the end of a news story with your curiosity not quite satisfied, with your questions not completely answered.

Newsweek tries to give you the angle the other magazines overlook, in every area of your news interest. Recent Newsweek stories asked, and answered, these thought-provoking questions:

Yes, Newsweek is a special kind of newsweekly for a special kind of reader. If your interests are wide -- Science and Space... Business and Finance...the Cities...Education...Medicine...Religion -- and your tastes are varied -- Sports...Theater...the Media... Life and Leisure...Books...Art -- you'll find a lot to look at and like in Newsweek. Over a dozen special sections each week divide the categories of news so you can quickly locate those you want.

By now you probably have some questions of your own about Newsweek. The best way I can answer them is to give you this special guarantee:

Try Newsweek. If it doesn't satisfy your special news needs, just let me know. I'll promptly refund your money for the remaining issues of your subscription.

The cost? A lot less than you'd expect.

If you'd prefer the convenience of Newsweek for a longer term, you have an opportunity to save even more:

But more important to you, this will give you a no-strings-attached opportunity to see for yourself what Newsweek can offer you as a newsweekly (especially in this exciting election year).

Just initial and return the enclosed order card in its own postpaid envelope...today.

Cordially,

Robert E. Riordan
Circulation Director

REB/ev

NEWSWEEK · THE NEWSWEEK BUILDING · LIVINGSTON, N. J. 07039

Newsweek *is noted for its effective use of direct mail. This letter uses "teaser" technique.*

Customer Letters

This semipersonal approach is most frequently used in letters sent to a list of customers. Since a definite relationship between buyer and seller is already established in such cases, it is only natural to take advantage of this relationship in direct mail letters. For example, *Time, Inc.* used the following approach in a letter from its book division:

> Dear Reader:
>
> Because you are one of the special (and fortunate!) people who own a copy of LIFE'S great Picture Cook Book, we feel sure that you will be fascinated by another wonderful cook book which is soon to be published . . .

In the retail field, there is often an even stronger buyer-seller bond which offers an opportunity to create a more personal tone for direct mail letters. An outstanding example is this letter sent to customers of Wellesley Auto Sales, Inc., a Massachusetts Chrysler-Plymouth dealer:

> Dear Customer:
>
> Something new has happened! For the eight years I have been with Wellesley Auto Sales, you have come to know me as a mechanic and later as the trouble shooter and shop foreman.
>
> As you know, one of my arms has been useless for two years, and it was operated on successfully in mid-January. I want to thank each of my customers for the sympathy shown me and the patience with me because of my working with one arm. However, the good news is this--I have been appointed to the Sales Staff of Wellesley Auto Sales. As you may understand, this is a big moment in my life and I hope to serve you in the future as well as I've tried to in the past.
>
> Please wish me well, and by all means contact me if you are considering a new or used car. I have enclosed my business card. Please keep it as a reminder, and if you are in the position to send me any business, I will greatly appreciate it.
>
> Very truly yours,
> Robert Morris

While few advertisers have a man who has had an arm in a cast for two years, the basic technique is still valid in a number of direct mail situations. Any time copy can be linked to a personal relationship, a highly effective letter can be developed.

Franklin Mint Letters

One of the key elements in the success of The Franklin Mint has been its ability to build a strong bond with its collector customers. A major role in maintaining this bond is through the letters which accompany product offerings. A letter announcing a new series of sterling silver collector's plates, for example, began:

> Dear Friend:
>
> I'm proud to be able to announce an important first in American collector's art--The Franklin Mint Bird Plates--and to notify you, as an established Franklin Mint collector, of your opportunity to obtain this exceptional series at the original issue price.

Later in the same letter, the Franklin Mint again took special note of the strong personal relationship it has with its customers:

> One of the important privileges reserved for you and other established Franklin Mint collectors is acquiring new collector's plates directly from the mint at the original issue price. Other collectors must obtain their plates from dealers. Since dealers are often sold out of their small allocations before they even receive shipment, few people other than established Franklin Mint collectors are able to obtain new collector's plates at the original issue price.

The success of this bond with customers was demonstrated by the letter illustrated on the facing page. Note the last paragraph:

> Since this offer is being extended only to registered purchasers of Franklin Mint Eyewitness Commemoratives, only a very small percentage of collectors will ever have the opportunity to obtain this limited edition issue.

This single letter didn't even have an illustration of the product—just the letter, an unillustrated order form and a business reply envelope. Yet it brought thousands of orders and must be considered by all standards an outstanding example of mail order success.

Another example of a personalized approach by The Franklin Mint was a letter to all shareholders. It was a short, one-page letter accompanying an attractive brochure and began:

> Dear Shareholder:
>
> On Sunday, October 31, the Bicentennial Council of the Thirteen Original States announced an extraordinary commemorative program of major historical significance. Since The Franklin Mint is deeply involved in this program, I am writing now to ensure that all Franklin Mint shareholders receive complete information about this program.

THE FRANKLIN MINT

FRANKLIN CENTER, PENNSYLVANIA 19063

May 26, 1972

Dear Collector:

Because the President's journey to Russia is an occasion of such historic importance, The Franklin Mint will strike an Eyewitness Commemorative to mark this event.

The Journey to Russia Commemorative will be available exclusively to registered purchasers of previous Franklin Mint Eyewitness Commemoratives.

By the time you receive this letter, our sculptors will be busy creating designs, based on events as they unfold in Russia and as witnessed through the miracle of satellite television. The design finally selected and recorded on precious metal will depict the most dramatic and significant moment of the President's journey.

Like the Presidential Journey to China Eyewitness Medal issued earlier this year, this unique commemorative will be available in several forms as outlined on the enclosed order certificate.

Because of the unusual nature of this offering, we can only accept orders postmarked by this coming Monday, June 5. Our total minting quantity will be strictly limited to those medals and pendant charms ordered by that date.

Since this offer is being extended only to registered purchasers of Franklin Mint Eyewitness Commemoratives, only a very small percentage of collectors will ever have the opportunity to obtain this limited edition issue. Your immediate decision will assure you of being able to include this commemorative in your collection.

Sincerely,

Charles Andes

Charles Andes
President

CA:lrt

The Franklin Mint is an independent, publicly owned corporation and is not affiliated with the U.S. Mint or any other governmental agency.

The Bicentennial Council has appointed The Franklin Mint to strike a unique series of silver commemorative medals -- the first in nearly 200 years of American history to OFFICIALLY HONOR the fifty-six Signers of the Declaration of Independence.

Autotyped Letters

The most personal of all direct mail letters are those which are individually typewritten. When the quantity is more than just a few letters, they are usually produced on an automatic typewriter. The operation of this machine is described in Chapter 40. The letter shown next is a typical example of an Autotyped letter. While there is nothing in the copy to indicate it is a personal letter, it stood out from the typical promotional letter just because it was individually typewritten.

There is something about the overall impression of a typed letter which brands it as genuine. Even if the recipient does not know the first thing about letter reproduction processes, he is quick to recognize an individually typed letter. Such letters create an interesting reaction, particularly in business offices. When a typewritten letter is received, the recipient usually has to make a more complicated decision than is required of a printed piece, which he can simply discard if he decides to take no action. But with a typewritten letter, the recipient often feels he must dictate or write an answer—even when all that has to be said is, "No, I'm not interested in what you propose."

Many mail order advertisers, who have previously received only an occasional complaint from nonbuying recipients of their usual printed letters, have been surprised to find a substantial number of replies from nonbuyers receiving Autotyped letters—letters saying, "Thanks for telling me your story. I'll keep your letter on file for future reference." And, true to their word, many of these nonbuyers do respond with an order at some future date, presenting evidence that Autotyped letters are indeed filed rather than discarded.

There are certain types of computer letters which closely approximate an Autotyped letter, but the majority of letters rushed through a computer are too obviously the product of an impersonal machine to yield the full personal touch captured by a regular Autotyped letter.

In a promotion booklet, "Profit and Prestige with Automatically Typed Letters," American Mail Advertising, Waltham, Massachusetts, explained the role of Autotyped letters:

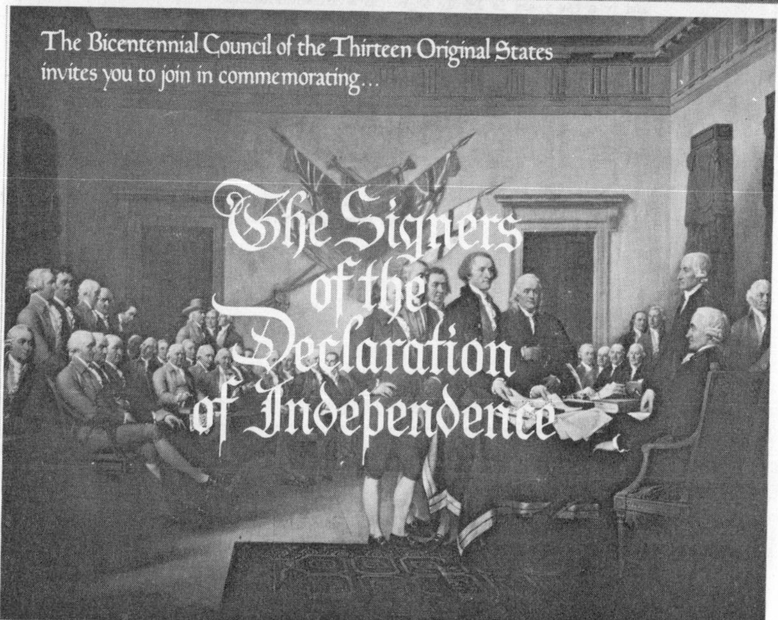

Cover and inside picture with overlay for Franklin Mint's elaborate and successful brochure.

Publishers of Books, Plays and Music · ESTABLISHED 1876

T. S. Denison and Company, Inc.

321 FIFTH AVENUE SOUTH MINNEAPOLIS 15, MINNESOTA

AFFILIATED COMPANIES: THE NORTHWESTERN PRESS, DENISON MUSIC COMPANY

July 12, 1960

Mr.Dick Hodgson,
27 Standford Road,
Wellesley Hills, Mass.

Dear Mr. Hodgson:

We are pleased to announce the private sale of a deluxe limited edition of two thousand copies of MINNESOTA HERITAGE which we consider the most comprehensive history ever done of our state. It is a beautifully designed book with an embossed leather cover done in our state colors, 9 by 12 inches, 430 pages, profusely illustrated with photos and line drawings. Each copy is numbered and will be registered in the purchaser's name. The price is $12.95 a copy.

The preface was written by Dr. James Morrill and the six-page introduction by Dr. Theodore C. Blegen. Over twenty scholars and authorities have contributed chapters to this book which has been three years in preparation. Every phase of Minnesota life and culture has been covered. It will be a good source book of Minnesota history for many years to come, and in a few years is likely to become a collector's item.

I am certain that you will be interested in securing one or more copies of this limited edition. We will appreciate your order by return mail, specifying the names in which you wish the copies registered. I anticipate that we will sell out this edition very quickly so I urge you to make a decision promptly.

Just jot your O.K. on this letterhead, stating the number of copies you want, and we will make a prompt delivery.

Very truly yours,

lmb-t

L. M. Brings, Editor-in-chief

An Autotyped letter stands out from the typical promotional letter.

There are two basic reasons for using automatically typewritten letters—profit and prestige. Profit is involved where a higher readership and a higher percentage of return will bring greater sales in proportion to advertising investment. Prestige is involved in all letter situations where good business taste calls for the finest letter reproduction process.

Generally speaking, automatically typewritten letters are used when the mailing is addressed by name . . . to officers of corporations, to influential business and social leaders, to key buying personnel, and to others who may be in a position to influence a business transaction.

Autotyped letters are nearly always used when a limited market offers a large potential—such as letters of solicitation by advertising agencies, space sales letters by national magazines, letters requesting large charitable gifts, letters selling engineering services or soliciting charge accounts for very exclusive shops.

Automatically typewritten letters are also used in credit collections, pre-call letters for salesmen, thank-you letters for past business, and nearly always in advertising correspondence addressed to present customers.

Many firms split their mailing list according to the potential of the prospect—if known. A firm selling machine tools, for example, might use automatically typewritten letters to solicit inquiries from firms in the manufacturing field, and form letters to announce new developments to the one-man machine shop. Other firms think that customers and past customers deserve special attention. A distributor selling to drugstores might use printed promotion pieces in its regular mailing pieces and reserve the more personal type letters for its long-established accounts.

Writing the Autotyped Letter

Because the Autotyped letter is designed to be more personal, it requires a different type of copywriting than most other direct mail letters. Copy for Autotyped letters should be as informal as a business relationship permits and should steer clear of mail order phrasing. Whenever possible, the Autotyped letter should duplicate the feeling of an individually dictated letter.

One way to give Autotyped letters a more personal touch is to include body fill-ins. You can set an automatic typewriter to stop anywhere in a letter so the operator can fill in special copy, such as the recipient's name, a date, amount of money, etc.

In its booklet on Autotyping, American Mail Advertising presented two dramatic examples which indicate how the results from use of Autotyped letters can offset their added cost:

A large, regional organization was soliciting memberships. A mailing list of 16,000 executives had been used over a period of years. The list had been "form letter milked." The last form letter mailing produced only one new member.

In a test, 500 people on the list were mailed automatically typed letters. These 500 executives had refused to join in the past. The mailing was made and produced over $8,000 in new memberships.

A typical reaction was summarized in a letter received from the president of a very large corporation. The letter said, "You have been sending me form letters for 13 years. Now that you have taken the trouble to invite my membership personally, my check is enclosed." The check was for $1,000.

The second example involves an alumni association of a prominent college. The association had accumulated a list of 400 "never heard froms"—alumni who had never contacted the school in any way since graduation.

An automatically typewritten letter was mailed to this group, and 80 of them joined the association by return mail.

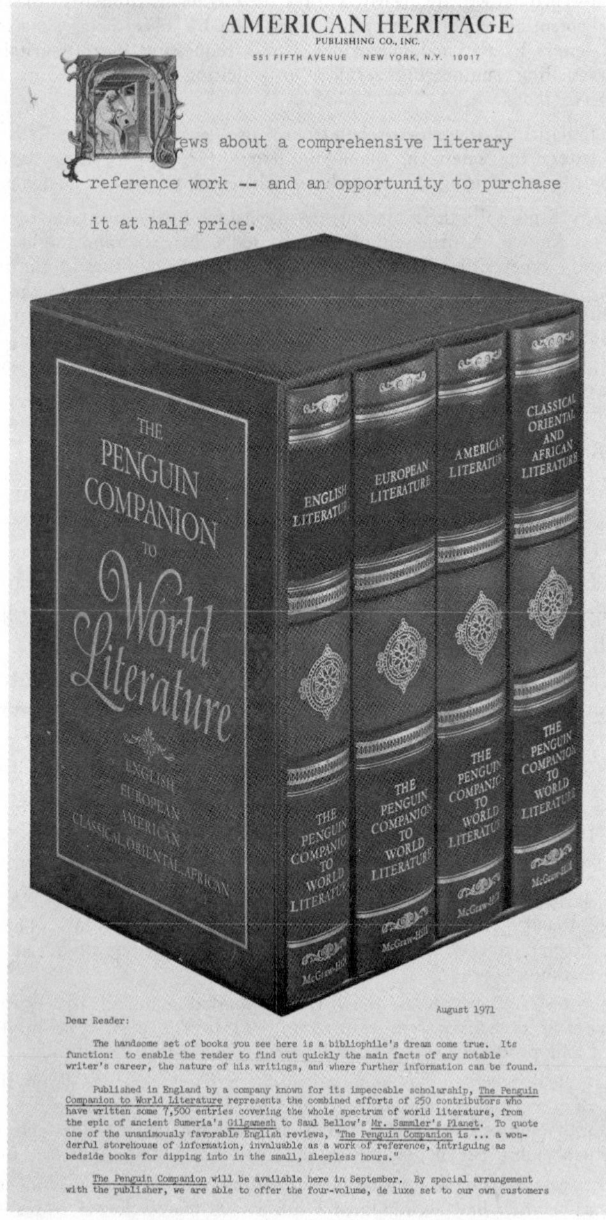

AMERICAN HERITAGE
PUBLISHING CO., INC.
551 FIFTH AVENUE NEW YORK, N.Y. 10017

News about a comprehensive literary reference work -- and an opportunity to purchase it at half price.

August 1971

Dear Reader:

The handsome set of books you see here is a bibliophile's dream come true. Its function: to enable the reader to find out quickly the main facts of any notable writer's career, the nature of his writings, and where further information can be found.

Published in England by a company known for its impeccable scholarship, The Penguin Companion to World Literature represents the combined efforts of 250 contributors who have written some 7,500 entries covering the whole spectrum of world literature, from the epic of ancient Sumeria's Gilgamesh to Saul Bellow's Mr. Sammler's Planet. To quote one of the unanimously favorable English reviews, "The Penguin Companion is ... a wonderful storehouse of information, invaluable as a work of reference, intriguing as bedside books for dipping into in the small, sleepless hours."

The Penguin Companion will be available here in September. By special arrangement with the publisher, we are able to offer the four-volume, de luxe set to our own customers

This elongated 9¼- by 18¼-inch letter from American Heritage had plenty of space to show a set of books. It was four-folded for mailing.

NEW YORK LIFE INSURANCE COMPANY

A Mutual Company founded in 1845

JOHN O. GAULTNEY, C.L.U.
VICE PRESIDENT

Mr.R.S.Hodgson
2040 Valley Lo Ln.
Glenview,Ill

Reserved for you -- the new RAND MC NALLY ROAD ATLAS and TRAVEL GUIDE.

This Atlas is truly the motorist's friend. It has 96 pages and gives beautifully clear new individual state maps, new individual Canadian province maps, new city maps, a new double page U.S. Interstate Highway map, a new double page feature on the Interstate Highway system, and includes a section on national parks.

We would also like to furnish you information about a New York Life plan for making your retirement years happy . . . years you will spend in leisure and comfort -- travelling, if you like, whenever and wherever you please on a guaranteed retirement income from New York Life.

Send in the post-paid card. We'll get your free "Road Atlas and Travel Guide" to you right away. There is, of course, no obligation.

Sincerely,

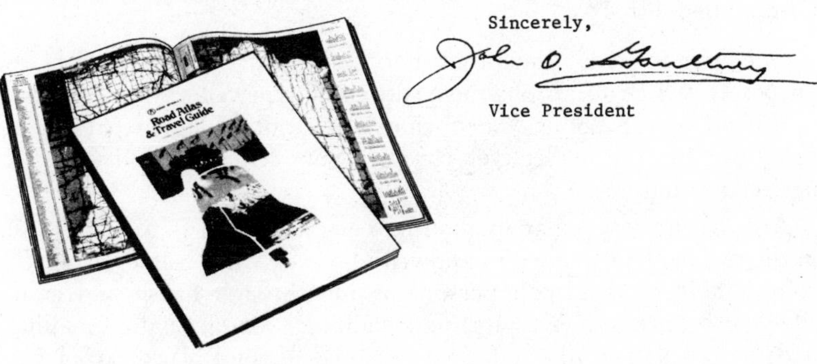

Vice President

RE (471)

Letters with a built-in reply card can be highly effective, particularly for premium offers. Life insurance companies are major users of this technique to attract leads for their agents.

Computer Letters

Next to the Autotyped letter in the degree of personalization is the increasingly popular computer letter. There is a wide variety of types of computer letters and related computer-personalized formats. Because of this variety and the multiple of applications of these formats, the following chapter is devoted entirely to this subject.

Other Personalized Letters

Personalization can be added to otherwise mass-produced letters in many ways. The most commonly used technique is the so-called matched fill-in. In such letters, the body is printed, while the address and salutation are added to each individual letter by typewriter. A number of methods for producing such letters are described in Chapter 40.

While it is possible to get a near-perfect "match," this ideal is seldom accomplished. In the majority of cases the letter comes out looking like exactly what it is—a printed letter with added personalization. Even so, the cost of personalization is often justified since it helps to set up a more personal relationship with the recipient. A man's name is still something very personal to him, and the use of it in direct mail can often lead to better results than a more nonpersonal approach.

But it is important to realize that you are not dealing with a strictly person-to-person communication. To try to deceive the recipient and make him believe the fill-in letter is an individual letter is to subject your entire letter to suspicion.

Unmatched Fill-Ins

One way to avoid the problem of poorly matched fill-ins is to purposely switch to an obviously different typewriter face or color of ribbon. By so doing, you obviously are not trying to put something over on the reader, yet you give your letter the full value of personalization.

An even more popular method of personalization is to simply fill in the recipient's name with handwriting. *Look's* Les Suhler achieved considerable success with personalization through brush and gold, silver or bronze ink. A typical personalized *Look* circulation mailing had the top half of the letterhead printed in solid black except for large reverse letters reading, "Did you know . . ." Atop the solid black area, the name of the recipient is painted in bold letters of bronze ink. The heading then consists of the recipient's name and the first few words of a sentence which continues into the body copy.

While both Les Suhler and *Look* are retired, many of the formats originated by Les Suhler are still recognized as the cornerstones for many of today's most frequently used direct mail pieces.

Personalization With Attachments

Sometimes it is more practical to personalize a letter with an extra element, rather than do the personalizing directly on the letters. Names are first applied to some easily personalized object, which is then attached to the letter. The most popular application of this technique is the Reply-O-Letter, which is the trade name of one type of pocketed letter. There is a variety of other brands now on the market. It uses an addressed reply card or envelope to add a degree of personalization to the letter. The addressed reply device is inserted in a pocket attached to the back of the letter. A die-cut opening at the top of the letter in the position where the address would normally be typed allows the address on the reply device to show through.

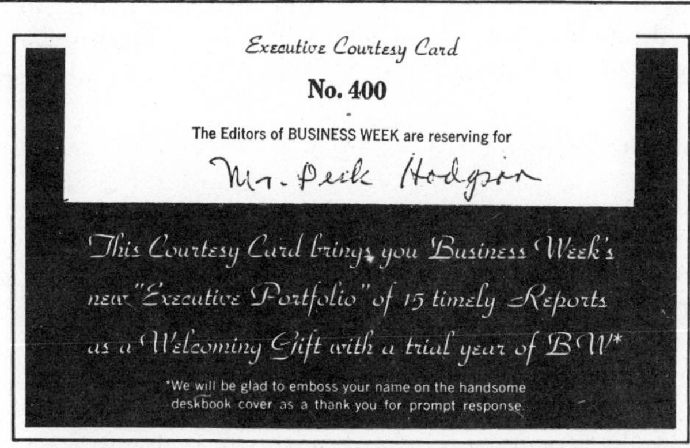

Executive Courtesy Card

No. 400

The Editors of BUSINESS WEEK are reserving for

Mr. Peck Hodgson

This Courtesy Card brings you Business Week's new "Executive Portfolio" of 15 timely Reports as a Welcoming Gift with a trial year of BW*

*We will be glad to emboss your name on the handsome deskbook cover as a thank you for prompt response.

The enclosed Courtesy Card brings you our 1962 EXECUTIVE PORTFOLIO fresh off the presses as a welcoming gift with a trial year of Business Week.

It includes 15 eye-opening Special Reports on major business problems and opportunities of vital interest to all of us.

Each of the Reports deals with vital factors a man must wrap his mind around for sound business decisions and long-sighted planning. Each of the 15 timely subjects is projected in depth -- researched, reported, digested, written, and edited by our world-wide network of news bureaus and headquarters staff of over fifty business and publication experts.

The handsome new PORTFOLIO will be embossed with your name in gold leaf if you accept my offer promptly. It is a most attractive deskbook.

All 15 Reports are packed with new key facts not generally known, eye-opening perspectives, interest galore. Their titles give you some idea:

A good example of personalizing a letter with an extra element. After many years, Business Week *still uses variations of this "Executive Courtesy Card" format.*

An ingenious variation of this technique was used by *Business Week* (see illustration). Recipients' names were handwritten on order cards. Then the letters had a die-cut slot—just the width of the order card—approximately 2 inches from the top of the letter. The cards were inserted in the slot after the letters had been folded, and they rested against the first fold. As a result, half of the card appeared at the top of the letter, with the filled-in name appearing just above the slot.

An increasingly popular device is to tip the order card or form to the letters. This serves a dual purpose—both to personalize the letter and to hold the addressed order form securely in the proper position so it will show through a window in the mailing envelope.

Many novelty items can be used for personalization. Some advertisers prefer a device such as a luggage tag which can be removed from the letter and used by the recipient. More often, a less-expensive item is used. One example is the "Tagged for You" letter shown opposite. A standard stringed tag carried the name of the recipient. The tags are filled out in advance and then the strings are simply inserted through a hole punched in the stock letterhead and taped to the back of the letter.

Combination Letters

Another method of obtaining personalization is by combining the letter with some other element of the mailing. *Newsweek,* for example, made the top half of a miniature letter the order form. The name and address were filled in on the order form, which showed through a window in the mailing envelope.

A number of direct mail advertisers use a combination invitation-letter. Such pieces usually devote the front page of a folder to a somewhat formal invitation, with the recipient's name filled in. The letter then appears on the inside pages of the folder.

Another commonly used combination is a four-page folder with the letter occupying the first page (and sometimes also the fourth page), with the inside spread devoted to illustrations and copy which would normally be printed in a separate enclosure. This offers economy both in production and inserting. In most direct mail circles, this combination of elements is considered less effective than mailings which use separate letters and enclosures, but some mailers have found no appreciable difference in results when testing this format against another. Therefore, it is advisable for any direct mail advertiser to test the comparative advantages of the two approaches before ruling out a letter-enclosure combination.

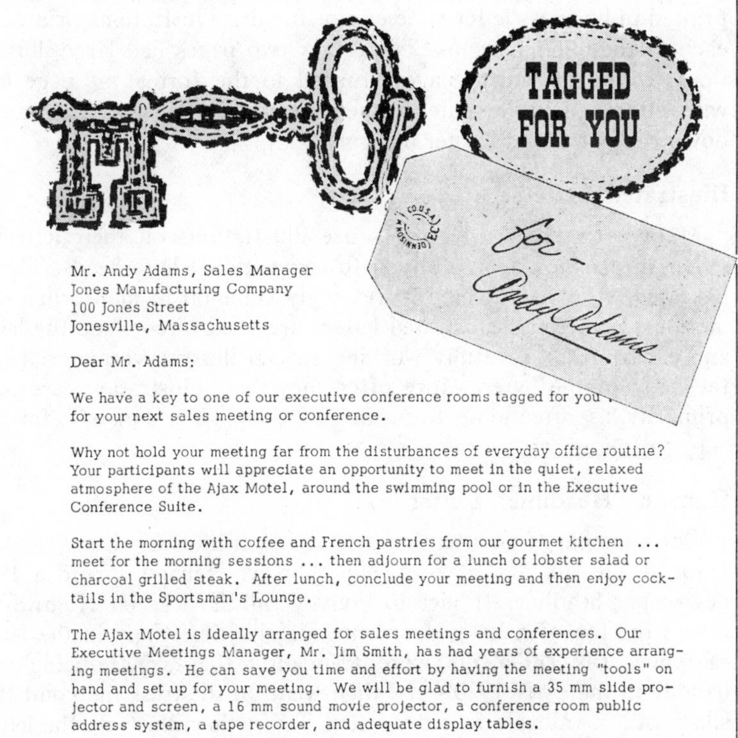

TAGGED FOR YOU

for – Andy Adams

Mr. Andy Adams, Sales Manager
Jones Manufacturing Company
100 Jones Street
Jonesville, Massachusetts

Dear Mr. Adams:

We have a key to one of our executive conference rooms tagged for you . . . for your next sales meeting or conference.

Why not hold your meeting far from the disturbances of everyday office routine? Your participants will appreciate an opportunity to meet in the quiet, relaxed atmosphere of the Ajax Motel, around the swimming pool or in the Executive Conference Suite.

Start the morning with coffee and French pastries from our gourmet kitchen ... meet for the morning sessions ... then adjourn for a lunch of lobster salad or charcoal grilled steak. After lunch, conclude your meeting and then enjoy cocktails in the Sportsman's Lounge.

The Ajax Motel is ideally arranged for sales meetings and conferences. Our Executive Meetings Manager, Mr. Jim Smith, has had years of experience arranging meetings. He can save you time and effort by having the meeting "tools" on hand and set up for your meeting. We will be glad to furnish a 35 mm slide projector and screen, a 16 mm sound movie projector, a conference room public address system, a tape recorder, and adequate display tables.

A change in atmosphere does remarkable things for creative thinking ... a change in locale enables you to hold the undivided attention of your audience. With the Ajax Motel handling all the bothersome details of arrangements, you can concentrate on your sales or conference presentation.

Why not telephone Mr. Smith right away and ask for his suggestions?

Sincerely yours,

AJAX MOTEL

John J. Green, Manager

Litho in U.S.A.

A comparatively inexpensive novelty such as the above will get attention. The stringed tag was personalized and then attached to the illustrated letterhead.

American Heritage Letter

A typical letter-enclosure combination was used by American Heritage Publishing Co., Inc. to introduce its twin offering of "The American Heritage History of Notable American Houses" and "An American Heritage Guide to Historic Houses of America." The first page of this four-page unit *(see illustration, page 702)* was printed in business letter style except for five illustrations printed on each of the outer margins. The center two pages had large illustrations, while the fourth page returned to the format of page one, with letter copy in the center of the page and five illustrations running down each of the two outer margins.

Illustrated Letters

Many direct mail advertisers use illustrations on their letters—either in place of or in addition to conventional letterheads. The illustrated letter has become increasingly common in mail order promotions. Sometimes illustrated letters are used to combine the letter and enclosure by carefully working special illustrative material into the body of the letter. More often, however, illustrations are used primarily as attention-getters and to establish a "mood" for the copy to follow.

Haband "Headline" Letter

One example of an attention getting illustration is a letter used by Haband Tie Co. of Paterson, New Jersey. Haband spread a 1921 newspaper headline, "Police to Convoy Silk Trucks on Highways," across the top of a letter promoting its silk ties. Copy in the letter told how silk shipments were frequently the target of highway bandits in the early 1920's and then went on to stress the point that silk is still a valuable fabric for ties. To further illustrate the letter, a reproduction of a 1921 newspaper clipping was included on page two of the four-page letter. The clipping told the story of a typical silk-truck hijacking. Another newspaper clipping was reproduced on the mailing envelope to gain special attention for the mailing.

Other Illustrated Letterheads

Columbia Record Club used a full-color reproduction of a typical travel scene as part of the letterhead which promoted its Panorama color slide programs. The illustration was positioned so it would show through a window in the mailing envelope.

Encyclopaedia Britannica, Inc., used a series of single color (blue) illustrations to contrast the old with the new in a three-page letter promoting "The Great Ideas Today" series. One row of illustrations showed portraits of great thinkers of the past, while a second row of illustrations included photos of contemporary events selected from the pages of the new series. A headline in black—"How can the great ideas of all time help us now?"—was printed between the two rows of illustrations.

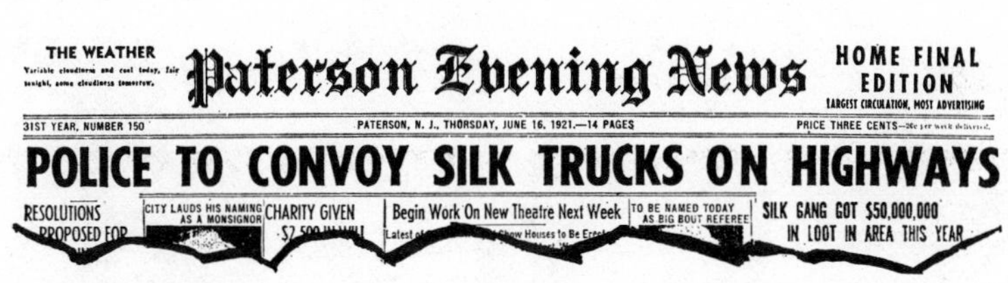

THE WEATHER
Variable cloudiness and cool today, fair tonight, some cloudiness tomorrow.

Paterson Evening News

HOME FINAL EDITION
LARGEST CIRCULATION, MOST ADVERTISING

31ST YEAR, NUMBER 150 — PATERSON, N. J., THORSDAY, JUNE 16, 1921.—14 PAGES — PRICE THREE CENTS

POLICE TO CONVOY SILK TRUCKS ON HIGHWAYS

RESOLUTIONS PROPOSED FOR

CITY LAUDS HIS NAMING AS A MONSIGNOR

CHARITY GIVEN

Begin Work On New Theatre Next Week

TO BE NAMED TODAY AS BIG BOUT REFEREE

SILK GANG GOT $50,000,000 IN LOOT IN AREA THIS YEAR

Dear Friend:

Our books show you as something of a stranger to us. Upward of a million conservative value-conscious men know us well. Now it is your turn.

You probably never got a letter like this before. It's possible you never will again. So right now is your chance to gain an "inside track" on certain money-saving methods that only our friends can enjoy.

And wait -- that's not all. Even if you turn down this chance, you will still be money ahead. You will be given a valuable Free Gift worth -- at the least -- $1.95. There is no "catch" to this. No strings attached. You don't have to buy a thing. It means exactly what it says. In fact I'd call it an understatement. This Gift would probably cost you more than the value we place on it, if you bought it -- as you very frequently do the year round -- on the open market.

Before telling you what this Gift is, I'd like to sort of "set the scene." So pause and reminisce with me a moment. Let me take you back to the Roaring Twenties -- and see if you remember how things were in those days.

LET ME TAKE YOU BACK 40 YEARS

It's a cool Thursday, in June, 1921. The Dodge automobile is still called the Maxwell and you can buy one for around $500 f.o.b. Detroit. The old Ford Model T "flivver" is selling for around $385. A music school is advertising "They Laughed When I Sat Down at the Piano." A chap named Arthur Murray is teaching the tango and the foxtrot by mail. Bernarr McFadden is glorifying the Body Beautiful. The $22.50 two-pants suit is an institution. ("Walk Up a Flight and Save $10!") Woodrow Wilson has made the world "safe for democracy." But has he? The war is over. But now there's another kind of war -- rum-running, bootlegging and hijacking of contraband booze. The bang of the hand grenade and the rattle of machine gun bullets are almost as loud here as they were on the Western Front.

But along the Pennsylvania and New Jersey roads leading into Paterson, the old "Silk City of America," another

Haband Tie Co. took advantage of a 1921 headline to sell its product.

The Peak House, c. 1676

Overhang and pendant, Parson Capen House, Topsfield, Mass.

AMERICAN HERITAGE
PUBLISHING CO., INC.
551 FIFTH AVENUE, NEW YORK, N.Y., 10017

May 28, 1971

Thomas Jefferson

Dear Reader:

If your house is much more than a century old, the odds are its bathrooms are an afterthought -- because its builders knew that "if a person should bathe in warm water every day, debility would inevitably follow...."

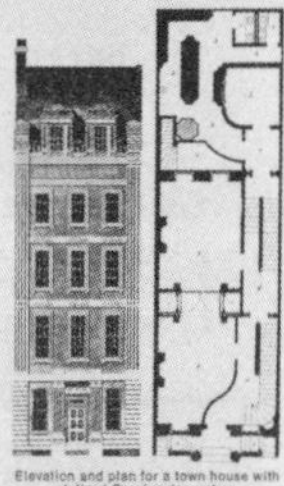

Elevation and plan for a town house with stylized Grecian decoration

If its style is modern, it may reflect an early 1900's dictum by Frank Lloyd Wright: "I declared the whole lower floor as one room, cutting off the kitchen as a laboratory....Scores of unnecessary doors disappeared and no end of partition...."

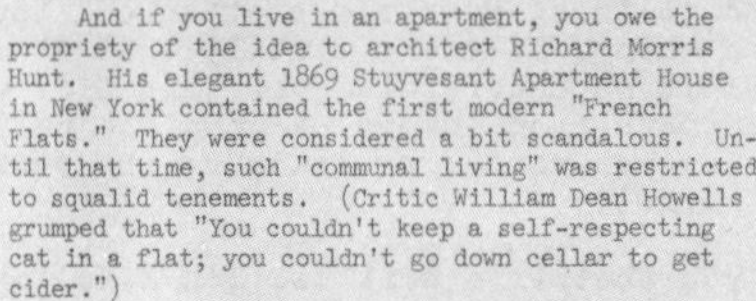

And if you live in an apartment, you owe the propriety of the idea to architect Richard Morris Hunt. His elegant 1869 Stuyvesant Apartment House in New York contained the first modern "French Flats." They were considered a bit scandalous. Until that time, such "communal living" was restricted to squalid tenements. (Critic William Dean Howells grumped that "You couldn't keep a self-respecting cat in a flat; you couldn't go down cellar to get cider.")

H. H. Richardson, architect

Sunnyside, home of Washington Irving

American homes, like American families, have mixed and interesting ancestries. Just as your own home expresses your character, the houses in our history speak accurately and eloquently of the times and tastes and ideals of their builders.

So if you like to explore historic houses -- to evoke their past, to admire their architecture and furnishings, to pick up adoptable ideas for a present or future home of your own ...

The Hermitage, whose cedars were planted by its owner, Andrew Jackson, and *Monticello*, embodiment of Jefferson's architectural genius

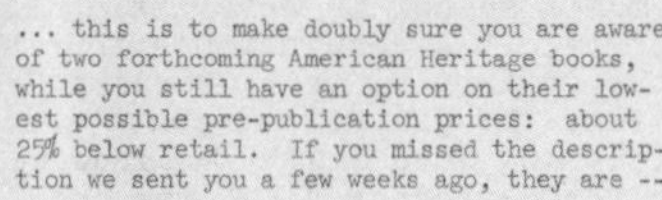

... this is to make doubly sure you are aware of two forthcoming American Heritage books, while you still have an option on their lowest possible pre-publication prices: about 25% below retail. If you missed the description we sent you a few weeks ago, they are --

Palladian window from Mount Vernon

Fred Smith House, Richard Meier architect

American Heritage used this attractive format to introduce two important books.

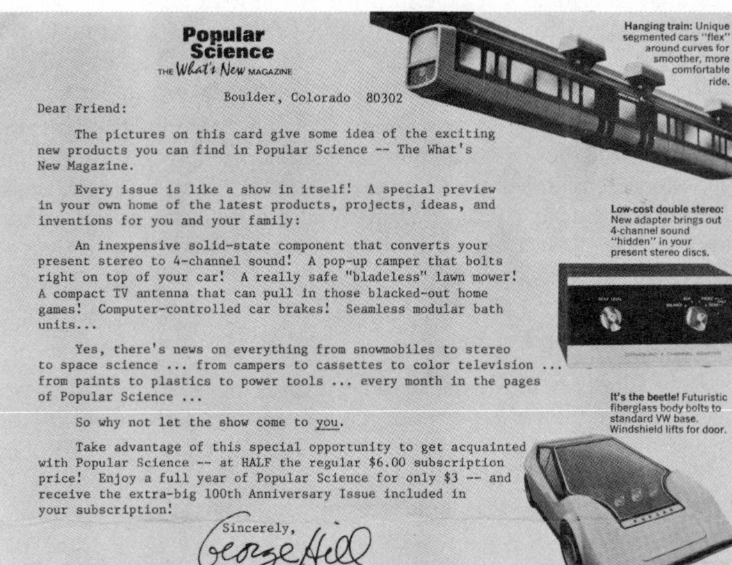

Popular Science
THE *What's New* MAGAZINE

Boulder, Colorado 80302

Dear Friend:

The pictures on this card give some idea of the exciting new products you can find in Popular Science -- The What's New Magazine.

Every issue is like a show in itself! A special preview in your own home of the latest products, projects, ideas, and inventions for you and your family:

An inexpensive solid-state component that converts your present stereo to 4-channel sound! A pop-up camper that bolts right on top of your car! A really safe "bladeless" lawn mower! A compact TV antenna that can pull in those blacked-out home games! Computer-controlled car brakes! Seamless modular bath units...

Yes, there's news on everything from snowmobiles to stereo to space science ... from campers to cassettes to color television ... from paints to plastics to power tools ... every month in the pages of Popular Science ...

So why not let the show come to you.

Take advantage of this special opportunity to get acquainted with Popular Science -- at HALF the regular $6.00 subscription price! Enjoy a full year of Popular Science for only $3 -- and receive the extra-big 100th Anniversary Issue included in your subscription!

Sincerely,

George Hill

George Hill,
Popular Science

1A72

Hanging train: Unique segmented cars "flex" around curves for smoother, more comfortable ride.

Low-cost double stereo: New adapter brings out 4-channel sound "hidden" in your present stereo discs.

It's the beetle! Futuristic fiberglass body bolts to standard VW base. Windshield lifts for door.

Discover over 100 new products & ideas...
...every month in Popular Science magazine!

Your 1/2 price offer inside!
MR RICHARD S HODGSON
2040 VALLEY LO LN
GLENVIEW IL 60025
Pull this tab to open!
Slide rule caddy: Precision 5-ring calculator doubles as a utility cup.

Letters can even be self-mailers. This 8½- by 11-inch card from Popular Science was folded once for mailing and had a tipped-on envelope containing the order form. The reverse side had full-color pictures illustrating the heading: "See the world's greatest new product show!"

McCall's printed a Christmas gift subscription promotion letter on salmon-colored stock, with a red, black, and green illustration of a decorated Christmas package in place of the letterhead. The package carried a tag with the heading, "Last Chance to Solve Your Christmas Problems with *McCall's*." The conventional letterhead was printed at the bottom of the second page of the two-page letter.

Fortune used a full-color painting showing the contents of a safety deposit box at the top of a four-page letter promoting subscriptions. The entire remainder of the four-page letter, except for the signature in blue on page four, was in simulated typewriter type printed in black. The illustration showed through a large window in the face of the mailing envelope.

Folders in Letter Format

Many times an illustrated letter becomes more of a product promotion folder than a letter, even though the copy is handled in letter style. For example, an illustrated mailing piece used by Mrs. Leland's Kitchens of Chicago to promote the use of its candies for fund-raising purposes is a letter only in that the piece carries a signature and most of the copy is printed in simulated typewriter type. The front page of the four-page piece (see illustration) has a long headline and a full-color illustration which occupies approximately half of the space on the page. The inside spread has copy in typewriter type (in red and black) plus five two-color line drawings to illustrate various points. Page four continues in letter style with two full-color illustrations of candy products in the top right hand and lower left corners.

Ambassador Leather Goods Folder

The letter doesn't necessarily have to be on page one of a letter-folder combination. A good example is the four-page piece shown on page 707. In this case, Ambassador Leather Goods used page one to emphasize the product through illustrations and short copy. The letter was confined to page two, while pages three and four gave more product details and offered additional illustrations.

Another advertiser using a similar technique was Fountain Hills, a McCulloch real estate development in Phoenix, Ariz. In this case, the four-page letter had an illustrated first page, the letter itself on pages two and three and illustrated selling copy on page four. The first page featured a full-color illustration of "the world's highest fountain" (McCulloch really likes to do things big—they're the people who moved the London Bridge to the American desert to

LAST CHANCE TO SOLVE YOUR CHRISTMAS PROBLEMS WITH McCALL'S

Dear McCall's Subscriber:

Christmas is just around the corner ... and if you are like most Christmas Shoppers, you still don't have most of your Christmas shopping done! So if you are busy bracing yourself for a last minute rush to the crowded stores, a last minute struggle to find appropriate presents for those "hard to suit" names on your list ... STOP! You can solve many of those problems right here, right now, with a few strokes of your pen ... by giving a Christmas Gift Subscription to McCall's!

Every woman on your gift list will be delighted to receive 12 big, beautiful issues of McCall's ... a reminder, once a month, of your friendly thoughtfulness, all during the New Year. You know yourself how <u>much</u> McCall's gives <u>you</u> -- it's one of the most <u>valuable</u> presents you can give, and you can give it now at a special Christmas gift rate:

SPECIAL CHRISTMAS GIFT RATE ... $2.50 PER GIFT

Whether you give one subscription, or twenty, each gift costs you only $2.50. And you order now, pay after January 10th!

Just write the names of your friends on the convenient gift order form, place your gift order in the enclosed business reply envelope, and mail <u>today</u> to McCall's. The minute McCall's receives your order, gift cards -- one for each gift -- will be mailed back to <u>you</u> to fill out and send to your friends! That way, you will be <u>sure</u> that an announcement of your gift arrives before Christmas. Each of the gift cards is beautfully decorated, expressive of the Christmas spirit, and will carry your personal message and Christmas greeting.

Your Christmas gift copies arrive gift wrapped! The first issue of McCall's that each of your friends receive comes in a

McCall's *obtained excellent results from this beautiful promotion letter.*

start another real estate development). Included on the front page copy was "See letter inside for the story of what Arizona and Fountain Hill can mean to you."

Esquire Format

A unique single color letter-folder combination was used by *Esquire* magazine *(illustration, page 709)*. This black and white piece capitalized on the nostalgia craze and featured a wash drawing of a gay blade of a past era, with little side bars such as "A gentleman removes his cravat only for sleeping" and "A gentlemen kneels only to pray or propose." The copy emphasized "Luckily, concepts change." The center spread was turned into a clever, selling checklist, while page four returned to letter format.

Webster's Unified Inc. Stamps

Another interesting technique of pulling the contents of a mailing together was used by Webster's Unified, Inc. The mailing package included a letter, brochure, sheet of picture stamps, Ecology I.Q. sheet on which stamps could be pasted and a business reply card with space for a "free book" stamp. *(See illustration, page 710.)* The letter drew primary attention to the enclosed sheet of stamps. The enlarged typewriter type heading read: "REMOVE BOOK STAMP AND AFFIX TO YOUR GIFT CERTIFICATE." Letter copy promoted a series of nature books published in cooperation with The American Museum of Natural History. The sheet of nature stamps provided reader involvement since they could be pasted on the back of the Ecology I.Q. sheet. Once accomplished, that left the large "free book" stamp ... and the only place to paste it was on the order card.

Holiday magazine used another approach (see illustration on page 711). It might be described as a letter, since it opens "Dear Reader": and closes with a printed signature, but an editorial-style format is used for illustrations and copy. There are 11 full-color, seven black-and-white, and two two-color illustrations on the four pages, mixed in with copy set in a conventional typeface. Most of the copy, although running continuously, serves as captions for the 20 illustrations.

Still another type of illustrated letter is one used by *Sports Illustrated* as a circulation promotion piece. The front page has a four-side bleed black-and-white photograph, with the salutation and first three paragraphs of copy in typewriter type reversed into the illustration (white on gray). The second page of the letter (the back

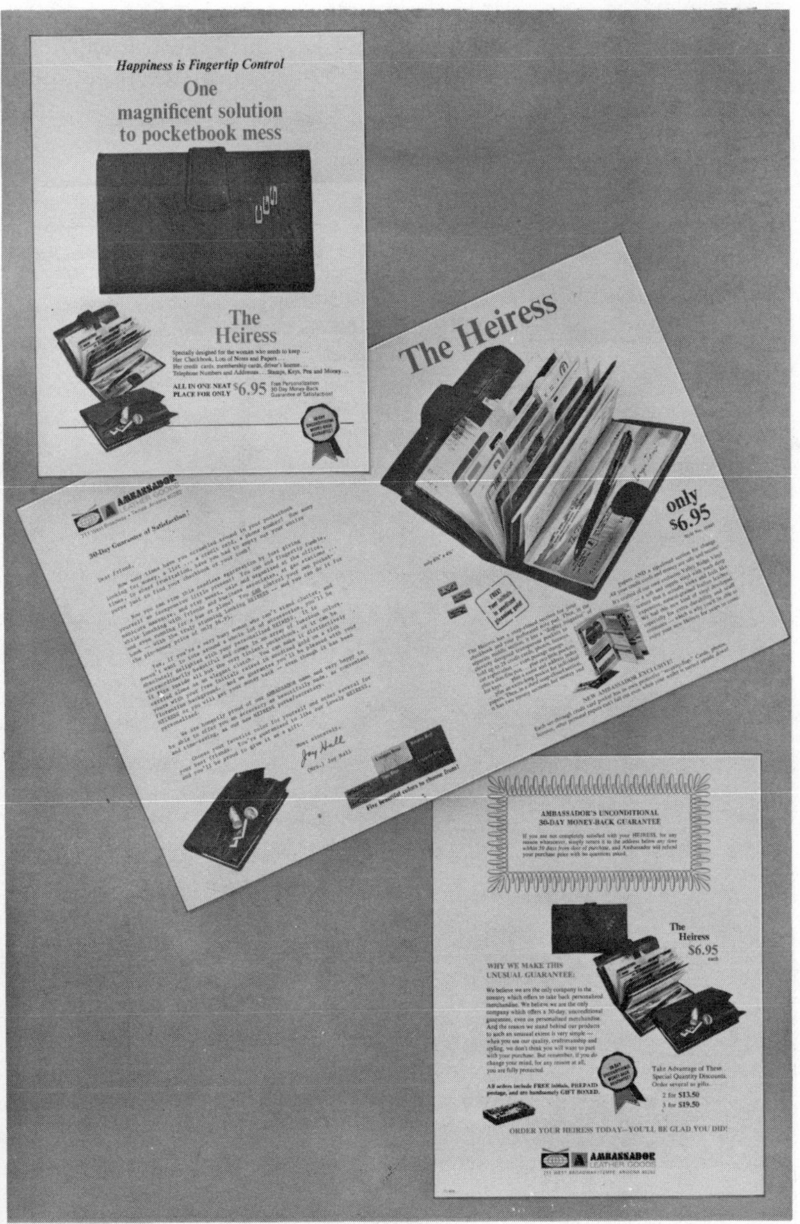

Aristocratic use of illustrations with the sales letter subordinated to the second page.

of the single sheet) is in black typewriter type against a screened background. Included in the background is a small illustration of a special premium plus the letterhead at the bottom of the page in a darker green.

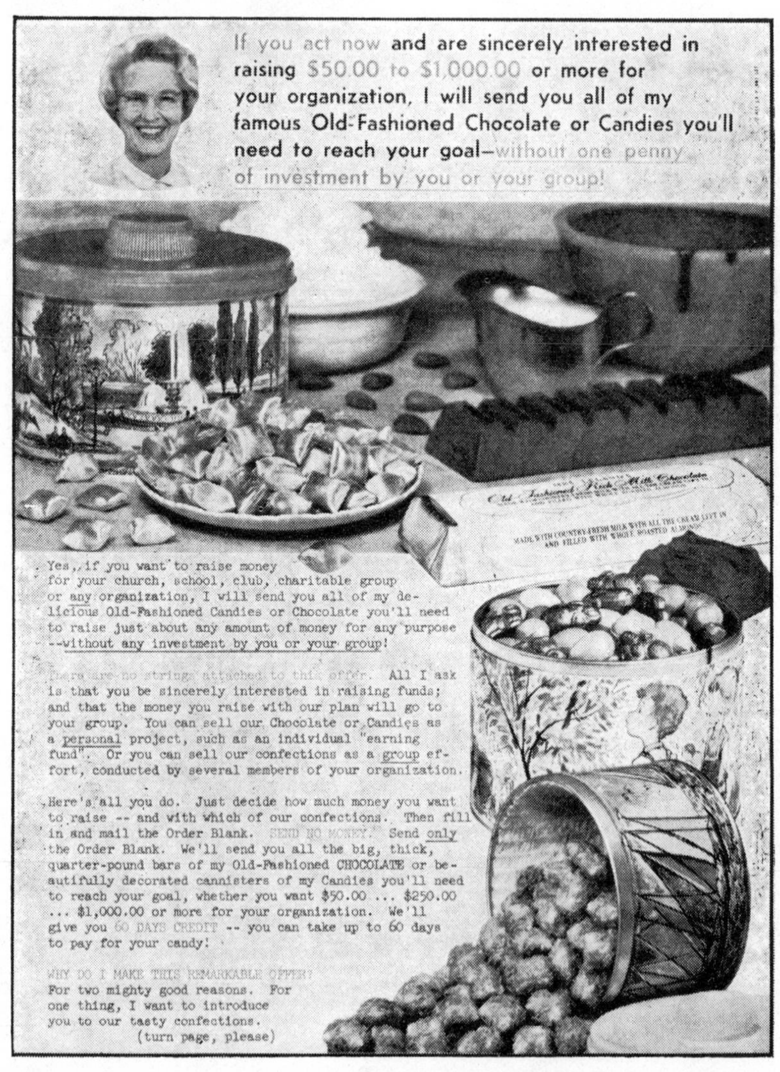

If you act now and are sincerely interested in raising $50.00 to $1,000.00 or more for your organization, I will send you all of my famous Old-Fashioned Chocolate or Candies you'll need to reach your goal—without one penny of investment by you or your group!

Yes, if you want to raise money for your church, school, club, charitable group or any organization, I will send you all of my delicious Old-Fashioned Candies or Chocolate you'll need to raise just about any amount of money for any purpose --without any investment by you or your group!

There are no strings attached to this offer. All I ask is that you be sincerely interested in raising funds; and that the money you raise with our plan will go to your group. You can sell our Chocolate or Candies as a personal project, such as an individual "earning fund". Or you can sell our confections as a group effort, conducted by several members of your organization.

Here's all you do. Just decide how much money you want to raise -- and with which of our confections. Then fill in and mail the Order Blank. SEND NO MONEY. Send only the Order Blank. We'll send you all the big, thick, quarter-pound bars of my Old-Fashioned CHOCOLATE or beautifully decorated cannisters of my Candies you'll need to reach your goal, whether you want $50.00 ... $250.00 ... $1,000.00 or more for your organization. We'll give you 60 DAYS CREDIT -- you can take up to 60 days to pay for your candy!

WHY DO I MAKE THIS REMARKABLE OFFER?
For two mighty good reasons. For one thing, I want to introduce you to our tasty confections.
(turn page, please)

Mrs. Leland's Kitchens sends out a combination letter and product folder.

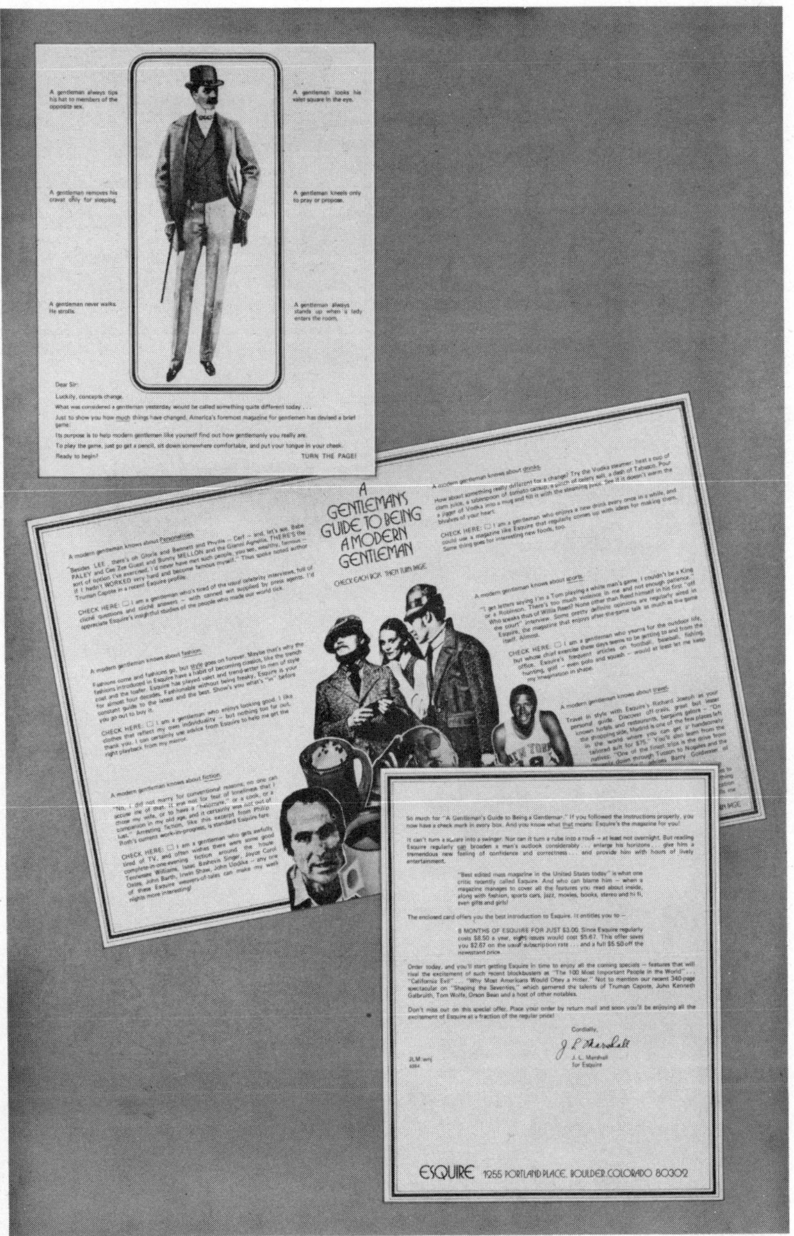

A gentleman always tips his hat to members of the opposite sex.

A gentleman looks his valet square in the eye.

A gentleman removes his cravat only for sleeping.

A gentleman kneels only to pray or propose.

A gentleman never walks. He strolls.

A gentleman always stands up when a lady enters the room.

Dear Sir:

Luckily, concepts change.

What was considered a gentleman yesterday would be called something quite different today . . .

Just to show you how much things have changed, America's foremost magazine for gentlemen has devised a brief game:

Its purpose is to help modern gentlemen like yourself find out how gentlemanly you really are.

To play the game, just go get a pencil, sit down somewhere comfortable, and put your tongue in your cheek.

Ready to begin? TURN THE PAGE!

A GENTLEMAN'S GUIDE TO BEING A MODERN GENTLEMAN

CHECK EACH BOX. THEN TURN PAGE.

So much for "A Gentleman's Guide to Being a Gentleman." If you followed the instructions properly, you now have a check mark in every box. And you know what that means: Esquire's the magazine for you!

It can't turn a square into a swinger. Nor can it turn a rube into a roué — at least not overnight. But reading Esquire regularly can broaden a man's outlook considerably . . . enlarge his horizons . . . give him a tremendous new feeling of confidence and correctness . . . and provide him with hours of lively entertainment.

"Best edited mass magazine in the United States today" is what one critic recently called Esquire. And who can blame him — when a magazine manages to cover all the features you read about inside, along with fashion, sports cars, jazz, movies, books, stereo and hi fi, even gifts and girls!

The enclosed card offers you the best introduction to Esquire. It entitles you to —

8 MONTHS OF ESQUIRE FOR JUST $3.00. Since Esquire regularly costs $8.50 a year, eight issues would cost $5.67. This offer saves you $2.67 on the usual subscription rate . . . and a full $5.50 off the newsstand price.

Order today, and you'll start getting Esquire in time to enjoy all the coming specials — features that will rival the excitement of such recent blockbusters as "The 100 Most Important People in the World" . . . "California Evil" . . . "Why Most Americans Would Obey a Hitler." Not to mention our recent 340-page spectacular on "Shaping the Seventies," which garnered the talents of Truman Capote, John Kenneth Galbraith, Tom Wolfe, Orson Bean and a host of other notables.

Don't miss out on this special offer. Place your order by return mail and soon you'll be enjoying all the excitement of Esquire at a fraction of the regular price!

Cordially,

J. L. Marshall

J. L. Marshall
for Esquire

JLM:wrj
4084

ESQUIRE 1255 PORTLAND PLACE, BOULDER, COLORADO 80302

Ingenious use that Esquire made of a single color capitalizing on the nostalgia craze.

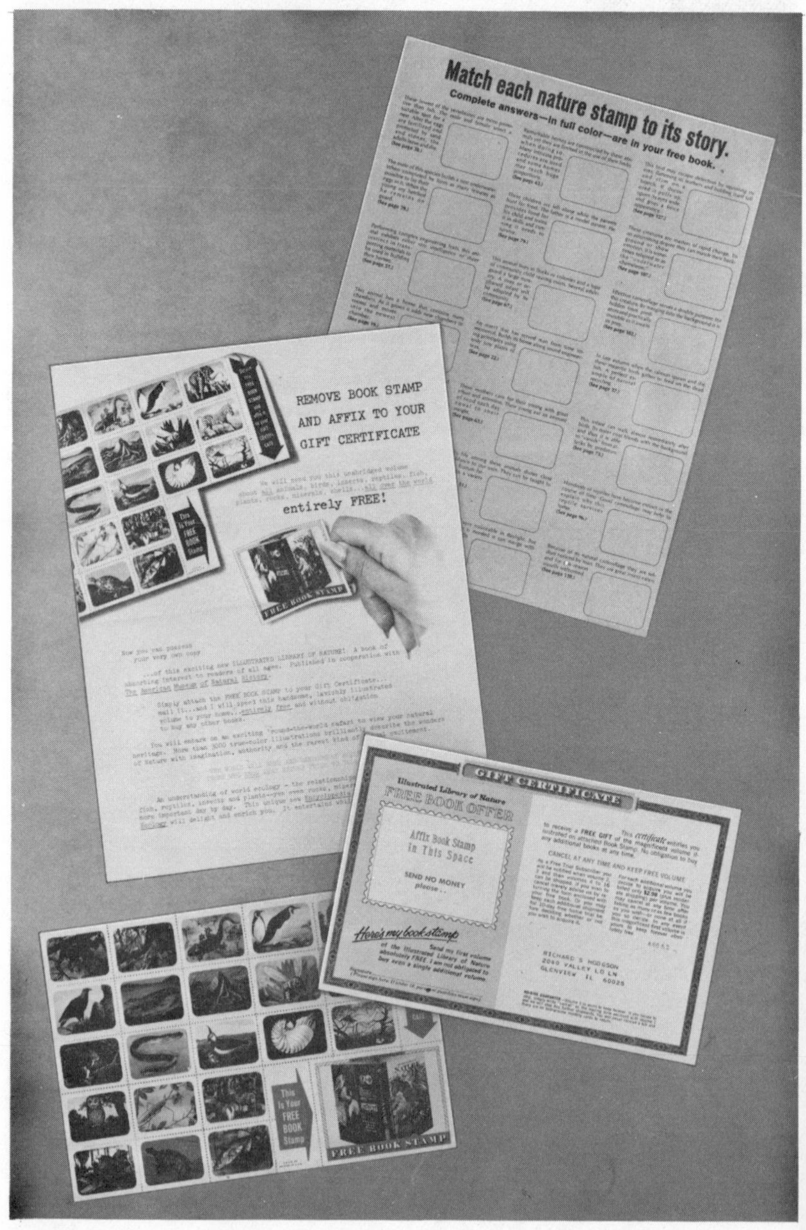

Attention—compelling use of illustrations and stamps emphasizing interest in ecology.

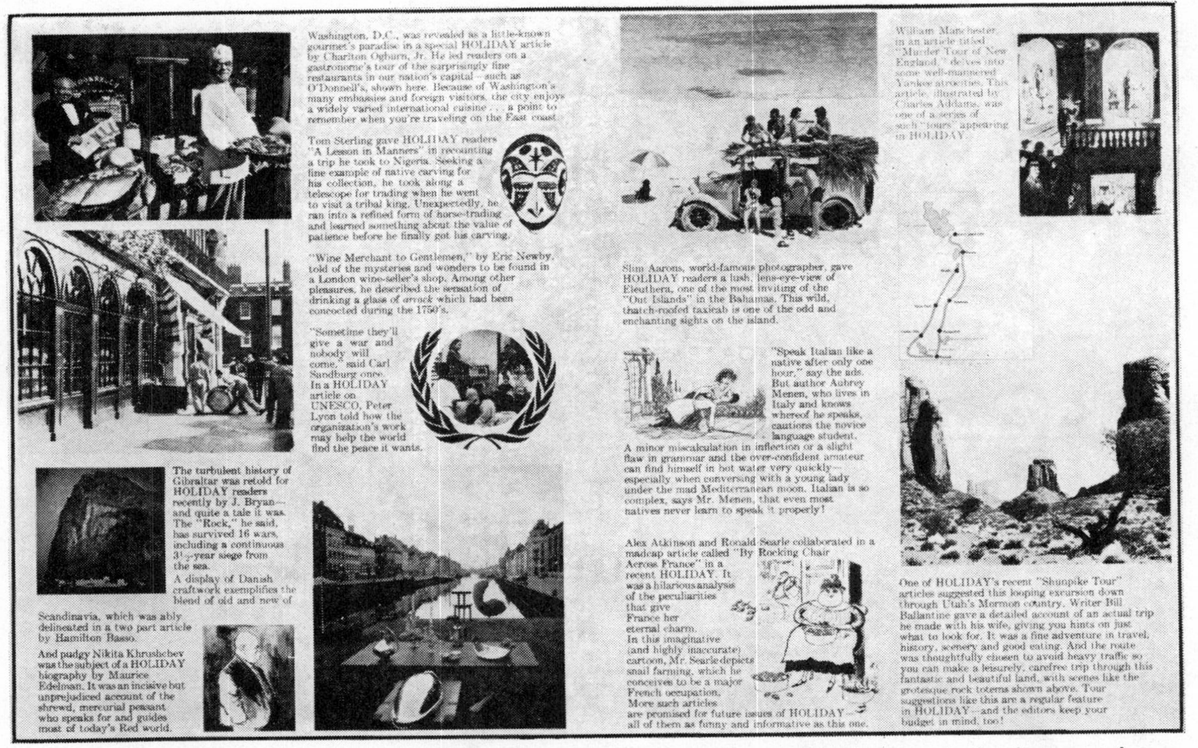

Washington, D.C., was revealed as a little-known gourmet's paradise in a special HOLIDAY article by Charlton Ogburn, Jr. He led readers on a gastronome's tour of the surprisingly fine restaurants in our nation's capital—such as O'Donnell's, shown here. Because of Washington's many embassies and foreign visitors, the city enjoys a widely varied international cuisine . . . a point to remember when you're traveling on the East coast.

Tom Sterling gave HOLIDAY readers "A Lesson in Manners" in recounting a trip he took to Nigeria. Seeking a fine example of native carving for his collection, he took along a telescope for trading when he went to visit a tribal king. Unexpectedly, he ran into a refined form of horse-trading and learned something about the value of patience before he finally got his carving.

"Wine Merchant to Gentlemen," by Eric Newby, told of the mysteries and wonders to be found in a London wine-seller's shop. Among other pleasures, he described the sensation of drinking a glass of *arrack* which had been concocted during the 1750's.

"Sometime they'll give a war and nobody will come," said Carl Sandburg once. In a HOLIDAY article on UNESCO, Peter Lyon told how the organization's work may help the world find the peace it wants.

The turbulent history of Gibraltar was retold for HOLIDAY readers recently by J. Bryan—and quite a tale it was. The "Rock," he said, has survived 16 wars, including a continuous 3½-year siege from the sea.

A display of Danish craftwork exemplifies the blend of old and new of Scandinavia, which was ably delineated in a two part article by Hamilton Basso.

And pudgy Nikita Khrushchev was the subject of a HOLIDAY biography by Maurice Edelman. It was an incisive but unprejudiced account of the shrewd, mercurial peasant who speaks for and guides most of today's Red world.

Slim Aarons, world-famous photographer, gave HOLIDAY readers a lush, lens-eye-view of Eleuthera, one of the most inviting of the "Out Islands" in the Bahamas. This wild, thatch-roofed taxicab is one of the odd and enchanting sights on the island.

"Speak Italian like a native after only one hour," say the ads. But author Aubrey Menen, who lives in Italy and knows whereof he speaks, cautions the novice language student. A minor miscalculation in inflection or a slight flaw in grammar and the over-confident amateur can find himself in hot water very quickly—especially when conversing with a young lady under the mad Mediterranean moon. Italian is so complex, says Mr. Menen, that even most natives never learn to speak it properly!

Alex Atkinson and Ronald Searle collaborated in a madcap article called "By Rocking Chair Across France" in a recent HOLIDAY. It was a hilarious analysis of the peculiarities that give France her eternal charm. In this imaginative (and highly inaccurate) cartoon, Mr. Searle depicts snail farming, which he conceives to be a major French occupation. More such articles are promised for future issues of HOLIDAY—all of them as funny and informative as this one.

William Manchester, in an article titled "Murder Tour of New England," delves into some well-mannered Yankee atrocities. This article, illustrated by Charles Addams, was one of a series of such "tours" appearing in HOLIDAY.

One of HOLIDAY's recent "Shunpike Tour" articles suggested this looping excursion down through Utah's Mormon country. Writer Bill Ballantine gave a detailed account of an actual trip he made with his wife, giving you hints on just what to look for. It was a fine adventure in travel, history, scenery and good eating. And the route was thoughtfully chosen to avoid heavy traffic so you can make a leisurely, carefree trip through this fantastic and beautiful land, with scenes like the grotesque rock totems shown above. Tour suggestions like this are a regular feature in HOLIDAY—and the editors keep your budget in mind, too!

Extensive use of color helped Holiday *dramatize its editorial product. This is the inside spread of a four-page letter.*

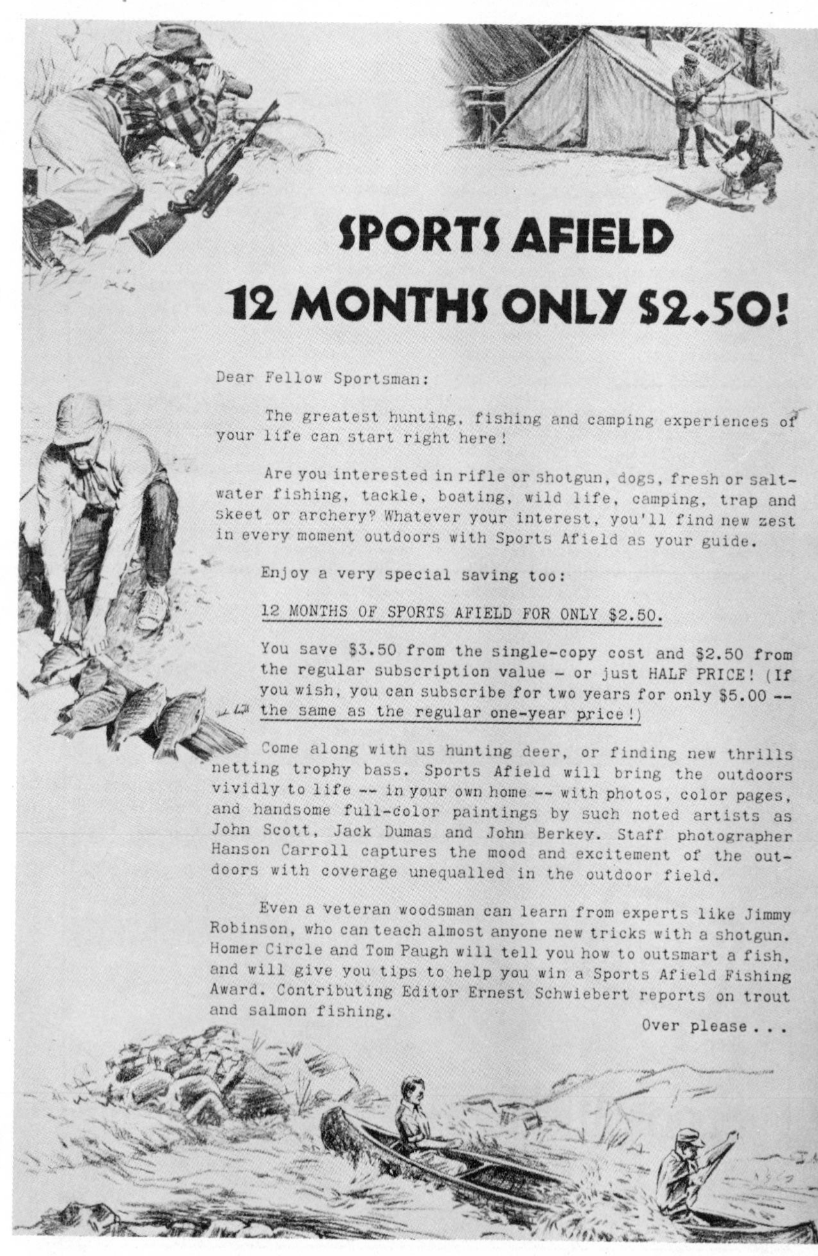
SPORTS AFIELD
12 MONTHS ONLY $2.50!

Dear Fellow Sportsman:

The greatest hunting, fishing and camping experiences of your life can start right here!

Are you interested in rifle or shotgun, dogs, fresh or salt-water fishing, tackle, boating, wild life, camping, trap and skeet or archery? Whatever your interest, you'll find new zest in every moment outdoors with Sports Afield as your guide.

Enjoy a very special saving too:

12 MONTHS OF SPORTS AFIELD FOR ONLY $2.50.

You save $3.50 from the single-copy cost and $2.50 from the regular subscription value - or just HALF PRICE! (If you wish, you can subscribe for two years for only $5.00 -- the same as the regular one-year price!)

Come along with us hunting deer, or finding new thrills netting trophy bass. Sports Afield will bring the outdoors vividly to life -- in your own home -- with photos, color pages, and handsome full-color paintings by such noted artists as John Scott, Jack Dumas and John Berkey. Staff photographer Hanson Carroll captures the mood and excitement of the out-doors with coverage unequalled in the outdoor field.

Even a veteran woodsman can learn from experts like Jimmy Robinson, who can teach almost anyone new tricks with a shotgun. Homer Circle and Tom Paugh will tell you how to outsmart a fish, and will give you tips to help you win a Sports Afield Fishing Award. Contributing Editor Ernest Schwiebert reports on trout and salmon fishing.

Over please . . .

Sports Afield uses sketches to clearly establish the type of contents it offers potential subscribers.

Cartoon Illustrations

A much more common illustration technique is to use a cartoon to dramatize the headline on the letter. This style is used frequently for collection letters, probably with the assumption that a clever cartoon will take part of the sting out of a dunning letter. With the widespread availability of cartoon illustrations at low cost through clip-art services, there is no problem in finding an instantly available cartoon to illustrate almost any headline.

In addition, you can buy a wide variety of illustrated flash bulletins, which come complete with cartoon illustration and headline to cover most any situation. All you need do is add letter copy of your choice, and you have a ready-to-mail piece with special attention-getting ability. (For additional details on flash bulletins, see Chapter 37—"Other Formats.")

Letter Gadgets

Another popular attention-getting device is the use of letter gadgets. You can buy hundreds of different plastic, metal, and cloth gadgets which are designed to be tipped onto a letter, or you can choose any small item which helps make a point. Typical examples of the use of letter gadgets are illustrated on page 715.

When using a letter gadget, it is important to select an item which will do more than just attract attention. Unless the gadget adds impact to your message as well, chances are the recipient will remember the attention-getter instead of the points you wanted to get across.

Trick Letter Formats

It is not necessary, of course, to produce your letter either in one of the standard dimensions (such as 8½ by 11 inches) or to print it on conventional paper stocks. Some of the most dramatic direct mail letters have utilized an unconventional format.

The easiest avenue of departure is to either enlarge or reduce the page size of your letter. Publishers Clearing House, for example, uses a 10½- by 13½-inch sheet for a two-page letter, with typewriter type blown up to about 1½ times its usual size. Using the re-

Prevention®
EMMAUS, PENNSYLVANIA, 18049
Robert Rodale, Editor
What Keeps
PREVENTION Magazine
Readers
So Spry and Perky?
Maybe it's the Good Food they Eat
Prevention
Maybe it's the Healthy
Exercise in the Outdoors
...and Maybe The Magazine Helps Too!!!

Dear Reader:

Here's a "No Risk" invitation to get you to see the NEW PREVENTION magazine. Discover first-hand why Rodale's unique health magazine can be so good for you. Here's our offer:

Mail the enclosed card today.

You will receive the latest issue of PREVENTION plus "PERK UP WITH PREVENTION!" -- a delightful, stimulating booklet about how you can actually enjoy living a healthier life.

And we will enter an introductory subscription for you to PREVENTION of 10 months for $2.87, a savings of $2.03 on the regular subscription price.

If -- and only if -- you decide that future issues of the magazine are worth getting, then you can pay the small subscription cost. YOU OWE US NOTHING -- AND MAY KEEP EVERYTHING WE SEND YOU" -- if you don't want future issues. All you need do is write "cancel" on the invoice you receive, and that's it. If you send payment now, your money will be refunded in full if you decide not to receive future issues.

(Please turn page)

Cartoons can put a letter reader in a good mood. This is how Prevention magazine sets the stage for a subscription promotion.

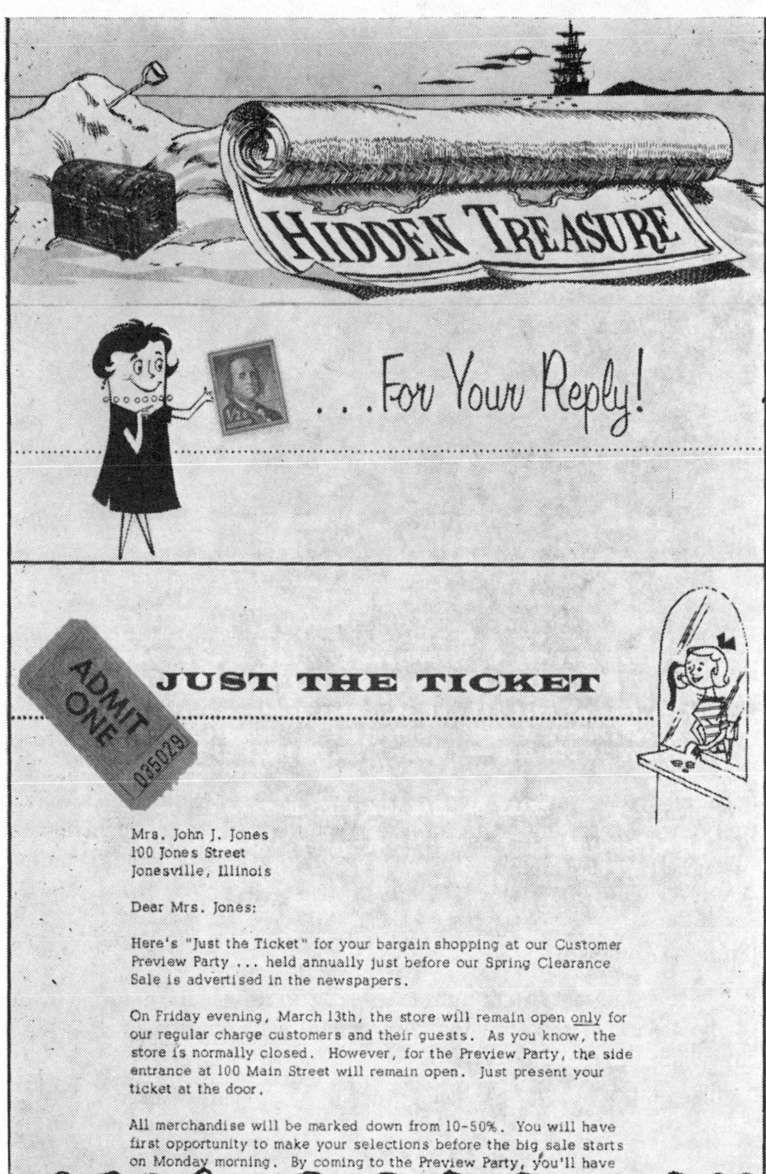

Mrs. John J. Jones
100 Jones Street
Jonesville, Illinois

Dear Mrs. Jones:

Here's "Just the Ticket" for your bargain shopping at our Customer Preview Party ... held annually just before our Spring Clearance Sale is advertised in the newspapers.

On Friday evening, March 13th, the store will remain open only for our regular charge customers and their guests. As you know, the store is normally closed. However, for the Preview Party, the side entrance at 100 Main Street will remain open. Just present your ticket at the door.

All merchandise will be marked down from 10-50%. You will have first opportunity to make your selections before the big sale starts on Monday morning. By coming to the Preview Party, you'll have

These three letters show how gadgets can attract attention. The treasure chest, stamp and ticket are pasted to illustrated letterheads.

Trick letter formats can be successfull in developing subscriptions, such as this miniature of a grocery bag used by The Ladies' Home Journal.

verse technique, a 5- by 7-inch letter with type reduced to about half the size used for conventional letters has proved effective.

The *Ladies' Home Journal* used an "It's in the Bag" theme for one of its circulation mailings. The mailing envelope, on brown kraft stock, was designed to look like a miniature grocery bag. The enclosed letter was on a 2- by 11-inch strip of white paper, which was rough perforated at the top to resemble the typical cash register tape. Copy on the "tape letter" was printed in light purple to imitate cash-register imprinting.

Unusual Surfaces

There is almost an unlimited variety of unusual surfaces which can be used effectively for direct mail letters. Some you might consider:

wallpaper	wrapping paper	gift wraps
cloth	canvas	metal foil
towels or washcloths	sandpaper	shingles
rubber sheets	blotter stock	lined paper

For more ideas on novelty letter techniques, see Chapter 31—"Showmanship Formats."

GOOD UP TO SEPT. 12, 1971	GOOD SEPT. 13 TO OCT. 12, 1971	GOOD OCT. 13 TO NOV. 12, 1971

Now, You Not Only Save By Dealing With Us Direct...

You Save By Dealing With Us Early!

We are sending you our Executive Pocket Planner to prove a point. That you can get a gift planner that looks like, feels like and works like a two dollar planner...but costs less than 84¢. And now with our Early Bird discount offer, you can save up to 10% simply by placing your order early, before our busy season begins.

It'll take you just two minutes to discover why most of our customers give this Planner to their customers and prospects year after year. And not just because they save money.

> First, notice the comfortable feel and expensive appearance of the cover. That's how it's going to look a year from now. Now tuck it into your coat pocket to try it on for size. Feels right, doesn't it?
> No wonder the U. S. Executive Pocket Planner is habit forming. It's the kind of gift a man keeps and uses -- for everything from jotting down a lunch date to recording car expenses to remembering an anniversary.

Here's everything you look for in a business gift...something to compliment your recipient while it speaks for your own good taste. All for about the price of a good cigar. And that includes your company name imprinted in gold.

As nice a gift as the Pocket Planner is, there may be certain V.I.P. customers or prospects on your list who deserve something even more 'special'.

> For them, we suggest the U. S. Executive Desk Planner -- a big, handsome 7-1/2 x 9-1/8" desk diary that's constantly in view to remind your recipient of your thoughtfulness. And just to make the selection more complete, both the Pocket Planner and Desk Planner are available in your choice of weekly or monthly planning editions.

So why not solve all your gift giving problems right now...and save money, too. Simply attach the discount stamp to the enclosed order card, fill it out and drop it in the mail. Do it today and save a full 10%!

Very cordially,

Robert Williams

Robert Williams
Vice President

RW:BB

P.S. Of course, every U. S. Executive Desk and Pocket Planner carries our iron-clad guarantee of complete satisfaction or your money back -- even if the Planners have already been imprinted!

Tipped-on discount stamps made an immediate point for U.S. Diary Company, encouraging early orders for its Executive Desk Planner.

John Plain

JOHN PLAIN & COMPANY • 444 W. WASHINGTON STREET • CHICAGO 60606

Please forgive me for not addressing this to you personally - too little time.
D. H.

Dear Friend and Customer:

I'm sitting here in my office -- long after everyone else has gone home -- wrestling with a problem, and I need your help.

I'm trying to stretch the dollars that my boss has allowed me for publishing our handsome new John Plain Book far enough to send one to every one of our customers -- but it doesn't appear as though I'm going to make it. It's sort of like trying to make the butter come out even with the bread.

I have a list before me that has your name on it, but it tells me that you have not placed an order in over a year. I've tried to find your name elsewhere on the list, perhaps at another address, showing you've ordered, but so far no luck.

So there's my problem...and here is my solution.

If I want you to have the new 700-page John Plain Catalog next August when it comes off the press, the two of us must find a way to do so.

If you will send me an order -- just one -- in the next sixty days, I can send you that catalog, and I've had an order form printed with your name and customer number, just to make it easier for you.

If you'll do your part, I'll do mine.

Will you send me that one order (and to my attention, please) so that I can put a green check after your name and send you your 1970 John Plain Book?

Sincerely,

Denzell Hale

Denzell Hale
Circulation Manager

P. S. If you've ordered from us recently, please disregard this letter -- you will be getting your catalog. (But save the order form and use it for your next order.)

A simulated hand-written note can add a personal touch to a letter. John Plain & Company used the technique to stimulate orders from "lost" customers.

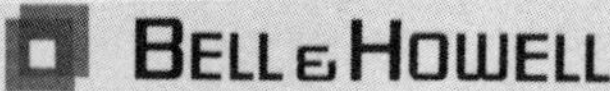
DITTO DIVISION
6800 McCormick Road Chicago, Illinois 60645
BELL & HOWELL

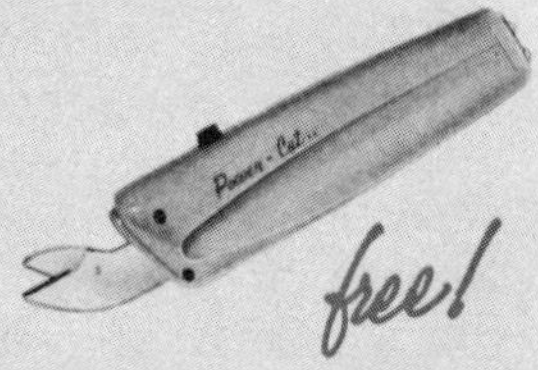

Dear Sir:

During this time period when many budgets are being cut and labor costs are increasing at a record rate, businessmen throughout the country are looking for ways to cut costs in all areas of their operation.

In the office, the high cost of making copies of correspondence, reports, etc. has usually been accepted. However, Bell & Howell now has a way to help you dramatically reduce this cost.

A recent national survey showed that 90% of all office copying required only 1 to 3 copies of each original. And the new Bell & Howell high-volume Statesman copier permits you to do just that--make a few copies from multiple originals in a minimum of time, with minimum effort, at minimum cost.

Your Bell & Howell representative would like an opportunity to demonstrate the Statesman copier to you. And for giving him a few minutes of your time, he will give you a Cordless Power Scissors for your office...absolutely FREE. It cuts paper, packages, cloth, string--even light cardboard...simpler and faster--just as the Bell & Howell Statesman makes copying simpler and faster.

Mail the enclosed postage-paid reply card today for a demonstration of the Statesman copier and your FREE "Power-Cut" scissors.

Sincerely,

Dean W. Berry, Jr.
National Sales Manager
Copier Products

the new Statesman

Bell & Howell illustrated both its product and a premium being offered to potential customers who would permit a demonstration.

Paper Selection

The choice of the right paper stocks for letterheads is highly important. Many advertisers make the mistake of trying to cut a few cents off the total printing cost by skimping on paper used for letterheads. Such an imagined savings can quickly backfire, however, since a small fraction of a cent more per letterhead can make a world of difference in the impression made by a mailing.

The most common letterhead size is 8½ by 11 inches, although the Executive size—7¼ by 10½ inches—is also popular. Substance weights of 24, 20, or 16 are the most common, and paper is usually selected with the grain running parallel to the writing direction—in an 8½- by 11-inch letter, the grain would run with the 8½-inch dimension.

For more details on paper selection see Chapter 46—"Paper and Envelope Guide."

Special Letterhead Techniques

One particularly useful special letterhead technique is to have a 2-inch flap at the top of the sheet. The normal letterhead is then printed on the face of the flap, while the area "hidden" below the flap is used for special information that would clutter the letterhead if printed "out in the open." This technique is particularly useful for associations and clubs which want to list all of their officers and directors or where a detailed product list or addresses of many branch offices and/or dealers are desired.

We have previously mentioned the combination letter where material usually printed in enclosures is featured on the center spread of a four-page folder, with the cover used for a letterhead. Many advertisers prefer to use an 8½- by 22-inch sheet folded in the center to yield four 8½- by 11-inch pages. This folding technique is particularly desirable when letters are to be individually typed since they can be fed into a typewriter without difficulty and have a more "personal" appearance.

LETTERHEADS

A well-designed letterhead can be highly important to the success of a direct mail program. In reality, the letterhead is to a direct mail program what a store front or a salesman's per-

You have been nominated for
membership as a

**National Associate in
The Smithsonian Institution**

Privileges for you and your family include:

- A year's subscription to SMITHSONIAN, the Institution's new monthly magazine of Man
- Eligibility for special members travel program
- Discounts on books and memorabilia purchased direct or by mail through the Smithsonian shops
- Preferential reception when visiting Washington, and the Smithsonian museums and galleries

Your numbered membership card is enclosed. *If you cannot use the card, please return it so that another person can be nominated in your place.* An envelope is enclosed for your early reply, with postage already paid, whether your answer is

Yes or No

Dear Nominee:

Call it voodoo, witchcraft ... or faith ...

... but when night falls on a tiny island in the New Hebrides, you and I are being worshipped with all the idolatry that Aztecs once lavished on the Sun.

> In the jungle, strips are periodically hacked back to guarantee our safe landing. Abandoned tin cans are monitored regularly in hopes of detecting our plane. Rows of crude wooden crosses are kept freshly painted to greet us.

Childish, innocent, touching, the cult of the people of Tanna grows out of World War II. A GI named John Frum -- who may or may not have existed -- is said to have promised to return

The Smithsonian Institution summarizes its sales story as part of the letterhead for a four-page letter which offers memberships and a subscription to its magazine.

sonal appearance is to other forms of marketing. European adman William Roderick Wilkinson in an article in *Industrial Marketing,* says:

> Some of your customers have never seen you. Some of them see your representative, talk to you on the telephone, write to you—they never *see* you or your premises or your plant or your people. Many of these customers form their impression of your company entirely by the only thing they *do* see regularly—your stationery. They read your letters, look at your labels, see your slips, pass your bills for payment—and their subconscious minds are ticking away, building a general impression of the kind of company you are. This general impression often tips the scales of selection one way or the other when they are considering your competitors' products.

What to Include

Not too many years ago, it was common practice to jam a letterhead full of every conceivable type of information about a company—from the names of the founders to a complete list of products and services. Good letterheads today, however, contain only essential information. This will generally include:

Company name
Street address
City, state, and zip code
Telephone number (including area code)

In addition, it may be desirable to add:

Principal product or service
Name of chief executive
Slogan
Trademark
Product illustration
Name of building
Room or suite number
Nature of business (if not indicated by name)
Founding date (if important competitively)

Designing the Letterhead

Letterhead design has become a highly specialized art, and most direct mail advertisers utilize the services of professional graphic designers to produce their letterheads. While some printers offer a professional design service, the majority have only limited ability in creating truly individual designs. Since a letterhead so often represents a company to its customers and prospects, it is advisable to entrust the design job only to the most skilled professionals.

Memo Flex Division,

515 Bannock Street, Dayton 4, Ohio

Here's the information you requested. I hope it is interesting and helpful. Please remember that Memo Flex is the really new method of visual control. It's simple, flexible and easy to use. It can save you time and money by eliminating mistakes.

After looking over the material I hope you will agree and send us your order. There's a bonus if you do it now.

Joan Cornelius
Sales Department

Memo Flex gave a personal touch to inquiry handling by including a simulated hand-written memo which included a photo of the writer.

While professional design adds to the cost of a letterhead—and buyers should always question any offer of "free design," for they are most likely to receive exactly what they pay for it—it is money wisely invested. Just as you would hire an architect to produce plans to be used by the contractor in building a new plant or home or in remodeling an old one, you should hire a designer to create a letterhead design for your printer to follow.

National Travel Club
Travel Building, Floral Park, N.Y. 11001
Over 65 Years Of Service To Our Members

J. F. SULLIVAN, President
H. W. SHANE, Vice President
SHELDON SHANE, Secretary

Rush memo!

November 16, 1971

Dear Member:

I have just been informed by our corresponding secretary that you have not yet renewed your membership.

Unless your dues are received before November 30, 1971, I must do the following:

✓ Notify the Insurance Company to cancel your accident insurance thus forfeiting your new maximum $35,000 coverage.

✓ Advise Fulfillment to discontinue your subscription to TRAVEL.

✓ Send a memo to all departments to discontinue all other membership benefits.

Why not mail your dues today and stay with us? It's only $8.50 annually, the lowest dues by the largest Travel Club in the world.

Cordially yours,

Vincent Durand

Vincent Durand
Auditor

SS:G

National Travel Club kept it simple in this "final notice" approach to renewals.

A good guide to letterhead design was presented by designer Lester Beall in a portfolio, "How to Design a Letterhead," published by Parsons Paper Co. of Holyoke, Massachusetts:

1. The letterhead should be an indication of the basic personality of the company rather than a tipoff on the eccentricities of the management.
2. Much thought should be given to the type of audience that will, in the main, receive your correspondence. Sometimes it is possible to inject dual personality in a letterhead design sufficient to adequately serve dual purposes. If this is not feasible, several different types of letterheads are used for different types of "audiences."
3. Regardless of whether a letterhead suggests formality or informality, the design should reflect a definite feeling of company integrity, a feeling that the company has been in existence a long time and will continue to be in existence indefinitely.
4. One of the functions of a letterhead is to act as an advertisement or salesman for the company. This does not, however, mean that a letterhead should be cluttered up by long listings of products or trade names or any other so-called advertising material that unfortunately is often included as part of a letterhead. The addition of this type of material to a letterhead serves only one purpose: it reduces the area of the correspondence and makes it harder to read.
5. The amount of space devoted to the design of a letterhead should be governed by the type of business that the letterhead serves, plus the average length of the correspondence.
6. The selection of typefaces or handlettering should reflect the business of the company and project a positive quality.
7. The choice of color as well as the character and texture of the typeface or lettering employed can psychologically project through the design itself almost any feeling or character that is desired.
8. The effectiveness and efficiency of a letterhead design can be tested by actually typing a letter on the layout.
9. The method of reproduction of the letterhead must be constantly kept in mind during the design process.
10. The use of an illustration or trademark on the letterhead should not be employed unless it (a) serves a definite functional purpose designwise and (b) adds to the psychological projection of the type of business concerned.
11. Paper, probably more quickly than any one other element, projects the inherent importance and character of the business involved.
12. In order to achieve a complete and efficient "design-package," it is essential to use matching paper stock for the envelopes. It almost goes without saying that one should employ the design characteristics and color of the letterhead on the corner card of the envelopes.

Chapter 27

COMPUTER FORMATS

JUST as the Computer Age has changed the entire complexion of handling mailing lists, it has spawned a whole new category of direct mail formats. Most obvious are the computer-generated letters which have made extensive personalization practical for even the largest lists. But the computer is also utilized to create a whole new arsenal of direct mail formats—order forms, special offer slips, booklets, etc.

In the beginning, direct mail advertisers had a tendency to go overboard in the personalization opportunities made possible by a computer. They often tried to insert the recipient's name into just about every line of a letter and every scrap of information stored in the computer was bound to be inserted somewhere in the copy.

But then as those same advertisers began to receive computer-generated pieces from other advertisers, the folly of this approach quickly became obvious. The simple rule which evolved was that overpersonalization actually destroyed the effect of personalization. Today, the most astute copywriters try to inject computer-generated personalization in the very same way they would personalize a piece of business correspondence if written on a one-to-one basis.

Bob Hanford's Guide

One of the best basic guides to the preparation of computer letters was prepared by Bob Hanford, Jr. and originally reproduced for the DMMA Direct Mail Manual.[1] While, like every guide to computers, it contains some details that have become outdated by the rapid progression of new generations of computers, his basic advice is still sound.

[1] "What Every Direct Mailer Should Know About Computer Letters" by Bob Hanford, Jr. DMMA Manual Release No. 4101.

In the 500-plus years since Herr Gutenberg invented movable type, men have been devising new ways to move words onto paper. The Age of the Computer (or EDPaleozoic Period) has brought still another way: the computer letter.

To communicate with its human operators, a computer must reproduce its digested data in some visible form. This usually is done by connecting the computer to a unit which "prints out" the data on continuous, fanfolded sheets of paper.

Some years back, someone got the bright idea of (1) programming a computer to print out words in a "letter" format; (2) adding name and address (i.e., mailing list) information to the computer's data storage; (3) printing letterheads on the continuous form sheets. Before you could say, "Thomas J. Watson, Junior" the computer letter was born.

Early computer letters had a major handicap. Their print-out was limited to CAPITAL LETTERS—which meant that they looked more like telegrams than everyday typing. In the past five years, however, major advances have been made in electronic hardware, including faster "chain" or "train" printers[2] with upper-and-lower case capability, and new (and less costly) "drum" printers. The "chain" or "train" printers are commonly called "on line" printers. The "drum" printers are usually run "off line" though some major mailers are using them "on line."

Since computer letters can be produced on both types of equipment, it's worth comparing the pro's and con's of "on line" and "off line" printing. For brevity's sake, we've simplified—perhaps oversimplified—the technical aspects of production. Mailers who *really* want to know the "how" of computer letters should visit a shop where they're being done. One minute's viewing time is worth 10,000 words.

On Line Letters. Produced by a printing unit connected directly to (i.e., "on line" with) a computer—e.g., an IBM 1403, Model 3 Printer driven by a System/360 computer. Printing done by a type "chain" or "train," roughly resembling a bicycle chain, on which all of the metal letters and numbers are mounted. This continuous belt of type moves at great speed *horizontally* to the lines of copy being printed. The printing impression is made by striking action of tiny hammers behind the continuous form paper which push the paper against a broad, inked ribbon—which, in turn, is pushed against the appropriate type character on the "train." Maximum printing speed: 775 lines/minute in upper-and-lower-case, and 1,100 lines/minute

2For reasons best known to computer engineers—and probably mostly to confuse us laymen—the type-carrying mechanism on the 775 line/minute printers is called a "chain"; on the 1,100 line/minute printers it is called a "train."

in all-capital letters;[3] (which means that the computer/printer is making—and translating into action—about 1,000 decisions per second).

Advantages: For a host of highly technical reasons, the print-out from "chain" or "train" equipment is cleaner and more sharply defined than "off line" or "drum" printing. In addition, several typefaces are now available, some of them matching actual typewriter typefaces.

Disadvantages: Since the printer unit is run by a computer, the time spent printing out computer letters must be counted as "computer time." This can range upwards of $50 per hour—or some $6,000 to $8,000 per month in rentals—which cost must be reflected in the cost of letters produced by this method.

Off Line Letters. Produced by equipment which *may* have rudimentary data storage capability, but which is not, in itself, a computer and which has *no direct connection to* a computer (e.g., Data Products Corp.'s Model LP M-1000 consisting of a "Tape Reader" unit and a "Printer" unit). Printing done by a cylindrical drum engraved, like a curved letterpress electro, with rows and rows of individual letters and numbers. This drum rotates at high speed, and the movement of the type is *vertical* to the line of copy being printed. Type impression made in essentially the same way as in on-line printing. Maximum printing speed: approximately 667 lines/minute.

Advantages: Since computers are used only to produce the tape for the printer—and since a drum printer rents for roughly one-fourth the cost of a computer—the cost of the resultant letters is considerably lower than those produced on-line.

Disadvantage: The complex combination of movements (of type drum rotating at 667 RPM and paper moving upwards at some 50 inches per second) produces a characteristic "ghosting" effect in which the horizontal elements in each letterform look blurred or thicker than the vertical elements (as if you typed a word on a regular typewriter, then turned the platen ever so slightly and typed right over it again). In brief, crisp, sharply-defined printing is not now possible with drum printers—although work on new "movement compensating" drums may lead to some improvement in the future.

Lists for Computer Letters. Obviously, to use computer letters at all, your mailing list has to be "on computer" too. This usually means magnetic tape—although some punched card and paper tape systems are in use.

---

[3]This, too, is subject to change depending on how the printer is used, and the type of print-out required. For example, with upper case, lower case, bold face *and* special characters (symbols) the maximum speed drops to 190 lines/minute.

A few years ago, converting a list involved key-punching names and addresses onto cards, then transferring the data from the punched cards to magnetic tape via a "card-to-tape" reader. Today, developments in direct-to-tape key-punching—and in the exciting field of electronic optical scanning from typed pages or other documents—have brought the price of conversions 'way down, the accuracy rates 'way up. So getting a list on computer isn't the costly, mistake-prone job it once was.

However, as computer communications grow more sophisticated, pure name-and-address data must be coupled with other personal or buying-habit information. Obviously, the more input you put in, the higher your conversion costs are going to be—by *any* conversion system.

Even with your list on tape, it still may not be able to give you everything you might wish in computer letter production. For example, it's perfectly acceptable for an *inside* address on a letter (and certainly on an envelope) to read "123 Parkway Cir., Stamford, CT 06905." But should you wish to refer to this address in the *body copy* of your computer letter, your programming and your equipment must be able to translate these address abbreviations into words. If it doesn't, you can end up with copy reading, "a service you'll enjoy receiving at your home on 123 Parkway Cir., Stamford, CT 06905"—which is definitely *not* the way it would be typed out in a personal letter. "On line" operations, incidentally, can store the necessary tables in memory to expand such abbreviations back to full length.

Supplies for Computer Letters. Since computer letters are the offshoot of computer print-outs for other purposes, the first paper suppliers in the field were business forms manufacturers. They were forms experts first, lithographers and direct mail suppliers second—which has meant problems in printing quality, innovation flexibility, delivery schedules.

Today, a few enterprising lithographers have entered the "forms" field. Some are doing excellent 4-color work—even die-cutting and blind embossing—on continuous form letterheads. But though the winds of change are blowing, the old rule of allowing a month for delivery of continuous form letterheads is worth following, at least temporarily.

Envelopes for computer letter mailings are another sticky problem. Unless you're mailing in window envelopes, your #10's, #9's, or whatever, must be supplied on continuous forms for computer addressing. Allow plenty of time to get the envelopes—also plenty of money. No. 10's on continuous forms still cost 3 to 4 times as much as the same envelopes in boxes. And don't forget to allow for the extra cost of detaching the envelopes from the forms *after* addressing.

Again, envelopes are an area where advances are being made fast, and where today's caveat can be tomorrow's no-problem. Best advice: watch for the breakthroughs sure to come as the use of computer letters grows.

Two other collateral points worth noting. First, your production budget should also allow a few bucks for trimming the completed letters to remove (at top and bottom) the "fuzz" left from the bursting operation. Second, you can pre-print your signatures, in position, as part of your letterhead printing. OR you can run them as a separate operation *after* the letters are done. (There is even one piece of equipment that applies a plate signature as the completed letters, still in continuous form, go through the burster.) There are advantages and disadvantages to each method. Work with your supplier and/or your own production people to determine which is best in your specific case.

Writing Computer Letters. Computer letters can be produced "one-up" (one at a time), "two-up" (side by side), or "three-up" (three in a row; mostly narrow forms and memos). Obviously, it's more economical to print two- or three-up, since you get two or three times as many letters or memos per minute for your money.

However, since the "chain" or "train" printer can only print out a maximum of 133 characters per line (160 characters, maximum, for the "drum" printer), doing letters two-up with an on-line printer means you are limited to copy lines with a maximum width of, say, 55-60 characters per line—assuming you want your letters centered on their pages, and with *some* right and left-hand margins. If you are willing to settle for uneven margins, or if (like some sophisticated computer letter users) you can fill the wider margin with art or printed copy, you can minimize the line-length problem. In either case, your copy must be carefully planned, cut and fitted—working closely with your computer people all the way.

Though the *normal* computer printer typeface is Elite in size,[4] the printer spaces these Elite-size letterforms at 10 characters-per-inch (or Pica *spacing*), not the normal Elite spacing of 12-per-inch. So, if you're accustomed to writing copy in Elite, you'll have to start thinking bigger—up to Pica size, anyway.

You *can* produce two-page computer letters (two separate pages, that is) with body personalizations on *both* pages. It's possible. But

[4]Some on-line printers are now available equipped with Pica-size typefaces.

it raises problems in collating and assembling the finished job so that the correct second page is with the correct first page. If you're making your mailing in computer-addressed (not window) envelopes, you've got a "double-matching" headache.

If you must go to two pages, try to avoid body personalizations on the second page. And if you can do that, you might as well go all the way and consider lithographing the second page. It can now be done skillfully enough so that it takes a pretty good eye to tell where the computer-printed copy leaves off and the lithography begins. Some major mailers are lithographing all but a few lines of their letters, using a computer to insert body personalizations in the spaces they've left for it, and getting away with it nicely.

Another solution we've seen—and one particularly suited to mail order and circulation solicitations—is to produce *four-page* folder/letters incorporating body personalizations (matched to lithography) on pages 1 and 4 and lithography, but *no* body personalization, on page 2 and 3.

Personalization of Letters. You can put it as an Axiom: body personalizations are most effective when they refer to known facts about the individual to whom the letter is addressed. The dollar amount of his last purchase or donation . . . the date of his order . . . the name of the individual he gave a gift to . . . the name of *someone else* in his family . . . the name of the company he works for . . . the city or state in which he lives or works . . . the make, or year of the car he drives . . . the college he attended and/or his year of graduation . . . his hobbies, favorite sport, political party, etc.

To date, the most glaring error made by computer letter users has been to insert the addressee's name in the body of the letter without rhyme or reason—and in places where it would not even be used in a personally-dictated, hand-typed letter. The result is that the name stands out like an orange shirt in a St. Patrick's Day parade—the surest possible signal to the reader that the letter is *not* the personal communication it purports to be.

What these name-droppers forget is that a letter's personal quality is not dependent upon, nor measured by, the number of times you can manage to squeeze an addressee's name into the body copy. Rather it is in the friendly, personal "tone" of the copy, the kinds of personal facts you use about your addressee, and the way you weave these facts into the copy fabric so that it seems perfectly natural for them to be there. When skillfully done, body personalizations can leave the reader with the feeling that you're writing directly to—and for—him. When badly done, the result is a letter that merely shows off the ability of the computer, not the copywriter.

Best rule of thumb: if you wouldn't write it that way in a letter dictated to a secretary, and with all the facts about your addressee at your fingertips, don't write it that way in your computer letter. Just because the computer *can* do it, doesn't mean it should be done.

Use of Computer Letters. Two obvious points are worth restating: (1) not every direct mail effort justifies the added cost of computer letter communication; (2) those that do still need to be evaluated from the standpoint of what *kind* of computer letter should be used.

There seems to be some evidence that in mailings to *consumer* lists even a minimum amount of personalization will greatly increase response. On the other hand, there is fragmentary evidence that, when mailing to *businessmen* at their offices, the higher the quality of computer letter production, the better the results. One practitioner suggests that this is because businessmen are accustomed to seeing, recognizing and giving greater attention to personally-typed letters than to "ordinary" direct mail—and that anything less than top-quality computer letter production won't get their readership. At least it makes another theory.

Like everything else in direct mail, the one sure way to tell if computer letters will work for you—and whether off line, on line or an offset/computer letter combination will work best—is to try them yourself, on your own lists, selling your own product or service.

The one clear fact about computer letters is that they are here to stay, and that they will call for a whole new way of thinking by direct mailers (and by marketing management) about lists . . . information acquisition, storage and retrieval . . . copy, enclosures and formats . . . and about the strategic role of the computer in the advertising and sales communications mix.

Perhaps the best testimonial to the kind of reader reaction a well-conceived and executed computer letter will elicit was contained in the O. E. McIntyre "Mail Marketing Newsletter" of some months back. Reporting on the use of computer letters by a major publisher, the "Newsletter" cited the comment one respondent penned on his reply card. "In this age of computers," he wrote, "it is refreshing to be treated once more as an individual."

Dick Trenbeth's Ground Rules

Another DMMA Manual release[5] featured a set of ground rules for computer letters prepared by Chicago fund raising expert,

[5]"Ground Rules for Computer Letters" by Richard P. Trenbeth. DMMA Manual Release No. 4102.

Richard P. Trenbeth. While, once again, it is important to stress that the rapidly changing computer field makes some of his "facts" out-of-date, his helpful suggestions still bear study by anyone considering the use of computer letters.

When anything is as hot and new as the computer letter, you can be sure the basic rules are subject to change without notice. But both beginners and seasoned professionals can take some comfort from the fact that it's relatively easy to build new experiences on top of a few fundamental ground rules.

1. COMPUTER-LETTER PRODUCTION REQUIRES COMPATIBLE MAGNETIC-TYPE RECORDS.

A surprising number of potential computer-letter users are still unaware that visual records and lists must be converted to magnetic tape in a format which will require minimum editing for upper-and-lower case application. Parts of records about each person on your list (title and name, street address, city, state, etc.) are known as "fields," which are ideally formatted in each tape record in a fixed position with a standardized number of characters for each field. Spacing in multiple titles (for example, Mr. and Mrs.) and in the complex "Mc" and "O'" names must be standardized and consistent. If your records are already on tape or you are renting compiled lists on tape, be sure to furnish your computer-letter supplier with a tape-record layout (a diagram of field positions and character counts for each field) and, if at all possible, a tape "dump" (a few pages of complete printout from the tape).

If you're planning to convert your own records to tape, be sure to invest in the services of an experienced consultant who can guide you in the most economical format for continued use on third-generation computers (the IBM System/360, Model 20, is in most general use for letter printing). Most conversions of visual data to magnetic tape are still accomplished by key-punching data on cards from which tape can be created, but a growing number of service bureaus and others are switching to less expensive optical scanning, which requires only accurate typists with special-font typewriters rather than scarce key-punch operators and costly punching equipment.

The average cost of converting an individual record to tape will run about 3.5 cents to 5.5 cents per name.

2. COMPUTER LETTERS CAN BE PRINTED ONLY ON FAN-FOLDED, CONTINUOUS-FORM LETTERHEADS.

Though a few commercial web-offset printers are now in the forms business, you will still have to deal with business-form printers for most of your requirements, and that means you must get used to much longer delivery, fewer colors, and sheet depths limited to the size of forms press printing cylinders. Sheets up to 11-inches in depth are relatively easy to get fairly quickly, but 12-inch and 14 inch depths may require waiting periods of up to seven weeks or more. Some of the newest forms presses are now capable of printing up to four colors on each side (including some four-color process work), perforating, spot gumming, die cutting, embossing, scoring, and corner cutting in a single pass through a press.

Paper stock for continuous letterheads can vary from inexpensive sulphite form paper up to 100% rag content or even light card stock (for membership cards, other identification cards, or personalized order cards). Special "heat-seal" forms with a coated back make it possible to computer print the customer's name and address on the right side and his account status on the left side, fold the sheet vertically, and run the folded sheet through sealing unit which bonds the coated back and converts the piece into a postcard (many public utility bills are now processed in this manner). Letterhead forms are converted to sheets by "bursting" (literally pulling apart the perforations separating the sheets while trimming off the pin-feed edges and slicing the sheets vertically). A more advanced machine, known as a "document converter," neatly trims all four sides, removing top-and-bottom perforation fringe in increments of sixths of an inch. Bursters have the advantage of merging two-up letters for bulk mailings, but there are also ways of overcoming this problem on the document converter.

Although there are some methods of printing signatures on computer letters after they are run, the best quality by far is obtained by printing the signature in its exact position at the same time as the letterhead is printed by the forms house. This means, of course, that you must determine the exact positioning of your letter copy when placing the order for the continuous letterheads.

Work closely with your computer-letter printer at all stages of planning your letterheads and envelopes. When you learn the strict linear requirements of printing on the computer, you'll be able to design your own letterheads and window envelopes but, even then, you'll prevent many costly errors by checking with your suppliers. Until someone solves the expensive riddle of hand-matching a personalized letter with a separately addressed envelope, you'll find by far the best solution is the cellophane window envelope with the window carefully positioned to show the inside address on the letter. Mailers accustomed to using brochures and reply envelopes in sizes too large to fit a monarch envelope can still use two-up computer letters by making sure that the windows in #9 and #10 are ½ inch from the left and ½ inch from the bottom, 1⅛ inches to 1¼ inches deep, and 4½ inches to 5 inches long. If the letter is shaken to the top of the sealed envelopes, usually the salutation will also show through the window, but this seems a minor penalty to pay for an otherwise satisfactory solution. If the letters are to be stamped and machine inserted, order your envelopes with the gum on the envelope flap stripped from areas under the stamp and the suction cups on the inserter.

3. PLANNING YOUR LETTER.

Most of the present computer-letter printing machines operating "on line" (directly connected with the computer) are limited to 132 print positions, 10 characters to the inch, or a total printing width of 13.2 inches. Translated to the most economical letter format, this means thinking in terms of printing letters "two-up" (side by side in the computer), resulting in 7 inches by 10½ inches trim size to fit a standard monarch envelope. Though you can use a variety of other formats, including 8½ inches by 11 inches and four-page folders within certain limits, all variations from the standard two-up format are going to cost you more money for programming and computer printing time. It's even possible to write 8½ inch by 11 inch letters two-up by slitting an 18 inch form and overlapping the two parts in the printer, but the most you can gain, aside from wider margins, is about one or two more characters per line. And the handling costs are substantially greater.

In most installations, the type resembles a standard typewriter elite type, but the letter spacing is pica spacing at 10 characters to the inch. Line spacing on most printers is six to the inch. A handy forms ruler—in tenths, sixths, fourths and sixteenths, showing standard-form depths and pin-feed spacing—can be obtained from your forms supplier.

In planning a letter in two-up format, limit your longest line to 58 characters, including spaces. On a 14⅞ inch by 11 inch form, the size most commonly used for two-up letters, your copy will safely hit all of the 132 print positions and leave you side margins of at least half an inch.

Personalization, the most exciting capability of the computer letter, introduces some mathematical problems you'll have to keep in mind in planning your letter and writing your copy. In relatively simple programs for completely computer-printed letters and in all preprinted letters with personalized lines filled in by the computer, it is important to remember that the line length will vary in proportion to the length of each personalization. A last name with 15 letters, for example, will require 12 more spaces, or 1.2 inches more than a last name with just three characters. Some sophisticated letter-writing programs now in use by advanced computer-letter printing houses make it possible to even out a personalized line by drawing up short words from the beginning of the next line. Ask your supplier if he can do this and then plan your copy to make it easier for him. Extremely long variables, such as names of banks, corporations, etc., are less obvious when positioned close to the beginning of the last line of a paragraph.

If you're in the habit of emphasizing by underlining, better get used to using capitals—or just stronger copy. On preprinted copy, printed at the same time as the letterhead, it is possible to underline manually with a pen or cold type rule when preparing the copy for camera. Also avoid too-frequent use of such special characters as ampersands, dashes, parentheses, quotes, etc., which appear only on the high-speed printing train and consequently slow down the printing speed substantially.

4. HOW TO THINK ABOUT PREPRINTS AND FILL-INS.

Some of the early users of computer letters in large quantities originated the preprinted letter body with matched computer fill-ins. Carefully handled, the fill-in comes reasonably close to matching the computer type on the preprinted form, but in many cases the technique is easily detectable. There are a few valid reasons for using preprints rather than full computer-printed letters—and all of them have to do with saving money at the expense of quality:

a. When the letter is to be part of a heavy third-class mailing package and the fill-ins can be limited to the type currently approved by the Postal Service (recently the Postal Service has approved for third-class mailing fully computer-printed letters in which the variables are limited to address information: name of the addressee, street, city or state).

b. When the run exceeds 100,000 letters and consequently the saving in computer time is appreciable.

c. When the length of the copy makes it desirable to preprint the back side of the sheet or pages 2 and 3 of a four-page folder. In runs under 100,000 the cost of the necessary quality control on matching can often equal the extra computer time required for a complete printout. If the mailer specifies the use of one-time mylar ribbons for both preprint and fill-ins, the cost of these more expensive ribbons can come close to offsetting any time saving on the computer. The major disadvantage to using preprinted letter bodies is the requirement that all copy must be ready for forms printing at least a month before the mailing date. If the fill-ins are not clearly permitted for third-class mailings by current Postal Service rulings, additional delays can be caused by waiting for decisions on specific rulings.

5. HOW TO ESTIMATE COSTS.

In talking about computer costs, it is always necessary to spell out certain basic requirements. For one thing, the potential user must furnish the letter printer with compatible magnetic-tape records. If modifications have to be made in the tape, count on a substantial extra charge. The same thing is true of any radical change in standard letter format. Whenever you hear that something unusual can be done on the computer, you can be sure the price is also going to be unusual. Handling costs will also vary greatly. A standard two-up letter, folded to fit a monarch window envelope, inserted, sealed, stamped and mailed first class, will cost far less than an oversized form, folded to fit a special window envelope, matched with an addressed reply card or envelope, collated with enclosures, sorted, bundled and tied for third-class bulk mailing.

The cost of your forms can also vary substantially. Continuous forms are always relatively expensive in quantities of less than 100,000. Additional colors, special sizes and other extraordinary requirements add to the cost. But all of these factors tend to level out in very large quantities. A special form that may cost as much as 3.5 cents per letterhead in quantities of 25,000 may drop to as low as 0.4 cents per letterhead in runs of a million or more. Form prices, incidentally, are usually quoted in "sheets," and in two-up format this means two letterheads.

Handy rule-of-thumb for determining the approximate cost of printing a letter two-up on the computer: $1 per thousand per line of computer-printed material plus $5 per thousand for set-up time.

A 27-line letter with date, three-line address, salutation, close and two lines of title will cost approximately $35 per thousand by line count, plus $5 for set-up, or a total of $40, bringing the unit cost to $4 per letter. In quantities of 50,000 or more, this estimated price is likely to be quite a bit higher than you'll be charged. Special requirements can raise the cost far above the thumb-rule estimate.

6. GOOD COPY IS STILL THE KEY TO SUCCESS.

Thoughtful computer-letter printers are just as concerned about the productivity of their customers' efforts as the customers themselves. Though there may be a few cases in which the basic capability of personalizing the salutation and mentioning the addressee's name or city once or twice in the body has substantially increased the pull, the most successful computer letters are still those with sparkling direct mail salesmanship throughout the copy and in which the personalization is raised to a higher level. Sweet as a person's name may be to his ears, he is still more impressed when you talk in a friendly, personal way about his most recent purchase or contribution by amount and date, the name of someone else in his family (children's names and ages seem to be effective), the college he attended and his class, his children's colleges, the make and year of his car, his political party, his line of work, the giving record of his class or others in his city, etc.

This points up the great desirability of capturing on the magnetic-tape record all data which you believe will be most effective in motivating people. Above all, don't personalize just to show off what the computer can do. Keep your personalizations on the same level as you would include in a truly personal letter, dictated to a secretary.

7. SOME TECHNICAL KNOWLEDGE OF THE EQUIPMENT AND ITS LIMITATIONS CAN BE HELPFUL.

In early days of computer letters (less than four years ago!), data-processing technicians who were usually grounded in accounting applications assumed the leadership in producing the letters without much awareness of the creative side of direct mail. More recently these technicians have become proficient in direct mail techniques, whereas most direct mail professionals still have a great deal to learn about data-processing equipment. A good introduction to the computer is a paperback book, *What the Manager Should Know About the Computer,* published in 1969 by the Business Education Division of Dun & Bradstreet, Inc., New York, and there are numerous operating manuals published by the manufacturers of computers, optical-scanning devices, business forms and handling equipment, inserting machinery, labeling and stamping devices, etc. Learn to work with a forms ruler and invest in a pica typewriter with ten characters to the inch and six-lines-to-the-inch spacing to speed up copy preparation. Talk with your data-processing people about ways to use the computer to accumulate marketing profile data for analysis and projections, list selection, and merging and purging. The computer is a marvelous instrument in the hands of a virtuoso.

8. BE WILLING TO LISTEN AND EXCHANGE EXPERIENCES WITH OTHERS.

Ask your forms supplier and computer-letter printers for advice on how to solve your problems. One highly successful mail order operator, by disclosing the large amount of hand-matching required by his past procedure became the beneficiary of a custom-designed form which in one pass through the computer will produce a truly personalized letter, an attached coded order form, and a tipped-on mailing label and should reduce previous costs by as much as 50%.

Everyone connected with computer-letter production is learning something new every day. Sharing your experiences with others can result in evolutionary breakthroughs which will benefit all.

Andy Andrews' Tips

One of the pioneer users of computer letters—and a master at effective use of computer formats for fund raising—is Frances "Andy" Andrews, president of American Fund Raising Services of Waltham, Mass. In a presentation at a computer seminar,[6] he offered a number of helpful suggestions for the preparation of effective computer letters.

There are, he said, two basic requirements for an effective personal letter: (1) it must *read* like a personal letter, and (2) it must *look* like a personal letter. The most effective personal letters are those which come closest to sounding like those which a writer would send to his personal friends. The aim of the personal letter is to duplicate the feeling of true correspondence. And, to be most effective, the letter should be written within the framework of normal, everyday personal communications.

The printed letter has the tendency to make the reader feel like a part of a small and unknown audience—a mass audience, and the personal letter is naturally associated with personal correspondence. The maximum effectiveness of personal letters is achieved when the copy is written in easy, friendly, believable style and without the polished construction of mail order writing or the use of mail order phraseology. The personal letter should be written in the same style normally used by a good correspondent. No attempt should be made

[6]"The Computer Letter" by Frances Andrews. A presentation at The Computer Seminar presented by Benson, Stagg & Associates. New York, September 1967.

to write a literary epic, or to demonstrate a command of the English language. A letter which represents personal warmth pulls best.

All of the "high-pressure-short-of-breath" mail order copy must be avoided. You don't tell a friend that the supply is so limited that he must tear out the handy coupon and rush it back in a postpaid envelope.

Writing Personal Letters

Andy Andrews pointed out that considerable skill is required to write personal letters which are suitable for mass production. The highest degree of believability is achieved when the letter is written on a person-to-person rather than a "speech to a crowd" style. The success of the personal letter is not the fact that it is typewritten or even looks typewritten but that it appears to be written to one individual only. The most effective sentence in your letter will be the one which contains the reader's name, because the old adage has it that the most beautiful sound in the world is the sound of a man's own name.

There are other personalizing inserts in a letter that take it out of the mass production look. You can use dates, amounts of money, references, street addresses, towns, colleges, classes, years of graduation, membership categories, your last year's contribution and so forth. It only takes one personalizing insert to take a computer letter out of the form letter class. Copywriters today are making a tremendous error in overdoing the use of computer's ability to personalize. I recently reviewed one letter which had a girl's name mentioned eighteen times in 28½ lines. This is unnecessary.

The mailing of a carbon copy follow-up a few weeks after the original can add an authentic touch because the reader who thinks he may have received a form letter in the beginning now has his fears dispelled.

The Personal Look

Andy Andrews also gave some tips on making sure computer letters have a "personal" look. The most effective personal letters, he said, are those which come closest to looking like that which a secretary would type, process and mail. The normal procedure in producing the personal letter for true correspondence is to type the letter, have the writer sign it, enclose it in either an addressed or a window envelope, stamp or meter it, then drop it in the nearest out-basket or mail box. Following this "secretary prepared" rule of appearance, the letter would certainly be typed in its entirety. The body of the letter would not be processed on a printing press then filled in by a secretary. Fill-ins have a certain attention-getting value but the reader is rarely tricked into believing the letter he received was either actually typed or signed by the writer.

To gain the complete effectiveness of the personal letter approach, all finishing operations will be exactly the same as the secretary would use if she were typing and mailing one letter only. For example, a secretary would not go to the addressograph file, pull out one plate and address one envelope--she would type it. The users of personal letters will do the same unless window envelopes are used. A secretary would not rubber stamp the signature of a personally dictated letter. Her boss would sign it with pen and ink. In mass production letters it is now possible to print a signature which is almost indistinguishable from the pen and ink signature. Any slight reduction in drawing power is more than compensated by the cost.

If a reply mechanism is used, the secretary might use a typewritten No. 9 envelope; address that to the writer and affix a postage stamp. The use of small folders, research reports, reprints of ads or other material which are referred to in the letter and are normally available in any office or business firm can be enclosed with beneficial results. In fact it's almost a necessity with computer letters because of the short copy space.

The outside envelope can either be metered or stamped without appreciable difference in return.

Every deviation from the normal secretary-produced letter will result in a reduction in return, and every production technique which makes the letter look more like a secretary-produced letter will increase the returns. But with each of those small variations you must balance return against cost.

EXAMPLES OF COMPUTER FORMATS

A complete book could be prepared showing nothing but different varieties of computer formats—and chances are it would be even larger than this volume. The following examples are intended only to give an indication of the vast range of formats available.

Reader's Digest

The first big user of computer formats was Reader's Digest Association and many of the innovations in computer formats have been developed by this leading publisher.

Advance Notice: One of the unique computer formats used regularly by the Digest is an advance notice of a mailing. Since Reader's Digest frequently uses a sweepstakes promotion approach, these advance notices usually emphasize the coming opportunity to win something. A variety of notification formats are used. One, for example, involves a 7 by 10 inch card folded to 7 by 5 inches. It makes no bones about being a computer-generated format since sprocket holes on the outer edges are left just where they are and not trimmed away. Personalization is on both sides of the card. The outer surface has both a computer-printed address and a name imprinted in a box beneath the heading: "Important advance notification to . . ." On the back of the outer surface is a second name fill-in within a printed "Annuity Contract." Personalization inside the piece includes two mentions of the recipient's name plus additional personalization of the street address, community and state.

Sweepstakes Letter: Reader's Digest uses a variety of methods to attract attention to their sweepstakes contests. One is a letter with two numbered coupons attached. One coupon carries the recipient's full address and is used with a window envelope; the other coupon just carries the name. Personalization sprinkled through the letter includes the recipient's name, community, other nearby communities and a repeat of the "lucky numbers" on the coupons, which are perforated for detaching from the letter and returning for entry into the sweepstakes competition.

Passport Letter: Another sweepstakes approach was a printed letter which had a "Passport" booklet attached at the bottom of the first page. The booklet has been personalized with name and address on the cover (used for mailing address in a window envelope) and a fill-in inside the booklet which used the now-common Digest technique of mentioning not only the recipient but two other "neighbors" who were among the "special" people in the community receiving the promotion. Inserted within the booklet were three "travel checks"—personalized coupons bearing two "lucky numbers" each.

Long Letter: The efforts of Reader's Digest to add elements of variety to its frequent mailings is demonstrated by a 7½ by 21 inch computer letter mailed in a transparent envelope. At the top of the letter were two perforated sections containing six sweepstakes numbers. The first 7 by 1½ inch section was a "save for your records" section and included a specific reference to the computer preparation: "Customer's Name Recorded By: IBM 360 COMPUTER." The second 7 by 4 inch section was in a variety of bright colors and again carried the six sweepstakes numbers plus personalization with the recipient's name and address. The body of the letter carried personalization both by name and community references.

Customer Service Mailings: The Digest also makes good use of the computer to maintain fine relations with its customers. A typical mailing is an order duplication card-letter. This piece, mailed in a window envelope, consists of a 6 by 8 inch card, folded and perforated in the center so the bottom half could be used as a business reply card. The computer-typed message reads:

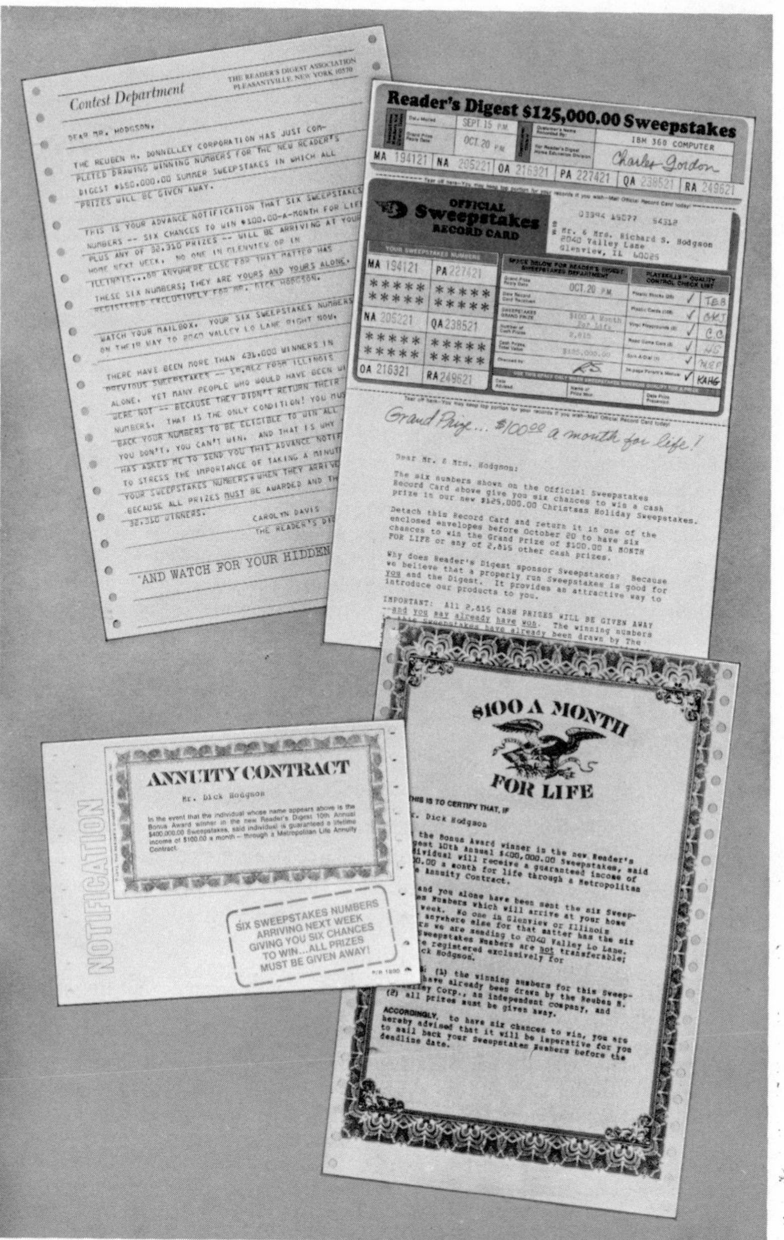

Contest Department

THE READER'S DIGEST ASSOCIATION
PLEASANTVILLE, NEW YORK 10570

DEAR MR. HODGSON,

THE REUBEN H. DONNELLEY CORPORATION HAS JUST COM-
PLETED DRAWING WINNING NUMBERS FOR THE NEW READER'S
DIGEST $150,000.00 SUMMER SWEEPSTAKES IN WHICH ALL
PRIZES WILL BE GIVEN AWAY.

THIS IS YOUR ADVANCE NOTIFICATION THAT SIX SWEEPSTAKES
NUMBERS -- SIX CHANCES TO WIN $100.00-A-MONTH FOR LIFE
PLUS ANY OF 32,310 PRIZES -- WILL BE ARRIVING AT YOUR
HOME NEXT WEEK. NO ONE IN GLENVIEW OR IN
ILLINOIS...OR ANYWHERE ELSE FOR THAT MATTER HAS
THESE SIX NUMBERS; THEY ARE YOURS AND YOURS ALONE,
REGISTERED EXCLUSIVELY FOR MR. DICK HODGSON.

WATCH YOUR MAILBOX. YOUR SIX SWEEPSTAKES NUMBERS
ON THEIR WAY TO 2040 VALLEY LO LANE RIGHT NOW.

THERE HAVE BEEN MORE THAN 436,000 WINNERS IN
PREVIOUS SWEEPSTAKES -- 18,462 FROM ILLINOIS
ALONE. YET MANY PEOPLE WHO WOULD HAVE BEEN WI
WERE NOT -- BECAUSE THEY DIDN'T RETURN THEIR
NUMBERS. THAT IS THE ONLY CONDITION! YOU MUS
BACK YOUR NUMBERS TO BE ELIGIBLE TO WIN ALL
YOU DON'T, YOU CAN'T WIN. AND THAT IS WHY
HAS ASKED ME TO SEND YOU THIS ADVANCE NOTIF
TO STRESS THE IMPORTANCE OF TAKING A MINUT
YOUR SWEEPSTAKES NUMBERS WHEN THEY ARRIVE
BECAUSE ALL PRIZES MUST BE AWARDED AND TH
32,310 WINNERS.

CAROLYN DAVIS
THE READER'S DI

AND WATCH FOR YOUR HIDDEN

Reader's Digest $125,000.00 Sweepstakes

Date Mailed	SEPT. 15 P.M.	Customer's Name Recorded By:	IBM 360 COMPUTER
Grand Prize Reply Date	OCT. 20 P.M.	For Reader's Digest Home Education Division	Charles Gordon

MA 194121 | NA 205221 | OA 216321 | PA 227421 | QA 238521 | RA 249621

Tear off here—You may keep top portion for your records if you wish—Mail Official Record Card today!

OFFICIAL Sweepstakes RECORD CARD

03394 15077 54312
Mr. & Mrs. Richard S. Hodgson
2040 Valley Lane
Glenview, IL 60025

YOUR SWEEPSTAKES NUMBERS

MA 194121	PA 227421
***** *****	***** *****
NA 205221	QA 238521
***** *****	***** *****
OA 216321	RA 249621

SPACE BELOW FOR READER'S DIGEST SWEEPSTAKES DEPARTMENT

Grand Prize Reply Date	OCT. 20 P.M.
Date Record Card Received	
Sweepstakes Grand Prize	$100 A Month For Life
Number of Cash Prizes	2,815
Cash Prizes Total Value	$125,000.00
Checked by	

PLAYSKILLS™ QUALITY CONTROL CHECK LIST

Plastic Blocks (28)	✓	TEB
Plastic Cards (108)	✓	CKJ
Vinyl Playgrounds (4)	✓	C.C.
Road Game Cars (4)	✓	HS
Spin-A-Dial (1)	✓	MEF
24-page Parent's Manual	✓	KAHG

Date Advised | Name of Prize Won | Date Prize Presented

Tear off here—You may keep top portion for your records if you wish—Mail Official Record Card today!

Grand Prize... $100.00 a month for life!

Dear Mr. & Mrs. Hodgson:

The six numbers shown on the Official Sweepstakes Record Card above give you six chances to win a cash prize in our new $125,000.00 Christmas Holiday Sweepstakes.

Detach this Record Card and return it in one of the enclosed envelopes before October 20 to have six chances to win the Grand Prize of $100.00 A MONTH FOR LIFE or any of 2,815 other cash prizes.

Why does Reader's Digest sponsor Sweepstakes? Because we believe that a properly run Sweepstakes is good for you and the Digest. It provides an attractive way to introduce our products to you.

IMPORTANT: All 2,815 CASH PRIZES WILL BE GIVEN AWAY --and you may already have won. The winning numbers in this Sweepstakes have already been drawn by The

NOTIFICATION

ANNUITY CONTRACT

Mr. Dick Hodgson

In the event that the individual whose name appears above is the Bonus Award winner in the new Reader's Digest 10th Annual $400,000.00 Sweepstakes, said individual is guaranteed a lifetime income of $100.00 a month — through a Metropolitan Life Annuity Contract.

SIX SWEEPSTAKES NUMBERS
ARRIVING NEXT WEEK
GIVING YOU SIX CHANCES
TO WIN....ALL PRIZES
MUST BE GIVEN AWAY!

$100 A MONTH FOR LIFE

THIS IS TO CERTIFY THAT, IF
. Dick Hodgson
the Bonus Award winner in the new Reader's
gest 10th Annual $400,000.00 Sweepstakes, said
dividual will receive a guaranteed income of
0.00 a month for life through a Metropolitan
e Annuity Contract.

and you alone have been sent the six Sweep-
es Numbers which will arrive at your home
week. No one in Glenview or Illinois
anywhere else for that matter has the six
rs we are sending to 2040 Valley Lo Lane.
Sweepstakes Numbers are not transferable;
e registered exclusively for
ck Hodgson.

: (1) the winning numbers for this Sweep-
have already been drawn by the Reuben H.
nnelley Corp., an independent company, and
(2) all prizes must be given away.

ACCORDINGLY, to have six chances to win, you are hereby advised that it will be imperative for you to mail back your Sweepstakes Numbers before the deadline date.

Reader's Digest was the first big user of computer formats.

Dear (name):

We appreciate your order for (product).

However, we recently filled a similar order and we do not know whether you intend to place another order for the same product. If you do, you need only initial the attached postcard and return it at our expense. Thank you very much for your interest—and for helping us do exactly as you wish!

Sincerely,
(signature)

Yes, please fill the additional order ....

Before the computer came along, it was generally considered uneconomical to make such follow-up mailings and a lot of strained customer relations developed. But with a computer checking every order, it is a simple matter to prepare a variety of standard formats which can be used with computer personalization to eliminate order difficulties in advance.

Sweepstakes Booklets: Computer-personalized booklets are used frequently for Digest promotions. These multi-page promotion pieces serve as the vehicle for entry in Digest sweepstakes. A typical example is a 7 by 3½ inch booklet titled "Book of Sweepstakes Certificates." The booklet had a die-cut cover with a window to expose the recipient's name and address for mailing. Inside were a series of certificates, each personalized in some way. The center pages of the booklet also carried the letter describing the sweepstakes and the product offer. It was personalized with name, address reference, and mention of similar products previously purchased. The back page of the booklet carried a repeat of the six sweepstakes numbers and full name and address personalization.

Longines-Wittnauer

Combination letter-order forms with computer personalization have become almost a trademark of Longines-Wittnauer. The letters carry a variety of personalization features—name, address, previous purchases, club membership, etc. But their most distinguishing feature is an endless variety of tip-ons and perforated sections. Some examples:

Perforated Certificates: A four-page letter, with computer fill-ins on pages one and four features a colorful certificate at the top third of page one. It is perforated and contains a space for affixing a "Free Record Album" stamp, which was tipped to page one. Personalization of the certificate includes the name and address plus a short blurb, with copy such as "The Hodgsons are to be among the few in the Glenview area to now receive this invitation" or "This confirms the Hodgsons of Glenview are entitled to an insider discount." Other varieties of this certificate-letter are shown in the illustration on page 000.

Tipped-on Certificates: In a somewhat similar vein, Longines uses a tipped-on certificate, rather than the perforated variety. The certificate, tipped to the top of the letter, is perforated for removal. Both the certificate and the letter carry computer personalization.

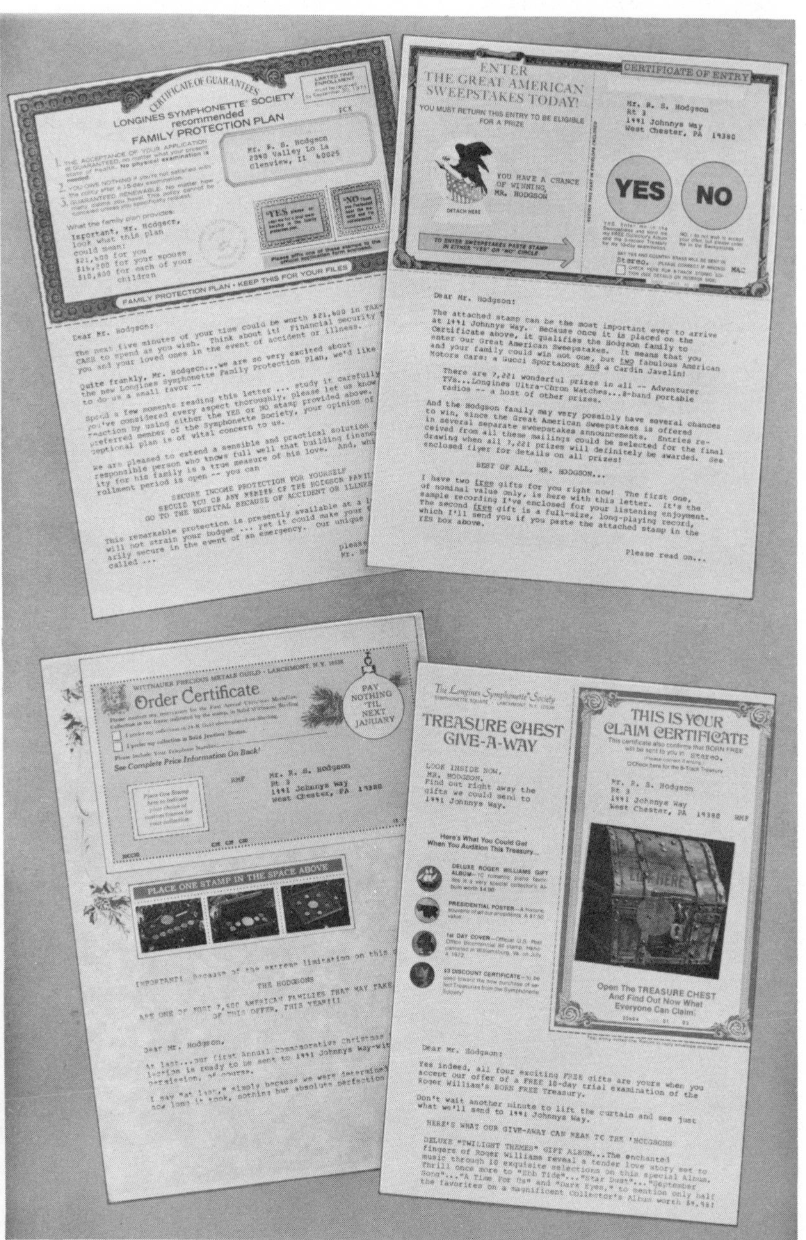
CERTIFICATE OF GUARANTEES

LONGINES SYMPHONETTE® SOCIETY recommended FAMILY PROTECTION PLAN

Mr. R. S. Hodgson
2340 Valley Lo La
Glenview, IL 60025

Important, Mr. Hodgson,
look what this plan
could mean:
$21,800 for you
$16,200 for your spouse
$10,800 for each of your
children

FAMILY PROTECTION PLAN • KEEP THIS FOR YOUR FILES

Dear Mr. Hodgson:

The next five minutes of your time could be worth $21,800 in TAX-
CASH to spend as you wish. Think about it! Financial security
you and your loved ones in the event of accident or illness.

Quite frankly, Mr. Hodgson...we are so very excited about
the new Longines Symphonette Family Protection Plan, we'd like
to do us a small favor --

ENTER THE GREAT AMERICAN SWEEPSTAKES TODAY!

YOU MUST RETURN THIS ENTRY TO BE ELIGIBLE FOR A PRIZE

YOU HAVE A CHANCE
OF WINNING,
MR. HODGSON

DETACH HERE

TO ENTER SWEEPSTAKES PASTE STAMP IN EITHER "YES" OR "NO" CIRCLE

CERTIFICATE OF ENTRY

Mr. R. S. Hodgson
Rt 3
1441 Johnnys Way
West Chester, PA 19380

YES

NO

Stereo.

MAC

Dear Mr. Hodgson:

The attached stamp can be the most important ever to arrive
at 1441 Johnnys Way. Because once it is placed on the
Certificate above, it qualifies the Hodgson family to
enter our Great American Sweepstakes. It means that you
and your family could win not one, but two fabulous American
Motors cars: a Gucci Sportabout and a Cardin Javelin!

There are 7,221 wonderful prizes in all -- Adventurer
TVs...Longines Ultra-Chron Watches...8-band portable
radios -- a host of other prizes.

And the Hodgson family may very possibly have several chances
to win, since the Great American Sweepstakes is offered
in several separate sweepstakes announcements. Entries received from all these mailings could be selected for the final
drawing when all 7,221 prizes will definitely be awarded. See
enclosed flyer for details on all prizes!

BEST OF ALL, MR. HODGSON...

I have two free gifts for you right now! The first one,
of nominal value only, is here with this letter. It's the
sample recording I've enclosed for your listening enjoyment.
The second free gift is a full-size, long-playing record,
which I'll send you if you paste the attached stamp in the
YES box above.

Please read on...

WITTNAUER PRECIOUS METALS GUILD • LARCHMONT, N.Y. 10538

Order Certificate

PAY NOTHING 'TIL NEXT JANUARY

See Complete Price Information On Back!

Mr. R. S. Hodgson
Rt 3
1441 Johnnys Way
West Chester, PA 19380

PLACE ONE STAMP IN THE SPACE ABOVE

THE HODGSONS

Dear Mr. Hodgson,

The Longines Symphonette® Society

TREASURE CHEST GIVE-A-WAY

LOOK INSIDE NOW,
MR. HODGSON.
Find out right away the
gifts we could send to
1441 Johnnys Way.

Here's What You Could Get When You Audition This Treasury...

DELUXE ROGER WILLIAMS GIFT ALBUM

PRESIDENTIAL POSTER

1st DAY COVER

$3 DISCOUNT CERTIFICATE

THIS IS YOUR CLAIM CERTIFICATE

Mr. R. S. Hodgson
Rt 3
1441 Johnnys Way
West Chester, PA 19380

Open The TREASURE CHEST And Find Out Now What Everyone Can Claim.

Dear Mr. Hodgson:

Yes indeed, all four exciting FREE gifts are yours when you
accept our offer of a FREE 10-day trial examination of the
Roger William's BORN FREE Treasury.

Don't wait another minute to lift the curtain and see just
what we'll send to 1441 Johnnys Way.

HERE'S WHAT OUR GIVE-AWAY CAN MEAN TO THE HODGSONS

DELUXE "TWILIGHT THEMES" GIFT ALBUM...The enchanted
fingers of Roger Williams reveal a tender love story set to
music through 10 exquisite selections on this special Album.
Thrill once more to "Ebb Tide"..."Star Dust"..."September
Song"..."A Time For Us" and "Dark Eyes," to mention only half
the favorites on a magnificent Collector's Album worth $4.98!

Longines-Wittnauer constantly sends out a variety personal certificates.

Hidden Message Tip-Ons: Another type of tip-on favored by Longines is a colorful miniature folder tipped to a certificate-letter. By peeking inside the sealed folder, the recipient discovers the special "goodies" he will receive as a bonus from Longines. Typical folders appear as a treasure chest, whose lid must be lifted, or a door which must be opened.

Double Card: Another certificate format involves the use of a 10½ by 8½ inch card, perforated in the center. The right half is a personalized certificate to be used as an order form. The left half is a computer-printed letter. Points of personalization include a salutation plus such body copy as:

> There's a very down-to-earth reason for making this offer to you rather than to certain other *Pennsylvania* residents.
>
> That's why a *Hodgsons'* membership would be so welcome to us.
>
> Now we'd be honored to name you as one of our 'paid' *West Chester* area representatives on the Preview Club panel.

Other techniques: In addition to letters, Longines-Wittnauer uses computer personalization in a variety of different ways. For example, a certificate with personalized name and address may be tipped to a folder and computer letters—complete with certificates—have been used as wrap-arounds for Longines catalogs.

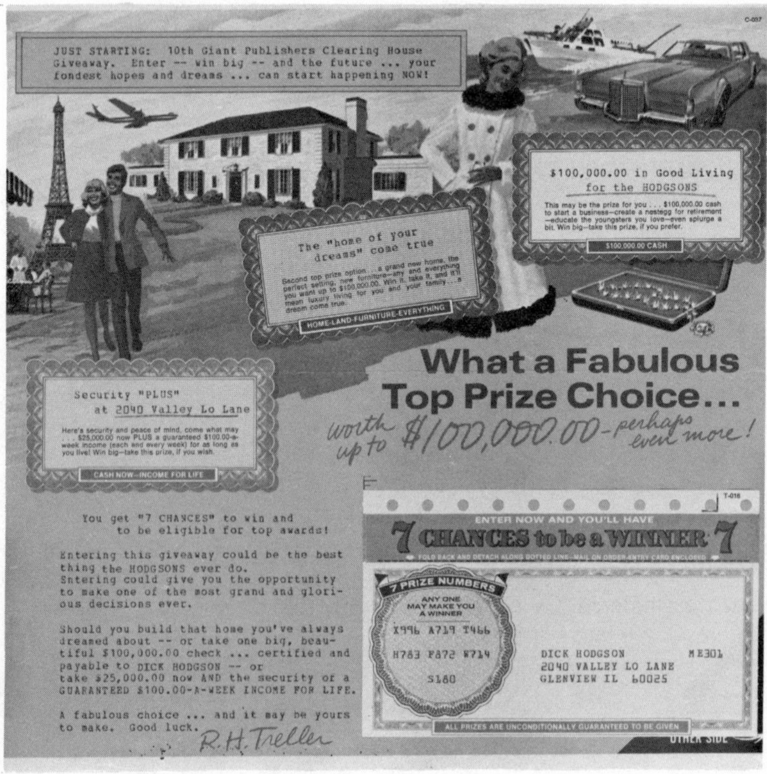

Publishers Clearing House

Another major user of computer formats is Publishers Clearing House, which generally uses an over-size horizontal mailing envelope loaded with an eclectic mixture of enclosures. At least two of the pieces are generally personalized by computer. For example, an illustrated letter, with tipped-on certificate-mailing label is personalized in a variety of spots with such copy as: "$100,000 in Good Living for the HODGSONS" . . . "Security 'PLUS' at 2040 Valley Lo Lane" . . . "Entering this giveaway could be the best thing the HODGSONS ever do." Enclosed with the letter is a memo with spot personalization, including name fill-ins on illustrations of prize checks. (See page 746.)

McCall's

The personalized certificate-letter gets a slightly different handling by *McCall's* magazine. Eight 5 by 2½ inch certificates with various values are attached to a two-page 6 by 10½ inch letter. Each of the certificates carries full name and address personalization. The letter also is computer personalized. *(See illustration, page 748.)*

Other Certificate Letters

Since the combination letter-certificate is one of the most versatile of the computer formats, a variety of examples are shown on the following pages.

Unique Personalization

While the ability of the computer to personalize letters with name, address and references to previous purchases is rather obvious, there are many other items which can be extracted from data files for personalization. Bankers Life & Casualty Co., for example, has utilized car owner lists and utilized the information about car ownership to add a personal touch to its letters. Copy for one letter, for example, started out: "You've read how hospital costs in the *(city)* area have been skyrocketing—like they have all over the country. The American Hospital Association says that the average cost of just a single day in *(city and/or state)* hospitals is now over *(actual dollar amount)*—and going up!" A few sentences later, the letter adds: "It's a dangerous financial situation to be in, *(name of recipient)*—especially if you're buying your new *(make of car)* on time, or have other financial obligations that you'd find hard to handle if you *also* had to shell out money for hospital bills."

McCall's

Mrs. R. S. Hcdgscn
2C4D Valley Ic Street
Glenview, IL 60C25

DETACH CERTIFICATES AND MAIL IN ENVELOPE PROVIDED

Dear Mrs. Hodgson:

Last year, thousands of doubting Thomasinas (see previous Winners List enclosed) entered the McCall's Sweepstakes, thinking they didn't have a chance to win.

BUT THEY DID WIN

And so can you -- because every one of the 25,023 prizes in the exciting new $175,000.00 McCall's "Diamond Jubilee" Sweepstakes will definitely be given away, Mrs. Hodgson.

In fact, one of the following prizes may already belong to you, and all you need do is claim it! If you're a winner, we'll send your prize direct to your home! Look at what you may have already won:

- The Grand Prize of $25,000.00 cash!
- A fully-equipped '72 Ford Pinto or $3,500 cash!
- A magnificent GE color TV console!
- A new Singer sewing machine with cabinet!
- McCall's cased set of "Diamond Trio" lipsticks!

Plus -- some wonderful Bonus Prizes, too, Mrs. Hodgson! Five stunning, $1,000 Diamond Dinner Rings will be given away in a separate random-prize drawing, and one of them may be yours! And if you reply by August 25, 1972, you may also win McCall's special "Early Bird" Bonus: $1,000.00 extra cash!

* * * *

WHAT'S IMPORTANT IS...
HOW YOU CAN WIN!

What must you do to win? Simply detach the eight personal Certificates made out in your name, and mail them in one of the enclosed envelopes right away. Yes, it's really that easy, Mrs. Hodgson.

OFFICE OF THE DIRECTOR
COLUMBIA RECORD CLUB
TERRE HAUTE, INDIANA 47808

Richard Hodgson,
we want you!

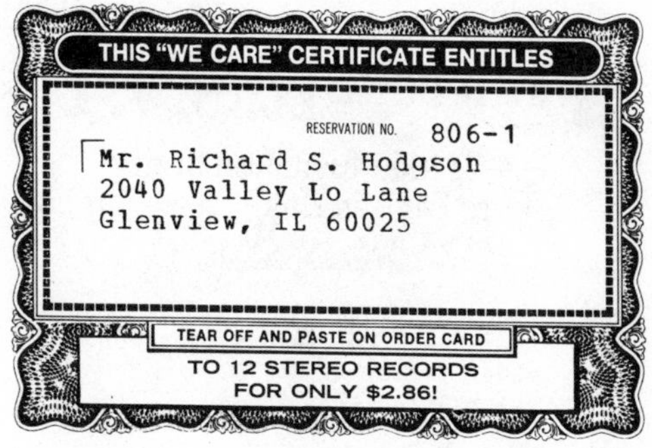

THIS "WE CARE" CERTIFICATE ENTITLES
RESERVATION NO. 806-1
Mr. Richard S. Hodgson
2040 Valley Lo Lane
Glenview, IL 60025
TEAR OFF AND PASTE ON ORDER CARD
TO 12 STEREO RECORDS
FOR ONLY $2.86!

PLUS an AM/FM radio for only $1.00 more!

We want you so much
we've put together this special
RICHARD S. HODGSON "WE CARE" PACKAGE
with your choice of up to
$81.76 worth of new records
-- for only $2.86 plus,
if you wish, a beautiful
AM/FM radio for just
$1.00 more!

Dear Mr. Hodgson:

We'd like a chance to show you how much money the Columbia Record Club can save you on the very latest hit records. To prove conclusively that you can't buy records for less regularly in any store in Glenview.

So, we will send you a special Richard Hodgson "We Care" Package. It will have your name on the outside. And inside ... any 12 records of your choice -- at a savings of up to $78.90 at regular Club prices, and if you wish, the handsome personal AM/FM radio shown on the next page. Truly a great bargain.

But bargains are what the Columbia Record Club is all about. As a member, you'll keep getting fantastic

10/1

Terre Du Lac **R.S.V.P.** Lake Development

THIS OFFER IS NON-TRANSFERABLE

A Cordial Invitation from
Terre Du Lac Lake Development

to enjoy Free Lodgings and Free Recreational Facilities for the 3 days and 2 nights selected by

12 0088925 A1
Mr. & Mrs. Richard S. Hodgson
2040 Valley Lo St.
Glenview, Ill. 60025

☐ Yes, we definitely want to come! Please confirm our reservations, as follows:

Arrival Date: 1st Choice:______
2nd Choice:______

_____ Adults and _____ Children

Phone us at:__________

YOUR RESERVATIONS WILL BE CONFIRMED BY MAIL OR PHONE, WITHIN SEVEN DAYS. IN ACCEPTING THIS FREE OFFER, YOU ASSUME NO OBLIGATION WHATEVER.

FILL IN, DETACH & MAIL IN POSTPAID ENVELOPE TODAY!

THIS OFFER IS NON-TRANSFERABLE

A

You're More Than Just
Another Name To Us, Mr. & Mrs. Hodgson

Though we don't know you personally, research tells us that you'll be more than impressed by what you'll discover at beautiful Terre Du Lac. You see, if we can have you spend a few days - free - as our guest, there's a good chance you'll choose to live your gradual retirement years down here in the clear and tranquil Ozark Foothills.

The enclosed folder helps you visualize the stability, investment potential and relaxing beauty of Terre Du Lac. Yet, we know you are not about to invest <u>in anything</u> by mail!

This is why we want you - and your family - as our guests at Terre Du Lac: To see our lovely "Lake-Land".

Important: We promise you that our guided tour of this sound investment in recreation and enjoyable living will not intrude on your 3-day, 2-night "Mini-Vacation" at Terre Du Lac. Indeed, you may make side trips to St. Louis or even down into the Ozarks.

To take advantage of this free vacation offer:

1. Study the calendar on the back of this letter and pick the open date most convenient to you. (Please also include a second choice.)

2. Fill in the attached R.S.V.P. ticket above and return in the postpaid envelope. We'll confirm your reservation for the number specified in your party right away.

(over, please)

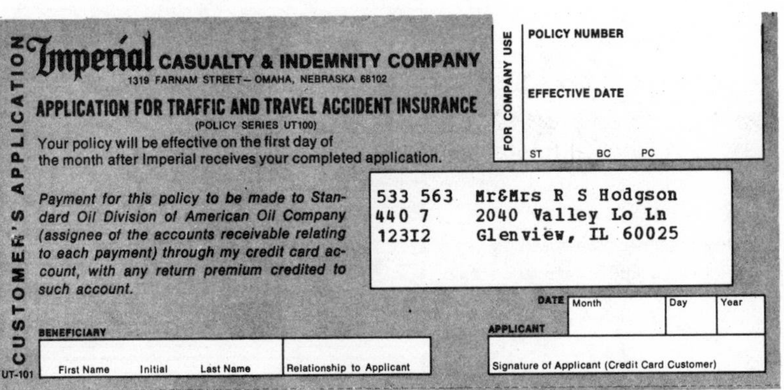

CUSTOMER'S APPLICATION

Imperial CASUALTY & INDEMNITY COMPANY
1319 FARNAM STREET— OMAHA, NEBRASKA 68102

APPLICATION FOR TRAFFIC AND TRAVEL ACCIDENT INSURANCE
(POLICY SERIES UT100)

Your policy will be effective on the first day of the month after Imperial receives your completed application.

FOR COMPANY USE
POLICY NUMBER
EFFECTIVE DATE
ST BC PC

Payment for this policy to be made to Standard Oil Division of American Oil Company (assignee of the accounts receivable relating to each payment) through my credit card account, with any return premium credited to such account.

533 563 Mr&Mrs R S Hodgson
440 7 2040 Valley Lo Ln
123I2 Glenview, IL 60025

DATE Month Day Year

BENEFICIARY
First Name Initial Last Name
Relationship to Applicant

APPLICANT
Signature of Applicant (Credit Card Customer)

UT-101

Mr&Mrs R S Hodgson
2040 Valley Lo Ln
Glenview, IL 60025

Dear Mr&Mrs R S Hodgson:

You're a modern person who believes in modern conveniences. Believing as you do, one of the conveniences you've enjoyed is your Standard Oil Credit Card.

It's only fitting that the credit card that has made it convenient for you to travel should now make it convenient for you to have modern travel protection.

For just $10 semi-annually -- automatically charged to your Standard Oil Credit Card -- you can get $25,000 worth of protection against traffic and travel accidents. Can you imagine a better bargain during these inflationary times?

Think for a minute —

Your membership in the Amoco Motor Club shows that you recognize the fine benefits offered to members.

You wouldn't hesitate about spending $10 for a dinner-for-two at your favorite restaurant.

You've probably spent $10 on "impulse". Now spend $10 on a carefully planned program of protection!

Read the enclosed folder to see exactly how valuable this protection really is. You're covered while you're driving or riding in any private passenger car -- while you're a passenger in a fare-paid vehicle (air liner, ocean liner, bus, train, taxi or airport limousine) -- while you are a

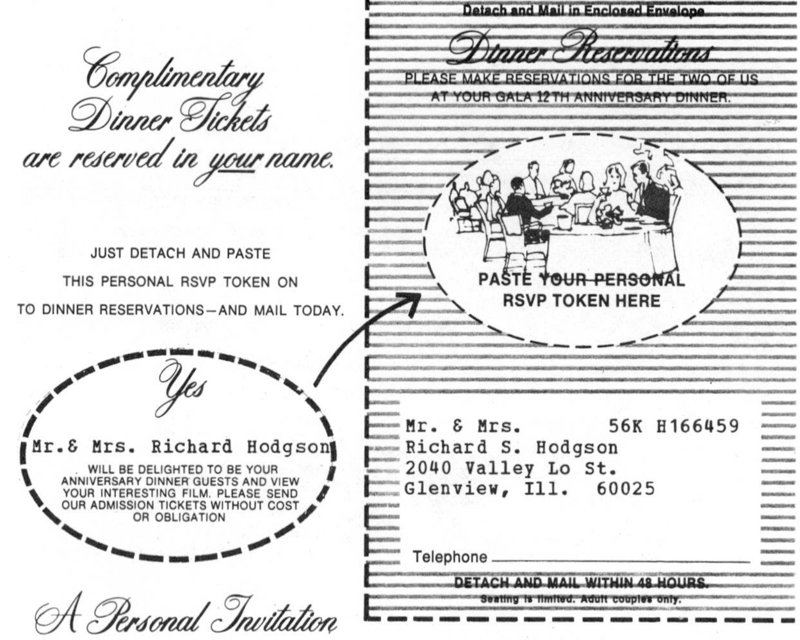
Complimentary Dinner Tickets are reserved in your name.

JUST DETACH AND PASTE THIS PERSONAL RSVP TOKEN ON TO DINNER RESERVATIONS—AND MAIL TODAY.

Yes

Mr.& Mrs. Richard Hodgson

WILL BE DELIGHTED TO BE YOUR ANNIVERSARY DINNER GUESTS AND VIEW YOUR INTERESTING FILM. PLEASE SEND OUR ADMISSION TICKETS WITHOUT COST OR OBLIGATION

A Personal Invitation

Detach and Mail in Enclosed Envelope

Dinner Reservations

PLEASE MAKE RESERVATIONS FOR THE TWO OF US AT YOUR GALA 12TH ANNIVERSARY DINNER.

PASTE YOUR PERSONAL RSVP TOKEN HERE

Mr. & Mrs. 56K H166459
Richard S. Hodgson
2040 Valley Lo St.
Glenview, Ill. 60025

Telephone ______

DETACH AND MAIL WITHIN 48 HOURS.

Seating is limited. Adult couples only.

Dear Mr. & Mrs. Hodgson:

Your names were given to me as a couple who might enjoy a sparkling evening as our Dinner and Movie guests.

There is no cost. The whole evening is yours to enjoy from beginning to end - with our compliments.

The occasion? It's GAC Properties' nationwide 12th Anniversary celebration - and we'd like you to help us celebrate.

You'll be treated to a full course dinner, given an interesting land sales presentation and see a fascinating color film showing Florida living, vacationing and investment opportunities that may enrich your lives.

I'm holding seats for you, Mr. & Mrs. Hodgson, but seating is limited and dinner arrangements must be completed. So please return above coupon at once. I'll mail your tickets as soon as I hear from you.

Sincerely,

Dinner Reservations

P.S. Don't miss this entertaining and rewarding evening. You're sure to have a wonderful time. Mail your Reservation today!

NOT TRANSFERABLE

WEEK'S FREE TRIAL INVITATION

YOURS ARE COMING SOON!

amazing new $30-look JB Shoes

QT3 00180720- MMQ1

You have been selected!

Mr. R. S. Hodgson
2040 Valley Lo
Glenview, Ill. 60025

HOW MANY PAIRS?	STYLE and COLOR		Write in SIZE see guide below	WHAT WIDTH? C, D or E
	BUCKLE STRAP BOOT	BROWN 94311		
		BLACK 94312		
	WING TIP BROGUE	BROWN 94321		
		BLACK 94322		
	MONK STRAP	BROWN 94331		
		BLACK 94332		
	MOC-TOE OXFORD	BROWN 94341		
		BLACK 94342		
	STRAP SLIP-ON	BROWN 94361		
		BLACK 94362		

WARREN, PENNA.:

MR. BLAIR: Those handsome new "John Blair" polymeric Shoes with PVC sole and heel sound terrific but you'll have to let me "walk test" them first. Send the 2 pairs I've marked for a week's Free Trial. If they're all you say after 1 week, I'll send only $15.95 for BOTH pairs, plus postage and handling, or return them and owe nothing.

P.S. If you send payment now, we pay all postage and handling costs. Your money instantly refunded if you aren't pleased. Shu-S2

PLEASE INITIAL HERE: ____________

SIZE GUIDE: WE CARRY ALL THESE SIZES: 7, 7½, 8, 8½, 9, 9½, 10, 10½, 11, 12

DETACH HERE AND MAIL TODAY!

Dear Mr. Hodgson:

Within the next few days, I am going to send two pairs of these amazing new JB Shoes to your Glenview address for a week's Free Trial!

I'm sending them, Mr. Hodgson, because words, pictures and even the actual sample enclosed cannot begin to tell <u>all</u> you should know about these fine shoes!

They are totally new and different from any you may now own! You must see, feel and actually wear them to appreciate their true value for they give you revolutionary new advantages ordinary Shoes never could ...

1. Uppers are constructed of an amazing new man-made polymeric material that neither scuffs nor cracks like leather. Shoes <u>stay</u> soft, supple and need no "breaking-in" -- feel like old favorites first time you wear them!

2. No more 40¢ Shoe-shines! Instead a damp cloth restores their permanently built-in finish to its full luster in just seconds!

3. Polyvinyl soles are waterproof and <u>guaranteed</u> to outwear uppers or you get new Shoes FREE!

4. They look like expensive $30 Shoes!... yet can be yours for under $8 a pair!

Picture <u>yourself</u> in these fine Shoes when yours come, Mr. Hodgson! Wear them anywhere, in any weather a full week Free! <u>Then</u> if you decide you

Shoe Headquarters for more than 9 Million Customers all over U.S.A.

Postagram Postagram Postagram Postagram Postagram

POSTAGRAM

FROM: HILLEGOM, THE NETHERLANDS
TO: ASHBURNHAM, MA U.S.A.

MRS. JOHN F. HESS
61 RUSSELL HILL RD
ASHBURNHAM, MA 01430

SPECIAL OPPORTUNITY.

HAVE ASSEMBLED OUTSTANDING MONEY-SAVING COLLECTION OF TOP QUALITY DUTCH BULBS.

GUARANTEED TO GROW IN ASHBURNHAM.

WAS ABLE TO CONCLUDE QUALITY PURCHASE ON SIX SPECIAL VARIETIES AND CAN OFFER FOR FALL DELIVERY TO **61 RUSSELL HILL RD** AT VERY ADVANTAGEOUS PRICE.

ENCLOSED BROCHURE DESCRIBES THIS SPRING GARDEN COLLECTION. **NOTE SPECIAL FREE BONUS.**

IF YOU ORDER BY SEPTEMBER 30, YOU CAN OBTAIN ALL 200 BULBS FOR JUST $19.95. SAVINGS OF 39%. TRULY AN OUTSTANDING BUY. **LESS THAN 10¢ PER BULB.**

AM PARTICULARLY HAPPY WITH DARWIN HYBRID TULIPS IN COLLECTION.

WILL DO ESPECIALLY WELL IN MASSACHUSETTS.

ALSO WAS ABLE TO ARRANGE SPECIAL PURCHASE BRECK'S COLOSSAL DAFFODILS. A LONG-TIME FAVORITE IN **FITCHBURG AREA.**

USE ENCLOSED ORDER FORM TO RESERVE YOUR SPRING GARDEN COLLECTION. SEND NO MONEY NOW. YOU'LL BE BILLED WHEN BULBS ARE DELIVERED AT PROPER FALL PLANTING TIME IN **WORCESTER COUNTY.**

SUPPLY LIMITED. ADVISE ORDERING PROMPTLY SO YOU CAN ENJOY THIS COMPLETE COLLECTION NEXT SPRING IN

HESS GARDEN.

WILLEM H. DEE
MANAGING DIRECTEUR
BRECK'S HOLLAND B.V.

Personalization by area can be useful in giving a mailing an "insider" feeling. The Franklin Mint, for example, has used computer letters with reference to the specific number of people in a state who are collectors of a relatively scare item (i.e. "You're one of just seven people in the state of Oklahoma who owns . . .").

Peoples Life Insurance Company effectively utilized a computer letter to sell student estate plans. The copy, prepared for Peoples by Guy Yolton, read:

> Right now, while your son (*name*) is attending college at (*name of college*), you can provide for his future security under circumstances that will never be so favorable again.
>
> Our Student Estate Plan—which (*son's name*) can qualify for now—as a (*year in college*)—provides a basic insurance program of $10,000 of convertible coverage at an annual premium of only $40. That's just $4 per thousand per year, a low rate that won't change until (*son's name*) is 28, when the policy converts to a permanent plan.
>
> Furthermore, there's no medical exam required now or at the time of conversion. And there are many other features to the Plan, such as the Additional Insurance Privilege. This guarantees options to purchase more insurance so that the policy can grow with the family it protects, providing coverage up to $30,000 if desired. What a wonderful way to insure (*son's name*) "insurability" for the rest of his life.
>
> Of course, this is probably not the first student insurance offer to arrive at the (*last name*) household. But chances are, none you have received, offer —at these low costs—such unusually liberal options extending beyond (*son's name*) graduation.
>
> The enclosed brochure includes details, plus an application form. Since (*son's name*) must sign the form, why not fill it out now so it will be ready next time he's home? Or to present delaying his coverage, you might send it to him today for his signature.

Sunset House

One of the first to personalize catalogs through computer-printed wrap-arounds or inserts was Sunset House. A 1968 cover wrap carried a letter starting on the back cover:

> Dear (*name*) Family:
>
> Tell me if I'm right, will you? I have an idea that nowhere in (*city*)— not even in (*county*)—is there a place where you can find as many unusual items of merchandise as there are in this little Sunset House Catalog.
>
> Right? Well, I hope so . . . because we do try! We really search the globe to discover new ideas that will make life a little easier and a little more fun for the (*name*) family.

Spencer Gifts

Another catalog house, Spencer Gifts, used a catalog wrap-around to tie-in with a sweepstakes promotion. The front cover had a computer-printed heading: "I Would Be Delighted To Send $25,000 or $10,000 or $2,500 to *(name)*." Below the heading was the following letter:

Will we add this name and this cash prize
(name) *(address)* $25,000
to this list of big prize winners . . .?
(list of names and addresses of previous winners)

> These lucky people . . . plus over 22,000 more . . . have already won prizes in previous Spencer Gifts sweepstakes. Is it the *(name)* turn to win a prize? All you have to do to find out is mail back your Round the World entry ticket opposite page 16. We will be adding 1033 more people to our ever-growing list of prize-winners . . . and we would be so delighted if one of the new names we added to this winners list was *(name)* of *(city)*.

Helen Gallagher-Foster House

A gatefold cover wrap was used by Helen Gallagher-Foster House for its catalog. The outside front cover had a personal salutation and mention of the community in copy, along with a personalized "Gift Certificate Claim Form." On the inside gatefold, the personalization was added to the illustration of a page from a simulated savings account book, showing monthly $100 deposits plus interest. The recipient's name was at the top of the bankbook page and inserted in the center of the page with the note: "After five years, *(name)*, you will have accumulated $6,780.01." The gatefold also contained two additional personalized "entry tickets." As an added note of personalization, the back cover of the wrap featured a bonus offer of personalized four seasons address labels, with an illustration of one of the labels with the recipient's name and address imprinted.

Another Helen Gallagher-Foster House catalog wrap contained a tipped-on "sweepstakes book." The booklet had a die-cut front cover through which the name and address of the recipient appeared. Inside were 16 computer-printed pages, with a letter running on right-hand pages and each lefthand page representing pages of a bankbook, showing the steady 10-year accumulation of the $100 a month being offered as top prize in a sweepstakes. Several of these pages had computer personalization (i.e. "Just look, *(name)*, your bankbook is now worth $10,160.54. should you win the grand prize."). There was, of course, spot personalization of the letter as well as the bankbook.

Hanover House

Another method of personalizing catalogs was used by Hanover House. Here, the catalog wrap was a reply envelope and order form. The recipient's name was already imprinted on the order form, which formed the back of the wrap. The reply envelope was the front of the wrap and contained a short letter on what would become the back of the reply envelope. It included an illustration of a package with the recipient's name and address imprinted. The letter read:

> Dear *(name)* Family:
>
> You have been chosen to receive a prize or free gift in The Hanover House triple bonus sweepstakes. This is a rare opportunity because very few families in *(city)* are eligible to enter this sweekstakes.
>
> We have assigned you the triple bonus number *(number)*. If this matches any of the winning numbers on the reverse side of this envelope, you have already won a valuable prize or will get a free gift.
>
> How happy your family will be to see a new Plymouth in front of *(address)* or a swimming pool in the back yard . . .

United States Purchasing Exchange

Even though it regularly uses envelopes for mailings, United States Purchasing Exchange has effectively used catalog overwraps to carry a computerized message. A gatefold cover on one catalog, for example, did triple duty. The front page had an illustrated letter with computer fill-ins to personalize the announcement of a sweepstakes. The gatefold contained the "Official Sweepstakes Certificates," each personalized with the last name of the recipient, with the name also included on matching stubs. The back of the wrap-around was also the back of an order blank and carried the name, address and customer code of the recipient, thus effectively keying orders.

Literary Guild

Syndicated mailings are a natural for computer personalization since this technique permits easy insertion of the name of the cooperating mailer. Literary Guild, for example, used a certificate-letter for a tie-in promotion with department stores. The heading on the certificate read:

> *(Name)*, you've been missing many important books in the months since you left the Book Club Family. On behalf of the Literary Guild, *(name of store)* invites you to now consider NO TIME LIMIT MEMBERSHIP.

Below the certificate was a letter, which began:

> It's true, *(name)*—because we recognize you as an old friend, we now invite you to renew membership on exclusive, "NO TIME LIMIT" terms. Once again you may enjoy the convenience of charging your purchases to your account at *(name of store)*.

Newsweek

A promotion letter from *Newsweek* magazine made effective use of the match code, which is almost automatically a part of a computerized mailing. This four-page letter had a standard center spread, but both localized and personalized copy on pages one and four. Consider this page one copy used for recipients in the Chicago area:

No one else in the Chicago
area has this number: *(match code)*
Call 800-243-6000 (free) at
any time of the day or night
and . . .

> . . . get 30 weeks of
> Newsweek for only
> $3.99 simply by giving
> this number *(match code)*

Dear *(name):*

A computer can do almost anything.

I repeat: *almost.*

It can devise a "match code" like the one above—that excludes the 6,711,200 other people in the Chicago area and identifies you, *(name)*, so positively that you can . . .

1. Pick up the phone and dial—absolutely free—800-243-6000.
2. When our special operator answers, do not give her your name and address. Instead read off your match code *(number)*—that's all!

A computer will then take your match code and, in microseconds, find out that *(number)* is the code for *(name)* of *(address)*.

And—presto!—Newsweek will be delivered to your home for 30 weeks at $3.99. It's the fastest way to order Newsweek. (The second fastest way is to send in the reply form I've enclosed.)

What else can a computer do?

Working with the information I feed into it, a computer can calculate what the probabilities are that you are one of the 453,711 in Chicago who get their world news from the *American*—or Huntley-Brinkley on WMAQ-TV . . . or what the chances are that you get most of your news of Chicago from the *Tribune* or from Fahey Flynn's late news on Channel 7.

The computer can tell me—from the list on which I found your name—that your education and income set you apart from the general population and make you a prime prospect for everything from magazines to mutual funds.

Business Week

Another computer format with growing popularity is the computer-personalized booklet. One user, for example, is *Business Week.* The cover of a 4 by 5 inch self-mailer booklet featured a picture of Colonel Sanders and was in the format of a miniature of a regular Business Week cover. A die-cut window at the bottom of the booklet cover showed a paragraph from the first page of a 12-page miniature letter bound into the booklet:

> Colonel Sanders seized an opportunity when he saw it.
>
> How many opportunities are you aware of these days,
>
> *(name)*?

A window in the back cover of the booklet contained the name and address of the recipient. This information was printed on a business reply card order form which constituted pages 11 and 12 of the booklet's body. The letter inside the booklet contained spot personalization with name and city of the recipient.

Redbook

Similar booklets—produced by Promotion Mail Associates of Farmingdale, N. Y.—were used by *Redbook* as part of a sweepstakes promotion. One, for example, had a die-cut front window in the shape of the "pot" at the end of a rainbow. From the heading of a letter inside the booklet, copy read:

> *(NAME)*
>
> You may have already won $25,000 in cash at the end of a $111,000 Prize Rainbow in Redbook's "Carefree Living" Sweepstakes!

The back cover of this 4 by 6¾ inch booklet had three die-cuts—one showing the address; the others showing computer-printed "lucky numbers."

A larger 7½ by 6½ inch booklet was used by Redbook for another sweepstakes promotion. Like the smaller booklet, it was designed to mail without an envelope. The name and address imprint showed through a front cover die-cut while another name and address imprint from a tipped-on order envelope showed through the back cover window. Copy on the eight inside pages was extensively personalized with spot use of name, address and the sweepstakes numbers.

Weekly Reader Record Club

Both the name of the parent and child were computer printed to show through the window of a computer-printed booklet used by Weekly Reader Record Club. In a 3¾ by 5 inch booklet, a front cover window contained the first paragraph from a letter inside:

(Parent's name), we'd like to send *(child's name)*—

FREE the Walt Disney record album, "Snow White!"

Both the child's name and the parent's name were spot printed throughout the body copy and the back cover showed the imprinted address: *"Child's name & Parents."* A larger 7½ by 6¼ inch computer-printed booklet for the same promotion used similar personalization. In this case, the window had a simple to-the-point message:

An enchanting Walt Disney record for *(child's name)* FREE.

Boise Cascade Properties

In a mailing for Boise Cascade Properties, the computer was used to print an entire invitation and attached, perforated reply card. The 5 by 10 inch card, which folded to 5 by 5 inches, had a standard four-color format on the outside, but the entire inside was computer printed:

> You and Mrs. *(name)* are cordially invited to join a small gathering of your neighborhood friends at a dinner party to be held at *(name and address of restaurant plus two optional dates)*.
>
> After you enjoy a pleasant dinner and a new color film, we will take a few moments to tell you about a new concept in family fun being created now by Boise Cascade Properties for this community.
>
> Of course, we will pick up the check, so we hope both of you will decide to come for an enjoyable evening.

Here are some examples of computer-personalized booklets.

Time

One of the most simple of all computer formats was a certificate-letter used by *Time* magazine. The 5 by 7 inch sheet, which folded to 5 by 3½ inches had just a 78-word computer-personalized letter and a certificate order form at the bottom, with name and address imprinted by computer. Copy read:

> Dear Mr. *(name)*:
>
> Just ask any of our readers in *(city)* about this special subscription offer—all the TIME you like for only 15 cents a week—and they'll tell you it's quite an invitation. Because TIME is regularly 29 cents a week by subscription, 50 cents at the newsstand.
>
> Try TIME—and see for yourself why there's no better news at any price.
>
> Simply use the pencil to fill in the number of weeks on the savings certificate below. We'll bill you later.

Also enclosed was a brief copy four-page 5¼ by 6¾ inch folder, a business reply envelope and one of those tiny little red pencils for which *Time* mailings have become famous over the years. The only copy on the white 5¾ by 4 inch window mailing envelope was *"An Invitation"* printed in wedding script.

Customer Goodwill Mailings

A variety of computer-generated formats have become the backbone of goodwill mailings to customers by auto dealers. Letters, service reminder cards, "birthday" (of the car's purchase) greetings, holiday greetings and gift coupons all are being personalized with the name of the buyer, the dealer and the salesman. For example, a typical anniversary letter from a Ford dealer reads:

> A Free Oil Change, *(customer's name)* . . .
> is our way of saying "Happy Second Anniversary" and to assist you in keeping your car properly serviced. Just present this letter to our Service Manager when you come in for your 24th-month service and inspection.
>
> Many of our customers, like yourself, who purchased a car from us two years ago are now seriously asking the question: "Should I keep my car or take advantage of its high trade-in value and buy a new one?"
>
> Your car will never have more trading value than it has TODAY. We are selling the finest new vehicles in the industry and I want to be sure you have an opportunity to test-drive one.

Please ask for me while your car is being serviced. We want to do all we can to guarantee your satisfaction, and trust you will permit *(dealer name)* to continue serving your automotive needs.

Very truly yours,
(name of salesman)

One of the more interesting computer formats used as an auto dealer's goodwill mailing was a 5 by 7 inch pocket edition of Rand McNally Interstate Highway Atlas. A letter on page one of the 20-page atlas read:

Let me say thank you for your recent purchase, *(name)*.

I have made arrangements with Rand McNally and Company to send you this Interstate Highway Atlas. It's a small token of my appreciation for your purchase a few months ago.

If you would like an additional map for the second car in the family, stop in, ask for me and I will try to obtain one for you.

Sincerely,
(salesman's name)

P.S. If a friend or relative would like an Atlas, have them ask for me.

Mead Dijit

One of the newer computer letter processes is a development called Mead Dijit. It involves a complicated process of placing droplets of ink on paper. It has two major advantages over more conventional computer printing—it is extremely fast and it permits the use of a wide variety of different styles and weights of type.

Laser Printing

Following close on the heels of Mead Dijit is the laser printing process utilizing an IBM 3800. Like Mead Dijit, it permits use of different styles, sizes and weights of type. While slower than the Mead process, laser printing has a number of advantages—particularly a wider printing width and greater flexibility.

At this writing, a number of other laser printing systems are being offered. However, all of the new "ink jet imaging" systems probably represent only the first generation of what may very easily become the printing system of the future. A good source of information about the latest developments in this growing field is the printer of forms who plays a vital role in the creation of direct mail pieces which are then personalized by jet imaging.

Chapter 28

DIRECT MAIL ENCLOSURES

SINCE direct mail is so completely flexible, there are hundreds of different types of items which can be enclosed with letters—or used separately. Most of them, however, fall within five basic categories—folders, broadsides, booklets, brochures and circulars. While there is often confusion in spelling out the differences between some of these types of printed material, a good guide has been offered by the Direct Mail/Marketing Association, in its book, *The Story of Direct Advertising:*

FOLDERS—

Folders are the most commonly used of all printed advertising forms, because they are comparatively inexpensive and most flexible. Size, shape, and style are unlimited. In format, *folders* bridge the gap between *personal letters* and the *booklet.* That is the best rule to remember when considering the use of folders. Use them to precede and follow the more elaborate forms, books, and presentations. Use them for the short, direct, printed messages that hammer home selling points in a quick, concise manner. Use them for single shots or for a series. Use them when the sales message should have a compact form that the reader can grasp quickly. Inject them with novelty and color, but never at the expense or interruption of the natural flow of the advertiser's story to the prospect. Folders can be used alone, or in conjunction with letters and other forms, to inform, instruct, persuade, remind, or bring home the order.

BROADSIDES—

Broadsides are large folders, used advantageously *when the average folder is not adequate* to convey the story and a booklet is not the form needed or wanted; *when a smash effect is sought,* particularly at the beginning of a campaign, or for a special announcement, or for a special emphasis of certain appeals; *when a large surface is required* for pictorial and bold copy expression; *when the psychology of bigness is desired.*

In designing broadsides, capture interest right at the beginning, and make sure that the interest is continued throughout, without confusion. Although large, a broadside should be designed for easy handling by the reader, with a physical makeup and layout that will lead the reader through in definite sequence quickly and impressively. Avoid smashing effects that confuse. They don't sell the reader. Broadsides are sometimes envelope-enclosed, but more often are self-mailers.

BOOKLETS—

From the brief explanations covering the use of folders and broadsides, it is quite evident that booklets should be used when these two other formats are not adequate to convey the longer story, or lack sufficient prestige value or appropriateness for certain printed promotion jobs.

The uses of booklets are almost as great and flexible as are the functions of their smaller brother, the folder. Usually designed for thorough reading and study rather than "flash" sales presentations, booklets must be attractive, interesting, and easy to read.

Booklets have a multiplicity of purposes. Booklets are to be used *when the story is lengthy; when it cannot be accomplished by a folder* or other lesser presentation; *when dignity of approach is desired; when desired elaborateness does not reach the "brochure" classification.*

Catalogs, house organs, sales booklets, instruction books, directories, price lists, etc., are some of the functional purposes of booklets (and books).

BROCHURES—

Brochures are for the glamorous phases of direct advertising and should be used *when an elaborate presentation* of company, product, or service is called for; *when there is a need or desire to go beyond the ordinary booklet and broadside format* for richness, power, and impressiveness in size, illustration, color, materials, bindings, etc.; *when the presentation of a story must match the bigness of the selling job,* must reflect the stature and dignity of the company responsible for its production.

CIRCULARS—

The circular, or flyer, is the usually inexpensive form to adopt when you want to get across a strong message in a flash. Circulars are generally flat pieces up to a size that stops at the broadside category. The circular provides an opportunity for big, smash headlines, black and white or full color. It can tell its story quickly, "loudly," and inexpensively.

"Standard" Formats

While the flexibility of direct mail encourages constant departure from any standardized formats, there is a handful of basic formats which are common. Most of them result from economies offered by certain "cuts" from paper stock, limitations of presses, the sizes of standard envelopes, and extended use considerations.

Like letterheads, enclosures are frequently 8½ by 11 inches in size. They may, however, be 11- by 17-inch folders or 22- by 17-inch broadsides folded to 8½ by 11 inches or 5½- by 8½-inch or 2⅔- by 8½-inch pieces folded from an 8½- by 11-inch sheet. Another very common unit is a 5- by 8½-inch sheet folded to four 2½- by 8½-inch pages. This makes an effective unit for enclosure in a standard No. 9 or No. 10 envelope. For No. 6¾ envelopes, a common enclosure is the 3⅛- by 6¼-inch folder. When folders (or single sheets) are designed for use as a busi-

I am pleased to send you this complimentary copy of Crain's Chicago Business together with an invitation to see this unique local business newspaper every week at a savings of 20%.

Rance Crain
Editor-in-chief

For 38¢ a Week
Crain's Chicago Business
Gives You In-Depth Coverage of:

- Retail Trade
- Manufacturing
- Banking, insurance and real estate
- Advertising and marketing
- Stock trades and tips
- Federal/state legislation affecting business
- Energy and the environment
- Earnings and dividends of leading Chicago firms

You are one of a select group of Chicago-area business executives receiving a copy of *Crain's Chicago Business* with our compliments.

This is your opportunity to check out *Crain's Chicago Business* with no obligation, at no cost. The risk is on us. We aim to prove that this new newspaper has the timely news, the hard data and the depth of insight into Chicago business that you can't find anywhere else. Or as fast!

If you like what you see and read, keep *Crain's Chicago Business* coming. It's easy. Just return the attached money-saving card today. We'll make sure you have your weekly *Crain's Chicago Business* there when you need it.

Return this card and save

$6.00

Pay just $24 for 52 weeks of the Chicago business news you need.

☐ **YES, KEEP CRAIN'S CHICAGO BUSINESS COMING.** Please enter my one year (52 issues) subscription for only $24—that's a 20% savings off the regular $30 rate and $15 off the $39 newsstand price.

☐ Payment enclosed ☐ Bill me ☐ Bill Company ☐ Charge it

SA1

☐ VISA ☐ Master Card—Interbank # ________

Card # ________ Expiration Date ________

Signature ________

Name ________ Title ________

Company ________

Nature of Business ________
☐ Home
☐ Business Address ________

City ________ State ________ Zip ________

☐ Send information on your group rate (40% off) for 5 or more subscriptions.

☐ I would prefer not to receive information or advertising by mail from companies not affiliated with Crain Communications Inc.

Not only did Crain Communications write top executives to subscribe to their new Chicago Business *but they sent three sample copies to prove its value.*

ness reply card, the maximum size is $3\frac{9}{16}$ by $5\frac{9}{16}$ inches. Larger units require postage at the straight first-class rate rather than the post-card rate.

Another consideration which often leads to use of a standard size is when the same material—artwork, engravings, typesetting, etc.—is planned for use in some other type of printed material. Many companies, for example, design direct mail pieces which are later incorporated into a catalog—or vice versa. In such cases, it is common to stick to the 8½- by 11-inch page size. This same size usually permits material to be quickly adapted to publication advertising.

FOLDERS

Of all types of enclosures, the folder is by far the most commonly used—and most versatile of formats. While the standard 11- by 17-inch sheet folded to 8½ by 11 inches, the 8½- by 11-inch sheet folded to approximately 5½ by 8½ inches, the 5- by 8½-inch sheet folded to 2½ by 8½ inches, and the 6¼- by 6¼-inch sheet folded to 3⅛ by 6¼ inches are most common, thousands of other variations are used with success by direct mail

Because of the tremendous variety of folder formats, it would be impossible to describe every possibility. However, a review of some typical direct mail folders will give a general idea of the directions which might be considered.

Invitation Format

A popular variation is the invitation, which usually has a somewhat formal appearance and is frequently personalized with the name of the recipient.

Crain's Chicago Business mounted a well-thought-out campaign when it was first launched. In addition to the four-page, invitational announcement of its debut, (8½ x 11 sheet folded twice) they sent out the 8½-by-11-inch sheet shown on page 766. This told a select group of Chicago-area business executives that they would actually receive a copy. As a follow-up three additional sheets were sent out, two of them offering a handsome poster of Chicago.

Discount Store News used a somewhat similar invitation format. The piece was printed in black on a 10½- by 8½-inch sheet of white laid stock, folded to four 5¼- by 8½-inch pages, then folded to 5¼ by 5¼ inches to fit a standard No. 5½ baronial envelope. Copy appeared only on the front cover and page three.

Page two and the back cover were blank. The invitation language on the cover was in formal style:

G. M. Lebhar and A. D. Friedman,
Publishers of Chain Store Age
are pleased to extend
to
(name handwritten)
an invitation to become
a
Charter Subscriber
to
Discount Store News
A new biweekly newspaper covering
discount store retailing

The American Museum of Natural History used a nonpersonalized invitation format to secure new members. An 11⅝- by 8½-inch sheet was short-folded to 6 by 8½ inches, with the front cover slightly narrower than page three, which carried a

The President and Trustees of
The
American Museum of Natural History
cordially invite you
to enjoy the privileges of
Associate Membership
and to accept
a full year's subscription to
Natural History Magazine

R. S. V. P.
Card Enclosed

Privileges of membership
are described inside

vertical band of gold ink along the right-hand edge which showed alongside the cover. The short fold helped to give the piece added dimension, even though the same gold ink was used as a second color on the cover itself.

Short Folds

The technique of short-folding a piece can be highly effective in direct mail enclosures. Most frequently it is used to gain added color without added cost on the cover of a folder. A typical procedure is to print a job in two colors but use a different second color on each side of the sheet. Then, when the piece is short-folded, the cover carries not only its own second color, but benefits from the second color of the inside spread as well. Additional color can be obtained through the use of duplex stocks, which are one color on the front and another color on the back. Appleton Coated Paper Co., Appleton, Wisconsin, has a set of interesting samples of special effects that can be achieved through trick folding of duplex stock; the set can be obtained by writing to the company.

Even full-color pieces can benefit from special folding. An example of a particularly effective short-folded piece is a 22½- by 12-inch broadside mailed by *American Heritage.* It was first folded to 11⅜ by 12 inches and then folded to 6 by 12 inches. This produced a 5⅜- by 12-inch cover with two edges protruding at the right. A bold red band was printed along the right edge of the cover. The first protrusion was white, while the second protrusion carried a bold band of blue. While copy was in invitation style (inviting enrollment in a Junior Library series), the piece used such lavish process color that it was far more dramatic then the more formal invitation formats described previously.

Another short-fold technique was used by A. B. Dick Company for a product bulletin. This time the short fold was a 2¾- by 8½-inch flap folded inside a four-page 8½- by 11-inch folder. The extra flap was used to call special attention to outstanding product features. A somewhat similar technique was used by The University of Michigan Press, which folded a 12- by 22-inch sheet to 8½ by 12 inches, which yielded a 5- by 12-inch flap to carry special copy.

Peek-Through Illustrations

This same University of Michigan Press piece also took advantage of the opportunity to add full color to a two-color envelope by the "picture window" technique. This is a favorite device of mail order advertisers and has wide application for all other types of direct mail. In this mailing, which promoted a book, *The Indian Journals,* a full-color painting of an Indian warrior peeked through a special acetate window on the face of the envelope (the reverse side was used for addressing).

There are hundreds of variations of this peek-through technique. International Graphic Society, for example, used a three-window envelope. On the front of the No. 68 catalog envelope were two windows—one for the address and another for a full-color illustration of the product being promoted—a series of books. Both of these items were on a perforated order card facing the front of the envelope. A third window on the back of the envelope showed two prehistoric birds, which appeared as a full-color illustration on the folder enclosed with the mailing. The back of the envelope carried the teaser: "What was this weird creature's amazing secret? See inside."

Many direct mail advertisers use the picture window as an economy device. The same envelope can be used for mailings for a variety of products with illustrations from the folders, showing through the envelope windows, converting this standard envelope to one "tailored" for each mailing.

Smaller Folders

Smaller folders are generally chosen when they will be used with a variety of different mailings or when they will accompany mailings which have a purpose other than that of the enclosure. For example, many utilities enclose house-organ folders with their monthly statements. Major telephone companies regularly use this public relations medium. New England Telephone & Telegraph Co., for example, encloses a four-page, 3- by 6-inch, black-on-colored-stock folder called *Between Ourselves* with each statement. Illinois Bell Telephone Co. has one of the most outstanding miniature house organs, a four-page 5⅞- by 6⅝-inch, black-and-white folder called *Telebriefs.*

Industrial Marketing used a four-page 5¼- by 7-inch sheet, folded in half to fit a standard window envelope. The brown-on-white folder described the contents of a book being offered as a subscription premium.

Harper and Row regularly uses six-page 3- by 5¾-inch folders for mail order book promotions. These are frequently printed in colored ink on colored stock. The cover and full inside spread usually promote the featured book, while the back cover and sometimes the front of the first fold promote additional books.

Built-in Reply Devices

Many folders contain built-in reply devices. One of the more common techniques is to use a double post card as an enclosure. The front cover and first inside page carry promotional copy, while the second inside page is the order form and the back cover is the face of the reply card. Time, Inc., uses this technique to produce "tag-along" promotion pieces, which are sometimes sent to subscribers of a given publication offering other publications. The colorful cards are 6 by 4¼ inches. Three examples are shown below.

Carte Blanche used a 7½- by 13-inch sheet folded to 3¼ by 7½ inches to promote group accident insurance. Half of the three-color piece (black and red on yellow stock) contained promotional copy, while the other half could be torn off and used as a business reply "envelope"—it contained a gummed strip at one edge so it could be refolded to form a 3¼- by 7½-inch open-end envelope after application information had been filled in.

Die-Cut Folders

Two types of die-cutting are frequently used to add drama and impact to direct mail folders. The most common technique is to cut some kind of "window" in the cover of the folder so a feature on

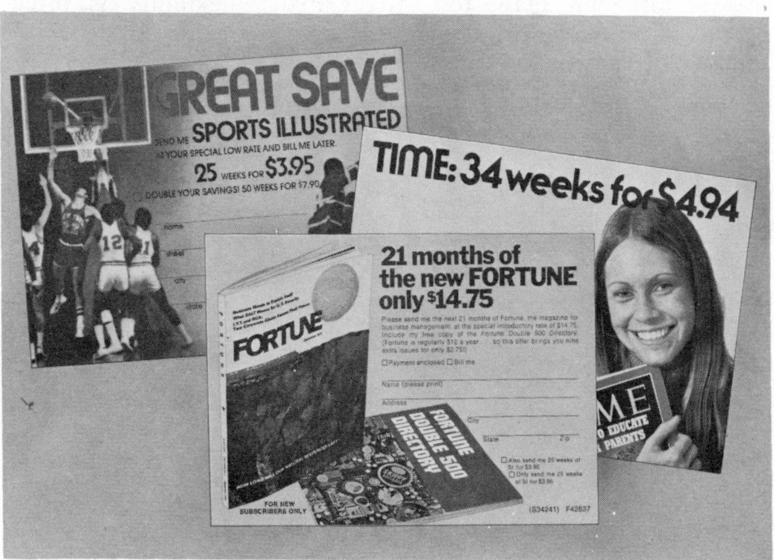

Many publishers, like Time, Inc., use "tagalong" promotion pieces similar to the above.

the inside spread will show through. Like the use of short folds, this type of die-cutting is used primarily to obtain color on the cover without the expense of additional press runs.

Another type of die-cutting is to trim the piece in the shape of a product or some featured item. This is often done after folding, although sometimes only the front cover is die-cut and then "framed" with the edges of the uncut third page. A typical outside die-cut piece is the Windsor Press folder illustrated next. It was a simple two-color job cut in the shape of a slice of bread.

BROADSIDES

While broadsides have long been used as mailing pieces in themselves, their popularity as enclosures is a relatively recent development. Broadsides have become particularly popular in the promotion of books, but they are also used by just about every type of direct mail advertiser.

The most common size is 17 by 22 inches, although many other sizes are also popular. Most frequently, the 17- by 22-inch broadside is folded to either 8½ by 11 inches or 5½ by 8½ inches, although here, too, direct mail's flexibility is often brought into play, with short folds used frequently to deliver a number of variations.

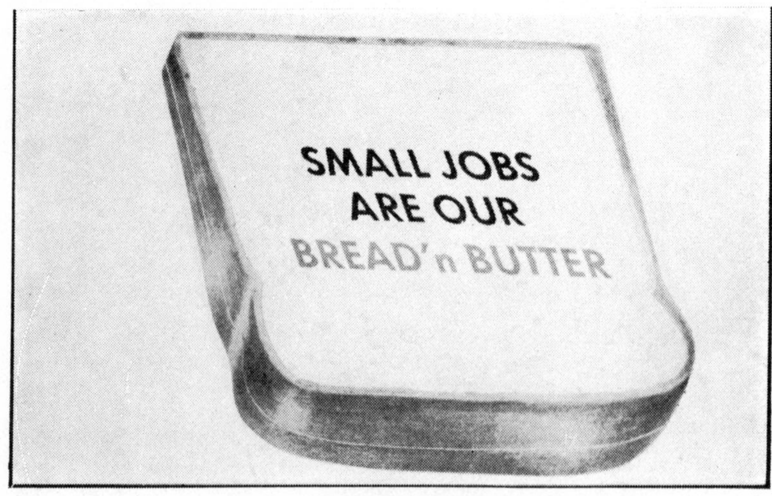

A clever die-cut piece sent out by Windsor Press to get more printing jobs.

Advantages of Broadsides

The major advantage of a broadside is its capability of handling large illustrations and masses of color. For many promotion purposes, this permits the advertiser to show his product in actual size or at least to use an illustration large enough to reveal important details which would be "hidden" in smaller illustrations.

Another advantage is on the cost front. With the broadside, no gluing, stapling, or trimming is required. This not only permits an initial saving in production costs, but it often yields a piece which is readily adaptable for a variety of different mailings. Broadsides are often designed so they can be mailed in a number of different envelope sizes. For example, a basic 17- by 22-inch piece may be folded to 8½ by 11 inches for mailing in a No. 9 booklet envelope (8¾ by 11½ inches), folded once again to 5½ by 8½ inches for mailing in a No. 6 booklet envelope (5¾ by 8⅞ inches), or given a letter fold to 3⅔ by 8½ inches for a regular No. 9 or No. 10 envelope.

Time-Life Books

The effectiveness of broadsides for colorful presentation is demonstrated by mailings to promote various Time, Inc. books. So effective have been these broadsides that advertisers in many fields have used them as a format guide for their own direct mail enclosures. Typical examples:

World Library—A 19- by 30-inch full-color broadside on coated stock was used to promote subscriptions to the World Library series. The giant-size sheet was folded four times to 8¼ by 10 inches. The large size permits display of an actual-size book opened to a typical spread plus a number of additional spreads shown in 3- by 4½-inch illustrations. Since the books have 8½- by 11-inch pages, these illustrations show the contents in graphic detail. The first fold across the bottom of the sheet is only 3 inches, so when the piece is opened to the full spread, the majority of the display is seen with a dramatic 3- by 30-inch strip presenting a display of six covers of representative titles in the series.

Treasury of American Folklore—An even larger broadside—16 by 39 inches—was used to present this popular book. The large dimensions not only permitted full-size display of a typical spread from the 8½- by 11¼-inch book, but 22 additional large-size, full-color illustrations from the book. Only three folds were used to yield an 8½- by 10-inch piece mailed in an 8¼- by 11-inch envelope. Since one of the chief features of the book being promoted was the lavish use of color to illustrate its contents, the colorful broadside stressed this point quickly and dramatically.

The Epic of Man—To promote this volume, *Time, Inc.* used a four-fold, 16¼-by 23½-inch broadside, designed for mailing in a No. 6 booklet envelope. Opening the first two folds produced an unusual 8- by 16½-inch piece. As usual, the book was presented in an actual-size reproduction, plus 22 addi-

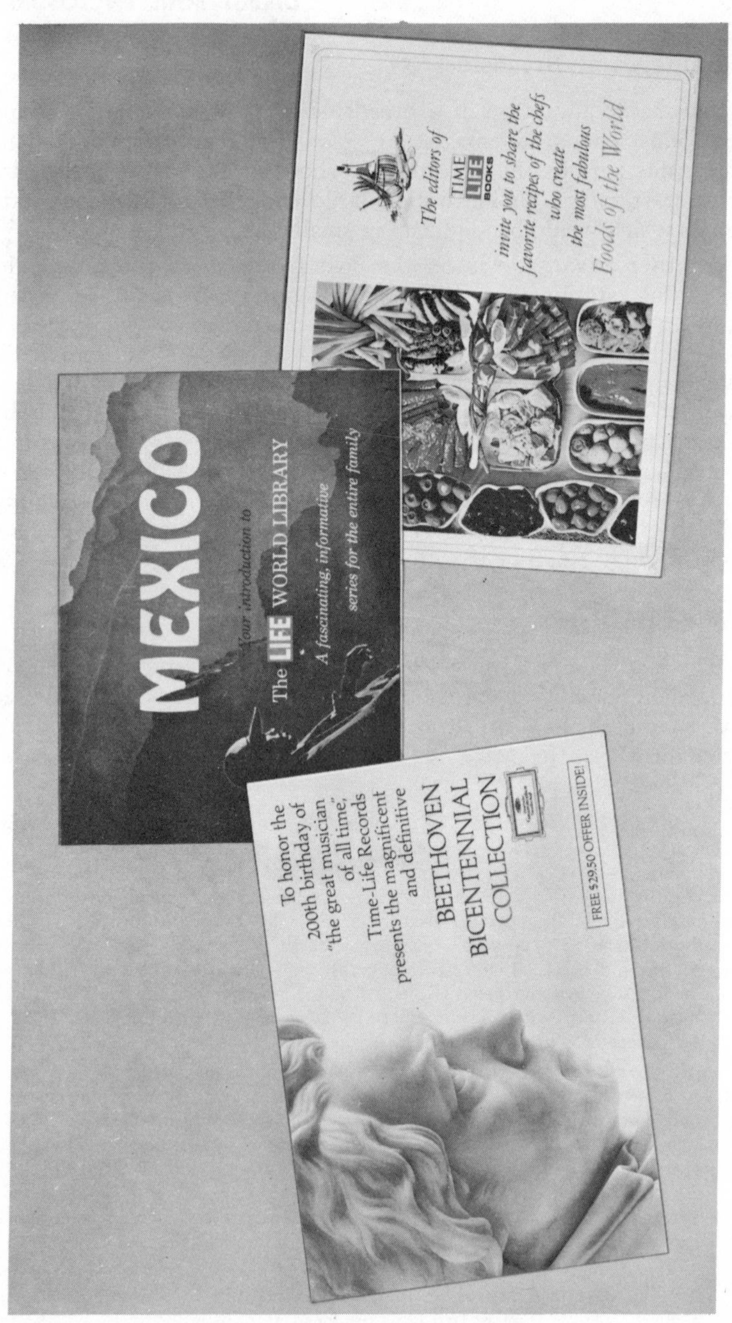

Noteworthy examples of Time, Inc.'s beautiful and effective four-color broadsides.

tional color illustrations. The long vertical folds served a functional purpose, dividing the full spread into three parts which were used to describe the three sections of the book.

The Kremlin—A 19½- by 23-inch broadside, three-folded to 5¾ by 9¾ inches, was used effectively to portray the beauty of this volume, published by the New York Graphic Society. Because of the quality of this book, it would have been difficult to portray it adequately without the large-size illustrations permitted by a broadside. For this piece, traditional folding was used—first to 11½ by 19½ inches, then to 9¾ by 11½ inches, and finally to 5¾ by 9¾ inches.

Birds of the World—A product-sampling was used for mailings to promote this Golden Books volume. A 15- by 20-inch broadside showed four actual pages from the book, with a 2½-inch strip running along the bottom of the sheet to provide added descriptive copy. A simple two-fold was used to obtain a 7½- by 10-inch piece.

The Story of Great Music—One of the most spectacular of all Time, Inc. mailings was used to promote Time-Life Records' "The Story of Great Music." The giant broadside opened to a full 22 by 34 inch poster. The upper quarter of the "poster" carried a giant headline—"Yours To Enjoy for 10 Days Free—This exciting introduction to great Baroque Music." The center half of the piece was a large bleed illustration of the book-record package being promoted. The bottom quarter contained copy in two columns of large type. The back of the "poster" also utilized large illustrations and big type to present various details about the offer.

Capitol Record Club

Another broadside technique was used by Capitol Records. This 14½- by 15-inch sheet was three-folded to 5 by 7¼ inches, with each of the 12 sections created by the creases treated as a separate page. The broadside promoted a special record sale, with from two to five albums illustrated and described on each of the "pages." Most mail order advertisers feel this broadside presentation technique is superior to a bound booklet, since the recipient can be exposed to so much of the promotion story at a single glance.

Sloan-Ashland

Broadsides are used regularly by Sloan-Ashland of Chicago to present products for mail order sale. To promote Bell & Howell motion-picture cameras and projectors, for example, Sloan-Ashland produced a colorful 16- by 23½- inch piece. This mailer, which was offered to a variety of different businesses to mail over their own lists, was three-folded to 6 by 8 inches. The "covers" contained teaser copy and illustrations. The first fold opened to show the product in use—a family and guests enjoying home movies. The second fold, opening to 11¾ by 16 inches, showed the camera and projector in full-color illustrations, which were large enough to reveal all important product details. The full spread promoted special

What Baroque Music is... and why music lovers find it so delightful

"BAROQUE" is the name given to a whole school of gay, fantastic music composed in the 17th and 18th Centuries—when the kings and queens of opulent Europe had their own court musicians and composers to create diverting music for their intimate drawing room parties and great balls . . . and when grand concerts in the elegant opera houses of London, Paris, and Vienna drew glittering audiences of lords and ladies who had the taste and leisure to enjoy great music.

The music of the Baroque Era was suited to its sophisticated, pleasure-loving audiences. It was light and sparkling, filled with surprises, extravagant combinations of instruments and tunes.

"The silver glint of Bach's trumpets, the brittle twang of Couperin's harpsichords, the sultry warbling of Telemann's oboes, the velvet throatiness of Purcell's violins: these are some of the musical sensations that *more* and *more* people are enjoying in this 20th Century—because of a great revival of *baroque* music. Filled with bright, primary tone-colors, these delightful sounds have been brought back into circulation after 250 years and more, not for crabbed antiquarian reasons but for sheer pleasure, because baroque music gives present-day listeners the kind of physical pleasure that makes the scalp tingle, makes feet tap and shoulders jive."*

As you and your family will discover when you listen to the four-record album of THE BAROQUE ERA, this is the most beautiful, *enjoyable* music ever written—music that was composed to give its audience sheer, lasting pleasure!

A growing desire among modern listeners to become explorers and adventurers in sound is one of the reasons for the phenomenal success of the so-called "baroque revival" that began shortly after World War II and by the mid-sixties threatened to sweep all before it in the world of music. It is no accident that this revival came at the time of the LP record and high-fidelity recording. The LP has made it possible for baroque music to get a hearing even if—because of many technical difficulties—baroque music is sometimes impractical for the modern concert stage. Most of the great multiple concertos of the baroque are rarely, if ever, heard in concert performances, because they require too many kinds of soloists—and it is impossible to assemble such a big group of featured musicians!

The great baroque chamber pieces which call for exotic combinations of strings and woodwinds could seldom find a convenient place in the usual repertory. But on discs they turn out to be ideally scaled to the proportions of a living room. In the same way, keyboard music originally created for the harpsichord in the most intimate surroundings was often inaudible in the back rows of a concert hall; but high-fidelity recording has put it in the home, where it belongs. And for all its intimacy, there is an air of pomp and pageantry, a sense of majestic self-confidence in much baroque music that appeals to modern listeners: we return to the baroque world for a sense of grandeur so lacking in our daily 20th Century lives.

We invite you now to join the growing rank of 20th Century music lovers who have discovered the most modern musical school of all—the music of the baroque era. By mailing the enclosed order card, you can secure a whole album of the greatest baroque music, superbly recorded by Angel Records, for 10 days *free* enjoyment.

TIME LIFE RECORDS

*From "The Baroque Era," the 60-page book accompanying the four-record set

One of the most spectacular of all Time, Inc. mailings was for "The Story of Great Music."

camera and projector features plus bonuses included in the "package" offered for $269.95—carrying case, light bar, free film, instruction book, screen, tripod, movie-making manual, an Abbott & Costello film, and discount coupons for additional feature films. The large dimensions of the spread made it possible to both illustrate and adequately describe all the special features and bonuses.

Columbia Record Club

A 15½- by 25-inch broadside, four-folded to 5 by 7¾ inches, was used by Columbia Record Club to promote its $179.95 mail order package of a stereo phonograph, record library, and record rack. The large spread permitted a very detailed illustration of the phonograph. A short fold yielded another large spread—10 by 15½ inches—on which 108 stereo record albums were described.

Golden Records

A five-fold broadside was used by Golden Records to promote its basic record library for young people. The 5½- by 7-inch mailer opened to 18½ by 21 inches. The large spread provided ample room to detail the full contents of the record library, which contained 12 albums, each featuring from 11 to 32 separate sections. By presenting the full list of 201 selections on the spread, an impact was achieved which would likely have been lost if the albums had been described on individual pages.

Doubleday Subscription Service

A unique broadside was used by Doubleday to promote magazine subscriptions. A 9½- by 18-inch sheet of gummed stock contained 96 perforated "stamps," illustrating and describing 48 magazines. Recipients were invited to tear off up to six of the stamps and attach them to an order card to order magazine subscriptions. The stamp broadside was two-folded to 4½ by 9½ inches for mailing in a 5¼- by 10-inch envelope.

The Franklin Mint

Enclosures tailored to individual products are used regularly by The Franklin Mint. Even though nearly every mailing is made by first class mail, the enclosures frequently have a "heavy" feeling—often created by effective use of color. For example, a 14½ by 11 inch piece, folded once to give an elongated 14½ by 5½ inch enclosure was used to promote a set of The Franklin Mint Zodiac Spoons.

Franklin Mint effectively used dark blue and enamel paper to give these promotions prestige and verisimilitude.

Printed on an enamel cover stock, the piece seemed much heavier than its actual weight through the use of a four-side bleed cover of dark blue, simulating the leather-like case in which the spoons are delivered. The inside 14½ by 11 inch spread was also a four-side bleed illustration showing the spoons in 9/10 actual size, with copy printed on an illustration of the white satin puff which lines the cover of the case.

Dark blue four-side bleed was also used to give a substantial feel to a 25¼ by 9 inch enclosure which folded twice to 8⅜ by 9 inches and announced the Official 1973 Inaugural Medals. The only illustration on the cover was a full-size picture of the reverse of the Inaugural Medal. The back of the folded piece also had a four-side dark blue with only the legend "The Inaugural Committee—1973, Washington, D.C. 20013" reversed out of the solid color. This use of a dark color and a minimum of illustrative or copy matter can give a minimum weight piece a feeling of substance.

Another variation of this technique used by The Franklin Mint was demonstrated in a mailing for "The Signers of the Declaration of Independence" medal series. In this case an 11 by 18¼ inch sheet of dark blue cover stock was two-folded to 11 by 8½ inch with only a large embossed gold eagle on the cover. Bound into this cover was an eight-page 10⅜ by 8⅛ inch folder on simulated parchment, with a tissue overwrap. When the cover—short-folded so the deckle edge at the bottom overlapped a bottom flap—was opened, the reader was exposed to introductory copy printed in gold on the tissue and showing through under the gold printing was a full-color reproduction of John Trumbull's famous painting "The Declaration of Independence." Six of the remaining pages carried the basic message in simulated hand-lettering with full-size illustrations of the medals in the series running down the right side. Since the piece opened vertically, the 16¼ inch long spreads gave a feeling of both substance and elegance. See page 691.

Another interesting vertical format was used to present Roberts Birds/1972, a set of five medals sculpted by Gilroy Roberts. This 8 by 5¾ inch piece opened to 8 by 16⅞ inches with an eight-page 7¼ by 4⅞ inch booklet bound into the bottom fold. Copy ran down the top two-thirds of the inside spread, while illustrations of the five individual medals were presented on the pages of the bound-in booklet.

GILROY ROBERTS CREATES FIVE NEW BIRD SCULPTURES

The only Roberts Birds to be issued in 1972.

This elaborate brochure and booklet was beautifully illustrated with the famous artist's birds.

BOOKLETS

The bound booklet has an important function in direct mail. The minute you fasten pages together in booklet form, a printed piece achieves a more permanent appearance and, therefore, quite frequently appears more important than the same amount of printed paper in an unbound format. Through pagination you can also organize complicated material effectively.

On the other hand, a booklet requires the direct mail advertiser to present his story in "short takes." The very necessity of having to turn a page can encourage the recipient to stop reading before he has received much of the story. Unlike the broadside, where you at least glimpse the full story at one time, the use of booklets requires special effort on the part of the recipient to get even partial exposure to the material being presented.

Generally, booklets are more costly to produce than unbound pieces. However, it is possible to use this format to reduce costs in certain cases. Through proper planning of color and folding, it is often possible to create a booklet with the appearance of lavish use of color, even though color printing has been restricted to just one side of the sheet.

Thing of Value

Another advantage of booklets is that they sometimes can be presented as a publication with monetary value. Some direct mail advertisers actually print a "price" on the cover of the booklets to create this impression. This, of course, must be limited to booklets that carry material of informational or entertainment value; it is not suitable, except in very exceptional cases, for booklets of a promotional nature.

One printer had the value of the "cover price" technique clearly demonstrated. For many years, the printer had been producing a booklet for a maker of building products. In addition to product listings, it carried "how to do it" material. One year, the advertiser decided to print a 50-cent cover price on the booklet. When the night crew had finished binding the first run of the new edition, it was discovered that a large quantity of the booklets were "missing." While never before had the printer's employees shown more than a passing interest in this job, the addition of the cover price convinced them here was something they should have for their own—and practically everyone on the night crew decided to take a copy home to study.

Club Booklets

Perhaps the most consistent users of booklets for promotion are the various "of-the-month" clubs. Like the older book clubs, the record companies try to create a "magazine" atmosphere for their monthly promotional booklets. This gives the clubs a chance to offer the booklet-magazines as a "membership service" rather than merely as a promotion piece.

American Heritage Sundry Department

Catalogs are frequently prepared in booklet form to serve as enclosures with mailings. An example is the 20-page, 5¼- by 7¼-inch booklet which was used by *American Heritage* to promote the sale of back issues and books to subscribers. Major books were given full-page promotion, while back issues and books of less sales potential were displayed in picture-caption treatment. Like so many catalog booklets, this one had a gatefold back cover which featured a perforated business reply order card. (By using a gatefold, the ordering device is always handy when the booklet is being studied.) For "double protection," *American Heritage* also printed a duplicate order form on the back cover of the booklet. Thus there was still an ordering device, even after the perforated gatefold reply card had been removed for use in sending an initial order.

Grolier, Inc.

Educational materials are frequently promoted with mailings which include a booklet. For example, Grolier, Inc., used an eight-page "Report to Parents" to tell the story of its teaching machines in a mailing made to parents of school-age children. In the 5½- by 8½-inch, two-color booklet, Grolier explained the background of teaching machines, their use and benefits, and Grolier's role in their development. Quotations from nationally recognized publications were heavily featured. The only out-and-out promotion in the booklet for the offer featured in the mailing was on the back cover.

Similar booklets are used by correspondence schools, publishers of reference sets, etc. Emphasis is usually on the benefits to be derived from the use of the products or services featured, and hard-sell promotion is usually left for the letter and other enclosures. A mailing from Conversation Studies of Chicago, for example, featured a 4- by 7-inch, 16-page booklet to promote the 12-lesson Ethel Cotton Conversation Course. The booklet discussed the value of improved conversation techniques and then outlined, in a soft-sell way, each of the 12 lessons. There was a one-page, inside-back-cover enrollment promotion, but more of the direct sell was in a two-page letter. A two-page flyer, also enclosed, promoted a special premium for enrollment. Details of the contents of the full course were contained on a 5½- by 8½-inch enrollment blank. A business reply envelope completed the package.

Book-of-the-Month Club

An extensive user of booklets for direct mail promotion is the Book-of-the-Month Club. A typical booklet was used to promote "Art Seminars in the Home." A 16-page booklet in the 7- by 10-inch size which the club uses regularly had its first nine pages devoted to selling the idea of home study of art. The next four pages presented a brief summary of each of the 12 portfolios offered in the program. The final spread showed a typical portfolio at three-fourths actual size.

A typical member's monthly mailing from Book-of-the-Month Club contains a variety of enclosures. The major piece is a booklet featuring the main selection plus many alternates. A typical booklet in a standard 7½ by 10⅛ inch format contains 32 pages plus covers and inserts. Standard typography is used from issue-to-issue to maintain continuity. Covers and inserts are in full-color, body pages in two colors. The featured selection usually receives the two front covers plus the first five or six pages of the body. Most alternate selections are presented rather briefly, but scattered through the booklet are promotions for a number of special alternates which receive one or two full pages. A four-page center insert, usually in full-color with multiple illustrations, gives special emphasis to a major alternate selection. The back covers, frequently with a gatefold and a bound-in special order card, also promote a major alternate.

A monthly BOMC mailing also contains a number of special enclosures promoting major alternate selections. These are usually the same size as the booklet, but with two or four pages each. Most often these special enclosures are two-color pieces, unless the book being promoted is a pictorial volume featuring color illustrations.

On occasion, the mailing package will also contain a separate "package" in its own envelope. For example, an enclosure promoting "The Visconti Hours" was packaged in a window envelope and contained a separate letter; four-color, four-page brochure; a two-page sample of the book, and a special business reply card order form.

Book-of-the-Month Club has found special enclosures advertising alternate selections very successful.

National Geographic Society

To promote memberships (which feature a subscription to *National Geographic Magazine*), the National Geographic Society frequently uses booklets to accompany its invitation format mailings. A typical booklet features 12 pages with brilliant color illustrations and text describing upcoming contents of the magazine. A simple two-color cover with the Society emblem blind-embossed is added to create a feeling of special dignity. The only printing is on the front cover, with the other three covers completely blank.

Prentice-Hall, Inc.

This publisher frequently uses an unusual portfolio technique to promote its books and services. These portfolio-booklets are prepared to resemble a special report. An unimprinted black portfolio is used, with a die-cut window on the cover through which shows the title from the first page of the "report." The inside pages are printed on lightweight stock with simulated typewriting, and follow a report-letter style. An order card is tipped or stapled to the inside back cover of the portfolio.

Newsweek

An unusual, unique booklet mailing was developed by S. Arthur Debner of *Newsweek*. Rather than enclosing the booklet in an envelope, a No. 6¾ envelope containing a letter-order form and business reply envelope was attached to the back cover of the 5½- by 8-inch booklet. The eight-page booklet was designed to look like a miniature issue of *Newsweek*. Five of the six inside pages were devoted to a digest of editorial material from the magazine. The only direct promotion of subscriptions was on the inside front cover, which included the note: "If you'd like all of *Newsweek* every week, see the '7-cents-a-copy' offer in the attached envelope."

BROCHURES

In direct mail terms, a brochure is simply a prestige printed piece. It may be a folder, a broadside, or a booklet, and is usually 8½ by 11 inches or larger in size. It may be used for almost any purpose which calls for prestige treatment. The account executive of a Pittsburgh advertising and public relations agency, which has prepared brochures for many of its clients, comments in an article in *Industrial Marketing:*

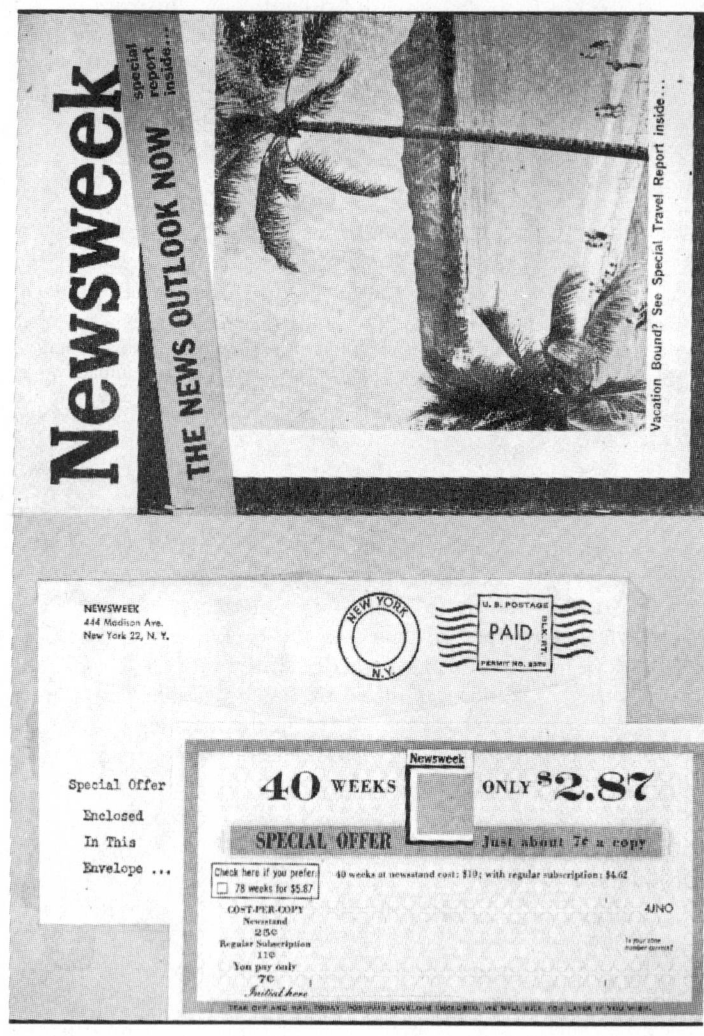

Newsweek used an eight-page miniature booklet to develop new subscriptions. (The illustration shows the front cover (right), back cover with its tipped-on envelope and the enclosed order form.)

Prestige brochures can be designed for a variety of purposes: telling company history, recruiting, capital goods sales, financial reporting. But regardless, they must fit one general set of specifications: they must read, feel, and look "top drawer."

Ideally, the prestige brochure should meet all of the six basic external sales objectives of a company:

1. Winning new customers
2. Holding present customers
3. Helping the salesmen
4. Strengthening distributor and dealer relations
5. Intensifying the advertising
6. Broadening the market

The prestige brochure also should be effective for use with more than one of the company's publics. For example, it should inspire retail salesmen, persuade the prospect, and comfort the stockholder. In most cases we shy away from doing normal-budget sales bulletins that attempt to be all things to all people in four or eight pages. But like a well-edited consumer magazine, we feel that a prestige brochure can be prepared to exert impact on a wide variety of people with diverse attitudes or interests. For example, its quality look and feel—even without a word of editorial—can create such impressions as financial solidity, progressive attitude, and confidence in a market or a product.

Single Market Brochures

While prestige brochures, as described above, are most often designed to "sell" a multitude of markets, direct mail brochures are sometimes aimed at creating a smash impact on a single market. Most often, they are used to promote products or services with a high price tag or a healthy continuing volume. Because of the cost per piece, however, such prestige brochures are usually mailed to carefully developed lists of customers and prime prospects.

Many companies count on elaborate brochures to spearhead a direct mail program for recruiting engineers or other personnel. Other advertisers use them primarily to help answer inquiries about products, services, etc.

Treatment of Enclosures

Andi Emerson of Emerson-Weeks offers these suggestions for treatment of the various elements in direct mail brochures:

Headlines. The brochures headline is usually featured on the front, with the exception of the letter brochure. The same rules apply for this headline as for newspaper headlines. It should be as wide and big as possible, clean, well-leaded characters, and printed in a very dark ink. (It can be reversed, but then the background must be very dark.) One thing to watch very carefully is that the folding of the brochure does not interfere with the reading! Never have the headline that can't be read without unfolding the brochure.

Main Illustration. Again, the same rules apply as for a newspaper. The main illustration should be of the product *in use,* if possible. It should be big, clean, and exciting.

Body Copy. The body copy rules are the same as for ads, except that the copy on the front of the brochure should be so interesting that it forces the reader to turn the page. This usually means putting the vitally interesting points on the front of the brochure, even though they will have to be repeated again inside.

Subheads. Good brochure writing uses a technique not used in other advertising writing. That is the double headline. One headline on the front page, another, different one inside the brochure. Regular subheads are a must inside the brochure and on the back page. Remember, the letter is personal, but the layout of the brochure is not, even when it's written in the first person. It is essential that the appearance of the brochure be a professional looking one. There is just no excuse for a sloppy job here.

Center Spread. Copy must be tightly written and copy blocks should be boxed off, subheaded, and separated out by the use of tints, screens, reversed and colors. Don't do *all* of these things in one brochure, or you will spend a lot of money to create a hodgepodge that will hurt sales. But your brochure must be exciting. Your center spread should carry the second headline across the entire space, if it is important and big enough. Otherwise, confine it to the first or second half, again making it big and bold. Usually this second headline is set in upper and lower, and it shouldn't be quite as big as the main head. Pictures in the center spread are very important. This is the place for little "technical" shots, showing the different features and points of interest. The more of these, the merrier, as long as the total cost doesn't rise too high.

Back Page. Subheads, guarantee, order coupon, testimonials and the closing sales pitch are all on the back page. Sometimes pictures are used, sometimes not. If you are using a coupon, make sure that the brochure remaining after the coupon has been deleted contains all the sales elements.

CIRCULARS AND FLYERS

The most simple of all enclosures are circulars or flyers. While they may be given many functional names—such as catalog sheets, product information sheets, etc.—their common characteristic is that they consist of a single sheet printed on one or both sides.

In many cases, these single-sheet enclosures are designed to meet some set of established standards. It is common, for example, to punch the sheets to fit into a binder. Or they may carry a filing code, such as those established by the American

Multiple Flyers

One frequently used technique is to prepare a mailing composed of a number of sheets, each promoting a different product or service. Unfortunately, such mailings often breed confusion, since the recipient may fail to recognize that there is no connection between the various promotion pieces other than that they share a common mailing envelope. When unrelated enclosures are used, it is advisable to add some coordinating piece, such as an order form listing every item featured on the enclosures or a letter which clearly explains the purpose of every enclosure.

Some mail order advertisers have found it highly effective to prepare a "matched set" of promotion pieces, with each piece promoting a different product or service and carrying its own order form. American Marketing Services, for example, uses an envelope-size portfolio into which is inserted a series of individual product slips. The portfolio serves to coordinate the individual slips and carries copy which establishes the relationship of the items. Precision Equipment Co. "packages" a set of 24 colorful business reply cards in an envelope. To provide continuity for the mailing, a similar design is used for each of the cards.

Product Promotion Flyers

The most common type of flyer is that promoting a single product or service. Frequently, magazine advertising layout techniques are used and, all too often, these enclosures are nothing more than reprints of a publication ad. While this is a simple and economical way of producing direct mail enclosures, it usually results in an inferior piece. A direct mail audience has little in common with a magazine or newspaper audience. The people may be the same, but the setting is different. The direct mail enclosure does not compete with a facing page possibly containing an ad for a competitive product. Instead, it stands on its own. If a person decides to read the copy and finds he or she is interested in the proposition, there is an immediate demand for as many details as possible and for answers to a host of questions.

A frequently used technique is to use the front of the sheet as an attention-getter, including only enough copy to develop an interest in the proposition. Then the back side of the sheet goes into enough detail to answer the majority of questions likely to be asked by interested recipients.

"Reader's Digest" Condensed Books

To promote its condensed books, *Reader's Digest* used a colorful single sheet enclosure. The front featured an oversize illustration of a condensed-books volume being offered without charge to encourage readers to try out a continuing subscription for the books. The only copy, in addition to that shown on the dust jacket of the book in the illustration, was a headline reading, "Regular Price $2.73—Yours Absolutely Free," and a two-line subhead at the bottom of the page, "This Beautifully Illustrated 576-page Volume of 'Best Sellers' from Condensed Books." A short "see other side" line and arrow pointed the way to the detailed copy. The reverse side was divided into three sections. One told the story of *Reader's Digest* condensed books, the second contained testimonials from well-known personalities, and the third section gave brief descriptions of the four books featured in the special condensed-books volume being offered.

Similar techniques may be used for one-side-printed sheets, too. In such cases, the top of the sheet usually is used to create interest, while the lower portion attempts to provide detailed information.

Providing Additional Information

Many times, special flyer enclosures are added to a mailing to cover subjects which either need special emphasis or might complicate the promotional story if included as part of the basic promotion pieces enclosed. One of the most frequently used "added flyers" is the "duplication slip." This is often included with mailings sent to lists likely to have a degree of duplication and adds a note of apology to those who receive duplicate mailings. An outstanding example of a duplicating slip is the Good News Publishers piece illustrated on page 792.

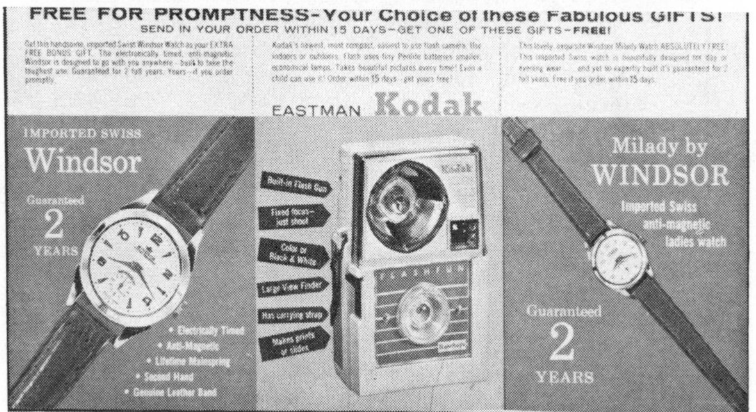

When a special premium is offered, it is common to describe it on a separate enclosure. Two examples of such flyers are shown above. Other frequently used "added information" flyers include reproductions of newspaper and magazine clippings, testimonial sheets, tie-in promotions for related products, pass-along order forms, lists of dealers and distributors, etc.

Don't Say No

Another type of special enclosure which has been growing in popularity is the "Publisher's Letter" or "Lift Memo." Typically, such an enclosure is in a sealed envelope with a teaser note such as, "Please open this if you decide *not* to accept this special offer." Some examples:

Reader's Digest inserts a note inside the "no" envelope of its twin envelope sets (one for a yes reply, the other for a no reply). The top of the note on a contrasting color stock is revealed when the recipient lifts the flap of the "no" envelope. Teaser copy says:

IF YOU HAVE
ALREADY RECEIVED
"SWORD OR THE SICKLE?"...

This is a special message for you. To acquaint as many people as possible with the Ministry of Good News, we use a number of mailing lists. Since there is a definite savings of the Lord's money by handling our lists in this separate manner, you may sometimes receive more than one mailing from us.

If you receive more than one copy of this folder, we hope you will understand. Perhaps you know of someone who would read this message just as you have. If so, we would appreciate your passing this folder along. It is another way of bringing the Word to the people of the world.

GOOD NEWS PUBLISHERS Westchester, Ill.

Pioneers in modern design of Gospel tracts for over two decades

An excellent sample of a "duplication slip."

"Please don't say 'NO' now!" When the note is pulled out of the envelope it contains copy emphasizing the free trial nature of the offer.

Weekly Reader Family Book Service uses a separate letter, folded and sealed with a blank Cheshire label. Teaser copy on the outside of the letter reads: "Do not open this unless you have already decided *not* to send for your Free Book!" The letter is headed: "A question from the publisher if you have decided not to send in for your free book." Copy starts: "As publisher of this encyclopedia I'm puzzled. I can't understand why everyone doesn't send in for the free first volume, since it is an outright gift (we even pay the postage). Perhaps you don't believe that it's really free. Then let me assure you . . ."

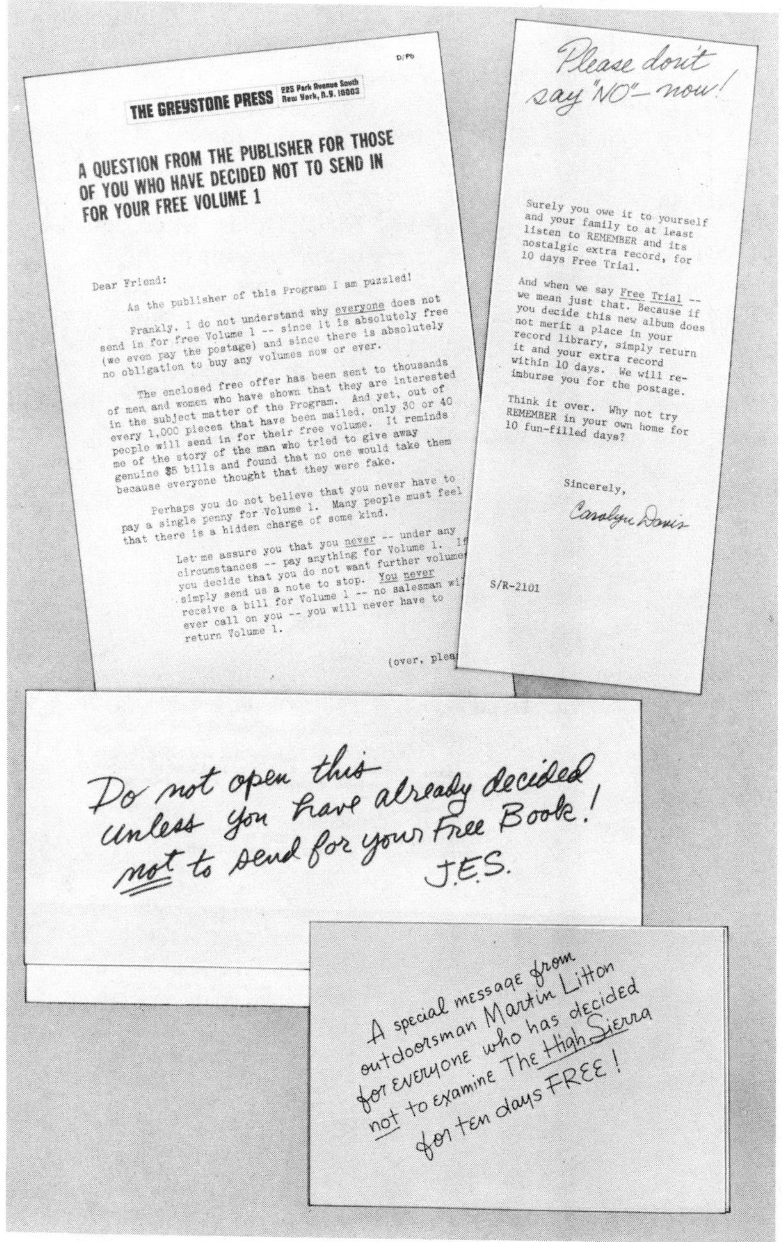

D/Pb

THE GREYSTONE PRESS 225 Park Avenue South New York, N.Y. 10003

A QUESTION FROM THE PUBLISHER FOR THOSE OF YOU WHO HAVE DECIDED NOT TO SEND IN FOR YOUR FREE VOLUME 1

Dear Friend:

As the publisher of this Program I am puzzled!

Frankly, I do not understand why everyone does not send in for free Volume 1 -- since it is absolutely free (we even pay the postage) and since there is absolutely no obligation to buy any volumes now or ever.

The enclosed free offer has been sent to thousands of men and women who have shown that they are interested in the subject matter of the Program. And yet, out of every 1,000 pieces that have been mailed, only 30 or 40 people will send in for their free volume. It reminds me of the story of the man who tried to give away genuine $5 bills and found that no one would take them because everyone thought that they were fake.

Perhaps you do not believe that you never have to pay a single penny for Volume 1. Many people must feel that there is a hidden charge of some kind.

Let me assure you that you never -- under any circumstances -- pay anything for Volume 1. If you decide that you do not want further volume simply send us a note to stop. You never receive a bill for Volume 1 -- no salesman wi ever call on you -- you will never have to return Volume 1.

(over, plea

Please don't say "NO"— now!

Surely you owe it to yourself and your family to at least listen to REMEMBER and its nostalgic extra record, for 10 days Free Trial.

And when we say Free Trial -- we mean just that. Because if you decide this new album does not merit a place in your record library, simply return it and your extra record within 10 days. We will reimburse you for the postage.

Think it over. Why not try REMEMBER in your own home for 10 fun-filled days?

Sincerely,

Carolyn Davis

S/R-2101

Do not open this unless you have already decided not to send for your Free Book!
J.E.S.

A special message from outdoorsman Martin Litton for everyone who has decided not to examine The High Sierra for ten days FREE!

Typical examples of Publishers' Letters which are included in mailings to pique the interest of the recipient.

The Greystone Press uses a miniature letter with a bold heading: "A question from the publisher for those of you who have decided not to send in for your free Volume 1."

Time-Life Books enclosed a separate letter with mailings for "The American Wilderness." The letter was two-folded and carried a teaser on its otherwise blank back: "A special message from outdoorsman Martin Litton for everyone who has decided *not* to examine *The High Sierra* for ten days FREE!" The letter signed by a member of the Board of Directors of the Friends of the Earth and the Sierra Club first explained why he was impressed with the Time-Life series and then added: "I would like to call your attention to the fact that the publisher, Joan Manley, means exactly what she says when she offers you a 10-day free trial of *The High Sierra.* There is no risk whatsoever on your part. You merely look the book over for 10 days. If you aren't as enthusiastic as I am about it, then simply send the book back. That's all there is to it."

20 WAYS TO IMPROVE CIRCULARS

Prepared by Robert Stone

Reprinted from *Advertising Age*, January 20, 1969

APPEARANCE

1. Is the circular in character with the market you are reaching?
2. Is the presentation in character with the product or service you are offering?
3. Is the circular in harmony with the rest of the mailing package?

CONTENT

4. Is there a big idea behind your circular?
5. Do your headlines stick to the key offer?
6. Is your product or service dramatized to its best advantage by format and/or presentation?
7. Are good quality drawings or photographs used to portray the product?
8. Do you show widely adaptable examples of your product or service in use?
9. Is your copy believable?
10. Is your copy easy to read—short words, sentences and paragraphs?
11. Are your statements backed up by proofs and endorsements?
12. Does your entire circular presentation follow a logical sequence and tell a complete story—including price, offer and guarantee?
13. Does your entire circular presentation build toward inducing the reader to take specific action?

PREPARATION

14. Does the layout have the feel of a good direct response circular?
15. Will the circular cut out of stock size paper?
16. Is the quality of paper stock in keeping with the presentation?
17. Is color employed judiciously to show the product or service in its best light?
18. Are typography, photography and art in keeping with the market and the proposition?
19. Has art been prepared in the best manner for the printing process to be employed?
20. Have color proofs been approved by the artist or art studio before going to press?

Chapter 29

CATALOGS AND PRICE LISTS

WHILE there are those who think of catalogs and price lists as media unto themselves, they more frequently are an essential part of the direct mail medium—and, even more often, of mail order advertising. To such organizations as Sears Roebuck and Montgomery Ward, of course, the catalog is widely recognized as *the* primary marketing tool. But to thousands of other companies, even though their owners and managers may not take time to realize it, the catalog is often the cornerstone around which their business is built.

Catalogs take all shapes and forms, ranging from the thousand-plus pages of the semiannual "dream books" published by major mail order houses to single sheets and simple folders listing the full product lines of small industrial companies. Some are filled with lavish color illustrations, while others are as simple as a series of typewritten listings reproduced by mimeograph or offset duplicator.

But most successful catalogs have one feature in common: they are designed for reference over an extended period—to provide essential information which will enable a customer to order without the aid of a salesman.

The Catalog as a Salesman

According to Wetzel Bros., Milwaukee printer, "a catalog must do what a good salesman does." In its guide to better catalogs, Wetzel offers the following suggestions for producing a "salesmanlike" catalog:

> *Plan the sale*—A salesman plans his campaign in advance. A catalog should do the same. The difference between an effective sales-producing catalog and an expensive, ineffective one is the planning that goes into it. Before producing a catalog, the advertiser should undertake a detailed analysis of the requirements of the persons who are most likely to use it. Only in this way can a company expect to devise an instrument which, because of its usefulness, will be more frequently used than other competitive catalogs.

It is not a job for the advertising department alone. Advertising should call on the services of the engineering department, production department, and the sales department. An effort should be made to discover which factors are most likely to influence the sale, when the presentation is made by a salesman. Conversely, an effort should be made to discover factors that act as deterrents to a sale.

Like a salesman, a catalog should be prepared to sell the company's products through promotion. It should be prepared to sell products other than those in which the buyer has an immediate interest. A recent survey discloses the fact that purchasing agents as a group are willing to have promotional material included in the catalog. In many cases they considered this material valuable to them to such an extent that they termed this information necessary. The chart below shows the extent to which various types of promotional material are accepted by purchasing executives.

TYPES OF PROMOTIONAL MATERIAL CONSIDERED ESSENTIAL OR ACCEPTABLE IN CATALOGS

Based on a survey of purchasing executives

	Essential	Acceptable	Disapprove
Explanation and illustrations of how to use products	78%	16%	6%
Description of manufacturing methods	43	45	12
Description of previous installations	39	48	13
Outline of company policies	36	45	19
Views of manufacturing equipment	16	57	27
History of the company	12	68	20
Views of the plant	11	59	30
Testimonials	4	37	59
Photographs of executives	1	24	75

Answer questions—Like a good salesman, a catalog is expected to answer many questions on various subjects. Unlike a salesman, the catalog cannot have this information at the tip of its tongue. A good catalog, however, can put this information at the tips of the buyer's fingers. This is done through good indexing and sectionalization. Almost every catalog should have an index. A complete index in the front of the catalog is preferred, but where the catalog is large or complicated, a section index should be placed in front and a complete index in back. Catalogs covering more than one line should have sections. These devices make it easy for the catalog user to find an answer to his questions. This is a service he appreciates, and his appreciation is demonstrated by his continued frequent use of your catalog.

Show the product—A good salesman likes to show the product he sells. A good catalog must show the product it sells. Because there is frequently a great similarity between competitive products, it is distinctly to the advantage of the catalog-salesman to show pictures of the products it discusses. Such illustrations should be as large and as clear as possible. They should satisfy every reasonable requirement the catalog user may have. Pictures should be accompanied by concise descriptions and, when necessary, by tables. The catalog-salesman must be very sure that the catalog user knows about which product it is talking.

Identify the company—A good salesman identifies himself and recalls the name of his company to his customer on every call. A good catalog should be designed to recall the name of the company as frequently as possible. This can be done through positive identification on the backbone so it may be selected from a long line of catalogs. It can also be done by adopting a design or cover that has a family association with the other promotional literature of the company producing it. The company trademark, if any, should be prominently displayed both on the backbone and the front cover.

Tell what it does—Like a good salesman, a good catalog will establish benefits. It establishes in the mind of the catalog user the way in which he will benefit from using the product illustrated. The catalog user must be told for what purpose the product is to be used.

Tell how it does it—Like a good salesman, the catalog must tell how the product performs its function. The explanation may be simple, but it must be complete. Wherever necessary, product-in-use illustrations should be carried with the other information. Such a description need not necessarily accompany every item in the catalog, but certainly provision should be made to show the catalog user how the product he contemplates buying will operate in his plant or office. Such illustrations may be accompanied by sketches, cutaway drawings, isometrics, schematic diagrams, or other devices to make this clear.

Give performance data—A good salesman is never satisfied to merely tell what his product will do and how it does it. He likes to offer proof, so his customer will be convinced of the merit of his product. The catalog performs this function by giving performance data. Your customer wants specific information, including all figures available, to show beyond doubt the economy or suitability of your product in his operation. This information is one of the most convincing sales arguments your catalog-salesman can provide.

Quote prices—A salesman is always ready to quote the price of his product. A good catalog should be ready to do the same thing. If it is practical, prices should be included in the catalog and related to the product on the same page. Because of frequent revision of prices, this is not always practical. When this situation exists, a separate, frequently-issued price list should be provided for inclusion in the catalog or for ready reference by the catalog user.

Ask for the order—A good salesman is always ready to accept an order for his product, even though he does not ask for it on every visit. Your catalog should be ready to accept an order or at least make it easy for the catalog user to place his order. In some instances, it is practical to include order blanks. When this is done, complete information should be provided so the user will know what information is required to fill the order. Where order blanks and business reply cards are not practical, directions should be given for placing an order by telephone, telegraph, or mail. If the nature of the product is such that it is necessary for a salesman or engineer to accept the order, the catalog should invite its user to call for such representation as he may need.

Keep calling—The successful salesman calls on his customers constantly. A good catalog is always on hand to make this contact for its sponsor. Proper identification, design, and color can serve as the calling card of the catalog-salesman. These can be factors that remind the catalog user time and time again that the catalog-salesman stands on the shelf, ready to answer any and every question.

Mail Order Catalogs

When most people think of catalogs, their minds first turn to the giants of the catalog field—the big books of Sears, Ward, and Spiegel. But mailboxes are also filled with thousands of other mail order catalogs ranging from the beautiful Christmas book published annually by Dallas' Neiman-Marcus department store to inexpensive booklets listing highly specialized products. In between are a host of other catalogs including the harbingers of spring, the seed and nursery catalogs; the multitudinous gift catalogs published by the trading-stamp companies; the "hidden price" books published by "wholesale" houses (now more commonly known as discount houses); sale catalogs distributed by all types of retail businesses; and hundreds of others.

To try and set forth any firm guidelines to the publishing of effective mail order catalogs is extremely difficult, because the product line, buyer audience, competition, and a number of other factors impose special requirements in nearly every case. However, a review of some of today's outstanding catalogs indicates some of the successful techniques which should be carefully considered in the publishing of any mail order catalog.

The Big Three

The original "Big Three" of the mail order field are Chicago-based Sears Roebuck, Montgomery Ward, and Spiegel, Inc. A thorough analysis of these three mail order catalog operations was developed in 1959 by Robert B. Konikow, consultant and author. While there have been some changes in these catalogs since that time, this analysis is still the most complete yet published. The following excerpts from Mr. Konikow's series of three articles give a general picture of these giants of the catalog field:

> Each of the three companies issues two general and six or so special catalogs a year. There is some catalog activity going on at all times. Schedules overlap, there is constant production, and, at any moment, you can find something at almost every stage of development.
>
> Basically, there isn't a great deal of difference among the three catalogs. Much of the merchandise is comparable, and there is much overlapping in customer population. One of the three, for example, figures that 40%

of its circulation is overlapped (by the catalog lists of the other two companies). In addition, each company keeps a sharp eye on what the competition is doing.

The major effort, in all three, goes into the two general catalogs, issued twice a year. The Fall-Winter edition, the larger of the two, comes out early in July; the Spring-Summer edition, about the first of the year. In addition to these, each company issues a varying number of special catalogs. Some of them, like those for the winter sales, are now regular fixtures. While much smaller than the generals, these specials have greater circulation, since the special values they offer make them a useful tool for winning new customers. They are also, and this is no small consideration, less expensive to print and mail.

Two of the three companies issue multiple editions. While Spiegel operates from its single warehouse in Chicago, both Sears and Ward have multi-city operations. Because merchandise emphasis and prices vary from branch to branch, each sales area must be supplied a separate catalog. This means that Ward issues nine different editions and Sears, eleven.

Since the catalog is a merchandising tool, it is with the merchandising people that each catalog starts. Preliminary meetings are held within each department, about six months prior to the release of each general catalog. Then the buyer and his opposite number from the sales promotion department decide on their section of the catalog. They make a presentation to top management, outlining their requirements in terms of total number of pages, specifying how many in full color. They also indicate estimated costs of the catalog pages they will use and sales expected to result.

This request is backed up with a layout sheet for each page in the department, which is called, variously, a pinup, merchandise pasteup, or rough layout. But regardless of the name, the word for this is "rough." It is not really a layout, but rather an allocation of space for each item to be presented. Where merchandise offered in a previous catalog is to be included again, clips are put in position. New merchandise is represented by rough sketches or parts of manufacturers' catalogs. The really essential information is the listing of the merchandise and its relative importance in the buyers' minds.

Top management weighs these requests, evaluates the estimates of each department, determines the overall budget, and adjusts the assignment of space. Sometimes more space, or more color, may be added to benefit the catalog as a whole, to make it more exciting or more fun to read, to increase the prestige of the company, rather than to benefit the individual department, or perhaps top management feels that one department has underestimated its potential sales.

There is a general feeling, within all three companies, that design is playing a more important role in catalog production. The trend in typography has been away from hollering out loud, from using heavy black letters, reverses, and other similar techniques. The typeface says something beyond the words which it spells; it has a personality of its own, gives a feel to the page, adds character.

Layout in general is cleaner and less cluttered. Fewer pieces of merchandise are shown, and the illustrations are bigger. Merchandise is shown in use rather than in isolation. This reflects, to some extent, an apparent increase in sophistication on the part of the buying public. Any mail order executive can match or top the story of the customer who sent in her money for a bedspread, and then complained because her $5.98 didn't get her the bed on which the spread was shown in the illustration.

This growth in understanding has permitted the showing of more interesting arrangements. A woman, for example, can be shown as one of a group of men on the page selling men's car coats. Another similar development is the use of related merchandise on a single page. This is somewhat unorthodox, since the tradition has been to allot the expense of each page to the department whose merchandise it shows. How do you divide the expense, and who gets the credit for the sale, when handbags are shown on the page devoted to shoes? But in spite of bookkeeping problems, it has been found that this not only sells more handbags, but also increases the sale of shoes.

This showing of merchandise in use creates a problem at times. Each of the companies has a rule, which is not surprising, that everything shown in a catalog picture must be purchasable. This has led to occasional dilemmas, when an artist wants a specific touch of color, but can't find it anywhere. An occasional answer has been to go out and get a manufacturer to supply the item, and add it to the catalog.

With the thousands of items included in a catalog—the latest Sears catalog includes an estimated 140,000 items—it is quite a problem to maintain coordination during the six- or seven-month period of production. Since any error or mistake made in a catalog has to be lived with for six months, great efforts are made to see that none occur.

Each of the companies has its own technique for checking and double-checking, but perhaps Sears has the most complete. Key to its process is a group of 40 advertising representatives. As soon as a layout is approved, it is turned over to one of this crew. He writes up the art instructions; sees that merchandise is delivered from the warehouse to the proper studio; checks catalog numbers, colors listed, sizes; and so on. He is the liaison between Sears and the printers, Sears and its studios.

This group is backed up by an editorial staff of 13, whose job is to go over every word of the copy to see that it is accurate. If somebody says "formerly $4.95," an editorial staff member checks to make sure that the item once was listed at that price; he sees that descriptions are accurate, that the proper nomenclature is used, and that the copy follows company policy, meets government requirements, and is clear and unconfusing.

Page by page, the catalog goes through the process of design, layout, typography, art, and photography. One at a time, it is checked off as complete, and is turned over to the printer. Now comes the process of printing as much as 38 million pounds of paper for a single issue.

These three houses use approximately 118,000 tons of paper each year. Gigantic four- and five-color presses roll almost continuously to meet edition deadlines. Block-long bindery machines gather forms to make complete catalogs. Massive, wicked-looking knives neatly trim the edges of four 1¼-inch-thick books at a time. Bundlers wrap the bulky catalogs, and they are sacked and sent on conveyer belts to waiting trucks and boxcars. It is an operation that, in its size and complexity, has no equal anywhere.

Planning for getting the big books on press starts at about the same time as planning for writing and designing them. The two aspects of preparation must go on simultaneously, and both are built around the demands of merchandising.

As soon as the buyers indicate what space each wants for his department, the printing experts go to work to plan the book. Knowing the capacities of each of the presses that is available, the demands of the merchandising people are broken down into forms and signatures. Here a great many factors must be taken into consideration. The most important, for all three companies, is the efficient use of the great presses, in particular the multicolor rotogravure presses.

Other forms will come, at varying rates, from full-color, heat-set letterpresses; from two-color and monotone rotogravure presses; from single-color letterpresses; from full-color offset presses. These must be timed and synchronized so that the signatures flow at the proper rate to keep the binders working steadily. On the other hand, such massive amounts of paper are used that the presses cannot get too far ahead of the binders. There is just so much storage space available for stockpiling of forms.

In the months of production the binderies are turning out three to four hundred thousand copies a day.

The problem of selecting the proper mailing list is a crucial one. Through the years, various criteria have been set up, but experience has boiled them down to three:

- Recency
- Frequency
- Amount

All three mail order organizations base their selections on the three factors, although, of course, their definitions, and the way they are applied, will vary.

Recency is the first of these three factors, and its import is simple. A buying season lasts for six months, the period between two successive general catalogs. What was the latest buying season which saw an order from a particular customer?

Frequency adds another dimension to the process of selection. In how many recent seasons has the customer ordered? In other words, how regular a customer is he?

The third factor is *amount,* for an obvious reason. A customer who spends a lot of money with a mail order house is a better customer than one whose order rarely goes over a dollar or two.

These three factors can all be obtained from the record of actual orders placed, although the three houses may use different methods in obtaining and recording the data. But all three share the approach that the best prospect is an existing customer. It is easier to get another order from somebody who has placed an order with you recently. A customer's past buying habits are the best guide to a prediction of the future.

Each of the houses has its own system for dividing its precious customer list into categories. Categories are based on the actual records of buying. As an order comes in, it is routed to a unit which pulls from the files the stencil card of that customer. Spiegel, with a single mailing point, has a single file, but the customer files of the other two companies are kept in the branch houses scattered across the country.

The most convenient customer card is one which has inserted a plate or stencil which gives the customer's name and address. Its first task is to run off as many shipping labels as are needed to handle the particular order. Ward uses Elliott stencils; Spiegel, Speedograph; Sears, Addressograph.

The minimum of information is posted on these cards, just enough to later establish which of the many categories this particular customer should be assigned to. Ward writes it in by hand, using a differently colored ink for each of the selling seasons with which it is concerned. Spiegel uses a system based on holes punched around the edge of the card. Sears punches holes in small cards held in the metal plate.

A careful check is kept of customer reaction and buying habits. Each of Ward's branch houses sends in a regular report of how the list varies as orders come in. These are collated at the Chicago office, so there is constant awareness of how many customers there are in each house in each of the categories which indicate sales potential.

Spiegel's centralized operation permits certain variations from this sampling procedure. This company has set up a carefully selected panel of customers, which is a mirror in miniature of the entire list. It runs between 3 and 4% of the entire list, and is statistically representative. The stencil card of each of these customers is flagged, so that when an order comes through, it is turned over to a special clerk who makes out a special IBM card for the transaction, using a special code.

While very simple data are recorded about the normal customer, this statistical guinea pig has many more facts jotted down. Such items as the source of an order (mail, visit to retail store, phone), number of departments involved, and so on, are indicated. Later, this information is transferred to the main IBM card for this customer.

This detailed sampling permits a great many different studies to be made on the relationship of buying and various factors, without the expense of taking a new sample, or of conducting expensive surveys.

One of the major problems, however, is of keeping this sample truly representative. For example, none of the customers whose names are included know that they are on a special list. This very knowledge could tend to introduce a bias in their purchasing habits.

As the planning for each catalog gets under way, the decision must be made as to who will get the coveted books. At Spiegel, the punched holes are the indicators for the selecting mechanism, which works automatically. The machine picks out those customers who meet the criteria that have been set up for that particular mailing, and prints labels for them.

Sears, too, selects its names automatically. The machine is set up to sense the punched holes in the cards on the plate, and to make labels only from those which have the specified characteristics.

At Ward's, the selection is done manually. The stencils are fed into a channel which runs along the front of the addressing machine. A girl glances at the records posted, and decides whether this customer meets the criteria of selection. If so, she prints a label. If not, she returns the card to the file without printing a label. And if the customer has not bought anything during the last five selling seasons, she touches a control that shifts the card to the inactive file.

The labels are generally large—at Ward's, for example, they are 3⅜ by 4⅜ inches—since they must contain, in addition to the name and address of the customer, the mailing permit.

Since the catalogs are heavy, and go by zone rates, it is usually more economical to ship them in bulk to various regional mailing points, and then hand them over to the U. S. Post Office. This results in no catalog ever paying more than a second-zone rate.

Boxcars are each loaded with 18,000 catalogs and truck trailers with 5,500, and they are hauled away to the regional distribution points. These are selected so that every point to which a catalog must go is within 150 miles of a regional distribution point. In addition, these post offices must have the capacity to handle the large volume which suddenly descends upon them.

Mailing isn't the only technique which is used to get catalogs into the hands of customers. In many communities, local parcel delivery services are called upon. Whether this method is adopted depends upon a number of factors, first of which being whether a community actually has such a delivery service. It also requires a fairly high concentration of recipients to make this special door-to-door service practical. Cost is always a factor, but unless parcel delivery also has the advantage of speed over the mail, the savings may not be worth achieving.

Since two of the three criteria of selection are frequency and recency, the list of customers is fairly accurate. The address is checked with each order. Less than 2% of the catalogs are returned because of poor addresses.

All three companies are constantly trying to add to their customer lists, using various techniques. Catalogs themselves are too expensive to use as a means of promotion. The greatest impact is made when a new catalog order store is opened in a community. Upon the opening of a new store, all the sales promotion tools are used. While the details vary, the aim is to make as much of an impact on the community as rapidly as possible, to add as many new buyers to the customer list as possible. And once a new name is added, a new stencil made out, the customer automatically falls in one of the categories considered for the list for the next catalog.

The Neiman-Marcus Christmas Catalog

Long considered the top "glamour gal" of the catalog field is the Christmas catalog of Neiman-Marcus, Dallas department store. This annual volume combines lavish displays of merchandise with interesting copy—often including subtle touches of humor. A recent issue had these features:

Size: 8¼ by 11 inches; 92 pages plus covers.

Color: 52 pages plus covers in full color; 40 pages black and white.

Contents: Over 500 different gifts were offered. A high percentage of the gifts were clothing and accessories, although there was a large selection of jewelry, housewares, decorative items, foods and candies, sporting goods, bathroom accessories, toys and other items.

Layouts: A variety of techniques were used to provide change-of-page throughout the catalog. Color and black-and-white were mixed throughout the catalog as were multiple illustration pages and single illustrations containing multiple gift suggestions.

Neiman-Marcus spares no expense in preparing its Christmas catalog. This cover was drawn by the famous artist, Ronald Searle.

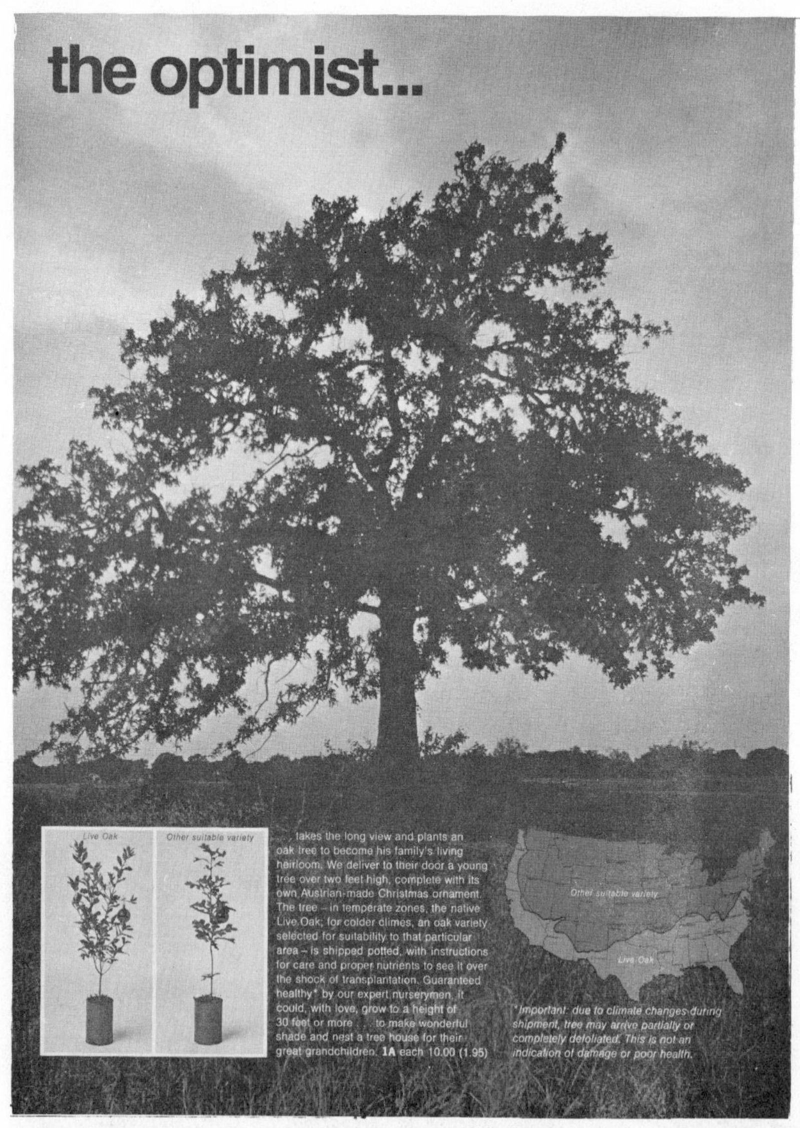

the optimist...
Live Oak
Other suitable variety
. . . takes the long view and plants an oak tree to become his family's living heirloom. We deliver to their door a young tree over two feet high, complete with its own Austrian-made Christmas ornament. The tree – in temperate zones, the native Live Oak; for colder climes, an oak variety selected for suitability to that particular area – is shipped potted, with instructions for care and proper nutrients to see it over the shock of transplantation. Guaranteed healthy* by our expert nurserymen, it could, with love, grow to a height of 30 feet or more . . . to make wonderful shade and nest a tree house for their great grandchildren. 1A each 10.00 (1.95)
Other suitable variety
Live Oak
*Important: due to climate changes during shipment, tree may arrive partially or completely defoliated. This is not an indication of damage or poor health.

Here Neiman-Marcus offered special gifts for the optimist—a slow-growing live oak tree with Austrian Christmas ornaments.

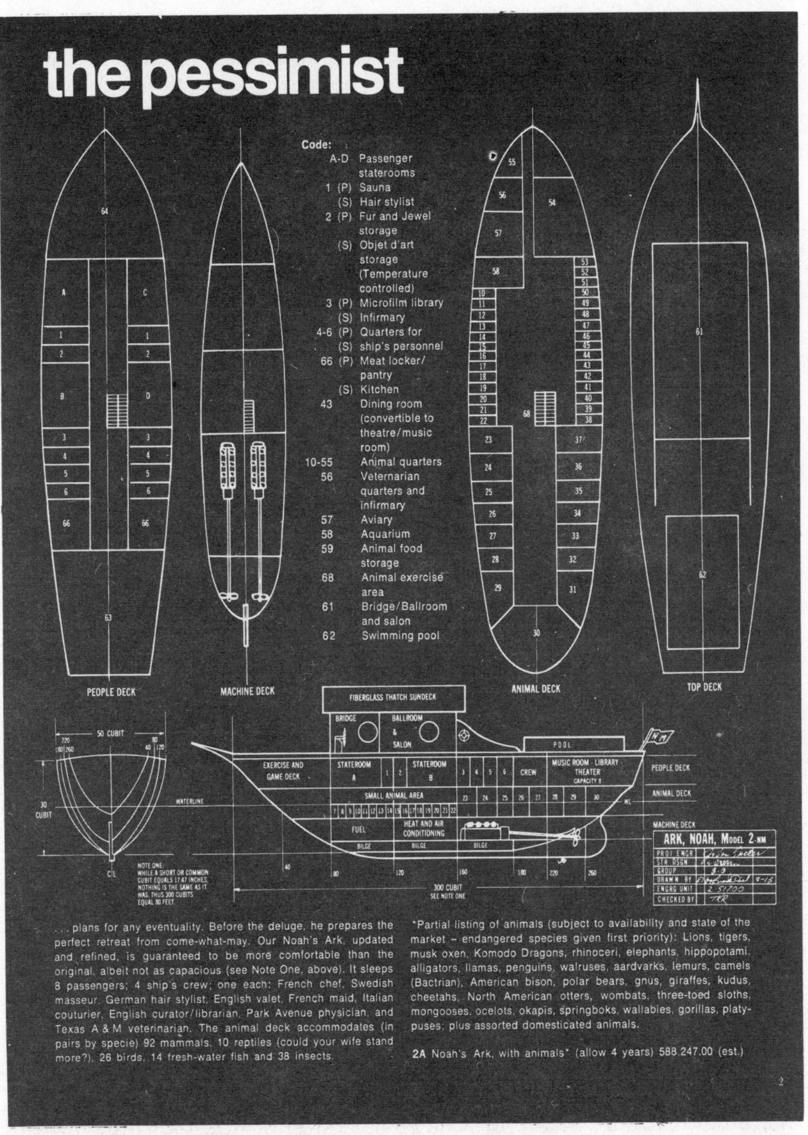

the pessimist
Code:
A-D Passenger staterooms
1 (P) Sauna
(S) Hair stylist
2 (P) Fur and Jewel storage
(S) Objet d'art storage (Temperature controlled)
3 (P) Microfilm library
(S) Infirmary
4-6 (P) Quarters for
(S) ship's personnel
66 (P) Meat locker/ pantry
(S) Kitchen
43 Dining room (convertible to theatre/music room)
10-55 Animal quarters
56 Veternarian quarters and infirmary
57 Aviary
58 Aquarium
59 Animal food storage
68 Animal exercise area
61 Bridge/Ballroom and salon
62 Swimming pool
PEOPLE DECK
MACHINE DECK
ANIMAL DECK
TOP DECK
FIBERGLASS THATCH SUNDECK
BRIDGE
BALLROOM & SALON
POOL
EXERCISE AND GAME DECK
STATEROOM A
STATEROOM B
CREW
MUSIC ROOM - LIBRARY THEATER
SMALL ANIMAL AREA
FUEL
HEAT AND AIR CONDITIONING
BILGE
PEOPLE DECK
ANIMAL DECK
MACHINE DECK
50 CUBIT
30 CUBIT
WATERLINE
NOTE ONE: WHILE A SHORT OR COMMON CUBIT EQUALS 17.47 INCHES, NOTHING IS THE SAME AS IT WAS. THUS 300 CUBITS EQUAL 80 FEET
300 CUBIT SEE NOTE ONE
ARK, NOAH, MODEL 2-NM
PROJ ENGR
STR DSGN
GROUP
DRAWN BY
ENGRG UNIT
CHECKED BY
. . . plans for any eventuality. Before the deluge, he prepares the perfect retreat from come-what-may. Our Noah's Ark, updated and refined, is guaranteed to be more comfortable than the original, albeit not as capacious (see Note One, above). It sleeps 8 passengers; 4 ship's crew; one each: French chef, Swedish masseur, German hair stylist, English valet, French maid, Italian couturier, English curator/librarian, Park Avenue physician, and Texas A & M veterinarian. The animal deck accommodates (in pairs by specie) 92 mammals, 10 reptiles (could your wife stand more?), 26 birds, 14 fresh-water fish and 38 insects.
*Partial listing of animals (subject to availability and state of the market – endangered species given first priority): Lions, tigers, musk oxen, Komodo Dragons, rhinoceri, elephants, hippopotami, alligators, llamas, penguins, walruses, aardvarks, lemurs, camels (Bactrian), American bison, polar bears, gnus, giraffes, kudus, cheetahs, North American otters, wombats, three-toed sloths, mongooses, ocelots, okapis, springboks, wallabies, gorillas, platypuses; plus assorted domesticated animals.
2A Noah's Ark, with animals* (allow 4 years) 588,247.00 (est.)

For the pessimist Neiman-Marcus suggested a modernized Noah's Ark, complete with animals, for $588,247.

Gift Identification: Each gift carried a boldface numeral-letter code carefully placed adjacent to the item and repeated with the caption. The numeral represented the page number.

Special Feature: Two features have long highlighted the annual Neiman-Marcus Christmas catalogs. A wide selection of special gift wraps is offered—ranging in price from $1 to $5 and gratis with gifts in the $100-plus range. A second looked-for feature is a high-priced gag gift. In the past this has included everything from "His and Hers" airplanes to a life-size stuffed lion with a diamond collar (and so the story goes, a buyer always seems to come along to shell out the thousands at which these gifts are priced). In its 1970 catalog, Neiman-Marcus offered special gifts for both "the optimist" and "the pessimist." For the optimist, it was a slow-growing live oak tree, two feet high and complete with its own Austrian-made Christmas ornament, priced at $10 each. For the pessimist, it was a modernized Noah's Ark—complete with animals: Said the copy: "The pessimist plans for any eventuality. Before the deluge, he prepares the perfect retreat from come-what-may. Our Noah's Ark, updated and refined, is guaranteed to be more comfortable than the original, albeit not as capacious. It sleeps 8 passengers; 4 ship's crew; one each: French chef, Swedish masseur, German hair stylist, English valet, French maid, Italian couturier, English curator/librarian, Park Avenue physician, and Texas A&M veterinarian. The animal deck accommodates (in pairs by specie) 92 mammals, 10 reptiles (could your wife stand more?), 26 birds, 14 fresh-water fish and 38 insects." Price, with animals, was "estimated" at $588,247.00, with four-years for delivery. For someone wanting something slightly less expensive, the catalog also offered "His and Hers" Thunderbirds. Loaded with Neiman-Marcus specified extras, the matched pair was priced at $25,000 plus tax.

Another special feature offered in a previous catalog was a new "Confidential Service." Copy explained:

> ***Many of our customers find themselves in the position of sending gifts to those in exceedingly high positions—kings, shahs, maharajas, prime ministers, and other heads of state. Obviously, such transactions must be kept completely secret and confidential.***

To assure such secrecy, Neiman-Marcus suggested sending confidential orders to a special address, where they would be handled by one of the three senior officers of the company: "No employee of Neiman-Marcus, other than one of the senior officers, will even know of the transaction. No written billing will be sent. Instead, billing will be by telephone." A 1% service charge was added for this service.

Yet another somewhat unique feature for a department store catalog is the inclusion of a large selection of non-gag high-price gifts. Typical: a $32,000 platinum and diamond necklace; a $6,975 ermine bathrobe; a $1,795 mink jacket; a $5,000 "wall of wine" (N-M offered only the wine racks but offered to furnish details on where to buy the proper wines to stock the wall); a

$495 cigarette box; a $110 woman's blouse; and dozens of other high-bracket clothing items.

While these special features add "spice" to the catalog, they have a possibly more important value—each year they generate reams of publicity for the catalog throughout the world.

Carl Forslund Furniture Catalog

One of the most beautiful mail order catalogs is the furniture book from Carl Forslund, Inc., of Grand Rapids, Michigan. A typical Forslund catalog contains 112 pages showing a wide variety of Colonial furniture, furnishings, and accessories. While only 16 pages of full color are used, they are well scattered through the monochrome pages and create the impression of a more colorful catalog than it actually is.

This 8½- by 11-inch catalog makes effective use of gravure to bring out the subtle details of the items featured. A variety of layout styles is used and copy is very informal and reads in almost storybook fashion. A typical item:

> *The Caxton Settle*—When you look at the swank model rooms in modern home magazines, do you notice how few decorators think that there is anyone left who ever reads a book? There are chairs without lights, and sofas have such low backs that you can't sit up (or sit back) to read. We found this real reader's couch in England, and photographed and measured it with the gracious permission of the owner of the White Hart Inn, a "rather-ing" but dashing retired Army officer. We modified it slightly (to make it perfect for *your* reading room), and the result is big and comfortable—75 inches wide, 21 inches seat depth, 42 inches high, with 27 inches back height inside. The price in A grade fabric, just like our own English brown linen in the picture (may we send you a good-size swatch so you can see the color and texture?) and shipped by freight prepaid is $337.10.

Throughout the catalog are many special illustrations and special copy to build a person-to-person relationship between the Forslund family and the company's customers. For example, along with the copy reprinted above and a 4½- by 6-inch illustration of the sofa is a small, 2- by 2-inch illustration showing Carl Forslund seated on the couch, with slippers and pipe, reading a good book. A short copy block says:

> On our own Caxton Settle at Drummond Island, we have electricity for reading but no phones to bother us (yet). We read what we like, and stop any time, and care not a whit to improve our minds, a most enjoyable plan. It's always surprising, though, to see one's self all double-chinned and baldish, just Grandpa . . . but that's real nice, of course!

Another informal touch is a letter on page three which introduces the catalog. It reads just like the personal "bringing-

The front and back covers of the Carl Forslund catalog, in attractive colors, are an excellent introduction to its personal, low-pressure selling.

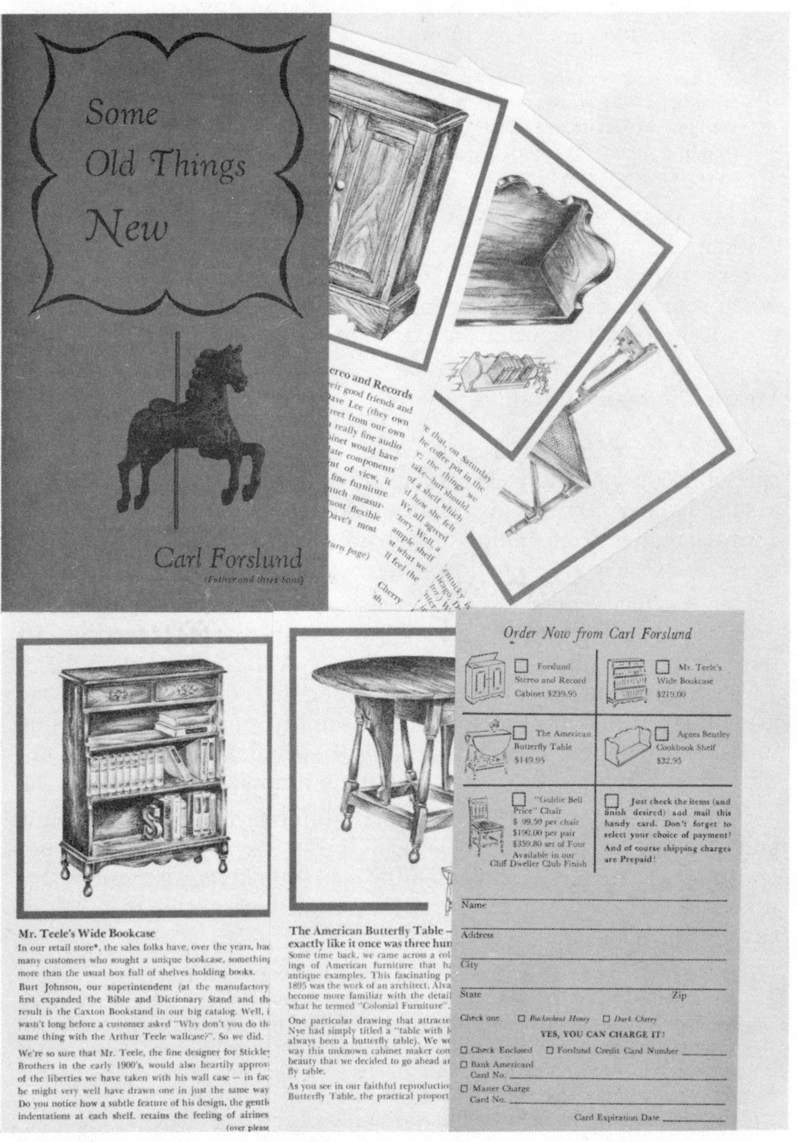

Some
Old Things
New
Carl Forslund
(Father and three Sons)
Mr. Teele's Wide Bookcase
In our retail store*, the sales folks have, over the years, hac
many customers who sought a unique bookcase, somethin
more than the usual box full of shelves holding books.
Burt Johnson, our superintendent (at the manufactory
first expanded the Bible and Dictionary Stand and th
result is the Caxton Bookstand in our big catalog. Well, i
wasn't long before a customer asked "Why don't you do th
same thing with the Arthur Teele wallcase?". So we did.
We're so sure that Mr. Teele, the fine designer for Stickle
Brothers in the early 1900's, would also heartily approv
of the liberties we have taken with his wall case -- in fac
he might very well have drawn one in just the same way
Do you notice how a subtle feature of his design, the gentl
indentations at each shelf, retains the feeling of airines
(over please
The American Butterfly Table –
exactly like it once was three hun
Some time back, we came across a col
ings of American furniture that h
antique examples. This fascinating p
1895 was the work of an architect. Alva
become more familiar with the detail
what he termed "Colonial Furniture".
One particular drawing that attracte
Nye had simply titled a "table with l
always been a butterfly table). We we
way this unknown cabinet maker con
beauty that we decided to go ahead a
fly table.
As you see in our faithful reproductio
Butterfly Table, the practical proport
Order Now from Carl Forslund
Forslund Stereo and Record Cabinet $239.95
Mr. Teele's Wide Bookcase $219.00
The American Butterfly Table $149.95
Agnes Bentley Cookbook Shelf $32.95
"Goldie Bell Price" Chair
$ 99.50 per chair
$190.00 per pair
$359.80 set of Four
Available in our Cliff Dweller Club Finish
Just check the items (and finish desired) and mail this handy card. Don't forget to select your choice of payment! And of course shipping charges are Prepaid!
Name
Address
City
State
Zip
Check one
Buckwheat Honey
Dark Cherry
YES, YOU CAN CHARGE IT!
Check Enclosed
Forslund Credit Card Number
Bank Americard
Card No.
Master Charge
Card No.
Card Expiration Date

In addition to its catalog, Carl Forslund sends out packets with each product shown on a separate sheet, printed in two colors.

friends-up-to-date" letters many families exchange at Christmastime. The final page in the catalog also uses informal language to explain the company's basic policies, ranging from shipping and payment terms to an invitation:

> This is a family business, and the best thing about families is their friends . . . so when you visit Grand Rapids (and my, how we love that!) you can expect to see Carl Jr. for sure, or if he's away, one of us will be standing in at the retail shop, 122 East Fulton Street. You're always welcome, as you know!

This page also explains the company's catalog schedule: "When do we publish new catalogs? At infrequent intervals (every two or three years), with some revisions and additions when reprints are necessary in between. So don't lend your copy promiscuously, but order an extra copy for your friend."

Heath Company Catalogs

A highly successful user of mail order catalogs to promote a special product line is Heath Company of Benton Harbor, Michigan, a subsidiary of Daystrom. Heath markets electronic products in kit form—ranging from radios to elaborate hi-fi sets and special electronic units such as an ignition analyzer and an electronic tachometer.

Heath's basic promotion piece is an annual catalog with approximately 56 pages. The 8½- by 11-inch catalog describes all the company's products in full detail. A typical catalog page (see illustration over) includes a detailed description of the kit; illustrations of the finished assembly, including an inside view; a schematic diagram; technical specifications; pricing details; and a reminder of the company's time payment plan.

Copy is designed both to stimulate interest in the specific unit and provide answers to technical questions. While explaining features so the nontechnical mind can quickly grasp their significance, all of the essential information desired by the technically minded is included. Typical:

> Why 70 watts? This is a question asked by many hi-fi enthusiasts. Serious audiophiles have felt the need for such an amplifier, and the Heathkit W-6M 70-watt amplifier is designed to fulfill that need. As the audio art progresses, so have the requirements of hi-fi components. Loudspeaker systems, for example, have vastly improved in bass response, necessarily decreasing their efficiency. Therefore, more amplifier power is required for the same acoustic output from the speaker . . .
>
> Silicon-diode rectifiers are used in the W-6M because of their compactness and long life. They have no filament to burn out or cause unnecessary heat. A heavy-duty transformer, coupled with the rectifiers, provides extremely good power supply regulation . . .

HIGH FIDELITY

25 Watt Amplifier KIT

Own One of the Finest

Specially Designed Peerless Output Transformer

Balance circuit requires only voltmeter for adjustment

Full 25 watt output with KT 66 tubes

Still a favorite in its power class, the W-5M represents one of the most outstanding high fidelity amplifiers available today at any price. It employs a specially designed Peerless output transformer and KT66 tubes to prevent loss of frequency response particularly at moderate volume levels, in addition to allowing increased power output. The circuit is rated at 25 watts and will follow instantaneous power peaks of a full orchestra up to 42 watts. Also featured is a "tweeter saver" which suppresses high frequency oscillation, and an easy-to-adjust balancing circuit to obtain "dynamic" balance between output tubes. In order to reduce harmonic distortion at low frequencies it is essential that the plate current of the output tubes be balanced. The exclusive balancing circuit in the W-5M makes this balancing operation easier and much more accurate. Precision balanced resistors are connected in the cathode circuits of the power output tubes. When the current in each tube is balanced, the voltage drop across each precision resistor will be the same as the resultant potential will be if measured at both cathodes at the same time. A great advantage is gained, since the current in both tubes is measured simultaneously instead of one at a time and only a voltmeter is required. A load limiting device is built into the amplifier to provide high frequency and transient stability. Rising impedance affects of speaker systems at higher frequencies will frequently cause oscillation in a feedback type amplifier, since the amplifier fails to match the load at these frequencies. To counteract this, a resistor and condenser have been installed in series across the output transformer secondary. The condenser is chosen to prevent loading of the amplifier throughout the audible portion of the spectrum and still provide loading above these frequencies. Results of this unique circuit arrangement add up to improved phase shift characteristics, reduced IM and harmonic distortion and improved frequency response with complete stability under all dynamic operating conditions.

All connectors and terminals are conveniently located on one side of the chassis apron. The circuit is fused, and two AC outlets are provided for accessory equipment. One outlet is switch-operated and can be used to automatically turn off record player motor when amplifier is turned off. Provision is made for matching 4, 8 or 16 ohm speakers at a terminal strip on the chassis. An attractive cover protects against tube breakage and accidental burns. The bottom plate has large rubber feet to prevent marring of furniture. Featuring stylish gold and black color harmony, the amplifier is suitable for built-in locations or as a bookshelf model. Conservatively rated, high quality components are used throughout to insure years of trouble-free performance. Easy to build and a thrill to use. **Shipped express only. Shpg. Wt. 31 lbs.**

MODEL W-5M $59^75

MODEL W-5: Consists of W-5M kit plus model WA-P2 preamplifier. Express only. Shpg. Wt. 38 lbs. **$79^50**

Specifications

Power output	25 Watts
Frequency Response	± 1 db from 5 to 160,000 cps at 1 watt
Harmonic Distortion	1% at 25 watts
Intermodulation Distortion	1% at 20 watts (60 and 3,000 cps, 4:1)
Hum	99 db below 25 watts
Damping Factor	40:1
Input voltage for 5 watts output	1 volt
Tube Complement	2—12AU7, 2—KT66, 1—5R4GY
Output Transformer	Peerless, Special Design
Power Requirements	105-125 volts, 50/60 cycles, 140 watts
Dimensions	13⅛" wide x 8⅛" deep x 8¼" high

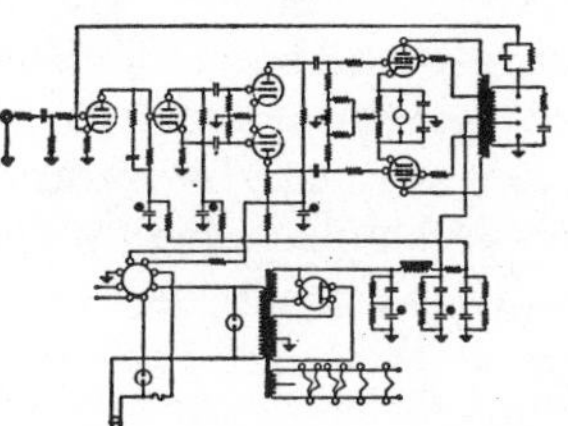

The Heath Company has been highly successful in using detailed, descriptive copy which has to provide answers to technical questions.

> You will not only thrill to the superb performance of the W-6M, but will take great pleasure in displaying the attractive styling and rugged construction of this top quality instrument . . .

Except for use of four colors on the cover and a second color on the first four and last four body pages, the catalog is black and white throughout. The majority of pages feature just a single kit. Order blanks and fold-them-yourself envelopes are bound into the saddle-stitched catalog.

Supplementary Catalogs

Heath supplements its annual master catalog with additional catalog units. Among them:

> *Ham Radio Market*—A 24-page, 7- by 10-inch supplementary catalog carries details on the full line of electronic kits of particular interest to ham radio operators. Two colors are used throughout and only a limited amount of copy, all carefully tailored to the interests of ham radio operators, is used.
>
> *Gift Catalog*—A Christmas gift catalog follows the same basic format of the Ham Radio supplementary catalog, except that copy is less technical and fewer products are included.
>
> *Stereo Special*—A special 12-page, two-color, 7- by 10-inch catalog aimed specifically at the hi-fi market was mailed to a group of prospects whose requests for information were received during a national hi-fi show. Featured was a four-page insert highlighting four key products illustrated in full color. Copy not only promoted the kits offered, but also sought to stimulate interest in hi-fi and in do-it-yourself assembly of stereo kits.
>
> *Test Facilities*—Another 24-page, two-color catalog promotes Heath's electronic test equipment. Copy is more technical than in the general catalog, but avoids an out-and-out technical approach.

Recognizing that the composition of its audience ranges from full-fledged "electronic bugs" to those who cannot tell an amplifier from a rectifier, Heath makes every attempt to serve the full range of prospects both through specialized catalogs and more detailed copy than would normally be used if the audience were more concentrated. In addition, Heath uses a number of supplementary techniques—both within the catalogs and as special printed pieces. For example, selector charts are frequently included in catalogs to help prospects choose complete high fidelity systems from among the vast variety of different units offered. To set aside fears of those who question their ability to assemble an electronic kit, Heath supplements catalog mailings with a four-page folder in question-and-answer format. Another highly successful supplementary piece is a 48-page booklet, "The How and Why of High Fidelity," which is offered for 25 cents through inserts included in catalog mailings. Over 160,000 of these booklets, which explain the ABC's of hi-fi, have been sold.

Allocating Catalog Costs

Writing in *Advertising Age,* Bob Stone states "Selling successfully via the catalog method is a combination of many things. But what really separates the men from the boys is a policy of ruthless analysis. The purist theory is: Every product offered must pay its way, or out it goes! In actuality the theory becomes watered down somewhat by several factors including (a) the need for enough selection to develop interest, (b) the need for enough pages to create a catalog appearance, (c) the need to test many new items to determine best sellers.

"But the more the purist theory is applied, the more profitable a catalog is likely to be. So let's examine the theory. Reduced to its simplest terms, the theory works like this:

"1. The total cost of the catalog in the mail is divided by the number of catalog pages. This establishes cost per catalog page.

"2. Then each item is 'charged' its cost of space based upon percentage of space allotted on a page. This establishes cost of advertising space for each item.

"3. When sales are all in, or projectable, a balance sheet is drawn for each item. The profit or loss for each item in the catalog is arrived at by taking total sales, less advertising cost, product and fulfillment cost and overhead.

"The merchandising director takes over after all figures are in, showing the winners and losers. And this is where wisdom comes into the picture. He doesn't simply repeat the winners and kick out the losers. Far from it. Let's look at two hypothetical cases through the merchandising director's eyes to illustrate the point.

"1. Here's an item that had half a page in the last catalog. The total sales came to $48,000. Advertising cost on a cost of space basis came to $6,000. All other costs, including merchandise, fulfillment and overhead, came to $24,000. It's a big winner. The merchandising director's decision is to give the item two-thirds of a page in the next catalog. He knows, based upon experience, an additional $2,000 investment on a 'hot' item will more than pay for itself.

"2. Here's another item which had a half page in the last catalog. But the balance sheet on this one showed a net loss of $1,000. The merchandising director decides against knocking this item out. Instead he decides to run the item again, but allotting one-fourth page instead of a half page. Experience tells him the item will make it with a lower advertising cost."

INDUSTRIAL CATALOGS

In terms of quantity of different catalogs, the industrial field is the out-and-out leader. There are but few industrial organizations in the country which do not issue some form of catalog. Sweet's Catalog Service Division of F. W. Dodge Corporation suggests there are four basic types of industrial catalogs in general use:

1. *The general catalog*—Probably the oldest industrial catalog form is the "general" or "company" catalog. Usually, it contains a "complete" description of every product the company makes. Because of its completeness, it frequently lacks flexibility in approach, making it difficult for different users to ferret out specific information they may require.

   Today, most general catalogs are used primarily for "internal" activities —salesmen, jobbers, dealers, distributors, warehousing, inventory, sales training, etc. Most companies, however, have adopted the loose-leaf form for greater flexibility.

   Sweet's observes: "If your company makes a *line* of products and sells to more than one market group, and the only printed product information you have for sales work, for answering ad inquiries, for use by potential customers, etc., is a general catalog, it is a hundred-to-one bet that your marketing program is very deficient in this respect."

2. *Promotion or institutional booklets*—While not a true catalog, such promotion pieces are frequently considered in the same breath as catalogs by many industrial marketers. They are usually attractive descriptions of the company, its history, facilities, contributions to industry and society, and often an account of its method of doing business with its customers.

   Such "catalogs" can be worthwhile primarily from a public relations standpoint. They are helpful and sometimes necessary in obtaining government contracts and in helping to introduce your company to important factors in new accounts. Sweet's observes, however, that the buyer wants information about products first, and information about the supplier second. "We have yet to see a case where an institutional booklet is a truly effective piece of *buying* promotion," says the memo.

3. *Product bulletins*—Generally speaking, these bulletins contain detailed technical data on single products or product lines. A highly efficient form for its purpose, the product bulletin can be timed with the introduction of products.

   "Product bulletins," says Sweet's, "afford great economy in that their limited number of pages makes them easy to revise, easy to mail, easy to file and easy to carry around. They are useful as components of a loose-leaf general catalog, and make it possible to sectionalize the loose-leaf general catalog." Two cautions are offered, however:

   Product bulletins are seldom specialized in their approach to the interests of buyers in different markets. Giving them the same catalog imposes a burden on each to translate the information into terms of their particular needs.

Because product bulletins give detailed information about a product or line, it is extremely difficult to organize the information to get the buyer to take a *specific buying action.*

4. *Market-specialized catalogs*—Such specialized catalogs are similar to the use of different ads in business papers aimed at different markets. They are planned to promote a specific buying action by potential customers with similar product interests. Each should contain information on all products of interest to buyers in the particular market, stated in terms of the specific interests of these buyers—and just enough information to induce the buyer to take the next buying step.

Three Types of Catalogs

Donald A. Dodge of Black-Russell-Morris, writing in *Sales Management,* describes three basic kinds of catalogs:

1. A high-priced, not-often-purchased product that demands technical knowledge and buying decisions by a team of engineering, management, maintenance, and purchasing men requires a technically oriented catalog that deals with *facts.* Here, concentrate on those details of your product that show exactly what it is, what it can and cannot do under a variety of conditions, its physical and chemical characteristics offering clues to its possible uses, and some typical current applications. Don't only tell, but *show* how it works with photos and diagrams.
2. Standardized, shelf-type maintenance supplies or replacement equipment requires another approach. Such items are comparatively low in cost, highly competitive, and normally available through local distributors or shipped on order from stock. Here, the catalog lists a composite of company products, gives all the facts for ordering, and, where possible, eliminates the need for a salesman's call. The product has, in large measure, been presold by other advertising methods, but complete information is still needed.
3. Engineered products, such as pumps, chemicals, metal shapes, and a variety of items meeting preset specifications, call for another form of catalog. Although price is a major consideration in selection, other factors have influence, too. Physical characteristics, chemical purity, uniformity of grain structure, delivery facilities, amount available, and your dependability should be stressed. In many instances, suitability for specific areas of application should be given to help narrow down the selection. Such catalogs place the burden of use responsibility on the buyer. The catalog should help him select the product that really meets his need, no matter how specialized his particular product may be.

Producing an Effective Industrial Catalog

W. M. Dickson, of the Douglas Fir Plywood Association, offers a nine-point guide to the production of effective industrial catalogs:

1. Divide your information into logical units.
2. Place these units in sequence—a sequence your buyer wants, needs, and will use.

3. Arrange your copy, illustrations and other pertinent data into close, well-knit groups.
4. Select a good type face—one that is readable, and one that has variety in its own family: bold, extended, italics, condensed, light, extra bold, and so forth.
5. Use two-page spreads. Be certain that information of a kind doesn't appear on the front of one page and the back of another. Instead it should appear well laid out, in the ideal visual unit, the two-page spread. (Normally, one visual unit is enough space to tell a factual story about any one element, phase or product.)
6. Use the most appropriate visual techniques. Make certain the pages have a good visual flow, that the eye is easily led from one area to another in a logical order. Keep the drawings three-dimensional or cross-sectional, and when dimensions are necessary, include *all* the important dimensions.
7. Use an index. It's important to the buyer. It saves him time.
8. Identify yourself on the cover. Be certain that it tells the buyer who you are, what your services or product are. Make it identify *you.* The back cover asks for the order. It lists branch offices or dealers. *Or* it contains sample specifications.
9. Use enough pages to tell your story. Avoid jamming. Balance the white space against the dark areas, and above all avoid coated stock. Glossy stock is out as far as many engineering design offices are concerned. It adds to the user's eyestrain by reflecting the glare of overhead lights usually found in most drafting rooms.

Sweet's Planning Checklist

Another excellent guide to the preparation of effective industrial catalogs is *Marketing Memo No. 17,* prepared by Sweet's Catalog Service after years of study by its research department:

1. *Front cover—does it quickly identify product and manufacturer?*

   As the front cover should be comparable to a poster in the brevity of its message, see whether it tells at a glance—by use of illustration, manufacturer's name, product name, trademark, or other means—what the catalog is all about.

2. *Index—if the catalog covers various products, are they easily found?*

   Check the index's value as an aid to the user in finding his way through the catalog by noting whether it shows the catalog's organization.

3. *Organization—is the catalog in clearly defined sections and visual units?*

   Observe whether the products are grouped according to specific uses and whether various types of information appear in the most logical sequence (according to importance of product to user, relative newness and oldness of products, etc.).

4. *Visual flow—is the catalog visually interesting?*

   See whether its visual techniques (use of pictures, color, charts, diagrams, shapes, etc., in preference to wordy texts) promote easy visual flow in and out of each visual unit and through the catalog.

5. *Content—is the information so developed that it promotes product selection?*

   Determine whether the information is sufficient for comparison and whether the catalog's presentation of product features, range of performance, applications, etc., facilitates comparison and promotes the intended buying action.

6. *Back cover—does it suggest the next buying step?*

   As the back cover should direct the user to sales offices, branches, representatives, or the manufacturer's special services, check for their inclusion, as well as telephone numbers and addresses.

Typography and Makeup

Still another effective guide to preparation of more effective industrial catalogs was prepared some years ago by B. M. Walberg, an account executive with John Mather Lupton Co., New York, for a series of articles which were published in *Industrial Marketing:*

1. *Are margins correct?* The best examples of bookmaking all show a graduated margin, the inside and upper margins being the narrower, and the bottom and outside the wider. Your catalog margins, perhaps cannot be as generous as those of handsome books, but still they can be attractive.
2. *Are reading lines short?* Catalogs are not read like newspapers. The reader's attitude is entirely different. We must, therefore, do everything we can to get the catalog read.
3. *Are columns right width to accommodate desired type and plates?* Large type in very narrow columns makes almost as uninteresting an appearance as small type in wide columns.
4. *Can indentations be improved?* The amount of indentation depends upon the width of the columns. Sometimes it is advisable not to have any indentation at all. Again, it may be better to set the first line flush and indent the rest of the paragraph.
5. *Do initials fit?* Initials are strong eye-attractors. They afford an introduction to the reading matter and should be used sparingly. They also serve to brighten what might otherwise appear to be a dull page by adding a pleasing touch of ornamentation.
6. *Are headlines balanced?* Headlines, since they are used for main features, are prominent and should harmonize with one another.
7. *Are running heads necessary?* Running heads tend to interrupt the reader's thought. The space taken up by these heads could be advantageously used for other purposes.
8. *Are subheads strategically placed to get attention?* It is an excellent selling point to put a subhead on a page every now and then, so that the reader's eye will focus on certain points or subjects that you wish him to notice. Subheads make reading easier.
9. *Is the most important item in the best position on the page?* The catalog page has an optical center, a point to which the eye naturally goes at first glance. Get your most important item in this space.

10. *Are borders economical?* Some pages which are loosely arranged need a border to give them compactness. When one is used it should be considered from the economical as well as from the artistic point of view.

11. *Is color properly placed?* The object in using color is not merely to make a better looking book, but also to make the reader more interested in the book. Color should be used to draw the eye to the reading matter. Color should be placed strategically so as to lead the reader along through the body matter.

12. *Has ornamentation been sparingly used?* The object of your catalog is to sell goods. Your only object in introducing ornamentation is to so dress up the catalog that your merchandise will show up to better advantage. Where the ornamentation is too elaborate, it diverts attention from the story, thus missing its object.

13. *Has allowance been made for special display?* In every catalog there are items of special importance. These should be arranged in the layout, so that they can be featured to good advantage. Special display also breaks up the monotony of the catalog and helps keep the reader's interest alive.

Organization of an Effective Catalog

Catalog consultant Norman Jervis, in an article which appeared in *Industrial Marketing,* claims organization of an effective industrial catalog can be reduced to three stages:

1. *Product information*—The product information we give in a catalog naturally varies with the type of product we are describing—it may be a piece of equipment, a material, or a service. In general, however, the information should include:

- *Identification of the product*—what kind it is, trade names, general advantages, codes or standards to which it conforms, the manufacturer's name, technical services, and distribution facilities.
- *Uses of the product*—recommended uses and limitations.
- *Forms of the product*—design principles, components and systems involved, sizes, appearance, composition and physical structure (in the case of materials).
- For materials, *properties* should be described.
- *Performance of the product*—installation, maintenance, durability.
- *Purchase of the product*—availability, specifying, location of sales representatives.

2. *Visual presentation*—This kind of information is best presented visually in the way that encourages and simplifies the use of your catalog.

   It is best to organize the information into "visual units," such as two facing pages self-contained in content, yet integrating with the other visual units in the catalog. These are points worth keeping in mind:

- Establish an *image* of your product. Whether you use photographs, drawings, or pictographs, you must convey to the reader what the product looks like.

- *Text,* whether in paragraph or caption form, should amplify the information conveyed pictorially, and should be both concise and factual.
- *Diagrams* may be charts, tables, and graphs, and these are more effective in presenting quantitative information than paragraphs of text.
- Type faces provide *accent.* They can effectively indicate *relationships* between elements of information—and they should always be selected for legibility.
- *Gradation* visually organizes catalog information so that the reader is instantly aware when an explanation or description applies to one or to a series of product types, applications, or characteristics.
- *Insulation* visually separates different groups of information from each other.

3. *A guide system*—Finally, to make it easier for the reader to find his way, we can speed reference to the specific items of information we have included with guide systems. These are simple, but effective, signposts that help the reader through the pages, pinpointing specific product information he is looking for.

   A guide system works as follows:

- The *selector guide* identifies major product information at the beginning of the catalog.
- It assigns a uniform *symbol* to each section.
- Combined with the product subject of the section, the symbol constitutes the *guidepost* throughout each section.

Utilization of these elements of good design can lead to an outstandingly successful catalog. They are tried and proved elements: tested for validity in thousands of catalogs and proved by continual studies of visual presentation for over 50 years.

Weaknesses of Industrial Catalogs

In 1956, with the cooperation of a leading industrial designer, Sweet's Catalog Service conducted a survey of catalog practices of nearly 1,000 leading U.S. firms. Analysis of catalog material from 748 of the companies disclosed three essential weaknesses common to a majority of the catalogs. These were described by Norman Jervis in his *Industrial Marketing* article:

1. They were not specifically tailored to the needs of design engineers. Much of the information was on products of no possible use or interest to the office which had asked for these catalogs. Also there was a lack of pertinent information on the very products this office was in a position to specify.
2. These catalogs were not designed with the buyer's need for *preliminary* product information in mind—to simplify and facilitate the first steps in selecting sources of supply. Too often, these catalogs contained a wealth of data that would be of interest only *after* the product had been bought and was in use; rather than the kind of data required at the time *buying* information was sought.

3. Most of the catalogs were not organized and arranged in a visual form to make it easy for industrial buyers to find the information.

Compiled Catalogs

Another important catalog group is the type which is compiled by a wholesaler or distributor. Such catalogs are generally produced by one of three basic methods:

1. Catalog compilers maintain a file of flexible units from which the wholesaler or distributor can select those units representing his product line. These units, containing illustrations and copy in a standardized format, are then combined into a tailormade catalog by the compiler.

2. Other wholesalers and distributors prefer to prepare their own catalogs. In most cases they depend upon illustrations and copy furnished by the manufacturers they represent, which are usually pasted up in page form for reproduction by photo-offset.

3. In a limited number of cases, catalogs are compiled by simply binding together preprinted catalog pages supplied by manufacturers.

While there has been a trend in recent years toward photo-offset catalogs compiled individually by wholesalers and distributors, this method generally results in an inferior catalog. While many attempts have been made to establish standards for manufacturers to follow in preparing catalog reproduction material to be used in such catalogs, the design, typography, and quality of furnished materials still vary greatly. As a result, many photo-offset catalogs present a disorganized appearance. Negative reaction on the part of customers has led many distributors to return to a quality catalog compiled and prepared by professionals after an unhappy experience with their own photo-offset substitute.

NWHA Catalog Standards

Among the groups which have prepared standards to guide manufacturers in the preparation of materials to be used in wholesalers' and distributors' catalogs is the National Wholesale Hardware Association. NWHA issued two sets of standards—one for material to be used for pages to be produced by photo-offset and the other for furnished catalog pages to be inserted in hardware wholesalers' catalogs. These standards are shown on pages 824 and 825.

PRICE LISTS

Although often excluded from the list of printed items requiring special design and copy consideration, the price list is a highly important part of many direct mail programs--and deserves far more consideration than it is usually given.

In the majority of direct mail pieces, prices are included as an integral part of the basic copy. However, there are some cases where special price lists are required. For example, there are occasions where different prices are offered to different groups, but it is impractical to prepare special printings of the basic literature for each of the groups. In other cases, it is desirable to have a quick-reference price list so prices for various items can be quickly compared. Such quick-reference lists are often valuable to supplement letters used for inquiry-answering so the letter can be kept unburdened with complicated pricing information.

Ideas for Price Lists

Lyndon E. Pratt, in an article which appeared in *Industrial Marketing,* suggests these ideas for preparing price lists:

> If pricing is considered from the standpoint of what is best for the prospective reader, certain things become obvious. The ideal pricing arrangement is for prices to be incorporated directly into the literature, whether specification sheets, brochures, or catalogs. But because prices change, this method may be impractical.
>
> Individual product price sheets are next in desirability. Any treatment where the individual product price sheet is attached to the product bulletin, in or out of the catalog, is an aid to the reader. It is often easier to be more specific in an individual product price sheet, for example, than in a general price sheet.
>
> On the debit side, the individual sheets involve extra cost and paper handling, and could, in a general catalog, add several pages. A compromise would be to use sectional price sheets, i.e., a price sheet for each catalog section (particularly where catalog dividers are used) to cover the products in that section.
>
> Normally, however, a general price sheet is necessary regardless of whether other types are used or not. It is important, then, that it be laid out carefully with particular attention to detail. General price sheets can be confusing if explanations are inadequate or exceptions not carefully spelled out for the reader.
>
> Finally, it is sometimes advisable to illustrate a general price sheet. This can be helpful where products or product type designations tend to be confusing because of complexity or similarity. Illustrations are one more factor contributing to quick identification for the reader.

STANDARDS FOR CATALOG PAGES FOR HARDWARE WHOLESALERS' CATALOGS WHICH ARE TO BE PRODUCED BY THE PHOTO-OFFSET METHOD

PAGE SIZE:	As selected by wholesaler.
PRINTED AREA:	7 by 10 inches.
MARGINS:	½ inch at top, ½ inch at bottom, ½ inch at outer edge. Binding edge as selected by wholesaler. Wholesaler's heading and page number to be placed in top margin.
COPY CONTENT:	Copy to be condensed, retaining only essential elements for buying data and interest. Generalized selling copy to be eliminated. Weights and packing to be included along with dimensions. Where various sizes are shown, they should be columned from top, with product numbers or sizes to left, prices at right, intermediate columns for size, packing, and weight.
UNIT SIZE:	Units should be made 1/5, 1/4, 1/3 or ½ column length.
ILLUSTRATIONS:	Line and halftone illustrations, with halftones in 100- to 120- and 65- to 80-line screen, from a direct letterpress proof.
SUGGESTED TYPE COMPOSITION:	
Heading of Items:	12- or 14-point Gothic bold, all caps.
Subheads:	10-point Gothic all caps.
Sub-subheads:	8-point Gothic all caps.
Numbers and Prices:	8-point Roman bold.
Body (Text) Copy:	8-point Roman light face, caps and lower case.
PRINTED SHEETS TO FURNISH FOR COPY:	All setups to be in black on white enamel or other glossy finish paper, letterpress printed clearly for best photographic copy. Printing on one side of the paper only. Size of sheet to be such as to permit mailing flat without folding.

STANDARDS FOR CATALOG PAGES FURNISHED BY MANUFACTURER TO BE INSERTED IN HARDWARE WHOLESALERS' CATALOG

PAGE SIZE:	12 by 12 inches.
PRINTED AREA:	7 by 10 inches. On color display pages space 1½ inches vertical and 2½ inches horizontal to be left at upper corner and outer edge for wholesaler use in pricing and furnishing special information.
MARGINS:	1 inch at top, 1 inch at bottom, ½ inch at outer edge, 4½ inches at binding edge.
PAPER WEIGHT:	Not to exceed equivalent weight of 16 to 20 pounds. Bond. Fewer pages—more items.
COPY AND LAYOUT:	Brief description—smaller cuts.
RECOMMENDATIONS:	Uniform arrangement. Print both sides of the page. Check copy to see that the following information is included where necessary. 1. Capacity or performance specifications 2. Material 3. Fabrication 4. Special Features 5. Operation 6. Color 7. Physical Dimensions 8. Packing 9. Weight 10. Number

Chapter 30

SELF-MAILERS AND POST CARDS

FROM a production standpoint, the self-mailer represents the least expensive of all direct mail formats. While the term is often used to describe any piece—card, folder, booklet, catalog, etc.—which is not mailed in an envelope, our reference here is to unbound pieces.

The most popular self-mailer is the post card. ("Postal card" refers to Government cards; "post cards," to cards produced by private manufacturers. Single and double postal cards are available through the post office.)

For some types of mailings—particularly those going to small lists—Government postal cards provide an economical, efficient medium. Since the printing surface is provided and they are already stamped, all that is necessary is to imprint and address them and a mailing is ready to go.

Picture Post Cards

For most direct mail purposes, however, picture post cards are a more popular medium. Because they are printed in standardized sizes, such post cards can be obtained economically.

Personal Medium

In addition to representing about the most economical type of full-color printing, the picture post card has another built-in advantage. To most recipients, a colored post card represents a friendly person-to-person contact, usually associated with happy times such as vacation trips. By taking advantage of this personal atmosphere, the post card can become an efficient direct mail tool. One of the major users of colored post cards is the automobile industry. Auto manufacturers regularly furnish their dealers color cards showing different models and colors. Some dealers imprint sales messages, while others have salesmen add a personal handwritten message.

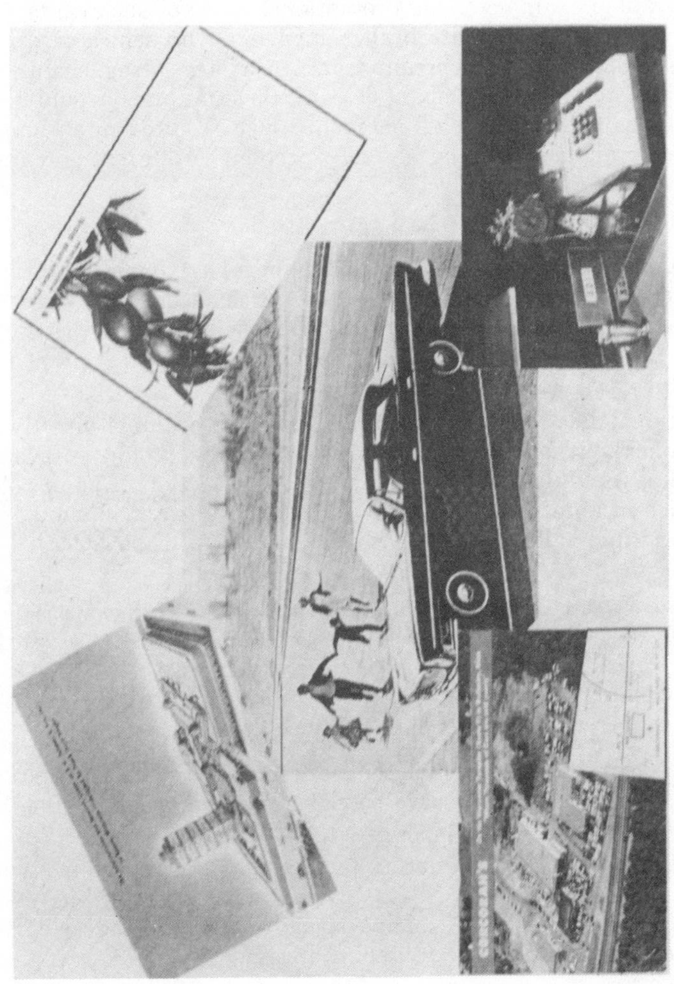

Multicolored post cards are an easy route to direct mail showmanship.

The White Motor Company used a series of eight post cards, each featuring a different White truck model owned by customers who transport everything from food products to steel. On the back of the cards was a brief description of the truck pictured and space for the salesman to pen a personal message.

A graphic example of the promotional value of such cards was demonstrated by a White branch manager who sent a card featuring a dairy and ice cream truck to a large drug chain. He simply noted on the back: "One of these Whites would look good in your colors." This personal touch resulted in an immediate sale and the opening of a new account with great potential.

Merchandising by Post Card

National Lead is one of many firms which have found color cards an excellent way to introduce point-of-purchase displays, magazine ads, and other promotional materials to dealers. Because the advertising material can be reproduced in full color quickly and at low cost, the cards do an excellent job.

National Lead also has used post cards to promote directly to consumers. It supplied paint dealers with a color post card showing its Dutch Boy Color Gallery, a collection of paint color samples in an attractive display unit. The message, in simulated handwriting, said:

> Yes, come in and see our "Dutch Boy" Color Gallery . . . filled with modern stylish colors to do that decorating job. You'll like the simple way your exact color needs can be filled. It's on display right now at..................

"I'm Coming" Announcements

Many traveling salesmen use picture post cards to announce their next visit to customers. While some salesmen use stock cards picked up en route, many firms have special post cards made up for this purpose.

A typical example is Ansco, which has cards printed with colorful shots "made from an original transparency on Ansco Color Film." These cards have space on the message side for the salesman to sign the following message:

> I expect to be in your city and plan to call on you on or about..................

There is also space for the recipient to use in making a list of items he will need to order when the salesman gets there.

Oster uses a similar technique with cards showing a variety of products used by barber and beauty shops. The message side says simply: "Will call (date)" and "Jot down your needs" (with several lines for fill-ins).

Detail men for the pharmaceutical firm, Pittman-Moore, use "will-call" cards with a humorous cartoon and message on one side.

Use of Stock Cards

Rockford (Illinois) *Morning Star* and *Register-Republic* sent out a series of stock picture post cards showing various local scenes. The messages, in simulated handwriting, pointed out that Rockford was a market of growing importance to advertisers.

The use of stock cards is a technique frequently overlooked by direct mail advertisers. Messages can often be adapted to fit any number of cards already available at low cost from local sources. Some producers of picture post cards make their complete picture or plate files available for use by advertisers wanting special subjects—thus eliminating the cost of photography and sometimes plate costs as well.

The reverse of this procedure is a technique which has been employed effectively by some advertisers. They make arrangements to have cards showing their plant or other facilities available through retail post card outlets. In some cases these cards are given free to retailers for resale; in other cases sold at a nominal fee. In still other instances the cards are placed in hotels, motels, transportation terminals, etc., for free use by tourists.

Post Card Showmanship

Many advertisers have turned to picture post cards as an easy route to direct mail showmanship. The dramatic promotional possibilities inherent in the color cards are limitless.

A Milwaukee printer, for example, sent prospects a series of picture post cards from vacation spots, all signed by a mysterious "Oscar." The first was sent from Amarillo, Texas, with a teaser: "Finally on that trip to the coast . . . Oscar." Another came from Tucson, Arizona, and read, "What a difference in climate—boy it's wonderful . . . Oscar." Similar messages arrived from Pasadena, California; Las Vegas; and finally one from Madison, Wisconsin. Immediately following this teaser series, prospects received a folder with the punch line: "Hey! I'm back . . . Oscar." Inside was a message from the until-then mystery man, who was finally identified as a pressman at Frank R. Wilke Printing Co.

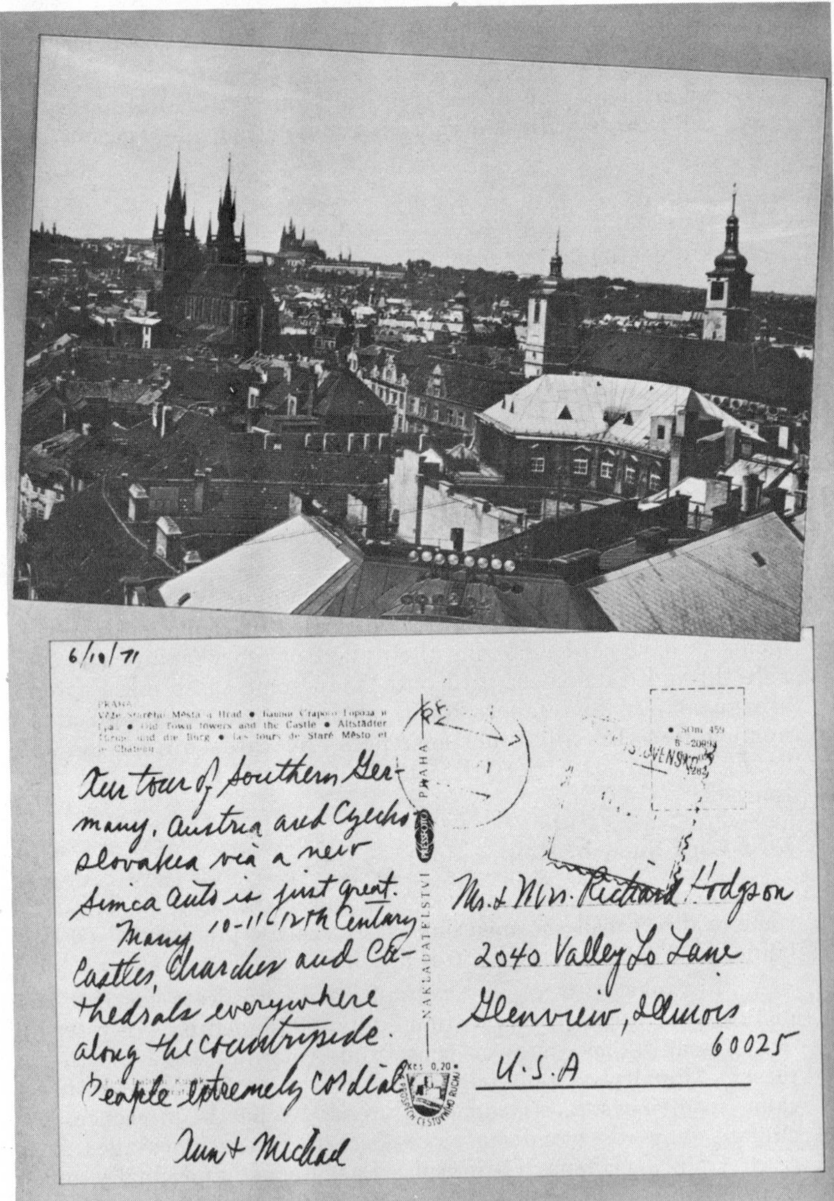

6/10/71

PRAHA

Old Town towers and the Castle

Our tour of Southern Germany, Austria and Czechoslovakia via a new Simca auto is just great.

Many 10-11-12th Century Castles, Churches and Cathedrals everywhere along the countryside. People extremely cordial.

Ann & Michael

PRESSFOTO PRAHA

NAKLADATELSTVÍ

Mr. & Mrs. Richard Hodgson
2040 Valley Lo Lane
Glenview, Illinois
60025
U.S.A

An excellent example of a "personal" picture post card with a subtle promotion for Simca automobiles. The author hasn't the slightest idea who "Ann & Michael" may be. In most foreign mailings such as this, the use of a colorful stamp enhances the total effect.

Lee Augustine's European Cards

Lee Augustine, president of Printing Machinery Company, takes promotional advantage of his trips to Europe by sending picture post cards to friends—business and personal—back in the U.S. But unlike most travelers, Mr. Augustine's personal mailing list numbers 1,500!

Before setting out on a trip, Mr. Augustine makes arrangements with scenic picture post card publishers in the countries he will visit to have selected cards ready and waiting for him when he arrives. He sends typed address labels directly to the publisher and has him affix both the addresses and postage before delivering the cards to his hotel. The publishers are instructed to use multiple stamps whenever possible.

Before he departs for his trip, Mr. Augustine has rubber stamps made up to convey his message from each country. He makes his first order of business upon arrival in each country the "stamping" of his message on the cards and getting them to the post office. Typical messages:

- *London* . . . "We like London. Supermarkets, central heating, hamburgers are all becoming a part of everyday English life. Printers are busy."
- *Paris* . . . "One thing that our out-of-the-country traveling does is to acquaint you of the fact that the world is full of many fine people. It has been our pleasure to meet such people in all of our travels. We find their interests and problems just like the ones that exist at home. Our friends may be interested in knowing that we have mailed 1,300 of these post cards from four different places in England and Europe. When traveling in this country we send cards to our friends abroad. It is part of our effort to promote international goodwill."
- *Stockholm* . . . "This is our first trip to Sweden. We hope during our stay to take many pictures depicting Stockholm in winter. We plan on spending some time with Olof Fridman, a participating member of the Craftsmen's Association. Olof had the pleasure of visiting the U. S. A. last year and met many craftsmen from coast to coast."
- *Heidelberg* . . . "This is a very interesting city. There are many Americans in this area—both military and civilian. We will drink to the health of our friends at one of the famous Heidelberg taverns."

Promoting Conventions

The Direct Mail/Marketing Association sent out a stock giant-size (6½- by 9-inch) card with a colorful picture of famed clown Emmett Kelly as "Weary Willie." Copy promoted a forthcoming convention. The picture was so appealing it was hard to throw away and became a constant reminder of the coming event to many recipients.

To tie in with a convention of the National Industrial Advertisers Association, *Industrial Marketing* magazine sent prospective advertisers a giant-size picture post card with an aerial view of San Francisco Bay.

Like so many other attractive stock picture post cards, these two giant cards provided added promotion mileage since they were frequently placed on office walls or bulletin boards.

Promoting a Meeting

The New York chapter of the Sales Promotion Executives Association picked probably the best attention-arousing postmark possible to promote a fall meeting—Moscow!

A picture post card showing the Kremlin was purchased at a New York bookshop. Then a message in simulated handwriting was imprinted. It read:

> Here gathering material for SPEA's big fall kick-off meeting at the American Exposition in Moscow.
>
> Look forward to seeing you on Sept. 16th at the Sheraton East. R. U.

The cards were then addressed and shipped to Moscow by Emery Air Freight (three days' transit time). A U. S. public relations firm which maintained an office at the American Exposition in Moscow affixed Russian stamps and airmailed the post cards back to the U. S. (return trip: eight days).

Neptune's "Fake" Post Cards

Neptune Storage of New York City also put picture post cards to showmanship use—but had to do a bit of faking to create the impression it wanted. Neptune started with black-and-white scenic views from various spots such as San Antonio's famed Alamo, San Francisco's Golden Gate Bridge, Washington State's Mount Rainier and a typical Florida scene.

The next step was to photograph a Neptune moving van from appropriate angles and strip the photos of the van into the photos of the scenic spots. (In the case of the Golden Gate Bridge and Florida scenes, it was necessary to "construct" roads where none really existed in order to work the Neptune vans into the pictures.) The black-and-white photos were converted to full-color shots by the Flexichrome method. The colored pictures were then printed as conventional picture post cards.

On the message side of the cards, simulated handwriting was used for "personal" messages from Neptune drivers. Addressing was done by hand by the same person who prepared the printed message copy. Typical copy (from The Alamo) read:

> Eating up the miles as usual, moving people . . . and hanging onto my safety record. Don't know whether you will be moving anyone out this way soon, but if you are, I'll be back in about two weeks, ready for another load.

Cards were signed by a Neptune driver and mailed about six weeks apart from appropriate post offices to traffic managers and real estate agents. While the messages and photos were "faked," the Neptune van drivers *did mail* the cards!

Mail Order Post Cards

While the conventional post card is not a common format for mail order advertisers, it has worked well for a number of companies. For example, Hale Indian River Groves, Wabasso, Florida, citrus packer, regularly mails double postal cards to its prospect list. One portion is printed in color with illustrations of fruit being promoted, along with appropriate sales copy, while the return portion contains a business reply order card.

More common in the mail order field are oversize cards and other self-mailer formats. The Butler Clinic, Mendota, Illinois, used a 5⅝- by 12-inch card to promote its line of publication handbooks. At one end of the card a 3-3/16-inch portion was perforated as a business reply order card. The remainder of the card contained promotional copy describing each of the handbooks.

A. A. Archbold, Burbank, California, publisher, uses an even more basic format—an 8½- by 11-inch sheet, printed on two sides (one color on colored stock). It is folded to a six-page self-mailer. The inside "spread" is used to promote a key publication, while two pages on the reverse side briefly describe as many as 17 additional publications with a coupon-type order blank. The remaining "page" becomes the address area.

Fidelity File Box, Inc., Minneapolis, uses a variation on this format. Its self-mailer is a 7¼- by 12¼-inch card folded to 3⅛ by 7¼ inches. Copy runs vertically on the card, with a perforated order form occupying the lower 3⅛-inch portion. The back side of card has additional promotion copy on the center half. The lower quarter is the address area, while the upper quarter is the face of a business reply card (backing up the perforated order form).

A somewhat similar format has been used by Better Letters Exchange, Howell, Michigan. This organization uses a 12- by 18-inch sheet folded to 4 by 9 inches. Opened to 9 by 12 inches, the first page is a letter; the inside spread contains basic promotion copy plus a coupon order form. The back page is used for the address area and some additional copy.

Disadvantages

The disadvantage of this type of format for mail order selling is that the respondent must furnish his own envelope. However, the low cost makes possible wider distribution for the same expenditure. In some cases this will yield the same return per dollar expenditure. Since there is no saving in postage, list rental, addressing, and some of the mailing costs, the advantage is usually with more conventional formats using envelopes.

Other Formats

Once you get beyond postal cards, post cards, and the other rather simple and basic formats just described, there is a vast variety of other self-mailer formats. Many people think first of the broadsides often used by retail stores—particularly supermarkets—for mailing to homeowners. These can be almost any size, and you just keep folding them down until you come to a convenient size for mailing. They are generally used to substitute for newspaper advertising in instances where no newspaper offers adequate economical coverage of a store's trading area.

Some mail order advertisers also use self-mailer broadsides. Brecks of Boston, for example, mailed a colorful 12- by 38-inch broadside from Holland, promoting flower bulbs. The piece was folded to 6½ by 9½ inches, and closed with a round paper seal. The sealing permitted insertion of a separate order form. To add to the impact, Netherlands postage stamps were affixed to the mailers.

Chapter 31

SHOWMANSHIP FORMATS

MOST effective direct mail involves the application of some degree of showmanship. Since one of the first jobs required of any mailing is to attract the recipient's attention, it is only natural to add an element of showmanship. But beyond the general use of showmanship in direct mail, there has been a growing use of formats which are out of the ordinary—formats which, by their very uniqueness, demand special attention.

This application of showmanship to direct mail deserves special attention. The very best showmanship formats will usually be items which have never before been used to convey direct mail messages to *your* audience. But while they may be new to most of your customers and prospects, chances are they have been used before to reach other groups. In fact, most of the best showmanship formats are based on ideas borrowed from some other medium and then applied in an unexpected way to direct mail.

The Role of Showmanship

There are four basic reasons for using showmanship in direct mail. Henry Hoke described them this way:[1]

1. It attracts attention, favorable attention when rightly handled.
2. It emphasizes the important points of your message.
3. It emotionalizes the appeal so that it strikes one or more of the basic human desires.
4. It creates *action* if the *impact* is appropriate.

In addition to its positive roles, showmanship in direct mail, if improperly handled, can have one very negative role—it can call attention to itself instead of achieving the purpose for which it was intended. Unless showmanship has a vital role, it should never be the key feature of any direct mail piece. Adroitly handled, however, it can be highly valuable in creating effective

[1]"How to Think About Showmanship in Direct Mail," by Henry Hoke. The Reporter of Direct Mail Advertising, Garden City, New York. 1961. $2.

direct mail. Henry Hoke suggested there are three basic reasons for using unusual mailing pieces:

1. To achieve a change of pace in a long or continuous campaign directed toward a more or less stabilized mailing list.
2. To demonstrate or visualize selling points. Unusual formats can be employed to add the "say it with flowers" technique to direct mail.
3. To dramatize consumer use or benefit in order to overcome: (1) human inertia; and (2) competition for the prospect's attention and patronage.

Mr. Hoke also offered seven basic problems to avoid in developing showmanship in direct mail:

1. Do not use any unusual or tricky format unless there is a real reason for it. Many advertisers are tempted to use so-called trick mailing pieces simply because they see something similarly clever used by someone else.
2. Be sure of your audience. Use same good taste and judgment in selecting unusual mailing pieces as you would use in your copy writing to a given audience.
3. Do not use unusual or tricky pieces on the spur of the moment, just to be different. Plan your unusual pieces carefully in advance, along with the rest of your merchandising campaign.
4. Be sure the finished job will look right when it reaches each recipient. Many good ideas go wrong due to amateur handling. For example, in die-cutting, be sure you use the right weight of stock. With tip-ons, be sure they will stay on. In sampling, be sure they are packaged right.
5. Realize that only a limited number of producers are equipped with machinery and experience to handle intricate, unusual formats properly. Some printers have discouraged the use of die-cuts because they are not equipped, or do not know how to handle them. Avoid disappointments by employing experienced production facilities.
6. Appreciate the limitation of tricky forms and abide by those limitations. Follow the advice of experienced designers who usually know what can and cannot be done.
7. A final rule of warning should be printed in large letters, framed and hung in clear view of every planning desk: *Do not make your unusual mailing piece so clever that the recipient will remember your cleverness rather than your offer.*

Seven Paths to Successful Showmanship

In their long-popular book, "Profitable Showmanship" (copyright Prentice-Hall, Inc., New York 1939), Kenneth Goode and Zenn Kaufman pinpoint seven general principles about successful business showmanship which can be applied to direct mail campaigns:

1. *Ideas are born right or wrong.* Showmanship calls for extremes—but the *right* extremes. Doing a thing differently may be doing it worse—no matter how differently! It does not help to be different when all the others are right.

2. *Find yourself a "natural."* The greatest danger in showmanship is the almost irresistible temptation to accept its traditional symbols—often threadbare and tawdry. Take hockey, for example. Red-white-and-blue uniforms look like showmanship. The idea of recruiting a whole Chicago team among American-born boys *is* showmanship.

3. *Think BIG.* Do not waste time on middle-sized elephants. There is no percentage in a "little-bigness," in second-bests. If you cannot get a Jumbo, the biggest of them all, don't compromise on a near-Jumbo. Reverse your attack completely and get a *baby* elephant, the smallest of them all. Lacking a whale, turn completely about and exploit a minnow. Take a lesson from the little tourist restaurant buried deep in the Alabama woods which courageously calls itself, "Swamp View."

4. *Do it surpassingly.* Sincerity in showmanship includes adequacy! Half a show is *not* better than none. It is worse! . . . Don't ever feel that because you have done your best you have done everything.

5. *Don't compete with yourself.* Do it surpassingly. But do not have more than one *it.* Circuses have six rings only to take care of 6,000 customers simultaneously. When the ringmaster seeks the climax of attention, he turns off everything but the spotlight, and speaks alone—quite softly. Advertisers, as a rule, give themselves more competition than their competitors do. You cannot get 300 percent attention by combining three 100 percent features.

6. *Make it crystal clear.* Sincerity in showmanship also includes absolute clarity of meaning. To avoid ambiguity may, in fact, be the greatest function of showmanship. True meanings must explode themselves—immediately, unmistakably, energetically to every mind.

7. *Keep it a game.* The genius of showmanship expresses itself in apt and picturesque play, sometimes quite unconsciously. Make your work interesting to people—and people will make it important for you.

Showmanship Checklist

While something unexpected is the ultimate in direct mail showmanship, most successful showmanship mailings fall into a relatively limited number of basic categories. For a Direct Mail Day speech in Detroit some years ago, the author prepared the following checklist of 20 basic ways to add an extra element of showmanship to direct mail:

1. *Magnify,* make it larger.
2. *Minify,* make it smaller.
3. *Adapt* something designed for another purpose.
4. *Add a color,* it is less costly than you might think.
5. *Change* colors, you can do this for "free."
6. *Add another dimension,* at least a third.
7. *Add another element* and a surprise.
8. *Add other uses* for prolonged impression.

9. *Modify,* the same thing done another way.
10. *Substitute* one element or more.
11. *Rearrange* the top at the bottom maybe.
12. *Reverse* the back at the front, too.
13. *Change time period* as it was back when or in the future.
14. *Change audience,* catch them by surprise.
15. *Personalize*—this is for YOU.
16. *Add quantity,* to emphasize quantity.
17. *Subtract quantity,* the other way around.
18. *Add fun*—for you, too.
19. *Split up,* for sustained impact.
20. *Get the recipient into the act*—always a good policy.

While this checklist establishes the basic points of departure for adding showmanship to direct mail, examples of direct mail showmanship in use are more easily divided with a different set of categories. This expanded checklist is shown on the following page and the examples of direct mail showmanship in action which follow have been presented in accordance with this 40-point checklist.

LETTER GADGETS

When many advertisers think of direct mail showmanship, their first thoughts are of letter gadgets—small plastic, metal, or cloth reproductions of various objects, usually in three dimensions. There are literally thousands of different letter gadgets available.

These letter gadgets have a flat back so they can easily be attached to printed material. While most commonly added to an illustration at the top of a letter, the dimensional objects have special impact when used in less common ways, such as on the covers of catalogs, as part of a reply card, and so forth.

A number of "working miniatures" are also available for use as letter gadgets. Gries Reproducer Corporation, 11 Second Street, New Rochelle, New York, for example, offers such items as tiny pliers, shears, wrenches, nutcrackers, jackknives, scissors, and tin snips which can actually be operated. Stegeman Specialty Manufacturing Company, Box 63, Newport, Kentucky, has miniature coil thermometers for use as letter gadgets.

AVENUES TO DIRECT MAIL SHOWMANSHIP

1. Letter gadgets
2. Other tip-ons
3. Unusual message surfaces
4. Magnification
5. Miniaturization
6. Unusual shapes
7. Unusual folds
8. Useful or unique items
9. Advertising specialties
10. Pieces designed for retention
11. Pieces designed for display
12. Games and toys
13. Historical items
14. Pieces designed for another audience
15. Unseasonal mailings
16. Unusual layouts and formats
17. Unusual copy styles
18. Unusual envelopes
19. Novelty packages
20. First day covers
21. Foreign mailings
22. Unusual postmarks
23. Unusual reply devices
24. Unusual mailing processes
25. Unusual art
26. Money and stamps
27. Phonograph records
28. Specialized stock materials
29. Special processes
30. Hard covers
31. Combining unrelated items
32. Product samples or parts
33. Check promotions
34. Clubs
35. Split-up mailings
36. Multiple mailings
37. Gag items
38. Teasers
39. Color
40. Personalization

OTHER TIP-ONS

While the letter gadgets specifically prepared for direct mail use are still very popular, there has been a growing trend to use of tip-ons which originally had another use. A trip to the local 10-cent store, for example, will yield hundreds of items which can be attached to direct mail pieces. Typical possibilities:

A button—"we're popping our buttons"

A key—"here's the key to . . ."

Feather—"you'll be tickled"

Brass fastener—"let's get down to brass tacks"

Piece of string—"no strings attached"

Toy watch—"it's time to . . ."

Calendar pad—"don't forget this date"

Blue ribbon—"it's a winner"

Magnifying glass—"take a close look"

Balloon—"you can expect big things"

Toothpick—"take your pick"

Aspirin—"no headaches"

Such a list, of course, is almost endless. Nearly every item small enough to be attached to a direct mail piece will suggest at least one possible copy theme.

Light & Power Utilities Corporation

To build interest in the opening of a new plant in Olive Branch, Mississippi, Light & Power Utilities Corporation of Memphis, Tennessee, prepared a series of five mailing pieces featuring tip-ons. Each was designed to represent a different stage of the building process:

1. *Cellophane bag filled with dirt*—"Here's the Real Dirt." Copy explained the dirt came from the first shovelful of earth at ground-breaking ceremonies.

2. *Length of steel wire*—"Hey—We've Got the Steel." The steel wire was bent in the shape of an "S" and used as the "S" in "Steel" in the headline. Copy poked fun at the fact that construction had been delayed by a steel strike.

3. *A piece of electrician's wire*—"We're Really Wired!" The "W" in the headline was formed by bending the wire, and copy explained the building was up and electrical wiring had begun.

4. *A cellophane bag with a lock of hair*—"Are We Tearing Our Hair!" Copy comically described woes of moving into the new plant. The hair was cut from switches bought at a local 10-cent store.

5. *Metal letter opener*—"Get the Point?" The letter opener was inserted through the cover of a folder so the point formed an arrow aimed at the location of the new plant on a map printed inside. The piece announced the formal opening of the plant and served as an invitation to attend the opening ceremonies.

Wolverine Tube

Probably nobody has ever produced such a continuing barrage of showmanship direct mail as H. A. "Hi" Harty of Wolverine Tube Division, Calumet & Hecla Inc., Allen Park, Michigan. Almost weekly, Mr. Harty mailed out something unusual to one of his company's lists. Letter gadgets, other tip-ons, and showmanship mailings of all kinds are included in the campaign. Typical mailings:

Sample package of chewing gum—"Here's a bit of sugar coating that you might like to chew on . . ."

Piece of stone—"You can't get blood from a stone . . ." The stone was integrated into an illustration so it appeared a needle had been stuck into the stone. A tube led from the needle to a plasma bottle.

Package of flower seeds—"How does your garden grow?"

Key chain hanging from an illustration of a vest—"Link your name to Wolverine"

Mousetrap—"We built a better one"

Tiny shoe-shine kit—"Finishes are important"

Stick of sealing wax—"Don't seal off condenser efficiency"

Piece of chalk—"Chalk up another for Wolverine"

Small metal snap—"It's a snap!"

Peanut—"It's what's in the shell that counts"

Miniature billboard—This piece, which is repeated frequently, has a clever saying on one side and product promotion on the other. Designed to stand on a desk, the clever saying is displayed to visitors while the product promotion stares at the original recipient of the mailing day in and day out.

For those who question the advertising value of gimmick mailings of this type, a couple of letters Mr. Harty has received from people on his mailing lists—typical of hundreds he received—are eye openers:

"This note is to compliment you on your sales promotion campaign carried on by mail during the last year. You have succeeded in keeping your company name clearly in front of us at all times. Quite often industrial selling lacks good and simple merchandising tricks."

"We certainly appreciate and thank you for your novel advertisements which you forward so faithfully. We would like to know where we may purchase your line in this city."

A most interesting aspect of the Wolverine mailings is the care which was taken to design "selling" mailing cartons. Most of the showmanship pieces were sent either in a paper tube, 1 inch in diameter and 6 inches long, or in a 4- by 4- by ½-inch miniature of Wolverine's product shipping cartons. The tube is a natural since

Wolverine manufactures tubes, but it has an additional advantage: Ever try stacking mail atop a round tube?

UNUSUAL MESSAGE SURFACES

Another of the more common direct mail showmanship techniques is to print the message on an unusual surface. Probably the most commonly used of the showmanship surfaces is a sheet of sandpaper. Hundreds of direct mail advertisers have chosen this technique to put across a sales message. It's so successful it is often repeated by the same advertisers.

Various cloth items are often used. Many of these, such as carpenters' aprons, newsboys' bags, chefs' hats, etc., are normally imprinted items. Perhaps more impact is obtained when a cloth item which is usually not imprinted is used. For example, a number of direct mail advertisers have printed their messages on beach towels, washcloths, dish towels, napkins; and at least one advertiser printed his message on a pair of ladies' panties! Swatches of unusual cloths are also used effectively.

Substitute Surfaces

There's no reason why your direct mail message *must* be printed on conventional printing paper. Some of the most outstanding showmanship mailings have been created simply by substituting another printing surface. Among the items you might consider:

A business machine company printed product information on an adding machine tape.

A radio network printed a colorful promotion message on a large beach towel.

The blank side of wallpaper has been used by a number of companies.

Sandpaper makes an attention-arousing surface with many logical copy themes.

A "We're Hanging Out Our Shingle" message was printed on a real shingle.

Fabrics used for unusual purposes create a lot of attention. One example: a letter printed on cloth used for making brassieres.

Aluminum foil can be very effective for special illustrations.

. . . and somewhat more common: sheets of acetate, plywood, thin sheets of metal, placemats, polyethylene bags, book jackets, bread wrappers, bottle labels, graph paper, formal invitations, decks of cards, shopping bags, wrapping paper, shelf paper, crepe paper, paper towels, napkins, children's bibs, and many other items.

Still another possibility is using items which have originally been imprinted for another use. For example, hotel or resort letterheads can often be used effectively. For some campaigns, lined paper from legal pads or school tablets is a natural. Graph paper, accounting forms, safety paper, and other preimprinted stock can also be useful.

MAGNIFICATION

The simple expedient of increasing the size of a mailing piece can often produce the desired element of showmanship. Lacking another idea, many direct mail advertisers have simply blown up their usual 8½- by 11-inch letters to 17 by 22 inches and created real impact. Giant-size telegrams, too, are a popular showmanship technique.

A particularly impressive mailing was a 10½- by 15-inch formal invitation sent out by the Rayon Information Center some years ago. The combination of formality with showmanship size was a real stopper. Another blowup which had real impact was "The Texan Scratch Pad," mailed by The Clegg Company of San Antonio. Its pages were 14 by 16 inches.

Die-cut product or package replicas in giant sizes also are an effective way of making a point. In a similar vein, Harris-Intertype Corporation mailed a replica of a dime 12½ inches in diameter printed on aluminum foil. Copy made this point:

> *Biggest Dime in Printing*—It represents the 2,000 extra impressions per hour you get with a Harris 14 by 20 inches . . . 2,000 more than you get with the next best press. Sure, a Harris costs a couple thousand more—with good reason. But you will keep it at least 10 years (only a fraction of its useful life). That is only $200 a year more. And if you run your Harris 2,000 hours a year (you will probably run it a lot more than that)—it amounts to only a dime an hour more. So, for this dime you get 2,000 extra quality impressions per hour! Can you think of a better way to make money in the printing business?

MINIATURIZATION

Even more popular than blowups are miniatures, which have long been a favorite direct mail showmanship technique. For some reason, big impact seems to come in small packages. Miniature letters, for example, are not only economical but often achieve better readership than their big brothers.

To be most effective, a showmanship miniature should be instantly recognized as a miniature of some object of established basic size. One popular technique is to send out a miniature of a 24-sheet poster—the common "billboard." Sharp & Dohme has used miniatures of record albums for mailing samples of its drugs.

One highly effective campaign featuring miniatures was used by The Reynolds & Reynolds Co., of Dayton, Ohio, to promote its specialized business forms. A series of four folders each had tiny reproductions of common business forms tipped inside.

UNUSUAL SHAPES

Die-cutting can quickly add an element of showmanship to an otherwise static mailing piece. This has long been a favorite showmanship technique for publishers promoting the sale of advertising space. *American Home,* for example, mailed a string of five giant-size, die-cut hot dogs. Copy read: *"American Home* said, 'Take a pound of frankfurters,' and within 30 days 7,043,200 dogs went down the hatch! . . . 768,800 women tried the recipes . . . 1,023,000 said they planned to . . ." and on into a sales pitch. A red string held the five weenies together.

Coronet magazine announced new advertisers by cutouts in the form of products sold by the advertisers. *Life* produced a red cardboard vest, which opened to tell the story of a promotion for men's clothing.

Aigner Index Company of Long Island City, New York, took a regular Government postal card and die-cut a filing tab, then laminated it, and used the piece to urge recipients to write in for a copy of the company's guide to indexing.

Message in a Slot

One of the most popular uses of die-cuts for direct mail showmanship is to cut a slot into an illustration and then insert the message—printed on a separate sheet—into the slot. Several stock "pull-out" formats are available for direct mail use. In addition to the stock formats, many direct mail advertisers create their own pull-out pieces. *American Girl* magazine, for example, prepared a folder which featured a cover illustration of a teen-age girl. From a slit in her hair protruded a tab reading "Pull Out Slowly." On a long strip of paper below the tab was a series of "the thoughts which go through a girl's head."

One of the best-remembered showmanship formats of all time was a piece created by Nick Samstag for *Time* magazine in 1956 using the "pull-out" technique. The piece was aimed at defining the type of reader who subscribes to the newsweekly. It was a giant piece mailed in an 8- by 14½-inch envelope with a hotel room key printed on it. The 7½- by 14-inch enclosure had a cover simulating the marble top of a hotel desk with the hotel's registration card atop the surface. The card contained the registration of an Edward Chandler, Jr., of White Plains, New York, an executive of the mythical Isoplast Corporation of New York City. He had been assigned to Room 608.

When the fourfold fanfold piece was opened, the recipient encountered the pigeonholes of the also-mythical Hotel Carleton-Cavendish in Chicago. Inserted into a die-cut slot in the box for Room 608 was the mail awaiting Mr. Chandler—all pieces were very realistic in appearance and revealed a lot about this *Time* reader. Included was a telegram which showed he was an important and successful businessman; a letter from his wife, which included a simulated clipping from the latest issue of *Time* concerning a spot they should consider for a vacation (the letter revealed more about the nature of the man); and a detailed hotel bill itemizing expenditures which proved Mr. Chandler to be the type of man potential *Time* advertisers should be interested in reaching.

Every attempt was made to create realism—right down to an actual canceled airmail stamp on the letter from Mrs. Chandler. Even the simulated *Time* clipping was printed on both sides for complete realism.

Time's promotional message was slipped into another die-cut slot —in the box for Room 584.

An obvious die-cut format is a multiple cut-out paper doll. This technique was used by the Premium Advertising Association of America, Inc. to promote one of its premium forums. The subject of the meeting was "Mrs. Customer." Details were printed on the upper halves of six pages of a 12-page fan-folded piece. The lower halves were die-cut in the shape of a lady paper doll—just the way a first-grader would cut it. When the piece was opened to its full 21 inch length, a string of six interconnected paper dolls was visible below the six pages of copy.

UNUSUAL FOLDS

Probably the least expensive way to add an element of showmanship to a direct mail piece is with a "trick" fold. In many cases, there will be no extra cost at all. Yet the technique can be highly effective—dramatic and, often, utilitarian.

The most common of the special folding techniques is to short-fold a sheet so one page extends beyond another. This is particularly effective with duplex paper stocks—those with a different color on each side of the sheet. With a short fold, the second stock color is visible along with the first and gives the impression of multicolor printing. Short-folding is also particularly effective when different colors of ink are used for printing on each side of the sheet.

Angle-folding is also an easy way to add showmanship to a direct mail piece. The usual technique is to dog-ear a corner of the sheet. Such folds can be used in a variety of ways. The Indianapolis Mail Box Sales Club, for example, used a letter with an illustration of an envelope in the upper-right-hand corner. The dog-eared corner was then folded down to form the flap on the envelope illustration. When the flap was lifted it revealed the contents of the envelope. The same technique is often used to "hide" the answer to a puzzle or question featured in the copy—"lift the flap for the answer."

Still another popular type of trick folding is the pop-up fold. This usually involves scoring the printed piece so a portion is folded over inside. Then, when the piece is opened, this portion pops up. The Union Pacific Railroad, for example, used a folder of this nature to promote a new style of dome lounge car. An illustration of the dome was die-cut at the top of a folder, then folded down inside the piece. When the two outside flaps of the folder were opened, the dome "popped up" into position at the top of a railroad car.

USEFUL OR UNIQUE ITEMS

There's no end to the showmanship possibilities when you build a mailing around some useful or unique item. Here is a handful of the thousands of possibilities:

Candy. Circulation Associates of New York mailed a box of Lifesavers candy to illustrate the theme: "Life savers—that's what Esso Standard Oil calls us." In another mailing in the same series, a box of Crackerjack illustrated the testimonial from another customer, who thanked the company for a "crackerjack job."

Shoelaces and razor blades. To urge its salesmen to push fuse links when selling other lines, General Electric mailed a variety of items usually considered tie-in sale items:

Shoelaces—*"Sell shoelaces with shoes"*

Razor blades—*"Sell blades with razors"*

Paint brush—*"Sell brushes with paint"*

Pen nib—*"Sell pen nibs with ink"*

Golf tee—*"Sell golf tees with golf clubs and balls"*

Calendar pads and thermometers. To encourage the recipient to display a direct mail piece on his desk or wall, a small calendar pad or thermometer can be tipped on.

Letter opener. To get its salesmen to pay more attention to the sales promotion material available for their use, Westinghouse added a letter opener to the cover of a brochure. Copy was written in an Oriental theme—a logical tie-in with the letter opener which was encased in a wooden sleeve with colorful Oriental decorations.

Simple printed pieces. A variety of simple, yet useful printed pieces can be used effectively to add showmanship to a direct mail piece. Wallet-size folders, for example, can be designed for use as a "dates to remember" record; phone number record; sports schedules; train, bus, and plane schedules; pocket calendars; baby-sitter logs; street directories; and so forth.

Picnic plates. A set of paper picnic plates, imprinted with a sales message, was used by the *Chicago Tribune* to promote advertising in a special summer issue.

Bra. The *St. Paul Pioneer Press-Dispatch* made media buyers really sit up and take notice when it mailed a real bra, mounted on cardboard. A ticket above the bra read, "If you have a sag in your St. Paul sales—pull." A gentle pull on the ticket produced a nice uplift in the bra.

Uranium. The Bureau of Advertising mounted a small piece of uranium on a card with the label: "You never know how loaded a little thing can be!" Copy went on to dramatize newspaper services in advertising and marketing.

Umbrella. Timing was highly important with a promotion piece once sent out by *Collier's*. To promote its "umbrella coverage," the now-defunct magazine had Western Union deliver real umbrellas to media buyers on the first rainy day.

Office plant. General Electric once sent a decorative plant to secretaries of its marketing managers. It was intended for display in their offices, serving as a reminder of a special program. For followup mailings, GE sent plant food tablets, a miniature cultivator, and a plastic plant trellis.

Nuts and bolts. A number of direct mail advertisers have grasped a special showmanship opportunity by mailing out sets of nuts and bolts for attaching license plates to cars—timing their mailings to coincide with a logical time for new licenses.

Pocket diary. When you have a special date, or series of dates, to emphasize, a pocket diary can be a natural showmanship item, perhaps with a special insert for the important dates.

Birdhouse. Philadelphia adman Harold M. Norman sent prospects a small wooden wren house with a promotional message on the roof.

Shopping bag. Seventeen magazine used a real shopping bag, imprinted with a fictional shopping list made out by a teenager after reading the magazine.

Flowers. When switching to a new format some years back, *American Weekly* boxed a copy of the first issue with the new look along with an artificial American Beauty rose.

Ties. To emphasize money-saving advantages, *Steel* magazine mailed a plaid bow tie.

Brushes. To illustrate "the difference in coverage," Mt. Washington TV Inc., in Portland, Maine, sent out a box containing two brushes—one large and one small.

ADVERTISING SPECIALTIES

A similar showmanship technique is to combine two media—direct mail and specialty advertising. Any advertising specialty jobber can show you hundreds of different items—either imprinted or unimprinted—which can be used to add showmanship to your direct mail pieces.

Lewis Shoe Stores

One of the best examples of the advertising specialty-direct mail combination is a mailing made by Lewis Shoe Stores of Waco, Texas, which sent ballpoint pens with a red ink filler to 1,200 schoolteachers (to use in marking tests and papers). An accompanying letter invited the teachers to visit Lewis for free refills and, if they desired, to open charge accounts. The mailing had amazing results: 63% of the teachers receiving the pens opened new accounts!

Matches by Mail

One of the most popular advertising specialty items for direct mail use is the book match. Hundreds of advertisers use this combination medium regularly. It is important to remember, however, that foil-lined mailing cartons are required for shipping matches through the mails.

A particularly popular showmanship idea, most frequently used by savings banks, is to send an attractively packaged box of 25 book matches imprinted with either "It's a Boy!" or "It's a Girl!" to new parents—usually accompanied by a gift certificate worth one dollar toward the opening of a new savings account for the newborn child.

Source of Supply

Your local advertising specialty supplier will usually turn out to be not only an excellent source of supply for the items you need for showmanship direct mail pieces, but often a fertile idea source as well. In most every major metropolitan area, there is at least one creative advertising specialty organization which is capable of assisting a direct mail advertiser in planning showmanship mailings.

The list on the following pages provides a good cross section of the items available through most any specialty jobber.

PIECES DESIGNED FOR RETENTION

It is not necessary to "add" something to a direct mail piece to achieve showmanship. A particularly effective showmanship technique is to create pieces with enough importance to make recipients want to save them for future reference.

One of the best campaigns of this nature has been developed by Sloves, the New York sales presentation and binding house. Some years ago, Sloves mailed an attractive 6- by 6- by 4-inch desk-top filing box with a hinged cover. Inside were a variety of samples of bindings offered by the company—useful miniatures. Also enclosed was a starter set of case histories describing effective sales presentations Sloves had designed. Each of the case histories was printed on a colored post card with a bleed full-color illustration on one side and detailed copy describing the presentation on the reverse.

But the file was just the start of a continuing direct mail campaign, which ran for several years. Periodically, Sloves sent out additional case history cards to be added to the file.

Similar continuing direct mail programs are built around loose-leaf binders and other "collection" devices.

PIECES DESIGNED FOR DISPLAY

Closely related to the showmanship technique of designing direct mail pieces for retention is to create items which can (and will) be displayed. This technique has the added advantage of extending the audience of your direct mail beyond the original recipient.

Perhaps the most famous of direct mail programs using this showmanship technique are the "Let's Have Better Mottoes" Association mailings created by the late Fred Gymer and now pub-

ADVERTISING SPECIALTIES

Here is a representative cross section of the thousands of different advertising specialties which can be integrated into a showmanship direct mail campaign:

Address Books
Almanacs
Animated Pictures
Appointment Books
Aprons
Arm Bands
Ash Trays
Auto Booster Plates
Auto Bumper Signs
Auto Clothes Hangers
Auto Dash Accessories
Auto License Frames
Auto License Holders
Auto Mirrors
Auto Record Books
Auto Reflectors
Auto Trouble Lights
Auto Visor Accessories
Baby Bibs
Baby Books
Baby Combs
Baby Forks & Spoons
Baby Rattles
Back Scratchers
Badges & Buttons
Baggage Tags
Ball-point Pens
Balloons
Bang Guns
Bank Bags
Bankbook Cases
Banners
Bar Accessories
Barbecue Aprons
Barometers
Baseball Schedules
Bill Hooks
Billfolds
Blankets
Blotter Packs
Bobby Pin Kits
Book Covers
Book Edge Protectors
Book Ends
Bottle Openers
Bowl Covers
Bowl Scrapers
Bowling Books
Box Openers
Bracelets
Bride's Books
Bridge Pencils
Brushes
Budget Keepers
Bullet Pencils
Cake Knives
Calculators
Calendar Cards
Calipers
Can Openers
Canes
Caps & Hats
Card Cases
Carpenters' Aprons
Carpenters' Pencils
Carving Sets
Catsup Dispensers
Ceramic Specialties
Change Pads
Change Purses
Christmas Cards
Cigarette Cases
Cigarette Dispensers
Cigarette Lighters
Cigarette Servers
Circuit Testers
Clipboards
Clocks
Coasters
Cocktail Forks
Cocktail Shakers
Cocktail Stirrers
Cocktail Trays
Coffee Measures
Coin Bags
Coin Holders
Coins & Tokens
Comb & File Kits
Comic Books
Commemorative Plates
Cook Books
Cooking Timers
Correspondence Clips
Crayons
Cutlery
Danger Signals
Decalcomania
Desk Accessories
Desk Calendars
Diaries
Dictionaries
Diet Guides
Dish Mats
Doodle Pads
Drink Pourers
Dust Pans
Egg Separators
Egg Timers
Emblems
Emery Boards
Envelope Moisteners
Eraser Shields
Erasers
Eyeglass Cases
Eyeglass Tissues
Eyebrow Pencils
Family Record Books
Fans
Farm Record Books
First Aid Kits

ADVERTISING SPECIALTIES (cont.)

Fishing Accessories
Flags
Flashlights
Fly Swatters
Folding Cups
Food Gifts
Four Leaf Clovers
Fruit Cakes
Fruit Picks
Games
Garden Markers
Gardening Accessories
Gear Gauges
Glare Shields
Golf Ball Markers
Golf Score Books
Golf Tees
Guest Books
Handkerchiefs
Headbands
Helmets
Historical Documents
Horoscopes
Hose Dryers
Hosiery Mending Kits
Hot Plates
Humidity Indicators
Humidors
Hunting Accessories
Ice Picks
Ice Scrapers
Inflatable Cushions
Inkstands
Invisible Ink Cards
Jar Openers
Key Holders
Key Racks
Key Rings
Key Tags
Kitchen Reminders
Kitchen Tools
Kites
Knife Sharpeners
Ladders
Lariats
Letter Openers
Levels
Library Sets
Lipstick Cases
Lipstick Tissues
Liquor Recipe Books
Litter Bags
Lollipops
Luggage
Luggage Tags
Magnetic Pencils
Magnets
Magnifiers
Maps
Marking Pencils
Match-Folder Specialties
Measuring Cups
Measuring Spoons
Mechanical Pencils
Memo Books
Memo Holders
Memo Pads
Memorial Books
Mending Kits
Meter Reminders
Mileage Calculators
Milk Bottle Covers
Miniatures & Replicas
Money Bags
Money Clips
Mugs & Steins
Musical Specialties
Nail Clippers
Nail Files
Name Plates
Napkins
Neckties
Needle Books
Needle Dispensers
Needle Threaders
Noisemakers
Note Books
Oil Reminders
Oilers
Optical Illusion Cards
Orchids
Paint Paddles
Paper Weights
Pass Cases
Pen Holders
Pencil Boxes
Pencil Clips
Pencil Sharpeners
Pennants
Perfume Dispensers
Perfume
Perpetual Calendars
Phone Book Covers
Phone Dial Caps
Phone Ear Pieces
Phone Holders
Phone Indexes
Picnic Kits
Pin Cushions
Place Mats
Plant Tags
Plaques
Play Money
Playing Cards
Pocket Calendars
Pocket Mirrors
Pocket Protectors
Pocket Secretaries
Poker Chips
Polishers
Polo Shirts
Portfolios
Postal Scales
Pot Holders
Pot Scrapers
Powder Puffs
Prayer Books
Preserves & Jellies
Puzzles & Tricks

ADVERTISING SPECIALTIES (cont.)

Rain Gauges
Rainwear
Razor Kits
Reading Racks
Recipe Books
Recipe Dials
Records
Ribbons
Ring Binders
Roast Holders
Rubber Money
Rulers
Salad Sets
Salt & Pepper Shakers
Savings Banks
School Bags
School Companions
Scissors & Shears
Scoops
Scotch Tape Dispensers
Screwdrivers
Seam Rippers
Self-Erasing Pads
Serving Trays
Sharpening Stones
Shoe Bags
Shoe Horns
Shoe Mitts
Shopping Bags
Signs
Sleeve Protectors
Slicers
Slide Rules
Slippers
Smelling Salts
Smoking Accessories
Soap Dishes
Soap & Soap Booklets
Song Books
Spark Plug Testers
Spice Racks
Sponges
Spoon Holders
Spot Removers
Spreaders
Squeegees
Stamp Dispensers
Stamp Holders
Staple Removers
Staplers
Stickers
String Cutters
Stud Finders
Styptic Sticks
Sun Visors
Tablecloths
Tank Gauges
Tape Measures
Thermos Bottles
Thimbles
Tie Clasps
Tissue Dispensers
Tobacco Pouches
Tool Kits
Tool Racks
Tooth Brushes
Toothpicks
Toothpick Dispensers
Tops
Towels
Toys
Trophies
Tumblers
Typewriter Brushes
Valuable Paper Holders
Vests
Wall Calendars
Want Books
Watch Fobs
Watches
Writing Portfolios
Yardsticks
Yo-Yo's

---

lished by John Yeck. The basic showmanship element in the "Mottoes" mailings is a small card punched for hanging. Each monthly card contains a lighthearted motto plus the name of the company making the mailing.

Many advertisers have adapted this syndicated technique to their own, specialized needs. For example, D. W. Onan & Sons, Minneapolis manufacturer of electric generating plants, sent out a series of "Confucius Say" cards to provide good working hints for their own, and their dealers' and distributors' salesmen. Typical examples:

> Confucius say: "Salesman who covers chair instead of territory always remain on bottom."

2222 Arbor Boulevard · Dayton, Ohio 45439 · 513/294-4000
THE LET'S HAVE BETTER MOTTOES ASSOCIATION, INC.

With back-to-school bells ringing in their ears, the judges this month happily declared Richard Hodgson president for the month as the result of his suggestion:

FOR THE MAN WHO HAS EVERYTHING
refinancing

Since our annual equinotique parade has been scheduled to begin early on the evening of the 21st, the president has suggested that we march very slowly northward, pausing for refreshments on the way, until the precise moment of the equinox, then reverse slowly, thereby remaining exactly in the same relation to the planet Jupiter for the entire proceedings. This should improve digestion.

English is funny: a fat chance and a slim chance mean the same thing.

Joe has spent the month in the confusing world of medical research, where he learned how to tell when kangeroos are sick (they don't feel jumpy); that even ulcers are good for something (they cut down the food bills) and that people who really have kleptomania can take almost anything for it.

English is still funny: if you're blunt enough they'll never think you're dull.

Other equinomical mottoes received from members this month include: KEEP OUR CITY CLEAN, HAVE A PIGEON FOR SUPPER, from Bud Savage; SELF PITY IS BETTER THAN NONE AT ALL, from Bob DeLay and the laconic LOOK BEFORE YOU LIP, from a member who mumbled his name too poorly to be identified.

Memory is what makes you recall what you forgot to do after it's too late.

Cordially,

John D. Yeck
Secretary
The Let's Have Better Mottoes Association

FOR THE MAN WHO HAS EVERYTHING

REFINANCING

"Better Mottoes"

"BETTER MOTTOES" ASSOCIATION, INC.
P.O. Box 225 Dayton, Ohio 45402

Zany, whimsical letters and separate mottoes create a friendly atmosphere.

Confucius say: "He who cut price best know true value of own equipment!"

Confucius say: "He who let pride get inflated someday have to swallow same."

Confucius say: "He who talk without thinking often cause commotion not motion."

Donnelley Framing Prints

R. R. Donnelley & Sons Company, Chicago, Illinois, printing company, has long made effective use of reproductions of fine paintings and other items suitable for framing. These prints not only serve the purpose of demonstrating the Donnelley abilities but most often are accorded a long-term "hanging" in office or home where they serve as a continuing reminder of the company's skills.

No advertising message appears directly on the Donnelley framing prints, except for a small type credit line in the lower margin. However, a booklet accompanies each of the prints and provides interesting background information about the subject plus copy which relates the skills used in creating the reproduction to the printing needs of the customer or prospect.

As an added element of direct mail showmanship, Donnelley creates impressive mailing containers for its framing prints plus special address labels which tie in with the theme of the print. These packages make the arrival of a Donnelley mailing a special event in the offices of the recipient. This helps to implant the Donnelley name in the minds of many who may never be directly exposed to the contents of the mailing.

Quotations for Framing

Another adaptation of the "Designed for Display" showmanship technique is a favorite device of Ken Nelson, Minneapolis adman. Mr. Nelson frequently selects a famous quotation and reproduces it on high-quality paper with attractive illustrations. While the quotations usually have a direct relationship to a sales point of a Nelson client, they are so attractively reproduced that a large number of recipients have them framed for continuing display.

GAMES AND TOYS

It is not necessarily child's play when toys and games are introduced into a direct mail program, for this showmanship technique often proves an ideal way to build desirable audience participation into an advertising program. Some advertisers find they can utilize an off-the-counter toy or game into their direct mail programs, while others create something original.

There are some who feel the use of toys and games is too undignified, particularly for a promotion aimed at top executives. However, the experience of those who have used this showmanship technique indicates that there is still part boy in the majority of those who now sit behind executive desks. In addition, there is usually a son, grandson, or favorite neighborhood youngster lurking in the background—and there are few businessmen who do not enjoy the opportunity to play the role of "hero" through the presentation of gifts which have originated as part of a direct mail program.

Off-the-Shelf Games

An excellent example of the use of off-the-shelf games to drive home key sales points was a showmanship mailing by a radio network. The featured item was one of those question-and-answer games where you must match the question and right answer by inserting two wires in holes. If you choose the right answer, a bulb lights up. This gadget had a stock set of question-and-answer cards to which were added a set of additional cards featuring the mailer's sales story.

Student Marketing Institute used two toy magnets to drive home a sales point. The horseshoe-shaped magnets were tipped inside a folder describing the "magnetic market"—a subject being promoted by the Institute. A paper clip was also enclosed. Recipients were instructed to place the clip vertically between the two magnets. Since one of the magnets was stronger than the other, the clip always was attracted to the one which represented the Institute's "magnetic market."

Columbia-Geneva Steel sent prospects a set of four wire puzzles—the kind where two identical pieces are linked together and you twist and turn the pieces trying to find the magical position which permits you to unlink them. The copy tie-in:

> "Wire problems can be as simple as these puzzles, or they can be very difficult. Whenever you find yourself faced with *any* wire problem, remember you can find an easy solution by calling in your Columbia-Geneva Steel Representative."

Children's Toys

All types of toys have found application in showmanship direct mail programs. Frequently, entire campaigns are built around a series of toy mailings. Probably the most frequently used theme is railroading, with all types of toy trains being put to direct mail use.

Even "live toys" are used for showmanship mailings. Live turtles and goldfish are the most popular. The turtles frequently have a promotional message painted on their backs. One use of small turtles has been for collection mailings. Said one mailer: "This is Slowpoke, he doesn't pay his bills on time. Don't be like Slowpoke, mail us a check." The technique worked wonders in collecting delinquent accounts.

Goldfish, mailed in transparent plastic bags, have also been used effectively by a number of direct mail advertisers. American Hammered, for example, mailed fish to prospects with a copy tie-in: "Fishing for instant oil control?"

Suppliers of materials have also used the mailing of toys to advantage. One plastics supplier, for example, sent industrial prospects a pair of roller skates made from its materials. For maximum impact, this mailing was sent just in advance of the Christmas season so recipients could utilize the sample skates as gifts to a favorite smallfry. As an added showmanship element, the skates came in a red open-mesh Christmas stocking.

Custom Toys and Games

One of the most popular applications of this showmanship technique is to print an advertising message on a sheet of hefty cardboard and then cut it up in the form of a jigsaw puzzle. One industrial company even went so far as to mail a jigsaw advertising message a piece at a time and then had salesmen present special prizes to any recipient who could exhibit an assembled puzzle after the mailing series had been completed.

You can also do a lot of interesting things through imaginative use of a folder. Northwest Orient Airlines created a paper airplane—the kind you used to sail across the room in grade school—and aimed it at a list of traffic managers. The 12-inch-long jet was printed in blue and red on silver stock. The message: "Put Northwest jet wings on your freight."

Other showmanship mailings have been based on interesting things the recipient can create by folding a sheet of paper himself. Air Express, for example, sent graphic arts executives a sheet of newsprint, with printed instructions on how to create a pressman's hat.

Poker by Mail

Still another form of audience participation is to send a series of playing cards—one at a time. The recipient saves each card until he has a complete five-card hand. Best hands then win prizes, usually awarded by salesmen making followup calls.

One user of this showmanship technique was Naugatuck Chemical Division of U. S. Rubber Company. The first of six mailings explained the rules of the direct mail contest:

> Rules: During the next several weeks, you'll receive five folders describing the many advantages of Kralastic MH.
>
> The highest hand wins! With each folder you'll receive a playing card. Keep this card until you have collected five cards and then return the five cards with your name, company, and address to the Sales Promotion Dept., U. S. Rubber, Naugatuck Chemical Div., Naugatuck, Connecticut. Winners will be announced within 20 days.
>
> "Loop Hole" Clause—If this contest becomes too complicated, all returns will be placed in a hat and winners selected. The winners are guaranteed to be selected fairly and squarely without preselection, favoritism, and other such malpractices that would incur the investigation of the FTC.
>
> Remember—Win with Kralastic MH—try it on your next design or molding job.
>
> Keep the cards—80 prizes to win!

A variation on this technique was used for an exhibit followup. An envelope company had visitors to its trade show exhibit draw a card and then register for a series of followup mailings. With each of four mailings was another card and holders of the best hands received prizes.

HISTORICAL ITEMS

Items of authentic historical interest have found many applications in showmanship direct mail. Both authentic antiques and reproductions have been used effectively.

One of the most common applications of historical showmanship items is for anniversary promotions. Many companies send reproductions of newspapers and magazines published on their founding date to draw attention to a major anniversary. Other items used include maps of historical vintage, reproductions of patent applications, reprints of vintage advertising and so forth.

Oxford Paper Company built an entire showmanship campaign around symbols of Early American salesmanship—to draw a comparison with present-day salesmanship techniques which utilize effective printed sales tools. Some of the items included in the Oxford campaign were reproductions of nineteenth-century advertising posters, an authentic piece of wampum, a pewter spoon like those sold by Yankee peddlers, and so forth.

Time magazine sent advertising prospects a folder entitled "Color Was in the Cards." The folder had an inside pocket containing matched ads—a half dozen full-color facsimiles of antique advertising cards and reprints of contemporary ads showing how these same advertisers promote their products today.

PIECES DESIGNED FOR ANOTHER AUDIENCE

Exposing a direct mail audience to an item usually associated with some other, dissimilar audience can be a highly effective showmanship technique. For example, sending press releases to an audience other than editors has been used effectively to add impact to a newsworthy sales story.

A consistent user of this showmanship technique is *Time* magazine. One of its most effective promotional mailings featured a copy of a small Texas weekly newspaper, *The Ralls Banner*. The newspaper was inserted in a booklet entitled "The Story of a Story." *Time* had featured the *Ralls Banner* editor, Ernest Joiner, in a story in its "Press" section. When the story pulled a sensational response, *Time* decided to make promotional capital of the situation. So it told the behind-the-scenes detail in the booklet—and for extra impact added an actual sample of the weekly newspaper. While any unusual hometown weekly newspaper is likely to get some degree of attention, the *Ralls Banner* couldn't miss. A typical editorial headline: "All Together Now—Let's Get Hysterical!" (about Khrushchev's visit to the U.S.).

Other advertisers have created showmanship in their direct mail by sending publications to audiences other than those who normally receive the publication. Some, for example, have run an ad in one of the more interesting weekly newspapers or smaller magazines and then have purchased an overrun of the entire issue for mailing to a direct mail audience—usually with a note added to call attention to the ad.

Another "extra audience" mailing by *Time* featured authentic golf scorecards from such unlikely spots as The Royal Hong Kong Golf Club; Club de Golf Anastacio in Sao Paulo, Brazil; Nyanza Club in Kisumu, Kenya, British East Africa; and Le

Club Laval-sur-le-Lac (the card didn't say where). In addition to the unusual scorecards, which were obtained by *Time* correspondents on-the-spot, the accompanying folder listed some of the more unusual local ground rules at eight widely scattered courses around the world. Typical: Nyanza Club water note: "If a ball comes to rest in dangérous proximity to a hippopotamus or crocodile, another ball may be dropped, at a safe distance, no nearer the hole, without penalty." The sales theme of the mailing: "The ground rules change from course to course but the game's the same all over the world and the same kind of people read *Time* all over the world."

A radio script was used effectively in a mailing from GRI Pharmaceuticals, Inc. The accompanying letter, in simulated hand-writing, was from noted radio personality Gabriel Heatter. Copy began:

> Dear Friend:
>
> Please read this friendly letter before you do another thing...
>
> BECAUSE
>
> I would like YOU, too, to have the opportunity to take advantage of the amazing FREE OFFER that I announced on my radio broadcast.
>
> Did you hear it?
>
> In case you missed hearing this important announcement, I am sending along a copy of my radio script exactly as broadcast.

Enclosed, of course, was a copy of a 60-second radio commercial with a promotional message about GRI's vitamins.

UNSEASONAL MAILING

There's nothing which says greeting cards have to be mailed at Christmastime or that vacation notices must be sent out in midsummer. Clever direct mail advertisers, looking for a showmanship theme, have taken advantage of this situation.

Agency Lithograph Company of Portland, Oregon, sent a "Christmas" card four months early—for reasons which were explained in copy:

> "Christmas comes a little early this year . . . because we have to get Gerry to school on time. We want you to meet Gerry Coigny. She is our Christmas present to you.
>
> "Last year we decided to say 'Merry Christmas' in a different way—by awarding an art scholarship to a deserving and promising young art student. Gerry is this student. The

Art Directors Club chose her to receive the one year's tuition and art materials scholarship sponsored by Agency Lithograph Company . . ."

Other effective uses of unseasonal mailings include use of New Year's, Thanksgiving, Birthday, Fourth-of-July, Valentine's Day, or even Halloween cards instead of Christmas cards. (It is important, in such "substitutions" to utilize the selected occasion because of some legitimate copy tie-in.)

Another "unseasonal" approach which has been growing in popularity is the mailing of July-to-June calendars instead of the traditional January-to-December variety.

UNUSUAL LAYOUTS AND FORMATS

It would take a volume the size of a Sears catalog to even begin to list a portion of the unusual layouts and formats which are available to the direct mail advertiser seeking an element of showmanship for his mailings. The almost unlimited flexibility of direct mail opens the door to a vast variety of possibilities.

Frequently, however, the greatest showmanship comes from the adaptation of some relatively common nondirect mail format to direct mail use. The Printing Products Division of Dayco Corporation has used a steady stream of such adaptations to promote its press rollers and other products to printers. Included in Dayco's bag of tricks:

A "Do-It-Yourself" Player Piano Roll. Dayco penned its own promotional words to the tunes of old-time favorite songs and then printed them upon a roll of heavy paper. On the reverse side were a series of numbered circles—"Cut them out," Dayco told the printers, "and you can play our sales message on your player piano."

A Sheet of Trading Stamps. "These trading stamps represent *extra value* at *no extra charge* that all users of Dayco products automatically receive with every purchase." A "trading stamp catalog" was included along with the sheet of stamps. The "catalog," of course, listed a number of Dayco products with accompanying selling copy.

Poker Chips. Dayco sales messages were printed on blue, white, and red circles which could be punched from a sheet of heavy card stock.

Coloring Book. Long before the coloring book craze hit the rest of the advertising world, John Yeck, of Yeck & Yeck, Dayco's agency (which created all of the unique formats in this continuing campaign), turned out a coloring book to promote Dayco products. Its title: "The Happy Printer and His Dog—a child's coloring book with a hidden message of profit for all printers."

Record Album. "Music to Make Money By" with The Happy Printer and his band. In addition to selling copy on the record jacket itself, there was a paper record inside the jacket with additional copy and a perforated reply card. (Interestingly, at the very same time Dayco mailed this showmanship piece, Harris-Seybold also send printers a mailing in the form of a record album—same size, same reply card insert in the shape of a record, and even the identical title, "Music to Make Money By"—probably direct mail's most amazing concidence since neither the advertisers nor their agencies were aware they had anything but an original idea until the twin mailings reached the same prospects at the same time.)

Book Jacket. A "whodunit," entitled "The Mystery of The Printer's Profits."

Gift Wrapping Paper. The design featured cartoons which had been used in Dayco publication advertising.

Checkbook. All but one check had been torn out, but the stubs told a story. Reading through them you discover how the printer obviously went from rags to riches following the purchase of Dayco products. The remaining check turned out to be a reply card on which the recipient could request additional information.

These are just a few of the possibilities you might consider. Among others which have been used successfully is the "report card" used by Macey Collators—the whole sales story was reported in the format of a grade school report card—and a sheet of "approvals" used by Bell & Howell. The approval sheet is the same format used by stamp dealers to send postage stamps to collectors. Some of the spaces on the approval sheet contained colorful stamps, while still others had selling copy for Bell & Howell.

Of course it is not necessary to imitate some common item to utilize an unusual layout or format for showmanship impact. Unusual sizes, folding arrangements, uses of color, etc., can all be put to good use to produce effective showmanship formats.

UNUSUAL COPY STYLES

While unusual copy was an important part of several of the effective showmanship formats just described, copy alone can sometimes be the best of all showmanship techniques.

For example, one of our all-time favorite direct mail pieces featured copy written by a 13-year-old schoolgirl. It was the story of "Wilbur," the rabbit who laid multicolored eggs. The author of this delightful piece was Mary Elizabeth Grimes, of Baltimore. The story fell into the hands of William Clawson, then advertising manager of Miller Printing Machinery Company, who converted it into an Easter mailing. Additional showmanship was added to the mailing by having it illustrated by a 13-year-old artist, and by having the type set by a 14-year-old typographer. (Although this piece was mailed in 1954, we still bring out our copy every Easter and let our children read the story once again—and think kindly of Miller Printing Machinery each year for having originally sent us the booklet.)

Story Book Village Letters

Harold M. Norman, Philadelphia advertising and sales promotion consultant, used copy aimed at children to win friends for his client, National Distillers Products Corporation.

As part of a sales-incentive program, National asked each of its salesmen for the names and nicknames of children up to ten years old. Then each child received a series of letters from "Story Book Village" in Green Lane, Pennsylvania. The animals which lived at the "Village" ostensibly wrote the letters and kept the children posted on their activities.

Meanwhile, the salesmen were involved in a baseball theme sales contest. So one of the letters (from "Geddy," the Story Book Village boxer dog) offered a bat or ball to the youngster who sent in the longest list of baseball words or terms. That was about as direct a tie-in as was contained in the letter series. In fact, no direct promotional value was sought for the children's letters. Instead, the program worked by indirection—helping to create an atmosphere of goodwill, which, in turn, resulted in greater sales effort.

Light Touch Letters

The light touch in copy has often been used effectively to add showmanship to a direct mail program. One of the best examples is a long-lasting campaign created by Helen Murray Hall, advertising and sales promotion manager of the Pacific Division of National Broadcasting Company, in Hollywood. It has involved a variety of different kinds of lighthearted letters, but the copy was so consistently good that NBC's letters became a special event upon arrival in the offices of many advertising time buyers.

Here's just one example. It was on regular NBC stationery but had a big, bold, handwritten headline reading, "I've got a gripe!" The letter read:

> I realize that this is the festive season and that I should feel all Santa Clausy. Believe me, I enjoy a Christmas greeting or friendly carol as much

as the next gal—but I'm a secretary who's got a problem. His name is John T. Williams, and he's driving me nuts.

For six weeks now I've been trying to finish "From Here to Eternity." I hear it's a good book, but I doubt if I'll ever find out. Every time I open the cover the noise starts: "Mary, get me the latest Nielsen ratings! . . . " "Mary, bring me the file on nighttime radio! . . ." "Mary, take a letter!" That's bad enough, but his crusades are a psychiatrist's delight.

This morning he turns on me with a wild look in his eye. "Mary," he says, banging the top of his desk, "do you know that one of the greatest buys in Western Network Radio has just become available?"

"That's nice," I reply.

"Ask me who it is!" he shouts.

"Who is it?" I say calmly, edging toward the door.

"ELMER PETERSON!" crows Mr. Williams.

He then goes into a frantic pitch about the fact that Elmer can *now* be bought Wednesday through Friday, as well as Tuesday, for only $668 time and program per show over all 14 NBC Western Radio Network stations. Pounding and hollering, he goes on to tell me why Elmer's 5:45 to 6:00 p.m. time is so ideal for advertisers who want both in-the-home and going-home listening, that Nielsen says that Elmer Peterson's news show averages a half-million listeners per broadcast, not counting the out-of-home tuner-inners, and what a terrific buy that is when you realize that a sponsor can cover all 14 major metropolitan coast areas for only $50 per market.

I tell you, this eager-beaver boss of mine has got me so nervous I've refused to hang up my stocking this Christmas for fear I'll find a memo in it. So how about giving a gal a break? Just pick up the phone and tell Mr. Williams you want to talk to him. Frankly, I don't care *what* you talk to him about—you might discuss Elmer Peterson since he's all steamed up over him right now—but at any rate it'll get the man out of my hair for a half-hour or so.

Do this for me, and I'll let you know how the book turns out.

Hopefully,
Mary Opie, Secretary
Network Sales

As an added showmanship element, this particular letter was mailed in an envelope with Gregg shorthand characters printed on the face. They read: "My boss is driving me nuts! How about yours?"

UNUSUAL ENVELOPES

It isn't only the contents of a mailing which hold showmanship potential. Often, the container in which it is sent can be the major impact builder. To begin with, there are many ways to add impact to a mailing envelope. *Sunset* magazine, for example, sent one of its circulation mailings in an envelope designed to resemble a picture post card. The back of the envelope had a full-color view of the magazine's scenic offices in Menlo Park, California. The address side was in typical picture post card fashion with a printed caption at the top of the left-hand half plus a simulated handwritten message below. The address was imprinted on the right-hand half.

Picture-window envelopes are frequently used for showmanship impact. A die-cut hole in the envelope reveals a portion of the copy or illustration on an enclosure. Some examples:

To merchandise its *Friends* external house organ to dealers, Chevrolet mails sample copies in specially designed window envelopes. Each of the envelopes features a dramatic illustration on its face—plus a die-cut window which allows a portion of the magazine's process color cover to become an integral part of the envelope illustration. For example, one envelope featured a July firecracker scene. A sky-burst from a fireworks display, which was the *Friends* cover illustration, showed through a small window to become the lighted fuse on the firecrackers. Another envelope illustration featured a football scene, die-cut so a full-color crowd from the magazine cover filled the stands.

Pfizer Laboratories built a series of mailings for its Renese polythiazide around the theme: "Distinguished in the response it produces." Each mailing featured a handsome folder, french-folded to 10 by 13 inches, with a 7- by 9½-inch die-cut opening in the front cover. Tipped under the opening in each folder was a full-color, embossed reproduction of such recognized art masterpieces as Vermeer's "The Seamstress" and Modigliani's "Gypsy Woman With Baby." The prints were removable for framing.

But art masterpieces are "old hat" in pharmaceutical direct mail. What especially distinguished Pfizer's mailings was the envelope. Its face had only a 5½- by 9½-inch window and the single word, "Distinguished," printed in gray. The art masterpiece appeared in the window, adding a note of showmanship impact even before the morning's mail was opened. The clear acetate of the window also helped intensify the colors of the painting. To maintain the high-quality appearance of the mailing, the return address, third-class indicia, and mailing address were restricted to as inconspicuous a position as possible on the back flap of the envelope, giving the art reproduction an opportunity to completely dominate.

Picture windows served another purpose in a truck tire promotion of B. F. Goodrich. Goodrich mailed prospects a series of items, each personalized with the name of the recipient. Interestingly, relatively common promotional items were used, but Goodrich made them distinctive by imprinting the recipient's name in big, bold type. Football and baseball facts' booklets were two of the items. These were then inserted in window envelopes so the bold personalized imprint caught the recipient's eye the minute the envelope was delivered.

Another effective application of envelope picture windows to add drama to mailings was a "Coin of the Realm" series from the National Fleet Department of Chevrolet. To dramatize Chevrolet's higher resale value, a series of mailing pieces was built around unusual historical forms of money, including Indian beads, rock salt, and German "shoe leather" money. To obtain maximum impact, each envelope had a picture window which revealed a portion of the "money" tipped on the front of a folder inside.

NOVELTY PACKAGES

In addition to envelopes, a vast variety of novelty packages have been used to deliver messages in a showmanship manner. Benjamin Moore & Company, for example, sent a series of mailings to dealers "packaged" in paint cans. Each of the four cans used in the campaign contained a point-making gimmick, a brief personal letter, reprints of national and local advertisements, and typical merchandising materials. Gimmicks included a roll of stage money to signify profits, a magic color trick to dramatize the color story, a mirror box reflecting the smiling face of "the happiest paint dealer," and a jigsaw puzzle map of the U. S. to show the cross-country coverage of Moore paints.

Southern Baptists' Radio & Television Commission also used a "product" to package a special mailing. In this case, it was a tape recording box which contained information about a tape-recorded radio series the Commission was offering to selected radio stations.

Trans-World Airlines used another approach, packaging material promoting European vacation trips in a clear vinyl pouch. The pouch had reuse by the travel agents to whom it was sent. Similar "reuse" items—such as billfolds, briefcases, filing boxes, etc.—have been used frequently to add showmanship to direct mail.

FIRST DAY COVERS

Collectors' items of all types have found showmanship applications in direct mail programs—but none quite fits the bill so completely as a First Day Cover. These are mailings made from a selected post office on the first day a new stamp is issued. A specially imprinted envelope is usually used and the newly issued stamps are canceled with a special postmark.

Some companies prepare their own envelope imprints. However, the majority of direct mail advertisers using this technique seem to prefer the steel-engraved first day covers which are issued for every new United States and United Nations stamp by such suppliers as The Washington Press, Maplewood, New Jersey.

The magic of the First Day Cover, of course, is that almost everyone is or knows a stamp collector, and any newly-issued stamp holds special interest. But even if there is no stamp collecting interest involved, a new stamp has an element of news value and thus adds special impact to a mailing.

James & Lamson First Day Cover Mailings

A typical longtime user of First Day Cover mailings is Jordan D. Wood of Jones & Lamson Machine Company, Springfield, Vermont. Once a month, Jones & Lamson sends a First Day Cover to its customers, prospects, and friends. The Cover envelopes contain an automatically-typewritten letter, usually with some copy link to the event, person, or place being honored by the new stamp. Typical Jones & Lamson letters:

100th ANNIVERSARY OF THE OVERLAND MAIL

When John Butterfield completed the first run of his new stagecoach service from Missouri to California a century ago, Jones & Lamson was 23 years old.

As we all know, tremendous advances have been made in transportation since that time. Progress is symbolized by new jetliners spanning the continent in 43 hours. In machining, too, a lot of things have been happening.*

*P.S. See our new machine tool catalog. I'll send you a copy upon request.

DEDICATION OF THE MACKINAC BRIDGE

This first day cover commemorates the opening of the Mackinac Bridge—the longest (over 5 miles, including approaches), most expensive ($100,000,000) span of its type in the world.

Of special interest to stamp collectors is the fact that the postmark, Mackinac Bridge, is used here for the first time, and will never be used again. (Reason is that the United States Post Office Department did not want to favor either Mackinaw or St. Ignace post offices, located at opposite ends of the bridge, and so created this postmark for one-time-only use.) This unique feature makes this cover an especially valuable one.

Unique features are of special value in the metal-working field, too. Witness the Jones & Lamson lines of machine tools and optical comparators, which incorporate important new engineering features found nowhere else.

UNITED NATIONS GENERAL ASSEMBLY OF 1959
(U.N. STAMP)

One reason why our friends like to continue getting these "First Day Covers" is that each one is new and different, yet fits into a pleasing, overall pattern.

The same things might be said of J & L's new "Certified Maintenance" Service which provides expert maintenance, testing and adjustment service for Jones & Lamson Optical Comparators located in customers' plants.

This valuable service,* assuring constant excellence of comparator performance, is indeed "new and different."

*Valuable, yes. Expensive, no.

Added Showmanship

Frequently it is possible to use a First Day Cover as a jumping-off point for more extensive showmanship. American-Standard, for example, used a First Day Cover mailing celebrating the opening of the St. Lawrence Seaway to introduce a new line of plumbing fittings. The mailing envelope carried a teaser: "It's new . . . it's revolutionary" plus copy calling attention to the value of the First Day Cover: "Do not destroy this envelope . . . The commemorative stamp on this envelope, postmarked on the date of issue, is a collector's item."

Inside the envelope was a gold-covered booklet containing copy which linked the Seaway—"revolutionary wonder of modern progress"—with the "new and revolutionary changes in the new fittings."

An interesting "plus" feature of the booklet was a block of four uncanceled stamps. Copy noted:

> "To commemorate the opening of this new 'sea route' to Europe, American-Standard has enclosed for you this block of first-issue stamps. These stamps, and the stamp on the envelope, canceled on the date of issue, are collector's items. If you *don't* save stamps, you may simply use them for

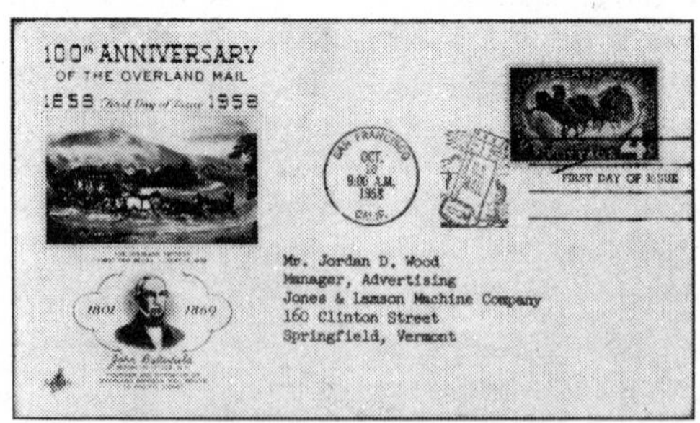

First Day Covers for Mackinac Bridge, United Nations, and the Overland Mail were successfully used by Jones & Lamson.

postage . . . or perhaps you have a friend who is a stamp collector. We hope, in any event, these new stamps emphasize the spirit of progress . . . the same progress demonstrated by the new and revolutionary changes you will find in the new American-Standard line of fixture fittings."

Anniversary Promotion

Another extended use of a First Day Cover was part of a centennial promotion by Seagram-Distillers in 1957. One of Seagram's mailings was in a 9- by 12-inch envelope carrying an Inauguration Day cachet and a first-day issue of the Atoms for Peace stamp. Inside the envelope was another collector's item—a reproduction of the front page and editorial page from the March 5, 1857, issue of the *New York Tribune.* The issue featured news of the inauguration of James Buchanan.

Not to be overlooked are First Day Cover mailings of foreign stamps—which carry the extra showmanship impact of mailings from abroad.

FOREIGN MAILINGS

In fact, any mailing from a foreign point carries extra impact. Whenever possible, foreign postage stamps—the more, the better—should be used and placed in a conspicuous place.

An example of how foreign mailings can be used effectively was a series of "hidden message" cards—where you dip a piece of blotter stock in water and a previously hidden message appears—used to promote Dynel, a synthetic fiber. Each of the cards featured an illustration of a native of the country from which it was mailed plus a printed message in the language of that country. If you did not understand the foreign tongue, you dipped your card in water and an English translation appeared.

UNUSUAL POSTMARKS

A closely related showmanship technique is making use of interesting postmarks to add impact to a direct mail program. This highly economical showmanship technique has proved particularly popular among industrial advertisers.

One company which has taken advantage of the opportunity to create showmanship through mailings from post offices with unusual names is Price Brothers Co., Dayton supplier of prestressed concrete building units, concrete blocks, and concrete sewer and pressure pipe. For many years, Price has been searching out post offices with names that fit the key selling features of its products. Among the mailing points have been Limestone, Tennessee; Waterflow, New Mexico; Strong, Mississippi; Economy, Indiana; Protection, Kansas; and Hundred, West Virginia.

Each Price postmark mailing discusses the selling features indicated by the town name. A typical letter, mailed from Limestone, Tennessee, read:

> "If the founding fathers of Limestone back in 1857 had mixed up a batch of concrete and buried it in the ground, it would be a better piece of concrete today than on the day they buried it . . .
>
> "The sand, gravel, water, and limestone in concrete all come from the ground, and when you put them back they're right in their own element. Concrete actually gets harder and harder the longer it is buried.
>
> "You can try this out for yourself. Next time you install a water line, use concrete pressure pipe. And if you care to dig it up for a look after 100 years, you'll find that it's harder and stronger and a better piece of pipe than the day you buried it . . . You can guess what pipe I recommend—Price pipe (made with limestone). If you want some, just drop us a line in Dayton, Ohio, or Hattiesburg, Mississippi."

Price takes no chances on the recipient missing the postmark because his secretary may have thrown away the envelope. The letters are self-mailers, with a sealed, perforated edge which can be quickly torn off—but the postmark remains to make its showmanship point.

Tips for Postmark Mailings

While the basic technique of creating "postmark mailings" is simple, there are some good ground rules to consider:

1. Send for an alphabetical index of the Directory of Post Offices from Superintendent of Documents, Washington, D. C. 20402. In it you will find post offices to "fit" most any theme. (For a representative selection of post offices with unusual names, see the list beginning on the next page.)

2. Before completing your plans, however, be sure to verify to make sure the post office of your choice is still in existence. Small post offices are often closed or consolidated by the Government on short notice.

3. If there are several post offices with the same name, choose the smallest because small post offices use hand stamps which are larger than machine stamps—and therefore have more attention value.

POST OFFICES WITH UNUSUAL NAMES

ALABAMA
Fairhope
Hurricane
Liberty
Summit
Midway
Three Notch
Duke
Buffalo
Five Points
Spring Garden
Service
Jack
Evergreen
Equality
Saint Bernard
Canoe
Chase
Harvest
New Market
Bucks
Magazine
Excel
Goodway
Reform
Banks
Holy Trinity
Empire
Prospect
Sunflower
Finegar Bend

ARIZONA
Maverick
Fry
Tombstone
Happy Jack
Parks
Globe
Inspiration
Young
Blue
Goodyear
Mobile
Show Low
Snowflake
Oracle
Superior
Skull Valley
Horn

ARKANSAS
Gentry
Pea Ridge
Zinc
Banks
Success
Twist
Union
Royal
Grapevine
Hope
Friendship
Umpire
Forty Four
Stamps
Magazine
Summit
Tomato
Story
Nimrod
Ink
Sweet Home
Snowball
Bonanza
King
Fiftysix
Flag
Fox
Rover
Wing

CALIFORNIA
Angels Camp
Associated
Five Points
Imperial
Death Valley
Laws
Bell
Wolf
Summit
Igo
Whiskeytown
Happy Camp
Standard

COLORADO
Wild Horse
Rush
Rifle

DELAWARE
Bear

FLORIDA
Shamrock
Midway
Bell
Venus
Knights
Day
Marathon
Baker
Jupiter
Clearwater
Frostproof
Enterprise

GEORGIA
Coffee
Dixie
Register
Ball Ground
Lovejoy
Rex
Council
Empire
Dial
Fry
Calvary
Center
Midway
Ideal
Juniper
Swords
Tiger
Good Hope

IDAHO
Eagle
Orchard
Star
Bear
Council

POST OFFICES WITH UNUSUAL NAMES (cont.)

IDAHO (Cont'd)
Atomic City
Sterling
Triumph
Banks
Bridge
Headquarters
Chilly
Squirrel
Sweet
Bliss
Dixie
Golden
Baker
May
Stone
Riddle
Gem
Page
Felt
Victor

ILLINOIS
Columbian
Golden
Liberty
Unity
Bureau
Cherry
Champaign
Assumption
Golf
Worth
Equality
Junction
Media
Zion
Triumph
Birds
Campus
Good Hope
Industry
Anchor
Normal
Bath
Lincoln's New Salem
Joy
Gays
Kings
Polo
Perks
Mark
Mohamet

INDIANA
Hope
Young America
Speed
Bath
Center
Star City
Santa Claus
Patriot
Battle Ground
Liberty
Universal
Petroleum
High
Middle
Victor
West
Hills
Lone Tree
Hale
What Cheer
Carpenter
Soldier
New Market
Story City

IOWA
Mystic
Beaver
Independence
Lost Nation
Superior
Whitten
Hardy
Pioneer

KANSAS
Bazaar
Bird City
Green
Rice
Rock
Enterprise
Hope
Severance
Sparks
Friend
Climax
Soldier
Holliday
Monument
Burns
Home
Liberty
Admire
Tyro
Ransom
Miles
Speed
Coats
Republic
Liberal
Zenith
Gem
Buffalo

KENTUCKY
Betsy Layne
Rush
Canoe
Little
Quicksand
Sample
Love
Quality
Enterprise
Globe
Soldier
Liberty
Pigeonroost
Plank
Wild Cat
Highway
Bow
Kettle
Huff
Green
Furnace
Pilot
Blue Moon
Bonanza

POST OFFICES WITH UNUSUAL NAMES (cont.)

KENTUCKY (Cont'd)

Cliff
Dock
Drift
Halo
Hi Hat
Price
Printer
Pyramid
Jett
Fancy Farm
Falls of Rough
Wax
Fry
Little Barren
Summit
Ages
Crummies
Bee
Bond
Parrot
Peoples
Bath
Decory
Mousie
Pippa Passes
Soft Shell
Spider
Talcum
Topmost
Vest
Cannon
Buffalo
Bunch
Cruise
Symbol
Victory
Banks
Crown
Day
Neon
Joy
Co Operative
Ever
Gypsy
Add
Beauty
Calf Creek
Job
Pilgrim
Tomahawk
Hope
Blaze
Holliday
Index
Zag
Narrows
New Liberty
Major
Mistletoe
Stay
Travellers
Busy
Butterfly
Daisy
Dice
Dunraven
Happy
Fishtrap
Goody
Greasy
Penny
Stone
Acorn
Drum
Keno
Farmers
Smile
Stamping Ground
Mac
White Rose
Windy
Flat
Midway

LOUISIANA

Branch
Supreme
Singer
Dixie
Oil City
Trees
Book
Acme
New Era
Pelican
Baker
Fort Necessity
Jigger
Dry Prong
Sunshine
Cut Off
Trout
Hilly
Diamond
Empire
Happy Jack
Triumph
Blanks
Mix
New Roads
Ball
Echo
Gardner
Start
Many
Noble
Welcome
Reserve
Sun
Independence
Water Proof
Point
Retreat

MAINE

Limestone
Perham
Oxbow
Strong
Sunset
Hope
Lookout
Winn
Liberty

MARYLAND

Fork
Granite
Sparks
Issue
Welcome
Rocks

POST OFFICES WITH UNUSUAL NAMES (cont.)

MARYLAND (Cont'd)

Street
Price
Hurry
Fair Play

MASSACHUSETTS

Buzzards Bay
Orange
Furnace

MICHIGAN

Bath
Atlas
Acme
Dollar Bay
Winn
Schoolcraft
Gay
Irons
Romeo
Chief
Republic
Skandis
Free Soil
Hope
Crystal
Cooks

MINNESOTA

Sleepy Eye
Young America
Fifty Lakes
Excelsior
Ball Club
Bigfork
Max
Regal
Viking
Triumph
Welcome
Climax
Plummer
Cotton
Iron
Zim
New Market
Savage
Staples
Buffalo
Echo
Porter

MISSISSIPPI

Liberty
Alligator
Pace
Banner
Reform
Enterprise
Rich
Walls
Leaf
Soso
University
Arm
Way
Strong
Union
Summit
New Site
Sledge
Star
Value
Panther Burn
Shivers
Burns
Bond
Independence
Savage
Tyro
Banks

MISSOURI

Liberal
Agency
Industrial City
Polo
Branch
Stet
Peculiar
Liberty
Bourbon
Buffalo
Cross Roads
Independence
Neck
Novelty
Zion
Safe
High Point
Holliday
Conception
Folk
Freedom
Hope
Rich Foundation
Foil
Duke
New Market
Fair Play
Half Way
Pleasant Hope
Black
Defiance
Blue Eye
Day
Cadet
Clubb
Diggins
Worth

MONTANA

Polaris
Wisdom
Belt
Peerless
Baker
Buffalo
Coffee Creek
Hungry Horse
Blackfoot
Cut Bank
Barber
Basin
Boulder
Big Arm
Circle
Pony
Silver Star
Twin Bridges
Superior

POST OFFICES WITH UNUSUAL NAMES (cont.)

MONTANA
(Cont'd)
Roundup
Pray
Cat Creek
Ledger
Zero
Victor
Paradise
Divide
Big Timber
Power

NEBRASKA
Royal
Surprise
Weeping Water
Wynot
Champion
Imperial
Broken Bow
Homer
Boys Town
Parks
Liberty
Republican
Star
Cook
Venus
Hardy
Superior
Friend

NEVADA
Blue Diamond
Searchlight
Gold Point
Mason
Silver City
Mercury
Steamboat
Baker

NEW HAMPSHIRE
Freedom
Sandwich
Union Bath
Unity

NEW JERSEY
Egg Harbor
Dutch Neck
Deal
Little Silver
Tranquillity
Hope

NEW MEXICO
Pie Town
Flying H
Hope
Loving
Silver City
Sunspot
Truth or Consequences
Dusty

NEW YORK
Deposit
Tunnel
Kill Buck
Sterling
Apex
Constable
Loon Lake
Owls Head
Climax
Hunter
Spectacular
Calcium
Grindstone
Limerick
Oxbow
Hunt
Sheds
Cold Water
Industry
Rush
Great Neck
Clay
Hall
Fine
Summit
Bath
Liberty
Neversink
Branch
Rose

NORTH CAROLINA
Fig
Husk
Bath
Ash
Old Trap
Marble
Spot
Kitty Hawk
Nags Head
Waves
Speed
Wood
Climax
High Point
Tuxedo
Comfort
Relief
Star
Alliance
Cash Corner
Liberty
Barber
Faith
Turkey
Wise

NORTH DAKOTA
Baker
Sterling
Wing
Price
Concrete
Crystal

OHIO
Frost
Mineral
Torch
Cable
Signal
Good Hope
Novelty
Buffalo
Charm
Aid
Outville

POST OFFICES WITH UNUSUAL NAMES (cont.)

OHIO (Cont'd)

Prospect
Fly
Diamond
Freedom Station
Continental
Franklin Furnace
Bath
Broadway
Dart

OKLAHOMA

Bunch
Jet
Gate
Blue
Mustang
Union
Sterling
Big Cabin
Bluejacket
Slick
Duke
Oscar
Bromide
Broken Bow
Cloudy
Jumbo
Snow
Lookout

OREGON

Halfway
Unity
Summit
Zigzag
Remote
Brothers
Sisters
Riddle
Sweet Home
Bridal Veil
Union
Friend
Timber
Fossil

PENNSYLVANIA

Large
Library
Presto
Freedom
Industry
Prospect
Republic
Brave
Crucible
Gypsy
Home
Childs
Bird in Hand
Paradise
Lawn
Cyclone
Effort
Skytop
King of Prussia
Limerick
Bath
Atlas
Strong
Fairhope
Liberty
Diamond
Oil City
Venus
Champion
Export
Railroad

RHODE ISLAND

Hope

SOUTH CAROLINA

Due West
Bath
Coward
Travelers Rest
Peak
Fair Play
Central
Liberty
Sunset
Trio

SOUTH DAKOTA

Parade
Interior
Deadwood
Lead
Tea
Faith
Wall
Summit
Wounded
Ideal

TENNESSEE

Neptune
Liberty
Prospect
Pressmen's Home
Only
New Market
Trade
Five Points
Greenback
Finger
Guys
Reliance
Algood
Model
Campaign
Daylight

TEXAS

Goodnight
Industry
Blanket
Cross Cut
Thrifty
Flat
Dawn
Ben Franklin
Spur
Telephone
Guy
Acme
Dial
Valentine
Venus

POST OFFICES WITH UNUSUAL NAMES (cont.)

TEXAS (Cont'd)
Telegraph
High
Earth
Sublime
Sweet Home
Buffalo
New Deal
Midway
Tarzan
Art
Star
Sunset
Cactus
Black
Imperial
Ace
Point
Pointblank
Happy
Grapevine
Nursery
Sunny Side
Royalty
Lawn

UTAH
Paradise
Price
Royal
Hatch
Tropic
Summit
Sterling
Enterprise
New Harmony

VERMONT
North Hero
South Hero

VIRGINIA
Evergreen
Smoky Ordinary
Valentines
Passing
Tiny
Minor
Supply
Upright
Narrows
Cash
Glass
Grand
Harmony
Noel
Rescue
Index
Ben Hur
Sterling
Mineral
New Point
Hurt
Triangle
Drill
Snowflake
Odd

WASHINGTON
Republic
Black Diamond
Midway
Mineral
Union
National
Urban
Gold Bar
Index
Sultan
Acme

WEST VIRGINIA
Junior Comfort
Exchange
Power
Duck
Shock
Auto
Points
Rig
Enterprise
Gay
Acme
Institute
Pinch
Sod
Tango
Man
Six
Superior
War
Woodwill
Rock
Speed
Justice
Pie
Frost
Stony Bottom
Buffalo
Hometown
Hurricane
Affinity
Odd
Pluto
Left Hand
True
Imperial
Hundred
Cyclone

WISCONSIN
Loyal
Superior
Fence
Hustler
Lily
Marathon
Unity
Pound
Wood
Winter
Victory
Embarrass
King

WYOMING
Emblem
Veteran
Freedom
Federal
Hell's Half Acre
Bright
Sunrise
Superior
Ten Sleep

4. After you've chosen your post office, write the postmaster and tell him of your plans. Ask to see a sample of his postmark—to make sure it isn't too worn to be legible. (Locating the postmaster may not be as easy as it sounds. Yeck & Yeck, the agency which prepares the Price postmark mailings, once tried to clear a mailing from a small Florida post office and it took the telephone company half a day just to locate the "town" and another day to get in touch with the postmistress, who not only had no telephone but was out fishing!)

5. Once you're sure the postmark will do, check again with the postmaster, describing your mailing in detail—size, quantity, desired mailing date, and so forth—and ask him the amount of time he will need to process the mailings. Some mailers consider two weeks about average for processing of a mailing by a small post office, although many small-town postmasters have been known to go all out to meet a tight deadline—even if it requires enlisting the aid of the local volunteer firemen, the Boy Scouts, or the Ladies' Aid Society.

6. Purchase your stamps from the post office which will do the mailing. Of course, you can use stamps purchased at any post office, but the post office that sells the stamps gets the credit and you can expect better cooperation from the postmaster who receives this credit. You will have to apply the stamps yourself, however.

7. When the mailing is ready to go to the post office from which it will be mailed, double-check on the type of transportation that serves the community. Many small post offices cannot be reached effectively by any means other than parcel post. When you have your shipping plans made, pass this information along to the postmaster so he can make all arrangements necessary to process your mailing on the schedule you want.

8. Don't forget to express your appreciation after your pieces have been mailed. It's not a necessity, but it's the least you can do to reward the sore-armed postmaster or postmistress who has hand-canceled (and those cancellation stamps are heavy!) your direct mail. A small gift will do the trick, but it is an even better gesture if you also send a letter to the editor of the nearest weekly newspaper with a word of praise for the postmaster (plus information about your use of the postmark).

UNUSUAL REPLY DEVICES

Showmanship does not have to be limited to the outgoing elements of your direct mail. You can also add impact by creating special reply devices. For example, a number of companies have found the use of preprinted collect telegrams an excellent showmanship reply device. All the recipient needs to do is to fill in his name and address on the telegram just as he would fill it in on a reply card, and call for a Western Union pickup. Western Union will even provide the telegram blanks for your reply.

Other effective showmanship reply techniques include affixing the proper postage in one-half cent stamps or using colorful commemorative stamps. One company even delivered homing pigeons to bring back the replies!

UNUSUAL MAILING PROCESS

The post office, itself, can provide a number of showmanship devices which, while common for regular correspondence, create special impact when used for direct mail purposes. Registered and certified mail and special delivery are good examples.

Or you may prefer to use a delivery service other than that of the postal service. Western Union, for example, offers a special service called Telegram-Plus. This service includes personal delivery of a telegram plus any other item you may want to circulate (i.e., samples, ad preprints, merchandising materials, and so forth). If your budget can stand it, you may want to arrange for costumed models to make your deliveries.

UNUSUAL ART

There is no end to the showmanship possibilities you can achieve through your selection of art and photographs. You may want to purchase or adapt art which many recipients will want to save for framing. Or you might turn to clever cartoons, which tickle the recipient's funny bone.

Some direct mail advertisers have made effective use of doodles; others have turned to drawings by children. Clever photos of babies and animals have both been used frequently for direct mail showmanship.

The possibilities are far too numerous to even try to list in detail. But this showmanship technique is one which certainly should be given special consideration.

MONEY AND STAMPS

Anyone who makes a collection of direct mail showmanship pieces soon finds that the most repeated "gimmick" is the penny. This is perhaps only logical since pennies are not only readily available, but they are also cheap (you will probably find it difficult to obtain any other dimensional gimmick for less than a cent each) and have readily recognized and appreciated value (even the prosperous business executive finds it difficult to resist stopping and picking up a stray penny he finds on the street).

Some of the many uses of pennies in direct mail include:

A number of banks have sent out mailings with the theme: "Here's a sample of our product" . . . the sample, of course, was a bright, new penny.

The Reader's Digest, among others, has affixed a couple of pennies to a mailing (usually positioned so they will show through a picture window in the mailing envelope) and suggested they are the recipient's "change" in advance. (A $2.98 offer, for example. The recipient sends in his check for $3.00 and keeps the two pennies as change.)

Engineering News-Record pasted pennies to mailing pieces it sent to advertisers to promote its Construction Costs Yearbook. One piece, for example, featured a drawing of a construction man with pennies pasted in position for his eyes. The theme: "Portrait of construction man looking at EN-R Costs Yearbook. That gleam in his eye is money—money he's ahead because of accurate costs information."

Another mailing from the same publication featured three pennies followed by "=$112,033." Copy explained how a 3 cents differential on per-item prices in a construction bid added up to a difference of $4,600, which won a $112,033 contract for the bidder.

Minnesota Paints used actual pennies to help merchandise its direct mail program for dealers. The pennies were made part of the headlines such as: "Introducing the super salesman you can hire for only a penny." In addition to United States pennies, the company included pennies from Switzerland and Yugoslavia for additional mailings.

Of course, you don't have to stop with pennies. A Chicago Chevrolet dealer, "Z." Frank, even went so far as to send real dollar bills to 10,000 prospects. The dollar had to do a lot of "talking," for the message accompanying it was just 15 words long: "You will be DOLLARS ahead . . . "Z." Frank before you buy! Our deal can't be beat." But the unexpected dollars did their job. "This was considered strictly institutional-type advertising, to impress upon the minds of the people in the neighborhood that they would be dollars ahead if and when they are ready to buy, if they purchase a car from "Z." Frank. The amount of comment created from this particular mailing was far beyond anything we ever anticipated, and the results proved to be most satisfactory," commented the dealer.

Flower Electrotype used two dimes to make a point. Positioned between the dimes was the headline: "What's the difference between these coins?" Copy continued: "Look closely at these coins. If you see a difference, call Uncle Sam. They should be identical. Now, just for the good sense of it, look closely at the electros you're buying. See any difference between them and your originals? . . . If you do see a difference, don't call Uncle Sam—call Flower."

Play Money

Sometimes "fake" money can be even more effective as a showmanship device. A Texas creative man, Luke Kaiser of Premier Printing & Letter Service, Houston, has created dozens of different kinds of "funny money" for use in direct mail campaigns. While the bills have an authentic appearance, close inspection shows that every design and copy element has been redesigned to help amplify the basic promotional theme—more often than not, with a humorous touch. Thus, the play money becomes not only an attention-attracting gimmick, but a promotion piece in itself.

Historical forms of money have also been put to showmanship use in many direct mail programs. The National Fleet Department of Chevrolet, for example, used a wide variety of historical "money" to emphasize a "savings" theme. Included were such items as Indian beads, German "shoe leather" money, rock salt. Oxford Paper Co. imbedded an authentic Indian wampum bead in a money clip. Union Bag mailed a genuine Piece of Eight from the Spanish Main plus a variety of other historical money items including a piece of cloth, similar to that used when trading with the Indians in the Massachusetts Colony.

Worthless Confederate currency, German marks, Chinese yen, and other no-longer-valued money still is being put to effective use to add impact to direct mail. Large quantities of such bills can usually be obtained at low cost. In addition, there is a number of foreign coins which, while still legal tender, can be obtained very cheaply.

There are numerous sources for money items and your local advertising specialty counselor can probably take care of most of your needs.

PHONOGRAPH RECORDS

With the advent of the so-called "printed record," sound has been added to many direct mail campaigns. Some of these printed records are created by laminating a preprinted piece and then stamping recording grooves into the lamination. More common, however, are clear plastic "Soundsheets," such as those produced by Eva-Tone.

Typical direct mail uses of printed records:

Metropolitan Life Insurance Co. sent 250,000 June brides-to-be a special recording, entitled "Getting Married?"

Buster Brown Shoes prepared a "Happy Birthday from Captain Kangaroo" record for mailing by shoe stores to children.

Direct Mail Advertising Assn. used the voices of its president and his assistant to tell prospective members about the association's services.

Warner Bros. plugged a new picture by sending theater operators a message from the star plus a new tune from the picture score.

Borden's Pharmaceutical Division sent medical information to doctors.

Encyclopaedia Britannica used the voice of its editor-in-chief to announce release of a new edition and pave the way for salesmen.

Ave Maria Radio Hour used a selection from its "Sermon on the Mount" program to help in fund-raising.

Squibb used records in four languages to introduce a new drug to doctors throughout North and South America.

Bahamas Development Board created a colorful four-page self-mailer with cooperative ads from 19 island companies and two recordings featuring native music.

United Fruit Co. previewed its radio advertising program to distributors and grocers with a 11- by 17-inch folder featuring a printed record.

Popular Club Plan used a recording to explain how a merchandise club could be formed.

Champion Spark Plug Co. offered dealers a variety of profit-making suggestions on its "Music to Sell More Spark Plugs By" record.

Columbia Record Club previewed two new releases for its members with a two-sided printed record.

Mailable Record Player

If you are concerned about the recipient of your mailing not having a phonograph on which to play your record, there is even a mailable record-and-player combination. Called a "Pop-Up Sound-o-Gram," the device folds to fit a No. 10 envelope. When removed, a cone-shaped horn pops into shape. On one corner is a steel needle. The recipient puts the needle in the groove of an attached 4-inch record and then turns the record and hears the message. The novelty item is available from Brownie Manufacturing Co., 55 Frankfort Street, New York, New York 10038.

SPECIALIZED STOCK MATERIALS

If you want direct mail showmanship in a hurry, there is a wide variety of "packaged" novelty mailings available for your use. A local lettershop should be able to provide details of what's currently available.

SPECIAL PROCESSES

Still another avenue to direct mail showmanship is available through the use of special production processes. These range from "invisible ink" to impregnating your mailing with the odor of a pine forest.

Invisible Ink

One of the most popular special production processes is the use of invisible ink. The message is usually printed on blotter stock and the recipient must dip the sheet into water before the words or illustrations appear. While many printers can produce such printing, many direct mail advertisers turn to a specialist such as M. E. Moss & Company, 119-H Ann Street, Hartford, Connecticut 06103, or Weck Process Co., 101 West 44th Street, New York, N. Y. 10036.

A variation on so-called invisible ink is the "strip tease" technique. This involves printing the message in waterproof ink and then overprinting with an opaque, water-soluble ink. The basic message then remains hidden until the piece is soaked in water, which will wash away the overprinting without affecting the basic message.

This technique was used by Mead Board Sales Inc. to introduce a waterproof outdoor sign material. A sample of the waterproof board was imprinted with a fully dressed cutie plus the caption, "Dip me in water—watch me change." And change she did. The water quickly washed away all clothing but a brief, brief bikini, which had been hidden beneath the dress.

Perfumed Inks

You can add the showmanship of "smell" to any printed piece by simply imprinting with a perfumed ink or compound. The leading source of odoriferous compounds is Fragrance Process Co. Inc., 667 Madison Avenue, New York, New York 10021. Fragrance Process offers more than 100 different aromatic printing compounds such as cinnamon roll, barbecue, pizza, grape, apricot, pickle, blackstrap molasses, coffee, juniper, rum, new-mown hay, lotus, jasmine, hickory, spruce, creosol, fire smoke, musk, leather, tobacco . . . even "Hospital Odor No. CR-12" and "Clean Odor No. 551." These colorless compounds are added simply by running printed pieces through the press again with the compounds in the fountain instead of ink. The cost is low—enough compound for 4,000 letter-size sheets, for example, averages about $10.

One of the classic stories of direct mail showmanship concerns the book publisher whose warehouse was damaged by fire. He sent out a mailing piece impregnated with the smell of smoke. The piece was so successful that the publisher not only sold all his smoke-damaged books, but even had to reprint certain titles to fill all the orders.

Another way to add the sense of smell to a promotion is with the microencapsulation process developed by 3M. This involves what is called a "sniff strip"—a pressure-sensitive label containing some 500,000 tiny bubbles per square inch. When the bubbles are broken by scratching the strip, they emit the unmistakable odor of the chosen fragrance. Among advertisers who have used this technique are A. O. Smith, which promoted its Harvestore silos with a piece containing a sniff strip with the smell of haylage; Nestle Co., with a chocolate-odor strip; E. R. Squibb & Sons, with a fruit odor to promote fruit-flavored antibiotic syrup, and Fleischmann's with the unmistakable smell of a freshly-mixed martini.

X-Ray Visuals

Another popular showmanship process is the "X-ray visual" or "take-apart" piece. The technique is relatively simple. A series of views are printed on clear acetate. Then, as each page is turned, a part is removed and exposes what lies beneath it. A watch company, for example, showed the inner workings of its watches by this technique. An automotive company explained key components of its cars' engines in a similar manner. A manufacturer of electric ranges showed how its products are built.

One of the most clever pieces of this kind opened to show an elevator full of people. As each page was turned, one of the passengers "left" the elevator—making some comment about the features of the elevator and thus promoting the products of the elevator manufacturer which sent out the mailing.

Smoldering Trails

A number of direct mail advertisers have created impact for their mailings by the use of specially treated paper. When a lighted cigarette is touched to a designated spot, it sets off a smoldering trail with a designated "path" turning to ashes. A trucking company used such a device to demonstrate the routes of its trucks. Others have used this idea to provide the previously hidden "signature" of the sender of a mailing.

HARD COVERS

One readily available, yet frequently overlooked, showmanship technique is adding hard covers to a booklet. This can be done for an entire mailing or to add a note of distinction to those copies being sent to special customers or prospects.

An excellent example is a reprint of a speech delivered by Paul J. Weber, marketing manager of the Instrumentation Division of Ampex Corp., Redwood City, California. Ampex took the text of Mr. Weber's talk, which was delivered to the Navy's Bureau of Ships, illustrated it with reproductions of slides which had been developed for the speech, and prepared a 76-page booklet called, "The Tape Recorder as an Instrumentation Device." The speech thus became a promotion device. The regular version had paper covers. But for key customers, prospects, and friends, Ampex added a set of hard covers and created a piece which was destined for permanent retention (who can throw away a hard-covered book?).

A number of companies issue their catalogs in two versions—soft covers for the regular list, hard covers for better customers.

COMBINING UNRELATED ITEMS

The unexpected combination of items which do not seem to belong together can often be a "winner" in achieving impact for a direct mail piece. For example, one company sent out a fishing plug in a plush-covered, satin-lined jewel case—a combination which was bound to attract special attention.

An all-time favorite of the author's was a colorful piece produced by the Paraffined Carton Research Council. It combined a 24-page booklet and a sample margarine carton. The booklet was attached to the sample carton so that the carton became the back cover of the booklet.

One of *Time* magazine's most outstanding advertising promotion pieces utilized two book-match packets. One was obviously a commercial packet, while the second was just as obviously a non-commercial packet designed for home use. The first was labeled "William Jones Corporation"; the second, "Sally and Bill Jones." The contrasting book-match packets helped *Time* emphasize the point that the magazine reaches "The Man in Two Positions to Buy."

PRODUCT SAMPLES OR PARTS

When all is said and done, there is probably no device with more effective showmanship potential than an actual sample of the product being promoted by direct mail. And when the product, itself, is too bulky to put into the mails, a part may do the trick.

Pharmaceutical manufacturers have been coming up with dramatic ways of presenting samples of their products by direct mail for many years. Pills and other drugs are made part of illustrations, packaged in all kinds of special boxes and packets, treated as jewels and generally made the "star" of the direct mail program.

One favorite technique of many advertisers is to place a plastic magnifying glass over a sample of a product or an important small part and urge the recipient to "Take a close look." Kaiser Aluminum used this technique to emphasize the fine detail which can be obtained in parts made of aluminum. A very small aluminum bushing—only .040 inch in diameter—was tipped to a card with the magnifying glass pasted atop the bushing.

Many other suppliers of raw materials create showmanship by distributing samples of products made with their products. Paper companies are masters of this technique, frequently distributing samples of items printed on papers they produce. A producer of glass beads sent out small packets of its product, offering prizes for the best suggestions on new uses. So many worthwhile entries were received the company had to expand its sales force to cover new prospects.

CHECK PROMOTIONS

An often-overlooked opportunity for direct mail showmanship comes with the mailing of checks to suppliers. Since checks are so often just mailed without any attempt at promotion, most any advertising tie-in is likely to gain special attention.

National Business Publications simply imprints this message on the reverse side of its checks:

Network of Business Know-How

> Technical, professional, scientific, industrial, merchandising, and marketing magazines in the United States and Canada—many of which make up the membership of National Business Publications, Inc.—constitute a network of specialized know-how unexcelled in communicating adult education and business information about new developments in product, method and service.

The Public Relations Board, Chicago public relations counseling firm, enclosed its checks in a folder imprinted with a simple, direct message:

> Here is our check.
>
> We hope you made a profit on us.
>
> For we like to do business with you
> and only by profitable transactions
> can you continue to prosper.
>
> As the occasion arises we trust you
> will recommend our services.
>
> For as we grow so will our need for
> what you sell.

Checks also made a good format for a value-oriented direct mail message. Creative Mailing Service, for example, took 35 of its most popular lists and put the essential information about each of them on a form resembling a bank check, complete with check stub. The 35 checks were bound into a checkbook holder. Each of the "checks" was actually a business reply card, so recipients of the mailing could request additional information about each list individually.

CLUBS

When a series of mailings is planned, you may be able to achieve greater reader interest and better continuity by creating a club atmosphere. This technique has proved particularly popular in industrial direct mail.

When Dewey and Almy Chemical Division of W. R. Grace & Co. started building a new plant in Owensboro, Kentucky, prospects for the plant's output were made members of the "Catwalk Superintendent's Club." At the beginning of the eight-piece mailing program, all recipients received personalized membership cards. Then the "members" were sent regular progress reports on the plant's construction progress. Finally, all "members" received a silver tie bar with the club emblem.

If you cannot think up a club of your own, there is always a syndicated series called the "Club-of-the-Month Club." "Members" receive membership cards in a new (fictional) club each month!

One of the most outstanding club promotions is the long-lasting "Executive Vice Presidents" promotion of Smith & Hemmings, Los Angeles direct mail firm. The first mailing to new names includes a laminated membership card identifying the recipient as an "Executive Vice President" of Smith & Hemmings. The letter, on a special illustrated letterhead, says:

You Have Been Elected an Executive Vice President!

The enclosed ID Card proves your new status . . . and will admit you to the meetings, if you ever find out where they are to be held.

> You will receive reports periodically from the management of YOUR company. And your dividends will be mailed to you irregularly as we make a profit in this crazy, wonderful business.
>
> Seriously, you are one of our "Vice Presidents" because we want to keep our personal acquaintance alive. In a big city like this—with things happening so fast—we want to make certain that we do not lose our friends through our own neglect.
>
> Soooooo, lean back, relax . . . and enjoy yourself. Watch your mail for your "Special Reports."

Typical Special Reports include dividends of one kind or another. One, for example, contained an actual Smith & Hemmings' check—for 13 cents. Another contained a sheet of S&H Red Stamps. Copy for the letter which accompanied this mailing is shown on the facing page. In addition to the letter and sheet of red stamps, there was a "catalog of collector's items available only with S&H 'RED' Stamps."

Items in the catalog included a "Campus Boy" raccoon coat; a live buffalo; an antique car, and a horse and wagon. (All, of course, required more stamps than were issued.)

SPLIT-UP MAILINGS

Spreading an attention device over a series of mailings can provide extra impact. One of the most frequently used applications of this technique is the "coffee break by mail." The first time we observed the technique in use, Thomas W. Bender, of McGraw-Hill Publishing Co., used it to promote space sales in *Electronic Buyers' Guide.* A more recent adapter of the idea was Claude F. Martin of Parlee Co., Indianapolis. The Parlee campaign, aimed at convincing church groups they should use a Parlee product to aid in fund-raising, involved seven mailings:

1. An announcement letter hinting at the unusual pieces to follow.
2. A folder with a wooden spoon attached—"Just to stir up thinking." Recipients were told to save the spoon for future use.
3. Another folder with a one-cup packet of instant coffee.
4. A folder with a package of powdered cream and a packet of sugar.
5. A paper cup was featured in mailing number five.
6. Then came a toothpick—"to pick out ideas."
7. Final mailing included a stick of gum—"chew over this idea."

Missing Link

Another popular "split-up" mailing is where a single cuff link is mailed. The first use of this technique was to draw visitors to an exhibit at a trade show (where they could pick up the matching link). Today, however, the technique is used more frequently to open doors for salesmen.

Chelsea Warehouses of New York sent a miniature door-knocker cuff link to customers and prospects with this letter on a Thanksgiving letterhead:

> At Thanksgiving time . . .
>
> We are giving "Thanks" for having such wonderful folks like you to do business with.
>
> We hope your holiday was most pleasant.
>
> In appreciation for letting us "knock on your door" during the past year, we'd like you

to have the enclosed gold door-knocker cuff link.

By the way, if it's O.K. with you, we'd like to "knock on your door" again and deliver the "mate" to give you a pair . . . but on one condition

NOT TO TALK BUSINESSE.

We'd just like to wish you "in person" the BEST for Christmas and New Year.

So, please, check and return the reply card.

P.S. One word was misspelled in the above letter. Do you know which word? Write the right answer on the reply card and we'll rush a Gold Door Knocker Tie Clip to you with your set of cuff links as your Genius Award.

While the letter emphasized the "not to talk business" contact, the enclosed reply card gave recipients an opportunity to request various pieces of promotional literature.

MULTIPLE MAILINGS

Just as you can add showmanship by splitting up a mailing, you can achieve impact by using multiple items. This is a particularly effective technique when you want to emphasize quantity.

A good example of how multiple units can be used to advantage is a mailing made by Reynolds Metals to impress its distributors and dealers with the numerous merchandising tools which had been prepared to support their efforts. To emphasize quantity, Reynolds mailed a full deck of playing cards. Copy explained:

> We're flabbergasted! When we began to count up the number of promotions that Reynolds has staged for you on behalf of Reynolds Wrap and other Reynolds consumer products, even we were surprised! By printing each one on a separate playing card we hope to show you how Reynolds' consistent advertising, merchandising, and promotion help you sell more . . .

Other advertisers have used the simple expediency of making each of their points on a separate sheet of paper, usually with a different color combination for each sheet.

GAG ITEMS

The real fun for most direct mail advertisers comes when they decide to use some kind of gag item to make a direct mail point with showmanship. Just walk into any novelty store and chances are you will find dozens of items which could be put to point-making use for your own product or service story. Some of the many items which have been used successfully include:

International Swimming Pool Corporation sent a packet of redwood seeds to "losers" in a prize drawing. The winner got a swimming pool. Copy with the seeds consoled: "All is not lost . . . for by planting the seeds attached, a redwood tree of the right size will be ready in about 800 years . . ."

Creative Mailing Service of Garden City, New York, sends prospects a plastic pass case containing 10 humorous "credit cards" for such establishments as "Morton's Mortuary—Satisfaction or Mummy Back"; "The Last Resort—within walking distance of all the good hotels"; "Sandy Acres Golf and Curling Club—on the Arabian Sea."

The Clegg Company of San Antonio sends friends its "Texan Scratch Pad"—with pages 14 by 16 inches.

Calcium Carbonate Co., Chicago, mails out a custom-made gag item each month. Mailings have included "Busy Executives' Coffee"—coffee candies in an instant coffee jar; "Desk-Top Foot Rest"—a plastic-covered piece of sponge rubber; a 5- by 5-inch metal sign, reading "Meter Out of Order—Officer: This meter did not register when I deposited a coin." (For more complete details on this ingenious campaign, see Chapter 24, "Direct Mail Spectaculars.")

A number of advertisers have used a "Do-It-Yourself Voodoo Kit" to put a "hex" on problems.

Another popular item used by numerous direct mail advertisers is a plastic "Panic Button."

Dy-Dee Diaper Service sends expectant fathers a lapel ornament in the shape of a golden diaper pin.

Wretched Mess News

Probably there isn't anyone who has more fun with direct mail than Dave Bascomb, alias Milford Poltroon, publisher of the "Wretched Mess News" of West Yellowstone, Montana (Genuine Zip Code: 59758). This San Francisco adman has turned a mimeograph machine, cheap paper and lovable copy into fun and games for everyone who receives one of his original mailings.

Like it or not, a mailing from Wretched Mess News will come in a real brown paper bag—not an imitation, the real thing. It will probably even have a smaller brown bag enclosed for reply (with the return address rubber stamped in red ink—you furnish your own stamp).

Here's one of his promotion letters, badly mimeographed on a piece of pink paper—heading rubber stamped in that same red ink:

> Why not let the Wretched Mess News bring Culture, Poise & Fish into your otherwise shabby life?
>
> The Wretched Mess is the ONLY periodical in the entire U.S.A. that DARES to completely ignore all vital, important news. Why? Because all vital, important news these days is foul, rotten & highly depressing.
>
> The Wretched Mess News instead concentrates on happy, fishy news. It proudly serves as America's last stronghold of Fearless Yellow Journalism.
>
> For a mere, wretched $2 you can have the next 6 fishues sent directly to your home, your yacht or your office. YES! An order form and a return bag are enclosed. SO WHY NOT?
>
> Wregards,
> Miss Ida Mae Poltroon
> Circulating Mgr.

P.S. If by fortunate circumstance you are already a Wretched subscriber, our heartiest congratulations on your apperception, foresight and Good Taste! Perhaps you have a "friend" you would like to pass this order form on to.

THIS IS A GENUINE
MIMEOGRAPHED LETTER

Another taste of the Milford Poltroon direct mail approach is a letter mimeographed on a piece of brown kraft wrapping paper, complete with a rough blade tear at the bottom. It promotes the annual, unbelievable Wretched Mess calendar, which comes complete with unfamiliar months and unfamiliar events:

> TREAT YOUR EYEBALLS
> to gleefully gazing at the accompanying page. It is one (1) of the swell months that make up our Wretched Mess Calendar. This pioneering work incorporates several long-needed calendar reforms:
>
> (A) a genuine Hole for hanging up By.
>
> (B) nicer paper.
>
> (C) complete renaming of all months, i.e., June is now SHIRLEY.
>
> It is lavishly illustrated WITH PICTURES including the graphic depiction of Termites Infesting Shirley Temple, National Shotgun Wedding Day, & many more, none of which are particularly suitable for framing.

This daring and original work makes a SWELL GIFT for all your friends, clients & anyone else a person such as yourself is likely to know. It is being advertised in a hellslew of national magazines for $1.50 EACH and well worth it. YES.

But because we tenderly think of you as a Special Needy & Deserving Person, we are making you this superspecial SECRET offer (do not tell NO ONE):

(price list)

These embarrassingly cheap low prices include plain envelopes for mailing.

You MUST use the enclosed handsome, good-taste order blank to be entitled to these ridiculous, rottenly low costs.

Only hurry.

Your swell friend,
Milford Poltroon

TEASERS

Many a direct mail campaign has been off to a fast start, with thanks to the showmanship of a "teaser mailing." R. R. Donnelley & Sons Co. paved the way for a sales-incentive program by mailing each salesman a bag containing three Brazil nuts and a simple, unexplained message: "Get set to crack some tough nuts." The details followed three days later after the sales force had had time to puzzle over the nuts.

Another advertiser cut his message into five parts and sent it a piece at a time. It wasn't until the fifth and final piece arrived that the entire message could be put together to make sense. (Rather than trust recipients to save each mailing, the preceding pieces were repeated with each mailing.)

COLOR

Color can be a vital showmanship element, particularly when it is used in some unusual way. Simply printing an item in an unexpected color often creates impact—red money, green sky, an orange Model T, a blue-faced or purple-faced person, and so forth.

A wide variety of unusual colors in printing papers has been developed primarily for showmanship mailings. One line, for example, features "impact" colors—unusually vivid hues.

Whenever you find one of your mailings lacks a desirable degree of showmanship, one of your first considerations should be the possibility of substituting a different color combination. Chances are it can be accomplished without spending any additional money.

PERSONALIZATION

Successful direct mail advertisers have long recognized that the greatest possible showmanship technique is personalization, particularly in this age of mass mailings and automation. The showmanship of personalization may come through computer letters, or it may involve adding the recipient's name in 14-carat gold.

Perhaps the ultimate in personalization is a series of one-of-a-kind promotion pieces used by Ad Agencies/Headliners of New York to sell advertising agencies on the use of the firms' graphic arts services. Each is the individual brain child of Creative Director Larry Ottino.

When the D'Arcy agency was awarded the Knox Gelatine account, for example, Ottino dreamed up the idea of sending D'Arcy executives a series of apothecary jars with their initials suspended in refrigerated gelatine. On a tag tied to the jar lid was the copy: "The perfect mixture—Knox Gelatine and D'Arcy. When your ideas have jelled and D'Arcy is ready to produce great advertising campaigns, may be suggest a helpful mixture that will guarantee the best results for Knox Gelatine: Blend equal proportions of D'Arcy copy and art direction with typography and lettering by Ad Agencies Services and The Headlines of New York. Result: Solid, but moving and vibrating ads. Call MU 7-0590 and Larry Ottino, coordinator of graphics for both companies, will be happy to help you mix the ingredients."

Another special promotion went to Young & Rubicam when it got the United Biscuit account. Special wrappers were printed for boxes of Butter Cookies. Copy on the box wrappers read: "United Biscuit Co. presents the newest old-fashioned butter cookies. Y & R Yellow & Rich Butter Cookies. These cookies baked especially for (name of recipient set in type). Packaged and distributed by ad Agencies'/ Headliners, suppliers of type/lettering/mechanical products that are definitely not half-baked. Chief baker, Larry Ottino, MU 7-0590."

Other individualized promotions in this program included a lunch box with a bottle of Rheingold beer to executives at Doyle Dane Bernbach when that agency was awarded the Rheingold account. The lunch box also had a ham and swiss sandwich with Levy's bread (another DDB account). When Grey agency picked up the Greyhound Bus account, Ottino sent out personalized tickets to Grey executives. Copy read: "Here's a ticket from the Headliners of New York, to your most exciting adventure since riding in a Greyhound. This ticket entitles you to $10.00 worth of the freshest process lettering you've ever seen." For Fuller & Smith & Ross when it got the Air France account, a personalized paper airplane was the copy carrier. And when Dancer, Fitzgerald & Sample hooked up with a toy account, in walked a mechanical dinosaur toy with a mounted knight carrying a personalized banner with a sales message.

"Cue" Magazine Introduction

A highly successful showmanship direct mail campaign, with considerable personalization, was used to introduce a new publisher's representative to prospects for *Cue* magazine advertising in western states. The new "rep," Bob Friedman, used six unusual mailings (sent for six continuous days):

1. *A split of champagne* plus a handwritten card proposing a special toast ("Join me in celebrating my new affiliation . . ."). The recipient's name was included on the card.
2. *Giant post card*—21 by 26 inches ("Big? You bet. *Cue* boasts a huge paid circulation . . ."). A special "P.S." to the individual recipients was handwritten.
3. *Shirt cuff.* Yes, an honest-to-goodness cuff, ripped off a shirt, with a special message handwritten with red-and-black ink ("A Special 'Off-the-Cuff' STARCH Report . . .").
4. *A phonograph record* with personalized messages.
5. *Tear sheet* from the *New York Times,* with mentions of *Cue* hand-circled in red.
6. *Copy of Cue magazine* with an attached note reading: "John, I thought you might be interested to see your name on page 40." On page 40, Bob Friedman penned this message atop the regular printed text: "John, your interest demonstrates how human nature compels people to be highly attracted by something that directly concerns them. The pages of *Cue* capture high readership."

Murphy & Miller Mailings

A different type of personalization was used by Murphy & Miller Inc., Chicago heating and air-conditioning firm. To sell complete home air-conditioning plants, Murphy & Miller attached an actual photograph of the recipient's home to their mailers. While these mailers cost 41½ cents each, a mailing of 1,240 resulted in 10 sales at a price of $1,350 each!

A variation of this technique is the use of newspaper and magazine clippings which include the name and/or photo of the recipient. Such items can be particularly effective when used with picture-window envelopes.

Harper's Personalization by Community

Still another type of personalization was put to good use by *Harper's* magazine, which created special mailings for residents in each of 53 top influential communities in the United States. At the heading of the *Harper's* letter was a special imprint in red: "Special to residents of (name of town)." Copy began: "Influence often runs contrary to bigness. Your community, for instance, is relatively small—but it is one of the 53 most influential communities in the United States . . ."

Other advertisers have created semipersonalized pieces by selecting often-repeated names on their lists (such as Jones, Johnson, Smith, and so forth) and imprinting the mailing pieces with the last name in large letters.

"Church Administration" Title Cards

Personalization by position was used to advantage by *Church Administration* magazine. The publication had the problem of trying to reach a dozen or two leading volunteer laymen in each Southern Baptist church. Unfortunately, names were available for only three or four key laymen in each church.

To solve the problem, promotion man Richmond O. Brown came up with the idea of a set of "title cards"—3¼- by 8½-inch table tents with standard church office titles imprinted on the face. Titles included Pastor, Church Secretary, Chairman of Deacons, Clerk, Brotherhood President, and so forth. Fine-quality gold stock was used to encourage actual use by the recipients.

The entire set for each church was mailed to the pastor, with a request that he hand them to the appropriate officers. While requesting similar distribution of a routine promotion piece would likely have been highly unsuccessful, offering a distinctive item worked wonders. The promotion message for the magazine was printed inside the "tent."

OUTSTANDING CAMPAIGN

If anyone were to pass out special honors for the finest continuing job of direct mail showmanship, the hands-down winner would be Exxon. Month after month over the years, Exxon has supported its dealers by showmanship mailings to motorists. While inexpensive gift items have been featured, they have individually and collectively created impact for the sales message and an atmosphere of goodwill for the dealers.

All of Exxon's gift items have three things in common:

1. They are useful.
2. They are easily mailed.
3. They are inexpensive.

Direct Copy Tie-Ins

Whenever possible, Exxon's copy has a direct tie-in with the monthly gift. For example, a plastic magnifying glass mailed in July was inserted into a folder headed: "Now's the time to take a closer look at your vacation plans . . ." Then, inside the folder, Exxon suggested, "Let *us* take a close look at your car before you leave." Copy also showed how the plastic magnifying glass could be used with Exxon road maps.

The campagin is based on a simple premise. Exxon feels that if it expects recipients to take time to read its messages it must repay them in some small way.

The success of the program is evidenced by the fact that not only do old dealers continue to resubscribe to the program each year, but by the fact that most new dealers take on the program. And never a month goes by but what the company receives numerous letters from customers and potential customers *asking* that their names be placed on the mailing list.

Typical Pieces

Each of the gifts is integrated into a colorful printed piece. Because the program is, in reality, the dealer's own direct mail campaign, each of the printed pieces is imprinted with the individual dealer's name and address. Typical mailings have included:

Soap-Gripper—a plastic sponge which can be wrapped around a bar of soap. Copy tie-in: "There's many a slip 'twixt the road and the grip. That's why, when it comes to tires, you can't afford less than the best!"

"Man's Best Friend"—a 16-page booklet with 25 full-color illustrations of leading breeds of dogs plus tips on care, feeding, and training of dogs. Copy tie-in: "You can be *dog-gone* sure when it comes to our lubrication."

Squeeze-It Key—a plastic key which can be used to squeeze the last ounce of toothpaste or shaving cream from the tube. Copy tie-in: "You'll make it easy on yourself with Atlas Bucron Tires."

Football Facts—a 64-page booklet of interesting information about football plus leading college and pro schedules. This annual volume tied in with Esso sponsorship of football games on TV. Many copy tie-ins are scattered throughout the handbook by applying football terms to promotional copy.

Twist-ems—a packet of tiebacks for flowers and vegetables. Copy tie-in: "Right from the ground . . . up . . . extra protection is yours with Atlas tires."

Poultry Lacing Pins—a November mailing included a set of six aluminum poultry lacers. Copy tie-in: "Time's getting near for 'turkey and all the trimmings' . . . but that's the time, too, for the start of winter-weather driving!"

Picture Hangers—a set of three picture hangers. Copy tie-in: "We'd like to hammer home this point . . ."

Easter Egg-Coloring Kit—a packet of transfers and egg dyes. Copy: "Some youngster you know will have fun with this Easter Egg-Coloring Kit. And . . . to make motoring more fun . . . let us give your car our special spring servicing!"

Paper Dolls—a cut-out paper doll of an Exxon serviceman with four additional suits of clothing. Each suit of clothing had a copy tie-in. For example, with a fire chief's suit: "Our *chief* aim is to serve you with three-alarm speed. Whatever service you're burning for, we ring the bell."

Packet of Seeds—copy: "Put new life and color in your garden and put new life in your winter-weary car . . ."

Stamp Book—a 12-page booklet containing a sports quiz. Quiz subjects were answered by pasting a colorful stamp in position on the page. Copy tie-in: ". . . and for the perfect answer to Happy Motoring . . ."

Sewing Kit—a little book containing thread, buttons, needles and pins. Copy tie-in: "You're in our book . . ."

Party Game Booklet—a clever little booklet containing five "safe tricks to liven up your next party." Copy tie-in: "There's no trick to safe driving when your car is equipped with Atlas tires."

Maps—many special maps are included in the program. Typical: "A Pictorial Map of Life in Colonial America."

Measuring Guide—a little plastic gadget to measure the right amount of butter or margarine for recipes. Copy tie-in: "Measuring can make the difference in safety, too."

Barbecue Recipe Cards—a set of cards containing recipes for popular outdoor barbecue dishes. Copy tie-in: "The best recipe in town for Happy Motoring!"

Why It Works

The Exxon "Gift of the Month" program is probably the classic example of simple, continuous direct mail showmanship. It has frequently been copied by other advertisers and regularly wins awards for its excellence.

One of the most important success factors is the skill with which the promotion theme is tied to the "gift." Not only are the items selected useful to the recipient, but as they are used they serve to remind the user of an important Exxon sales story. Another secret of Exxon's success has been the company's ability to turn up "gift" items which have a direct relationship to travel and automobile care.

Chapter 32

DIRECT MAIL SPECTACULARS

THE direct mail spectacular, while another showmanship technique, has several distinctive characteristics. It represents the most elaborate—and frequently the most costly—use of the direct mail medium. Designed primarily to call special attention to something, the spectacular is almost always directed to a highly select audience.

Perhaps the spectacular's most distinguishing characteristic is its dimensional nature. While some spectaculars are flat, ultra-high-quality printed pieces, the majority feature three-dimensional objects and are mailed in specially prepared boxes rather than envelopes. As a result, direct mail spectaculars are frequently called "dimensionals."

Spectaculars are sometimes used independently, but more often they are part of a multimailing campaign. Frequently, spectacular mailings are integrated into a campaign which includes pieces of a more conventional nature. Another distinguishing characteristic is that the dimensional objects featured in spectacular mailings are usually designed for retention over an extended period. Often the objects are specially tailored for some functional use by the recipient.

Age of the Spectacular

While not completely new, the direct mail spectacular has come into popularity during the past decade along with advertising spectaculars in other media. Nearly everyone has neglected his regular high-rated TV show to devote an hour to one of the spectaculars used by TV advertisers when they have a special story to tell. Magazines and newspapers, too, have come in for their share of advertising spectaculars. In magazines you find fold-out covers, multiple-page insertions, tear-out booklet inserts. In newspapers, advertisers resort to pages printed on foil, colorful "wallpaper-type" inserts, special tabloid sections, and other spectacular techniques. Outdoor posters are adorned with giant-size cutouts, animation, and other devices. Car cards and posters are decorated with dimensional objects. Trade-show exhibits grow more spectacular each year. One advertiser even employed a whole fleet of skywriting planes to cover the heavens with multicolored spectacular messages.

These are all symptoms of the intensive effort to hurdle the attention-barrier which surrounds every potential buyer of any product or service. A survey by General Foods showed that the average American is exposed to 1,518 promotional messages each day of his life. Thousands more go unnoticed because a dial was on a different spot, a newspaper or magazine page wasn't turned—or the prospect just didn't see them because he was too busy or took a different route.

While direct mail has the advantage of being directed to the specific audience an advertiser wishes to reach, and survey upon survey has proved almost 100% of all direct mail at least gets opened, there is no assurance the message will make any kind of impression. So direct mail advertisers, too, have turned to the spectacular technique when they have a special story to tell and do not want to take a chance that it might get lost in the din of the more than 1,500 promotional voices with which it must compete on the day of its arrival at the prospect's home or office.

For the most part, the direct mail spectacular technique is reserved for campaigns directed at limited audiences. Most frequently, it is aimed at busy executives or businessmen who are known to be recipients of large quantities of other direct mail advertising.

Planning a Direct Mail Spectacular

A great deal of creativity goes into the successful direct mail spectacular. Seldom is one of these attention-winning dimensional mailings a spur-of-the-moment idea. Instead, a great deal of careful planning goes into each piece. Among the factors which must be fully considered are:

- How can the mailing secure immediate attention, yet do a *primary* job of dramatizing the sales message?
- Can the dimensional objects be obtained at a reasonable price with guaranteed quality and delivery?
- Can the object be packaged to assure delivery in *perfect* condition?

- Will this mailing fit naturally into the campaign, adding its weight to the promotional impact made by preceding and subsequent mailings?
- Can the theme be sustained over a series of mailings?
- Does the theme have potential for use in other promotion media?
- Will the point of the mailing be obvious?
- Will the dimensional object be offensive to any of the recipients?
- Can the mailing be handled by regular direct mail service organizations or will it be necessary to arrange for special handling?
- Will the mailing meet all postal requirements?
- Is the same technique being used or has it recently been used for other mailings to the same audience? (To be most effective, a spectacular mailing should have the stage pretty much to itself.)

But the most important factor of all:

- *Will the mailing piece be so clever the recipient will remember the cleverness rather than the company which sent it and the story it was trying to tell?*

Advantages of Spectaculars

The direct mail spectacular has a number of inherent advantages. For instance, it usually gets first attention in the morning's mail. It is almost impossible to ignore a box with unknown contents. If the dimensional object is clever enough, it usually is shown to others—thus multiplying its impact and making a more indelible impression on the original recipient as he explains why he received it. Since few people are willing to just discard an item of intrinsic value, the dimensional mailing piece usually has an extended period of longevity during which it reminds the recipient again and again of the message it accompanied.

An added advantage of the spectacular is its ability to build a favorable corporate image for the sender. Many advertisers have used spectaculars primarily to emphasize the fact that they are creative organizations capable of providing more than just the routine in products and services.

Salesmen find another added value in the use of spectacular promotions. When they must make repeated calls upon customers and prospects, the customer inevitably wants to know "what's new?" All too often, unfortunately, there is no legitimate answer which provides real meat for a sales conversation. But the salesman supported by a spectacular promotion program has a valuable conversational aid. While the spectacular promotion may not represent a new product or service to talk about, it makes "news" in itself and thus leads to sales conversation of mutual interest.

Still another plus value of spectaculars is the interest they can create within the advertiser's own organization. Too frequently, a company's promotion passes right over the heads of executives, sales force, and others in the company. "We've heard it all before," is the usual reaction, even though this is often far from the truth. A spectacular approach, however, makes them sit up and take notice; the fact that it generates comments from recipients—and, frequently, even from competitors—makes them more conscious of the value of the promotion program which supports their selling efforts.

Much the same thing can be said of distributors and manufacturers' agents, although here the spectacular approach can produce even greater dividends. Within every multiline distribution organization there is the problem of giving adequate attention to each of the hundreds or thousands of products handled. Some are bound to receive greater attention than others—some because they carry a higher profit margin; some because they are easier to sell; still others because they are exciting products to talk about. But if products or services do not automatically fit any of these qualifications, the spectacular promotion approach may be what wins "equal attention" for a line. It can help make the line more exciting to talk about and can dramatize a sales story in a way which implants product features and benefits more deeply in a salesperson's mind and thus makes the product easier to sell.

How Union Bag-Camp Uses Spectaculars

Direct mail spectaculars can be used to accomplish a variety of promotional objectives. Their versatility is illustrated by some of the campaigns of Union Bag-Camp Paper Co., which has twice won the direct mail industry's top award—DMMA's Gold Mail Box. Probably the best known of the Union Bag spectaculars was the famed Yoon Yun campaign, which established benchmarks for many outstanding direct mail spectaculars used today. This 1953 campaign has been described as "the most impressive campaign in the history of direct mail."

The aim of the Yoon Yun campaign was to accelerate acceptance for a relatively new Union Bag product. While the company had been known for over 75 years as a leading supplier of paper containers, it wanted to dramatize the fact that it was now manufacturing corrugated shipping containers.

The campaign, aimed at 2,000 potential customers, was built around legends involving a mythical Chinese character, Yoon

Yun, and used a mixture of dimensional mailings and elaborate printed pieces. The first two mailings were "teasers," with no identification of the mailer. They featured Chinese Linking Rings, one of the favorite illusions of magicians. Two of the metal rings were included in each of the mailings, which, in addition, featured colorful printed folders relating an interesting Chinese legend concerning Yoon Yun. The third mailing, a folder headed "The *Real* Secret of Yoon Yun's Magic Rings," revealed the reason for the campaign and the advertiser. Copy linked the magic rings to the special features of the product. Subsequent mailings continued in a Chinese vein and included a variety of dimensional objects—a colorful puzzle, miniature foods, a set of magnetic "pick-up sticks," and a box of Chinese litchi nuts.

Typical of the reaction from prospects was an unsolicited letter from a major potential buyer of corrugated cartons: "As a purchasing agent with years of experience, I thought we had seen every possible means of attracting attention by advertising, but it was refreshing to see a completely new and interesting method of bringing to our attention the quality of the product you are selling . . . Such individuality of thinking reflects very highly on your company and makes us most receptive to the idea of some day doing business with you."

Four years later, Union Bag came up with another spectacular, which once again won a DMMA Gold Mail Box. This time a money theme was used for a campaign designed to accomplish nine specific objectives:

1. Increase brand preferences for Union multiwall bags.
2. Demonstrate that although original cost, quality, and production facilities are comparable among major multiwall manufacturers, there are major dollar-and-cent differences when all costs are evaluated.
3. Spell out the areas of service which, individually or collectively, can constitute this difference.
4. Demonstrate and document Union's superiority in each of these areas.
5. Build stature of Union representatives as packaging consultants and specialists—help them gain an audience in companies where competition is solidly entrenched.
6. Reach top executives whom salesmen usually do not have a chance to see personally.
7. Help unearth new prospects for Union multiwall bags.
8. Act as a continuing reminder—between and after salesmen's calls—of how Union Value Analysis works to multiwall users' advantage.
9. Sell a complete packaging concept that can be implemented by and coordinated with trade advertising and publicity.

To accomplish these objectives, Union used a 16-unit mailing series. As in the Yoon Yun campaign, a mixture of dimensionals and colorful printed pieces were featured. All had a money theme designed to hammer home the campaign's message: "Money has value and usefulness only in terms of what it will buy. The test of an expert buyer is not alone the price he pays. The real standard is value received." For most of the mailings, a historical tale of a medium of exchange was told and illustrated. Dimensionals included a real Greek tetradrachmon coin minted over 16 centuries ago; a miniature bolt of cloth similar to those used by native traders in American colonial days; a genuine piece of eight from the Spanish Main attached to a money clip, a salarium disc (common salt once used to pay Roman soldiers), and a trick money-making machine into which the recipient inserted blank paper and out came a real United States dollar bill, a simulated check for $129,000 representing money saved by a Union multiwall customer, and a bill-size recap of the campaign story.

A more recent Union Bag-Camp Paper campaign utilized still another basic direct mail dimensional technique--product demonstration. In this 1960 campaign aimed at top executives, Union Bag promoted bleached packaging board with a series of miniature containers produced from the company's product. The colorful designs illustrated the printability and versatile properties of the board. Included in the series were such items as a 6½- by 3-inch mailbox; a 2- by 2-inch snuff box; an 8- by 4-inch mummy case; and miniature match, bakery, freezer, and cigarette cartons.

GETTING THROUGH TO TOUGH AUDIENCES

While these three spectacular campaigns cover a variety of objectives, all had one objective in common. They were aimed at a "tough audience"—busy executives who are subjected to hundreds of promotional messages daily. The majority of direct mail spectaculars have such an objective as at least one of the reasons for their use.

Advertising Space Buyers

Probably no audience is tougher than advertising space buyers. It is composed of men and women who not only are recipients of a tremendous quantity of promotion material, but who also are extremely critical of each piece they receive. Spectacular mailings are used quite frequently to reach this audience. Among the best have been the elaborate pieces developed some years ago by Jess Hadsell for Curtis Publishing Company's *Holiday* and *American Home* magazines. The majority were created by unusual paper constructions, although other dimensional items were also used—but always incorporating printed messages directly with the dimensional object. Typical pieces have included:

- A box in the shape of a Buckingham Palace Guard House, with a die-cut guard standing in the doorway. When the guard is removed, an accordion-folded message comes out of the little house telling the *Holiday* story.
- A die-cut parrot "standing" on a metal ring (with a string attached for hanging as a mobile).
- Dimensional paper replicas of a Paris kiosk, a lighthouse, the Leaning Tower of Pisa, rocket ship, Spanish galleon, Christmas tree.
- A popgun. When fired, the cork pops out trailing a paper streamer bearing a promotion message.
- A bottle of champagne in a bucket imprinted with a promotion message.
- A wooden pants hanger holding a simulated pair of trousers imprinted with a message.
- A string of imprinted paper hot dogs.

One of the major advantages of the Curtis dimensional pieces were that they had a great deal of longevity as displays. They were hung in offices, tacked on bulletin boards and displayed on bookcases, desks, and filing cabinets where they could be seen by hundreds who were not original recipients of the mailings. This amounts to getting prospects to help advertise your products for you.

The Medical Profession

Another tough audience is the medical profession. The average American doctor receives around 5,000 direct mail pieces each year, including some of the most elaborate printed specimens which can be produced. But when there is a special story to be told, the advertiser trying to get through to the doctor frequently turns to dimensional mailings.

Abbott Laboratories, for example, faced a major marketing problem with its Pramilets prenatal supplement. There was a big potential market, but other major pharmaceutical houses had already established their products before Abbott got started. So Abbott turned to a spectacular direct mail campaign which included simulated birth announcements, elaborate sample packages, an expensive cigar "in honor of the doctor's next blessed event," and a simulated book containing samples. The campaign moved Abbott from eighth place with just 3% of the total market into second place with a 120% sales increase in just six months.

Hoffman-LaRoche used another spectacular technique to get through to doctors. It reduced the number of its mailings and combined them into a series of elaborate packages, each including a letter, reply card, product information booklet, and eight samples—plus a colorful replica of an antique map—all inserted in a large, beautifully designed presentation box. Hoffman-LaRoche made a special point of calling its revised promotion technique to the doctors' attention and asked for their comments. As many as 15,000 favorable comments and more than 8,000 requests for additional copies of the antique maps followed a single mailing to 55,000 general practitioners.

Bank Executives

Bankers constitute still another tough audience which has been successfully "cracked" by spectacular mailings. International Business Machines, for example, wanted to tell the story of its data-processing systems to the presidents of 500 of the nation's largest banks. It was a detailed story and required a number of consecutive mailings. To sustain interest in the subject over an extended period, IBM developed a special wooden frame into which special tiles could be fitted. When completed, the frame became either a desk tray or a colorful piece to be displayed on the wall. The initial mailing featured the tray and first tile, plus a personalized letter explaining the campaign. Five subsequent mailings brought the additional tiles needed to complete the design—accompanied, of course, by the story of IBM's systems. By the time the campaign had ended, over half of the 500 bank presidents receiving the mailings had written unsolicited letters of commendation and approval. It is interesting to note that all of these men could easily have afforded to buy dozens of similar trays and are under constant pressure in their work. Yet the majority took time not only to acknowledge the receipt of the IBM promotion campaign but also to see the IBM salesmen who followed up the mailings.

While the IBM approach was steeped in dignity throughout, a more whimsical approach can also be used successfully to reach bank executives. The Bank of America, for example, promoted its traveler's cheques to New England bankers with a tale of a mythical Captain Silas Trevelyan who made a trip into uncharted waters of the Caribbean in 1668 and survived pirates, storm, shipwreck, and other harrowing experiences—thanks, of course, to his Bank of America travelers cheques. To kick off the campaign, each of the bank presidents received an automatically typewritten letter outlining what was to follow:

> It is not a regular procedure for an advertiser to alert the recipient of his program. However, that is what we are going to do with this letter.
>
> To bring to your attention our Bank of America Travelers Cheques, we have devised a direct mail campaign which we believe to be most unusual. We trust that you will enjoy the campaign both as a promotion for our Travelers Cheques and as interesting reading for its own sake.
>
> We have selected the Caribbean as an area where many of your clients will be cruising and vacationing in the coming season. The subject matter of the campaign is a mythical journey undertaken in the 1600's by a sea captain on behalf of you who have commissioned him to explore the region to ascertain general local trading conditions. The locations and incidents of his alleged journey are, basically, authentic. He finds hidden treasure and temptation beckons him along the way. He will report back to you each of his adventures. Of course, he travels with Bank of America Travelers Cheques.
>
> We hope at the conclusion of this unique program, you will have become more familiar with our service.

Six spectacular mailings followed. Each contained a letter from Captain Trevelyan in simulated handwriting printed on parchment stock. The first included a map of the Caribbean. The second arrived in a hollow bamboo tube encased in a burlap mailing bag. The third was tucked into a seashell cushioned with dried seaweed, and was also in a burlap bag. The fourth arrived in a rum bottle. The fifth was sealed in a heavy paper packet and included a rough treasure map and an antiqued traveler's cheque stained with Captain Trevelyan's blood. The sixth and final mailing included a ceramic replica of an ancient Spanish coin designed for use as a paperweight. The campaign drew over 600 unsolicited letters of praise from the 1,802 bank presidents receiving the mailings and opened many previously closed doors for Bank of America representatives. In addition, many of the recipients adapted the mailings for special displays in their bank lobbies and windows.

Editors

Editors constitute still another hard-to-reach audience. Since they receive as many as 500 press releases in a single day, it takes a special mailing to get more than a quick spot decision as to the editorial worthiness of a given story. A technique which has been used suc-

The first in a series of six spectacular mailings by the Bank of America was a pirate's map of the Caribbean and a parchment letter.

cessfully to gain special attention from editors is the "press party by mail." One of the best examples is a spectacular mailing sent out by Knipco Inc. to farm publication editors to announce a new portable farm heater. The boxed mailing was labeled, "Dinner Party Inside," and contained a letter from Knipco's president explaining, in a lighthearted manner, that rather than bring the editors to a press party, Knipco was bringing the press party to them. Included in the package were a bagful of colorful confetti; a 1½-ounce bottle containing a whisky-colored fluid (it was maple syrup, since postal regulations forbid the mailing of the real thing); a cocktail napkin "imprinted" with a wet-bottomed martini glass; a martini-soaked olive wrapped in Saran; plus a collapsible slide-viewer kit with two colored slides showing the product, and the usual press release, glossy photo, and product literature.

Retailers

Many retailers constitute a particularly tough audience since they have such a wide variety of responsibilities, each of which usually involves receipt of direct mail promotions. Certified Metals Co. got its share of attention from jewelers for a new line of ring mountings with a series of dimensionals, each emphasizing a product feature:

- Paper tulip . . . "new and fresh as spring"
- Art print . . . "only an old master could create"
- Letter in legal portfolio . . . "certified gold content"
- Miniature padlock and key . . . "special Hide-a-Way lock"
- Children's sunglasses . . . "brighter finish"
- Toy handcuffs . . . "don't be handcuffed by a limited line"
- Model Cadillac . . . "style"
- Piggy bank . . . "you'll save"

Schulze & Burch Biscuit Co. used a wedding theme for a spectacular series which merchandised a new cracker product to grocers. Included were wedding invitations, marriage certificates, and a wedding gift box containing a split of champagne and a sample box of the new crackers.

To get retailers interested in a special merchandising approach for over-the-counter fabrics, Burlington Mills used a variety of dimensional devices, including a compressed plastic sponge ("expanding market"), a matchbook ("hot fabric"), an egg timer ("right timing"), a toy pistol ("repeat business"), a horn ("advertising"), and a plastic nutshell which opened to reveal miniatures of Burlington's own promotion materials "in a nutshell."

A more sophisticated spectacular mailing program helped Christian Dior Stockings introduce its new line to buyers. The campaign's theme was "Holiday in Paris" and dimensionals took a Parisian theme. They included a jar of pink caviar and a jeweled cobblestone paperweight.

Auto supply dealers came face to face with an unusual dimensional mailing when American Hammered Division of Sealed Power Corp. sent out plastic bags containing two live goldfish to illustrate a "fishing for profits" theme.

Industrial Executives

Top industrial executives, too, can frequently be tough to reach. Probably more spectacular direct mail campaigns have been designed to get through to this market than any other. An outstanding example is the model train mailing created by Minneapolis-Honeywell Regulator Co. in 1959, and adapted by other advertisers since that time. Honeywell kicked off the campaign with a telegram to 115 carefully chosen executives of companies which manufacture water heaters. It read:

> HONEYWELL IS SHIPPING YOU WHOLE TRAINLOAD OF INFORMATION ON NEW LINE OF WATER HEATER CONTROLS. BE WATCHING FOR FIRST CARLOAD SHIPMENT WITHIN NEXT FEW DAYS.

The telegram was followed by five dimensional mailings at two-week intervals. Each featured a Lionel HO model railroad car "loaded" with Honeywell's sales story based on a "Switch to the Honeywell Line" theme. The fifth mailing, which featured the locomotive, told the executives a Honeywell representative would call soon to deliver the transformer and track. The highly successful campaign resulted in two major manufacturers switching to Honeywell controls, while the doors of 94 percent of the recipients of the mailings were wide open for presentation of the full product story by Honeywell representatives.

Another impressive spectacular campaign designed to reach key industrial executives was created by Canadian National Railways for the heads of 1,200 United States manufacturing companies considered likely candidates to build Canadian plants. To tell its story, CNR mailed an engraved chrome-plated railroad spike, a unique screwdriver-flashlight, a handsomely boxed collection of 12 Canadian minerals, a personalized laminated luggage tag, and maple-leaf cuff links.

Engineers

But probably the toughest audience of all to try to influence through direct mail was reached with amazing success by Servo Corporation. Servo, wanting to recruit top engineers for its Long Island laboratories, mailed spectaculars to 4,000 carefully selected prospects. The first was a jigsaw puzzle which, when completed, told Servo's story. Another mailing contained an unusual information booklet with a slide chart built into the front cover. Both mailings offered an unusual record which contained a range of test signals engineers could use to check their hi-fi systems—and, on the flip side, a recruiting message from Servo. The two spectacular mailings drew 2,000 requests for the record—a 50% response from this usually hard-to-reach market. The end result was that Servo was able to hire the 30 engineers it needed at a total recruiting cost of $333 each—compared to the usual cost of $4,000 each when more conventional methods are used.

The Epaulet Men

A very special kind of direct mail spectacular has been created by a unique organization in Westport, Conn., Avery, Hand & Co. In describing its brand of spectaculars, the company focuses on a quotation from Colonel Daniel Morgan, commander of "Morgan's Rifles," at the Battle of Saratoga in 1777: "Forget the poor fellows who fight for sixpence a day. Concentrate your fire on the *Epaulet Men!*"

Avery, Hand has created a highly effective format which has been used to reach management audiences by such firms as American Broadcasting Co., The Greenbrier, National Geographic Society, Great Northern Paper, duPont and Eastern Airlines.

The typical Avery, Hand promotions generally consist of two basic elements for each mailing:

- A portfolio of highly-provocative subject matter—often of a unique historical nature keyed to a recipient's business interest—which projects subtly, yet unmistakably, a powerful contemporary sales message.
- A strategically-worded covering letter on the client's executive stationery, individually typed and hand-signed, which evokes a positive, calculated response.

Eastern Airlines

Typical of Avery, Hand's direct mail spectaculars was a campaign from Eastern Airlines "to the 5,000 men who run America," designed to position Eastern as the leader and spokesman for the aviation industry. The campaign was titled "Ionosphere" and had a "The Nearness of Distance" theme.

The first mailing included a handsome blue box, covered with rich leather, lavishly gold stamped and personalized with the recipient's initials. Inside was a personal letter from Eastern's chairman:

> "Too low they build
> who build beneath the stars."
>
> These words, written over 200 years ago by the English poet, Edward Young, express a concept as old as man—and as new as the age of space.
>
> For thousands of years, men of aspiration have sought to extend their reach—building upon the accomplishments of previous generations—until now the stars themselves are almost at our finger tips.
>
> As commercial aviation enters its fourth decade, we find ourselves living in a new world created by the airplane. True, it is a world almost without distance, but it is by no means a world without challenge. "Nearness of Distance" is the greatest challenge of all. And we of Eastern welcome it.
>
> By means of this portfolio you have before you (and additions to it which you will receive from time to time) we hope to explore the dimensions of the past as a means of expressing our faith in the future of air transportation. I hope our effort to define the proper perspective of the airplane in the service of mankind will prove interesting and pertinent to you.
>
> And I hope also that you will find this portfolio a worthy expression of man's constant quest to extend his reach.

Also included in the blue box was the first of Eastern's document-laden portfolios. Entitled "Man Learns to Find His Way," it incorporated faithful replicas of manuscripts dating back to 1269 which documented the development of navigational instruments. It included an actual astrolabe, an early form of compass.

Three other mailings followed—all crafted into dramatic expositions on man's key efforts to extend himself. The third volume, for example, was titled "The Nearness of Distance: Man Learns to Multiply his Strength." Featured was an 8½ by 11 inch portfolio with a parchment overwrap bearing the program title, "Ionosphere."

The portfolio was made of heavy blue cover stock. On the front was a simulated memo from James Watt reading:

> I had gone to take a walk on a fine Sabbath afternoon. I entered the Glasgow Green and passed the old washing house. I was thinking upon the engine at the time; and I had not walked further than the golf-house, when the whole thing was arranged in my mind.

The memo was printed in simulated handwriting on foxed paper. It had a red wax seal in the lower left. This 4½ by 5½ inch memo was mounted first to a piece of gold foil with 1/8 inch borders extending beyond the memo on all four sides. This, in turn, was mounted on a piece of gold-tan text stock with 1/4 inch borders visible. This triple-piece was, in turn, mounted directly to the blue cover stock. A caption below it was printed in black on a piece of light blue text stock, affixed to a larger piece of red stock, both mounted on the dark blue portfolio cover.

When the portfolio was opened, two gatefold flaps carried captions. On the left was a part of the Watt quotation, printed on foxed paper and mounted first to a piece of red text stock, then to a piece of gold text. All were then mounted to the blue portfolio cover. On the opposite flap was the "Ionosphere" logo in black on ivory, mounted to a slightly larger piece of light blue text, both affixed to the portfolio cover.

When both flaps were opened, the portfolio spread out to 27½ by 11 inches. Four elaborate attachments were tipped in. On the left was a 5¼ by 10¼ inch folder on blue cover stock (lighter in color than the portfolio). It had a re-creation of a drawing which Watt made to submit along with his patent application for the steam engine. The folder was mounted to a piece of foil, which provided a 3/8 inch gold border around the folder. Inside the folder was a 9¾ by 9¾ inch sheet of foxed stock with a replica of a section design for a stationary steam-engine built for Henry Cotes & Co. in 1784, with notations in Watt's handwriting.

The next section of the portfolio's spread had a sheet of gold-colored text to which was tipped a 10-page booklet titled, "Notes of James Watt—18 November 1774—10 March 1786." The cover was red, with black decorations, and title and border gold stamped. Each lefthand page inside the booklet had a note in simulated handwriting —again printed on foxed paper and then mounted to colored text stock. On the facing lefthand pages were the notes set in type.

The third section of the spread had a pocket containing three folders. The pocket was printed in black on a sheet of distinctive green text stock, and then mounted to a sheet of red paper. The three folders, printed in black on light blue stock, were slipped into the pocket, and the entire set was secured with a red ribbon. Copy on the pocket explained:

"Revolutions never go backwards!"

Quickly following the news of Watt's revolutionary invention, steam power spread from the factory to the outdoor world. Man's dream of high-speed transportation was on the brink of reality.

1. In 1803 Richard Trevithick built his "portable steam engine," forerunner of the railway locomotive.

2. By 1805, the revolution had spread to America, and Oliver Evans of Philadelphia invented the first powered vehicle which would run on land and on sea.
3. And man's ingenuity soared. Steam power was soon considered for flight, and in 1842 one William Henson actually applied for and received a patent from Queen Victoria for an "Aerial Steam Carriage."

Enclosed are three brief chapters on man's expanding knowledge of mechanical power as a means of transportation—over land, over sea, and above the earth.

The first folder described "Trevithick's Portable Steam Engine." There were three foxed paper tip-ons: a clipping from an 1808 newspaper; a simulated ticket for a ride on the steam engine, and a patent drawing.

The third folder about Evans' steam carriage also had three tip-ons—a cover from *The Mechanic* magazine; an old woodcut showing Evans steaming down the Delaware in his "Orukter Amphibolos," and a July 1805 letter in Evans' handwriting.

The third folder had two tip-ons—a colored engraving showing Henson's proposed steam airplane in flight and a patent drawing of the proposed plane.

The fourth panel was again bordered in gold and contained a black-on-white portrait of James Watt tipped to a colored sheet of text stock with additional copy.

When folded, the elaborate portfolio bulked to ½ inch. It was, of course, accompanied by a personalized letter from Eastern's board chairman.

Even though the Eastern spectacular campaign went to what was considered a list of the 5,000 men "who run America," it averaged an 80% response, with a high of 96%—each an unsolicited personal letter response.

OVERCOMING LACK OF PRODUCT DIFFERENCES

One of the most revealing studies of industrial buying was conducted for Penton Publishing Co. by Dr. F. Robert Shoaf, motivation research consultant. Dr. Shoaf set out to determine the extent psychological factors extend into the industrial buyer's business life. One of his key findings was: "As industrial products become more alike, emotional factors become important in the selection of brand or suppliers . . . The more your product tends to be like that of someone else, the more your customers and prospects will tend to buy the 'sizzle' as well as the steak." In many cases, that "sizzle" must be provided by the promotion given the product. Thus, many industrial advertisers have turned to direct mail spectaculars to overcome the difficulties of building an image for their products with few demonstrable differences.

General Electric's "Hidden Values"

Perhaps the classic example of this type of direct mail spectacular was the highly successful "Hidden Values" campaign created by General Electric to promote its fluorescent lamp ballasts. GE's ballasts looked like anybody else's product, which led prospects to think they were alike. But GE was convinced its ballasts offered "hidden values" in the form of extra service and extra performance. To convince prospects of these advantages, GE mailed a series of seven direct mail spectaculars, each featuring a clever analogy. The campaign started with a colorful theme-establishing piece featuring a full-color treasure map on parchment stock suitable for framing. The authentic map showed known treasure locations off the Florida Keys.

The next six pieces featured dimensional items which might or might not have great value. In each mailing, a certain number of the pieces did carry items whose value ranged from $15 to $40. Unless the recipient was an expert, however, the value remained "hidden" until he contacted a GE salesman (who had been given clues to identify the valuable items). The campaign included Indian-head pennies, synthetic and real sapphires, commemorative postage stamps, poker chips, arrowheads, and gold nuggets—real and fool's gold. All of the items had the advantage of being relatively easy to mail; available in sufficient quantities at a reasonable price; ranging in value from a few cents to as much as $40, without obvious differences—plus all fitted into a consistent campaign treatment. By the time the campaign had ended, 65 percent of the recipients had responded to one or more of the pieces. In all, a total of 2,700 customer-originated contacts were made by GE salesmen.

Oxford's "Symbols of Guidance"

Another outstanding example of how direct mail spectaculars are used to promote products with few demonstrable differences is the award-winning "Symbols of Guidance" campaign developed by Oxford Paper Co. to promote a new North Star line of coated printing papers. For this campaign directed to the nation's 3,000 largest volume buyers of coated printing papers, Oxford combined Autotyped letters and boxed dimensionals. Each of the dimensionals featured an ancient legend of the North Star, which was a symbol of guidance in most early cultures. To dramatize the Norse legend, which held the North Star was a golden spike driven into the heavens to guide seafarers, Oxford sent a gold-plated railroad spike with a crystal star on its head. An Indian legend was dramatized by an authentic arrowhead; a Chinese legend by three Chinese fortune cookies containing Oxford sales messages; a Grecian legend by a replica of an early Greek coin imbedded in a key-chain fob; and an Egyptian legend by an authentic model of a clay tablet covered with hieroglyphics.

An interesting aspect of the Oxford campaign, which was the first in a projected 5½-year series of spectacular campaigns aimed at large-volume paper buyers, is how the basic campaign theme was tailored to less elaborate mailings designed to reach an additional 15,000 smaller volume paper buyers. Oxford commissioned renowned artists to recreate the legends and reproduced these paintings as covers on promotional folders which demonstrated the printability of Oxford papers. The paintings, in turn, will become a traveling "fine art in advertising" exhibit.

Continuing Campaigns

Two long-term campaigns also demonstrate the ability of direct mail spectaculars to do a continuing job of overcoming the promotional handicap of little demonstrable product difference. For nearly 30 years, Foote & Jenks had used dimensionals to promote its line of food flavorings. The objects are usually relatively common items, but each is used to dramatize a sales point, such as a miniature world globe ("finest anywhere in the world"), an artificial carnation ("we're courting your business"), a set of children's watercolors ("claims are easy to color"), miniature suitcase covered with colorful foreign resort labels ("why travel the world?"), oversized billfold ("your dollar is bigger").

But probably the most unusual direct mail spectaculars are those used by Calcium Carbonate Corp., which mails a monthly gift package to its key customers and prospects. Each gift dramatizes a sales point in some offbeat way. The gifts are all specially designed items, usually with a humorous twist, such as:

- Desk-Top Foot Rest . . . A plastic-covered piece of sponge rubber imprinted: "Keep your feet up to keep your blood pressure down."
- Busy Executives' Coffee . . . An instant coffee jar filled with coffee-flavored candies so the executive can enjoy coffee without interrupting work.

Some of the dimensionals that Foote & Jenks has used to promote its flavoring materials: an oversized billfold, a miniature suitcase, shoehorn, children's watercolors, etc.

- The Sport of Millionaires . . . A fancy box containing a black-and-red *velvet* shoe-shining mitt, decorated with a gold button, and a can of shoe polish.
- Hunter's Emergency Kit . . . Another fancy box containing such items as Sen-Sen, Alka-Seltzer, aspirin, bottle opener, jigger, lipstick remover, and a universal blank check.
- Meter Sign . . . A 5-inch-square metal sign for the executive to carry in his car. It is imprinted: "Meter Out of Order—Officer: This meter did not register when I deposited a coin."

An interesting aspect of the Calcium Carbonate program is how it was budgeted. Before the campaign was initiated several years ago, the company was spending about $10 each year for a Christmas gift for each key customer and prospect. On reflection, the company decided a better use could be made of this expenditure and came up with the idea of spending $1 per prospect each month for the spectacular "gift" mailings.

OTHER USES FOR SPECTACULARS

While these examples illustrate the most common applications of the direct mail spectacular, there are many other promotion problems which find a solution in dimensional mailings.

Competing With Giants

One of the toughest promotion problems is when the small manufacturer with a limited advertising budget must compete against industry giants, whose promotional spending runs into millions of dollars annually. In such cases, a program of direct mail spectaculars is often closely coordinated with salesmen's calls. Not only does the use of a spectacular promotion make a company seem larger than it really is, but it can quickly establish key sales points while opening doors for the salesmen.

Hess Inc., an independent oil refinery competing with the giants of the industry in supplying oil dealers for home heating, used a series of long-remembered boxed dimensionals including a fake faucet with a suction cup which could be attached to any unlikely place ("one billion gallons on tap"), a pocket watch ("any time"), a phony hypo ("shot in the arm for your business"), and a miniature Early American "Don't Tread on Me" flag in a desk stand ("independence").

Pennsylvania Transformer, which competes with big names like General Electric and Westinghouse in selling distribution transformers to utilities, has long used a trade character,

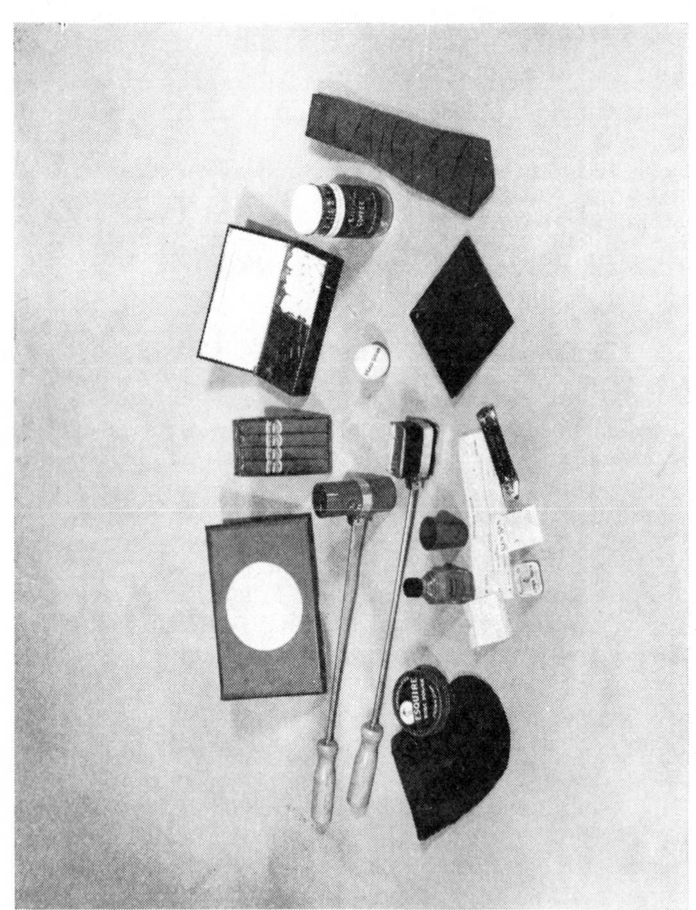

Here are some of the unusual direct mail spectaculars used by the Calcium Carbonate Corp.: coffee for busy executives, golf ball with the words "head down" stamped on it, velvet shoeshining mitt, meter sign, etc.

"Petey," around whom it has built dozens of spectacular mailings. Petey travels the world, sending back point-making mementoes, and serves in many other imaginary promotional roles. One of the most spectacular of the Petey mailings was built around an imaginary fraternity, Pi Sigma Rho, into which prospects were initiated. The Latin initials stood for Pole Star Regulator, one of Pennsylvania Transformer's products. In addition to a series of clever letter mailings which initiated each prospect into the fraternity, the campaign included a number of items bearing the fraternity crest—ceramic beer mugs, mechanical pencils, billfolds, beanies, and even fraternity songs.

Paving the Way for Salesmen

Many spectacular mailing programs have no role other than paving the way for sales calls. The basic objective in such cases is usually to speed up the time required to complete a sale by arousing prospects' interest in a product or service before salesmen call. Raytheon, for example, mailed industrial distributors a series of four red velvet bags containing a pair of loaded dice ("can't be beat"), a roll of stage money ("better profit picture"), a deck of cards ("new deal"), and a pair of opera glasses ("watch for the man with the red velvet bag"). When the salesman arrived, he carried a large red velvet bag containing a gilded flip-chart which told the full story of a new promotion program.

General Mills' Mechanical Division turned premiums used for the company's breakfast cereals into a highly successful direct mail spectacular campaign which paved the way for salesmen calling on industrial executives. The program featured four books on satellites and space travel by Willy Ley, and do-it-yourself models of a rocket, a space station, and a moon ship. Like many spectacular programs, the use of child-oriented items made a big hit. Advertising manager Lloyd E. Pearson, explained: "Every man has a son, grandson, nephew, boy-next-door, or other young friend who would be delighted to receive these items."

Stimulating Salesmen's Interest

The generating of enthusiasm among salesmen for a special marketing program is another promotion problem which frequently is solved by spectacular mailings. General Electric, for example, promoted a "Jack Pot" sales incentive contest with a letter with two small dice attached, a packet of gold-foil-wrapped chocolate coins, a toy slot machine, a small plastic numbers game, and a packet of miniature playing cards.

Minnesota Paints Inc. concentrated on salesmen's wives in a campaign to open more sales outlets. For each new store a salesman sold, the wife received a check with which she could buy a new item for her wardrobe. To build interest, the wives received miniature hats, dresses, handbags, and a vial of perfume. The salesman, himself, received an unusual item—a diamond-studded tie tack to be returned when he sold his first new outlet and used as a map pin to show the store's location.

Moving Into an Entrenched Market

When a new supplier moves into a market already served by others who have established their products, it takes a special promotion effort to get a foothold. Such was the case of television station WLW-I, which came into the Indianapolis market after two other major network-affiliated TV stations were already on the air. To attract sponsors, the new station mailed a variety of spectaculars at six-week intervals. Included were a miniature suitcase containing a 6-foot-long simulated railroad ticket, giant-size cartoons suitable for framing, colorful paintings of local scenes, a strip of movie film, a miniature gold award cup, an imprinted baker's hat, and a miniature TV set holding salt and pepper shakers.

Change of Pace

Sometimes a spectacular campaign is used primarily to provide a change of pace which will stimulate renewed interest in a long-term campaign. Penton Publishing Co. injected a number of dimensionals into its continuing campaign to promote advertising in *Steel* magazine. One of the most effective items was a bow tie in a Scotch plaid pattern to emphasize a moneysaving theme.

Selling a Complete Line

There are times when a company becomes so well known for one product that its other products more or less get lost in the shuffle. At such times, a spectacular promotion approach may be required to develop full interest in the complete line. Allis-Chalmers developed an outstanding direct mail spectacular under such circumstances. To sell a series of related components to 3,000 key prospects, the company sent a miniature working motor. It was mailed piece by piece through a series of seven mailings, along with instructions on how to assemble the motor and make it work. This single spectacular campaign is given credit for laying the groundwork for literally millions of dollars in sales.

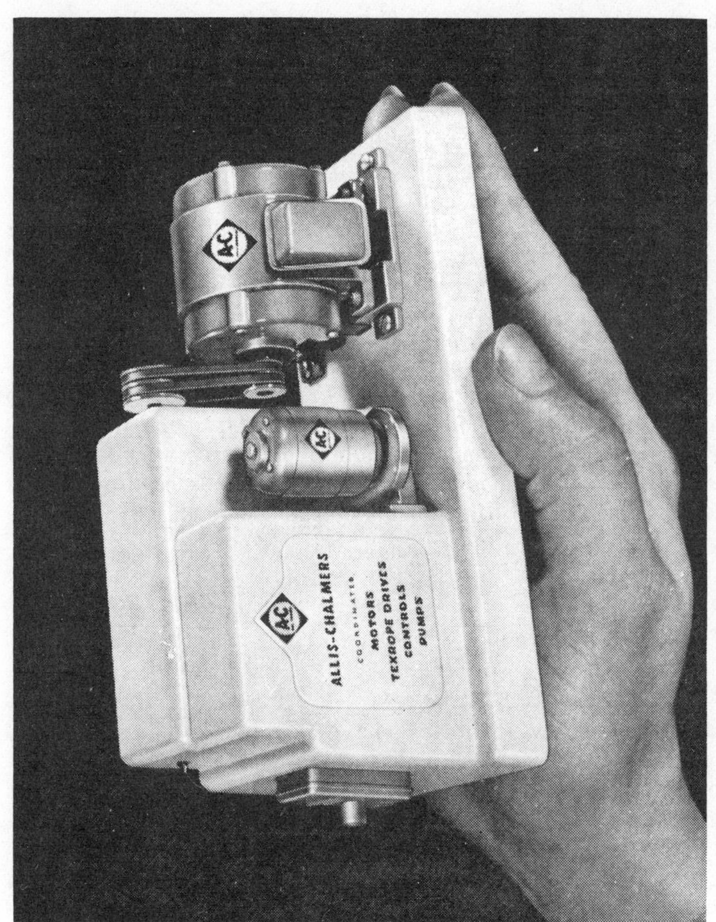

This miniature working motor was dramatically mailed out piece by piece in seven mailings to 3,000 key prospects.

Impact on a Small Market

Direct mail spectaculars are a natural when there is a relatively small market which can be pinpointed. Alcoa, for example, had a new aluminum cap for ketchup bottles and recognized that just 25 ketchup bottlers represented a market potential of $3,600,000. To dramatize its new product story to 150 key executives controlling this market, Alcoa sent a series of eight specialty caps—the kind you wear on your head. Each cap was designed for use in a different sport—golf, fishing, cardplaying, hunting, skating, skiing, sports cars, and baseball. Each mailing included a ticket for a monthly drawing for a valuable prize. The tickets had to be picked up in person by an Alcoa salesman to be eligible for the drawing. The salesmen had no trouble getting in to see the busy executives, and one immediate sale for more than a million Alcoa bottle caps was directly traceable to the campaign.

To Build Traffic and Attendance

Direct mail spectaculars have also been used successfully to draw crowds where normal promotion programs could be expected to produce only routine response. Readily available items were effectively adapted by Raytheon to the job of promoting attendance at a special preconvention sales meeting in Chicago. A special promotion theme was tied to each of the items obtained without cost:

- A picture post card of the Palmer House, the meeting's location . . . "Reserve now"
- A United Air Lines ticket envelope . . . "Be sure you're aboard"
- A Pennsylvania Railroad timetable . . . "Time your arrival"
- A copy of the *Chicago Tribune* . . . "News will be made"
- A pocket travel itinerary planner . . . "Plan now"

Many trade-show exhibitors have adapted a "missing link" approach to draw crowds to their exhibits. A single cuff link—or some other object which requires a mate to be useful—is sent to prospects. To pick up the matching unit, the prospect is required to put in a personal appearance at the designated location. This same technique is used to open doors for salesmen (who deliver the "missing link"), to build store traffic, to stimulate attendance at meetings, to encourage prospects to send in for literature, and for other purposes.

Dramatizing a Special Event

Seagram-Distillers Company is typical of advertisers that have used direct mail spectaculars to help dramatize special events. For its 1957 centennial, Seagram sent out a number of spectaculars including a reproduction of an 1857 edition of the *New York Tribune,* a full-color map of the U.S. in 1857, a Currier & Ives print, a set of authentic menus from famous restaurants of 1857 plasticized for use as placemats, and two intriguing guessing games.

To Introduce New Facilities

The construction of new facilities often requires quick development of customers in areas or fields which previously have not been served. Again, the direct mail spectacular can play a vital role. P. H. Glatfelder Co. built a new plant campaign around a series of dimensional mailings related to new construction—a miniature trowel letter-opener, a brick-shaped ashtray, a palette of children's watercolors, a carpenter's pencil, right down to a pair of scissors to "cut the ribbon." In a similar campaign, Dewey & Almy made prospects for the output of a new chemicals plant members of a "Sidewalk Superintendent's Club" and sent regular progress reports, many accompanied by dimensional items related to construction. "Members" also received membership cards and a special tie clip bearing the club's emblem.

Dramatize Results

To present dramatic evidence of reader response, *Hitchcock's Machine & Tool Directory* sent advertising prospects a miniature mailbag containing 500 quarter-size reproductions of unsolicited testimonial letters from readers.

Teasers to Build Interest

Direct mail spectaculars are used in a variety of ways to build advance interest in promotion items to follow. Frequently, the initial mailings contain no identification of the advertiser, but are used to "tease" the prospect so he will be anxious to find out what they are all about. This technique was used, for example, by an advertising agency which first sent an empty frame with spaces for three picture tiles. Two of the three tiles arrived in the next two mailings and, like the frame, carried no identification of the sender. The third tile accompanied a detailed brochure which presented "the complete picture" of the agency's services.

One of the most intriguing teasers was developed by Pepperell Fabrics, which mailed a locked miniature safe with a message reading: "Guard this safe! It is securely locked to protect its valuable contents until you open it. As an added precaution, the combination is being sent separately. You will have it soon."

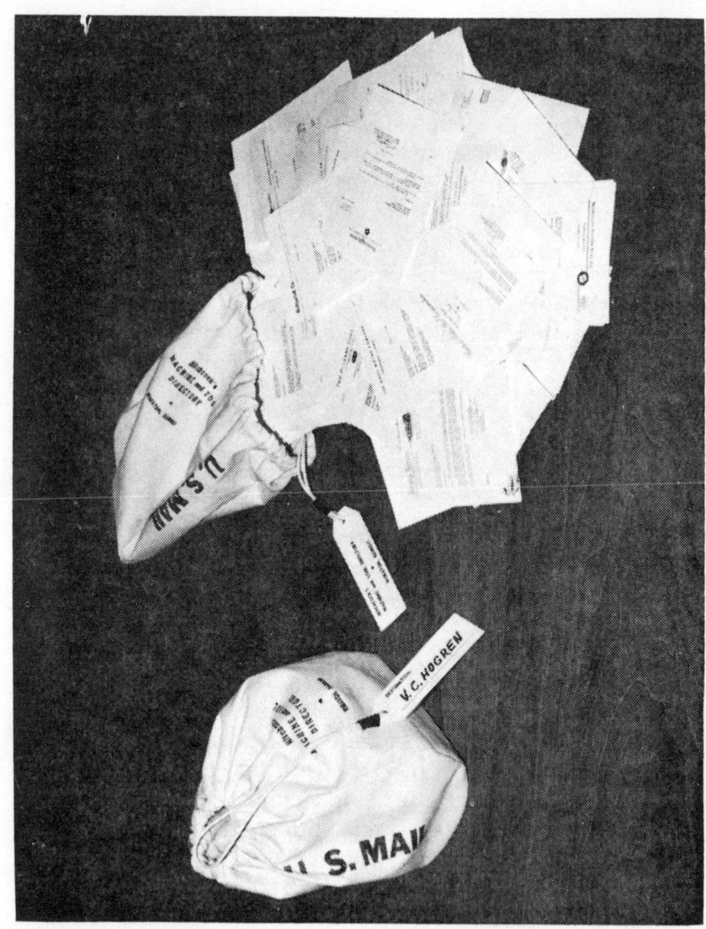

Samples of the miniature mailbag containing 500 testimonial letters from readers of Hitchcock's Machine & Tool Buyer's Directory.

The three-number combination was then sent one number at a time along with promotional messages. When the safe was finally opened, it contained a battery-operated alarm which went off as soon as the door was opened. Also inside were a packet of simulated money carrying a detailed promotion message, stock-like certificates telling about "extra dividends" and showing fabric swatches, and a paperweight with the Pepperell emblem. The paperweight was added so the safe would "rattle" when recipients received it.

To Make A Single Point

While the author has made extensive use of direct mail spectaculars, none was more effective than a campaign for R. R. Donnelley & Sons Company in 1965. At that time, Donnelley had made the decision to enter the roadmap business. Hundreds of thousands of dollars were being spent to develop a completely new set of base maps—the first which had been created by anyone since the advent of the Interstate Highway System. A veteran sales force was busy in the field seeking customers for the new maps. But they were encountering a natural reluctance—major customers were afraid to shift from their regular sources to try a "pig in a poke." The competition was busy fanning the flames of this reluctance—suggesting that Donnelley was just seeking some guinea pigs for a market test.

Time was drawing short. Most commitments for roadmaps are made in the final quarter of the year and only 16 weeks remained before the key buyers would have their orders for 1966 penned to a contract. The problem: to convince the key buyers and influence factors among the 30 major oil companies who represented the bulk of the roadmap business that Donnelley was deadly serious about the map business and had a product well worth their serious consideration.

The answer: bombard the 180 decision makers with a once-a-week mailing for 15 weeks and keep hammering home a single point—Donnelley was deadly serious about its entry into the roadmap business. No routine mailing program, no matter how elaborate, could be expected to reach and convince busy men like the presidents and board chairmen of major oil companies, nor their equally busy subordinates who were old hands in dealing with persistent sales pitches from everyone in the roadmap business.

The campaign consisted of 15 mailings—five personal letters; nine deluxe packages, each containing a collector's miniature of a famous automobile, and another package containing a shadowbox in which the cars could be displayed.

Because this campaign represents result-producing spectacular direct mail in its most basic form, a study of the elements may prove helpful for any mailer considering the use of this technique.

Mailing No. 1

The campaign opened with an autotyped letter sent to each of the 180 decision makers. It read:

> It may seem like carrying coals to Newcastle for me to tell you about the history of highway travel in America . . . and the way the automobile has changed our economy, geography and entire social structure. But, with your permission, I'd like to do just that.
>
> Over the next several weeks, I plan to send you a series of miniature automobiles—each representative of an era in the development of motoring. And, along with the models, I'll include a short vignette on motoring history.
>
> We've planned this series to dramatize the fact that rapid changes in highway travel have created a need for new approaches to road maps and that Donnelley has developed a complete new generation of maps featuring new techniques of design and styling to fill that need.
>
> We sincerely hope you'll enjoy being on the receiving end of this series. I'd like to urge you to save the models since the complete series will graphically portray the history of motoring. If you'd like to display these authentic replicas in your office or home, I'll be glad to provide a special shadowbox designed for this purpose.
>
> In any event, you'll receive the first of these mailings in a few days. If you would prefer not to receive the rest of the series, just let me know and I'll make sure your name is removed from the select list. But since your company is one of the important buyers of road maps, we are anxious to present the story of our complete new generation of maps. We hope the series of miniature car mailings will make this not only possible but an enjoyable experience for you.
>
> The first of your models, which will illustrate the first decade of the automobile in America, is in the mails now and should reach you in a day or two.

Mailings No. 2 and 3

This letter was followed by two packages, one mailed the same day as the letter; the second mailed a week later. The mailing carton was a 7 by 3 by 3½ inch oyster-white corrugated mailer with a distinctive label. Labels were individually typed and postage stamps were used to give the package a personal touch. Inside the mailer was a Kromekote-wrapped two-piece gift box containing a custom-made foam filler, with a die-cut opening to protect the collector's miniature.

Mailing No. 2 had a miniature of an 1898 Hautier, representing the decade of the 1890's. Enclosed was a six-page brochure discussing the beginnings of the automobile industry and the forerunners of today's roadmaps. A simple two paragraph sales message was on the back cover of the brochure *(see illustration on following page for an example of the cover design and typical sales messages).*

Mailing No. 3 had a miniature of a 1908 Model T Ford, representing the decade of the 1900's. Like all of the miniatures, it was a true collector's item and not a toy. The six-page brochure continued the story of the development of highway travel in the U.S. and had only a very brief sales message.

Mailing No. 4

The second autotyped letter was mailed three weeks after the first. It read:

> By this time, I hope the first two cars in our series illustrating "The Changing World of Highway Travel" have arrived safely in your office. If, for some reason, you haven't received the 1898 Hautier and the Model T Ford, be sure to let me know so I can put a tracer on them.
>
> Very shortly, I'll be sending you the third miniature in this series—a 1912 Packard Landaulet representing the development of motoring during the important decade of 1910-1919. Meanwhile, however, I'm sending along that special shadowbox designed for displaying these authentic replicas, which I mentioned in my letter of July 21.
>
> When you receive your shadowbox, you'll note that each of the shelves has three diagonal grooves. These have been cut to fit the front wheels of the miniature cars and have been planned so the cars can be displayed from upper left to lower right in chronological order. Thus, the 1898 Hautier will fit in the upper left, with the Model T in the center of the top shelf and the 1912 Packard Landaulet at the right.
>
> The other six cars in this series will follow at regular intervals, each accompanied by a short vignette on the development of highway travel during the decade each model signifies. I hope you're finding time to read these capsule histories . . . and possibly finding an additional minute to read our brief sales message included in each folder.
>
> We're mighty proud of our new roadmaps and honestly feel they represent a substantial improvement over previously available maps. I had a good chance to check out our Southern New England map the past week as I drove my family to Cape Cod for a bit of vacation. Didn't get lost once!
>
> I'm most anxious to provide you with more details on this new generation of roadmaps if you have any questions. Meanwhile, I hope you're enjoying these little models and will be able to find a nice spot for the shadowbox.

This letter, like the other four in the campaign, was signed by Road Map Sales Manager Warren L. Gabler, who frequently added a handwritten postscript to make each of the letters even more personal.

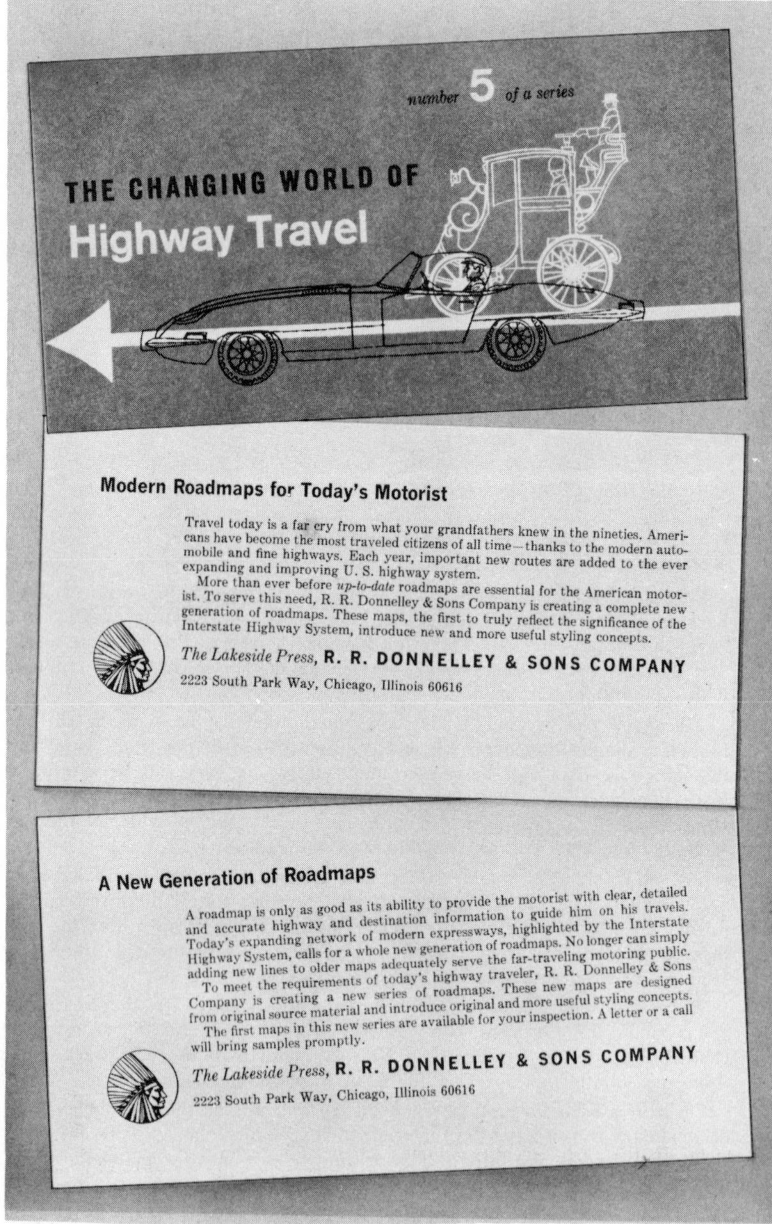

number 5 of a series
THE CHANGING WORLD OF
Highway Travel
Modern Roadmaps for Today's Motorist
Travel today is a far cry from what your grandfathers knew in the nineties. Americans have become the most traveled citizens of all time—thanks to the modern automobile and fine highways. Each year, important new routes are added to the ever expanding and improving U. S. highway system.
More than ever before up-to-date roadmaps are essential for the American motorist. To serve this need, R. R. Donnelley & Sons Company is creating a complete new generation of roadmaps. These maps, the first to truly reflect the significance of the Interstate Highway System, introduce new and more useful styling concepts.
The Lakeside Press, R. R. DONNELLEY & SONS COMPANY
2223 South Park Way, Chicago, Illinois 60616
A New Generation of Roadmaps
A roadmap is only as good as its ability to provide the motorist with clear, detailed and accurate highway and destination information to guide him on his travels. Today's expanding network of modern expressways, highlighted by the Interstate Highway System, calls for a whole new generation of roadmaps. No longer can simply adding new lines to older maps adequately serve the far-traveling motoring public.
To meet the requirements of today's highway traveler, R. R. Donnelley & Sons Company is creating a new series of roadmaps. These new maps are designed from original source material and introduce original and more useful styling concepts.
The first maps in this new series are available for your inspection. A letter or a call will bring samples promptly.
The Lakeside Press, R. R. DONNELLEY & SONS COMPANY
2223 South Park Way, Chicago, Illinois 60616

One of the covers and two of the sales messages that Donnelley created for its new map series.

Mailing No. 5

The custom-made shadowbox was the fifth mailing in the series. It was shipped fourth class mail the same day as the second auto-typed letter was mailed first class. The shadowbox, filled with all nine cars in the series, is illustrated on page 932. It should be noted that nowhere on the shadowbox (or on the cars) is there any Donnelley identification—an important element in the program. Since it was anticipated (and correctly so) that the majority of the recipients would display the car collection in their office or home for many years, the lack of "source" was bound to encourage visitors to ask where the unique collection had come from. When the recipient mentioned Donnelley, it seemed logical that the next question would be, "How come?" And this question, of course, could only be answered by a repetition of at least some portion of the basic sales message. Thus, the collection would serve as a continuing promotion for many years to come.

Mailings No. 6 and 7

Two more cars followed at one-week intervals. First, the 1912 Packard Landaulet mentioned in the second letter and representing the decade of the 1910's; then, a 1928 Mercedes SS, representing the 1920's. The Mercedes shown in the illustration on page 933 is typical of the detail of the collector's miniatures. It was handmade in Europe from dozens of individual parts. The doors could be opened. The seats were hinged to tilt forward. And the wire wheels even had spring suspension.

The copy in the little brochure which accompanied the Mercedes is typical of the chapter for each decade:

> With the return of the Doughboys from World War I, America was ready to take off on a travel splurge that once-and-for-all put the nation on wheels. Wartime experience convinced a previously somewhat dubious public that the automobile, rather than just an expensive hobby, was a vehicle which could be counted on for a variety of transportation tasks. Fortunately, the war period brought about much needed improvements in tires, which had been one of the biggest headaches for pre-war motorists.
>
> Once the public took the automobile to its heart, it was inevitable that pressure would develop for better roads. Local, state and national governments in the early twenties adopted plans and began making funds available to build networks of all-weather roads on which the growing armada of motor vehicles could travel. The slogan, "Get the Farmers Out of the Mud," spearheaded the public's Good Roads Movement.
>
> In 1925, the Secretary of Agriculture created the Joint Board on Interstate Highways which set to work creating a 75,884-mile U.S. highway system. One of the major achievements of this period was the adoption in 1926

THE CHANGING WORLD OF HIGHWAY TRAVEL

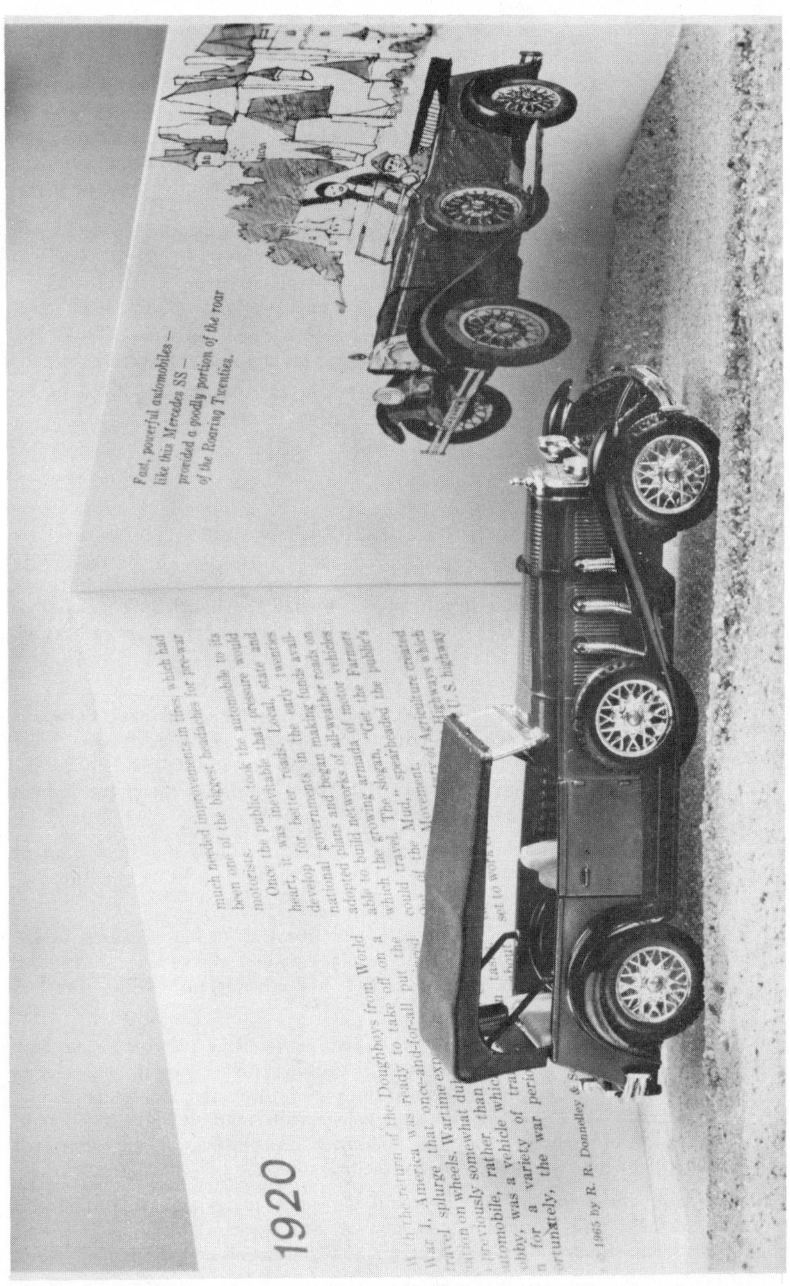

One of the cars in the custom-made shadowbox at the left—a 1928 Mercedes SS' in Europe.

of a coordinated Federal-State highway numbering system. Until that time, only some two dozen of the individual states had numbered their major through roads.

With improved and better marked highways now identified by a consistent numbering system, and mechanically improved cars being produced in rapidly increasing numbers, the American tourist industry boomed in the late twenties. And with Americans taking to the highways in record numbers, there was a constant demand for roadmaps. Virtually all major oil companies adopted the free map practice initiated by Gulf in 1914 and America became a nation of map readers.

Each "chapter" in the copy traced the development of roadmaps in the U.S., building a base for the need of a "modern day" map to serve the needs of today's highway travellers—the new product being introduced by Donnelley.

Mailing No. 8

The eighth mailing was a third autotyped letter, accompanied by actual samples of two of Donnelley's new roadmaps. The letter read:

By now, your mailman should have delivered the fourth in our series of miniature cars—the 1928 Mercedes SS, which represents The Changing World of Highway Travel in the Twenties. It's one of my favorites in this collection.

In each of the little folders which have accompanied the cars, there has been a short story about our new generation of roadmaps. Among other things, we've mentioned the new and more useful styling concepts of the Donnelley maps. I'll have to admit that those words, in themselves, sound pretty much like just "advertising talk."

So, I thought it might be a good idea to let our new maps do a bit of speaking for themselves. I'm enclosing two of them for your personal inspection. I hope you'll have a moment or two to look them over.

In particular, I would like to call your attention to our handling of the Interstate Highway System and major place names. We've done everything possible to make immediately obvious these and other features which travelers use most frequently.

While these maps are fully detailed, I think you'll be pleased to note how readily you can find specific features. One thing we've done to achieve this ease of use is to "stratify" various kinds of information. All place names, for example, are printed in the same color, while other features consistently appear in different colors. Even the most unsophisticated map user can quickly find the kind of information he seeks.

While you're looking, I hope you'll glance at the reverse side. The size and detail of the metropolitan area maps may surprise you. This is one of the special values we've built into our new generation of roadmaps.

One more point: even though these maps have the size and great detail of custom-made special maps used by some oil companies, they are Donnelley's *stock* maps, available without extra charge to every map buyer.

We're putting the fifth miniature car in the mails today and you should receive it shortly. Finding a detailed miniature of a car of the Thirties turned out to be a major problem. For some unexplained reason, none of the makers of precision miniatures has yet seen fit to reproduce a model of any of the American classics of that decade. We finally did locate a representative miniature of the period, produced by a small plant in Italy. When you get it, open one of the doors and take a look at the realistic reproduction of the car's interior.

I hope you're continuing to enjoy these miniatures and that you've found a spot for the shadowbox. Be sure to let me know if I can provide you with any additional information about our maps.

Mailings No. 9 and 10

What the letter had to say about the car of the Thirties was only too true. Searching out the nine cars was a major job. They came from five different manufacturers in four different countries. Conducting a search such as this is a job for a real professional. In this case, it was handled by K-Promotions of Milwaukee. Since it is such a time-consuming chore, it is usually best to place the job in the hands of a supplier organization which already has extensive files and experience in tracking down hard-to-find items.

The car finally chosen to represent the Thirties was a 1932 Fiat. It was selected because, even though European in vintage, it had the appearance of a typical U.S. car of the period. A caption in the brochure explained, "By the thirties, automobiles were edging into an era of conformity. Millions of cars—all looking more or less like this 1932 Fiat—were providing dependable transportation for the rapidly expanding legion of motorists."

The selection of a car for the Forties was easy—a World War II Jeep. But finding a model which would fit with the collection was even more difficult than finding the Fiat. There were plenty of toy jeeps—but all of the miniatures in the collection were far more than toys. Finally, K-Promotions located a true collector's miniature in Denmark.

Mailing No. 11

The fourth autotype letter explained the problems of finding the Jeep, a device calculated to build a strong feeling of involvement on the part of the recipients:

By now, two of the three shelves of your shadowbox should be filled with miniature cars representing The Changing World of Highway Travel from the 1890's through the 1940's.

Your sixth car—the miniature Jeep representing the war years—went in the mails to you a couple of weeks ago. We had to fudge a bit on this model.

As you may have recognized, the model was of an advanced mid-fifties Jeep. We tried our best to find a good miniature of World War II vintage, but progress has come to the model field along with the automobile industry. So, to keep our series complete, we had to settle for the little Danish-made model, which we felt was the most detailed of the miniatures currently in production.

A somewhat similar fate befell us when it came to your next model—a Ford Thunderbird representing the developments in highway travel during the fifties. We didn't like the quality of the early vintage T-Bird models presently available, so we picked a more recent model for your shadowbox. It will be in the mails to you shortly and we hope you like it.

A number of my friends have asked who created this series of mailings. I'm happy to report the whole job from concept through production and mailing was handled by our Creative Services staff. This same staff is working closely with us in our entire roadmap development program.

While we've made a point that our new generation of roadmaps is a stock map series comparable to the special custom maps which many companies have been using, we fully expect every buyer to individualize the maps to fit his company's specific needs. Our Creative Services staff—including idea men, designers and copywriters—is readily available to work with your own creative people in producing a map series to meet all of your requirements.

If I can provide any special information about this Donnelley service, be sure to let me know.

Mailing No. 12 and 13

Next came the Thunderbird and one week thereafter a Volkswagen to represent the Sixties. Brochure copy accompanying the little VW brought the story of the development of the roadmap right up to the new product being introduced by Donnelley:

> While the speed with which many states can be crossed on the new expressways has brought about a demand for large area maps, there is a growing legion of "shunpikers"—tourists who prefer to bypass the turnpikes and seek out the colorful and interesting historic and scenic attractions along less traveled routes. Their interests call for even more detail than many previous maps have offered. And even the turnpike traveler's most frequent map need comes when he leaves the uninterrupted ribbons of concrete to complete his journey or to seek relief from the monotony of non-stop driving. Thus, today's motorist seeks a modern map to serve his needs—one which clearly indicates expressway networks, yet includes complete, easily interpreted detail of the network of feeder roads which reach beyond the main traffic arteries.

Mailing No. 14

The fifth and final autotyped letter in the campaign followed the VW mailing and had an enclosed booklet which recapped the entire story of "The Changing World of Highway Travel." The booklet contained a reprint of each of the "chapters" which had accompanied the first eight car mailings, thus giving each recipient a handy reference booklet to keep with his miniature car collection. Letter copy read:

> By this time, your "Changing World of Highway Travel" shadowbox should be eight-ninths full . . .and the miniature car to fill the missing spot will be in the mails to you today. It represents the future for highway travel.
>
> The future, of course, is very important to us since we have created our new generation of roadmaps to meet the changing patterns of highway travel—not just as they exist at this moment, but to facilitate accurate, up-to-the-moment changes as they occur in the years ahead.
>
> With this letter, I'm enclosing a little booklet reprinting the copy from each of the "Changing World of Highway Travel" folders which accompanied your first eight miniature cars. I thought you might like to have this historical record for future reference. The booklet will also serve as a permanent guide to the cars on your shadowbox since each is illustrated and described.
>
> All of us at Donnelley sincerely hope you have enjoyed being on the receiving end of this mailing series. While we have now "filled" your shadowbox, I'll plan to drop you a note from time to time to keep you posted on our expanding roadmap program. Meanwhile, I hope you'll let me know if I can provide you with any details about our new maps. I won't be disappointed, of course, if you can take a minute right now to glance over the brief commercial on pages 34 and 35 of the enclosed booklet.
>
> By the way, please be sure to give your final car a close inspection when it arrives. It has some interesting features. Like a good TBA salesman, be sure to check under the hood and in the trunk . . . and then open and close the doors and test the steering and spring suspension. I hope it meets with your approval.
>
> P.S. If you'd like another copy or two of "The Changing World of Highway Travel" booklet, just drop me a note and I'll be glad to see that you get them.

The postscript was a subtle way of telling recipients that there were no additional sets of cars available, but that the numerous people who had asked to "get on the list" could at least receive a copy of the story which went with the cars.

Mailing No. 15

The last mailing in the campaign was a particularly outstanding collector's miniature—a sleek Jaguar, with a lot of special details as indicated in the letter. There was a miniature motor under the hood and even a spare tire in the trunk. So detailed was this miniature that you could open the door, turn the steering wheel and the front wheels would turn. Encouraging personal involvement with this final miniature was considered a good way to wrap up the program.

Results

Even before the campaign was half finished, there was no question about it having done its job in convincing key map buyers that Donnelley was indeed very serious about the roadmap business and a long way beyond just making a market test.

Some of the side benefits are worth noting. Many of the top company officials who received the mailings asked the map buyer to introduce "the guy who's sending me these cars" when he came on a sales call. And in at least eight companies where such a request was made, the Donnelley sales manager found "his" cars proudly displayed on the president's or board chairman's office wall.

There appears to be no question but that the shadowbox and its miniature cars will be on display in recipients' offices and homes for many years to come.

And, most important of all, the campaign was a key factor in many sales—not just of roadmaps but other creative products from Donnelley.

Lessons for Spectacular Users

This comprehensive campaign points the way to a number of valuable lessons in planning the most effective use of direct mail spectaculars:

1. One of the most important uses for direct mail spectaculars is to drive home a single sales point. By concentrating on a single theme, there is little chance that the dimensional items used in the mailing will become the only focus of attention.
2. The more closely a spectacular program can be tied to the personal interests of the recipient, the more likely it will be warmly received and long remembered. (Obviously, automobiles are of very special interest to those in the oil industry—the primary buyers of roadmaps.)
3. Continuity is an important element in direct mail spectacular campaigns. To parlay the effect of each mailing, it's important to utilize graphics and copy in a way which will blend all mailings into one total picture.
4. Recipient involvement is a highly desirable element in an effective spectacular program. The more the recipient can be made to feel an "insider," the more he is likely to respond.
5. Just because a lot of money is being spent on dimensional mailings is no reason to think you can eliminate other important elements of effective direct mail. Letters, in particular, shouldn't be overlooked.

6. In most cases, lengthy sales messages and dimensional mailings don't fit together. If you have a complicated story to tell, chances are that some other technique may work better.
7. If you're sending dimensional items with a potential long-term display, go easy on seller imprints. The larger you make your name, the less is the chance your dimensional piece will be put out in the open.
8. Lay the groundwork for reciptivity of your mailings. There are cases where you can tease the recipient and sneak your sales message in during the campaign or at the end. But in the majority of cases you'll be better off to tell the recipient what you'll be sending him and why.
9. And wrap the whole program together at the end. If you've been able to maintain interest throughout a campaign—and have sent something which has had a warm reception—few will object to hearing a repeat of the point or points you set out to establish.
10. If your dimensional items are designed to be saved together, go the extra mile and provide the recipient with an easy way to save the collection.

Chapter 33

HOUSE ORGANS, NEWSLETTERS, AND BULLETINS

A PROMOTION technique of continually growing interest to direct mail advertisers is what is generally called an "external publication." Included under this broad heading is a variety of different formats ranging from slick magazines to simple newsletters and bulletins.

While some externals have been published regularly for nearly a century, this promotion technique has seen its greatest growth and acceptance in the years since the end of World War II. While estimates vary considerably, it is safe to say that today there are well over 10,000 different external publications issued regularly by United States businesses and institutions, and many of these are as well-edited and printed as the finest of general consumer publications.

The real growth of external publications was an outgrowth of the internal (employee) house organ. At first, many companies simply began sending copies of their employee publication to customers, prospects, and others outside the company. This, naturally, led to a change in editorial emphasis for many publications, with the net result that many became a confusing mixture of advertising and employee news. Neither of the two separate publics, with entirely different viewpoints, could be served very well.

Internal-External Publications

The problems inherent in the internal-external publication were outlined by Robert Newcomb and Marg Sammons, company communications consultants, in an *Industrial Marketing* article, "How to Please (Almost) Everyone with an External-Internal Publication":

The majority of companies agrees that there is a distinct difference between the internal and external audience, that it is difficult to blend the interests of employees and external readers in the same literary bucket. The principal objection to internal-externals, even in the minds of many who produce them, is that they are neither fish or fowl. In the publisher's zeal to aim his conversation in several directions at once, he finds that too few are actually listening.

There are, however, some useful signposts along the way, which should prove helpful both to the new—and the established—internal-external editor:

1. *Decide why you want an internal-external.* If it is a caprice of the board chairman, who wants a means of reaching shareholders, maybe it would be cheaper and more practical to originate a stockholder external, instead of expanding the employee paper and thereby weakening its local appeal.

2. *Determine the interests of the reading group.* Spend some time learning the preferences of your audience. No editor living can create an internal-external without having the pulse of his readers. It is not easy but it is possible to determine reader interests through a sample survey, made in advance of publication.

3. *Avoid the snob appeal.* Plush layouts, excessive use of color and too-sophisticated copy will quickly alienate the basic employee audience. If it is too snobbish, stockholder readers whose favorite company literature is a dividend check may suggest more appropriate uses for the publication's budget. The middle-of-the-road approach is safer and more considerate of the audience.

4. *Look into the experiences of others.* Publishing a successful internal-external can be treacherous, so learn from the humbling experiences of companies that have tried it. Let the company's communications man visit the plants of other publishers, armed with questions and eager for answers.

5. *Survey the publication frequently.* Even if it is only a once-over-lightly sampling, try to determine how well (or how poorly) you are doing. An annual checkup is as good for a publication as for a human being.

There still are a large number of internal-external publications being published today—many of them highly successful. But in the majority of cases greater success can be achieved by producing separate publications for internal and external audiences.

External Formats

There are six basic formats used for external publications: (1) Magazines, (2) Booklets, (3) Newspapers, (4) Newsletters, (5) Bulletins, (6) Unique Printed Pieces.

Of course, there also is the possibility of combining two or more of these basic format types. For initial planning, however, it is usually best to start with just one of the formats and build within this basic framework.

Magazine Formats

Usually the most elaborate externals are published in the magazine format. The basic size is 8½ by 11 inches, although an 8¼- by 11¼-inch trim size (standard business publication format) is frequently used. Other popular sizes include:

Pocket size—No standard dimensions but ranging from 3¾ by 5⅛ inches to 5 by 7 inches. Probably the most popular pocket size is 5 by 7 inches.

Digest size—5⅜ by 7½ inches.

"Large" size—9 by 12 inches.

Life size—10½ by 14 inches.

Post size—10¾ by 13¾ inches.

Booklet Formats

There are few size standards for external publications published as booklets. In most cases, they closely resemble pocket-size magazines, the difference being the handling of editorial material.

The popularity of different sizes changes frequently. At this writing, one of the most popular sizes is the 4- by 9-inch vertical format. Tomorrow an entirely different format may be in vogue.

Newspaper Formats

There also is little standardization in sizes used for newspaper style externals. In most cases, however, the external newspaper is a baby brother to the common daily or weekly newspaper. Probably the most frequently used size is 8½ by 11 inches, with three columns to the page.

Other popular sizes for externals published in newspaper format are 9¼ by 12⅛ inches, 10 by 13 inches, 10¾ by 15½ inches, 17 by 22 inches, and 19 by 25 inches.

Newsletter Formats

Newsletters almost invariably stick to 8½ by 11 inches, with about the only flexibility being in the choice between one or two columns to the page. The one-column (letter) format is the most popular, with copy typewritten and unjustified. When newsletters are typeset, however, the two-column format is generally used since shorter lines are easier to read.

Bulletin Formats

The basic difference between the newsletter and bulletin formats is in the handling of copy. Whereas newsletters usually contain relatively short paragraphs, each devoted to a single subject, the bulletin frequently is devoted to a single subject. In addition, bulletins are frequently illustrated, while the newsletter very seldom makes use of illustrative matter.

Unique Printed Pieces

Unique formats, of course, refuse to stand still for any standardization. This is only logical since the main purpose of such formats is to achieve recognition through distinctive styling. In many cases, these "unique" publications are essentially newspapers, magazines, or newsletters treated in a special way. Some examples:

Imp—Described as the "world's smallest house organ," *Imp* was an external published by Orville E. Reed, Howell, Michigan, the late direct mail expert. Essentially a newspaper format applied to a regular government postal card, each issue contained two 8½-pica columns.

Telebriefs—This is another miniature newspaper. Published by Illinois Bell Telephone Co. as a monthly bill enclosure, each issue has four 5⅞- by 6⅝-inch pages, each containing either three 10-pica or four 7-pica columns. It is interesting to see how halftone illustrations appear to be "big" even when they may be only 7 picas wide when used in this miniature format.

Dole Doings is the elongated monthly publication of Dole Valve Co., Chicago. It contains sixteen 4½- by 11¾-inch pages. There is only one column of type per page.

Calendar house organs—A number of companies combine their external house organ with a monthly calendar. One paper company, for example, features a monthly calendar and illustration on the front of an 8½- by 11-inch sheet of heavy cover stock and then publishes a magazine-style story on the back of the sheet. The story each month is related to the calendar illustration.

According to Lithoplate, Inc.—That's the title of the unique external published by "the company of the same name." Each issue is printed on an 11- by 16-inch sheet, which is then accordion-folded to yield twelve 2⅝- by 11-inch pages, each carrying a single 14-pica column.

Galley Format. At one time, the Film Council of America issued a regular publication in galley format—long, narrow strips of newsprint printed on one side only (ideal for bulletin board posting and clipping).

Format Checklist

When it comes to deciding which format best fits your needs, the following checklist[1] may prove helpful:

1. *Budget, time, talent.* As in most promotion media, the major consideration must always be the amount of money

[1]Checklist from "Selecting a Format for External Publications," by Dick Hodgson. *Advertising Requirements.*

available to do the job, the time which can be allocated to doing it, and the talent of the people who will do it.

One of the biggest mistakes made by many external publishers is trying to work one or two steps beyond their budget-time-talent limitations. You frequently see a mediocre newspaper or a downright poor magazine being published by those who have the money, time, and talent to publish an excellent newsletter.

Since one of the main jobs of an external is usually the building of a company personality, it only stands to reason that you should do everything possible to make sure that you will be able to turn out a publication of the highest quality—with whatever format is decided upon.

2. *Material to be used.* Different kinds of material will call for different types of formats. If, for example, you want to convey company or industry news, the obvious choice will be either a newspaper or newsletter. On the other hand, if the basic content will be photographs, a magazine format will probably work best.

Whatever the content, there is a tried-and-proved format to fit the job. A factor which should not be overlooked, however, is that it is sometimes possible to achieve special impact by adapting your material to an unexpected format.

3. *Who will read it.* As in all advertising, the intended audience must always be given primary consideration when determining the form your material will take. Nowhere is this more true than with externals.

4. *Where will it be read.* Some externals are designed for reading by commuters—a pocket size, of course. Others are intended for busy executives to read at their desks—frequently the newsletter is chosen. At least one external house organ is designed for reading by customers in barbershops—anything but a magazine format would quickly get lost in the shuffle. This list is endless, but the point should be clear—the chosen format should be compatible with the "point-of-reading."

5. *End use.* Many externals are expected to have a life beyond the first reading. The most obvious example is material intended for office filing. In such cases, of course, an 8½- by 11-inch size is almost mandatory.

6. *Distribution method.* If the external is simply to be mailed by itself, there may be no major format problem. But if it is to be an invoice enclosure, distributed by salesmen, placed in pickup racks, or handled in some other "non-standard" way, the booklet format is usually the logical choice.

7. *Competition.* There are really two forms of competition which must be considered when selecting a format. First of all, of course, is business competition. It is important to analyze the types of externals being used by your competitors to reach the same audience. In most cases, you will probably stand to gain more by selecting a different format —unless you can be sure that you can provide better quality and achieve distinctive identity with the use of a similar format.

But just as important, however, is competition from other publications. Whatever format you choose, you can be sure that your external will be compared, at least subconsciously, with all other publications in the same format, not just those of your competitors, and not just other externals.

If you are publishing a magazine, for example, you must face the sometimes bewildering fact that your publication will be compared with consumer and business magazines, and other externals, using the same basic magazine format. This does not mean that your readers will expect you to produce a combination of *Life, Fortune,* and the *Saturday Evening Post* just because you have chosen to publish a magazine, but they will make comparisons nevertheless. If you cannot hope to be at least at the midpoint in the quality standards of all magazines received by your average reader, you will probably do well to consider another format.

8. *Production economies.* As in the case of all printed material, it is important to keep in mind certain basic guides to economic production such as standard paper sizes, press limitations, and so forth. While this should be obvious, it is amazing how often non-standard sizes are chosen without stopping to consider paper waste, necessity for using larger (and more costly) presses, breaking points in postal rates, and many other important factors.

9. *Reuse of material.* While this is really part of checkpoint number eight, it deserves special attention. Many times material originally developed for use in an external house organ can be reused for other purposes, with impor-

tant economies resulting. The most obvious example, of course, is reuse of engravings in direct mail, annual reports, sales aids, and so forth.

Another good example is reuse of feature material developed for externals as part of the firm's publicity program.

This works both ways, of course. Externals can frequently use material developed for publication advertising, catalogs, direct mail, and other purposes.

In both cases, however, it is important to select a format which will easily accommodate available material.

10. *Speed of production.* A final point to consider is the "lead time" required for the format you select. If speed is of the essence, a newsletter can often be produced on simple duplicating equipment and be in the mails within a few hours after the first line is written. At the other end of the scale, slick magazines produced in full color may require several months for complete production.

When to Publish an External

One of the best checklists for analyzing the desirability of publishing an external was featured in a Canadian external, *Bulman's Sales Trails,* Winnipeg, Manitoba:

1. Do you depend to any considerable extent on "repeat" business to keep your yearly volume at a profitable level?
2. Can your salesmen readily locate probable sources of future business? (Essential for building a good mailing list.)
3. Do you believe your volume would be higher if your salesmen could make more frequent calls on your customers?
4. Are your salesmen overloaded? That is, do they have more customers and "prospects" to call on than they can satisfactorily service—and "sell"?
5. Does your company "line" include a number of *different* major products? (A distinction is made here between *different* major products and *similar* major products. A steel company might be selling a number of special alloys which would be *similar* major products, whereas sheets, plates, and beams would be *different* major products—and hence in need of extra-special promotion.)
6. Are your products sold in so many different markets that you simply can't afford a budget big enough to buy advertising space in *all* relevant trade and business magazines?
7. Alternatively, do you have a number of profitable "fringe" markets where you would like to get coverage of the chief buyers—but *without* going to the expense of buying *complete* advertising space?
8. Does your "line" include more minor products, deserving of advertising support, than you can afford to advertise adequately in existing trade and business publications?

9. Is your company's "line" of products such that "educational" work would tend to stimulate an increase in sales volume? That is, "educational" work like articles on "How to Install," "How to Apply," "How to Service," and so on.

10. Do you often feel that regular trade publications do not give as much editorial attention to your type of products as you believe they should?

11. Do you ever feel that your salesmen—whether representatives directly employed by you, dealers, or jobbers—need to be better informed about your products, their uses, and so on?

12. Is yours a company which sells through exclusive dealers, or representatives—the kind of people who would appreciate and benefit from having their names or advertisements appear in copies of ***your*** "external" going to *their* list of customers and "prospects"?

13. Finally, is it your company's policy at the present time to capitalize on the goodwill you already enjoy by introducing *new* products or additional lines? An "external" of long standing is an excellent vehicle for giving them a free initial ride!

Purposes of Externals

In its excellent handbook, *The Company Publication,*[2] S. D. Warren Co. points out there are certain definite things that a well-edited house organ can do to improve relations with the people who constitute the market for a product or a service. Specifically it can:

> Make readers aware of the character and integrity of the institution it represents.
>
> Excite interest in a product or a service by means of romance articles and dramatized stories of the product in use.
>
> Acquaint customers with facts about merchandise or services—facts that will help customers to use the product with greater satisfaction.
>
> Inform customers of *all* of the use possibilities of the product, thus extending the opportunities for use, and consequently for sale.
>
> Prove to prospects, by means of testimonials and pictured reports of installations, the worth of a product or service.
>
> Invite inquiries and questions that may exist in the minds of customers regarding a product or service.
>
> Present pertinent articles on technical or statistical subjects that will establish the magazine (and its publisher) as an authority in the field.

[2]"The Company Publication"—Booklet 5 of a series: Managing a Business with the Help of Printing. S. D. Warren Co., Boston.

Keep readers informed of the new trends and product developments.

Show intimate glimpses of the workings of the organization so that readers may feel well acquainted with the company.

Aid immeasurably in the building of favorable relations.

Typical Externals

In its guide to company publications, S. D. Warren Co. presents some typical external publications:

Boeing Magazine is published monthly by the Boeing Co. A typical issue discussed advances in space exploration and Boeing's part in the program. The back cover carried a company advertisement. Size 8½ by 11 inches, 16 pages, self-cover, lithographed in black and white, duotone, and solid colors on wove offset paper. Boeing also publishes *Boeing News* for employees and *Plane Talk* for employees and customers.

Comment is published for the interest and information of business executives by J. W. Clement Co., manufacturer of quality printing. The publication truly reflects this claim. Subjects treated have to do with printing in one phase or another. Design is modern and the printing is in four-color letterpress on double-coated paper. Size 8½ by 11 inches, 16 pages and cover.

Fluor-o-scope is published quarterly for employees, customers, and shareholders by The Fluor Corp., Ltd. Informative articles discuss Fluor's place in industry. A typical issue is devoted to helium and its applications. Size 8½ by 11 inches, 24 pages including cover, lithographed in four-color process and duotone on dull-coated fluorescent paper.

Hercules Chemist is published two times a year by Hercules Powder Co. Discusses products and applications in industry. Articles are informative and well illustrated. Size 8½ by 11 inches, 24 pages and cover, printed letterpress on glossy coated paper, four-color cover and three colors inside. Hercules also issues a number of other publications for employees and customers.

Abbottopics is published eighteen times a year by Abbott Laboratories for the medical profession. Contains informative articles on medical and related subjects written under the direction of a medical editor. Abbott advertisements are also used. Size 8⅝ by 11½ inches, 32 pages and cover, lithographed in four colors, inside on pigmented offset paper, cover on coated offset paper.

Progress Thru Research is published by the Central Research Laboratories of General Mills Inc. It points up the accomplishments of research in developing the products of General Mills. Includes stories of company personalities—also company advertisements. Size 8½ by 11 inches, 20 pages and cover, printed letterpress in two colors on glossy coated paper. General Mills also publishes *Horizons* for stockholders and *Modern Millwheel* for employees.

Dow Diamond is published by The Dow Chemical Co. in the interest of the company's business friends, stockholders, and employees. It presents interesting and informative articles relating to the fields where Dow prod-

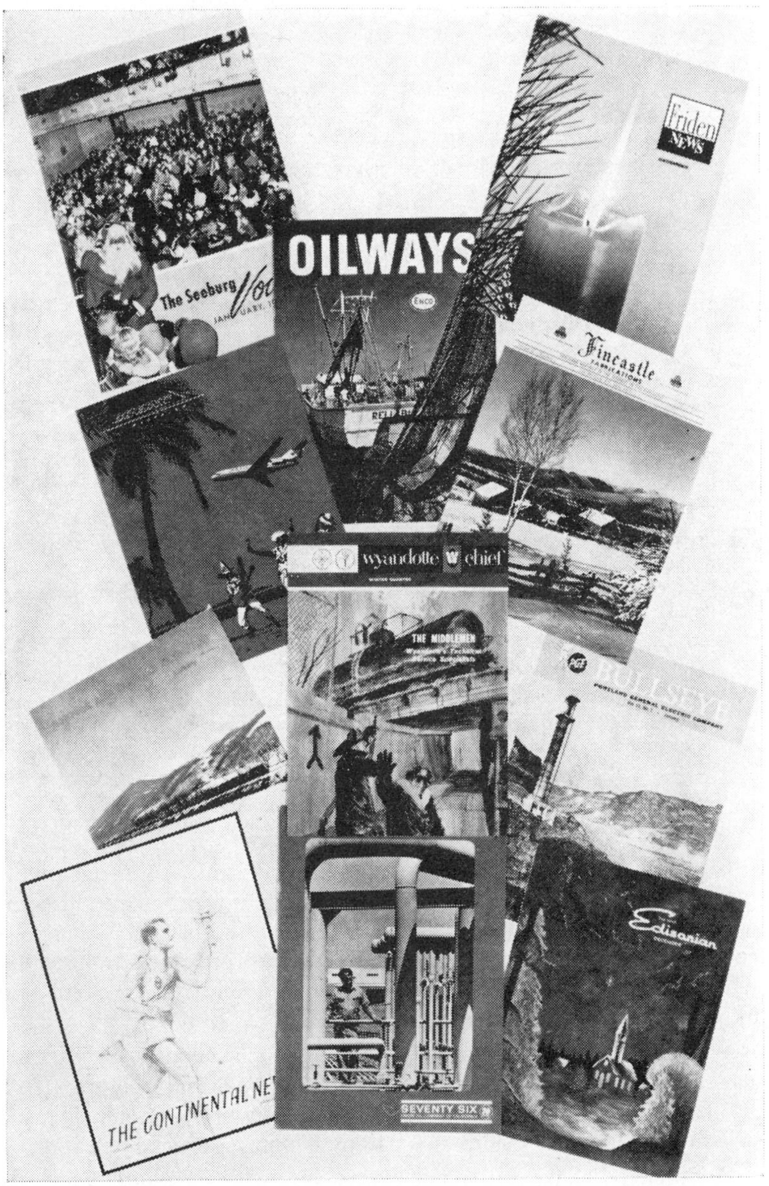

House organs have become increasingly valuable in direct mail circles. Among those shown here are Union Oil's, Boeing's, and Norfolk & Western's.

ucts are used. Also contains a progress report of recent developments in the news. Size 8½ by 11 inches, 32 pages and cover, lithographed in four-color process, black-and-white and duotone on glossy coated offset paper. Dow also issues other publications for customers, for employees, and for dealers.

Walworth Today is published in the interest of industrial progress by Walworth Co. Presents news about the company, interesting and informative stories of product applications and of company research. Size 8½ by 11 inches, 16 pages including cover, lithographed in three colors—some duotones.

The Orange Disc is the magazine of the Gulf Companies. It is published bimonthly for employees and stockholders. Contains interesting articles about oil producing areas and industries where oil is essential to operation. Also offers Gulf news in pictures and a page of headline news. Size 9 by 12 inches, 40 pages and cover, lithographed in four colors on glossy coated paper. Gulf Oil Corp. also publishes *Gulf Oilmanac* for employees.

Pneumatic Packaging is published monthly by Pneumatic Scale Corp. Ltd. Each issue contains stories about customers and users of Pneumatic Scale equipment. Methods of packaging various products are illustrated in these articles. Some issues include a four-page Service Section. The back cover carries a Pneumatic advertisement. Size 7½ by 10½ inches, 16 to 20 pages, printed letterpress in three colors, glossy double-coated paper.

Monsanto Magazine is published monthly by Monsanto Chemical Co. It presents a wide range of articles relating directly and indirectly to the many products and fields served by Monsanto. Lithographed in four-color process, both cover and inside. Size 8½ by 11 inches, 32 pages and cover, coated paper throughout.

Bausch & Lomb Today is published by Bausch & Lomb Inc. for the ophthalmic professions. Content includes articles of general interest to these groups and also items of specific interest relating to ophthalmic products. A reply card for ordering literature and requesting more information is included. Size 5¾ by 7¼ inches, 32 pages, lithographed on dull coated offset paper, cover in four-color process.

Ford's "Publishing Empire"

Probably the best-known publisher of company-sponsored publications is the Ford Motor Co., which regularly turns many different publications, all of topnotch quality. Heading the list of Ford publications is the much-honored *Ford Times,* a pocket-size monthly which has been published continuously since 1908. It has a circulation of 1,700,000.

While it does not carry advertising as such, about 25% of each a wide variety of non-automotive reading material ranging from recipes to stories about interesting vacation spots. Color is used lavishly, with water colors and paintings getting special attention.

Another popular Ford publication is *Ford Farming,* which is circulated quarterly to 1,200,000 farmer-customers of Ford tractor dealers. It is produced in regional editions, tailored to the agricultural specialties of each region.

Other Ford Publications

Newsletters are also a part of Ford's publication program. "High Dollar Farming," which was started in 1958, goes to 30,000 county agents, vocational agriculture teachers, and other farm leaders. Another newsletter is "Ford Farm Management," which reaches 75,000 farmers each month.

Other publications include magazines, newsletters, and bulletins for Ford's marketing organization. Some of these are:

American Road, public service magazine addressed to employees and retirees.

Continental Magazine, published quarterly and sent to 500,000 owners of American luxury cars.

Ford Industrial Tractor Power, a quarterly sent to 175,000 industrial customers.

Ford News, gives news about division programs, policies and employees' activities.

Ford Truck Times, covers items with Ford truck tie-in and sent to 2,500,000 truck owners.

Ford World, a biweekly newspaper containing industry news.

Tieline, published ten times a year in the interest of public service.

Up-to-Date, published three times a year and sent to retired, salaried employees.

John Deere's Furrow

Probably the longest running external house organ in the country is *The Furrow* published continuously since 1895 by John Deere & Company of Moline, Illinois. It is published in 22 different editions and mailed bi-monthly to 1,700,000 farmers. Each copy carries a dealer imprint.

Because farming has become a highly specialized activity, Deere maintains a selective mailing list which categorizes farmers by crop, farm animals and size of farm. Dealers have the responsibility for updating the list to make sure that it includes all major farms in their areas plus key influentials in their communities.

Since mailing is handled from Deere headquarters, a special coding system has been developed to make sure each recipient gets the right edition. The list is first broken down by Deere branch office and then by the proper edition within each branch. Next come dealer codes within each branch. Deere uses a combination of the three-digit sectional center number from postal zip codes and an additional two digits for each dealer within a sectional center area. Then, each name is filed by zip code for mailing purposes.

Plan for an External

Any publication to be issued on a regular basis should have a carefully detailed plan. An example of a typical plan for an external was included in "The Company Publication," published by S. D. Warren Co., Boston.

In presenting its outline, Warren noted: "This plan is not offered as a model, but merely to show in a general way how many organizations go about the building of a house organ plan. It can be made much more comprehensive. A plan helps everyone who takes part in building a house organ. It helps the house organ editor to remember the basic purposes behind the publication. And this is most important if greatest returns are to be realized for money expended."

A PLAN FOR A PUBLICATION FOR USERS AND PROSPECTIVE USERS OF BLANK PRODUCTS

PURPOSE: To make customers and prospects more fully conscious of Blank Products—what they are, what they will do and where they can be bought. To inform customers how to use the products profitably.

NAME: *The Blank Magazine.*

TO BE CIRCULATED TO: All known customers and prospects; the office people and sales force of the Blank Company; all dealers who may request it.

DATE OF PUBLICATION: Quarterly.

DATE FOR CLOSING: First of every third month.

PERSONNEL OF STAFF:

Advisory Committee—Public relations manager, sales manager, advertising manager.

Editor-in-Chief—To be appointed by the advisory committee.

Associate Editors—The manager of each division or branch office. Heads of different sales divisions in home office.

DUTIES OF ADVISORY COMMITTEE: To confer with and to advise the editor on matters of general policy.

DUTIES OF EDITOR: To supervise production of each issue; to select and edit material submitted for publication.

DUTIES OF ASSOCIATE EDITORS: To write articles and report items of news that may be interesting to customers. To procure photographs and information regarding installations or unusual use of the product that may be adaptable to a story. To help keep the mailing list up to date.

INSTRUCTIONS TO EDITOR: Write in language that customers will be sure to understand. Do not harp on the products too much. Soft-pedal straight sales talk. Stick to discussion of subjects that have the quality of genuine interest. Make the publication representative of the whole field of endeavor of the Blank Company. Use lots of pictures.

General Instructions About Copy: Write plainly or type on one side of paper. Be sure of your facts. Spell names correctly. Make each story or writeup as brief as possible without slighting the subject. Photographs must be accompanied by complete descriptions of what they represent, when and where they were taken and by whom.

What to Write About: The following should be referred to constantly by editors and contributors: (1) Accounts of results obtained from use of the products that might have testimonial value. (2) Stories or pictures of the product in use that give testimony of use values. (3) Items or incidents that have a romantic, dramatic or humorous appeal to help add color to the magazine. (4) New or unusual applications for the product. (5) Information about new products, developments and trends. (6) Facts about the company and its performance in terms of interest to investors.

Content of Externals

The editorial content of external publication is as varied as the thousands of companies which publish them. *Printer's Ink* ("The External House Organ Matures," March 3, 1961) surveyed 20 companies publishing externals and came up with these observations:

While the sales and image-building aspects of their publications are important, almost without exception the companies queried said the goal of their external house organs was to provide a *service.* Henry Hecht, managing editor of Merrill Lynch, Pierce, Fenner & Smith's "Investor's Reader," described his firm's house organ as "one more service to investors—we want to humanize and dramatize business news, get more people interested in the market."

Likewise, Ciba hopes its "Clinical Symposia" "provides material doctors can't get elsewhere," while Allstate says its "Home & Highway" (boasting a circulation of 4.5 million) is geared "to extend our service into related areas of family life."

This refrain of service to the reader is one in which all producers of successful external house organs seem to join. Another: "Our only chance of being read is to provide the audience with something he cannot get elsewhere. Swamped as he is with reading material he has paid for, we have to be extra good to get him to read something he receives free."

Almost without exception, all house-organ publishers agree in principle with Allstate: "We give the reader what he wants to read in 85% of the space, and what we want him to read in 15% of the space."

While a hard-sell approach is generally frowned upon, most companies do make the reader aware throughout the magazine of who has paid for its publication. This may be done by running only articles that have something to do with the company, or by tieing all articles to the company, but not in an obvious way (Standard of New Jersey, among others, does this).

IBM is one of the most vehement in its attitude toward hard sell in external house organs. "We *never* mention the company," it declares.

Most external house organs utilize a magazine-type format, and most of them carry articles on a wide variety of subjects in each issue. Travel, fashion, art, international problems, space exploration and other typical consumer-magazine themes are increasingly common fare.

But while the trend in the field is to this diversity of articles in each issue, a few publications do confine themselves to one theme. Sargent's new "Architectural Beacon" does this, and Grey Advertising's "Grey Matter" does, too.

Performance of Externals

Wetzel Bros., Milwaukee printer, suggests that "the performance or success of a house magazine depends on blending all of its tasks into one harmonious whole. The salesman and his counterpart, the house magazine, must work as a team, each striving for the same ultimate goal."[3]

They plan their calls on companies who have a reason to buy your product.

They try to tell your story to the right man; the salesman by questioning and interviewing, the magazine by techniques that attract the attention of the man for whom the message is intended.

They hold the interest of your prospects by speaking clearly, and presenting the advantages of your product in an interesting and informative manner.

They make an effort to be familiar with your prospects' problems and the requirements of his industry.

They present information and sales messages with the familiarity of a friend, and do not confine their discussion to a tabulation of selling points.

They earn and keep respect of your prospects through their appearance. The salesman through a wise choice of clothes and neat grooming, the house magazine through its appearance and the quality of its printing.

The salesman proves his worth by quick thinking and adjusting himself to conditions. The house magazine presents preevaluated ideas, illustrated and balanced to achieve the friendly spirit of a visit and the value of a sales call.

Editing the External

In "The House Magazine" Wetzel Bros. offers six basic guides for effective editing of externals:

[3]"The House Magazine" published by Wetzel Bros., Milwaukee.

1. *Edit for management.* Your house magazine is the voice of management. It is the most effective way for the president or other officers to send a message to the prospect or customer. It gives you a chance to voice official support of the salesman, and be sure that the salesman is conveying the business philosophy of the company to the prospect. The house magazine also permits you to repeat vital business concepts which may be overlooked by your salesman.

2. *Tell the whole story.* Your salesman frequently finds it difficult, or impossible, to tell the whole story of his company or product. He is seldom given enough time to tell it all at once, and serialization in personal interview is not effective. Your house magazine has an opportunity to supplement the words of your salesman with appropriate pictures, charts, and graphs. It can tell the story in as many installments as you choose, each complete in itself, with back copies available for reference. Your magazine has the great, added advantage of being able to employ experts at this type of narration. This can result in a series of articles, effectively expressed and illustrated, interesting to your prospects, customers, stockholders, and employees—the whole story of your company or product.

3. *Tell the story behind the story.* Frequently, even such a series as this—articles on the company, product, plant, and equipment—does not cover all the stories of interest to prospects and customers. There are many anecdotes, personal histories, and other stories which can be of great value to the firm issuing a good house magazine. Word and picture articles about the men who make the product, the men who run the business, histories of raw material, the founders, and so forth, are of interest to most readers. The house magazine lets you introduce your personnel to prospects and customers, and (on the assumption that the salesman himself would be too modest to do it) offers a splendid method of telling readers something about the salesman who calls in person.

4. *Edit to hold interest.* To be successful, your house magazine must take advantage of advanced thinking in layout and art techniques, for not even the finest writing and most interesting articles will compensate for a drab, uninteresting appearance. Layouts should be clear and eye-catching. Art and type should offer a pleasing change of pace as the reader progresses from page to page. At the same time, a family kinship must be retained to hold the magazine together. General publications and trade papers depend on editorial layouts to provide family association, and on advertising for variety. The average house magazine must do both jobs and do them well, without a host of advertisers. Remember: to be of real value to you and your company, carefully planned articles and features must reach the audience for which they are written—layout and art techniques can get them there, or stop them.

5. *Edit to sell the product.* You do not need to be reluctant about advertising your company and product in your own house magazine. The American businessman expects your house magazine to be used as a selling tool. Advertising messages here will not compete for attention with those of other firms. You can make a friend and tell your sales story without interruption from other advertisers. Your sales story can be told with factual sales articles in the general copy, or may be put across in straight advertising.

6. *Edit to become a welcome visitor.* The acceptance of your house magazine will increase as its regularity becomes more apparent. While business executives have expressed a preference for monthly house magazines, many are successfully published at other intervals. This expressed preference for monthly magazines is an indication of your prospect's willingness to accept an advertising message, if it is accompanied by good editorial writing. The important thing is to appear regularly.

Questions for External Editors

In an *Industrial Marketing* article, "How to Produce a Good External Publication," by Robert Newcomb and Marg Sammons, April 1961, Merrick Jackson of Hill & Knowlton poses eight important questions for editors who wish to produce outstanding external publications:

1. *Are you keeping tabs on your mailing list?* Be sure you have a live, responsive audience. Periodic checks of your mailing list will help keep the undeliverables or the disinterested to a minimum.

   How much does it cost you to reach a reader six times a year? If you edit a free circulation job, it may amount to $3 annually. One thousand undeliverables mean a loss of $3,000 to the magazine and its sponsor, a sizable chunk of any external budget.

2. *Do you maintain your mailing list by occupations?* This quiz question will not apply to all externals, since breakdowns by occupation may not always be necessary. However, by ascertaining the occupation of each reader and then keeping totals, you can learn at any time how many persons you have in a profession and determine whether this is enough.

   It will help, too, in determining in advance, reader interest in specific articles, i.e., an external editor was weighing the possible reader interest in a contribution tied to chemical engineering; upon checking, he found he had only 11 chemical engineers on his whole list, so he dropped it.

   Checking the mailing list by occupations may show that you are low in a few key occupations. Finally, an occupational breakdown makes it possible for you to reach any group speedily.

3. *How well do you actually know your audience?* Through continuing surveys, it is possible to find out more about the tastes of your readers and what they think of your sponsor and work. This is simply two-way communication on a regular rather than a one-shot basis. It enables the editor to correct weak spots and to forge personal links with his readers.

4. *Do you present your material in familiar terms?* You can best attract busy people by "talking" to them in terms of *their* interests, not primarily in yours. Convince them by the way you present your material that you are earnestly offering them something you believe is a fair exchange for the reading time they are willing to give you.

5. *Do you assist the reader in getting to the point quickly?* The title of your story should excite the reader, and the headline and the leading paragraph should hold him. Accompanying illustrations should be simple but dramatic. The entire page or pages should be a cohesive pattern of concise and consistent storytelling.

6. *Do readers believe what you say?* After all, you represent a special interest and readers know it. But your special interest need not show annoyingly. It should not, if people are to respect what you say, read it with understanding and, you hope, arrive at a favorable conclusion. This is true whether you are discussing an economic attitude or machine tools.

7. *Are you building a secondary readership?* Do you prepare press releases on major stories and send them out with the appearance of the issue? Do you try to key-in any of your contents with radio and television newscasts? Do you work up any special features for magazines or Sunday supplements? Do you offer reprints at cost to groups possibly interested in a specific feature? Do you stimulate other editors to reprint or digest, and offer to supply prints or mats?

8. *Are you selling your publication to the boss who pays the bills?* He is busy, too, and if you want him to appreciate the value of the external you are producing for him, you should let him know periodically—by conversation, by visual presentation, progress report, nonpartisan endorsement or any other legitimate means—how well you are doing. Some publications catch cold when adverse economic winds start to blow. The better the editor has built up his resistance, the less likely the illness will prove fatal.

NEWSLETTERS

During recent years, with a tremendously expanded volume of printed material of all types clogging business communications routes, the newsletter has become an extremely popular format. Few businessmen receive less than a dozen newsletters every month—most of them sent without cost to promote the senders' products and services.

The big advantage of the newsletter is that it *appears* easy to read—a publication which will give a maximum amount of information in a minimum amount of reading time. Another advantage, of course, is that a regular newsletter can be published for a modest amount of money.

When to Consider a Newsletter

There are some pretty well established guidelines to help evaluate the advisability of publishing a newsletter. In "How to Produce an Effective Newsletter" (American Marketing Services, 1960), the author suggested these five reasons for *not* publishing a newsletter:

1. If you plan to use lots of photos, a newsletter is *not* for you. Photos and newsletters are seldom compatible. While one or two photos may be used to add a change of pace to a newsletter, the use of a large number of photos tends to destroy the basic newsletter format and thus diminishes its effectiveness.

NEWSLETTER

THE RISE OF NEWSLETTERS

With the demand for simplified methods to convey information quickly to large audiences, the newsletter format has become one of the most important tools of business communications. This economical format is rapidly growing in use throughout the U.S., particularly in business and industry. Today, few American business executives fail to receive at least one regularly published newsletter. Even publishers of top business magazines frequently turn to the use of newsletter formats to provide their readers with material of special importance.

Something of Value . . . Behind the growth of newsletters lies a problem which plagues all businessmen -- how to keep abreast of the many important developments which affect their operations. It would literally take a 40-hour week devoted entirely to reading for the average executive to keep up with the tremendous volume of printed material issued each week in most fields. Obviously, such time is not available ... so the businessman turns to those media which can provide the greatest volume of information for the least reading time expended. In such a pattern, the newsletter has special value.

WHAT'S AHEAD: While newsletters are already extremely popular, look for the idea to enter new areas -- particularly increased use for internal communications. Possible applications:

* Combined bulletins ... Rather than sending a series of bulletins, each covering a single subject, many companies are digesting the material and putting the highlights in a widely distributed newsletter. Recipients are urged to request the full bulletins covering subjects of special interest to them.

* Reader's reports ... Another application of growing popularity is an internal newsletter which digests material of special interest to the company. A special "reader" is employed to follow all publications containing material of possible interest and prepare a newsletter report on what's appeared in print. Newsletter recipients can obtain copies of the original articles from the company library.

Footnote: As newsletters continue to make their appearance, the next development may be a newsletter containing highlights from newsletters -- a "Reader's Digest of Newsletters."

The big advantage of the newsletter is that it appears *easy to read.*

2. If you plan to regularly run long articles, a newsletter is *not* for you. The newsletter format is designed for short, to-the-point items. If the reader finds himself face to face with lengthy discussions, the basic conception of the newsletter is destroyed and he will very likely look at your publication as a second-rate job in comparison with the magazines and newspapers he receives, since these other media can handle a long item so much better.
3. If there is nothing "newsy" about your material, a newsletter is *not* for you. The reader expects a newsletter to be a carrier of up-to-the-minute items. Disappoint him on this score and you will have a hard time gaining a share of his limited reading time.
4. If you cannot give your readers the feeling of letting them in on something special, a newsletter is *not* for you. This is one of the key "tricks" of successful newsletter editing. If you are not adequately staffed to handle this kind of writing, you will probably be better off looking for some other format.
5. If you look upon a newsletter as simply the cheapest way to produce a regular publication, a newsletter is *not* for you. While, in most cases, the newsletter *is* the most economical method of publishing, costs alone should not be the reason for selection of a newsletter format. *No publication is inexpensive unless it can achieve readership from its recipients.*

Reasons for Selecting a Newsletter Format

These negative aspects are balanced out by six major advantages of the newsletter format:

Simplicity. Just as simplicity is one of the advantages in gaining acceptance among readers for a newsletter, it is also one of the big advantages to the publisher. There are fewer decisions to be made. No questions about how to treat each subject; about which subjects to illustrate; about selection of typefaces, headline styles, layout, and so forth. Once the format is established, the issue-by-issue decisions are limited almost entirely to what items to include and the relative importance of these items.

Economy. While we have pointed out that economy should not be the only reason for deciding upon any format, it is certainly a major advantage of newsletters. You can produce the best possible newsletter for only a fraction of what it usually costs to produce a good newspaper or magazine.

Speed. Another major advantage of a newsletter is that it can be produced in a matter of hours. Thus, your "hot" stories can be on their way to readers before they have a chance to cool off.

Control. The simplicity of a newsletter operation makes it possible for effective editorial control with a minimum of effort. Since fewer people are usually involved in a newsletter operation than in other types of publications, tighter control can be maintained. There are also fewer steps to production, thus less opportunity for things to go wrong.

Facilities. Production of a newsletter can be handled by more different production methods than most any other type of publication. Thus, production facilities are more readily available. While an outstanding newsletter requires competent, professional handling, these skills are readily available in most areas.

In this regard, it should be pointed out that many are misled by the thought that a newsletter is so simple a production job that it can be handled easily by any person who knows how to type. This misconception, unfortunately, has ruined many otherwise acceptable newsletters. As in the production of any type of printed material, there are tricks of the trade which frequently spell the difference between success and failure. By all means, you should seriously consider having a printer or lettershop experienced in newsletter production handle the production of your newsletter for you.

Acceptance. As we noted at the very beginning, one thing which has boomed the newsletter in recent years is its acceptance as a publication which gives a maximum amount of information in a minimum amount of reading time. This established acceptance is certainly a major advantage for those who are about to embark on a newsletter publishing project. While each new newsletter must deliver editorial material worthy of the recipient's time in order to retain a position on the "must reading list," it starts off with the odds in its favor—thanks to the pioneering work done by the many outstanding newsletters already being published.

SIZES FOR EXTERNAL PUBLICATIONS*

	Trimmed Publication	*Standard Paper Without Bleed*	*Standard Paper if Pages Bleed*
Envelope Enclosure Sizes	3⅜ x 6¼	28 x 42	28 x 44
	4 x 9⅛	25 x 38	28 x 42
Pocket Sizes	3¾ x 5⅛	32 x 44	35 x 45
	4¼ x 5⅜	35 x 45	38 x 50
	4½ x 6	25 x 38	28 x 42
	5¼ x 7⅝	32 x 44	35 x 45
	5½ x 8½	35 x 45	38 x 50
Intermediate Sizes	6 x 9⅛	25 x 38	28 x 42
	7¾ x 10⅝	32 x 44	35 x 45
File Size	8½ x 11	35 x 45	38 x 50
Small Magazine and	9¼ x 12⅛	25 x 38	28 x 42
Small Newspaper Sizes	10 x 13	28 x 42	28 x 44
Large Magazine Size	10¾ x 13¾	28 x 44	....
Large Newspaper Sizes	10¾ x 15½	32 x 44	35 x 45
	17 x 22	35 x 45	38 x 50
	19 x 25	38 x 50	....

*From "The Company Publication"—S. D. Warren Co., Boston.

A Study of More Than 100 External Publications

The following statistics resulted from a survey conducted by *Advertising Requirements:*

FREQUENCY OF ISSUE

Monthly	31 percent
Quarterly	28 percent
Bimonthly	26 percent

CIRCULATION

Under 5,000	13 percent
5 to 20,000	29 percent
20 to 100,000	18 percent
Over 100,000	10 percent

FORMAT

Magazine	78 percent
Newspaper	11 percent
Newsletter	7 percent

SUPERVISION

Advertising manager	46 percent
Public relations director	14 percent
Manager of public relations & advertising	10 percent
President	7 percent
Sales manager	6 percent

BUDGET

Advertising	62 percent
Public relations	16 percent
Sales	7 percent
Sales promotion	6 percent

METHOD OF REPRODUCTION

Letterpress	56 percent
Offset	30 percent
Combination	10 percent
Rotogravure	4 percent

OTHER DUTIES OF EDITOR

None	27 percent
Advertising manager	22 percent
Assistant advertising manager	15 percent
Public relations & Advertising manager	7 percent
Public relations director	4 percent
President	4 percent
Copywriter	3 percent
Ad planner	3 percent

OUTSIDE SERVICES BOUGHT

Reproduction	71 percent
Photography	43 percent
Design	36 percent
Writing	19 percent

SOURCE OF CIRCULATION LIST

Company salesmen	32 percent
Distributors	14 percent
Dealers	13 percent
Customer lists	13 percent
Requests	10 percent
Advertising department	4 percent

CONTENT

General features	53 percent
Industry news	50 percent
Company news	49 percent
Product news	7 percent

GENERAL PURPOSE

Public relations	70 percent
Sales promotion	70 percent
Product news	25 percent

Chapter 34

ANNUAL AND SPECIAL REPORTS

WHILE many people fail to recognize it, annual reports and other material sent to stockholders are really forms of direct mail advertising. The only basic difference is that the "product" being advertised is the company itself.

Not too long ago, the typical annual report was a dry, uninteresting compilation of statistical information. But in recent years there has been a very decided trend toward making the annual report a colorful, inspiring promotional tool which includes not only the required statistical information but a complete story of what has been happening within the company.

Annual Report Formats

Most annual reports are published in the standard 8½- by 11-inch size—primarily because this is considered the easiest size to file. Some companies do come up with a variation simply by binding along the 8½-inch length, producing a horizontal booklet rather than the more common vertical format.

To gain greater impact, some firms occasionally use a larger size, but generally recognize that they are sacrificing the potential of having their report kept on file. In a number of cases, however, both impact and fileability have been achieved by producing an oversize report which includes a pocket containing a standard-size statistical summary. Thus, the basic financial information can be quickly removed and kept on file by those who need it for future reference.

Pocket-size reports, while tried from time to time, have generally proved undesirable since it is difficult to present complicated statistical material on a page smaller than 8½ by 11 inches.

Contents

A comprehensive checklist of suggested contents of the modern annual report was presented in "Checklist for a Well-Balanced Annual Report," by Twentieth Century Press Inc.:

FRONT COVER DESIGN:

........Product in Use
........Industry Represented
........Pattern-Repetition
........Symbolic Treatment
........Trademark or Brand

Reproduction of:

........Photograph
........Drawing—Pastel
........Water Color
........Oil Painting

Number of Colors:

........Four Colors
........Three Colors
........Two Colors—Duotone
........One Color
........Metallic Ink

Essential Information:

........Corporate Name
........Fiscal Year End
........Consecutive Year
........Anniversary (if any)

INSIDE FRONT COVER:

Choice of:

........List of Subsidiaries of Products
........Industries Served
........Map Locating Plants, etc.
........Management—Policy
........Pledge for Future Progress
........Photo of Main Plant—Home Office
........Leading News Development
........Other Selection

INTRCDUCTORY PAGE:

........Corporate Name
........Executive Office Address
........Industry (if not obvious)
........Table of Contents:
.... Editorial—Narrative
.... Charts—Maps
.... Financial Statements
........Transfer Agent
........Registrar
........General Counsel
........Independent Auditor
........Market—Stock exchange

HIGHLIGHTS PAGE:

........2-Year Comparatives
........Percentage Change Column

Choice of Content:

Millions of Dollars:

........Sales—Total or Net
........Federal Taxes on Income
........Dividends Declared
........Plant and Equipment
........Expenditures for New Plant
........Depreciation of Plant, etc.
........Net Working Capital
........Working Capital Ratio
........Long-Term Debt (if any)
........Invested Capital
........Net Worth—Book Value

Per Share of Common Stock:

........Federal Income Taxes
........Net Income
........Dividends Paid
........Working Capital
........Shareholders' Equity

Other Information:

........Units Produced—Breakdown
........Number of Plants, Dealers, Stores, Sales Outlets, etc.
........Number of Employees—Year end
........Number of Stockholders

ANNUAL REPORT

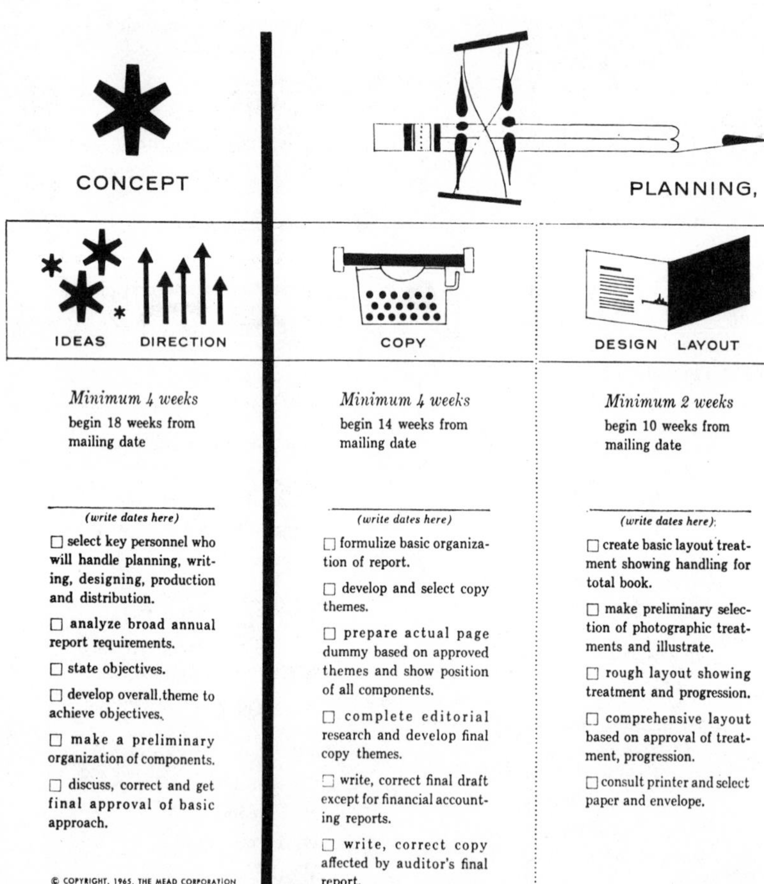

CONCEPT — IDEAS, DIRECTION

Minimum 4 weeks
begin 18 weeks from mailing date

(write dates here)

- ☐ select key personnel who will handle planning, writing, designing, production and distribution.
- ☐ analyze broad annual report requirements.
- ☐ state objectives.
- ☐ develop overall theme to achieve objectives.
- ☐ make a preliminary organization of components.
- ☐ discuss, correct and get final approval of basic approach.

PLANNING, — COPY

Minimum 4 weeks
begin 14 weeks from mailing date

(write dates here)

- ☐ formulize basic organization of report.
- ☐ develop and select copy themes.
- ☐ prepare actual page dummy based on approved themes and show position of all components.
- ☐ complete editorial research and develop final copy themes.
- ☐ write, correct final draft except for financial accounting reports.
- ☐ write, correct copy affected by auditor's final report.

DESIGN LAYOUT

Minimum 2 weeks
begin 10 weeks from mailing date

(write dates here)

- ☐ create basic layout treatment showing handling for total book.
- ☐ make preliminary selection of photographic treatments and illustrate.
- ☐ rough layout showing treatment and progression.
- ☐ comprehensive layout based on approval of treatment, progression.
- ☐ consult printer and select paper and envelope.

PLANNING CHART

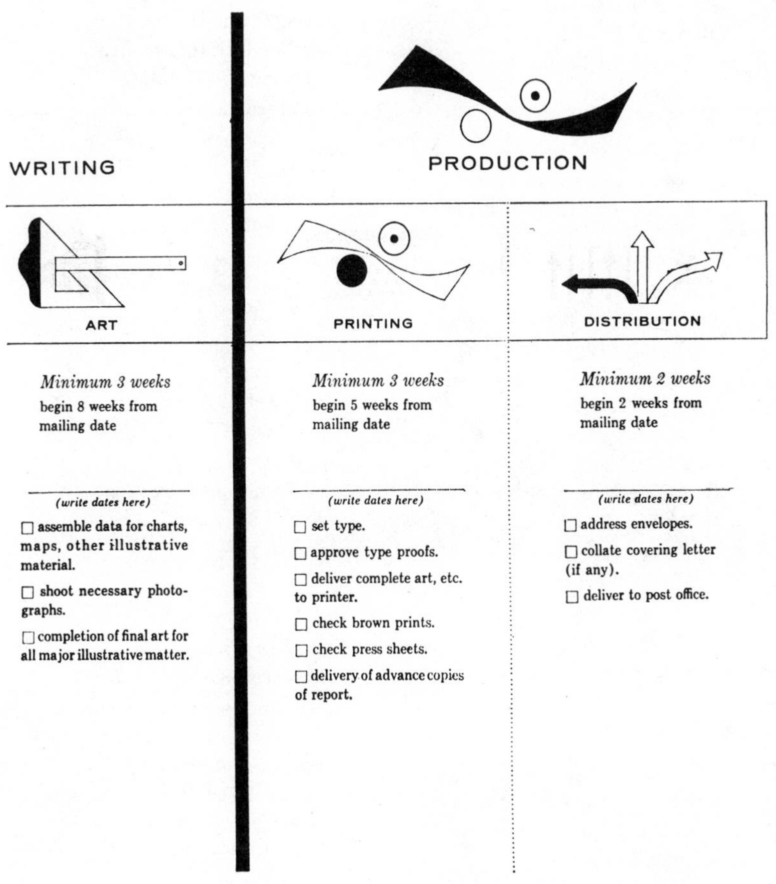
WRITING
PRODUCTION
ART
PRINTING
DISTRIBUTION
Minimum 3 weeks
begin 8 weeks from mailing date
Minimum 3 weeks
begin 5 weeks from mailing date
Minimum 2 weeks
begin 2 weeks from mailing date
(write dates here)
☐ assemble data for charts, maps, other illustrative material.
☐ shoot necessary photographs.
☐ completion of final art for all major illustrative matter.
(write dates here)
☐ set type.
☐ approve type proofs.
☐ deliver complete art, etc. to printer.
☐ check brown prints.
☐ check press sheets.
☐ delivery of advance copies of report.
(write dates here)
☐ address envelopes.
☐ collate covering letter (if any).
☐ deliver to post office.

Chart:

........Breakdown of Sales Dollar:
........Income—Outgo

PRESIDENT'S LETTER:

........One-Page Summary
or
........Two-Page Review
........Informal Photograph:
.... Portrait of President
.... Board of Directors
........Friendly Salutation:
.... To Our Stockholders
.... Fellow Shareholders
.... To Share Owners and the Public
.... To the Friends of Our Company
........Sales and Per Share Earnings
........Financial Position
........Capital Additions (if any)
........New Products or Services
........Acquisitions and Mergers
........Unfilled Orders—Backlog
........Research—New Products
........Outlook or Prospects
........Appreciation:
.... Officers' Cooperation
.... Employee Loyalty
........Facsimile Signature
........Date of Letter

NARRATIVE SECTION:

........Sales Trend—Percent Change
........Earnings Trend—Percent Change
........Explanation for Change
........Federal Taxes
........Dividend Policy
........Earnings Reinvested
........Property, Plant & Equipment
........Expansion—Plant Additions
........Mergers and Acquisitions
........Subsidiaries—Branches
........Imports and Exports
........Inventories—Price Trends
........Research and Engineering
........Capital Investment
........Change in Capital Structure
......New Financing Planned (if any)
........Financial Position—Comparison
........Working Capital Analysis
........Stockholders' Equity—Book Value
........Long-Term Debt (if any)
........Stockholder Information:
.... Number—Trend
.... Classification
.... Geographical Distribution
.... Sex and Average Holdings
........Employee Information:
.... Length of Service
.... Worker Productivity
.... Pensions—Insurance
.... Health and Safety
.... Training—Promotions
........Management Changes:
.... Board of Directors
.... Officers
.... Obituaries
........Advertising—Promotion
........Public Relations
........Industry

Choice of Illustrations:

........Products Being Manufactured
........Products in Use
........Buildings and Plant Facilities
........Raw Material Sources
........Employee Activities
........Shareholders' Annual Meeting
........News Events of Year
........Awards and Commendations
........Advertisements—Booklets

Choice of Charts & Graphics:

........Sales
........Earnings and Dividends
........Federal Taxes
........Breakdown of Sales Dollar

........Income vs. Outgo ("Highlights")
........Working Capital
........Long-Term Debt (if any)
........Net Worth—Book Value
........Trend of Number of
.... Stockholders
.... Employees

FINANCIAL STATEMENTS:

........Comparative Balance Sheets
........Comparative Earnings Statements
........Profit and Loss Account
........Surplus Analysis
........Working Capital Changes
........Cash-Flow Tabulation
........Analysis of Funded Debt (if any)
........Footnotes—Readable Type
........Auditor's Certification

BACKGROUND STATISTICAL TABULATION:

........Fifteen Years
........Ten Years
........Five Years

Financial—Ratios:

........Sales—Gross or Net
........Net Before Taxes
........Profit Margin
........Federal Taxes
........Net After Taxes
........Earnings per Share of Common
........Dividends Paid per Share
........Current Assets
........Current Liabilities
........Net Working Capital
........Working Capital Ratio
........Working Capital per Share
........Long-Term Debt (if any)
........Land, Buildings and Equipment
........Accumulated Depreciation
........Expenditures on New Plant
........Shares Outstanding:
.... Preferred (if any)
.... Common (par value)
........Stockholders' Equity:
.... Share Capital
.... Earnings Re-invested
.... Capital Surplus
.... Reserves
.... Book Value per Share
........Number of Stockholders
........Number of Employees—Year end:
.... Capital Investment
.... Average Weekly Wage

Efficiency Indexes:

........Turnover of Fixed Capital
........Turnover of Inventories
........Turnover of Accounts Receivable
........Average Collection Period

Operating Statistics:

NOTE: Depends on Industry

MANAGEMENT TABULATION:

........Board of Directors—Identify Directors who are not officers
........Executive Committee
........Finance Committee
........Officers—Titles—Indicate Department of each Vice President

INSIDE BACK COVER:

Choice of Subjects Not Used for Inside Front Cover:

........List of Subsidiaries or Products and Services
........Industries Served
........Map Locating Plants, etc.
........Management Organization Chart
........Pledge for Future Progress
........Photo of Main Plant—Home Office
........Leading News Development
........Other Selection

BACK COVER:

Optional Choice:

........Leading Product—Brand Name

........Trademark—Hallmark

........Slogan—Logotype

........Continuation of Illustration from Front Cover—Full or Part

........Other Selection

Planning an Annual Report

The Annual Report Council produced a filmstrip[1] which offered a 17-point plan for producing more effective annual reports:

1. *Get started early.* Three to four months before your fiscal year ends. You can schedule and design without all the financial data.
2. *Plan an overall theme.* This helps to get your thinking organized early, and adds impact to the report.
3. *Set up a schedule.* This should cover every step in production, but it is not any help unless you stick to it.
4. *Collect ideas.* See that all department or division heads get their opportunity to contribute early.
5. *Set a budget.* Build this on firm estimates for all subcontracted work: graphics, photography, printing.
6. *Organize your graphics.* Decide which data will need charts and graphs, and develop rough sketches.
7. *Select your photos.* Go through your files, find what you can use, and schedule for the missing shots.
8. *Develop a preliminary dummy.* This should show general format, copy approach, color, illustrations, and so forth.
9. *Get the dummy approved.* Don't delay in getting top management's reaction to the preliminary dummy.
10. *Build your distribution list.* Don't forget employees, suppliers, press, etc., for greater public relations mileage.
11. *Discuss production problems.* See your printer, engraver, mailing house to avoid costly errors.
12. *Finish sections early.* Don't wait until the last minute to finish sections that do not need final figures.
13. *Distribute mailing list early.* Give your printer and mailing house a clean and complete list.

[1]"How to Plan and Produce a Prizewinning Annual Report." This filmstrip is available through Graphics Institute, 42 West 39th Street, New York, New York 10018.

14. *Give management a final opportunity.* Let them check a dummy while changes may still be made.
15. *Set up accountant's report.* Rush it to the typesetter, and see that everybody okays proofs.
16. *Abandon false dignity.* If it can speed final production, get down to the printers during the final stretch.
17. *Stimulate interest in the report.* Send out press releases, take out ads for the maximum impact.

Variations in Format

One of the most common variations in annual report formats is use of a gatefold—either on one of the covers or within the body of the report. These elongated pages (some of them double gatefolds extending to 34 inches or more) offer an opportunity to present material of special importance with considerable impact. Some of the uses of gatefolds include:

Comprehensive product spread.

Maps showing location of company plants, service facilities, customers, distributors, and so forth.

Manufacturing flow charts.

Picture stories of all kinds.

Aerial photographs of extensive manufacturing layouts.

Many other format variations and special graphic techniques are also used to add impact to annual reports. While the possibilities are relatively unlimited, some idea of the things which can be done to make reports more interesting can be seen by considering the following roundup of ideas from just a small sample of reports ("44 Ideas for More Interesting Annual Reports," by Peg Miller, *Advertising Requirements):*

PICTURE STORY FORMAT

1. A Canadian food store chain, Dominion Stores Ltd., copied *Life* magazine's format—complete to size, *Life* red on cover, etc.—it could be mistaken for a copy of that magazine. Inside, the same theme is carried out. In *Life* picture story style, a "typical" stockholder is taken through the stores, warehouses, and so forth. Photographs were all crisp black and whites with exception of cover. *Life* style type faces also were used.

   Before deciding to copy a specific magazine, it is essential to secure the publisher's permission.

2. "The Story of an Order" was Stone Container's method of unfolding operational activities for stockholders. In picture story style, an order for a corrugated shipping carton was followed through each department at Stone. Again only black-and-white photos were used with a bright orange color block to liven each page.

3. Employees of Chesapeake & Ohio Railroad were the central figures in its picture story report. On each page were pictures of employees of one division—freight dispatchers, conductors, porters, flagmen, office and yard workers. Each told his role in the railroad's operations and the total effect is a complete picture of the railroad's workings for the year.

4. Caterpillar Tractor built its picture story around the theme, "Caterpillar machines move the earth." A series of full-color photos showed Caterpillars at work around the world. A different machine was shown doing a different job in a different part of the world in each photo. In this way all current models and what each was used for were presented. A full-color picture symbol map was included.

USE OF COLOR AND FULL-COLOR PHOTOS

5. The last page of a Greyhound Bus report unfolded like a travel folder. Full-color photos showing many of the famous tourist spots across the United States with a Greyhound bus conspicuously in the foreground made up the "travel folder."

6. Five colors were used by one company to divide a simulated coin and show how the corporation's dollar was spent. Stockholders could tell at a glance the percentages of money invested, taxes, money paid out in dividends, etc., by examining the color separators on the drawing of a coin.

7. Eastman Kodak used a number of full-color, full-page reproductions of Kodachromes in a yearly report. Reprints of the photos were offered to stockholders in a note on the title page of the report.

8. Duotones—yellow and black—of various wheat field scenes form the backgrounds for Sunshine Biscuit's financial story. The duotones were full-page, bleed, and some covered two-page spreads. A copy block and a graph block were mortised into each page. Balance sheets on plain white paper were found on the last pages of the report.

9. A number of companies' yearly reports were in two colors only and many of these used columns of color to separate columns of figures on a white page. Popular colors were the so-called "earth" colors—yellows, greens, blues, rusts—tinged with a touch of brown.

10. A strip of color across the bottom of each page successfully added a note of continuity to another report.

11. Several companies achieved unusual effects with the use of two colors by overprinting one color on another—creating the appearance of three colors.

12. Distillers Corporation uses the same cover each year but prints it in different colors.
13. Acme Steel's sales dollar was shown by dividing a mock dollar bill, printed in yellow. The divisions were shown with white strips.
14. A painting of timber-covered mountains and a mountain goat was reproduced in full color on the cover of Weyerhaeuser Co.'s report. Inside similar wildlife studies in duotones decorated each page.

GRAPHS, CARTOONS, LINE DRAWINGS USED TO EXPLAIN FINANCES

15. A magazine format with "situation"-type cartoons by well-known cartoonists sparked a Girard Trust Corn Exchange Bank report.
16. Cartoons in an American Type Founders' report showed who gets how much of the company's money for doing what.
17. A series of six line drawings was used by Union Oil Co. to represent the division of net profit.
18. Increasingly larger cartoon figures of Uncle Sam presented a picture of how taxes grew over years in Champion Papers Inc.'s report.
19. Dominion Stores inserted a broadside folder into one of its reports. Inside the first fold were seven line drawings representing expenditure of company income. When the broadside was fully opened, complete balance sheets and auditors' report were revealed.
20. Graphs decorated nearly every page of Acme Steel's latest report. They showed which department contributed the most volume of sales over a seven-year period; income before and after taxes for the same period; earnings invested and expended on building and equipment; growth of shareholders, and statistical data on earnings for a 10-year period.

SPECIAL DEVICES

21. Onionskin sheets inserted in the middle of each two-page spread in a Girdler Corporation report not only provided an interesting contrast with the glossy opaque stock used for the body of the report, but served as indexes and introductory pages dividing the various sections. In several instances, the onionskin sheets contained copy to accompany photos printed on the adjoining body pages.

    Design on onionskin pages harmonized and complimented design on pages beneath it. A lot of white space was used on both glossy and onionskin. Two different shades of warm brown with black alternated on both glossy and onionskin pages.
22. Several companies have used two or more different-colored stocks to divide various sections of reports. One report, for example, used gray stock throughout except for the center spread which contained balance sheets—they were printed on white.

23. Entire reports have been printed on graph paper. Brown & Bigelow used an art version of graph paper in red, gold, black, and gray to form the cover and as decorative background for many pages in its report.

24. A number of reports had figure sheets printed on glossy paper while the operational story was printed on non-slick stock. Reversal of the same procedure also has been used.

25. Another idea is printing balance sheets on heavy bristol and inserting them in the center of the report.

26. Texaco Inc.'s golden anniversary report incorporated a gold foil cover with white deckle embossed overlay. Gold color was repeated on each page.

27. Another report (Dominion Stores) also used the overlay idea. Title of the report, "Parable of the Three Peas," plus a drawing of a dinner plate and place setting were printed on white ripple stock overlay. The overlay had a triangular cut at the bottom. The cover, a brown-and-white duotone of a huge crowd of faces, showed around the overlay edges. When the overlay was lifted, a copy line mortised in the center of the duotone illustration read, ". . . and how they fed a vast multitude." The three peas idea was used to divide various sections of the report.

28. Reports to employees have been printed on newsprint with a series of cartoons, comic-book style, used to explain figures.

29. Plastic binding has been used successfully by many companies to give their reports a distinctive touch.

30. A die-cut red-and-black "battery" formed the cover of a Burgess Battery's report. Stone Container has used a die-cut box as the cover for its report.

31. Laminated acetate covers add a special note of quality to a number of annual reports. Shellmar Products Corporation, for example, used one of its own acetate products for covers.

32. Die-cut windows on covers and inside have been used to dramatize the theme of "look" at the record or figures, and so forth.

33. The majority of annual reports for a number of years have been 8½ by 11 inches. Variations in size are likely to attract attention. One company simply reversed its 8½- by 11-inch dimensions every other year.

34. Covers that extend ¼ to ½ inch on all sides of the inside pages create a "dignified" portfolio effect for reports.

35. Brown & Bigelow tipped in a miniature reproduction of its most popular product—the famous Boy Scout calendar—in an annual report.

36. A new wallpaper design was the cover of United Wallpaper's reports for many years. Reports were bound between actual sheets of wallpaper.

37. Capitol Records used a record—an LP—to report to stockholders. The disc narrated history of the company and accompanied a regular annual report.

38. Many companies include reprints of ads in reports. Some bind them into the book; a Sunbeam report had reprints of all its ads for the year inserted into pockets in the back cover.

39. An issue of its house organ telling employees about Westinghouse Electric's fiscal operations was in the form of a check book. Eleven checks disposed

of one year of the company's sales. On the page facing each check was an explanation for each item paid.

40. Motorola's employee report was a "space opera." Drawings of space ship characters romped through the pages explaining company finances.
41. Two different booklets are frequently used to separate financial data and other details. In most cases, the booklet containing the financial information is a cut-and-dried financial report, while the second (and in some cases, third and even fourth) booklet contains information covering research, products, advertising. In other cases, both the financial report and supplementary booklets get a full design treatment with effective use of color, illustrations, and so forth.
42. Separate booklets covering operations other than strictly financial ones have been enclosed in a back-cover pocket of the annual report by several companies.
43. One company used an oversized booklet that had been prepared as a promotional piece and converted it into an annual report by binding balance sheets, auditors' report, and a letter from the company president into the volume. The original booklet contained a picture story of the company's products, machinery and other operations.
44. Hard-bound books have also been used effectively as annual reports. Such treatment is generally limited to anniversary occasions or when the company feels it particularly important that the report be retained for an extended period of time.

Annual Report Kit

One of the finest guides to assist both beginners and professionals in preparing more effective annual reports is a four-part kit produced by The Mead Corporation. Of special interest is Booklet No. 2 in the kit, "Planning and Writing the Annual Report." Among the contents is the Annual Report Planning Chart shown on the following two pages.

Also included in the booklet is a contents checklist:

1. Cover . . .

The cover should interest the prospective reader at first glance. This is basically a design problem—one for your artist. A good cover may mean the difference between a read or an unread report.

Many things can be done to make it arresting and inviting.

1. Photos or illustrations
   a. bleed
   b. dramatic art treatment
2. Color

3. Embossing
4. Die-cutting
5. Special folds
6. Cover stock

2. Highlights . . .

Purpose of this section is to present a quick picture of the year's operation. This technique is especially useful in cases where the complete corporate story might run as many as 32 or more pages. Corresponding figures for the previous year should also be presented. Consider inclusion of these subjects:

1. Sales
2. Earnings
   a. net income
   b. net income as a percent of sales
   c. earnings per share of common stock
   d. dividends per share of common stock
3. Taxes
   a. per share of common stock
   b. per dollar of net income
   c. per dollar of dividends
4. Employment
   a. number of employees
   b. average weekly earnings
5. Shareholders
   a. total
   b. increase over previous year
6. Plant facilities
7. New products

3. Management . . .

Duties of each officer of the corporation and identification of each member of the board of directors with notation of length of service is important to demonstrate management's qualifications and competence. New appointments should be handled in a way that will draw attention to their background, experience and the positions they occupy. Here are some of the things that might be added:

1. Pictures of each
2. Information regarding management depth
3. Management recruitment and in-service development policies

4. The President's Letter . . .

It should be short—never more than two pages—crisp and to the point. It should be warm, friendly and conversational. Think of it as a personal presentation of all the material in the report, as a preamble, an introduction, a pace-setting narrative. Above all it should:

1. Invite interest
2. Promote readership of the report
3. Explain present conditions
4. Describe the future
5. Illustrate important points with bar graphs, pictures or drawings

5. Narratives . . .

This is by far the largest single writing assignment in the book. It should be essentially a step-by-step description of the operations of the company during the fiscal year, and divided by sub-headings with pictures, illustrations and graphs emphasizing every important subject. Here is a list of possible subjects you might wish to include:

1. Sales
2. Industry position
3. Trade recognition
4. Future outlook
5. Expansion, new equipment
6. Branches
7. Subsidiaries
8. Products
9. New products
10. Market prospects
11. Customer relations
12. Dealer relations
13. Distribution facilities
14. Advertising and sales promotion
15. Inventories
16. Unfilled orders
17. Employee relations
18. Employee benefits
    a. pensions
    b. insurance
    c. disability

d. training
e. recognition

6. Income-Outgo Chart . . .

The source and distribution of income is best explained graphically —usually in the form of a pie chart. However, the chart is not to be considered as a substitute for the actual listing of figures. Information should include the following:

1. Receipts
   a. net sales
   b. other income such as interest on receivables, dividends from subsidiaries, etc.
2. Distribution of receipts
   a. cost of materials, etc.
   b. wages, salaries, pensions, insurance, etc.
   c. taxes (federal, state, local)
   d. dividends
   e. amount re-invested in company

Notes to the financial statement might include:

1. Principle of consolidation
2. Employee pensions
3. Accounts and notes receivable
4. Inventories
5. Employees' bonus
6. Contingent liabilities, etc.

7. The Balance Sheet . . .

The most essential component of the annual report is the balance sheet. And the most essential thing about it is simplicity. Although it is a standardized form determined by accounting practice conforming to various legal requirements it is, nevertheless, not readily understood by the majority of stockholders. For this reason "Notes to the Financial Statement" may be added to clarify certain points.

The balance sheet should include:

1. Current assets
2. Investments and miscellaneous assets
3. Capital stock in the treasury
4. Real estate, plants, equipment
5. Total assets
6. Current liabilities

7. Other liabilities (bonuses, taxes, misc.)
8. Reserves
9. Capital stock and surplus
10. Total liabilities

8. Statistical Comparisons . . .

Year to year comparisons—running as far back as possible—but covering at least the past ten years, enable readers to judge company business trends. This material should include:

1. Sales
2. Earnings
3. Dividends
4. Taxes
5. Reserves
6. Financial progress
7. Market value of stock

9. Stockholder Information . . .

A complete, comparative table showing the number of stockholders, average size of holdings, etc., for a number of years should be presented. This provides a basis for year-to-year comparisons by financial analysts and professional shareholders. It should:

1. Classify stockholders
   a. age
   b. occupation
   c. educational level
   d. geographical distribution
2. Categorize shareholders
   a. men-women
   b. insurance companies
   c. brokers and nominees
   d. estates and trusts
   e. educational institutions
   f. charitable institutions
   g. others
3. Account for shareholders
   a. owning less than 100 shares
   b. owning more than 100 shares
4. Illustrate organizational structure
   a. corporate structure including subsidiaries
   b. management authority

5. Describe products or services
   a. markets
   b. trend of distribution
   c. other industries served
   d. per capita consumption, etc.
6. Stockholders
   a. trend of average number
   b. trend of average holding
   c. trend of holdings by number of shares, etc.
7. Employees
   a. trend of average number
   b. trend of wages
   c. cost of pensions, insurance, etc.

10. Table of Contents . . .

Index or listing of all material in the annual report.

SPECIAL REPORTS

The annual report format is also used for a variety of other direct mail purposes—particularly by companies and institutions which are not required to report their financial picture but wish to provide select audiences with some kind of progress report.

In addition, many companies supplement their annual report with special reports to key audiences such as employees, suppliers, customers, distributors. In some cases the basic content of the regular annual report is retained but supplemented with additional information of special interest to the nonfinancial audiences. More commonly, however, a completely revised report is issued since the language of financial audiences is sometimes difficult for the average layman to appreciate.

Employee Annual Reports

The judges in a nationwide contest to determine the best annual reports to employees made these observations about such reports[2]:

1. *The employee annual report is taking on an identity of its own.* In the past, many companies have preferred to distribute to employees, if they distributed anything at all, the actual stockholder report. The employee was invited to read it if he felt like it, and understand what he could of it, which was generally little. Recently an impressive percentage of managements have begun to issue tailor-made reports for the employees.

[2] "Should Companies Publish Annual Reports for Employees?" by Robert Newcomb and Marg Sammons, *Industrial Marketing.*

(In the contest, six of the nine companies whose reports rated highest devoted an entire publication to the report, not just a portion of an employee magazine.)

2. *The new type of employee report shows planning.* In the contest, a slapped-together version of the stockholder report, milked down for employee consumption, did not rate too high. The high scorers were those that had clearly been planned for a long time ahead.
3. *While the language is simpler, management still talks stuffily to employees.* It doesn't show up in the higher-scoring entries too much, but farther down the line a tendency reveals itself to write pontifically, and the judges spotted it.
4. *The newer, better reports are lively and pictorial.* In its conversion to the kind of report employees read and apparently prefer, the product today seems much livelier, more colorful and pictorial. Some of the more extreme entries go to cartoon techniques and similar methods (with results both good and bad), but in general the visual acceleration is in the direction of better pictures, simpler graphs.

Getting Readership for Employee Reports

Simply publishing and distributing an employee annual report may not be enough. It often takes a well-planned and carefully executed program to assure satisfactory attention from an employee group for company communications of all types. The following tips are offered by two leading authorities on company communications[3]:

1. If it's an insurance booklet, employee report, retirement manual—or any piece of literature of that type—let the people know in advance that it is coming. Use every possible means to promote it: articles in the employee paper prior to introduction and from time to time after it has been distributed; through announcements on the bulletin board, and through newsletters to employees.
2. Get the supervisors briefed on the literature, first by explaining it all carefully to them (as a matter of sound policy); then encourage them to talk about the literature to their own people.
3. Develop means for getting a "playback" on the information the literature contains. Quiz contests and other participating affairs can help the authors determine whether their messages "got through" or whether no dent was actually made.
4. If it's an employee annual report, change the form of presentation each year. If the company does it the same way, year in and year out, the audience starts walking out on the show.

Los Angeles Police Report

An example of a nonfinancial annual report is the publication issued annually by the Los Angeles Police Department. A few years ago, the department simply released a Statistical Digest. Then the department decided it could make its report do a real communica-

[3]"How Do You Get Employees to Read an Annual Report?" by Robert Newcomb and Marg Sammons, *Industrial Marketing*.

tions job if it followed the lead of the business world and produced a report using pictures and easily understood copy.

While working on a limited budget, the Los Angeles Police annually turn out a highly informative report which has done an excellent job both in building appreciation and support from Los Angeles citizens and in strengthening morale of members of the department.

The 32-page, one-color report contains a variety of information, mostly in picture-and-caption style. While it is impossible to cover all activities of the department each year, judicious planning makes it possible to build a complete story by concentrating on different activities each year. Thus, in about three issues a complete story can be unfolded with adequate attention to each phase of the department's activities.

The report gets widespread distribution throughout the Police Department, where it serves as an extension of the indoctrination given personnel when they first join the force. Distribution to the public includes those on a chamber of commerce list of prominent civic personalities; public relations firms and advertising agencies; all California legislators; heads of all city and state departments; colleges; cities and police departments around the country; and all schools in Los Angeles. This distribution is supplemented by giving the report to influential visitors to the police administration building, students who have assignments to write reports on the police department, and the press.

Interim Reports

Many companies supplement their annual reports to stockholders and the financial community by publication of special interim reports.

The most common interim report is the quarterly. The Borden Company, for example, publishes "Borden Quarterly Memo to Stockholders." This 6⅞- by 3¼-inch report has eight pages with reports on meetings, elections of officers, information on new products and facilities, and other developments since the last annual report.

General Motors publishes a "GM Stockholders' Quarterly"—a 16-page 7- by 9-inch report with both financial and general information. General Electric's quarterly report has eight 7½- by 9¾-inch pages with magazine-style presentation.

In addition to regular quarterly and annual reports, various companies issue special reports on events of spot interest such as the annual meeting, announcements of a new product line, opening of a new plant, and so forth.

Chapter 35

STATEMENT AND LETTER STUFFERS

CONSIDERABLE debate has raged over the value of direct mail pieces enclosed with nonpromotional mailings such as monthly statements and routine business correspondence. In the retail field, statement and letter stuffers have been widely accepted. But in other fields such as industrial and mail order, there are many who have serious doubts as to the value of such devices.

The bulk of the evidence, however, is that this inexpensive promotional device has more than just a little merit. A great many of those who argue against this device, it turns out, have either never tested stuffers or have gone no farther than to miniaturize some other type of promotion so it will fit an envelope.

Department Store Stuffers

Probably the strongest advocates of statement stuffers are the major department stores. While most smaller stores content themselves with using stuffers furnished by the manufacturers whose goods they sell, the larger stores usually create their own stuffers.

One of the finest store-produced stuffers is published monthly by Marshall Field & Company and enclosed with all statement mailings. Over the years, the Field stuffer format has changed and at this writing a 16 page, 3 by 6½ inch booklet is being used. Each issue includes a variety of items plus an order blank for mail orders. The booklet is full color throughout. Mail order catalog techniques are followed for displaying and describing the merchandise.

Jordan Marsh of Boston uses the packet technique for its statement stuffers. Sixteen 3⅛- by 5½-inch slips, printed in a single color on both sides, are inserted into a 3½- by 6-inch portfolio. The two-color portfolio is formed by folding a 1½-inch flap at the bottom of a 7- by 7½-inch sheet, which is given a second fold to 3½ by 6 inches.

Typical stuffers used by department stores, oil companies and travel companies.

Other Retail Stuffers

Many other stores create individual slips or small folders to accompany their statement mailings. These custom-designed pieces often accompany other stuffers prepared by manufacturers and imprinted with the store's name. While there is a great variance in sizes for stuffers, the majority is around 3 by 6 inches since this size is compatible with almost every type of statement envelope.

While both the format and subject matter of retail stuffers vary all over the landscape, the following stuffers are typical:

Carson Pirie Scott & Co. prepared a six-page 4¼- by 6¼-inch black-and-white folder to promote its women's raincoat specials. Five different coats were promoted, one to a page, with the sixth page used as an order blank.

R. H. Stearns used a 3¾- by 5½-inch single sheet stuffer to promote summer storage for furs. A cartoon with an Eskimo riding a flower-sniffing polar bear plus the heading, "Stearns for Summer Storage," was printed on one side and promotional copy on the reverse. The piece was in deep red ink on pink stock. Stearns regularly uses single-color printing on colored stock to give a change of pace to its custom stuffers.

Scott's Lawn Products are promoted in a series of 3- by 5¾-inch, four-page folders printed in green and black. The folders, which Scott supplies dealers, each concentrate on promotion of a single basic product, but additional Scott products receive mention. The order blank imprinted on the backs of the folders lists several Scott products.

Judy Bond women's fashions are promoted in a typical apparel stuffer. It is a six-page, 3- by 6-inch piece in full color, with one item of clothing featured on each page plus an order blank (with the store's name imprinted) on the back page.

Bloomcraft uses a single sheet 3⅜ by 5⅜ inches, full-color stuffer to promote its decorator pillows. An illustration on the front shows a model amidst 11 pillows. Each pillow is described in brief on the reverse side along with other order information and order blank with the individual store imprint.

Reefer-Galler is one of many manufacturers which uses reply post cards as stuffers. Reefer-Galler lists and illustrates nine household moth killers and push-button insect sprays on one side of the card which is printed in red and black. There is space for writing an order, and a store imprint. The address side is in traditional business reply format with the stores' names imprinted.

Crane's, plus most every personal stationery maker, converts its own products into envelope stuffers. A traditional format, for example, has promotional copy on the inside spread plus order blank and store imprint.

These and other retail statement stuffers are shown in the illustrations on the following pages.

Old Equity Life Insurance Co.

Among the most consistent users of stuffers are insurance companies. Almost every company in the field uses this promotional device along with their billing notices. And among insurance companies there is probably no stronger advocate of stuffers than William J. McKenna, vice president of Old Equity Life Insurance Co., Evanston, Illinois. In a magazine article[1], Mr. McKenna explained why:

"For every $1 we spent on printing inserts last year we got back $45.87 in annualized premiums on new business—not to count the lapse prevention and goodwill we built among our present policyowners.

"Our envelope stuffers have three major purposes:

1. To sell further insurance to present policyholders
2. To create a good image and build goodwill for Old Equity
3. To service and hold on to our customers

"We have developed four major types of stuffers to serve these purposes. They are:

1. A series of information cards
2. A quarterly magazine, *The Policyowner*
3. A miniature annual report
4. A series of lapse-prevention reminders

"The best source of new business for any company is from satisfied customers. Three times a year we enclose an information card with our premium notices. The information card might feature a general program review or a specific request for a policy, such as our hospital and surgical protection. We find that our return on these information cards averages 3 percent. In other words, for every 100,000 cards (which we enclose with our premium notice billing—at no extra postage!) we obtain 3,000 'hot' leads from our present policyowners.

"The card stimulates our policyowners to thinking about additional coverage, and the business reply card brings action. Our insurance counselors

[1]"Bill Inserts—How to Hitch-Hike Your Way to More Business and Good Will," by William J. McKenna. *The Reporter of Direct Mail Advertising.* May 1960.

have a very high closing ratio on these particular leads. Their average sales run about three for every five cards called on.

"Our information cards are always mailed with the spring, summer and autumn issues of *The Policyowner,* thus allowing us to run a companion article on the policies or services offered on the card.

"The quarterly magazine, *The Policyowner,* is our chief ambassador of goodwill to our policyowners. *The Policyowner* (4 pages, 5½ by 7 inches, two colors) keeps the individual informed of company policies and practices, explains new forms of coverage, reprints third-party endorsement of Old Equity, and provides public service features. Our annual report mailing accompanies the spring issue of *The Policyowner.*

"Since our policyowners may pay premiums on a monthly, quarterly, or yearly basis, the fastest way to handle the inserts is to place them in each billing. It means that monthly premium-payers receive more than one copy of *The Policyowner* and the current inserts. Contrary to the majority of thinking in the direct mail field, we have discovered there is no resentment on the part of the policyowner from this practice.

"Perhaps the greatest advantage to us as an insurance company in the use of enclosures is that it does help us prevent a loss of business from persons allowing their policies to lapse.

"Our most successful inserts have been simple 3½- by 7½-inch fliers, printed on only one side, that hit home to the policyowner the importance of his insurance protection. We use statistics on accidents and health levels, the listing of 'extras' in his policy with Old Equity, and the angle of security and peace of mind to keep the policyowner paying his premium."

Other insurance companies have also found stuffers valuable. The Mutual Life Insurance Company of New York uses a quarterly miniature (3½ by 5-inch) 12-page house organ, *MONY Topics.* Printed in two colors on coated stock, it includes features about the company, insurance in general, and such public service features as "Social Security and You" and "How to Keep From Growing Old."

John Hancock Mutual Life Insurance Company for many years converted its institutional magazine ads for use as premium notice stuffers. The John Hancock ads feature paintings of famous Americans and outstanding copy describing their contributions to our way of life. The full-page magazine ads run in full color but the 3½- by 6-inch stuffers are printed in black and white with the painting and headline from the ad plus the start of the copy on the face of the stuffer and the remainder of the copy and signature on the reverse side.

The Equitable Life Assurance Society of the U. S. frequently encloses 5½- by 10½-inch cards, folded to 3½ by 5½ inches, with its premium notices. These cards, printed in two colors on both sides, generally promote some special kind of insurance. One of the folds is a business reply card on which the policyowner can request additional information.

Illinois Bell Telephone Co.

Another group of consistent users of bill stuffers are the nation's telephone companies. Most often they use miniature external house organs and the best of the lot is Illinois Bell's *Telebriefs*.

Telebriefs is mailed monthly to each of the more than 2 million subscribers in the company's territory—and readership studies show well over 85% readership. Each issue consists of four-5⅞- by 6⅝-inch black-and-white pages in newspaper format. An amazing amount of material manages to fit into the small format. The average issue features more than 10 different editorial items and about 10 halftone and cartoon illustrations.

Any direct mail advertiser considering a miniature bill-stuffer house organ would do well to write for sample copies of *Telebriefs* to Illinois Bell Telephone Co., 208 West Washington Street, Chicago, Illinois 60606.

Exxon

Another user of a bill-stuffer house organ is Exxon, which publishes monthly issues of *Happy Motoring News*. This 6⅛- by 9½-inch, two-page, newspaper-style piece is folded to 3⅛ by 6⅛ inches and mailed to several million Exxon customers with their monthly invoices. Full color is used throughout the folder. Editorial content concentrates primarily on company news and industry developments, although occasional travel items are included.

Most other oil companies include stuffers of one kind or another with their bills. Among other items, stuffers frequently are used to merchandise advertising in other media—particularly advance promotion of television shows.

Mail Order Stuffers

Stuffers are frequently used by mail order sellers to promote additional products or services. American Marketing Services, for example, included two tag-along promotions with its regular mailings. A standardized 3½- by 8½-inch slip was used. The upper two-thirds illustrated and described the items while the lower one-third was an order coupon. Experience with this form of stuffer indicates no reduction in orders for the basic item being promoted, while it brings in a substantial quantity of multiple orders.

Other mail order companies use business reply card order forms for stuffer purposes. Still others use small-size folders for tag-along promotions.

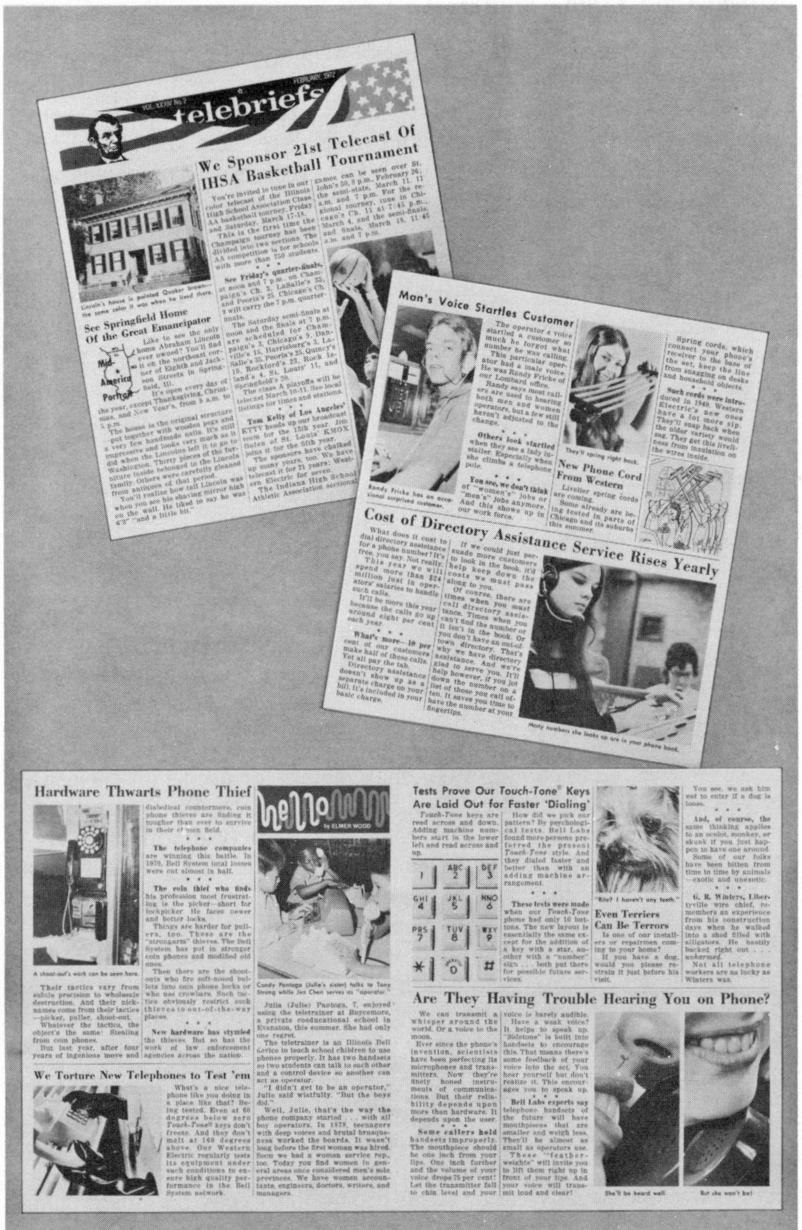

VOL. XXXIV No. 2 telebriefs FEBRUARY, 1972

We Sponsor 21st Telecast Of IHSA Basketball Tournament

You're invited to tune in our color telecast of the Illinois High School Association Class AA basketball tourney, Friday and Saturday, March 17-18.

This is the first time the Champaign tourney has been divided into two sections. The AA competition is for schools with more than 750 students.

* * *

See Friday's quarter-finals, at noon and 7 p.m. on Champaign's Ch. 3, LaSalle's 35, and Peoria's 25. Chicago's Ch. 9 will carry the 7 p.m. quarter-finals.

The Saturday semi-finals at noon and the finals at 7 p.m. are scheduled for Champaign's 3, Chicago's 9, Danville's 15, Harrisburg's 3, LaSalle's 35, Peoria's 25, Quincy's 10, Rockford's 23, Rock Island's 4, St. Louis' 11, and Springfield's 20.

The class A playoffs will be telecast March 10-11. See local listings for times and stations.

* * *

Tom Kelly of Los Angeles' KTTV heads up our broadcast team for the 13th year. Jim Bolen of St. Louis' KMOX joins it for the 5th year.

The sponsors have chalked up many years, too. We have telecast it for 21 years; Western Electric for seven.

The Indiana High School Athletic Association sectional games can be seen over St. John's 50, 8 p.m., February 26; the semi-state, March 11, 11 a.m. and 7 p.m. For the regional tourney, tune in Chicago's Ch. 11 at 7:45 p.m., March 4, and the semi-finals and finals, March 18, 11:45 a.m. and 7 p.m.

Lincoln's house is painted Quaker brown—the same color it was when he lived there.

See Springfield Home Of the Great Emancipator

Mid-America Portrait

Like to see the only home Abraham Lincoln ever owned? You'll find it on the northeast corner of Eighth and Jackson Streets in Springfield, Ill.

It's open every day of the year, except Thanksgiving, Christmas, and New Year's, from 9 a.m. to 5 p.m.

The house is the original structure—put together with wooden pegs and a very few handmade nails. It's still impressive and looks very much as it did when the Lincolns left it to go to Washington. Thirty pieces of the furniture inside belonged to the Lincoln family. Others were carefully gleaned from antiques of that period.

You'll realize how tall Lincoln was when you see his shaving mirror high on the wall. He liked to say he was 6'3" "and a little bit."

Man's Voice Startles Customer

The operator's voice startled a customer so much he forgot what number he was calling.

This particular operator had a male voice. He was Randy Fricke of our Lombard office.

Randy says most callers are used to hearing both men and women operators, but a few still haven't adjusted to the change.

* * *

Others look startled when they see a lady installer. Especially when she climbs a telephone pole.

* * *

You see, we don't think of "women's" jobs or "men's" jobs anymore. And this shows up in our work force.

Randy Fricke has an occasional surprised customer.

They'll spring right back.

New Phone Cord From Western

Livelier spring cords are coming.

Some already are being tested in parts of Chicago and its suburbs this summer.

Spring cords, which connect your phone's receiver to the base of the set, keep the line from snagging on desks and household objects.

* * *

Such cords were introduced in 1949. Western Electric's new ones have a lot more zip. They'll snap back when the older variety would sag. They get this liveliness from insulation on the wires inside.

Cost of Directory Assistance Service Rises Yearly

What does it cost to dial directory assistance for a phone number? It's free, you say. Not really.

This year we will spend more than $24 million just in operators' salaries to handle such calls.

It'll be more this year because the calls go up around eight per cent each year.

* * *

What's more—10 per cent of our customers make half of these calls. Yet all pay the tab.

Directory assistance doesn't show up as a separate charge on your bill. It's included in your basic charge.

If we could just persuade more customers to look in the book, it'd help keep down the costs we must pass along to you.

Of course, there are times when you must call directory assistance. Times when you can't find the number or it isn't in the book. Or you don't have an out-of-town directory. That's why we have directory assistance. And we're glad to serve you. It'll help however, if you jot down the number on a list of those you call often. It saves you time to have the number at your fingertips.

Many numbers she looks up are in your phone book.

Hardware Thwarts Phone Thief

A shoot-out's work can be seen here.

Their tactics vary from subtle precision to wholesale destruction. And their nicknames come from their tactics—picker, puller, shoot-out.

Whatever the tactics, the object's the same: Stealing from coin phones.

But last year, after four years of ingenious move and diabolical countermove, coin phone thieves are finding it tougher than ever to survive in their chosen field.

* * *

The telephone companies are winning this battle. In 1970, Bell System total losses were cut almost in half.

* * *

The coin thief who finds his profession most frustrating is the picker—short for lockpicker. He faces newer and better locks.

Things are harder for pullers, too. These are the "strongarm" thieves. The Bell System has put in stronger coin phones and modified old ones.

Then there are the shoot-outs who fire soft-nosed bullets into coin phone locks or who use crowbars. Such tactics obviously restrict such thieves to out-of-the-way places.

* * *

New hardware has stymied the thieves. But so has the work of law enforcement agencies across the nation.

We Torture New Telephones to Test 'em

What's a nice telephone like you doing in a place like that? Being tested. Even at 60 degrees below zero *Touch-Tone®* keys don't freeze. And they don't melt at 160 degrees above. Our Western Electric regularly tests its equipment under such conditions to ensure high quality performance in the Bell System network.

hello by ELMER WOOD

Candy Pantoga (Julie's sister) talks to Tony Strong while Jen Chen serves as "operator."

Julia (Julie) Pantoga, 7, enjoyed using the teletrainer at Roycemore, a private coeducational school in Evanston, this summer. She had only one regret.

The teletrainer is an Illinois Bell device to teach school children to use phones properly. It has two handsets so two students can talk to each other and a control device so another can act as operator.

"I didn't get to be an operator," Julie said wistfully. "But the boys did."

Well, Julie, that's the way the phone company started . . . with all boy operators. In 1878, teenagers with deep voices and brutal brusqueness worked the boards. It wasn't long before the first woman was hired. Soon we had a woman service rep., too. Today you find women in general areas once considered men's sole provinces. We have women accountants, engineers, doctors, writers, and managers.

Tests Prove Our Touch-Tone® Keys Are Laid Out for Faster 'Dialing'

Touch-Tone keys are read across and down. Adding machine numbers start in the lower left and read across and up.

How did we pick our pattern? By psychological tests. Bell Labs found more persons preferred the present *Touch-Tone* style. And they dialed faster and better than with an adding machine arrangement.

* * *

These tests were made when our *Touch-Tone* phone had only 10 buttons. The new layout is essentially the same except for the addition of a key with a star, another with a "number" sign . . . both put there for possible future services.

"Bite? I haven't any teeth."

Even Terriers Can Be Terrors

Is one of our installers or repairmen coming to your home?

If you have a dog, would you please restrain it just before his visit.

You see, we ask him not to enter if a dog is loose.

* * *

And, of course, the same thinking applies to an ocelot, monkey, or skunk if you just happen to have one around.

Some of our folks have been bitten from time to time by animals—exotic and unexotic.

* * *

G. R. Winters, Libertyville wire chief, remembers an experience from his construction days when he walked into a shed filled with alligators. He hastily backed right out . . . *unharmed*.

Not all telephone workers are as lucky as Winters was.

Are They Having Trouble Hearing You on Phone?

We can transmit a whisper around the world. Or a voice to the moon.

Ever since the phone's invention, scientists have been perfecting its microphones and transmitters. Now they're finely honed instruments of communications. But their reliability depends upon more than hardware. It depends upon the user.

* * *

Some callers hold handsets improperly. The mouthpiece should be one inch from your lips. One inch further and the volume of your voice drops 75 per cent! Let the transmitter fall to chin level and your voice is barely audible.

Have a weak voice? It helps to speak up. "Sidetone" is built into handsets to encourage this. That means there's some feedback of your voice into the set. You hear yourself but don't realize it. This encourages you to speak up.

* * *

Bell Labs experts say telephone handsets of the future will have mouthpieces that are smaller and weigh less. They'll be almost as small as operators use.

These "featherweights" will invite you to lift them right up in front of your lips. And your voice will transmit loud and clear!

She'll be heard well. But she won't be!

One of the most effective bill stuffers, with 85% readership, is Illinois Bell's Telebriefs.

Credit Card Billing Stuffers

One of the major group of users of statement stuffers consists of the credit card companies. Each month, most credit card billing statements are accompanied by a variety of different stuffers. Some promote the credit card itself and special services offered by the credit card company, but many of the credit card companies also offer outside advertisers a chance to ride along with their statements for a fee.

An example of a stuffer from a credit card company itself is the bi-monthly newsletter enclosed with BankAmericard statements from the First National Bank of Chicago. The four-page 7¼ by 9¾ inch newsletter is printed on lightweight stock. The first and fourth pages generally carry three columns of news-type items, while the inside spread is composed of six coupons offering special bargains when a BankAmericard is used at various merchants.

Because bankers usually are reluctant to provide special promotion opportunities to anyone who might compete with their business depositors, bank-oriented credit card statements are generally not open to mail order stuffers. However, the big national credit card organizations such as American Express, Diners Club and Carte Blanche actively promote the use of their statements as a vehicle for mail order promotions.

Promotional Envelopes

An especially effective promotional vehicle for use as an enclosure is the promotional envelope designed for use by the customer in paying his bill. Such envelopes come in a variety of different formats and any major envelope company will be happy to supply a variety of samples to illustrate the different kinds you might want to consider. Probably the most popular is the so-called "bangtail" envelope, which has a perforated second flap which can be removed before mailing and used as an order blank for the product or service being promoted. This second flap folds beneath the regular flap and usually contains a continuation of copy from the reverse side of the envelope. The front of such envelopes, of course, has the mailing address of the company doing the billing.

Another very effective promotional envelope for enclosures involves a special construction developed by U.S. Envelope Co. The reply envelope usually contains no promotional copy on either front or back but a message and/or order blank is mechanically inserted into the envelope so that the unit is delivered as one piece for inserting purposes.

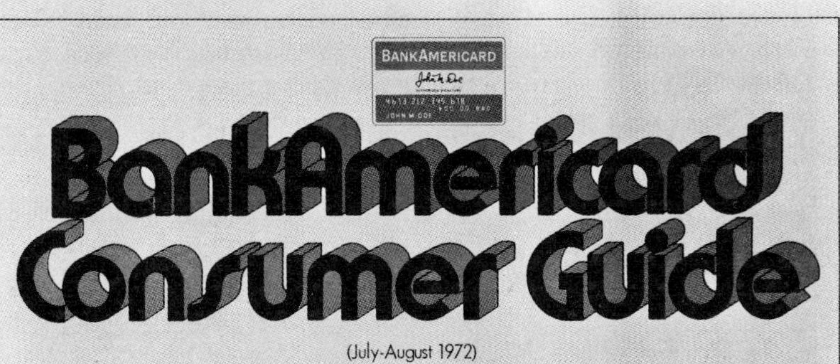

(July-August 1972)

WHAT'S NEW FOR YOU

Introducing the *BankAmericard* Check!

These are your personal checks from *BankAmericard* and you can use them for any amount up to $500, provided you do not exceed your available credit.

Write a *BankAmericard* Check to pay bills — insurance premiums, doctor and dentist bills, auto payments and repairs, rent or mortgage loan payments, taxes, furniture, house repairs and improvements, utility bills, etc.

You can also deposit up to $500 in your personal checking account by making your *BankAmericard* Check payable to your bank.

Going on vacation? Take *BankAmericard* Checks with you or cash one and take the money.

Here's how it works. You write a *BankAmericard* Check for an amount determined by your needs. Keep your credit limit and balance in mind so you don't write the check for more than your available credit.

The checks are charged to your account as a Cash Advance and returned to you with your monthly statement.

Send for your *BankAmericard* Checks by filling out the request form inside. The *BankAmericard* Check gives new meaning to the word convenience by allowing any bill to be charged to your account and by providing instant cash for your checking account.

Another New Service

You can now charge travelers cheques to your *BankAmericard* account. Check with your local *BankAmericard* bank for details.

CREDIT TIPS

Making installment payments on a car, furniture or even a home? Read this.

These installment contracts often have fairly stiff penalties or late charges of between 2% and 5% on payments received past due dates.

The best way to avoid these added costs is to pay on time, but emergencies, unexpected bills or inconvenient payments dates sometimes make this impossible.

In these cases, save on penalties and late charges by making your payments on time. Take advantage of the convenient Cash Advance feature of your *BankAmericard* or make your payment with a *BankAmericard* Check (see "What's New for You" for details).

INFORMATION PLEASE

When you sign a sales slip to charge merchandise or service on your *BankAmericard,* be sure to keep those white tissue copies the merchant gives you. Here's why.

What if you charge an item and later decide to return it? That little tissue copy is your proof of purchase when you return merchandise.

Keeping receipts serves as a handy budget reminder because you always know how much you have charged and what your balance is.

The most obvious reason for retaining tissue copies is to check the accuracy of your monthly statement by matching them against the hard copies *BankAmericard* sends you.

Have you ever forgotten what you charged by the time your monthly statement arrives? To avoid any confusion, make specific notations on your copy at the time you sign the sales slip. For instance, on airline receipts, note your destination.

When you pay your *BankAmericard* bill, include the large right-hand stub of the payment card with your check. We strongly recommend that you write your account number on your check to insure speed and accuracy in crediting your account.

An attractive example of a stuffer, which is also a newsletter, sent out by a credit card company.

Duplication Slips

Another type of enclosure is the "please excuse us if this is a duplicate mailing" slip which is used by mail order and fund raiser mailers when outside lists are utilized. Five examples of such slips are shown in the illustration on page 991.

Stuffers in Business and Industrial Mailings

The overall picture of the use of stuffers in mailings to businesses and manufacturers was summed up by the editors of *Industrial Marketing* ("Envelope Stuffers—Do They Produce Sales, or Other Values?" January 1961), after polling a panel of advertising and sales promotion men:

> "Practically all of the marketing, advertising and sales promotion men that we asked about this 'problem' agreed that you'll make few actual sales through the use of envelope stuffers. However, many of them felt that this type of promotion should not be abandoned because it might have considerable hard-to-measure promotional value . . .
>
> "If you were to predicate the use of envelope stuffers on the record of actual sales results by industrial companies or distributors, your best move would be to forget about them. If, however, you wish 'to keep your name before your customers,' or to announce a new product line or unusual application in the hope of provoking interest or additional inquiries, envelope stuffers may be an economical way to do it."

American Hospital Supply Corp.

One reader responding to the *Industrial Marketing* article, however, provided clear-cut evidence that stuffers, properly used, do have a place as a *sales* tool in business and industrial sales promotion. Warren F. Holl, merchandising manager of American Hospital Supply Corp., Evanston, Illinois, told of a two-year study on stuffers by his company[2]:

> "Among various approaches tried during our survey to find what type of envelope stuffer was best were: offering to send the customer information, reducing the price, and offering free goods. We tried these approaches both on equipment items and consumable items. We found only one really successful approach and have been concentrating on it. Each month we put out an envelope stuffer featuring a consumable or repeat item, and each month we offer free samples.
>
> "Prior (to the adoption of the selected approach) we used envelope stuffers from various manufacturers from whom we purchase products for resale, but each supplier used a different style of circular so that our program had no continuity. Therefore, we began printing our own stuffers

---

[2] "Reader Tells of Recent Successes With Envelope Stuffer Technique." Letters to the Editor, *Industrial Marketing,* June 1961.

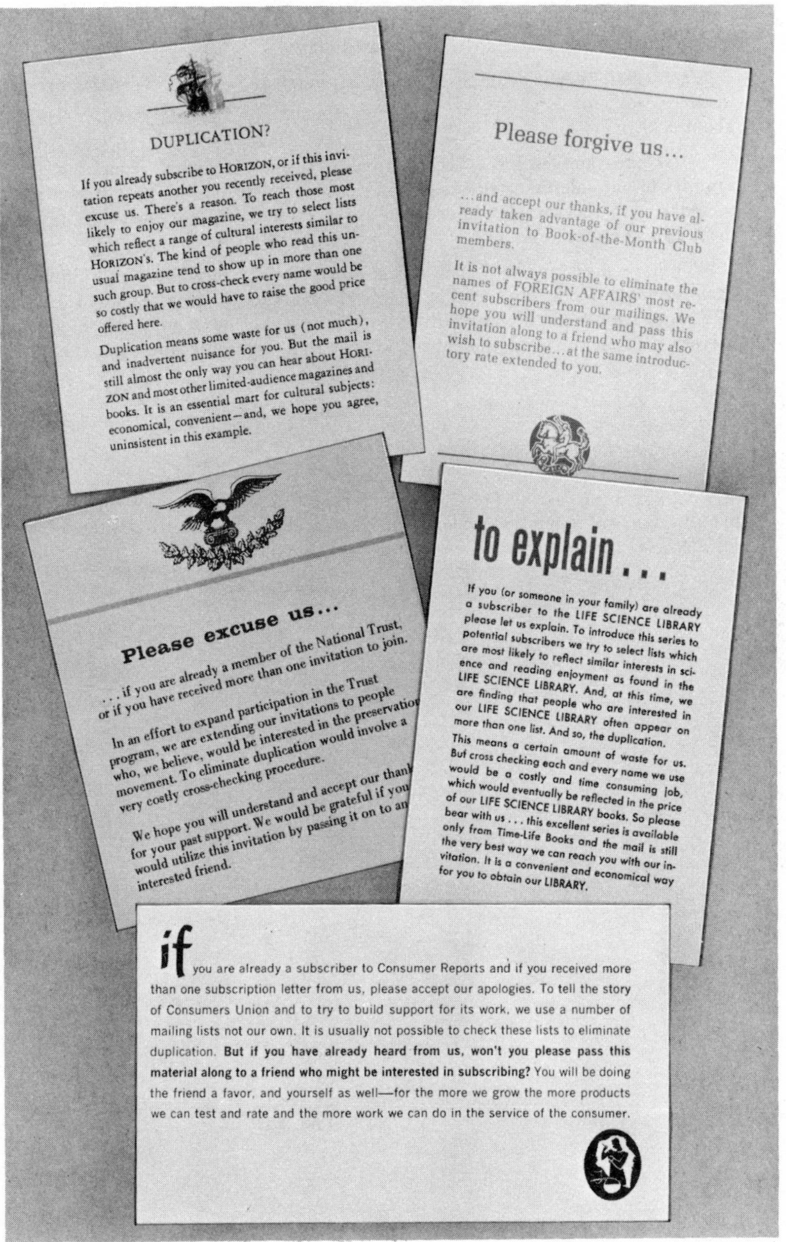

DUPLICATION?

If you already subscribe to HORIZON, or if this invitation repeats another you recently received, please excuse us. There's a reason. To reach those most likely to enjoy our magazine, we try to select lists which reflect a range of cultural interests similar to HORIZON's. The kind of people who read this unusual magazine tend to show up in more than one such group. But to cross-check every name would be so costly that we would have to raise the good price offered here.

Duplication means some waste for us (not much), and inadvertent nuisance for you. But the mail is still almost the only way you can hear about HORIZON and most other limited-audience magazines and books. It is an essential mart for cultural subjects: economical, convenient—and, we hope you agree, uninsistent in this example.

Please forgive us...

...and accept our thanks, if you have already taken advantage of our previous invitation to Book-of-the-Month Club members.

It is not always possible to eliminate the names of FOREIGN AFFAIRS' most recent subscribers from our mailings. We hope you will understand and pass this invitation along to a friend who may also wish to subscribe...at the same introductory rate extended to you.

Please excuse us...

. . . if you are already a member of the National Trust, or if you have received more than one invitation to join.

In an effort to expand participation in the Trust program, we are extending our invitations to people who, we believe, would be interested in the preservatio movement. To eliminate duplication would involve a very costly cross-checking procedure.

We hope you will understand and accept our thank for your past support. We would be grateful if you would utilize this invitation by passing it on to an interested friend.

to explain . . .

If you (or someone in your family) are already a subscriber to the LIFE SCIENCE LIBRARY please let us explain. To introduce this series to potential subscribers we try to select lists which are most likely to reflect similar interests in science and reading enjoyment as found in the LIFE SCIENCE LIBRARY. And, at this time, we are finding that people who are interested in our LIFE SCIENCE LIBRARY often appear on more than one list. And so, the duplication.

This means a certain amount of waste for us. But cross checking each and every name we use would be a costly and time consuming job, which would eventually be reflected in the price of our LIFE SCIENCE LIBRARY books. So please bear with us . . . this excellent series is available only from Time-Life Books and the mail is still the very best way we can reach you with our invitation. It is a convenient and economical way for you to obtain our LIBRARY.

if you are already a subscriber to Consumer Reports and if you received more than one subscription letter from us, please accept our apologies. To tell the story of Consumers Union and to try to build support for its work, we use a number of mailing lists not our own. It is usually not possible to check these lists to eliminate duplication. **But if you have already heard from us, won't you please pass this material along to a friend who might be interested in subscribing?** You will be doing the friend a favor, and yourself as well—for the more we grow the more products we can test and rate and the more work we can do in the service of the consumer.

Large mailers utilize slips like the above to avoid irritating their potential customers.

so that there is continuity of layout, size, etc. Each offers free samples or the opportunity to place an order immediately.

"Each mail department uses these stuffers daily with all statements, invoices, etc., for a period of a month. We average 700 returns, which is about 5%.

"After the samples have been mailed, we send the card requesting the samples to our salesman who calls on the account. He follows up our mailing to make sure the samples have been received and the customer has given them full consideration.

"We have measured our sales and find that in the three months following each promotion our sales on the featured item go up from 20% to 50%. We can attribute the increase to this program, as we have purposely avoided all other promotions on these products so that we could measure results."

Chapter 36

SURVEYS AND QUESTIONNAIRES

ONE of the most important applications of direct mail is to obtain research information through the use of questionnaires. Not only do many research organizations use this technique, but it is the survey mechanism most often used directly by advertisers.

There is nothing really complicated about preparing direct mail surveys. Good common sense and application of proved direct mail principles are the primary ingredients. Nevertheless, a great many users of this research technique fail miserably in their efforts.

Preparing the Questionnaire

Probably the greatest failing of those who try to do research by mail comes in the preparation of the questionnaire itself. Since there will be no researcher present to help the respondent interpret the questions, the copy must be kept simple and easily understandable. And, of special importance, the questions should be made easy to answer.

Far too often, questions are framed in such a way that they cannot be answered in a straightforward way. In most cases multiple choice type of questions are best—but only when all of the possible answers are included among the choices. If there is any question, it is usually best to include an "other" choice, with a blank in which the respondent can fill in his alternate answer.

Another common failing of direct mail research is the tendency to ask leading questions which are designed to affirm some preconceived conclusion. This may be helpful for some promotion purpose, but it is seldom honest research.

Make It Look Simple

Another common failing of much direct mail research is that the questionnaires look too complicated and time-consuming. In addition to cutting down on the number of returns, there is an always-present danger that the bulk of the returns will come from "research bugs" who take delight in answering any and every questionnaire they come across. The danger is that such respondents will not represent a true cross section and thus your replies will be heavily weighted in one direction.

Perhaps the ideal questionnaire is one that contains just one short question which can be answered by simply checking "yes" or "no." From a practical standpoint, however, such questionnaires seldom fit the research needs. But every effort to make the questionnaire *look* easy to answer will pay off in better returns.

Make It Look Important

In addition to keeping your questionnaire easy to answer, it should look "important," as if the respondent will be performing a worthwhile service if he takes time to answer it.

One business publication sent a double post card questionnaire to a large list and received a wholly inadequate 7½% return. Then an expert research organization came into the picture and suggested the addition of three elements which created an atmosphere of importance:

1. An introductory question on a subject of little interest to the magazine but of great interest to the people being asked to respond.
2. A reply envelope which helped to imply that the returns were considered of greater importance, and offered more anonymity to the replies.
3. A shiny new quarter with each questionnaire.

The revised questionnaire was mailed to a random sample of the original large list and drew a 46% return from the same respondents who had paid so little attention to the original "unimportant" questionnaire.

In another test, a mailer drew less than 20% return on a mimeographed questionnaire to a select audience. So the next time around he made two basic changes:

1. He printed the questionnaire rather than mimeographing it.
2. He included a few simple line drawings from a stock art service.

The same type of questions were asked and the questionnaires were sent to the identical audience which had yielded less than a 20% response a short time before. This time, with the more impressive questionnaire, a 68% response was received.

12-Point Law of High Returns

Dr. Paul L. Erdos of Erdos and Morgan Research Service, in the article "How to Get Higher Returns from Your Mail Surveys" *(Printer's Ink),* suggests there are 12 basic factors in building high returns into a survey mailing:

1. *Prestige of organization doing survey.* If you mail a questionnaire to architects, it is desirable, in the interest of high returns, to do so in the name of or at least in cooperation with a recognized association of architects, such as the American Institute of Architects. Similarly, subscribers to *The Wall Street Journal* will answer in greater numbers if the request comes from the publication itself.

   On occasions we have tested returns from subscribers to a prestige publication when surveyed by mail from the publication as against mail from a "blind" or actual research house. We found a 10% to 20% difference in returns in favor of the use of the publication's own stationery. Frequently publications want to be able to state that an independent organization has had exclusive control of the questionnaires. In order to do so while still utilizing the prestige of the publication to get higher returns, the reply envelope may be addressed to the name of the publication, market research department, at the address of the research house.

2. *Interest respondents have in subject of survey.* Obviously, if you were to send a questionnaire about shoe polish to an engineer, he would not be too interested. He is much more likely to be interested in answering a survey on engineering problems.

   The interest factor very often is a sample-distortion problem, as people who are most interested in a given subject are most likely to answer. Motorboat owners will be more likely to answer motorboat surveys than nonowners, therefore special precautions must be taken to get answers from the nonowner group or to evaluate ownership questions properly. However, our problem right now is not the bias factor but getting higher returns. We have often found that the addition of a question or a set of questions which while actually of no interest to the client were of great interest to the respondent, successfully beefed up an otherwise boring questionnaire and resulted in much better returns.

   The subscriber to a magazine who is less than fascinated by the prospect of answering two pages of questions on the ownership of household products might more readily be persuaded to start working on the questionnaire if the first question asks for suggestions for articles the editors could include in the magazine to make it more interesting *to him.* Of course, it must be weighed in each case whether such additions might bias answers to subsequent questions. It is a general rule, though, to try to have a subject that will interest the respondent.

Perhaps best results can be expected when surveying people about the great interest in their lives. In a survey done among 3,500 subscribers to *Road & Track,* a sports-car magazine, a two-page questionnaire on sports cars was mailed. Results: 70% of them replied and 5% more sent in questionnaires too late to be included in the tabulations. A single mailing, without inducement or premium, did it.

3. *The questionnaire should be easy to read,* from the point of view of copy and of layout. The phrasing of questions obviously is important, as in all research, but the paper, layout, and type are perhaps even more important as far as high returns are concerned. If a questionnaire *looks* difficult it will often end in the wastebasket before the potential respondent has had a chance to find out that it is not difficult.

   The type should not be too small for reading or too large to give an airy, uncrowded page. The layout should get all possible white space, because the more print there is on a page, the more difficult it seems to wade through it. We found that an easy-looking questionnaire is much more important for good returns than a "pretty" one. We found that illustrations (except where needed for better understanding) very seldom help returns, especially when they take up a lot of space.

4. *The questionnaire should not be too long.* Too many executives (especially if they are not research men) feel that since all that money is being spent, they should find out everything in one survey. But there is an inverse ratio between the length of the questionnaire and the percentage of returns. There is only so much information you can get at one time. We even found that the size of the paper we print the questions on makes a difference: We get better returns on note-paper size questionnaires than on letter-size sheets. Of course, they cannot be illegible or crowded-looking.

   We think (although we never tested this specifically) that a four-page, letter-size questionnaire would pull better than the same copy in a 12-page, smaller-size booklet. One more thing: If you have a lot of questions, either don't number them or else divide the questionnaire into sections and start numbering again with each section. When the busy executive receives a questionnaire that ends with question 58(c) he may very well decide to throw it away.

5. *Letter and questionnaire should convince the respondent* that either: (a) he is a very important person, therefore the survey will be of little value without his answer; or that (b) this is a very important survey, therefore he should be flattered by having a chance to take part in it. We have found that we can often help returns by giving titles to our questionnaires. Such a title as "Survey Among Leading Industrialists" helps when sending a questionnaire to upper-echelon people in industry.

6. *The letter should be short*—very few people bother reading long letters enclosed with questionnaires—and it should emphasize that it takes but a short time to answer the few simple questions.

7. *The letter should read and look like a personal letter.* We always personalize it with at least a one-line matched fill-in, use ink-blue printing for signatures, and write it in a person-to-person tone.

8. *The letter should tell why the survey will benefit the recipient.* If there is obviously no such benefit, don't try to fool him—you are better off if you just ask the respondent's help as a favor. The letter should *not* emphasize that the survey will be a wonderful promotional gimmick to get lots more advertising for a publication, or that it will enable a manufacturer to increase his profits. This kind of letter promptly raises this question in the respondent's mind: "What do *I* get out of this windfall?"

9. *The letter should assure the respondent* that all information will be handled confidentially, or assure him of anonymity if questionnaires are not keyed.

10. *A report should be offered* to repliers, many of whom will be interested in how their fellow respondents are thinking on the same subjects. They should always be given the choice either to write their names and addresses on the questionnaire or to send in their requests on separate letterheads or cards, so their answers will remain confidential. These offers often help returns.

11. *The reply envelope should be stamped and processed*—it looks less like a commercial mail-out piece than a printed business-reply envelope does, and many people dislike to throw away "money," even if it is only a stamp. It should be stated in the letter that a stamped reply envelope is enclosed. This is assurance that it will not take any time or cost any money to mail back the filled-in questionnaire.

12. *It often helps returns to use airmail postage:* It adds urgency and importance to the mailing. However you must be careful *not* to put an airmail stamp on outgoing or reply envelopes going to nearby places. In such cases the feeling of urgency is replaced by one of futility and inefficiency. Being in New York, we often send our surveys airmail (and enclose airmail reply envelopes) either south and west of Pennsylvania or west of the Mississippi. But in any case we make sure no respondent will have to feel foolish mailing a questionnaire back to us from the Empire State Building (four blocks away) "by air."

It also helps to ask respondents in the letter (in a very polite way) for a prompt answer. If they do not answer soon they may not respond at all. An actual deadline is, however, a somewhat double-edged weapon. If speed is actually of paramount importance it will get the bulk of your returns in sooner than normal. However, you will probably lose some returns from those who discard it entirely because they were too busy when it first came.

Use of Premiums

Many different kinds of premiums have been used to boost returns in direct mail surveys. Probably the two most frequently used items are money and ballpoint pens. Use of money, while probably the most simple of all premiums, creates a basic problem. If you imply that the money represents the entire worth of the respondent answers, you are likely to insult him (unless, of course, you are rich enough to enclose $100 bills with your questionnaires). A typical handling of this problem was this postscript in a survey conducted by Erdos and Morgan for Associated Business Publications:

> P.S. The enclosed brand-new dollar bill, while not intended as reimbursement for your valuable time, is sent along as a token of appreciation for your kind cooperation. You might want to give it to a favorite charity, or perhaps a favorite youngster.

Test after test has proved that premiums do increase returns—often by large percentages. A Marsteller Inc. survey of oil field equipment and service companies, for example, made a split test using the same letter and questionnaire, but enclosing a new 25-cent piece in the second set of mailings (and adding a P.S. on the letter explaining that the quarter was *not* sent as a means of paying the respondent for his time). The returns:

Letter and Questionnaire Only	20.2%
Letter, Questionnaire, and Quarter	52.1%

A survey conducted for *House & Home* involved 3,752 questionnaires directed at builders, split 50-50 with the first half receiving no premium and the second half receiving a quarter. In this case the mailings with the quarters pulled 56%, while the non-premium mailing drew only 34%. An almost identical result was shown in a split mailing test of questionnaires sent to business and professional men as part of a readership survey. This time 58% responded to the mailings which included quarters; only 35% to the non-premium mailings.

Three-Way Test

An even more conclusive test was conducted for the Martin K. Speckter Agency by Erdos and Morgan Research Service. It was described in *Printers' Ink* in the article "Successful Mail Surveys: High Returns and How to Get Them," by Dr. Paul L. Erdos:

> The Martin K. Speckter Agency wanted to check the penetration of various publicity and slogans aimed at advertising executives by a media client. Advertising men are tough to survey: those in high positions and working for large agencies or companies get bombarded by more questionnaires than most other groups.
>
> Because we felt it was important to get at least a 50% return, we suggested a pilot study to establish the method to be used. We took a random sample of 600 names from the total list of advertising executives to be surveyed. We divided this list into three random groups of 200. Each group received the same one-page, two-side questionnaire with a letter and a reply envelope. The first group received no premium, the second group received a new 25-cent coin, the third group a new $1 bill. On the second

mailing we sent a $1 bill to those who received no premium the first time and no premium to those who received one before. We sent this followup mailing to every second non-replier and weighted their answers by a factor of two. Airmail was used both ways south and west of Pennsylvania. Here is what we found:

	GROUP 1	GROUP 2	GROUP 3
First mailing (Nov. 16)			
Premium	None	25 cents	$1
Returns (% of total mailing)	23%	40%	54%
Second mailing (Dec. 7)			
(To every second non-replier)			
Premium	$1	None	None
Returns (weighted)	27%	3%	6%
Total returns (weighted)	50%	43%	50%
Cost of premium	$77	$50	$200

Money vs. Merchandise Premiums

On the basis of this and many other tests his organization has conducted, Dr. Erdos concludes: "We have found that of all possible premiums, coins or $1 bills are most advisable in many cases. We also found that a shiny new quarter or a crisp new $1 bill are better for our purpose than used money."

However, there are many cases where merchandise premiums are much more practical than using money. In this same article, Dr. Erdos offers four important considerations for choosing a premium:

1. It should be something the prospective respondent will find desirable. Obviously you will not gain many extra returns by sending potholders to Wall Street executives or a fancy set of stock market charts to housewives.
2. It should be something that does not introduce bias. If you offer 24-inch shillalahs, you may run into the problem of having your sample overweighted with returns from Gaelic midgets. A premium should be the kind of thing everybody in a given universe could be interested in.
3. It should be small and light enough to be easily mailed—shillalahs of any length are out for this reason, too.

4. It should not be too expensive. There are two ways of using premiums: either as inducement to answer, accompanying the questionnaire, or as a reward to respondents only.

Showmanship Approach

Several researchers have used a favorite direct mail showmanship technique to combine both of the ways of using premiums which Dr. Erdos mentions. This is to send half of "a pair" along with the questionnaire and offer to send the other half when the completed questionnaire has been received. Cuff links, earrings, salt and pepper shakers, and take-apart toys are favorite items to use for such mailings.

Advance Buildups

Another popular technique for boosting survey response is to send an advance notice of a survey about to be conducted. Post cards are the favorite device for this approach. *Time,* for example, sent a post card with this message:

> You are one of a representative group of Time subscribers whom we are asking to take part in a special survey. In a few days you will receive an envelope from Time containing a simple keyed questionnaire. It will take less than 10 minutes to fill out—and your answers will be very valuable to us. I hope we can count on your cooperation.

The mailing which contained the questionnaire was imprinted: *"This is the survey we wrote you about."*

Followup Mailings

Post cards are also used to remind those receiving a survey mailing that the time has come to return their questionnaires. Others prefer simply to wait a reasonable time and then send all nonrespondents a second, third, and sometimes even a fourth copy of the original questionnaire. Still others use telegrams or phone calls for followups.

Preparing the Copy

The handling of the copy in both your covering letter and the questionnaire can play a major role in determining the percentage of response you can expect.

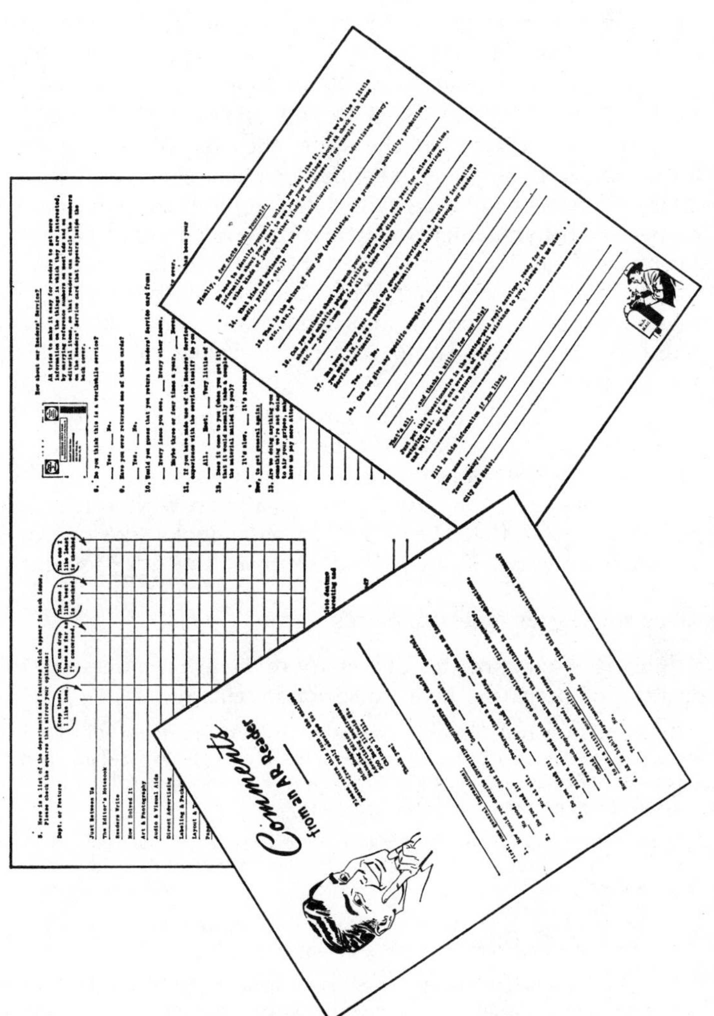

A typical questionnaire sent out by a magazine to ascertain its readers' interests and opinions.

In a DMMA "Research Bulletin," Phil Ross of Philip I. Ross Company, New York agency, makes these observations[1]:

> "Many considerations affect the rate of reply. Perhaps most important of all is the factor which also seems to be of first importance in gaining high readership for a direct mail advertisement. This factor is interest. If people are interested in you and your product, they will read your advertisement, and they will reply to your questionnaire.
>
> "It follows, then, that the style, the quality, the interest-arousing 'feel' of your questionnaire makes a great difference one way or another. After all, people read mail because of personal involvement, which simply means that the mere problem of disposing of the letter, or the folder, or card, involves the recipient physically and mentally. He has to make a decision about it, and it may well seem like an easy out for him to simply do what he is asked to do—answer the questions.
>
> "The first hurdle in a questionnaire is probably either the first question or perhaps the first paragraph of the accompanying letter. This is the point at which you either get him or lose him. It seems that a letter is a must with a questionnaire; it seems that the letter, or what looks like one, will be most effective if it is separate from the questionnaire."

Ten Tips for Better Questionnaires

Dr. John R. Young, of the University of Houston, offers the following tips for preparing better questionnaires:

1. *Be Brief.* In a typical survey, we asked only 10 questions, all of which were placed in two columns on one side of an 8½- by 11-inch sheet of paper. Judicious use of white space was also incorporated in order to avoid the appearance of a crowded page.
2. *Make Answering Easy.* It was not necessary for respondents to write answers to questions. Only check marks or letter designations were necessary.
3. *Avoid Ranking.* Too many mail surveys ask respondents to rank as many as 10 or 15 items "in order of importance."
4. *Use Special Interest Questions.* Several questions of particular interest to respondents should also be useful to the surveyor, but they can be included even if of marginal value.
5. *Avoid Confidential Areas.* Instead of asking for the amount of advertising expenditures, include a listing of dollar classifications, and ask respondents to check the one in which their expenditures fall.

---

[1]Research Bulletin. Vol. I No. 5, April 1960. Issued by the Direct Mail/Marketing Association, 6 E. 43rd St., New York, New York 10017.

6. *Don't Use Technical Talk.* Define those terms which are likely to be interpreted differently by respondents.
7. *Include Cover Letter.* The letter should be brief, friendly, and personalized. The letter should explain the purposes of the study and should stress reasons why the recipient (not the surveyor) should be interested in the study.
8. *Offer Benefits.* If information sought is of interest to those surveyed (which is generally true), promise a summary of findings, and by all means live up to this promise as soon as possible.
9. *Protect Your Sources.* Assure the respondent that neither his name nor information he provides will appear in any published statement of findings.
10. *Provide a Return Envelope.* Some researchers believe that the stamp is better than business reply imprints.

Aided Recall

An often effective technique in research by mail is to use aided recall techniques. A typical use of this technique was described by James W. Brown, of Detroit Diesel Engine Division, General Motors Corp., in an *Industrial Marketing* article, "What Do Your Customers Read?":

> "The survey we conducted was of the 'aided recall' type. The survey consisted of an 8½- by 11-inch folder with an addressed 'personalized' letter on the first page and with miniature reproductions of magazine covers on the inside. In the letter we asked the recipient to place an X in a small box adjacent to the magazine or magazines he reads regularly and to circle the box beneath the magazine for which he has a special preference or in which he 'would be most likely to read our advertising.'
>
> "It was sent out to 5,571 buyers of GM diesel engines or equipment powered with a GM diesel engine. Surveys returned and tabulated came to 2,094—a 37.6% overall return."

For Continuing Reference

If you plan to make extensive use of mail surveys, you will want to obtain a copy of "Professional Mail Surveys" by Paul L. Erdos. This 1970 book from McGraw-Hill, Inc. is by far the most valuable reference work on the subject ever prepared. It illustrates sample questionnaires, letters, instruction sheets and cost-estimating forms and has a particularly helpful 56-point summary of standards for good surveys.

Chapter 37

OTHER FORMATS

IN addition to the more common direct mail formats which have wide application, there is a large number of more specialized formats. While it is impractical to describe the majority of these in any detail, there are some which deserve special consideration.

Many of these specialized formats are primarily the tools of the sales promotion and public relations men and are covered in great detail in two previous handbooks published by The Dartnell Corporation—*Sales Promotion Handbook,* edited by Ovid Riso, and *Public Relations Handbook,* by Richard W. Darrow, Dan J. Forrestal and Hill & Knowlton.

Publicity Releases

While the subject of publicity releases is covered in great detail in Dartnell's *Public Relations Handbook,* this represents a highly important direct mail format and deserves special mention here.

There is little variety in press release formats—and indeed there should not be. The standard format is to mimeograph or print typewritten copy on one side only of white 8½- by 11-inch sheets of paper. The heading should contain the name, address, and phone number of the organization or individual sending the release; a person who can be contacted for additional information; the date of the mailing; and the date upon which the information can be published (or "For Immediate Release" if it can be published as soon as received). Copy should always be double-spaced and there should be ample margins so that an editor using the release can mark desired changes and instructions to the typesetter.

It is helpful to suggest a headline for the release—something which sums up the contents. By all means allow enough space at the top of the release (below your heading) so the editor can add his own headline.

Preparing Better Releases

Some years ago, the author conducted a survey of over 300 editors of business publications to determine just what they preferred in press releases[1]. From that survey came the following tips for better releases:

DO'S

...mark your release with date of issue and release date.

...use standard 8½- by 11-inch sheets for your releases—smaller or larger sizes are a headache for an editor.

...double space all releases.

...leave room at the top of the first page for editor's use.

...leave margins around release copy for editing.

...use only one side of paper.

...give a source for additional information (name, address, phone number), and make sure he knows the score—is not just an executive who has to check with someone else to find the answers.

...give complete information about the subject of the release—including what it is, who makes it, where it can be obtained, price, specific applications, advantages, how it is different from previous models, etc.

...include a brief summary of long releases.

...remember that an editor is a busy person.

...give full address of the firm involved and make sure it isn't buried in the release.

...make sure that your release is really *news*—not just a rehash of something you've sent the editor before.

...get the release right the first time. If it is necessary to send a correction —and this should be limited as much as possible—send an entire new release, with any changes clearly indicated.

...avoid superlatives. If they are warranted, the editor will add them.

...keep your releases to the minimum length necessary to present the facts of interest to the editor.

...know the subject about which you are writing—particularly its applications in the publication's field of coverage.

...keep your mailing list up to date. You are not going to be on the best side of an editor when your releases are addressed to one of his predecessors—particularly one who may have left 10 or 20 years before (and this is actually being done).

...include a copy of literature with all releases which mention or describe literature.

---

[1] "Do's and Don'ts for Better Press Releases," by Dick Hodgson. *Advertising Requirements.*

DO'S

...consider the deadlines of weekly and monthly magazines and see that they get releases far enough in advance to reasonably compete with newspapers.

...take an editor's name off your mailing list when he requests it.

...give background information when necessary to amplify a release.

...keep a tab on your releases by checking published versions against the original release. This should provide a good guide to the acceptability of your material.

...familiarize yourself with the editorial closing dates of publications and meet these deadlines. Otherwise, don't expect your material to be used.

...send your releases to the editor, not to the advertising director, publisher, etc. As Al Hattal, managing editor of *Geyer's Topics,* put it, "The padded sledgehammer is not a good tool for cementing good relations with editors."

...when making a personnel change announcement, lead off with the name of the person involved, not the name of the one making the announcement.

...have something to say! The simple desire to "get in the paper" is not enough.

...follow *news* style in all releases.

...remember that it is an editor's prerogative to arrive at a different evaluation or interpretation than your own.

...remember that just *one* attempt to "pull the wool" over an editor's eyes will make him skeptical of all of your releases for a long time.

...*completely* identify everyone mentioned in releases.

...if you send an electro, always enclose a proof and indicate what release it illustrates. In the majority of cases, however, you will be better off to forget about the electro—unless you know the editor uses them.

...avoid dating your releases ("Today, John Doe announced," or "Last week, the Jones Co. . . .") when sending to monthly magazines.

...title your releases for quick identification.

...be prepared to give prompt attention to requests for additional information, special photographs, etc.

...write the best possible release. Don't consider the job as something of secondary value. If you want publicity, you have to "pay" for it in your best release writing effort.

DON'TS

...use all caps anywhere in a release—not even for the trade name of your product.

...send carbon copies.

...send hectograph releases unless you are sure that your machine will turn out copies which are as clear as the original typing.

DON'TS

. . . use onionskin paper for releases.

. . . ask that the editor send you tearsheets if the material is used. If it is the publication's policy, you will get them anyway.

. . . use highly technical language unless your release goes only to technical publications.

. . . try to get too much into a single release. If you have several subjects, send separate releases.

. . . try to get tricky in your releases—stick to the facts and present them clearly.

. . . give a far-in-advance release date and expect the editor to hold your material until that date. If you want to brief editors in advance of a certain event, send something that is strictly a briefing . . . and then follow up with the release itself, closer to release time.

. . . expect the editor to use your releases just because you are an advertiser or a potential advertiser. Nothing will alienate an editor quicker than this kind of pressure.

. . . call or write the editor to find out when and if he is going to use a stock release you sent out.

. . . expect the editor to notify you if he plans to use your release.

. . . overuse trade names. Once or twice in the average release is probably enough.

. . . expect the editor to use your release just as you send it. That is why they call him an "editor."

. . . use press releases in lieu of advertising. If this is the case, it is usually obvious to the editor and your release will get a quick rejection.

. . . try to pass off something as an "exclusive" if it isn't. If the editor ever gets caught on this one, you have "had it!"

. . . try to inject the president of the firm into all of your releases—only those which are about him.

. . . bury the principal subject in the body of the release. Get it up front where it belongs!

. . . expect the editor to prepare his material from catalog sheets alone. Send the catalog sheets, but attach them to a press release.

. . . take pot shots at competitors in releases.

. . . try to include everything in the first paragraph.

. . . try to pass off the same releases to business publications, consumer magazines, and newspapers.

. . . release a story to a favored publication at one time and then send a general release to competing publications at a later date. If it is an "exclusive," keep it that way!

. . . accumulate several different stories and fling them at the publication for release in one issue.

DON'TS

... release news *after* it has appeared in your advertising.

... claim that your particular brand is "the best made" or better than someone else's—just admit that it is good.

... include a return post card with your releases, expecting the editor to commit himself to use of your material in a particular issue.

... expect the editor to be able to recall—or even see—every release received by his publication.

... invite inquiries for more information unless you are fully prepared to provide it promptly.

... accuse an editor of being unfair or negligent if he does not use your release; and don't remind him that he has used "less important" items on competitors.

... use the overworked (and grammatically incorrect) phrase, "new innovation," to describe a mediocre product change.

... insist on specific length of item to be published, particular wording, etc. This is one of the surest ways to assure non-use by the editor.

... *tell* the editor that his readers will be interested in your story. If they will, no one knows better than the editor, who is paid to know his audience.

... try to send a release a week, or meet a similar schedule. Wait until you really have something important to say.

... send additional copies of a release just because the editor did not use the first one.

... send mats—very few editors will go to the trouble and expense to have them cast for printing.

... complain if you are charged for making a cut to illustrate a new product release. While this is a standard practice with only a limited number of magazines, you will have to accept it if you want to reach their audiences.

... ask to check galley or page proofs on a story.

Photo Releases

Just as there are standardized formats for press releases, there are basic requirements for photo releases. In the majority of cases, photo releases accompany press releases, and this leads to one of the major mistakes committed by mailers of such material. Assuming that the press releases make the subject matter of the photo releases perfectly clear, too many publicity people just enclose unidentified photos with their press releases.

In all cases, each photo should have an individual caption. The best method is to mimeograph or print captions on white paper and then attach them by rubber cement to each photo. An excellent idea is to use perforated paper so the caption can be quickly and easily removed from the photo without chance of damage. The caption can also be "printed" on the back of the photo, but most editors consider this inferior to captions attached on separate sheets. However, it is always worthwhile to supplement the separate caption with some kind of matching information on the back of the photo. This is particularly important when photos of individuals are sent since editors receive hundreds of such photos for each issue and there is always a chance the photos will get mixed up after the separate caption has been removed.

The survey of business paper editors brought forth some additional "do's and don'ts" for handling photo releases:

DO'S

...caption your photographs, regardless of whether or not they are accompanied by a press release.

...hire a good photographer.

...leave a white border around your photos so that the editor can use it for instructions to the engraver.

...use imagination in your photographs. A little extra thought may be the prime factor in getting your photo into print.

...go easy on retouching photos. Probably the best guide is: If the retouching is obvious, you have gone too far.

...make sure all head sizes are the same when sending a group of portraits for use with the same release.

...limit cheesecake photos to those publications which use such material. If you are not sure, your best bet is to include a straight photo.

...make your pictures believable—do not put a fashion model in the latest Paris creations in a kitchen, etc.

...indicate the source on the back of pictures sent with releases—even if captions are attached.

...indicate "which end is up" when sending a photo in which this point is not completely obvious.

...use stiffeners when sending photos.

...make captions easy to remove from photographs. Best bet is to have caption sheets perforated so that they can be neatly torn from photos.

...identify *everyone* in a photograph.

DON'TS

...use paper clips or staples on your photographs.

...request that photos be returned, except in special cases where you have supplied the editor with pictures at *his* own request.

...ask the editor to request photographs "if he wants them." If your release requires photographs for illustration, invest enough money in the project to include photos with the original mailing.

...send group photos where everyone is looking at the camera, unless this kind of pose is specifically requested.

...try to plaster your brand name all over photos.

...overprint identifying material on photographs, unless it is in an area which will obviously be cropped by the editor.

...furnish product data on back side of photo unless the same data is included in a separate release.

...send photos separately from releases they are intended to illustrate.

...send matte prints.

...use the same photo for releases which will be used in ads.

Press Kits

A variation on the press release is the more comprehensive press kit. It is most generally used to provide detailed information for those who will write about subjects of more than routine interest—new product introductions, open-houses, new buildings.

A typical press kit was created by Parsons, Friedmann & Central, Boston advertising agency, for a Smithcraft Lighting Division of A. L. Smith Iron Co. new plant opening. Inserted in a two-pocket portfolio were the following items:

A printed program outline for the plant opening day.

A background release giving an historical chronology of the company.

A list of significant Smithcraft developments.

A seven-page general release.

A separate release on the architectural details of the new plant.

Another separate release on the electrical contracting involved in the new plant.

A six-page release on the plant opening aimed at business and financial editors.

A separate release on the processes used in the plant.

A panoramic view of the new plant.

A photo showing officials of Smithcraft and local officials participating in the "start up" of the new plant.

A portrait of the company president.

An "action photo" of the Smithcraft management team.

Seven photos showing various stages of plant construction.

Ten photos showing plant facilities and the manufacturing process.

A diagram showing the flow of production through the new plant.

Two diagrams which were to accompany the release on electrical contracting.

Two photos showing typical installations of the company's products.

Facts Book

Another variation on the publicity release is a facts book. While too seldom used, this type of format represents a very worthwhile mailing. An example of a publication of this nature is the "Editors' Facts Book," published by Union Carbide Corporation. This plastic-bound book contains a complete list of public and industrial relations contacts (including office and home phone numbers); an index of the company's products (so comprehensive it required 16 printed pages); a 40-page discussion of the company's products and processes, plus a copy of the corporation's latest annual report.

Industry Handbooks

Many companies have made lots of friends through the publication of a helpful industry handbook. Such publications come in a variety of formats and with varying contents. Generally, however, they feature basic reference material required by a specific industry or occupation. They can range from simple pocket folders to giant, hard-bound encyclopedia volumes.

A typical industry handbook was published by the Frank G. Hough Co. Known as the *Bulk Material Handbook,* it combined the company's basic knowledge of the industry with an analysis of the industry's problems, a series of tables providing basic weight and physical property information on all bulk materials, specific cost-factor formulas for determining actual operations plus other formulas by which the cost of operating the company's equipment could be figured. All of this material was included in the 60-page, 4- by 7-inch plastic-bound handbook.

The reasons for publishing such a handbook were outlined by the company's advertising manager[2]:

1. Establish the first authentic text on the subject of handling loose materials.
2. Establish recognition for the company as the authority on bulk material handling.
3. Educate our markets on the full potentials of mechanized bulk handling.
4. Perform an important customer service.
5. At the same time create a greater demand for our product among our customers.
6. Simplify the selling job for our salesmen in the field.
7. Help break down the barrier of "price."
8. Increase the effectiveness and range of our basic advertising program.

Warren's Handbooks

A company which has made exceptional use of the industry handbook route to promotion is the S. D. Warren Co., Boston paper manufacturer. A recent listing of some of the Warren-published handbooks included the following titles:

- *Business—Its Nature and Its Functions*
- *Management—Its Functions and Responsibilities*
- *Management and Its Corporate Society*
- *Printing—The Essential Aid to Management*
- *Printing—Its Forms and Designations*
- *Printing—Types & Typography*
- *Printing—The Processes of Reproduction*
- *Printing Papers and Their Uses*
- *Mailing Lists and Regulations*
- *How Will It Print by Offset*
- *Estimator's Book*
- *A Workbook for Planning Printing*
- *Better Yearbooks Through Better Planning*
- *The Company Publication*
- *The Employee Manual*
- *Sales Training and Direction*
- *The Sales Catalog*

[2]"How to Prepare an Industry Handbook," by Raymond P. Wiggers. *Advertising Requirements.*

These actually are just a few of the many handbook-type publications issued by Warren. A typical handbook contains well over one hundred 8½- by 11-inch pages, featuring a substantial quantity of halftone illustrations. The material and illustrations used in the handbooks are constantly being up-dated.

Syndicated Direct Mail Formats

Probably no field offers so much ready-to-use and semi-prepared promotional material as is available to direct mail advertisers. There are literally thousands of different types of syndicated or "stock" mailing formats available. The majority of the completely ready-to-use pieces are designed for specific types of retailers or institutions. They are supplied by manufacturers for use by their dealers and distributors, by many trade associations and by "outside" organizations which specialize in syndicated formats.

Most of the syndicated direct mail formats fall into one of six basic categories:

1. Complete mailings which require only imprinting of the advertiser's name and address.
2. Semicomplete mailings to which a specified amount of custom copy can be added.
3. Stock formats which have a limited amount of art preprinted.
4. Blank formats, usually involving special die-cuts, to which illustrations, headings and copy must be added.
5. Novelty formats of every size, shape and description.
6. Reproduction material which can be adapted to a number of different formats.

Complete Mailings

Perhaps foremost among the mailings which require only imprinting are those already described in detail in Chapter 10—"Dealer-Identified Direct Mail." In addition to these manufacturer-supplied formats, however, is a wide selection of complete mailings produced by specialist service organizations and/or trade associations. In most cases, the service organizations concentrate on a single field—such as banking, hardware, building suppliers, etc.

One of the most popular types of ready-to-use mailings is the syndicated external house organ. These are available both for specific fields and with more generalized editorial content for use by different types of advertisers. (For additional details, see Chapter 33—"House Organs, Newsletters, and Bulletins.")

"Let's Have Better Mottoes" Association

Another popular type of ready-to-use mailing is the novelty format. The best known of these are the whimsical mailings of the "Let's Have Better Mottoes" Association developed by the late Frederick E. Gymer of Cleveland and now published by John Yeck of Dayton. This relatively simple format is used for monthly mailings by dozens of companies in various fields throughout the world. Each mailing consists of a simple 3¾- by 6¼-inch motto card and a mimeographed letter (see illustration on page 853.)

Recipients are made "members" of the association and the letters are designed so names of several "members" can be inserted into the copy each month. The letters report on the fictional monthly activities of the association and the antics of Joe, the association's parade horse. Typical of the zany copy:

> "The February parade of members will form at Chez Nick Hot Dog & Root Beer Stand near Rocky River and the procession will take place on the river ice to avoid paying a city street parade permit fee. Joe, our parade horse, cannot march because he is recovering from being hit in the face with a wet fish while doing the town with Elmer, a horse pal who works the swing shift hauling garbage."

All of the mottoes are on the zany side and anyone who suggests a truly inspirational motto is automatically "ousted" from the association. Typical mottoes:

> "Do it tomorrow—you made enough mistakes today."
>
> "If you want a quick decision—NO!"
>
> "Whistle while you work—it will drive everyone nuts."
>
> "THINK! It may be a new experience."
>
> "If you can keep your head while others are losing theirs—maybe you don't understand the situation."
>
> "Come in—everything else has gone wrong today."
>
> "I never get lost—everyone tells me wheie to go."
>
> "Coming to work doesn't hurt—it's the long wait to go home."
>
> "Here's the solution—now what's the problem?"
>
> "I like my job—it's the work I hate."

No hard sell is included with the motto mailings. One of the subscribers to the service, Edward D. Muir of Muir Investment Corp., San Antonio, Texas, explains, for example, that his company uses the mailings to create a friendly climate in a situation where most competitors feature the same service, price and quality. The business, he feels, goes to the company and salesman on the friendliest terms with the prospect.

Stock Formats

The most frequently used of all syndicated formats are the so-called "stock formats"—cards, bulletins, folders, etc., on which headings and/or illustrations have been preprinted. Thousands of different items are available from the following basic sources:

Goes Lithographing Co., 42 W. 61st Street, Chicago, Illinois 60621

Idea Art, 30 E. 10th Street, New York, New York 10003

National Creative Sales, 1030 Leggett Avenue, New York, New York 10055

Arthur Thompson & Co., 109 Market Place, Baltimore, Maryland

Flash Bulletins

Of all stock formats, flash bulletins are the most popular. Most of them are published on 8½- by 11-inch sheets with a catchy headline and a colorful illustration. There is such a selection of different designs available that you can usually find a preprinted flash bulletin to fit—or at least come close to—any theme you might dream up.

While flash bulletins are designed primarily for those who want interesting and effective mailing pieces, but whose mailing lists are too small to warrant the cost of original art, plates and color printing, these syndicated pieces are also used by major direct mail advertisers with large lists. Most often they are called into play when a fast-approaching deadline suggests use of something instantly available.

In addition to flash bulletins with promotional headings, there are many designed for special situations such as Christmas messages, welcoming messages, awards, certificates, newsletters, sales bulletins, news releases, inquiry answering, price lists, etc.

Some years ago it was common for syndicators to offer matching envelopes with tie-in art and copy, but the trend in recent years is to offer picture-window envelopes designed so a portion of the flash bulletin art is visible through the window.

Flash Cards

Also popular are flash cards, usually about 5 by 7 inches in size, which carry designs similar to those used for flash bulletins. These cards are useful for the situation where fast, short messages are required, and where enclosures or reply cards are unnecessary. In addition to advertising, these cards are used widely for announcements, sales notices, dealer and salesman mailings, contests, meeting notices, price change announcements and similar direct mail applications.

Blank Formats

Another popular type of syndicated format is the blank piece to which the advertiser adds all copy—including artwork and headings. The most common of these formats is the combination letter and reply device. While the majority of suppliers usually supply a complete package, including printing and often all of the creative work, such formats are also available unprinted.

Among the leading suppliers of this type of syndicated format are:

Ansa-letter, 200 Hudson Street, New York, New York 10011

Direct Mail Printing Co., 15 West 20th Street, New York, New York 10011

Reply-O-Letter Co., 7 Central Park West, New York, New York 10023

In addition, many regular envelope companies supply such formats.

Of these combination formats the best known is the letter with a pocket holding the reply card. The recipient's name is typed on the reply card which shows through a die-cut window at the top of the letter (and often again through a window in the mailing envelope). This format was made popular by Reply-O-Letter Co., but is now available through dozens of sources.

Other formats use a variety of die-cutting and folding techniques to combine the reply device and the outgoing piece into a single unit. One of the widest ranges of such units is offered by Direct Mail Printing Co. of New York, which is one of the major sources for *unprinted* formats of this nature. This company offers a comprehensive catalog and guide to the use of combination formats.

Novelty Formats

There is a wide range of syndicated novelty formats available for direct mail use. Since they come and go with various whims of the suppliers and buyers, it is difficult to describe those available at any given time. Some of these pieces are highly ingenious, while others are highly functional.

One usually excellent source for novelty formats is Brownie Manufacturing Co., 261 Broadway, New York, New York 10007. Among the popular formats offered by Brownie are:

- *A pop-up parasol,* which springs open when a folder is opened.

- *A pop-up viewer,* which contains a disc with a number of miniature slides for viewing through a built-in magnifier.
- *A window curtain piece,* with a message that rolls up or down as a folder is opened and closed.

A number of suppliers offer mailable viewers—both for stereo and regular transparencies. Two primary sources are Visual Data Corp., 3 Edison Avenue, Chesterfield, Mo. 63017, and Curtin & Pease Mail Marketing, 2725 N. Reynolds Rd., Toledo, Ohio 43615.

Another frequently used format is the three-dimensional pop-up developed by Nicholas Jannes of Jannes Associates Inc., 222 West Huron Street, Chicago, Illinois 60610. This patented cardboard device folds flat but contains rubber bands which cause it to pop into a dimensional piece when it is removed from an envelope. Pop-ups are also available from Graphics 3, Inc., 150 Toney Penna Drive, Jupiter, Fla. 33458.

Syndicated Reproduction Material

A sixth type of syndicated format in popular use is less "complete" than the others. It consists of reproduction art which can be used to prepare a variety of direct mail formats. The major sources for such material are:

Art-Pak Clip-Art Service, Box 1142, Pomona, California 91769

Dynamic Graphics, Inc., 6707 N. Sheridan Rd., Peoria, Illinois 61614

Volk Corp., 1401 N. Main St., Pleasantville, N.J. 08232

Dynamic Graphics, for example, supplies a monthly reproduction art service which regularly includes formats for direct mail flyers and folders. In most cases, these formats are used to provide second-color art, with "open" spaces to add headlines, illustrations and copy in the basic color.

Chapter 38

ORDER FORMS AND REPLY CARDS

ONE of the greatest mysteries in the direct mail field is why so few advertisers—including many who know better—pay such scant attention to the design, copy, and production of their order forms and reply cards. It is not unusual to find a beautiful mailing featuring a fancy full-color brochure; letter on top-quality stock; an imaginative, impressive mailing envelope; a well-designed reply envelope—and a downright sloppy order form or card.

Yet the order form or reply card can be the most important element in a mailing. It is like the salesman's "closer"—it has to bring in the order or other desired response.

Methods for Securing Response

There are nine basic formats used to secure response from a direct mail offer: (1) Order card, (2) Order blank, (3) Invoice to be okayed, (4) Coupon, (5) Imprinted reply envelope, (6) Extra copy of letter to be initialed, (7) Packet of order forms, (8) "Gimmick" approaches, (9) Combination order form-letters.

ORDER CARDS

For the majority of mailings, the business reply card is the preferred response device. Unless the mailer expects the respondent to enclose payment with his order, the card is usually designed so that it may be mailed without an envelope. However in cases where payment with the order is desired, most mailers include a business reply envelope even if the order card has a business reply face.

The primary ingredient of a good order card is a summary of the offer. This may be on the return card itself or printed on a tear-off portion which the respondent will keep.

There is a growing trend toward the use of address-imprinted reply cards which are inserted in a window envelope for original mailing. The advantage is that the respondent does not have to fill in his name and address on the order card. This not only simplifies the process of responding, but is of tremendous aid to those who have to handle the orders since a great many respondents otherwise provide hard-to-decipher addresses.

The Importance of Order Cards

Lewis Kleid, a leading mail order expert, in an article, "Mail Order Markets and Methods" (*The Reporter of Direct Mail Advertising,* March 1963), offers these observations on the importance of order forms:

> "The reply device can make or break your chance of getting an order. At the moment when the prospect is ready to sign—after having examined the letter and circular—a poorly designed device or confused statement on the form could interrupt and kill the decision to buy.
>
> "An order form should not be jammed with options and stipulations in solid six-point type. It should be easy to read and understand and easy to act upon. *Look* magazine knows how to do it. With certificate borders, check background, and good design their forms project an image of great value, stimulate action, and require no effort.
>
> "Addressing the form instead of the envelope has several benefits:
>
> 1. It's faster. You can print and ship forms while the envelopes are being manufactured.
> 2. Clerks can read preaddressed order cards easier than forms which have been handwritten.
> 3. Ordering is easier. The card needs only be mailed (initials or signatures are sometimes required).
>
> "When planning a mailing, start with the order form first and build your mailing around it. The easier you make it to order—the greater your chance of getting the order."

Double-Window Envelopes

With preaddressed order forms, a mailing envelope with a double window on its mailing face is often an effective approach. The right-hand window is for the address, while the left-hand window can be used to reveal an illustration or special copy on the order form.

The following illustration shows how this approach has been applied by American Marketing Services. To simplify its mailing problems, the mail order company used a basic double window envelope for the majority of its offers. The envelope involved only one-color printing, but variety was achieved by using three different paper stocks (gray, light blue, and white) and three different colors of ink (dark blue, dark green, and maroon). By combining the inks and papers, nine "different" envelopes were obtained at very little added cost over a single style.

Then to "tailor" these basic envelopes to each offer, special order cards were prepared. The basic design was a 3¼- by 8½-inch card with a perforated 3-inch stub on the left-hand side. On this stub was a special design highlighting some feature of the product being offered. The cards were frequently printed on colored stock in either one or two colors of ink. When the colors on the cards were "combined" with the colors of the envelopes, each mailing took on a distinctive appearance.

In some cases an additional imprint was added to the envelopes to supplement the show-through illustration from the order card.

Order Card Stubs

The use of perforated stubs on order cards has been growing in popularity, particularly in the mail order field. These stubs serve a variety of purposes:

As a "receipt" or "record" of an order.

As a convenient place to restate the offer.

As a method for making the order card a "self-contained" promotion vehicle (particularly for inclusion with mailings featuring some other product or service).

As a convenient spot to give instructions for filling out the order form.

As a guarantee certificate.

As a device to make an order card large enough to hold in position in a window envelope, yet easily convertible to a smaller size to get within the requirements for minimum return postage rates.

To provide an area for applying glue so the card can be tipped to another part of the mailing (such as to the letter).

Examples of AMS' mailings featuring double-window envelopes. Illustrations on the left side of the order cards show through "picture window" in the face of the envelopes.

As an area to promote a premium.

As an area for special illustrations.

Typical users of order card stubs include:

The Heritage Club. One side of the stub on this two-color 5½- by 8½-inch reply card features an illustration of three bonus books being offered with a trial membership. On the reverse side there is an outline of some of the advantages of membership in the Club. The stub occupies a 4½- by 5½-inch area.

Panorama Colorslide Programs. This red, white, and blue 5¼- by 8⅛-inch card with a 5- by 5¼-inch stub features an illustration of the materials being offered on one side and an illustrated outline of typical subject material on the reverse.

Grolier Enterprises, Inc. Another red, white, and blue card promotes a home-teaching machine. The 5¼- by 8-inch card has a 5- by 5¼-inch stub which features an illustration of the teaching machine in use on one face and a list of 12 basic courses being offered on the opposite face.

Rodale Books, Inc. This 5½- by 8½-inch order form is printed in black and yellow on white enamel stock and on one side only, since a business reply envelope was enclosed with the mailing to encourage payments with orders. The 5¼- by 5½-inch stub features an "unconditional money-back guarantee" with a space for inserting the date and the amount of the order.

Columbia Record Club. This 8¼- by 5⅝-inch two-color order card has a horizontal stub (8¼ by 2¾ inches) across the top. One side of the stub quickly summarizes a special offer while the reverse side carries a listing of "advantages of membership."

Book-of-the-Month Club Inc. Still another red, white, and blue order form, this one is 5¾ by 8½ inches with a 3¼-inch stub at the left-hand side. The copy on the stub simply says: Please use the order card at the right if you wish to receive the material being offered. The rapid reading study program package, which is the featured offer, is illustrated in a full bleed photo on the reverse side of the stub.

Better Homes & Gardens. This 9¼- by 7½-inch jumbo card is designed for return in a business reply envelope so is printed one side only (orange and blue on white). The stub is headed: "Customer's Receipt" and summarizes the offer.

Popular Club Plan. A full-color illustration of a special premium (a French purse) is featured on the 3⅜- by 3⅞-inch stub of this 3⅞- by 9-inch order card. Respondents are told to "save this stub" as a reminder of the premium offer (which is sent after the first order is received from a catalog offered for return of the reply card).

Moody Monthly. The red and black on yellow 3⅜- by 7¼-inch reply card has a 1¾-inch stub at the left offering a bonus book with a year's subscription to the magazine. Small type describes the book (*Great Sermons by Great Preachers*) plus the magazine's money-back guarantee.

Sports Illustrated. A 3¼- by 7⅞-inch two-color reply card has a 2⅛-inch stub with copy suggesting that subscribers pass the card along: "Next time, why loan your copy of *Sports Illustrated*? . . . just pass this special introductory offer along to your sportsminded friends."

USA-1. This short-lived magazine utilized a 3- by 3⅝-inch stub on its elongated (10½-inch) order card for a brief letter summarizing the kind of magazine charter subscribers would receive. The reverse side of the stub carried a two-color illustration of the magazine's cover.

American Heritage. The 3⅜- by 1⅝-inch stub on *American Heritage's* renewal order card (3⅜ by 7 inches) contains a blank on which the subscriber can record the date on which he mailed his order.

The National Observer. An attractive 8⅜- by 3⅜-inch single color-on-color (dark brown on tan) order card featured a 2¾-inch stub on the right-hand side with copy in reverse outlining just what the subscriber would receive and what his options were.

Consumers Digest. This 8½- by 3⅜-inch order card had a 2⅝-inch stub on the right-hand side outlining the details of a money-back guarantee. The reverse side explained the limited nature of a "charter membership" offer being made.

Precision Equipment Co. Another guarantee was featured on the 3¾- by 4-inch stub of a 4- by 9-inch reply card. The face of the stub was designed to carry a certificate appearance—including a printed signature. Copy read: "The sender of this card has the irrevocable and unconditional guarantee that if for any reason he is not 100% delighted in every way with the Bennett Wireless Intercom he may return it at Precision Equipment Company's expense and owe absolutely nothing. No explanation will be required as to reason for the return." (*This incidentally, is an outstanding example of copy for a mail order money-back guarantee.*) The reverse side of the stub showed an illustration of the wireless intercom being offered, plus a space for filling in the date ordered.

Other Stub Applications

Although difficult to illustrate, the "promotion piece" stub deserves special comment. In many cases, the "stub" is really the basic promotion piece. For example, *Life* prepared a 17- by 3-inch promotion piece for insertion with a cooperative couponing mailing. The piece was folded to 6 by 3 inches and included a 5¼- by 3-inch reply card. The 11¾-inch "spread" facing the reply card had a miniature letter on one side and illustrated promotion copy on the reverse.

A somewhat larger piece was used by The Better Reading Program. A 6⅞- by 9¾-inch card was folded to 6⅞ by 3½ inches yielding a reply card plus a four-page "stub" with complete promotional copy for the company's Rapid Reading Kit. One page featured a teaser illustration and headline, another had rather detailed copy on what could be accomplished with the kit, the third featured an illustration of the kit's contents, and the fourth page provided details of a special seven-day free trial offer.

American Heritage makes particularly effective use of folded flaps on its order cards. These flaps are perforated for removal before mailing the order card. Among the approaches which have been used:

A 5- by 3¾-inch order card for *The American Heritage History of Flight* had a 2½- by 3¾-inch black on yellow flap folding atop the order form from the left side. The flap was a miniature reproduction of an early-day air circus. The back side of the flap contained a summary of the details of the book offer.

A 6- by 3⅜-inch order card for *The American Heritage Picture History of the Civil War* featured a 2-inch fold-down top flop with a vintage Civil War illustration in black on dark blue plus the title of the book reversed from the blue. The back side outlined terms for advance orders.

A four-page 3½- by 5½-inch folder was used for *The Horizon Book of the Renaissance.* The third and fourth pages were the order card. The "front page" contained a black photo of a statue against a deep red background and reverse copy: "Reservation Card—The Horizon Book of the Renaissance." The remaining page carried copy promoting advance orders and outlining the special terms being offered.

Copy for Order Forms

While the copy to be used on your order form will depend upon the offer you are making, there are a few basic essentials for nearly every good order or inquiry device.

1. Restate your offer as simply, yet clearly as possible.
2. If there is a choice of terms, make sure each choice is clearly indicated and give the respondent a very specific place to indicate his choice. (Beware of the tightly spaced line of choices with a little spot between each item for checking. Too often the respondent gets confused as to whether he should place his checkmark before or after his choice.)
3. Clearly indicate what additional action will be expected of the respondent.
4. Clearly indicate just what action you will take upon receipt of the order or inquiry.
5. Allow sufficient room for the respondent to fill in all of the information you request. The very minimum space

should be that required for typing the information on a pica-size typewriter—and this may be too small a space for many respondents.

6. Indicate any time limits to the offer.
7. Make sure your own name and address are included on the card even if you are providing a return envelope with the mailing. (Order cards frequently get separated from other elements of a mailing or are put aside for ordering at a later date.)
8. Explain any guarantee you are extending.
9. Explain any premium which is being offered.
10. If the offer is not being limited to the original addressee, include a line of copy suggesting the order form be passed along to someone else if it is a duplicate.

An example of how order card copy can cover a complicated situation without presenting undue confusion to the prospect is found in a mailing for the Life World Library:

> "*YES . . . I am interested.* Please send me, for 10 days' free examination, a copy of the limited edition volume, *Japan.* If I decide to keep this book, I will pay only $2.95 (plus shipping and handling). You may then confirm my reservation to receive future volumes in the Life World Library, which I understand are being issued a volume at a time at 2-month intervals, at the same price of $2.95. It is understood that these future volumes are also to be sent to me on approval, and I may return any volume within 10 days after receiving it, and may cancel my reservation at any time. It is also understood that if, after examining this first volume, I do not choose to keep the book or become a subscriber, I may return the volume within 10 days, my reservation for future volumes will be canceled, and I am under no further obligation."

ORDER BLANKS

Order blanks win preference over order cards when one or more of three basic circumstances are present:

1. Several different items are being offered.
2. More information is required of a respondent than could be expected to "fit" on a reply card format.

3. It is anticipated that the respondent will use an envelope for reply so he can enclose payment or to make the order "confidential."

Since there are fewer limitations on size and format of order forms, a much wider variety is to be found. In fact, it is difficult to find two direct mail advertisers using similar order forms, whereas there is often a great similarity of order cards.

Sears' Catalog Order Blanks

The basic "reference source" for many direct mail advertisers who wish to design effective order forms is their latest copy of the Sears, Roebuck & Co. catalog. A typical Sears' order blank is shown on page 1027. The full-page, two-side form has eight basic elements:

1. *Address Information.* This includes space for the respondent's name and address, instructions if the shipment is to be made to an address other than that of the respondent, and the respondent's old address if he has moved since his last order.

2. *Order Information.* Ruled spaces are included for ordering 12 different items. Headings include: catalog number, how many, name of item, color (number and name), size, unit price, total price, and shipping weight.

3. *Tax Information.* Detailed instructions are included for computing state sales taxes.

4. *Shipping Instructions.* The respondent is given an opportunity to choose his preferred method of shipment—parcel post, express, or freight.

5. *Credit Instructions.* The buyer is given the opportunity to order on credit by checking one of two boxes. One for Sears' "Easy Payment Plan" requires completion of a mail order retail installment contract form on the reverse side of the order blank. The second choice is for use by customers having a revolving charge account. In addition to a box for the checkmark, there is a blank to enter the account number and to indicate at which retail store his records are maintained.

6. *Order Summary.* The final section on the face of the order form has lines for computing the total cost of the order, the amount for sales tax, postage, previous balance, total, and amount enclosed with the order. Additional spaces are provided for totaling up the shipping weight and entering the parcel post zone.

7. *Credit Application.* Most of the space on the reverse side of the Sears' order blank is devoted to an installment credit application.

8. *Shipping Information.* The remainder of the reverse side has detailed information on parcel post, truck, freight, or express shipments and how to send money.

Date________________ 19__

SEARS, ROEBUCK AND CO.
CHICAGO, IL 60607

Sears

PLEASE BE SURE TO INCLUDE ZIP CODE IN YOUR ADDRESS

SATISFACTION GUARANTEED OR YOUR MONEY BACK

PLEASE GIVE COMPLETE DELIVERY INFORMATION

Be sure to give complete mailing address at the right, filling in the correct information on the lines provided. ON FREIGHT ORDERS, IF YOU DO NOT HAVE A STREET ADDRESS, additional information is needed for delivery by truck. The name and/or number of the road or highway, landmarks such as a church, gas station, fire house or bridge are important guides. Please give these details on the lines provided.

PLEASE DO NOT WRITE IN SPACE BELOW

PLEASE PRINT PLAINLY

All members of the same household should order under one name

NAME________________
(FIRST NAME) (MIDDLE INITIAL) (LAST NAME)

Mailing Address________________

Post Office________ State________ ZIP CODE

Telephone Number________________

SHIP TO ANOTHER ADDRESS? If you want this order shipped to another person or to a different address, freight or express station, give address here:

NAME________________

Mailing Address________________

Post Office________ State________ ZIP CODE

IF YOUR ADDRESS HAS CHANGED since last order, please give your old mailing address here:

Mailing Address________________

Post Office________ State________ ZIP CODE

TEAR OUT ORDER BLANK ON THIS LINE

STATE COLOR OR PATTERN CHOICE BY NUMBER IF REQUESTED

	CATALOG NUMBER	HOW MANY	NAME OF ITEM	COLOR Pattern, Finish, Etc.	SIZE Measure to be sure	PRICE Ea., Yd., Pr., Etc.	TOTAL PRICE Dollars	Cents	SHPG. WT. Lbs.	Oz.
1										
2										
3										
4										
5										
6										
7										
8										
9										
10										
11										

ILLINOIS customers add 5c tax for each dollar of goods (4c state, 1c city).
IOWA or MISSOURI customers add 3c tax for each dollar of goods.
KENTUCKY customers add 5c tax for each dollar of goods.
INDIANA, MICHIGAN, OHIO or WISCONSIN customers add 4c tax for each dollar of goods.
If your county in **OHIO** has a tax, include the additional tax required.
Tax rates based on information at printing and subject to change.

HOW SHALL WE SHIP? Parcel Post ☐ Express ☐ Freight (Rail or Truck) ☐ | In Metropolitan areas, merchandise can be delivered by fast package delivery service at higher cost. ☐ PACKAGE DELIVERY SERVICE

Add this to my
☐ **SEARS REVOLVING CHARGE ACCOUNT,**
☐ **SEARS EASY PAYMENT PLAN** or
☐ **MODERNIZING CREDIT PLAN RETAIL INSTALLMENT CONTRACT AND SECURITY AGREEMENT,** which is incorporated herein by reference.

MY ACCOUNT NUMBER________ At what Sears store?________ (DO NOT SEND IDENTIFICATION CARD OR PLATE)

Signature of the Head of Household________________ (WRITE—DO NOT PRINT)

TOTAL FOR GOODS		
← AMOUNT FOR TAX		
If credit order, we will figure and fill this in for you. POSTAGE		
Amount I owe Sears on previous order		
TOTAL CASH PRICE		
AMOUNT ENCLOSED — Sears Checks		
AMOUNT ENCLOSED — Money Order or Check		

Total Pounds | Total Ounces

Total Weight in Pounds

Enter Parcel Post Zone No.

See yellow pages for shipping information

C

Sears 273

Through its long experience Sears has evolved this basic order form.

Jackson & Perkins Order Blanks

More common in the mail order field are order blanks with the available items prelisted for easy ordering. While this order blank format is most common among advertisers which are promoting a limited number of items, it has been used effectively by a number of catalog publishers including Jackson & Perkins Co., which used tearout order forms bound into its catalog. A typical Jackson & Perkins order form listed more than 300 different roses on its two sides (see illustration on the next page).

All the buyer needs do is to fill in his name and address, the nearest express office, and the amount enclosed at the top of the order blank and then indicate the quantity and total cost of each selection he wants. The roses are listed in three columns on both sides of the form. They are grouped under such headings as Hybrid Teas, Floribundas, Perennials, and so forth. Each line includes a space for entering quantity, code number, name of rose, single unit price, price in units of three, and space for entering total price for quantity ordered. A blank for a subtotal is included at the bottom of each column. Then at the bottom of the third column on the back page is an area for computing total cost: Total for back page, total for first page, shipping and handling charges (this is a standard 50-cent fee and is preprinted), and total enclosed.

A flap facing the order blanks gives complete details on how to order, how to remit payment, shipping dates, and so forth.

Jackson & Perkins uses even more simplified order blanks to accompany special offer mailings.

M. P. Brown Envelope Co.

Another basic type of order form combines promotional material with space to order items. M. P. Brown Envelope Co., for example, uses a two-page, 8- by 11-inch order form which describes seven different types of business envelopes and a shipping label. Opposite the illustration and description of each item is a bold box printed in red. The buyer simply writes in the box the quantity of each item he wants. At the bottom of the back page is a space to fill in the name and address to be imprinted on the envelopes or labels and a line for a signature.

Another application of this technique is a handy inquiry-answering order form used by American Marketing Services. An 11- by 8½-inch sheet was accordion-folded to 3⅔ by 8½ inches. The first fold became a short letter thanking the ad-

Quan.	Code No.	CLIMBERS continued	Each	3 For	Total
	361	White Dawn	$2.00	$5.25	
		Group #452 .$ 5.25			
		Group #462 . 10.50			
		Group #472 . 7.85			
		Group #482 . 6.75			
		Group #492 . 7.00			
		Group #502 . 6.55			
		Group #512 . 7.85			
		Common Roses			
	280	Better Times	$1.75	$4.65	
	880	Condesa de Sastago .	1.75	4.65	
	881	Countess Vandal	1.75	4.65	
	282	Crimson Glory	1.75	4.65	
	204	Dicksons Red	1.75	4.65	
	404	Eclipse	1.75	4.65	
	284	Etoile de Hollande ..	1.75	4.65	
	S-391	Frau Karl Druschki ..	1.75	4.65	
	380	K. A. Viktoria	1.75	4.65	
	480	Lydia	1.75	4.65	
	411	McGredy's Sunset ..	1.75	4.65	
	481	McGredy's Yellow ...	1.75	4.65	
	482	Mrs. P. S. DuPont ...	1.75	4.65	
	180	Numa Fay	1.75	4.65	
	285	Poinsettia	1.75	4.65	
	883	President Hoover ...	1.75	4.65	
	182	Radiance	1.75	4.65	
	286	Red Radiance	1.75	4.65	
	115	Signora	1.75	4.65	
		Group #232 .$18.35			
		Group #242 . 12.25			
		Group #252 . 6.10			
		ROSES FOR SPECIAL PURPOSES			
	S-192	Baby Betsy McCall ..	$1.25	$3.30	
	S-291	Baby Masquerade ..	1.25	3.30	
	S-292	Dwarfking	1.25	3.30	
	S-191	Max Graf	1.50	3.90	
	S-290	Oakington Ruby	1.00	2.50	
	S-193	Opal Jewel	1.25	3.30	
	S-293	Red Imp	1.50	3.90	
	S-190	Rosa Rouletti	1.00	2.50	
	S-392	Twinkles	1.25	3.30	
	S-390	Wichuraiana	1.50	3.90	
		Group #312 ..$6.35			
		Group #322 .. 6.55			
		TREE ROSES		2 For	
	324	Americana	6.75	12.50	
	278	American Home	6.75	12.50	
	475	Arlene Francis	6.75	12.50	
	279	Avon	6.75	12.50	
	490	Diamond Jubilee	6.75	12.50	
	191	Enchantment	6.75	12.50	
	192	Fashion	6.75	12.50	
	137	Gail Borden	6.75	12.50	
	497	Golden Masterpiece .	6.75	12.50	
	325	Hawaii	6.75	12.50	
	829	Ivory Fashion	6.75	12.50	
	830	King's Ransom	6.75	12.50	
	187	Kordes Perfecta	6.75	12.50	
	293	New Yorker	6.75	12.50	
	238	Orchid Masterpiece ..	6.75	12.50	
	891	Pageant	6.75	12.50	
	495	Peace	6.75	12.50	
	894	Personality	6.75	12.50	
	135	Pink Duchess	6.75	12.50	
	198	Queen Elizabeth	6.75	12.50	
	294	Red Pinocchio	6.75	12.50	
	188	South Seas	6.75	12.50	
	322	Spartan	6.75	12.50	
TOTAL				$	

Quan.	Code No.	TREE ROSES continued	Each	2 For	Total
	186	Sterling Silver	$6.75	12.50	
	893	Tanya	6.75	12.50	
	391	White Queen	6.75	12.50	
				3 For	
	3080	Lilac: Edith Cavell ..	$3.00	$7.50	
	1081	Mme. A. Buchner ...	3.00	7.50	
	6081	Paul Hariot	3.00	7.50	
	2080	Paul Thirion	3.00	7.50	
	6080	Pres. Fallieres	3.00	7.50	
	5080	Pres. Grevy	3.00	7.50	
		Group #522 .$15.00			
				2 For	
	1103	Magnolia Soul	$3.50	$6.50	
		PERENNIALS		3 For	
	4090	Achillea, G. Plate ...	$1.00	$2.50	
	5091	Anchusa, Myoso. ...	.75	2.00	
	1092	Aster, Adorable	.75	2.00	
	5092	Frikarti	.75	2.00	
	2090	Astilbe, Fanal	.85	2.25	
	2091	Koblenz	.85	2.25	
	3091	White Gloria	.85	2.25	
	1093	Bleeding Heart, Pink.	.85	2.25	
	3092	White	1.00	2.50	
	5094	Campanula, Blue Car.	.75	2.00	
	3112	White Star	1.00	2.50	
	5095	Catananche	.85	2.25	
	2093	Centranthus Ruber ..	1.00	2.50	
	3004	Chrys. Bob White ...	1.00	2.50	
	2016	Brown Crain	1.00	2.50	
	2024	Canada Jay	1.00	2.50	
	2019	Chestnut Warbler .	1.00	2.50	
	1007	Chickadee	1.00	2.50	
	2015	Chimney Swift ...	1.00	2.50	
	1006	Desert Quail	1.00	2.50	
	4016	Golden Cockatoo .	1.00	2.50	
	4020	Golden Tern	1.00	2.50	
	2017	Horned Lark	1.00	2.50	
	1016	Humming Bird ...	1.00	2.50	
	3003	Iceland Gull	1.00	2.50	
	2023	Myrtle Warbler ...	1.00	2.50	
	2012	Painted Bunting ..	1.00	2.50	
	2018	Pine Siskin	1.00	2.50	
	2021	Purple Finch	1.00	2.50	
	2010	Redpoll	1.00	2.50	
	2014	Sandpiper	1.00	2.50	
	3002	Seagull	1.00	2.50	
	3005	Snowy Egret	1.00	2.50	
	2022	Song Sparrow	1.00	2.50	
	1008	Titmouse	1.00	2.50	
	2025	West. Meadowlark	1.00	2.50	
	1015	Wood Peewee	1.00	2.50	
	4018	Yellow Warbler ...	1.00	2.50	
	4091	Coreopsis, Gol. Shower	.75	2.00	
	3070	Delph. Debutante ..	.85	2.25	
	5070	Delightful	.85	2.25	
	5071	Enchantment	.85	2.25	
	3071	Freedom	.85	2.25	
	5072	Gayety	.85	2.25	
	6071	Glorious	1.00	2.50	
	8070	Happiness	1.25	3.15	
	6072	Loveliness	1.50	3.75	
	3072	Peace	1.50	3.75	
	1071	Pink Glow	1.50	3.75	
	2102	Dianthus, Caprice ...	1.25	3.15	
	1107	Coral Gem	1.25	3.15	
	1095	Irene	1.00	2.50	
	1104	Lacy Lass	1.25	3.15	
	1109	Marcella	1.25	3.15	
	3097	Silver Mine	.85	2.25	
TOTAL				$	

Quan.	Code No.	PERENNIALS continued	Each	3 For	Total
	3098	Funkia, Sub. Alba ...	$ .85	$2.25	
	3111	Gypsophila, Fairy Perf.	1.25	3.15	
	1096	Rosy Veil	.85	2.25	
	4093	Heliopsis, Patula ...	.75	2.00	
	5096	Lavender, Hidcote Bl.	1.00	2.50	
	3100	Lily-of-the-Valley ...	.65	1.75	
	1106	Lythrum, Hy. Robert .	1.00	2.50	
	2096	Monarda Ca. Scarlet .	1.00	2.50	
	1099	Croftway Pink	1.00	2.50	
	7090	Pachysandra T. 10 for	$3.00	1.00	
	8090	Penstemon, Ruby King	.85	2.25	
	2097	Phlox, Brigadier	1.00	2.50	
	3101	White Admiral	1.00	2.50	
	2098	Poppy Salmon Glow .	.85	2.25	
	4097	Rudbeckia, Sul.	1.00	2.50	
	1100	The King	.85	2.25	
	6094	Salvia Sup., Pur. Gl.	1.25	3.15	
	1108	Sedum, Autumn Joy ..	1.25	3.15	
	2099	Brilliant	.75	2.00	
	2100	Fire Glow	.75	2.00	
	4098	Golden Carpet ...	.75	2.00	
	1105	Rosy Carpet	1.00	2.50	
	4101	Shasta: Gobham Gold	1.50	3.75	
	3103	Esther Read	.85	2.25	
	3105	Wirral Supreme ...	1.25	3.15	
	5097	Stokesia, Lav. Queen	.85	2.25	
	4102	Trollius Golden Queen	1.00	2.50	
	7092	Vinca Minor ..10 for	$3.00	1.00	
	6060	Viola, John Wallmark	.85	2.25	
	6061	Purple Heart	.85	2.25	
	6062	Purple Wallmark .	.85	2.25	
	3109	White Heart	1.00	2.50	
	4060	Yellow Vixen	.75	2.00	
	6092	Violet, Double Russian	.75	2.00	
	1102	Rosina	.75	2.00	
	6093	Royal Robe	.75	2.00	
	3107	White Wonder ...	.75	2.00	
	3106	White Veronica	1.25	3.15	
		Group #532 ..$5.70			
		Group #542 .. 3.80			
		Group #552 .. 3.80			
		Group #562 .. 5.00			
		Group #572 .. 4.20			
		Group #582 .. 4.40			
		Group #592 .. 3.30			
		Group #602 .. 3.30			
		Group #612 .. 3.00			
		Group #622 .. 7.15			
		Group #632 .. 5.80			
		Group #642 .. 3.80			
		Group #652 .. 3.20			
		Group #662 .. 6.65			
		Group #672 .. 4.95			
		Group #682 .. 7.50			
		Group #692 .. 4.95			
		Group #702 ..14.15			
		Group #712 .. 4.95			
		Group #722 .. 6.65			
		Group #732 .. 4.80			
		Group #742 .. 4.25			
		Group #752 .. 9.15			
				Total for the page $	
				Total from other side $	
				Shipping and Handling Charges $	.50
				TOTAL ENCLOSED $	

When ordering Merchandise Please use Order Blank on Page D of Garden Supply Pages.

This second page of a Jackson & Perkins' order blank uses all space effectively.

dressee for his inquiry. It was personalized by simply handwriting the addressee's name at the top of the page.

The remaining two pages constituted the order form. Five publications were illustrated and described. Below each description were boxes for the respondent to check to indicate which items he wanted and to select optional terms. Name and address information was entered at the bottom of these two pages (see illustration following).

INVOICE TO BE OKAYED

One of the danger areas in mail order selling is the use of a preprinted invoice which a respondent simply okays to place his order. While this technique is widely accepted for renewals of magazine subscriptions, it has been subjected to sharp attack when used for other mail order purposes.

The ethics of this order form format are certainly open to question. If the recipient *clearly understands* that the "invoice" is simply a handy order device, there is little chance of criticism. Unfortunately, however, such an understanding is not always present. This is particularly true in dealing with business concerns since the "invoice" order blank may be routed to the accounting department, where it is considered a request for payment. A check is sent, the merchandise is received, and confusion reigns as the recipient insists he never ordered the items he received. Net result: ill-will for the mailer and often the trouble and expense of handling returned merchandise and reimbursement to the "buyer."

When it comes to renewals of magazine subscriptions, the use of the invoice format is so widely used that it is accepted for what it is. A typical renewal invoice is shown on the facing page.

COUPONS

Coupon order forms are usually integrated into other promotional formats. In most cases they follow the copy styles of order cards. One advantage of the coupon is that it is easily keyed to the promotion since it is printed at the same time. The disadvantage is that the respondent must tear or cut it out before he can return it.

In many cases, both a coupon and another order device are included in the same mailing. The advantage to this dual ap-

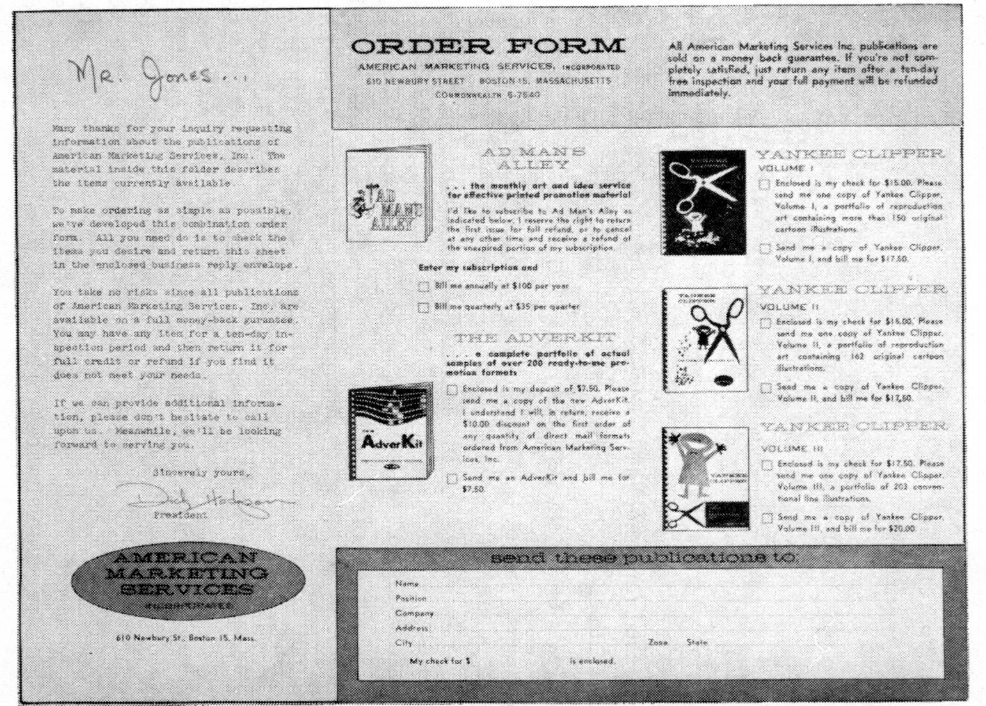

Mr. Jones . . .

Many thanks for your inquiry requesting information about the publications of American Marketing Services, Inc. The material inside this folder describes the items currently available.

To make ordering as simple as possible, we've developed this combination order form. All you need do is to check the items you desire and return this sheet in the enclosed business reply envelope.

You take no risks since all publications of American Marketing Services, Inc. are available on a full money-back gurantee. You may have any item for a ten-day inspection period and then return it for full credit or refund if you find it does not meet your needs.

If we can provide additional information, please don't hesitate to call upon us. Meanwhile, we'll be looking forward to serving you.

Sincerely yours,

President

AMERICAN MARKETING SERVICES INCORPORATED

610 Newbury St. Boston 15, Mass.

ORDER FORM

AMERICAN MARKETING SERVICES, INCORPORATED
610 NEWBURY STREET BOSTON 15, MASSACHUSETTS
COMMONWEALTH 6-7640

All American Marketing Services Inc. publications are sold on a money back guarantee. If you're not completely satisfied, just return any item after a ten-day free inspection and your full payment will be refunded immediately.

AD MAN'S ALLEY

. . . the monthly art and idea service for effective printed promotion material

I'd like to subscribe to Ad Man's Alley as indicated below. I reserve the right to return the first issue for full refund, or to cancel at any other time and receive a refund of the unexpired portion of my subscription.

Enter my subscription and

☐ Bill me annually at $100 per year

☐ Bill me quarterly at $35 per quarter

THE ADVERKIT

. . . a complete portfolio of actual samples of over 200 ready-to-use promotion formats

☐ Enclosed is my deposit of $7.50. Please send me a copy of the new AdverKit. I understand I will, in return, receive a $10.00 discount on the first order of any quantity of direct mail formats ordered from American Marketing Services, Inc.

☐ Send me an AdverKit and bill me for $7.50.

YANKEE CLIPPER
VOLUME I

☐ Enclosed is my check for $15.00. Please send me one copy of Yankee Clipper, Volume I, a portfolio of reproduction art containing more than 150 original cartoon illustrations.

☐ Send me a copy of Yankee Clipper, Volume I, and bill me for $17.50.

YANKEE CLIPPER
VOLUME II

☐ Enclosed is my check for $15.00. Please send me one copy of Yankee Clipper, Volume II, a portfolio of reproduction art containing 162 original cartoon illustrations.

☐ Send me a copy of Yankee Clipper, Volume II, and bill me for $17.50.

YANKEE CLIPPER
VOLUME III

☐ Enclosed is my check for $17.50. Please send me one copy of Yankee Clipper, Volume III, a portfolio of 203 conventional line illustrations.

☐ Send me a copy of Yankee Clipper, Volume III, and bill me for $20.00.

send these publications to:

Name
Position
Company
Address
City Zone State
My check for $ is enclosed.

This inquiry-answering form is casually personalized.

proach is that a reply device remains with the basic material when filed—even if an order card or form has already been used.

IMPRINTED REPLY ENVELOPES

An economical way of handling order forms is to make them a part of your business reply envelope. A number of suppliers offer syndicated order form-reply envelope formats, or you can prepare your own quite easily.

Two basic formats are used:

1. *A "V-Mail"-style format,* similar to the letter forms used for overseas mailing during World War II. Here the order form is printed on a flat sheet which is then die-cut and gummed so it can be folded into an envelope and sealed.
2. *Imprinted envelope.* An order form is simply printed beneath the flap or on the back of an envelope.

John Plain Order Blank

One user of the "V-Mail" format is John Plain & Co., which binds a number of envelope-order forms into its catalogs. One side of the form has blanks for filling in order information, while the reverse side contains the face of the envelope plus order instructions and change-of-address space (see illustration on page 1034).

A somewhat more complicated fold-up-and-seal order form is used by The Marine Corps Association to solicit subscriptions to *Marine Corps Gazette.* This is a 16¾- by 6¾-inch sheet plus die-cut flap, which is folded to 7⅜ by 3⅜ inches both for original mailing and return. The recipient simply reverse-folds the piece to convert it into a reply envelope. One side of the piece contains a multicolored, two-page promotion piece. The reverse side is divided into four sections, plus two flaps (see illustration across). One of the sections is the front of the reply envelope, another the back. A third section constitutes the order blank, while the fourth section is designed to be used by the association as a shipping label for a bonus premium being offered.

Imprinted Envelopes

Many different styles of imprinted envelopes are used for reply purposes. Most of them have a large flap which seals along the bottom of the envelope. This permits almost full utilization of both the back of the envelope pocket and the back of the flap for order

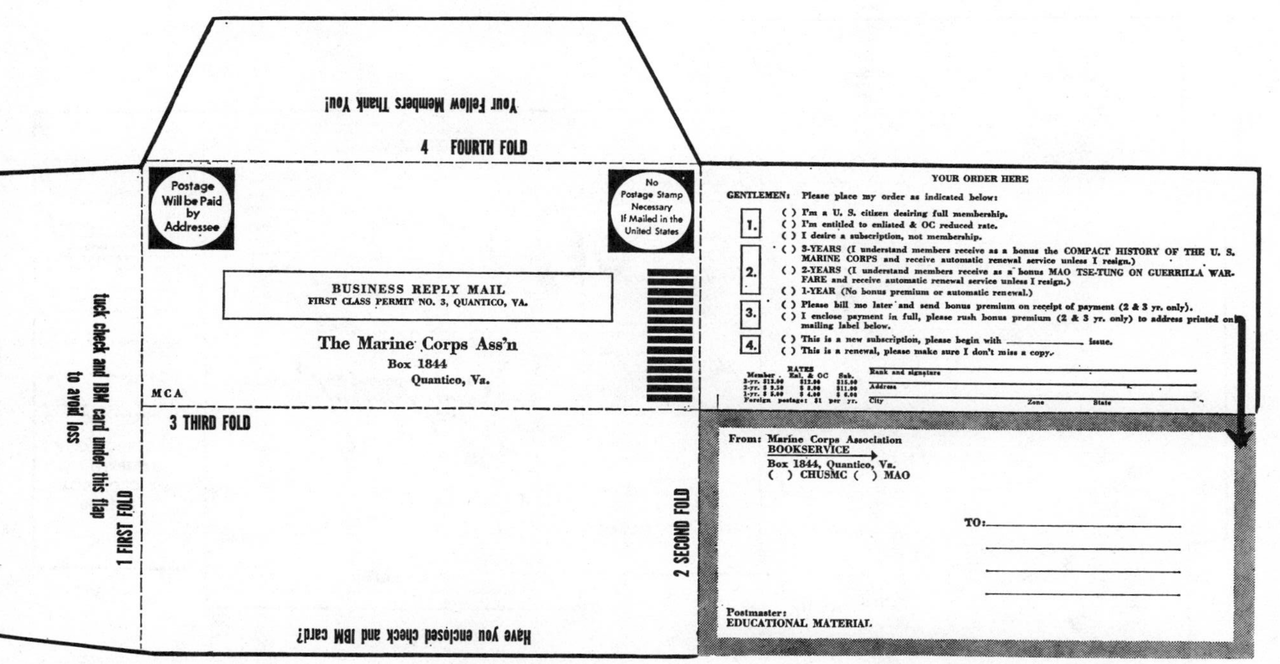

Your Fellow Members Thank You!

4 FOURTH FOLD

Postage Will be Paid by Addressee

No Postage Stamp Necessary If Mailed in the United States

BUSINESS REPLY MAIL
FIRST CLASS PERMIT NO. 3, QUANTICO, VA.

The Marine Corps Ass'n
Box 1844
Quantico, Va.

MCA

3 THIRD FOLD

1 FIRST FOLD

tuck check and IBM card under this flap to avoid loss

2 SECOND FOLD

Have you enclosed check and IBM card?

YOUR ORDER HERE

GENTLEMEN: Please place my order as indicated below:

1.
( ) I'm a U. S. citizen desiring full membership.
( ) I'm entitled to enlisted & OC reduced rate.
( ) I desire a subscription, not membership.

2.
( ) 3-YEARS (I understand members receive as a bonus the COMPACT HISTORY OF THE U. S. MARINE CORPS and receive automatic renewal service unless I resign.)
( ) 2-YEARS (I understand members receive as a bonus MAO TSE-TUNG ON GUERRILLA WARFARE and receive automatic renewal service unless I resign.)
( ) 1-YEAR (No bonus premium or automatic renewal.)

3.
( ) Please bill me later and send bonus premium on receipt of payment (2 & 3 yr. only).
( ) I enclose payment in full, please rush bonus premium (2 & 3 yr. only) to address printed on mailing label below.

4.
( ) This is a new subscription, please begin with ______ issue.
( ) This is a renewal, please make sure I don't miss a copy.

RATES

	Member	Enl. & OC	Sub.
3-yr.	$13.00	$12.00	$15.00
2-yr.	$ 9.50	$ 8.00	$11.00
1-yr.	$ 5.00	$ 4.00	$ 6.00

Foreign postage: $1 per yr.

Rank and signature ______
Address ______
City ______ Zone ______ State ______

From: Marine Corps Association
BOOKSERVICE
Box 1844, Quantico, Va.
( ) CHUSMC ( ) MAO

TO: ______

Postmaster:
EDUCATIONAL MATERIAL

The Marine Corps Association obtains many subscriptions with this complicated fold-up-and-seal order form.

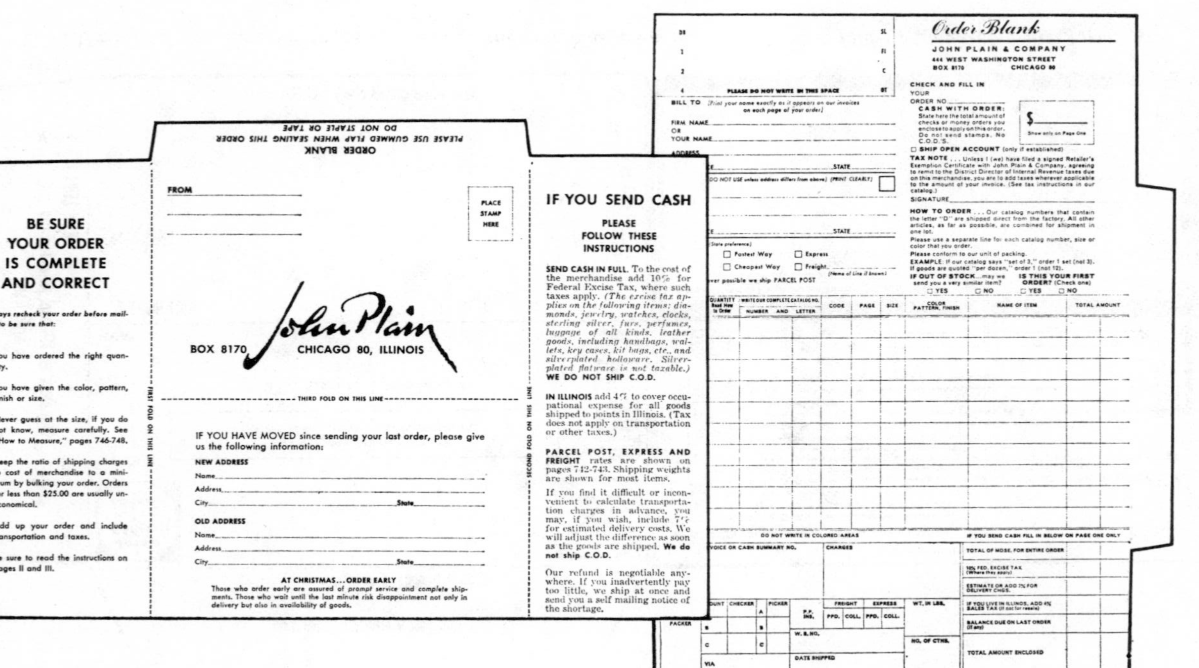

BE SURE YOUR ORDER IS COMPLETE AND CORRECT

Always recheck your order before mailing to be sure that:

1 You have ordered the right quantity.

2 You have given the color, pattern, finish or size.

3 Never guess at the size, if you do not know, measure carefully. See "How to Measure," pages 746-748.

4 Keep the ratio of shipping charges to cost of merchandise to a minimum by bulking your order. Orders for less than $25.00 are usually uneconomical.

5 Add up your order and include transportation and taxes.

6 Be sure to read the instructions on pages II and III.

FIRST FOLD ON THIS LINE

ORDER BLANK
PLEASE USE GUMMED FLAP WHEN SEALING THIS ORDER
DO NOT STAPLE OR TAPE

FROM ______

PLACE STAMP HERE

BOX 8170 John Plain CHICAGO 80, ILLINOIS

THIRD FOLD ON THIS LINE

IF YOU HAVE MOVED since sending your last order, please give us the following information:

NEW ADDRESS
Name ______
Address ______
City ______ State ______

OLD ADDRESS
Name ______
Address ______
City ______ State ______

AT CHRISTMAS...ORDER EARLY
Those who order early are assured of *prompt* service and complete shipments. Those who wait until the last minute risk disappointment not only in delivery but also in availability of goods.

SECOND FOLD ON THIS LINE

IF YOU SEND CASH

PLEASE FOLLOW THESE INSTRUCTIONS

SEND CASH IN FULL. To the cost of the merchandise add 10% for Federal Excise Tax, where such taxes apply. *(The excise tax applies on the following items: diamonds, jewelry, watches, clocks, sterling silver, furs, perfumes, luggage of all kinds, leather goods, including handbags, wallets, key cases, kit bags, etc., and silverplated holloware. Silverplated flatware is not taxable.)* **WE DO NOT SHIP C.O.D.**

IN ILLINOIS add 4% to cover occupational expense for all goods shipped to points in Illinois. (Tax does not apply on transportation or other taxes.)

PARCEL POST, EXPRESS AND FREIGHT rates are shown on pages 742-743. Shipping weights are shown for most items.

If you find it difficult or inconvenient to calculate transportation charges in advance, you may, if you wish, include 7% for estimated delivery costs. We will adjust the difference as soon as the goods are shipped. **We do not ship C.O.D.**

Our refund is negotiable anywhere. If you inadvertently pay too little, we ship at once and send you a self mailing notice of the shortage.

Order Blank

JOHN PLAIN & COMPANY
444 WEST WASHINGTON STREET
BOX 8170 CHICAGO 80

DB 1 2 4 PLEASE DO NOT WRITE IN THIS SPACE SL FI C BT

BILL TO *(Print your name exactly as it appears on our invoices on each page of your order)*

FIRM NAME OR YOUR NAME ______
ADDRESS ______
STATE ______
DO NOT USE *unless address differs from above)* (PRINT CLEARLY)
STATE ______
(State preference)
☐ Fastest Way ☐ Express
☐ Cheapest Way ☐ Freight ______ (Name of Line if known)
...ever possible we ship PARCEL POST

CHECK AND FILL IN
YOUR ORDER NO. ______

CASH WITH ORDER: State here the total amount of checks or money orders you enclose to apply on this order. Do not send stamps. No C.O.D.'S.

$ ______ Show only on Page One

☐ SHIP OPEN ACCOUNT (only if established)

TAX NOTE . . . Unless I *(we)* have filed a signed Retailer's Exemption Certificate with John Plain & Company, agreeing to remit to the District Director of Internal Revenue taxes due on this merchandise, you are to add taxes wherever applicable to the amount of your invoice. (See tax instructions in our catalog.)

SIGNATURE ______

HOW TO ORDER . . . Our catalog numbers that contain the letter "D" are shipped direct from the factory. All other articles, as far as possible, are combined for shipment in one lot.

Please use a separate line for each catalog number, size or color that you order.

Please conform to our unit of packing.

EXAMPLE: If our catalog says "set of 3," order 1 set (not 3). If goods are quoted "per dozen," order 1 (not 12).

IF OUT OF STOCK...may we send you a very similar item? ☐ YES ☐ NO

IS THIS YOUR FIRST ORDER? (Check one) ☐ YES ☐ NO

QUANTITY Read How to Order	WRITE OUR COMPLETE CATALOG NO. NUMBER AND LETTER	CODE	PAGE	SIZE	COLOR PATTERN, FINISH	NAME OF ITEM	TOTAL AMOUNT

DO NOT WRITE IN COLORED AREAS

INVOICE OR CASH SUMMARY NO. | CHARGES | COUNT | CHECKER | PICKER | P.P. INS. | FREIGHT PPD. COLL. | EXPRESS PPD. COLL. | WT. IN LBS. | NO. OF CTNS. | PACKER | W. & NO. | DATE SHIPPED | VIA

IF YOU SEND CASH FILL IN BELOW ON PAGE ONE ONLY

TOTAL OF MDSE. FOR ENTIRE ORDER
10% FED. EXCISE TAX (Where they apply)
ESTIMATE OR ADD 7% FOR DELIVERY CHGS.
IF YOU LIVE IN ILLINOIS, ADD 4% SALES TAX (If not for resale)
BALANCE DUE ON LAST ORDER (If any)
TOTAL AMOUNT ENCLOSED

Front and back of the "V-Mail" format which John Plain & Co. binds into its catalogs.

purposes. If an increased area is required, the flap may be extended and perforated so the additional area can be torn off and inserted into the envelope. Several examples of imprinted order envelopes are shown.

An interesting application of this envelope technique is used by *Advertising Age.* While a conventional order blank is included with promotions for the magazine, the business reply envelope has an imprinted back which offers the respondent the opportunity to enter subscriptions to two additional publications—*Industrial Marketing* and *Advertising & Sales Promotion.*

This tagalong use of envelopes is sometimes used with reply envelopes enclosed with retail store monthly bills. Impulse items are most often featured in such promotions. Mail order companies sometimes use imprinted envelopes to request names to whom catalogs can be sent. Others use envelopes of this type to permit handy transmittal of changes of address.

EXTRA COPY OF LETTER TO BE INITIALED

When autotyped letters are used for promotion, some companies enclose a carbon copy of the original letter and then request respondents simply to initial the copy and return it to the sender in order to receive whatever is being offered. This technique has proved particularly effective in business and industrial promotions.

PACKET OF ORDER FORMS

Another approach to providing order forms with promotions of multiple items is to describe and illustrate one or a few items on a slip of paper and then enclose a number of such slips in a packet. Each slip has an order form printed on it.

An example of this technique is the "Ideas and Aids" packet illustrated on page 1039. The 3¾- by 9-inch packet is a miniature portfolio containing about a dozen 3⅔- by 8½-inch slips promoting items published by American Marketing Services. A variety of different colors of paper stock is used to add impact to the packet. However, a basic design is used for each of the slips to add continuity.

This same technique is also used by department stores for statement stuffers. (See Chapter 35, "Statement and Letter Stuffers.")

Nation's Business | 1615 H ST., N.W., WASHINGTON 6, D. C.

RENEWAL INVOICE

Is your address correct

DICK HODGSON
27 STANFORD RD-WELL H
BOSTON 81 MASS
MIA4150 N2A 274 11 C
AMERICAN MARKETING SERV

AMOUNT ENCLOSED:

☐ $6.75 for 1 year

☐ $18.00 for 3 years

☐ Bill me later

Initial__________

PLEASE RETURN THIS UPPER HALF TO INSURE PROPER RECORDING OF YOUR ORDER

Continuation of Nation's Business for one year -- subscription to include two complimentary management reports. See bonus slip enclosed For maximum savings, continue your subscription for 3 years at $18.00... saves you $2.25	$6.75

IF YOU HAVE ALREADY RENEWED, PLEASE DISREGARD THIS REMINDER

Nation's Business • 1615 H ST., N.W., WASHINGTON 6, D. C.

Retain bottom half for your records. Subscription fee is tax-deductible.

Nation's Business *sends out this renewal invoice with excellent results.*

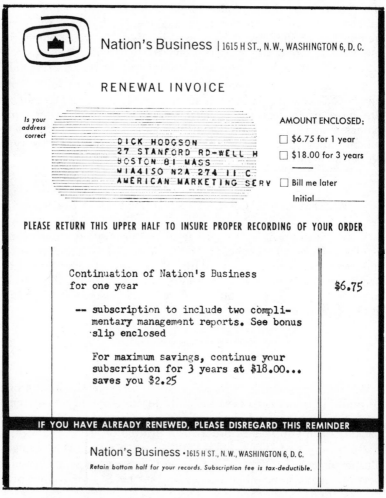

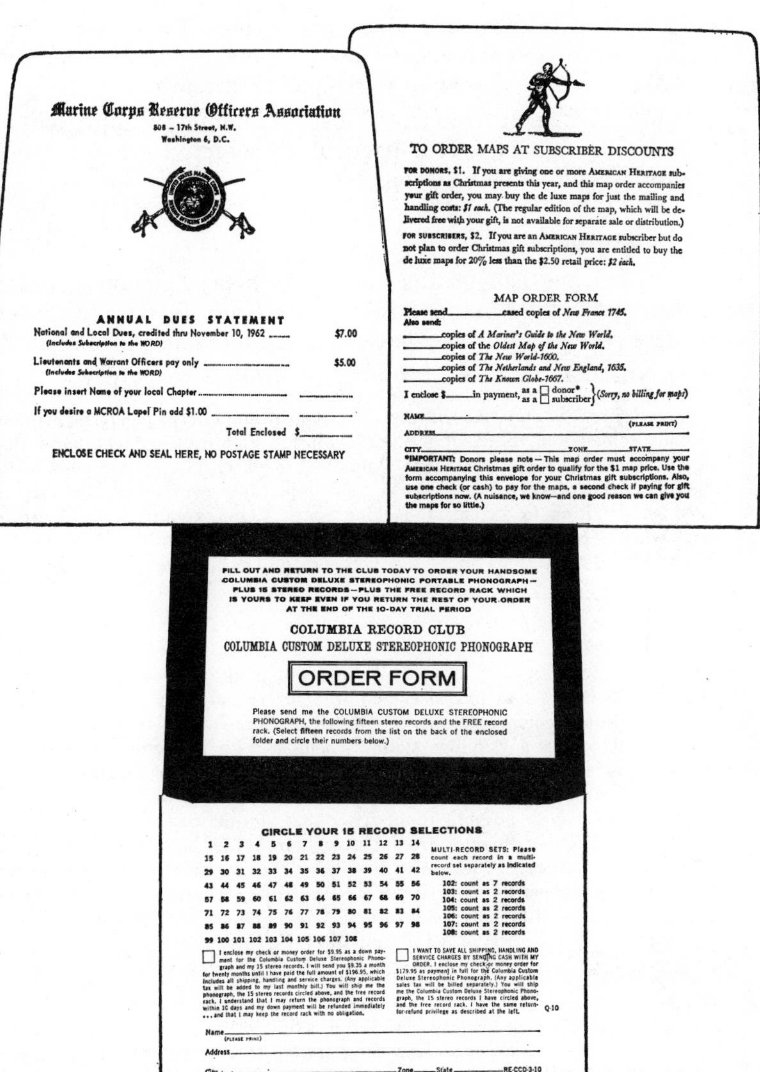

Marine Corps Reserve Officers Association
808 – 17th Street, N.W.
Washington 6, D.C.

ANNUAL DUES STATEMENT

National and Local Dues, credited thru November 10, 1962 ______ $7.00
(Includes Subscription to the WORD)

Lieutenants and Warrant Officers pay only ______ $5.00
(Includes Subscription to the WORD)

Please insert Name of your local Chapter ______ ______

If you desire a MCROA Lapel Pin add $1.00 ______ ______

Total Enclosed $______

ENCLOSE CHECK AND SEAL HERE, NO POSTAGE STAMP NECESSARY

TO ORDER MAPS AT SUBSCRIBER DISCOUNTS

FOR DONORS, $1. If you are giving one or more AMERICAN HERITAGE subscriptions as Christmas presents this year, and this map order accompanies your gift order, you may buy the de luxe maps for just the mailing and handling costs: *$1 each.* (The regular edition of the map, which will be delivered free with your gift, is not available for separate sale or distribution.)

FOR SUBSCRIBERS, $2. If you are an AMERICAN HERITAGE subscriber but do not plan to order Christmas gift subscriptions, you are entitled to buy the de luxe maps for 20% less than the $2.50 retail price: *$2 each.*

MAP ORDER FORM

Please send ______ cased copies of *New France 1745.*
Also send:
______ copies of *A Mariner's Guide to the New World.*
______ copies of the *Oldest Map of the New World.*
______ copies of *The New World-1600.*
______ copies of *The Netherlands and New England, 1635.*
______ copies of *The Known Globe-1667.*

I enclose $______ in payment, as a ☐ donor* / as a ☐ subscriber } *(Sorry, no billing for maps)*

NAME ______ (PLEASE PRINT)
ADDRESS ______
CITY ______ ZONE ______ STATE ______

*IMPORTANT: Donors please note—This map order must accompany your AMERICAN HERITAGE Christmas gift order to qualify for the $1 map price. Use the form accompanying this envelope for your Christmas gift subscriptions. Also, use one check (or cash) to pay for the maps, a second check if paying for gift subscriptions now. (A nuisance, we know—and one good reason we can give you the maps for so little.)

FILL OUT AND RETURN TO THE CLUB TODAY TO ORDER YOUR HANDSOME COLUMBIA CUSTOM DELUXE STEREOPHONIC PORTABLE PHONOGRAPH—PLUS 15 STEREO RECORDS—PLUS THE FREE RECORD RACK WHICH IS YOURS TO KEEP EVEN IF YOU RETURN THE REST OF YOUR ORDER AT THE END OF THE 10-DAY TRIAL PERIOD

COLUMBIA RECORD CLUB
COLUMBIA CUSTOM DELUXE STEREOPHONIC PHONOGRAPH

ORDER FORM

Please send me the COLUMBIA CUSTOM DELUXE STEREOPHONIC PHONOGRAPH, the following fifteen stereo records and the FREE record rack. (Select fifteen records from the list on the back of the enclosed folder and circle their numbers below.)

CIRCLE YOUR 15 RECORD SELECTIONS

1 2 3 4 5 6 7 8 9 10 11 12 13 14
15 16 17 18 19 20 21 22 23 24 25 26 27 28
29 30 31 32 33 34 35 36 37 38 39 40 41 42
43 44 45 46 47 48 49 50 51 52 53 54 55 56
57 58 59 60 61 62 63 64 65 66 67 68 69 70
71 72 73 74 75 76 77 78 79 80 81 82 83 84
85 86 87 88 89 90 91 92 93 94 95 96 97 98
99 100 101 102 103 104 105 106 107 108

MULTI-RECORD SETS: Please count each record in a multi-record set separately as indicated below.
102: count as 7 records
103: count as 2 records
104: count as 2 records
105: count as 2 records
106: count as 2 records
107: count as 2 records
108: count as 2 records

☐ I enclose my check or money order for $9.95 as a down payment for the Columbia Custom Deluxe Stereophonic Phonograph and my 15 stereo records. I will send you $9.35 a month for twenty months until I have paid the full amount of $196.95, which includes all shipping, handling and service charges. (Any applicable tax will be added to my last monthly bill.) You will ship me the phonograph, the 15 stereo records circled above, and the free record rack. I understand that I may return the phonograph and records within 10 days and my down payment will be refunded immediately . . . and that I may keep the record rack with no obligation.

☐ I WANT TO SAVE ALL SHIPPING, HANDLING AND SERVICE CHARGES BY SENDING CASH WITH MY ORDER. I enclose my check or money order for $179.95 as payment in full for the Columbia Custom Deluxe Stereophonic Phonograph. (Any applicable sales tax will be billed separately.) You will ship me the Columbia Custom Deluxe Stereophonic Phonograph, the 15 stereo records I have circled above, and the free record rack. I have the same return-for-refund privilege as described at the left. Q-10

Name ______ (PLEASE PRINT)
Address ______
City ______ Zone ______ State ______ RE-CCD-3-10

Three examples of imprinted order envelopes. Note how much information can be put into these areas.

"GIMMICK" APPROACHES

Direct mail showmanship does not bypass the order form. Hundreds of devices have been used to make doubly sure the reply device does not escape the recipient's attention.

Probably the most frequently used "gimmick" approach is the simulated certificate. It is particularly effective when a "special value" theme is being promoted.

"Look" Certificates

Probably no one had greater success with the "gimmick" order form than Les Suhler of the now defunct *Look.* In fact, his order forms were so successful they have spawned thousands of imitators.

Three typical *Look* order forms are shown on page 1042.

Special Look Savings Certificate. This certificate is typical. It is printed in four colors—red, blue, and black against a light-green background designed to resemble the safety paper used for bank checks. It is loaded with special touches designed to make it look important—everything from simulated handwriting to an official looking eagle. Copy explains: "This certificate, when returned to *Look* magazine, along with an additional $3 remittance, constitutes full payment for 39 issues of *Look* at the regular $6 subscription rate."

Reservation Certificate. Another frequently used *Look* order form technique distinguishes this order form—the use of gold ink. Other colors are magenta, light-blue, and black. Like the other forms shown, it measures 6¾ by 10⅛ inches and has a tear-off stub for retention by the buyer. Two other techniques commonly used by *Look* are present—a certificate border and a spot to affix a "savings stamp" enclosed with the letter. Basic copy: "You, as a *Look* subscriber, are cordially invited to use the attached certificate to reserve a 10-day free examination of this book *(The Story of America's Religions)* with no obligation. After that you may either keep the book at the special $3.00 discount from the regular $14.95 bookstore price (plus a few cents postage) . . . or return it without charge. Money-back guarantee: You don't risk a penny (and you save the postage charge) when you send your remittance with your reservation. You must be pleased, or you may return the book and receive a full refund check."

Prepublication Certificate. This order form was used for another *Look* book—*The Story Behind the Painting.* The four colors were red, dark-orange, deep-blue, and black. Again a savings stamp was used. Copy: "Please send me *The Story Behind the Painting* in rich buckram binding for 10 days' examination. I must be completely delighted by its splendor, beauty and clarity, or I will return the volume to you within 10 days and owe nothing. Otherwise you will bill me at the special prepublication price of only $11.95 (regular price, $14.95) plus a few cents' postage and handling." This certificate form has a blank for the buyer's signature. In almost every case, *Look* includes at least one feature which requires the buyer to take some specific action other than just returning the certificate to complete an order.

American Marketing Services promotes multiple items on different colors of paper stock. For continuity, the same basic design is used.

"Reader's Digest" Tip-ons

Another strong believer in the "gimmick" approach to order forms is *Reader's Digest.* Six typical *Digest* order forms are shown on page 1041.

Dividend Certificate. This 3¼- by 6-inch certificate in red, blue, green, and black was printed atop a 7½- by 13-inch letter. Adjacent to the certificate were two perforated "stamps"—one contained a full-color illustration of a record album with "yes" superimposed; the other had "no thank you" printed in red atop a gray background. Copy explained: "This Dividend Certificate will bring you the *Digest's* delightful new three-record album, 'The World's Greatest Waltzes,' for only $6.79 (plus a small postage and handling charge). You might expect to pay as much as $14.95! (To obtain ***your*** album for 5 days' free examination—*without obligation*—return this certificate with the Album Stamp pasted on the enclosed bill.)" This mailing was made to members of the Reader's Digest Condensed Book Club and accompanied the invoice for the then-current quarterly book. A spot was imprinted on the invoice for pasting one of the two "stamps."

Reservation Certificate. This order form for the waltz album is more typical of the *Digest* approach. A cardboard "Waltz Medallion" was tipped to the stub on the 5¾- by 10¼-inch order form. Then there was a die-cut slot with a paper pocket pasted on the reverse side of the card. Copy read: "To receive your Album, place 'Waltz Medallion' in this pocket and mail card today." The card was printed in gold, lavender, light-blue, and black.

Subscriber's Gift Certificate. This 6⅝- by 10½-inch order form has two punch-out tokens, one reading, "Yes please," the other, "No thank you." Copy explains: "To enter your Digest Gift Subscriptions at this reduced price, place 'Yes' token in slot at left. Fill in names and addresses below. Mail card in reply envelope—no postage necessary. No need to pay now—we'll bill you next year at only $2.97 per gift (instead of the regular price of $4.00). Because we must soon determine how many Gift Copies of the special Christmas issue to print, please send back one token to tell us whether you accept this offer or not."

Popular Music. One token and two slots were used on this multicolor order form. The "token" was a reproduction of the record album with a simulated code number superimposed. Copy adjacent to the first slot read: "Yes! Please send me 'Popular Music That Will Live Forever' for 5 days' free examination! To receive your album for 5 days' free trial, place special 'Album' Token in pocket above and mail today! If not delighted, you may return it after 5 days, and owe nothing." Copy with the alternate slot read: "No, thank you. I do not wish to examine an album at this time. (Use this pocket only if you do not even want to see and hear this beautiful, 10-record album.)"

Paid in Full Token. This card headed, "Reservation Certificate," was used with an offer of a free sample copy of "Best-Sellers from Reader's Digest Condensed Books." It has a certificate border printed in light-green plus two slots into which the gold "Paid in Full" token can be inserted. The first is labeled, "Yes . . . To secure your free volume, place your 'Paid in Full' Token here." The second: "No, thank you . . . Use this pocket only if you do not wish to receive a free book at this time."

One can hardly resist ordering when he receives these colorful order forms which Reader's Digest *mails out regularly.*

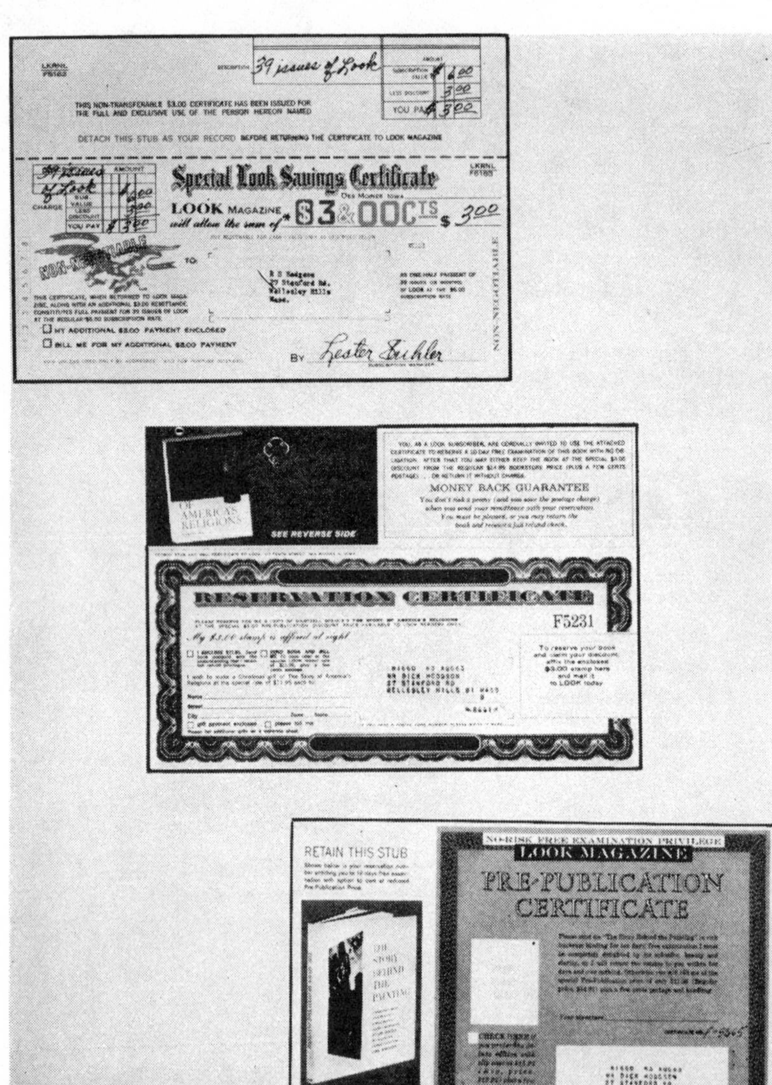

These "gimmick" order forms originated by Les Suhler of Look *have had thousands of imitators.*

New Member's Reservation Card. The *Digest* is a great believer in the use of pennies in its mailings. Two shiny new pennies were tipped to this card, and, like the tokens on other cards, were positioned to show through a picture window in the mailing envelope. This card was used with a mailing offering four RCA Victor records for only 98 cents to those "joining" the RCA Victor Record Club. Copy: "Send no money now. Just select your four records from the enclosed folder, tear off the four corresponding stamps, paste them in place on this card and mail today! We'll bill you later for just $1 plus handling and postage—you keep 2 cents as your 'change' *in advance!*"

COMBINATION ORDER FORM-LETTERS

With the growing use of computer-printed direct mail formats, the combination order form-letter has become the standard format for many mailers. This format is described and illustrated in Chapter 27—"Computer Formats."

HOW TO KEY ORDER FORMS

Most direct mail advertisers using order forms and reply cards in their mailings prefer to have them "keyed" so returns can be properly attributed to the mailing or list responsible for the returns. There are several methods for such keying.

The most frequently used method is to simply imprint a code letter or number on the card or form. This can be part of the original printing or can involve a separate imprinting step. Some inserting equipment has an attachment which automatically imprints a key number on the card, form, or reply envelope as material is being processed. This technique permits use of the same reply device for all mailings and eliminates the necessity of inventorying quantities of separate reply devices for each key. Other useful techniques include:

Use a different color of paper stock for each key.

Use a different ink color combination for each key.

Trim off corners to identify different keys.

Print consecutive serial numbers on reply devices and assign a series for each key.

Trim order cards to different lengths and widths.

If your return address is in a town or city that does not have postal zones, you can add a fictional zone number. This has an added advantage over some other keying systems since the zone number is likely to be used even if replies are not made on your prepared reply device.

Request that replies be made to a specific individual—using a different name for each key.

Use IBM tab cards with punched codes. Even if you don't have IBM processing equipment, you can "read" the punched codes to identify different keys.

Date the reply device, using a different date for each key.

A particularly economical method for keying reply cards or order forms is to include a row of typographical ornaments, letters, or numbers at the bottom or side. The complete row will represent the first key. For subsequent keys, have your printer route or wipe the ornaments from his plate one by one as the press run progresses. For example, if you want 10 different keys, a full row of 10 ornaments will represent the first key; nine ornaments, the second key; eight, the third key; and so forth. If you do not know quantity requirements for various keys in advance, you can use a paper drill to cut a hole through various ornaments.

Virgil Angerman's Tips

One of the best guides to the preparation of effective order forms is "The Psychology of Wording an Order Form" prepared by Virgil D. Angerman, Sales Promotion Manager of Boise Cascade Envelope Division:

> The order form, whether it is printed on card stock, a slip of paper, or as a coupon at the bottom of a sales letter, bridges the gap between the buyer and the seller. It is an agreement or contract between two parties, one the buyer and the other the seller. This can be the most crucial part of your sales package. Many a sale has been lost because the order form did not clearly state the terms of the offer.
>
> In planning the order form, special consideration should be given to the format. Will you use a reply card or an order blank? If you use a reply card, the standard size is 3¼ by 5½ inches. Postal regulations specify (See Section 131.222b of the Postal Manual) that reply cards having a thickness of less than 0.006 or more than 0.0095 of an inch (micrometer measurement) are non-mailable. In paper terminology this means a minimum basic weight of 70 lb. high bulk stock. A flimsy feeling card does not inspire confidence for it may be damaged in the mails.
>
> Many advertisers use an oversize reply card, usually 3½ by 8½ inches if it is pre-addressed and enclosed in a No. 10 (4⅛ by 9½ inches) window envelope. This keeps the card or order form from "floating." The extra portion of the card may be used as a perforated stub to feature your refund guarantee, illustrate the merchandise, describe a premium, or for your cus-

tomer to record the date of purchase, check number, amount, etc. Maximum mailing portion is 4¼ by 6 inches.

Order forms enclosed in catalogs vary in size depending upon the size of the page and the number of items offered. Ample space is needed for the customer's name and address, where shipment is to be made, catalog number, description of items ordered, price, amount of tax, shipping and handling charges, total amount enclosed, and other details needed to fill the order. Obviously, all of this information cannot be included on the average reply card if there are many items to be ordered. Hence, the choice of a format depends entirely upon your individual requirements.

PLANNING THE ORDER FORM LAYOUT

There are other considerations in planning the format that will help to stimulate sales. An important point is to allow ample space for the customer to fill-in his name and address and other needed information you may require such as: Title, Name of Firm, Type of Business, Home or Business Address, Bill Company, Bill Me, and a place for signature or initials. A cramped order form discourages sales. If possible, arrange the order form for typewriter spacing.

The layout and typography of the order form should be inviting, easy to read and look important. Rules and borders can add attractiveness. A stock certificate type of border inspires confidence. Use a good quality of paper stock for it commands respect.

If possible, order forms should be designed to fit the reply envelope without folding. This saves time at the mail opening desk.

THE ADDRESS YOU USE CAN BE IMPORTANT

Should you use a street address, a building address or a Post Office Box address? Obviously, a street address makes it easier for a customer to call at your place of business if he desires. Building addresses are used by many advertisers for their prestige value or to use a Room Number for keying purposes. Post Office Box addresses are being used more and more by many firms as a way to sort their mail or for pick-up convenience. In either case, you should always include your Zip Code number for speed-up delivery.

The response to offers in certain types of businesses can be increased by using addresses that have a relationship to the product or service. For example, Hollywood, California, is considered the entertainment center of the country. A proposition in the entertainment field pulls better if a Hollywood address is used. An aviation publication or school enjoys added prestige if located at the airport. An address in the Wall Street district is helpful to a financial service. A firm selling meat specialties by mail finds that an address in a packing house location is an advantage.

4 STEPS IN WRITING AN ORDER FORM

The order form is probably the most important enclosure in a direct mail package. It is "Where the Action is!" Therefore, keep it simple and spell out the terms of the offer in easily understood language. The following steps will help you organize your order form.

1. How to Start an Order Form

The opening words of an order form should express a REQUEST; make a DEMAND; or state a FACT. Here is how a REQUEST can be worded: "Please send me . . ."; or "I'd like to examine . . ." A DEMAND starts this way: "Sign me up. Send me . . ."; or "Rush me your newest . . ." To state a FACT one merely says: "I enclose . . ."; or "Attached is my order . . ."; or "As a new subscriber . . ."

When you have decided which approach you prefer to use, perhaps one of the following 27 ways to start an order form may prove helpful.

1. As a new subscriber . . .
2. Attached is my order . . .
3. Before the price goes up . . .
4. I accept your invitation . . .
5. I am taking you up . . .
6. I enclose . . .
7. I want to examine . . .
8. I want to find out . . .
9. I want to own . . .
10. I want to save . . .
11. I wish to sponsor . . .
12. I'd like to examine . . .
13. If my reservation is received in time . . .
14. Please accept my . . .
15. Please enroll me . . .
16. Please mail, postage prepaid . . .
17. Please rush my . . .
18. Please send me . . .
19. Please supply me . . .
20. Rush me your newest . . .
21. Send postpaid . . .
22. Sign me up. Send me . . .
23. Send me your . . .
24. Yes! I am interested . . .
25. Yes! Please send me . . .
26. Yes—We want to give . . .
27. Yes, I want to try . . .

2. Specify Product or Service

Next, the order form should specify what the customer is ordering. Is it a book? A subscription to a magazine? Nursery stock? A hunting jacket? An electric drill? Or, whatever you are selling. Allow space for quantity, catalog number, etc., if needed.

3. State Prices and Terms

The terms of the offer should be clearly stated. Tell the absolute truth. There should be no trick phrases, no hidden meanings, just a straight forward statement of the price of your product or service, the delivery charges if any, the amount of the down payment and a schedule of monthly payments if sold on the installment plan. This is one phase of the selling process where you can build confidence and avoid misunderstandings.

4. Emphasize Your Guarantee

A strongly worded guarantee of "complete satisfaction or money back" will strengthen your offer and help to break down sales resistance. Here is how Sturbridge Yankee Workshop word their guarantee: "OUR IRONCLAD GUARANTEE! You must be satisfied. If any item you buy from us does not please you, you may return it, postage or shipping charges collect, within 10 days, for a complete and instantaneous refund. No reason is necessary." There are no loop-holes in that guarantee!

FIVE METHODS OF SELLING

Now let's consider the various "Methods of Selling." Are you going to use the "Free Examination" plan of no payment unless satisfied? Or, "Cash in Advance Subject to Refund?" Or, the "Positive Order—Not Subject to Cancellation or Refund?" Or, "C.O.D.—Pay Upon Arrival?" Or, the "Negative Option Plan"? The wording for each of these methods of selling must be clearly stated to avoid confusion. If you raise a doubt in the mind of the prospect, you may lose the order or have difficulty in collecting the account. Here are typical examples of the five methods of selling:

1. Free Examination—No Payment Unless Satisfied

You have the choice of five methods of selling. First, the "Free Examination" or the approval plan which gives the prospect the opportunity of seeing or using the product for 10 days or more before paying for it. Here is how one publisher words his "Free Examination" offers:

Please send me, for free trial examination, a copy of the revised, up-to-date HANDBOOK OF BUSINESS LETTERS by L. E. Frailey, I understand that I may use this Handbook for 10 full days. After that time, if I find the 761 model business letters contained in this book will save me hours of time and effort spent in letter writing, I will send you $17.95 plus postage and packing. Otherwise I will send it back and pay nothing, owe nothing.

☐ SAVE MONEY: Check here if you prefer to enclose payment (plus sales tax where applicable) now, in which case we pay postage and packing charges. Same return privilege, full money-back guarantee.

Note that the above order form spells out in easy-to-understand language the terms of the offer. There is no money down, no obligation to buy unless the customer is satisfied. The free examination period is definitely spelled out. Also, note the saving to be made by sending cash with order with a money-back guarantee.

2. Cash In Advance Subject to Refund

Second, a variation of the "Free Examination" offer is where a cash-in-advance or deposit is required, with the understanding that payment will be refunded if the customer is not satisfied. The Acme Dress Form Co. asks for a deposit of $4.95 as evidence of good intentions. They word their order form this way: "I understand that I may use for full 30 days—make as many outfits as I please! If I am not absolutely delighted, I may return form for full and immediate refund." This phrase breaks down all sales resistance as the customer can return the form and get her money back if not satisfied.

Please rush my Acme MIRACLE S-T-R-E-T-C-H DRESS FORM! I enclose deposit of $4.95 in check or money order. I understand that I may use for 30 full days—make as many outfits as I please! If I am not absolutely delighted, I may return form for full and immediate refund. Otherwise, I agree to pay $3.00 for 5 months until full payment of $19.95, plus shipping charges, is made.

Name

Address

City State Zip

3. Positive Order—No Cancellation Or Refund Privilege

Third, is the "Positive" plan which calls for payment upon receipt of bill or the remittance is enclosed with the order. The Wall Street Journal word their "Positive" order form this way:

> I accept your invitation to try THE WALL STREET JOURNAL, with its reports of important developments and trends. Please send it to me daily for the next Ten Weeks for $5.
>
> ☐ Check attached ☐ Bill me ☐ I prefer one year at $26

A "Positive" order is not subject to cancellation or refund. Note in the copy above, there is "sell" in the wording: "—with its reports of important developments and trends." This is what the customer expects to get from The Wall Street Journal. Your order form should read as though the customer were writing to you.

4. C.O.D.—Pay Upon Arrival

Fourth, is the C.O.D. plan where the customer agrees to pay the postman upon receipt of the merchandise. Many firms require a small deposit to ensure that the customer will accept the shipment when it arrives. This helps to cut down refusals. In the copy below you will note that Information, Incorporated, offers the choice of sending full payment with the order or a "Goodwill deposit" of $1.00 and the balance C.O.D. plus postage and handling charges. In either case, the money-back guarantee applies. The wording of this order form is exceptionally well thought out.

Gentlemen: Yes, I want to try a copy of Gertrude Enelow's BODY DYNAMICS entirely at your risk. I am enclosing the low introductory price of only $4.98, complete. I will use this book for a full ten days at your risk. If I am not delighted . . . if this book does not do everything you say, I will simply return it for every cent of my money back.

☐ If you wish your order sent C.O.D. CHECK HERE! Enclose $1 goodwill deposit. Pay postman balance, plus postage and handling charge. Same money-back guarantee, of course!

Name (please print)

Address

City

State *Zip Code*

5. Negative Option Plan

This method of selling is used by the record clubs, book clubs and others having a continuing program of releases, usually monthly. The customer enters a trial order for his first release at a reduced price with the understanding that additional releases will be shipped and billed unless the customer wishes to refuse the automatic shipments. In that case, all he need do is to return the dated card provided in advance giving him the option of accepting or refusing the shipment. If the card is not returned by the date on the card, it is understood the shipment is to be made and billed. Note how the RCA Music Service explain their Negative Option Plan in the coupon at the right.

YES, please accept my application for trial membership in the RCA Music Service, and send me the 4 selections I have chosen for only 99 cents. I understand I may refuse the automatic shipment of each month's Main Selection, or order other selections by returning the dated card always provided. I agree to buy as few as four more selections at regular Service prices within a year to fulfill my trial membership. Then, under the Music Service's dividend plan, I may choose one selection FREE for every two I buy at regular Service prices. (A small shipping-service charge is added to each order.)

10 SALES TECHNIQUES THAT STIMULATE RESULTS

1. Use a Numbered Order Form

A numbered order card or form adds a feeling of exclusiveness to your offer. Print the number in red ink to call attention to the personalization.

2. Avoid Legal Phrases

You may have seen order forms that read like they were written by a Philadelphia lawyer. The wording discourages prospects from ordering. Certain offers require detailed phraseology. The International Correspondence Schools in wording their order form formerly said: "I agree" to certain requirements. Now they say: "I understand," which has the same meaning without the legal phraseology. This helps to break down sales resistance.

3. List Highest Price First

When offering the choice of three price units such as $3.00, $4.00 or $5.00, list $5.00 first, $4.00 second, and $3.00 last. You can get more orders at the higher unit which increases the dollar volume per thousand letters mailed.

4. Indicate "Best Buy"

Look magazine in listing three price offers, $4.00, $6.00 and $8.00, overprints the $8.00 price with a simulated rubber stamp impression reading "Best Buy." Half of the orders received are at the $8.00 price. An excellent idea to increase the unit of sale.

5. Non-Transferable Order Form Adds Appeal

When pre-addressed order forms are used, you can give the offer added value by stating that the order form is "Non-Transferable" and is to be used only by the person whose name appears on the form.

6. Personal Checks Accepted

Another way to get more cash with order is to state that Personal Check will be accepted. This eliminates the buying of a money order or cashier's check. Saves time and costs less. Also, a check is a safe way to remit.

7. "Credit Approved" Stimulates Orders

An idea that stimulates more orders is to print on your order form the words, "Credit Approved" or "Credit O.K." This gives the prospect a feeling of good credit.

8. Definite Time Limit Gets Action

Put a definite time limit on your order forms when making a special offer. For example, you can say: "This offer is Void after (mention the date). That helps to get action.

9. What to Say Instead of "Sign Here"

When you ask a prospect to "Sign" the order form, it implies the customer is going to be involved. A better way to get the "Signature" is to say: "Write your name here."

10. No Salesman Will Call

Many people abhor the idea that a salesman may call and hence hesitate to answer direct mail solicitations and advertisements. If you sell exclusively by mail, mention in your copy, "No salesman will call." This has increased results up to 50% more.

74 SUGGESTED HEADINGS FOR ORDER FORMS

Every order form or coupon should have a heading that urges ACTION, offers a BENEFIT or makes a PROMISE. For example, the heading: "Tear Off and Mail The Card—NOW!", is ACTION compelling. Another example of ACTION is: "Don't Delay! Mail This Card Today!".

Good examples of headings offering BENEFITS are: "Special Saving Certificate." "Use This Order Form for Greater Profits," "I Accept Your Bargain Offer" and "Free Gift Certificate."

A heading that makes a PROMISE is: "Examine a Copy at Our Expense —Just Return This Card." Also, a PROMISE is indicated in these headings: "Guaranteed Order Form," "Order Now for Immediate Shipment" and "No Money Down—18 Months to Pay."

Here are 74 suggested headings for your consideration:

1. Acceptance Card
2. Act Now! Mail Card—Send No Money
3. Air Mail Coupon Today
4. Certificate of Decision
5. Check and Return This Form Promptly
6. Discount Certificate
7. Don't Delay! Mail This Card Today!
8. Enrollment Application
9. Examine a Copy at Our Expense—Just Return This Card
10. 15-Day Free Examination Offer
11. 50th Anniversary Offer
12. Fill in and Mail TODAY!
13. Free Book Certificate
14. Free Examination Card
15. Free Gift Certificate
16. Free Information Certificate
17. Free Inspection Card
18. Free 10-Day Trial Reservation
19. Free Trial—Send No Money
20. Guaranteed Order Form
21. I Accept Your Bargain Offer
22. Introductory Certificate
23. Investment Certificate
24. Just Mail Coupon—No Salesman Will Call
25. Just Mail This Card Today
26. Mail Card at No Risk—Send No Money
27. Mail Coupon for Giant Free Catalog
28. Mail for "On Approval" Examination
29. Mail Free-Trial Coupon Today
30. Mail No-Risk Coupon Today
31. Mail Now for Free Book
32. Mail This Card for 14-Day Free Trial
33. Mail This Card Today—No Stamp Needed
34. Money-Back Coupon
35. Money-Saving Certificate
36. New Subscription Application

37. No Money Down—18 Months to Pay
38. No Risk Enrollment Application
39. No Risk Inspection Request
40. No Risk Special Order Form
41. Non-Transferable Certificate
42. Official Enrollment Form
43. Order Form with Return Privilege
44. Order Now for Immediate Shipment
45. Order with Confidence
46. Personal Reservation Form
47. Renewal Certificate
48. Reservation Certificate
49. Rush Coupon for Your Free Outfit
50. Send for Free Catalog
51. Send for Illustrated Brochure
52. Send for The Facts Today
53. Send No Money—Just the Card
54. Send Now for Free Trial
55. Send This Money-Saving Card Today
56. Special Discount Coupon
57. Special Enrollment Form
58. Special Gift Offer
59. Special Half-Price Certificate
60. Special Introduction Offer
61. Special No-Risk Offer
62. Special Offer Certificate
63. Special Pre-Publication Offer
64. Special Savings Certificate
65. Special Trial Form No. 1021
66. Subscription Certificate
67. Subscription Reservation Card
68. Tear Off and Mail The Card—NOW!
69. This Blank Makes it Easy to Renew
70. This Coupon Answered Within 24 Hours
71. Use This Order Form for Greater Profits
72. Use This $5 Gold Certificate
73. Will You Examine This New Book if We Send it FREE?
74. Yours for 10 Days FREE!

Chapter 39

ENVELOPES

SINCE the envelope is the first element in most direct mail "packages" which comes face to face with the recipient, it plays a vital role in the success of any mailing program. So widely recognized is this fact of direct mail life that a very high percentage of today's mailings go forth to do their work in envelopes which have been specially designed to work in harmony with the other mailing elements.

Gone is the day when the successful direct mail advertiser simply goes into the stockroom and pulls a few boxes of the "standard" company envelopes off the shelf and uses them for his mailings. Even the business reply envelope included with many mailings—particularly in the mail order field—often gets special treatment to coordinate it with other elements in a given mailing.

And while there has been an accelerating trend toward use of dramatic envelopes, often featuring attractive color illustrations and attention-getting gimmicks, it is well to remember that there are many cases where a conventional business or personal envelope style will be the most appropriate envelope for a mailing. Certainly this is true when you are trying to make your message a highly personal one.

Picture Window Envelopes

Of special interest to direct mail advertisers is the so-called "picture window" envelope. Since 1955, the post office has permitted the use of windows in envelopes for uses other than addressing. While direct mail advertisers—except for a handful of ingenious pioneers—were slow to take advantage of this opportunity, the use of display window envelopes has been growing.

Picture window envelopes have several advantages:

They can convert an otherwise drab envelope into a colorful showpiece without added printing cost—just the more economical cost of die-cutting a window.

They make it possible to quickly tailor a "stock" envelope to a custom design for each mailing.

They can be used to tease the recipient into examining the contents by revealing only a portion of what is inside the envelope.

They permit a special showmanship gimmick to do double duty—both as a part of the enclosure and as an element of the envelope.

They can be a showmanship element in themselves.

The illustration shown here shows how a number of different direct mail advertisers are using picture window envelopes to add impact to their mailings:

Popular Club Plan. A premium offer is dramatized by having a full-color illustration show through an envelope window. Copy alongside the window says: "Reserved for you. Genuine leather French purse . . . *free*!"

Jackson & Perkins. To promote a new experimental "Sunshine Mum," a 1¾-inch-diameter round window was added to this two-color envelope. Above the window was printed: "We have just hybridized a new plant with blooms so brilliant that we call it *Sunshine!*" A sunburst of golden yellow appears around the window and through it you see a portion of a full-color illustration of the new mum.

TV Guide. A simple little picture window at the left side of this very plain, official-looking manila envelope reveals the words, "Cash Voucher," printed on the enclosed order form. The only printing on the envelope is the postage indicia—not even a return address.

Best-in-Children's Books. A genuine butterfly attached to an enclosed letter is plainly visible through the window on the face of this envelope.

Outdoor Cookbook. The envelope also features a large back-of-the-envelope picture window. This window reveals a dramatic full-color illustration of a table setting.

Life Picture Cookbook. Elegant is the best way to describe this envelope which features an oval window inside an illustration of a picture frame. The background of white and light gold gives the feeling of a distinctive wallpaper. Inside the picture window is a full-color illustration featuring a cock pheasant, a skillet, and various grains and vegetables—all of which become the picture on the wall.

Panorama Colorslide Programs. The picture window in this envelope becomes a screen upon which a travel picture is being projected. The illustration printed on the envelope shows a family in a darkened room viewing

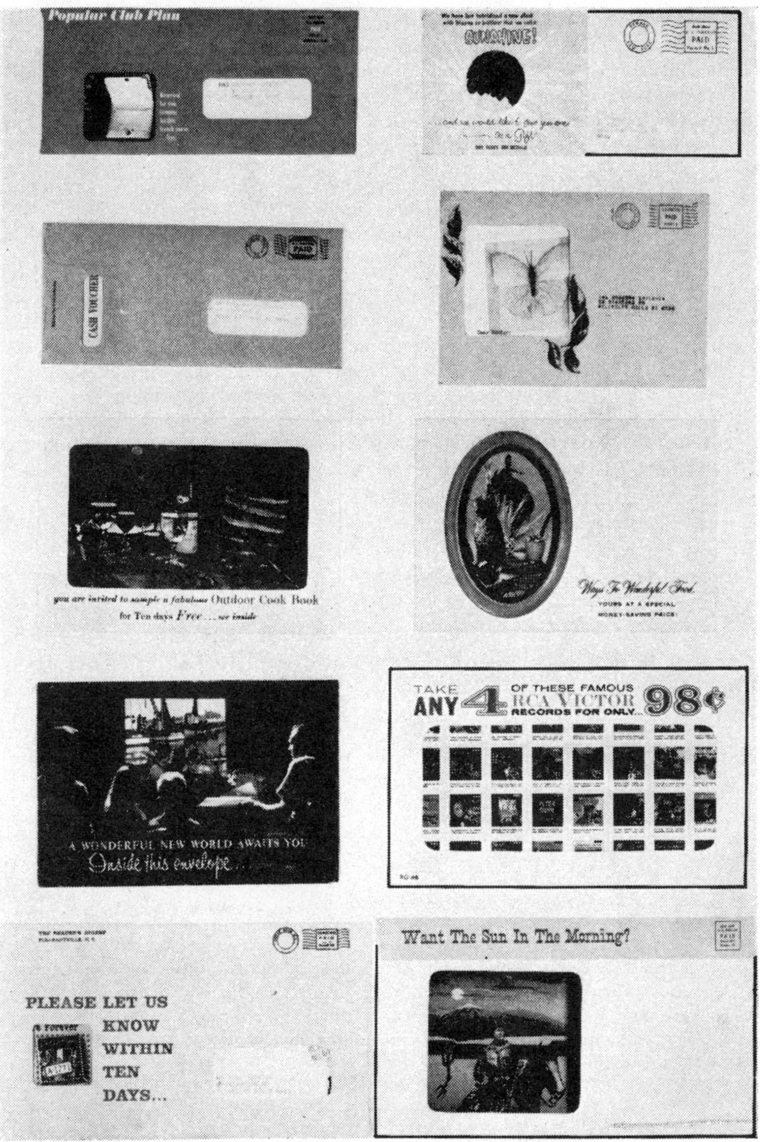

These "picture window" envelopes permit the wonderful four-color printing to make its sales impact.

the screen. The picture on the screen is a full-color illustration from a folder inside the envelope.

RCA Victor Record Club. A large (8¾- by 3½-inch) picture window on the back of this envelope shows a portion of a sheet of full-color stamps which are enclosed. Each stamp features an illustration of a record album. The buyer pastes his selection of stamps on the order card to identify the records he wants. The mailing side of this 10½- by 6¼-inch envelope has two windows—one for the address and the second showing two new pennies.

The Reader's Digest. A frequent user of picture window envelopes, *Reader's Digest* often features three-dimensional tokens as the "picture-in-the-window." The envelope illustrated has a dimensional replica of a record album, the product being featured.

Gaw-O'Hara Envelope Co. To promote the use of envelope picture windows of colored acetate, Gaw-O'Hara created a dramatic demonstration piece. The mailing envelope had an amber acetate window below the heading: "Want the sun in the morning?" Through the window appeared an illustration of a cowboy riding the desert beneath a blazing sun—or at least so it seemed. When the enclosed folder was removed from the envelope, the illustration turned out to be a picture of the cowboy riding the desert on a moonlit night. Copy on the folder carried through the teaser line on the envelope by adding: ". . . Or the moon at night?"

Personalizing Through Windows

Another effective use of a picture window envelope is to add a special note of personalization. Many different techniques have been used successfully. Several direct mail advertisers have used photos tipped to an enclosure and positioned so the entire photo or a portion of it shows through a window in the envelope. Applications of this effective attention-getter include:

Homes. To welcome new homeowners to a community, retailers have had pictures of the homes tipped to a "welcome" folder or letter. Others, seeking business opportunities such as installation of air conditioners, remodeling work, and so forth, use pictures of all homes in an area.

Children. Promotional-minded businesses have arranged to have snapshots or portraits taken where groups of children gather—schools, churches, playgrounds, and so forth. The resulting prints are then attached to mailing pieces which are sent to parents—with their children's pictures peeking through an envelope window to guarantee special attention to the mailing.

Conventioneers. Another good spot for taking pictures which can be used for mailings is at a convention or trade show. Highlighting the photo in a direct mail followup is a natural. Pictures of both individuals and convention groups have been used in this way.

Open Houses. An excellent added touch to an open house event is to take pictures of all visitors and then send prints as souvenirs. The same idea can be applied to other events such as store and plant openings.

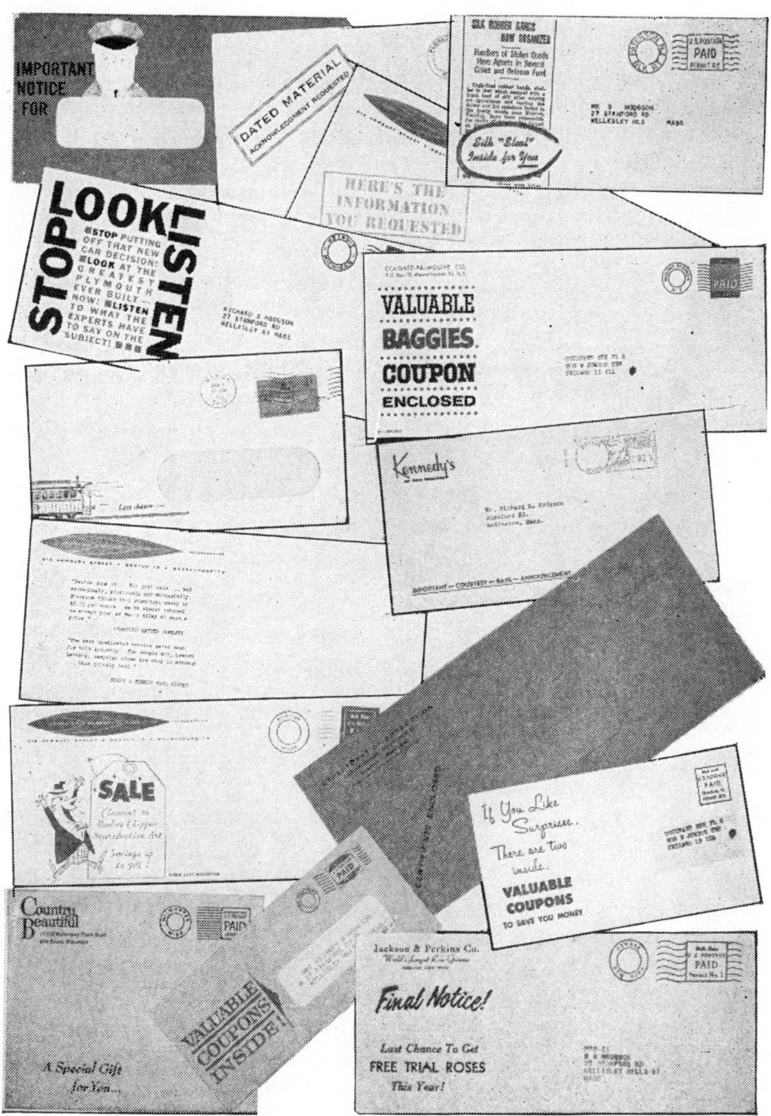

Experience shows that teaser messages often increase readership of contents.

Tie-ins. Photo mailings provide an effective method to tie in with special events such as club meetings, golf outings, company picnics, graduation ceremonies, banquets, awards ceremonies, major social events, and so forth.

Visitors. One Chicago advertising agency executive takes candid pictures of all of his visitors and then attaches prints to his followup letters.

Salesmen's Followups. A number of enterprising salesmen carry cameras with them on sales calls. They take pictures of the offices, plants, or homes they visit and use them to demand special attention for material sent as a followup.

Automobiles. Even the family car can make a good subject for a picture mailing. Service stations and garages can take pictures of cars brought in for servicing and then attach them to service reminder mailings.

While a photograph is probably the most effective personalizing method used with window envelopes, other direct mail advertisers have followed the same principles but used newspaper and magazine clippings or special gadgets with the recipient's name imprinted. The next illustration shows how a newspaper clipping was used to personalize a picture window envelope mailing.

(For additional examples of effective picture window techniques see Chapter 31, "Showmanship Formats.")

Teaser Copy

Experience has generally indicated that some type of teaser message on an envelope increases readership of the contents. A selection of envelopes with typical teaser messages is shown on page 1057. The techniques range from a quick summary of the message to reproductions of newspaper clippings and testimonials.

In inquiry handling, it is particularly important to identify the mailing to inform the recipient that the enclosed material is what he has requested. This distinguishes it from unsolicited material and assures increased attention.

Some advertisers have gone overboard in the use of teasers and implied that the contents of the envelope were something other than the recipient finds when he obeys the impulse created by the teaser. In many cases this technique backfires by creating such a strong feeling of disappointment—or even disgust—that an immediate negative reaction results, creating little but ill-will for the mailer.

13 Teaser Techniques

Virgil D. Angerman of Boise Cascade Envelope Division has developed a list of 13 basic envelope teaser techniques:

1. *To make your mail appear important* . . . If the message on your envelope convinces the prospect that the contents are important, you have won the first round in the battle for the order. You can do this with a phrase such as "Important Message Inside This Envelope;" a simulated rubber stamp impression with the words "Contents Important," or words such as "Last Reminder."

2. *Individualized teaser copy* . . . You can get greater acceptance of your mail if it carries an individual appeal to the prospect. Individualizing is breaking down the total list into groups of people with similar backgrounds or interests. You should give the reader the impression that he is reading a letter that was written with *him* in mind. An insurance company individualizes its appeal by saying "For California Families Only." Grolier Enterprises mails its list of encyclopedia buyers and puts "A Special Announcement for Encyclopedia Owners" on the envelope. To reach mothers of children, you can use "For the Mother of" above an address containing a child's name.

3. *Simple phrases to get action* . . . That's what you want—action! You can get action by using simple phrases in your teaser copy that motivate people. One of the most compelling pieces of teaser copy we have ever seen is used by an investment service. It reads: "Return Collect Telegram Enclosed." The copy is in the form of a simulated rubber stamp and appears immediately above the window in the envelope. A variation of the collect telegram idea is to use a simulated rubber stamp impression with the copy, "Return Air Mail Envelope Enclosed." This suggests urgency. *Flower and Garden* gets action on a renewal letter with teaser copy reading, "Last Chance to Renew Your Flower and Garden Subscription." Beaver Shoe Company uses, "Reply Requested within 24 Hours," with the copy in a circle, printed in red.

4. *The profit motive attracts customers* . . . Everyone is interested in ways to make or save money. Hence, this appeal will command immediate attention for your mail. In writing your teaser copy, be as specific as possible. For example, copy reading: "This Envelope Contains a Valuable Certificate worth $5.00" is a definite offer of a saving that ties in with the theme of a sales letter. Another advertiser used the profit appeal: "Here's how to *save* $150 on your Federal Income Tax." Offers of a million dollars in prizes is a profit motive used most successfully in sweepstakes mailings. "Boom and Inflation Ahead" is a profit motive appeal that Kiplinger uses in introducing its *Washington Letter.*

5. *News headlines create anticipation* . . . People are so accustomed to reading the headlines in newspapers that if you write your teaser copy in newspaper headline style, you will capture the reader's interest. An interesting example is the way one advertiser printed a teaser message in a style which simulated a clipping from *The New York Times.* Just the words, "THE NEW," appeared at the top, suggesting that the item was indeed clipped from the *Times.* Below that was a *Times*-style headline reading, "Amazing New Invention Doubles Your Reading Power." A sub-head and two paragraphs of newspaper-style copy followed. Another advertiser uses one of his best pulling ads as teaser copy. The headline is set in newspaper style. Another advertiser uses a background with a "washed-out" reproduction of an old newspaper for atmosphere. Then, a

simulated clipping starts a news story which can be completed only by opening the envelope.

6. *Questions will stimulate readership* . . . When you meet a friend and ask him a question, you expect an answer. If you are contacting prospects by mail and ask them a question, you hope that it will stimulate a reply. Questions should have a "soft sell" approach, for if they are not expressed in a friendly way, they can irritate the prospect and you may lose a customer. Questions often are intriguing. One advertiser puts his questions in handwritten form to give them a personal appearance. Here is how the copy reads:

   "How can you pay as little as 1% tax?"
   "How can you legally avoid the 25% gain tax when you sell your house?"
   "Can a broker charge you a 50% markup?"

   Another advertiser uses an envelope with a beautiful color picture of cut glass and then asks the question: "Are you the Kind of Woman Who Loves Beautiful Things?"

7. *Use interesting facts to pave the way* . . . Offer the prospect information that pertains to his health, business, social, religious, or financial status and you have an eager listener. For example, one teaser read: "Information About Your Income Enclosed." Another said: "Find out how you can get paid for staying well." A teaser reading "Tax-Free Income Plan" has a strong appeal to prospects with money to invest.

8. *Seasonal appeals will win attention* . . . An often overlooked sales opportunity is the seasonal appeal. If your proposition lends itself to a gift promotion, a fashion angle, or a holiday offer, very effective teaser copy can be written. A catalog gift house dresses up its envelope with an illustration of a gift-wrapped package and ties in with the copy, "Coming up for Christmas." Easter is a happy time of year. One advertiser dramatizes his teaser saying, "Just in time for Easter." Another uses the teaser: "If you're tired of chipping ice and shoveling snow."

9. *Use curiosity to arouse interest* . . . There is an old saying that "curiosity killed the cat." But people are curious, too. Appeal to this impulse and you are sure to get action. How many women could resist opening an envelope with: "Please do not open until after 8 P.M.?" And here is a real stopper: "—about your appointment in Washington, April 15." And if you received an envelope with big letters "HA" and "PRI" on the face, wouldn't you be curious? This was used for a "half price" offer and the remainder of the words was printed on the back of the envelope.

10. *The sympathy appeal opens envelopes, hearts and pocketbooks* . . . Picture an abandoned child crying for food, or an orphan boy or girl in need of shelter, clothing, food, or an education, and you have an appeal that gets action. The sympathy appeal is used chiefly to raise funds for religious missions, hospitals, schools for orphans, institutions for the mentally ill, etc. Illustrations are frequently used instead of a message, for, as a Chinese philosopher once said, "A picture is worth more than ten thousand words." As an example, the Jesuit Missions of New York dramatizes its appeal for funds by illustrating a child crying for help. If you received a mailing with an illustration of a lonely boy looking through a window at Christmas time with this copy on the envelope: "Give him the warmhearted joy of a happy Christmas this year," wouldn't you open the envelope?

11. *Use suspense to hold the reader's attention* . . . Webster defines "suspense" as a condition of mental uncertainty, anxiety or apprehension. The suspense appeal can start on the envelope as the beginning of a letter, the opening paragraphs of a thrilling novel or an important message, which are continued from the envelope to the sales letter. *Atlantic Monthly* started its teaser copy on the back of one of its envelopes: "Suddenly, a woman's piercing shriek resounded through the club. Such unseemly noises in the well-mannered quiet were unbelievable. Out of the ladies' drawing room rushed the ladies; out of the men's smoking room ran the gentlemen. In the hall, they found (continued inside)." The Ave Maria Press in promoting the sale of one of its pamphlets starts its teaser copy with an excerpt from the booklet: "It was shortly before midnight in the death row of an eastern penitentiary . . ."

12. *Appeal to civic pride for action* . . . A powerful appeal to use if your community needs a library, a swimming pool or a playground is civic pride. Everyone wants others to know that his community is progressive, that it has all the advantages that make it a good place to own a home. Cities, too, are proud of their cultural and recreational facilities or historical places to visit. Civic pride can be featured on envelopes in the promotion of cities and institutions. The Lion Court Motel, St. Augustine, Fla., shows its civic pride by illustrating its envelope with scenes of early Spanish explorers who settled in its city. The San Francisco Convention & Visitors' Bureau features the city's cable cars. And Lycoming College used an illustration as teaser copy—a picture of a bronze nameplate for The Alumni Lecture Hall with a $25,000 price tag hanging from it, thus dramatizing its appeal for funds from the alumni.

13. *Play up special interests* . . . Almost everyone has a hobby. It may be golf, boating, fishing, hunting, skiing, crafts, athletics, music, investments, gardening or scores of other leisure-time activities. Tap your prospect's special interests and he will want to know more about your offer. Show me the fisherman who could resist opening an envelope with the teaser copy: "How the buzz of a dying bee triggered a great idea for fishermen!" *Golf Magazine* used a color photo of Arnold Palmer and the teaser: "Now . . . the great champion reveals his tournament-winning secrets to you."

These examples show how teaser copy on the envelope can be used to get the prospect's attention and then get the prospect to open your mail. A word of caution: Postal regulations require that you leave at least 3½ inches of clear space from top to bottom, the right end of the address side of envelopes, folders or labels. This space will be used for address, postage, postmark, and other endorsements such as airmail and special delivery. On large envelopes, a clear rectangular space on the right-hand side of the envelope of not less than 3 by 4¼ inches for the address, stamps, postal imprint, postmark, etc. is acceptable. To play it safe, it's a good idea to submit a rough layout of your envelope for postal approval *before* you prepare any finished art or proceed with the manufacturing.

The important thing to remember in using teaser copy is that the theme must be carried over from the envelope to the letter, otherwise you lose the impact.

Reservations About Teasers

While envelope teasers can prove highly effective, there are times when they don't fit a mailing. If, for example, you are trying to create the impression of a truly personal letter, it's best to eliminate any envelope copy that you wouldn't normally put on a personal letter.

If you use duplicates of mailing pieces for follow-up, chances are that you will get higher readership if the piece comes in an envelope that looks different than the original. It's too easy to react: "I've already seen this" . . . and just discard the mailing without reading it. If you start with a different envelope, there's a good chance the entire mailing will take on a new character and thus stimulate the recipient to take another look at what you have to say.

Illustrated Envelopes

An increasing number of mail order advertisers have been using colorfully illustrated envelopes for their mailings. The most common technique is to use colored photos of featured merchandise. Book publishers have led the way in developing this promotional technique by adapting colored illustrations from their books to decorate envelopes.

Illustrated envelopes are not limited to the mail order field, however. Many businesses take advantage of the "unused" surfaces on their envelopes to do a little extra promotion. One of the favorite techniques is to feature a photograph or drawing of a plant, store, or institution on the full back side of the envelope. Several envelope manufacturers offer special creative services to design and produce envelopes of this nature.

On-Envelope Promotions

Still another use for illustrated envelopes is to utilize the surface for a complete promotion—frequently something which differs from the basic promotion included within the envelope.

For example, Jackson & Perkins Co. uses its catalog envelopes to offer a special assortment of four roses. Copy explains that "this offer available only on this envelope." The roses are illustrated in full color, along with descriptive copy. The envelope flap serves as the order form for this special offer.

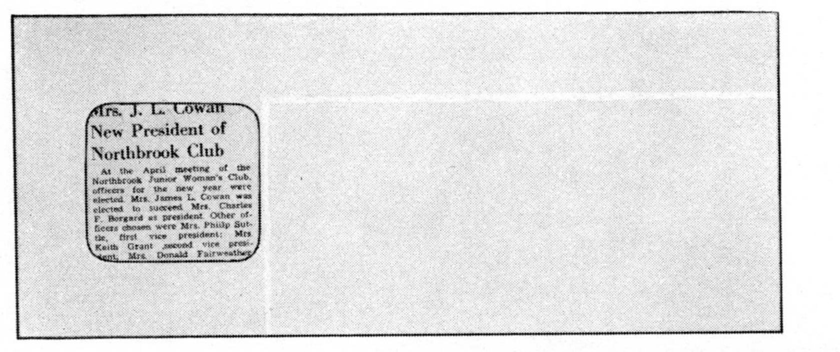

Mrs. J. L. Cowan
New President of
Northbrook Club

At the April meeting of the Northbrook Junior Woman's Club, officers for the new year were elected. Mrs. James L. Cowan was elected to succeed Mrs. Charles F. Borgard as president. Other officers chosen were Mrs. Philip Suttle, first vice president; Mrs. Keith Grant ,second vice president; Mrs. Donald Fairweather

Mrs. J. L. Cowan
New President of
Northbrook Club

At the April meeting of the Northbrook Junior Woman's Club, officers for the new year were elected. Mrs. James L. Cowan was elected to succeed Mrs. Charles F. Borgard as president. Other officers chosen were Mrs. Philip Suttle, first vice president; Mrs. Keith Grant ,second vice president; Mrs. Donald Fairweather, third vice president; Mrs. Richard Saunders, recording secretary; Mrs. Leonard Dettmers Jr., corresponding secreatry; and Mrs. George Martin, treasurer. Chairmen of standing committees elected were Mrs. Richard Hammond, Mrs. David Hagues, Mrs. William Howett, Mrs. Howard Davis, and Mrs. William G. Butler.

The officers will be installed at the May meeting.

How a newspaper clipping can be used to personalize a "picture window" envelope mailing.

Burstein-Applebee Co. uses its catalog envelope to promote three "specials"—an electric drill, an automatic timer, and a transistor portable radio kit. The flap is used to provide an "order blank" on which recipients can request that catalogs be sent to other interested parties.

Letter-on-the-Envelope

A somewhat similar approach is the printing of the basic sales message on the envelope. This has even been carried to the extent that envelopes have been used *without contents*—the entire message being printed on the front or back of the envelope.

More common, however, is to print a summary of the sales story on the envelope. *Look* magazine, for one, has found this a worthwhile direct mail technique.

Good Housekeeping used a variation of this technique and printed the start of its message on the mailing envelope. The heading said: "31 Ways to Save Money!" Eight of the ways were listed on the envelope, along with a note that 23 more ways could be found inside the envelope. Then the letter picked up the list, starting with idea number nine. (See illustration on the next page.)

Gimmick Envelopes

The showmanship approach to direct mail has not escaped the mailing envelope. A wide variety of special attention-getting techniques has been created to add impact to envelopes.

The transparent carrier has proved highly effective for many direct mail advertisers. These see-through envelopes can be made of a variety of materials, but the most popular and easiest to handle is the polyethylene bag. Pfaelzer Brothers, for example, mailed its Christmas gift catalog in a "poly" bag. The attractive colored illustrations on the covers of the catalog were completely visible, except for a small area occupied by the mailing label. (In using transparent carriers, it is important to check with postal authorities to make sure your addressing device is acceptable.)

Another showmanship device for envelopes is a special opening device. One type of envelope has a pull-string. Another clever approach was used by Nationwide Mutual Insurance Co., which cut two diagonals on the end of its reply card to form a point. The point was then inserted so it protruded from a die-cut opening at one end of the envelope. Copy on the envelope (see illustration,

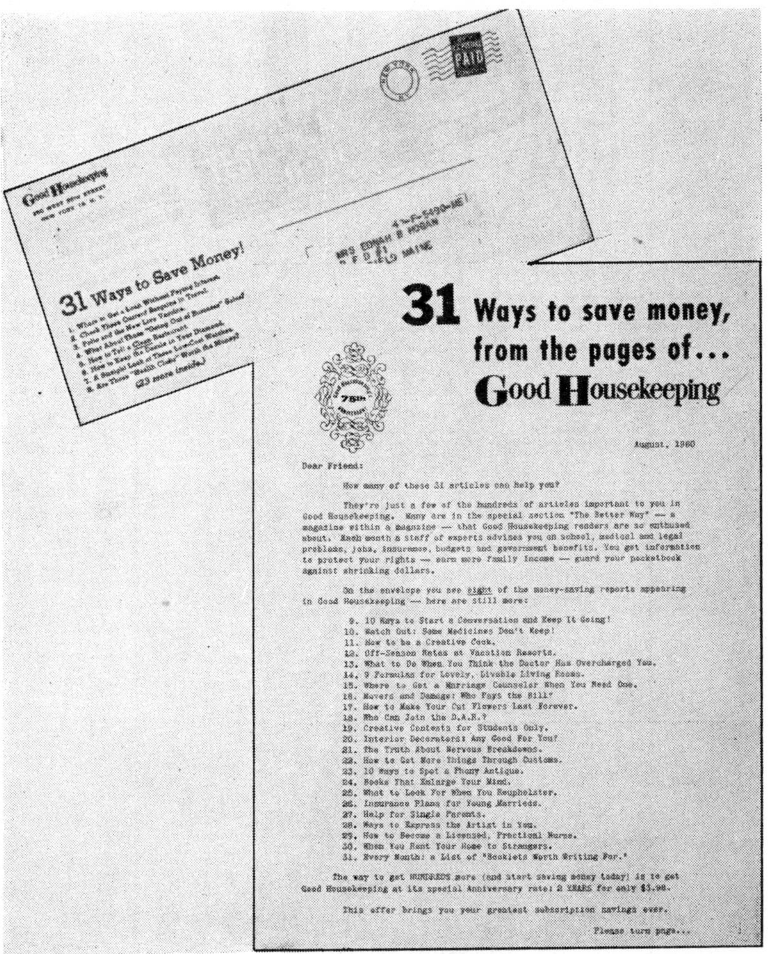

31 Ways to save money, from the pages of... Good Housekeeping

August, 1960

Dear Friend:

How many of these 31 articles can help you?

They're just a few of the hundreds of articles important to you in Good Housekeeping. Many are in the special section "The Better Way" — a magazine within a magazine — that Good Housekeeping readers are so enthused about. Each month a staff of experts advises you on school, medical and legal problems, jobs, insurance, budgets and government benefits. You get information to protect your rights — earn more family income — guard your pocketbook against shrinking dollars.

On the envelope you see eight of the money-saving reports appearing in Good Housekeeping — here are still more:

9. 10 Ways to Start a Conversation and Keep It Going!
10. Watch Out: Some Medicines Don't Keep!
11. How to be a Creative Cook.
12. Off-Season Rates at Vacation Resorts.
13. What to Do When You Think the Doctor Has Overcharged You.
14. 9 Formulas for Lovely, Livable Living Rooms.
15. Where to Get a Marriage Counselor When You Need One.
16. Movers and Damage: Who Pays the Bill?
17. How to Make Your Cut Flowers Last Forever.
18. Who Can Join the D.A.R.?
19. Creative Contests for Students Only.
20. Interior Decorators: Any Good For You?
21. The Truth About Nervous Breakdowns.
22. How to Get More Things Through Customs.
23. 10 Ways to Spot a Phony Antique.
24. Books That Enlarge Your Mind.
25. What to Look For When You Reupholster.
26. Insurance Plans for Young Marrieds.
27. Help for Single Parents.
28. Ways to Express the Artist in You.
29. How to Become a Licensed, Practical Nurse.
30. When You Rent Your Home to Strangers.
31. Every Month: a List of "Booklets Worth Writing For."

The way to get HUNDREDS more (and start saving money today) is to get Good Housekeeping at its special Anniversary rate: 2 YEARS for only $3.98.

This offer brings you your greatest subscription savings ever.

Please turn page...

Good Housekeeping *obtained considerable readership by starting its sales message on the outside of envelope.*

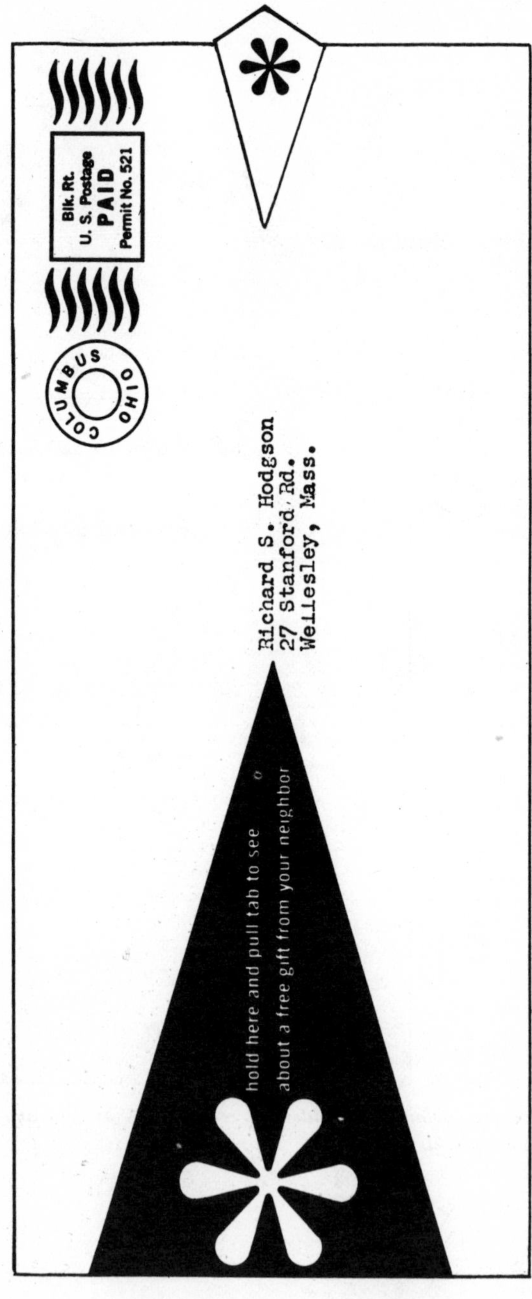

Blk. Rt.
U. S. Postage
PAID
Permit No. 521
COLUMBUS OHIO
Richard S. Hodgson
27 Stanford Rd.
Wellesley, Mass.
hold here and pull tab to see
about a free gift from your neighbor

Pulling the extended tab on the right rips open the envelope in a dramatic manner.

preceding page) read: "Hold here and pull tab to see about a free gift from your neighbor." Pulling the extended reply card point ripped open the envelope.

Any envelope manufacturer can show you dozens of showmanship approaches which have been created for direct mail advertisers.

Closed Face vs. Window Envelopes

Lewis Kleid, Inc. offers these considerations in deciding whether to use a window envelope or a closed face envelope:

Window envelopes are used heavily in mail order selling because:

1. It is faster to print and ship order forms for rental addressing. No time is lost waiting for envelopes to be manufactured.
2. Anything that makes it easier for the customer to order improves results. No need to write the name and address on the order. The customer merely checks the pre-addressed form and returns.
3. Internal processing is more accurate. Clerks have no problem in reading stencil or typewriter addressed order forms.
4. Spoilage in envelope manufacture or packing methods reduces the quantity —sometimes substantially. A box of 500 envelopes does not always contain 500 envelopes. You can be more accurate in shipping order forms than in shipping envelopes.
5. Window envelopes save sales tax on rental addressing for New York City companies. By a strange quirk in the regulations, addressing on a preprinted form is not taxable. Sales tax is chargeable if the addressing is done on envelopes.

Closed face envelopes are used by some companies because:

1. You can stockpile. No need to design envelopes for each job.
2. Closed face envelopes lend themselves better for label addressing. (It must be noted, however, that with the use of IBM labels and Cheshire affixing, labels on order forms are not obstrusive.)
3. Closed face envelopes are cheaper. A plain window (without cellophane or glassine) adds roughly 35 cents per M to the cost.
4. A standard order form might slide around in a large window envelope. (This can be corrected by using the spot-o-gum attachment on the inserting machine to hold the form in position—or by using a perforated order card to occupy the full size of the envelope.)

New machinery now permits envelopes to be slotted and cellophane affixed in one operation. This has cut the cost of window envelopes—particularly when picture windows and other double window formats are used.

Use of pre-addressed order forms in mailings to house lists facilitates file location and reduces the possibility of cutting duplicate customer plates.

Reply Envelopes

The Postal Service has established a number of hard and fast rules concerning the design of Business Reply Envelopes. However, even with these regulations, it is still possible to create reply devices with a unique personality.

It is important, however, to check any design departure in reply envelopes with your local postmaster. Even if a particular design has been approved for some other direct mail advertiser, your postmaster may consider it unacceptable and not permit its use.

A basic rule which should be followed by everyone is "when in doubt, ask." If your postmaster doesn't have an answer, United States Postal Service headquarters in Washington will.

Window Messages

Virgil Angerman of Boise Cascade suggests 13 ways you can utilize the space that shows through a window of an envelope:

1. *"Thank You" Messages* . . . The most widely-used idea is the "Thank you" message. When acknowledging orders, this message printed under the window is a thoughtful way of showing your appreciation for a customer's business. Typical messages: "Thank you for banking with us." "Thank you. It is to good friends like you that we owe whatever success we have achieved."

2. *Reminder Notices* . . . When action is needed, a "Reminder Notice" under the window helps to get a prompt response. This idea is used very effectively by companies asking for signed proxies. Could be used in requesting customers to include their zip code when ordering, or enclose stubs of invoices, etc. Typical messages: "Would you do us the favor of signing and mailing your proxy today." "Please renew your membership promptly."

3. *Feature Trademarks* . . . Your firm's trademark makes excellent "copy" for an overall pattern or design for inside printing. Not only does it build acceptance for your company's trademark but it makes the envelope more opaque for confidential enclosures. Easy to use.

4. *Announce Anniversaries* . . . If your firm is going to celebrate an anniversary soon, you can publicize it at a minimum of cost by printing the anniversary message or design under the envelope window where your customers will see it the second they open the envelope. Or, you could say, "In the field since 1937" as one firm does and create additional confidence in your company.

5. *Getting Changes of Address* . . . Every firm has the problem of keeping its mailing list up-to-date. One way to get the changes of address is to ask for them in a message under the envelope window. This will help cut your mailing costs. Typical messages: "For your convenience change of address may be reported on the back of the enclosed check." "Change of Address: Please advise (address) of any change in your address."

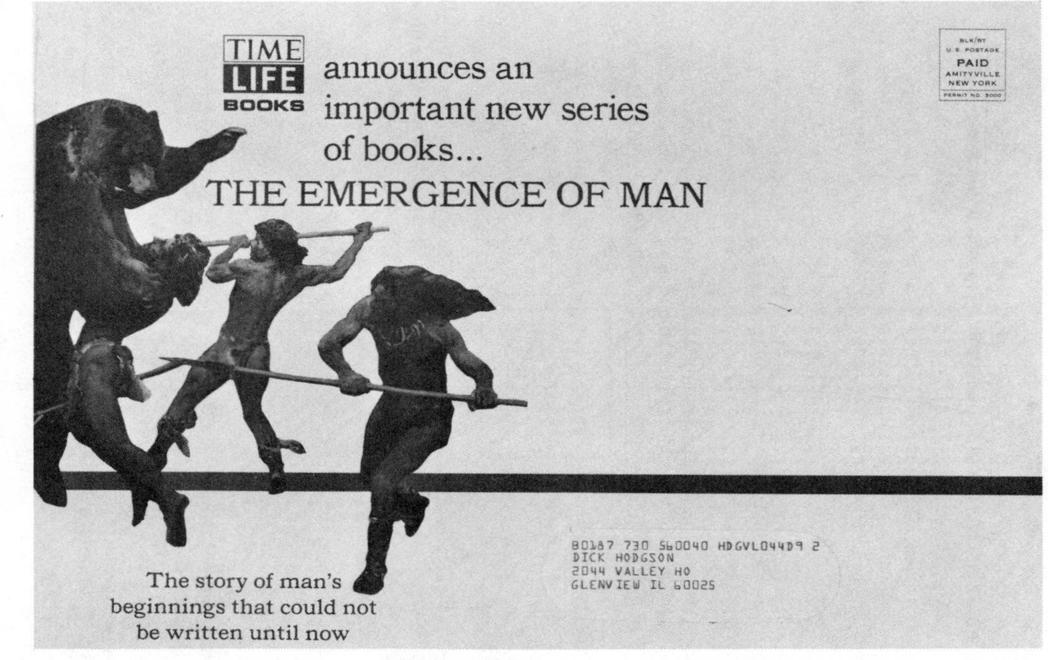

Colorful envelopes are an important element in mailings for ***Time-Life Books.*** ***In addition to the*** *full-color illustration on the face of the envelope shown above, the back of the envelope had color illustrations of four of the volumes in this book series.*

6. *Promote Economic Advantages* . . . This idea can be used to recruit new employees or to point out economic advantages of a city or state. Here is how the Public Service Electric & Gas Co., Newark, N. J. extolls the advantages offered by New Jersey with a window envelope message: "New Jersey's position as a national leader in research means a continuing flow of new products, new industries and new jobs . . . a guarantee of an ever-expanding economy."

7. *Publicize Safety Campaigns* . . . A safety campaign requires constant publicity. One oil ocmpany mails millions of pieces of mail every year with simple automotive safety messages in window envelopes.

8. *Consumer Services* . . . To emphasize their desire to be of service in answering inquiries and correspondence, The Swiss Colony, Monroe, Wisconsin, dealers in food specialties uses the space under the windows of one of their envelopes to say: "Happy to be of service!" Efengee Electrical Supply Co. uses a window message to call attention to five convenient locations "for everything electrical."

9. *Feature Company Slogans* . . . United Airlines ties in with its advertising slogan, "Fly the friendly skies of United" by printing the same message under the window of its envelopes.

10. *Charity Appeals* . . . Messages appealing to religious or charity instincts prepare the recipient for the request about to be made. Here is how one appeal was worded: "The warm hand of true charity enriches all men it touches . . . rewarding those who give in still greater measure than those who receive."

11. *"Sell" Your Services* . . . Your customers and prospects may not be aware of the various facilities or services your company offers and can perform. Tell them about them in the free space under the windows in your envelopes.

12. *Specialized Messages* . . . You may wish to convey a special message to your customers in a subtle way. Here are six examples of how this idea can be put to practical use under the windows of your envelopes:

    "You make your own credit rating. We only keep the record."

    "Your advertising today is your best insurance for good business tomorrow."

    "This check made possible by your continued use of our products and services."

    "If it's made by Kodak—you know it's good! This window is made of our Kodacel sheet."

    "Our greatest asset—your goodwill."

    "Business goes where it is invited . . . stays where it is appreciated."

13. *Mini-Ads* . . . Department stores that mail monthly statements to charge account customers have an excellent opportunity to call attention to special sales coming up by printing the details so they show through an envelope window. Insurance companies can offer booklets on health. Savings and Loan Associations can promote the opening of new savings accounts. There are many ways "sales" messages can be used under the windows in your envelopes.

Chapter 40

BASIC PRODUCTION TECHNIQUES FOR LETTERS

THERE are many different techniques for producing direct mail letters—ranging from individually typed letters to those turned out by the millions on high-speed printing equipment. Essentially there are three basic categories of letters from a production standpoint:

1. Individually personalized letters
2. Mass-produced, semipersonalized letters
3. Mass-produced, nonpersonalized letters

The type of letter production technique chosen depends primarily on two factors: (1) the job to be done, with special consideration of the relationship between the sender and the recipient, and (2) the budget available.

In campaigns where personalization is of special importance, it is essential to select one of the first two techniques listed above. These, however, are considerably more costly than mass-produced letters. Unfortunately many direct mail advertisers, facing budget limitations, make the mistake of trying to do a highly personalized job with an obviously nonpersonal technique. There are times, however, when special copy techniques can give a mass-produced letter a more personal touch. But American direct mail audiences have long since become sophisticated to the point where they recognize when nonpersonal production techniques are used that a mailing is sent to them as a member of a large audience, rather than as select individuals. This is particularly true with mailings sent to business audiences.

INDIVIDUALLY PERSONALIZED LETTERS

There are really only two types of completely personalized direct mail letters—those which are individually typewritten (or, in a limited number of cases, handwritten) and those which are automatically typewritten.

Personally Typewritten Letters

If the quantity of a mailing is less than 50 letters, you may want to consider having them typed individually. However, most direct mail users wanting a quality, personal letter turn to automatic typing when the quantity required starts running above the ten mark.

For small "runs" of typewritten letters, the job is usually handled internally by the secretarial staff. However, nearly every lettershop provides typewritten letter service—and many will even prepare quantities of handwritten letters. In addition, home workers are available in many communities to handle such projects.

If close supervision of letter production is required and the job must be handled internally, the use of temporary manpower services is often the ideal solution. Additional typewriters can be rented to handle the overload.

Automatically Typewritten Letters

In recent years there has been a substantial increase in the use of automatically typewritten letters for direct mail purposes. For all intents and purposes, autotyped letters are identical in appearance to personally typewritten letters—with one important exception: they are *error free,* without erasures and strikeovers, unless, of course, such "errors" are purposely included to add to the "individual" appearance of the letters.

Autotyped letters are produced on regular typewriters, one at a time. Rather than being completely controlled by a typist, however, these typewriters are connected to an activating unit which operates on much the same principle as the old-time player piano. A "master" tape or roll is originally "cut" either on the automatic typing unit or with a separate machine, and this tape or roll is then "played back" to produce multiple copies of letters on the typewriter.

When producing an autotyped letter, the operator inserts a letterhead and as many carbons as desired in the typewriter and types in the heading and salutation by hand. With a flip of a switch, the automatic mechanism takes over and begins typing the letter at speeds up to 160 words a minute. If special, individualized information is required in the body of the letter, a stop signal is included in the master tape or roll. When this point is reached, the typewriter stops automatically and the operator can type in a special price, date, name, or other item. A flip of the switch starts the automatic typing again. At the end of the letter, another stop perforation turns off the machine and the operator removes the completed letter and inserts the next letterhead.

In commercial operation, a single operator may handle a battery of as many as six automatic typewriters. In some cases a "slave unit" is used to type the address on an envelope or label at the same time this information is typed on the individual letters. In other cases tapes with names and addresses punched on them are used to type this information on the automatic units. Another variation is the "selector" unit which can handle dozens of different paragraphs. This works on much the same principle as a jukebox. The different paragraphs are typed on the master tape or roll. The operator selects the paragraphs desired by punching a series of numbered buttons. The machine then takes over and types the paragraphs in the sequence selected.

Signing the Letters

To carry out the completely personal appearance of autotyped letters, individual signatures are usually used. Depending on the quantity needed, these are usually added either by expert "forgers" —skilled operators who can duplicate any signature in a matter of a few seconds—or by an AutoPen. This machine, originally designed for signing government documents, can sign up to 450 letters an hour. It requires a specially prepared control disk which activates a fountain pen and guides it to duplicate any specific signature.

When large quantities of autotyped letters are produced, the signature may be preprinted in the appropriate position by offset—usually at the same time letterheads are printed. Skilled Autotypist operators can make sure the letter "fits" the signature exactly. If the printing is handled with skill it is almost impossible to detect the fact the signature was not individually signed.

Rubber plate signatures, however, are seldom used with autotyped letters, since it is seldom possible to create an "authentic" appearance with this reproduction method.

Carbon Copy Followups

One of the special advantages of individually typewritten letters is that carbon copies can be turned out at the time the original is prepared for little more than the cost of materials. These are then used both for followup and merchandising purposes. The usual followup process is to keep the carbons for a period of ten days to two weeks. As replies are received from the original mailing, carbons are pulled and destroyed. At the end of the control period, the remaining carbons are mailed, usually with either a note attached or a simulated message imprinted on them. When imprinted messages are used, they are usually preprinted on the sheets to be used before the carbons are prepared.

Interestingly, the response from the mailing of carbons is frequently greater than from the original mailing.

An important cost consideration in planning autotyped letters is to remember that they *must* be mailed first class.

Computer Letters

In recent years, there has been an ever-increasing use of computer-generated letters, including those where the message is created by jet ink imaging. In fact, the advent of computer letters is considered by many direct mail people as the factor which really made mass personalized mailings practical. With today's advanced techniques, the computer letter often has the look of an individually-typed letter. Computer companies are constantly working to improve these.

For long runs, computer letters are considerably less expensive than any other form of personalized letter.

Additional details concerning computer letters are included in Chapter 27—Computer Formats.

MASS-PRODUCED, SEMIPERSONALIZED LETTERS

When lists are large and budgets are tight, many direct mail advertisers turn to semipersonalized letter techniques to bridge the gap between the completely impersonal message and one individually prepared for the recipient. In many cases these less costly techniques produce results to rival those from completely personalized mailings. This is particularly true when the message is *obviously* intended for a large audience.

It is sometimes possible to create the appearance of an individually personal letter through one of the mass-production techniques for semipersonalized letters—but the odds are working against the direct mail advertiser. The most common techniques involve "fill-ins"—printed letters with the address and salutation added with a typewriter or by computer. While close matches are possible, the majority can't pass a close scrutiny test.

Direct mail audiences are much smarter than many direct mail advertisers give them credit for being. And the more direct mail they receive, the less likely they are to be fooled by a semipersonal letter attempting to masquerade as an individually typed letter. This is not to suggest, however, that the addition of individual names and addresses to letters is always worthless. Everyone's name is important to him or her. The fact that you have taken the time and trouble to add it to a message and done so in a neat, orderly way indicates a desire to approach the recipient on a personal basis. This, in itself, often more than compensates for the added cost of personalization.

Beware the Clumsy Match

A poor "match" can backfire, however. If it becomes obvious that you are trying to trick the recipient into believing a form letter is a personal one, it immediately puts up a danger signal in his mind saying, "Watch out for this advertiser. He's trying to trick me and isn't giving me credit for being very smart."

Fill-ins in the body of a letter are much more dangerous than just adding addresses and salutations. Not only must you try to match the "color" of the type, but alignment must be perfect. One way to overcome this handicap is to completely avoid the problem of matching. This is accomplished by such techniques as using obviously different colors of typewriter ribbons or making fill-ins by handwriting.

This is one area where extensive testing is highly desirable. Do not take anyone else's experience as a guide for your mailings. Test all types of personalized and nonpersonalized mailings and evaluate the results against the costs before deciding on the technique most satisfactory for your needs. And if long-range prestige is important to you, remember that a greater degree of personalization may easily carry with it plus values through image building which do not show up immediately in direct results.

Personalized Flatbed Letters

Many trade names are given to letters printed on a flatbed letterpress with matching fill-ins by typewriter. Techniques vary from producer to producer, but the results are usually the closest possible to an automatically typewritten letter at about half the cost or less.

What makes these letters stand out from those prepared by other mass-production techniques is the special "makeready," which permits individual characters to be adjusted to create a typewriter-like appearance. Periods, for example, can be built up so they punch through the paper as they do when letters are individually typed. Other "imperfections" can also be created through careful makeready.

But not all flatbed letters come out looking like the twin of a typewritten letter. In its *Letter Reproduction* research report, the Direct Mail Advertising Association comments:

> With absolute production controls between the mechanical production of the body of the letter and the fill-in work of the typist, the flatbed letter will be as close to the individually typed letter as possible. But it takes effective methods, expert supervision, skilled craftsmen and an established policy of not accepting less than perfection as a standard of the shop.

Flatbed letters are particularly adaptable for long runs. Printing is usually done through a ribbon to assure a close resemblance to typing. Most any basic typewriter typeface can be selected. For fill-ins, it is desirable to use an electric typewriter, since it gives a more even stroke which will most closely resemble the original printing.

Personalized Offset Letters

A number of direct mail firms have developed special techniques to produce letters for fill-ins using offset presses. The original copy for the letter is typed with the same machine which will be used for fill-ins. It is then carefully photographed and printed from metal plates. The fill-ins are made with one-use carbon ribbons. Since no punch-through is possible in offset printing, it is difficult to create a typed "feel," but the even match possible with carbon ribbons can produce a pleasing appearance.

It takes real skill to produce personalized offset letters and there are relatively few lettershops which can do a topnotch job with this technique. Costs, particularly for short runs, are usually considerably less than for flatbed letters.

Personalized Multigraphing

Multigraphing (described in more detail in the next chapter dealing with nonpersonalized letters) can also be used with fill-ins. Few producers, however, are able to create a true match, although it is possible to come close if the equipment and operators are of the highest caliber. However, since special makeready cannot be accomplished, it is not possible to come up to the quality of good flatbed letters.

In most cases, however, the cost is less than for flatbed letters, with the added advantage of being able to print signatures in a second color on the same run.

Generally, you will find there is a distinctive multigraph appearance to letters produced by this process. Since it is so widely used for nonpersonalized mailings, this is a distinct drawback.

Penscript

A technique used primarily by retailers is to print a handwritten letter by letterpress or offset and then personalize it with the name of the recipient in matching handwriting. This is a relatively slow process, useful primarily for short runs, since it is almost imperative that the individual who writes the original copy for printing individually write in each name to personalize the letters. It is difficult to provide a rule of thumb for costs on penscript letters, and good services for matching are not available in all areas.

Grams

Another technique for semipersonalized "letters" is to use a simulated telegram. These can be prepared by either flatbed or offset printing, with fill-ins handled on typewriters with faces similar to those used on Teletype machines. Such techniques, of course, are generally limited to short messages.

Reply Form Letters

One of the most popular techniques for semipersonalized letters is the Reply-O-Letter and other similar combination reply cards/letters. Such letters avoid the necessity of attempted matching of address with the body of the letter, which is printed by any available process. Instead, there is a die-cut opening where the salutation of the letter would normally appear. In a pocket behind this opening a reply card is inserted. It carries the name and address of the recipient, which shows through the opening (and usually through a window in the mailing envelope as well).

The big advantage of this technique is that all the recipient needs do to reply is remove the reply card from its pocket and drop it in the mail, since it already carries his name and address. Costs run about the same as other semipersonalized letters with fill-ins. A number of companies offer complete services for the preparation of these reply form letters, including special copywriting services and other counseling. You can also buy the diecut letter forms blank for your own imprinting.

MASS-PRODUCED, NONPERSONALIZED LETTERS

There are dozens of different methods for producing direct mail letters when personalization is not required—ranging from the time-honored Hectograph duplicator to Triplehead Multigraphing. Some processes make it possible to closely approximate an individually typed appearance, while others are designed simply to put words on paper economically.

Experience in most cases has indicated that greater readership can be obtained when a letter looks like a letter, rather than just another printed piece. For this reason most direct mail advertisers use typewriter typography even for printed pieces which could just as easily and economically use "fancier" typography.

Multigraphed Letters

The Multigraph machine, developed in the early 1900's by the Addressograph-Multigraph Corp.'* was long the most commonly used reproduction machine for direct mail letters which were designed to resemble individually typed letters. The Multigraph has a curved drum onto which typewriter type is clipped and then covered with an inked ribbon. The type can be set either by hand or machine.

An attachment on the Multigraph permits imprinting a signature in a second color. In addition, illustrations can be printed along with body copy.

Quality of multigraphing varies greatly. Unfortunately many of the Multigraphs in use today have long since outlived their ability to produce a quality letter; and too many lettershops have a tendency to continue to use ribbons after they are worn and to fail to replace broken type. Another problem is that many paper stocks are not suitable for multigraphing. Hard-finished, rag-content bonds, for example, often produce a fuzzy appearance, as the ribbon impression has a tendency to "run" and "spread."

But, with careful attention to detail, a very high quality can be obtained by multigraphing.

**now AM International Inc.*

Triplehead Letters

A popular variation on standard multigraphing is Triplehead reproduction, which involves use of what amounts to a combination of three multigraph drums. With this Rube Goldberg device, three colors can be printed at one time—plus a fourth color from the signature attachment.

The most common application of Triplehead reproduction is to print a two-color letterhead, plus the body of the letter in a third color (sometimes with special paragraphs in one of the colors used for the letterhead) and the signature in a fourth color.

The operation of the Triplehead Multigraph definitely requires special skill, and even so, direct mail advertisers should not expect the quality of reproduction they can obtain by more conventional letterpress or offset printing. But where maximum quality is not a requirement, the economies of Triplehead reproduction can make the process ideal for many direct mail letters.

Mimeographed Letters

For short-run, low-cost letters, mimeographing is one popular reproduction method. And in recent years the quality of mimeographing has been improved to the point where casual observers often cannot detect the difference between it and letterpress or offset printing.

To prepare copy for mimeographing, you simply type or draw the message on the wax coating of a fibrous stencil. Pressure from typing or drawing pushes aside the wax from the area to be printed and permits ink to pass through the fibers of the stencil onto the paper. Stencils can also be "cut" electronically.

The maximum practical run for mimeographing is 5,000 copies, although as many as 10,000 impressions can be obtained under special circumstances. It is possible to obtain multicolor mimeographing in a single run, but usually separate runs are desirable for each color. Absorbent stocks are a must for best results and electric typewriters are best for cutting stencils.

Like multigraphing, quality varies greatly in commercial mimeographing. Good equipment and special skills can produce excellent work, while a great bulk of the mimeographing which goes into the mails is far down the quality scale. DMMA's *Letter Reproduction* manual comments: "Unfortunately, much mimeographing is produced with inadequate equipment and unskilled employees and many users never see the process at its best."

Costs vary greatly depending upon the service delivered but, in general, mimeographing is considerably less costly than any other letter process except spirit duplicating. One big advantage is the speed with which a job can be produced. It is possible to start from scratch, cut a stencil, and run off as many as 5,000 copies in an hour's time.

Direct-Image Offset Letters

Next in line on the cost scale (and sometimes even less costly than mimeographing) is the direct-image offset letter. It is produced from paper, plastic, or light metal plates which can be inserted in a typewriter for direct typing or produced directly from copy through a transfer machine.

In the most common method, the copy is typed directly onto a special paper plate which is then run immediately on a Multilith or other small offset press. Usually copy is typed on an electric typewriter with a one-use carbon ribbon. With the growing use of "office-type" offset presses, this method of preparing direct mail letters has replaced mimeographing in most instances. One advantage is the ability to use a greater variety of paper stocks. As yet, however, the offset duplicators require greater skill than mimeographs to produce consistent results. However, when masters and printing are handled skillfully, the results can be superior to the best mimeographing.

Costs are slightly higher than mimeographing, but less than multigraphing. The usual maximum number of copies from a paper plate is around 5,000 although experienced operators regularly obtain 10,000 or more impressions of good fidelity.

Offset Letters

When greater quality is required, the most frequent choice—particularly for long runs—is the regular offset letter. These can be produced on either large or small presses and involve the photographing of copy and preparation of a metal printing plate To most closely duplicate the appearance of typing, copy is frequently screened to "gray it down." On the other hand, when really "crisp" appearance of the typewriter characters is desired, original typed copy is reduced from 10 to 20%. Copy is normally prepared by electric typing with a carbon ribbon on a hard paper surface.

When long runs are required, it is most common to print letterheads and copy at the same time. Signatures are usually printed in a second color used for the letterhead. (Many mail order firms adopt a blue and black letterhead so the blue second color can be used for signatures, "handwritten" postscripts, and marginal notes, while the black is used for typewritten material.) Two attachments for small presses are particularly useful for the preparation of direct mail letters. The T-51 head, an additional printing cylinder, permits two-color printing on standard Multiliths in a single run. Another useful attachment is a signature device like the one used on Multigraph machines.

Offset printing permits use of both line and halftone illustrations on letters. Costs, of course, vary just as they do for all other types of offset printing.

Letterpress Letters

Except for the special flatbed letters described previously, most letterpress-printed letters make little or no attempt to duplicate a typewritten appearance, other than possibly to use a typewriter typeface. Letterpress letters are usually used interchangeably with offset letters for long runs.

Facsimile Handwritten Letters

When a short message is required, many direct mail advertisers turn to printed reproduction of a handwritten message. Such messages can be produced by either offset or letterpress. They are frequently referred to as either "penscript" or "pencilscript" letters. A number of printers have developed special skills in reproducing such letters, giving them a highly authentic appearance. Various trade names are used to describe these special techniques.

One common use for these "letters" is for printing memos to be attached to carbon or duplicate copies used in followup mailings. In preparing copy for penscript letters, a fountain pen with black ink is used. However, reproduction is usually in blue ink. A soft, black lead is required for pencilscript letters, with reproduction usually in a gray ink.

Spirit Duplicated Letters

While a highly inferior process from a quality standpoint, spirit duplicating is often used for short-run direct mail letters, primarily for intracompany use. The master is prepared simply by typing, writing, or drawing on treated sheets with a special "carbon paper" underneath. An aniline dye is transferred from the "carbon paper" to the back of the master. Paper is then moistened as it is fed into the spirit duplicator and "picks up" a portion of the dye from the master.

The maximum number of copies possible varies considerably, but the process is seldom used for more than 350 copies. While the purple color is most common, other colors are now available.

Many variations of the spirit duplicating process are available. The most common is the Hectograph, which involves a gelatin to which the dye is transferred before printing. A more recent development is the azo process, which uses an azo rather than aniline dye. Costs are extremely low and copies can be turned out rapidly.

Chapter 41

PRINTING PROCESSES

THREE basic printing processes account for the bulk of direct mail advertising—offset lithography, letterpress, and gravure. In recent years offset lithography has taken a commanding lead from letterpress as the most frequently used direct mail reproduction process. However, during the period when the letterpress-to-offset switch was being made, the two processes have drawn closer and closer together in terms of the basic advantages each offers a direct mail advertiser.

At one time, for example, letterpress could definitely be counted upon to provide sharper, more accurate color reproduction, while offset looked to reduced makeready time as one of its chief advantages. Today, however, outstanding color reproduction is being accomplished with offset lithography, while the development of new types of printing plates and special makeready systems have brought letterpress closer to offset in this area.

Today any list of comparative "advantages and disadvantages" of different printing processes is almost worthless, for the differences are not primarily from one printing process to another but from one printer to another. Nevertheless special circumstances often suggest first consideration of one process. Therefore it is important for a direct mail advertiser to understand the basics of each of the primary processes—plus a number of secondary processes which can often solve special reproduction problems.

Five Printing Methods

Before analyzing each of the primary and secondary printing processes, it is important to understand the five methods for imprinting multiple images on paper or other surfaces:

1. *Relief Printing*—The oldest of the printing processes involves spreading ink over a raised surface, which is then pressed against paper, leaving an inked impression on the paper. In everyday terms this is the same as using a rubber stamp. In printing the principle is used by such processes as letterpress and flexography.

2. *Planograph Printing*—This process involves transferring an image from one flat surface to another flat surface. A common analogy is using a blotter on a signature of "wet" ink. In printing the most common planograph process is lithography. Here the image is first applied to a flat surface in a way so it will attract a greasy ink, while the rest of the surface without the image is receptive to water, which is applied to the printing plate before ink is applied. Since the water repels the greasy ink, it "sticks" only to the image area. Thus when paper is brought into contact with the entire surface it picks up ink only from the image area.

3. *Intaglio Printing*—A direct opposite of relief printing, intaglio involves depositing ink in depressions on the printing surface and then "lifting" the ink from these depressions onto the paper. The most common intaglio process is gravure, but the same basic principle is used by collotype, engraving, and other processes.

4. *Offset Printing*—Rather than being one of the basic processes, offset printing involves the addition of an intermediate step in the transferring of an image from a printing plate to paper. A blanket—most commonly of rubber—is brought into contact with the inked plate, picking up the ink and holding it until paper is brought into contact with the blanket. When the paper is pressed against the blanket, it picks up the ink. The most common use of offset is in conjunction with lithography, although there has been growing use of dry offset, which utilizes relief plates, and the technique is also used as part of some intaglio printing processes.

5. *Screen Printing*—The fifth basic reproduction method involves squeezing ink through openings forming an image in an otherwise solid surface so that it is deposited on paper passing or held in position below the screened surface. The most common process is screen process printing, which is also called "silk-screen printing," and really this same basic process is used in mimeographing.

OFFSET LITHOGRAPHY

The emergence of offset lithography—generally referred to only as "offset" as *the* basic printing process for direct mail purposes is a post-World War II development. As late as the early 1950's, letterpress was still considered by many as the workhorse of direct mail printing processes. But then, while the letterpress craftsmen and their suppliers rested on the thought that offset was inferior in most ways to their time-honored process, the lithographic industry, led by the pace-setting Lithographic Technical Foundation, was busy conducting ambitious research projects which rapidly overcame previous handicaps and resulted in new techniques and equipment.

Today, most of the guides to selection of printing processes are woefully out of date when it comes to offset. In progressive offset plants, it is possible to obtain just about every quality offered by competitive printing processes. However, that word *progressive* is highly important, for there is a much wider variation in quality and versatility from printer to printer with offset than in most other processes. Because of the rapidity with which new offset techniques have been developed, there is only a small percentage of offset printers who can deliver the maximum in quality and versatility.

How the Process Works

Photography is the key to modern offset printing. All copy, with the exception of halftone illustrations, is pasted in position and then photographed to size for platemaking. Halftone negatives are then made of continuous tone copy such as photographs and wash drawings, and these are fitted into position along with the line negative. This is called "stripping." When both the line and halftone negatives are joined together, they are placed in contact with a thin, sensitized sheet of aluminum and exposed to an arc light. Areas exposed to light become hardened. The plate is then processed and is instantly ready for use on an offset press.

Because the thin aluminum plate is highly flexible, it can be wrapped around a cylinder on an offset press. In the printing process, water is first applied to the plate. It adheres only to the unhardened areas which are not to be printed. Next the plate comes in contact with ink rollers. Since the ink has a grease base, it is repelled by the water on the nonprinting areas, but sticks to those areas which have previously repelled the water.

Next, the plate is brought in contact with the resilient blanket on the press. While the plate continues to revolve and repeat the dampening and inking process, the paper is squeezed against the blanket by impression rollers and picks up the printing image.

Types of Offset Printing

Like all printing processes, there is a number of variations of offset. For direct mail purposes, the two chief classifications are sheet-fed offset and web offset. In sheet-fed offset, paper is fed one sheet at a time. Recently, however, there has been a rapid growth in web offset, which involves feeding paper from a roll at very high speeds.

Another area of variation is in the type of plate used for printing. Plates range all the way from direct-image paper plates, on which copy is directly typed or drawn as described in Chapter 40, to deep-etch plates, which involve acid etching and add a degree of intaglio printing to the basic lithographic process.

Because of the many variations of offset possible, it is important to work closely with your lithographer in selecting the one which is appropriate for any given direct mail printing job.

Reproducing Color

One of the areas where offset has become extremely important to direct mail advertisers is in the reproduction of full-color illustrations. Not too many years ago lithographers had difficulty obtaining consistent results in process color reproduction, but improved techniques have been developed which now afford excellent results.

It is important, however, to recognize that two basic types of full-color reproduction are offered—fidelity color and "pleasing" color. Like letterpress and gravure, offset can produce faithful reproduction of original colors. But the work of Eastman Kodak in the early 1950's led to a simplified color reproduction system which, while producing "eye-pleasing" full-color printing, is not designed primarily to yield exact matches of original colors. Because the system is so highly mechanical and uses only the three primary colors, rather than four colors required in most full-color reproduction, it can be purchased at low cost—often no more than that charged for two-color printing using duotones.

The preparation of color plates for offset is primarily a photographic process and the camera is called upon to accomplish much work that is normally performed by hand in the preparation of process color plates for letterpress. Not only does this mean less costly platemaking, but speeds up the process in many cases.

Advantages of Offset

Perhaps the best way to evaluate the potential of offset printing for any direct mail piece is to consider some of the basic advantages of the process. (However, it is important to keep in mind the fact that recent developments—particularly plastic plates and new wrap-around presses—are rapidly bringing to letterpress many of the abilities which have been previously almost exclusively found in offset printing.)

Work from pasteups—Since offset plates are made from "mechanicals" which include both type and illustrations pasted in position, they eliminate much costly handwork usually required for other processes. Makeup on a drawing board is less costly than on the printer's stone, with its higher hourly rates. This advantage disappears, however, when large quantities of type are involved, since a typographer must still make up the type matter and then proof it for use on the pasteups. But when most of the space is occupied by illustrations, ornamentation, hand-lettering, or other non-typographic material, there is a definite cost advantage for offset.

More economical plates—When many or large illustrations are required, offset is considerably less expensive than other processes. As previously pointed out, this is a particular advantage in reproducing full-color illustrations, but it is also important in single and simple color reproduction. Line illustrations are handled at the same time as type matter is photographed. They are just pasted in position along with the type. While halftone negatives are made separately and then stripped in on the line negatives for platemaking, these negatives and the stripping are generally less expensive than the high-quality photoengravings used for letterpress. And when special effects—such as outlining, vignetting, opaquing, dropouts, and overprints—are required, the cost can be considerably lower, since all handwork is done on the negatives rather than on the plates.

Reuse of color separations—Once color-separation negatives have been produced for offset platemaking, these same separations can be used again not only for same-size reproduction but for reductions and blowups. This can be of special importance to the direct mail advertiser who wishes to use the same illustrations in different mailing pieces.

Elimination of makeready—Since positioning of elements for register is done right on the offset plate and printing will be done on a resilient rubber blanket, little time is required to get an offset press rolling. This can result in major cost savings.

Inexpensive duplicate plates—Duplicate platemaking for offset is a simple matter. The original negatives are simply used to prepare the duplicate plates. This is considerably less expensive than preparing electrotypes or producing duplicate letterpress engravings. In addition step-and-repeat cameras are used to duplicate material on the same negative for jobs that are to be printed in multiples on a single press run.

Low-cost reprints—Since offset plates have little bulk, they can be stored easily and are instantly ready for use when a direct mail piece must be reprinted. Even if the plates are not retained, offset printers usually retain negatives for extended periods so it is a simple matter to have new plates made economically with little time required.

Fewer limitations in papers—Because paper is printed from a resilient rubber blanket, a wider variety of paper stocks is suitable for offset printing. Even fine-screen halftones can be reproduced successfully on relatively rough-surfaced papers such as newsprint, text papers, fancy finishes, etc. In many cases a less expensive stock can be used with comparable quality of reproduction.

Finer halftone screens—Halftone screens as fine as 400-line can be reproduced by offset and it is relatively common to use 175-line screens. This is particularly important to direct mail advertisers who wish to use very small illustrations of their products, particularly in multi-item catalogs.

Self-contained shops—Most offset printers offer a complete service under one roof. Unlike letterpress where engraving and electrotyping are usually done separately from the printing operation, offset printers usually make their own plates. This affords more specific control and usually makes possible faster deliveries when required.

Web Offset

In recent years there has been an amazing growth for webfed, heat-set offset. The basic difference between web offset and the more common offset process is that paper is fed from rolls instead of sheets. The big advantage was explained by Bernard Green of Majestic Press Inc. in an article in *Graphic Arts Buyer:*

> Press speeds of 1,200 feet per *minute* are possible with the newest publication units and 800 f.p.m. is an acceptable standard for other kinds of equipment. Simple arithmetic shows that this speed is the equivalent of *25,000* 22¾- by 35-inch sheets an hour, and good sheet-fed offset production is figured at 6,000 sheets an hour. More impressions per hour usually means lower cost per unit, but web offset offers many other money-saving features as well. Most presses are equipped with cutting and folding attachments so that the printed web can be delivered in the form of flat sheets or signatures ready for trimming. Pasting units enable the web offset printer to deliver completed booklets directly from the delivery end of the press, and the larger publication units have bundling and tying machines attached to minimize subsequent handling operations.

To these advantages must be added the fact that paper in rolls is less expensive than sheets, although much of this saving may be lost due to spoilage, which is generally much greater in web offset.

The quality of the work turned out by these fast, economical units is excellent and the web offset process is being used for an increasing number of direct mail jobs—particularly in the long-run catalog field.

LETTERPRESS PRINTING

While offset has taken the lead in the direct mail reproduction field, letterpress is still highly important for many types of jobs, and with new developments may regain its once secure lead.

Unlike offset, where the total printing job is combined on a single plate by photographic means, letterpress usually involves the combination of a number of different printing elements—type, engravings, rules, ornaments, spacing material, etc.—which are locked together in metal forms for printing. Once forms are ready for the press, they may be electrotyped or stereotyped to provide a one-piece printing unit. Such units, however, are usually only in page size; if a job has multiple pages, these electrotypes and stereotypes must be combined to form a complete printing unit.

Types of Presses

Most letterpress printing is done with three basic types of presses:

1. *Platen press*—This is the original form of letterpress printing and involves squeezing a piece of paper between the type form, which is held in a vertical position, and a flat metal impression plate. While the platen press (often called "the job press") is the workhorse of the letterpress printing industry, it is limited in size. It is a highly versatile unit in most ways, but is limited to smaller jobs. The largest form which can be handled by common platen presses is 14 by 22 inches. And since operating speed is limited, the platen press is generally used only for relatively short runs or special types of jobs such as perforating, numbering, blind embossing, etc., where slower speeds are required.

2. *Cylinder press*—Like the platen press, this letterpress unit uses a flat printing form, but instead of being held vertically, it is laid horizontally on a flat metal bed. As a result, it is often called a "flatbed press." Paper, however, is placed around a cylindrical drum and brought in contact with the printing form on the flatbed as the drum revolves. The bed moves back and forth as the drum revolves. Two revolutions of the drum are required for each sheet printed since the type form must be reinked and returned to its "starting position" after each impression. Because of this reciprocation, the speed of cylinder presses is relatively slow.

There are three basic types of cylinder presses. In addition to the reciprocating press described above, there are two-color and perfecting presses. The two-color cylinder presses use two cylinders and two type forms—one for each color. The paper is automatically transferred from one cylinder to the other, ending up with two colors on one side of the sheet. The perfecting press, like the two-color press, has two printing cylinders and type forms, but turns the paper over when it transfers from one cylinder to the other, printing one color on both sides of the sheet in a single press run.

3. *Rotary press*—Instead of flat printing forms, rotary presses require a curved printing surface. This is usually obtained by making electrotypes or stereotypes of the original type form. These duplicate plates are clamped onto the cylinder and come in contact with the paper, which is fed between the plate cylinder and an impression cylinder. Paper can be fed from a roll or as individual sheets.

Like reciprocating cylinder presses, there is a number of different types of rotaries, including many designed to perform specific kinds of printing. The basic press makes one impression for each revolution of its cylinders, with inking being performed on the plates not in contact with the paper as the cylinder revolves. Multicolor units are of two types. One involves a single impression cylinder but multiple printing cylinders. As the paper goes around the impression cylinder, each of the printing cylinders apply ink. More common is a series of complete printing units, each having its own printing and impression cylinders. The paper simply travels from one unit to the other as the different colors of ink are added.

There are also perfecting rotary presses, which turn the paper so it will be printed on both sides in one press run. One of the most common types of rotaries is a five-color unit which delivers finished sheets printed in four colors on one side and a single color on the reverse side, although these presses often can be adapted to deliver full color on both sides of the sheet.

Because of the expense involved in making curved plates and in making the presses ready for printing, rotary presses are generally limited to long runs of 25,000 or more. They are often used for catalogs and other multiple-page direct mail units. It is quite common for a number of attachments to be added to rotary presses so they will deliver semicompleted jobs which have been folded to page size and pasted.

Advantages of Letterpress

Even before new developments are taken into consideration the letterpress process offers several basic advantages:

Wide range of press equipment—There are literally hundreds of different types of letterpresses in use, each having special advantages to offer. This means that a direct mail advertiser can usually find a press which is "tailored" to his job requirements, rather than having to settle for restrictions imposed by less versatile equipment available for other processes.

More mechanical—Letterpress is more mechanical than any other major process. It is less dependent upon close control of heat, humidity, and chemical elements and thus produces more consistent results.

Better solids—The heavier ink film of letterpress, the direct application of ink from plate to paper, and the elimination of water produce much better solids at faster speeds than with offset printing.

Direct-from-type printing—When jobs involve extensive typesetting, letterpress offers the advantage of being able to print directly from type matter. This advantage is partially wiped out when long runs are required and electros must be prepared to overcome type wear.

Flexibility—When changes in elements of a job are required, letterpress offers extreme flexibility since individual elements can quickly be changed without the necessity of remaking the entire page or form. This can be especially important in direct mail printing when special coding or imprinting of material is required.

Additional operations—Many specialty operations, such as scoring, die-cutting, numbering, and perforating may either be done along with the printing or on the same letterpress equipment. In addition, letterpresses are often equipped to deliver folded signatures, which are pasted or stapled. This not only reduces costs in many cases, but also speeds up deliveries.

Closer register—In color printing, it is usually easier to maintain close register on letterpress equipment. Not only can the individual elements be adjusted as necessary, but letterpress is less likely to be affected by changes in humidity or because of paper stretching or shrinking from the water used in lithography.

Specialty Plants

There are many specialty printers who are equipped—most often with letterpress equipment—to handle special types of printing jobs. One type of specialty printer which should be investigated by every direct mail advertiser is the tag company. This type of printer utilizes specially designed machines which generally print from stock in rolls and combine as many as a dozen different operations in one printing run. For example, the tag presses can turn out a finished product which is printed on two sides in multiple colors, numbered, die-cut, perforated, punched, special material pasted in position, trimmed, and folded—all in a single run. While not usually designed for top-quality printing, these tag printing units can often be used to meet complicated requirements combined with budget restrictions.

OTHER PRINTING PROCESSES

While there are many specialized printing processes, only four additional processes are used to any appreciable extent for direct mail—gravure, flexography, collotype, and screen process.

Gravure

This intaglio process is used only for long-run jobs, since the initial cost of preparing printing cylinders is relatively high. To prepare the large copper cylinders, copy is first photographed and then "printed" on a sensitized gelatin transfer medium called "carbon tissue." The carbon tissue is first screened to provide partitions around the cells which are later etched into the cylinder to hold the ink. This screen is just the reverse of conventional screens, in that the lines are transparent and the dots opaque. The exposure hardens the lines so they will remain firm when the cylinder is etched.

After being screened, the carbon tissue is exposed to a continuous-tone positive of the copy. The gelatin of each of the dots hardens in proportion to the amount of light passing through the positive. Thus, the lightest tones produce a relatively hard gelatin, while the dark areas produce softer gelatin.

After this exposure, the gelatin is transferred, in position, to the copper cylinder, which is acid etched. A complete tonal range is achieved with dots representing dark areas etched to a maximum depth and those for lighter areas etched to lesser depths. When the cylinder is placed on the press for printing, it passes through an enclosed ink fountain and the cells are filled with ink. The rest of the cylinder also becomes coated with ink, but this is removed by a "doctor blade" which wipes surface ink from the cylinder before it comes in contact with paper.

Because of the wide tonal range possible and the ability to deposit substantial quantities of ink on paper, gravure is particularly useful for direct mail pieces requiring colorful illustrations. Gravure lends itself to high-quality reproduction of continuous-tone illustrations, even on the most inexpensive paper. Reproduction of type—particularly smaller sizes or those with delicate details—is not as sharp, however, since screening is required.

One general rule of thumb used in evaluating the possible practicability of gravure is a minimum of 100,000 impressions for one-color printing or 250,000 copies for process color. Shorter runs can be handled on sheet-fed gravure, but this slower process is seldom used for direct mail printing.

Flexography

Basically a letterpress process, flexography (formerly known as aniline printing) is frequently used for jobs where minimum quality is required or where printing must be on a hard surface such as cellophane, acetate, or foil. It differs from conventional letterpress in that liquid rather than paste-type inks are used and plates are of resilient rubber rather than metal.

Flexographic presses print at extremely fast speeds and the use of rubber plates eliminates most conventional makeready. Because the fluid ink has a tendency to spread, coarse screens are required.

In direct mail, flexography is most frequently used for envelopes and reply cards, although larger pieces are sometimes printed on flexographic presses when quality requirements are low and budgets are tight.

Collotype

Basically a short-run process, collotype (also called photogelatin printing) is only infrequently used for preparation of direct mail materials. Its primary direct mail use is when extreme fidelity of reproduction is required. Collotype is an intaglio process, but instead of using a metal cylinder with holes to receive the ink as does gravure, a gelatin printing surface is used. This gelatin surface is hardened by photographic exposure in proportion to the density of the material to be reproduced. The gelatin absorbs ink—with dark areas receiving larger amounts of ink and lighter areas absorbing lesser amounts of ink. Because no screens are needed to break up the subject into dots, reproduction can be extremely fine and come close to a photographic print.

While platemaking costs are relatively low, their press life is limited and press speeds are slow. The usual rule of thumb for the maximum collotype run is 5,000 impressions, although jobs are frequently ganged up to deliver a greater total count.

Screen Process

Like collotype, screen process (also called silk-screen printing) has only limited use for direct mail. Usually it is called upon only when irregular surfaces must be printed or for special covers used on fancy brochures. The basic process is simple. A tightly stretched silk screen, part of which has been coated to close up the pores in the silk, is placed in contact with the surface to be printed and a thick, pigmented ink is squeezed through the silk. Originally, the basic procedure was to completely coat the silk and then cut away by hand areas to be printed. Today, however, photographic methods are used.

The big advantage of the screen process is that very heavy deposits of ink or paints can be deposited on the printing surface.

Comparing the Processes

An analysis of the comparative advantages and disadvantages of the three processes most used for direct mail—letterpress, offset and gravure—has been prepared by The Printing Industry of Illinois. The following chart shows the various rankings given on ten basic characteristics that affect both quality and price.

	Letter-press	Offset	Gravure
Flexibility	1	2	3
Proofing, corrections and alterations	1	2	3
Reproduction of tone	3	2	1
Reproduction of line work	1	2	3
Image size and continuous image	3	1 or 2	1 or 2
Press makeready	3	2	1
Material to be printed	2	1	3
Color control	1	2	3
Plate or cylinder 'life'	2	3	1
Register control	1	2	3

Flexibility

1. *Letterpress*—Can be run from original type and engravings. Duplicate plates (electros) can be made for longer runs on either cylinder or rotary presses. Electros can be made from plates sent from other printer or engravers. Individual plates can be removed from press and others substituted on split run jobs.

2. *Offset*—Photographic step always necessary in offset. Portions of plate difficult to remove and re-etch. In most cases, the entire plate must be remade.

3. *Gravure*—Same limitations as in offset with even greater limitations in time and cost factors. Not suitable for short runs.

Proofing, Corrections and Alterations

1. *Letterpress*—Proofing can be made quickly and inexpensively at every step of the process. Corrections can also be made at every step, even to the repair of damaged areas while the plate is on the press.

2. *Offset*—Proofing is an extra operation. Proofs are not "samples" of the original image as in letterpress. Corrections and alterations must be made on photographic image before plate is made. Corrections to offset plates are limited.

3. *Gravure*—Proofs are not obtainable until cylinder is nearly complete. Cylinder must be proved on large equipment which is costly. Corrections can be made to cylinders but major corrections and alterations are difficult, time consuming and costly. Often, it pays to make a new cylinder.

Reproduction of Tone

1. *Gravure*—Has the longest tone range resulting from the uniformity of ink coverage in the shadow or dark end of the scale. This, coupled with an inconspicuous screen (150 line or more), gives fine detail and "photographic quality" to the reproduction. The depth of the dot, rather than the area (as in relief and offset) determines the tone.

2. *Offset*—Cannot reproduce the darker end of the scale as well as gravure. Offset is limited to the conventional screen, which is more noticeable than gravure. Offset however, can reproduce subtle highlights with good fidelity.

3. *Letterpress*—Shortest tonal range resulting from limitations of the etching process. Dot is sharp which gives "brilliance" to the reproduction when printed on coated papers. However, hard edges may result during printing when copy contains vignette or water colored artwork.

Reproduction of Line Work

1. *Letterpress*—In sharpness of line copy reproduction, letterpress holds a slight edge. This is because the image is transferred directly to the paper. As the impression takes place, a slight "squeeze out" occurs, forming a sharp edge on the line or type being reproduced.

2. *Offset*—Plates are installed quickly. Some packing needed under the plate. very sharp line work. The introduction of chromed plates with minute grain has also sharpened line reproduction. However, the offset blanket cylinder still has some grain which "softens" the edges on line work.

3. *Gravure*—Type and line work is impaired by the screen. Some compromises can be made by using a finer screen for type but this necessitates additional operations in cylinder making.

Image Size and Continuous Image

1. or 2. *Offset*—Press equipment is available with large cylinders to print large, unbroken areas such as might be used for outdoor advertising billboards.

1. or 2. *Gravure*—Although presses could be designed with large cylinders and offer the same size feature of offset, such presses are not common. This is because the length of run is limited and would not justify the higher cost of gravure cylinder making on such jobs. Gravure does offer a "continuous image" on overall patterns for packaging materials that are run on web presses. In the other two processes, it is necessary to have a "break" in the image to lock on plates.

3. *Letterpress*—Definitely limited to relatively small plate sizes which restricts the total area that can be printed. On some types of press equipment, space must be provided at intervals for "hook room."

Press Makeready

1. *Gravure*—Cylinders are quickly installed and lined up. No special preparation needed on printing surface or impression cylinder.

2. *Offset*—Plates are installed quickly. Some packing needed under the plate. Blanket needs some attention but makeready is simplified because of blanket flexibility.

3. *Letterpress*—Plates must be processed in a "premakeready" operation. Often, "spot" underlays must be made. Packing may need extra thickness in spots "overlays." Plates are locked up individually. Makereadys often run into several hours, especially on color work.

Material to be Printed

1. *Offset*—Generally conceded to reproduce on the widest variety of materials. Flexibility of blanket enables printing on uneven surfaces. Some problems occur on certain types of coated (glossy) papers. Linty papers can cause lint to stick to the inked portion of the blanket causing specks in the solid areas.

2. *Letterpress*—Best quality on coated (glossy) paper but can print on dull uncoated paper. Poor on uneven surfaces and lightweight stock.

3. *Gravure*—Prints well on even surfaces or lightweight papers. Extreme pressures on press "iron out" textured papers and destroy effects. Can print on glossy surfaces if stock is made for the process.

Color Control

1. *Letterpress*—Good makeready and good ink distribution with color set to match progressive proofs will give consistent color throughout press run. Color variations occur mostly as a result of plate and packing wear.

2. *Offset*—Color control in offset compares favorably with letterpress except for one problem. The pH factor (acidity-alkalinity) of the dampening solution affects color. As plates "wear," oxidation takes place in the dampened areas of the plate. This causes non-printing portions of the plate to print. Acid can be added to the dampening solution which eliminates this fault. In doing so, the image area of the plate is made less ink receptive which causes color to fade.

3. *Gravure*—Gravure inks are thin and volatile and tend to "settle out" unless kept under constant agitation. Pigments adaptable to gravure inks are somewhat inferior to those of relief or offset.

Plate or Cylinder "Life"

1. *Gravure*—Cylinders are capable of producing several million impressions. It is often possible to "dechrome" and "rechrome" offering the possibility of extremely long runs.

2. *Letterpress*—Chromed electros also offer long runs although the chances of damage to individual plates is greater. Chief failure is due to cracks caused by crystallization of the metal.

3. *Offset*—The introduction of trimetal (chrome, copper and aluminum) offset plates was a significant contribution to greater plate life. However, it is conceded that offset plate life cannot compare with gravure cylinders although trimetal plates are nearing letterpress runs in some instances.

Register Control

1. *Letterpress*—Individual plates can be moved on the press to obtain and maintain precise register. Constant control of the web or sheet as it travels through the press presents the same problem in all three processes. However, penetration of the paper (by ink vehicles or dampening solutions) is minimized in letterpress.

2. *Offset*—Although precise register can be obtained in photo composing, dampening solutions tend to swell or stretch the paper making register more difficult. Offset pressrooms are usually air conditioned to maintain constant humidity levels and minimize register problems.

3. *Gravure*—A share of gravure register problems can be traced to the paper quality inherent to gravure printing. Some ink solvents penetrate the paper. This, coupled with extreme pressures used (between the cylinder and the impression cylinder) contribute to register problems. Atmospheric conditions that affect paper is another factor in register on color web presses.

PRINTING TRADE CUSTOMS

Standard trade practices for the graphic arts industry have been established by various trade associations. Direct mail advertisers are affected primarily by the standards established by the Printing Industry of America (generally followed by most letterpress printers) and the National Association of Photo-Lithographers.

Printing Industry of America

Adopted by Printing Industry of America, Inc., in convention at Pittsburgh, Pennsylvania, October 4-5, 1945:

ORDERS regularly entered cannot be canceled except upon terms that will compensate against loss.

EXPERIMENTAL WORK performed at customer's request, such as sketches, drawings, composition, plates (including lithographic plates), presswork, and materials shall be charged for at current rates.

SKETCHES, COPY, DUMMIES, and all preparatory work created or furnished by the printer, shall remain his exclusive property and no use of same shall be made, nor may ideas obtained therefrom be used, except upon compensation to be determined by the owner.

ART WORK, TYPE, PLATES (including lithographic plates), engravings, electrotypes, negatives, positives, and other items when supplied by the printer shall remain his exclusive property, unless otherwise agreed in writing.

ALTERATIONS—Proposals are only for work according to the original specifications. If through customer's error, or change of mind, work has to be done a second time or more, such extra work will carry an additional charge, at current rates for the work performed.

STANDING TYPE MATTER—Plates (including lithographic plates and negatives) will not be held after completion of the order except by special agreement and charge therefor.

PROOFS—Two proofs shall be submitted with original copy. Corrections, if any, to be made thereon and to be returned marked "O.K." or "O.K. with corrections" and signed with name or initials of person duly authorized to pass on same. If revised proofs are desired, request must be made when proof is returned. Printer is not responsible for errors if work is printed as per customer's O.K.

PRESS PROOFS—An extra charge will be made for press proofs, unless the customer is present when the form is made ready on the press so that no press time is lost. Presses standing awaiting O.K. of customer will be charged at current rates for the time so consumed.

OVERRUNS or underruns not to exceed 10% of the amount ordered shall constitute an acceptable delivery and the excess or deficiency shall be charged or credited to the customer proportionately.

Customer's Property—The printer shall charge the customer, at current rates, for handling and storing customer's stock or customer's printed matter held more than thirty (30) days. All customer's property that is stored with a printer is at the customer's risk, and the printer is not liable for any loss or damage thereto caused by fire, water leakage, theft, negligence, insects, rodents, or any cause beyond the printer's control. It is understood that the gratuitous storage of customer's property is solely for the benefit of the customer.

Delivery—Unless otherwise specified the price quoted is for a single shipment, F.O.B. customer's local place of business. All proposals are based on continuous and uninterrupted delivery of complete order, unless specifications distinctly state otherwise.

Terms—Net cash thirty (30) days. All claims must be made within five days of receipt of goods.

Delays in Delivery—All contracts are made contingent upon wars, strikes, fires, floods, accidents, or other contingencies beyond the printer's control.

Repairs, Changes, trimming, mortising, anchoring, special proving, or similar work required by the customer, including, but not limited to, drawings, engravings, electrotypes, and negatives shall be billed at current market rates.

Paper Stock furnished by the customer shall be properly packed, free from dirt, grit, torn sheets, bad splices, etc., and of proper quality for printing requirements. Additional cost due to delays or impaired production on account of improper packing or quality shall be charged to the customer.

Color Proofing—Because of the difference in equipment and conditions between the color proofing and the pressroom operations, a reasonable variation in color between color proofs and the completed job shall constitute an acceptable delivery.

National Association of Photo-Lithographers

Adopted by National Association of Photo-Lithographers, 1934, and reconfirmed every year in annual conventions.

Orders—Regularly entered orders cannot be canceled except upon terms that will compensate the lithographer against loss.

Experimental Work performed at customer's request, such as sketches, drawings, composition, plates, presswork, and materials will be charged for.

Sketches and Dummies—Sketches, copy, dummies, and all preparatory work created or furnished by the lithographer, shall remain his exclusive property and no use of same shall be made, nor any ideas obtained therefrom be used, except upon compensation to be determined by the owner.

Drawings, Negatives, and Plates—Art work, drawings, negatives, positives, plates, and other items when supplied by the lithographer shall remain his exclusive property, unless otherwise agreed in writing.

Alterations—See PIA Trade Customs.

Approval of Proofs—If proofs are submitted to the customer, corrections, if any, are to be made thereon and the proofs returned to the lithographer marked "O.K." or "O.K. with corrections" and signed with the name or initials of the person duly authorized to pass on same. If revised proofs are desired, request must be made when proof is returned. The lithographer is not responsible for errors if work is completed as per customer's O.K.

Press Proofs—An extra charge will be made for press proofs, unless the customer is present when the plate is made ready on the press so that no press time is lost. Presses standing awaiting O.K. of customer will be charged at current rates for the time so consumed.

Color Proofing—See PIA Trade Customs.

Quantities Delivered—Overruns or underruns not to exceed 10% of the amount ordered shall constitute an acceptable delivery and the excess or deficiency shall be charged or credited to the customer proportionately.

Customer's Property—The lithographer shall charge the customer, at prevailing rates, for handling and storing customer's paper stock or customer's lithographed matter held more than thirty (30) days. All customer's property that is stored with a lithographer is at the customer's risk, and the lithographer is not liable for any loss or damage thereto caused by fire, water leakage, breakage, theft, negligence, insects, rodents, or any other cause beyond the lithographer's control. It is understood that the gratuitous storage of customer's property is solely for the benefit of the customer.

Delivery—Unless otherwise specified the price quoted is for a single shipment, F.O.B. customer's local place of business. All estimates are based on continuous and uninterrupted delivery of complete order, unless specifications distinctly state otherwise.

Terms—Net cash thirty (30) days unless otherwise provided in writing. All claims must be made within five days of receipt of goods.

Delays in Delivery—All agreements are made and all orders accepted contingent upon strikes, fires, accidents, wars, flood, or other causes beyond the lithographer's control.

Paper Stock Furnished by Customer—Paper stock furnished by the customer shall be properly packed, free from dirt, grit, torn sheets, bad splices, etc., and of proper quality and specifications for the lithographer's requirements. Additional cost due to delays or impaired production on account of improper packing or quality shall be changed to the customer.

Chapter 42

PRELIMINARY PRODUCTION PROCESSES

BEFORE a direct mail piece can be printed, there is a number of preliminary processes which must be completed. While there are dozens of operations which may be performed, the three most important are artwork, typography, and plate-making.

ARTWORK

In all printing processes, the first production step is preparation of copy and illustrations to be reproduced. Each year there is an increasing number of techniques which can be used to accomplish this preliminary work. And with the new developments comes a constant change in taste. Just as women's fashions change from year to year (and often repeat themselves from time to time), graphic design fashions are subject to constant change and revivals.

For this reason, among others, it is important to utilize the services of progressive graphic arts firms and art studios in the planning, design, and production of direct mail. In addition to helping keep your direct mail advertising in tune with contemporary tastes, utilizing the latest knowledge of developments will often result in improved quality and lower costs.

Buying Artwork

Buying artwork is a complicated matter. There are few standards to follow—from either a quality or a cost standpoint. What constitutes good art is difficult to say, for what is best in the eyes of one is highly inferior in the eyes of another. Therefore, it is best to determine just what any piece of art is intended to do and then let this purpose be the primary determining factor in the selection of the type of art.

There are six primary sources of artwork for direct mail printed matter, each with its advantages and disadvantages:

1. *Internal art staff*—Direct mail advertisers requiring a large volume of artwork—and particularly those who operate their own reproduction departments—often maintain an internal art staff. This offers the advantage of close control, instant availability, and, often, economy. But these advantages are generally far outweighed by the many disadvantages.

Perhaps the major disadvantage of an internal art staff is limitation in skills. No artist is ever skilled in more than one or two of the dozens of basic art techniques. A good cartoonist, for example, is seldom capable of producing realistic illustrations. A good layout man seldom produces the best finished art. A good water colorist is usually lost when working with pen and ink or scratchboard. As a result, most internal art departments are staffed by jacks-of-all-trades who turn out acceptable, but mediocre, work in a number of different art media.

Even if the internal art staff is large, with specialists in different media, it is difficult to command the services of the best artists in any one medium. The creative personality skilled in a given art medium usually seeks an opportunity to work on a variety of different jobs and, as a result, shies away from the typical internal art department where his assignments are usually highly similar in nature.

Other disadvantages include the problem of peak-and-valley workloads, which involve periods of high activity followed by uneconomical periods when there is little legitimate work to be done. Then, too, there is a tendency for an internal art department to fall into a set pattern which produces a monotony in graphic design and often fails to keep up with changing tastes in graphics.

2. *Agency art staffs*—Direct mail advertisers who utilize advertising, sales promotion, or direct mail agencies to handle their creative work often find agencies with their own finished art staffs. The advantages and disadvantages follow the same pattern as those for the internal art staff, although the added volume handled by these agencies usually means that there is less of a peak-and-valley problem and also, that these agencies will attract more creative artists because of the opportunity to work on a wider variety of jobs.

An interesting "hybrid" has developed in recent years. It is a combination art studio/direct mail agency. Such organizations are primarily art studios which have added additional creative personnel to handle all details of direct mail production. Some of the best direct mail art has come out of these agencies. There is a danger, however, that too great an emphasis will be placed on the artwork and that other elements of the creative task will suffer. As these agencies develop direct mail experience, they will deserve increasing consideration by advertisers.

3. *Printer or lettershop art staffs*—Many producers of direct mail materials maintain art staffs to provide the illustrations and design required by their customers. Some of the staffs are highly skilled, but beware the direct mail producer who suggests such a service is available as a "free bonus" when you use his facilities for your production needs. The best rule of thumb is to expect to get just exactly what you pay for. Good art and design are not inexpensive, and no printer or lettershop can afford to give them away. As a result, you will either get inferior work or increased prices.

The major advantage of art services provided by printers or lettershops is that their art staffs usually have a superior knowledge of the equipment and techniques which will be used to handle your direct mail printing. Thus, they can tailor the art and design to "fit" the mechanical aspects of the production. This often can result in substantial printing economies and improved quality.

But, like internal and agency art staffs, there is likely to be a limited range of skills available in a printer or lettershop art department. The most successful departments usually limit their services to layout and design and then turn to more specialized outside sources for finished art.

4. *Art studios*—The surest bet in obtaining quality artwork is to turn to the art studio where a wide range of skills is available. While studio prices have a tendency to be higher than any other source, the quality of the work often makes these added costs well worthwhile. But remember, there is a wide variation in the capabilities of different art studios. It takes careful research to select the art studio which is most capable of doing the work you need and you will generally find you will need more than one studio if your requirements are broad.

In working with an art studio, an advertiser generally deals with a contact man, who is not an artist himself. However, the skills of these contact men can be just as important as those of the artists, since they must interpret your requirements and see they are placed in the hands of the artists best able to turn out the work. Since the art buyer seldom deals directly with the artist, it is usually wise to make periodic visits to art studios to see firsthand the type of work being turned out and to get a good idea of the capabilities and limitations of the personnel.

5. *Free-lance artists*—In most areas there are many free-lance artists available to handle almost any type of art or design work —and many direct mail advertisers fulfill most of their art requirements through mail contact with free-lance artists scattered throughout the country and even abroad. The usual procedure in working with free lancers is to ask them to bring a portfolio of samples of their work to your office (or to submit samples through the mails). In some areas, free lancers work through brokers who act in the same capacity as an art studio's contact man.

In general, you will find that free lancers produce comparable quality at less cost than any other art source. But are costs can seldom be given a price-list treatment. Naturally, the more skilled an artist becomes—and the more his work is in demand— the higher the price he can command. In working with free lancers, it is usually best to establish the price in advance. The artist will then be able to judge the amount of time he can afford to devote to the project. For maximum economy, it is usually best to give a free lancer a number of jobs at one time. Since this will reduce his nonproductive contact time, the price per piece will generally be lower.

6. *Syndicated artwork*—One of the most important developments in the art field in recent years has been the rapid growth of syndicated art services. Many direct mail advertisers depend almost exclusively upon these services to provide the bulk of the illustrations they use for printed matter. Costs are low, but there is wide variation in quality.

There are three basic types of syndicated art available: (1) clipbooks containing a number of illustrations at a cost of pennies each; (2) continuing services, which provide a steady flow of syndicated art for a monthly, quarterly, or annual fee; and (3) semicustom art-by-mail services, which will create material to your specifications within a certain limited range. In addition to reproduction art, some of these services will provide mats, electrotypes, or engravings for letterpress use.

Since the nature of the material supplied by these services varies so widely, it is best to obtain samples from each of the individual services if you are interested in syndicated art.

One common mistake in considering syndicated artwork is to think of it only in terms of direct reproduction. Most of the syndicated artwork available has been specifically designed so it can be tailored to fit varying circumstances. With very little effort, most illustrations can become semicustom art.

A Code of Ethics for Art

Dealing with artists and art studios can sometimes become a complicated process. To simplify some of the points of confusion, a code of ethics covering practices in the buying of art was established. While the original code was intended primarily for use in the New York area, it has since been used as a guide throughout the country.

1. INTRODUCTION—In 1945 a group of artists and art directors in the City of New York, concerned with the growing abuses, misunderstandings, and disregard of uniform standards of conduct in their field, met to consider possibilities for improvement. They reached the conclusion that any effort, to be successful, must start with the most widespread backing, and further that it must be a continuing, not a temporary, activity. On their recommendation, three leading New York art organizations together established and financed a committee known as the Joint Ethics Committee. This is published in response to the many requests for information about operations and scope of the Committee.

2. PERSONNEL—The Joint Ethics Committee is composed of three members each from the Society of Illustrators, the Art Directors Club, and the Artists Guild, appointed by the directing bodies of each of these organizations, but serving jointly in furtherance of the purposes for which the Committee was founded.

   Members of the Joint Ethics Committee are selected with great care by their respective organizations. Their selection is based upon their experience in the profession, their proven mature thinking and temperament, and their reputation for impartiality.

3. CODE OF FAIR PRACTICE—The Code of Fair Practice, as established by the Joint Ethics Committee and endorsed by the National Society of Art Directors, was conceived with the idea of equity, not alone for the artist but for the art representative and the buyers of art.

   The Committee zealously upholds the ethical standards set forth in the Code and invites with equal readiness any and all reports of violations on the parts of artists, art representatives or buyers of art.

4. ACTION—The Committee meets one or more times a month to read and act upon complaints, requests for guidance, and reports of Code violations. The proceedings and records of the Committee are held in strict confidence. In the interest of the profession, typical cases are published periodically without identification of the parties involved. However, in the case of flagrant violation, the governing bodies of the parent organizations may be fully informed. All communications to the Committee must be made in writing. When a complaint justifies action, a copy of the complaining letter is sent, with the plaintiff's permission, to the alleged offender. In the exchange of correspondence which follows, matters are

frequently settled by a mere clarification of the issues. Further action by the Committee becomes unnecessary, and in many instances both sides resume friendly and profitable relationships. When, however, a continued exchange of correspondence indicates that a ready adjustment of difference is improbable, the Committee may suggest mediation or offer its facilities for arbitration.

5. MEDIATION—Both parties meet informally under the auspices of a panel of mediators composed of three members of the Committee. If the dispute requires guidance in a field not represented in the committee's membership, a specially qualified mediator with the required experience may be included. The names of members of the panel are submitted to both parties for acceptance.

   The conduct of a panel of mediators is friendly and informal. The function of the panel members is to guide; not to render any verdict. The panel's purpose is to direct the discussion along such lines and in such a manner as to bring about a meeting of minds on the questions involved. If mediation fails, or seems unlikely to bring about satisfactory settlement, arbitration may be suggested.

6. ARBITRATION—A panel of five arbitrators is appointed. One or more is selected from the Committee, and the remainder are chosen by virtue of their particular experience and understanding of the problems presented by the dispute. Names of the panel members are submitted to both parties for their approval. Both parties involved sign an agreement and take oath to abide by the decision of the panel. The panel itself is sworn in and the proceedings are held in compliance with the Arbitration Law of the State of New York. After both sides are heard, the panel deliberates in private and renders its decision, opinion, and award. These are duly formulated by the Committee's counsel for service on the parties and, if the losing side should balk, for entry of judgment according to law.

   So far, every award has been fully honored. The decisions and opinions of this Committee are rapidly becoming precedent for guidance in similar situations. The Committee's Code has been cited as legal precedent.

7. COMMITTEE SCOPE—The Committee acts upon matters which can be defined by them as involving a violation of the Code or a need for its enforcement.

   Upon occasion, the Committee has been asked to aid in settling questions not specifically covered by the Code of Fair Practice. The Committee gladly renders such aid, providing it does not exceed the limitations of its authority.

8. COMMITTEE LIMITATIONS—The Committee offers no legal advice on contracts, copyrights, bill collecting, or similar matters. But its judgments and decisions as to what is fair and ethical in any given situation are supported by the entire profession represented by the Committee.

   The Committee's influence is derived from widespread moral support, and while it has neither judicial nor police powers, and cannot punish offenders nor summon alleged violators to its presence, still, its growing prestige and dignity of operation have made it a highly respected tribunal to which few have ever failed to respond when invited to settle their differences.

9. Committee Maintenance—No fees or expenses are charged to anyone requiring the services of the Committee. The Committee's facilities are not limited to members of its supporting groups. They are freely offered to any individual, business, or professional organization.

   The operating expenses of the Committee are defrayed by three organizations represented. The time and services of the members and legal counsel are voluntarily contributed without any form of personal gain.

RELATIONS BETWEEN ARTIST AND ART DIRECTOR

1. Dealings between an artist or his agent and an agency or publication should be conducted only through an authorized art director or art buyer.

2. Orders to an artist or agent should be in writing and should include the price, delivery date and a summarized description of the work. In the case of publications, the acceptance of a manuscript by the artist constitutes an order.

3. All changes and additions not due to the fault of the artist or agent should be billed to the purchaser as an additional and separate charge.

4. There should be no charge for revisions made necessary by errors on the part of the artist or his agent.

5. Alterations to artwork should not be made without consulting the artist. Where alterations or revisions are necessary and time permits and where the artist has maintained his usual standard of quality, he should be given the opportunity of making such changes.

6. The artist should notify the buyer of an anticipated delay in delivery. Should the artist fail to keep his contract through unreasonable delay in delivery, or nonconformance with agreed specifications, it should be considered a breach of contract by the artist and should release the buyer from responsibility.

7. Work stopped by a buyer after it has been started should be delivered immediately and billed on the basis of the time and effort expended and expenses incurred.

8. An artist should not be asked to work on speculation. However, work originating with the artist may be marketed on its merit. Such work remains the property of the artist unless paid for.

9. Art contests except for educational or philanthropic purposes are not approved because of their speculative character.

10. There should be no secret rebates, discounts, gifts, or bonuses to buyers by the artist or his agent.

11. If the purchase price of artwork is based specifically on limited use and later this material is used more extensively than originally planned, the artist is to receive adequate additional remuneration.

12. If comprehensives or other preliminary work are subsequently published as finished art, the price should be increased to the satisfaction of artist and buyer.

13. If preliminary drawings or comprehensives are bought from an artist with the intention or possibility that another artist will be assigned to do the finished work, this should be made clear at the time of placing the order.

14. The right of an artist to place his signature upon artwork is subject to agreement between artist and buyer.

15. There should be no plagiarism of any creative artwork.

16. If an artist is specifically requested to produce any artwork during unreasonable working hours, fair additional remuneration should be allowed.

RELATIONS BETWEEN ARTIST AND REPRESENTATIVE

17. An artist entering into an agreement with an agent or studio for exclusive representation should not accept an order from, nor permit his work to be shown by any other agent or studio. Any agreement which is not intended to be exclusive should set forth in writing the exact restrictions agreed upon between the two parties.

18. All illustrative artwork or reproductions submitted as samples to a buyer by artists' agents or art studio representatives should bear the name of the artist or artists responsible for the creation.

19. No agent or studio should continue to show the work of an artist as samples after the termination of their association.

20. After termination of an association between artist and agent, the agent should be entitled to a commission on work already under contract for a period of time not exceeding six months.

21. Original artwork furnished to an agent or submitted to a prospective purchaser shall remain the property of the artist and should be returned to him in good condition.

22. Interpretation of this code shall be in the hands of the Joint Ethics Committee and is subject to changes and additions at the discretion of the parent organizations.

PHOTOGRAPHY

Much the same "rules" can be applied to purchasing photography for direct mail advertising as were suggested for other types of artwork. Above all, however, place a high value on the services of *professional* photographers. While there are thousands of good amateurs, very few have a real understanding of reproduction requirements. This is an important "plus" you should expect—and demand—from a professional.

How to Order Commercial Photography

The following 17 suggestions to aid advertisers in ordering commercial photography have been prepared by Todd Studios of St. Louis:

1. Plan ahead as far as possible. Don't rush your photographer or any other supplier.

2. Check your production costs before you sell your idea or layout to your boss or client.

3. Before ordering important or expensive photographic work, discuss your plans with the person who will give the final okay. Be sure you know what he wants and that you can convey his wishes to the photographer.

4. Prepare a layout. Artistic ability is of little concern. On this layout show:

   - Position and angle of the subject to be photographed.
   - Indicate the desired background. Keep it simple and uncluttered. Hold properties or number of models to a minimum. Not many subjects can be shot on a pure white background. State whether the photographer is to opaque or "block out" the background or whether you, the engraver, or the printer will handle it.
   - Show the space allotted to the subject to be shot and the space allotted to the copy.
   - Write all specific instructions on the border of the layout—not on the purchase order.
   - Order the print to the desired size—size of layout, size of final reproduction, or a size large enough to be retouched. Actual size of layout plus 50% is usually large enough for retouching. Remember, an engraver cannot effectively enlarge a print more than twice size or reduce it more than six times size.
   - State whether additional print paper (black or white) is needed around the borders.
   - If your layout cannot be released to the photographer, either make an onion skin tracing or have it photocopied.
   - State the type of print paper you require. Glossy paper is usually standard, but for some special purposes semimatte or matte prints are better. Prints come in two basic weights, and a variety of surfaces. Prints can also be toned to various colors which may be a definite aid.
   - State what type of proofs are necessary. This is especially important in model work where quite a few negatives are made. Usually, contact glossies or red portrait proofs are sufficient for you to make your selection.

5. Prepare your purchase order completely—*and issue it at the time you give out the work.* Do not use it for minute instructions to your photographer. It should merely identify the job and the time needed. When specifying the time needed, do not say "as soon as possible" or "rush." Tell the specific hour and day that you will use it. *Don't give false deadlines—but do allow enough time for retakes.*

6. Select a commercial photographer who is fully equipped and who has the correct man to handle your job. Then, trust his judgment in assisting you.

7. Call in the photographer's service representative. Show him your layout. Discuss the job, pick out the models (if needed), *and get the price question settled at this point.*

8. If several photographers are asked to bid on the job, a good general rule is to throw out the highest bidder because he is usually a one-order man, and throw out the lowest bidder because he must cut corners somewhere to make a profit.

9. Be sure that the merchandise you give the photographer to shoot is a select article—finish in good shape, labels on straight, etc.

10. If it is necessary to gather properties, state whether you will secure them or whether the photographer is to collect them. This can be expensive to you.

11. If several photographs are to be reproduced together, specify that the print tones be even and that correct size or proportion be held.

12. If models are to be used, hire professional, *photogenic* men or women. Many beautiful girls do not photograph *well.* Avoid using your client's family. It will almost always cause trouble.

13. When buying color photography, reproduce from color transparencies if no retouching or additional artwork will be needed.

14. When buying black-and-white work, order an additional print to serve as a guide to the retoucher, or as a spare in case of damage to the original. After the retoucher has finished with it, file for future reference.

15. State how the photograph is to be reproduced. The photographer can make a print which is best for the various types of media—newspaper, magazine, TV, etc.

16. Bunch your orders when possible. Avoid too frequent pickups and deliveries.

17. Think of overall costs when buying photographs, including retouching and engraving costs. It is false economy to attempt to save a dollar on the photograph and lose many dollars on added retouching or engraving expenses—or even several thousand dollars in wasted media space.

Special Photographic Services

Many direct mail advertisers make regular use of photo reporting services which have photographers located throughout the country (and even worldwide). To make use of these services, the advertiser just gives his basic instructions to the headquarters office and the organization arranges for local reporter-photographers to take the necessary photographs on location and obtain any type of information which may be needed to accompany the pictures.

Stock Photographs

Just as you can obtain stock artwork for far less than custom-tailored art, there are thousands of low-cost "stock" photos available to meet a variety of direct mail requirements. Most sources can supply catalogs showing subjects they have available. While there are hundreds of sources, the following list represents some of the best-known suppliers:

Alpha Photo Associates, 251 Park Avenue, New York, New York 10013

The Associated Press, 50 Rockefeller Plaza, New York, New York 10020

Atoz-Van Cleve Photography, 7067 N. Glenwood, Chicago, Illinois 60626

The Bettmann Archive, 136 East 57th Street, New York, New York 10022

Black Star, 450 Park Avenue South, New York, New York 10016

Collectors Series, 161 West Harrison Street, Chicago, Illinois 60605

Ewing Galloway, 342 Madison Avenue, New York, New York 10017

Globe Photos Inc., 404 Park Avenue South, New York, New York 10016

Image Bank, 415 West Superior Street, Chicago, Illinois 60610

Harold M. Lambert Studios, 2801 West Cheltenham Avenue, Philadelphia, Pennsylvania 19150

Frederic Lewis Inc., 35 East 35th Street, New York, New York 10016

Magnum Photos Inc., 15 West 46th Street, New York, New York 10036

Piles & Files of Photos, 1030 North State Street, Chicago, Illinois 60610

Publix Pictorial Service Inc., 4711 West Byron Street, Chicago, Illinois 60641

Rapho Photo Researchers, 60 East 56th Street, New York, New York 10022

H. Armstrong Roberts, 4203 Locust Street, Philadelphia, Pennsylvania 19104

Shostal Associates, Inc., 60 East 42nd Street, New York, New York 10017

Sickles Photo-Reporting Service, 410 Ridgewood Avenue, Maplewood, New Jersey 07040

Three Lions Inc., 150 5th Avenue, New York, New York 10011

United Press International Newspictures, 220 E. 42nd Street, New York, New York 10017

Wide-World Photo, 50 Rockefeller Plaza, New York, New York 10022

TYPOGRAPHY

Setting type for direct mail material follows most of the basic rules of advertising typography. However, a great deal more "cold type" is used for direct mail than for almost any other type of printing. Cold type is prepared primarily by photographic means, rather than from molten metal used in hot-type processes. Also in the area of cold-type composition is that done on typewriters and typewriter-like machines.

To best understand the variations possible in typography, you should first understand the basic typesetting methods:

Hand Composition

When just a few words are required or when a highly unusual typeface is wanted, type is usually set by hand. A composing stick is held in one hand while the typographer picks up individual type characters from a type case with the other hand and places them in the stick. Various size spaces are used to fill out the line to the length required. The primary use for hand composition is for display headlines. It takes very little training to set a line of type, but best results come when the typographer is a real type artist, with years of experience. While the differences added by the typographic artist are subtle, they can turn a routine job into one of beauty.

Linotype and Intertype

These machines produce one-piece lines of type. An operator sits at a keyboard and as he depresses each key, a matrix is released from a large magazine. Wedge-shaped bands are inserted between matrices wherever spaces are to appear. Once a line has been filled, the space bands are pushed upward. Their wedge shape opens up the spaces between words equally and pushes the line to the right to completely fill whatever length of line has been chosen. Once the line is "tight," molten metal is poured into the assembled matrices and casts a complete line of type, called a slug. The operation is a relatively fast one, but has been speeded up in recent years by what is known as a teletypesetter. This involves producing a punched tape on a typewriter and then feeding the punched tape into an operatorless Linotype machine.

There are limitations both in size of type and length of line in the use of Linotype. Most machines can produce a line of only 30 picas (5 inches), and two lines must be butted together if longer lengths are required. (Some machines are equipped to handle 42-pica lines but are not available in many shops.) While it is possible to set large sizes of type on the Linotype, most typographers limit Linotype production to the smaller sizes up to 14- or 18-point, unless a considerable quantity of large-size composition is required.

Leading between lines is automatically included when a line is cast. For example, an 8-point type can be cast on a 10-point slug, giving 2-point leading between each line. Corrections must be made a full line at a time, and careful proofreading is required to make sure corrections are made properly.

Most printers and typographers offer a limited range of typefaces for Linotype composition, and if large amounts of typesetting are required, it is important to make sure the proper magazines of matrices are both available and not committed to some other job. If a large volume of repeat typography using the same typeface is planned, a printer or typographer will usually arrange to obtain the necessary matrices if they are not already on hand.

Photosetting

While "hot metal" composition was long the basic method of setting type for direct mail pieces, it has become uncommon today. Instead, computerized equipment which utilizes one of several forms of photographic composition is in general use. There is a vast array of different makes and models of computerized photocomposition equipment on the market and they offer great flexibility combined with simplified operation, which means they can generally be operated by less costly personnel.

This "anyone can operate one" attitude, however, can work to your disadvantage. Far too often, the operation of the new generation of photocomposition machines is placed in the hands of untrained personnel who don't understand the finer points of good typography. As a result, the finished typesetting often lacks the finishing touches which give a quality appearance to professional typography.

The best rule of thumb to follow if you want top quality composition is to look to an advertising typographer rather than a "secretarial service" which happens to have typesetting equipment. Generally, the typographer will have several different typesetting methods available and will select the one most appropriate for the job you want done. The above photocomposition equipment, of course, has replaced Linotype the way the automobile replaced the horse and buggy.

Monotype

Another method for producing body copy is the two-machine Monotype process. In this process, the operator sits at a keyboard which produces a perforated paper tape. This tape is then fed into a casting machine, which turns out individual type characters composed in lines. As the operator nears the end of each line, he feeds information to the tape which, in effect, tells the casting machine how much space to insert between each word.

While Monotype composition is generally a bit more expensive than Linotype, it has several advantages. Generally, Monotype produces a higher quality. A harder metal can be used so the type has longer wearing characteristics. Since each character is set individually, corrections are made a character at a time, rather than a line at a time. Another advantage is the ease with which different typefaces and special characters can be mixed. Monotype is not as widely available as Linotype, however.

Ludlow

The Ludlow system combines hand and machine composition. Individual matrices are assembled in a stick by hand and then inserted in a casting machine which turns out lines of type. While smaller sizes are available, Ludlow is generally used for setting display type from 18-point to 96-point, although its range is from 4-point to 240-point. The advantage of Ludlow over hand composition is that "new" type is always available. It also offers definite cost advantages whenever the same line is needed more than once, since as many lines as required can be cast from the assembled mats.

Phototype

To set display type photographically, several machines are available. These generally use master fonts which are negatives on a continuous roll of 35mm. film or a disk. This is a hand operation, although some of the machines have a degree of automation built in. The operator selects each character desired and then immediately exposes it on photographic paper or another film. An extremely wide range of typefaces and hand-lettering styles is available for this process, and special effects—such as screening or superimposing a pattern—can be added while a line is being "set."

While manufacturers of these machines have widely promoted the belief that "anyone" can quickly be trained to operate them, best results generally come from highly skilled operators. Unless a large volume of display composition is required, it is generally best to buy phototype from service organizations, which frequently offer rapid service at low cost. In fact, if only a limited number of words is required, phototype composition will probably be considerably less expensive than hot-type display composition. Its primary use is for offset or when complete page-size plates are planned for other processes.

Varitype

When a tight budget is a major factor, body composition is often "set" on one of the typewriter-like devices which can produce justified lines (lines which are flush left and right). The most popular of these machines is the Varityper, which has changeable typefaces. The amount of space between words is varied to produce lines of common length. Some of the machines require two typings to produce the finished copy. The operator first types the copy without variable spacing to determine how much added space will be required and then retypes the finished copy. Other machines produce a byproduct tape which is then used to operate the machine automatically to produce the finished copy with variable spacing.

Typewriter Composition

Since a lot of direct mail printing does not require justified lines, straight typewriter composition is often used. This is particularly common for letters to be reproduced by offset. Copy is generally typed with a one-use carbon ribbon. To obtain particularly crisp, sharp reproduction, the original typewritten matter is often reduced from 10 to 20% at the time negatives are made. Electric typewriters are generally used because they produce an even weight for all characters.

When carbon ribbons are not available, it is possible to achieve approximately the same results by eliminating the ribbon and typing directly through a sheet of carbon paper onto a hard-surfaced paper. Extreme care must be taken, however, to avoid smudging.

Pasteup Type

Another method for producing display composition is to use individual "pasteup" letters. Many different makes are available in three basic styles. The most common consists of transfer sheets. The individual letters are printed on the reverse side of a transparent sheet and each has a wax backing. When the face of the sheet is burnished, the letter below the burnished area is transferred from the back of the transparent sheet to whatever surface is below it. The second style consists of letters imprinted on clear acetate sheets which have an adhesive backing. Each letter is cut from the sheet and pasted into the appropriate position. Another basic style involves letters printed on opaque paper, either with or without adhesive backing. These paper letters are provided both on sheets and on individual one-letter tabs, which can be assembled in a "stick" much like the one used by a Ludlow compositor. When a line of these tabs has been composed, a strip of adhesive tape is pressed across their backs to produce a continuous line.

List Cameras

One supplementary process which deserves special consideration is the automatic list camera. Several makes are available. What they do is to take material prepared on cards and automatically photograph it line by line to produce what amounts to a galley of type. These cameras are particularly useful for preparing directories, price and parts lists, and some types of catalogs.

Selecting Typefaces

One of the best "starter" guides to selecting typefaces is *How to Select Typefaces,* published by Intertype Co. This manual points out:

> Typography—like architecture, fashion, or any of the arts—is a reflection of a way of life. The flourishes of older faces are reminiscent of the elegance of days gone by. The crisp, straight lines of modern types reflect our age of speed. The new, wide extensions mirror the expansiveness of the times in which we live.
>
> Every typeface designed has a message as certain as that of a symphony or a painting. Some say "hurry, hurry, hurry," in the urgency of their strokes. Some say "rest a while and reflect upon the good things around you." Some say "fashion, fickle, fragile, foolish"; and others, "here I am, as sound as the gold in Fort Knox."
>
> Typography has character and spirit—sometimes intangible and invisible as the force of gravity, but, like the force of gravity, the character is ever present. The force we see—the only force—is the effectiveness of type in printed, finished form. If type is right, it accomplishes our purposes; if it is wrong, it is often detrimental.
>
> There is no chart that outlines when to use which typeface. There is no catalog that lists which faces will blend with others. The choice, as with the choice of art techniques and layout, must be left to the designer. As with other forms of art, the same understanding of principles that lie beneath design is the determining factor. Typography *is* a form of art. Its use determines the effectiveness of transmitting one person's thought to another. The manner in which it blends with other art forms with which it is combined is of the utmost importance.
>
> As with art techniques, typography is largely a matter of feeling and spirit. Choice of a typeface can no more be worked out by a slide rule than a painting can be created by consulting a table of what colors go well together.
>
> Another important consideration in the selection of a typeface is legibility, for what good is the printed message that no one will read? If the layout calls for type in wide measure, the choice should be a face that can be read when it is set according to design—not one which the eye cannot absorb.

There are faces—especially scripts—that are meant to be used sparingly, as a single emphatic word or headline. There are faces, especially those in schoolbooks, which are inviting to the eye in solid printed mass and lead the reader on.

Color, either of stock or of ink, affects the legibility of typefaces. Many typefaces that are easily read when printed black on white become difficult to read when color is introduced. Choice of stock is another element that should control choice of type; absorbency and reflection are very definite factors affecting readability. Because of the vast range of both stock and ink, it is advisable to see a sample of the selected face on the stock and in the color to be used.

In combining typefaces, it is generally safe to assume that the members of one group of designs will go reasonably well with one another; by the same general rule, they will not be harmonious with members of another group. A delicate, feminine type, such as Garamond, has nothing in common with block Beton; free, open-air-loving Bookface is uncomfortable in the company of citified Cairo.

Characteristics of Type

James M. Secrest, writing in *Advertising Requirements,* says there are five basic typeface characteristics which must be considered in making type selections:

1. *Color*—Each individual typeface has a definite weight or color. Some faces such as Futura Light, Lightline Gothic, Stymie Light, and similar ones have a minimum amount of color. Others are much bolder and carry a large amount of color. Some of the faces in this category would be Futura Ultra Bold, Cooper Black, Airport Black, Futura Display, and Ultra Bodoni. Garamond, for instance, was once called a "white letter" in differentiating it from the more common "black letter" of that period. Type color plays an extremely important part in the balance of an ad. When type is set en masse, as in the text matter, the selection of a face too light or too heavy for the other elements in the layout can result in throwing the entire composition out of balance. It is important to think of text matter as similar to a benday screen of a like tone when making the type selection.

2. *Texture*—It has only been during the last couple of decades that the texture of type has been given the consideration it now enjoys. Before the Bauhaus movement in Germany, and its fine efforts toward a "New Typography," type was selected on the basis of color and legibility alone. As you know, texture plays an important part in modern art . . . the intermingling, blending, contrasting, and overlapping of textured surfaces in collages and paintings strive to affect the tactile senses through the eyes. It was soon recognized that type also had texture, each face different from the next. Thus, type texture was soon incorporated in the work of the modern artists by the use of torn scraps of newspapers in their collages and drawing facsimiles of these scraps in their paintings.

3. *Directional Movement*—All typefaces, whether we are conscious of the fact or not, have movement. This movement can be horizontal, as in the case of Century Schoolbook, Paragon, Ionic, Textype, and others that feature very short ascenders and descenders. Or it can be vertical, as

found in the faces that have long ascenders and descenders like Bodoni Book, Piranesi, Bernhard Modern, etc. Italics, by the very nature of their design, have a diagonal flow which, in turn, can be fast, lazy, or erratic.

The importance of these flow lines cannot be overemphasized. It is important because, like any other lines in the ad, if they intersect either actually or by implication, they set up a tension at and adjacent to this intersection. This area is thus considered to be the scene of conflicting forces and results in great attention-arresting possibilities.

The directional movement of type can also be used to guide the reader's eyes through the ad to some extent in much the same manner as lines and spots of color employed by the illustrator. Very often, if the illustration features a vertical structure, a display line with horizontal movement is chosen to lead into it purely for the sake of the dynamic possibilities inherent in the two conflicting movements.

4. *Historical Association*—Consciously or not, certain typefaces do have historical association in the minds of readers. For instance, the "black letter" faces like those more commonly known in this country as "Old English," are associated with ecclesiastical work. In the same manner, many of the faces with a Venetian ancestry, such as Medieval, Benedictine, and similar designs, as well as those like Hammer, Unical and Libra, suggest antiquity. The prime example of historical association insofar as this country is concerned is Caslon. Caslon is usually associated with the American Revolutionary period because the Declaration of Independence was printed from this type as well as practically all other printing up to the year 1800. This fact has been taken advantage of by many advertisers stressing an early American product.

5. *Mood*—Rightly or wrongly, many readers place typefaces in definite categories of their own. They think of a given face as a "fashion" type, an "industrial" type, or possibly as a "primer" face. This fact can be taken advantage of in two ways. First, by using it for the products with which it is commonly associated to create a fashion or an industrial mood, or secondly, by employing these faces with a touch of "reverse English." In other words, instead of using Stymie Black for a heavy industry client, which is the rather prosaic approach, try it for your next lingerie ad. The very fact that it seems so out of place to the casual reader makes it worth its weight in gold for its attention-arresting value.

Basic Rules for Good Typography

While there is no area in typography where there is one hard-and-fast rule to cover every situation, some generally accepted rules of thumb have been developed over the years. While they certainly cannot be applied in every case, they deserve consideration in the preparation of effective direct mail pieces.

The first basic rule is "keep it simple." This is often easier said than done, however. The first step is to consider the typography from a reader's standpoint, rather than primarily from a designer's standpoint. To best serve your reader, make it easy for him by doing such things as putting all captions adjacent to the illustrations they describe. Keep the length of lines no longer than an alphabet and a half of any given typeface. Put some leading between lines of type—particularly all sizes over 8-point. But never put more space between lines than the height of the type itself. The following chart is often suggested as a basic guide:

Type Size	*Minimum Leading*	*Maximum Leading*
6 point	solid	1 point
8 point	solid	2 point
10 point	solid to 2 pt.	4 point
11 point	1 point	4 point
12 point	2 point	6 point
14 point	3 point	8 point

Some other basic rules are: (1) Avoid "all caps," except for a minimum number of words needing special emphasis; (2) in most cases, it is best to avoid masses of type set in sans serif faces, since serifs help to hold the reader's eye on the type line; (3) if you have page upon page of type matter, do not choose a face with too even a weight, since this makes reading monotonous.

One of the most important lessons to learn is to utilize "white space" effectively. Do not crowd type matter to the edges of the page or right up to illustrations. Nothing can discourage a potential reader more rapidly than to see a page jammed full of "black ink." Also, to best organize material, use white space to separate thoughts and reduce the amount of white space (in comparison with the rest of the page) to help connect related elements.

Preparing Copy for Typesetting

There are 10 basic rules for preparing copy for typesetting which are highly essential both for reasons of economy and to assure best results:

1. All copy should be typewritten double- or triple-spaced with either *standard* pica or elite type. Avoid, when possible, the use of some of the more modern typewriter faces which do not have the same width of characters as the standard faces. Elite produces 12 characters per inch; pica, 10 characters per inch.
2. Send the typographer the original. Carbon copies smear and often an "e" looks like an "o," or a comma comes out looking like a period. If a lot of changes or corrections have been made on the original copy, have

it retyped before sending it to the typographer. The cost of retyping is a lot cheaper than paying a high hourly rate to a typographer, who is slowed down considerably by hard-to-follow copy—and you will end up with fewer errors.

3. Key your copy so the typographer will know exactly where each unit of type will go, and supply an accurate layout so all units will "fit" the space intended for them. When giving dimensions, always designate the reading direction first—8½ by 11 inches always should mean 8½ inches wide by 11 inches in depth.

4. Use printer's measures whenever possible. Type is always measured by points and picas. There are six picas to the inch and 12 points to a pica or 72 points to an inch. And do not be confused by "em" or "en" measures—they vary with each type size. An "em" is a square of type—for example, 12 points wide by 12 points high or 6 points wide by 6 points high—and an "en" is half the width of an "em." But leave "em" and "en" talk to the printers and concentrate on picas. If you specify type by the inch system, you are apt to run into trouble and higher costs. For example, if you ask for type to be set 1-7/8 inches wide, it will come out 11 picas and three points. Since typesetting is done in picas or half picas, the typographer will have to set his measure for 11½ or 12 picas and then fill in the extra space by hand on each line.

5. Be sure to *write* instructions in full. Do not count on verbal or incomplete instructions. A piece of copy has to be handled by quite a few people as it goes through the typesetting process and every misunderstanding adds up to more cost and poorer quality.

6. When making corrections or giving instructions, use standard printers' symbols. They are as old as the hills, and every printer and typographer understands them. The most important marks are one line under a word for italics, lower case; two lines under a word for small caps; three lines, all large caps; a wavy line, bold face. Any other type instructions should be written out. On copy keep your marks and changes as close to the basic copy involved as possible, since the typographer keeps his eyes on the line as he sets copy. If he has to switch his view to some other place on the page, time will be lost and chances for errors increase.

7. In making corrections on proofs, however, corrections should be made out in the margins where they can be seen and easily understood. Stick to standard proofreader's marks.

8. If possible, give your typographer a little leeway in setting type. He often can make simple changes which will improve both quality and economy. For example, if you have a series of words (such as "available in red, brown, midnight blue, and green"), the typographer may be able to eliminate awkward letterspacing or tight lines if he can switch the order of the words.

9. Make sure all typefaces specified will mix properly. Just because every face you have selected is 12-point does not mean that all of them will line up perfectly. Some faces are set to run along the bottom of the line, some along the center of the line, and others near the top of the line. Matching types of uneven alignment is a complicated, time-consuming operation.

10. The most important rule of all is to consult with your typographer before you prepare your layouts and type specifications. You will often find

you can save money and get more nearly the effect you want by choosing alternates to the typefaces which come originally to mind. For example, you might choose a hand composition face for the heads in a booklet. Perhaps, however, the typographer has a very similar Ludlow face. If it can be substituted you will not only save money, since Ludlow composition is usually less costly than hand composition, but chances are you will get better quality, since Ludlow assures all new type.

Typographic Trade Customs

Every direct mail advertiser should be acquainted with the basic trade customs followed by typographers. While your typographer may have a few special "ground rules" of his own, most typographers follow this basic list of trade customs prepared and adopted by members of the Advertising Typographers Assn.:

1. ORDERS—Regularly entered orders cannot be canceled except upon terms that will compensate the typographer for work already done. Written instructions are required with all orders. Instructions given orally or by telephone, dealing with work in process, must be confirmed immediately in writing, otherwise the typographer will not be held responsible for errors or misunderstandings.
2. ESTIMATES—When estimates are furnished, it is understood that they are only approximate.
3. TYPOGRAPHY—All typography is charged on a time basis—by the hour. Each six minutes or fraction thereof constitutes a unit and ten units equal one hour.
4. SPECIAL SERVICE, LAYOUTS, ETC.—To be charged as time work.
5. CUT WORK—All work pertaining to cuts such as notching, mortising, trimming, cropping, blocking, reblocking, jobbing, etc., charged as time work. Removing and reinserting cuts in type forms charged as time work.
6. AUTHOR'S ALTERATIONS—Charged on a time basis the same as typography.
7. PROOFREADING—Minimum charge of 10% on all operations except press and foundry lockup.
8. PASTEUP PROOFS—Charged as time work.
9. PRESS LOCKUP—Charged as time work on the same scale as foundry lockup shown in schedule furnished customers. Press lockup of electrotypes or complete engravings will be proportionately less, according to labor involved.
10. PRESS PROOFS—As in schedule, exclusive of press lockup. Color proofs and strike-in proofs charged as time work.
11. OVERTIME—All work requested to be done outside of regular working hours shall be charged for at overtime rates.
12. SPECIAL MATERIAL—All type, rules, special material, etc., bought at request of customer shall be paid for by him.
13. MINIMUM CHARGE—No individual job will be charged at less than five units.

14. PRINTING FROM TYPE—A limit of 200 impressions may be taken from foundry type forms. If more than 200 proofs are required, type must be electrotyped.

15. PROOF PAPER—For ordinary proofs, a regular proof paper will be used. If a special paper is desired by the customer, the charge for proofs shall be based on stock selected.

16. IMPRINTING PROOF PAPER—A regular printing charge will be made if client desires his special imprint on proof paper.

17. STEREOTYPING—Under no circumstances will it be permitted to make mats from foundry type unless charge is made for the value of the type. The stereotyper as well as the customer will be held responsible for value of type if form is stereotyped.

18. FOUNDRY AND PRESS FORMS—Type forms returned from electrotyper after plating and also forms proofed for reproduction are assumed to be dead and will accordingly be distributed.

19. MOLDING—Not more than four molds will be allowed from any type form. Pattern plates must be made for more than four molds. The electrotyper and the customer will be held responsible for value of type if more than four molds are made.

20. ELECTROTYPES AND ENGRAVINGS—All artwork, photographs, electrotypes, and engravings ordered through the typographer will be billed at not less than 20% above net invoice cost. The same care in protecting customer's property as the typographer's own will be exercised, but the typographer will not be held responsible for engravings, electrotypes, artwork, or photographs being stored without charge over six months, or that may be lost or damaged by causes beyond his control.

21. SENDING TYPE FORMS OUT OF PLANT—No foundry type will be sent to outside firms for printing without the guarantee that all foundry type will be electrotyped or a charge will be made for the value of the type.

22. LIEN—It is understood that all *type, plates, cuts, paper, or other material belonging to the customer,* may remain in the possession of the typographer as security until all just claims of the typographer shall be paid.

23. RESPONSIBILITY FOR ERRORS—In the final lockup of form for foundry *or proofs for reproduction* entails no other penalty than resetting the ad correctly without charge.

24. WRAPPING AND MAILING—If typographer is required to wrap and mail proofs, cuts, etc., a charge will be made to cover cost of this work, plus postage or express.

25. AGREEMENTS—All agreements are made and all orders accepted contingent upon strikes, fires, acts of transportation companies, or causes beyond our control; the seller shall not be responsible.

26. CHANCE ORDERS—No work will be produced on a chance or speculative basis.

PLATEMAKING

If your direct mail material is to be printed by letterpress, the advertiser frequently takes the basic responsibility for preparation of printing plates. In offset, gravure, and other processes, platemaking is usually handled by the printer. Some letterpress printers run an "integrated shop," which involves preparation of photoengravings and duplicate plates, and some advertisers prefer to let the printer handle ordering of such material from outside sources.

However, since most direct mail advertisers get involved in plate buying at one time or another, it is important to have a basic understanding of the factors involved. Most engravers have excellent reference guides available, and it is well to obtain and study this material.

Types of Photoengravings

There are two ways to describe differences in types of photoengravings—by the end result or by the engraving materials and processes used. In terms of end result, the basic types of engravings are line, halftone, and combination.

Line Engravings—The least expensive and most simple type of engraving is the line plate or line cut. It is usually etched on zinc or magnesium and contains no continuous-tone areas, except those which are artificially added. To make a line plate, copy is photographed—with any enlargement or reduction in size handled at this time. The resulting negative is then placed atop a sensitized sheet of metal and exposed to a strong light. The printing portions of the plate are affected by the light and become acid-resistant. Then the plate is exposed to acid which eats away the nonprinting portions to a specific depth, leaving the printing portions raised for relief printing. Actually, there are several operations in the etching of the plate, and results can vary depending upon the skill of the engraver and his attention to detail.

Halftone Engravings—Halftone plates are used for reproduction of continuous-tone copy such as photographs or wash drawings. The basic engraving process is similar to that used in making line cuts, except that a screen must be used to make the photographic negative. This is done by inserting a glass screen between the camera lens and the sensitized film. The screen is composed of fine diagonal cross-hatched lines. These lines break down the original copy into dots on the negative. The dots will vary in size according to the intensity of the tone they are to reproduce. Thus, in light areas the dots will be so small they almost disappear, while dark areas will have dots which join together to make a practically solid surface. Various size screens are used depending primarily upon the type of paper and press to be used in printing the plate. Screens for letterpress usually range from 55 to 150 lines per square inch. For rotary printing on newsprint stock, an engraving from 55 to 85 lines is generally used; for magazine work, a screen of 85 to 120 lines; and for printing on fine coated stock, the finer screens may be selected. Plates coarser than 100-line are usually etched on zinc or magnesium, while finer screens are almost always etched on copper.

Combination Engravings—Combination plates involve etching both black-and-white line work and halftones on the same plate. There are other variations such as the dropout or highlight halftone, where dots are eliminated from portions of the halftone in which perfectly white areas are desired; outline plates, where the halftone subject is "outlined" by cutting away dots outside the basic subject area; vignetting, where a soft edge is given to a halftone; etc.

Special Effects

There are special engraving techniques which are frequently used to achieve special effects. The most common is the use of benday screens to give a continuous-tone effect to a line engraving. There is a variety of designs which the engraver can add to specified areas of a drawing to achieve a screened or pattern effect. While once very popular, engraver-added bendays have pretty much been replaced by artist-added screens and patterns. This can be accomplished either by applying the selected designs from preprinted, adhesive-backed sheets to the drawing or by preparing the drawing on special boards which have built-in patterns.

Dropout effects can also be obtained by use of special materials. The most common is the fluorographic highlight process.

Engraving Costs

Costs of photoengravings vary greatly. The primary basis for determining costs is on a unit basis. A standard chart is used to determine the number of units in any size engraving. While the units increase primarily by the number of square inches, long and narrow engravings demand a premium. But the cost per unit is just a starting point in figuring costs, for "extras" quickly multiply charges. There is a variety of operations which call for extra charges—oversize or undersize copy, outlining, dropouts, benday work, "difficult copy," etc. Some engravers with a low unit rate balance out their total charges by "extras," while higher unit rate engravers frequently make fewer charges for extras.

Quality can also vary considerably. Photoengraving is far from being a completely mechanical process. Even before plates are made, the skill of the engraver's photographer can play a major role in the end results. After the initial engraving, considerable handwork is usually done on better plates and some handwork is required on nearly every plate. Since photoengraving is a highly competitive field, you can generally count on getting just about what you pay for—and a really good engraving is nearly always worth the extra cost.

Color Plates

Reproduction of subjects in color is obtained by preparing two or more printing plates. The two most common letterpress methods are duotones—which involve printing in two colors; and process color —which involves printing in four colors. Duotones, of course, do not produce a full-color reproduction, but for some subjects may result in a highly realistic substitute. In addition, there are several "fake duotone" processes, such as printing the same plate in two different colors, with the dots slightly off-center, and printing a plate atop a solid color or an evenly screened plate. A true duotone, however, involves two different plates which carry different tone values. (This should not be confused with duotone inks, which are used with one printing impression but create both a hard image of the dot and a spreading of ink beneath the dot in a lighter tone—much as ink will spread when writing with a fountain pen on a porous surface.)

To prepare process color plates, the original full-color subject is photographed through filters and screens are placed at different angles for each plate. The resulting plates are printed in the three primary colors—red, yellow, and blue—plus black, which is used to obtain strength in detail and to produce neutral shades of gray, which are difficult to obtain with any combination of the three primaries. When printing, the dots are not placed atop one another, but laid side by side. Unless viewed with a magnifying glass, however, the dots blend together to produce a single hue. The size of the dot of each of the colors determines the hue which hits the eye. Strong dots of blue and yellow, for example, will produce green; blue and red, purple; etc.

For some types of color reproduction, more than four plates are used. When gold or some other metallic color is important, for example, such colors are generally added through a fifth plate. Reproduction of some art subjects have required as many as 12 different plates, although modern printing techniques have usually eliminated the need for more than five colors. Considerable handwork and re-etching are usually done on color plates to achieve maximum fidelity to the original, although modern electronic and photographic equipment has reduced the amount of handwork required.

In some process color work, the black plate is eliminated and only the three primary color plates are used. Generally, this three-color printing is limited to inexpensive printing where the aim is to achieve a pleasing color effect rather than high fidelity to the original subject.

Photoengraving Specifications

There have been many checklists prepared for guidance in ordering photoengravings. The most detailed is contained in the *Photoengraving Specifications Manual* issued by Printing Industry of America. While the task of adhering to the specifications lies primarily with the engraver, it is well for a direct mail advertiser to understand them and cooperate with his printer in seeing they are followed. The following summary, from the *Photoengraving Specifications Manual,* pertains primarily to four-color engravings, but many of the individual specifications apply equally to black-and-white and duotone engravings:

1. Paper—Be sure specified paper is used for proofing.
2. Makeready—None should be used when proofing originals. Proof with correct impression sufficient only to firmly print entire plate.
3. Ink—Be sure specified inks are used.
4. Color Sequence—Be sure specified sequence (to be used by printer) is followed in proofing. There are two accepted sequences in common use:

A	B
1. Yellow	1. Yellow
2. Red	2. Red
3. Blue	3. Black
4. Black	4. Blue

5. Ink Quantity and Proofing—Use normal inking. Do not over- or under-ink. Use four-color presses if possible.
6. Color Bars—Always use color bars full width of engraving and parallel to ink rollers.

7. Screen Density—There are fairly definite limits to the density which can be successfully and cleanly reproduced in production printing, printed four colors at a time, wet. The maximum screen density in an engraving should be kept to a limit of 85%. Beyond this limit ink tends to fill up plates and prints muddy. A solid plate will print smoother than one which has a tone of 95% or more. If a solid is desired, dense tone, 90% or 95%, should be avoided by instructing the engraver to "paint in" such areas to make them solid.

8. Trapping—Trapping, in color printing, is the affinity of one ink for another when superimposed, or printed together wet, at production press speeds. The greater the density in each plate, the more difficult it is to print four colors wet and to avoid muddiness. Experience indicates that in an area where colors overlap a total of 200% for all four engravings is the density limitation for best results. Any combination totaling 200% is practicable. Superimposition of two solid colors, however, is impracticable and unsatisfactory.

9. Solid Blacks—When a rich solid black area is required in a four-color subject, engravings must be etched as follows, no stronger:

   Black: solid

   Blue: 50% density

   Red: 20% density

   Yellow: 10% density

   The red plate especially must not exceed 20%, otherwise the reproduction will have a reddish tinge.

10. Etching—Engravings should be etched deep and clean, without undercutting, pitting, etc. Engravings which are shallow or ragged will produce unsatisfactory electrotypes. While the depth will vary with different screens, typical is the recommended standard depth for 120 screen highlights, .0032 of an inch; middletones, .0022 of an inch; shadows, .0015 of an inch. Different papers, however, require different etching depths.

11. Vignettes—The dots in a vignetted edge should be graduated in size within at least one-half inch of the edge and until they almost disappear at the edge. Vignetted effects cannot be obtained merely by makeready; this is poor practice and cannot be duplicated successfully in production printing. To obtain good vignetted effects by the use of two or more colors, arrange to terminate the lighter color plate slightly inside the darker. Avoid vignettes in very small, completely enclosed areas.

12. Thin Rules and Type—Use only one color whenever possible for thin rules and type in color. Do not use more than two colors on thin rules or small type, or reverse type.

13. Surprinting Type on Screen—Use a halftone screen of not more than 30% density where type is surprinted, and preferably only 20%. Surprinting breaks up type and makes it difficult to read. Avoid the use of type which has thin lines or fine serifs.

14. Metal—Original copper halftones should be supplied for best results. Combinations of copper engravings for some of the colors of a set, and zinc engravings for others, are not acceptable. Line engravings should also be made on copper for best results.

15. Each Plate in One Piece—Each color engraving should consist of one complete unit. Pieces are not acceptable, as a rule. "Patched" plates may be distorted under molding pressure when electrotypes are made.

16. Screen—While each printer will generally have a specified standard, the following are most common:

    For English finish, super or lower grades of machine coated—100 or 110 screen.

    For better grades of machine coated or brush coated—120 screen.

    Finer screens should be used with caution and only at the introduction of the printer.

17. Corrections—Preferably none. If important corrections are made in engravings, the entire set should be reproofed. Otherwise progressives will not be an accurate guide for color matching. When time does not permit making corrected progressives, supply a proof of each corrected plate in its own color and *indicate* corrections on each color and on the four-color proof as well.

18. Routing, Dead Metal, Trimming—Rout close to printing area, leaving one-eighth inch routed line around live matter, .030 of an inch deep. Leave all other metal in plate, including 1-inch bearers all around. If routing is necessary due to proofing conditions, replace dead metal with metal before shipping to printer. Mark dead metal with an "X." Trim shoulders deep and as nearly vertical as possible.

19. Backs of Engravings—Backs of engravings must be smooth, without holes or scars. If back is scarred, a defective electrotype may result.

20. Burnishing—Avoid burnishing large areas. Burnishing produces mushroom dots which may break off in electrotyping, causing a loss in tonal value. Depth of etching is reduced and dots become uneven.

21. Identification—Each engraving should be steel-punched with the name of the color in two places—top and side bearers.

22. Electrotypes for Insertion—Electrotypes of type matter to be inserted into original engravings should be nickel-faced and have a shell of .015 of an inch thickness, backed up with hard metal to .063 of an inch thickness.

Do's and Don'ts for Engravings

The following checklist, adapted from "Do's & Don'ts for Better Engravings," by Richard Hodgson, which originally appeared in *Advertising Requirements,* provides an effective guide when ordering engravings:

Do's

...mount all artwork and copy on *even* board.

...have sizes marked in a conspicuous place on either front or rear of all art and copy (in addition to specifications on purchase orders).

...always include instructions for handling of finished engravings, proofs and original artwork (i.e., ship to ...., hold for o.k., etc.).

. . . include instructions for mounting of all engravings.

. . . mark desired cropping clearly on all copy.

. . . remove all old sizes and crop marks used on previous orders.

. . . protect artwork with acetate or paper flap.

. . . make all layouts as complete and accurate as possible. Paste up photostats of each element or be sure art will scale to the correct proportion and size.

. . . make keyline drawing with linework and type pasted in position for one shot if possible.

. . . clearly outline portions of photographs desired, using Chinese white.

. . . specify ink number or send printed sample or swatch when special ink or color effect is desired.

. . . use tissue flap to indicate areas to be dropped out pure white, or painted solid black.

. . . draw register marks on artwork and flaps for accuracy when two or more pieces of art are required to register one upon the other.

. . . use thin guidelines to indicate extent of benday or halftone. Draw in red if they are to be removed; in black if they stay on.

. . . use sufficient retouching for contrast on artwork intended for newspaper reproduction.

. . . use key letters or numbers to identify various elements, and mark both artwork and layout.

. . . draw base lines on artwork for mounting cuts on angles.

. . . specify "width" dimension first, "height" last when ordering definite plate size.

. . . know advantages and limitations of reproductive processes *before* ordering engravings.

. . . specify the line screen wanted.

. . . give the engraver complete information as to final use of plates—type of printing, paper stock, etc.

. . . select a typeface suitable for such reproduction when it is to be overprinted on screen panels.

. . . include color swatches for matching purposes.

. . . if deviation from color of copy is desired, supply engraver with a proof, swatch, or sample that shows actual shade desired.

. . . with color plates that are to be proofed with special inks and special stock, give the engraver several days' notice while art is being prepared so that ink and paper will be on hand at proofing time.

. . . in four-color reproduction take into consideration limitations imposed by ink colors specified by publisher.

. . . keep rubber cement off face of reproduction copy.

. . . check proportions of insert copy to make sure it will fit.

. . . furnish engraver with accurate stripping layouts.

...specify whether plates are to be made for electros, mats, metal base, or wood base.

...specify if bleed size is included in marked size.

...when using benday or tint blocks, specify both screen and tone value.

...when marking overlays for benday or color separation, be accurate.

...get printers to wash plates thoroughly after they're used, and store carefully.

...code or symbol each ad for future reference, especially if it is a portion of a campaign.

...on intricate jobs, give the engraver a dummy with complete detail as to stripping, slant, positioning, etc.

...be cautious in making your own color separations.

...double check on mechanical requirements of publications for which engravings are to be used. Give complete instructions to the engraver.

...consult your engraver whenever in doubt.

...*(most important of all)* give the engraver enough time to do the quality work your order deserves. Be sure to tell him *exactly* when the engravings are required.

ENGRAVING CHECKLIST

When ordering photoengravings, include the following information:

1. Size—"width" first; "height" second.
2. Type of plate—copper, zinc or magnesium.
3. Screen of halftone.
4. Mounted or unmounted—with or without bearers.
5. Mortises.
6. Number of proofs and type of stock in certain cases.
7. Color proofs and sample of ink or in numbers.
8. When wanted.
9. Delivery instructions.
10. Tints or benday desired. Order by number or letter from your engraver's tint chart—never by percent.

Don'ts

...take any previous discussions or instructions for granted.

...attempt to prepare art on intricate jobs without consultation with your engraver.

...send art to engraver without complete instructions.

...ship plates without checking proofs for errors.

...use paper clips to attach instructions to art (particularly photographs).

...write on back of unmounted photographs.

...mark crop marks on the face of a photo (use margins or an overlay).

...use fine serif typefaces when double-printing, especially on halftones.

...use too deep a blue wash for indicating benday or tint laying, as the blue will photograph.

...use cracked, torn, or damaged artwork without first retouching or repairing imperfections.

...rush your engraver if top quality is necessary.

...use anything other than typographer's etch proofs for type that is to be engraved for reproduction. Small type should be replaced by an electrotype patch.

...mix colors of paint when retouching, as they photograph differently.

...specify percentage tones of benday or halftone tints without first consulting a tone chart.

...change your mind about color without correcting color guide for engraver.

...expect more in the engraving than is in your copy.

...forget that copy prepared for fine screen rarely reproduces as well in coarse screen for newspaper reproduction.

...overlay crop marks so they become a part of the wanted area of a halftone.

...be afraid to write a complete note of instructions, criticisms of artwork, and so forth.

...surprint type on dark or confusing areas—it won't be legible.

...guess that copy will insert into a certain area. Use a proportion scale and be accurate.

...send brown or gray stats and expect clean reproductions.

...expect clean etchings from newspaper clippings.

...send a dummy that is obviously well prepared and later tell the engraver certain changes have been made unless the changes are indicated.

...submit art layouts with sloppy pasteup work. The camera picks up everything and work that is not neat results in opaquing and handwork by the engraver for which an additional charge is made.

..."cry wolf" on deadlines.

...submit copy too large for normal reduction. Time and money can be saved by furnishing reduced prints with original artwork.

Photoengraving Trade Customs

The following trade customs have been adopted by members of the American Photoengravers Association:

Orders. Orders regularly placed and entered cannot be canceled except upon terms that will compensate the photoengraver for work and services performed and materials consumed.

Alterations. All alterations or changes directed by the buyer or his agent, subsequent to the acceptance of the order, are charged additional in accordance with the time and materials consumed therein.

ARTWORK, SKETCHES, DUMMIES, LAYOUTS, ETC. All artwork, dummies, layouts, sketches, etc., submitted with estimates, are considered as having been made upon order and are charged according to the time and materials employed in their creation.

EXPERIMENTAL WORK. Experimental work performed at the request of the buyer or his agent is charged according to the time and materials consumed.

CUSTOMER'S PROPERTY. All drawings, photographs, and copies used in the making of photoengravings are received, held, and returned at the owner's risk and the photoengraver assumes no responsibility for loss or damage thereto beyond reasonable care. Paintings, copies, and merchandise of value should be insured by the owner and at his expense.

NEGATIVES. All negatives and positives used in the reproduction of originals are the property of the photoengraver, unless specifically invoiced to the buyer.

CONTINGENT LIABILITY. In the interest of a common understanding and mutual protection, a true proof of each photoengraving and set of color plates are furnished to the buyer or his agent for approval and acceptance. No responsibility attaches to the photoengraver for delays or expenses caused by holding press, waiting for plates, corrections, changes, reprinting, electrotypes, paper, etc., incurred after proof has been accepted.

PROGRESSIVE COLOR PROOFS. Progressive proofs furnished by the photoengraver show the colors used and the sequence of printing upon paper stocks specified. All changes of color, printing sequence, or paper stock in the subsequent printing of the plates are at the risk of the buyer.

DELIVERY. No responsibility is assumed by the photoengraver after photoengravings, copies, and merchandise have been duly delivered to designated points or common carriers.

REPAIRING PHOTOENGRAVINGS. Repairs upon damaged plates are made at the owner's risk and expense.

MAGAZINE STANDARDS. All extra operations performed in making photoengravings to conform to the special requirements of publishers or others shall be charged additional in accordance with the time and materials consumed.

TERMS. Net cash, ten days after delivery unless otherwise provided in writing. Interest charged on past due accounts from the fifteenth of the month following delivery. All claims must be made within five days of receipt of goods and plates.

Duplicate Plates

Duplicate printing plates are required for direct mail printing under the following circumstances:

1. When long runs are required and the original printing materials will wear out before the run is completed;
2. When a reprinting is anticipated and the original material will become too worn for a reprinting or will be too difficult to store;

3. When a job is to be printed in more than one plant or on more than one press;
4. When the job is to be run 2-up, 3-up, etc;
5. When there are strict deadlines and it is dangerous to gamble on damage to the original material during the press run.

There are several methods for duplicating the original material. One is to have duplicate engravings made along with the originals. This is practical when little handwork is required, since a duplicate is considerably less expensive when ordered along with the original. But this method is useful in only a limited number of cases.

Electrotypes

The most common method of duplicating letterpress plates and forms is through electrotypes. The basic method is to make a mold of the original material with wax or some other substance. Copper is then deposited electrolytically on this mold and is later backed with lead. When long press runs are anticipated, the electro is nickel-plated.

Stereotypes

A less expensive method of making duplicate plates is by stereotyping. In this process a paper matrix ("mat") is forced down over the type and/or engravings and makes a mold. Molten metal is then poured into this mold to produce a duplicate of the original form. This method is used most commonly for preparing plates for newspapers printed on rotary presses.

Chapter 43

FINISHING PROCESSES

ONCE printed sheets come off the presses, there are dozens of additional operations which may be required before a direct mail piece is ready for delivery to the post office. Very often, these finishing operations are just as important as the printing itself.

While it would be impossible to cover all of the possible processes for handling direct mail printed material, several of the basic processes deserve special consideration.

Folding

Dozens of different folds can be handled by conventional folding machines. However, folding techniques vary depending upon equipment available and speed and economies required, so it is highly important to determine just how folding is to be handled *before* any job is printed. For long runs, folding is usually "ganged," so the machines can fold two or more pieces at one time. Many folders will automatically cut the folded pieces as part of the folding operation. Whenever possible, presses should be utilized which have folding attachments to permit delivery of a folded signature as part of the printing run. This eliminates at least one handling operation.

While most printers and lettershops have some basic folding equipment, it is quite common to send printed sheets to outside binderies whenever complicated folding is required. One thing to keep in mind when planning folded pieces is the grain direction in the paper. When heavy stocks and some kinds of coated stocks are used, a common practice is to score the paper to facilitate folding. This may be accomplished during the press run —particularly on letterpress—or as a separate operation.

One handy piece of equipment for office use which is often overlooked is the small folding machine. In recent years, a number of accurate, versatile desk-top folders have been developed and can prove highly worthwhile if even a modest volume of direct mail is handled internally. Most any office equipment dealer can provide details on these small folders. If your personnel average as little as an hour a week folding letters and other items, it will probably be both advantageous and economical to obtain a small folder.

Die-Cutting

Many direct mail pieces are cut into special shapes. Simple jobs can be handled by a letterpress printer, but die-cutting is more commonly handled by firms organized to specialize in such finishing operations. Often a standard die can be used, thus eliminating the cost of special dies, and some types of cuts on a standard paper cutter will result in a die-cut effect.

There are two types of dies—high dies and steel-rule dies. High dies resemble a heavy-duty cookie cutter and can cut through many sheets of paper at one time. Steel-rule dies are made by cutting the basic pattern out of a ¾-inch sheet of plywood on a jigsaw, then bending steel rule to fit the pattern. The plywood with its steel rule insert is then placed on a regular letterpress and cuts one sheet at a time (although several sheets of lighter weights of paper may be cut with one impression).

When you intend to include die-cutting in a direct mail piece, check with a diemaker during initial planning, since there are many limitations as to what can be done and many materials cannot be handled efficiently and economically. In all cases, it is best to avoid die-cutting which calls for hairline registry between the cutting die and the printed image; be doubly careful if the die-cut area is printed on both sides.

Punching and Perforating

Punching is usually handled by a paper drill, which is very much like the common power drill used in machine shops. In addition to drilling holes for binding purposes, holes are sometimes used by direct mail advertisers to add a showmanship element to their pieces—a simulated die-cut. Large stacks of paper can be drilled at one time. The paper drill can also be fitted to cut round corners on sheets.

Perforating may be handled in three basic ways—on the press while printing (usually on a letterpress, although special perforating tape is available for use on offset presses), on the folder while folding, or as a separate operation either on a press or on a special perforating machine.

Binding

Binding is generally divided into four categories:

1. *Pamphlet binding*—This title is somewhat misleading, since so-called pamphlet binding is used not only for small pamphlets, but also for booklets, magazines, and soft-covered books. The most common variety is saddle-stitching, which is accomplished by stapling through the center fold of the paper sheets. Many presses and folders are equipped to perform this type of binding automatically and also a related process which eliminates the wire staples and instead places a strip of adhesive on the center folds of the sheets so they may be glued together.

   For thicker pieces (usually those over ¼ inch thick), side-wire binding is used. Instead of stapling through the fold, wire staples are placed along the left-hand side of the sheets. While providing a secure binding, this method has the disadvantage of preventing the bound publication from being opened flat. To overcome this disadvantage, a special binding method called "perfect binding" is often used. This method involves trimming the folded sides and roughing the edges, then applying a special adhesive which both holds the pages together and attaches the body to the cover. This type of binding is commonly seen in telephone directories.

2. *Book binding*—While not frequently used for direct mail material, some elaborate pieces are given hard-cover binding. The body of such books is frequently bound with the perfect binding technique, and then placed inside hard covers. A more expensive technique is to sew signatures with thread. A number of different bookbinding techniques are used in sewing operations. After signatures are attached together, they are rounded and prepared for covering on a back-lining machine which glues the body to supporting strips of crash cloth and paper and adds head- and foot-bands.

   Covers are made by gluing cloth or other covering material to boards. The title and designs are stamped either on a printing press or a die-stamping press. The body is attached to the covers on a casing-in machine. Other operations may include tinting or gilding the edges of the paper and covering the books with book jackets.

3. *Mechanical binding*—There has been constantly increasing use for special mechanical binding methods—such as loose-leaf plastic and spiral binding. There are two basic reasons for the popularity of this type of binding: (1) the pages lie flat when opened and (2) because individual sheets are most often used, it is possible to make variations in contents from book to book with little effort.

   There are three basic types of mechanical binding used by direct mail advertisers. Perhaps the oldest of the mechanical binding methods is *spiral binding,* which uses a corkscrew or coil of nickel-plated wire that is inserted through holes in the left-hand side of the sheets and covers. In addition to nickel-plated wire, brass, stainless steel, and plastics are sometimes used.

   By far the most popular type of mechanical binding in use today is the piece of plastic which has been die-cut in the shape of a comb or rake, and then rolled up onto itself so the teeth tuck under the backbone.

Slots are cut into the left-hand edges of the body and covers, and the teeth of the comb are held open while the sheets are slipped over them. Then, when once again released, these teeth recoil and hold the pages securely. A variation has a backbone which is a separate piece, that can be slipped off the teeth of the comb so pages can easily be removed or added.

The third type of mechanical binding utilizes *closed rings*. A number of different types are available, with the most popular being Wire-O and Cercla. Wire-O has parallel wire loops, which are connected continuously. Cercla features enameled metal rings connected by a backbone. Both types are crimped in the bindery to close them securely.

4. *Loose-leaf binding*—Loose-leaf binding is used by direct mail advertisers primarily for material designed for retention over extended periods or when substitutions and additions will be made frequently. The most frequently used type of loose-leaf binding is the standard three-ring binder, although a wide variety of page-holding mechanisms are available. Covers are generally prepared by specialized manufacturers, and pages are inserted by hand. Almost any manufacturer of loose-leaf binders can provide detailed information on the preparation of material for this type of binding.

Collating

Two types of collating are required by direct mail advertisers: (1) gathering sheets and signatures for binding and (2) gathering individual elements for insertion in envelopes for mailing. At one time, collating was primarily a hand operation, and for small jobs, hand collating is still commonly used.

Hand collating can be done in a variety of ways. For small jobs with few elements, sheets or signatures may simply be stacked in front of an individual who picks them up one at a time and stacks the collected items in a crisscross pile, so one set can be identified from the others above and below it.

Quite a few semimechanical devices are available to speed up this operation. One type involves placing each of the elements in a separate bin. When a pedal or lever is depressed, one copy of each of the elements slides forward in the bin and can quickly be gathered by hand. Sometimes a revolving table is used. Individual elements are stacked around the table which revolves in front of the collectors, who gather each item as it passes by and assemble these items into sets.

For longer runs, automatic gathering equipment is used. In lettershops and small printshops, an eight-station gathering machine is the most common, but as many gathering stations as necessary can be included on the more complex machines. The availability of appropriate collating equipment is an important factor in selecting a producer of direct mail material.

Inserting

When it comes to collating material for insertion into envelopes, an inserting machine is commonly used for the larger jobs. This machine not only collates the pieces to be inserted, but opens the envelopes, inserts the material into them, seals the envelopes, and, if required, meters them with the appropriate postage. These machines can also be equipped to key reply cards, envelopes, or order forms.

If a job is to be machine-inserted, it is highly important to make sure all of the material will fit the stations on the machine and not jam the mechanism or skip. One mistake frequently made by direct mail advertisers is that printed material is too large to be inserted into the envelopes by machine. Inserting machines just cannot handle a "tight fit." So be sure to check the requirements of the machine which will handle your inserting *in advance*, to make sure your enclosures "fit." Also make sure the inserter can handle the size of envelope you plan to use. Many printers and lettershops can handle no envelope larger than a standard No. 10 on their automatic inserters, while others are equipped for larger mailing elements.

Since mechanical inserting is much less costly than hand inserting, it should be used wherever possible. When a number of items are to be hand-inserted, they are frequently "nested" so all of the elements fit inside the letter or basic printed piece and the person doing the inserting needs pick up only one item and place it inside the envelope. On hand inserting, envelopes are usually sealed and metered on mechanical equipment.

Chapter 44

ADDRESSING METHODS

OF ALL the "production" areas in direct mail, none is more important than addressing. Yet, in spite of recent developments, including the application of computers, direct mail is often addressed by machines and techniques which leave much to be desired. One basic factor is still lacking in all of the most modern systems—producing an address which is attractive to the eye.

Where there is considerable debate over whether or not the physical appearance of an address has any important function other than informing the postman where to deliver a piece of mail, most every direct mail advertiser secretly (or openly) yearns for a system which is both fast and selective and, at the same time, produces a printed appearance of the highest quality.

Factors in Choosing an Addressing System

There are many factors which must be considered in choosing an addressing system to fit the needs of any direct mail advertiser. And these factors are important, whether the addressing system is to be maintained internally or placed in the hands of a lettershop or service firm.

Among the factors to be considered are:

- The size of the list.
- How many different variations of the list must be used.
- How often the list will be used.
- How frequently names and addresses must be changed, added, or deleted.

- The speed required in addressing.
- How easy it will be to maintain the list properly.
- The quality of the impression needed.
- The maximum length and number of lines needed for addressing.
- The initial cost of equipment.
- The cost of the address plates, stencils or computer data input.
- Cost of preparing address units.
- How much floor space will be required—both initially and as the list grows.
- Who will operate the equipment.
- Who will service the equipment.
- What types of material will be addressed.
- Uses for the list equipment other than for addressing.

While all of these factors may not be important at the time a system is chosen, it is important to remember that once one system is in use, it is extremely difficult to change to another. If there are doubts about future needs, it is probably well to turn to an outside addressing service initially and use the least expensive method compatible with basic needs.

Basic Types of Systems

There are several ways to categorize addressing systems. First of all, there are hand, mechanical, and computer systems. Second, systems may be divided according to the medium used for addressing—ranging from hand-typing on envelopes, cards, or labels to fiber stencils, metal and plastic plates, spirit duplicating, heat transfer, etc. But as you analyze various systems, you will inevitably come to the fact that each make of machine must be weighed on its own merits, regardless of the category into which it falls.

There are several sources for information on addressing systems. Both the Direct Mail/Marketing Assn. and Mail Advertising Service Assn. have publications on the subject, and manufacturers of each of the systems have copious literature. Trade magazines can also provide reprints on the subject.

After you have studied the literature available, the next best move is to call in representatives of the addressing systems which seem to offer the best solution to your needs, and have them analyze your requirements and make recommendations. Keep in mind that nearly every addressing system has many variations, with dozens of "extras" available to tailor it to meet the specifications of different kinds of mailing jobs. And then, *before* you spend any money for a system, also call in representatives of local direct mail service organizations to see if perhaps they can offer the service you need for less cost and with greater efficiency than would be possible with an internal system.

While it would be impossible to fully describe all of the possible variations of all of the addressing systems, the following brief descriptions of the major systems available at this writing will indicate the scope of what is available.

Addressograph

Probably the best-known mechanical addressing system is the Addressograph. In fact, all addressing machines are often erroneously called "addressographs." The basic characteristic of this system is a multipiece metal plate, consisting of a frame with an insert on which the name, address, and other information can be embossed. As the plates pass through the addressing machine, their embossed letters print through an inked ribbon.

Plates for the Addressograph are punched on a typewriter-like machine called a Graphotype. The plates can be embossed by hand or the addresses can be prepunched on a paper tape, which is then fed into an automatic Graphotype that operates continuously at maximum speeds. Frequently, these tapes are prepared as a byproduct at the time envelopes or labels are addressed or when data cards are typed.

There are three basic Addressograph plate styles. Two consist of frames which carry an embossed metal insert; the other is a one-piece plate which is embossed directly. The plates are long enough to carry full names, addresses, and other information without a great deal of abbreviation.

There are three basic Addressograph plate styles. Two consist of frames which carry an embossed metal insert; the other is a one-piece plate which is embossed directly.

Selectivity is obtained by the addition of tabs to the frame of the plate. There are 12 basic positions when the full tab is used, but by use of notched or perforated tabs the selectivity can be increased to as many as 60 different possibilities.

The major advantages of the Addressograph are the extreme flexibility which is possible through the addition of special features and a high-quality address imprint. Because this equipment is so widely used and has a long record of performance, it is easy to obtain maintenance service, and operators familiar with its operation are widely available. The major disadvantage is a high initial cost, both for the machines and their extras and for plates and storage equipment. Another disadvantage is that the plates are heavy and require a large amount of floor space for storage.

Speedaumat

A variation of the Addressograph is the Speedaumat, which uses a small metal plate prepared on an embossing machine. The Speedaumat operates on the same principle as the Addressograph and plates are prepared on a Graphotype, although a special model is required and it cannot be used interchangeably to prepare Addressograph plates. Automatic models operated by prepunched tape are available.

Plates for the Speedaumat are one-piece and smaller than those used for the Addressograph. Because of their smaller size, the length of the line is limited and it is often necessary to abbreviate portions of a name and address. Addressing can be done at speeds up to 12,000 an hour; and the machines, while not as flexible as the Addressograph, can address most every type of material used in direct mail, including dickstrips, gummed labels, envelopes, self-mailers, and wrappers. One model addresses from a roll of stock and delivers full wrappers.

The machine is equipped with an expirator, which pulls out coded plates when required. Selectivity is obtained by a series of 24 notches which can be cut into the top and/or bottom edges of the plate. The notches may be cut by hand or gang-notched on a special machine. They can also be purchased prenotched.

The Speedaumat is often considered the workhorse of the noncomputer addressing field, with special popularity in the lettershop and publishing field. Its advantages are flexibility, speed of addressing, and lighter weight of plates. The plates are over four times lighter than Addressograph plates and are smaller, so a much larger number can be stored in the same amount of floor space. A good impression is obtained in addressing. The main disadvantage is the limited address area and the limitation of selector spaces to 24 positions.

Elliott

Long the favorite of the direct mail advertiser with a small list, yet one of the most versatile of all addressing systems, is the Elliott. The distinguishing feature of the Elliott addressing system is its fiber stencil—a miniature mimeograph stencil in a cardboard mount or imbedded in a Remington Rand punched card.

Perhaps the biggest advantage of the Elliott system is the ease with which stencils can be prepared. Any standard or electric typewriter can be used, although it is best to obtain specially equipped models if a large quantity of stencils is to be cut. These special typewriters automatically feed stencils and hold them in the proper position for typing. The addressing equipment itself is also relatively simple to operate.

Different colors of mounts are available for identification of different sections of a list. The mount can be punched in as many as 44 positions for selective addressing. When more selective addressing is required, the Remington Rand punched card stencil is used.

The basic disadvantage of the system is that the quality of the addressing varies greatly. While it is entirely possible to obtain very sharp, clear addresses, poorer quality is often obtained, particularly when machines are operated at top speeds—which range up to 8,000 addresses an hour, although the average speed is between 1,000 and 1,500 an hour on most models. On the advantage side, it is possible to obtain highly distinctive addressing through the use of special typewriter faces. Quite a few direct mail advertisers, for example, use a script face to obtain the appearance of simulated handwriting.

Another disadvantage is the difficulty of reading the addresses on the stencils after they have been inked a number of times, thus making list changes difficult. It is common to type filing information on the cardboard mount, but the space is limited and only a portion of the address can be included.

Pollard-Alling

The Pollard-Alling addressing system features metal plates linked together into reels of 2,500 addresses, which can be run at speeds up to 60,000 addresses an hour. The one-piece aluminum plates are embossed on a Reliefograph, which has a standard typewriter keyboard. Plate embossing is generally faster than on Addressograph, Speedaumat or Elliott.

Only a limited amount of selectivity is possible with the Pollard-Alling system. One of the disadvantages is that the plates will handle a length of only 22 characters, although five lines are available on each plate. Another disadvantage is that list changes are somewhat more complicated than with most other systems, since the reel must be unrolled to the proper position, the old plate detached from the roll, and the new one added. On the advantage side, as many as 20 names are visible at one time. But the biggest advantage is the high speeds attainable in addressing.

Scriptomatic

Scriptomatic is based on the spirit-duplicating principle. Like Dittotype spirit duplicating, the quality of reproduction is at the low end of the quality scale, and there is a limit to the number of impressions which can be obtained satisfactorily from a single master, although the normal life is sufficient for most requirements. After repeated handling, there is a tendency for the address to become blurred. Several improvements have been made in the Scriptomatic system, so a direct comparison with conventional spirit duplicating is perhaps unfair.

But the system has many advantages. It is frequently used in conjunction with electronic sorting machinery—including IBM, Remington Rand, and McBee. The master address is imprinted directly on the punched card. Addressing is normally accomplished by typing on the face of the card, while the address is automatically picked up on the back of the card by use of a special process ink. One of the disadvantages is that this special ink sometimes stains the operator's hands.

Addressing can be done with a hand roller or with a variety of different high-speed automatic addressing units. Speeds as high as 40,000 addresses an hour can be obtained and 20,000-an-hour speeds are comparatively common. Cost of address masters varies, depending upon the selection system used, but are generally comparatively low in cost. The masters can be produced at high speeds. Another advantage is that the masters require very little storage space.

Scriptomatic installations are most frequently tailored to the specific requirements of the user and are most commonly used for large lists requiring rapid addressing of a relatively low quality.

Computer Addressing

By far the most common method for direct mail addressing is through the use of computers. Computer addressing was still the subject of great debate in direct mail circles when the Post Office announced mandatory Zip Coding. Almost overnight, every reluctant major mailer stopped debating and made the switch to computerized lists.

Detailed information about the use of computers for direct mail lists will be found in Chapters 18 and 19.

Label Addressing

There are several methods to produce addresses on labels. While the most common "system" is to type individual addresses on perforated sheets of labels, often in snap-out carbon sets, copying machines are also used frequently. One of the most popular copying systems is through the use of Diazoprinters manufactured by GAF Corp.'s Office Systems Division. Other popular methods include use of Xerox and Thermofax copying machines.

Home typists are often used to handle such addressing. They are generally housewives who utilize spare time to handle the overload for direct mail advertisers. Lettershops often serve as "middlemen" in arranging for home typists' services, although large direct mailers often deal directly.

Other Systems

Some mailers still address from printed galleys of type, which are printed on strips of paper and then attached to the mailing piece with devices such as the Wing mailer. Other advertisers print addresses on envelopes in advance and then sort the envelopes into sets for future use.

Another method is to prepare punched tapes, which are used to operate automatic typewriters. While extremely slow, a very high quality of address can be obtained, as envelopes are inserted into typewriters individually.

Cheshire Addressing

Probably the single most common factor in direct mail addressing—particularly for longer lists—is a little slip of paper with half of a hole at its center top and center bottom called a Cheshire label. Even before the computer came along, direct mailers had discovered they could print names and addresses on a roll of paper at much greater speeds than directly onto the material being mailed. These printed rolls were then fed into a Cheshire machine for high speed label application to mailing pieces.

Mechanical addressing machines printed addresses onto a strip of labels one label wide. Classified as north-south strip listers, these one-up strips are still in common use.

Until Cheshire developed a special computer labeling head which allowed the direct use of the multiple width computer printout to be cut and applied directly to mailing pieces, computer printouts were cut up into individual north-south lists similar to those generated by mechanical addressing systems. The development of the new Cheshire head brought about a major revolution in the use of computers for name and address printing and allowed the full use of the computer for list maintenance and selectivity.

An interesting Cheshire development was the marriage of Xerox and Cheshire technology. It resulted in Cheshire's Address Card Lister which can be utilized economically for smaller lists. It involves the use of tab cards which are automatically fed into a Xerox copying machine which produces a Cheshire strip list.

Additional information on Cheshire systems can be obtained from the company at 408 Washington Boulevard, Mundelein, Ill. 60060. Cheshire is also a good source for information about the comparative advantages of different types of addressing systems since their equipment is used with all major kinds of addressing machines.

Chapter 45

SPECIAL EQUIPMENT AND SERVICES

DIRECT mail is one of the last strongholds of *individual* creativity in the advertising field—and a high percentage of the annual direct mail volume is turned out by advertising and sales promotion managers who jealously guard this opportunity to put their creative ability on display. Unfortunately, the net result is often an inferior product, for the day of the specialized service has long since entered the direct mail field—just as it has every other form of advertising.

There are extremely few cases where a superior product will not be the result when an advertiser turns to one of the numerous staffs of skilled specialists who service the direct mail field. By selective buying, a direct mail advertiser can obtain an excellent mailing package at less cost than he can produce it internally.

The best rule of thumb to use is to always buy your direct mail services from outside suppliers—unless you have idle time or facilities you must utilize.

Scarcity of Personnel

It is becoming increasingly difficult to find and hold qualified creative people—and the problem will grow in the years ahead. Good direct mail copywriters, in particular, are in very short supply to meet the growing demand for their services. And the graphic arts field is growing so complex that a whole crew of specialists may be required to handle all the requirements of a given job.

The more skilled personnel are being attracted to agencies and other service organizations where they can become vertical specialists in a position to command increased income. When employed by an individual direct mail advertiser, there is seldom an opportunity to concentrate on a single specialty—except in large organizations such as major mail order firms which, in effect, operate their own internal direct mail agencies.

The Captive Plant

This same basic philosophy applies not only to personnel, but to equipment as well. There has been a growing tendency to develop large internal duplicating and addressing departments. As new, simplified offset duplicating equipment is developed, more and more advertisers have decided to "cut down" on outside expenditures and handle much of their production internally.

This is a marked reversal of a trend which brought about the demise of most large internal printing plants, which were once quite common among large direct mail users. As this larger equipment became outdated, it was discovered that replacement costs had skyrocketed and it was no longer practical to try to maintain these departments. In addition, it had become increasingly difficult to obtain and hold skilled personnel in competition with regular printers and lithographers. Still another problem was the graphic arts labor unions, which often demanded wages and fringe benefits out of line with those offered to other types of employees. To meet the demands of the graphic arts unions would have led to difficulty with other employees.

But probably the most important factor in the demise of the old-time captive plant was the widespread use of more accurate cost accounting, which uncovered dozens of previously "hidden costs," such as time required for supervision by executives and basic overhead. So the big captive plant did a disappearing act.

Bigger Duplicating Departments

While the big presses were being scrapped, the Mimeograph and Ditto machines remained and gradually were replaced by offset duplicating machines. The next step was inevitable—more and more auxiliary equipment was added, including cameras for platemaking, folders, cutters, etc. And suddenly the captive plant was back, although utilizing smaller presses.

As the duplicating equipment grew, the demand for jobs to keep the equipment and personnel busy once again began to draw direct mail jobs back into the plant from outside producers. And once the printing was "back at home," it was only natural to try to handle other direct mail operations, such as addressing, internally.

Usually, an internal duplicating department has a definite role in producing office forms and internal communications. But it seldom can be utilized to advantage if quality direct mail is required. To evaluate the comparative advantages of handling direct mail internally or externally, the following factors should be fully considered:

Quality—Is the right equipment available to turn out the best possible quality; are the operators truly skilled in all aspects of quality control?

Cost—What are the true costs of internal production—including supervisory costs, depreciation, storage, fringe benefits, all overhead factors, and allowances for peak-and-valley production, resulting in either overtime or nonproductive hours which should be prorated against all jobs?

Timing—Can you get jobs when you need them, or must you tailor your mailing schedules to available production time?

Advice—Can your internal production department properly advise you on alternate processes, mailing requirements, cost-saving techniques, sources for special materials, etc.? (And can you afford the loss of creative ideas furnished as a "plus" by outside service organizations?)

Attitude—This is probably the most important factor of all. Are your requirements given "customer" treatment internally, with a sincere desire to "meet competition" by turning out the best possible quality at the lowest possible cost?

Other Services

While most of the preceding suggestions are designed for evaluating production operations, much the same checklist can be used in evaluating creative services, such as original planning, list building, copywriting, layout, artwork, etc. But since ideas are so important in these creative areas, it is more difficult to make an accurate comparison, and it is generally best to assume you will benefit when you use the services of outside organizations.

TYPES OF DIRECT MAIL SERVICE ORGANIZATIONS

There are eight basic types of organizations from which direct mail services can be obtained:

1. Advertising agencies
2. Sales promotion agencies
3. Direct marketing agencies.

4. Lettershops
5. Printers
6. List suppliers
7. Free lancers
8. Specialized services

In many cases, you will find combination organizations which really fit into two or more of the above categories, but each deserves special consideration.

Advertising Agencies

Perhaps the strangest paradox of modern advertising is the reluctance of advertising agencies to actively seek the opportunity to handle direct mail for their clients. Only a limited handful of the major advertising agencies show real interest in direct mail, even though it may constitute a major portion of the advertising effort of their clients.

In the past, the major objection of agencies to handling direct mail was based on difficulty in obtaining adequate compensation to cover costs and yield a profit. Publication and broadcast media extend a 15% commission to agencies on all space and time advertising, upon which a simplified accounting system can be based, and costs of preparing advertising for these media fall into a limited number of categories easily understood by most clients. Direct mail, on the other hand, is surrounded by variable cost factors and, except in a limited number of cases, there are no automatic commissions.

Rather than become involved in dual accounting procedures, most agencies have preferred to limit their activities to commissionable media. But this "excuse" for avoiding direct mail is no longer valid in the majority of cases, since most agencies now have standard cost-accounting procedures which can be applied just as easily to direct mail as to other types of advertising. However, the resistance to direct mail built up over the years continues to reign paramount in the minds of agency management, and few have made any real effort to serve their clients fully by providing professional direct mail services.

Agency Compensation

Agencies which have become active in preparation of direct mail for clients usually favor compensation based on an hourly rate formula, plus a surcharge on all outside purchases (such as art, photography, typography, printing, mailing services, etc.—but usually excluding postage). The foremost exponent of this method of compensation is Ira Rubel, agency financial consultant, who offered this explanation of the system in an article in *Industrial Marketing:*

> Agencies should determine the value of their work on the basis of the cumulative time spent by employees, whose services are variously valued at a stipulated amount per hour. In the advertising agency, as in other personal service businesses, experience has shown that hourly rates equal to between 2¼ to 2¾ times salary cost usually will cover all costs and produce a reasonable profit. This assumes that all time used on clients' advertising is included and that the full time worked is reported. The exact factor (2¼ to 2¾) will depend on such variables as the employees' habits of reporting time and which employees charge time to client work.
>
> For example, a copy chief receiving $15,000 annually will account for about 1,500 hours of work a year. The hourly cost rate, then, is $10 per hour. A reasonable billing price for such a copywriter's service is about $25 an hour. Now such a multiple of prime cost may seem excessively high to advertising managers who are not accustomed to computing personnel costs to include overhead and profit. Advertising agencies, like other businesses, have a considerable amount of indirect salary cost and overhead expense. In addition, it must be remembered that a part of every man's time must be devoted to study, research, administration, and other matters; also that there are many employees in agencies who devote some or all of their time to work that benefits clients, but which cannot be charged to any of them.
>
> Possibilities of adjustment can, therefore, be provided for . . . If the various hourly rates are computed fairly and the work is well done, the hourly rate principle will always function justly.

The major alternate to the hourly rate method of compensation is through a standard markup of outside purchases. While this method is still used by many agencies, and may have a tendency to balance out over a number of jobs, it often results in abuses. For example, a job involving low production costs may be slighted because the markup will not be sufficient to cover adequate creative treatment, while production treatments more costly than justified may be given other jobs to provide enough markup to cover costs.

What Agencies Offer

The major advantage of having an advertising agency handle direct mail in addition to other media is that best results are usually obtained when all promotion efforts are carefully coordinated. There is usually a substantial saving in time and cost, since the same basic research, instructions, discussions, and often much of the creative and production effort can be used for all media.

At the present, the major drawback to having direct mail handled by agencies is that most agencies are not oriented to a direct mail viewpoint and are seldom staffed to handle direct mail with skill. There is a tendency to make direct mail take a back seat to other media, with which the agency is more at home. It is common to assign only junior copywriters to direct mail or to place jobs in the hands of creative people who have little or no direct mail training and who, as a result, tend to treat it like a stepchild. Arthur P. Hall, Aluminum Company of America's director of advertising, points out:

> There is a term in professional advertising circles which is frequently used. The term is "collateral," and it is usually applied to any media other than space or time. Direct mail is generally tarred with this brush. It is called a *collateral* medium, something other than primary. Granted, there is much advertising strategy in which direct mail is properly considered as a collateral force. But there are many other effective strategies in which space or time become collateral to direct mail as the primary medium.

Before deciding to have your advertising agency handle direct mail, it is well to check to make sure there are personnel available who have a thorough understanding of the medium and specific experience with the type of direct mail you plan to use. Ask for concrete evidence of previous accomplishments and carefully evaluate this evidence against similar material obtained from other types of service organizations which are available to handle your account.

Affiliated Direct Mail Agencies

Some agencies, recognizing that their regular organizational structure couldn't provide the specialized service required by mail order advertisers, have established a separate organization to concentrate on direct response advertising. In many cases, these affiliated direct mail agencies have creative staffs equal to those of completely independent direct mail agencies.

While these affiliated agencies frequently handle the direct response advertising needs of the agency's regular clients, they frequently also serve an independent list of clients as well.

Sales Promotion Agencies

In recent years, a crossbreed between the advertising agency and direct mail agency has developed. While it may be known by a variety of titles, it can best be described as a "sales promotion agency." This organization's distinguishing characteristic is that the bulk of its work for clients is outside the area of time and space advertising.

Many sales promotion agencies do handle publication and broadcast advertising, but their main skills are usually in dealing with printed matter of all types—including point-of-purchase displays, incentive programs, catalogs, sales manuals, and, of course, direct mail. Frequently, these agencies started as art studios, although many have been set up as subsidiaries by advertising agencies which have found it difficult to mix sales promotion media with publication and broadcast media.

In general, sales promotion agencies will be staffed with specialists skilled in many forms of direct mail. However, it is important to carefully analyze this factor, since many of these organizations have a tendency to concentrate major effort on a single type of promotion service or on a specific production technique.

Direct Marketing Agencies

It is often difficult to draw a dividing line between the direct marketing agency and the lettershop. The difference is primarily a matter of business emphasis—while the lettershop places major concentration on the production aspects of direct mail, the agency concentrates on the creative aspects. Most direct marketing agencies have at least some internal production facilities, while most lettershops at least make a pretense of offering creative services.

Much of the best direct mail each year is turned out by direct marketing agencies. Their major advantage over both advertising and sales promotion agencies is that both management and the creative staff are fully indoctrinated on the finer points of direct mail and can call upon years of experience to help solve the advertiser's direct mail problems.

The role of the direct mail agency was well explained in a booklet, *How to Get More for Your Direct Mail Dollar,* published by Dickie-Raymond Inc.:

> Probably the quality that is most helpful to our clients is our *specialized ability.* Specialized ability, growing from our exclusive concentration on direct mail advertising.
>
> Dickie-Raymond's varied experience can broaden the horizon of your sales and advertising thinking, yet keep it on tested paths.
>
> Whether the project at hand is a continuing campaign, a letter, a folder, a booklet, or a mail research effort, specialized experience brings into play techniques, methods, and approaches that have been tested and retested hundreds of times, and that can make all the difference in results.
>
> In direct advertising, particularly, the basic truths and lessons learned in serving one industry or branch of business have equal application to other fields. And in no division of advertising and selling are method and tech-

> nique more vitally important. This is not to suggest the prescribing of hard-set formulas—but rather the application of experience-born judgment and proven direct mail theory. This way of working takes a great deal of the guesswork out of promotional planning. It oftentimes saves you the waste motion and lost money of expensive trial-and-error . . .
>
> Few companies can afford to establish or maintain an internal staff capable of supplying the constant flow of ideas, the diversification of thinking, the thousands of creative and supervisory man-hours that are necessary to the planning, writing, and production supervision of an active (direct mail) program . . .
>
> The work we do does not compete with that done by general advertising agencies . . . Almost without exception, the companies we serve are also served by general advertising agencies.

While the explanation is of Dickie-Raymond's own service, the same basic description can be applied to nearly every major direct mail agency.

Lettershops

The lettershop is the most versatile of all direct mail service organizations—and the most important to the majority of direct mail advertisers. While primarily a production organization, it may also offer a number of excellent creative services, although, as a general rule, most lettershops are likely to claim credit for more creative ability than they can deliver—particularly in the area of copywriting and design.

Lettershops come in all sizes and degrees of capability. Many are little more than secretarial services with mimeographs and addressing machines. Others are giant organizations offering comprehensive services ranging from creation of campaigns, list compilation, list maintenance, art, and design to printing, addressing, inserting, and mailing. The long-established title of "lettershop" is abhorred by many in the field, for it usually falls far short of describing the range of services offered.

In its *Purchasing Guide for Direct Mail Advertising,* the Mail Advertising Service Assn. lists the following basic services offered by its member lettershops:

Artwork	Automatically Typed Letters
Direct Mail Agency	Hand Addressing
Letterpress (Platen)	Letterpress (Large Cylinder)
Machine Folding	Mailing Lists
Mechanical Addressing	Mechanical Inserting
Mechanical Collating	Mimeographing
Multigraphing	Occupant Lists
Offset Composition	Packaging and Shipping

Photo Copy	Photo Offset
Platemaking	Spirit Duplicating
Telephone Answering	Typesetting
Typewriter Addressing	Secretarial Service

Xerography

Dealing With Lettershops

In dealing with lettershops, it is well to remember that no two shops offer exactly the same combination of abilities. Many are highly skilled in one area, but offer only mediocre service in other areas. In general, however, the larger shops offer a relatively wide range of skills and are competent to provide valuable consulting services on most direct mail problems.

Costs of lettershop services are relatively standard, although they will vary from one geographical area to another. Standards of quality, however, vary greatly. Once you have located a lettershop which meets your requirements for quality and service, work closely with that organization and do not try to scatter your work among a number of different shops. This will usually result in better service and lower costs.

Printers

Many printers offer a variety of direct mail services. In general, however, they are less skilled in the finer points of direct mail than those who specialize in the medium. No general rules can be offered to cover the value of printers' direct mail services. Many lettershops have complete printing facilities, and many printers offer extensive lettershop services. The main difference is the emphasis given direct mail by the management of the business.

List Suppliers

A somewhat similar situation presents itself in a comparison of lettershops and list suppliers. Many lettershops offer extensive list services, while some list suppliers maintain at least a minimum lettershop service. As a rule, however, list suppliers will be of value in the area of creativity and production mainly in providing consulting services. Many of the truly outstanding direct mail experts are to be found in the mailing list field.

Free Lancers

In many areas of direct mail creativity, the best source of service is a free lancer. This is particularly true of copywriting. There are many copy specialists who operate primarily on a free-lance basis. Many concentrate their efforts on a particular type of copy, such as sales letters, mail order, catalogs, company histories, etc. Most of the free lancers usually concentrate on a single geographical area, although a number—such as noted letter specialist, Paul Bringe of Hartford, Wisconsin—serve clients throughout the world.

There are also direct mail consultants, usually operating on a free-lance basis, who specialize in developing or analyzing direct mail programs, without necessarily performing any of the actual work in carrying out the campaigns.

Specialized Services

The direct mail field abounds with specialized services which are offered on both a syndicated and a custom basis. Most of these services are vertical in nature, and the biggest difficulty in using them for creative planning is that their operators are highly prejudiced about the value of the individual service they offer. Nevertheless, there are many occasions when one or more of these specialized services is the best possible answer to a direct mail advertiser's needs. The important point is to always analyze these specialized services in comparison with other possible approaches on *your* own terms.

HOW TO WORK WITH AN OUTSIDE AGENCY

One of the best presentations on how to work with an outside agency in preparing effective direct mail was prepared not by an agency man but by an advertiser—Paul Goldberg, promotion director of Consumers Union, Mt. Vernon, N. Y. It originally appeared in the DMMA Direct Mail Manual and is included here in full:

Creative Thinking

I think today there is general agreement that the single most important contribution an agency can make to the marketing function is *creative* thinking. One good creative idea can influence corporate profits more than virtually any other factor. One creative advertising campaign can produce greater revenue than years of cost-reducing programs.

For smaller companies, creative ideas are the only means of offsetting the impact of the huge advertising expenditures of their bigger competitors. For any size company, creative advertising can do more to make similar products distinctive, and to gain a product a share of its competitive market, than anything else in the total marketing function.

The problem, then, is how the advertiser—or client—can best get this kind of creativity from his advertising agency. Assuming you've been careful to select an agency that's demonstrated creativity, the way to get the best ideas from it is to understand the client-agency relationship, and particularly *your* function in it.

First Responsibility

Your first responsibility is to establish your own goals, define your overall strategy, and supply your agency with adequate information to develop a program that suits both. The only person who knows what you hope to accomplish through advertising is you. No agency can define your goals for you, and no agency can read your mind—so don't make it waste time trying.

Next, let the agency educate itself about your business. Explaining your product or operations is a fine introduction, but yours is strictly a client's-eye view. The client lives so intimately with his own business that he usually can't see the forest for the trees. Plant tours, inspections of facilities, or any kind of first-hand exposure to your business that you can provide give the agency a chance to see it all with fresh eyes. Your agency is thinking *with*—and *like*—the consumer, and being impressed by things that will, in turn, impress potential customers.

You may know—and take for granted—that every widget manufacturer employs 27 different hand operations to make a first-class widget. But if the consumer doesn't know it, that fact can be turned into an advertising campaign that will establish you as *the* quality widget-maker. In fact, some of the most successful advertising campaigns ever created began with a client saying, "But *everybody* does that"—only to have the agency answer, "Sure. But nobody *knows* it."

Collaboration

Once you've determined your goals and strategy and let the agency become thoroughly familiar with your operations, the important thing in establishing a good creative climate becomes collaboration. Information and ideas should flow freely *between* you and the agency, with a minimum of formality and fiat.

Actually, *collaboration* may be a dangerous word. Don't infer from it that you're supposed to be creating the ads, because that isn't your function. Your job is to use *your* expertise where it applies, and not in areas where the agency people are the professionals.

For instance, you're the ultimate authority on matters of fact. If an idea is based on an invalid assumption about your product, or if a piece of copy contains factual errors, it's your job to set the agency straight. If you know from past experience that a certain *kind* of advertising has been unpopular with your sales force or your major retailers, let the agency know about it. If you know that your retailers or dealers would rather see one ad in *Life* than six ads in the local newspapers—or *vice versa*—bring the point up. The agency respects your experience and judgment in these areas, and wants to utilize it.

Just bear in mind that rewriting headlines or redoing layouts *isn't* your function. In that area, the agency wants *its* experience and judgment respected.

Keep Things Simple

This inevitably leads to the next point: KEEP YOUR COLLABORATION WITH THE AGENCY AS SIMPLE AS POSSIBLE. One of the most famous animals on Madison Avenue is a strange creature with the trunk of an elephant, the neck of a giraffe, the body of a camel, the legs of a gazelle and the tail of a monkey. As any advertising man can tell you, it's a horse designed by a committee!

The lesson is implicit. Remember that you're working toward a common goal, and view your agency as an integral part of your corporate marketing effort. Set up a situation where a compact, responsible team from your organization can work closely with an opposite-number team from the agency. If they can blend compatibly and informally—work together, succeed together, or even occasionally get shot down together, you'll get a better creative output and a much higher ratio of successes to failures than you'll get by any other system.

Don't Copy-Cat

With that out of the way, let's remember that getting the highest possible creativity from the agency means, by definition, getting advertising that is *original* as well as *arresting.* That, in turn, leads to another cardinal rule: Don't ask your agency for copy-cat ads!

Outside our own business hours, we're all consumers of other people's products, and we all respond to other people's advertising. When we encounter an ad or a commercial that *we* like and react to, we have a terrible tendency to ask our agencies to "give me something like that." Nothing is more dangerous.

No reasonable man would tell his doctor what to prescribe for him because he read an article in *Reader's Digest,* or tell his lawyer how to handle his affairs because he always reads the legal page of *Time.*

By the same token, no sensible advertiser will tell his agency how to advertise because he saw a great ad or heard a great radio spot. The fact that a terribly clever or witty or funny ad sold *you* a can of tuna fish or a pizza mix or some other inexpensive, mass-market item doesn't mean that it will sell *your customer* on a higher priced product that's an investment instead of a whim.

The hard sell that got *you* to invest $5.95 in a mail-order book or subscription could be completely wrong for a product aimed at a status or fashion-conscious market. And the beautiful "reason why" approach that convinced you to buy an expensive product or to change stock brokers *could* be a total disaster where *your product* is concerned.

Any good agency can give you clever ads, hard-selling ads, reason-why ads. *Any* good agency can give you whatever you ask for as easily as pushing a button. But *no* good agency wants to give you ads that are *wrong* for you and your product. Ask for a copy-cat ad and you may get it, but you won't get creativity, which is, in essence, the best possible ad for *your product.*

Trust the Agency

When we rule out copy-catting, we bring in something of truly major importance—*trusting* your agency to create the kind of campaign that will do the job best for you. This is, in essence, the sum total of everything we've considered up until now.

Your business is making widgets. Whether you elect to make the world's finest widgets, or the world's cheapest widgets, or the most competitive widgets you possibly can, you're a professional widget-maker, and your agency respects you as such.

Your agency's business is to *sell* your widgets, and the people who are doing *that* job will do it much better if you don't step on their toes. Getting the ultimate in creativity ultimately depends upon getting the ultimate from creative people. And that, in today's parlance, brings us all down to the nitty-gritty.

If you want the best possible advertising, if you want real creativity, if you want *all* that the creative people at your agency are capable of giving you, respect them, appreciate them, and deal with them on their own level—the professional level.

If you've done all the things we've considered up to now, your agency will never create a piece of advertising for you that isn't based on a good, solid reason.

Your Role

What the agency submits for your approval is the product of a lot of thinking about the goals, strategy, facts, markets, media, knowledge and information you've collaborated on. And it's the original creation of people who've absorbed and digested all that and turned it into an advertising campaign by means of their special talents. Now it's in your hands—or the hands of your advertising manager—and the question is: What will *you* do with it?

At this point, the *negative* possibilities are infinite, so I think we'd better limit ourselves to the *positive* approaches that will guarantee you the best creative results.

First, *don't try to take over the agency's* function. The philosophy of advertising people is very simple: We don't tell *him* how to *make* widgets, so why should he tell us how to make ads? Don't try to do the advertising yourself.

Second, *try to be objective.* Remember *your* function—checking for factual accuracy. Don't fall into the subjective judgment pit of assuming that an ad won't do a job with a housewife in Terre Haute because it doesn't appeal to *you.* And *don't* ask your friends and relatives for their opinions about your upcoming advertising campaign. If someone from your agency said, "My mother-in-law thinks you make lousy widgets," you'd probably wonder who made his mother-in-law an expert on widgets. Your agency will be pretty upset if you offer *your* mother-in-law as an expert on advertising!

Third, *criticize constructively.* The bane of every copy writer and art director is the client who says, "I don't like it." No reason why, no alternative, just thumbs down. Remember that the agency had a reason for doing what they did. You need a reason for saying nay.

Fourth, *give credit where credit is due.* If you like something, *say so.* This gives creative people a tremendous lift, and inspires them to do even better for you.

The Golden Rule

And there, as the saying goes, you have it. If you think that you'll have trouble remembering all the fine points and generalizations, may I suggest the Golden Rule: Do unto others as you would have others do unto you. Treat the professionals at your agency *as professionals.* Let them know about it when you like what they do. Let them know why you don't like it when you don't.

Remember that the client who creates an atmosphere of professionalism and proper division of labors and due appreciation will get a 24-hour effort from creative people—they'll live and breathe and dream about your account and make selling *your* product their number-one function in life.

Remember, too, that when you undermine, snipe at and downgrade the creative people at your agency, they're going to get surly. They'll still do their jobs, but they'll do them at a minimal level. Your account will become a chore to be gotten through as quickly as possible, as opposed to a labor of love.

And, in extremis, give the agency the benefit of the doubt. If you just don't know—and can't determine by testing—what will or won't be the best possible campaign for you, trust the agency's judgment. And if you blow one, try to work out the reasons why you did—objectively—before you change agencies or ask for a new creative team.

Remember that your agency's best interests lie in doing the best possible job for you. The more you *sell,* the more you can spend on advertising. The more you can *spend,* the more your agency profits.

That simple fact may explain why the most successful marketers in the country have the lowest agency turnover rate. It may even explain why you sometimes catch yourself saying, "Whatever became of Zilch Widgets? They used to be a big name before they started changing agencies every six months."

Chapter 46

PAPER AND ENVELOPE GUIDE

OF all the ingredients in any direct mail "package," two of the most tangible are the paper and the envelope. Yet, while highly important to the success of a direct mail piece or campaign, paper and envelopes are often given the least and last consideration. Too few direct mail advertisers completely analyze the things which are accomplished through careful paper and envelope selection for *every* mailing.

Selection of paper has many results. Proper selection can enhance the mood of the printed material or can destroy it. It can make illustrations "sing out" or can ruin them. Paper can be restful to the eyes or can cause headaches.

Envelopes, the first part of most mailings to create an impression, are more than just a method for conveying material through the mails. While their "transportation" capabilities must be carefully considered, thought must also be given the image they will create for your mailing.

Selecting Papers

There are many factors which will determine the right paper for any direct mail job. The following checklist, prepared by the author for *Advertising Requirements,* will help make the job of selecting that right paper easier:

- *What process is to be used?* . . . Generally speaking, papers for offset lithography are made differently from those designed for letterpress.
- *What kind of printed piece is it?* . . . If it is mostly composed of text matter, an antique book paper will probably be selected. But if it is for general promotional work, and will be used for halftones, then a machine coated sheet would be better if the job is to be printed by letterpress.

- *Is weight a factor?* . . . Many times a considerable saving in postage can be made in large runs by using a lightweight sheet. Some types and brands of papers have definite advantages over others in certain weights. In lightweight stocks, for example, opacity is tremendously important.
- *Will the job be folded?* . . . Since most printed pieces are folded, the paper selected must rate high on this point, unless the job is to be scored.
- *How much paper is involved?* . . . While cost is not a major factor in small runs, it can account for as much as 50% of the total cost of such jobs as big publications with enormous press runs. A careful analysis of all suitable stocks can frequently result in vast savings.
- *What is the mood to be created?* . . . Some papers whisper softly of music and candlelight while others help create a circus atmosphere; some breathe elegance, others speak of economy. If your job is aimed at creating some special mood, it is important to select a paper which will help do this job.
- *How will the piece be used?* . . . There is a vast difference in papers suitable for fast, one-time reading and those which fit a job which will be frequently folded and unfolded, handled by greasy or dirty hands, hung on walls for months at a time, etc.
- *What finishing processes will be required?* . . . If a job is to be stapled, punched, die-cut, varnished, sewed, glued, or handled by any of the hundreds of special processes used to finish a printed job, it is important to select a stock which is adaptable to such handling.
- *What colors are required?* . . . Not all papers come in the same range of colors. If a specific color—even a special "shade" of white—is desired, the choice may be limited.
- *What is the size of the finished job?* . . . There are different standard sheet sizes for different kinds of paper. If economy is a factor, it is important to select a stock from which your job can be cut with as little waste as possible. In this regard, it is important to know the paper size limitations of the presses on which the job is to be printed.
- *Is it necessary to "match" papers?* . . . Perhaps you're planning to use one stock for the cover of your job and another for the remainder. If it is important to match them accurately, for either texture or color, you must select the papers very carefully.
- *How soon do you need the paper?* . . . Don't just assume that because the stock you plan on using is a "standard" item it is always instantly available in the size, weight, color, and quantity you require. Before going ahead and making a definite decision on the paper you need, check with your local sources of supply to determine its availability.
- *Will another paper work just as well?* . . . Okay, now you've decided on just what paper is needed. But the task of paper selection is not necessarily ended. A comparison of similar stocks may reveal that you can get the same results with another paper which can save you money.
- *Can the paper supplier fill the order?* . . . Even after you've made a final decision, you must still check another point. It is not unusual for an artist to create, an art director to approve and a printer to accept a job

which demands a piece of paper that a mill cannot make as described. So it is important to know the minimum and maximum requirements of a mill source for any deviation from a completely "standard" item.

Paper Characteristics

Although there are thousands of different papers available for direct mail printing, all printing papers have certain characteristics in common. An understanding of these characteristics is essential for efficient ordering of paper. An excellent discussion of these characteristics was given by Thomas N. Cook, of Hamilton Paper Co., at a Philadelphia seminar:

1. *Dimension and weight* . . . Little need be said about paper dimension, for everyone knows paper has length and width measured either in inches or centimeters. But weight is another matter. Do you know, for instance, what is meant when the weight of a particular paper is described as 25 by 38—70/500? This means that 500 sheets of this paper cut to size 25 by 38 inches when put on a scale will weigh 70 pounds. By simple arithmetic, you can easily see that we can project a weight for 1,000 sheets of the same size. Obviously, 1,000 sheets would weigh 140 pounds and this would be described as 25 by 38—140M.

   To carry the thought further, 1,000 sheets in double the size (38 by 50 inches) would weigh 280 pounds.

   Do not confuse weight with thickness. Weight refers to actual scale weight which is determined by *controlling the amount of raw material per square foot of paper.*

   Of course, there are other basic sizes commonly used as basis weights. Bond grades use 17 by 22 as the basic size; cover grades commonly use 20 by 26 as the basic size. However, once you grasp the arithmetic principle you need not be confused by different basic sizes.

   Remember that basis weight simply means actual scale weight of 500 sheets of paper in a standard basic size. And remember that by simple arithmetic, you can find the weight for other quantities in that size or a multiple of that size.

2. *Grain direction* . . . If you have ever seen paper being manufactured, you know that it is made at relatively high speeds in a continuous strip. You also know that paper is composed of a mat of tiny cellulose fibers. Because of the speed at which paper is manufactured, the majority of these fibers lie in a direction parallel to the flow on the paper machine. Cross grain, of course, refers to the direction across the paper machine.

   Grain direction is important to you, as a paper buyer, because it influences the dimensional stability of the paper. It is a characteristic of the cellulose fiber that, as long as it exists, it will be affected dimensionally by changes in moisture content or humidity. Because this cellulose fiber changes in diameter rather than length, the principal change in dimensional stability takes place across the grain rather than with the grain.

   You must consider grain direction particularly if the paper is to be lithographed. The lithographer can compensate for changes in dimension of the paper lengthwise around his cylinder, but not across the cylinder of his press. Therefore, paper to be lithographed is normally ordered grain long.

Grain direction will also affect fold and stiffness of paper. It is obviously easier to fold with the grain than across the grain because to fold across the grain more fibers will have to be broken. The stiffness will be greater with the grain than across it. As an experiment in determining grain direction, simply take a piece of paper and fold it each way.

3. *Laid and wove* . . . Paper must be either laid or wove. You are probably familiar with the traditional laid design consisting of parallel lines visible when the paper is held up to light. This pattern originated with the earliest papermaking in China where the paper was manufactured on a screen made from fine strips of split bamboo sewn together, crosswise, at intervals of approximately one inch. This screen imparted to the paper a design which persists to this day in fine papers. A wove sheet is simply paper without this pattern of laid marks and the accompanying crosswise chain marks

4. *Deckle edge and plain edge* . . . Just as paper must be either laid or wove, it must also have a plain or deckle edge. If the paper has a deckle edge, remember that the deckle can only be on two opposite sides, not on all four, and the deckle must be parallel to the grain. This is because deckle edges on modern papermaking equipment are made by cutting the edge of the paper with a fine jet of water as the continuous strip of paper flows along the machine.

5. *Color* . . . Color, of course, is an obvious characteristic except for one area: Remember that white is no longer a sufficient description of a color. There is an almost unlimited variety of shades of white—pink whites, green whites, blue whites, even purple whites and—of course—the new fluorescent whites.

6. *Finish* . . . All paper has some sort of a finish. The finish may have been imparted right on the paper machine or in a separate process. Ordinary machine finishes include smooth, vellum and antique. The term "smooth" refers to just what it implies; antique is another term for rough; vellum is a term which covers the middle ground between the two.

   Special finishes include felt, supercalendered or embossed. When paper has a felt finish it means that the paper, during manufacture and while it was still wet, was brought into contact, under pressure, with a woolen blanket felt of a distinctive weave. This felt imparts a three-dimensional design to the surface of the paper.

   Supercalendered paper goes through an additional smoothing operation accomplished by running the paper, under pressure and with moisture present, between alternate rolls of chilled steel and fiber. This polishes the surface to a high smoothness.

   Paper with an embossed finish has a design pressed into the paper after it has been removed from the papermaking machine. It is run dry but under pressure between two rolls, one or both of which are engraved with a special design.

7. *Caliper* . . . There is, of course, a correlation between weight and caliper (thickness), but, again, do not confuse one with the other. A heavier, smooth-finish paper may have less caliper than a rough-finish paper, yet

it may weigh more. In ordering paper, caliper is particularly important in book work, where a uniform number of pages per inch may well be of critical importance.

8. *Sizing* . . . If paper is surface sized it means it has been treated, probably with a starch solution, much as the collar of a shirt is starched. Sizing is used in papers intended for offset printing in order to give surface strength. Otherwise, fragments of the surface would pick off during printing. In letterpress printing, paper performs better if it is not surface sized, although it is possible to print almost all papers by letterpress. For offset printing the paper must be surface sized.

9. *Packaging* . . . Paper is packed either guillotine trimmed on four sides or untrimmed. It must be either ream marked or sealed in packages. It can come packed in cartons, on skids, or in wooden cases.

10. An additional characteristic, not to be specified but of importance, is the fact that paper, being obviously two-sided, has a felt side and a wire side. The felt side is the side which is up as the paper is being manufactured. The opposite side—or wire side—is so called because it is the side which is in contact with the wire screen on the machine during manufacture. The felt side is considered the right side of a sheet of paper.

How to Use Paper Classification Charts

At the end of this chapter are paper classification charts prepared by The Dartnell Corporation to give a quick-reference guide to the various printing papers available for direct mail use. The descriptions, suggestions, and recommendations are, of necessity, general, but cover most of the basic details a direct mail advertiser needs for his initial paper selection analysis. Points covered:

Major group classifications: the five divisions of book papers, cover papers, writing papers, newsprint papers, and thin papers which, together, probably constitute well over 95% of the paper requirements of the average direct mail printing program.

Kinds of paper: the various subdivisions of the major groups, such as sulphite bond, rag-content bond, ledger, wedding paper, etc., in the case of writing papers.

Basic size: the size sheet established by trade custom for figuring the basis weight for each kind of paper. Often the basic size is also the one in which that paper is most frequently used and therefore most easily available from paper merchants.

Basis weight (sometimes referred to as "substance"): the weight in pounds of one ream of the basic size of that particular paper. All commercial papers are figured 500 sheets per ream except tissue and wrapping, which are figured 480 sheets per ream. Each kind of paper is stocked only in certain weights set up by the paper industry as standard. Regular weights of English Finish, for example, are 40, 45, 50, 60, 70, and 80 pounds per ream of 500 sheets; and the weights of coated papers are 70, 80, 100, 120, and 150 pounds. Intermediate weights must be made to order at the paper mill, usually at additional cost. The charts show the usual range of weights, but it is always a good plan to consult a paper merchant for the weights available in the size required. If the quantity is large enough, most paper can be made to special order in almost any weight, sheet size, or roll width at regular pound rates.

Presses most often used: a section of the chart cross-indexing the various papers according to their suitability for the different printing processes. It is not absolute, of course, because too much depends on the skill or limitations of individual printers to draw hard-and-fast conclusions, but it represents the average of printing buying experience. In order not to place the printer at a disadvantage, it is always wise to consult him regarding the most suitable paper for the job, especially if there is a variance from these recommendations.

Recommended halftone screen: again represents averages rather than absolutes. Since good halftone reproduction on letterpress equipment depends upon the quality and adaptability of the engravings, the condition of the press, the craftsmanship of the presswork, and the character of the ink, as well as upon the paper, a range of two or three screens is given. In general, however, the smoother and more even the paper finish, the finer the screen it will effectively reproduce.

There are, of course, other stocks the production man is frequently called on to buy which are not listed in the paper classification charts—such as blotting stock, bristols, and other heavy papers used as card stock, for fancy finish covers, and for a few other specialties. Samples of these unusual papers are easily obtained from printers and paper merchants, and they do not constitute the direct mail advertiser's everyday stock in trade. It is well, however, to keep a fairly complete file of cover paper samples, so that when there is a mailing to be produced, the selection can be made in the office rather than working through the printer or paper merchant.

General description and common uses: this is the column heading under which are listed the characteristics of each paper that distinguish it from the others. At the risk of oversimplification, the descriptions and uses are kept brief, although entire chapters might be written on each one. Literature is readily available to direct mail advertisers who are interested in studying the intricacies of paper manufacture and use more thoroughly.

Controlling Paper Costs

Following the paper classification chart are a series of tables which will assist the direct mail advertiser in selecting the most economical paper sizes by avoiding waste. The first chart, on page 1182, "How to Select the Right Page Size to Avoid Wasting Paper Stock," covers the standard sizes of bond and ledger papers and lists 39 different page sizes which can be printed in practical and economical units from the three sheet sizes of 17 by 22 inches, 17 by 28 inches, and 19 by 24 inches. It illustrates the wide variety of sizes available without going outside the range of standard sheets. It is important to remember, however, that particular stock may not be available in all three sizes.

A chart, "Amount of Paper Required," (page 1183), covers the most economical sheet size to obtain specific furnished sheets for three basic types of direct mail—broadsides and folders, booklets and catalogs, and envelope enclosures. The chart also shows envelope requirements for the most common trimmed sizes of direct mail.

The third chart, "Comparison of Cost of Standard Sizes and Special Sizes," shows how economies occur when standard sheet sizes are used, rather than ordering special sizes to accommodate printing requirements. (See page 1188.)

Ordering Paper in Rolls

With the growing use of web-fed rotary equipment for all basic types of printing, many direct mail advertisers are, for the first time, finding themselves face to face with a new paper problem—ordering paper in rolls. One of the best guides to handling this problem was prepared by Charles Morris, noted paper authority, for *Advertising Requirements.* He offers those guides on the next page to follow when writing orders for paper in rolls.

- Be sure to indicate weight of paper as maximum—not to do so cheats you of yardage.
- Caution—remember weight of roll includes outside wrapper and non-returnable core. Weight of returnable core is not charged.
- Remember, you are billed for gross weight of roll—paper, wrapping and nonreturnable core.
- When estimating, be sure to allow for spoilage. Most operators say 5 percent covers loss of paper weight.
- Be sure to instruct supplier to number and show weight of each roll on outside wrapper and on shipping and billing papers.
- Be sure to indicate when printing is to be produced with heat-set or other special inks. Extreme care is given the "pick" factor, and splices are properly treated for processing.

Arithmetic Help

Here is an approved method of figuring the approximate weight of paper in rolls:

Example: To determine the weight of a roll of bond paper that is 30 inches in diameter and 12 inches wide: square the diameter, 30 x 30 = 900; multiply by the width, 900 × 12 = 10,800; multiply by the factor .027, 10,800 × .027 = 291.6

Answer: 291.6 pounds.

These are the factors to use to help you determine the approximate weight of a roll for papers most often purchased in rolls: antique finish, .018; machine finish, English finish, offset, bond, ledger, writing, manifold, onion skin,

- *Indicate clearly*

........speed of press
........exact roll width
........minimum and maximum diameter
........machine roll
........rewound roll
........wire side out
........felt side out
........for letterpress
........for lithography
........for gravure
........one color
........two colors
........three colors
........four colors
........one side of sheet
........both sides of sheet
........directional arrows on wrappers of large rolls

- *Core specifications*

........inside diameter
........fiber ....metal
........returnable
........nonreturnable
........slotted
........width of slots
........not slotted
........slots in juxtaposition

- *Be sure to insist upon high-quality hard rolls*

........tight wound
........even wound
........free from slitter dust
........load on side
........on end
........on skids
........minimum of splices—indicate how many splices-per-roll are acceptable
........flag splices

.027; super, .030; coated two sides, .034; coated one side, .030. These factors —average among paper manufacturers—apply for all weights.

For any given diameter, lighter-weight papers will bulk less. More of it, therefore, will be wound on a roll.

ENVELOPES

Envelopes for direct mail are ordered in two ways. For smaller mailings, blank made-up envelopes are ordered and imprinted with the return address, printed indicia if desired, and promotional information. For longer runs, envelopes are imprinted before being made up. Flat sheets may be printed by a regular printer and then delivered to an envelope maker for manufacturing, or the envelope company may do the entire job.

Whenever possible, envelopes for an extended period should be ordered at the same time for maximum quantity discount. Envelope companies are generally happy to work on an annual contract basis, producing and delivering envelopes as needed, but offering reduced prices in return for a firm contract.

It pays to be extremely careful in choosing an envelope manufacturer. There are wide variances in both quality and price. If you are looking for quality, you will generally want to avoid envelopes printed by high-speed flexography. While some envelopes printed by this method have a reasonable degree of quality, the average flexographic envelope printing is of low quality. (For more detailed information on envelopes, see Chapter 32.)

Glossary of Envelope Terms

The following glossary prepared by The Dartnell Corporation will guide direct mail advertisers in selecting the proper envelopes to fill their needs:

Airmail Envelopes. While any envelope may be used for airmail if endorsed "Via Airmail," most regular users of this class of postal service adopt special envelopes for the purpose. Designs for printed airmail envelopes are of two types: "A," a border consisting of alternating red and blue oblique parallelograms which must be printed on white paper and thus produce a red, white, and blue design 5/32 of an inch wide around the edges of both the address side and the back of the envelope; and "B," two ¼-inch stripes, one of red and the other of blue, extending horizontally across the center of the envelope with a ¼-inch band of white between. Both envelopes should be imprinted "Via Airmail."

Booklet Envelopes. Special envelopes to fit any size of booklet are available in either regular or postage saver style, usually with open sides or diagonal seams. In the selection of envelopes for booklets, it is wise to consider the durability and folding qualities of the booklet stock before ordering envelopes to match. Frequently the paper used for the booklet is not suitable for envelopes. In many cases a contrasting or harmonizing color is preferable to a matching color, particularly when a matching color would involve an unsuitable paper stock.

Business Reply Envelopes. Concerns which have obtained permits from their postmasters are privileged to use business reply cards and business reply envelopes. The address side of such envelopes bears the following information: Permit number; name of post office issuing the permit; the words, "Business reply envelope"; the inscription, "No postage stamp necessary if mailed in the United States"; the words "Postage will be paid by addressee" (whose name may be inserted if desired) over the name and complete address of the person or concern to whom the envelopes are to be returned. A space of at least 1⅛ inches shall be left for postmarking at the top of the envelope on the left of the indicia in the upper right corner. Such indicia shall be prominently printed and not obstructed or surrounded by any other matter. All of the foregoing shall be arranged in one of the standard forms provided by the post office. No extraneous matter may appear on the address side. Applications for permits should be addressed to the postmaster on Form No. 3614. No deposit is necessary.

Catalog Envelopes. The same considerations which govern the selection of booklet envelopes also apply to those for catalogs except that catalogs, being usually larger and heavier, generally call for a stronger and heavier paper stock. Most catalog envelopes are made in the open-end style with a center seam, giving strength and durability. They are available in all sizes.

Color. The use of color for envelopes has been steadily growing in recent years. Not only color printing for the design of the corner card, but colored stocks for the envelope itself have become popular. There should be some relationship between the colors of the inks and stock on the envelope and the colors of the mailing piece itself. Matching, harmonizing, or contrasting colors may be chosen for the envelope if appropriate to the contents.

Corner Cards. Originally conceived simply to meet postal requirements of a return address, the term "corner card" has come to embrace all the various types of design employed by advertisers and others to register an advertising impression on the recipient before he even opens the envelope. Good typography, artistic designs, the use of color, all contribute to the effectiveness of the envelope as a miniature poster. Care should be taken, however, not to violate postal regulations concerning the amount of space which should be left for addressing and stamping, and to include all pertinent information.

Counter and Package Envelopes come in a wide variety of special sizes and styles, depending upon the nature of the product to be packaged. Some are designed for their display value in retail stores; some for customers' convenience in carrying merchandise away. In either case, such envelopes are styled for packaging rather than for mailing purposes.

Envelope Paper is a general term descriptive of paper suitable for making envelopes for mailing. It should be strong, opaque for commercial uses, with good folding qualities and writing surface, and should lie flat without curling. While papers of nearly all types have been used for envelopes, often inappropriately, the best papers for the purpose are white wove writings, bonds, ledgers, manilas, ropes, krafts, and colored papers.

Fasteners. There are four principal styles of fasteners for open-end, catalog, booklet, and other styles of envelopes: (1) Gummed flaps; (2) ungummed flaps, to be tucked in; (3) metal clasps; and (4) string and button.

Filing and Expansion Envelopes range all the way from plain open-side envelopes with thumb cuts to accordion-pleated expansion envelopes of great strength and durability. Ordinary filing envelopes are made to contain standard 8½- by 11-inch material, although many are made in smaller sizes for other types of filing equipment. Kraft and jute manila are the stocks principally used. For expansion envelopes, red rope, jute, and heavy kraft are preferred.

Flaps. In general, flaps of envelopes are of four styles: (1) The regular flap which is most popular but which, for reasons of extra strength or unusual appearance, is not always suitable; (2) the pointed flap, which imparts an air of distinction to the envelope and also provides a slightly larger gumming surface, frequently being used for executive correspondence; (3) the wallet flap, which is extremely strong, extending well down below the center of the envelope, with a very large gumming surface; and (4) the bankers flap, which is extremely deep.

Order-Blank Envelopes. Various types of the business reply envelopes have been developed to carry order forms on the inside. The order form is printed on one side of the sheet and the address and reply form on the other; the recipient simply fills in the order, folds and seals the envelope, and mails it in.

Payroll Envelopes are small containers for coins and bills which are bought in bulk by banks for distribution among their customers or by individual companies. Sizes range from 3 by 4½ inches upward.

Postage Saver Envelopes are like regular envelopes in appearance and construction, the only difference being that they have a loose flap at one end which is simply tucked in without being sealed. In another style of postage saver envelope, one end is stuck with a spot of gum instead of being sealed full length, and the words, "Pull out for postal inspection," are printed on or adjacent to the loose flap. Postage saver envelopes enable the advertiser to send out a third-class mailing in keeping with post-office regulations with the back flap of the envelope sealed in the same way as first-class mail.

Return Envelopes are simply self-addressed envelopes, either stamped or unstamped, as distinguished from business reply envelopes. The latter, of course, bear a printed insigni a and permit number obligating the mailer to pay the postage on their return.

Special Delivery Envelopes, made according to the new ruling and specifications of the Post Office Department, embody a special design and special colors which get immediate recognition from postal clerks and insure special delivery handling. Around the borders of special delivery envelopes appear alternating yellow and green dots. On the right side—1⅜ inches from the top of a No. 10 envelope, for example, ¼ inch from the right-hand side, and 1⅞ inches from the bottom—are two yellow horizontal rules enclosing the words, "Special Delivery," which are printed in green. The design of smaller special delivery envelopes is reduced in proportion.

System Envelopes. For practically every office, store, and factory system, there is a special system envelope available. The variety of sizes, styles, and functions of such envelopes is so great that a general description becomes practically impossible, but some conception of their range may be obtained from a brief mention of a few of them: Books of envelopes for installment payments, imprinted with blanks for filling in the amount due, the sender's name, address, etc.; sets of calendar envelopes, with space for shopping lists, telephone lists, etc.

Two-Compartment Envelopes. This term refers to any sort of envelopes which carry first-class mail in one compartment and third- or fourth-class mail in another, with the resultant saving in postage and the assurance that both the letter and the literature arrive together. (Envelopes of this type are handled in the mail as matter of the third- or fourth-class, depending on the nature of the contents of the lower class compartment.)

Window Envelopes, so called because they permit the name and address typed on the enclosure to be read through the envelope itself, are of three main types: (1) Open-face, consisting of a plain, uncovered, die-cut opening; (2) one-piece, in which the window is made in the body of the envelope by impregnating that portion of the paper with a suitable oily material; and (3) two-piece type, with a piece of glassine, cellophane, or some other kind of transparent material affixed over the panel. To be mailable, any type of window envelope must have a panel running parallel to the length of the envelope, and windows must not be closer than 1⅜ inches from the top, or closer to the bottom or either side than ⅜ of an inch. No "border" around this "window" portion may exceed 5/32 of an inch in width. Window envelopes are covered by particular restrictions as to printing. These envelopes *must* bear the return card of the sender, which must consist of the name and address, or post office box number, and city from which mailed. The name of a building will not suffice unless the mailer occupies that building in its entirety.

STYLES OF ENVELOPES USED IN DIRECT MAIL

1. High Cut Open Side
2. Low Cut Open Side
3. Side Seams Open Side
4. Square Flap Open Side
5. Reverse Face Wallet Flap
6. Open Side Pointed Flap
7. Two Fold Imperial
8. Baronial Open Side
9. Bankers' Safety Open Side
10. Wallet Open Side, Side Seams
11. Penny Saver
12. Columbian Clasp
13. Pamphlet
14. Open End Catalog
15. Open End String & Button
16. Safety Express
17. Single Metal Tongue Reversible
18. Coin
19. Cabinet
20. Tag Envelope

Standard Sizes of Envelopes

PAY

No. 2	2½x4¼
No. 1½	2 9/16x4

COMMERCIAL

No. 5	3 1/16x5½
No. 6	3⅜x6
No. 6¼	3½x6
No. 6¾	3⅝x6½

OFFICIAL

No. 7	3¾x 6¾
No. 7½	3⅞x 7½
No. 8½	3⅝x 8⅜
No. 9	3⅞x 8⅞
No. 10	4⅛x 9½
No. 11	4½x10⅜
No. 12	4¾x11
No. 14	5 x11½

BARONIAL

No. 4	3⅝x4 11/16
No. 5	4⅛x5⅛
No. 5½	4⅜x5⅝
No. 6	5 x6

POLICY (Open and Official)

No. 9	4 x 9
No. 10	4⅛x 9½
No. 11	4½x10⅜

CATALOG

No. 0	2½x 4¼
No. 3	3 x 4½
No. 5	3⅛x 5½
No. 9	4 x 9
No. 9½	4⅛x 9½
No. 10	3⅜x 6
No. 11	4½x10⅜
No. 12	4¾x10⅞
No. 14	5 x11½
No. 15	4 x 6⅜
No. 20	3⅞x 7½
No. 25	4⅝x 6¾
No. 30	4⅞x 7¼
No. 35	5 x 7½
No. 40	5⅜x 7½
No. 45	5¼x 8
No. 50	5½x 8¼
No. 55	6 x 9
No. 60	6¼x 9½
No. 63	6½x 9½
No. 65	6½x10
No. 68	7 x10
No. 70	7 x10½
No. 75	7½x10½
No. 80	8 x11
No. 83	8½x11½
No. 90	9 x12
No. 93	9½x12½
No. 95	10 x12
No. 97	10 x13
No. 105	11½x14½

Major Group Classification	Kind of Paper	Substance (basis weights) Usually Available	Type of Press This Paper Most Often Used On: Letterpress: Job Press	Letterpress: Cylinder	Letterpress: Rotary	Offset	Rotary Gravure	Recommended Halftone Screen for Letterpress Printing
BOOK PAPERS BASIC SIZE 25 x 38	Machine Finish Book	45 to 70	x	x	x	x		75 to 100 Line
	English Finish Book	40 to 80	x	x	x	x		85 to 110 Line
	Super-Calendered Book	45 to 80	x	x	x	x	x	100 to 120 Line
	Offset Book	50 to 150		x		x		
	Text Paper	60 to 80	x	x		x		55 to 85 Line
	Coated (Enameled) Book	60 to 100	x	x		x		120 to 150 Line

GENERAL DESCRIPTION AND COMMON USES

Lowest grade of book or halftone paper having a medium finish which is obtained from the calender stack on the paper machine. Often called by its abbreviation—M.F. Used on low-quality books, catalogs, and circulars. When hard-sized, may be used for label printing and inexpensive jobs run on offset presses.

This type of paper has a smoother, more even finish than M.F., and is more heavily loaded with mineral fillers, though it is still finished on the paper machine. Available in several grades to suit various requirements of finish, whiteness and folding strength. The cheaper grades are widely used for package inserts, publications, and catalog work. Better grades for schoolbooks, pamphlets, etc.

Commonly referred to as S. & S.C.; this sheet has a higher, glossier finish (obtained after leaving the paper machine by passing through a series of hot and cold rolls called the calender stack), has less bulk and is more transparent than E.F. of the same weight and quality. Like E.F., Super also comes in various grades for particular requirements. Super is usually used in books, catalogs and pamphlets that require a fairly smooth surface for halftone illustrations.

An uncoated paper specially made for offset lithography, particular efforts being taken to build into the sheet qualities that minimize distortion from stretching, shrinking, and curling. The sheet must be clean, free from fuzz and have a hard-sized surface. Generally available in three grades and can be obtained in white and several pastel colors in regular, antique, and a large variety of "fancy" finishes such as linen, crash, stucco, handmade, etc. Though it may be run letterpress or sheet-fed gravure successfully if properly sized, Offset paper is used almost exclusively on offset presses for practically all types of work from single color leaflets to multicolor books and broadsides.

A high grade paper of good texture and appearance, often made with some rag-pulp. Available in white and colors with rough finishes such as eggshell, antique, felt, wove, and laid; sometimes watermarked and deckle-edged. Widely used for books, fine brochures, announcements, mailing pieces, etc.

Coated or Enamel paper comes in a number of grades of "folding" and "printing" qualities. Some grades are available in pastel colors. Enameled book can be had in gloss or dull finish. As indicated by its name, the paper is covered or "coated" with fine clay in combination with other materials. The smoother and more even the surface, the finer the screen halftone that can be reproduced upon it. Halftone screens on dull-coated sheets should be 120-line or coarser. This is the most practical and most commonly used paper where good color process or black halftone reproduction is to be obtained. The "folding" grades are used for folders, pamphlet and catalog covers, etc., where strength is an important factor. "Printing" grades are used for brochures, color inserts, direct-mail pieces, and other jobs requiring maximum smoothness for fine halftone reproduction. Coated paper specially sized and coated for offset lithography is available. Coated-one-side is used for label work, box-wraps, and printing or lithographing of sheets later to be mounted on heavy board for window displays.

Major Group Classification	Kind of Paper	Substance (basis weights) Usually Available	Type of Press This Paper Most Often Used On: Letterpress — Job Press	Letterpress — Cylinder	Letterpress — Rotary	Offset	Sheet-Fed Gravure	Rotary Gravure	Recommended Halftone Screen for Letterpress Printing
COVER PAPERS BASIC SIZE 20 x 26	Coated Cover		x	x		x			120 to 150 Line
	Rag-Content Cover	25 to 50 (Light) 50 to 65 (Medium)	x	x		x	x		
	Handmade Cover	65 to 130 (Heavy)	x	x		x	x		
	Metallic Cover		x	x		x			85 to 110 Line
WRITING PAPERS BASIC SIZE 17 x 22	Railroad Manila	14 to 20	x	x		x			65 to 85 Line
	Mimeo Paper	16 to 28	x						65 to 85 Line
	Sulphite Bond	13 to 28	x	x		x			85 to 110 Line
	Rag-Content Bond	13 to 28	x	x		x			
	Ledger	24 to 40	x			x			85 to 110 Line
	Wedding Paper	28 to 40	x						

GENERAL DESCRIPTION AND COMMON USES

In the heavier weights, the coated book papers also serve as excellent cover papers when a surface is sought to take a fine halftone screen or color process plates. The covers may be glossy coated, dull coated, duplex coated, or coated for offset.

Like rag-content bond, cover stocks are made of a furnish having 25 per cent to 100 per cent rag. Surface without special finish is known as antique surface, but many rag-content covers are specially embossed with so-called "fancy finishes."

Materials generally are rag, and each sheet is made individually with a deckle on all four sides. Handmade covers are limited largely to type and line cuts unless they are engraved or embossed, or printed by offset or sheet-fed gravure.

Metallic covers are fashioned by affixing a pigment composed of metal flakes such as aluminum or bronze powder to regular cover paper by means of either casein or lacquer. They have a smooth printing surface, but one that requires special inks and craftsmanship.

Usually a groundwood grade of writing paper, sized for pen-and-ink writing. Available in 2 or 3 colors—of which yellow is most popular. Used for school tablets, second sheets for typewriting, order blanks, and sales books.

A special type of soft sized, semiabsorbent writing paper available in several colors and grades ranging from sulphite to rag content with wove or laid finish. Used almost exclusively for letterheads and other forms which are to be processed on the Mimeograph machine.

Sulphite Bond papers are made of bleached chemical pulps, hard sized, and usually have a fairly smooth finish similar to E.F. Some bonds are available in linen, ripple, and other finishes, and often in 10 to 12 colors. They are made in four grades, of which the two higher grades may be watermarked. Used for office forms, letterheads, envelopes, and other commercial purposes.

Rag Bonds contain from 25 per cent to 100 per cent rag fibers, are hard sized, and some of the better grades are loft dried. All grades are usually watermarked. The outstanding characteristics are: Rich feel and appearance, "crackle," permanence, and strength. Originally made for government bonds and insurance policies, they are now also used in fine stationery and better grades of commercial letterheads and envelopes. Printing halftones on rag bond by letterpress is not recommended. Much of this paper is used in lithographing and steel engraving.

Like Bond papers, Ledger is available in rag, rag-content, and sulphite grades; usually white or buff. Though often used for ledger and other bookkeeping forms, its folding qualities and excellent writing, ruling, and typewriting surface make it suitable for maps, wills, certificates, bankbooks, and other items requiring unusual permanency and handling qualities.

A fine quality writing paper available in several finishes—kid, plate, and linen. Particularly suited to steel engraving and fine commercial and wedding announcements; often used for social correspondence.

Major Group Classification	Kind of Paper	Substance (basis weights) Usually Available	Type of Press This Paper Most Often Used On						Recommended Halftone Screen for Letterpress Printing
			Letter-press						
			Job Press	Cylinder	Rotary	Offset	Sheet-Fed Gravure	Rotary Gravure	
NEWS-PRINT BASIC SIZE 24 x 36	Standard Newsprint	32 to 35	x	x	x	x			55 to 65 Line
	Halftone News	32 to 55	x	x	x			x	65 to 100 Line
	Colored Poster	32 to 35	x	x	x				65 to 85 Line
	Catalog News	19 to 30			x			x	65 to 100 Line
	Novel News	32 to 35		x	x				55 Line
THIN PAPERS	Bible Paper Basic Size 25 x 38	20 to 40		x					100 to 110 Line
	Onionskin Basic Size 17 x 22	7 to 10	x						100 to 110 Line
	French Writing Basic Size 17 x 22	9 to 10	x	x					

GENERAL DESCRIPTION AND COMMON USES

This paper is made largely of mechanical wood pulp. As the name implies, it is used principally for newspapers and other short-lived printed pieces. It is available in white and pastel shades of pink, peach, green, and salmon.

Similar to Standard Newsprint but has a somewhat harder, smoother finish produced by the addition of mineral fillers and a higher machine finish. Used where a finer halftone screen is required than can be effectively printed on Standard Newsprint.

Resembles Standard Newsprint, though somewhat stronger. Usually used in a range of six colors (deeper than Standard Newsprint) for printing sales bills, throw-aways, circulars, and other pieces requiring inexpensive colored stock.

A lightweight, opaque paper with fair strength for its weight. Made principally of groundwood pulp and is machine finished. Used for seed and mail-order catalogs and directories of wide circulation where mailing weight and paper bulk are a major consideration.

This sheet is made with a rough finish to lend bulk to the finished book; approximately 25 per cent thicker than Standard Newsprint of the same weight. Sometimes called "Bulking" News. Used in cheap novels or "pulp" magazines such as western or detective thriller stories.

A thin, opaque book paper of relatively good strength, sometimes called India or Oxford India paper. Usually made with a percentage of rag pulp to withstand considerable handling. Originally developed in England for use in Bibles. Used in books, dictionaries, encyclopedias, insurance rate books, and other purposes where small bulk, strength and opacity are important. An excellent paper for use where the dual qualities of lightness and opacity are prime requisites in jobs printing on both sides of the sheet.

Onionskin is a thin, lightweight and somewhat transparent paper having typical Bond paper characteristics. Printing qualities in this sheet are not quite as essential as strength and smoothness. Available in several colors. Principally used for manifold purposes where several copies are made at one time by interleaving carbon paper on such work as shop orders, schedules, copies of reports, etc. Also coming into wide use for air-mail correspondence and manuscript copies, to save postage.

A thin, evenly finished writing paper also known as French Folio. It is somewhat transparent. Available in white and several colors; hard sized for writing. Used for pulling printers' proofs and for make-ready on printing presses. Also suitable for price lists, carbon copies, lightweight circulars, and other material requiring the use of only one side of the sheet.

How to Select the Right Page Size to Avoid Wasting Paper Stock

Economical Page or Form Sizes (Inches)	Standard Bond and Ledger Sizes (Inches)	Number of Pages Which May Be Cut from Full Size Sheets	Number of Pages or Forms to Ream
2⅛ x 2¾	17 x 22	64	32M
2⅛ x 3½	17 x 28	64	32M
2⅛ x 5½	17 x 22	32	16M
2⅛ x 7	17 x 28	32	16M
2⅜ x 3	19 x 24	64	32M
2⅜ x 6	19 x 24	32	16M
2¾ x 4¼	17 x 22	32	16M
2¾ x 8½	17 x 22	16	8M
3 x 4¾	19 x 24	32	16M
3 x 9½	19 x 24	16	8M
3½ x 4¼	17 x 28	32	16M
3½ x 8½	17 x 28	16	8M
4 x 8½	17 x 28	14	7M
4 x 9½	19 x 24	12	6M
4¼ x 5½	17 x 22	16	8M
4¼ x 7	17 x 28	16	8M
4¼ x 11	17 x 22	8	4M
4¼ x 14	17 x 28	8	4M
4¾ x 4	19 x 24	24	12M
4¾ x 6	19 x 24	16	8M
4¾ x 8	19 x 24	12	6M
5½ x 8½	17 x 22	8	4M
5½ x 17	17 x 22	4	2M
6 x 9½	19 x 24	8	4M
6 x 19	19 x 24	4	2M
7 x 8½	17 x 28	8	4M
7 x 17	17 x 28	4	2M
8 x 9½	19 x 24	6	3M
8 x 19	19 x 24	3	1½M
8½ x 11	17 x 22	4	2M
8½ x 14	17 x 28	4	2M
8½ x 22	17 x 22	2	1M
8½ x 28	17 x 28	2	1M
9½ x 12	19 x 24	4	2M
11 x 17	17 x 22	2	1M
12 x 19	19 x 24	2	1M
14 x 17	17 x 28	2	1M
17 x 22	17 x 22	1	½M
17 x 28	17 x 28	1	½M

Amount of Paper Required

Broadsides and Folders

Flat Size	Cuts out of	Sheets required for 1,000 copies
22½ x 35	35 x 45	500
22 x 32	32 x 44	500
22 x 28	28 x 44	500
21 x 28	28 x 42	500
19 x 25	25 x 38	500
17½ x 22½	35 x 45	250
16 x 22	32 x 44	250
14 x 22	28 x 44	250
14 x 21	28 x 42	250
12½ x 19	25 x 38	250
11¼ x 17½	35 x 45	125
11 x 16	32 x 44	125
11 x 14	28 x 44	125
10½ x 14	28 x 42	125
9½ x 12½	25 x 38	125
8¾ x 11¼	35 x 45	63
8 x 11	32 x 44	63
7 x 11	28 x 44	63
7 x 10½	28 x 42	63
6¼ x 9½	25 x 38	63
5⅝ x 8¾	35 x 45	32
5½ x 8	32 x 44	32
5½ x 7	28 x 44	32
5¼ x 7	28 x 42	32
4¾ x 6¼	25 x 38	32

NOTE: The above figures are net requirements of paper with no allowance for spoilage. For broadsides and folders, they are based on the assumption that no trim is required; for booklets, catalogs and envelope enclosures, trim area is included. No allowance is made for bleed.

—Compiled by *Advertising Requirements*

Booklets—Catalogs

Trimmed Size	Cuts out of	Sheets required for 1,000 copies: 8 pages	16 pages	32 pages
9¼ x 12⅛	38 x 50	250	500	1000
8½ x 11	35 x 45	250	500	1000
7¾ x 10⅝	32 x 44	250	500	1000
6 x 9⅛	25 x 38	250	500	1000
5½ x 8½	35 x 45	125	250	500
5¼ x 7⅝	32 x 44	125	250	500
4 x 9⅛	38 x 50	84	167	334
4½ x 6	25 x 38	125	250	500
4¼ x 5⅜	35 x 45	63	125	250
3¾ x 5⅛	32 x 44	63	125	250

Envelope Enclosures

		Cuts out of	Sheets required for 1,000 copies
4-pages	3½ x 6¼	28 x 44	42
4-pages	3 x 6⅛	25 x 38	42
6-pages	3½ x 6¼	28 x 44	63
6-pages	3 x 6⅛	25 x 38	63

Envelope Requirements

PAGE SIZE TRIMMED	STANDARD ENVELOPE SIZE	
3⅛ x 6¼"	3⅝ x 6½"	(No. 6¾ Commercial)
4 x 6"	4¾ x 6½"	(No. 3 Booklet)
5 x 7"	5½ x 8⅛"	(No. 5 Booklet)
5½ x 8½"	6 x 9"	(No. 1 Catalog)
6 x 9"	6½ x 9½"	(No. 1¾ Catalog)
7 x 10"	7½ x 10½"	(No. 6 Catalog)
7¾ x 10⅝"	8¼ x 11¼"	(No. 8 Catalog)
8½ x 11"	9 x 12"	(No. 10½ Catalog)
9 x 12"	9½ x 12½"	(No. 12½ Catalog)
11 x 14"	11½ x 14½"	(No. 14½ Catalog)

Comparative Weights of Paper Sheets

Figured to Nearest Half Pound of Standard Sizes

BOOK PAPERS, COATED AND UNCOATED

25 x 38 Basis	30	35	40	45	50	60	70	80	90*	100	120*
22 x32	22	26	29½	33½	37	44½	52	59½	66½	74	89
24 x36	27	32	36	41	45	55	64	73	82	91	109
25 x38	30	35	40	45	50	60	70	80	90	100	120
26 x29	24	28	32	36	40	48	56	63	71	79	95
26 x40	33	38	44	49	55	66	77	88	99	109	131
28 x42	37	43	50	56	62	74	87	99	111	124	149
28 x44	39	45	52	58	65	78	91	104	117	130	156
29 x52	48	56	64	72	80	96	112	126	142	158	190
30½x41	39	46	53	59	66	79	92	105	118	132	158
32 x44	44	52	59	67	74	89	104	119	133	148	178
33 x46	48	56	64	72	80	96	112	128	144	160	192
34 x44	47	55	63	71	79	94	110	126	142	157	189
35 x45	50	58	66	75	83	99	116	133	149	166	199
36 x48	54	64	72	82	90	110	128	146	164	182	218
38 x50	60	70	80	90	100	120	140	160	180	200	240
41 x61	78	92	106	118	132	158	184	210	236	264	316
42 x56	74	86	100	112	124	148	174	198	222	248	298
44 x56	78	90	104	116	130	156	182	208	234	260	312
44 x64	88	104	118	134	148	178	208	238	266	296	356

***Applies only to coated papers.**

BOND, LEDGER, AND FLAT WRITING PAPER

17 x 22 Basis	13	16	20	24	28	32	36	40	44
16 x21	11½	14½	18	21½	25	28½	32½	36	39½
17 x22	13	16	20	24	28	32	36	40	44
18 x23	14½	17½	22	26½	31	35½	40	44½	48½
19 x24	16	19½	24½	29½	34	39	44	49	53½
17 x28	16½	20½	25½	30½	35½	40½	46	51	56
19 x26	17	21	26½	31½	37	42½	47½	53	58
22½x22½	17½	21½	27	32½	38	43½	48½	54	59½
22½x24½	19	23½	29½	35½	41½	47	53	59	65
20 x28	19½	24	30	36	42	48	54	60	66
22 x25½	19½	24	30	36	42	48	54	60	66
24½x24½	21	25½	32	38½	45	51½	58	64	70½
22½x28½	22½	27½	34½	41	48	55	61½	68½	75½
21 x32	23	29	36	43	50	57	65	72	79
16 x42	23	29	36	43	50	57	65	72	79
24½x28½	24½	30	37½	45	52½	59½	67	74½	82
24½x29	24½	30½	38	45½	53	61	68½	76	83½
22 x34	26	32	40	48	56	64	72	80	88
23 x36	29	35	44	53	62	71	80	89	97
18 x46	29	35	44	53	62	71	80	89	97
24 x38	32	39	49	59	68	78	88	98	107
28 x34	33	41	51	61	71	81	92	102	112
25½x44	39	48	60	72	84	96	108	120	132
34 x44	52	64	80	96	112	128	144	160	176

COVER PAPER

20 x 26 Basis	25	35	40	50	65	80	90
20x26	25	35	40	50	65	80	90
23x33	36½	51	58½	73	95	117	131
26x40	50	70	80	100	130	160	180
33x46	73	102	117	146	190	234	262

Chart of Paper Characteristics

TYPE OF PAPER	SURFACE		COLORS	DENSITY	STRENGTH
	1-rough 10-smooth	1-soft 10-hard	1-white only 10-wide range	1-loose 10-firm	1-weak 10-strong
BOOK					
Antique	1	1	3	3	3
Laid	2	2	3	4	3
Eggshell	2	2	3	3	3
Plate	4	5	3	4	3
Machine F.	3	4	3	3	3
English F.	4	4	3	4	3
Super-Cal'd	5	5	3	5	4
Bible (India)	4	5	3	7	6
R-gravure	5	5	1	4	5
Offset	2	4	3	4	4
Newsprint	2	1	1	2	1
Coated Gloss	9	7	3	5	4
Coated Dull	8	6	3	5	4
Coated Cast	10	7	5	5	5
Coated Offset	9	7	3	5	5
Coated Folding	9	7	3	5	7
COVER					
Antique	3	3	10	6	7
Plate	5	6	10	6	7
Coated	9	7	8	6	6
OFFICE					
Bond-Sulph.	6	8	10	8	6
Bond-Rag	6	8	5	8	9
Ledger-Rag	7	8	3	8	9
Duplicator	3-5	2-5	5	5	5
Bristol-Index	7	6	5	6	6
Bristol-Rag	7	6	5	6	8
Manifold	6	7	10	8	8
SPECIAL					
Blotting	2	1	5	1	2
Poster	2	1	5	2	1
Kraft	1	5	3	7	9
Tracing	8	9	1	9	4

NOTE: Ratings apply to general types of paper, not to specific brands. Their purpose is to aid the planner of printing to select a suitable kind of paper for the specific job.

Chart of Paper Characteristics—Continued

OPACITY 1-low 10-high	REFLECTIVITY 1-low 10-high	HALFTONE Screen Scale Maximum	COMMENTS	TYPE OF PAPER
				BOOK
9	1	50		Antique
9	1	50	Surface pattern	Laid
9	1	65		Eggshell
9	2	65	Plate; Linen; Ripple	Plate
8	3	100		Machine F.
8	3	110		English F.
8	4	120		Super-Cal'd
6	2	110	Very thin; opaque	Bible (India)
8	3		In rolls	R-gravure
8	1	65		Offset
7	1	65-85		Newsprint
9	9	200		Coated Gloss
9	4	150		Coated Dull
9	10	200	Also coated 1 side	Coated Cast
9	9	200		Coated Offset
9	9	200		Coated Folding
				COVER
10	1	65		Antique
10	4	85-100	Plate; Ripple	Plate
10	7	150		Coated
				OFFICE
6	3	100		Bond-Sulph.
6	3	100		Bond-Rag
7	3			Ledger-Rag
5	2			Duplicator
10	4			Bristol-Index
10	4		Drawing Board	Bristol-Rag
3	3		Thin; low opacity	Manifold
				SPECIAL
10	1			Blotting
7	1		Like newsprint	Poster
10	1			Kraft
1	3		Nearly transparent	Tracing

(Prepared by Frederic Kammann for *Advertising Requirements*)

Equivalent Weights

OF VARIOUS TYPES OF PAPER IN REAMS OF 500 SHEETS

EQUIVALENTS FOR	BOOK 25 by 38	BOND 17 by 22	COVER 20 by 26	BRISTOL 22½ by 35	INDEX 20½ by 24¾
	30	12	16	25	16
	40	16	22	33	21
	45	18	25	37	24
	50	20	27	41	27
	55	22	30	46	29
	60	24	33	50	32
Book	65	26	36	54	35
	70	28	38	58	37
	75	30	41	62	40
	80	31	44	66	43
	90	35	49	75	48
	100	39	55	83	53
	120	47	66	99	64
	33	13	18	27	18
	41	16	22	34	22
	51	20	28	42	27
Bond	61	24	33	51	33
	71	28	39	59	38
	81	32	45	67	43
	91	36	50	76	49
	102	40	56	89	54
	46	18	25	38	24
	64	25	35	53	34
	73	29	40	61	39
	91	36	50	76	49
Cover	100	40	55	83	54
	110	43	60	91	59
	119	47	65	98	63
	146	58	80	121	78
	164	65	90	136	88
	183	72	100	151	98
	133	52	73	110	71
	151	59	83	125	81
Bristol	181	71	99	150	97
	211	83	116	175	113
	241	95	132	200	129
	271	107	149	225	145
	110	43	60	91	58½
Index	135	53	74	112	72
	170	67	93	141	91
	208	82	114	172	111

The above table shows standard basis weights and indicates what those weights become when translated from one basis to another basis. For example, a reference to the Writing or Bond shows that 24-pound Bond is the equivalent of a 60-pound Book paper, a 33-pound Cover and a 33-pound Index paper.

COMPARISON OF COST OF STANDARD SIZES AND SPECIAL SIZES

Book Papers—2,000 to 5,000 pounds

The differential for special sizes in lots of 2,000 to 5,000 pounds is 10 percent. In many cases the adding of this differential makes a special size order cost more than the same number of sheets in the next larger standard size. Often, therefore, it is cheaper to order the next larger standard size.

The following table will be of help to you in arriving at the advantageous size to buy:

Standard 38 by 50

If you require a special size in between these two, buy 38 by 50. For example: 36½ by 48½ with the 10 percent differential added will cost more than 38 by 50.

Standard 36 by 48

The standard size 36 by 48 is cheaper than a special size 35½ by 45½.

Standard 35 by 45

If you need 32½ by 44½ you can buy 35 by 45 for the same price or slightly less.

Standard 32 by 44

If you require a special size 29 by 44 you can buy 32 by 44 for the same price. 29½ by 44 will cost more than 32 by 44.

Standard 28 by 44

The 28 by 44 is cheaper than any special size down to the next standard 28 by 42.

Standard 28 by 42

A special size 26½ by 41 will cost as much as the standard size 28 by 42. For sizes between 26½ by 41 and 28 by 42 buy the 28 by 42 for a savings in money.

Standard 26 by 40

Any special size in between 26 by 40 and 25 by 38 will cost more than 26 by 40. Buy 26 by 40 as a saving.

Standard 25 by 38

Buy the 25 by 38 size as more economical than any size in between these two.

Standard 24 by 36

(From *Printing Papers and Their Uses*, published by S. D. Warren Co., Boston)

Chapter 47

TIPS ON COST CUTTING

ONE of the biggest advantages of the direct mail medium is its extreme flexibility—particularly in regard to costs. While certain minimum costs are fixed, due to such items as postal rates and list charges, the area of production presents wide latitude.

The following list of cost-cutting factors is by no means complete. In fact, each of the 175 suggestions included may automatically suggest other avenues for reducing costs. For convenience in reference, we have tried to group the ideas into basic production categories. However, there is a great deal of overlap between categories, and a thorough review of the complete list is suggested for those who are seeking opportunities to extend their direct mail budgets.

PLANNING

1. **Plan in advance:** By far the most important avenue for controlling direct mail costs is to plan all details carefully, well in advance of the mailing date, being sure to make allowances for emergencies and upsets. It is almost inevitable that a job planned and produced against tight deadlines will not only require sacrificing a certain degree of quality but will involve extra charges.

2. **Bring in suppliers:** The direct mail expert has yet to be born who knows all of the angles about both quality and economy. It is most advantageous to discuss each job in detail with *all* suppliers during the early planning stages. One mistake often made by direct mail advertisers is to limit planning discussions to only one or two suppliers, instead of seeking every ounce of help from everyone who will become involved in the eventual job. Among those who should be included in initial planning stages are:

Printer	Typographer
Artist	Photographer
Paper Supplier	Envelope Supplier
Lettershop	Copywriter
Art Director	Production Supervisor
Photoengraver	Binder
List Supplier	Postal Officials

3. **Seek suggestions from all:** When seeking planning help from suppliers, do not limit this help to the specific area of production in which these suppliers are involved. Very often, for example, the best ideas on art will come from the printer, the paper supplier, or the photoengraver, while the artist may offer valuable tips on printing, paper, and engraving. By all means, inform each of the suppliers of all contemplated production plans so they can tailor their help to the conditions under which they will work.

4. **Check the post office:** It is amazing how many seemingly wonderful direct mail jobs hit a sudden snag when arriving at the door of the local post office. The safest rule to follow is to check every planned mailing with the postal officials before a single sheet has been printed. Never assume a mailing meets postal requirements or can be handled properly. Take a few moments to make this check during planning stages, and, in the long run, you will save yourself a lot of headaches.

5. **Keep planning:** Do not assume all your planning is completed when you have a finished layout in hand and every supplier has furnished his bid. Continually check with suppliers as a job progresses. For example, before the art is sent off to the engraver, check with the printer and paper supplier to make sure it is "right" for the job. (On the other hand, do not make these control checks a major project requiring an undue amount of time on the part of your suppliers. Some direct mail advertisers have been known to call full-blown production conferences requiring hours of time every few days. Time is an expense to most suppliers, and it will show up as an added cost somewhere if the buyer is unreasonable in his demands.)

6. **Set a schedule:** Once a job has been planned, set a specific production schedule, with deadlines for all concerned. Make sure the deadlines are realistic and acceptable to everybody—and then make sure each supplier sticks to what he has promised.

7. **Assign a liaison man:** Establish a single liaison man within your organization for each job, and then insist all suppliers work through this individual. This will not only save time for suppliers, but will avoid contradictory decisions and make sure no important factor falls between two members of your staff—each believing the other has taken care of it.

8. **Do not be too rigid on specifications:** When asking quotations from suppliers, make your specifications clear, but not too rigid. Allow them to make suggestions for changes which can introduce economies without affecting the quality or utility of the job, or which will yield better results within the same budget limitations.

9. **Project future needs:** Whenever possible, project your future needs for a given direct mail piece. In almost every case, it is much less expensive to order larger quantities during the initial production, rather than to plan on reprints at a later date.

10. **But do not overstock:** On the other hand, it is often false economy to just guess you *might* need additional quantities and then let them gather dust on stockroom shelves, forgotten, because no specific plans have been made for future utilization of the material.

11. **Keep inventory records:** Be sure to set up an active inventory record and control system which will always tell just what materials are on hand which can be utilized for any direct mail project.

12. **Avoid dating material:** Unless it is absolutely necessary, do not "date" direct mail material. An "old" piece can often be used again if it is not made obsolete by dating in original production. Some of the factors to consider are clothing and hair style on models, calendars or identifiable issues of publications in illustrations, copyright or "cover" dates, etc.

13. **Check additional uses:** Every element of direct mail production and individual finished pieces can have possible additional uses if such planning is considered in advance. Art, typography, and engravings, for example, can often be utilized for other printed material. Folders, brochures, and booklets may provide excellent aids for salesmen.

14. **Establish standards:** If you frequently repeat different types of direct mail material, an established set of basic standards can often provide substantial economies. Basic typography standards, for example, not only permit reuse of much material

but they reduce time required for specifications and also aid in planning other elements. The same is true of other production factors such as artwork, engravings, paper, envelopes, etc.

ARTWORK AND PHOTOGRAPHY

15. Gang orders: In dealing with artists and photographers, it is wise to make multiple assignments whenever possible. Contact and delivery time is an important cost factor. Anything which can be done to reduce such time expenditures will result in reduced costs.

16. Build a file: Always keep a well-indexed file of art and photography used for previous jobs. Even if it is not possible to use a given illustration "as is," it can often be used as a starting point and revised to meet a specific requirement at less cost than completely new art.

17. Consider stock art and photos: If your direct mail does not absolutely require completely original illustrations, always consider the use of stock illustrations. Such material is considerably less expensive than originals. Even if an original touch is required, stock materials may very easily be the starting point. Again, revisions are usually less costly than completely original material. An additional advantage is that you can save time because you know in advance what the finished illustration will look like.

18. How about "free" art and photos? There are hundreds of sources for art and photography at no cost to you. Many firms maintain a large library of illustrations which are available just for the asking. One of the best sources is the Federal Government. Almost every Government agency has an impressive file of illustrative material available at little or no cost. Other excellent sources are trade associations, chambers of commerce, airlines and railroads, travel bureaus, public relations agencies, and public libraries.

19. Veloxes and conversions: Consider the use of "screened veloxes" or line conversions of continuous-tone photographs. Both techniques can produce special art effects economically, in addition to reducing costs of engravings and making printing on less expensive paper stocks practical. A screened velox is simply a photograph which has a halftone screen included in the print. These are particularly useful when it is necessary to drop out certain areas of an illustration, paint in solid areas, or outline the illustration—jobs which can be costly in the platemaking process, but which can often be handled inexpensively by an artist.

Line conversions have the same advantage but utilize designs other than halftone dots for converting a continuous-tone illustration such as a photograph to black-and-white "lines." Both types of illustrations can utilize line engravings rather than more costly halftones. *Caution:* Be sure to check requirements with your printer and/or engraver in advance and select a photographer who is experienced in handling conversions.

20. Use shading tints: You can often obtain continuous-tone effects by utilizing shading tints or special artists' drawing boards with built-in shading effects. If you are not acquainted with this cost-cutting method, have your artist show you the wide variety of effects possible.

21. Keep layouts clean: A clean layout, without any extraneous markings, will help reduce costs up and down the line.

22. Use tissue overlays: When instructions are required—and they should be kept as simple and as few as possible—put them on a tissue overlay. In this way, instructions can be directed to the specific area involved. Marking up an original layout just confuses everybody.

23. Avoid close registration: Whenever possible, avoid close registration of colors or different elements. This will save considerable time in all phases of production and frequently will eliminate costly extra charges. It also reduces rejects in printing.

24. Know the printing process: Decide the printing process to be used for reproduction before preparing final artwork. Then the artist can work within the limitations of the chosen process and tailor his work to obtain the highest possible quality and the lowest possible cost.

25. Establish a budget: When dealing with artists, it is always best to clearly establish all budget limitations—not only what can be allowed for artwork, but the money limitations for the entire job. An experienced artist can tailor the design and artwork to achieve the best possible effect for the dollars available.

26. Consider finished art finished: Do not make changes in finished art. The time to make changes is in the initial layout or rough art stage.

27. **Pre-separate art**: For multicolor artwork, have the artist prepare colors on acetate overlays. In most every case, it will be less costly for the artist to do the color separation than to assign this task to the platemaker.

28. **Use standard reductions**: When a number of pieces of art will be required for a job, ask the artist to prepare all material either same size or for a standard percentage reduction. This will permit economies in platemaking and layout.

29. **Use cartoons**: One of the least expensive types of artwork is the cartoon. You can buy excellent cartoons for as little as $10 each, even from many established cartoonists. (Like all artwork, however, you should expect to pay more for work from "name" cartoonists or if your requirements are strict and considerable contact time is required.) An additional advantage of cartoons is that they can usually be reproduced less expensively. Cartoons also lend themselves well to extensive reuse and revised treatments.

30. **Build reuse into art**: A single piece of artwork can often be converted into dozens of *different* illustrations through reductions, enlargements, cropping, color changes, different engraving techniques, etc. Such multiple uses are most practical if they are planned in advance and the art is tailored to adaptation.

TYPOGRAPHY

31. **Choose the right process**: Type can be set in a variety of different ways. But there is usually one right way for any given job. Consult with your typographer to tailor your specifications to the most economical typesetting process for your job.

32. **Give clear instructions**: Nothing can increase costs of typography as rapidly as confusing instructions. Take time to spell out specifically what you want and check with your typographer to make sure everything is clear before the job is put into production.

33. **Prepare clean copy**: One of the most important rules of thumb in direct mail production is to always remember that you can hire a typist for at least an hour for what you would spend for ten minutes of a typographer's time. Thus, clean copy can be a major economy. Always retype a heavily corrected manuscript before sending it out for typesetting.

34. Proper copy style: All manuscripts should be typewritten on 8½- by 11-inch sheets with two- or three-line spacing. Leave ample margins for revisions and instructions. Number pages to preserve correct order, and place the numbers in the same place on each sheet. If clippings or other odd-size materials are to be included in copy, paste them on 8½- by 11-inch sheets which can be included in order in the manuscript. Be sure to indicate the end of the manuscript. And type with a good, black ribbon.

35. Master copy: Always maintain one master copy of a manuscript. If a number of people are responsible for checking copies of the manuscript, transfer their corrections to this master copy (usually with identification marks to indicate who called for the correction). Retype copy with changes before ordering typesetting and read the retyped copy against the master.

36. Duplicate copy: Always retain an exact duplicate of copy sent to the typographer, complete with instructions. This will enable accurate and quick reference if questions arise.

37. Duplicate copies for the typographer: When a manuscript calls for more than one type of typesetting, it is usually advisable to furnish the typographer with extra copies of the manuscript, so each individual typesetter will have a copy with which to work. This is particularly important when time is a factor, since it enables two or more typesetters to work on the copy at the same time. Be sure all copies are completely legible.

38. Colored instructions: Use colored pencils for instructions to the typographer and save the black pencil for corrections on the copy. It is often helpful to use different colors for instructions for different types of typesetting. Check with your typographer to determine his preference in this matter.

39. Rubber stamps: If you tend to order the same typefaces in the same style frequently, have a set of rubber stamps made to cover the more common situations. This will not only speed up the job of preparing copy for the typographer, but will make sure all information is clear and complete.

40. Copy sheets: If your volume of standardized typography is even greater, have printed copy sheets prepared. Proper design will save time in estimating copy, specifying typefaces, and in avoiding mistakes. Your printer or typographer can probably supply you with sample designs.

41. Develop a style manual: Establish a standard style for your copy. The best starting point is to adopt one of the standard style manuals, such as those published by the *New York Times,* University of Chicago Press, Government Printing Office, etc. Then add to this standard manual your own list of preferred spellings of words that occur frequently in your copy and a list of deviations, if any, from the manual. Make sure your typographer has a copy of this complete style guide. This procedure will not only simplify copy preparation but produce substantial economies in typesetting, proofreading, and eliminating expensive alterations.

42. **Deal with one typographer:** In the long run, you will probably save money by sticking to a single typographer or a limited number of typographers. As they become familiar with your special requirements, they can reduce time required to handle your copy. This is particularly important if you have many special style requirements.

43. **Cast copy accurately:** Do not just guess how much copy it takes to fill a given space. There are plenty of methods for tailoring copy to fit a space—or for determining the amount of space required for a given amount of copy set a certain way. Learn one of these systems and use it regularly.

44. **Make alterations in manuscript:** Any alterations in type cost money. So the right time to make alterations is while copy is still in manuscript form.

45. **Get layout approved:** If your final layout requires approvals, be sure to obtain them before copy is sent out for typesetting.

46. **Avoid telephone alterations:** Unless tight deadlines offer no alternative, never make alterations over the telephone. Not only is it time-consuming, but the chance for additional errors is great. Send back proofs with changes clearly marked.

47. **Use galley proofs:** Many direct mail advertisers make the mistake of thinking they will save money by having the typographer make up copy to fit a specific layout before reproduction proofs are pulled. In most cases, it will be less expensive to just have the typographer pull galley proofs and then have an artist paste material into position. This is not always true, however, so be sure to check the best procedure for each job. Remember, too, that you will generally get better alignment of horizontal material on the typographer's stone or in a camera than on a drawing board, particularly if a lot of material requiring special spacing is involved.

48. Get a "style" approved: When a lot of typesetting is involved and the style must be approved by several people, it is usually a good idea to have a trial sample set for approvals. Then use this sample as a basic guide for typesetting once it has received an okay.

49. Control proof ordering: Do not order more proofs than you need. Typographers have a standard number of proofs which they provide at no additional charge. Extra proofs entail additional charges. So do not fall into the trap of ordering extra proofs unless they are absolutely essential.

50. Get approvals before repros: When reproduction proofs are to be the end product from the typographer, it is usually best to first get a set of rough proofs, check them for typographic errors and alterations, and then order reproduction proofs after copy has been fully okayed.

51. Group jobs: A lot of little jobs always cost more when ordered one at a time. Whenever possible, gang as many jobs as possible—both in ordering and on proofs.

52. Avoid super-rush jobs: Give your typographer as much time as possible to complete your job. This will enable him to handle it in the most economical way possible—avoiding overtime and reducing the chance for errors.

53. Consider photo-lettering: When just a few words of display type are required, it is often less expensive to order photo-lettering rather than regular display typography. And with the wide variety of photo-lettering styles available today, you can usually use it in place of much more costly hand-lettering for the majority of jobs. If you do not already have one, get a book of styles available from a convenient photo-lettering organization and keep it handy for reference on all jobs.

54. Take advantage of type ornaments: An often overlooked avenue of production economy is the use of typographic ornaments. Your printer or typographer probably has hundreds of them available for your use, and often they can substitute for much more costly artwork.

55. Avoid vertical rules: When preparing charts, you can save a lot of money and time by having the typographer insert only the horizontal lines. Vertical lines can then be added by an artist. Or if the job is to be run in two colors, use the basic color for copy and horizontal rules and have the vertical rules set to run in the second color. If both horizontal and vertical rules are handled by the typographer for one color printing, it requires setting each column of material separately or sawing slugs apart to allow insertion of vertical rules. The net result is not only greater cost, but greater chance for error and poorer quality. Even if you are printing by letterpress, it may easily be more economical to have an artist draw in the vertical rules on a reproduction proof and then have an engraving made, rather than to have the whole job handled by a typographer.

56. **Allow typographer options:** The typographer can be of special assistance if given the latitude to alter copy slightly to achieve best results. For example, if you want to avoid widows (single words or short lines at the end of copy), you can indicate optional words which can be "cut if necessary." And when you have a series of words where the exact order is unimportant, the typographer can do his job better and faster if he has the option of changing the order to suit typesetting convenience. It is far better to note these options in the beginning rather than to send back proofs for resetting with alterations.

57. **Use proper marks:** Learn and use the accepted copyreaders' and proofreaders' marks. Do not make the typographer guess what you want. The time he takes for guessing ends up on your bill—plus the cost of alterations required when he does not come to the right conclusions.

58. **Check sources in advance:** Not every typographer will have all the specific typefaces your job may require. Whenever possible, work within the limits of the type selection offered by a single typographer. If he has to send out for some of the elements of your job, there are bound to be delays and increased cost.

59. **Consider typewriter composition:** For many types of direct mail jobs, typewriter composition is just as practical as more costly "hot-type" or photo composition.

60. **Build a proof file:** Save extra reproduction proofs of frequently used material such as your company name, address, and phone number; product names; logotypes; etc. These will come in handy for future jobs and are particularly valuable when they are set in a different face than will be used for other copy.

61. **Double-check the obvious:** One of the most common mistakes is to overlook careful checking of frequently repeated material such as the company name and address. Since such copy is so "automatic," it may be overlooked on the original

copy and in the first proofreading. Thus, there is great chance for errors to creep in. So make a mental note to *always* double-check the obvious.

PLATEMAKING

62. Gang engravings for economy: When ordering engravings, always try to combine same-reduction copy. For line copy, it is best to paste up all items with common reductions, have them prepared as one engraving, and then cut them apart. For half-tones do not try pasting up material for later sawing apart, since chances are there will be differences in tonal range which can be easily handled in the camera when "shot" individually. If the material is pasted up together, expensive handwork is likely to be required to get the best quality. But most engravers will allow discounts when "same focus" copy is sent in the same order.

63. Same-size copy: For top economy, offer the engraver material to be reproduced in its original size.

64. Avoid oversize and undersize copy: When copy must be greatly enlarged or reduced, it is usually most economical to handle the initial enlargement or reduction by photostats or photocopies. Check with your engraver for the maximum reduction and enlargement he will allow without premium prices. And compare his extra charges for reductions and enlargements with the cost of having this job handled elsewhere.

65. Let printer saw apart: In many cases, you will find it more economical to have your printer saw apart ganged engravings. There are times when the printer will handle this task without charge. But check first and analyze comparative costs.

66. Clear instructions: Be sure your engraving instructions are completely clear. Most engravers will provide gummed labels to be attached to copy. These labels have spaces for filling in all basic information required.

67. Send platemaker the best copy: Do not skimp on copy sent to a platemaker. Poor copy requires extra time—and time is money. It will be a lot less expensive to have a photographer prepare a better print or an artist touch up rough work rather than to turn over the responsibility for quality upgrading to a platemaker.

68. **Use understandable marks:** Indicate crop marks and mortises clearly and properly. If you are not sure of the best procedures, check with your engraver and follow his instructions.

69. **Do not overbuy:** Order the least expensive type of engraving that will produce the quality and press run you require. If your halftone screen is 100 or less, you will probably be perfectly safe with zinc or magnesium halftones. Unless there is some tricky copy, you seldom require copper halftones for line work. Tell your engraver the details of the job and let him advise you on the most practical engravings.

70. **Duplicate plates:** For multicolor line work, it is often economical to have duplicate plates made and then have the appropriate areas routed off each of the plates so only the material to be printed in each color remains. This can be a tricky process, but it deserves consideration.

71. **Avoid odd sizes:** While basic charges for engravings are on a square area basis, you pay premium prices for long and narrow engravings. For example, a ½- by 17-inch engraving costs just as much as a 5½- by 17-inch engraving.

72. **Hitchhike on engravings:** Whenever a line engraving does not use the maximum area allowed in a given price bracket, consider including an item of frequently used copy, such as a logotype. You can then have it sawed off the plate for use when needed, and the only extra charge will be for the saw-apart.

73. **Avoid strip-ins:** When preparing copy for platemaking—particularly for offset—try to combine as much material as possible on a single "flat." Each item which must be stripped in on the negative before the plate is made involves added cost. As mentioned previously, it is usually less costly to have an artist handle the positioning of material rather than to have the task handled by a platemaker.

74. **Furnish spreads:** For offset work, it is usually most economical to provide spreads of facing pages already pasted into position rather than having the engraver strip individual pages into spread position. However, be sure you know the limitations of the engraver's camera. If the camera cannot handle a spread, he will have to cut the pasteup apart and shoot it as individual pages; you will have wasted your artist's time and added an operation for the platemaker. And be sure you know the imposition of the pages as they will be printed. Just because page two faces page three in a booklet does not mean they will be printed side by side.

75. Strive for simplicity: When it comes to halftones, avoid outlines, silhouettes, and vignettes if costs are a factor. You will save at least 50 percent by sticking to square halftones—those with all square corners.

76. Consider standard tint blocks: When your job calls for areas with a colored background—either screened or solid—consider the use of stock materials. Most printers can furnish plastic or metal tint blocks to fill your needs, and there is no necessity to have special engravings made.

77. And stock cuts, too: Thousands of illustrations are available as stock cuts. Many printers carry a wide variety in inventory, and there are at least a dozen sources with extensive catalogs (graphic arts trade magazines regularly carry ads identifying these suppliers). The cost of these stock cuts is often less than just the cost of engravings alone, with the artwork as a "bonus."

78. Offset conversions: If you have original letterpress copy and are reprinting a job by offset, you can usually get by without having to order halftone strip-ins. Just paste up a proof of the original letterpress halftone in position with line copy and have the entire job handled as a line shot. If a skilled cameraman is on the job, the results should be highly satisfactory. In addition, there are a number of special conversion processes available. Check with your offset platemaker to see what he offers. If you know in advance that a job will have to be reprinted at a later date, ask your printer to pull a set of reproduction proofs while the type and engravings are still "fresh," and then save these proofs for your conversions.

79. Do not order unnecessary mounting: Be sure to check with your printer to determine if he wants plates mounted. He may prefer to use a special metal base to which he will attach the plates himself. If they are mounted by the platemaker, he will have to strip off the base material—an added cost to you, in addition to the original cost of mounting.

80. Combine mounting: On the other hand, the printer may not only prefer to have the plates mounted, but he may want to have two or more cuts mounted in position on a single base. If such is the case, it may be most economical to have the platemaker handle this job before sending the plates to the printer.

81. Avoid double shipping: There are a number of ways to handle transmittal of plates to the printer. It may be most economical to have the engraver ship them direct, rather than sending them to you and then having you pay the additional cost of routing them to the printer. On the other hand, if he has to make two deliveries—proofs to you and plates to the printer—you may find yourself with added delivery charges. You will have to check your specific situation, but it is a matter deserving special consideration.

82. **Use photostats for reverse copy:** If you want your copy reversed (white on black rather than black on white), it is usually more economical to have a negative photostat prepared than to let the platemaker handle the job.

83. **Avoid combination cuts:** Whenever possible, avoid combining halftones and line copy on the same letterpress plate. This requires a costly photoengraving operation.

84. **Adopt standard sizes:** The adoption of a set of standard basic sizes for engravings can often save time and money. While there will always be exceptions, the majority of illustrations used in printed material can usually be restricted to a relatively limited number of basic sizes—particularly in routine direct mail jobs, such as catalog sheets, house organs, catalogs, etc. Then, by saving artwork, cropped photos, engravings, offset negatives, etc., you can build an instantly available file of material which can be quickly adapted to new jobs as they come along. With the standard sizes in mind, it is also easier to plan layouts.

85. **Pick a platemaker:** In the long run, you will save time and money if you pick a platemaker who can handle *all* of your jobs for you. While most areas have "standard unit prices" which are supposedly charged universally, most engravers will be more than willing to give you a special price if you provide them with a quantity of work. This is only reasonable, since contact, pickup and delivery time, and accounting will be reduced.

86. **Watch "extra" charges:** Do not be misled by the engraver offering the lowest unit rate. The big charges for platemaking often come when the extras are billed, and there are great differences in what different platemakers will charge for extras. You will only learn your lesson in this area by experience (or from the experience of others), but it is worthy of serious study.

87. **Beware of false economy:** Economy can be a dangerous thing in platemaking. Remember, the job does not end with the engraving—it still must be printed. Consult with your printer

frequently to be sure the plates you furnish are not causing costly headaches on the press. Many direct mail advertisers have learned too late that a few pennies saved on platemaking have been wiped out by extra dollars spent for printing which was complicated by inferior plates.

PRINTING

88. Select the right process: The most important factor in printing economy is to choose the right process for a given job. No general rules can be offered, except that each printed piece should be analyzed separately and then assigned to the type of printing which promises the greatest economy without sacrificing quality.

89. Select the right printer: Once the process has been selected, you cannot just turn to any printer offering that process. He has to have the right equipment, the right craftsmen, the right press availabilities, and the right attitude. Even the largest printer in the world cannot handle every job efficiently and economically.

90. Work closely with the printer: While it is important to bring all suppliers into the act when you begin planning a direct mailing, special attention should be paid the printer. Since it is up to him to produce the end product, he should be consulted at all steps in the production process. By following his advice, you will frequently be able to save money on every production operation.

91. Gang-printing jobs: One of the greatest avenues for printing economy comes through the ganging of jobs. In many cases, you will be able to combine two or more jobs for a single press run. This is a possibility which should always be considered.

92. Use trim space: More often than not, you can get a special bonus with your printing jobs at very little extra cost. Before any job goes to press, check to see (1) if the full capacity of the press is being utilized and (2) if there will be "waste" trimmed from the paper being used or if another larger standard size sheet could be used. If both checks indicate there will be room for additional printed material, consider working in an "extra" job in that "trim space." The cost will be low—usually just a little extra for trimming, packaging, delivery, and additional platework. Some of the items you might consider for that trim space are memo pads, routing slips, thank-you notes, envelope enclosures, letter tip-ons, business cards, salesmen's giveaways. It is an excellent idea to build a file of trim space possibilities and then put them in the works whenever the opportunity arises.

93. **Split-fountain printing:** In multicolor letterpress printing, it is wise to consider split-fountain printing. This involves dividing the ink fountain on the press so it holds more than one color of ink. With special equipment which most printers have available, you can have more than one additional color at very little over the two-color cost. It will require special planning to utilize this possibility effectively, so be sure to check with your printer in advance to determine all limitations. One important caution: You will have to allow a "neutral" space between colors, so be sure to determine just how closely your printer can split his fountain.

94. **Low-cost color:** There is a number of special color processes available which offer dramatic economies. For example, picture post cards are normally printed by specialists who work with standard sizes printed in gang runs, using special color-reproduction techniques. If your requirements fit within the range of these standard sizes, you can often obtain color printing of excellent quality at substantially reduced cost. Other printers offer special automated color-reproduction techniques with built-in economies. While most printers in the low-cost color field concentrate on so-called pleasing color rather than high-fidelity color, their work is satisfactory for many direct mail purposes. In most cases, you will find these low-cost color techniques most satisfactory for relatively limited quantities, since most of the economies come in the original preparation of material rather than during the press runs. As the size of the press run increases, you will generally find that you can obtain the same prices from other printers who may offer superior quality and substantially more versatility.

95. **Consider tip-ons:** When you wish to add color to a job that has little more than a black-and-white budget, consider the possibility of tipped-on illustrations. For example, you might tip picture post cards to an otherwise black-and-white job. The effect can be dramatic and the added cost of tipping may be well worthwhile.

96. **Stock printed materials:** One way to extend a direct mail production budget is to use stock printed materials to which you add your copy. A number of suppliers offer a wide variety of preprinted, colorful bulletins, folders, flashcards, certificates, and other formats at far less than it would cost to prepare simi-

lar materials yourself. Generally, these materials are used for relatively short runs, since the cost advantages disappear as quantities are extended.

97. Watch color positioning: Be sure to select color position for press economy. Proper planning may avoid extra press runs. For example, you may require color on only one side of a sheet, reducing the press runs from four to three—two runs for the side with a second color and just one for the backup. It is particularly important to consider how the job will be folded in planning your color positioning.

98. Avoid special inks: In picking colors, try to stay within the range offered by your printer or regular ink supplier. You can expect more consistent color and lower cost if you pick a color out of a swatch book, rather than asking for a special match.

99. Do not get ahead of yourself: Make sure your printer has received all the elements required for the job—type, engravings, paper, etc.—before demanding he get started on the job. Missing elements will only cause costly delays and unnecessary headaches.

100. Give your printer a complete dummy: Written and verbal instructions are no substitute for a detailed dummy of the printing job. Paste all engraver's and typographer's proofs, plus pickup material, in exact position in your dummy. Do not just indicate them with a penciled note. Then be sure your dummy is folded as you want it and that each page is carefully numbered.

101. Provide color samples: Always provide your printer with a sample of the exact color you desire. Instructions such as "Use a reddish brown" or "Add a little yellow to the ink shown on the enclosed sample" only lead to costly confusion. There are dozens of excellent guides available from which you can select your colors, and it may prove helpful to build a file of interesting color samples from printed pieces which cross your desk.

102. Complete instructions at the beginning: The right time to give your printer all of his instructions is when you submit the dummy. Instructions "to come" only lead to trouble later. If some details, such as shipping instructions, must be delayed, be specific as to when and how they will be supplied.

103. Stick to standard sizes whenever possible: There is a good reason why so much printed material falls into standard sizes such as 5 by 8 inches, 6 by 9 inches, 8½ by 11 inches, and

9 by 12 inches. Standard paper sizes, printing equipment, folders, envelopes, and other items have been designed to economically handle the basic sizes. So, whenever possible, give first consideration to one of the standard sizes.

104. Beware of three-color jobs: Most printing equipment is designed to print in one, two, four, or five colors. This means a three-color job is usually a misfit. While there are ways, such as the split-fountain printing already described, to obtain three colors economically, it will usually be best to leave this "in between" number out of your original color planning.

105. Watch those bleeds: Bleeds—areas where printing runs off the edge of the paper—are often a costly headache. Four-side bleeds are out of the question for most jobs, unless you want to buy oversize paper and have the sheets trimmed after printing. An area must always be allowed for the grippers—metal fingers which hold the paper in place during the printing operation. Be sure to consult with your printer every time you plan to use bleeds.

106. Consider repeats in the same job: An effective cost saver is to plan a job so you can use the same art, engravings, and/or typography in two or more places. For example, you may have a key illustration on the cover, which can be effectively reprinted in the body of a booklet. Of course, this means that the cover and body must be printed separately, and sufficient time must be allowed to move the repeated material from one form to another. It is not always necessary to repeat the material in its original form. You may want to crop away certain portions from an engraving, drop words from a line of type, or change colors. While this technique can be highly effective as a cost saver, it must be carefully planned or you will run into extra charges which wipe out any potential savings from the repeats.

107. Set up jobs for simple changes: When you have a piece requiring special copy for limited markets in addition to a long run for regular use, it is not necessary to handle the situation as two completely separate jobs. When planning the piece, include copy or design panels which can be eliminated after the regular run, replacing the eliminated material with the copy required for the special markets. Or, after the initial run, you may simply remove the copy or design panels and continue the run with these areas blank. When you have sufficient sheets for the special markets, simply put them back on the press for imprinting the special copy in the blank areas. This method is particularly useful for multicolor jobs. On black-and-white jobs, chances are the savings in plate costs and makeready time will more than offset the cost of the additional press run for imprinting.

108. Consider self-covers: When preparing booklets or other multipage units, always give special consideration to self-covers —covers which are the same as the body of the "book." To add covers of a different stock involves additional press runs and added folding and binding costs. Very often, for the same amount of money, you can dramatically upgrade the entire piece by applying the extra costs for separate covering to the materials and printing in a self-cover job.

FINISHING

109. Plan folding carefully: Proper planning can turn a difficult folding operation into a simple one. Always plan all details of folding in the very early planning stages, and never wait until a job is printed before deciding on the folding technique.

110. Use press folding: Many printers have special folding and binding equipment built into the delivery end of their presses. Such equipment is generally used only for long-run jobs, but should always be given consideration, since its use can provide substantial cost advantages.

111. Avoid hand-folding: Folding equipment is available somewhere to handle nearly every job mechanically. Since hand-folding is a costly, inferior process, always seek out mechanical folding first. If your own printer is not equipped to handle the folding mechanically, it may prove to be most economical to have the job farmed out to a trade bindery.

112. Consider press scoring: When heavy stock must be folded or when folding must be done against the grain of the paper, you may improve quality and reduce costs by having scoring (indenting the paper's surface by rules which are higher than the rest of the matter to be printed) done on the press. If you have wide, unprinted margins, you may be able to achieve blind scoring by using the split-fountain technique and eliminating all ink from the scoring area. Scoring, of course, may be handled as a separate operation and, even so, can prove to be a cost saver if unscored material will present folding complications resulting in slower speeds and considerable spoilage.

113. Fold double: Many jobs can be printed and folded two-up and then cut apart after the folding has been completed. Simple cuts (slitting) can be accomplished on many folders during the basic folding operation.

114. Die-cutting without dies: Many special effects can be obtained by straight-blade cutting, eliminating the need of more costly die-cutting. By watching the order of folding and cutting, you will be able to come up with a wide variety of effective novelty results.

115. Simulate die-cuts: Another economical technique for obtaining die-cut effects without dies is through the use of paper drills, round cornering, and special folding. A couple of hours spent with a creative printer or binder will produce dozens of useful ideas.

116. Do not overlook tag companies: When it comes to special finishing, do not overlook the facilities offered by so-called tag companies. These firms have a variety of ingenious pieces of equipment which can produce a wide range of effects economically. A visit to one of these plants will set your sights on many ideas you have probably never previously considered.

117. Consider pasting instead of stapling: For many multi-page jobs, you may be able to reduce costs by having pages glued together by a narrow strip of adhesive applied along the folding edge of pages during the folding operation. Signatures are delivered already bound, rather than requiring a separate binding operation.

118. Simplify tip-ons: If you plan to attach a gimmick to a direct mail piece—such as a coin, plastic letter gadget, colored illustration, etc.—consider printing an actual-size illustration of the item exactly where it is to be attached. This will not only serve as a guide for tipping the item into place, but frequently makes it possible to utilize the piece and/or original artwork without the gimmicks.

119. Extra trim area for small pieces: If you are binding a miniature booklet or folder, you will probably find it best to allow a substantial trim area when printing the material. This not only permits more accurate folding and easier binding, but also makes possible the use of bindery equipment which might not be able to handle smaller folds. Losses in additional paper costs are quickly made up in savings in bindery charges.

120. Look beyond the graphic arts: When direct mail pieces involve considerable handwork, you may find it advisable to go beyond normal graphic arts channels to complete the finishing operations. Many companies have found that special tipping, hand-folding, packaging, and other time-consuming operations can be accomplished during idle time in other industries—often on their own production lines. While skilled supervision may be required, most of these operations require only a limited amount of training.

121. Watch inserting requirements: Automatic inserting equipment can introduce considerable economy in preparing mailings, but only if material has been designed to fit the limitations of this automatic equipment. Be sure to check all inserting requirements before a job is produced.

122. Keep an eye on postage costs: Postage costs should always be kept in mind during finishing operations. Trimming as little as an additional 1/64 of an inch off the edges of a piece may result in a substantial postage saving if the weight is reduced to the next lower bracket. Other factors to consider include the number and kind of staples used in binding, gluing in place of stapling, and even the weight of adhesives used in tipping operations.

PAPER AND ENVELOPES

123. Use standard paper sizes: Always give first consideration to standard paper sizes for any printing job. Almost without exception, they will be less expensive than odd sizes.

124. Design to eliminate waste: Design your direct mail printed materials to use the full area of a sheet of paper, and shift to other standard sizes of different types of stock if you cannot get an economical "cut" from the sheet originally chosen.

125. Check weight carefully: Determine the total weight of your printed piece before a final decision on paper is reached. A minor change in paper specifications may result in major mailing economies.

126. Do not forget the extra weight: When figuring the weight, don't forget to consider ink that will be applied, staples or adhesive, and other things which will be added to the paper in processing. These may be enough to throw the piece into the next higher postage bracket, and a change in paper specifications may bring the piece back into a lower bracket.

127. **Consider colored stocks:** A wide variety of beautiful colored paper stocks is available—and the varieties are increasing yearly. By choosing a colored stock, you may be able to obtain the effect you want with fewer press runs for additional colors.

128. **Do not forget duplex stocks:** In addition to regular colored stocks, you can obtain certain papers with a different color on each side of the sheet. Use of these stocks may provide a desired effect of multicolors at the cost of one-color printing. These sheets are particularly effective when folded off center or die-cut so both sides of the sheet are seen at the same time.

129. **Be sure paper meets your printer's requirements:** You cannot use any type of paper on every type of printing equipment. Selection of the wrong stock can result in substantial increases in printing costs through slower press runs, higher rates of spoilage, etc. Always consult with your printer during the early planning stages about your paper choice.

130. **Check folding qualities carefully:** Be sure to check the folding qualities of your paper—including what happens to the printing on it when it is run through a folder. Many otherwise "perfect" jobs have been ruined when it came to folding the printed signatures.

131. **Watch grain direction:** Many paper stocks are offered with a choice of grain directions. Be sure to check all printing, folding, and use requirements before selecting grain direction.

132. **Consider odd lots:** Particularly when only limited quantities of paper are required, you may be able to save considerable money by taking advantage of odd lots of paper already in your printer's inventory or available through paper merchants who specialize in handling this type of order. By taking advantage of such arrangements, you may be able to obtain the stock you need at a substantial discount.

133. **Combine paper orders:** If you can project your paper orders, you may be able to come up with substantial savings by ordering in multiple cartons or carloads. Quantity discounts add up quickly in paper purchasing.

134. **But watch storage costs:** When buying for future requirements, be sure to consider the cost of storage. If you are not careful, storage costs can quickly wipe out any savings you might have produced. And also make sure storage is under con-

trolled conditions. Your paper stock can be damaged or ruined if it is not stored properly. In particular, consider humidity. A paper that is too wet or too dry may cause major difficulties in printing and binding . . . and it is amazing what added moisture can do to postage costs.

135. Consider use of the printed piece: Do not overlook the end-use factor in selecting paper. If a piece will wear out quickly and require a replacement, it may be more economical to select a better stock in the beginning. The cost of mailing replacements alone may provide enough dollars to buy the finest stock possible for the original shipment.

136. Watch opacity: The amount of show-through may be a definite deciding factor in economical paper selection. Too transparent a sheet may require more costly printing to achieve the results you desire.

137. Select right packaging: Paper can generally be obtained in cartons, in cases, or on skids. Be sure to check with your printer for his preferences.

138. Beware too big or too heavy skids: The graphic arts industry is full of stories of jobs gone wrong because paper skids were too large for doors, elevators, or available storage space... or because the weight was too great for elevators, floors, or handling equipment. Double-check these factors in advance . . . and be sure to check on the proper direction for skid legs or runners.

139. Buy envelopes from a specialist: Unless your quantity requirements are very small, always buy envelopes from an envelope manufacturer rather than from a printer or lettershop. There are few trade discounts in envelope buying which you cannot obtain directly. In addition, an envelope-maker can generally provide a wider choice and offer special help which will result in envelope economies.

140. Anticipate requirements: You can obtain substantial savings by quantity buying of envelopes. So determine your needs for an extended period and gang your envelope orders. You usually can arrange to have your envelopes shipped as you need them and still take advantage of bulk-order economies.

141. Use standard sizes: Special sizes of envelopes require tailormade dies and often cannot be produced economically. Every major envelope-maker offers a wide range of standard sizes, so stick with these for the majority of your requirements.

142. **Imprint small quantities:** For large envelope orders, it is usually most economical to do the printing on flat sheets which are then made up into finished envelopes. But for smaller orders, you will generally save money by buying finished envelopes and having them imprinted with the necessary copy.

143. **Consider lighter weights:** Always check the weight of stock used for envelopes if mailing costs are a consideration. A wide variety of stocks is available, and by switching to a lighter weight you may be able to maintain the quality you desire but save postage and paper costs.

144. **Consider window envelopes:** You may be able to save money on envelope imprinting by using die-cut windows which permit printed matter on the enclosures to show through the openings.

145. **Use open windows:** Glassine or one of the other transparent materials may give your envelope window a quality touch, but if costs are a major problem you can save money by just using a die-cut window without a transparent covering.

146. **Stock envelopes:** If you use the same envelopes for repeated mailings, you can save money by ordering in bulk. Even if you change mailing envelopes, you may want to buy your business reply envelopes in bulk.

147. **Check envelopes for inserting:** When choosing an envelope size, be sure to check to make sure it can be used with automatic inserting equipment. If it is too tight a fit, you may have to insert enclosures by hand at a substantial jump in costs.

148. **Or trim enclosures:** If the envelope you are planning to use won't work on the inserter, don't just automatically order a larger envelope. First give consideration to the possibility of trimming your enclosures slightly. This will reduce your mailing weight and often permits you to use less costly standard size envelopes.

149. **Let the buyer pay the postage:** Some tests have shown no substantial reduction in orders when a regular reply envelope was used in place of a business reply envelope. Don't just assume you have to pay the return postage to get the order. Test first. Then if your customers don't object to using their own stamps, you'll save a pile of money by eliminating BRE's.

POSTAL SERVICES

150. Use Government Postal Cards: If you're making a first class mailing which can fit on a standard postal card, why not let the government pay for the paper? Use of standard postal cards also eliminates the necessity of metering the mail since the "stamp" is already printed on the card.

151. Mixed class mail: If only a portion of your mailing is first class mail, you don't have to pay the first class rate for the entire weight. You can enclose first class material with other class mailings if you properly mark the mailing and pay an extra one-ounce first class fee. But remember that your mail will be handled in accordance with the lowest class postage involved.

152. Check mailability in advance: If there is any question about the mailability of your piece, be sure to check with your postmaster *before* having it produced. You may end up having to scrap a lot of valuable material or mail at a higher cost which could be avoided by a little advance research.

153. Check your postal scales regularly: A lot of mailers have gone over budget because their scales told a little lie. It's a good procedure to check your postal scales regularly to make sure they're accurate.

154. Keep abreast of postal regulations: There's nothing static about postal regulations. What may have been permitted a few weeks ago may no longer be okay for mailing. And what is eligible for mailing at a particular rate is always subject to change. Keeping abreast of postal regulations can be a major budget factor.

155. Use "Address Correction" for list cleaning: At least two or three times a year, use the "Address Correction" services of the post office for your mailings. This is one of the most economical ways to get address change information for your list.

156. Use First Class occasionally: If you mail regularly by Third Class mail, you can benefit by making an occasional First Class mailing to get your material forwarded automatically to those who have moved. Asking for change of address information in such mailings can be another economical way to help with list cleaning.

MAILING LISTS

157. Keep your lists clean: One of the biggest money savers for any direct mail advertiser is constantly cleaning his mailing lists. There's no way to waste money faster than to mail undeliverable pieces.

158. Exchange lists: To save on list rental costs, consider the possibility of even exchanges of lists with other mailers.

159. Date your list entries: Be sure to include a "create date" for each name on your list. Names which have been on a list for a long time deserve special checking to make sure they're still productive and that mailings are actually being delivered.

160. Eliminate duplicate list entries: Every list should be given a purge treatment regularly. Duplicate mailings can be terribly expensive both in terms of actual cost and decreased returns.

161. Analyze list response: Analyze the response to your mailings by different list categories (i.e. geographical, demographic characteristics, etc.) and eliminate unproductive categories in subsequent mailings.

162. Keep track of "bad" names: When a name is pulled from a list because of credit problems, inadequate response, etc., be sure to keep that name on file to prevent it from being reentered on the list at a later date.

163. Merge lists: When more than one list is being used for a mailing, consider merging the lists to eliminate duplicate mailings.

164. Seek advice of list experts: A good mailing list broker or list compiler can frequently save you a lot of money by steering you away from unproductive lists and providing you with "free" services that are an automatic part of their operations.

MISCELLANEOUS

165. Economical keys for reply cards: There are quite a few ways to key your reply cards or order forms without having to order a special printing for each key. One economical method is to include a row of typographical ornaments or numerals at the bottom or side of the piece. The complete row represents the first key. For subsequent keys, the printer simply removes the ornaments from the plate or type form one by one as the press run progresses. The remaining number of ornaments or numerals establishes the key. Another economical method is to use a paper drill to cut a hole through various ornaments. Or you can trim off one of the corners.

166. **Control inventories**: When direct mail printed materials are carried in inventory, it is dangerous to find yourself face to face with an empty bin. This may result in costly rush jobs for replacements or in holding up mailings beyond deadlines. An effective control system is to establish minimum quantities required and then have your suppliers wrap that amount in a brilliant color of paper. Instructions are then issued that these specially wrapped items must never be opened without special permission. You are thus automatically warned when reorders are necessary.

167. **Take advantage of discounts**: Most suppliers offer discounts for prompt payment and quantity orders. Keep a careful check on these discounts.

168. **Check bills carefully**: Your production bills can often indicate possibilities for substantial economies on future jobs. Be sure to check each extra charge carefully. Frequently, proper planning will eliminate such a charge on future jobs.

169. **Submit "kill" orders promptly**: Material being held by any of your suppliers awaiting possible reorders can cause a variety of problems. While this may seem unimportant to you, it is a headache for the supplier and eventually will result in added costs for you. This is particularly true in letterpress printing from original type. If type metal and handset type must be kept in an inactive status, it cannot be used for other jobs.

170. **Schedule for economy**: Give your suppliers an opportunity to handle your requirements during their off-seasons and you can arrange better prices.

171. **Consider cooperative mailings**: You'll reach a lot more people for the same money if you include your mailing piece in a cooperative mailing.

172. **Let your promotions ride piggy-back**: You can get a "free ride" for your promotion message if it can be included with bills, invoices, packages, etc.

173. **Keep an inventory:** Be sure to keep an accurate inventory of all of the items you use in your mailings. You may even want to adjust your mailing quantities to the minimum quantity of something already in inventory.

174. **Build a direct mail team:** Select reliable suppliers carefully and then stay with them. You will save money in the long run. It not only costs money to conduct a supplier search, but by building a strong relationship with your supplier team, you'll build economies into your programs through better communications and a cooperative effort to see that your mailings do the job for which they are intended.

175. **Analyze each job thoroughly:** One of the most important cost savers of all is to analyze each job thoroughly, making special effort to seek out previously overlooked economies. Do not try to do this alone, but invite all of your suppliers to offer their suggestions.

Chapter 48

TESTING AND PROJECTING

ONE of the major advantages of direct mail over most other advertising media is the ease and economy with which you can both test the potential effectiveness of a mailing and project the probable returns.

Thus, it is possible to approach advertising situations with greater confidence. While there is always a certain gamble in any direct mail promotion, if you have pretested, the chances are you will be able to predict results with far more accuracy than is possible in any other medium.

Types of Testing

There are eight basic types of testing conducted most frequently by direct mail advertisers:

1. The complete mailing package
2. Lists
3. Copy
4. The offer
5. The price
6. Format of the individual elements in a mailing package
7. Reply devices
8. Miscellaneous details

Many direct mail advertisers feel there are really only three basic areas for testing: (1) the offer, (2) the lists, and (3) the physical components of a mailing—and, indeed, all of the eight basic types of testing listed above can be grouped under these three headings. But it can be misleading to consider testing under such broad categories. In fact, if you are about to consider direct mail testing for the first time you will probably want to consider test possibilities on an even more detailed basis than the eight most frequently used types we are including as reference points.

To get a good idea of the hundreds of legitimate test possibilities, you may want to refer back to Chapter 7, "Mail Order," in which we have included a list of "tips" from mail order experts. Nearly every one of these ideas indicates a possible area for testing before you can go about direct mail advertising for your products or services with confidence.

Complete Mailing Package

There are many highly successful direct mail advertisers who insist the only legitimate way to conduct a test is on a "complete package" basis. To try to vary any single element for comparison testing, they insist, is to pit a coordinated "package" against a less adequate "package."

This theory is probably more applicable to the experienced direct mail advertiser, who has already learned through trial-and-error answers to many of the things which lead to testing of elements by those in search of foundation stones upon which to build direct mail confidence. Nevertheless, even the beginner in direct mail should never overlook the importance of complete package testing as at least part of his research program.

Self-Mailer vs. Letter + Enclosure Package

A good example of a test of complete mailing packages was a three-way test conducted by New Holland Machine Co.[1] A list of 64,500 farmers was divided into three approximately equal groups. The first group received the self-mailer alone. The second group received the self-mailer in an envelope with a 3- by 4-inch memo in simulated handwriting enclosed, The third group received the self-mailer plus a printed letter in an envelope. All three mailings offered a demonstration of a machine and/or a free booklet.

In this test, the mailer with a memo pulled twice as many returns as the self-mailer alone, while the mailer with a letter pulled nearly four times the number of returns produced by the self-mailer alone.

A somewhat similar test was conducted by United Business Service. Here a self-mailer was tested against a Multigraphed letter plus a two-color circular, a two-color reply card, and a

[1]This example—and the majority of other examples of direct mail tests described in this chapter—was digested from a Case Study Report prepared by the Direct Mail /Marketing Assn. DMMA stresses that the conclusions reached by any single test do not necessarily apply in any future mailing either by the same or different direct mail advertiser. Repeated testing is the only reliable procedure for reference.

business reply envelope. Both mailings offered a special report plus a four-week trial subscription to an investment advisory service for $1. The test was made to nine different lists, using samples of approximately equal size for each mailing package.

In this test, the self-mailer pulled a return of 2.14% while the letter-plus enclosures package pulled 2.48%. However, the cost per trial was only $1.00 for the self-mailer, while the more expensive package had a cost-per-trial of $1.68. (The cost-per-order is an important factor in any test of mailing packages and is usually more revealing than a simple percentage of return consideration.)

Other Package Tests

A test by U.S. Envelope Co. involved an offer of samples. Two mailings were used. The first consisted of a letter, a few samples of a new type of envelope, plus a reply card. Additional samples and price information were offered. The second mailing included a letter and a reply card with which to request samples —but had no samples enclosed in the mailing.

The sampleless mailing pulled a 15% response, while the mailing with samples drew only 1.2%. Since one of the objectives was to produce leads for salesmen, the sampleless mailing, with 13 times the response, was considered the most successful. In a case like this, however, it should be remembered that the entire list receiving the mailing with samples was directly exposed to the product, while only 15% of the other list ended up getting samples.

Another typical test was conducted by National Research Bureau, which tested the mailings of a catalog with and without an enclosed sales letter. The mailing which included a letter drew 47% more sales volume than simply a catalog alone.

List Testing

By far the most common type of testing in the direct mail field is on lists. Mail order firms, for example, will test nearly every list—including their own—before making extensive mailings.

The usual procedure is to send a mailing which has already been tested and found satisfactory to a representative cross section of a list. If the test pulls a profitable response, the mailing is then sent to the entire list. While there is considerable difference of opinion as to what constitutes a "representative cross section," the most commonly accepted rule of thumb is to use a minimum of 2,000 names or 10% of the list. When large lists are involved, tests are often conducted on a two-flight basis. This involves mailing to less than 10% to begin a test, and then if this proves successful—or has at least an indication of possible success—a second (and sometimes a third) quantity is mailed.

An example of a list test is a mailing made by The Macmillan Co. to sell books to newly-promoted executives. Since available names were broken down by year of promotion, the test involved three lists:

1. Executives promoted a year ago or less.
2. Executives promoted a year to two years ago.
3. Executives promoted two to three years ago.

The tests showed approximately the same percentage of returns from lists one and two, but there was a definite deterioration in returns from list number three.

Copy Testing

Every direct mail advertiser, at one time or another, questions the effectiveness of his copy. Fortunately, it is relatively easy to make a copy test. The usual technique is to mail two versions of copy on an every-other-name basis.

While some direct mail people go overboard and make copy tests on every small detail, the majority prefer to concentrate on testing either complete versions of letters or just variations in headlines and lead paragraphs.

An example of how advertisers can get bitten by the copy-testing bug is the direct mail manager of a Chicago correspondence school who made extensive tests to determine how to close a letter—"Sincerely yours," "Very sincerely yours," "Sincerely," and dozens of other variations. When he had completed his tests, he proudly proclaimed he had discovered that he could increase his returns from a certain section of one southern state if he closed his letters to names in that market with "God bless you."

Testing of this minute nature generally causes more harm than good. Not only does it require time and effort which might better be applied to more important projects such as testing entire new approaches, but it also results in creating ill-founded "rules" which have little validity except as they apply to the specific mailing involved in the original test. Vary any other element in a mailing and it is necessary to test again.

The Offer

Perhaps the most important test is the offer you make in your mailings—and the way in which the offer is made. All too often, there is a tendency to decide upon a specific offer before any work begins on a mailing. Then, when testing is decided upon, no consideration is given the possibility of changing the offer itself.

There is almost no end to the number of variations which can be made in an offer. Old American Insurance Co., for example, made a test to determine whether the offer of a personal record book in conjunction with an inquiry about older age life insurance would bring more inquiries *and* subsequent direct-by-mail sales than a standard inquiry-producing offer without any special inducement. Just under 100,000 pieces were mailed, split about equally between the two offers.

The booklet offer brought back a 4.6% response, while the standard offer produced only 3.3% returns. But when it came to converting these inquiries to sales, the percentage of closure was reversed. Although there were roughly one-third more inquiries from the booklet offer, this list ended up pulling sales totaling only 93.1% of those made to the smaller standard offer inquirers' list.

This example clearly indicates the importance of withholding judgment on any test until all the results are known. In addition to needing evidence about percentage of closure, it is often important to determine such factors as the collectibility of accounts, the number of items returned for credit or refund, and so forth.

Number of Products

National Research Bureau made a test involving the offering of one product or two in a single mailing. The basic offer was for collection stickers used by business firms. Another portion of the list received not only the collection sticker offer but also a "tag-along" offer for collection envelopes. The single offer was mailed to a list of approximately 17,000, while the dual offer was made to 38,000.

The single offer pulled a response of 1.19% with a revenue of $74.00 per thousand pieces mailed. The dual offer resulted in a return of 1.24%, but a revenue per thousand of only $73.78. In this case, the percentage of return was the most important factor since profit depends primarily on repeat business from previous purchasers.

In a test conducted by American Marketing Services, it was determined that including offers for a variety of products in answers to inquiries about a specific product, rather than just sending literature about the product or service generating the original request, could increase dollar revenue as much as 100%, although the total number of orders remained approximately the same.

"Billboard's" Offers

The *Billboard* magazine has conducted a number of unusual tests to determine how many different subscription rates should be offered. One test involved an order coupon listing six subscription rates vs. an order coupon listing 45 rates (including the six rates on the first coupon). The cost per copy remained the same on all rates. All other materials used in the mailing remained the same. Three lists totaling just over 10,000 names were used, with testing on an every-other-name basis.

The 45-rate coupon pulled a 1.34% response, while the six-rate coupon pulled 1.16%. And not only did the 45-rate coupon pull more returns than a six-rate offer, but previous tests had shown that the 45-rate offer outpulled single rate offers.

Another *Billboard* test involved a comparison of offering from eight to 52 issues as compared to offering a subscription of eight to just 36 issues. Both offers involved cut rates. Approximately 14,000 pieces were mailed with the split on an every-other-name basis. The eight to 52 issue offer drew a return of 1.63%, while the eight to 36 issue offer drew 1.58%. While the percentage of return was about equal, the offering of a maximum of 52 issues at cut rates produced a profit of $1.47 per order, while the maximum of 36 issues offer yielded only 37 cents profit per order.

Price Tests

While price is usually considered a key element in a direct mail offer, it deserves special consideration from a testing viewpoint. One of the biggest mistakes made by many mail order advertisers is to assume that the lowest possible price is bound to yield the best returns. There have been many cases when it has turned out that $12.50 is a better price than $10.00 or $19.95 is better than $17.50. The key, of course, is the net profit per order unless a primary objective is to add new customers to the list for their repeat purchases value. Even then, however, a higher price will sometimes yield the greatest *number* of orders. The answer, of course, is to test.

One area often tested is the comparative returns between an even money amount and odd amounts. This is particularly true in lower price offers. In some cases, for example, it turns out that a $3.33 offer will outpull a $3.00 offer. But in other cases, particularly to lists where there is a high percentage who will enclose cash with the order, an even amount will definitely up returns.

Plotting Demand Curves

One use for price testing is to plot a "demand curve"—the economist's term for the relationship between the selling price and the quantity sold. This is a technique used by Time, Inc. and described by researcher Orlan Gaeddert:[2]

> By testing both higher and lower prices than we expect to use in our immediate practice, we can plot the demand relationship on a graph. When the data from many tests on different lists and in different economic and seasonal climates are combined, we have a powerful tool for aiding management in evaluating the probable impact of any proposed price change. This same body of experience can also be an invaluable aid in selecting the right price level for a new venture.
>
> In plotting demand curves for our products I have found it useful to work with relative return percentages rather than absolute response levels. In other words, use the response on the control or standard offer as a base equalling 100. Then express the responses to test offers as ratios to this base. This manipulation removes much of the extraneous variation caused by seasonal or list effects when comparing groups of tests run at different points in time.
>
> The proper interpretation of a price test involves a consideration of long run as well as short run effects. This in turn implies getting beneath the surface. Thus, we should ask not only how much business is obtained from each price level, but also we should question the quality of that business. The pertinent measure of quality would ordinarily be the proportion of repeat customers or the cost of obtaining a repeat customer. This information too, can be obtained from tests plus historical experience.
>
> Some things cannot be tested satisfactorily. For example, competition is encouraged by wide profit margins. So a high price might look good on paper, but work out poorly in the long run if adopted. Thus, the proper interpretation of a test, and the proper decision, depend on business sense as well as technical expertise.
>
> Many old wives tales have sprung up in this field about magic numbers, price barriers, etc. If there really is something special about the number 7, or an even dollar price, or some particular combination of units and dollars, this would show up on a demand chart as an unusually high (or low) demand as compared with other points on the curve. Occasionally, I have found test results that are appreciably off the curve, but I suspect that most of the so-called magic numbers are flukes of testing rather than repeatable results.

[2] "Testing Price Effects in Mail-Order Marketing" by Orlan Gaeddert. *The Reporter of Direct Mail Advertising*. October 1965.

Often there are two prices of interest—the unit price and the gross dollar price. Ordinarily both variables have a critical influence on the response rate. The reaction to the unit price may be modified to some extent by the copy treatment. In other words, price testing overlaps copy testing. Fourteen cents or five dollars can be made to sound like a bargain, but another phrasing for either price might sound too high.

Multiple choice offers are quite common in trade practice. If you test these things carefully, you will probably find that they are very tricky. The first offer, a type face, a change in just one of the prices can bring an important change in the total response pattern. Thus, for multiple choice offers we find both layout and copy elements influencing the reaction to different price schedules.

"Town Journal" Test

Often it is desirable to test to determine whether or not it is desirable to offer a range of prices. Farm Journal Inc. has made several tests along this line. One for *Town Journal,* for example, involved testing on an every-third-name basis offers for four years at $5, two years at $3, and a combination offer including both rates.

The four-years-at-$5 offer produced 275 orders and $1,375. The two-years-at-$3 offer produced 384 orders and $1,152. The combination offer produced 365 orders and $1,351.

In commenting on the test, Farm Journal Inc. reported:

> We've tested this pricing problem many times. The results are always the same. The lower price when offered alone will bring in the greatest volume of orders, but the least amount of money. The higher price when offered alone will give the greatest dollar return, but fewer orders. The mailing offering both prices will pull more orders than the offer quoting only the higher price and almost as many orders as an offer quoting just the lower price. Also, the two-choice price offer will result in a greater dollar return than the offer quoting only the lower price and almost as great a dollar return as the offer quoting just the higher price.

Free vs. Token Payment

Another interesting type of price testing is shown in a test conducted by Doubleday & Co. when launching its "Best in Books," a club offering a bimonthly hardcover omnibus volume of both abridged and unabridged books. To attract new members, three basic offers were tested. The first offer involved giving the first selection free. The second offer asked 10 cents for the first selection. There were 50,000 pieces mailed for each offer.

Using returns from the free offer as a base of 100, the 10-cent offer drew 160 and the 25-cent offer drew 140. This is one of many tests which have indicated that free offers are looked upon with suspicion and distrust. People do not expect to *really* get something for nothing. However, they appreciate a true bargain such as the 10-cent and 25-cent offers made by Doubleday.

Charging Postage Costs

Many mail order advertisers have conducted tests to determine if adding cost of shipments has any material effect on returns. The National Wildlife Federation tested two offers—one which involved specific amounts of postage to be added to each item ordered; the other with a flat 15-cent postage charge for orders of less than $5 and orders over $5 postage prepaid. A 20,000 list was split 50-50.

The first offer, requiring specific amounts of postage for each item ordered, drew a 7.9% response; the second offer drew 8.1%. There was an even greater difference in dollar sales, however, with the second offer producing $3,601 in revenue compared to only $3,104 for the first offer. The conclusion drawn from the test was that complicating an offer with the addition of specific postage charges lowered returns sufficiently to offset any advantage gained through added revenue to cover postage costs.

Another area frequently tested by mail order advertisers is the potential of obtaining payment with orders by offering to prepay postage on cash orders, with shipping and handling charges added to credit orders.

Terms of Payment

Still another element of pricing which requires careful testing is the offering of alternate terms of payment. An example of a test of this type was described by Bob Stone:[3]

> National Research Bureau offered alternate terms of payment to purchasers of our "Direct Mail Manual":
>
> 1. $25.00—if paid within 10 days
> 2. $7.50 in 10 days and four monthly payments of $5.00, making a total of $27.50.
>
> An analysis of the first thousand orders received disclosed that 32% chose the one-payment plan (saving $2.50), whereas 68% chose the installment-payment plan. Obviously we in-

[3]"How to Profit From Direct Mail Testing," by Robert C. Stone. *Envelope Economies* No. 151. Published by Tension Envelope Corp.

creased our total results by offering installment terms (and purchasers were willing to pay for the privilege).

Format of Elements

Every element that goes into a direct mail package can be subjected to testing. Keeney Publishing Co., for example, conducted a test to determine the effectiveness of an envelope with the corner card giving the name of the magazine *(American Artisan)* as compared with an envelope with the corner card giving the name of the publishing company. A list of approximately 17,000 was used, split on an every-other-name basis.

The test indicated that the use of the name of the magazine was more productive, drawing 1.2% returns compared with just 1.0% when the publishing company name was on the envelope.

Use of Color

One of the most frequently tested items is the value of additional color in the elements of direct mail packages. There have been many cases where tests have shown that spending additional money to add color to mailings more than pays off in dollars returned. But, on the other hand, tests in other cases have shown that it is sometimes possible to eliminate costly color pieces and still produce profitable returns.

National Wildlife Federation tested the comparative effectiveness of two promotion folders—one printed in six colors on one side and one color on the reverse, while the second was printed in two colors on both sides. Ten different lists were split on a 50-50 basis. The total test mailing was just over 26,000.

The two-color folder brought 444 returns with an average sale of $1.58, while the six-color folder produced 478 returns with an average sale of $1.81. Thus, while there was not a substantial difference in the number of returns, the six-color folder more than paid for itself in the increased dollar volume it produced.

Reply Devices

Of all of the elements in a mailing, the reply devices probably receive more testing than any other. Reply cards are tested against order forms and envelopes. Business reply (postage paid by the advertiser) is tested against devices requiring the recipient to add his own stamps. Certificate-type forms are tested against conventional order blanks. In fact, there are hundreds of different types of tests possible.

Sooner or later, it seems, just about every direct mail advertiser decides to test the advantage of airmail reply devices against straight first-class mail. *Atlantic Monthly* made a series of tests to determine if enclosing an airmail business reply envelope in its renewal solicitations would increase returns over conventional business reply envelopes. Oddly enough, in three different tests the regular business reply envelope actually outpulled the airmail reply envelopes. The total for all three tests was a return of 16.8% for the regular envelopes against only 15.5% for the airmail envelopes.

Look magazine tested airmail reply envelopes against airmail special delivery reply envelopes, after having determined that airmail reply envelopes would often outpull regular reply envelopes on its renewal mailings. Two tests came up with similar results—fewer returns when the special delivery feature was added. In the combined results, the airmail special delivery envelopes pulled only 83% of the returns produced by the straight airmail envelopes.

Separate Order Forms

The American Medical Association tested the comparative advantage of having a separate addressed order form vs. an addressed order form attached to the letter in promotional mailings for *Today's Health* magazine. Approximately 150,000 pieces were mailed, with an every-other-name sort.

The separate order forms pulled 6.2% returns compared to only 5.2% for the attached order form. There was an additional advantage in using the separate order forms since they were slightly cheaper to produce. The end results showed a cost-per-order of $1.04 for the separate order form and $1.19 for the attached order form.

Another test by *Today's Health* involved comparing pre-addressed order forms against those which required the buyer to fill in his name and address. Approximately 30,000 pieces were tested with a 50-50 split. In this test the addressed forms produced a 6.3% return, while the unaddressed forms drew only 4.9%. (An added advantage to using preaddressed order forms is that fulfillment personnel do not have to worry about illegible handwriting and missing information. It often amazes beginners in the mail order field how many people will send in an order complete with cash payment and forget to include their name and/or address.)

Non-Mail Order Reply Devices

While most of the examples of testing refer to companies selling something by mail order, the same type of testing is valid for those using direct mail for other purposes. Unfortunately there is less testing done by non-mail order companies and little available information about results of those tests which have been conducted.

An example of a non-mail order test was conducted by Provident Mutual Life Insurance Co. of Philadelphia, which wanted to find out if a business reply card was necessary when a valuable premium was being offered. The offer was for a portfolio of 12 paintings to be sent along with information about a special life insurance programming service. The mailings were identical except that one had a reply card enclosed and the other asked recipients to "just write me today."

Of 580 pieces mailed with the reply card, 124 replies were received. Of 585 pieces without card, only 29 replies were received.

Miscellaneous Details

There are many other details which can be tested. For example, the type of postage for the outgoing mailing is frequently studied. McGraw-Hill Publishing Co. tested renewal mailings using window envelopes with stenciled impressions from the renewal order blank providing the address and mailed with printed third-class bulk indicia against plain front envelopes with typed addresses and first-class metered postage imprints.

While the first-class mailings pulled a 16.3% response against a 15.6% response for the third-class mailings, the added cost of the first-class mailings more than offset the added income from the returns.

Look magazine came up with a different conclusion from similar tests with its credit collection mailings. *Look* had been mailing its first billing effort first class to speed delivery so maximum collections were received before the second effort. This first billing pulled nearly 50% pay-ups. Then subsequent efforts were mailed third class. These third-class mailings were tested against first-class using stamps and it was discovered that returns could be upped by an average of 21.4% by using first-class mail throughout the billing series. The results were considered to more than offset the added cost of first-class postage.

A somewhat similar test was conducted by *Atlantic Monthly* to determine the comparative advantage of Pitney-Bowes meter impressions vs. metered indicia and printed indicia. Four lists totaling over 200,000 were split three ways for the test. Results showed the Pitney-Bowes meter impression outpulled the other two types of third-class postage. With an index of 100 for the meter impression, results showed 92.92 for the metered indicia and 87.61 for the printed indicia.

Letterheads

An area which invites frequent direct mail testing is letterheads. Hundreds of tests have been conducted to determine such things as the comparative advantages of using the regular company letterhead against a specially designed letterhead . . . using illustrated vs. non-illustrated letterheads . . . using one-color letterheads vs. multicolor letterheads, etc.

The use of letterhead gadgets is also subjected to frequent testing. In one test, the *Billboard* compared an illustrated letterhead with a piece of string attached ("The Ties Are Stronger Than Ever") against the same illustrated letterhead without the string. The use of the string increased returns from 3.85% to 6.85%.

Preprints vs. Reprints

Another example of the multitude of different kinds of tests which can be conducted is shown by a report in the "Let's Make Direct Mail More Profitable" series by Edward Mayer and Earle Buckley. These outstanding direct mail experts reported on a continuing series of tests to determine the comparative effectiveness of preceding a trade magazine advertisement with a preprint of the ad vs. following the insertion with a reprint.

Several lists were divided on a 50-50 basis. Half of each list received a preprint accompanied by a simulated handwritten memo and reply card mailed to arrive one week prior to the magazine in which the ad would appear. The other half of the list received the same basic mailing package, except that the ad was in reprint form and arrived one week after the publication in which it appeared. Tests were made over a two-year period for four firms whose products varied from heavy and costly machinery to inexpensive office and factory appliances, generally nonconsumer items.

The total number of coupons from the ads and reply cards from the mailings were added together to compare preprint vs. reprint results. For the first client, preprints outpulled reprints by an average of 7%; for client No. 2, preprints had an 11%

advantage; with client No. 3, preprints had a 6% advantage; and for the fourth client, preprints outpulled reprints by an average of 21%.

Some other results of this testing are revealing:

> Coupons received from magazine advertising of all four clients increased by an average of 14% when the preprint combination was used.
>
> Readership studies of the magazine advertisements showed an increase in "noted and/or read most" of 18% in favor of the preprint.
>
> Fourteen percent more inquiries were converted into sales with the preprint-insertion combination than with the insertion-reprint combination.

Determining Direct Mail Profitability

An example of a unique test to determine the profitability of specific direct mail programs was reported by Bruce Murray:[4]

> Several years ago McIntyre developed a "sales search" program for a major client, an automobile manufacturer, to determine the relationship between the cost of specific mail promotions and the profit they brought to the company in increased sales.
>
> Several matched panels were selected, all but one of which received mail promotions; the remaining one, the control panel, received no mail. Of course, all panels were exposed equally to the regular print and broadcase advertising. Subsequently the number of additional cars bought by the panels that had received the mail promotions was calculated, and the cost of obtaining these additional sales through direct mail.
>
> As long as this cost was less than the company's profit from each sale, the promotion was considered a success, but whenever the cost exceeded the profit, the promotion was dropped.
>
> An example of a typical sales search was one that followed a mailing of 20 million mailing pieces in January 1960. Four different promotions were mailed in that campaign, and the marketing areas of San Jose, Calif., St. Louis, Mo., and Buffalo, N. Y., were chosen for the sales search.
>
> In these three areas, five panels were chosen on an alternate household basis. Panels 1 through 4 received the different mailings, while Panel 5 remained the control panel. Each panel contained more than 350,000 households, and the total sample ran to 1,750,779 names.
>
> Names of new-car buyers in these areas were all forwarded to McIntyre for a full year after the mailing, and McIntyre determined to which of the panels each purchaser belonged. The number of cars sold to each of the first four panels above the number sold to the control panel was determined and matched against the cost of the mailing program to determine the cost to the company of obtaining each additional sale. Since the profit on each sale ran around $200, any cost per additional sale that fell below that figure

[4] "Test-market by Mail and Save" by Bruce W. Murray. *Media/scope*. September 1964.

was profitable—although, as the chart below reveals, some promotions were more profitable than others:

Panel	Promotion	Total Car Sales	Addl. Sales	Cost of Promotion per 100 M Names	Cost per Addl. Sale
1	Mailing A	10,001	255	$12,372	$169
2	Mailing B	9,998	252	14,338	199
3	Mailing C	9,963	217	7,898	127
4	Mailing D	9,699	-47	11,669	neg.
5	Control	9,746	—	—	—

The results of this sales search revealed Mailing A as moderately profitable and Mailing C as highly successful—due mainly to its low cost. Mailing D which stimulated no additional sales, was dropped. Mailing B, which barely broke even at $199 per sale, represented a modification of A's approach and was also dropped as unprofitable.

Testing Mailing Techniques for Surveys

How testing can help improve returns from direct mail surveys was demonstrated by John W. DeWolf of G. M. Basford Company. In his *Research News* letter, he reported on 25 "split-run" tests of mailing techniques:[5]

> In connection with the Basford-conducted Advertising Exposure Ratio studies, we made 25 "split-run" tests of mailing techniques. In 12 of the cases, the test was based on mailings of 1,000 letter-questionnaires—half using one technique, half using another. Most of the rest of the tests were based on mailings of 400 to 500 letter-questionnaires—again split on a half-and-half basis.
>
> In each test, the outgoing letter was a 200-word request for help in determining what publications the respondent reads. The questionnaire was a standard "AER" questionnaire—a list of publications, with a place for the respondent to indicate his chances (in percent) of seeing an outstanding ad had it appeared within the last six months. Returns averaged 46% from the original mailing, and 37% from the follow-up mailing to non-respondents.
>
> In the following tables, a value of 100 is given to the percent of returns from a "standard" mailing. Except where indicated, this consists of a letter on Basford letterhead, with the questionnaire appearing on the reverse side; a full matching fill-in; a salutation of "Dear Mr."; the letter mailed in a No. 10 window envelope, with a regular 5-cent stamp; and the return envelope carrying a regular 5-cent stamp. Except for the test of mailing dates, both halves of each test were mailed on the same day—usually on a Monday.
>
> The cost shown represents the cost per letter for a mailing of 1,000 letter-questionnaires.

[5]"How Stamps, Envelopes and Addressing Affect Returns of Mailed Questionnaires." G. M. Basford Research News. No. 20. June 22, 1964.

Test of Letterhead	*4 Tests*	*2 Tests*	*Cost/Letter*
G. M. Basford	100	100	28.1c
Industrial Research Associates		96	28.1
Client	96		28.1

Test of Stamps, Outgoing Letter	*3 Tests*	*2 Tests*	*Cost/Letter*
Regular 5c	100		28.1c
Commemorative 5c	87	87	28.1
Postage Meter—1st class		85	27.7
Postage Meter—3rd class	(Being Tested)		26.7

Test of Outgoing Envelopes	*1 Test*	*Cost/Letter*
Regular No. 10	100	30.4c*
Window No. 10	94	28.1

*Regular envelopes are cheaper but require addressing; costs are based on letter carrying full fill-in.

Test of Full-In, Salutation	*3 Tests*	*2 Tests*	*1 Test*	*Cost/Letter*
Full Fill-in, Dear Mr.	100*	100*	100*	30.4c*
Full Fill-in, Dear Sir	94			29.4 *
No Fill-in, Dear Mr.			79	25.6 *
No Fill-in, Dear Sir		76		23.9 *

*These tests and costs are all based on using regular envelopes, not window envelopes.

Test of Return Stamp	*1 Test*	*1 Test*	*Cost/Letter*
Regular 5c	100		28.1c
Commemorative 5c		93	28.1
Postage Meter	(Being Tested)		27.7
Business Reply	87	87	24.5 *

*Costs for postage reply are based on a 40% return.

Test of Mailing Date	*2 Tests*	*Cost/Letter*
Mailed on Friday	100	28.1c
Mailed on Monday	94	28.1
Mailed on Wednesday	(Being Tested)	28.1

Test of 25c Incentive	*1 Test*	*Cost/Letter*
No Incentive	100	28.1c
Incentive	173	56.1

Test of Questionnaire	*2 Tests*	*Cost/Letter*
Questionnaire on back of letter	100	29.7c
Questionnaire on separate sheet	85	30.7

"Cost/Letter" includes stationery and envelopes; flat-bed printing of letter from monotype through a typewriter ribbon—with matching fill-in; signature in blue ink; multilithing questionnaire on back; folding, collating, and inserting letter and return envelope; sealing and mailing; and affixing stamps to both the outgoing and return envelope.

DANGERS IN TESTING

While direct mail testing is definitely desirable, there is a danger of going overboard and becoming "test happy" or of putting too much stock in results of individual tests.

Perhaps an even greater danger lies in the tendency of some direct mail advertisers to try and apply test results developed by some other advertiser to provide answers to their own problems. While there are many cases in which the tests of two different advertisers will turn up the same answers, there is little guarantee that this will happen. Just the name and reputation of the mailer alone will bring a substantial variation in results. Add to this a difference in products, price, mailing schedule, markets, and other factors and there is little sense in trying to draw conclusions from the tests of others.

Error Factors

Another danger in testing is a failure to allow a sufficient factor for variations in test results. A number of leading direct mail advertisers have sent *identical* mailing pieces to large lists and keyed reply cards on an every-other-piece or every-third-piece basis. In such "tests" it is not unusual to come up with variances of as high as 10% to 25%.

To prevent misinterpretation of results, it is desirable to retest wherever possible to confirm any answers which appear to have been pinned down in an initial test.

Waiting Until the Full Results are Known

One of the biggest dangers in testing is the tendency for direct mail advertisers to try to read too much into the initial stage of a testing period. A good example of why it is important to wait until the whole story has developed is shown in a case study reported by Lewis Kleid, Inc. This study involved a $1.00 trial offer with the objective of converting these trials into full-price magazine subscriptions:

List	Initial Return %	Conversion %	Net Return %
1	6.86	23	1.58
2	6.17	13	.80
3	5.91	13	.77
4	5.86	24	1.40
5	5.29	26	1.37
6	5.22	12	.63
7	5.14	23	1.18
8	5.00	18	.90
9	4.90	15	.74
10	4.57	26	1.19
11	4.20	34	1.43

In commenting on the returns, Lewis Kleid noted that the list which pulled the lowest initial return was the second highest on net return and had the highest conversion percentage. Said Kleid: "Lists which produce an exceptional return on a free or low-unit offer must be checked carefully since the percentage of conversions and poor credit may make them unprofitable. On the other hand, lists which produce a low initial response may surprisingly end up with a high conversion and pay-up rate."

Fallacy of Fallacious Testing

In a speech some years ago at the Hundred Million Club, New York's association of mail order advertisers, Maxwell Sackheim talked of "The Fallacy of Fallacious Testing":

> I have come to the conclusion that mail order people generally are addicted to the insidious habit of *overtesting*. So serious is this disease that, where it exists in its most pernicious form, the unsuspecting victim loses his ability to think for himself, to judge, to make decisions, to act. He believes the easy way out of any selling problem is to test. Why think when it is so easy to get the correct answer by mailing a couple of thousand or by running an ad or two?
>
> If every test could be safely projected, much of the fallacy of testing would be eliminated. But we all know how much difference there can be between the result of a test and the result of a mailing. Too many things can happen to destroy the projection of a test. Within the span of a season, a month, or even a week, marked economic, competitive, or psychological changes can take place, and when they do—blooey go your expectations. And the element of elapsed time is only one of the dangers.
>
> I have known of campaigns based on the results of a 200-test mailing—of weighty decisions arrived at by virtue of an infinitesimal difference of results between the use of half-cent stamps instead of metered mail, between colored envelopes and white, between No. 10 envelopes and No. 6. You would think, after so many years of recorded experience, we would have learned that tests do not always tell the whole truth—that we will never

completely formularize advertising as long as there are changes in the weather, in world conditions, in domestic affairs, and even in local conditions from month to month and from week to week. That we will never be able to project a test with absolute assurance that the final result will be true to our original projection as long as an interval of time elapses between our test and our campaign.

I am not arguing against testing, but against *fallacious testing;* and against faulty interpretations of tests. I object to tests which determine the best day of the week on which to mail; to tests which are intended to prove whether a price of $1.98 is better than $1.99; to tests of half a dozen or more slightly different letters; and to tests of 500, or even 1,000, to determine whether a proposition or a list is worth going ahead with on a large scale.

Tests that tell you nothing or actually mislead you are worse than none. Divide any list into units of 1,000 and after the results are in, check the percentages of orders against each of those units. You'll be startled by the difference between your "best" thousand and your "worst."

The cure for indiscriminate testing is judgment. Disregard, ruthlessly and boldly, and without regret or reservation, any idea that you are not confident has a chance to pay. Don't toy with "fringe" or "lunatic" ideas that you would disregard at once if they came out of someone else's head, or if their cost came out of your pocket. The reason for failure is not a lack of ideas, but a lack of discrimination in their use.

There are many who agree wholeheartedly with Max Sackheim—and a lot of direct mail experts put it in even stronger language. Howard Dana Shaw, for example, says in an article, "Beware of Tests" in *The Reporter of Direct Mail Advertising:*

The disease "test-mania" costs mailers millions, because most tests are worthless and most test statistics reported by experts are all wet. And that means that every day somebody in direct mail is jumping at conclusions and spending money in the wrong direction.

Value of Testing

But while there are those who constantly warn of the danger of overtesting, the majority of successful direct mail advertisers —particularly those in the mail order field—never stop testing. Their thinking is best typified by some words from Boyce Morgan[6]:

There has been a lot written and said about "too much testing," "testing minor details," and "judgment is better than testing." Yet a lot of us stubborn mail order people go right on testing every chance we get.

Why do we do it? Are we just spineless poltroons, with no confidence in our own judgment?

6Quoted in "How to Think About Mail Order" by Henry Hoke. *The Reporter of Direct Mail Advertising Inc.* Garden City, New York.

Could be! I think I have about as much confidence in my own judgment as the next mail order man, and when I can't test—or until I *can* test—I rely on it with few misgivings.

But in a couple of cases, I've relied on my judgment first, and tested later—and been badly burnt. After you've done that a few times, and thrown away several thousand dollars of your own money doing it, you soon go back to a "constant testing" policy—and let the accusations of cowardice fall where they may.

I've just avoided making that same mistake again. Here's the story:

Our best pulling letter on "Better Business by Telephone" has been our "Stop and Think" letter. A few months ago I wrote a new one, which we called the "New Questions" letter. It was my judgment that it should pull better than the old letter—but experience has taught me to stick to the old and tested letter until a new one proves itself, no matter what my personal judgment is.

At the same time, I had the feeling that on a comparatively high-priced business service like ours a two-page letter should work better when printed on two separate sheets, than when printed on both sides of a single sheet. But again, I wanted to know for sure.

So over the past couple of months we have run a series of tests, both to make sure that the "New Questions" letter *really was* better than the old "Stop and Think" letter, and also to settle the "minor point" as to whether we should run them on a single sheet both sides, or on two sheets.

Now these are all small tests, but note their beautiful consistency. And also note how the Morgan judgment got kicked in the pants. (*See table on the next page.)*

Two things seem pretty obvious. First, the old "Stop and Think" letter is still a lot better than the new letter. Second, both letters work a lot better on both sides of a single sheet than on two sheets.

In fact, the one-sheet treatment is actually a bigger factor affecting returns than the difference in the letters. In no case does a two-sheet letter pull better than one sheet both sides. But by putting the weaker letter on one sheet, you can make it outpull the stronger letter on two sheets!

I challenge any expert to forecast this outcome on the basis of his judgment alone. And wouldn't I be crazy now to follow my original judgment—which would have been to use the new letter instead of the old—and on two sheets instead of both sides of the same sheet? It turned out to be the worst possible combination I could have used!

Of course, we'll make a few more tests. But I've never seen results reverse themselves when they've been as definite and consistent as these have been.

And, again of course, we are not generalizing about the comparative value of *all* letters run on one and two sheets. The results are convincing for *these* letters, on *our* service—and that's all. But it is certainly a "minor detail" that I'm going to test on every future letter I use.

The Tempered Viewpoint

Between these two extremes, you will find a more tempered viewpoint. It was well expressed by Ed Mayer in the third edition of his very valuable book, *How to Make More Money With Your Direct Mail* (National Foremen's Institute. New London, Connecticut 1960). Ed used to make a lot of speeches on the subject of "Seven Cardinal Principles of Direct Mail." The seventh of his principles was: "Test every mailing you make." Now Ed says:

Boyce Morgan's Test of Two Letters

		"Stop & Think" Letter 1 sheet, both sides	"New Questions" Letter 1 sheet, both sides
List A		19 orders	15 orders
List B		34 orders	22 orders
	Total	53 orders	37 orders
		"Stop & Think" Letter 1 sheet, both sides	"New Questions" Letter 2 sheets
List C		26 orders	13 orders
List D		16 orders	5 orders
	Total	42 orders	18 orders
		"Stop & Think" Letter 2 sheets	"New Questions" Letter 1 sheet, both sides
List E		20 orders	22 orders
List F		18 orders	32 orders
	Total	38 orders	54 orders
		"New Questions" Letter 1 sheet, both sides	"New Questions" Letter 2 sheets
List G		18 orders	8 orders
List H		13 orders	3 orders
	Total	31 orders	11 orders

The principle was wrong because you not only can't test every mailing you make, but furthermore, and much more important, it is a sinful waste of money if you do.

There are four almost obvious reasons why you should not test all your mailings:

1. You shouldn't test unimportant things and minor details.
2. The timing of your tests may make your final mailing results completely impossible to judge.
3. The overall size of your mailing market may be such that you cannot possibly test legitimately without using the entire list.
4. The great majority of direct mail neither asks for, nor expects, either an order or an inquiry.

M. P. Brown, one of the real mail order "greats" has, in one short paragraph, given the whole picture of why unimportant things are not worth testing. He says: *"If the success of a mail order operation is dependent upon testing the little things like underscoring key phrases, such an operation is built upon sand."*

What to Test

An indication of the limitless number of things which can be tested in direct mail was given in a column by Thomas L. Collins in *The Reporter of Direct Mail Advertising.*[7] In this column, Tom Collins reported on the answer he got when he asked Sol Blumenfeld for some of the possibilities he considered in seeking to create or improve a winning direct mail package. The answer:

Should we test a jumbo 9 by 12 inch envelope? A baronial-size envelope? Maybe our present envelope in four color?

How about testing a self mailer? A reply-velope package? A booklet mailing? A simple postcard mailing?

Should we try cutting a display window in the envelope for a four-color circular show-through?

Could we try a Kraft paper envelope? A colored stock envelope? A test paper or metallic foil envelope?

Would embossing the envelope or watermarking the inside of our envelope help our package? And how about using scented ink or stock?

Should we try the new zippered, heat-sealed polybag envelopes?

Should we test letting the premium, involvement device or trial offer on the order form show through the envelope?

What about envelope copy? Should we test teaser copy? Flashing the offer? Or should we leave copy off the envelope altogether?

Should we use heat transfer addressing on the envelope? Direct addressing? Or should we cut a window in the envelope and address the order form or letter?

Shall we develop a 2-color circular test? A 4-color circular? How about testing a giant 22 by 36 inch poster-spectacular circular?

[7]"Excedrin Headache No. 246852" by Thomas L. Collins. *The Reporter of Direct Mail Advertising.* June 1968.

Should we design a "non-tracking" circular instead of a "tracking" circular? It would give us more room for big displays.

How about circular vs. booklet or multiple inserts?

Should we try a die-cut circular? Perhaps a circular with 3-dimensional pop-up devices like those on greeting cards?

Should we use photographs instead of illustrations? Or add line drawings to the copy panels?

How about enclosing some transparencies of our product with a low cost viewing device?

Should we create a combination letter-circular? Combination letter-order form? It could save us $10 per M.

Should we test a fully computerized letter? A computer matched fill-in letter? Maybe a highly personalized Nelco or automatic type-written letter.

Shall we do a multigraphed letter? Screened type? IBM Executive?

Should we test the use of illustrations in the letter? Photographs down the side of the letterhead? Or how about a rebus-type picture letter or a jumbo typewriter letter?

Should we test a long copy, six-page letter? A short memo-type letter? A completely handwritten letter? A telegram-type letter?

Should we use supercaptions and subcaptions in letter copy? Should we use two colors in the body of the letter? How about double-spacing the type for increased legibility?

Should we test enclosing samples of our product? Fabric swatches? Press proofs? Lithographs? Or how about enclosing an inexpensive plastic long-playing record promoting our product?

Should we test enclosing a separate insert of testimonials? A separate guarantee insert? A separate premium insert?

How about involvement devices? Yes-No tokens?" Stamps? Record tokens? Book tokens? Sweepstakes tokens?

Instead of a punchboard token, how about a grab-bag of 50 or 60 loose tokens representing our offer?

Should we test a piggy back offer?

Why don't we test a game format? Book Club Bingo? Record Club Crosstic? Art I.Q.? How about using an invisible ink novelty?

Should we test a BRE against a BRC? Air mail return vs. first class return? Should we enclose a postage stamp?

Should we use heavier stock on the BRC? Should we print on safety paper?

Should we enclose an extra Pass-along order form?

Should we test a letter written from a woman's point of view? A letter written by a corporate officer?

Should we test copy that is more anecdotal and humorous? More bargainy and value oriented?

Should we use understatement? Or emphasizing our claims more?

Should our copy be more locally oriented? Would a letter from our Topeka, Kansas salesman or post office box prove a better puller than one from New York? Or would a mailing from Paris, France test out better than the one from New York?

12 RULES FOR DIRECT MAIL TESTING

The "rules" for any particular direct mail test must depend principally upon the objective of the test. However, there are 12 basic guidelines which will apply to the vast majority of testing situations:

CHECKLIST FOR DIRECT MAIL TESTING

1. Test one thing at a time—or everything.
2. Make sure your test lists are representative of the entire list.
3. Keep track of the portion of any list used for testing.
4. Be sure to use a sufficient quantity to obtain reliable test results.
5. Consider two-flight testing.
6. Mail all pieces at the same time.
7. Don't make any *major* decisions based on *minor* results.
8. Don't follow results blindly.
9. Don't get test happy.
10. Don't try to read non-tested factors into your results.
11. Follow up quickly.
12. Continue to keep tab on your results.

1. *Test one thing at a time—or everything.* There are only two valid types of direct mail tests. The first involves the "package" testing concept wherein you test one complete mailing unit against another complete mailing unit and send both to lists which can reasonably be considered "equal." The more common type of testing, however, involves evaluation of elements of a mailing—copy, lists, reply devices, offers, prices, format of various elements, etc. In such cases it is important to test just one thing at a time—with all other factors the same.

If, for example, you wish to determine the relative value of window envelopes against full-face envelopes, all other elements of the mailing should be the same. Or if you want to test first-class vs. third-class postage, you will destroy the validity of your test if you try two different types of copy at the same time.

The one exception to this "rule" is that you must keep elements in harmony with one another. You cannot very well make a reasonable test of different prices if both your selling copy and reply device do not carry complete pricing information. In fact, one cardinal rule of testing is to evaluate all elements of the mailing package to make sure you have not confused your offer by introducing a test element into one part of the mailing without changing other items which are in conflict with such an offer.

2. *Make sure your test lists are representative of the entire list.* This rule has two important applications. First of all, when making a comparison test, be sure that all lists being used are equals. The easiest method is to simply split your list on an every-other-name, every-third-name, etc., basis. This may present some mechanical problems, but they are usually quite easily solved.

Probably the best method to handle this type of list division is to run the two or more versions of the item to be tested through a collating machine so they will be stacked in proper test order. For example, if your test will involve three different reply cards you can have them stacked on a 1-2-3-1-2-3-1-2-3-1, etc., basis before they are run through the addressing machine. Of course, if the reply device is not one of the basic variables in the test, it is still important to have it properly coded so you will be able to quickly analyze test returns.

If it is not practical to pre-sort in test order, it will usually be to your advantage to keep each of the lists being used in identical geographical order so that they can be quickly inter-filed before mailing to take advantage of bulk mailing economies. (And in this regard, it is important to remember that the Post Office does not care if you vary features of your mailing just as long as all pieces are of the same size and weight. Size and weight are the things the Post Office considers when it requires pieces to be "identical" to qualify for bulk mailing rates.)

The other application for this rule involves testing of lists. If you want to determine the pulling power of a given list, it is highly important to make sure the portion you choose to test is representative of the entire list. It may not be practical to conduct list tests on an every-other-name basis. This creates problems in making extension mailings without a lot of duplication. If there has been just a single change in a list between the time of the test and the extension, it becomes almost impossible to obtain the portion of the list which has not already been mailed since the 1-2-1-2-1, etc., sequence is no longer the same.

One common method of selecting a segment of a list for testing is to choose equally spaced portions. For example, if the list is on Addressograph plates you may want to use every fifth or seventh drawer of plates. Or you may want to use an inch system wherein you measure off the list and address to those plates which fall within the first inch of space in every foot (or every 6 inches, 10 inches, and so forth).

When it comes to very large lists, you will have to settle for a less representative cross section in many cases. Since most large lists are arranged geographically, you will want to make sure your test sample includes names from all of the areas covered by the list. One of the most common methods of testing such lists is to select a *major* state in each of the five basic regions—South, East, Central, Mountain, and Pacific—and then establish a consistent pattern for that section of the lists for those states you will include (or which additional states you wish to add if any of the chosen states will not provide sufficient names to make up a representative sample segment for a given region). If possible, you will want to make sure your sample portion from any region is in the same proportion to the total sample as the total number of names from that region is in proportion to the entire list. In such testing, you will also want to double-check to make sure you have not, by accident, come up with a list that represents only major cities or only nonmetropolitan areas. This will introduce a certain amount of bias into your test sample.

Another type of bias you will want to avoid, if possible, is that which shows up if your sample represents only a small part of the alphabet. In the DMMA Report, "Testing—The Scientific Approach in Direct Mail," Dr. W. A. Doppler points out:

> Family names are more than tags. They tell about origin, family traditions, customers, etc. In the language of testing, common names indicate clusters, and clusters produce bias in a sample.
>
> Suppose you need a 6,000 sample. You could take any 6,000 names in alphabetical order. Suppose you did. Suppose your list is large. You would bias your sample with an undue share of Browns, Caseys, Cohens, Daniels, Diamonds, and all the other high-frequency names in the early part of

the ABCs. You would miss the Schiffs, Schultzes, Schwartz's, Smiths, and Turners at the tail end.

If you are renting lists, you'll want to do everything possible to make sure you are getting a true cross section of the total list. It is not at all an uncommon practice for many list renters to introduce bias into samples by including a higher percentage of their "best" names than will be found in the entire lists. Only experience—both your own and that of list brokers with whom you work—will protect you from the "loaded" list sample.

List expert Ed Burnett recommends using the last one or two numbers of the Zip Code, rather than every Nth name, to develop test lists. His reasoning:

1. Nth number samples (every 100th, or every 125th, or every 150th name) are one of the most talked of (but least used) methods of test selection.
   a. If the computer service doesn't have an Nth number selection capability, a new program must be provided, and tested and debugged.
   b. Computer services often find it easier to "take the first so many of" as the first 200 in a state, or the first 300 in a 3 digit SCF.
   c. The "Nth number sample" while statistically ideal, is too much trouble.
   d. The average user cannot by inspection determine if the test sample has been drawn on an "Nth number" basis or not—so supposedly "Nth number" tests are easily fudged.
2. Nth number samples in most cases *cannot* be skipped on continuations. (A continuation is additional use of the same list after a successful test.)
   a. Unless the computer service has a quite sophisticated program which tags each record used for a test, there is almost no way that "Nth number" test quantities or prior continuations can be identified. If the computer cannot identify such records, it cannot skip them.
   b. Very few mailers involve themselves in such sophisticated programming.
   c. Most if not virtually all "continuations" must by their very nature incorporate duplication of records already run before.

d. If a list between uses is updated, in any way—even by the removal or addition of just one record—this kills any possibility of guaranteeing to skip the prior test sample.

3. The use of last digit of zip, or last two digits of zip is safe, sure, economical, and simple.

a. If you run all (or most) records ending in a given digit, or pair of digits, for your test, you can make certain of skipping the test simply by omitting such digits in your continuation.

b. If you wish to see what a 2nd mailing to the *same* records will do, you select records with the same last digit or last two digits. True, a few new names may now be in file due to an update, but even a 10% or 20% increase or decrease in the file will not obviate the validity of such a test.

It should be clear that you hardly ever can get the *same* Nth number sample for a test of 2nd use of the same names.

c. Last digit zip is a good reasonable cross-section of any file. As the chart on page 1245 indicates, on business lists and service lists (and this will hold for consumer lists as well) last digit zips range from 6% of a typical file to 16%—with 7% of the 10 last numbers of zip being within a small fraction of covering an even 10% of the list.

d. Where a 1 for 10 or a 1 for 15, or a 1 for 20 selection will not provide sufficient sampling thru the whole list, use of last two digits of zip will guarantee this. (If a list has 100,000 records, and a test of 3,000 is desired, taking all "2's" (i.e.—1 for 10) will produce 3,000 records when ⅓rd thru the list. Taking all "O2's," plus "22's" (a little over 3% of all zip records) will produce a solid sample thru the entire list.

e. It is easy to record usage by last digit of zip—and easy for the list owner to comply with such selection and omission.

Even the bugaboo of leaving records unused in a file can be solved. Let us assume you have tested zip records ending in 2 with a 5,000 sample—and the list has 200,000 on it. From the chart, zips ending in 2 equal 10% of the file, or 20,000. You can call the balance of these records ending in 2 either by stipulating "start at 5 digit XXXXX," or by stipulating (if such was the case) "skip the first 5,000 zip records ending in 2, and take the balance."

If you are a list owner, and paying the costs of providing reasonably adequate test samples from a large list or a large list universe, you may find it expedient to establish test sample lots.

1. Such test samples should be drawn off periodically—say once per quarter—to obviate obsolescence.
2. Such test samples should be of sufficient size to provide unduplicated test samples for all similar offers.
3. It is a good idea to draw off samples of differing size—to make possible modest continuations without recourse to the main file. For a frequently tested list in the 300,000 to 500,000 class we recommend unduplicated sample lots be drawn of 50,000, 25,000 and 15,000. A user who moves from 5,000 to 20,000 can easily be accommodated within the first two blocks . . . without recourse to the main file.
4. These sample lots should be selected on the basis of last two digits of zip—with each quarterly selection utilizing a different group of 2 digit groups. In this way access to the main file, without duplicating one record on the current test sample file, is assured.

The following charts show statistical data, based on analyses of large files of businesses (all Beauty Shops) and services (all Schools) . . . by last digit of zip, and last two digits of zip.

LAST DIGIT ZIP ANALYSIS

Digit	All Beauty Shops	All Schools	Average
1	17%	16%	16½
2	10	10	10
3	9	9	9
4	9	9	9
5	8	9	8½
6	9	9	9
7	9	8	8½
8	7	8	7½
9	6	6	6
0	12	13	12½

LAST-TWO DIGIT ZIP ANALYSIS

Digits	All Beauty Shops	All Schools	Average
01	9.41%	7.61%	8.01
02	3.04	2.10	2.57
03	2.08	2.22	2.15
04	2.07	2.19	2.13

Digits	B. S.	S.	Avg.	Digits	B. S.	S.	Avg.
05	2.07%	2.24%	2.16	49	.53%	%	
06	2.43	1.95	2.19	50	1.42	1.55	1.49
07	1.08	1.51	1.29	51	.71	.96	.84
08	1.07	1.30	1.19	53	.70	.84	.77
09	1.62	1.16	1.39	54		1.05	
10	2.10	1.96	2.03	56	.60	.84	.72
11	1.07	1.59	1.33	57	.60	.82	.71
12		1.38		58	.46		
13	1.23	1.68	1.46	59	.13		
18	1.30	1.01	1.16	60	.16	1.67	.92
19	1.10	.90	1.00	62	.73		
20	2.20	2.05	2.13	66	.73		
22	1.22	1.25	1.24	67	.63		
25	1.10			68		.66	
26	1.14	1.08	1.11	69	.50	.63	.57
27	.84	.91	.73	71		.69	
28	.71	.93	.82	72		.69	
29	.61	.80	.72	73		.63	
30	1.63	1.78	1.71	74	.47	.63	.55
31	1.06	1.14	1.10	75	.41	.53	.47
32		1.12		77	.52	.66	.59
33	.80	1.04	.92	79		.47	
34	1.09	.88	.99	80	.74	.82	.78
35	.96	1.08	1.02	81		.53	
36	.80	.90	.85	82	.11	.49	.30
38	.75	.86	.81	83	.44	.53	.49
39	.60	.73	.67	85	.23	.45	.34
40	1.07	1.87	1.47	89	.10	.29	.19
45	.75			95	.21	.28	.25
47	.64			96	.16	.17	.17
				98		.13	

NOTE: Zip Codes are comprised of 5 Digits: The first 3 Digits describe the Sectional Center, while the final 2 Digits are assigned to individual post offices and/or neighborhood areas within cities.

You will note that the preponderance of the use of 01 (for virtually every zip area) makes two-digit zip "01" by itself the equivalent of any last digit zip. (01=8%, last digit zip 2 thru 0 range from 6% to 12%). As is logical, 02, 03, 04, 05, 06 are next largest, and are indeed the only 2-digit numbers other than those ending in zero with 2% or more of the records. There is a strong correlation between the business file and the professional file—which were zipped by two different organizations. The variance, except for 18 small 2 digit zips which appear in one list and not the other, are in the neighborhood of + or -10 to 15%. Over 95% of the records in each list can be directly compared by 2 digit zip.

3. *Keep track of the portion of any list used for testing.* Unless you would just as soon remail to names on a test list, you will want to keep records of the portion of any list tested so those names can be eliminated when making subsequent tests or when mailing to the entire list.

There is a number of methods for keeping such records, depending primarily on how the sample was selected. If you have used equally spaced portions of a list, a simple mathematical record will provide the information you need. However, you may want to supplement this with more detailed information such as the first and last name in each test segment so you can double check when making subsequent mailings. Most mailers do not worry too much whether or not there is a slight duplication unless, of course, the mailing pieces are particularly expensive. In such cases, it may well pay to even keep a duplicate record of *all* names involved in a test.

As pointed out previously, it is almost impossible to make unduplicated followup mailings when selection has been on an every-other-name basis. If this type of test is desired, it may well pay to have the entire list addressed when the sample list is prepared and then hold "unused" names pending results of the tests.

4. *Be sure to use a sufficient quantity to obtain reliable test results.* If you hope to obtain valid information from a direct mail test, you must make sure your test quantity is large enough to produce reliable information. Far too often, inexperienced direct mail advertisers will try to draw hard-and-fast conclusions from small tests.

It is important to remember that it is not only the quantity of pieces mailed, but also the quantity of returns which is important in determining whether you have made a large enough test to produce reasonably reliable results.

There are many differences of opinion among experienced direct mail advertisers about what constitutes a sufficient quantity for the average test. The most commonly used rule of thumb for list tests is to use a minimum of 2,000 names or 10% of the list, up to a maximum of 10,000 names. When a list is larger than 100,000 names, the usual procedure is to conduct a series of tests in increments of 10,000 until a full 10% has been tested. However, if the list is particularly large and results from the first one or two tests indicate probable success, subsequent tests are usually made in quantities considerably larger than 10,000.

When you are making comparison tests, a common rule is to keep mailing until you have a minimum of 200 replies upon which to base your comparisons. In many cases, however, this will prove to be far too small a quantity of returns to really prove a point. A number of scientific guides will be presented later in this chapter to help you determine the quantity you will need to obtain reliable information.

5. *Consider two-flight testing.* We have already mentioned the desirability of making a continuing series of tests when large lists are involved. This same principle can be applied to nearly every type of test unless, of course, the available lists are too small to permit additional test mailings.

A good rule of thumb for all direct mail testing, however, is to follow the "two-flight" principle, wherein you follow up your initial test with another identical test to make sure that some extraneous factor has not prejudiced test results.

6. *Mail all pieces at the same time.* One of the surest ways to introduce bias into test results is to mail your samples on different days. Direct mail results can be drastically affected by current events. Weather can be a major factor, and newspaper headlines and other factors can cause major variations in results.

So be sure to deliver all pieces in your sample to the post office at the same time—not just the same day, but preferably intermixed in the same bundles and/or mailbags. Just an hour's difference in delivery of mailings to some post offices can mean as long as a week or 10 days' difference in eventual delivery of the pieces.

It is important to recognize that all control of your tests stop the minute you deliver your mailings to the post office. Therefore, it is important to do everything possible to control them to the very last minute they are in your hands. It often pays to make an advance check with your local postmaster to determine the best possible time to drop your mailing so it can be handled in one lot without a great deal of delay.

7. *Do not make any major decisions based on minor results.* We have already mentioned the importance of having a sufficient quantity of returns to enable you to make valid judgments as to the results of your tests. If you want your direct mail testing program to be of real value, you will want to avoid making any major decisions until you have a quantity of returns large enough to present clear-cut evidence.

In his "Beware of Tests" article, Howard Dana Shaw gives this example:

> One of the best jobs of scientific testing being done is at the Kiplinger Washington Agency. Boyce Morgan, who runs that end of the business, showed the Philadelphia Direct Mail Club the charts they keep to determine how many letters must be mailed before you can rely on the results.
>
> Factors being tested are plotted on the graph by lines representing return results. If one letter brings 3% on a small test and another 2½%, one line starts out a little above the other. They find these lines perform strange antics of crossing and uncrossing through mailings of 1,000 and 2,000 (quantities believed by many to give conclusive answers)—yes, and through mailings of 5,000 and 10,000.
>
> When the lines settle down and behave themselves so that one stays above the other, then they know which letter or other factor being tested is superior. They find that it takes 25,000 to 30,000 before the question is settled, leaving no possibility of the result figures reversing themselves.

8. *Don't follow results blindly.* As the Kiplinger example shows, you don't want to trust any initial results until all evidence is in. But even when all the evidence appears to be at hand, you will still want to keep your eyes and mind open to the possibility that you may not really have found the hard-and-fast rule you seek.

This world is full of direct mail advertisers who are convinced they have come up with some uncontestable "rules" for success in their mailings . . . and they follow them year in and year out —often right into bankruptcy. Too many circumstances change —and often change quickly—to make it advisable to accept the results of any test as the final word. The only sure way is to use the information you do develop, but keep testing to find out if there might not be new circumstances which require a new approach.

9. *Don't get test-happy.* Yes, keep testing—but do not get so bogged down in testing your mind becomes closed to the possibility of following your intuition and getting on with the business of advertising and/or selling your products.

Testing should always be a *secondary* activity for direct mail advertisers. If time and money are available for tests, fine. But never let them dominate your direct mail program.

And do not get involved in testing minor details. Go back and read those words of Max Sackheim's on page 1234. Think about them. And then forget all about trying to test whether a blue envelope and an orange reply card will outpull a purple envelope and a yellow reply card. Such tests may provide interesting conversational tidbits to toss around at direct mail meetings, but chances are they will not mean a blasted thing when you try to apply the results to another mailing.

Test the big things—copy approaches, complete packages, lists, major variations in reply devices, different offers, etc. And test them as often as your schedule and budget will permit. Then you will not have time to worry about minor things such as the color of ink for your postal indicia.

10. *Do not try to read non-tested factors into your results.* An always-present danger is the tendency to try to find answers to questions which were not subjected to controlled testing. Whenever there is a variation in results, a lot of direct mail advertisers immediately try to find out "why" by studying their mailing package.

There are just too many "outside" factors which can influence results to make such a search very profitable. However, if you do come across something which might suggest a route to success, make it the subject of a test under controlled conditions. And do not trust your hunch until you have some reliable evidence to back it up.

11. *Follow up quickly.* When you have completed a test and are convinced you have the basic answers you need, follow up quickly with your regular mailings and/or list extensions. Outside factors can change rapidly and make your subsequent mailings subject to a whole new set of circumstances.

12. *Continue to keep tab on your results.* This is particularly important when it comes to extensions on rented lists. It will pay to always suspect rented test lists as being at least slightly loaded with better-than-average names. By keeping close track of your results on extensions you can get a good picture of the reliability of those from whom you rent your lists plus evidence with which you can do a better job of projecting probable returns when making future tests.

THE MATHEMATICS OF TESTING

Direct mail testing is by no means an exact science. However, it is helpful to apply as much science to testing as possible. Most important is to apply some of the established mathematical formulas to aid in interpreting your results. There are many formulas and mathematical tables which can be used, but probably the most helpful are the two tables shown here.

Law of Probability as Applied to Evaluation of the Results of Test Mailings

If— the size of the test mailing is:	and— the % return on the test mailing is:	then 95 chances out of 100, the % return on the identical mailing to the whole list will be between	If— the size of the test mailing is:	and— the % return on the test mailing is:	then 95 chances out of 100, the % return on the identical mailing to the whole list will be between
100	1	0 & 2.99	250	1	0 & 2.26
100	2	0 & 4.80	250	2	.23 & 3.77
100	3	0 & 6.41	250	3	.84 & 5.16
100	4	.08 & 7.92	250	4	1.52 & 6.48
100	5	.64 & 9.36	250	5	2.24 & 7.76
100	10	4.00 & 16.00	250	10	6.20 & 13.80
100	20	12.00 & 28.00	250	20	14.94 & 25.00
500	1	.11 & 1.89	1,000	1	.37 & 1.63
500	2	.75 & 3.25	1,000	2	1.12 & 2.88
500	3	1.48 & 4.52	1,000	3	1.92 & 4.08
500	4	2.25 & 5.75	1,000	4	2.76 & 5.24
500	5	3.05 & 6.95	1,000	5	3.62 & 6.38
500	10	7.32 & 12.68	1,000	10	8.10 & 11.90
500	20	16.42 & 23.58	1,000	20	17.48 & 22.52
2,000	1	.55 & 1.45	5,000	1	.72 & 1.28
2,000	2	1.37 & 2.63	5,000	2	1.60 & 2.40
2,000	3	2.24 & 3.76	5,000	3	2.52 & 3.48
2,000	4	3.12 & 4.88	5,000	4	3.45 & 4.55
2,000	5	4.03 & 5.97	5,000	5	4.38 & 5.62
2,000	10	8.66 & 11.34	5,000	10	9.15 & 10.85
2,000	20	18.21 & 21.79	5,000	20	18.87 & 21.13
10,000	1	.80 & 1.20	100,000	1	.94 & 1.06
10,000	2	1.72 & 2.28	100,000	2	1.91 & 2.09
10,000	3	2.66 & 3.34	100,000	3	2.89 & 3.11
10,000	4	3.61 & 4.39	100,000	4	3.88 & 4.12
10,000	5	4.56 & 5.44	100,000	5	4.86 & 5.14
10,000	10	9.40 & 10.60	100,000	10	9.81 & 10.19
10,000	20	19.20 & 20.80	100,000	20	19.75 & 20.25

Note: The size of the test mailing, not the size of the list being tested, governs the reliability of the test results.

The easiest to use is the one showing the law of probability as applied to evaluation of results of test mailing. This table was worked out for DMMA by E. L. Quenon in *Research Techniques for Direct Mail.* In using this table it is important to remember that it automatically allows for a 5% chance of error. This is a gamble readily accepted by most advertisers since to even try for greater accuracy is impractical.

Table of Minimum Sample Size

PLUS OR MINUS ERROR on Expected % of Return	Expected Percentage of Return from Mailing										
	1.0%	1.5%	2.0%	2.5%	3.0%	3.5%	4.0%	4.5%	5.0%	5.5%	6.0%
.05	152,100	227,000	301,200	374,600	447,200	519,000	590,100	660,400	729,900	798,700	866,700
.1	38,000	56,800	75,300	93,600	111,800	129,800	147,500	165,100	182,500	199,700	216,700
.2	9,500	14,200	18,800	23,400	27,900	32,400	36,900	41,300	45,600	49,900	54,200
.3	4,200	6,300	8,400	10,400	12,400	14,400	16,400	18,300	20,300	22,200	24,100
.4	2,400	3,500	4,700	5,900	7,000	8,100	9,200	10,300	11,400	12,500	13,500
.5	.....	2,300	3,000	3,700	4,500	5,200	5,900	6,600	7,300	8,000	8,700
.6	.....	.....	2,100	2,600	3,100	3,600	4,100	4,600	5,100	5,500	6,000
.7	.....	.....	.....	.....	2,300	2,600	3,000	3,400	3,700	4,100	4,400
.8	.....	.....	.....	.....	.....	2,000	2,300	2,600	2,900	3,100	3,400
.9	.....	.....	.....	.....	.....	.....	.....	2,000	2,300	2,500	2,700
1.0	.....	.....	.....	.....	.....	.....	.....	.....	.....	2,000	2,200

To pick a single example from the table, consider the case of a test mailing of 2,000 pieces which yields a 2% return. This will indicate that, according to the law of probability, there are 95 chances out of 100 that an identical mailing to the whole list from which the test sample was drawn will produce a return of between 1.37% and 2.63%.

The second table is considerably more complicated, but is designed to provide a wider range of information. It was compiled by Richard Ostheimer of Time Inc. for the DMMA Research Committee and was originally presented as part of a valued report on testing by Dr. Doppler. The following explanation of how to use the "Table of Minimum Sample Size" was included in the DMAA Report:

> The size of the sample does not depend upon the universe to be tested. It makes no difference whether your total list, the statistical universe, is 50,000 names or 500,000 names or 5 million names. The sample size will be the same for each list.
>
> *A sample must be large enough to produce statistically significant results and it need not be larger than the smallest number which will do that very thing.* Making a sample larger than necessary does not improve the test—it only adds to the labor and makes unnecessary expense. How then do we determine the sample size?
>
> 1. Make up your mind how *confident* you want to be. Mathematical statisticians have a measure they call "level of confidence." They have compiled tables, curves, and graphs of confidence levels. The two most often used levels of confidence are 99 chances in 100 and 95 chances in 100. In list-testing the 95 level will do. The table of sample size is figured on the 95 confidence level. In other words, when you use the table you know that if you ran many tests, chances are that 95 times out of 100 your sample would be representative of the whole list. You also know that five times in 100 you can expect to be wrong. Sampling is gambling. No getting away from that. No harm done either, so long as you know the size of the gamble you take.
>
> 2. Make up your mind how much *error* due to chance you can permit. Do you have to work very closely, say one-tenth of 1 percentage point plus or minus? Are you able and willing to accept .9% and 1.1% as the same figure, namely 1% plus or minus .1%? Or is one-half of 1 percentage point sufficiently accurate? The decision is up to you. The table gives you per-

missible errors from .05 to 1 percentage point in steps of one-tenth of 1 percentage point.

3. Make up your mind regarding the *expectancy* of your list. A list with an expected return of one reply out of 100 letters requires a different size sample than a list with an expected return of five out of 100. The expectancy is listed at the head of the columns. You will find expectancies from ½% to 6% in steps of ½% of expected returns from the list.

4. Select the sample size by going down the expectancy column until you meet the percentage-of-error row. This is your minimum sample.

How to Use the Table

You can use it to *find the permissible error.* Suppose you mailed 10,000 names, and got 1% returns. Go into the 1% column. The nearest figure there is 9,500. Go to the left until you are in the error column. There you find .2 percentage points. Now you can say the return from the mailing was 1% plus or minus .2. This means you may expect from the entire list a return somewhere between .8% and 1.2%.

Or you can use the table to *find the size of the minimum sample.* Suppose you have a list where you expect a return of 3.5%. You want to run a very close test, permitting yourself an error of .2%. In other words you are willing to accept returns of 3.7% and 3.3% as identical results, namely 3.5% plus or minimum .2. How large is the minimum sample? Start with the error column. Find the error of .2. Follow this row until you are in the 3.5% expectancy column and you find the figure 32,400. This is your minimum sample size.

There is a third way you can use the table to find significance. Suppose for some practical reason you must confine your mailing to 5,000 names. You did mail 5,000. The returns are in. You got 2%. Enter the table in the 2% column. The nearest sample size of the 5,000 is the 4,700 figure. Go to the left until you hit the error column. There you find .4 percentage points. Therefore you can say your mailing brought you 2% plus or minus .4 returns. If you had pulled a pair of samples for a comparison test and one brought 1.6% returns and the other brought 2.4% returns, there is nothing to choose between the two results. Statistically they are identical.

A System for Testing

For those who want to do a highly sophisticated direct mail testing job, a series of articles by Dr. C. L. Jain in *Direct Marketing* is an absolute must. Dr. Jain is on the faculty of the School of Business at St. John's University in Brooklyn and has an extensive background in direct mail. He has developed a number of formulae which will prove most helpful to the mathmatically inclined. For the average mailer, however, one of his *Direct Marketing* articles provides a good starting point in developing a testing program:[8]

> How can you be absolutely sure that any decision you make about offers, copy and package on the basis of test results is the right one? You can't. Absolute certainty is an impossible goal given the vagaries of testing and the statistical tools available to the researcher.
>
> However, you can come close enough to the goal of certainty to take much of the guesswork out of test results. All that is needed is a willingness to take the time to structure a test so that the response brings in meaningful data and a willingness to make the effort to analyze the data thus obtained with the use of statistical tools which have proved worthwhile to many mailers.
>
> The aim of this article is to outline a procedure for conducting a package (copy, offer, etc.) test and analyzing the data.
>
> The two most important things in the science of testing are: (1) how a test is conducted and (2) how data are analyzed. Testing is the basis of sampling analysis where a small number of items are used to acquire knowledge about the characteristics of the whole group, the universe. An error, no matter how small and in what direction it is made—either in constructing a test or analyzing data, adversely affects the quality of results.
>
> As in any form of research the best place to start is to spell out objectives as clearly as possible. Are we trying to find the best copy, offer, circular or anything else? Such information helps in making an appropriate test plan. While structuring a test one rule should be kept in mind—"Never test more than one thing at a time." This rule is not something which is required in statistical theory, but one is less likely to fall in an erroneous trap in interpreting data if it's followed. Anyone who wishes to test several variables may do so by pulling several pairs of samples, and determining, in each pair, the effect of one and only one variable.
>
> After the objective is set, one is ready to structure a test. Below are the steps to be followed:
>
> 1. Select five different samples from a list which meets the market profile of a mailer. It is not always necessary to conduct a package test on more than one list, particularly, where the objective is to develop one standard package. However, where the objective is to develop different packages for different markets, more than one list will be required.

8"Which Copy or Offer is Best?" by Dr. C. L. Jain. *Direct Marketing*. December 1968.

The size of each sample should be 5-10 thousand times the number of different packages to be tested. Although the reliability of results improves with the increase in the size of the sample, the use of too many names raises costs. To the author, a quantity of 5 to 10 thousand offers fairly reliable information. Whatever quantity is decided upon, it should be identical in each segment of a test.

Testing a copy or offer on different samples (as we will see later) enables the researcher to perform a consistency test—to see whether the results derived from each sample are relatively consistent with one another. Similarity in results implies that results are pretty conclusive and reliable.

2. Split names of each sample into as many equal segments as the number of packages. It is not necessary, though desirable, that each sample selected is representative of the whole list, because here the objective is to discover which package pulls relatively more than others and not to infer the performance of a list from a sample test. What is important, however, is that the names of each sample are split into homogenous segments, which can be achieved by an X-way split. Where four different packages are to be tested, the homogeneity in segments can be accomplished by dividing each sample by a four-way split. Assign a separate key to each segment of each sample.
3. Mail all the segments on the same day and from the same place.
4. When all the responses are in, list their cumulative return as shown in Table 1.

TABLE 1

Hypothetical Response

Package	Sample I		Sample II		Sample III		Sample IV		Sample V	
	Responses	%	Responses	%	Responses	%	Responses	%	Responses	%
A	300	3.00	360	3.60	290	2.90	325	3.25	350	3.50
B	250	2.50	200	2.00	190	1.90	245	2.45	210	2.10
C	260	2.60	800	8.00	270	2.70	290	2.90	280	2.80
D	280	2.80	290	2.90	300	3.00	50	.50	310	3.10

There is no single method for analyzing data from a test. Various tests, depending upon the objective, can be made for gathering information about the nature of data. However, in many cases, with three tests—test of average, test of consistency and test of significance—sufficient information can be obtained to draw a conclusion.

The most frequently used method in analyzing test data is the arithmetic average where the returns of all segments using the same packages are lumped together and then divided by the number of segments. The arithmetic average return of all four packages is given in the last row of Table 2, on page 1257. It shows that if the cost of each package is same, "C" is the

TABLE 2

Test of Arithmetic Average

Sample	PACKAGE			
	A (Responses)	B (Responses)	C (Responses)	D (Responses)
I	300	250	260	280
II	360	200	800	290
III	290	190	270	300
IV	325	245	290	50
V	350	210	280	310
Total	1625	1095	1900	1230
Arithmetic Average	325	219	380	246
Arithmetic Average in Percentage	3.25	2.19	3.80	2.46

Note: Quantity mailed on each segment is assumed to be 10,000.
Source: Table 1.

best package. On the average, it pulled 3.80% response, the highest of all. Other packages in descending order of average return are "A," "D" and "B."

It is not unusual for the data to exhibit extreme variations not only in the return of different packages but also of the different segments of the same list with the same package. Under such circumstances, conclusions will be distorted by the use of an arithmetic average. Extreme variations in response do not generally reflect the characteristics of packages—that is, extremely high response is attributable to an exceptionally bad package—though they certainly affect the computed average. Looking at Tables 1 and 2, one finds that package "C," when examined with respect to other packages within each sample, does not appear to be the best package. Extremely high response in one segment (8.0% in sample II) made its overall average the highest. Similarly, extremely low response of package "D" in sample IV adversely affected its overall average.

To exclude the influence of extreme values from the overall averages, a *modified* average is used. To compute the modified average, responses of each package are listed in descending order, and the average of each is calculated by eliminating the extreme values. In Table 3 (page 1258), the average of three central values were computed, eliminating one value at the top and one at the bottom. This shows that "A" rather than "C" is the best package. (There is no hard and fast rule about how many values should be eliminated from top and bottom. This depends upon the number of total observations available and the number of extreme values—values which appear to be out of line.)

TABLE 3

Test of Modified Average

Rank	PACKAGE A (Responses)	B (Responses)	C (Responses)	D (Responses)
1	360	250	800	310
2	350	245	290	300
3	325	210	280	290
4	300	200	270	280
5	290	190	260	50
Total of three central values	975	655	840	870
Modified Average	325	218	280	290
Modified Average in Percentage	3.25	2.18	2.80	2.90

Note: Quantity mailed on each segment is assumed to be 10,000.
Source: Table 1.

The best package is not necessarily the one which pulls the highest can be used, where the position of each package within each sample is likely to do well. The distortions in data which are clear and distinct can be taken out by computing a modified average, while others which are not visible, at least, on the surface, have also to be accounted for in the selection of the best package. Because of invisible distortions, any package may perform well on one or two samples, but the best one is that which does well test after test.

To examine the repetitive quality of a selected package, a consistency test can be used, where the position of each package within each sample is ranked, and then their frequency (number of times each package comes in first, second, third and fourth) is determined. In Table 4 (page 1259), a frequency of package "A," "B," "C" and "D" by rank are given in column 2, 5, 8 and 11 respectively. It shows that package "A" ranked first in three out of the five cases (60%—Column 4). Where it did not get the first position it attained the next position (that is, the second position). Package "B" failed to achieve the first rank even for once (Column 5). Both packages "C" and "D" attained the top rank only in 20% of the cases (Column 10 and 13). As a rule of thumb, according to this test, the best package is one which scores first position in fifty, or more, percent of the cases. This implies that if the same test is repeated, the odds are 50% or better in your favor that the selected package will come in on top. However, where neither one of the packages attains the top rank by such a percentage, any selection made will be poor and unreliable.

It is always desirable to conduct a test of significance on the two best packages, particularly where the difference between them is rather small. This enables the mailer to determine whether the variation between them arose because of chances or of characteristics inherent in the packages. If the difference is attributable to chance, then the best package may not be the real best one. On subsequent tests, its position may change. Under such circumstances, it will be desirable to arrange another test to check the validity of a selected package.

TABLE 4

Test of Consistency

Rank	PACKAGE											
	A			B			C			D		
	Frequency	Cumulative Frequency	Cumulative Frequency in %	Frequency No.	Cumulative Frequency No.	Cumulative Frequency %	Frequency	Cumulative Frequency No.	Cumulative Frequency %	Frequency	Cumulative Frequency	Cumulative Frequency in %
(1)	(2)	(3)	(4)	(5)	(6)	(7)	(8)	(9)	(10)	(11)	(12)	(13)
1	3	3	60	0	0	0	1	1	20	1	1	20
2	2	5	100	0	0	0	1	2	40	2	3	60
3	0	5	100	1	1	20	3	5	100	1	4	80
4	0	5	100	4	5	100	0	5	100	1	5	100

Source: Table 1.

Based upon tests of modified average and consistency, the two best packages, in our example, are "A" and "D" ("A" is the best package and "D" is the second best). Chi-square test (or test of significance) can be used to see whether or not the difference between them is significant. Observed responses of these two packages (originally shown in Table 1) are reproduced in Table 5 (page 1261). (Because of the distortion in data of sample IV, package "D," the responses of both packages on this sample have been excluded.)

In testing for significance, it is necessary to state a hypothesis. The statistical procedure is for the purpose of testing whether this hypothesis is right or wrong. Hence, in this instance, we start with the hypothesis that both packages are equal, i.e. that the response to each is the same. If this is true, the expected response from each would be shown in Table 6.

The expected response of each sample is derived by averaging the responses of both packages. The expected response of package "A" or "D" is equal to: $300 + 280/2 = 290$, and so on. The value of chi-square can be obtained by using the formula:

$$X^2 = \sum \frac{(F_o - F_e)^2}{F_e}$$

Where X^2 stands for chi-square, for sumtotal, for observed responses and for expected responses. By substituting the values of observed and expected responses in the formula, we get:

$$X^2 = \frac{(300 - 290)^2}{290} + \frac{(280 - 290)^2}{290} + \frac{(360 - 325)^2}{325} + \frac{(290 - 325)^2}{325} + \frac{(290 - 295)^2}{295} + \frac{(300 - 295)^2}{295} + \frac{(350 - 330)^2}{330} + \frac{(310 - 330)^2}{330}$$

$$= 10.80.$$

For test of significance we also need to know the degrees of freedom. This is computed by this formula: df = (c-1) (r-1)—where df stands for degree of freedom, c for number of columns and r for number of rows of the table. In data, given in Table 5, c = 4 (because results of four samples are included) and r = 2 (because we want to test the difference between two best packages "A" and "D"). By substituting these values, we get: df = (4-1) (2-1) = 3.

The final step is to find the table value of chi-square corresponding to 3 degrees of freedom at 95% level of confidence (meaning we will be right

TABLE 5
Observed Responses

Package	SAMPLE			
	I (Responses)	II (Responses)	III (Responses)	V (Responses)
A	300	360	290	350
D	280	290	300	310

TABLE 6
Expected Responses

Package	SAMPLE			
	I (Responses)	II (Responses)	III (Responses)	V (Responses)
A	290	325	295	330
B	290	325	295	330

TABLE 7
Critical Values of Chi-Square

Degrees of Freedom	Probability (0.05)	Degrees of Freedom	Probability (0.05)
1	3.84	6	12.60
2	5.99	7	14.10
3	7.82	8	15.50
4	9.49	9	16.90
5	11.10	10	18.30

Source: Mason, Robert D., *Statistical Techniques in Business and Economics* (Home Wood, Illinois: Richard D. Irwin, Inc., 1967). p. 501.

95 times out of 100). This value is 7.82% as given in Table 7. As a rule, if the calculated value is greater than table value, the hypothesis is wrong—meaning that the difference between the two packages is significant—and vice versa. In our example, the calculated value (10.80—computed earlier) is greater than table value (7.82). Thus our hypothesis—there is no difference between package "A" and "D"—is wrong. Variations between them resulted from differences in characteristics rather than chance.

These three tests have given enough information to make a decision. According to the test of modified average, "A" is the best package because it pulled the highest average return after the allowance for extreme values were made.

Consistency test confirms this conclusion as it reveals the nature of this package to repeat its best performance. The test of significance shows that the difference between "A" and "D" (second best package) is significant, meaning "A" came on the top because of its good quality rather than chance variation.

PROJECTED RETURNS

As you develop a sufficient quantity of results from different mailings, you will probably want to work out a timing schedule so you can project probable final returns on the basis of early returns. While there is no way you can work up a schedule which has any real degree of built-in accuracy, it is still worth the effort so you will have a continuing picture of how your returns are progressing and when you can reasonably expect to have reached a plateau in returns so you can start tabulating results.

First of all, it is important to recognize that a lot is going to depend upon the service you receive from the post office. Since this is not consistent, it does little good to try to base a schedule on the basis of the day you put your pieces into the mails. Instead, you will want to start with the first day on which you receive returns from scattered points representing a reasonable cross section of the list used. (You will usually find you get a small handful of returns from some single location several days ahead of the start of your real returns—so wait until scattered points are represented.)

Once returns start coming in, begin recording totals on a day-by-day basis. Then all you have to do is to convert your cumulative total for each day into a percentage of the total return. As soon as you have done this for several lists, you will have the raw material from which you can develop a timing chart which will prove useful in projecting returns from future mailings.

If your results are typical, you will probably find that you receive 25% of your total returns during the week following the day of receipt of the first returns in quantity. You will probably hit the 50% mark by the end of the second week. Then things will slow down a bit. It may take a week and a half or two weeks more to hit the 75% level. Then the last 25% will drift in relatively slowly. Chances are, however, that by the end of the first month of receipts you will have at least 85% of your total return.

This is an area where it is important to develop your own chart. Those developed by other advertisers will probably be of little value to you since much will depend upon factors which vary from advertiser to advertiser, product to product, and list to list.

PROJECTING TOTAL PROBABLE RETURNS

A lot of charts have been developed to help direct mail advertisers estimate results on the basis of early returns. Unfortunately, no single chart ever proves of lasting value for more than a handful of advertisers (if for any). However, such a chart can be almost a necessity for any advertiser who must project his probable returns to extend a test or make mailings on a regular basis.

The charts shown here and on the following pages serve two purposes. First of all, by their differences they show the folly of trying to apply someone else's charts to your own business and the folly of using an old chart, particularly in these days of erratic postal service. But more important, they will provide a guide to help you in setting up your own chart based on the actual records of your own mailings.

Chart No. 1

Source: Lawrence G. Chait & Co., Inc. Results from a 14 million mailing for a relatively big-ticket, non-impulse mail order item. Mailed third class bulk mail.

Week	Percentage of Total Orders	Cumulative Percentage By Week	Week	Percentage of Total Orders	Cumulative Percentage By Week
2	1.3	1.3	11	2.8	92.3
3	6.3	7.6	12	1.9	94.2
4	21.5	29.1	13	1.2	95.4
5	27.2	56.3	14	.9	96.3
6	13.4	69.7	15	.6	96.9
7	7.9	77.6	16	.6	97.5
8	5.9	83.5	17	.5	98.0
9	3.2	86.7	18	.4	98.4
10	2.8	89.5	19	.2	98.6
			20	1.3	99.9

Chart No. 2

Source: *Business Week.* Results on more than four million subscription solicitations during a three-year period in early 1960's.

Week After 1st Orders	% of Total Orders Received	% of Total Orders To Come
1st	30	70
2nd	58	42
3rd	75	25
4th	84	16
5th	88	12
6th	91	9
7th	93	7
8th	95	5
9th	96	4
10th	97	3
12th	98	2
17th	99	1
26th	100	—

Chart No. 3

Source: *Business Week.* Results based on more than one million subscription solicitations mailed during a three-month period approximately 10 years after the mailings charted in Chart No. 2 above.

Week	Average % of Total Orders Received	Percentage Range of Orders Received	Median Percentage of Orders Received	Mode of Orders Received
1	3.9	0.3- 24.7%	17.7%	1.3%
2	27.0	6.5- 77.3	39.5	31.4
3	54.6	13.6- 96.4	66.2	75.0
4	67.2	18.9-100.0	74.9	68.9
5	77.8	36.5-100.0	82.5	81.4
6	82.8	46.9-100.0	87.8	100.0
7	85.8	58.1-100.0	89.2	100.0
8	92.6	74.3-100.0	92.2	100.0
9	95.3	87.5-100.0	93.8	100.0
10	96.2	88.0-100.0	96.8	100.0
12	99.4	92.0-100.0	99.7	100.0
17	100.0	100.0-100.0	100.0	100.0

DEFINITIONS

Time intervals are weeks from the day the first order was received.

Average number of orders may be deceptive because of the wide variation in size of keys mailed.

Percentage range of orders received indicates limit of tolerance one way or the other.

Median column is a standard measurement indicating that 50% of all responses will be greater and 50% lesser.

Mode is the percentage figure of total orders occurring most frequently.

Geographical Variations

List broker Lewis Kleid calls attention to the need for geographical analysis of list testing. He reported on the state-by-state response for a magazine subscription mailing sent to over 400,000 selected prospects. (See following page.)

In commenting on these returns, Lew Kleid noted: "If 1½% were considered 'break-even,' the total mailing would have been unrewarding since it pulled only 1.37%. However, 14 out of the 35 states pulled over 1½% and if only these states had been used, the list would have been considered good."

State	Quantity Mailed	% Return
Delaware	1,352	2.29
Texas	7,855	2.19
Louisiana	2,008	2.09
Washington	10,667	2.05
Oklahoma	3,471	1.93
Kansas	5,510	1.83
Tennessee	1,583	1.96
California	38,250	1.72
Georgia	3,731	1.80
Rhode Island	1,964	1.73
Minnesota	5,545	1.55
Missouri	10,143	1.37
Mississippi	1,436	1.60
South Carolina	2,857	1.58
Wisconsin	10,751	1.40
North Carolina	9,161	1.42
Maryland	9,629	1.40
Connecticut	12,814	1.40
Colorado	4,177	1.41
Virginia	12,135	1.38
Washington D. C.	1,760	1.48
Ohio	35,796	1.28
Indiana	16,750	1.25
New Jersey	28,211	1.27
Michigan	26,152	1.22
New York	59,242	1.27
Kentucky	7,604	1.22
Massachusetts	14,840	1.29
Pennsylvania	39,072	1.20
Alabama	3,241	1.20
Arkansas	2,050	1.22
Illinois	32,143	1.11
Maine	4,163	1.13
Florida	5,313	1.11
Iowa	7,962	1.02
TOTAL	438,798	1.37

Chapter 49

INQUIRY HANDLING

THE handling of inquiries presents one of the most amazing paradoxes in advertising. Millions of dollars are spent each year for advertising which has a primary aim of producing inquiries and then those millions are allowed to go to waste because no system has been established for efficient inquiry handling.

A study by the Research Department of Potts-Woodbury Inc. for Tension Envelope Corporation showed just how poorly inquiries are being handled. Potts-Woodbury answered 273 ads in *Better Homes & Gardens, Farm Journal,* and *Practical Builder.* Each of the ads selected contained an invitation to write for more information. Yet one firm out of nine completely ignored the inquiry. Of the others, 75% of the non-mail order advertisers did not tell how or where to buy and 70% made no followup.

Even the mail order firms, to whom inquiries represent boom or bust, failed to come through with a good record—14% failed to enclose either an order blank or return envelope. The replies took as long as 10 weeks to arrive and nearly 50% did not include even a form letter. Of those who did use letters, only 17% used typewritten replies—most of them from the business paper advertisers.

Actually, the Potts-Woodbury study showed much better results than most similar research projects. One of the largest tests was made by a Washington, D. C., advertising executive who sent inquiries to 1,200 national advertisers. One year later, only 424 advertisers had replied, and of the 424 only seven made any kind of followup.

Format of Replies

The author conducted a minor scale research project aimed at studying the format of replies to inquiries in the home building, home furnishing, and accessories fields. Of the 80 reply packages analyzed:

Only eight had any type of personalization. One of these was an autotyped letter, the other seven used filled-in letters. Two of the fill-ins utilized forms which had been designed for another purpose, destroying the value of personalization and creating confusion.

Only 34 of the pieces had any kind of covering item, such as a letter, to indicate that the enclosed literature was being sent in answer to a specific request. Four of these had imprints on the outside of the envelope to say that the contents represented material which had been requested.

Nine of the 80 replies used material originally designed for promotion to dealers or distributors (instead of to homeowners)—although all of the requests were directed to companies advertising the availability of consumer literature (all of the ads appeared in *consumer* magazines).

A high percentage of the returns utilized unrelated pieces, which were just tossed into an envelope with nothing to show the interrelationship of the enclosures.

There were only five followups—one by the manufacturer originally sending the literature, the other four from local dealers. All followup contacts were by mail—including one which was nothing more than a local dealer's business card mailed in an envelope.

Some of the reply mailings are worthy of study since they involve ideas which have wide application.

Resistane Coating Corporation

A particularly effective inquiry-answering package was used by Resistane Coating Corporation of Yonkers, New York, which makes a protective coating material for wallpapers. The reply package included four items—a printed "thank you" letter, a folder with before-and-after samples, a 12-page booklet telling the Resistane story in language oriented to the homeowner, and a "test card" containing two wallpaper samples—one with and the other without Resistane.

The letter copy read:

Thank you for your interest in RESISTANE as expressed in your response to our advertisement.

We believe the enclosed printed matter will give you a clear understanding of our custom service of RESISTANING wall coverings before they are hung.

Do not be misled into believing that all wallpapers labeled "Plastic Coated," "Vinyl Sealed," etc., etc., are well protected against staining. Most of those so labeled are not resistant to greases and oils.

A simple way of determining how much they are protected against staining is to apply a little lighter or cleaning fluid on them. If the fluid goes through the colors and wets the paper you can be sure anything oily or greasy will do the same. This kind of test can be done to papers right in the sample books. When the fluid evaporates there will be no evidence of it having been on the paper. If you can get a sample piece from your dealer, take it home and give it the test we suggest on our test card enclosed.

Should you have any questions not answered by the literature herewith, be free to write us.

Yours very truly,
Resistane Coating Corporation

The test card mentioned in the letter was an 8¾- by 3¾-inch card on which had been mounted two samples of the same wallpaper—one with and the other without Resistane treatment. The suggested test was to smear a line from one end of the card to the other with butter, lard, bacon, or any other household material likely to get on wallpaper. Then attempt to remove the smear from both pieces of wallpaper. Then recipients were advised to make a second test with crayon or lipstick. The punchline: "We believe you will convince yourself that a Resistaned wallpapered wall is easier to keep clean than a painted wall."

The sample folder contained before-and-after samples of seven different types of wallpaper. This demonstration piece was designed to show how little difference in appearance there is when Resistane coating is applied.

The booklet contained product information, testimonials, a listing of some of the famous homes and institutions which have Resistaned wall coverings, and information on how the homeowner can obtain the coating service.

Save Space.
Add color,
style,
convenience
and comfort.

You'll be happy with the "New Look" a Dormalux Nook will give your kitchen.

For further information:
Fill in and mail the attached reply card.
No postage required.

TEAR ON DOTTED LINE

Gentlemen:

I received your literature and am interested in purchasing a DORMALUX NOOK. Without obligation please send me the following information:

- ☐ **Color Swatch Card**
- ☐ **Name and location of nearest distributor**
- ☐ **My cost on a** ______________ (Give model name) **Kitchen Nook** ________ (Give size)
  with a ______________ (Give size) **Table.** ☐ **Also on a matching chair.**
- ☐ **Other** ______________________________

____

Name ______________________________

Street ______________________________

City ______________ **Phone** ______________

A reply card can serve as both a covering device and a reply device.

Dormalux Reply Card

The only advertiser in this study of inquiry handling to enclose a reply card of any type was The Dormalux Co., Inc., of Buffalo, manufacturer of furniture for dining nooks. The reply package had just the reply card and an eight-page, full-color 8½- by 11-inch booklet. An address label was stapled to the booklet in a position which would show through the window of the mailing envelope. The reply card served both as a covering device and a reply device. It was a double 3½- by 5½-inch card. The face carried this message:

THANK YOU!

Thank you for asking about Dormalux Kitchen Nooks. We hope our literature will be helpful to you in planning an attractive and comfortable eating area.

Cordially yours,
Dormalux

The reply card is shown in the illustration on page 1270.

Formica's Packet of Cards

One of the most unusual inquiry-handling devices included in the study was mailed by Formica Corporation. It consisted of an envelope containing 38 3¼- by 5⅝-inch cards. All except one of the cards contained black-and-white illustrations of furniture. The backs of the cards were designed to enable the recipient to request additional information from the manufacturers of the pieces of furniture illustrated (see illustration on the next page).

The thirty-eighth card was the cover to the packet. Its face was printed in black, red, and gold, and carried the title: "Shoppers' Guide to Formica Surfaced Furniture." Copy on the reverse side explained:

> This packet contains a small sampling of the many types of Formica laminated plastic-surfaced furniture available to you.
>
> Information on the complete line of Formica surfaced furniture of each manufacturer is listed on the back of the pictures. If your favorite furniture dealer does not have your particular choice in stock, ask him to order it for you . . . or use these preaddressed post cards to find out the name of your nearest dealer.

Woodard Double Mailing

The one manufacturer to follow up was Lee L. Woodard Sons, Inc., Owosso, Michigan, wrought-iron furniture maker. The first mailing contained four 4- by 6½-inch eight-page booklets, each describing a different line of wrought-iron furniture. The folders were accompanied by a 5½- by 7-inch note reading:

Dear Customer:

Enclosed is the Woodard Literature you requested. We are using this form letter to expedite mailing the data to you and will write you shortly with the name and address of your nearest dealer.

Some of the 38 cards mailed by Formica as an unusual inquiry-handling device.

Your interest in Woodard is indeed sincerely appreciated.

Lee L. Woodard Sons, Inc.

Then, 37 days later, a filled-in letter was received. It was on a regular 8½- by 11-inch letterhead and read:

Your recent request for literature on Woodard wrought iron suggests that you are considering decorative changes in your home.

The literature mailed cannot completely answer your questions. However, the experienced staff at the dealer listed below would be most helpful to you in the selection of Woodard and the development of a coordinated scheme.

They would be pleased to be of assistance to you.

Masonite Portfolio

A method of coordinating possibly unrelated materials was used by Masonite Corporation, Chicago, to handle its inquiry response. An 8¾- by 11½-inch four-page folder was wrapped around the requested literature. On its face it had a simulated file tab reading, "Idea File," plus a letter (see illustration on the following page).

The inside spread of the "Idea File" portfolio contained descriptions of various Masonite products plus a section on the advantages of Masonite materials and another section describing the manufacturing process. The back cover offered free remodeling plans.

Case's Wholesale Reference

When a manufacturer's outlets are primarily wholesalers, suggesting a point-of-contact can be difficult. Case Manufacturing, Robinson, Illinois, maker of plumbing supplies, handled the situation with this paragraph in the fill-in letter sent with its product brochure:

We are listing the wholesale distributor nearest you where you may see Case items on display. Your inquiry to them will be most appreciated—no doubt your plumber will help you arrange such a visit.

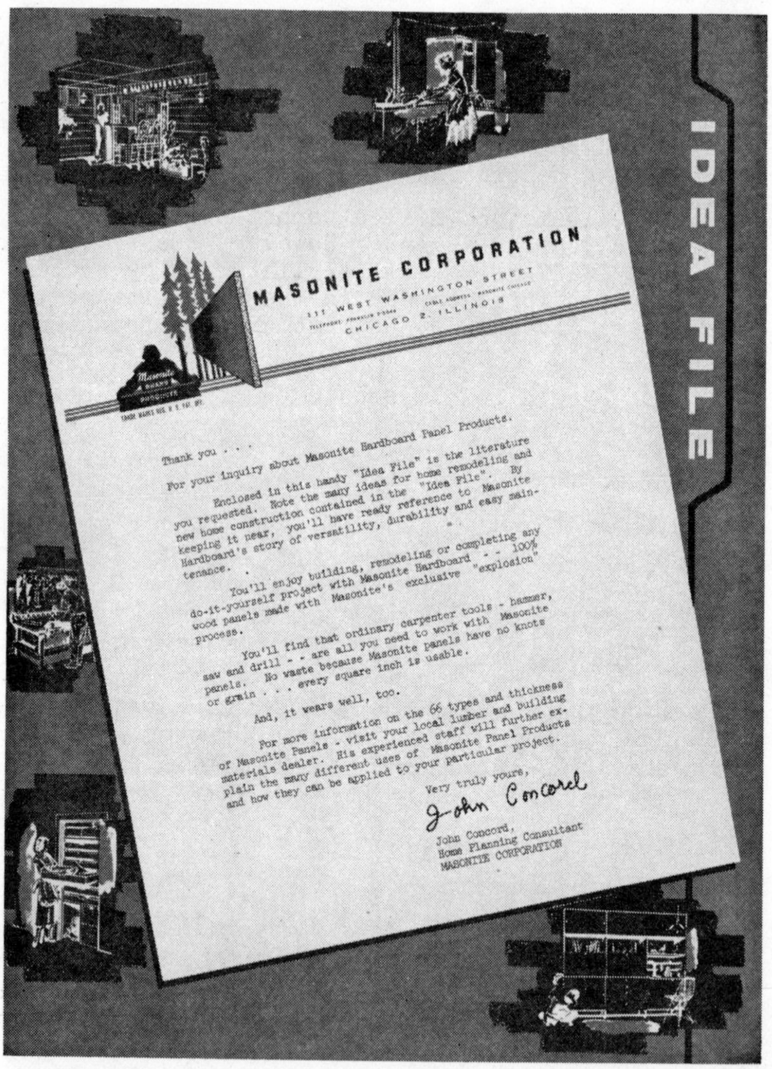

MASONITE CORPORATION
111 WEST WASHINGTON STREET
CHICAGO 2, ILLINOIS

Thank you . . .

For your inquiry about Masonite Hardboard Panel Products.

Enclosed in this handy "Idea File" is the literature you requested. Note the many ideas for home remodeling and new home construction contained in the "Idea File". By keeping it near, you'll have ready reference to Masonite Hardboard's story of versatility, durability and easy maintenance.

You'll enjoy building, remodeling or completing any do-it-yourself project with Masonite Hardboard - - 100% wood panels made with Masonite's exclusive "explosion" process.

You'll find that ordinary carpenter tools - hammer, saw and drill - - are all you need to work with Masonite panels. No waste because Masonite panels have no knots or grain . . . every square inch is usable.

And, it wears well, too.

For more information on the 66 types and thickness of Masonite Panels - visit your local lumber and building materials dealer. His experienced staff will further explain the many different uses of Masonite Panel Products and how they can be applied to your particular project.

Very truly yours,

John Concord

John Concord,
Home Planning Consultant
MASONITE CORPORATION

Masonite Corporation evolved a clever method of combining possibly unrelated materials.

Value of Inquiries

Inquiries are the life blood of many advertising programs. While used in many ways, they serve three principal purposes:

1. To separate those with special interests from a larger audience.
2. To provide leads for sales followup.
3. To test reaction to selling themes and determine interest in products and services.

Inquiries requiring direct mail followup can come from many sources—newspaper, magazine, radio and television advertising; inquiry-seeking direct mail programs; trade shows, fairs and other events; via salesmen, service personnel, and other employees; telephone calls and letters—and dozens of other ways. Some are very specific, others are general. Some are from serious buyers, others from those with a casual interest or "file-builders."

But regardless of the source inquiries can be one of the most valuable assets of any business. They should never be treated lightly. Even what may appear on the surface to be "nuisance" inquiries deserve the courtesy of a reply—even if it is just to say you are sorry you cannot supply the information requested.

A case in point: Some years ago, a number of leading universities received a short letter asking them what they would do if someone were to give them a million dollars to use as they saw fit. Only one of the universities went to the bother to answer the letter. This school told its plans for a new, well-equipped engineering center. It said it would use the million dollars to help get the center underway. That reply paid off handsomely for the letter had been sent by the secretary of a millionaire who did not want his identity known. The end result was that the university not only got the million dollars it needed to get the engineering center underway, but the rest of the money the project required—all because it treated a seemingly casual inquiry with respect.

Organizing an Inquiry-Handling Program

Organizing to handle inquiries efficiently is not necessarily a simple project. It deserves the same degree of consideration given all other phases of the advertising and sales program.

The most productive systems are usually those which include some form of automation—at least so obviously routine inquiries can be handled without individual analysis and decision.

In many cases, the inquiry-handling program only begins with the sending of information. From that point, it involves support from salesmen, distributors, and/or retailers.

15 Steps to Success

In discussing inquiry-handling problems in a previous publication[1], the author developed a 15-step guide. It was not offered as a sure-fire formula since no single system could possibly fit all types of businesses, but the basic steps are adaptable to the majority of inquiry-handling situations.

1. *Analyze every inquiry.* All inquiries are not alike, even if they stem from the same source and request the same information. For example, even a technical magazine may produce inquiries from large companies and small companies; good credit risks and bad credit risks; active prospects and curiosity seekers; professionals and students; domestic concerns and foreign prospects . . . to name just a few of the possible variations.

   Then, too, requests for the same information may come from a variety of sources and arrive in a number of different ways. In most cases, inquiries will originate in one of the following ways:

   —Direct correspondence.

   —Requests forwarded by salesmen, distributors and/or retailers.

   —Telephone requests.

   —Coupons from advertisements.

   —Non-coupon responses to offers in advertisements.

   —"Bingo-cards"—the circle-the-number cards included in many business publications.

   —Responses to publicity items.

   —Business reply cards sent with direct mail pieces.

   —Miscellaneous.

   Depending upon the nature of your business, you should analyze every request first on the basis of its source—usually a simple matter—and then on the basis of the estimated sales and/or goodwill potential of the inquirer. One major caution should be observed: do not be misled by assuming that all inquiries have the same basic value just because they look similar on the surface. For example, responses via the so-called "bingo cards" will vary considerably. Some publications will draw a high percentage of active prospects—particularly in fields where this type of inquiry mechanism has become well established and is accepted as a basic method of obtaining information quickly. On the other hand, requests from other publications may consist primarily of "file builders" —people who like to obtain reference information against the day when they might need it in a hurry.

2. *Answer every inquiry promptly.* Every inquiry should be answered within 24 to 48 hours—regardless of the estimated sales potential. Do not allow inquiries to drift around from one interested party to another (with a few disinterested parties in between). Even if you cannot provide

[1] "A Basic Guide to Effective Inquiry Handling," by Dick Hodgson. American Marketing Services, Waltham, Massachusetts. 1960. $1.

immediate service on all the information being requested, at least inform the inquirer of the receipt of his request and tell him when he'll have the information he is seeking.

It is good business manners, of course, to reply promptly to any communication and inquiries are no exception. If you have properly analyzed the inquiries, you will be able to spot those which require special treatment—such as a wire, phone call, or airmail reply. But do not assume that all others can be handled at will. You can never be sure just when there is an important sale awaiting . . . and the same request has gone to a competitor.

3. *Answer personally.* Don't fall into the trap of looking at a stack of inquiries and missing "the trees for the forest." Each inquirer is an individual and deserves to be treated as such.

   If your volume of inquiries is relatively low and your potential sale is more than pennies, think *only* in terms of typewritten, personally signed letters. However, if you are one of those companies which must handle thousands of inquiries each month, you may want to consider dividing inquiries into two basic types: (1) those which have arrived in an "impersonal" manner and represent relatively low sales potential, and (2) others.

   Only if the cost of completely personal inquiry handling is absolutely prohibitive should you consider a semipersonal reply to those in the first category above. But even these should have some degree of personalization such as a fill-in on a form letter or at least a handwritten name on a "thanks for your request" attachment.

   By "impersonal" manner, we mean such devices as the "bingo" cards, a list of students sent in by an instructor, etc. However, if the inquirer has sent a personal request, even if it is just a filled-in coupon from a magazine ad or the return of a business reply card, he deserves a personal reply. If you say it is too expensive, you certainly ought to reevaluate your entire promotion program to see if you really want inquiries.

   Actually, the cost of personal replies may not be as high as you think. With automatically typewritten letters, you should be able to prepare a reply for only a fraction of the cost of obtaining the inquiry originally. (You will find details on the use of automatically typewritten letters for inquiry handling in the inquiry-handling case histories which follow.)

4. *Be friendly.* Treat inquirers as though you were visiting them on a first sales call. Take advantage of the opportunity to lay the groundwork for a lasting friendship. Say thanks for the inquiry and make it sound like you mean it.

5. *Reply fully.* Take a good look at each and every inquiry and make sure you fully understand just what is being requested. If there is any confusion, tell the inquirer about it and assure him that you want to make sure he gets all the information he is seeking.

   If you do fully understand what is being requested, make sure that everything is sent or explain why not. If there must be a delay, say so . . . and then make sure whatever you have promised is sent as soon as possible. If what is being requested is too expensive to be sent to an unqualified prospect, send what you can and give the inquirer an opportunity to qualify himself for the additional material. And again, be friendly about it.

6. *Have a system.* This is the most important step of all.

While there is no single inquiry-handling system which will fit every situation, whatever system you choose should be as automated as possible. At the far extreme are systems which utilize electronic data-processing machines. But unless you just happen to be blessed with lots of available time on such equipment, you will find that a relatively simple system will suffice.

Your first step will be to review the types of inquiries you have been receiving. And at the same time, take a long and hard look at what treatment you have been giving them—not just in your office but right down to the followthrough which results in sales.

This review will enable you to organize inquiries by types. Some of the factors you might consider:

—Source of inquiry.

—Type of inquirer.

—Product or service about which inquiry is made.

—Short-range potential.

—Long-range potential.

(And don't overlook the importance of long-range potential. Many companies just discard inquiries from students or those at a low level on a company organization chart. We know of one company, which shall go nameless, which has lost well over a quarter-million dollars in sales because it failed to respond to inquiries sent in by members of just one class of trade-school students. Its major competitor did respond to such requests and gained friends for life.)

After you have studied the types of inquiries received regularly, make a complete analysis of what treatment they are presently receiving. Consider:

—How long it takes to complete initial servicing of an inquiry.

—The number of executive-hours being devoted to inquiry handling.

—The number of clerical hours being devoted to inquiry handling.

—How much followthrough is being given to each type of inquiry.

—What is being done to qualify different degrees of potential in inquiries.

—What records are being kept of inquiries (and are they complete enough to give you such simple facts as cost-per-inquiry, percentage of inquiries being converted to sales, areas producing the greatest volume of useful inquiries, and so forth).

These are but a few of the items you will want to consider. But they are typical of the factors which must be considered before you can put an automated inquiry-handling system into operation.

Several actual examples of proved inquiry-handling systems will be explained later.

7. *Assign responsibilities.* Once you have decided on the system you will use, assign clear-cut responsibilities for each step in your inquiry-handling procedure. By all means, see that a single individual is charged with basic responsibility for keeping the system operating.

Then you will want to pin down just who (or at least what department) will have responsibility of each element of the handling procedure. This should be clearly spelled out and put in writing.

8. *Make sure your system is understood at all levels.* Do not just take for granted that even the most simple system will be understood by everyone involved. To work properly, an inquiry-handling system must be carefully explained to everyone who will be affected by it. This is particularly true of new employees who are brought into the system after it is in operation.

   The best place to start is at the point of mail delivery and the telephone switchboard. Since these are the points where inquiries usually make their first direct contact with the advertiser, it is particularly important that all personnel understand just what they are to do with each type of inquiry as it arrives.

   One of the best methods is a simple wall chart covering all basic types of inquiries. On such a chart go instructions naming the specific individual to whom each type of inquiry is to be routed. Copies of the chart can be made available to everyone concerned with any phase of inquiry handling—including branch offices, distributors, salesmen, etc., who may have occasion to need fast response to a given type of information request.

   It is also helpful to have a single verbal inquiry-recording form which can be used by secretaries, clerks, and others who may receive phone inquiries when the individual responsible for handling them is absent. Frequently, this same form can be used by field personnel who must route inquiries to headquarters.

9. *Have a practical method for recordkeeping.* Some form of standardized record should be kept for all inquiries. The actual form will depend upon many factors, but regardless of its details it should be designed for long-term use and not just something which is set up to fit each situation as it develops.

   Among the features you may want to include in your record system are:
   —Sources of inquiries.
   —Cost of fulfillment.
   —Cost of obtaining inquiries.
   —Assignment of responsibility for followthrough.
   —Percentage converted into sales.
   —Cost of conversion into sales.
   —Geographical distribution
   —Actual items sent in response to inquiries.
   —Individual or department processing inquiries.
   —Inventory controls for material used in processing inquiries.

   You will find such records useful not only in making periodic analyses of your inquiry-handling system but also a valuable guide to evaluating relative value of different types of advertising and publicity and/or different media.

10. *Quality inquiries.* No matter what quantity of inquiries you receive, you should develop a definite technique for qualifying the best prospects. One of the most effective methods is the use of a business reply card with the first response you make to an inquiry.

    Of course there will be many instances where an inquirer can immediately be identified as a key prospect. In such cases, you will want to bring up your big guns right away.

But the average inquiry for most advertisers will be an unknown quantity until some qualification has been made. If you can get the prospect to qualify himself, so much the better. Therefore, many companies have successfully used the business reply card technique.

In these cases, basic literature is sent immediately upon receipt of an inquiry, along with a letter offering additional material. A business reply card (or questionnaire and business reply envelope) is enclosed. It will usually contain questions calling for answers which will help to qualify prospects, although in many cases just getting a prospect to return the reply card represents sufficient qualification.

11. *Set followthrough in motion.* There are few instances where merely answering an inquiry represents completion of the inquiry-handling process. Even mail order firms should generally expect to make followup contacts before producing orders.

Among the steps to be considered:

—Adding inquirers' names to mailing list.

—Planning specific additional mailings at regular intervals.

—Notifying salesmen, distributors, and/or retailers for personal followup.

—Analysis of inquiries for possible interest in additional products, services, and/or literature.

12. *Enlist support of field forces.* Most "outside" personnel cast a jaundiced eye at inquiries—unless they are part of a proved, sales-producing system. This is particularly true in companies where every inquiry is sent into the field with instructions to make a personal followthrough.

Most salesmen firmly believe that they know their territories, and the potential of prospects within those territories, far better than "the brass at headquarters." In most cases they are probably right. Therefore, inquiries coming down from "the brass" represent an imagined insult to many salesmen and are quickly branded as "worthless."

Then along comes a concentrated push to "follow up on those inquiries." So John Q. Salesman sorts through the batch gathering dust in the glove compartment of his car, picks out the least likely possibilities, makes a few token (and half-hearted) sales calls . . . and sends back a stack of smoking call reports proving that "inquiries are no damn good."

Far from being fiction, this is an all-too-common situation in companies where the field forces have not been enlisted to support a workable inquiry-handling system. For many companies faced with this problem, the answer has turned out to be surprisingly simple.

The first step is to *keep routine inquiries out of salesmen's hands.* Wait until some kind of qualification has been made. Then demand prompt followup and reporting on all qualified inquiries. Once the salesmen fully understand that every effort is being made to eliminate a lot of blind leads, they quickly respond to the very real assistance an inquiry can give them in making their sales quotas.

One important caution: Never give an inquiry the credit for a sale if any form of contact has been made by the salesman. Salesmen seldom like to share credit with anyone or anything when they send back a signed order. It is good psychology to let them have the full credit.

13. *Identify best leads.* When you have what you consider a "hot" lead, identify it as such and give it special treatment. This is particularly true in the case of leads passed along to salesmen.

One of the most common methods for handling such inquiries is to have a bright red sticker which is prominently attached to the report routed for handling either internally or in the field. A demand for a special followup report in a specified period of time can also be used and, in itself, frequently assures special handling.

Some companies consider all inquiries arriving by phone, wire, or personal letter as deserving such special attention. When such leads are routed for action, it is worthwhile to consider attaching an actual copy of the original inquiry.

14. *Screen copy.* Before any inquiry-handling system will work, you should consider just what is prompting the inquiries in the first place. Far too often, advertisers have picked up the "inquiry bug." As a result, they have gone overboard in turning out advertising and publicity designed primarily to produce large quantities of inquiries, with very little thought being given to trying to limit response to those individuals and/or companies who really should reply.

If you love to see stacks of inquiries roll in from everywhere, just run an ad or send out a bunch of publicity releases offering a free sample. Play the free sample up big. You'll get inquiries all right. Oh, how you'll get inquiries! But chances are there will be a lot of chaff with the wheat—and even the best inquiry-handling system will be strained to cull out the real prospects among the respondents.

Actually, a very high percentage of inquiry-stimulating ads fail to do an effective screening job. A report prepared by the Industrial Advertising Research Institute points out:

It is almost axiomatic that "the best screening is in the copy." Companies which were receiving an excessive number of casual inquiries usually resorted to broad claims in their advertising. Thus inquirers were attracted who could not use the products featured or had only a passive interest in them. Copy which produced the highest percentage of worthwhile sales leads presented, as a rule, specific, factual details which clearly established the limitations as well as the advantages of the product.

Copy that calls for a statement of interest on the part of the inquirer is an excellent basis for screening. For example, a request for price and delivery data is evidence of immediate intent to buy. An indication of possible future needs would suggest adding the inquirer's name to the mailing list.

The conventional have-a-representative-call screening device is not always advisable because it may close the door to a personal call if not checked, or may generate ill-will if a prompt call does not follow an affirmative check.

15. *Treasure inquiries.* Inquiries can be the life blood of your entire marketing operation. If treated with respect, they can become the primary catalyst for an ever-ascending curve on your sales chart.

But inquiries are fickle. Treat them badly and they can turn on you and help to destroy the foundation upon which a successful company is built. Inquirers demand and deserve respect . . . the kind of respect which comes through an efficient, properly functioning inquiry-handling system.

INQUIRY-HANDLING SYSTEM

There are many approaches to setting up an efficient inquiry-handling system. It can be done internally, or you may prefer to turn the entire project over to an outside service organization. But no matter which approach you take, you will likely find the real clue to success is the degree to which you can make the whole thing automatic.

Any system which requires the making of a lot of individual decisions—particularly if the decisions are the responsibility of busy executives—is little better than no system at all.

Six Basic Questions

Before you decide to set up an inquiry-handling program, you will want to ask yourself some basic questions. McGraw-Hill Inc. suggests these:

1. *Do we want inquiries?* Is our product suited to the inquiry sales approach? Is our company so well known that our salesmen are welcome without inquiries? Is our distribution chain so elaborate that our distributors generate their own inquiries? Do we want to sell to a few large companies or to many smaller firms?

2. *Can we handle inquiries properly?* Do we have catalogs, brochures, and letters ready to send to prospects? How quickly can we get material on the way to inquirers? Do we have a system through which every inquiry is screened and answered automatically?

3. *Will our inquiries produce sales calls?* Do our salesmen know all about our inquiry program? Are they enthused about its possibilities? Do they get word of inquiries from their area almost as soon as we receive them?

4. *Do we record inquiries systematically?* Can we relate inquiries to specific advertisements and the magazines by which they were stimulated? Can we relate inquiries to sales on a cost-accounting basis? Do we analyze our markets by cross referencing inquiries by respondents' industries and functions?

5. *What kind of advertising program should we plan?* Is it safe to focus strongly on inquiry-producing advertising? What size advertisement produces the most inquiries? What frequency should we plan, and how often should we change our offer? What kinds of copy and format draw the best prospects?

6. *Can we coordinate advertiser, agency and publication efforts?* Does every member of our team know how to provoke, screen, and deliver high-yield inquiries most effectively for our sales goals?

Basic Inquiry-Handling System

McGraw-Hill has also offered a basic eight-point system for handling inquiries.

1. *All inquiries are delivered promptly* to the processing department.

2. *Every inquiry is read in full.*

3. *Inquiries are screened for quality.* Send your salesmen after the 10% of your inquiries that really mean business—those from responsible industrial executives.

4. *Each inquiry is recorded,* by date, publication, issue, and the inquirer's name, company, title, and industry. This lets you tally the literature you have sent to the prospect, the sales calls made on him, the sales volume developed, the magazine that produced the inquiry. Importantly, it helps you to find prospects by cross indexing inquiries—if a production engineer in one aircraft plant asks about your product, chances are that other production engineers in other aircraft plants will be interested, too.

5. *Every inquiry is answered.* Acknowledge receipts of the inquiry by a letter or card that thanks your respondent for his interest, tells him that the information he wants is on the way, gives him the name and address of your nearest salesman or distributor, and asks him to specify if he wants your product information for reference or for a specific application. Since every company is fighting the talent war, route student inquiries to the personnel department for recruiting purposes.

6. *The sales force is fully informed.* Tell your salesmen specifically what information the prospect requested, what pieces of literature you have sent. Emphasize how carefully you have screened the prospect, underscore the fact that personal sales calls increase the rate at which inquiries become sales, stress that the salesman, not the advertising department, will be credited with the sale.

7. *Literature is sent to the inquirer*—if possible, the same day his request is received. It often takes two weeks for the inquirer to get his information, and by that time he may be irritated, uninterested, or both—out of the market. Make it easy for your prospect to investigate your product further by enclosing a stamped letter and request form, or a stamped card with your literature.

8. *Sales call results are recorded.* This helps you make sure that your salesmen are actually making sales calls on inquirers, and allows you quick, accurate analysis of the sales volume your inquiries produce.

"Printers' Ink" Model System

A more detailed inquiry-handling plan was developed by *Printers' Ink.* It involves 17 steps for processing inquiries ("How to Follow Leads That Result From Advertising," by Carroll J. Swan):

1. All mail time-stamped when it arrives at the plant.
2. Inquiries segregated from such other mail as bills, mail for the purchasing agent, etc.
3. Inquiries keyed as to source. This can be done with special colored cards to attach to the inquiry. The cards can be filed so as to build a mailing list. Colors would indicate whether the inquirer was an individual prospect, a company prospect, a prospective dealer, a schoolteacher, etc.
4. Keyed as to demands of the inquirer. Numbers 1, 2, 3, etc., can indicate in that order: Asked for shipment of merchandise advertised, asked for name and address of local dealer, asked for information only, etc.
5. Inquiries sorted into those that require a personally dictated answer and those that can be answered by prefabricated form letters or printed literature.
6. These two categories delivered within two hours after arrival, one to the department that sends out personal replies, the other to the routine mailing department.
7. Personally dictated replies mailed within 36 hours, or a post card sent at once saying that the inquiry has been received and will be answered in .... days when sufficient data can be compiled for a proper answer. Then answer within that time.

8. Prefabricated answers handled by sufficient personnel in a department organized to have them in the mail in 24 hours, as follows:

9. Inquiries keyed for prefabricated answer that best suits the inquiry. This can be done by letters A, B, C, etc., to indicate booklet offered in national ad, form letter saying that salesman will call, post card giving local dealer's name and address, etc.

10. Inquiries keyed as to geographic location. This does two things. It localizes the inquiry so that it can be checked against local advertising as an indication of regional response. It localizes the inquiry as to dealer or to a group of dealers and as to distributor. Or for a company whose contact is direct through its own salesman, it indicates what salesman's territory the inquiry comes from.

    At this point, too, the inquiry can be keyed for the advertisement that produced it. Then at a later time a check can be made to relate inquiries to advertisement, media, sale, etc.

11. Name of dealer, distributor, salesman or geographic locality entered on card to be kept as a permanent record of the inquiry and its disposition.

12. Name and address of inquirer and any other data that are to be saved for permanent record typed on the card.

13. Any other typing done that is necessary: envelopes addressed, personalized salutations on those form letters that call for it, name and address of local dealer typed into reply if called for.

14. Inquiry time stamped again when answer is placed in the mail.

15. Distributor, local dealer, or salesman notified of the action taken, either with a special mailing or by forwarding the inquiry itself (now of no further use).

16. File the permanent record card.

17. Have a definite procedure for followup if that is worth the additional effort.

Handling Consumer Inquiries

The inquiry-handling systems described thus far were designed primarily to handle industrial or business requests. How about consumer inquiries? Another model system was suggested by *Printers' Ink* for handling this type of inquiry:

1. Have a definite office or desk assigned to job of receiving the inquiries.

2. Acknowledge receipt of inquiries on the same day with at least a thank-you post card.

3. Avoid every possible delay in fulfilling a promise made in an advertisement. Be sure to include name, address and telephone number of nearest dealer or type of store where your product is sold. Urge consumers to take a look at it.

4. Notify nearest dealer about inquiry at once.

5. If personal followup is in order, give dealer full information he needs to handle inquiry intelligently.

6. Make sure your dealer's followup does credit to your own advertising and promotion. If necessary, supervise his letters to see that they're neat, properly processed and well written and that they create a good impression for both parties.

7. Ask dealer to report the result of personal followups. Give him a return card already filled out as completely as possible so that it will be easy for him to report the results.

8. Use quick forms to record inquiry in a permanent file, to send thank-you to new prospect, to notify dealer. If distributors are also a factor in followup, send them a note.

9. Prepare reports for top management as a guide to prospect interests—and variations of it—as well as proof of job being done by advertising.

10. Prepare result summaries from permanent inquiry file (a) for use of advertising department in judging media and appeals and (b) for use of sales department in keeping followup boys on the job—and sold on advertising.

11. Study value of inquiries received—either by surveys in the field or reports received after followup. Don't judge returns in terms of numbers only; it's numbers of good prospects you're after.

12. Set up a system for screening inquiries if that seems advisable. This can be done through correspondence, through a second more selective offer made at the same time that you answer the inquiry, in person by junior salesmen, by checking name, address or business connection of person sending in the inquiry against directories in some cases.

13. Send a second followup. Put the hottest inquiries on your list for regular direct mail; tell them where they can see or hear other advertising of yours.

14. Convince salesmen and dealers of value of leads from advertising. Include case histories in house organs and bulletins of specific new business developed by ads. Use sales meetings to tell salesmen the value of these leads to them. Provide incentive for followup.

15. Weed out your permanent inquiry file on a periodic basis. If no indication of action taken by prospect is obtained, use another followup to find out if person who inquired is still a prospect, now a satisfied customer or out of the running. If still a prospect, light a fire under the salesman or dealer to go after him again in person.

External Inquiry Handling

Lettershops and other service organizations frequently handle the entire task of processing inquiries. Methods vary depending upon the equipment and personnel available and the requirements of the clients.

A typical external inquiry-handling system involves same-day processing using automatically typewritten letters, personally signed. The system has eight steps:

1. An analysis is made of inquiries received by a client. The vital inquiries, which must be handled by top management, are left for the client's individualized attention. The balance are classified into standard types.
2. Once inquiries have been classified, master letters with variations are composed. The master paragraphs are punched into a "memory" tape for the IBM-Autotypist machine.
3. Each variation of a letter is coded. When an inquiry is received, it is coded. For example, a code such as 1-8-11-60—$80.00 might mean that standard paragraphs 1, 8, 11, and 60 would be used and the amount of $80.00 inserted as the quotation price in paragraph 60.
4. Each day, the client sends his inquiries to the lettershop. They are received directly by an inquiry followup girl who is assigned to the client's project. This girl punches the indicated codes into the machine, inserts the letterhead, types in the name and address and salutation. The automatic typing device takes over.
5. At the same time the original letter is being typed on the Autotypist, several carbon copies are made for the client's files and for mailing to the sales force or the distributor organization.
6. Each inquiry followup girl operates her own "lettershop." Personal signatures are applied using the Auto-Pen—another automation marvel which produces actual pen-and-ink signatures at high speed. In the self-contained "lettershop," the label or envelope is typed, the appropriate literature is drawn from the client's rack, the mailing is assembled and tabulated.
7. The inquiry followup girl prepares carbons to be mailed to the field sales organization. She prepares the mailing to be sent back to the client, containing the permanent records of the inquiry. The prospect, the salesman and the company receive their information at about the same time.
8. At the end of the month, the client is given a summary report. The client is billed at a predetermined, flat rate per inquiry.

Globe Industries' System

Globe Industries Inc., Dayton, Ohio, manufacturer of precision miniature electric motors, uses a six-piece carbon snap-out set as the key element in its inquiry-handling program. The first "page" of the form is a gummed sheet with four perforated sections. On these sections are typed the name and address of the inquirer and the Globe representative. These then become mailing labels, yet the information is automatically added to the five other sheets in the snap-out set. Another of the perforated sections is a label imprinted, "Hot Prospect." This label is affixed to reports of inquiries which have come in via letterheads, telegrams and telephone and immediately lets the representative know that the inquiry is more than routine.

The other five pages of the set carry such information as:

Inquirer's capital rating,

Record of previous purchases,

What product was inquired about,

Source of the inquiry,

What was sent to the inquirer and when, plus additional information.

There is also space at the bottom of the form in which the representative can indicate if the name should be added to the mailing list or if he should not be considered a good prospect.

Sales representatives are sent the first two copies of this form, one of which must be returned to Globe with the required followup information. If no reply is forthcoming from the salesman, or if the inquirer returns the reply card which is automatically sent with literature, the third copy is sent to the representative. The fourth copy is retained in the advertising files and the fifth accompanies correspondence or order paperwork.

To simplify the handling of inquiry mailings, Globe uses a simple flap attachment (see illustration below). The inquirer's name is filled in in ink at the top of the flap to add a personal

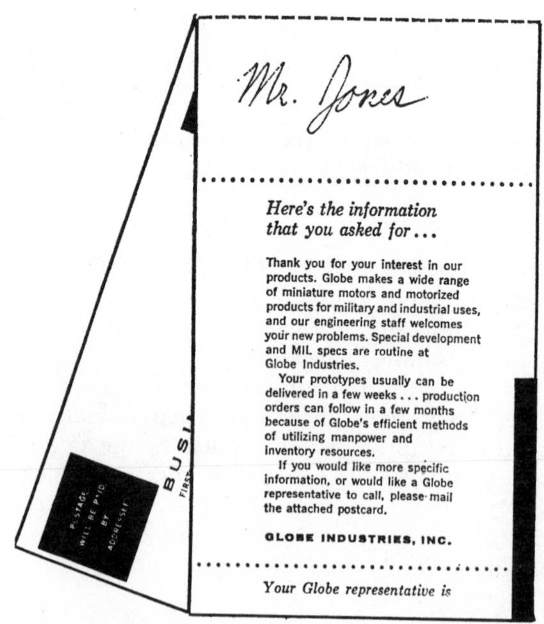

Globe Industries, Inc., usually receives a 15% return on this reply card.

touch. The name of Globe's nearest representative goes at the bottom. The back of the flap consists of a business reply card on which the inquirer can ask to be added to the Globe mailing list, or can indicate if he wants more specific information or to have a representative to call. Globe generally receives a return of about 15% of these reply cards, including 3% who specifically ask for a salesman to call.

Koppers' System

Another snap-out form user is the Wood Preserving Division of Koppers Co., Pittsburgh. Paul A. Schweibinz explained the system in *Industrial Marketing:*

> It only takes a few minutes after the mail arrives in the morning to code each letter, post card, or coupon with a letter and a number—one identifying the appropriate literature which will answer the inquirer's request and the other identifying our nearest sales outlet. Advertisers Associates, a local direct mail house that handles the processing from this point, provides a twice-daily messenger pickup.
>
> The key feature of our inquiry-handling system is located at the direct mail house. A five-part carbon-interleaved form, devised by our advertising agency, takes care of our distribution problem. The top sheet is a printed form letter, reproduced on our letterhead, thanking the respondent for his inquiry. Advertisers Associates types in his name and address, refers to the product or service he expressed interest in, and lists the name and address of his nearest Koppers' sales office or licensee. The fill-in matches the body copy of the letter.
>
> When the letter is filled in, the top sheet is removed and gathered with the literature indicated by the coding. The package is then inserted in a Koppers' envelope and mailed to the inquirer. The second copy of the form is sent to the sales manager for information only, and the third copy, on pink paper, is returned to the advertising department. We use this copy for reference and followup.
>
> The fourth copy, on green stock, goes to the appropriate field sales office for possible followup or distribution to the retail dealer outlet nearest the customer. The yellow copy is used when we wish to simultaneously alert our licensee wood treaters or pole building contractors about a particular inquiry.

A unique feature of the Koppers' system is that the green or yellow copies merely alert field forces of customer interest. Followup at this point is not requested but left to the field personnel's discretion. With each letter, Koppers encloses a reply card inviting the inquirer to request specific details, terms, data, and so forth. When one of these cards is returned, field personnel are informed that the inquirer has become a qualified prospect, requiring immediate followup.

Plymouth Traveler

A snap-out form designed to do four important jobs was developed to handle inquiries received from readers of *Plymouth Traveler,* a dealer-sponsored owner's magazine published by Chrysler Corp. Each issue of the magazine offered readers travel reference information from tourist attractions featured in the magazine's editorial sections.

Since each issue of the magazine drew between 1,000 and 10,000 requests for travel literature, it was important to have a quick-and-easy system to process those requests. The three-page carbon set illustrated on the facing page was the answer.

Page one had three fill-ins:

1. The name and address of the Plymouth dealer sponsoring the magazine sent to the inquirer.
2. The name of the travel organization which would actually mail out the requested travel information.
3. The name and address of the owner sending in the inquiry.

This first page of the carbon set was sent to the organization which would fulfill the request for literature. The top third of the 5¾- by 6¾-inch sheet, which was printed on perforated gummed label stock, was designed for attaching to the literature. The fill-ins for both the dealer and the organization sending the literature were included on this enclosure. This allowed the dealer to get credit for handling the inquiry, which if sent without the enclosure would come directly from the tourist organization without any reference to the fact that the material was being sent in response to the request made via *Plymouth Traveler.*

The middle third of the gummed stock form was designed to serve as a mailing label. It contained only the filled-in name and address of the inquirer, plus the simple legend, "Here is the material you requested." Because it was assumed that the tourist organization would be using pre-packaged material which al-

Plymouth Traveler

THE PLYMOUTH TRAVELER Magazine, Box 4778, Chicago, Ill. 60680

This material is sent to you with the best wishes of the PLYMOUTH TRAVELER and your PLYMOUTH dealer:

Mainline Chrysler-Plymouth
1234 Main Boulevard
Metropolitan, Ohio 34567

Courtesy of: The Atlanta Chamber of Commerce

Here is the material you requested.

To:

Mr. John J. Johnson
5678 Walnut Court
Anytown, Ohio 34577

How to use these handy gummed labels:
Detach upper label and attach to literature
Detach middle label and affix to mailing envelope
Discard this lower piece.

...go, Ill. 60680

...PLYMOUTH dealers by the

...th

...Chamber of Commerce

...ar Mr. Dealer:

Mr. John J. Johnson
5678 Walnut Court
Anytown, Ohio 34577

Who receives the PLYMOUTH TRAVELER MAGAZINE, thanks to you recently wrote us requesting additional travel information. Perhaps this reader is planning a trip and needs service, accessories ... or even a new car! A call or letter from you might prove worth while.

The Plymouth Traveler

...by the

...678 Walnut Court
Anytown, Ohio 34577

Who receives the PLYMOUTH TRAVELER MAGAZINE, thanks to you recently wrote us requesting additional travel information. Perhaps this reader is planning a trip and needs service, accessories ... or even a new car! A call or letter from you might prove worth while.

The Plymouth Traveler

ready had its return address imprinted, no *Plymouth Traveler*-oriented imprint was included.

The lower third of the form contained instructions to the travel organization.

The second page of the snap-out set served as a letter notifying the dealer that one of his customers had requested travel literature. Included in the copy was the reminder: "Perhaps this reader is planning a trip and needs service, accessories . . . or even a new car! A call or letter from you might prove worthwhile."

The third page—a duplicate of the second—was used to inform district offices of the requests being handled—important information in convincing dealers that their sponsorship of the magazine was a valuable promotion expenditure.

General Electric's Verified Inquiry Program

Probably the most highly developed program of inquiry qualification has been developed by the Industrial Sales Operation of General Electric Co. Each week, this GE unit receives some 2,600 inquiries from all sources—advertisements, news releases, trade shows, letters, and direct mail. Since it is highly unlikely that all of these inquiries—or even a major portion of them—represent "hot prospects," G.E. had to develop a method of screening the inquiries so that only those which could reasonably be assumed to be bona fide sales leads would be sent to salesmen for followup. The resulting program is called the "Verified Inquiry Program."

This program was described by George M. Robertson, advertising services manager of GE's Industrial Sales Operation:

> A few of the daily flow of inquiries request prices or application information. These go immediately to field sales offices for followup. The others simply ask for product literature, which is mailed with dispatch—90% within 24 hours and the remaining 10% within 48 hours.
>
> A copy of each inquiry is stamped with the date filled and is sent to the appropriate advertising account manager. He, in turn, sends the inquiry to the product department concerned. Thus, everyone interested is kept posted and knows immediately the inquiry performance of any promotion.
>
> The requested product literature is sent to customers and prospects with a short "thank you" letter directing the respondent to the nearest GE sales office, a list of which ap-

pears on the reverse side of the letter. The material is mailed in a specially identified envelope.

Also enclosed is a "May we help you further?" form, which folds into a business reply envelope. The form is really a product application data blank which asks the respondents these questions:

> Do you have a specific application with which we might help you? Please outline your needs below.
>
> For this application, about how many units would you require?

The idea back of the questionnaire is to determine whether the respondent's interest is casual or serious. If he is not in the market now, or if he wanted the publication for information only, the chances are pretty good he will not reply. If, on the other hand, he is serious and ready to do business, he will either call our sales office or take the time and effort to answer the questions and, presumably, we will have a lead on a bona fide prospect.

When a reply is received, the information is sent immediately to the nearest district sales office via a verified inquiry form. The sales manager retains one copy and sends another to the proper salesman. Other copies are retained for recordkeeping purposes. The verified inquiry form includes the prospect's name and address, what literature has been mailed to him, what prompted the original inquiry, and a suggestion where additional information for followup can be found in the vast library of product information published by GE.

After contacting the prospect, the salesman fills in information concerning the call on the form. This information is then routed back to the advertising department for analysis and use in evaluation of inquiries.

Is this program effective? The composite view of our field sales managers points up this noteworthy fact—72% of the verified inquiries represent immediate or long-range business.

12 Tips From GE

George Robertson notes that this effective program is based on 12 guideposts. He credits the Industrial Advertising Research Institute's report, "A Study of Methods for Handling and Evaluating Industrial Advertising Inquiries," as the source for these guides:

1. The inquiry must be answered promptly—ideally within 48 hours.
2. The inquirer should receive an acknowledgment, preferably a letter.
3. Competent personnel should be in charge of the inquiry-handling system.
4. A simple, practical method for recordkeeping is needed to permit quick analysis.
5. The system must be understood at all levels, clerical through sales management.
6. The system must provide for careful screening.
7. The system must insure followup to make sure that the inquirer has received what he asked for.
8. Large, promising sales leads should be plainly labeled.
9. The salesman—the man who knows best—should have the option of selecting the method and time of followup of routine inquiries.
10. And, this is just common sense—all personnel should be educated as to the cost of, value of, and benefits to be expected from efficient inquiry handling.
11. Salesmen should be credited for obtaining orders, regardless of the contribution made by inquiries.
12. Administrative control should not be divided if you are to reap some real benefits.

Coding Inquiries

An important feature of the inquiry-handling systems of many companies is a special system for coding all inquiries. For example, Hitchiner Manufacturing Co. uses a series of numerals which quickly provide information on how the inquiry was received and how it was handled. A typical code might read 6/14X66-201-34 4. This would mean:

6/14 = The date on which literature is sent and the salesman is notified.

X = If one "X" precedes the number, the inquirer is not on the mailing list but at least one person from this company or branch is. If two "X's" (XX) precede the number, no one from the inquirer's company is on the mailing list.

64 = the month and year of the promotion which drew the inquiry (in this case it would mean June 1966).

201 = the specific ad, direct mail piece, or other promotion which promoted the inquiry.

34 = the number of the specific literature sent in answer to the inquiry.

4 = the last number is a designation of the sales territory in which the inquirer is located.

Buchanan Coding System

A more elaborate coding system is used by Buchanan Electrical Products Corporation. The next illustration shows the record card which is sent to sales representatives. It is part of a three-part snap-out set. The first part of the set is the mailing label used to forward the literature. The second part goes to the salesman, while the third part is retained for followup purposes by the advertising department.

1. *Representative*—Every Buchanan representative is given a numerical designation, which is entered in the first box at the top of the card.

2. *Type of Account*—Whenever the type of account represented by the inquirer is immediately obvious, a letter designation is entered in the second box. Typical designations include "A" for Aircraft, "AR" for Architect, "C" for Contractor, "CE" for Consulting Engineer, "U" for Utility, etc.

3. *Product(s) of Interest*—Specific products involved in each inquiry are entered in the third box by letter codes. For example, "BU" means Bushends, "CF"=Conduct Fittings, "SC"=Splice Caps, "WT"=Wire Terminals, etc.

4. *Source of Inquiry and How Received*—Three different codes are entered in the "Source of Inquiry" boxes. The first of these boxes is for either trade shows or publication advertising. If a trade show, the letter code "Z" is used followed by a code for the particular trade show ("ZEI"= Electrical Industry Show, Chicago; "ZMC"=Massachusetts Electrical Contractors Assn.; "ZTF"=International Trade Fair, Toronto; etc.). In addition, Buchanan has designated letter codes for more than 300 publications which carry the company's advertising and/or publicity ("AA"=*Aviation Age,* "AUM"=*Automation,* "FBS"=*Forbes,* "JN"= *Jobber News,* "SAJ"=*Southern Automotive Journal,* "WW"=*Wireless World,* etc.) If the source is unknown, an "X" is entered in this box.

   The second of the Inquiry Source boxes is for the date of the publication issue or trade show as applicable.

   The third of these boxes indicates the type of item which drew the inquiry—"A"=Advertisement, "P"=Product Item, "L"=Literature Item, "E"=Editorial Article.

   The "Via" box indicates the nature of the inquiry—"C"=Coupon (from a publication), "L"=Letter, "T"=Telephone, "P"=Post card; "V"=Verbal, "W"=Wire.

5. *Literature Sent*—Designations similar to those used to indicate "Products of Interest" are used in this box to designate types of literature sent. If a distributor is involved, distributor discount sheets are included in the inquiry-answering package and an asterisk (*) is added to the code.

6. *Date of Handling*—In the final box is entered the date on which the inquiry was handled.

REPR.	ACCT.	PRODUCT	SOURCE OF INQUIRY	VIA	LIT. SENT	DATE

Inquiry has been received from and literature sent to:-

Please indicate follow-up action and results on reverse side of this card and return to Hillside as soon as possible.

OFFICE COPY

Buchanan Electrical Products Corporation, Hillside, N. J.

INQUIRY FOLLOW-UP REPORT

ACTION TAKEN—

PERSONAL CALL / / | PHONE CALL / / | LETTER* / / | ☐ SEE CORRESPONDENCE* | ☐ SEE FIELD REPORT*

REFERRED TO DISTRIBUTOR / /

DATE | NAME | CITY | STATE

RESULTS OBTAINED—

ORDER PROCURED* / / DATE | NO. | $ VALUE | QUOTED* / / DATE | $ VALUE | ☐ QUOTATION REQUESTED*

☐ EXCELLENT POTENTIAL | ☐ POSSIBLE FUTURE SALES | ☐ KEEP ON MAILING LIST | ☐ NO PROSPECT—TAKE OFF MAILING LIST

Type of account___

Products of interest___

Remarks___

Will follow up on __ / / __ Per___ / /

*ATTACH TO THIS CARD

Buchanan Electrical Products Corporation uses an elaborate coding system.

Followup Systems

Most effective inquiry-handling systems will have some device to procure followup information either from the inquirer or from field selling organizations. The Buchanan inquiry form, has a report which the representative fills out and sends in to the company (see illustration on page 1296).

A less complicated report form is used by The Pfaudler Co. (see illustration on next page). All the sales representative needs do is to write in the date on which the followup is made and check appropriate boxes to indicate whether the inquirer is a customer, a prospect, or neither; and whether he should be added to the mailing list, and, if so, for which product line.

Racine Hydraulics McBee System

For more rapid retrieval of information, Racine Hydraulics uses a McBee Keysort card, which has a series of numbered holes around all four sides. These holes can be notched to indicate the number of the ad pulling the inquiry, the magazine in which it appeared, credit rating of the inquirer, S.I.C. number of the inquirer's firm, plus additional information.

On the face of the card, Racine Hydraulics furnishes the dealer information about the inquiry—name and address, type of business, Dun & Bradstreet rating, the company's rating of the sales potential of the inquirer (1 = Potential appears good, 2 = Potential does not appear good, 3 = Unable to appraise potential), and the source of the inquiry.

On the back of the card, the dealer fills in the following information if Racine has given the inquiry a No. 1 rating.

Customer contacted on..
Date

☐ Sold: see order No..................................	☐ Equip. not in price range
☐ Quoting: Will advise in .... days	☐ Equip. not in pressure range
☐ Catalog Collector	☐ Equip. not in size range
☐ Not planning to purchase in near future	☐ Other reasons..............................
☐ No longer interested in this item	....

Comments..

....

Signed...Date...............................

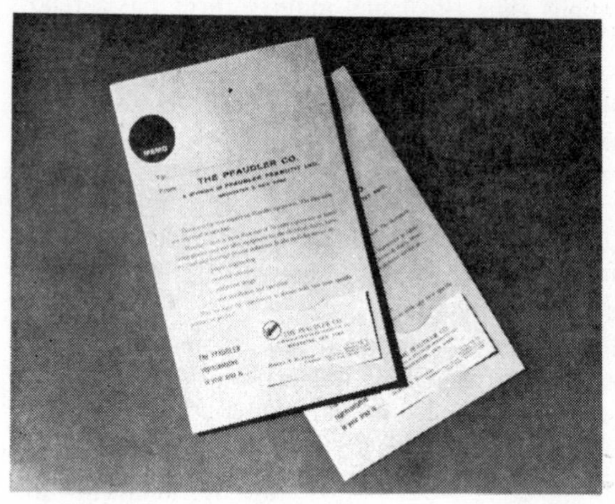

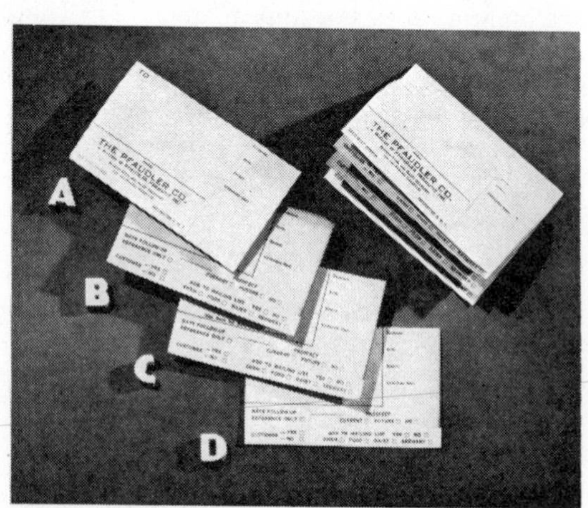

The Pfaudler Co. developed a simple report form for inquiry handling.

Bruning Letter Form

The Charles Bruning Company makes use of one of its own products—diazotype copying machines—as part of its inquiry-followup system. All inquiries are originally answered with an autotyped letter, composed from a standard selection of paragraphs. As these letters are typed, three additional carbons are made on translucent paper, which can be used as masters for the copying machines.

These copies are on oversize sheets which have a form down the right-hand side and across the bottom. The right-hand form has space for providing salesmen with information concerning the nature of the inquiry. Then along the bottom is a form for the salesman to fill out. It includes a record of sales calls and an area to check results: Product sold; Good prospect for future sale; Bought or is buying competitive product; "Coupon clipper"—no need for product.

When the salesman has completed his sales followup, he fills in the information requested and then makes a print of the finished form and returns it to the advertising department.

Followup Via the Inquirer

Many companies contact the original inquirer directly to obtain information by which to evaluate inquiry handling. Reflectal Corporation, for example, used a double post card. The outgoing message side said:

WILL YOU GRADE OUR "REPORT CARD"?

A month ago, in answer to your request, we sent you some literature on ALFOL Insulation. At the same time, we promised that a representative would be contacting you soon to answer any further questions you might have.

Naturally, we hope your inquiry has been serviced to your full satisfaction. If it hasn't, however, if we have "flunked out" somewhere along the line, we'd like to know about it. And only you can tell us.

So won't you give us our "grades" by checking the four short questions on the attached reply card. It takes but a minute and it helps so much in providing you—and others like you—the kind of thorough service we want you to have. Thank you very much.

On the reply side, Reflectal asks the recipient to check either true or false for these questions:

1. Your answering letter, together with the literature you enclosed, gave us the basic product information we requested.
2. We were contacted, just as you indicated, by an ALFOL salesman.
3. Your representative answered our questions, gave us the buying information we needed.
4. We decided to give ALFOL a chance to "do its stuff." Your representative (has supplied) (will be supplying) us with .... sq. ft.

Universal Followup Card

New Equipment Digest suggests using a business reply card along with literature mailed in answer to inquiries. The following form is suggested:

SAMPLE REPLY CARD

THANKS FOR YOUR INQUIRY

1. Was the information in the enclosed literature adequate? ( ) Yes ( ) No
   If not, what additional information do you desire?

   ....

2. Is purchase of this type equipment contemplated? ( ) Yes ( ) No
   If yes, for what application?

   ....

3. When do you anticipate this purchase? ( ) 1-3 mos. ( ) 3-6 mos. ( ) over 6 mos.
4. What quantity do you anticipate using?..
5. Comments..

Thank you,
John Smith, Sls. Mgr.

*Name..

Company..

Address..

*You may find it advisable to type or stencil the individual's name and company, or to numerically code each card. This will insure proper identification of those cards which are returned.

A Word of Warning

A final word of warning is in order on the handling of inquiries. It comes from S. E. Voran, sales promotion manager of Parker-Hannifin Corporation, who reported to *Industrial Marketing:*

> Some years ago, we maintained elaborate records on inquiries and the followup of them, but eventually discovered we were spending a lot of time maintaining these records, and decided they were not that beneficial to us. In other words, cutting out an elaborate recordkeeping system is about the only way I can think of for cutting costs in inquiry handling.

As for any other aspect of direct mail and mail order operations, the cost of keeping inquiry records should be watched carefully to insure that added sales or goodwill justify the expense. But even a minimal system should insist on answering the prime question: "Is every inquiry being handled?" Any consumer who takes the trouble to make an inquiry deserves—and expects—a followup of some kind.

The initial followup should be made as promptly as possible, and should provide as much information about the product or service as possible. Subsequent followups, made for the purpose of closing a sale, should not be made too quickly or too frequently. Many consumers are quite deliberate about making purchases, particularly through the mail, and will delay their order long after they made a firm decision to purchase. Followups that seem too frequent and urgent only serve to annoy.

APPENDIX

Appendix A

Media/scope's Check List for Direct Mail Advertising*

Considerations for the media strategist contemplating use of the direct mail medium.

GENERAL OBJECTIVES

Direct Mail as Advertising

Advertising which attempts, through the mail, to influence people favorably toward a product or service. This kind of direct mail has the same goals as other advertising—that is, to inform, to influence, to build an image.

Direct Mail Marketing

Effective marketing strategy may call for—

1. the use of the direct mail medium alone.
2. the use of direct mail in calculated coordination with other media to reach a desired sales objective. Such coordination involves a reasoned division of prospecting or selling responsibilities; first, so that each medium is assigned the selling function it performs best; and, second, so that the communications in each medium work to reinforce the selling messages conveyed through other media. (Example: a couponing or sampling program conducted in conjunction with newspaper, radio, and spot TV advertising to introduce a new product.)

Direct Mail Selling

The sales approach and the sale, itself, is made through the mail, without the use of other media, salesmen or dealers. The use of the term "mail-order selling" is avoided here because that term includes selling in which the purchase is initiated via mail-order ads in newspapers, magazines, radio, TV, car cards.

WHEN TO USE DIRECT MAIL

1. When sampling would be both practical and desirable.
2. When the advertising message is too complicated or too detailed to be conveyed efficiently in other media.
3. When a specific, selected market is desired and other media can provide it only at the cost of waste circulation.
4. When personal, personalized, or confidential communication is desired.
5. When the format or color that an advertiser's marketing strategy requires can't be carried in other media.

*Reprinted through the courtesy of Standard Rate and Data Service, Inc.

6. When a specific market area needs to be covered with a minimum of slop-over into adjacent areas.
7. When specific timing or frequency of contact is desired.
8. When couponing is desirable.
9. When controlled research is called for (e.g.: measuring of effectiveness within certain markets; ascertaining prospect profiles; or testing price, packaging, or logical users for new products).
10. When a controlled mailing is desirable (mailings will go only to certain income groups, owners of certain makes of cars, boat owners, etc.).
11. When mail order (sale of the product directly to the prospect, without retailers, dealers or other media) is desirable.
12. When you want to accomplish the following jobs in the marketing process:

    A. Obtain responses indicating interest (as in "securing leads")—

        a. to be followed up by more direct mail.

        b. to be followed up by salesmen.

    B. Put the prospect into position for personal selling (as in "traffic building")—

        a. in a retail outlet or showroom.

        b. in front of an exhibit of products—particularly those which salesmen cannot take to the prospect for demonstration.

    C. Create a receptive atmosphere for salesmen—

        a. through cordial-contact mailings which build an "image."

        b. through institutional types of direct mail (for example, mailings such as the paper and printing companies use to illustrate the product features or the company's abilities).

        c. through the "impact" created by any type of mailing sent out. Any mailing will create some kind of impression. Well-executed mailings will identify the advertiser favorably.

    D. Influence selected groups to action—

        a. building salesman incentive.

        b. obtaining credits and collections.

        c. building mailing lists.

        d. developing political campaigns.

    E. Make more effective the impact of advertising in other media—

        a. by gaining the cooperation and building the enthusiasm of all persons involved with your advertising efforts, through keeping them properly motivated and informed.

        b. by helping to convert impressions created by other advertising media into sales through—

            (1) bringing the prospect and product together at the point of sale.

            (2) following up inquiries developed by other media.

            (3) using ads from newspapers or magazines as a mailing piece or part of a mailing unit to precede or follow up the issue of the magazine or newspaper in which the ad appears.

CHARACTERISTICS

1. Selectivity

Direct mail is the only advertising medium which permits the pinpointing of advertising to a pre-selected individual person. There is almost no classification of the American population that cannot be isolated and reached by direct mail, whether the market is national (and numbers in the millions) or the prospects number 100 in a particular dealer's territory.

2. Person-to-Person Character

The personal letter is the oldest direct mail format of all. The personal nature of direct mail remains today one of the medium's primary assets. You can be personal and confidential in direct mail even when trying to reach large numbers of prospects. Modern equipment makes possible the production of apparently personally-typed letters at a fraction of former costs. Even mass mailings are accorded personal mail privacy and receptivity at point of receipt.

3. Long Copy Treatments

They are well suited for direct mail.

4. Competition

Less, or no, competition for the recipient's attention from other advertising and/or editorial matter.

5. Format Variety

Almost unlimited opportunity for creative ingenuity in expressing an advertising idea. Budget, talent, and U.S. postal regulations are the only restrictions. Selection of format, colors, shapes, sizes, etc. are virtually unlimited.

6. Variety of Reproduction Processes

Direct mail offers greater flexibility in format choice because of the wide variety of reproduction processes available. All forms of the graphic arts can be adapted to direct mail.

7. Attention-Attracting Techniques

Cutouts, folds, odd shapes, pop-ups, and many others are possible in direct mail.

8. Testing

The individual, personal qualities of direct mail are ideal for research. With small, carefully selected samples of lists, copy approaches, and advertising ideas can be tested before an entire ad effort is thrown in one direction.

9. Timing

You can produce direct mail as you need it. There are no restrictions to publication dates. Direct mail can be timed with reasonable accuracy to hit a market when you want it to (important when direct mail is coordinated with other media in a campaign, emergency situations, and seasonal products and services).

10. Reply Devices

Business reply mail is an important postal service for advertisers. Business reply envelopes are easily mailable. They permit responses to be returned to the advertiser without the respondent having to pay the postage.

LIST SOURCES

1. Internal

Compiled by advertiser from his own sales records, credit records, shipping records, general correspondence, sales force recommendations, trade show registrants, etc.

2. External

a. List brokers: The list broker acts as an agent between the list owner and the advertiser seeking lists which correspond to his market profile. The list user normally rents lists for one-time use; the broker is paid by the list owner. It is the list broker's job to keep abreast of all developments in the list field. Many brokers have experienced staffs searching for "new" lists, and for more detailed information about known lists. A list broker, in addition to arranging list rentals, can help direct mail users in many other ways. For example, on list maintenance, keeping direct mail records, and in testing procedures.

b. List compiler: Specialists in compiling specific kinds of lists such as industrial, birth lists, automobile registration lists, and other select markets. They are in business to compile practically every kind of mailing list for which there is a market. A list compiler may already have the list needed and will either rent or sell it for less than cost of compilation. If an advertiser wants a completely new list compiled, he may deal directly with a compiler or he can work through a list broker.

c. Specialized list houses: A small number of compilers maintain multimillion specialized lists from which selection can be made according to geographic location and by many demographic characteristics. These organizations offer comprehensive services encompassing all phases of direct mail marketing.

d. Occupant lists: a kind of compiled list comprising just addresses, no names. Occupant lists are often used when saturation mailings are desired and the direct mail message is not of a personal nature. Occupant mail is delivered to whomever lives at a given address, with no problem of non-delivery if someone has moved.

FORMATS

1. Letters

Direct mail at its best is a person-to-person communication. The personal, or personalized letter, is the oldest direct mail format.

2. Letter with Enclosure

There are hundreds of different types of items which can be enclosed with letters—or used separately. Most of them, however, fall within five basic categories: Folders, broadsides, booklets, brochures, and circulars.

3. Self-Mailer

A self-mailer can range from a postcard or single page to a multi-page presentation of a product or service.

4. Catalogs and Price Lists

Catalogs take all shapes and forms, ranging from the thousand-plus pages of the major catalog houses to single sheets and special price lists, and simple folders listing the full product lines of small industrial companies.

5. House Organs, Newsletters, and Bulletins

6. Annual and Special Reports

7. Statement and Letter Stuffers

8. Showmanship Formats

Out of the ordinary formats which by their very uniqueness, demand special attention. Possibilities are wide, including unusual message surfaces, historical items, unusual layouts, copy styles and envelopes, foreign postmarks, gag items, product samples or parts.

9. Spectaculars

The most elaborate use of the direct mail medium. The spectacular is almost always directed to a highly select audience. Its most distinguishing characteristic is its dimensional nature. Most spectaculars feature three-dimensional objects and are mailed in specially prepared boxes rather than envelopes. Spectaculars are sometimes used independently, but more often they are part of a multi-mailing campaign, and the dimensional objects featured in such mailings are usually designed for retention by the recipient over an extended period.

10. Product Sampling

11. Couponing

A certificate with stated value (in money or merchandise) which the recipient presents to a retailer to receive a price reduction on a specified item.

12. Co-operative Mailings

The sharing of the same envelope for advertising messages by non-competing advertisers.

13. Sweepstakes

A prize offer where the winners are determined on the basis of chance. This is an attention-attracting device to motivate the recipient to: (1) open the envelope, (2) read the offer, and (3) make a response decision. The latter takes the recipient closer to the point of purchase (e.g. into an automobile dealer's showroom).

MEASURING EFFECTIVENESS

The usual yardstick for media (i.e. cost-per-thousand), is not the primary yardstick for direct mail; but, rather, how much it costs per response generated in terms of:

1. a sale
2. an inquiry
3. a visit to a store

WHO DOES WHAT?

1. Advertising Agency

The extent of agency involvement in the direct mail medium depends on the extent to which direct mail has been integrated into the normal agency organization. Agencies often work in cooperation with one or more of the following outside supplier and or specialist sources:

2. Direct Mail Agency

Exclusive concentration on direct mail medium.

3. Sales Promotion Agency

Main skills usually in printed matter of all types, including direct mail, point of purchase, incentive programs and so on.

4. List Suppliers

(see LIST SOURCES)

5. Direct Mail Consultants

Specialize in developing or analyzing direct mail programs.

6. Free Lance Specialists

In the copy area, for example, there are many specialists who concentrate on a particular type of direct mail copy.

7. Lettershops

Primarily production organizations, but may also offer a variety of creative services.

8. Printers

Primarily production, but may offer a variety of creative and other direct mail services.

COMPENSATION

1. Publishers' Concept

Mailing house allows agency commission.

2. Publishers' Concept Plus Agency Fee or Added Commission

This is a commission plus fee concept similar to some arrangements made on individual accounts when space commissions do not cover agency expenses and reasonable profit.

3. Agency Fee

APPENDIX B

DIRECT MAIL ORGANIZATIONS

THE ASSOCIATION OF DIRECT MARKETING AGENCIES—342 Madison Avenue, New York, NY 10017.

CANADIAN DIRECT MAIL MARKETING ASSOCIATION—150 Consumers Rd., Suite 405, Willowdale, Ont. Canada M2T 1P9

CHICAGO ASSOCIATION OF DIRECT MARKETING—221 N. La Salle St., Chicago, IL 60601.

DIRECT MAIL/MARKETING ASSOCIATION, INC. (DM/MA)—6 E. 43rd St., New York, NY 10017.

DIRECT MAIL/MARKETING CLUB OF ATLANTA—c/o Atlanta Magazine, 62-85 Barfield Rd., Atlanta, GA 30328.

DIRECT MARKETING CLUB OF ST. LOUIS—P.O. Box 2093, St. Louis, MO 63158.

DIRECT MARKETING CLUB OF TORONTO—P.O. Box 3000, Station A, Toronto, Ont., Canada M5W 1A5.

DIRECT MARKETING CLUB OF WASHINGTON—608 H St., S.W. Washington, DC 20024.

DIRECT MARKETING IDEA EXCHANGE—475 Park Ave. S. (Room 3500), New York, NY 10016.

DIRECT MARKETING WRITERS GUILD—516 5th Ave., New York, NY 10036.

FULFILLMENT MANAGEMENT ASSOCIATION, INC.—224 W. 57th St., New York, NY 10019.

THE HUNDRED MILLION CLUB—c/o Accredited Mailing Lists, Inc., 3 Park Ave., New York, NY 10016.

LONG ISLAND DIRECT MARKETING ASSOCIATION—c/o Four Star Associates, 260 Duffy Ave., Hicksville, NY 11802.

MAIL ADVERTISING SERVICE ASSOCIATION INTERNATIONAL—7315 Wisconsin Ave., Suite 818E, Washington, DC 20014.

MAIL MARKETING CLUB OF DETROIT—c/o R. L. Polk & Company, 6400 Monroe Blvd., Taylor, MI 48180.

MAIL MARKETING CLUB OF NEW ENGLAND—c/o Direct Marketing Concepts, 1661 Worcester Rd., Framingham, MA 01701.

NATIONAL MAIL ORDER ASSOCIATION—5818 Venice Blvd., Los Angeles, CA 90019.

NEW JERSEY DIRECT MAIL MARKETING CLUB—20 Nassau St., Princeton, NJ 08540.

OHIO VALLEY DIRECT MARKETING CLUB—c/o Nielsen Lithography Company, 3731 Eastern Hills Lane, Cincinnati, OH 45209.

PHILADELPHIA DIRECT MAIL CLUB, INC.—222 Lancaster Ave., Devon, PA 19333.

SAN FRANCISCO ADVERTISING CLUB—681 Market St., San Francisco, CA 94105.

THE WOMEN'S DIRECT RESPONSE GROUP—P.O. Box 5134 F.D.R. Station, New York, NY 10022.

APPENDIX C

DIRECT MAIL BIBLIOGRAPHY

Advertising & Sales Promotion. *Direct Mail: Principles & Practice,* Crain Communications Inc.

Alexander, Ralph S., et al. *Industrial Marketing,* Irwin, 3rd edition, 1967.

American Association of Advertising Agencies. *Direct Mail Advertising: New Marketing Tool for Media Planning,* 1967.

Andrews, Francis. *Fund Raising: Marketing for Human Needs,* Direct Mail/ Marketing Assn. 1976.

Arnold, Edmund C. *Ink on Paper,* Harper & Row, 1963.

Association of National Advertisers. *Advertisers Practices in Pre-Testing and Evaluating Effectiveness of Promotion Materials.*

Association of National Advertisers. *Applying Today's Computer Technology to Advertising and Marketing.*

Association of National Advertisers. *Coupon Promotions.*

Association of National Advertisers. *Practical Guides and Modern Practices for Better Advertising Management.* Seven volumes, 1957-1959.

Baker, Stephen. *Visual Persuasion,* McGraw-Hill, 1961.

Ballinger, R. A. *Direct Mail Design International,* Van Nostrand Reinhold, 1963.

Barban, Arnold M. and Sandage, Charles H., eds. *Readings in Advertising and Promotion Strategy,* Irwin, 1968.

Barton, Roger. *Advertising Agency Operations and Management,* McGraw-Hill, 1955.

Barton, Roger. *Media in Advertising,* McGraw-Hill, 1964.

Bedell, Clyde O. *How to Write Advertising That Sells,* McGraw-Hill, 2nd edition, 1952.

Birren, Faber. Color: *A Survey in Words and Pictures,* University Books, 1963.

Birren, Faber. *Selling Color to People,* University Books, 1956.

Black, George. *Listen, Mr. President,* Chilton, 1960.

Blanding, W., and Hopper, W. S. *Common Carrier Advertising Handbook,* Traffic Service Corp., 1960.

Borden, Neil H., and Marshall, Martin V. *Advertising Management: Text and Cases,* Irwin, revised edition, 1959.

Borden, Neil H. *Economic Effects of Advertising,* Irwin, 1942.

Boyd, Harper W., Jr.; Fryburger, Vernon; and Westfall, Ralph L. *Cases in Advertising Management,* McGraw-Hill, 1964.

Boyd, William P. and Lesikar, Raymond V. *Productive Business Writing,* Prentice-Hall, 1959.

Brann, Christian. *Direct Mail and Direct Response Promotion,* Wiley, 1972.

Brantley, C. Owen. *How to Sell Printing by Mail,* The Druillard Press, 1962.

Brink, Edward L. and Kelley, William T. *The Management of Promotion,* Prentice-Hall, 1963.

Britt, Steuart Henderson. *Marketing Manager's Handbook,* Dartnell, 1973.

Brown, Lyndon O.; Lessley, Richard S.; and Weilbacher, William M. *Advertising Media, Creative Planning in Media Selection,* Ronald Press, 1957.

Brown, Milton, and others. *Problems in Marketing,* McGraw-Hill, 3rd edition, 1968.

Brown, Russell A. and Edwards, C. M., Jr. *Retail Advertising and Sales Promotion,* Prentice-Hall, 3rd edition, 1959

Buckley, Earle A. *How to Increase Sales With Letters, McGraw-Hill,* 1961.

Buckley, Earle A. *How to Write Better Business Letters,* McGraw-Hill, 4th edition, 1957.

Burnett, Leo. *Communications of an Advertising Man,* Leo Burnett Co., 1961.

Burns, Aaron. *Typography,* Van Nostrand Reinhold, 1961.

Bursk, Edward C. *Text and Cases in Marketing: A Scientific Approach,* Prentice-Hall, 1962.

Bursk, Edward C. and Chapman, John F., eds. *Modern Marketing Strategy,* Harvard University Press, 1964.

Butterfield, William H. *Common Sense in Letter Writing,* obtainable from author.

Caples, John. *Making Ads Pay,* Harper & Row, 1957.

Caples, John. *Tested Advertising Methods.* Prentice-Hall, 4th edition, 1974.

Carnegie, Dale. *How to Win Friends and Influence People,* Simon & Schuster, 1936.

Chas, Cochrane and Barasch, Kenneth L. *Marketing Problem Solver,* Chilton Book Company, 2nd edition, 1977.

Cherry, David. *Preparing Artwork for Reproduction, Crown Publishers Inc.* 1976.

Cheskin, Louis. *Secrets of Marketing Success,* Trident, 1967.

Clarke, George Timothy. *Copywriting: Theory & Technique,* Harper & Row, 1959.

Cogswell, Harry. *Find a Career in Advertising,* Putnam, 1960.

Colley, Russel H. *Defining Advertising Goals for Measured Advertising Results,* Association of National Advertisers, 1961.

Collier, Robert. *The Robert Collier Letter Book,* Prentice-Hall, 6th edition, 1950.

Consolidated Papers, Inc. *Dimensions in Lithography.*

Cornell, James. *The People Get the Credit,* Spiegel, Inc., 1964.

Cossman, E. Joseph. *How I Made $1,000,000 in Mail Order,* Prentice-Hall, 1963.

Craig, James. *Production for the Graphic Designer,* Crain Books.

Crawford, John W. *Advertising: Communications for Management,* Allyn & Bacon, 2nd edition, 1964.

Crisp, Richard D. *Marketing Research,* McGraw-Hill, 1957.

Crisp, Richard D. *Sales Planning and Control,* McGraw-Hill, 1961.

Dair, Carl. *Design with Type,* Pellegrini & Cudahy, 1952.

Darrow, Richard W. and others. *Public Relations Handbook,* Dartnell, 2nd edition, 1979.

Dembner, S. Arthur and Massee, William E., eds. *Modern Circulation Methods,* McGraw-Hill, 1968.

DeVoe, Merrill. *Effective Advertising Copy,* Macmillan, 1956.

Dexter, Lewis Anthony and White, David Manning, eds. *People, Society and Mass Communications,* The Free Press, 1964.

Dichter, Ernest. *Handbook for Consumer Motivations,* McGraw-Hill, 1964.

Dierson, Frank T. *Planning for Chance Promotions,* Promotion Marketing Association of America, Inc.

Dillman, Don A. *Mail and Telephone Surveys,* John Wiley & Sons, 1978.

Dillon, John. *Handbook of International Direct Marketing.* McGraw-Hill, 1976.

Direct Mail/Marketing Assn. *Direct Mail/Marketing Manual,* revised, 1979.

Direct Mail/Marketing Assn. *Fact Book on Direct Response Marketing,* published annually.

Direct Mail/Marketing Assn. *DM/MA Catalog Directory,* 1978.

Dirksen, Charles J., and Kroeger, Arthur. *Advertising Principles and Problems,* Irwin, 1960.

Dodge, B. F. *Industrial Marketing,* McGraw-Hill, 1970

Doppler, Dr. William Arkwright. *Testing—The Scientific Approach in Direct Mail,* Research Committee of the Direct Mail/Marketing Association, revised edition, 1960.

Dunn, S. Watson. *Advertising Copy and Communication,* McGraw-Hill, 1956.

Egner, Frank. *Letters for Special Occasions,* McGraw-Hill, 1957.

Engel, James F. et al. *Cases in Promotional Strategy,* Irwin, 1971.

Erdos, Paul L. *Professional Mail Surveys,* McGraw-Hill, 1970.

Evans, Bergen and Cornelia. *Dictionary of Contemporary American Usage,* Random House, 1957.

Fellows, Margaret M., and Koenig, Stella A. *Tested Methods of Raising Money: for Churches, Colleges and Health and Welfare Agencies,* Harper & Row, 1959.

Fenvessy, Stanley J. *Keep Your Customers (And Keep Them Happy),* Dow Jones-Irwin, 1976.

Flesch, Rudolph. *The Art of Readable Writing,* Harper & Row, 1960.

Flesch, Rudolph. *How to Speak and Think More Effectively,* Harper & Row, 1960.

Fortune Editors. *The Amazing Advertising Business,* Simon & Schuster, 1957.

Frailey, L. E. ("Cy"). *Handbook of Business Letters,* Prentice-Hall, 1965.

Frailey, L. E. ("Cy"). *The Sales Manager's Letter Book,* Prentice-Hall, 1951.

French, Benjamin I., Jr. *Customer Service Manual,* Prentice-Hall Inc. 1976.

French, Elbrun R. *The Copywriters' Guide,* Harper & Row, 1959.

Frey, Albert W. *Advertising,* Ronald Press, 4th edition, 1970.

Frey, Albert W. and Davis, Kenneth R. *The Advertising Industry,* Association of National Advertisers, 1958.

Fried, Robert P. and Meredith, George. *Incentives in Marketing,* National Premium Sales Executives, 1977.

Fruehling, Rosemary T. and Bouchard, Sharon. *The Art of Writing Effective Letters,* McGraw-Hill, 1972.

Gaw, Walter A. *Advertising Methods and Media,* Wadsworth, 1961.

Glim, Aesop. *How Advertising Is Written,* Dover, 1961.

Graham, Irvin. *How to Sell Through Mail Order,* McGraw-Hill, 1949.

Graves, Richard. *Creating Customers,* Tri-Ocean, 1967.

Green, Paul E. and Frank, R. E. *Manager's Guide to Marketing Research,* Wiley, 1967.

Groesbeck, Kenneth. *The Advertising Agency Business,* Advertising Publications Inc., 1964.

Harding, D. R. *Customer Value Analysis in Direct Marketing and General Direct Mail Concepts,* Center for Direct Marketing, 1972.

Hayakawa, S. I. *Language in Thought and Action,* Harcourt, 1972.

Hilary House. *The Direct Marketing Market Place,* Hilary House Publishers, 1979.

Hodgson, Richard. *A Basic Guide to Effective Inquiry Handling,* American Marketing Services, 1960.

Hodgson, Richard. *Direct Mail in the Political Process,* Direct Mail/Marketing Assn. 1976.

Hodgson, Richard. *Direct Mail Showmanship,* American Marketing Services, 1961.

Hodgson, Richard. *How to Produce an Effective Newsletter,* American Marketing Services, 1961.

Hodgson, Richard. *How to Work with Mailing Lists,* Direct Mail/Marketing Assn., 1976.

Hoffman, Armin. *Graphic Design Manual,* Van Nostrand Reinhold, 1965.

Hofsoos, Emil. *What Management Should Know About Industrial Advertising,* Gulf Publishing Co., 1970.

Hoge, Cecil C. Sr. *Mail Order Moonlighting,* Business Studies, Inc., 1976.

Hoke, Henry. *Direct Mail,* Oceana, 1966.

Hoke, Henry, Library. *Reporter of Direct Mail Advertising.* This set includes 10 volumes: *Dogs That Climb Trees; How to Get the Right Start in Direct Advertising,* by Harrie Bell; *How to Think About Direct Mail; How to Think About Letters,* by Howard Dana Shaw; *How to Think About Readership in Direct Mail; How Direct Mail Solves Management Problems; How to Think About Showmanship in Direct Mail; How to Think About Mail Order; How to Think About Production and Mailing; How to Think About Industrial Direct Mail.*

Hotchkiss, George Burton. *An Outline of Advertising,* Macmillan, 1950.

Howard, James E. *How to Use Mail Order for Profit,* Grosset & Dunlap, 1963.

Huey, Craig A., Makepeace, Clayton, and Gama, Michael. *The Direct Marketing Executive's Workbook,* Craig A. Huey, 1979.

Hymes, David. *Production in Advertising and the Graphic Arts,* Holt, 1958.

Industrial Advertising Research Institute. *Building and Maintaining Industrial Direct Mail Lists,* Report No. 10, 1961.

Industrial Advertising Research Institute. *Measuring the Effectiveness of Industrial Direct Mail,* Report No. 14.
Study No. 2: *Planning More Productive Mailings,* 1964.
Study No. 3: *Pretesting Industrial Direct Mail,* 1965.

International Paper Company. *The Pocket Pal for Printers, Estimators & Advertising Production Managers.*

Intertype Co. Division of Harris-Intertype Corporation. *How to Select Type Faces.*

Jain, Chaman L. and Migliaro, Al. *An Introduction to Direct Marketing,* AMACOM.

Joffe, Gerardo. *How You Too Can Make at Least $1 Million in the Mail-Order Business,* Advance Books, 1978.

Jones, Duane. *Ads, Women and Box Tops, Printers' Ink,* 1955.

Ketcham, Howard. *Color Planning for Business & Industry,* Harper & Row, 1958.

Kirkpatrick, C. A. *Advertising Mass Communication in Marketing,* Houghton Mifflin, 1964.

Klein, Bernard. *Guide to American Directories,* Klein, revised regularly.

Klein, Bernard. *Mail Order Business Directory,* Klein, revised regularly.

Kleppner, Otto. *Advertising Procedure,* Prentice-Hall, 5th edition, 1966.

Kobs, Jim. *Profitable Direct Marketing,* Crain Books, 1979.

Laird, Donald A. and Eleanor. *Psychology,* McGraw-Hill, 4th edition, 1967.

Lane, Edward. *The Beginner's Guide to Selling Information by Mail,* The Green Tree Press, 1976.

Lasker, Albert D. *The Lasker Story, As He Told It,* Crain Communications, Inc., 1963.

Latimer, Henry C. *Preparing Art and Camera Copy for Printing,* McGraw-Hill.

Lesley, Philip, ed. *Lesly's Public Relations Handbook,* Prentice-Hall, 2nd edition, 1971.

Levitt, Theodore. *Innovation in Marketing: New Perspectives for Profit & Growth,* McGraw-Hill, 1962.

Levy, Harold P. *Public Relations for Social Agencies,* Harper & Row, 1956.

Lucas, Darrell B., and Britt, Steuart Henderson. *Advertising Psychology and Research,* McGraw-Hill, 1950.

Lucas, Darrell B. and Britt, Steuart Henderson. *Measuring Advertising Effectiveness,* McGraw-Hill, 1963.

Luick, John F. and Ziegler, William Lee. *Sales Promotion & Modern Merchandising,* McGraw-Hill, 1968.

Mahoney, Tom and Sloane, L. *Great Merchants,* Harper & Row, 1966.

Martineau, Pierre. *Motivation in Advertising,* McGraw-Hill, 1971.

Martyn, Sean. *How to Start and Run a Successful Mail Order Business,* McKay, 1971.

Mayer, Edward N., Jr. *How to Make More Money with Your Direct Mail,* Printers' Ink, 3rd edition, 1960.

Mayer, Edward N., Jr. and Ljungren, Roy G. *The Handbook of Industrial Direct Mail Advertising,* Business/Professional Advertising Assn. 1972.

Mead Corporation. *Annual Report Kit,* 1960.

Melcher, Daniel, and Larrick, Nancy. *Printing and Promotion Handbook,* McGraw-Hill, 3rd edition, 1976.

Menning, Jack H., and Wilkinson, C. W. *Communications Through Letters and Reports,* Irwin, 5th edition, 1972.

Meredith, George. *Premiums in Marketing,* National Premium Sales Executives, Inc., 1971.

Messner, Frederick R. *Industrial Advertising,* McGraw-Hill, 1963.

Messner, Richard. *How to Sell Printing & Lithography,* Fred W. Hock Associates, Inc., 1963.

Milton, Shirley *What You Should Know About Writing Advertising Copy,* Oceana, 1969.

Murphey, Robert W. *How & Where to Look It Up,* McGraw-Hill, 1973.

National Institute of Real Estate Brokers. *How Realtors Sell by Mail,* 1957.

National Retail Merchants Assn. *Direct Mail Advertising & Selling for Retailers,* National Retail Merchants Assn., 1978.

Nauheim, Fred. *Business Letters that Turn Inquiries into Sales,* Prentice-Hall, 1957.

Norins, Hanley. *Compleat Copywriter,* McGraw-Hill, 1966.

Ocko, Judy Young and Rosenblum, M. L. *The Specialty Store and Its Advertising,* National Retail Merchants Assn., 1976.

Ogilvy, David. *Confessions of an Advertising Man,* Atheneum, 1963.

Omega Press. *How to Think About Computer Marketing,* 1968.

Paro, Gary R. *Winning in Mail-Order,* G. R. Paro, 1976.

Pease, Otis. *The Responsibilities of American Advertising,* Yale University Press, 1958.

Peel, J. D. *Anniversary Celebrations Made Easy,* Chilton, 1959.

Pinney, Roy. *Advertising Photography,* Hastings House, 1962.

Prentice, Robert M. *Coupon Promotions: How to Plan, Execute, and Evaluate Retailer-Redeemed Coupon Programs,* Association of National Advertisers, Inc., 1962.

Printing Industries of America. *Trade Customs and Printing Contracts,* Printing Industries of America.

Quenon, E. L. *Direct Mail Research Techniques,* a Direct Mail/Marketing Association research bulletin, April 1961.

Reeves, Rosser. *Reality in Advertising,* Knopf, 1961.

Reibel, John P. *How to Write Successful Business Letters in 15 Days,* Prentice-Hall, 1953.

Reibel, John P., and Robert, Donald R. *Ten Commandments for Writing Letters That Get Results,* Printer's Ink, 1957.

Reporter of Direct Mail Advertising, The, "How to Think About Direct Mail," 1951.

Reporter of Direct Mail Advertising, The, "How to Think About Mailing Lists, July, 1963.

Ris, Thomas F. *Promotional & Advertising Copywriter's Handbook,* TAB Books, 1971.

Risley, George. *Modern Industrial Marketing,* McGraw-Hill, 1972.

Riso, Ovid. *Sales Promotion Handbook,* Dartnell, 7th edition, 1979.

Robertson, Horace O., and Carmichael, Vernal J. *Business Letter English,* McGraw-Hill, 2nd edition, 1957.

Roman, Kenneth and Maas, Jane. *How to Advertise,* St. Martin's Press, 1976.

Roman, Murray. *Telephone Marketing: How to Build Your Business by Telephone,* McGraw-Hill, 1976.

Rosen, Ben. *Type and Typography, The Designer's Type Book,* Van Nostrand Reinhold, 1967.

Rosenblum, M. L. *How to Design Effective Store Advertising,* National Retail Merchants Association, 1961.

Ross, Maxwell C. *How to Write Successful Direct Mail Letter Copy,* Direct Mail/Marketing Assn., 1976.

Rowland, Carrie Mills. *Advertising in Modern Retailing,* Harper & Row, 1954.

Rubin, Robert. "What You Should Know About Selecting the Market," in *Mail Order Strategy,* published by The Reporter of Direct Mail Advertising, 1956.

Ryan, Bernard, Jr. *So You Want to Go Into Advertising,* Harper & Row, 1961.

Sackheim, Maxwell. *How to Advertise Yourself,* Macmillan, 1978.

Sackheim, Maxwell. *My First Sixty Years in Advertising,* Prentice-Hall, 1970.

Sandage, Charles H. *The Promise of Advertising,* Irwin, 1961.

Sandage, Charles H. and Fryburger, Vernon, eds. *The Role of Advertising: A Book of Readings,* Irwin, 1960.

Sandage, Charles H., and Fryburger, Vernon. *Advertising: Theory and Practice* Irwin, 8th edition, 1971.

Sawyer, Howard G. ("Scotty"). *Business-to-Business Advertising,* Crain Books, 1978.

Schellhase, Betsy A. *How to Be a Successful Copywriter,* Arco, 1965.

Schlemmer, Richard M. *Handbook of Advertising Art Production,* Prentice-Hall, 2nd edition, 1976.

Schreier, Fred T. *Modern Marketing Research,* Wadsworth, 1963.

Schutte, William and Steinberg, Erwin R. *Communication in Business and Industry,* Holt, Rinehart & Winston, 1960.

Schwartz, Eugene M. *Breakthrough Advertising: How to Write Ads That Shatter Traditions and Sales Records,* Prentice-Hall, 1966.

Seil, Manning D. and Senger, Frank B. *Advertising Copy & Layout,* Interstate, 1966.

Sheppard, Mona. *Plain Letters,* Simon & Schuster, 1960.

Shieele. *A Short History of the Mail Service,* Smithsonian Institution Press, 1970.

Shimek, John Lyle. *Billions of False Impressions,* Concepts of Postal Economics, 1970.

Shoaf, Dr. F. Robert. "Here's Proof—The Industrial Buyer is Human," *Industrial Marketing,* June 1959.

Shurter, Robert L. *Written Communication in Business,* McGraw-Hill, 3rd edition, 1965.

Simon, Julian L. *How to Start and Operate a Mail-Order Business,* McGraw-Hill, 2nd edition, 1976.

Simon, Morton J. *The Law for Advertising and Marketing,* Norton, 1956.

Skelly, Florence R. *Consumer Trends Affecting Your Business,* Direct Mail/ Marketing Assn., 1976.

Skillin, Marjorie and Gay, Robert M. *Words Into Type,* Prentice-Hall, Inc. 3rd edition, 1974.

Small Business Administration publications with applications to the direct mail and mail order field:

Starting and Managing a Small Duplicating and Mailing Service, The Starting and Managing Series, Vol. 8, 1963.

Selling By Mail Order, Small Business Bibliography, No. 3.

National Mailing List Houses, Small Business Bibliography, No. 29.

Direct Mail Advertising for the Small Manufacturer, Management Aids for the Small Manufacturer, No. 172.

Direct Mail Advertising for Small Retailers. Small Marketers Aids, No. 72.

Smart, Walter Kay; McKelvey, Louis William; and Garfen, Richard Conrad. *Business Letters,* Harper & Row, 4th edition, 1957.

Smith, Abbott P. *How to Sell Intangibles,* Prentice-Hall, 1958.

Smith, Roland B. *Advertising to Business,* Irwin, 1957.

Squire, Elizabeth. *Mail-Order Shopping Guide,* Barrows.

Stacey, N. A. and Wilson, A. *The Changing Pattern of Distribution,* Pergamon, 1965.

Stanley, Thomas Blaine. *The Technique of Advertising Production,* Prentice-Hall, 2nd edition, 1954.

Starch, Daniel. *Measuring Advertising Readership & Results,* McGraw-Hill, 1966.

Stebbins, Harry A. *Copy Capsules,* McGraw-Hill, 1957.

Steckel, Robert C. *Profitable Telephone Sales Operations,* Arco Publishing Co.

Steinhoff, Dan. *Small Business Management Fundamentals,* McGraw-Hill, 1978.

Steinkamp, Wilbert H. *How to Sell and Market Industrial Products,* Chilton, 1970.

Stephenson, William. *The Study of Behavior,* University of Chicago Press, 1953.

Stern, Alfred. *How Mail Order Fortunes Are Made,* Arco Publishing Co., 3rd edition, 1979.

Still, Richard R. and Cundiff, Edward W. *Essentials of Marketing,* Prentice-Hall, 2nd edition, 1972.

Stone, Bernard and Eckstein, Arthur. *Preparing Art for Printing.* Van Nostrand Reinhold, 1965.

Stone, Robert. *Successful Direct Mail Advertising and Selling,* Prentice-Hall, 1955.

Stone, Robert. *Successful Direct Marketing Methods,* Crain Books, 2nd edition, 1979.

Strauss, Victor. *The Printing Industry,* R. R. Bowker, 1967.

Strunk, William J. and White, E. B. *The Elements of Style,* Macmillan, 1979.

Stuart, Lyle. *Mailer's Guide to Postal Regulations,* revised regularly.

Swan, Carroll J. *Tested Advertising Copy,* Printers' Ink, 1955.

Taplan, Walter. *Advertising—A New Approach,* Little Brown, 1960.

Taylor, J. L. and Robb, J. F. *Fundamentals in Marketing,* McGraw-Hill, 1971.

Tillman, Rollie and Kirkpatrick, C. A. *Promotion,* Irwin, 1972.

Turner, Howard M. *Sales Promotions That Get Results,* McGraw-Hill, 1959.

Wales, Hugh G.; Gentry, Dwight; and Wales, Max. *Advertising Copy, Layout & Typography,* Ronald Press, 1958.

Wales, LaRae H. *A Practical Guide to Newsletter Editing & Design,* Iowa State University Press.

Watkins, Julian. *The 100 Greatest Advertisements,* Dover, 2nd edition, 1959.

Webster, Frederick E., Jr. *Marketing Communication:Modern Promotional Strategy,* Ronald, 1971.

Weiner, Richard. *Professional's Guide to Public Relations Services,* Prentice-Hall, 1971.

Weir, Walter. *Truth in Advertising and Other Heresies,* McGraw-Hill, 1963.

Weiss, E. B. and Weiss, Richard E. *1010 Tested Ideas That Move Merchandise.* McGraw-Hill, 1962.

Weiss, E. B. *Merchandising for Tomorrow,* McGraw-Hill, 1961.

West Virginia Pulp & Paper Company. *Production Notes.*

Wilkinson, C. W.; Menning, J H.; and Anderson, C. R. *Writing for Business,* Irwin, 3rd edition.

Wilson, John M. *Open the Mind and Close the Sale,* McGraw-Hill, 1953.

Wirsig, Woodrow, ed. *Principles of Advertising.* Pitman.

Wolfe, Harry D. and Twedt, Dik W. *Essentials of the Promotional Mix,* Appleton, 1970.

Wood, James Playsted. *The Story of Advertising,* Ronald Press, 1958.

Wyckham, Robert G. et al., eds. *Images & Marketing: A Selected & Annotated Bibliography,* American Marketing Association, 1971.

Yeck, John D. *How to Get Profitable Ideas for Creative Problem Solving,* McGraw-Hill, 1965.

Yeck and Maguire. *Planning and Creating Better Direct Mail,* McGraw-Hill, 1961.

Young, James Webb. *How to Become an Advertising Man,* Crain Communications, Inc., 1963.

Zacher, Robert V. *Advertising Techniques and Management,* Irwin, 1967.

Publishers Listed in Bibliography

ADVANCE BOOKS, Box 7584, San Francisco, California 94120.

AMACOM, Division of American Management Associations, 135 W. 50th St., New York, New York 10020.

APPLETON-CENTURY-CROFTS, 292 Madison Avenue, New York, New York 10017.

ARCO PUBLISHING COMPANY INC., 219 Park Ave. S., New York, New York 10003.

ART DIRECTION, 19 West 44th Street, New York, New York 10036.

ASSOCIATION OF NATIONAL ADVERTISERS, INC., 155 East 44th Street, New York, New York 10017.

R. R. BOWKER CO., 1180 Avenue of the Americas, New York, New York 10036.

BUSINESS/PROFESSIONAL ADVERTISING ASSN., 205 E. 52nd Street, New York, New York 10017.

BUSINESS STUDIES, INC., 104 Arlington Ave., St. James, New York 11780.

BUTTERFIELD, WILLIAM H., Box 4343, Tech Station, Lubbock, Texas 79400.

CHILTON BOOK COMPANY, Chilton Way, Radnor, Pennsylvania 19089.

CONSOLIDATED PAPERS, INC., 1 Pennsylvania Plaza, New York, New York 10001.

CRAIN COMMUNICATIONS, INC., 740 North Rush Street, Chicago, Illinois 60611.

DARTNELL CORPORATION, THE, 4660 Ravenswood Avenue, Chicago, Illinois 60640.

DIRECT MAIL/MARKETING ASSOCIATION, 6 East 43rd St., New York, New York 10017.

DOVER PUBLICATIONS, INC. 180 Varick Street, New York, New York 10014.

DOW JONES-IRWIN, 1818 Ridge Road, Homewood, Illinois 60430.

FREE PRESS, THE, 866 Third Avenue, New York, New York 10022.

GRAPHICS INSTITUTE, 42 West 39th Street, New York, New York 10018.

GREEN TREE PRESS, THE, 615 Carroll Street, Akron, Ohio 44304.

GROSSET & DUNLAP, INC., 51 Madison Avenue, New York, New York 10010. (Mail orders go to Kingsport, Tennessee 37662.)

GULF PUBLISHING COMPANY, Box 2608, Houston, Texas 77001.

HARCOURT, BRACE, JOVANOVICH, INC., 757 Third Avenue, New York, New York 10017.

HARPER & ROW, PUBLISHERS, INC., 10 East 53rd Street, New York, New York 10022.

HARVARD UNIVERSITY PRESS, 79 Garden Street, Cambridge, Massachusetts 02138.

HILARY HOUSE PUBLISHERS, INC., 1033 Channel Drive, Hewlett Harbor, New York 11557.

HOLT, RINEHART AND WINSTON, INC., 383 Madison Avenue, New York, New York 10017.

HOUGHTON MIFFLIN COMPANY, 1 Beacon Street, Boston, Massachusetts 02107.

CRAIG A. HUEY, 708 Silver Spur Road, Rolling Hills Estates, California 90274.

INDUSTRIAL ADVERTISING RESEARCH INSTITUTE (Marketing Communication Research Center), 15 Chambers Street, Princeton, New Jersey 08540.

INDUSTRIAL MARKETING, 740 North Rush Street, Chicago, Illinois 60611.

INTERNATIONAL PAPER COMPANY, 220 East 42nd Street, New York, New York 10017.

INTERSTATE PRINTERS AND PUBLISHERS INC., 19 North Jackson Street, Danville, Illinois 61832.

INTERTYPE COMPANY DIVISION OF HARRIS-INTERTYPE CORPORATION, 360 Furman Street, Brooklyn, New York 11201.

IOWA STATE UNIVERSITY PRESS, South State Ave., Ames, Iowa 50010.

RICHARD D. IRWIN, INC., 1818 Ridge Road, Homewood, Illinois 60430.

KIMBERLY-CLARK CORPORATION, North Lake Street, Neenah, Wisconsin 54956.

B. KLEIN PUBLICATIONS, P.O. Box 8503, Coral Springs, Florida 33065.

ALFRED A. KNOPF, INC., 201 East 50th Street, New York, New York 10022.

LITTLE BROWN AND COMPANY, 34 Beacon Street, Boston, Massachusetts 02106.

MACMILLAN, INC., 866 Third Avenue, New York, New York 10022.

McGRAW-HILL BOOK COMPANY, INC., 1221 Avenue of the Americas, New York, New York 10020.

DAVID McKAY COMPANY, INC., 750 Third Avenue, New York, New York 10017.

MEAD CORPORATION, 118 West First Street, Dayton, Ohio 45401.

WILLIAM MORROW & COMPANY, INC., 105 Madison Avenue, New York, New York 10016.

NATIONAL RETAIL MERCHANTS ASSN., 100 West 31st St., New York, New York 10001.

NATIONAL SAVINGS & LOAN ASSN., 3350 West Diversey Avenue, Chicago, Illinois 60618.

W. W. NORTON & COMPANY, INC., 500 Fifth Avenue, New York, New York 10036.

OCCUPANT MAILING LISTS OF AMERICA, INC., 239 North 4th Street, Columbus, Ohio 43215.

OCEANA PUBLICATIONS, INC., 75 Main Street, Dobbs Ferry, New York, New York 10522.

G. R. PARO, 750 N. Salina Street, Syracuse, New York 13208.

PARSONS PAPER DIVISION OF NATIONAL VULCANIZED FIBER COMPANY, 84 Sargeant Street, Holyoke, Massachusetts 01040.

PERGAMON PRESS, INC., Maxwell House, Fairview Park, Elmsford, New York, N.Y. 10523.

PLANNED CIRCULATION, 1300 Route 46, Parsippany, New Jersey 07454.

PRENTICE-HALL, INC., Englewood Cliffs, New Jersey 07632.

PRINTING INDUSTRIES OF AMERICA, INC., 1730 N. Lynn Street, Arlington, Virginia 22209.

PROMOTION MARKETING ASSOCIATION OF AMERICA, INC., 420 Lexington Avenue, New York, New York 10020.

G. P. PUTNAM'S SONS, 200 Madison Avenue, New York, New York 10016.

RANDOM HOUSE, INC., 201 East 50th Street, New York, New York 10022.

REALTORS NATIONAL MARKETING INSTITUTE, 430 N. Michigan Avenue, Chicago, Illinois 60611.

REPORTER OF DIRECT MAIL ADVERTISING (DIRECT MARKETING), 224 Seventh Street, Garden City, New York 11530.

SIMON & SCHUSTER, INC., 630 Fifth Avenue, New York, New York 10020.

SWEET'S DIVISION, McGRAW-HILL, 1221 Avenue of the Americas, New York, New York 10020.

TAB BOOKS, Blue Ridge Summit, Pennsylvania 17214.

TRAFFIC SERVICE CORPORATION, 815 Washington Building, 15th and New York Avenues, Washington, D.C. 20005.

TRIDENT PRESS, 1230 - 6th Avenue, New York, New York 10009.

UNITED STATES GOVERNMENT PRINTING OFFICE, Washington, D.C. 20402.

UNIVERSITY BOOKS, INC., 120 Enterprise Avenue, Secaucus, New Jersey 07094.

UNIVERSITY OF CHICAGO PRESS, 5801 Ellis Avenue, Chicago, Illinois 60637.

VAN NOSTRAND REINHOLD COMPANY, 135 West 50th Street, New York, New York 10001.

WADSWORTH PUBLISHING COMPANY, INC., 10 Davis Drive, Belmont, California 94002.

S. D. WARREN COMPANY, 225 Franklin Street, Boston, Massachusetts 02101.

WEHMAN BROS., 158 Main Street, Hackensack, New Jersey 07601.

WETZEL BROTHERS INC., 112 North Broadway, Milwaukee, Wisconsin 53202.

JOHN WILEY & SONS, INC., 605 Third Avenue, New York, New York 10016.

Appendix D

DIRECT MAIL GLOSSARY

A.A.: Printer's or proofreader's abbreviation for author's alteration/s.

A.A.A.A.: Abbreviation for the American Association of Advertising Agencies; also called "the 4 A's."

ABSORBTION: Process whereby ink is dried by soaking into paper fibers.

ACCENT FACE: Type used for contrast with basic typography of a printed piece.

ACCENTS: Marks in different positions on certain type characters to indicate pronunciations.

ACCESS TIME: (C) The time interval between the call for and the delivery of information from a storage unit or device.

ACCORDION FOLD: A series of folds in a printed piece with each being in opposite direction of previous fold.

ACCUMULATOR: (C) A register in which the result of an arithmetic or logic operation is stored.

ACCURACY: (C) The degree of freedom from error.

ACETATE: Transparent sheet placed over artwork to carry instructions and/or carry additional art detail.

ACHROMATIC: Black, white and gray "colors."

ACTIVES: Customers on a list who have made purchases within a prescribed time period, usually not more than one year; subscribers whose subscriptions have not expired.

ADDER: (C) A device that can supply the sum of two or more quantities placed into it.

ADDITIONS: New names, either of individuals or companies, added to a mailing list.

ADDRESS: Individual listing on a mailing list.

ADDRESS: (C) An identification for a register, location in storage, or other data source or destination; the identification may be a name, label or number.

ADDRESS CODE: (C) Instruction codes used to locate a specific item of data within the storage units of a computer.

ADDRESSING: The process of imprinting names and addresses on labels and/or mailing pieces.

ADDRESSOGRAPH: A method of addressing mailings through the use of metal plates with embossed letters.

ADP: (C) Automatic Data Processing. Data processing performed by a system of electronic or electrical machines so interconnected and interacting as to reduce to a minimum the need for human assistance or intervention.

ADVANCE RENEWAL: A subscription which has been renewed prior to the expiration of a previous subscription.

AFA: Advertising Federation of America.

(C) denotes a term used in data processing (computer terminology).

AIR: Artists' slang for the white space within a layout.

AGAINST THE GRAIN: Applied to paper folding when fold is made at right angles to the grain of the paper.

AGATE: An old name in the U.S. for a size of type measuring 14 lines to an inch and slightly smaller than 5½ points. An agate line is a standard used for measuring newspaper advertisements.

AIA: Acronym for Association of Industrial Advertisers.

AIDA: The most popular formula for the preparation of direct mail copy. The letters stand for Get Attention, Arouse Interest, Stimulate Desire, Ask for Action.

AIR BRUSH: An instrument operating by compressed air, for spraying ink or liquid colors onto photographs or other illustrations.

AIRMAIL ENVELOPES: While any envelope may be used for airmail if endorsed "Via Airmail," most regular users of this class of postal service adopt special envelopes for the purpose. Designs for printed airmail envelopes are of two types: "A," a border consisting of alternating red and blue oblique parallelograms which must be printed on white paper and thus produce a red, white, and blue design 5/32 of an inch wide around the edges of both the address side and the back of the envelope; and "B," two ¼-inch stripes, one of red and the other of blue, extending horizontally across the center of the envelope with a ¼-inch band of white between. Both envelopes should be imprinted "Via Airmail."

ALBUMEN PLATE: Printing plate commonly used for offset lithography.

ALGOL: (C) Algorithm Language. A programming system used for scientific applications which translates mathematical type terms into computer language.

ALGORITHM: (C) A prescribed set of well-defined rules or processes for the solution of a problem in a finite number of steps.

ALIGNMENT: Lines of type are in alignment when the top, bottom, right or left edges of the letters are in a straight line.

ALPHANUMERIC: (C) Pertaining to a character set that contains both letters and numerals, and usually other characters. Synonymous with Alphameric.

ALTERATIONS: Changes made on proofs by the customer or author, not due to printer's error. They are usually chargeable to the customer by the printer or typesetter.

ALUMINUM FOIL: A thin, lightweight metal stock which can be used as a printing surface.

ALUMINUM PLATES: Thin plates of aluminum used for lithographic printing.

AMPERSAND: The technical name of the symbol (&) used for "and" in company names, etc. Also called "short and."

ANALOG COMPUTER: (C) A scientific type computer which operates on measurable physical quantities such as the rotation of a shaft, the amount of voltage, the size of a displacement, etc.

ANALOGOUS: Color harmony involving two colors adjacent on color wheel.

ANALYST: (C) A person who defines problems and develops alogrithms and procedures for their solution.

ANIMAL SIZE: Gelatin employed for sizing surface of rag-content grades of paper.

ANNOUNCEMENT: A printed piece giving notice of special events, change of address, appointments of personnel, etc.

ANNOUNCEMENT PAPER: Papers intended for announcement (advertising or social). Usually supplied with matching envelopes.

ANNOUNCEMENTS: (1) Paper or cards, plain or paneled, which are cut to size or folded so as to fit envelopes made from the same stock and usually sold in sets. (2) A mailing piece, most commonly a self-mailer, which announces a specific event.

ANPA-AAAA: Abbreviation for American News Publishers' Association - American Association of Advertising Agencies; used to refer to standard colors of inks identified by a conventional code.

ANSA-LETTER: A patented mailing device used to facilitate replies to direct mail promotion letters.

ANTIQUE: A typeface similar to Roman faces, but heavier and without hair lines.

ANTIQUE FINISH: Paper with slightly rough finish. Similar to eggshell finish.

AQUATONE: Method of printing combining fine screen on gelatin plates with offset lithography.

ARITHMETIC UNIT: (C) The section of a data processing system which contains the circuits for performing arithmetic operations.

ARREARS: Subscribers whose names are retained on an active subscription list after the period for which they are paid has expired.

ART: (1) Illustrative material prepared by an artist. (2) Original copy for platemaking.

ART SERVICE: An organization which supplies artwork on a commercial basis.

ARTWORK: (Printer's copy) All drawings, paintings, photographs, special ruling, hand-lettering, etc.

ARTYPE: Preprinted letters on transparent, self-adhesive plastic.

ASCENDER: That part of the type which projects above the upper shoulder of the type.

ASCII: (C) American Standard Code for Information Interchange.

ASSEMBLE: (C) To prepare a machine-language program from a symbolic program by substituting machine codes for symbolic codes; to put together subroutines and routines into a main program.

ASSOCIATION SUBSCRIPTIONS: Publication subscriptions which are obtained as part of a membership service of an organized group. In some cases members of the group may have the option of deducting a portion of their dues and choosing not to receive the publication.

ASYNCHRONOUS COMPUTER: (C) A computer in which each event or the performance of each operation starts as a result of a signal generated by the completion of the previous event or operation, or by the availability of the parts of the computer required for the next event or operation.

ATCMU: Acronym for Associated Third-Class Mail Users.

AUDIENCE: The total number of individuals reached by a mailing.

AUDIENCE, PASSALONG: The additional individuals exposed to a mailing piece originally sent to others.

AUDIT: Examination of a publisher's records and corroborative data in order to check for correctness of the Publisher's Statements covering the period audited.

AUTHOR'S ALTERATIONS: Changes marked in a proof by the author (or editor), as contrasted with corrections made by a proofreader.

AUTHOR'S PROOF: The proofs which are to be or have been sent to the author or editor.

AUTO LIST: A mailing list compiled from automobile registration records.

AUTOMATIC CHECK: (C) A check performed by equipment built specifically for checking purposes.

AUTOMATIC CODING: (C) The machine-assisted preparation of machine language routines.

AUTOMATIC COMPUTER: (C) A computer that can perform a sequence of operations without intervention by a human operator.

AUTOMATIC GRAPHOTYPE: A machine used to emboss stencil plates from information previously punched on paper tape.

AUTOMATIC PROGRAMMING: (C) The process of using a computer to perform some stages of work involved in preparing a program.

AUTOMATIC TYPESETTING: Setting type by machine activated by a prepunched tape or other signal mechanism.

AUTOPEN: A device which individually signs letters or other documents with a pen activated by a master disc created for any individual signature.

AUTOTYPED LETTERS: Individually prepared letters produced on a typewriter activated by a pre-punched roll.

AUTO-TYPIST: Trade name of an electric typewriter used especially for facsimile letters.

AUXILIARY EQUIPMENT: (C) Equipment not actively involved during the processing of data, such as input/output equipment and auxiliary storage utilizing punched cards, magnetic tapes, discs or drums; data processing equipment which directly supports or services a computer.

AUXILIARY OPERATION: (C) An operation performed by equipment not under continuous control of the central processing unit.

AVAILABILITY BOOK: A mailing list count in report form for given geographic areas, specific markets, etc. Also called a Prospect Availability Book or a Count Book.

AVERAGE OUT: The process of using rented list and setting a quota for desired profit or acceptable loss and then continuing to mail to available lists until this quota is reached on a cumulative basis.

BACKBONE: The back edge of a bound book.

BACK COPY: Any issue of a magazine or book series prior to current issue.

BACKING UP: Printing one side of a sheet after the other side has been printed.

BACK LINING: A paper cemented to the backbone of sewed books to bind the signatures and to allow space between the backbone of the book and the backbone of the cover.

BACK MARGIN: The white space between the inside edge of the printing material of a page and the fold or bound edge.

BAD BREAK: A difficulty occurring in printing makeup, as when a break line falls at the bottom or top of a page or when an illustration falls above or below a break line or in a space too small for it, etc. Also refers to word incorrectly divided.

BAD COPY: Manuscript or illustration copy that is indistinct, illegible, weak (as with poor photographs), or otherwise difficult to read or to reproduce.

BAD LETTER: A letter that does not print clearly or fully.

BALLOON: A circular, oblong, or other space indicated as emerging from the mouth of a speaker and conventionally used in comic strips to show speech.

BANK ENVELOPE: An envelope style with a pointed flap, available in sizes from 3¾ by 5¾ to 5½ by 8¼ inches.

BANK PAPER: High-grade writing paper made of rag or chemical wood pulp with bond characteristics and durability.

BANKERS FLAP: An envelope style available in sizes from 3⅞ by 7½ to 6 by 12 inches.

BANKERS SAFETY: A style of envelope with an attached gummed tab, available in sizes from 3½ by 6 to 4⅛ by 9½ inches.

BANNER LINE: A large headline which extends across an entire page or spread.

BARONIAL ENVELOPES: An envelope for formal-appearing mailings; generally more nearly square than commercial types of covers.

BASE: Wood or metal upon which printing plates are mounted to hold securely at type height. Also called "block."

BASE COLOR: First color used in printing as a background over which other colors are printed.

BASIC PRICE: The price at which a product is regularly offered, as contrasted with a special or discount price.

BASIC SIZE: A specific size established by trade custom for each type of paper and upon which its basis weight is figured.

BASIC WEIGHT: (Paper) The weight of 500 sheets, or one ream, of standard size paper. Basic standard size of bond, ledger and writing papers is 17 by 22 inches; book and magazine papers; 25 by 38 inches; cover papers, 20 by 26 inches; foil laminates, 24 by 36 inches.

BASTARD: Referring to size or form, one which is not standard and must be specially prepared and handled. Referring to a book title, a short title appearing alone on a separate page preceding the title page.

BATCH PROCESSING: (C) A system approach to processing where similar input items are grouped for processing during the same machine run.

BATH NOTE: A folded writing paper, 8½ by 14 inches.

BATTERED: Type or printing plates which have been damaged in a way so that imperfections are visible in the printed image.

BAUD: (C) A unit of signaling speed in data transmission. The speed in bauds is equal to the number of bits per second.

BAUDOT CODE: (C) The standard five channel paper tape code used extensively in telegraphy and teletypewriter services.

BEARERS: Strips of metal or wood placed around a form, or the "dead metal" left on an engraving, type high, to protect the material during electrotyping.

BENCHMARK PROBLEM: (C) A problem used to evaluate the performance of computers relative to each other.

BEN DAY: (From the name of the inventor.) Sheets of transparent shadings, screens, dots, lines, and other designs which can be pasted on an illustration, either to fill in or to form a background. The use of Ben Day saves many hours of artists' time.

B.F.: Boldface type.

BIBLE PAPER: A strong, opaque, thin book paper, used to reduce the bulk of a book.

BILLHEAD: Printed form used for bills or statements.

BIMETAL PLATES: Press plates on which the printing image is on one metal with the nonprinting areas on a second metal, usually the printing image is on copper with the nonprinting area of chromium or stainless steel.

BINARY CODE: (C) A code that makes use of exactly two distinct characters, usually 0 and 1.

BINARY NUMBER SYSTEM: (C) An internal numbering system used by computers which uses the number two as a base (as opposed to the decimal system which uses the number ten); a characteristic or property involving a selection, choice or condition in which there are only two possibilities.

BINARY SEARCH: (C) A search in which a set of items is divided into two parts, one part is rejected, and the process is repeated on the accepted part until those items with the desired property are found.

BINDER: Craftsman who works in a bindery.

BINDER BOARD: A paper board usually covered with cloth and used for the cover of books. Thickness generally ranges from 3/10 to 3/1,000 of an inch.

BINDERY: A place where books, magazines or pamphlets are bound; an edition bindery devotes itself to publishers' work in quantities; a job bindery to miscellaneous work; a pamphlet bindery to paper-covered publications, magazines and self-covered catalogs. A trade bindery generally serves printers.

BINDERY REEL: The dick strip when it is a finished product ready to be cut apart into individual labels and affixed or heat-transferred to individual envelopes, cards of packages for mailing.

BINDING: The method in which a booklet, book, catalog, or brochure is fastened together. The method varies with the job and may consist of simple wire staples, a patented wire or plastic binding in more elaborate jobs, or a sewed binding in the base of permanent books.

BINDING EDGE: The edge of a printed signature where the piece will be bound.

BINGO CARD: A reply card inserted in a publication and used by readers to request literature and samples from companies whose products and services are either advertised or mentioned in the editorial columns.

BIT: (C) A contraction meaning a binary digit; a single pulse in a group of pulses; a single hole in a punched tape or punched card. Bits comprise a character; characters comprise a word.

BITE: The attribute of printing paper which causes it to accept ink.

BLACK AND WHITE: One color printing.

BLACK-AND-WHITE LINE EDGE: An illustration framed with an outer black line inside of which is a white line of the same thickness.

BLACK FACE: A heavy typeface; also called boldface.

BLACK LETTER: A term originally used for Old English and similar text letters which followed the lettering of the old manuscripts. Now commonly used to describe any heavy typeface.

BLANK: A pre-printed format to which custom copy is to be added.

BLANKET: A sheet of rubber or composition material which covers the printing cylinder of an offset press, receiving the impression from the plate and transferring it to paper.

BLEED: When the margins of any printed piece have been trimmed so as to cut into the printed area, the piece is said to bleed; if a page is printed to the fold, it is said to bleed to the fold.

BLIND: A light spot on a proof, wherein the dots were not completely opaque.

BLIND EMBOSSING: Impressing a design into the back of a sheet of paper so it appears in bas-relief on the front side. No ink is used.

BLIND PERFORATING: Adding perforations to paper without any printed perforation marks.

BLIND PLATE: A lithographic plate containing an image which will not accept ink, and, therefore, will not print.

BLOCK: The wood or metal base on which is mounted a printing plate. Also called "base."

BLOCK: (C) A set of things, such as words, characters, or digits, handled as a unit.

BLOCK DIAGRAM: (C) A graphic representation showing the logical sequence by which data is processed.

BLOCK LETTERS: A designation for sans-serif type characters.

BLOCKING OUT: Obscuring part of an illustration.

BLOCK INPUT/OUTPUT: (C) A section of internal storage of a computer reserved for the storing and processing of input and/or output information.

BLOCK PRINTING: Printing from engraved or carved wooden blocks.

BLOTTING PAPER: Absorbent, unsized stock used for blotters. One side may be coated for printing.

BLOWUP: Any type matter or illustration which has been enlarged, usually several sizes, from the original. Also the process of enlarging.

BLURB: A short, concise summary used to introduce an article or story in the issue in which it appears or in a forthcoming issue. Also the type matter describing book and/or author on the dust jacket.

BMF: Business Mail Foundation.

BODY SIZE: The size of type in points, measured from the "nick side" to the opposite side.

BODY STOCK: Foundation stock for any coated board or paper.

BODY TYPE: The kinds of type used for ordinary composition in paragraphs or pages of one face, as distinguished from display type or headings.

BOGUS: (1) Papers and boards manufactured principally from old papers or low-grade stock in imitation of grades using higher quality raw material. (2) Copy set by newspaper typographers and not intended for use, usually due to union contract conditions.

BOILER PLATE: Features and illustrations made up in advance of other material to be used as filler in newspapers, magazines, and similar publications.

BOLDFACE: Heavy-faced type, in contradistinction to light-faced type.

BOLT: The uncut edge of a folded signature of printed material.

BOND PAPER: Originally, paper made entirely from rags and coated, for use in printing bonds and stock certificates. Now generally refers to any hard-surfaced paper.

BONDING STRENGTH: The property of a sheet of paper which resists the removal of coating, fibers or plies.

BOOKBINDER'S CLOTH: A fabric used in making the case or cover of a book. This material varies in quality and finish.

BOOK JACKET: A paper cover placed over the board covers of a book, usually printed in a fashion to attract readers. Also called "Dust Jacket."

BOOKLET: Any small book, but especially one with a self-cover.

BOOKLET ENVELOPES: Special envelopes to fit any size of booklet; available in either regular or postage-saver style, usually with open sides or diagonal seams. In selection of envelopes for booklets it is wise to consider durability and folding qualities of booklet stock before ordering envelopes to match. Frequently paper used for booklet is not suitable for envelopes. In many cases contrasting or harmonizing color is preferable to matching color, particularly when matching color would involve unsuitable paper stock.

BOOK PAPERS: A class of paper used for books, catalogs, periodicals, booklets, etc.; includes various finishes such as antique, EF, supered or coated stocks.

BOOK SIZES: The designation of book sizes originally based on their relation to a sheet of paper measuring 19 by 25 inches.

BOOK SYSTEM: Method of proofreading which requires two marks for every correction—one to denote place of error; the other to indicate correction to be made.

BOOK WORK: Printing work involved in the production of books.

BOOTSTRAP: (C) A technique or device designated to bring itself into a desired state by means of its own action.

BORDER: Ornamental types of connecting designs which can be made to surround or enclose type matter; also includes straight line rules.

BOTTOM: Lower edge of a page.

BOTTOM LINE: The last line of type on a page.

BOUNCE BACK: An offer enclosed with fulfillment of an offer.

BOUND-IN: A signature, page or enclosure securely attached at the binding edge of a printed piece.

BOURGES GRAYS: Halftones of black printed on film; broken down into certain percentages.

BOURGES SHEETS: Transparent sheets of various colors with a self-adhesive backing used for preparing artwork.

BOX: Unit of type copy enclosed by a border.

BRACKETS: Typographic devices used to set off matter grammatically in apposition.

BRANCH: (C) A sequence of instructions executed as a result of a decision instruction; to depart from the usual sequence of executing instructions in a computer; synonymous with jump or transfer.

BRANCHING: (C) A method of selecting the next operation for the computer to execute while the program is in progress, based on the computer results.

BREAK LINE: A line of type which is shorter than the full measure.

BRE: Business Reply Envelope.

BREAK: The place for ending or dividing a line of type.

BREAKDOWN: The division of categories within a mailing list.

BREAK-UP: The operation of distributing the components of type forms for jobs which have already been printed; to separate the parts of a form which will print in different colors; to divide into two or more printings; to identify the different signatures and inserts for correct binding pagination.

BREVIER: A name for 8-point type.

BRIDGE: A proofreader's mark indicating that two letters or words should be connected.

BRIGHTNESS: Term designating the amount of light reflection from the surface of a paper.

BRILLIANCE: Color property which makes an ink stand out or appear strong.

BRILLIANT: A name for 4-point type.

BRISTOL BOARD: Heavy or extra-heavy index or announcement paper.

BROAD: A name for 48-point measure.

BROADBAND: (C) As applied to data transmission, to denote transmission facilities capable of handling frequencies greater than those required for voice communications.

BROAD FOLD: A printed sheet folded so as to make pages wider than the usual shape or of greater width than depth.

BROADSIDE: A single full sheet or half sheet of paper, printed on one side or two, folded for mailing or direct distribution, and opening into a single, large advertisement. Especially used for door-to-door distribution.

BROCHURE: Strictly a high-quality pamphlet, with especially planned layout, typography, and illustrations. The term is also used loosely for any promotional pamphlet or booklet.

BROKEN BASTARD: A name for 32-point type.

BROKEN MATTER: Type composition with a mixture of short paragraphs, headings, etc.

BROKEN PACKAGE: Quantity of paper less than normally packaged amounts.

BRONZING: Printing with a sizing ink and applying bronze powder while still wet to secure the effect of metallic inks.

BROWN PRINT: See Red Print.

BRUNING: Photocopying process used to prepare proofs.

BUCKET: (C) A slang expression used to indicate some portion of storage reserved for accumulating data, or totals.

BUFFER: (C) A device usually located between the main memory and an input/output source to provide temporary storage of data until called for by the central processor or the output device.

BULK: A term which may refer either to sheet thickness or to the relation of a thickness of a sheet to its substance weight.

BULLET: Large, bold dot used for decoration.

BULK MAIL: A category of Third Class Mail involving a quantity of identical pieces which are specially processed for mailing by the mailer before delivery to the post office.

BULLETIN: (1) News or announcements published periodically. (2) A statement of policy, an instruction, or a news item for posting on a bulletin board and/or for distribution.

BUNDLING: The tying up of signatures of a book.

BURN IN: The process of baking photo-sensitive resist to produce a hard acid-resistant coating in making printing plates.

BURNISHED: A plate on which some area has been rubbed with a burnishing tool to make it darker when printed.

BURN OUT: A photographic method of removing one color in a set of color printing plates so it will not affect a second color to be printed on the same area.

BURSTING: (C) Separation of continuous forms on which computer letters are printed. The process also strips off the pin-feed margin which contains the sprocket holes used to feed forms through the computer printer.

BURSTING STRENGTH: A characteristic of paper involving its strength, measured in pounds per square inch.

BUSINESS FORMS: Special printed forms such as billheads, interoffice message forms, and other more or less standardized forms.

BUSINESS PAPER: A periodical published for business audiences.

BUSINESS REPLY MAIL: Concerns which have obtained permits from their postmasters are privileged to use business reply cards and business reply envelopes. The address side of such envelopes bears the following information: permit number; name of post office issuing the permit; the words,

"Business Reply Mail"; the inscription, "No postage stamp necessary if mailed in the United States"; the word, "Postage will be paid by addressee" (whose name may be inserted if desired) over the name and complete address of the person or concern to whom the envelopes are to be returned. A space of at least 1⅛ inches shall be left for postmarking at the top of the envelope on the left of the indicia in the upper right corner. Such indicia shall be prominently printed and not obstructed or surrounded by any other matter. All the foregoing shall be arranged in one of the standard forms provided by the post office. No extraneous matter may appear on the address side. Applications for permits should be addressed to the postmaster on Form No. 3614. No deposit is necessary.

BUTTED LINES: Two or more lines of type placed side by side to create a single line of type.

BUTTERFLY FOLDER: A mailing piece from which a portion "jumps up" when the piece is opened or unfolded.

BY-LINE: A line giving the name of the author of an article, book, etc.

BUYER: A name on a mailing list representing a customer.

BYTE: (C) A sequence of adjacent binary digits operated upon as a unit and usually shorter than a word.

C. & L.C.: Capital and lower case letters.

C. & S.C.: Abbreviation for capital letters and small capital letters.

C.O.D.: Collect on delivery or cash on delivery.

C.Q.: An instruction that a word as spelled in copy is correct—even though incorrectly spelled—and should not be changed in typesetting.

CABOT LETTER: A patented type of reply letter used in direct mail advertising and promotion.

CALENDARS: Printed cardboard backs to which calendar pads are to be attached; also the calendars themselves. (Note difference in spelling between "calendar" and "calender.")

CALENDER: (Verb) To press between rollers for the purpose of obtaining a smooth, glossy surface. (Noun) The machine used for calendering.

CALENDERED PAPER: Any paper which has been smoothed in manufacture; there are various degrees of calendering.

CALIFORNIA JOB CASE: Receptacle in which foundry type is stored and from which type is set.

CALIPER: Thickness of paper.

CALLIGRAPHIC TYPE: Typefaces based on styles of handwriting.

CALLIGRAPHY: The art of beautiful handwriting usually involving unconnected characters.

CALLITYPE: A method of producing printing plates by photoengraving from typewritten copy.

CAMEO PAPER: A dull smooth-finished coated paper.

CAMERA LUCIDA: A device used by artists with which an opaque image can be projected onto a drawing surface, permitting enlargement, reduction and/or reproportioning for tracing. Frequently called a Lucie.

CAPS: Abbreviation for "capitals." The large letters of an alphabet (upper case) as opposed to the small letters (lower case).

CAPTION: The title or description at top of an article or illustration. Ordinarily a caption does not take a period; other punctuation is usually as elsewhere. Improperly but often misused to mean "legend."

CAPTIVE PLANT: A printing and/or duplicating facility operated by a company whose major business is in an unrelated field.

CARBON TISSUE: Paper coated with gelatin which contains an inert colored pigment used as a resist material to transfer the image from a printing positive to a gravure cylinder. Originally this pigment was carbon and the name is still used.

CARBRO: A lamination of thin color separation positives mounted on a reflective white surface.

CAR CARDS: Sheets of cardboard intended for advertising in buses, subway cars, etc.

CARDBOARD: Stiff, sturdy sheet containing several layers of low-quality paper pasted together.

CARD CODE: (C) A combination of punches used to represent alphabetic and numeric information on a punched card. The most-used is called the Hollerith code, after IBM founder Dr. Herman Hollerith.

CARLOAD LOT: The minimum amount of paper required for individual freightcar shipment at the carload rate; generally 36,000 or 40,000 pounds.

CARRIER, COMMUNICATIONS COMMAND: (C) A company furnishing communications services.

CARRIER SYSTEM: (C) A means of obtaining a number of channels over a single path by modulating each channel upon a different carrier frequency and demodulating at the receiving point to restore the signals to their original form.

CARRY FORWARD: An instruction to transfer type matter to the next column or page.

CARTOGRAPHY: Drawing or compiling maps.

CARTON: A shipping unit of paper equivalent to one-fourth of a case, or about 125 pounds.

CASE: A wooden tray with a number of small compartments wherein type is laid.

CASE BOUND: A book with a stiff cover which is made separately, the sewed book being inserted.

CASE LOT: A quantity of flat paper, usually from 500 to 600 pounds, packaged in a fiberboard or wooden box.

CASH RIDER: Also called "a cash up" or "cash option" wherein an order form offers installment terms, but a P.S. offers the option of sending full cash payment with order, usually at some saving over the credit price as an incentive.

CASH WITH ORDER: A requirement for full payment at the time order is placed.

CAST OFF: A typographer's term for estimating the amount of space required for a given amount of text or copy. (Also CASTING UP.)

CATALOG: A book or booklet showing merchandise, with descriptive details.

CATALOG ENVELOPES: The same considerations which govern the selection of booklet envelopes also apply to those for catalogs except that catalogs, being usually larger and heavier, generally call for a stronger and heavier paper stock. Most catalog envelopes are made in the open-end style with a center seam, giving strength and durability. They are available in all sizes, with gummed or ungummed flaps.

CATALOG PAPER: Lightweight paper with a machine or English finish, usually manufactured with substantial proportions of mechanical pulp, which is suitable for good fidelity reproduction of illustrations.

CATTIE: Printer's slang for an ink smudge on a printed page.

CELL: (C) Storage of one unit of information, usually one character or one word.

CENTER SPREAD: A double spread appearing in the exact center of a bound or stapled book or booklet.

CENTERED HEADING: A line of display type centered on a block of body type or on a page.

CENTRAL PROCESSING UNIT (CPU): (C) The group of components of a data processing system which contains the logical, arithmetic, and control units for the basic system.

CERTIFIED MAIL: First Class Mail of no intrinsic value sent with a receipt which the recipient must sign.

CHAD: (C) The piece of material removed when forming a hole or notch in a storage medium such as punched tape or punched cards.

CHADLESS: (C) Pertaining to the punching of tape in which chad does not result.

CHANGEOVER: The act of revising a catalog page used for one edition to prepare it for use for another edition.

CHARACTER: (C) One of a set of elementary symbols such as those corresponding to the keys on a typewriter.

CHARACTER: (Printing) The term applied to a single printed or typewritten letter.

CHARACTER COUNT: A method of estimating type sizes and space by counting the number of characters in the text or copy.

CHARACTERS-PER-PICA (CPP): System of copyfitting.

CHARACTER RECOGNITION: (C) The technique of reading, identifying and encoding a printed character by optical means.

CHARGEABLE TIME: Number of hours or hour units (six minutes) required to complete a typesetting or printing job.

CHASE: The metal frame in which type is locked for printing.

CHECK: (C) A means of verification of information during or after an operation.

CHECK BINDING: A book side stitched with board sides, covered with marble paper, cloth back, cut flush.

CHECK FOLIO: Size of paper, 17½ by 24 inches.

CHECK PAPER: A bond or ledger paper made of rag or chemical wood pulps and used for checks.

CHECKPOINT: (C) A place in a routine where a check, or a recording of data for restart purposes, is performed.

CHECK ROYAL: Size of paper, 19 by 26 inches.

CHEMITYPE: A process for producing maps, charts, etc. by etching lines in a zinc plate covered with wax, filling them with fusible metal, and then eating away the zinc with an acid and leaving the lines in relief.

CHROMA: Quality of intensity of a color.

CHROMA: The purity of a color determined by its degree of freedom from white or grey—color intensity.

CHINESE PAPER: Very thin, soft paper prepared from bamboo bark.

CHIP BOARD: Single ply board of low density made from a mixture of papers to a maximum thickness of 72 points.

CHIROGRAPH: Handwritten document.

CHROMATIC: True colors.

CHROMART PRINTS: High-quality custom color print on paper made especially to serve as art copy in the production of printing plates.

CHROMATIC PRESS: Printing press especially designed for color printing.

CHROMED PLATE: (1) For letterpress printing, an electrotype, either copper or nickel faced, that has been plated with chromium to a thickness usually not over .0001″ to give longer press life; (2) For gravure printing, a rotogravure cylinder similarily coated.

CHROMO: A color photographic print.

CHROMO PAPER: Any paper especially suited to color printing.

CHROMOTYPE: A picture reproduced by any kind of chromatic process.

CIRCUIT: (C) A physical, metallic connection between two points, also called a channel.

CHUNKS: Various elements—illustrations, borders, initials, etc.—proofed up together without being organized into proper order.

CIRCLED CORRECTIONS: Corrections in a printer's proof that are to be charged to the author, publisher or advertiser.

CIRCLES OF CONVENIENCE: A method of charting areas from which the bulk of customers is drawn for a store or institution.

CIRCULARS: General term for printed advertising in any form, including printed matter sent out by direct mail.

CLAMBSHELL: Colloquialism for platten press.

CLAPPER: Colloquialism for platten press.

CLASP ENVELOPES: An envelope with a metal fastener.

CLASS MAGAZINES: Magazines which through their editorial appeal are designed to reach distinct classes of people. In the case of some magazines the class is very comprehensive, such as women's magazines or farm papers. In the case of others, such as trade papers, sporting publications, etc., the group is more limited.

CLEAN PROOFS: Printer's proofs containing few or no typographical errors.

CLEAR: (C) To put a storage or memory device into a state denoting zero or blank.

CLIP ART: Syndicated art intended for reproduction.

CLIP SHEET: Syndicated collection of printable copy.

CLOSE MATTER: Type set without line spacing.

CLOSE PUNCTUATION: Type matter containing an excessive amount of punctuation.

CLOSE TO THE PAPER: Lithographic terms referring to the amount of ink being run; relatively small amount of ink being used in printing.

CLOSE UP: Instruction to printer to bring type matter or illustrations closer together.

CLUBS: Two or more subscriptions to the same publication obtained by solicitors, not part of a publisher's organization.

COATED BLANK: A blank card coated on one or both sides; made of low-grade pulp.

COATED LITHO: Hard-coated book paper usually used for label work.

COATED ONE SIDE: Printing paper with only one side coated.

COATED PAPERS: Any paper to which a surface coating has been applied by the manufacturer or converter.

COATING: Mineral substances used to cover the surface of paper or board.

COBOL: (C) Common Business Oriented Language. A programming system which uses basic English language and then translates the English phrases into computer code programs which can be understood and executed by the computer.

COCKLE: Paper finish with surface ripples.

COCKUP: Larger than text initial letter which aligns with the bottom of other type but extends above the normal type line.

CODE: (C) A set of characters or symbols used in the alphabet or decimal numbering system or for special purposes.

CODER: (C) A person who prepares computer instruction sequences from detailed flow charts, as contrasted with a programmer who prepares the procedures and flow charts.

CODING: (C) A list, in computer code, of the successive computer operations required to solve a given problem.

CODING: (1) Identifying reply devices to identify list on which name originally appeared. (2) A logical structure of letters and numbers used to classify characteristics of a name on a list.

COILS: Paper slit to a desired width from a roll of paper and rewound on cores for web printing.

COIN ENVELOPE: Style of small envelope with a side gummed flap, available in sizes from 1 11/16 by 2¾ to 3½ by 6½ inches.

COLD CANVASS: To solicit business from a general group of suspects without qualifying them as prospects, as in house-to-house canvassing.

COLD EMBOSSING: Embossing without use of heat.

COLD TYPE: Type set photographically or by a means which does not utilize metal (hot type).

COLLATE: (C) To take two or more sets of related information already in the same sequence and merge them in sequence into a single group.

COLLATE: (Printing) To examine the gathered sheets, or signatures, to see that the order or sequence is correct.

COLLATE: (Mailing) To assemble individual elements of a mailing in sequence for inserting into a mailing envelope.

COLLATE: (Binding) To assemble sheets or signatures in sequence for binding together as a book or booklet.

COLLATING MARK: An identifying mark printed on the backbone of a signature to show by inspection if it is in the correct volume and in proper sequence.

COLLATING SEQUENCE: (C) An ordering assigned to a set of items, such that any two sets in that assigned order can be collated.

COLLATOR: (C) A device to collate or merge sets of cards into a new sequence.

COLLOTYPE: Continuous tone printing through use of plates with a gelatin coating. Sometimes called Photogelatin Printing.

COLOPHON: A trademark, usually placed on the title page or at the back of the book with inscription of author, publisher and printer.

COLOR: Typographic term to identify overall tone of massed of type.

COLOR BARS: A conventional method of showing color rotation on four-color process proofs.

COLOR BUILDUP: When more than one color of a similar nature is printed one on top of another—for example, two different reds and a pink in one area.

COLOR CHART: A paper, booklet, or book showing various colors of ink for selection in color printing. Also called "tint chart."

COLOR CORRECTION: Any of various methods such as masking, dot-etching, re-etching intended to promote improved color renditions. Can be done on screened or continuous tone separation negatives, or by corrective work on the halftone printing plate.

COLOR FLAP: A transparent or translucent sheet placed over illustration copy to show color separation or other layout details.

COLOR KEY PROOF: A set of proofs made chemically, usually on acetate, to show the approximate final result of four color printing. Also used to provide quick color proofs for jobs with uess than four colors.

COLOR SEPARATION: The division of the many colors of original color copy into the required number of separate plates, usually four or fewer. Different color separation filters are used to make each of the plates.

COLOR PROOFS: Proofs showing the finished reproduction of a color illustration.

COLOR SEQUENCE: The order in which colors are printed.

COLOR SWATCH: (1) An air brushed sample, or preferably, printed example of a special color, not available from standard color selections, prepared by the artist to specify that color to the printer. (2) The color bar which appears along one edge of a proof sheet, showing the color inks used in printing the sheet.

COLOR TRANSPARENCY: A full color photographic positive on a transparent support.

COLOR WHEEL: Diagrammatic arrangement of primary and secondary colors as a visual aid in determining relationship and harmony among colors.

COLUMN: One, two or more vertical series of lines of type printed side by side.

COLUMN INCH: Advertising unit one column wide by one inch deep.

COLUMN RULE: A vertical rule used to separate columns of type or other matter, as in bill forms and tabular work.

COLUMN WIDTH: Width of a printed column, usually expressed in picas.

COMBINATION PLATE: A printing plate which includes both halftone and line illustrations.

COMBINATION SALE: Subscriptions to two or more different publications or products sold at a special combination price.

COMBINED AUTO POSITIVE: Where two or more auto positives are sandwiched together and one positive is reproduced with the combined elements on it.

COMMERCIAL A: The symbol (@) used to designate the word *at* or *to* in price quotations.

COMMERCIAL ABBREVIATIONS: Printing abbreviations used to represent business phrases, words, etc.

COMMERCIAL ENVELOPES: Oblong envelopes available in sizes from 3 1/6 by 5½ to 3⅝ by 6½ inches.

COMMERCIAL LETTER: Size of paper, 11 by 17 inches.

COMMERCIAL NOTE: Size of paper, 5½ by 8½ inches.

COMMERCIAL POST: Size of paper, 11 by 17 inches.

COMPARE: (C) To check information against related information, to determine whether it's identical, larger or smaller.

COMPILE: (C) To prepare a machine language program from a computer program written in another programming language.

COMPILED LIST: A mailing list prepared to include all names meeting certain specifications but not composed exclusively of those who have responded to previous mailings and/or a specific activity of a business firm or other single organization.

COMPLEMENTARY HARMONY: Color combinations using two colors directly opposite each other on a color wheel.

COMPOSE: To set type by hand or machine.

COMPOSING MACHINE: A mechanical device for typesetting.

COMPOSING ROOM: The department in which all activities from the first setting of type to the final preparation of forms for the press are carried on.

COMPOSING RULE: A piece of metal against which type is set and which can readily be removed from behind the type after justification is completed.

COMPOSING STICK: Metal receptacle into which type is placed when set by hand.

COMPOSITION: Material set in type, or the art of setting type.

COMPREHENSIVE: Complete and detailed dummy. Also: Comp, Compre.

COMPUTER: (C) A device capable of solving problems by accepting data, performing prescribed operations on the data, and supplying the results of these operations.

COMPUTER CODE: (C) A machine code for a specific computer.

COMPUTER INSTRUCTION: (C) A machine instruction for a specific computer.

COMPUTER LETTER: (C) A letter "written" by a computer.

COMPUTER NETWORK: (C) A complex consisting of two or more interconnected computing units.

COMPUTER PROGRAM: (C) A plan or routine for solving a problem on a computer.

CONCURRENT PROCESSING: (C) The ability to work on more than one program at the same time.

CONDENSED TYPE: Typefaces that are narrow or slender.

CONSOLE: (C) That part of or unit in a data processing system which provides facilities for manual control and observation of the system.

CONTACT PRINT: A photographic print exactly the same size as the negative. Made with the firm negative and sensitized paper in contact.

CONTACT SCREEN: A halftone screen made on a film base and used in contact with the film to be exposed in making printing plates.

CONTINUOUS FORMS: (C) Forms which are connected using a fanfold method and are fed into a computer printer.

CONTINUOUS TONE COPY: Illustrative or decorative copy with gradually increasing or diminishing tones resulting from varied pigment thicknesses. To print by relief or offset tone copy must be made into halftones which simulate the copy.

CONTRAST: Accentuated detail in both dark and light areas of art.

CONTROLLED CIRCULATION: Publications of any kind which are sent regularly to a list of persons who do not pay any direct subscription price. The term applies especially to association magazines, to which the subscription price is included in the membership fee.

CONVERSION: The method of manufacture by which a printed job can be changed from one printing process to another. For example, making offset positives from letterpress engravings or rotogravure positives.

CONVERT: (C) To change the representation of data from one form to another such as from cards to tape.

COOL COLORS: Colors which tend to recede from the viewer, usually greens and blues.

COPPERPLATE PAPER: Good quality unsized paper, calendered on one side only.

COPY: (C) To reproduce information in a new location replacing whatever was previously stored there, leaving the source of information unchanged.

COPY: Matter (manuscript, typewritten, artwork, or photography) to be reproduced in printed form.

COPY BOARD: Frame in which art is placed to be photographed in camera.

COPY CHIEF: Person in charge of a group of copywriters.

COPPERPLATE GOTHIC: A family of sans-serif type.

COPY COUNT: Any one of several methods for estimating the space needed for a given amount of text in a given type size.

COPYHOLDER: One who reads manuscript, reprint or typewritten copy to the proofreader.

COPYRIGHT: An exclusive right secured by law to authors and artists. A copyright is effective for 28 years and may be renewed one time only.

COPYWRITER: Person who creates advertising copy.

CORE STORAGE: (C) A form of magnetic storage that permits high-speed access to information within the computer.

CORNER CARDS: Originally conceived to meet postal requirements of a return address, the term "corner card" has come to embrace all the various types of design employed by advertisers and others to register an advertising impression on the recipient before he even opens the envelope. Good typography, artistic designs, the use of color all contribute to effectiveness. Care should be taken to observe postal regulations concerning the amount of space which should be left for addressing and stamping, and to include all pertinent information.

CORRECT: To mark errors on a proof.

CORRESPONDENCE: Size of card, 4½ by 3½ inches.

COST PER INQUIRY: A simple arithmetical formula—total cost of mailing or advertisement divided by number of inquiries received; of limited usefulness, since it excludes overhead and other cost factors and cannot anticipate delayed or indirect effects.

COST PER ORDER: Similar to COST PER INQUIRY.

COUCHE PAPER: Coated one-side enameled book paper.

COUNT: Total of pieces printed and/or mailed.

COUNT BOOK: See Availability Book.

COUNTER CARD: Advertising cards intended for display on the counters of stores.

COUNTER-ETCH: The preliminary treatment of a grained offset plate with an acid to sensitize the metal grain so that the plate will be cleaned to accept ink or grease.

COUNTER AND PACKAGE ENVELOPES: These come in a wide variety of special sizes and styles, depending upon the nature of the product to be packaged. Some are designed for their display value in retail stores; some for customers' convenience in carrying merchandise away. In either case, such envelopes are styled for packaging rather than for mailing purposes.

COUPON: A portion of a promotion piece or advertisement intended to be filled out by inquirer and returned to advertiser.

COUPON ENVELOPE: Style of envelope with an attached coupon in sizes from 3½ by 6 to 3⅝ by 6½ inches.

COUPON PREMIUM: Item of merchandise sent in response to mailing of a coupon, usually at no or little cost to the recipient.

COURT: Size of cut card. Standard size is 4½ by 3½ inches. Large Court is 4⅞ by 4 inches.

COVERAGE: The extent to which a mailing is made to the individuals or companies constituting the total universe available for mailing.

COVER: Synonym for envelope; also refers to any type of outside wrapping for mailing.

COVER STOCK: Heavy paper used for single fold cards or cover pages.

CRAFTINT: Patterns similar to those of Ben Day which are pre-printed on transparent self-adhesive sheets and applied to artwork for line engraving.

CRAFTYPE: Trade name for letters pre-printed on a transparent self-adhesive sheet.

CRASH FINISH: A finish which gives paper the appearance of linen.

CREASABILITY: Property of a sheet of paper to resist cracking when sharply bent.

CREATIVE DIRECTOR: Person responsible for supervising idea development, copywriting, design and layout of advertising material.

CREDIT LINE: A line accompanying an article or illustration giving credit to the originator or copyright holder.

CRIMPING: Creasing the binding edge of ledger sheets so that book will open freely.

CRISSCROSS DIRECTORIES: Special publications issued by telephone companies in which names are listed by street address rather than alphabetically.

CROP: To cut off or trim the parts of an illustration which are not to be included in the finished printing. Cropping of photographs is usually done by lines made with a grease pencil or with a cut-out paper mask overlay.

CROP MARKS: Indications which inform the engraver as to where artwork is to be cut or as to where a bleed page will be cut.

CROSSLINE: A single line of type, usually boldface, which serves as a sub-heading within a column of text matter.

CROWN: Size of paper, 15 by 19 inches.

CURL: Tendency of a sheet of paper to curve upward, usually as a result of excessive moisture.

CURRENCY PAPER: Paper used for printing paper currency, bonds and other securities.

CURSIVE: Type which resembles handwriting but with unconnected letters.

CURVED PLATE: A printing plate which is curved to fit the cylinder of a press.

CUSTOMER: An established buyer on a mailing list.

CUSTOMER LIST: A list of people or businesses who have purchased a particular product or service.

CUT: Photoengraving plate.

CUT-IN: An illustration, note, or heading printed within the text matter of a page or form, as when small type or a small cut is placed in a space between words of a regular text.

CUT CARDS: Small sizes of cards cut in standard sizes.

CUT FORM: A printing form consisting entirely or primarily of illustrations.

CUT LINES: Identifying lines for illustrations.

CUTOFF RULE: Hairline that marks the point where continuous copy moves from one column to another.

CUTOUTS: Printed pieces cut into irregular shapes by steel dies.

CUTTING: Trimming stock or printed materials along one, two or three edges.

CUTTING RULE: Steel rule more than type high, locked into a printing form. Used for cutting envelopes, cards, guide edges, etc. on press.

CYAN: The color sensation produced by the simultaneous reception of blue and green light. Often called "process blue."

CYBERNETICS: (C) The theory of control and communication in the machine and the animal.

CYCLE: (C) (1) An interval of space or time in which one set of events or phenomena is completed. (2) Any set of operations that is repeated regularly in the same sequence.

CYLINDER: That part of a cylinder press on which the sheet is carried over the form. On rotary presses the plates are curved and are carried on the plate cylinder. The cylinder carrying the paper is called the impression cylinder.

CYLINDER MACHINE: A principal type of papermaking machine.

CYLINDER PRESS: A press in which the type form is flat but the printing is done against a revolving cylinder.

DAMASK PAPER: Paper having a finish resembling linen.

DANDY ROLL: Portion of a papermaking machine which creates special surface designs or is used in creating a watermark.

DASH LEADERS: Dashed or hyphenated type printed in lines to guide the eye to a certain position on the page.

DATA: (C) Facts or information that can be used or handled by data processing equipment.

DATA, ANALOG: (C) A physical representation of information such that the representation bears an exact relationship to the original information. The electrical signals on a telephone channel are analog representations of the original voice.

DATA COLLECTION: (C) The act of bringing together data from one or more points to a central point. May be in-plant, a short distance, or thousands of miles.

DATA COMMUNICATION: (C) The transmission or transferring of data from one point to another.

DATA, DIGITAL: (C) Information represented by a code consisting of a sequence of discrete elements.

DATA-PHONE: (C) A term used by AT&T to describe any of a family of devices used to permit data communications over telephone channels.

DATA PROCESSING: (C) Any operation or combination of operations on data. Broadly, work performed on computer equipment.

DATA PROCESSING SYSTEM: (C) A network of machine components capable of accepting information, processing it according to man-made instructions, and producing the computer results.

DATA PROCESSOR: (C) Any device capable of performing operations on data.

DATA REDUCTION: (C) The computer job of bringing large masses of raw data to their simplest form, and then organizing them in a useful manner.

DATA TRANSMISSION: (C) The sending of data from one place to another or from one part of a system to another.

DATA SET: (C) A modulation/demodulation device designed to provide compatibility between input/output equipment and communications facilities. Also called modem.

DATELINE: The name of the city or town and the date placed at the beginning of a news story not of local origin.

DAY-GLO INK: A brilliant fluorescent ink. These inks contain phosphorescent material which have a remarkable saturation and brilliance.

DEADBEATS: Customers who fail to pay amounts due.

DEADLINE: A time set for the delivery of work.

DEAD MATTER: (1) Copy, type or plates which will not be used again and may be distributed or destroyed; (2) printing height portions of plates or type form used only for support during molding, and removed or routed out before printing.

DEALER IDENTIFIED: A type of direct mail prepared by a manufacturer and then imprinted with the name of a dealer.

DEBUG: (C) To detect, locate and remove errors from a programming routine or malfunctions from a computer.

DECIMO: A book size between twelvemo and octavo, considered to be about 5⅜ by 8 inches.

DECISION TABLE: (C) A table of all contingencies that are to be considered in the description of a problem, together with the actions to be taken.

DECK: A secondary line or group of lines in a multiple-unit headline.

DECK: (C) A collection of punched cards.

DECK HEAD: A heading having two or more groups of type.

DECKLE EDGE: Paper with one or more feathery edges.

DECODE: (C) To ascertain the intended meaning of the individual characters or groups of characters in the program.

DECORATED TYPE: Typefaces with special designs added to the basic type forms.

DECOY: A dummy name inserted into a mailing list to detect misuse of the list.

DEEP ETCHING: Etching a printing plate extra deeply to give more contrast to the lights and shadows.

DELETE: Proofreader's mark to remove material.

DELIVERABILITY: Mailing pieces actually delivered to addressees.

DELUXE RIDER: A P.S. offering a deluxe version of what is being sold at a somewhat higher price.

DEMOGRAPHIC: Social, economic and geographic characteristics.

DEMY: Size of paper, 16 by 21 inches.

DENSITY: Percentage value in terms of black; for example 50% density refers to a 50% tint of solid black.

DENSITY, PACKING: (C) The number of useful storage elements per unit of dimension, e.g., the number of bits per inch.

DENSITOMETER: An electrical instrument designed to accurately measure optical density or tone values.

DESCENDER: That part of the type which extends below the shoulder of the type.

DESCENDING LETTERS: Lower-case letters with portions which descend below the body of the letter, as g, p or q. The portion below the body of the letter is known as the "descender."

DEVELOPING INK: A liquid, greasy ink which is applied to the plate after exposure for the purpose of protecting the hardened albumin during the washing off process in platemaking.

DIAGNOSTIC ROUTINE: (C) A programming routine designed to locate and explain errors in a computer routine or hardware components.

DIAMOND: Name for 4½-point type.

DIAMOND FLAP: Envelope shape where the flaps are cut from the corners to a point in the center.

DIAZO: Photocopying machine used to produce proofs.

DICK STRIP: A roll of paper on which mailing addresses are printed.

DIE CUT: A sheet, cover, or other printed piece which has been specially cut into other than standard forms or shapes.

DIAPER: Small ornament or pattern repeated in geometrical form.

DIE EMBOSSING: A process whereby a brass or steel die, with a design cut into its surface, is used to raise a design from the surface of a sheet of paper.

DIGIT: (C) A character used to represent one of the non-negative integers smaller than the radix.

DIGITAL: (C) Data in the form of digits.

DIGITAL COMPUTER: (C) A computer that operates on discrete data by performing arithmetic and logic processes on these data.

DIGITAL DATA: (C) Information expressed in discrete symbols.

DIMENSIONAL: Mailing piece which has a three-dimensional enclosure.

DINGBATS: Typographic decorations.

DIODE: (C) An electronic device used to permit current flow in one direction and to inhibit current flow in the opposite direction.

DIRECT ADVERTISING: A broad term encompassing all the diversified forms of advertising directed to specific audiences selected by the advertiser.

DIRECT HALFTONE: A halftone negative or positive that is made by the camera direct from the article itself.

DIRECT IMAGE: A printing plate on which the image has been drawn, typewritten or printed without photomechanical operations.

DIRECT MAIL: Use of the postal service to deliver common messages to a selected audience.

DIRECT LITHOGRAPHY: Lithographic printing wherein the paper comes in direct contact with the image-carrying plate, as opposed to Offset Lithography.

DIRECT MAIL AGENCY: A business organization which specializes in the creation of direct mail material for advertisers.

DIRECT MARKETING: Selling accomplished as a result of a direct response to an individually delivered seller-to-buyer message.

DIRTY PROOF: A printer's proof with a multitude of errors.

DISK STORAGE: (C) A method of storing information in code, magnetically, in quickly accessible segments on flat rotating disks.

DISPLAY: (C) A visual presentation of data.

DISPLAY FACE: Type composition in which various sizes and faces of type are used to attract attention, as in cover and title pages, catalogs, and various kinds of advertising.

DISPLAY TUBE: (C) A tube, usually a cathode ray tube (CRT), used to display data.

DISTORTION: Press sheets sometimes tend to increase or fan out in size in the direction away from the press gripper and guide corner of the sheet, diagonally toward the back edge corner opposite the guide and gripper corner.

DITTO: Duplicator for office use.

DMAA: Acronym for the Direct Mail Advertising Association.

DOCTOR BLADE: The knife blade which removes excess ink from a gravure cylinder, leaving ink only in the wells.

DOCUMENTATION: (C) The collecting, organizing, storing, citing, and disseminating of documents or the information recorded in documents.

DODGER: A small sheet of advertising matter for enclosure with letters or for hand distribution. Also called "handbill."

DOT AREA: The percent of the area of a halftone which is occupied by the dots.

DOT ETCHING: The process of altering the dots on a halftone for corrections and changes.

DOT LEADERS: A series of dots or periods designed to guide a reader's eye to a certain position on the page.

DOUBLE CAP: Size of paper, 17 by 28 inches.

DOUBLE COPY: Size of paper, 20 by 33 inches.

DOUBLE DEMY: Size of paper, 21 by 33 inches.

DOUBLE DEMY OBLONG: Size of paper, 16 by 42 inches.

DOUBLE DOUBLE CAP: Size of paper, 28 by 34 inches.

DOUBLE DOUBLE CROWN: Size of paper, 30 by 40 inches.

DOUBLE DOUBLE FOLIO: Size of paper 34 by 44 inches.

DOUBLE ELEPHANT: Size of paper, 27 by 40 inches.

DOUBLE ENGLISH: Name for 28-point type.

DOUBLE FLAT FOOLSCAP: Size of paper, 16 by 26 inches.

DOUBLE FOLIO: Size of paper, 22 by 34 inches.

DOUBLE FOUR POUND: Size of paper, 22 by 31 inches.

DOUBLE IMPERIAL: Size of paper, 30 by 44 inches.

DOUBLE IMPERIAL CAP: Size of paper, 29 by 44 inches.

DOUBLE LARGE: Size of card, 4½ by 6 inches.

DOUBLE LARGE POST: Size of paper, 21 by 33 inches.

DOUBLE-LEADED: Type with 4-point spacing between lines.

DOUBLE LEADING: Matter with two leads, or strips of metal, inserted between the type lines.

DOUBLE LETTER: Size of paper, 16 by 20 inches.

DOUBLE MEDIUM: Size of paper, 23 by 36 inches.

DOUBLE MEDIUM OBLONG: Size of paper, 18 by 46 inches.

DOUBLE-PAGE SPREAD: A display—usually an ad—which covers two facing pages. Also called "double spread." If in center of book, called "center spread."

DOUBLE PACKET: Size of paper, 19 by 24 inches.

DOUBLE PARAGON: Name for 40-point type.

DOUBLE PICA: Name for 22-point type.

DOUBLE POST: Size of paper, 32 by 20 inches.

DOUBLE POTT: Size of paper, 25 by 15½ inches.

DOUBLE PRINT: Superimposing a line negative on a halftone background.

DOUBLE ROYAL: Size of paper, 24 by 38 inches.

DOUBLE ROYAL LONG: Size of paper, 19 by 48 inches.

DOUBLE RULE: Printing rule which creates two parallel lines.

DOUBLE SMALL: Size of card, 3½ by 5 inches.

DOUBLE SMALL PICA: Name for 22-point type.

DOUBLE SMALL POST: Size of paper, 19 by 30½ inches.

DOUBLE SUPER ROYAL: Size of paper, 20 by 56 inches.

DOUBLE THICK: Cover paper made by pasting two sheets together.

DOUBLE TRUCK: Two pages at the center of a printed piece that are made up as a single unit.

DOUBLE WINDOW ENVELOPE: An envelope having one window for the address and another to display some portion of the printed material enclosed.

DOUBLETONE: Drawing paper with two shading patterns made visible by application of developing fluid.

DOWN STYLE: Style preference which uses a minimum of capital letters. Most newspapers prefer down style.

DOWN-TIME: (C) The period during which a computer is malfunctioning or not operating correctly due to machine failures.

DOWN-TIME: (Printing) The period during which equipment is not producing due to lack of copy.

DRAG: Sometimes used to describe the fact that a press is printing double dots or the appearance that a sheet is being dragged over the blanket of an offset press, causing the dotst to elongate.

DRAGON'S BLOOD: Resin powder used to protect from acid those portions of a photoengraving that are to remain as printing surfaces.

DRAW DOWN: Smear of ink on paper, used to match ink to color specification, when preparing special colors.

DROP FOLIO: A folio placed at the bottom of a page, usually centered.

DROP LETTER: Large capital letter which extends below a line of body type.

DROPOUT: Creating white areas in the reproduction of a halftone by eliminating part or all of the screen on the plate.

DRUG ENVELOPE: Envelope with a rounded flap, available in sizes from 1¾ by 2⅞ to 2 5/16 by 3⅝ inches.

DRY BRUSH: An art technique wherein the brush is used with pigments in a moist—not wet—manner.

DRY FINISH PAPER: Paper with a high finish which has been surfaced without moistening.

DRY FOIL: A foil surface that is substantially free from oily films, suitable for lacquering, printing or coating with adhesives.

DUCHESS: Folded note paper and matching envelope, usually 6 by 4¼ inches.

DULGEN PROCESS: A refinement of the gravure cross line screen, in which the halftone dot is incorporated into the gravure process. Thus, the dots vary both in size and in depth. This process permits the duplication or syndication of gravure color work; used most often in newspaper gravure and comic sections.

DULL COAT: A smooth-finish, enameled paper; contrasted to glossy.

DUMMY: A mock-up giving a preview of a sheet, booklet, book, or other unit intended for production, showing the placement and nature of the various elements as a guide for the artist, printer, or others concerned.

DUMP: (C) To transfer all or part of the contents of one section of computer memory into another section or to an output device.

DUOTONE: Printing produced by two plates, usually one with dark ink and another with a lighter ink.

DUOTONE INK: An ink which, after drying, gives the job an appearance of having been printed in two different tones of the same color.

DUPLEX: (1) Paper with a different color on each side. (2) Typesetting matrix with two character molds. (3) The type character which occupies the secondary position of a matrix.

DUPLICATE: A repeated name on a mailing list.

DUPLEX ENVELOPE: Double envelope with a letter-size envelope affixed to the face of a larger envelope.

DUPLEX FINISH: Paper having a different finish on each side.

DUPLICATORS: Machines for reproducing printing in small quantities.

DUPLICATE ORIGINALS: Duplicate mechanical layouts or printing plates used when a job is to be run in two or more locations or at two different times.

DUPLICATING CHECK: (C) A check based on the consistency of two independent performances of the same task.

DYCRIL: Photopolymer printing plate.

DYETONE: A process in which a black photo image is printed in modulated color.

DYE TRANSFER: A colored print made from a color transparency.

DYNAMIC DUMP: (C) A dump that is performed during the execution of a program.

E.F.: Abbreviation for English Finish paper.

EAM: (C) Electrical Acclunting Machines. Pertaining to data processing equipment, such as key punches, sorters, collators and tabulators.

EAST/WEST LABELS: Mailing labels arranged to read from left to right and generally applied to mailing pieces with high speed Cheshire equipment.

ECHO CHECK: (C) A method of checking the accuracy of transmission of data in which the received data are returned to the sending end for comparison with the original data.

EDIT: (C) To rearrange information; deletion of unwanted information, selection of permanent data, etc.

EDITORIAL: All matter in a publication which is not advertising.

EDITION: Number of copies of a printed piece printed at one time.

EDITION BINDERY: Bookbinding plant which turns out work in large quantities.

EDITION WORK: Printing or binding work done in large quantities.

EGGSHELL FINISH: A smooth, antique finish with a pitted effect, similar to an eggshell.

EGYPTIAN: Square serif typeface.

EDP: (C) Electronic Data Processing. Pertaining to data processing equipment that is predominantly electronic.

EIGHTEENMO: (18mo) A book size measuring approximately 4 by 6¼ inches with 36 pages.

EKTACHROME: A color transparency.

ELECTROTYPE: General term used for a metal plate employed in printing. Frequently called merely "electro."

ELEPHANT: Printer's slang for a sheet measuring 23 by 28 inches.

ELEPHANT FOLIO: Book size approximately 14 by 23 inches.

ELITE: Style of typewriter type equivalent to 10-point printer's type.

ELLIOTT: A method of addressing mailings through the use of cards containing an imbedded fiber stencil. Addresses are typed with a regular typewriter on the stencil and ink is forced through the stencil to create the address on mailing pieces.

ELROD: Casting machine which produces rules, borders and spacing material in a continuous strip.

EM: The square of a body of any given typeface.

EM DASH: A dash one em long.

EM QUAD: Metal less than type-high, one em square, used for spacing.

EM-SPACE: Spacing material less than a quad.

EMBOSSING: Relief printing by means of dies after color printing is done by letterpress. When no printing is done on the area to be embossed it is called "blind embossing."

EMERALD: Size of type about 6½-point.

EMPEROR: Size of paper, 40 by 60 inches.

EMULSIFICATION: The suspension of very finely divided oily or sensitive matter in a printing ink.

EMULSION: Photographic term for gelatin solution holding light sensitive silver salts in suspension, used as a light sensitive coating on photographic plates or film, or on metal plates in photo-mechanical printing processes.

EN: One-half the width of an em.

ENAMELED STOCK: Coated blanks, book paper, and other papers with a hard finish. Used for fine printing, especially of color illustrations.

ENCLOSED MORTISE: That part of a plate or cut, completely enclosed on all sides, which has been sawed out to permit the insertion of type or other matter.

ENCLOSURE: Any item inserted into a mailing envelope or package.

ENCODE: (C) To apply the rules of a code.

END MATTER: Part of a book that follows the main body of text.

END-OF-TOWN MARK: Mark applied to a dick strip for purpose of separating cities for mailing purposes.

END PAPERS: Paper used for covering the inside of book covers.

ENGLISH FINISH: A book paper surface which is smoother than machine finish and not as smooth as supercalendered.

ENGRAVER'S PROOF: Fine proof of an engraving, usually suitable for reproduction.

ENGRAVING: (1) The art or process of making letters, illustrations, or designs on wood, metal, or other substances by cutting or etching, for the purpose of printing or stamping on paper or other materials. Closely related to typography in modern practice are wood engravings, line etchings, and halftone etchings. Engravings of these kinds are in a relief, and when made on blocks which bring their surfaces to height of type, they may be printed in the same forms with type, or in separate forms, on ordinary typographic presses. Other common forms of engraving are the intaglio, copper and steel plates, made by several methods— hand work, machine work and acid etching—and printed by various kinds of machines. (2) An engraved plate, or an impression made from an engraved plate. (3) An engraved inscription. (4) Any letterpress plate produced by photoengraving methods.

ENGROSSING: Hand-lettering, usually with embellishments, applied to diplomas, certificates, etc.

ENTRY: (C) A statement in a programming system; usually each entry is written on one line of a coding form and punched on one card.

ENVELOPE CORNER CARD: Return address printed in the upper left-hand corner of an envelope.

ENVELOPE PAPER: A general term descriptive of paper suitable for making envelopes for mailing. It should be strong and opaque for commercial uses, with good folding qualities and writing surface, and should lie flat without curling. While papers of nearly all types have been used for envelopes the best are white wove writings, bonds, ledgers, manilas, ropes, krafts, and colored papers.

ENVELOPE STUFFER: Any advertising or promotional material enclosed in an envelope with business letters, statements, or invoices.

EQUIVALENT WEIGHTS: The difference in weight between quantities of the same kind of paper in two different sizes of sheet.

ERASE: (C) To remove information from a memory unit of a computer by replacing it with zeros or blanks.

ERRATA: Errors discovered after a piece has been printed and called to the attention of a reader through a separate printed piece.

ERROR: (C) Any discrepancy between a computer, observed, or measured quantity and the true, specified, or theoretically correct value or condition.

ESPARTO: Pulp for papermaking from Esparto grass from Spain or North Africa.

ETCH PROOFS: Black proofs made from a form which has been locked up in a chase with bearers.

ETCHING: (1) Removing non-printing areas from relief plates by acid. (2) Intaglio process used to create fine art.

ETCHING DOTS: Hand process of enlarging or reducing lithography dots to proper size for best printing quality.

EVEN PAGE: The left-hand pages of a book or booklet, which carry even numbers (2, 4, 6, etc.). Also called "verso."

EXCEPTION PRINCIPLE SYSTEM: (C) An information system which reports on situations only when actual results differ from planned results.

EXCHANGES: An arrangement whereby two mailers exchange equal quantities of mailing list names.

EXECUTE: (C) To perform a data processing routine or program, based on machine-language instructions.

EXECUTIVE ROUTINE: (C) A routine which controls loading and reloading of routines and in some cases makes use of instructions which are unknown to the general programmer.

EXIT: (C) A way of momentarily interrupting or leaving a repeated series of operations in a program.

EXPANDED TYPE: An extra-wide face of type.

EXPIRE: A former customer who is no longer an active buyer.

EXPIRATION: A subscription which is not renewed.

EXPIRATION DATE: Date on which a subscription expires.

EXTENSION: (1) Mailing of additional names after testing a portion of a mailing list. (2) Continuance of a subscription beyond its original expiration date.

EXTERNAL: A publication for customers of a company.

EXTERNAL MEMORY: (C) A storage unit (such as a magnetic tape) which is external to the computer.

EXTRA CONDENSED TYPE: Typeface of extreme narrowness.

EXTRACT: (C) To remove from a set of items of information all those items that meet some arbitrary criterion.

F.C.: Abbreviation for "Follow Copy."

FACE: Style of type.

FACSIMILE: The exact reproduction of a letter, document, or signature; also printed letters simulating typewritten letters.

FACTOR: (C) Any of the elements or quantities which, when combined by any of the four arithmetic processes, form a total.

FAIR REGISTER: The degree of register applicable to printing, scoring, perforating and numbering jobs where under normal conditions there is a maximum variation of 1/32 of an inch. Acceptable only for black-and-white and non-critical two-color work. Fair register is not acceptable for multicolor reproduction.

FAKE COLOR: Simulation of the effect of process color printing by manual modification of black-and-white negatives.

FAMILY: Subdivision of type with a trade name as identification.

FAN-FOLD: Same as Accordion Fold.

FARM OUT: Allocating a part or a whole job to a subcontractor.

FASTENERS: There are four principal styles of fasteners for open-end, catalog, booklet, and other styles of envelopes: (1) gummed flaps; (2) ungummed flaps, to be tucked in; (3) metal clasps; and (4) string and button.

FAULT: (C) A physical condition that causes a device, a component, or an element to fail to perform in a required manner.

FAX: Facsimile. Transmission of pictures, maps, diagrams, etc., by wire.

FEATHERWEIGHT: Extremely light printing papers.

FEEDER, AUTOMATIC: A mechanical device which automatically feeds materials into a press, binder or similar machine. Pile Feeder: An automatic device that feeds material into the machine from a pile. Cross Feeder or Stream Feeder: An automatic device that feeds a continuous stream of closely spaced sheets into the machine. Web Feeder: A method of feeding into a machine from a continuous roll.

FELT SIDE: That side of the paper which has not been in contact with the wire during manufacture. It is the top side of the sheet, and usually presents a better printing surface than does the wire (bottom) side.

FIBER LIFT: Lifting or loosening of fibers from the surface of a sheet during printing, most easily noticed in solids as fine white lines.

FIELD: (C) A specified area in a record used for a particular category of data.

FILE: (C) A collection of data. A group of records each of which usually contains the same type of information.

FILE GAP: (C) An area on a storage medium, such as tape, to indicate the end of a file.

FILE MAINTENANCE: (C) The processing of information in a file to keep it up to date.

FILING AND EXPANSION ENVELOPES: These range from plain, open-side envelopes with thumb cuts to accordion-plated expansion envelopes of great strength and durability. Ordinary filing envelopes are made to contain standard 8½- by 11-inch material, although many are made in smaller sizes for other types of filing equipment.

FILLER: Minerals used to improve the printing quality of paper.

FILL-IN: (C) Computer letters where the bulk of the body is pre-printed and the computer fills in personalization details.

FILL-IN: A name, address, or other words added to a form letter. A fill-in is generally typed manually in automatic-typed letters, although in some operations mailing plates may be used to individualize form letters.

FILLED-IN: A term used to describe the result when too much ink is used in printing an illustration, resulting in areas which are printed too heavily. When the dots in a halftone screen are too close together for the quality of paper on which the cut is printed there is danger that the illustration will be filled in.

FILM: Transparent sheeting used for contact plates in art in photography, covered with a photo-sensitive emulsion, a transparent or translucent membrane or base supporting photographic emulsions.

FILM NEGATIVE: Film showing art reverse of original.

FILM POSITIVE: A black positive image of a design on clear film.

FILTER: A transparent color film placed between the subject being photographed and the photographic film to prevent light of certain colors from reaching the sensitive film.

FILTER: (C) A device or program that separates data, signals or material in accordance with specified criteria.

FINAL COPY: When copy is sent to the printer in several installments, final copy is the last installment sent. Final copy should be plainly marked as such, in order that the printer may know when to proceed with makeup.

FINE PAPERS: Broad term used to distinguish papers used for printing, writing and covers from wrapping and other non-printing paper

FINISH: (Art) The term applied to completed artwork.

FINISH: (Paper) There are six major categories of finish for printing papers. In order of increasing smoothness they are: Antique, Eggshell, Vellum, Machine, English and Super-calendered.

FINISHING LINE: Thin black line surrounding a square halftone.

FIRST CLASS MAIL: Mail receiving priority treatment. May contain individual messages.

FIRST DAY COVER: An envelope carrying a newly-issued stamp which has been cancelled on the date of issue at the point of issue of that stamp and usually bearing a special commemorative cachet.

FIRST REVISE: Proof pulled after errors marked on a galley proof have been corrected.

FIT: The accurate rendering and/or printing of two or more colors which occupy the same space in a design so that none shows along the edge.

FIVE-LINE NONPAREIL: Name for 30-point type.

FIVE-LINE PICA: Name for 60-point type.

FIXED WORD LENGTH: (C) Pertains to a computer system whose storage devices may contain words of one fixed length as opposed to other systems which allow words of variable length; i.e., a fixed word length of five would represent 125 as 00125, and a variable word length would store only the 125.

FLAG: Title plate on the first page of a periodical.

FLAGWAVER: A newspaper insert with reply cards along an outer edge which have been slit along their horizontal dimension and perforated along the vertical dimension which adjoins the main body of the insert.

FLAPS: In general, flaps of envelopes are of four styles: (1) The regular flap which is most popular but which, for reasons of extra strength or unusual appearance, is not always suitable: (2) the pointed flap, which imparts an air of distinction to the envelope and also provides a slightly larger gumming surface, frequently being used for executive correspondence; (3) the wallet flap, which is extremely strong; extending well down below the center of the envelope, with a very large gumming surface; and (4) the bankers flap, which is extremely deep.

FLASH BULLETINS: Pre-printed direct mail formats usually 8½ by 11 inches.

FLASH CARDS: Pre-printed direct mail formats on a card stock suitable for use as a self-mailer.

FLAT: Group of engraver's negatives exposed and etched as a single unit before being sawed into individual cuts.

FLATBED PRESS: A press which prints from a flat, horizontal type form.

FLAT CUTTER: A machine for trimming or cutting paper with a diagonal downward action. The long knife is fixed into a stock, which has a long, sliding motion.

FLAT FOOLSCAP: Size of paper, 13 by 16 inches.

FLAT LETTER: Size of paper, 10 by 16 inches.

FLAT PACKET: Size of paper, 12 by 19 inches.

FLAT PAPER: Printing paper which comes from the mill in flat sheets.

FLAT PLATE: An etched printing plate showing poor contrast.

FLAT PROOFS: Individual proofs made from each plate in a color series.

FLAT TINT: A continuous tone resulting from the use of positive or negative dots of regular spacing and size.

FLAT TONES: Lithograph areas of dot formation containing a single tone value, without graduations.

FLEXOGRAPHY: Relief printing process using rubber plates and special inks. Frequently used for adding dealer imprints to pieces printed by other processes.

FLEXOWRITER: Typewriter used for cold type composition.

FLEXOWRITER: A special typewriter which can be operated by punched paper tape. It is frequently used to prepare letters which appear to be individually typed but have a common message. The address and salutation are typed mechanically and then the machine takes over and automatically types the remainder of the letter.

FLINT PAPER: Paper with highly polished surface.

FLIP-FLOP: (C) A circuit or device containing active elements capable of assuming either one of two stable states at a given time.

FLOP: To reverse an illustration so that the right side of the original becomes the left side in the final printing, and vice versa.

FLOWCHART: (C) The graphic representation of the logical flow of information in a data processing system.

FLOWLINE: (C) A line representing a connecting path between symbols on a flowchart.

FLUOROGRAPHIC: Process to produce highlight halftones photographically.

FLUSH BLOCKING: Trimming a plate so that the printing surface comes flush with one or more edges of the block on which the plate is mounted.

FLUSH COVER: A cover that has been trimmed to the saze size as the text pages.

FLUSH HEAD: Short for flush-left head, a style in which each line is aligned to the left.

FLUSH PARAGRAPHS: Paragraphs having no indentation.

FLYER: A small advertising circular.

FLYLEAF: Page which is free from printing but which is part of a printed signature.

FOLDER: A printed piece with one or more folds in which, when folded, each panel constitutes a separate page.

FOLDING MACHINE: Machine used for folding printed sheets.

FOLIO: (1) The figure or numeral placed on a page to denote its sequence. (2) A sheet of paper size 17 by 22 inches.

FONT: Complete assortment of all the different characters of a particular style and size of type.

FOOLSCAP: Size of paper, about 13 by 16 inches.

FOOLSCAP AND HALF: Size of paper, 13 by 24 inches.

FOOLSCAP AND THIRD: Size of paper, 13 by 21 inches.

FOOT: Bottom edge of printed piece.

FOOTNOTE: A note of explanation or reference at the bottom of a page, apart from the regular body type. Footnotes are usually set in smaller type than the text matter.

FORE EDGE: Edge of a book that is opposite its backbone.

FORM: Type and material locked in a chase and ready for the press or electrotyping.

FORM LETTER: Any letter, whether produced in quantity or individually, used to fit a specific situation likely to be encountered frequently. *See also* GUIDE LETTER.

FORMAL BALANCE: Layout pattern that balances elements of equal size in exact mathematical relation to a vertical axis.

FORMAT: Strictly, the size, shape, and general makeup of a publication; loosely applied to the appearance of any printed material.

FORTRAN: (C) Formula Translation. Any of several specific procedure-oriented programming languages.

FORTY-EIGHTMO: (48mo) Book size measuring approximately 2½ by 4 inches with 96 pages.

FOTOSETTER: A typesetting machine which uses matrices carrying an imbedded negative from which lines of type can be prepared photographically.

FOTOREX: Machine for producing cold type in display sizes.

FOUNDRY PROOF: A proof made of a locked form intended for plating, but before making it into a plate.

FOUNDRY SEPARATION: When all printing elements of a two-color page can be placed in one type form, the foundry is asked to make a "foundry separation." For each set of press plates required two press plates are molded from the type form. The plate to be used for the first color is routed so that all second color elements are removed. The plate to be used for the second color is routed so that all first color elements are removed. Where elements come within 1/16" of each other, foundry separations cannot be made.

FOUNDRY TYPE: Individual characters of hard metal used for handset typography.

FOUNTAIN SOLUTION: A slightly acidic mixture which bites into the metal plate. It is used to repeatedly replenish the film on the water-receptive, non-printing area on lithographic plates.

FOUR-COLOR: The exact name for the common term "full-color" and which is the number of plates used in most full-color printing.

FOURDRINIER MACHINE: A machine employed in the manufacture of paper and board. Named for its inventor.

FOUR-LINE BREVIER: Name for 32-point type.

FOURTH CLASS MAIL: Packages sent at parcel post rates.

FREE LANCE: In the art and writing fields, the name applied to an independent artist, photographer or writer who does work for different organizations.

FREE SHEET: Paper free from groundwood.

FRENCH-FOLD: A type of fold for pieces printed on only one side, thereby doubling their bulk. Usually makes an eight-page mailing piece, only four of which are printed.

FRENCH FOLIO: A thin paper with an even finish, used for lightweight circulars, printing proofs, etc.

FREQUENCY: How frequently a buyer makes a mail order purchase from a given advertiser, usually number of times per year.

FRISKET: Protective paper to shield areas of printing plates from ink or photographic paper from light.

FRONTISPIECE: The illustration facing the title-page of a book.

FTP: Abbreviation used by a binder to designate folded, trimmed and packed printed pieces.

FUGITIVE COLORS: Colors or inks which are not permanent. Such colors fade or change when exposed to light.

FULL BOUND: A binding completely covered with leather.

FULL COLOR ART: Artist's finished illustration complete, in actual colors in which it will be reproduced.

FULL COLOR PROCESS: Usually refered to as the reproduction of all colors by utilizing the three primary colors—yellow, red and blue—plus a black key plate. This is achieved by separation of a finished piece of art by camera, usually into process colors—magenta, cyan, yellow plus black.

FULFILLMENT: A general term applied to the processing and servicing mail orders.

FULLFACE: Normal design of a typeface in regard to weight and width.

FULL PAGE: Printed page filled from top to bottom with type matter.

FULL PRINT: When the image on the paper has been printed heavier than the image on the plate. All dots are slightly enlarged.

FUMING: The discoloring of paper on the reverse side of the printed image caused by weight which generates heat by drying and reacts with the fluorescent chemicals in the paper causing a yellow stain.

FURNITURE: Pieces of wood or metal used to fill out the blank spaces in a printing form.

FUZZ: Loose fibers or lint appearing on the paper surface in printing.

GADGET LETTER: A letter containing an item fastened to or enclosed with the letterhead; such items, called gadgets, may be bits of string, miniature tools, coins, etc.

GALLEY: A long tray for holding type after it has been set.

GALLEY PROOF: A proof pulled after type has been composed or set and before it has been compiled or made up into pages.

GANG RUN: Printing from a form containing a group of typed pages or plates to be run at one printing. Applied, for example, to several different letterheads or bill forms printed simultaneously, to be cut apart later.

GAP, INTER-RECORD: (C) An interval of space or time deliberately left between recording portions of data or records. Used to prevent errors through loss of data and permits tape stop-start operations.

GATE: (C) A circuit with one output and many inputs designed so that the output is activated only when certain input conditions are met.

GATEFOLD: Page wider than normal pages of a printed piece which is folded so that it must swing out gatewise when unfolded for reading.

GATHERING: The operation of collating folded signatures in consecutive order.

GEAR STREAKS: Ghostlike, lighter-appearing parallel streaks or images that show on halftones and solids and look like the teeth marks of gears.

GENERAL PURPOSE COMPUTER: (C) A computer designed to solve a wide variety of problems.

GENERATOR: (C) A program for a computer which generates the coding of a problem.

GENERATOR, PROGRAM: (C) A program which permits a computer to write other programs automatically.

GENERATOR, REPORT: (C) A technique for producing complete data processing reports giving only a description of the desired content and format of the output reports and certain information concerning the input file.

GET-A-FRIEND: The technique used in direct mail to obtain prospect names by asking present customers to recommend their friends. Also called MGM—"Member-Get-A-Member."

GHOSTED: Background which has been lightened by application of ink with an airbrush or of plastic shading sheets.

GHOSTING: The appearance of a faint image on a halftone or solid caused by ink being removed from the form rollers.

GIANT LETTERS: A letter blown up to larger than standard 8½- by 11-inch size. Giant letters generally measure 11 by 17 inches or 17 by 22 inches.

GIGO: (C) Garbage In-Garbage Out. A slang acronym used to indicate that if you input faulty material, you get poor results.

GIMMICK: Attention-getting device, usually dimensional, attached to a direct mail printed piece.

GLARE: High reflection from a glossy, enameled, or polished paper surface.

GLASSINE: Glazed, semitransparent paper.

GLAZED PAPER: Paper with high gloss.

GLOSSARY: Definitions of technical or otherwise unfamiliar terms listed alphabetically.

GLOSS INK: Ink containing an extra quantity of varnish.

GOLD STAMPING: Process of stamping or impressing a printing surface with a design in gold.

GONE TO BED: Ready to be printed.

GOOD COPY: Clear, readable and well-edited copy.

GOOD MATTER: Type matter ready for reuse.

GORDON PRESS: Small, upright platten press.

GOTHIC: A synonym for sans serif type.

GRADE: Relative quality of a specific type of paper.

GRAIN: Grain, as applied to paper, refers to the parallel lay of fibers in machine-made paper. It runs in the direction the paper moves through the Fourdrinier machine.

GRAINING: Preparing a printing plate (lithographic) to be water-receptive.

GRAINY: Referring to the printed image, a sandy-textured appearance, rough—as against a smooth-appearing image.

GRAMS: Simulated telegram formats used for short direct mail messages.

GRAND EAGLE: Size of paper, 27 by 40 inches.

GRANITE FINISH: Paper mottled by the addition of fibers of a different color.

GRANITE PAPER: Paper which clearly shows two or more contrasting colors of pulp on its surface.

GRAPHIC ARTS: Comprehensive term which includes printing, engraving, painting, drawing, lettering, writing and all other arts using lines or marks on a surface; frequently applied to the printing industry.

GRAPHOTYPE: A machine for preparing Addressograph and Speedaumat address plates.

GRAVURE: An intaglio printing process.

GRAVURE SCREEN: A cross line screen, ruled 80 to 300 lines to the inch, forming spaces or cells between the lines. The screen has uniform spaces, never varying.

GRAY SCALE: A series of ten graduated values used in platemaking.

GREASEPROOF: Class of wrapping papers impervious to oil and grease.

GREAT PRIMER: Name for 18-point type.

GRIPPER: A space allowed at the end of a printing sheet beyond the bounds of the image to be printed; used as a gripper edge for feeding sheets into presses.

GRIPPER EDGE: Edge of paper which is fed into the press gripper or clamps which grip the paper and guide it through the press. Most offset presses, for example, require a minimum of ⅜" as a gripper margin along the length of the sheet in which area no printing can appear.

GRIPPERS: Mechanical fingers that hold paper onto an impression cylinder of a printing press.

GROTESK: Gothic type.

GROTESQUE: Any typeface which is odd or fanciful.

GROUNDWOOD: A mechanically prepared coarse wood pulp generally used in the manufacture of low-priced grades of paper.

GUARANTEE: A pledge of satisfaction made by the seller to the buyer and specifying the terms under which the seller will make good his pledge.

GUIDE COLOR: Sketch or color indication used when making plates from uncolored copy.

GUIDE EDGE: Edge of paper which lines up the sheet against a side guide or is pushed to a guide by a push guide to insure the proper positioning of a sheet in register from left to right as it is fed into the grippers of the press.

GUIDELINES: Guidelines for Ethical Business Practice of the Direct Mail Advertising Association, Inc. designed to establish standards of good business conduct for direct mail advertisers.

GUIDELINE SYSTEM: Method of proofreading in which the error is circled and connected by a line to marginal instructions.

GUIDE LETTER: A form letter in which one or more sentences or paragraphs change to meet individual circumstances, but in which most of the form is the same for all recipients.

GUIDE MARKS: A method of using crossline marks in the press plate to indicate trim centering of plate, etc., as well as press register in multicolor work. Not to be confused with Register Marks used for stripping elements to register.

GUILLOTINE: An instrument for trimming paper with a downward cutting action.

GUM ARABIC: Gum from acacia trees used in graphic platemaking.

GUMMED LABELS: Address labels with a moisture-sensitive adhesive.

GUMMED PAPER: Paper treated with a moisture-sensitive adhesive.

GUMMING THE PLATE: Protecting the non-printing areas of a plate with a solution of gum arabic to prevent oxidation and to protect the metal.

GUTTER: The division between two facing pages.

GUTTER MARGIN: The page margin at the binding edge of a book or pamphlet.

HACKER PROOF: A proof pulled carefully on enamel stock or transparent acetate, suitable for reproduction. (Also called "reproduction proof.")

HADEGO: Machine for producing display type photographically.

HAIRLINE: A very fine line used in engraving or printing.

HAIR-LINE REGISTER: Register of dot-for-dot or line-for-line accuracy in printing, scoring, perforating and numbering.

HALF: Term used in reference to paper sizes generally meaning half the long side of the sheet.

HALF-BOUND: A binding of which only the back and corners are covered with leather.

HALF-TITLE: (1) The title of a book preceding the first page of text matter. (2) The brief title which precedes the main title page, usually a single line in plain type. (3) The bastard title.

HALFTONE: A reproduction (usually of continuous tone copy) made by photographing through a halftone screen. The term also is applied to the plate or to the printed impression made from such a plate.

HALFTONE SCREEN: A lined screen used in a camera to break up a continuous-tone image into dots. The screen may be fine or coarse depending upon the paper upon which the completed halftone will be printed. (*See* SCREEN.)

HALO: Term used to describe a hickey in printing.

HANDBILL: *See* DODGER.

HANDBOOK: Small, compact guide or reference book.

HAND FOLDING: Folding of printed pieces accomplished by hand rather than a folding machine.

HANDLE: Sensation obtained when handling a sheet of paper.

HAND-SET TYPE: Type matter set by hand; contrasted to machine-set type, as with the Linotype, Monotype, Ludlow, etc.

HANDWORK: Engraver's term referring to any work on a plate, copy or negative done by hand rather than photomechanically.

HANGING INDENTION: Style for body and headline composition in which the first line is set full measure and all succeeding lines are indented.

HARD COPY: (Printing) Typewritten copy produced simultaneously with perforated tape to actuate typesetting machines.

HARD COPY: (C) A business form. Usually called this when associated with another type of output such as tape or cards.

HARD DOT: A halftone dot, positive or negative, characterized by a sharp, clean edge.

HARDWARE: (C) A term used to describe the mechanical, electrical and electronic elements of a data processing system.

HEAD: (1) Display line or lines at the top of printed matter. (2) Top of a printed piece.

HEAD: (C) A device which reads, records, or erases information in a magnetic storage medium.

HEADBAND: Small, ornamental cloth band fastened to the inside of the back of a book.

HEADINGS: Headlines as distinguished from body type.

HEAD MARGIN: White space above the first line on a printed page; usually half the width of the bottom margin.

HEADPIECE: Small ornament or illustration at the beginning of a printed piece.

HEAD TO HEAD: Sheets printed on both sides with the head of each side at the same end of the sheet.

HEAT-ACTIVATED LABELS: Labels with a chemical on back which, when heateo, stick to a mailing piece.

HEAT-SET INKS: Quick-drying inks with solvents which are vaporized through the application of heat after a piece has been printed.

HEADLINER: Machine to produce display sizes of cold type.

HEAT TRANSFER: Addressing method whereby printed addresses are transferred from a carrier to the mailing piece by a heat process.

HEAVY IMPRESSION: Extra boldness achieved in printing when the printing plate or type is squeezed too heavily against the paper.

HECTOGRAPH: Lithographic duplicating machine for low-cost, low-quantity reproduction.

HICKIES: The result of dirt or other foreign matter falling on the blanket of an offset press or paper before printing. Causes a hollow halo or ring-like appearing spot of ink on the paper or the reverse, or a non-printing halo or ring in the solids or halftones area of the printed image.

HIGHLIGHT: The lightest or whitest parts in a single color picture represented in a halftone by the finest dots or by the absence of all dots or tones in that portion of the picture.

HIGHLIGHT HALFTONE: Eliminating the screen from portion of a halftone.

HIGH KEY PHOTOGRAPHY: Photographs in color or black and white made under brilliant illumination.

HOOVEN: Trade name of automatic electric typewriters, used in tandem, for making multiple copies of facsimile letters.

HORSING: Reading proof by one man without assistance of a copyholder.

HOT METAL: Hot type. Type set in metal.

HOT STAMPING: Impressing heated type or stamping dies against thin metal leaf to produce a metallic image on a printed piece.

HOUSEKEEPING: (C) Operations in a routine which do not contribute directly to the solution of a problem but do contribute directly to the execution of a program by the computer.

HOUSE ORGAN: A periodical published by a company for its employees and/or customers.

HUE: (1) Quality which makes colors as we recognize them. (2) Product of mixing two colors together.

IDP: (C) Integrated Data Processing. A system that treats as a whole all data processing requirements to accomplish a sequence of data steps, or a number of related data processing sequences, and which strives to reduce or eliminate duplicating data entry or processing steps.

IDLE TIME: (C) The time that a computer is available for use, but is not in operation. Similar term used in printing.

ILLUMINATION: (1) Decorations applied by hand to printed material. (2) Type decorated with small pictures.

IMITATION PARCHMENT: Paper resembling parchment but generally made from hydrated sulfite pulp.

IMPERIAL CAP: Size of paper, 22 by 29 inches.

IMPOSITION: The process of arranging the pages in a form so that when printed and folded they will fall in proper numerical order.

IMPRESSION: The pressure, or effect of pressure, between the printing surface and the paper surface.

IMPRIMATUR: Official endorsement of a product, service or publication by an "outside" organization.

IMPRINT: The name of the publisher or the printer of a publication. The publisher's imprint is usually at the bottom of the title page and at the bottom of the backbone on bound books. The printer's imprint, if on a book, is generally at the bottom of the page backing the title page or on the last page of the book.

IMPRINTED: A printed piece which has had the name of the advertiser added in a separate operation such as a dealer's name added to a brochure prepared by a manufacturer.

INCENTIVE: Something of value offered to encourage mail order action.

INDENTION: (1) The setting of a line or lines from the margin. (2) The resulting blank space.

INDEX BRISTOLS: Bristols used principally for index records and business cards.

INDEX-WORD: (C) A storage position or register the contents of which may be used to modify automatically the effective address of any given instruction.

INDIA PAPER: A very thin bible paper used principally for books.

INDICATOR: (C) A light or other signal, generally on the computer console, which is used to indicate that a particular condition has occurred in the computer.

INDICATORS: Special printed marks added to pieces to facilitate collating and binding.

INDIRECT ADDRESSING: (C) A method of cross reference. A memory location which, when addressed, will tell you where to find the correct location of the fact being sought.

INDIRECT COLOR SEPARATION: The making of color separations on a continuous tone film before it is photographed through the halftone screen.

INFERIORS: Subscripts. Small letters or figures cast on the lower part of type to denote certain values in chemical and mathematical formulae.

INFORMAL: Layout pattern in which approximate balance is achieved by gree distribution of elements around an imaginary pivot at the optical center of the page.

INFORMATION PROCESSING: (C) The processing of data that represents information.

INFORMATION RETRIEVAL: (C) A method of cataloging vast amounts of related data so it can be called up any time it is needed, with speed and accuracy.

INQUIRER: A person who answers an offer of information about a product or service.

INITIAL: A large single type, often ornamented, used at the beginning of a chapter. An initial is always several times as large as the body type.

INK RECEPTIVITY: That property of a sheet of paper (or other material) which causes it to absorb ink. It is considered one of the important properties of paper as regards printing quality.

INLINE: Describes a roll-fed set-up where, in addition to printing, other operations are performed on one "pass," such as die-cutting, sheeting, folding, embossing or laminating.

INLINE: Ornamented type in which a white line runs down the middle of the main strokes.

INPUT: (C) (1) Data to be processed. (2) The device used for putting data into a computer. (3) The process of transferring data from external to internal storage.

INPUT OUTPUT: (C) Commonly called I/O. A general term for the equipment used to communicate with a computer; the data involved in such communication.

INQUIRY: (C) A request for information from storage. e.g., a request for the number of available airline seats.

INQUIRY STATION: (C) A device, generally a typewriter keyboard, used to "talk" to the computer, usually to get quick answers to random questions.

INSET: The pages cut off in folding and placed in the middle of the sheet.

INSET INITIAL: Large letter used for decorative effect dropped into an area normally occupied by body type.

INSERT: A term used broadly to indicate an item inserted into some other item. A special advertising section inserted into a newspaper. A minor element inserted into a direct mail package.

INSIDE FORM: A term applied to one of the forms used in the printing of a signature, containing the next lowest folio of that signature when folded.

INSTRUCTION: (C) A statement that calls for a specific computer operation.

INTAGLIO: A process of printing from lines or dots recessed into the surface of a metal plate. Gravure, an intaglio process, is printed from cells recessed into the surface of a metal cylinder.

INTEGRATED CAMPAIGN: Advertising campaigns which use various media to achieve a single result.

INTERCOUPLE: (C) To connect two machines or machine components mechanically, electrically, or electronically.

INTERFACE: (C) A common boundary between automatic data processing systems or parts of a single system.

INTENSITY: The quality of a color which we identify as brightness or brilliance, a low-intensity color is a dull color, a color of high intensity is a brilliant color—though both may be of the same hue and value.

INTERLEAVE: (C) To insert segments of one program into another program so that during processing delays in one program, processing can continue on segments of another program; a technique used in multiprogramming.

INTERLEAVING: Inserting separately printed sheets within the body of another printed signature.

INTERLOCK: (C) A device to prevent the reading of two characters at the same time, or to prevent accidental depression of an operating control.

INTERMEDIATE COLOR: A color produced by mixing a primary color with a secondary color.

INTERNAL: A publication for employees of a company.

INTERNAL-EXTERNAL: A publication for both employees and customers of a company.

INTERTYPE: A typesetting machine similar to the Linotype but differing in some details.

INTERRUPT: (C) A break in the normal flow of processing. The normal job flow can be resumed from that point at a later time. An interrupt is usually caused by a signal from an external source, e.g., a terminal unit.

INTIMATION: Size of card, 6 by 3⅝ inches.

INVERTED HALFTONE: Another name for the Dultgen process in gravure printing.

INVERTED PYRAMID: Heading with successive lines each shorter than the one above it.

INVISIBLE INK: Ink which is not visible under normal conditions but which becomes visible when water, a chemical or a special light source is introduced.

INWATS: Incoming Wide Area Telephone Service. Used by mail order firms to receive orders by long distance phone calls, without the caller having to pay for the call.

I/O: (C) Input/Output.

ITEM: (C) A set of one or more fields containing related information; the contents of a single message.

ITERATE: (C) To repeat, automatically, under program control, the same series of processing steps until a predetermined stop or branch condition is reached; to loop.

ITALIC: A style of letter that is slanted, in distinction from upright Roman.

IVORY: Paper finish produced by beeswax coating which is calendered.

JACKET: An extra protective cover of a book. Also called "book jacket" or "dust jacket."

JIM DASH: Short, centered line used to separate sections of a heading or body copy.

JOB: Any piece of work to be printed.

JOB BINDERY: Bindery specializing in small lots.

JOB PRESS: Small printing press.

JOB SHOP: Commercial printing plant.

JOG: To push or shake printed sheets to bring into alignment in a compact pile.

JUMP: (C) An instruction signal which specifies the location of the next instruction and directs the computer to find that instruction.

JUNK MAIL: Mailing pieces which are dishonest, misleading, immoral, salacious or offensive.

JUSTIFY: (1) To write the exact number of words or letters to fill a given space. (2) To set one line or more of type to fill a given space.

JUSTOWRITER: Typewriter that produces justified lines of cold type.

JUTE MANILA: A wrapping paper suitable for cards, envelopes, tags, etc.

KEMART: A photomechanical reproduction process in which sketches are made with nonfluorescing pigments on fluorescing drawing surfaces.

KERN: That part of certain letters or types which projects beyond the body, as in italic *j* or *f*.

KERNING: Adjusting type character so that portions of one letter overlap portions of another letter.

KEY: (C) A group of characters usually forming a field, utilized in the identification or location of an item.

KEY: (Artwork) Identification of positions of copy or art in a dummy or on a "comp" by use of letters or other symbols.

KEY DRAWING: The drawing which will be the master to which other drawings, in separation art, will be drawn for correct registration when printed. Usually the drawing for black.

KEYLINE: A mechanical diagram of reproduction copy for the guidance of the platemaker.

KEY PLATE: The plate of a set of color plates which carries the most detail and to which the other plates are registered.

KEY POSITIVE: The single positive of a set of color positives that has the most detail. This is usually the black positive to which all of the other positives are registered. (Also Key Negative.)

KEYPUNCH: (C) A keyboard actuated device that punches holes in a card to represent data.

KEYED: Advertising is said to be keyed when an identifying letter or number is so used as to show the advertiser which mailing or publication brought a given response. Thus a coupon, order, or inquiry addressed to "Department A" indicates that a certain magazine or list pulled this reply.

KICKER: Short line in smaller type above the main line of a heading.

KILL: To strike out words from copy or on proofs; also to destroy type or cuts.

KISS IMPRESSION: Ideal printing impression so that ink is applied to paper without leaving an impression of the type itself.

KODACHROMES: A specific brand name of the Eastman Kodak Company with reference to their transparencies and/or reproduction of same. Often used to refer to all types of color transparencies.

KRAFT: A sturdy paper (from German for "strong").

KRAFT PAPER: A high-strength wrapping paper made from sulfate pulp. It is usually brown but may be dyed to other colors.

KROMEKOTE: Coated paper rolled under pressure against a polished, heated cylinder to produce a highly glossed enamel finish. A brand name.

KROMECOTE: Coated paper of extremely glossy finish.

KROMOLITE: Method of producing drop-out halftones photographically through use of filters and combination of line and halftone negatives.

LABEL: (1) Gummed piece of paper applied to a mailing and containing the name and address of the recipient. (2) One section of a dick strip.

LABEL PAPER: Paper specially sized for printing labels; may be coated or uncoated.

LACQUERING: Applying transparent coating to protect the surface of a cover or page or to give a glossy finish. Also called "varnishing."

LAID PAPER: A paper which shows a pattern of finely spaced parallel lines and widely spaced cross lines when held up to the light; contrasted to woven paper.

LAMINATING: The process of uniting two materials, such as foil and paper, with an adhesive, using pressure, heat, or both.

LAMPBLACKING: Printing with a sizing ink, and while still wet, applying lampblack. Sometimes done with proofs made on transparent material to assure that the printing is opaque. Proof is then used in the same way as a photo positive.

LANGUAGE: (C) A defined set of symbols that can be converted to machine language, e.g., ALGOL, FORTRAN, COBOL, etc.

LARGE: Size of cut card, 4½ by 3 inches.

LARGE CHECK: Size of paper, 19 by 24 inches.

LARGE DOUBLE POST: Size of paper, 21 by 33 inches.

LARGE-PAPER EDITION: Book printed with wider margins than usual.

LARGE POST: Size of paper, 16½ by 21 inches.

LAYDOWN: The application of the resist containing the image to the copper gravure cylinder preparatory to etching the image into the cylinder.

LAYOUT: Positioning subject matter on press sheet for most efficient production. Artist's sketch showing relative positioning of illustration, headline and copy.

LEAD (pronounced "ledd"): A less-than-type-high strip of metal used primarily to space between lines of type. Standard widths are one pt., two pt., and three pt., but they may be even wider. Also spelled LEDD.

LEAD (pronounced "leed"): A suggestion from any source that an individual, company, or group may be prospective buyers.

LEADERS (pronounced "leeders"): Rows of dots or dashes, such as used on contents pages between words and page numbers.

LEADING (pronounced "ledding"): The white space between printed lines.

LEAF: In books, generally considered as two pages, front and back, as, for example, pages 3 and 4. Pages 2 and 3 would be on separate leaves.

LEAFLET: Generally a printed piece folded once and containing four pages; sometimes a small booklet with as many as 16 pages.

LC: Lower case. Small letters of alphabet.

LCA: Lower case alphabet length.

LEDGER: Paper with smooth writing surface that withstands folding.

LEGEND: Descriptive matter under or beside a cut as distinguished from caption (title above cut). Often mistakenly called "Caption."

LEGIBILITY: The quality of type that, involves the quickness of perception of groupings of words.

LETTER GADGETS: Dimensional items affixed to direct mail pieces.

LETTERHEAD: The printing on a letter which identifies the sender.

LETTER PAPER: Paper cut and finished for correspondence use.

LETTERPRESS: Any printing which is done direct from type. The term is used in contrast to printing done by the offset process.

LETTERSHOP: A business organization which handles the mechanical details of mailings such as addressing, imprinting, collating, etc. Most lettershops offer printing facilities and many offer some degree of creative direct mail services.

LETTER SPACING: The allowance of more space between letters in type setting than would be normal in setting the type.

LIBRARY ROUTINE: (C) A special-purpose program which may be maintained in storage for use when needed.

LIFT: The maximum number of sheets of paper stock that can be placed under the knife of the cutting machine at one time for efficient cutting.

LIGATURE: Two or more letters joined together and cast on the same body of type, like fi, ff, ffl, etc.

LIGHTFACE: A description given to type having a face with thin lines which prints a light tone, in contrast to bold or black-face type.

LIGHT TABLE: A table or drawing board with a frosted glass plate inset into the table. Underneath are lights to shine up through the glass.

LINE: Artwork which has no tonal variations and which is, therefore, usable for the making of line cuts.

LINECASTER: Machine that casts full lines of type.

LINE COPY: Copy which is solid color throughout and obtains tonal variations by changing the size and spacing of areas of color with lines, stipple, etc.

LINE CORRECTIONS: Corrections made or to be made within a line of type, involving changes in characters or resetting the type.

LINE CUT: Engraving made from copy in which the tonal variations, if any, result from the size or spacing of solid areas of color and not from the use of a halftone screen. Also called "Line Engraving."

LINE DRAWINGS: Artwork with solid black lines which can be reproduced without introduction of halftones.

LINE GUAGE: A pica ruler used by printers.

LINE NEGATIVE: Negative with clear lines with a photographically opaque background.

LINEN FINISH: A finish applied to paper to give the appearance of linen.

LINE PRINTING: (C) The printing of an entire line of characters as a unit.

LINESPACING: Adding space between lines of type.

LINES-TO-THE-INCH: Crossline halftone screens are made up of opaque lines ruled at right angles to each other. Some screens have more lines to the inch than others and are classified accordingly. Screens commonly used by lithographers, for example, are 133-line and 150-line. The number of dots to the square inch created by these screens are equal to the square of the lines—thus a 133-line screen will produce 17,689 dots to the square inch.

LINING SYSTEM: Placement of letters on the body of type so that all faces of the same point size will align to a common baseline.

LINOFILM: Phototypesetting system.

LINOTYPE: A typesetting machine in which the letters set from a keyboard somewhat similar to that of a typewriter emerge on lead slugs of various lengths. Term used in contrast to Monotype and hand-set type, in which each letter is separate from the rest.

LIST ARRANGEMENT: Order in which addresses are maintained on a mailing list (e.g. by ZIP codes, alphabetically, by states, etc.).

LIST BROKER: A business organization which arranges the rental of mailing lists compiled by others.

LIST CLEANER: A mailing to ask help of recipients in keeping a list up to date.

LIST COMPILER: A business organization which compiles special mailing lists for sale or rental to direct mail advertisers.

LIST MINIMUM: Minimum number of names which a list owner or compiler will rent.

LIST RENTAL: To rent another's mailing list for one-time use.

LIST SOURCE: Source from which names were obtained for a mailing list.

LITHOGRAPHY: In contrast to letterpress printing, a printing process which does not print from type but from plates made from photographs. Offset lithography is usually called simply "Offset."

LIVE MATTER: (1) Type composition or pages that have not yet been printed or molded for electrotyping. (2) Matter in type forms or plates which is to print in the final product in distinction from dead matter—which will not print.

LOAD: (C) To place data into main core storage.

LOAD UP: Used in mail order when the original order has been for a series purchase and the buyer is offered an opportunity to buy the entire series at one time.

LOCATION (type): Term applied to the galley on which type is stored before use or reuse; galleys are numbered for storage and corresponding numbers are placed on proofs to show location.

LOCATION: (C) A unit storage position in the main internal storage.

LOCKUP: Tightening a form securely in a chase by means of quoins or clips to prepare it for the press or the foundry.

LOGOTYPE: Originally meant to describe a word on a single type body. Now used to designate the characteristic signature of a firm or product. Also two or more letters cast together as ligatures.

LOOP: (C) The repetition of a series of instructions.

LOOSE-LEAF: Binding of single sheets of paper so that any individual sheet may easily be removed.

LOWER CASE: Small letters, as distinct from capitals (upper case) and small capitals.

LTF COLOR BLOCKS: Stripe or band colors printed on the edge of a sheet in certain sequence, used to test and maintain color standards in lithographic printing.

LUDLOW: A patented typesetting process, generally used for larger sizes and special faces of type.

M.F.: Abbreviation for machine finish (paper).

MACHINE-COATED PAPER: A type of coated paper generally used in magazines.

MACHINE CODE: (C) An operation code that a machine is designed to recognize.

MACHINE INSTRUCTION: (C) An instruction that a machine can recognize and execute.

MACHINE LANGUAGE: (C) The set of symbols, characters, or signs, and the rules for combining them, which conveys to the computer instructions or information to be processed.

MACRO INSTRUCTION: (C) A single instruction that causes the computer to execute a predetermined sequence of machine instructions.

MAGENTA: The color sensation produced by the simultaneous reception of red and blue light. Often called "Process Red."

MAGNETIC CARD: (C) A card with a magnetic surface on which data can be stored by selective magnetization of portions of the flat surface.

MAGNETIC CORE: (C) Main Core. A configuration of tiny doughnut-shaped magnetic elements in which information can be stored for use at extremely high speed by the Central Processing Unit.

MAGNETIC DISC: (C) A flat circular plate with a magnetic surface on which data can be stored by selective magnetization of portions of the flat surface.

MAGNETIC DRUM: (C) A circular cylinder with a magnetic surface on which data can be stored by selective magnetization of portions of the curved surface.

MAGNETIC INK: An ink that contains particles of a magnetic substance whose presence can be detected by magnetic sensors.

MAGNETIC INK CHARACTER RECOGNITION: (C) (MICR) The machine recognition of characters printed with magnetic ink.

MAGNETIC STORAGE: (C) A storage device that utilizes the magnetic properties of materials to store data.

MAGNETIC TAPE: (C) A plastic tape with a magnetic surface on which data can be stored in a code of magnetized spots.

MAGNETIC THIN-FILM: (C) A logic or storage element coated with an extremely thin layer of magnetic material, usually less than one micron thick (about four hundred-thousandths of an inch).

MAILABILITY: Qualities of a product which make it suitable for shipment via the postal service.

MAILER: (1) A direct mail advertiser. (2) A printed direct mail advertising piece. (3) A folding carton, wrapper or tube used to protect materials in the mails.

MAILING MACHINE: A machine which attaches labels to mailing pieces and otherwise prepares such pieces for deposit in the postal service.

MAIL ORDER: A method of conducting business wherein merchandise is offered by mail, orders are received by mail and/or merchandise is shipped by mail.

MAIL ORIENTED: The characteristic of an individual wherein he responds to mail order offers.

MAKEREADY: Material used on a printing press to bring all type matter and illustrations to exactly the same height so that the printed impression will be even. Also the process of preparing material on the press.

MAKE READY SHEETS: Sheets used to get lay and color when starting a production press run. These sheets are generally waste. Also referred to as start up.

MAKEUP: The arranging of type lines and illustrations into page form.

MAKING ORDER: A quantity of paper sufficient to be scheduled by a papermarker as a special run.

MALE DIE: A die for embossing in which the design is raised above the surface, the raised portion fitting into the depressed areas of the female or counter die.

MANIFOLD: Thin paper.

MANILA ENVELOPE PAPER: A finished paper especially made for envelopes.

MANUAL INPUT: (C) The entry of data by hand into a device at the time of processing.

MANUSCRIPT: Copy for typesetting. MS (singular). MSS (plural).

MARBLED PAPER: Stock which has been decorated with a marble finish.

MARGIN: The space between pages or plates or between the edge of the printed matter and the edge of the paper.

MARK-SENSE: (C) To mark a position on a card or paper form with a pencil. The marks are then interpreted electrically for machine processing.

MARKUP: The amount added to the cost psice of a mail order product or service to determine the selling price.

MASA: Acronym for Mail Advertising Service Association, International.

MASK: Unsharp or diffused—in the masking method of color correction used in color lithography, an unsharp photographic mask is sometimes made in a printing frame by placing a thin sheet of acetate between the separation negative, and the material for the positive, with the illumination placed off center, and the frame whirled during the exposure. Done to promote better halftone reproduction and color rendition.

MATCH: A direct mail term used to refer to the typing of addresses and salutations onto letters with a printed body.

MATCHED INSERTING: (C) Multiple items personalized by computer and combined for inserting into an envelope for mailing.

MATHEMATICAL MODEL: (C) A set of mathematical expressions that describes symbolically the operation of a process, device or concept.

MATTE: Textured finish of paper.

MATRICES: The molds on Monotype, Linotype, Intertype, or Ludlow machinery which are filled with molten lead to form the letters of type.

MCBEE KEYSORT: A filing method which permit selection of all units with a common identifying factor by inserting a rod through holes with punched notches.

MCEI: Acronym for Marketing Communications Executives, International.

MCKEE TREAT: The physical deformation of a printing plate to adjust for the various printing pressures required by the corresponding tonal areas with consideration of the type of paper and the overprint characteristics.

MEASURE (type): The length, usually expressed in picas or ems, of a single line of type.

MECHANICAL: Finished artwork ready for printing production.

MECHANICAL SCREEN: Any dot or line pattern used by the photoengraver for reproducing an illustration.

MECHANICAL SEPARATIONS: Copy for a platemaker prepared by an artist with separate overlays for each color to be used in printing.

MEDIA: Publications, broadcasting stations, etc. which accept advertising.

MEMORY: (C) Any device into which units of information can be copies, which holds this information and from which it can be obtained at a later time (interchangeable with storage).

MERCHANDISING: A method of increasing the effectiveness of advertising by (1) translating it into terms of advantages for dealers, retailers, salesmen, etc.; and (2) by projecting the advertiser's message beyond the audience of the media in which it originally appeared.

MERGE: The process of intermixing two or more mailing lists into a single list.

METALLIC INKS: Sheen inks composed of metal and color.

METALLIC PAPER: Paper with a coating giving the effect of metal. Also special coated paper which can be marked with metal letters or designs.

MEZZOTINT: Form of fine-art etching in which the entire surface is burred to act as intaglio wells.

MICR: (C) Magnetic Ink Character Recognition. A check-encoding system used by banks for purpose of automating. Also used for coupon and direct mail coding.

MICROENCAPSULATION: Microscopic beads containing fragrances. When a beaded surface is scratched the fragrance is released.

MICROSECOND: (C) One millionth of a second. A time measurement used to measure the operating speed of a computer.

MIDDLETONE: Any neutral tone intermediate between the highlight and shadows of the original and reproductions therefrom.

MILLINE RATE: The cost of advertising space based on one agate line reaching one million in circulation.

MILLISECOND: (C) One thousandth of a second. Another time measurement for operating speed of computers.

MIMEOGRAPH: Originally the trade name of a duplicating machine for reproducing bulletins, form letters, etc., by means of a typed stencil; now loosely applies to any of several stencil-operated reproduction machines.

MIMEOGRAPH PAPER: Paper specially made for mimeograph reproduction.

MINIATURE LETTERS: Letters which have been reduced photographically so that both the size of the sheet or letterhead and the printing or typing are smaller than normal. Miniature letters are usually 4¼ by 5½ inches in size.

MINION: Name for 7-point type.

MINIONETTE: Name for 6½-point type.

MINNIKIN: Name for 3-point type generally used for piece fractions, accents, etc.

MISPRINT: Deviation from copy; typographical error.

MITERING: The cutting of a rule at an angle so as to make perfect corners.

MNEMONIC: (C) Aiding the memory. A group of letters or symbols with a sound or appearance suggesting that for which they stand.

MODERN NUMBERS: Numbers which align at the baseline.

MODERN ROMAN: Typeface distinguished by thin, straight serifs and a marked variation between thick and thin strokes.

MODIFIED SILHOUETTE: Halftone engraving with only one to three sides outlined.

MODIFIED VIGNETTE: Halftone engraving in which one or more sides are straight, the others blending into the white of the paper.

MODULATION: (C) The process by which some characteristic of one wave is varied in accordance with another wave. This technique is used to make business machine signals compatible with communications facilities.

MOIRE: Undesirable pattern which results when a cut is made from the print of a halftone or certain other types of printed illustrations; i.e., by photographing a printed illustration.

MONARCH: Style of envelope with a pointed flap and corners, available in a 3⅞ by 7½ inch size.

MONEY ORDER: A method for transmitting payment wherein the buyer deposits cash with an issuing organization and the issuing organization reimburses the seller for the amount deposited upon presentation of the transmitted receipt of the buyer's deposit.

MONOCHROMATIC: Harmony achieved by using tints and shades of only one color.

MONTAGE: Single illustration produced by using multiple pictures.

MONOTYPE: A typesetting machine on which words and sentences are formed from individual type letters *See also* HAND-SET AND LINOTYPE.

MOONLIGHTER: A free-lance artist, photographer or writer who has a regular source of employment but does free-lance work for others in his spare time.

MORGUE: Collection of reference material.

MORGUE: Printer's designation for place where cuts or copy are stored after use or pending future use.

MORTISE: A hole or other space cut in the surface of a plate or in a printing block to accommodate type. Also the process of making such holes.

MOSQUITOS: Non-decorative elements such as trademarks used in a letterhead.

MOTTLING: Grainy, speckled, uneven appearance of solid printing areas. Surface of solids look like a mass of dark ink islands separated by irregular rivulets of lighter or less dense ink.

MULTICOLOR PRESS: A press which prints two or more colors in rapid succession.

MULTIGRAPH: Trade name of a small printing press, used especially for multiple copies of printed letters, bulletins, circulars, etc.

MULTIPLEX: (C) To interleave or simultaneously transmit two or more messages on a single channel.

MULTIGRAPH PAPER: Paper especially suited for use on the Multigraph machine.

MULTIPROCESSING: (C) Two or more processors executing programs residing in a system memory. In multiprocessing, one of the processors acts as a system control processor, and the other processors on the system are subordinate to it.

MULTIPROGRAMMING: (C) The interleaved or simultaneous execution of two or more programs by a single computer.

MUNSELL SYSTEM: Method of designating colors by numerical gradation.

MUSIC DEMY: Size of paper, 14⅜ by 20¾ inches.

MUTTON: An em quad. Mutt.

NAME PLATE: Name of a periodical as it appears on the first page and at the top of other pages.

NANOSECOND: (C) A billionth of a second. A time measurement used to measure the operating speed of a computer.

NATURAL: Paper color such as cream, white or ivory.

NEGATIVE: A photographic image of originals on paper, film or glass in reverse from those of the original copy.

NEGATIVE OPTION: When a mail order buyer must notify the seller that he does *not* wish to purchase an item. Generally used for book and record clubs.

NESTING: Placing one enclosure within another before inserting into a mailing envelope.

NETWORK: (C) A series of points interconnected by communications channels.

NETWORK, LEASED LINE OR PRIVATE WIRE: (C) A series of points interconnected by telegraph or telephone channels, and reserved for the exclusive use of one customer.

NETWORK, PRIVATE TELEPHONE: (C) A series of points interconnected by leased voice-grade telephone lines, with switching facilities or exchange operated by the customer.

NETWORK, PRIVATE TELEGRAPH: (C) A system of points interconnected by leased telegraph channels and providing hard-copy and/or five-track punched paper tape at both sending and receiving points.

NEWSLETTER: A publication which contains newsworthy material in the form of a letter. Most newsletters are 8½ by 11 inches in page size with copy in typewritten form. Generally just one or two paragraphs are devoted to any single news item.

NEWSPRINT: Paper of the kind generally used for newspapers and comic books.

NICKELTYPE: Electrotype which has been nickel plated for long life.

NICKS: Parallel groves in the side of a piece of type to identify it by font.

NIXIE: Mailing returned by the Post Office as undeliverable as addressed.

NOISE: (C) Any disturbance tending to interfere with the normal operation of a device or system.

NONDESTRUCTIVE READ: (C) A read process that does not erase the data in the source.

NONPAREIL: A unit of measure: ½ of a pica (six points).

NORTH/SOUTH LABELS: Mailing labels which read from top to bottom and can be affixed with Cheshire equipment.

NOTE PAPER: Size of paper one-half the size of letter paper.

NOVELTIES: Ornamental type.

NOVELTY FORMAT: An attention-getting direct mail format frequently dimensional in nature.

Nth NAME: Method of selecting a portion of a mailing list for test mailings (e.g. every 5th, 10th, 20th name).

NUMERICAL CONTROL: (C) Pertaining to the automatic control of processes by the proper interpretation of numerical data.

NUT: An en quad.

O.K.: Proofreader's mark to indicate a proof is without error.

O.K. w/c: Proof is okay except for indicated corrections.

OBJECT PROGRAM: (C) The machine-language program that is converted to electrical pulses which actually guide operation of a computer.

OBLIQUE: Letters, other than Romans, which slant to the right.

OBLONG: A book bound on the shorter dimension.

OBLONG: Rectangle of 2x3 proportions.

OBLONG BOOK: A book where the backbone dimension is less than the length.

OCCUPANT LIST: Mailing lists which contain only addresses (eliminating names of individuals and/or companies).

OCR: (C) Optical Character Recognition. Machine identification of printed characters through use of light-sensitive devices.

OCTAVO: (8vo) (1) Book size measuring approximately 6 by 9 inches. (2) Printed form folded three times to make a 16-page signature.

OCTODECIMO: (18mo) Printed form folded into 18 leaves, 36 pages.

ODDMENT: Sections of a printed piece not included in the text proper (e.g. table of contents, flyleaves, etc.).

ODD PAGE: Right-hand pages, which carry odd folios (3, 5, 7, etc.).

OFF COLOR: Paper or ink which do not match a specified sample.

OFFER: The exact terminology used to describe the product, price, terms, etc. in mail order.

OFFICIAL ENVELOPE: Number 10 envelope.

OFFICIAL ORGAN: Periodical owned by an association organized for purposes other than publishing or a commercial periodical given special status by an association and mailed to members of that association.

OFF-LINE: (C) Pertains to operating devices not under the direct control of the central processing unit.

OFFSET: A smudge resulting from ink on one page smearing onto another. (Not to be confused with "Offset," referring to offset printing.)

OFFSET PAPER: Specially coated paper which can be used for offset lithography.

OFFSET PRINTING: A term used in contrast to letterpress. Offset printing is a kind of lithography in which the impression is made from the surface of a roll (usually rubber) to which an image has been transferred from a photographic plate.

OLD ENGLISH: Heavy black type with hand-lettered characteristics.

OLD STYLE NUMBERS: Type numerals in which the 3, 4, 5, 7 and 9 project below the baseline.

OLD STYLE ROMAN: Typeface distinguished by bracketed serifs, minimal difference between thick and thin stroks.

ON: Term indicating the number of illustrations or pages printed on a single sheet.

ON-LINE: (C) Pertains to operating devices under the direct control of the central processing unit.

ONE-UP: (C) Single letter printed on computer. Two-Up, Three-Up, etc. indicate the number of letters printed simultaneously on the computer.

ONIONSKIN: A thin paper, generally translucent, with characteristics of bond paper.

OPACITY: Quality of paper that prevents printing on back of sheet or on another page from showing through.

OPAQUE: Referring to paper, not permitting passage of light, in contrast to translucent or transparent. In photoengraving, to paint out areas not wanted in the final illustration.

OPAQUE: (1) In art, paint with a non-transparent quality. (2) In photoengraving and platemaking, the painting out of areas, on the negative, which are not desired on the printing plate.

OPAQUE WHITE: A pigment used to white out areas on original illustration copy.

OPEN ACCOUNT: Shipment of merchandise without payment in advance.

OPENENDED: (C) A process or system that can be augmented.

OPEN PUNCTUATION: Type matter containing the minimum of necessary punctuation.

OPEN UP: To render less opaque so that more light may pass through areas intended to appear more open.

OPERATING SYSTEM: (C) An integrated collection of computer instructions that handle selection, movement and processing of programs and data needed to solve problems.

OPERATION: (C) A defined action; the action specified by a single computer instruction.

OPTICAL BLUE: A shade of blue which will not be picked up in photographing illustration copy unless a special filter is used.

OPTICAL CENTER: A point 10% above the mathematical center of a paper or layout.

OPTICAL CHARACTER RECOGNITION: (C) See OCR.

OPTICAL READER: (C) A device used for machine recognition of characters by identification of their shapes.

OPTICAL SCANNER: (C) (1) A device that scans optically and usually generates an analog or digital signal. (2) A device that optically scans printed or written data and generates their digital representations.

OR: (C) Operations Research. The use of analytic methods adapted from mathematics, for solving operational problems, to provide management with a more logical basis for making sound predictions and decisions.

ORDER-BLANK ENVELOPES: Various types of business reply envelopes have been developed to carry order forms on the inside. The order form is printed on one side of the sheet and the address and reply form on the other; the recipient simply fills in the order, folds and seals the envelope and mails it in.

ORDER CARD: A return card similar to a coupon in effect, to be filled out, checked, or initialed by the inquirer or customer and mailed back to the advertiser. Order cards are often self-mailers.

ORDER FORM: Similar to an order card except that it is printed on paper rather than on card stock; may require being sent in an envelope or may be sealed to form a self-mailer.

ORNAMENT: Rule, border of decoration cast in type and used to embellish printed matter.

ORNAMENTED: Type in which the basic form is embellished or extremely altered.

OUTLINE: Ornamented letter with only its outline defined.

OUT OF REGISTER: When two or more colors are not printed in the proper relationship to one another.

OUTPUT: (C) (1) The final results after data is processed in a computer. (2) The device or set of devices used for taking data out of a computer system and presenting them to the user in the form he desires. (3) The process of transferring data from internal to external storage.

OUTSERT: An item attached to the outside of a mailing package.

OUTSIDE FORM: The side of a sheet which when folded contains two outside pages of the signature. These are always the lowest and highest folios in the form. The inside form is the reverse side of the sheet. These terms also applied to the form of type or the plates from which the sheets are printed.

OVERFLOW: Type for which there is insufficient space in page make-up. It is placed outside the printing page and keyed to its proper position within the page. Sometimes called "overset."

OVERHANG COVER: A cover larger in size than the enclosed pages.

OVERLAY: Any material on which artwork may be done and which will be transparent enough to show other related artwork. Drawings for secondary colors, etc. are often done on overlays, usually on acetate.

OVERLAY: Transparent flap over artwork to provide mechanical color separation or instructions to the platemaker.

OVERPRINTING: (1) Adding additional printing to an already completed printed piece. (2) Application of a varnish or lacquer to printed matter.

OVERS: Surplus left after the required number of pieces have been mailed.

OXFORD RULE: Printing element that produces two parallel lines, one thick and one thin.

OXIDATION: Process whereby ink dries on paper.

OXIDATION: A form of rusting of the non-image area of offset plates which will hold ink and print. Caused by improperly protecting the plate with gum when the press is stopped.

OZALID: Photocopying machine used to produce proofs.

OZALID PROOFS: Chemical proofs on acetate in which single colors are overlayed to get a quick result of approximate final color values without press proofing. Used extensively in color process work for quick checking.

PACK: (C) To include several brief or minor items of information into one machine item or word.

PACKAGE: All of the elements of a mailing.

PACKAGE TESTING: Mailing two or more different direct mail packages to determine the comparative results of each.

PACKING DENSITY: (C) The number of useful storage cells per unit of dimension (e.g. the number of bits per inch stored on a magnetic tape).

PADDING: Simple method of binding sheets of paper by applying a flexible adhesive on one edge of sheets.

PAGE PROOF: A proof of type matter which has been made up from galleys into pages.

PAGINATION: Arranging type so it will print pages in proper sequence.

PAID CIRCULATION: Copies of a publication which have been paid for by their purchasers, not for resale, and are distributed in the field served.

PAINTING UP: Method of preparing one-color original to be used as copy for two-color plates.

PAMPHLET BINDING: Simple binding which involves a minimum number of folds.

PAPER GRAIN: Grain of paper runs parallel with length of paper as it is received from the mill.

PAPER-TAPE READER: (C) A device which senses and translates the holes in a roll of perforated paper into machie-processable form.

PAPER WEIGHT: *See* BASIS WEIGHT.

PARAGRAPH OPENERS: Typographic elements to direct the reading eye to the start of a paragraph.

PARALLEL: (C) Handling simultaneously in separate facilities.

PARAMETER: (C) A quantity in a program whose value specifies or partly specifies the process to be performed.

PARCEL POST: Fourth Class mail.

PARCHMENT: Type of paper stock, somewhat translucent in character. Originally parchment was produced from animal skins.

PARITY CHECK: (C) A check in which the number of 1 bits in a character is determined and the sum checked for an odd or even number.

PASSALONG: Additional readers reached when a direct mail piece or publication is passed along to others by the original recipient.

PASTE-UP: Affixing elements into position for platemaker.

PASTEUP TYPE: Preprinted letters which can be cut apart and then pasted onto layouts for use in preparing printed pieces.

PATCH: (C) Section of coding inserted into a routine to correct a mistake or alter the routine.

PATCH: (Printing) A section of type set as an alteration to an existing form. The patch is either placed into a mortised plate, or is reproduced as a plated patch, or as a cello to be used in an overall cello of a form yet to be produced on a plate or cylinder.

PATENT BASE: A metal base, sometimes used to take the place of wood for mounting electrotypes.

PATTERN: A pattern plate consists of all printing elements of any one color soldered together in relationship to one another so that when molded they will provide a complete press plate of that color. Elements may consist of original engravings and/or electrotypes of halftones, zincs, type portions, etc. Example: The blue plate of a four-color set would contain all printing elements to appear in the blue press plate, all being so placed that they will register with similar press plates made from patterns of the black, red, and yellow.

PAYROLL ENVELOPES: Small containers for coins and bills which are bought in bulk by banks for distribution among their customers or by individual companies. Sizes range from 3 by 4½ inches upward. Sometimes used as enclosures for gadgets in gadget letters.

PBX: (C) Private Branch Exchange. A manual or dial exchange, connected to the public telephone network, located on a customer's premises and operated by his employees.

PDS: Paid During Service. Subscription plans wherein customer pays as he receives merchandise.

PEBBLE: Paper finish with tiny surface dimples.

PENSCRIPT: Letters written in script, either by hand, processed, or printed.

PERCENT OF RETURN: Results of a direct mail program in terms of number of respondents vs. total quantity mailed.

PERFECTING: A sheet printed on the second side is said to be perfected or completed. A rotary press that delivers a signature printed on both sides of the sheet is said to be a perfecting press. There are also flatbed presses with two cylinders and two beds that print on both sides ot the sheet. These are known as "flatbed perfectors."

PERFECT BINDING: Machine binding method wherein the back folds are cut off, leaf edges roughed, glue applied and a cover then attached without the use of binding wire or sewing.

PERFECTING PRESS: Rotary printing two sides of paper during one operation.

PERFECTING PRESS: A press which prints both sides of the paper at one passage through the machine.

PERFORATING RULE: Sharp, dotted steel rule, slightly higher than type, and used in conjunction with type forms to perforate the sheet when printing.

PERFUMED INKS: Regular printing inks to which a concentrated scent is added to impart a desired aroma or fragrance on the printed sheet.

PERIPHERAL EQUIPMENT: (C) Units or devices that are part of an entire data processing system, but not actually part of a computer; i.e., a Flexowriter functioning off-line, card sorter, reproducer, a forms burster, forms encoder, etc.

PERSONALIZATION: (C) Including material from the data file which relates to an individual in a computer-printed letter.

PERSONALIZING: The individualizing of direct mail pieces by adding the name of the recipient.

PERT: (C) Program Evaluation and Review Technique. A program which solves specific problems related to management control.

PETIT: German name for 8-point type.

PETIT ROMAIN: French name for 10-point type.

PHONE LIST: Mailing list compiled from names listed in telephone directories.

PHOTO COMPOSING MACHINE: A step-and-repeat machine which makes it possible to repeat the same image, from one negative or positive, any number of times on a printing plate.

PHOTOCOMPOSITION: Typographic material produced and arranged by a photo method rather than by metal type.

PHOTOENGRAVING: Printing plate produced by photochemistry for relief printing.

PHOTOGELATIN: Collotype printing.

PHOTOGRAVURE: Intaglio printing that doesn't use a screen but projects light between minute granules of resin.

PHOTOLETTERING: Display type lines created by photographically printing individual characters on photosensitive paper or film.

PHOTOMECHANICAL: A process in which photography is an aid or an auxiliary to some mechanical process.

PHOTON: Phototypesetting machine.

PHOTO SENSITIVE RESIST: A coating material which, when properly processed, leaves a resist pattern on a plate, highly resistant to chemicals.

PHOTOSTAT: Trade name. A positive reproduction of a piece of art on paper.

PHOTOTYPESETTING: Cold type composition by photographic means.

PI: To mix up type.

PIA: Acronym for Printing Industries of America.

PICA: The standard for measuring type matter width or depth—1/6 of an inch, or 12 points.

PICK: When small portions of the surface of a sheet of printing paper are torn away by inked printing rollers.

PICKING: The dissolving of dry ink on a printed sheet by wet ink of a succeeding cylinder, leaving small unprinted areas on the completed job.

PICKUP: A standing page or part of a page picked up to be worked on and used again.

PICOSECOND: (C) One thousandth of a nanosecond (one trillionth of a second).

PICTURE WINDOW ENVELOPES: Envelopes which have an opening through which a portion of the contents can be seen before the envelope is opened.

PIGEONHOLE: Unduly wide space showing between words set in type.

PIECE FRACTIONS: Numerical fractions composed by use of two linecasting matrices.

PIGGY-BACK: An offer that hitches a free ride with another offer.

PIGMENT: Substances which provides the color in ink.

PINPOINT DOT: The finest halftone dot used in photoengravings.

PLANOGRAPHIC: Lithographic printing.

PLASTIC BINDING: Use of loops of plastic for binding.

PLATEN: Flat surface upon which paper rests when it comes in contact with printing surfaces. Also short for platen press.

PLATEN PRESS: Any press that gives a printed impression by bringing together two flat surfaces, one of which is called the bed and the other a platen.

PLATES: Flat, smooth pieces of metal which have been treated to create a printing surface.

PLOTTER, XY: (C) A device used in conjunction with a computer to plot coordinate points in the form of graphs and charts.

PLUGBOARD: (C) A removable panel which, through external wiring patterns, activates the operation of a specific application. When placed in a machine, the wires are interconnected with terminals within the machine causing this program activation.

PLY: One of several pieces of paper pasted together.

POINT: The unit of type measurement—0.0138 of an inch, 12 points to the pica.

POLLARD-ALLING: A method of addressing mailings through the use of aluminum plates which are linked together into reels of up to 2,500 addresses. The system is normally used for large mailing lists.

POLYWRAP: To package materials in thin sheets of polyethylene which are sealed by heat.

POLYWRAP LABELS: Labels which adhere to polyethylene wrappings.

POST: Size of paper, 17 by 22 inches.

POSTCARD PAPER: Smooth, even-surfaced paper approximately 0.009 inch in thickness; basis size, 22½ by 28½ inches; weight range 94 to 105 pounds.

POST CARDS: Single sheet self-mailers on heavy stock.

POSTAGE SAVER ENVELOPES: Like regular envelopes in appearance and construction, the only difference being that they have a loose flap at one end which is simply tucked in without being sealed. In another style of postage saver envelope, one end is stuck with a spot of gum instead of being sealed full length and the words, "Pull out for postal inspection," are printed on or adjacent to the loose flap. Postage saver envelopes enable the advertiser to send out a third-class mailing in keeping with post-office regulations with the back flap of the envelope sealed in the same way as first-class mail.

POSTAL CARDS: Mailing cards with postage pre-printed. Sold by USPS.

POSTMARK: Cancellation marking applied to stamps by the postal service and usually containing the date of mailing and the point of entry into the mail service.

POSTMORTEM: (C) Analysis of an operation after its completion.

POSTSCRIPT: Additional matter added to a letter following the signature of the sender.

POTT: Size of paper, 13 by 16 inches.

POWDERLESS ETCH: A method of etching plates which reduces side-etching and almost completely eliminates dimensional loss of the dots.

PRELIMINARY: The portion of a printing job which preceeds presswork.

PRELIMINARY MATTER: All the pages which precede the regular text of a book.

PREMAKEREADY: (1) The proving and leveling operation which is done to adjust for uneven plates prior to delivery of such plates to the production printing press. (2) Inspection and correction of submitted advertising material in a composing room.

PREMIUM: An item offered to a buyer, usually free or at a nominal price, as an inducement to purchase or obtain for trial a product or service offered via mail order.

PREPRINT: An advertising insert printed in advance and supplied to newspaper for insertion.

PRESS: Any machine for making impressions, especially on paper, from an inked surface.

PRESS PASTED: Binding of pages of a signature during regular printing operations and requiring no stitching or sewing.

PRESS PROOF: A proof which has been printed on a regular press (not a proof press) after makeready.

PRESS SHEET: The printed sheet.

PRICELIST: A printed list of prices which is published separately from descriptive material.

PRIMARY COLORS: The red, yellow and blue of printing inks. Often called "process" colors.

PRIMARY COLORS: Red, blue and yellow.

PRIMARY LETTERS: Lowercase characters which have no ascenders or decenders.

PRIMARY OPTICAL AREA: Focal point near the upper left corner of a sheet where the reader's eye first looks at a printed piece.

PRIMER: Old name for 10 and 18-point type.

PRINCE OF WALES: Size of paper, 3 by 4½ inches.

PRINTER: Man or firm which produces printing.

PRINTER: (C) An output device for printing out computer results as numbers, words, or symbols. They can be anything from electric typewriters to high speed printers operating at thousands of lines a minute.

PRINTER'S DEVIL: Apprentice or helper in a printing shop.

PRINTER'S OBLONG: Rectangle whose length is 1.73 times its width.

PRINTS: Fine art produced by various printing processes.

PRIVATE LINE SERVICE: (C) A channel or circuit furnished a subscriber for his exclusive use.

PRIVATE MAIL: Mail handled by special arrangement outside the postal service or regular commercial delivery organization.

PROCESSING: Developing, fixing, washing and drying exposed film.

PROCESS COLOR: Method of printing which duplicates full-color continuous tone original copy by optically mixing primary colors.

PROCESS FOUR-COLOR PRINTING: The use of yellow, red, blue and black positives for reproducing almost any color.

PROCESS PLATES: Color plates, two or more, used in combination with each other to produce other colors and shades. Usually involves the application of the primary pigments of yellow, magenta, cyan, and black.

PROCESSOR: (C) (1) In hardware, a data processor. (2) In softfare, a computer program that includes compiling, assembling, translating and related functions for a specific programming language.

PROGRAM: (C) A plan for the solution of a problem.

PROGRAM LIBRARY: (C) Collection of available computer programs and routines.

PROGRAMMED CHECK: (C) A check procedure designed by the programmer and implemented specifically as a part of the program.

PROGRAMMER: (C) A person who prepares instruction sequences without necessarily converting them into detailed codes.

PROGRAMMING LANGUAGE: (C) Language used to prepare computer programs.

PROGRESSIVE PROOFS: See PROGRESSIVES.

PROGRESSIVES: A set of proofs showing each color plate separately and then in combination, run in the proper color rotation on the paper and inks specified.

PROJECTING: To estimate total returns from a mailing based on returns during the first few days or weeks.

PROOFING: Denotes the operation of pulling proofs of plates for proof-reading, revising, trial, approval of illustration, and other purposes prior to production printing.

PRO FORMA INVOICE: A mailing piece designed to look like an invoice but which is actually a selling piece.

PROOFREADER: One who reads proofs of copy for accuracy.

PROOF PRESS: A small printing press, usually hand operated, for pulling proofs.

PROOFS: A trial printing on paper.

PROSPECT: A name on a mailing list who is considered to be a potential buyer of a given product or service but who has not previously made such a purchase.

PROSPECTING: Mailing to get leads for further sales contact rather than to make direct sales.

PROTECTED LOCATION: (C) A storage location reserved for special purposes in which data cannot be stored without undergoing a screening procedure to establish suitability for storage therein.

PROTYPE: Manually operated machine for cold typesetting.

PROVE: To pull a proof.

PSEUDO-CODE: (C) An arbitrary code, which must be translated into computer code.

PUBLICITY: Obtaining editorial coverage in media without expenditure of advertising funds.

PUBLISHER'S STATEMENT: Certified statement of circulation and distribution data made by a publisher and issued unaudited, but subject to audit.

PULL-OUT: An attention-getting direct mail format which involves inserting a message into a printed piece, with a portion exposed. The recipient must pull the exposed portion to release the message for reading.

PULL SHEETS: Sheets removed from the run after every press stop. These sheets may or may not have variations in color, but are usually acceptable. Considered as good sheets.

PULLING A PROOF: Printer's term for making a copy of a cut or type matter on a proof press.

PUNCHED CARD: (C) A card punched with a pattern of holes to represent data.

PUNCHED TAPE: (C) A paper tape on which a pattern of holes or cuts is used to represent data.

PURGE: The analysis of a group of mailing lists to eliminate duplicate names and addresses.

PYRAMIDAL: Layout pattern that has elements in a regular or inverted V shape.

QUAD: Blank printing unit to create spacing. Quadrat.

QUAD: A piece of type metal less than type high used in filling out lines.

QUAD CROWN: Size of paper, 40 by 30 inches.

QUAD DEMY: Size of paper, 35½ by 45 inches.

QUAD FOOLSCAP: Size of paper, 34 by 27 inches.

QUAD POST: Size of paper, 32 by 20 inches.

QUAD POTT: Size of paper, 31 by 25 inches.

QUADRANT MAKE-UP: Layout pattern in which the page is divided into quarters, each designed independently of the others.

QUAD REAM: Package of printing paper containing 2,000 8½ by 11 inch sheets, wrapped in individual package of 500 sheets each.

QUAD ROYAL: Size of paper, 40 by 50 inches.

QUANTITY: (C) A plus or minus number in the mathematic sense.

QUARTER-SHEET CARD: Cardboard one-quarter of the size 22½ by 28½ inches.

QUARTO: (4to) Book size measuring approximately 9 by 12 inches with eight pages.

QUEEN NOTE: Size of paper, 3½ by 5⅜ inches.

QUERY: A small q. or an interrogation mark (?) made by proofreader to call author's attention to possible error. Question of spelling: ?sp.; question of fact: ?F.; question of grammar: ?G; illegal copy: ?C.

QUESTIONNAIRE: A printed form mailed to a specified audience to solicit answers to specific questions.

QUIRE: 1/20 of a ream. A quire of fine paper consists of 25 sheets; or coarse paper, 24 sheets.

QUOIN: An expanding device (usually matching, toothed iron wedges) used to lock a form in a chase.

RADIX: (C) The base of a numbering system. The total number of distinct marks or symbols used in the numbering system, i.e., decimal system radix is 10:0, 1, 2, 3, 4, 5, 6, 7, 8, 9. Binary system radix is 2:0; 1.

RAG CONTENT PAPER: Bond and ledger papers containing from 25% to 100% rag fibers.

RAILROAD: To hurry copy through the composing room, eliminating or reducing proofreading.

RAILROAD BOARD: Clay-coated board tinted to give a variety of colors. Basic size, 22 by 28 inches; standard thickness, 0.018 to 0.024 inches.

RANDOM ACCESS: (C) A storage device wherein access to the next position from which information is to be obtained is in no way dependent on the position from which information was previously secured. Also called Direct Access Storage.

RANGE: (C) All the values which a function may have.

RATE CARD: A card issued by a publisher giving advertising rates and other information of interest to advertisers.

RATTLE: Stiffness of printing paper.

READ: (C) To copy, usually from one form of storage to another, i.e., read magnetic tape.

READ: (Printing) Short for proofreading or copyreading.

READABILITY: Quality which affords maximum easy and comfort in reading type matter over a sustained period.

REAL-TIME: (C) A method of processing data so fast there is virtually no passage of time between inquiry and result. Technique of computing which a process is taking plase so results can be used to guide operation of the process.

REAM: Conventional unit for quantity of sheets of paper. Fine and printing papers run 500 sheets to a ream; coarse, tissue, and wrapping papers run 480 sheets to a ream.

REAM WEIGHT: The weight of one ream of any given paper.

RECENCY: Last previous order from a mail order buyer.

RECORD: (C) A collection of related items of data treated as a unit.

RECTANGULAR: Layout pattern where total area is subdivided into smaller units which have a harmonious relationship with each other.

RECTO: The right-hand page of a book or booklet, as opposed to verso, the left-hand page. Recto pages are always odd numbered (1, 3, 5 etc.).

RED PRINT: Proof of the rotogravure positive, which is sent to customer by printer. Comparable to page proof in letterpress. Also called Brown Print. Seldom red in color.

REDUCTION: Decreasing the density or opacity of a negative by removing some of the metallic silver forming the image.

RE-ETCHING: (1) Supplementary or local etching of halftone plates to reproduce the detail, tones and color values of the original. (2) Lightening a tone or local area by additional etching. (3) In gravure, re-etching darkens a tone instead of lightening it.

REFLECTION COPY: Original copy which is viewed and must be photographed by light reflected from its surface.

REGISTER: (C) Device used in a Central Processing Unit for temporary storage of small amounts of data or intermittent results during processing.

REGISTER: A term referring to the accuracy of placement of printing; printed lines which do not fall exactly where they should are "out of register."

REGISTER MARKS: Small marks for guiding engravers in obtaining proper register in color separation printing.

REGISTERED MAIL: First class mail with a declared value which involves signature by recipient upon receipt.

RELEASES: Written permission for the use of an individual's name, likeness or statement for use in advertising.

RELIABILITY: (C) The probability that a device will function without failure over a specified time period or amount of usage.

RELIEFOGRAPH: A machine for preparing address plates for the Pollard-Alling address system.

RELIEF PRINTING: Printing wherein ink is applied to a raised image and then transferred to paper.

RELOCATE: (C) In programming, to move a routine from one portion of storage to another and to adjust the necessary address references so that the routine, in its new location, can be executed.

REMOVALS: Names of individuals or companies removed from a mailing list.

RENEWAL: A subscription which has been renewed prior to or at expiration or within six months thereafter.

RENEWAL: Order from a buyer for continuation of a service.

REPEAT MAILING: Sending a second mailing to the same mailing list.

REPERFORATOR: Machine that perforates tape used for automatic typesetting.

REPLATE: To rearrange elements in a type form and prepare a new stereotype or electrotype. Frequently used in catalog printing for price changes, etc.

REPLY CARD: A sender-addressed card included in a mailing on which the recipient may indicate his response to the offer.

REPLY-O-LETTER: One of a number of patented direct mail forms for facilitating replies from prospects.

REPRINT: (1) Separate printing of material originally appearing in a periodical. (2) New printing of a work previously printed.

REPRODUCTION PROOF: A proof of illustration or type matter, pulled on a special proof press, which can be photographed for offset reproduction or engraving. Abbr.: Repro. (Also called "Hacker Proof.")

RERUN: (C) To repeat all or part of a program on a computer.

RESET: (C) To restore a storage device to a prescribed initial state.

RESPONSE RATE: Percent of returns from a mailing.

RETURN: (C) To go back to a specific point in a program, usually when an error is detected, for the purpose of re-running or re-starting the program.

RETURN ENVELOPES: Self-addressed envelopes, either stamped or unstamped, as distinguished from business reply envelopes, which bear a printed insignia and permit number obligating the mailer to pay the postage on their return.

RETURN REQUESTED: An indication that a mailer will compensate the postal service for return of an undeliverable mailing piece.

RETURNS: Responses to a direct mail program.

REVERSE: White letters on a black background in printing.

REVERSED POSITION: A plate which has been reproduced facing one way is "reversed" when reproduced facing the opposite. For example, a portrait which has been facing "out" (toward the edge of page) is reproduced to face "in" (toward the gutter). Also called "flopping."

RFMR: Acronym for Recency-Frequency-Monetary Ratio, a formula used to evaluate sales potential of names on a mail order mailing list.

RIGHT SIDE: Felt side of printing paper.

RING BINDER: Most common form of loose-leaf binding wherein sheets are punched with holes which fit around rings in a binder.

RIPPLE: Paper finish.

RISING INITIAL: Initial letter which aligns with the baseline of body type.

RIVER: In typesetting, a river is a white channel in a block of body type caused by wide word spacing near the same point in each of several succeeding lines.

ROBOTYPER: An automatic typewriter used for the preparation of letters in quantity.

ROLL-FED: Printing from rolls of paper instead of single sheets.

ROLLOUT: To mail to a full list of names after making a test mailing to a portion of that list.

ROMAN: Generic name for the type commonly used in all ordinary reading matter.

ROP: Run of paper. Usually refers to color printing in a newspaper or magazine which can be placed on any page.

ROTARY PRESS: Letterpress in which paper fed from a continuous roll is printed as it passes between an impression cylinder and a curved printing plate.

ROTOGRAVURE: A printing method in which inkwells are etched into copper cylinders. Ink from these wells is then deposited on paper or other printing surfaces to create an image. Especially suitable for fine color reproduction.

ROTOGRAVURE PAPER: A specially finished paper used for rotogravure newspaper supplements, catalogs, etc.

ROUGH: Dummy or layout in sketchy form with a minimum of detail.

ROUND-FLAP GLOVE: Style of envelope with a rounded flap, available in sizes from 4 to 6 to 3⅞ by 7½ inches.

ROUNDOFF: (C) To delete the least significant digit or digits of a numeral and to adjust the part retained in accordance with some rule.

ROUTINE: (C) A sequence of instructions which perform a definite function within a larger program. Also Subroutine.

ROYAL: Size of paper, 26 by 20 inches.

ROYAL OCTAVO: Book size measuring 6½ by 10 inches.

ROYAL PACKET: Size of paper, 6 by 9½ inches.

ROYALTIES: Sum paid per unit mailing or sold for the use of a list, imprimatur, patent, etc.

ROUTING: Removing non-printing metal from printing plates.

ROUTING: (rhymes with "outing.") Cutting away any metal from the surface of a printing plate. Applied both to printing surface and nonprinting areas.

ROYALTYPER: An automatic typewriter which permits the punching of a control stencil and use of that stencil to duplicate letters in quantity.

RULE: Type-high typographic element that prints as a line.

RULE-UP TABLE: A squared light table used in lithographic platemaking.

RUN: (C) One performance of a program on a computer.

RUN: (Printing) The total quantity of pieces required in a printing job.

RUNAROUND: Type matter which is set in narrow measure to pass along the side of a cut.

RUNNING HEAD: Name of book and/or chapter title at the head or foot of each page.

RUN OF PAPER: A term applied to color printing on regular paper and presses as distinct from separately printed sections made on special color presses. Abbr.: R.O.P.

RUN OF PRESS: Order to a printer to run off all the paper on hand for a specified job.

RUNOVER: Type which must be run over from one line to another.

S.I.C.: Standard Industrial Classification.

SADDLE STITCHING: Wire staples driven through the back fold of a booklet and clinched in the middle, enabling it to open out flat.

SAFETY PAPER: Paper treated to make visible any attempt to erase or change anything that has been written or printed on its face.

SAFEWAY MAILER: Style of envelope in which the flap is cut into tabs made to fit into slits in the envelope; available in sizes from 6¾ by 9½ to 12¾ by 15½ inches.

SALES PROMOTION: Techniques used by a company to promote the movement of its products and services toward the customer (as contrasted to advertising which is aimed at moving the customer toward the products and services). Sales promotion media are usually distinguished by the fact an advertiser controls the format and the audience, rather than working within the limitations imposed by a publisher or broadcaster.

SALES PROMOTION AGENCY: A business organization which specializes in the creation of all types of promotion material except magazine, newspaper, radio and television advertising.

SALUTATION: Method used at the beginning of a letter to address recipient of a mailing piece.

SAMPLING: Distributing samples of a product to a mailing list.

SANS SERIF: Letters without serifs. Gothic styles of type are sans serif.

SATIN FINISH: Paper with a special smooth finish suggesting satin.

SCALING: Determining dimensions of artwork which is to be enlarged or reduced from the original.

SCAN: (C) To examine sequentially part by part.

SCANNER: A device which color separates and color corrects electronically and records this information on photographic film as continuous tone or halftone. Scanners also may be used to engrave dot structures on materials suitable for printing.

SCANNING: (C) Method of by-passing punch cards for feeding information into the computer. Typewritten or printed characters are read by an electronic device and recorded on magnetic tape.

SCARF ENVELOPE: Style of envelope available in sizes from 4⅝ by 6¾ to 5½ by 8¼ inches.

SCORE: Impressing a line into a sheet of paper or card to facilitate folding.

SCRATCHBOARD: An art technique which involves scratching away portions of a black coating on white board so that the image is formed by the scratched lines.

SCREEN: A term used to indicate the number of dots per inch in a halftone. Coarse screens (60-line, 65-line, 80-line or 85-line) are used for newsprint and other soft-finish paper; screens of 100, 110, 120, 133, 150, and 175 lines and finer are used for smoother and enameled papers. The term "screen" is also used for Ben Day, according to a special numbering code.

SCREENING: Hardening portions of the sensitized carbon tissue by passing light through the transparent lines of the screen in gravure.

SCREEN PROCESS: Silk screen printing.

SCREEN RULING: The number of lines per inch on a halftone screen.

SCREEN SEPARATION: The distance the halftone screen is placed from the light sensitive plate.

SCREEN TINT: A screened appearance or lighter shade of color than the solid. A light value of any color.

SCRIPT: Type similar in appearance to handwriting.

SCRIPTOMATIC: A method of addressing based on the spirit-duplicating principle. Addresses are typed directly onto cards with a special carbon. The system is most frequently used in conjunction with electronic sorting systems such as IBM, Remington Rand and McBee.

SCRUB NEGATIVE OPTION: When the premium offered for a club-type program is so large that the buyer is required to take a minimum number of units without a negative option choice.

SDA: (C) Source Data Automation. A method of recording information in coded forms on paper tapes, punched cards, or tags that can be used over and over again to produce other records without rewriting.

SEARCH: (C) To examine a set of items for those that have a desired property.

SECOND COMING TYPE: Big, black headline type used by newspapers only for the most important stories.

SECONDARY COLOR: Violet, orange, green produced by mixing two primary colors.

SECTIONAL CENTER: A postal facility serving a specified geographical area represented by the first three digits of a zip code.

SECURITY ENVELOPE: Style of envelope with gummed fastenings, available in sizes from 2½ by 4½ to 5 by 9 inches.

SECURITY PAPER: Paper with bond characteristics similar to currency paper. May contain distinctive features and safety features to protect against counterfeiting.

SEE COPY: Proofreader's mark instructing printer to compare proof with original copy.

SELECTRIC: Trade name for a typewriter for which many different kinds of type can be used interchangeably.

SELF-COVER: A cover of the same paper as the inside text pages.

SELF-MAILER: A direct mail piece mailed without an envelope or special binding. Advertising post cards, for example, are self-mailers.

SELF-SEAL: An envelope with special adhesive requiring no moisture for sealing.

SENSE: (C) To read a code mechanically, electrically or electronically.

SENTINEL: (C) A symbol marking the beginning or the end of some element of information.

SEPARATION BY CAMERA: The photo-mechanical isolation or division of colors of an original piece of artwork into their primary hues; each record or negative used for the production of a color plate. See COLOR SEPARATION.

SEPARATION NEGATIVE: A negative made from any single color of a multicolor illustration.

SEQUENTIAL OPERATION: (C) Pertaining to the performance of operations one after another.

SERIAL: (C) Time-sequencing of two or more processes.

SERIAL ACCESS: (C) The process of obtaining data from, or placing data into, storage when there is a sequential relation governing the access time to successive storage locations.

SERIAL OPERATION: (C) An operation whose processes are performed in a time sequence.

SERIF: The fine lines at the end of a type letter, particularly the corners at top and bottom.

SERIGRAPHY: Silk screen printing.

SERVICE BUREAU: (C) An organization with one or more computers that does data processing work on a commercial basis.

SET: The measurement of the length of a line of type.

SET-OFF: Smudging caused by transfer of ink from one printed sheet to another.

SET SIZE: Refers to the width of the body of type (i.e., "8 point, 8 set" means that an em of 8 point type will measure exactly 8 points horizontally; an em of "8 point, 8½ set" means that an em of 8 point type will measure 8½ points in width. Eight point letters in both 8 set and 8½ set are exactly the same in size and appearance, but the 8½ set letter will have more spacing at the sides).

SET SOLID: To set type without spacing between lines.

SEVENTY-TWOMO: (72mo) Book size of 72 leaves or 144 pages.

SEXTO: Book size consisting of 6 leaves or 12 pages.

SHADE: The gradations of a color with reference to its degree of darkness of a color, or gradation of a color with reference to its mixture with black.

SHADOWS: The dark solid and almost solid portions of a picture represented by the largest dots or the solids in a halftone.

SHARPEN: To decrease in strength, as when halftone dots become smaller, opposite of thicken.

SHEET: Cut size or trimmed size of a finished paper.

SHEET FED: Gravure printing produced on separate sheets of paper (in contrast to rotogravure which is done on a continuous web, or roll, of paper).

SHEET AND HALF CAP: Size of paper, 13½ by 24½ inches.

SHEET AND HALF DEMY: Size of paper, 22½ by 26½ inches.

SHEET AND HALF FOOLSCAP: Size of paper, 13¼ by 24½ inches.

SHEET AND HALF POST: Size of paper, 19½ by 23½ inches.

SHEET AND HALF POTT: Size of paper, 12½ by 22½ inches.

SHEET AND THIRD FOOLSCAP: Size of paper, 13¼ by 22 inches.

SHEETING: The process of cutting sheets from a roll of paper.

SHEETWISE: A sheetwise form is one of two forms which lock up separately and run separately on opposite sides of a sheet. Example: A four-page fold printed from two forms of two pages each, pages 1 and 4 (outside form) being printed from one form, and pages 2 and 3 (inside form) being printed on the opposite side of the sheet. Each sheet makes one complete copy, and 2,000 impressions are required to make 1,000 copies. (*See:* WORK AND FLOP, WORK AND TURN, AND WORK AND TWIST.)

SHINGLING: Staggered position of type and halftones on single pages of a saddle-stitched book; the uneven outer edges of pages when a book is opened.

SHORT AND: Proofreader's term for the ampersand. (&)

SHORT FOLD: A method of folding a piece so one or more pages are shorter than other pages.

SHORT DEMY: Size of paper, 14⅜ by 20¾ inches.

SHORT FORM: A form which does not fill an entire lithographic plate.

SHOULDER: (1) Space on the bottom of a piece of type to allow space for descenders and to separate lines. (2) A depressed ledge of metal that surrounds image area in an engraving.

SHOW-THROUGH: Visibility on one side of a piece of paper of the printing on the opposite side or on another sheet.

SIDEHEAD: A headline placed in the margin instead of within the type body.

SIDE SEAM OPEN END: Envelope style available in sizes from 4 by 6¼ to 7½ by 10½ inches.

SIDE STITCHING: Wire staples driven through the side of a book, or a number of signatures, as they lie flat. Also SIDE WIRE.

SIGNATURE: A section of a book, ordinarily obtained by the folding of a single sheet into 8, 12, 16, or more pages.

SIGNATURE CUT: A cut bearing the device or name of a firm or individual.

SILENT READING: A reading of a proof as a check for grammar, continuity and clarity; read without the copy.

SILHOUETTE: An illustration from which the background of the image has been cut or etched away.

SILK SCREEN: A printing process in which ink is transferred to the paper through stretched silk.

SILVERPRINT: Photocopy used as a proof.

SIMULATE: (C) To represent the functioning of a system or process by a symbolic (usually mathematical) analogous representation of it.

SIMULATOR: (C) A computer or model which represents a system and which mirrors or maps the effects of changes in the original, enabling the original to be studied and analyzed by means of the behavior of the model.

SIXTEENMO: (16mo) Book size measuring approximately 4¼ by 6¾ inches with 32 pages.

SIXTY-FOURMO: (64mo) Book size measuring approximately 2 by 3 inches with 128 pages.

SIZING: Rosin or other material incorporated into paper to give water-resisting properties.

SKID: A platform used for storage and movement of printing paper and printed pieces.

SKID: Quantity of paper amounting to approximately 3,000 pounds.

SKIP CHARGE: Special charge for skipping certain names on a mailing list.

SLIP SHEETS: Paper sheets fed between sheets being printed to prevent ink from smearing.

SLITTING: Cutting printed sheets into two or more sections during the printing or folding operations.

SLUG: (1) Line of typeset matter produced on a Linotype or Intertype machine. (2) A blank metal line 6 points in height used for spacing.

SLUGGING: A check of printed lines on a proof against appropriate copy wherein only certain parts of the lines, usually the end words, are identified against the copy. To object is to be sure that a line was not dropped, repeated or transposed.

SLURRING: Smears in the screen formation of halftones.

SMALL CAPS: Printers' language for smaller capital letters of the same font as the regular capital letters of the font.

SOCK: Excessive pressure in printing.

SOFT PAPER: Antique; egg shell; and other low-finish, lightly sized papers of soft body.

SOFTWARE: (C) (1) The collection of man-written solutions and specific instructions needed to solve problems with a computer. (2) All documents needed to guide the operation of a computer (e.g., manuals, programs, flowcharts, etc.).

SOLID (TYPE): Type matter is said to be set solid when no leading has been added.

SOLIDS: One hundred percent tones or colors which have no dots in them when printed.

SOLID-STATE COMPONENT: (C) A component in a computer whose operation depends on electrical activity in solids (e.g., performance of a transistor or crystal diode).

SORT: (C) To arrange data in an ordered sequence.

SORTS: Type kept in storage or ordered as the need arises to replenish type cases used for hand composition.

SOURCE LANGUAGE: (C) A language nearest to the user's usual business or professional language, which enables him to instruct a computer more easily.

SPACE: (C) A place intended for the storage of data (e.g., a place on a printed page or a location in a storage medium).

SPACING: Separation between characters or groups of characters in type. Letterspacing between individual characters. Wordspacing between words. Linespacing between lines.

SPACES: Small pieces of type metal, less than type high, used for spacing between letters and words.

SPECIAL DELIVERY: Mail delivered as received by a post office.

SPECIAL-DELIVERY ENVELOPES: Envelopes embodying a special design and special colors. Around the borders of special-delivery envelopes appear alternating yellow and green dots. On the right side—1⅜ inches from the top of a No. 10 envelope, for example, ¼ inch from the right-hand side, and 1⅞ inches from the bottom—are two yellow horizontal rules enclosing the words, "Special Delivery," which are printed in green. The design of smaller special-delivery envelopes is reduced in proportion.

SPECIAL HANDLING: First class handling enroute of package mail.

SPECIFIER: A name on a mailing list representing one who is in the position to specify the buying of a particular product or service but who does not necessarily place the order.

SPECS: A specific description of work to be processed.

SPEEDAUMAT: A variation of the Addressograph which uses a smaller metal plate.

SPINE: Backbone of a book.

SPIRAL BINDING: A technique involving the threading of a continuous spiral of wire through pre-punched holes.

SPLIT FOUNTAIN: Color printing of two different colors simultaneously.

SPLIT RUN: Division of a generally similar promotion piece into two or more variations, enabling the advertiser to test different copy appeals.

SPONSOR SYSTEM: A method of controlling names on a mailing list by assigning each name and address to a sponsor who is responsible for keeping that listing up to date.

SPOT COLOR: Use of any color which does not attempt to simulate the full spectrum.

SPOT CORRECTIONS: Corrections made or to be made on portions of a form which will not cause a replacement of type or cuts, etc.

SPOTS: Decorative typographical units.

SPOTTING: Removing black and white dots from the photoengraved plate to open up solids or to build up white spots.

SQUARE HALFTONE: A finishing style in which the halftone screen runs to the edge of the printing plate, which is trimmed straight both vertically and horizontally.

SQUARE SERIF: Type in which serifs are the same weight, or heavier than, the main strokes.

SQUEEZE-OUT: A thicker ridge of ink at the outside edges of dots or characters, typical of letterpress printing. It is caused by the pressure of the printing surface against the paper.

STACKING: Placing one enclosure atop others for inserting into a mailing envelope.

STAGING: Application of acid resisting varnish or staging solution to local areas of line or halftone etchings so as to permit further etching of the untreated surface of the plate.

STAMP: A gummed paper device used to show payment of postage.

STAMPING: Printing by impressing type through metal foil and into the surface of the printing surface. Blind stamping uses no foil or ink.

STAMPING DIE: A solid block, usually of brass, but also made of other materials upon which has been engraved the design or lettering to be stamped.

STANDARD INDUSTRIAL CLASSIFICATION: A numerical coding system developed by the Bureau of the Budget used in the classification of business establishments according to the principal end-product made or service performed at that location.

STANDING AD: One which runs in several issues without change.

STANDING TYPE: Type which has been set and is ready for use, or which has been used and is stored for possible future use.

START-UPS: Same as Make-Ready Sheets. Sheets used to get color and register.

STAT: Printer's slang for a Photostat.

STATEMENT STUFFER: A small printed piece designed to be inserted in an envelope carrying a customer's statement of account.

STATIC: An excessive positive or negative electrical charge in a sheet of paper or foil which causes the sheet to be attracted to other sheets or materials.

STEEL ENGRAVING: A printing plate made manually by cutting away non-printing areas, leaving only thin lines in relief.

STICK: A typographer's composing stick.

STEP-AND-REPEAT: A photocomposing technique which makes it possible to repeat the same image from one negative or positive any number of times on a printing plate.

STEP UP: The use of special premiums to get a mail order buyer to increase his unit of purchase.

STEREOTYPE: Reproduction plates made by impressing a form into a pliant mold or matrix and then making a cast of this with type metal.

STET: A proofreader's term meaning "let it stand." Used when a word or sentence has been marked out (deleted) and then the decision is made not to delete it, after all. The material marked for deletion is underlined by a series of dots, and the word "stet" is written in the margin, to instruct the printer to disregard the deletion marks.

STOCK ART: Art sold for use by a number of advertisers.

STOCK CUT: Printing engravings kept in stock by the printer or publisher for occasional use (in contrast to exclusive use).

STOCK FORMATS: Direct mail formats with illustrations and/or headings pre-printed and to which the advertiser adds his own copy.

STOPPER: Advertising slang for a striking headline or illustration intended to attract immediate attention.

STORAGE: (C) A device in which data can be entered and stored and from which it can be retrieved.

STORED PROGRAM: (C) A program stored internally in a data processing system for control of machine function. The normal manner in which EDP systems are controlled.

STORED PROGRAM COMPUTER: (C) A digital computer that stores instructions in its main core and can be programmed to alter its own instructions as though they were data and can subsequently execute these altered instructions.

STRIKE SHEETS: Sheets used to get the lay or position on a press.

STRIP: A paper tape on which a group of names and addresses has been printed.

STRIP: To combine two or more negatives into one illustration.

STRIP FILM: Gelatin process emulsions for line and halftone photography coated on a temporary support, which permits stripping or removal of the negative after fixing and washing of the developed image.

STRIP-IN: To insert additional material into a photographic negative or positive used for platemaking.

STRIP TEST: A method for determining the direction of grain in paper.

STRIPRINTER: A machine for setting cold type in display sizes.

STUBS: A perforated attachment to an order form which the buyer removes for his records before forwarding the order.

STUD HORSE: Large black display type.

STUDIO: A commercial organization which prepares artwork or photography for advertising.

STUDY, APPLICATION: (C) The detailed process of determining a system for using a computer for definite functions or operations.

STUFFER: Advertising enclosures placed in other media (i.e., newspapers, merchandise packages, mailing for other products, etc.).

STYLE: Rules of uniform usage in a printing plant or publishing house. Style refers to such details as capitalization, compounding, punctuation, preferred spelling, etc. *See* DOWN STYLE AND UP STYLE.

SUBROUTINE: (C) A routine that can be part of another routine.

SUBSCRIBER: Individual who has paid to receive a periodical.

SUBSCRIPTION: Contractual agreement by an individual or a firm to purchase one or more copies of a publication for a given period.

SUBSET: (C) Contraction of "subscriber set," refers to a modem installed on a subscriber's premises.

SUBSTANCE: Basic weights adopted to designate regular sizes of various kinds of papers; may refer to a ream or to 1,000 sheets.

SULPHATE: Pulp produced by using sodium sulphate in cooking the wood.

SULPHITE: Pulp made by cooking chips of wood in a sulphite acid.

SUPERCALENDERED PAPER: Paper with a high, glossy surface.

SUPERIMPOSE: Process of printing on a sheet which previously has been printed.

SUPERROYAL: Size of paper, 20 by 28 inches.

SUPPLEMENTARY LIST: Address list which contains names and addresses not in regular mailing sequence.

SURPRINT: Print made from one negative superimposed upon a print from another negative.

SWATCHING: Attaching samples of material to a printed piece.

SWITCHING, MESSAGE: (C) The technique of receiving a message, storing it until the proper outgoing circuit is available, and then transmitting it.

SYMMETRICAL: A layout pattern consisting of two vertical halves which are mirror images of each other.

SYNDICATED MAILING: Mailings prepared for mailing by firms other than the manufacturer or syndicator.

SYNDICATOR: One who makes available prepared direct mail promotion pieces for mailing to its own lists by a list owner. Product fulfillment services are also usually offered.

SYNTHESIS: The process of creating all colors of the spectrum by printing only three primary colors.

TABLE, DECISION: (C) A table of all contingencies that are to be considered in the description of a problem together with the action to be taken.

TABLOID: A pre-printed advertising insert of four or more pages, usually about half the size of a regular newspaper page, designed for inserting into a newspaper.

TABLE SHEETS: Same as pull sheets. Those removed from the run while the press is in operation, checked and then left on a table to be placed back on the stack with the rest of the run.

TABULAR WORK: Composition involving columns with vertical lines and horizontal rules.

TAG ENVELOPE: An envelope punched to serve also as a tag.

TAPE: Perforated paper which directs the action of automatic typesetters.

TAPE: (C) Magnetic tape on which data is recorded.

TEAR SHEET: A page torn from a book or magazine and sent to an advertiser, inquirer, or other person.

TEASER: An advertisement or promotion planned to excite curiosity about a later advertisement or promotion.

TEMPERA: Poster paint, opaque, water-soluble paint; artwork produced using tempera paints.

TELECOMMUNICATIONS: (C) Any transmission or reception of signals or intelligency of any nature, by wire, radio, visual or electromagnetic systems.

TELEPRINTER: (C) Trade name used by Western Union to refer to its telegraph terminal equipment.

TELEPROCESSING: (C) Trademark used by IBM in referring to their equipment used in the data communications field.

TELETYPE: (C) Trademark of the Teletype Corp. A system for transmitting messages over a distance, employing keyboard or paper tape sending and printed receiving.

TELETYPEWRITER: (C) Trade name used by AT&T to refer to telegraph terminal equipment.

TELEX: (C) An automatic Teletype exchange service provided domestically by Western Union.

TERMINAL: (C) A point in a system or communication network at which data can either enter or leave.

TERMINAL UNIT: (C) A device, such as a key-driven or visual display terminal, which can be connected to a computer over a communications circuit and which may be used for either input or output from a location either near or far removed from the computer.

TERTIARY COLORS: Colors produced by mixing two secondary colors.

TEST LISTS: A portion of a mailing list used to test response to a mail order offering.

TEST ROUTINE: (C) A routine which shows whether or not a computer is functioning properly.

TESTING: A preliminary mailing or distribution intended as a preview or pilot before a major campaign. Test mailings are used to determine probable acceptance of a product or service and are usually made to a specially selected list.

TEXT: (1) Editorial material. (2) Body matter set in type. (3) A book paper made with a variety of finishes and used primarily for brochures, booklets, announcements and other commercial printing. (4) A bold typeface based on the handwritten form of the alphabet as developed in Germany.

TEXT TYPE: Body type.

TF: Until Forbid. Entering an order which will continue to be fulfilled until the buyer requests that service be stopped.

THERMOGRAPHY: A method of obtaining raised letter printing by applying a resin powder to fresh ink, heating it to melt and then cooling to form a raised image.

THIN SPACE: Copper spacing material used in typography. Much thinner than regular type metal spacing material.

THIRD CLASS MAIL: Non-personalized mail with delayed handling. Most direct mail advertising is sent Third Class.

TERMS: Methods by which a mail order buyer is required to pay for merchandise or services ordered.

TEXT PAPERS: Printing papers specifically made for use in the manufacture of books.

THIRTY-TWOMO: (32mo) Book size measuring 3¼ by 5 inches; 64 pages.

THREE-COLOR PROCESS: The reproduction of a full-color original by using three colors, usually red, yellow and blue.

THROUGHPUT: (C) Productivity based on all facets of an operation, e.g., a computer with capability of simultaneous operations.

THROWAWAY: An advertisement or promotional piece intended for widespread free distribution. Throwaways are usually printed on cheap stock and delivered by hand, either to passersby or house to house. Broadsides are sometimes referred to as throwaways.

THUMBNAILS: (1) Miniature sketches or dummies of a proposed direct mail piece. (2) Small size portrait engravings.

TIE-IN: Cooperative mailing effort involving two or more advertisers.

TIME, IDLE: (C) Time in which machine is in good operating condition and attended, but not in use.

TIME, PRODUCTION: (C) Good computing time, including checks, and reruns caused by misinformation.

TIME SHARING: (C) The use of a computer for two or more purposes during the same overall time interval.

TINT: A slight trace of color. The presence of a small amount of color usually diffused throughout as white tinged with blue.

TINT BLOCK: A solid plate, without etching or engraving on it, used for printing a color. The density of the color is described in percentages: a 25% tint would be ¼ as strong as the full color, and a 50% tint would be ½ as strong as the full color, etc.

TINT CHART: A paper, booklet, or book showing various colors of ink for selection in color printing. Also called "color chart."

TIP-IN: To paste or glue one or more pages into a bound or stapled book or booklet. Color plates of less than page size may be tipped in by pasting them onto bound pages. The item tipped in is called a "tip-in."

TIP-ON: An item glued to a printed piece.

TITLE PAGE: First full page of a book, bearing its name and that of the author and publisher.

TOENAIL: Quotation mark.

TONE: The shade or degree of a color. A quality or value of a color. The slight modification of a particular color or hue, as true of green.

TONE VALUE: Intensity of a color or a mass of type, as compared to black, white and gray.

TOOLING: Cutting grooves in the photoengraved plate to produce white lines, or cutting away printing surfaces to produce white areas.

TOOTH: Texture of paper wherein it has some degree of roughness to the touch.

TOUCH PLATE: A special plate made to run an additional color or to add portions of a design to gain a more finished or professional look.

TOWN DOTTING: A system for designating the end of one city or town on a mailing list and the beginning of the next. Usually takes the form of a large dot on the last stencil impression or in the space following the last stencil impression.

TRADE CUSTOMS: Standard practices in the graphic arts field, affecting every phase of work.

TRADE PUBLICATIONS: Magazines edited to reach a specific trade, profession or business and not intended for general circulation.

TRAFFIC BUILDER: A direct mail piece intended primarily to attract recipients to the mailer's place of business.

TRANSPARENCY: A transparent positive photograph in color or black and white, in contrast to a negative.

TRANSDUCER: (C) A device which converts energy from one form to another.

TRANSPARENCY: A photographic image to be viewed by transmitted light, usually full-color.

TRANSPOSITION: A typographic error in which two or more characters are transposed (i.e., hte instead of the).

TRIAD: Color harmony achieved by using three colors equidistant from each other on the color wheel.

TRICESIMO SECUNDO: Book size about 3½ by 5½ inches.

TRIM: To cut the edges of a book or other job. Folded forms are trimmed to open the pages.

TRIMETALLIC: An offset plate combining aluminum, copper and steel or zinc.

TRIPLEHEAD LETTERS: Printed letters created on a special Multigraph machine which permits printing of a two-color letterhead, letter body and signature in a single operation.

TRUNCATE: (C) To drop digits of a number of terms of a series, thus lessening precision.

TRUTH TABLE: (C) A table that describes a logic function by listing all possible combinations of input values and indicating all the logically true output values.

TTS: Teletypesetter. A typesetting machine actuated by perforated tape.

TWELVEMO: (12mo) Book size measuring 5 by 7½ inches with 24 pages.

TWENTY-FOURMO: (24mo) Book size measuring 3½ by 6 inches; 48 pages.

TWO COMPARTMENT ENVELOPES: Any envelopes which carry first-class mail in one compartment and third- or fourth-class mail in another, with the resultant saving in postage and the assurance that both the letter and the literature arrive together. (Envelopes of this type are handled in the mail as matter of the third or fourth class, depending on the nature of the contents of the lower class compartment.)

TWO-FLIGHT TESTING: Making a test mailing of one portion of a list and following with a second test of another portion to verify results from the first portion.

TWO-LINE DOUBLE PICA: Name for 44-point type.

TWO-LINE ENGLISH: Name for 28-point type.

TWO-LINE GREAT PRIMER: Name for 36-point type.

TWO-LINE INITIAL: Initial letter with the depth of two lines of text matter.

TWO-LINE PICA: Name for 24-point type.

TWO-ON: Printing jobs where the material to be reproduced is duplicated on the printing plate so that two copies are printed on each sheet. Also: Three On, Four On, etc.

TWO-PIECE SIMPLEX: Loose-leaf binding consisting of two pieces of cover material, hinged and punched so sheets may be inserted between them and held with fasteners.

TWO-UP: Duplicated pages printed at the same time and designed to bind two at a time. Also: Three Up, Four Up, etc.

TWO-TONE: Paper with a different color on each of its sides.

TWX: (C) Teletypewriter Exchange Service. A switched network providing means for interconnecting AT&T Teletypewriter subscribers.

TYPE C PRINT: A color print made directly from a color negative.

TYPE HIGH: A plate which has been mounted to exactly the same height as the printing surface of type, 0.918 of an inch.

TYPE METAL: Usually an alloy of lead, antimony, tin, and brass used in typemaking.

TYPESETTER: A phototypesetting machine.

TYPEWRITER ENVELOPE: Style of envelope with rounded flap, available in sizes from 3⅝ by 6½ to 4⅛ to 9½ inches.

TYPOGRAPHIC ERRORS: Mistakes made when type is set.

TYPOGRAPHY: The process of setting material in type for printing.

TYPRO: Machine for setting display type by cold type composition.

U.C.: Upper case or capital letters.

U&LC: Upper and Lowercase. Capital and small letters.

UNDERCOAT: A clear coating sometimes applied to foil during printing, but before laying on ink. Frequently used under white ink.

UNDERCUTTING: Action of acid in the photoengraving process when it cuts sideways rather than straight down, thus undercutting dots.

UNDERLAY: Pieces of paper pasted under type or cut to bring it to the proper level for printing.

UNDERLINES: Captions appearing below an illustration.

UNIT OF SALE: Description of average dollar amount spent by customers on a mailing list offered for rental.

UNIT RECORD: (C) A term often used to mean a punched card.

UNIT RECORD EQUIPMENT: (C) Electromechanical machines used to process data recorded on punched cards.

UNIVERSAL FRACTIONS: Fractions designed to harmonize with all families in a type category.

UNIVERSE: Total number of individuals which might be included on a mailing list; all those which fit a set of specifications.

UNPACK: (C) To separate diverse information which has been included into one machine item or word.

UPDATE: (C) To put into master file changes required by current information or transactions.

UP FRONT: Securing payment for a product offered by mail order before the product is sent.

UPPER CASE: Capital letters, as distinct from lower case and small caps.

UPRIGHT: A book bound on the longer dimension.

UPS: United Parcel Service.

USP: Unique Selling Proposition. Key selling points in an advertisement.

USPS: United States Postal Service.

UP STYLE: Printing style which prefers maximum use of capital letters.

UP-TIME: (C) Time during which a computer has the power turned on, is not under maintenance, and is known or believed to be operating correctly.

USASCII: (C) United States of America Standard Code for Information Interchange.

UTILITY ENVELOPE: Style of envelope ranging from 3½ by 6¼ to 7½ by 10½ inches in size.

VALIDITY: (C) Correctness.

VALUE: The quality of dark or light in color. Pure values are represented by grays from white to black.

VANDYKE: A proof in the form of a positive print made from a film negative.

V-MAIL: A mailing format developed during World War II and adopted by direct mail advertisers.

VARIABLE DATA: (C) Data or information which is, or is assumed to be, changing.

VARIABLE WORD LENGTH: (C) Refers to a storage device in which the capacity for digits or characters in each unit of data is of variable length.

VARITYPER: Trade name for typewriter for which many different kinds of type can be used interchangeably.

VARNISHING: *See* LAQUERING.

VELOX: A halftone print, made by an engraver, of a photograph. Retouching may thus be done without defacing the original photograph.

VELLUM PAPER: A high-grade ledger paper which imitates parchment.

VERIFICATION: The process of determining the validity of an order by sending a questionnaire to the customer.

VERSO: The left-hand pages of a book or booklet, as opposed to recto, the right-hand page. Verso pages are always even numbered (2, 4, 6, etc.).

VERTICAL PRESS: A printing press on which the type forms are locked vertically, in contradistinction to a flatbed press.

VIGNETTE: An illustration in which the background gradually fades away, in contrast to a silhouette or an illustration with a full background.

VIGNETTE: A halftone in which the tone of the engraving blends almost imperceptibly into the white of the paper.

W.F. Proofreader's abbreviation for Wrong Font.

WALLET FLAP: Style of envelope with a wide, straight flap, available in sizes from 3⅜ by 5⅜ to 3⅞ by 7½ inches.

WARM: Colors which seem to move forward in the viewer's vision, usually reds, oranges and some yellows.

WASH: A drawing done in a wet medium as opposed to a line drawing.

WASH DRAWING: Drawing in which a water-soluble color is applied as a wash.

WASHED OUT: A weak, dissipated, diluted color.

WASTE SHEETS: Printed sheets completely spoiled to the point where they can't be salvaged.

WATS: (C) Wide Area Telephone Service. A service providing a special line allowing the customer to call a certain zone, on a direct dialing basis, for a flat monthly charge.

WATERMARK: A marking pressed into paper in the manufacture; consists of letters, words, or designs.

WEB: Printing paper which comes in rolls.

WEB PRESS: A rotary printing press which prints on rolls of paper.

WEDDING BRISTOLS: Deluxe bristol board made by gluing sheets of all-rag paper together. Basis size, 22½ by 28½ inches; standard weight range, 100 to 180 pounds.

WEDDINGS: Superfine writing paper.

WEIGHT: May refer to the unit weight of a ream, or of 1,000 sheets, or of a specified quantity or substance number of sheet.

WEIGHT: Color density, strength or the ink film thickness printed on the surface of a sheet of paper, foil or other material.

WET PRINTING: Any process of printing where wet ink is printed on top of wet ink of another color.

WHITE MAIL: Incoming mail that is not on a form sent out by the advertiser.

WIDOW: A short line ending a paragraph and appearing at the top of the next column of type. By extension, any short line which ends a paragraph.

WINDOW ENVELOPES: So called because they permit the name and address typed on the enclosure to be read through the envelope itself. They are of three main types: (1) open-face, consisting of a plain, uncovered, die-cut opening; (2) one-piece, in which the window is made in the body of the envelope by impregnating that portion of the paper with a suitable oily material; and (3) two-piece type, with a piece of glassine, cellophane, or some other transparent material affixed over the panel. To be mailable, any type of window envelope must have a panel running parallel to the length of the envelope, and windows must not be closer than 1⅜ inches from the top, or closer to the bottom or either side than ⅜ inch. No "border" around this "window" portion may exceed 5/32 inch in width. Window envelopes are covered by particular restrictions as to printing. These envelopes must bear the return card of the sender, which must consist of the name and address, or post office box number, and city from which mailed. The name of a building will not suffice unless the mailer occupies that building in its entirety.

WING MAILER: Label-affixing device which uses strips of paper on which addresses have been printed.

WIRE SIDE: The under side of a sheet of paper as it comes off a paper-making machine. Opposite of Felt Side.

WIRE STITCHING: The fastening of pages together with wire staples. *See* SADDLE STITCH AND SIDE-WIRE STITCH.

WOODCUT: Printing plate made by carving non-printing areas out of a type-high block of wood.

WORD: (C) A set of characters, occupying one storage location, which is treated as a unit.

WORDSPACING: Additional space added between words in typography.

WORD-TIME: (C) The time required to transport one word from one storage device to another.

WORKING STORAGE: (C) In programming, storage locations reserved for intermediate results.

WORK AND FLOP: Work-and-flop forms are identical to work-and-turn forms except the sheet is turned toward the gripper (or lower) guides. Work-and-flop forms are used when the number of pages, lengthwise of the cylinder, is an uneven number. For example, a 16-page form could be printed work and turn, while a 20-page form would be printed work and flop. If a 20-page form should be run work and turn, the middle pages would back themselves.

WORK AND TUMBLE: Same as Work and Flop.

WORK AND TURN: Work-and-turn forms are those which, when run on one side, back themselves up after the sheet has been turned over, so that the original side guide edge is on the opposite side of the press. Example: In place of printing two forms of two pages each (as described under sheetwise form), the four pages are arranged in one form and printed. The sheets are then turned end for end and printed on the opposite side. If 1,000 folders are to be printed work and turn, the same size as described under sheetwise, a sheet twice the size will be used and 500 sheets printed on both sides, or 1,000 impressions. This will make 1,000 folders, as each sheet when cut will make two folders.

WORK AND TWIST: Work-and-twist forms are those that require two impressions on each half of the sheet to complete the sheet. The second impression is made after twisting the sheets so that new edges are at both the side and gripper (or lower) guides. Used principally in printing double-blank or cross-rule forms.

WORK-UP: Unwanted deposit of ink caused when spacing material is type-high.

WOVE: A paper finish which resembles tightly knit cloth.

WRITE: (C) To transfer information to an output medium; to copy, usually from internal storage to external storage.

WRITING: Paper with a smooth surface, sized to prevent ink from being absorbed.

W.F.: Proofreader's abbreviation for wrong font.

WRONG FONT: Letters of one series (or font) mixed with those of another. In proofreading, indicated by w.f.

XEROGRAPHY: Inkless printing method utilizing static electricity.

X-HEIGHT: The height of primary letters such as a, o, m and x.

X-LINE: The line which marks the top of primary letters.

ZERO SUPPRESSION: (C) The elimination of nonsignificant zeros in a numeral.

ZINC: Synonym for a line cut, in contrast to a halftone.

ZIP-CODE: A five-digit number used to identify areas of postal delivery.

ZIP-A-TONE: Transparent sheets imprinted with various patterns and used to create tonal effects in line engravings.

ZONE: (C) A portion of internal storage set aside for a particular purpose.

Appendix E

COPYRIGHT LAW OF THE UNITED STATES

What Is a Copyright

A copyright is a form of protection given by the law of the United States (Title 17, U.S. Code) to the authors of literary, dramatic, musical, artistic, and other intellectual works. The owner of a copyright is granted by law certain exclusive rights in his work such as:

- the right to print, reprint, and copy the work.
- the right to sell or distribute copies of the work.
- the right to transform or revise the work by means of dramatization, translation, musical arrangement, or the like.
- the right to record the work.
- the right to perform the work publicly, if it is a literary, dramatic, or musical work.

The rights granted by the copyright law are not unlimited in scope. For example, recording rights in musical works are limited by the so-called "compulsory license" provision, which permits recordings upon payment of certain royalties after the initial recording has been authorized by the copyright owner of the musical composition. In the case of nondramatic literary works and musical compositions, the performance right is limited to public performances for profit.

Who Can Claim Copyright

Only the author or those deriving their rights through him can rightfully claim copyright. Mere ownership of a manuscript, painting, or other copy does not necessarily give the owner the right to copyright. In the case of works made for hire, it is the employer, and not the employee, who is regarded as the author.

There is no provision for securing a blanket copyright to cover all the works of a particular author. Each work must be copyrighted separately if protection is desired.

Minors may claim copyright. However, state law may regulate or control the conduct of business dealings involving copyrights owned by minors; for information on this subject, it would be well to consult an attorney.

What Can Be Copyrighted

The copyright law (Title 17, U.S. Code) lists 14 broad classes of works in which copyright may be claimed, with the provision that these are not to limit the subject matter of copyright. Within the classes are the following kinds of works:

Books (Class A). Published works of fiction and nonfiction, poems, compilations, composite works, directories, catalogs, annual publications, information in tabular form, and similar text matter, with or without illustrations, that appear as a book, pamphlet, leaflet, card, single page, or the like.

Periodicals (Class B). Publications, such as newspapers, magazines, reviews, newsletters, bulletins, and serial publications, that appear under a single title at intervals of less than a year. Also contributions to periodicals, such as stories, cartoons, or columns published in magazines or newspapers.

Lectures or similar productions prepared for oral delivery (Class C). Unpublished works such as lectures, sermons, addresses, monologs, recording scripts, and certain forms of television and radio scripts.

Dramatic and dramatico-musical compositions (Class D). Published or unpublished dramatic works such as the acting versions of plays for the stage, for filming, radio, television, and the like, as well as pantomimes, ballets, operas, operettas, etc.

Musical compositions (Class E). Published or unpublished musical compositions (other than dramatico-musical compositions) in the form of visible notation, with or without words. Also new versions of musical compositions, such as adaptations, arrangements, and editing when it represents original authorship. The words of a song, unaccompanied by music, are not registerable in Class E.

Maps (Class F). Published cartographic representations of area, such as terrestrial maps and atlases, marine charts, celestial maps, and such three-dimensional works as globes and relief models.

Works of art; or models or designs for works of art (Class G). Published or unpublished works of artistic craftsmanship, insofar as their form but not their mechanical or utilitarian aspects are concerned, such as artistic jewelry, enamels, glassware, and tapestries, as well as works belonging to the fine arts, such as paintings, drawings, and sculpture.

Reproductions of works of art (Class H). Published reproductions of existing works of art in the same or a different medium, such as a lithograph, photoengraving, etching, or drawing of a painting, sculpture, or other work of art.

Drawings or sculptural works of a scientific or technical character (Class I). Published or unpublished diagrams or models illustrating scientific or technical works, such as an architect's or an engineer's blueprint, plan, or design, a mechanical drawing, an astronomical chart, or an anatomical model.

Photographs (Class J). Published or unpublished photographic prints and filmstrips, slide films, and individual slides. Photoengravings and other photomechanical reproductions of photographs are registered in Class K.

Prints, pictorial illustrations, and commercial prints or labels (Class K). Published prints or pictorial illustrations, greeting cards, picture postcards, and similar prints, produced by means of lithography, photoengraving, or other methods of reproduction. A print or label, not a trademark, published in connection with the sale or advertisement of articles of merchandise also is registered in this class.

Motion-picture photoplays (Class L). Published or unpublished motion pictures that are dramatic in character, such as feature films, filmed or recorded television plays, short subjects and animated cartoons, musical plays, and similar productions having a plot.

Motion pictures other than photoplays (Class M). Published or unpublished nondramatic motion pictures, such as news films, travel films, nature studies, documentaries, training or promotional films, and filmed or recorded television programs or nontheatrical motion pictures having no plot.

Sound recordings (Class N). Published sound recordings, such as phonograph discs, tape cassettes and cartridges, player-piano rolls, and similar material objects in which a series of sounds are fixed. The copyright law covers only those sound recordings that are fixed and first published on or after February 15, 1972. Registration in Class N is not a substitute for registration for the music or other copyrightable matter recorded, and is not appropriate for a sound track when it is an integrated part of a motion picture.

What Cannot Be Copyrighted

Even though a work does not fit conveniently into one of the 14 classes, this does not necessarily mean that it is uncopyrightable. However, there are several categories of material which are generally not eligible for statutory copyright protection. These include among others:

- Titles, names, short phrases, and slogans; familiar symbols or designs; mere variations of typographic ornamentation, lettering, or coloring; mere listings of ingredients or contents.
- Ideas, plans, methods, systems, or devices, as distinguished from a description or illustration.
- Works that are designed for recording information and do not in themselves convey information, such as blank forms to be used as time cards, account books, diaries, bank checks, score cards, address books, report forms, and the like.
- Works consisting entirely of information that is common property and containing no original authorship. For example: standard calendars, height and weight charts, tape measures and rulers, schedules of sporting events, and lists or tables taken from public documents or other common sources.

Unpublished Works

An unpublished work is generally one for which copies have not been sold, placed on sale, or made available to the public. Unpublished works are eligible for one or the other of two types of protection:

Common Law Literary Property. This type of protection against unauthorized use of an unpublished work is a matter of state law, and arises automatically when the work is created. It requires no action in the Copyright Office. It may last as long as the work is unpublished, but it ends when the work is published or when statutory copyright is secured by registration.

Statutory Copyright. This is the protection afforded by the federal law upon compliance with certain requirements. Only the following types of works can be registered for statutory copyright before they have been published: musical compositions, dramas, works of art, drawings and sculptural works of a scientific or technical character, photographs, motion pictures, and works prepared for oral delivery. There is no requirement that any of these works be registered for statutory copyright in unpublished form, but there may be advantages in doing so. If they are registered in their unpublished form, the law requires that another registration be made after publication with the copyright notice affixed to the copies (see page 7).

The following types of material *cannot* be registered for statutory protection in unpublished form: books (including short stories, poems, and narrative outlines), prints, maps, reproductions of works of art, periodicals, commercial prints and labels, and sound recordings. These works secure statutory copyright by the act of publication with notice of copyright.

Copyright Procedure for an Unpublished Work

Statutory copyright for unpublished works is secured by registering a claim in the Copyright Office. For this purpose it is necessary to forward the following material:

Application Form. The appropriate form may be ordered from the Copyright Office from the list printed on pages 10 and 11. Forms are supplied without charge.

Copy. In the case of manuscripts of music, dramas, lectures, etc., one complete copy should accompany the application. It will be retained by the Copyright Office. For photographs, deposit one photographic print. Special requirements concerning motion pictures, and certain graphic and artistic works, are stated on the application forms.

Fee. The registration fee for unpublished works is $6.

Published Works

Published works are works that have been made available to the public in some way, usually by the sale or public distribution of copies. The copyright law defines the "date of publication" as "the earliest date when copies of the first authorized edition were placed on sale, sold, or publicly distributed by the proprietor of the copyright or under his authority, . . ."

No specific number of copies or method of distribution is required for a general publication. However, it is sometimes difficult to determine the dividing line between a general publication and a limited distribution (such as sending copies to agents, publishers, or some other limited group for a specific purpose). If you are in doubt about publication in a particular case, it may be advisable to consult an attorney.

The rights in a work will be permanently lost unless all published copies bear a notice of copyright in the form and position described on pages 7 and 8. When a work has been published without notice of copyright it falls into the public domain and becomes public property. After that happens it serves no purpose to add the notice to copies of the work, and doing so may be illegal.

In the case of works that cannot be registered before publication, it is the act of publication with notice of copyright, rather than registration in the Copyright Office, that secures statutory copyright. While the Copyright Office registers claims to copyright, it does not grant copyright protection.

Copyright Procedure for Published Works

Three steps should be taken to secure and maintain statutory copyright in a published work:

- *Produce copies with copyright notice.* Produce the work in copies by printing or other means of reproduction. It is essential that all copies bear a copyright notice in the required form and position (see pages 7 and 8).
- *Publish the work.*
- *Register your claim in the Copyright Office.* Promptly after publication, you should send the following material to the Copyright Office:

  APPLICATION FOR REGISTRATION. The appropriate form may be requested from the Copyright Office from the list printed on pages 10 and 11.

  COPIES. Send two copies of the best edition of the work as published.

  FEE. The registration fee for published works is $6.

NOTE: The law requires that, after a work is published with the prescribed notice, two copies "shall be promptly deposited," accompanied by a claim of copyright (that is, an application for registration) and the registration fee.

The Copyright Notice

Form of the Notice. As a general rule, the copyright notice should consist of three elements:

- *The word "Copyright," the abbreviation "Copr.," or the symbol ©.* Use of the symbol © may have advantages in securing copyright in countries that are members of the Universal Copyright Convention.
- The name of the copyright owner (or owners).
- The year date of publication. This is ordinarily the year in which copies are first placed on sale, sold, or publicly distributed by the copyright owner or under his authority. However, if the work has previously been registered for copyright in unpublished form, the notice should contain the year date of registration for the unpublished version. Or, if there is new copyrightable matter in the published version,

it is advisable to include both the year date of the unpublished registration and the year date of publication.

These three elements should appear together on the copies. Example:

© John Doe 1973

Optional Form of Notice. A special form of the notice is permissible for works registrable in Classes F through K (maps; works of art, models or designs for works of art; reproductions of works of art; drawings or sculptural works of a scientific or technical character; photographs; prints and pictorial illustrations; and prints or labels used for articles of merchandise). This special notice may consist of the symbol ©, accompanied by the initials, monogram, mark, or symbol of the copyright owner, if the owner's name appears upon some accessible portion of the copies. A detachable tag bearing a copyright notice is not acceptable as a substitute for a notice permanently affixed to the copies.

Position of the Notice. For a book or other publication printed in book form, the copyright notice should appear upon the title page or the page immediately following. The "page immediately following" is normally the reverse side of the page bearing the title. For a periodical, the notice should appear upon the title page, upon the first page of text, or under the title heading. For a musical composition, the notice may appear either upon the title page or upon the first page of music.

Notice for Unpublished Works. The law does not specify a notice for unpublished works. Nevertheless, to avoid the danger of inadvertent publication without notice, it may be advisable for an author to affix notices to any copies that leave his control.

How Long Does Copyright Protection Last

The first term of statutory copyright runs for 28 years. The term begins on the date the work is published with the notice of copyright, or, in the case of unpublished works registered in the Copyright Office, on the date of registration. A copyright may be renewed for a second term of 28 years if an acceptable renewal application and fee are received in the Copyright Office during the last year of the original term of copyright, which is measured from the exact date on which the original copyright began. Recent Acts of Congress have extended second-term copyrights that would have expired on or after September 19, 1962; however, these extensions have no effect on the time limits for renewal registration. For further information about renewal copyright and these extensions, write to the Copyright Office.

International Copyright Protection

If a work is by an author who is neither a citizen nor a domiciliary of the United States, special conditions determine whether or not the work can be protected by U.S. copyright. Specific questions on this subject, and questions about securing protection for U.S. works in foreign countries, should be addressed to the Register of Copyrights, Library of Congress, Washington, D. C. 20559.

Transfer or Assignment of Statutory Copyright

A copyright may be transferred or assigned by an instrument in writing, signed by the owner of the copyright. The law provides for the recordation in the Copyright Office of transfers of copyright. The original signed instrument should be submitted for the purpose of recording. It will be returned following recordation. For the most effective protection, an assignment executed in the United States should be recorded within 3 months from the date of execution. Assignments executed abroad should be recorded within 6 months. For information about assignments and related documents, request Circular 10.

Application Forms

The following forms are provided by the Copyright Office, and may be obtained free of charge upon request:

*Class A	Form A: Published book manufactured in the United States of America.
*Class A or B	Form A-B Foreign: Book or periodical manufactured outside the United States of America (except works subject to the ad interim provisions of the Copyright Law of the United States of America; see Form A-B Ad Interim). Form A-B Ad Interim: Book or periodical in the English language manufactured and first published outside the United States of America and subject to the ad interim provisions of the Copyright Law of the United States of America.
*Class B	Form B: Periodical manufactured in the United States of America. Form B: Contribution to a periodical manufactured in the United States of America.
Class C	Form C: Lecture or similar production prepared for oral delivery.

Class D	Form D: Dramatic or dramatico-musical composition.
Class E	Form E: Musical composition by an author who is a citizen or domiciliary of the United States of America or which is first published in the United States of America. Form E Foreign: Musical composition by an author who is not a citizen or domiciliary of the United States of America and which is not first published in the United States of America.
*Class F	Form F: Map.
Class G	Form G: Work of art; model or design for work of art.
*Class H	Form H: Reproduction of a work of art.
Class I	Form I: Drawing or plastic work of a scientific or technical character.
Class J	Form J: Photograph.
*Class K	Form K: Print or pictorial illustration. Form KK: Print or label used for article of merchandise.
Class L or M	Form L-M: Motion picture.
*Class N	Form N: Sound recording. Form R: Renewal copyright. Form U: Notice of use of musical composition on mechanical instruments.

Mailing Instructions

Address. All communications should be addressed to the Register of Copyrights, Library of Congress, Washington, D. C. 20559.

Fees. Do not send cash. Fees sent to the Copyright Office should be in the form of a money order, check, or bank draft, payable to the Register of Copyrights.

Mailing. Processing of the material will be more prompt if the application, copies, and fee are all mailed in the same package.

Available Information

This information attempts to answer some of the questions that are frequently asked about copyright. For a list of other material

*Not to be used for unpublished material.

published by the Copyright Office, write for "Publications of the Copyright Office." Any requests for Copyright Office publications or special questions relating to copyright problems not dealt with here should be addressed to the Register of Copyrights, Library of Congress, Washington, D. C. 20559.

The Copyright Office cannot give legal advice. If you need information or guidance on matters such as disputes over the ownership of a copyright, getting a work published, obtaining royalty payments, or prosecuting possible infringers, it may be necessary to consult an attorney.

Appendix F

PRINCIPAL BUSINESS DIRECTORIES

AB FUN RIDE SURVEY. Lists U.S. ride manufacturers showing type of unit, capacity, and price. Also includes importers and foreign manufacturers of the equipment. Arranged alphabetically. 40 pp. AMUSEMENT BUSINESS, 2160 Patterson St., Cincinnati, Ohio 45214.

ACCOUNTING INFORMATION SOURCES. Complete listing of current accounting literature. Three sections: background of modern accounting; associations which represent the entire profession; literature covering the regulation of accounting and auditing practices by U.S. Federal agencies. Alphabetically arranged by entry. Includes listing of Basic Accounting Library. Appendixes. Author and subject indexes. 420 pp. GALE RESEARCH CO., Book Tower, Detroit, Mich. 48226.

AD CHANGE. Designed to give subscribers up-to-the-minute news of changes in the national advertising field. Issued weekly giving agency appointments and changes in personnel in the field. NATIONAL REGISTER PUBLISHING CO. INC., 5201 Old Orchard Rd., Skokie, Ill. 60076.

ADVERTISERS ANNUAL. An alphabetical list of all British Firms engaged in advertising and selling, covering newspapers and magazines, outdoor publicity and posters, commercial television, radio, and cinema, advertising agents, consultants and public relations; direct mail agents; marketing specialist; etc., 1,260 pp. Annually. INTERNATIONAL PUBLICATIONS SERVICE, 114 E. 32 St., New York, N.Y. 10016.

ADVERTISING, EDITORIAL, AND TELEVISION ART AND DESIGN ANNUAL. Contains an alphabetically classified directory of products and services in the graphic field. Also other illustrated information is included. 576 pp. Annual. WATSON-GUPTILL PUBLICATIONS, One Astor Plaza, New York, N.Y. 10036.

ADVERTISING SPECIALTY REGISTER. Directory contains entries of approximately 1,000 names and addresses of firms selling through advertising specialty distributors and jobbers—names of executives, products, and trade names. Published by ADVERTISING SPECIALTY INSTITUTE, 4730 Chestnut St., Philadelphia, Penn. 19139. Available to trade members only.

AERONAUTICAL ENGINEERING—A SPECIAL BIBLIOGRAPHY. A selected bibliography on aeronautical engineering. 132 pp. NATIONAL TECHNICAL INFORMATION SERVICE, Springfield, Va. 22151.

AGENT, THE. Lists suppliers of fabrics, trimmings, services and equipment used in the garment manufacturing industry. Semi-Annual. HALPER PUBLISHING CO., 300 W. Adams St., Chicago, Ill. 60606.

AGING, DIRECTORY OF NATIONAL ORGANIZATIONS WITH PROGRAMS IN THE FIELD OF. An alphabetical listing of 300 private, nongovernmental agencies representing a broad spectrum of organizations—social welfare, unions, professional groups, churches—whose programs directly or tangentially serve the interests of older people. 95 pp. NATIONAL COUNCIL OF THE AGING, INC., 1828 L St., N.W., Washington, D.C. 20036.

AGRICULTURE HANDBOOK 305. PROFESSIONAL WORKERS AND STATE AGRICULTURE EXPERIMENT STATIONS AND OTHER COOPERATING STATE INSTITUTIONS. Published by the UNITED STATES GOVERNMENT PRINTING OFFICE, Supt. of Documents, Washington, D.C. 20402.

AIA GUIDE TO NEW YORK CITY. Describes thousands of architecturally interesting buildings in New York City. Produced by the American Institute of Architects. 464 pp. MACMILLAN & CO., 866-3rd Ave., New York, N.Y. 10022.

AIR CARGO GUIDE. An index of all cargo airlines, their routes, flights, freight charges, etc. 186 pp. Monthly. REUBEN H. DONNELLEY CORP., 2000 Clearwater Dr., Oak Brook, Ill. 60521.

AIR-CONDITIONING & REFRIGERATION WHOLESALERS DIRECTORY. A list of 740 member air-conditioning and refrigeration wholesalers with their addresses, telephone numbers, and official representatives. Arranged alphabetically by region, state, and city. 52 pp. Annually. AIR-CONDITIONING & REFRIGERATION WHOLESALERS, 22371 Newman Ave., Dearborn, Mich. 48124.

AIR FORWARDER. A listing of air freight forwarders and cargo agents. Annual. REUBEN H. DONNELLEY CORP., 711 W. 3rd Ave., New York, N.Y. 10017.

AIRLINE INDUSTRY DIRECTORY OF PUBLICATIONS. Lists members of the Air Transport Association of America, and bibliography of Association publications. 20 pp. Published by the AIR TRANSPORT ASSOCIATION OF AMERICA, 1000 Connecticut Ave., N.W., Washington, D.C. 20036.

AIRPORT EQUIPMENT REDBOOK DIRECTORY. Information on airport ground support equipment, materials, supplies and services. Annual. AIRPORT SERVICES MANAGEMENT, 731 Hennepin Ave., Minneapolis, Minn. 55403.

AIRPORT REFERENCE. Describes manufacturers and their airport equipment products. Annual. OCCIDENTAL PUBLISHING CO., 1411½ Kenneth Ave., Glendale, California 91201.

AIR SHIPPERS MANUAL. Manual contains a list of American and foreign offices of domestic and international airlines: I.A.T.A.—authorized cargo agents and C.A.B.—registered air freight forwarders. Listing of airline services to all parts of the world, and including air freight statistics, tables, charts, and graphs pertaining to the air cargo industry. 164 pp. Annually. REUBEN H. DONNELLEY CORP., 711 W. 3rd Ave., New York, N.Y. 10017.

AMATEUR CHAMBER MUSIC PLAYERS. Roster contains 5,000 amateur players of chamber music in the United States and players in 70 foreign countries, giving names, addresses, telephone numbers, instruments played, and a grading of relative abilities of each player. 56 pp. Biennially. Published by AMATEUR CHAMBER MUSIC PLAYERS, Box 66A, Vienna, Va. 22180.

AMERICAN APPAREL MANUFACTURERS' ASSOCIATION DIRECTORY OF MEMBERS AND ASSOCIATE MEMBERS. Contains data on approximately 800 member firms of the American Apparel Manufacturers Association, listing personnel by title. Also provides information on purchasing agents, merchandise manufactured, number of plants, and lists suppliers to the trade. Annually. AMERICAN APPAREL MANUFACTURERS' ASSOCIATION, INC., 1611 N. Kent St., Arlington, Va. 22209.

AMERICAN ART DIRECTORY. Describes activities of over 3,300 U.S. and Canadian museums, art schools, and art organizations arranged alphabetically by state, province and city. Museums listings include names of key officials and data on special collections and publications. Name of head and registration data are shown for the art schools. 536 pp. R. R. BOWKER CO., 1180 Ave. of the Americas, New York, N.Y. 10036.

AMERICAN BANK DIRECTORY. Consists of an alphabetically arranged list of 14,000 national, state, savings, private banks and trust companies—telephone number, address, date established, transit number, officers, directors, principal correspondents, condensed statement of condition, and out-of-city branches. Semiannually. McFADDEN BUSINESS PUBLICATIONS, 6364 Warren Dr., Norcross, Ga. 30071.

AMERICAN CRAFTS GUIDE. A nationwide directory listing 3,000 craft shops, studios, museums, galleries, workshops, supply houses, places of instruction and sources of Indian work and folk art. Also lists major crafts, fairs and festivals in the U.S. 222 pp. THE H. M. GOUSHA CO., 2001 the Alameda, P.O. Box 6227, San Jose, Calif. 95150.

AMERICAN INSTITUTE OF AERONAUTICS AND ASTRONAUTICS ROSTER. 23,000 professional members, aerospace scientists and engineers, of the AIAA. Arranged alphabetically by names and organizations. 340 pp. Biannually. AMERICAN INSTITUTE OF AERONAUTICS AND ASTRONAUTICS, 1290 Avenue of the Americas, New York, N.Y. 10019.

AMERICAN NEEDLE TRADES DIRECTORY. A classified list of manufacturers and suppliers of fabrics, machinery, trimmings and factory equipment for the men's and women's garment manufacturing industry. KOGOS PUBLICATIONS CO., 77 Maple Drive, Great Neck, N.Y. 11021.

AMERICAN SOCIETY OF APPRAISERS—DIRECTORY OF MEMBERS. Directory contains a complete roster of the approximately 3,000 certified regular and senior members of the American Society of Appraisers. Annually. AMERICAN SOCIETY OF APPRAISERS, Dulles International Airport, P.O. Box 17265, Washington, D.C. 20041.

AMERICAN STOCK EXCHANGE, INC. DIRECTORY. Publication consists of entries of regular and associate members of the American Stock Exchange—officials. Member organizations, Exchange staff, and executives of member organizations. Semiannually. COMMERCE CLEARING HOUSE, INC., 4025 W. Peterson Ave., Chicago, Ill. 60646.

AMEX DATABOOK. Provides a membership, company list, trading volume, administration and information services of the exchange, with data on each. Also a list of publications is included. 60 pp. AMERICAN STOCK EXCHANGE, 86 Trinity Pl., New York, N.Y. 10006.

AMUSEMENT BUSINESS BUYERS' GUIDE. Directory contains an alphabetically arranged, classified listing of approximately 2,500 amusement and recreation equipment manufacturers, suppliers and service firms. 120 pp. Annually. BILLBOARD PUBLISHING CO., 1917 West End Ave., Nashville, Tenn. 37203.

ANIMALS NEXT DOOR, THE. A guide to over 400 zoos and aquariums of the Americas published in cooperation with the National Recreation and Park Assoc., Washington, D.C. Describes the contents of each, visiting hours, fees, etc. Also describes factual material about zoos, endangered species and other important information. 170 pp. FLEET ACADEMIC EDITIONS INC., 160 Fifth Ave., New York, N.Y. 10010.

A.O.P.A. AIRPORT DIRECTORY. Lists 11,500 airports, seaplane bases, heliports in the U.S. geographically and alphabetically. 475 pp. Annual. AIRCRAFT OWNERS AND PILOTS ASS'N., Air Rights Bldg., 7315 Wisconsin Ave., Washington, D.C. 20014.

APPAREL TRADES BOOK. Publication contains a grouping of entries providing a listing of approximately 110,000 retail and wholesale apparel enterprises, with financial ratings noted for each. Published by CREDIT CLEARING HOUSE DIVISION of DUN AND BRADSTREET, INC., 99 Church St., New York, N.Y. 10007.

ARCHITECTURE, MEMBER AND ASSOCIATE MEMBER SCHOOLS OF THE ASSOCIATION OF COLLEGIATE SCHOOLS OF. Directory provides material on 95 American and Canadian schools that are members and associate members of the Association of Collegiate Schools of Architecture, noting name of school, address, and name of head or dean of each. ASSOCIATION OF COLLEGIATE SCHOOLS OF ARCHITECTURE, INC., 1735 New York Ave., N.W., Washington, D.C. 20006.

ART BIBLIOGRAPHIES. A new international reference service covering the literature published in Art and Design and comprised of three bibliographical series: Art bibliographies Modern: Art bibliographies Current Titles: are Art bibliographies Historical. Consult publisher for further information. ABC-CLIO INC., 2040 A.P.S., Santa Barbara, Calif. 93103.

ASSOCIATION OF DIESEL SPECIALISTS MEMBERSHIP DIRECTORY. A list of over 200 service and supply specialists in diesel parts. Listed alpha-geographically. Published in the September issue of FLEET MANAGEMENT NEWS, 300 W. Lake St., Chicago, Ill. 60606.

AUDIO-VISUAL CATALOG DIRECTORY. Information on motion pictures, film strips, slides, sound recordings and video tapes that the federal government produces and either sells or loans for educational purposes. NATIONAL AUDIO-VISUAL CENTER, National Archives and Records Service, General Services Administration, Washington, D.C. 20409.

AUDIO-VISUAL COMMUNICATIONS ANNUAL BUYING GUIDE TO AV EQUIPMENT AND SERVICES. An alphabetical listing of products and services to the audio-visual communications industry. Listed are still projects, silent and sound, motion picture supplies and equipment, color labs, etc. 118 pp. Annual. UNITED BUSINESS PUBLICATIONS INC., 750 Third Ave., New York, N.Y. 10017.

AUDIO-VISUAL EQUIPMENT DIRECTORY. A list of 2,200 items of audio-visual equipment, alphabetically by company within 67 categories. 512 pp. Annually. NATIONAL AUDIO-VISUAL ASSOCIATION, INC., 3150 Spring St., Fairfax, Va. 22030.

AUDIO-VISUAL MARKET PLACE. Provides company names, addresses and key personnel and product lines for all active producers, distributors and other sources of AV learning materials. Also includes: national, professional and trade organizations concerned with AV; educational TV and radio stations; manufacturers of AV hardware, with full address, key personnel, etc.; AV dealers, contract production services; a bibliography of reference works on AV materials; etc. 293 pp. R. R. BOWKER CO. 1180 Avenue of the Americas, New York, N.Y. 10036.

AUDIO-VISUAL RESOURCE GUIDE, THE. Designed for use in religious education, this cumulative edition includes classified evaluations of more than 2,500 current church-related audio-visual materials. Materials include under such headings as The Bible-Old Testament background, history of the Scriptures, contents of the Old Testament, concepts of God, historical and narrative literature, ethics, mental health, parent training, intergroup relations, problems of war and peace. FRIENDSHIP PRESS, P.O. Box 37844, Cincinnati, Ohio 45237.

AUTO SUPPLIES AND HARDWARE CHAINS. Publication names approximately 1,900 chain stores operating over 38,000 stores in the United States; includes listings of buyers' names, products handled, number of stores operated, and executive personnel. Annually. CHAIN STORE GUIDE, 425 Park Ave., New York, N.Y. 10022.

AUTO TRIM NEWS DIRECTORY OF PRODUCT SOURCES. Lists manufacturers and their products servicing the auto trim industry. Annual. NATIONAL ASSOC. OF AUTO TRIM SHOPS, 129 Broadway, Lynbrook, N.Y. 11563.

AUTOMOTIVE YEARBOOK, WARD'S. Contains 600 automotive equipment and accessory industry executives listed alphabetically by company. Included are company and product listings and other statistical information. 284 pp. Annually. WARD'S COMMUNICATIONS, INC., 28 West Adams St., Detroit, Mich. 48226. Free to subscribers to "Ward's Automotive Reports."

BANK DIRECTORY, AMERICAN. Consists of an alphabetically arranged list of 14,000 national, state, savings, private banks and trust companies—telephone number, address, date established, transit number, officers, directors, principal correspondents, condensed statement of condition, and out-of-city branches. Semiannually. McFADDEN BUSINESS PUBLICATIONS, 6364 Warren Dr., Norcross, Ga. 30071. National edition.

BANK MARKETING BIBLIOGRAPHY. A selected bibliography of books and other materials to aid those in bank marketing. Listings are annotated with pertinent information. THE AMERICAN BANKERS ASSN., Marketing Division, 1120 Connecticut Ave., N.W., Washington, D.C. 20036. 125 pp.

BASIC BOOKS IN THE MASS MEDIA. Contains an annotated by subject booklist of 665 publications covering publishing, general communications, broadcasting, film, magazines, newspapers, advertising, indexes, scholarly and professional periodicals. 252 pp. UNIVERSITY OF ILLINOIS PRESS, Urbana, Ill. 61801.

BEAUTY AND BARBER BUYING GUIDE. A directory of manufacturers, their products and brand names, alphabetically according to categories. Also includes beauty and barber supply dealers and schools. Over 5,000 listings included. 186 pp. Annual. SERVICE PUBLICATIONS INC., 100 Park Ave., New York, N.Y. 10017.

BEAUTY AND BARBER SUPPLY DEALERS, DIRECTORY OF. Contains listings of approximately 1,600 beauty and barber shop suppliers—owners' names, number of salesmen, territory covered and type of customers. Maintained in current condition by issuance of Supplements every 3 to 4 months. NATIONAL BEAUTY AND BARBER MANUFACTURERS' ASSOCIATION, 100 Park Ave., New York, N.Y. 10017.

BEST REFERENCE BOOKS. Contains a selected 818 substantial reference titles from over 12,000 reviews in the seven volumes of ARBA. 448 pp. LIBRARIES UNLIMITED, P.O. Box 263, Littleton, Colo. 80160.

BIBLIOGRAPHIC GUIDE TO BUSINESS AND ECONOMICS. Includes comprehensive cataloging and bibliographic information for Business and Economics including Economic theory, population, demography, economic history, land, agriculture, transportation and communication, commerce, business administration, finance, etc. 1,935 pages, 3 volumes. G. K. HALL & CO., 70 Lincoln St., Boston, Mass. 02111.

BIBLIOGRAPHIC GUIDE TO CONFERENCE PUBLICATIONS. A comprehensive guide for acquisitions, cataloging and research for locating proceedings, reports and summaries of conferences, meetings, and symposia, as well as collections or partial collections of papers presented at conferences in all languages and subjects. G. K. HALL & CO., 70 Lincoln St., Boston, Mass. 02111.

BIBLIOGRAPHIC GUIDE TO LAW. Reference source for new publications in the legal field including United States Law, International law, International arbitration, Treaties and foreign law, etc. 1,254 pp. 2 volumes. G. K. HALL & CO., 70 Lincoln St., Boston, Mass. 02111.

BIBLIOGRAPHIC INDEX. Bibliographies in English and foreign languages, including those published separately as books of pamphlets and those appearing as parts of books or pamphlets are covered. In addition over 2,200 periodicals are regularly examined for bibliographical material. Material is listed by name of author under subject headings. H. W. WILSON CO., 950 University Ave., Bronx, N.Y. 10452.

BIBLIOGRAPHY OF PUBLICATIONS OF UNIVERSITY BUREAUS OF BUSINESS AND ECONOMIC RESEARCH. A reference guide to those publications of schools of business and economics which do not appear in traditional library indexes. Lists books, bulletins, monographs, working papers and periodicals covering a wide range of subjects—from economics, pollution and environment, business management, etc. UNIVERSITY OF COLORADO, Business Research Division, Boulder, Colo. 80302. Annual. 200 pp.

BIBLIOGRAPHY ON PHYSICAL DISTRIBUTION MANAGEMENT. An annual publication supplementing the 1967 bibliography with entries in nine categories such as physical distribution concept, legal and public policy sources, handbooks and general reference, etc. NATIONAL COUNCIL ON PHYSICAL DISTRIBUTION MGT., 222 W. Adams St., Chicago, Ill. 60606.

BIOGRAPHICAL DICTIONARIES AND RELATED WORKS. Entries of 4,829 who's who's, directories, encyclopedias, rosters, histories, professional guides, portrait and biography indexes and catalogs, registers, dictionaries of anonyms and pseudonyms and other sources of biographical information about persons of note throughout the world. Includes title, subject and occupational indexes. 1056 pp. Published by GALE RESEARCH CO., Book Tower, Detroit, Mich. 48226.

BLACK ENTERPRISE—LEADING BLACK BUSINESSES ISSUE. Contains a listing ranked by financial size of 100 Black-owned or Black-controlled businesses with sales of $2 million or above, 49 banks with total assets of $2 million or more, 41 savings and loan associations with total assets of $100,000 or more, and 41 insurance companies with total assets of about $200,000 or more, includes company name, city and state, name of chief executive, year founded, financial data, etc. EARL G. GRAVE PUBLISHING CO., 295 Madison Ave., New York, N.Y. 10017.

BLACK GUIDE. Directory of black members of Congress, major Washington-based black organizations and associations and African and Caribbean embassies. 128 pp. WASHINGTON BOOKS, 1828 L St., N.W., Washington, D.C. 20036.

BLUE BOOK OF MAJOR HOMEBUILDERS. Information on more than 700 major homebuilders, home manufacturers, mobile home manufacturers and new town community developers—the leaders of the home building industry. Lists names of principals, corporate structure, financial data, areas of operation, etc. 500 pp. Annual. CMR ASSOCIATES INC., 1559 Eton Way, Crofton, Md. 21113.

BOOK TRADE OF THE WORLD, THE. A three volume symposium provides an international and country-by-country survey of bookselling and publishing today. Lists important information such as: book clubs, literary agents, import-export, etc. Published by R. R. BOWKER CO., 1180 Avenue of the Americas, New York, N.Y. 10036.

BOOKMAN'S YEARBOOK. Lists antiquarian book dealers, libraries with antiquarian collections, individual collectors and publishers. Annual. 470 pp. ANTIQUARIAN BOOKMAN, P.O. Box 1100, Newark, N.J. 07101.

BRIEFING PAPERS COLLECTION, THE. Contains a bibliography of over 1,000 articles and books on government procurement and contracting. Main section of books is a collection of 35 articles on key Government Contract topics, authored by practicing experts. FEDERAL PUBLICATIONS INC., 1725 K St., N.W., Washington, D.C. 20006. Annual subscription includes bi-monthly "Briefing Papers" service plus annual "Briefing Papers Collection."

BRUSH MANUFACTURERS BUYING GUIDE. Lists manufacturers, distributors, importers and export agents of all types of materials, equipment and machinery used in the manufacture of all types of brushes. BROOMS, BRUSHES AND MOPS, P.O. Box 694, Milwaukee, Wis. 53201.

BRUSHWARE'S BUYERS' GUIDE. Consisting of approximately 2,000 entries arranged alphabetically by product and by company, publication contains a listing of sources of all material, equipment and supplies used in the manufacture of brushes, brooms and mops. Listings are cross-indexed by name of supplier. 99 pp. Annually. BRUSHWARE PUBLICATIONS, INC., 1629 K Street, N.W., Suite 509, Washington, D.C. 20006.

BUILDERS' COMMERCIAL AGENCY CREDIT REFERENCE BOOK. Publication contains the names, financial ratings and classifications of 15,000 firms and individuals directly connected with construction in the Chicago, Illinois area. Annually with supplements by BUILDERS' COMMERCIAL AGENCY, 105 N. Oak Park Ave., Oak Park, Ill.

BUILDING OFFICIALS AND CODE ADMINISTRATORS INTERNATIONAL—MEMBERSHIP DIRECTORY. An alpha-geographical list of architects, engineers, municipalities, code enforcement officials. Approximately 3,000 listings. 120 pp. Annually. BUILDING OFFICIALS AND CODE ADMINISTRATORS INTERNATIONAL, 1313 E. 60th St., Chicago, Ill. 60637.

BULLINGER'S POSTAL AND SHIPPERS GUIDE FOR THE U.S. AND CANADA. Presents an alphabetically arranged listing of approximately 200,000 American and Canadian towns and counties and their post offices and railroad stations, and mailing and shipping information. Guide supplies zip code numbers for towns or villages that do not have a post office. 1,500 pp. Annually. BULLINGER'S GUIDES, INC., 63 Woodland Ave., P.O. Box 501, Westwood, N.J. 07675.

BUSINESS BOOKS IN PRINT. Contains bibliographic information on virtually every in-print business book available in the U.S. Fields covered are banking, advertising, research and many other subjects. Arranged in three sections; subject, author and title. Annual. R. R. BOWKER CO., P.O. Box 1807, Ann Arbor, Mich. 48106.

BUSINESS MEETINGS SELECTOR FOR MARKETING EXECUTIVES. A semi-annual insert in "Advertising and Sales Promotion" magazine, lists sites, services and techniques for upcoming business meetings. ADVERTISING AND SALES PROMOTION, 740 Rush St., Chicago, Ill. 60611.

CAMP BUYING GUIDE. Consists of entries of 200 major suppliers of 1,700 children's camp products. Annually. The March issue of "Camping" Magazine by AMERICAN CAMPING ASSOC., Bradford Woods, Martinsville, Ind. 46154.

CEMENT DIRECTORY, AMERICAN. Publication provides an alpha-geographically arranged grouping of entries on approximately 300 North, Central and South American cement manufacturing companies; also includes listings of officers and operating personnel. 270 pp. Annually. BRADLEY PULVERIZER CO., 123 S. 3rd St., Allentown, Penna. 18105.

CEMETERY DIRECTORY, INTERNATIONAL. A geographic listing of approximately 10,000 cemeteries including telephone numbers, type of corporations and style of cemetery. Buyers' Guide section lists cemetery suppliers and type of merchandise handled. 260 pp. Published every six to eight years by the AMERICAN CEMETERY ASSOCIATION, 250 E. Broad St., Columbus, Ohio 43215.

CERAMIC COMPANY DIRECTORY. Publication presents alphabetical listings of approximately 1,600 companies in or allied to the ceramic field. Listings detail name, address, telephone number, TWX, Telex and cable numbers, company description, names of officials and their titles, and number of employees. 150 pp. Annually. American Ceramic Society "Bulletin" by THE AMERICAN CERAMIC SOCIETY, 65 Ceramic Dr., Columbus, Ohio 43214.

CERAMIC DATA BOOK. Contains a list of approximately 3,000 ceramic equipment and raw materials manufacturers and supplies. Annually. CAHNERS PUBLISHING CO., 89 Franklin St., Boston, Mass. 02110.

CHEMICAL GUIDE TO THE UNITED STATES. Directory consists of listings of approximately 600 major American chemical concerns, providing name, address, principal officers, representative annual sales figures, plant locations and products; foreign subsidiaries and affiliates are noted, as well. Biennially. NOYES DATA CORP., Noyes Bldg., Park Ridge, N.Y. 07656.

CHEMICAL INDUSTRY HANDBOOK. A guide to the chemical industry in the United Kingdom and European industries such as paint, oil, plastics, pharmaceuticals, etc., with information on each firm listed. 390 pp. INTERNATIONAL PUBLICATIONS SERVICE, 114 East 32 St., New York, N.Y. 10016.

CHEMICAL MARKET ABSTRACTS. Provides in-depth coverage of all domestic and foreign information significant for the chemical, plastics, paper, metals, fibers, rubber, petroleum and other process industries. Over 14,000 digests annually are obtained from more than 100 key foreign and domestic sources. Monthly. PREDICASTS, INC., 200 University Circle Research Center, 11001 Cedar Ave., Cleveland, Ohio 44106.

CHEMICAL WEEK BUYERS' GUIDE ISSUE. The complete guide to sources for chemicals and packaging. This Guide lists 1,600 manufacturers and distributors; home branch and district offices; telephone numbers; 6,500 office listings. It is made up of a Catalog Section; Chemicals, Raw Materials and Specialties Directory with over 6,000 product listings and 50,000 individual listings of major producers with distributors. There is also included a Tradenames Directory of over 6,500 names. In the Packaging Area there is a Company Directory of manufacturers of all types of packaging containers, accessories and bulk shipping equipment; also a Packaging Catalog Section. Included are 400 different categories of packaging items with 4,000 listings of all major suppliers. In addition there is a Packaging/Shipping Trade names directory of over 300 names. Published annually in October by CHEMICAL WEEK, McGRAW-HILL, INC., 1221 Avenue of the Americas, New York, N.Y. 10021. Available only to subscribers of *Chemical Week* magazine.

CITIZEN'S ENERGY DIRECTORY—A GUIDE TO ALTERNATIVE ENERGY RESOURCES. Provides a geographical listing of 500+ citizen groups, manufacturers, gov't agencies, researchers and private individuals with expertise on alternative energy technologies. 150 pp. Annual. CITIZEN'S ENERGY PROJECT, 1518 R St., N.W., Washington, D.C. 20009.

CITY DIRECTORY CATALOG. Presents a listing of every city directory in North America. Contains a census, county list, listings of auto owners, farmers, householders, property owners, telephone numbers, rural routes, taxpapers; wives' names detailed in each listing. Annually. ASSOCIATION OF NORTH AMERICAN DIRECTORY PUBLISHERS, 270 Orange Street, New Haven, Conn. 06509.

CIVIL RIGHTS: A GUIDE TO THE PEOPLE, ORGANIZATIONS AND EVENTS. An alphabetical guide to names of individuals and organizations prominent in the civil rights movement between 1954 and the present. Also a list of states with civil rights legislation and state agencies with civil rights responsibilities, and a list of black elected officials in the United States, 194 pp. Published by R. R. BOWKER CO., 1180 Avenue of the Americas, New York, N.Y. 10036.

CIVIL SERVICE HANDBOOK. A complete guide to federal, state and local positions in the U.S. Civil Service. It tells you how to apply and includes other information on jobs available. 128 pp. ARCO PUBLISHING CO., INC., 219 Park Ave. South, New York, N.Y. 10003.

COLLECTION AGENCIES, AMERICAN DIRECTORY OF. Lists professional collection agencies and collectors throughout the U.S., Canada and parts of Europe. 255 pp. Annual. THE SERVICE PUBLISHING CO., 168 Washington Blvd., 15th & New York Ave., N.W., Washington, D.C. 20005.

COLLECTORS, DIRECTORY OF BONDED. Consists of approximately 2,500 collection agency members of the American Collectors Association, with name of owner or manager, address and telephone number. 596 pp. Annually. AMERICAN COLLECTORS ASSOCIATION, INC., 4040 W. 70th St., Minneapolis, Minn. 55435.

COLLEGE PLACEMENT ANNUAL. An alphabetical by state listing of 1,500 employers who recruit college graduates. Each entry includes pertinent information about employers and types of positions available during the next year. 456 pp. Annually. COLLEGE PLACEMENT COUNCIL, INC., P.O. Box 2263, Bethlehem, Pa. 18001.

COLLEGE PLACEMENT DIRECTORY. Contains listings of approximately 1,500 companies and government agencies hiring American college graduates—information on business firms hiring college graduates; information on all levels of government; cross-indexes of companies and government agencies arranged by types of job opportunities offered and by location; listing of most American and Canadian colleges including name of placement director, and other information. Published by INDUSTRIAL RESEARCH SERVICE, INC., Dover, N.H.

COLLEGE STORE BUYERS GUIDE. Contains entries of approximately 1,000 products sold in college stores, with names of manufacturers. Published by THE NATIONAL ASSOCIATION OF COLLEGE STORES, Oberlin, Ohio.

COLLEGE STORE PRODUCTS AND MANUFACTURERS DIRECTORY. Lists manufacturers of products sold in college stores. COLLEGE STORE NEWS, 735 Spring St., N.W., Atlanta, Ga. 30308.

COLLEGIATE WOMAN'S CAREER MAGAZINE, THE. Alphabetical listings of companies offering jobs to college graduate women. Three issues per year. EQUAL OPPORTUNITY PUBLICATIONS, INC., P.O. Box 202, Centerport, N.Y. 11721.

COMMUNICATION DIRECTORY. Lists communication associations, communication centers, meetings, data sources, career sources, education sources, books and other publications and other sources and data on the communications field. COUNCIL OF COMMUNICATION SOCIETIES, P.O. Bpx 1074, Silver Spring, Md. 20910.

COMMUNICATION IN ORGANIZATIONS. A bibliography and sourcebook of information on all aspects of organizational communications, arranged by topics of interest. 286 pp. GALE RESEARCH CO., Book Tower, Detroit, Mich. 48226.

COMMUNICATION RESEARCH IN U.S. UNIVERSITIES: A DIRECTORY. An alphabetical list of 109 universities and colleges which teach communications or journalism. 30 pp. INSTITUTE OF COMMUNICATIONS RESEARCH, University of Illinois, 1207 West Oregon, Urbana, Ill. 61801.

COMMUNICATIONS GRAPHICS. This directory features a bibliography listing 300 books, periodicals, directors, suppliers, manufacturers and articles dealing with communications graphics. Also includes a "how-to" guide and a point-by-point coverage of facilities-planning. 240 pp. VAN NOSTRAND REINHOLD CO., 450 West 33rd St., New York, N.Y. 10001.

COMMUNICATIONS/SOURCE. Describes the politics, activities, and how to get in touch with more than 500 groups at work reinventing the social and humane uses of printing, publishing, art, music, theatre, libraries, film, newspapers, television and computers. Also includes descriptions of 400 books, periodicals, films, and tapes useful as communication resources in social change. 125 pp. THE SWALLOW PRESS, INC., 211 W. Junior Terrace, Chicago, Ill. 60613.

COMMUNICATIONS, SOURCE NO. 1. A guide to 1,000 print and media groups, books, films, periodicals useful as communications resources for initiating social change. 120 pp. THE SWALLOW PRESS, INC., 211 W. Junior Terrace, Chicago, Ill. 60613.

COMMUNITIES, SOURCE NO. 2. A bibliography of reference material on tenant housing problems, active groups, community programs, etc. 256 pp. THE SWALLOW PRESS, INC., 211 W. Junior Terrace, Chicago, Ill. 60613.

COMMUNITY DIRECTORY. Provides a complete and up-to-date listing of intentional communities and communes published in the last several years. Contains approximately 300 names and addresses plus information on diet, government, size, spiritual preferences and which communities are looking for new members. SCHOOL OF LIVING, P.O. Box 3233, York, Pa. 17402.

COMPUTER AND INFORMATION SYSTEMS. Devoted to complete and comprehensive coverage of the world literature in this field. CAMBRIDGE SCIENTIFIC ABSTRACTS, INC., 6611 Kenilworth Ave., Suite 437, Riverdale, Md. 20840.

COMPUTER-ASSISTED INSTRUCTION: A SELECTED BIBLIOGRAPHY. A computer print-out bibliography of articles and books on computer-assisted instruction. 235 pp. ASSOC. FOR EDUCATIONAL COMMUNICATIONS AND TECHNOLOGY, 1201-16th St., N.W., Washington, D.C. 20036.

COMPUTER DISPLAY REVIEW. Contains in four volumes information on cost, availability and application of all types of Display terminal equipment. 2,000 pp. Annual with supplements. G. L. M. CORPORATION, 594 Marrett Rd., Lexington, Mass. 02173.

COMPUTERS AND DATA PROCESSING INFORMATION SOURCES. Twelve sections covered: General Orientation, Planning and Organization, Personnel (staffing), Equipment, Supplies, Facilities, Communication and Records, Comptrollership, Operating, Directing, Front Office References, The Future, broken down into 79 subheads. Appendixes. Author and Title index. Subject index. 275 pp. Published by GALE RESEARCH COMPANY, Book Tower, Detroit, Mich. 48226.

COMPUTER YEARBOOK AND DIRECTORY. Publication contains entries on manufacturers of data processing equipment and services, colleges and universities offering data processing courses, private business schools, private and public institutes, associations with interest in data processing, computer-user organizations, audio-visual aids. Also provides information on flow charting symbols and techniques, computer manufacturers, computer and computer systems, insurance companies' data processing usage, federal government ADP installations inventory and a list of data processing abbreviations. Annually. AMERICAN DATA PROCESSING, INC., 401 N. Broad Street, Philadelphia, Pa. 19107.

CONCISE HANDBOOK OF OCCUPATIONS. Describes the different occupations, and job and career opportunities in each. 320 pp. J. G. FERGUSON PUBLISHING CO., 111 E. Wacker Dr., Chicago, Ill. 60601.

CONCRETE INSTITUTE DIRECTORY, AMERICAN. Directory's approximately 15,000 listings provide a complete membership roster of the American Concrete Institute. Biennially. AMERICAN CONCRETE INSTITUTE, P.O. Box 19150, Detroit, Mich. 48219.

CONCRETE INSTITUTE—MEMBERSHIP DIRECTORY, PRESTRESSED. Directory contains information on approximately 2,100 company members (producers), associate company members (suppliers), and affiliate members (non-register personnel), and professionals and students (architects and engineers) in the field, affiliated with the Prestressed Concrete Institute. All technical and other committee personnel listed by committee. Annually. 96 pp. PRESTRESSED CONCRETE INSTITUTE, 20 N. Wacker Dr., Chicago, Ill. 60606.

CONSUMER DISCOUNT PRICE GUIDE. Information on over 10,000 products; automobiles, appliances, hi-fi stereo equipment, televisions, air conditioners, etc. 386 pp. Annually. PUBLICATIONS INTERNATIONAL, LTD., 3841 W. Oakton, Skokie, Ill. 60076.

CONSUMER EDUCATION BIBLIOGRAPHY. Lists with brief annotation, 2,000 books, booklets, pamphlets, films, filmstrips, etc., designed as a guide to the knowledge and information necessary to make intelligent choices in the marketplace. 170 pp. SUPT. OF DOCUMENTS, U.S. GOVERNMENT PRINTING OFFICE, Washington, D.C. 20402.

CONSUMER HELP. Lists the names, addresses and phone numbers of City, County, State and Federal agencies, as well as important business organizations. Including information regarding consumer rights in mobile homes, condominiums, auto repairs, auto sales, landlord/tenant problems, television repairs, food, retirement and other facets of everyday concern. THE BROWARD COUNTY DIVISION OF CONSUMER AFFAIRS, 200 S.E. Sixth St., Fort Lauderdale, Fla.

CONSUMERISM, CAPITAL CONTACTS IN. Provides information needed for contacts to solve consumer problems, including every government consumer affairs office with address and phone number and a description of each of the offices, etc. FRASER/RUDER & FINN, 1701 K Street, N.W., Suite 906, Washington, D.C. 20006.

CONSUMER INDEX TO PRODUCT EVALUATIONS AND INFORMATION SOURCES. Provides a listing of product tests and evaluations from more than 110 sources—tests refer to general consumer, business, educational and library products—grouped into 121 categories—includes alphabetical index with subject index to categories. 263 pp. Quarterly with annual cumulation. PIERIAN PRESS, P.O. Box 1808, Ann Arbor, Mich. 48106.

CONSUMER PRODUCT INFORMATION. Lists federal publications aimed at assisting the consumer in the purchasing, usage and care of products. Areas covered include appliances, automobiles, child care, health, food, housing, etc. 16 pp. PUBLIC DOCUMENTS DISTRIBUTION CENTER, Pueblo, Colo. 81009.

CONSUMER PROTECTION DIRECTORY. Contains a listing of national, state and local governmental and private organizations offering information, protection, or assistance on consumer problems. 466 pp. MARQUIS ACADEMIC MEDIA, 200 E. Ohio St., Chicago, Ill. 60611.

CONSUMER'S REGISTER OF AMERICAN BUSINESS. Provides a listing of 51 business classifications alphabetically with trade names including 12,500 advertisers along with the products they produce. 1,100+ pp. Yearly. NATIONAL REGISTER PUBLISHING CO., 5201 Old Orchard Rd., Skokie, Ill. 60076.

CONSTRUCTION DIRECTORY. Lists 8,000 contractors, sub-contractors and services connected with the construction industry in Texas, Louisiana, Oklahoma, Arkansas and New Mexico. 224 pp. Annual. CAPS OF THE SOUTHWEST, 3108 W. 6th, Ft. Worth, Texas 76107.

CONSTRUCTION EQUIPMENT BUYERS GUIDE. Lists 10,000 makers and local distributors of construction equipment; includes complete product and trade names listings. 400 pp. Annually. CAHNERS BOOKS, 221 Columbus Ave., Boston, Mass. 02116.

CONSTRUCTIONEER DIRECTORY. Lists manufacturers and distributors serving the construction industry. 330 pp. Annual. REPORTS CORP., 1 Bond St., Chatham, N.J. 07928.

CONSTRUCTOR—DIRECTORY ISSUE. Provides an alphabetical listing by company name of more than 8,000 member firms engaged in building, highway, heavy, industrial, municipal utilities, and railroad construction. 330 pp. Annually in July. ASSOCIATED GENERAL CONTRACTORS OF AMERICA, 1957 E. St., N.W., Washington, D.C. 20006.

CONTRACTORS REGISTER. Publication contains listings of 10,000 architects, general contractors, subcontractors, construction material and equipment suppliers and dealers. 90 pp. Biennially. SERINA PRESS, 70 Kennedy St., Alexandria, Va. 22305.

CONVENTIONS, DIRECTORY OF. Provides a geographical and industrial listing of 18,000 association conventions, trade/industrial and public shows. 360 pp. Semiannual. SUCCESSFUL MEETINGS MAGAZINE, 1422 Chestnut St., Philadelphia, Pa. 19102.

CRUSADE FOR EDUCATION. Published nine times per year, "Crusade for Education" describes professional openings in the United States and abroad for teachers, librarians, administrators and scientists; information on undergraduate scholarships, current graduate awards, summer opportunities, teachers' discount services; educator's bookshelf, writing, and part-time work. Published by ADVANCEMENT AND PLACEMENT INSTITUTE, 169 N. 9th St., Brooklyn, N.Y. 11211. Subscription included in annual membership fee.

DECISION JOB DIRECTORY. Contains a listing of 1,500 American companies offering engineering or scientific employment opportunities to technical personnel, and 7,500 key executive and engineering contacts. Entries detail company name, address, phone number, industry and/or products; year established, sales, total number of professional and non-professional employees; name of president, director of engineering, directory of research, name of technical employment manager, listed alphabetically and cross-indexed. Revised and published annually. DECISION, INC., 4500 Summerside Rd., Cincinnati, Ohio 45244.

DICTIONARY OF PERSONNEL AND GUIDANCE TERMS. An alphabetical listing of terms for the personnel and guidance worker. Also includes associations, agencies and professional organizations in the U.S. and Canada. J. G. FERGUSON PUBLISHING CO., 111 E. Wacker Dr., Chicago, Ill. 60601.

DIRECTORY OF CAREER PLANNING AND PLACEMENT OFFICES. Contains information on placement personnel and interview dates on 1,900 four-year and two-year campuses. 228 pp. COLLEGE PLACEMENT COUNCIL, INC., P.O. Box 2263, Bethlehem, Pa. 18001.

DIRECTORY OF DIRECTORS. An alphabetical list of over 13,000 key executives with their titles, directorships, business and home addresses plus a list of over 2,400 leading Canadian companies with head office addresses and the names of officers and directors. 770 pp. Annually. FINANCIAL POST DIVISION, MACLEAN-HUNTER LTD., 481 University Ave., Toronto M5W 1A7, Ontario, Canada.

DIRECTORY OF DIRECTORS IN THE CITY OF NEW YORK. Contains a listing of approximately 15,000 executives and directors of 3,000 New York corporations, and a cross-index of companies by executives and firm names. Annually. DIRECTORY OF DIRECTORS CO., 350 Fifth Ave., New York, N.Y. 10001.

DIRECTORY OF GOVERNMENT AGENCIES SAFEGUARDING CONSUMER AND ENVIRONMENT. Contains state-by-state listings of federal and/or state officials with jurisdiction in each state over food and drugs, meat and poultry, pesticides, air pollution control, water pollution control, consumer protection: Fraud and deceptive practices, weights and measures, environment and narcotics control, etc. Also includes local officials. 90 pp. Biennially. SERINA PRESS, 70 Kennedy St., Alexandria, Va. 22305.

DUN AND BRADSTREET REFERENCE BOOK OF CORPORATE MANAGEMENTS. Contains a biographical sketch of each officer and identifies all directors in the 2,400 companies of greatest investor interest in the United States. Each biographical sketch includes the following: name, marital status, age, education and career description. Contains approximately 30,000 listings. 1,400 pp. Annually. DUN AND BRADSTREET, INC., 99 Church St., New York, N.Y. 10007.

ECOL: BOOK CATALOG OF THE ENVIRONMENTAL CONSERVATION LIBRARY. A bibliography of books, documents, papers and related materials from all subjects which have a bearing upon the physical environment and man's impact on it. Includes subjects as resource management, pollution, environmental policy and law, conservation, population and many more. 208 pp. AMERICAN LIBRARY ASSOC., 50 E. Huron St., Chicago, Ill. 60611.

ECOTECHNICS: AN INTERNATIONAL ECOLOGY DIRECTORY. Contains information on 900 product categories and provides manufacturers and service organizations in the U.S., Canada, Japan, and Western and Eastern Europe, lists more than 35,000 sources: names, addresses, telephone, and telex numbers on major areas of environmental concern. 480 pp. FAIRCHILD BOOKS AND VISUALS, 7 E. 12th St., New York, N.Y. 10003.

EDITOR AND PUBLISHER INTERNATIONAL YEARBOOK. Consists of alpha-geographically arranged entries of approximately 250,000 international daily and weekly executive newspaper personnel; detailed information on all American and Canadian daily and weekly newspapers—giving circulation, advertising, rates; also contains material on equipment, syndicates, schools of journalism, and press galleries. Annually. 626 pp. EDITOR AND PUBLISHER CO. INC., 575 Lexington Ave., New York, N.Y. 10022.

EDITOR AND PUBLISHER MARKET GUIDE. Entries on approximately 1,500 newspaper market areas, including data on population, income, sales, transportation, housing and banking, etc. List of newspapers in each area giving circulation data and name of advertising representative or contact personnel. 540 pp. Annually. EDITOR AND PUBLISHER CO., INC., 575 Lexington Ave., New York, N.Y. 10022.

EDUCATION INDEX. A cumulative author subject index to 241 educational publications in the English language. Although primarily a periodical index, proceedings, yearbooks, bulletins, monographs and material printed by the United States Government are included. Subject areas indexed include administration; pre-school elementary, secondary, higher and adult education; teacher education, counseling and guidance; curriculum and curriculum materials. Subject fields indexed include the arts, applied science and technology, audio-visual education, business education, comparative and international education, exceptional children and special education, health and physical education, languages and linguistics, mathematics, psychology and mental health, religious education, social studies and educational research relative to areas and fields indexed. Published monthly (except July and August) with annual cumulations by THE H. W. WILSON CO., 950 University Ave., Bronx, N.Y. 10452. Specific service basis rates available on request from publisher.

E.I.A. GUIDE, THE. Publication provides entries on where to buy for approximately 25,000 national manufacturers of electronic, industrial and aerospace equipment and supplies and their western representatives. Classified product and service section included. 580 pp. Annually. DIRECTORIES OF INDUSTRY, INC., 9371 Kramer-Unit I, Westminster, Calif. 92683.

EEM-ELECTRONIC ENGINEERS MASTER. Contains entries of approximately 6,300 electronics manufacturers—with names, addresses, telephone numbers, sales managers, plus sales office locations; 3,000 product headings with manufacturers' names, addresses and 6,000 trade names. Catalog section of 661 manufacturers included. 1,500 pp. Annually. UNITED TECHNICAL PUBLICATIONS, 645 Stewart Ave., Garden City, N.Y. 11530.

ELECTRONIC MARKET DATA BOOK. Lists electronic products and information on their sales and production. 110 pp. Annually. Published by ELECTRONIC INDUSTRIES ASSOCIATION, 2001 Eye St., N.W., Washington, D.C. 20006.

EMERITI FOR EMPLOYMENT. Provides information on approximately 500 recently or soon-to-be retired professors emeriti available for teaching, consultation and research appointments, listing for each the degrees held, institutional affiliations, and year of retirement; field or specialty of each included. Published by THE NATIONAL COMMITTEE ON THE EMERITI, P.O. Box 24451, Los Angeles, Calif. 90024.

ENERGY ATLAS. Listing of 52 Federal Departments and agencies including Regional Offices and Laboratories, 100 Congressional committees, subcommittees and organizations, 500 State energy related agencies. Legislative organizations and city energy office, 150 Federal, Regional and National non-Government organizations at the State and local level, and 600 energy publications, periodicals, guide-books and directories and government publications, etc. FRASER/RUDER AND FINN, 1701 "K" St., N.W., Washington, D.C. 20006.

ENERGY DIRECTORY, THE. Provides information on thousands of energy organizations, trade associations, professional societies, state governments, or corporations, etc. Including 12,000 officials and executives, their addresses and phone numbers. 500 pp. EIC ENVIRONMENT INFORMATION CENTER, INC., 292 Madison Ave., New York, N.Y. 10017.

ENERGY INDEX. Contains 12,000 abstracts of key articles, documents and reports on all aspects of the energy crisis and power technology since 1970. Covers consumption, usage, energy resources, plant sitings and other information. 400 pp. Annual. ENVIRONMENT INFORMATION CENTER, INC., 292 Madison Ave., New York, N.Y. 10017.

ENGINEERING AND MINING JOURNAL, MARKETING DIRECTORY GUIDEBOOK. Classified listing by product of companies supplying machinery, equipment and supplies used in the industry. Annual. McGRAW HILL, INC., 1221 Ave. of the Americas, New York, N.Y. 10020.

ENGINEERING EDUCATION IN THE U.S. A guide for foreign students to engineering institutions in the United States. 60 pp. IIE, 809 United Nations Plaza, New York, N.Y. 10017.

ENGINEERING INDEX ANNUAL. Annual volume consists of an annotated bibliography of articles involving engineering concepts and methods abstracted, listed alphabetically, cross referenced and indexed by subject and author from periodicals and society transactions, bulletins and reports of government agencies, universities, institutes and research organizations. Indexed by subject, giving title, author of the article; listed by author, listing all the authors and co-authors of the articles listed in the subject index. Published annually by ENGINEERING INDEX, INC., 345 E. 47th St., New York, N.Y. 10017.

ENVIRONMENT INDEX, THE. Lists 60,000 entries representing coverage from scientific, technical trade and general magazines, government reports, conference papers and proceedings, nationally-read newspapers, books and films. Also listed are environmental control patents, major legislation introduced and names and addresses of state and federal pollution control officers. 800 pp. Published by ENVIRONMENTAL INFORMATION CENTER, INC., 292 Madison Ave., New York, N.Y. 10017.

ENVIRONMENTAL DIRECTORY WORLD. Provides an alphabetical listing by country of 30,000 companies, organizations, personnel involved in environmental activities throughout the world. 1,600 pp. Biennially. BUSINESS PUBLISHERS, INC., P.O. Box 1067, Blair Station, Silver Spring, Md. 20910.

ENVIRONMENT U.S.A. A guide to 5,400 agencies, people and material concerned with environmental activities in the U.S. with descriptions and information on each. Over 1,500 sources listed: agencies, consultants, libraries, conferences and meetings in the field, newspapers, periodicals, etc., including a comprehensive bibliography of 1,500 publications and books. 451 pp. R. R. BOWKER CO., P.O. Box 1807, Ann Arbor, Mich. 48106.

ENVIRONMENTAL PROTECTION DIRECTORY. Provides a listing of national, state, and local government and private organizations where users can seek information about current programs or receive assistance on solving current problems. 526 pp. MARQUIS ACADEMIC MEDIA, 200 E. Ohio St., Chicago, Ill. 60611.

EQUIPMENT GUIDE BOOKS. 18 volumes of information on construction equipment. 5 books are guides to new and used values for construction equipment, and to rental rates. 13 volumes contain current specifications for one type or class of construction equipment. Approximately 75,000 listings. 25,000 pp. Published by EQUIPMENT GUIDE BOOK CO., 3980 Fabian Way, Palo Alto, Calif. 94303.

EXECUTIVE DEVELOPMENT PROGRAMS IN UNIVERSITIES. Lists executive development programs conducted by 50 U.S. universities. Detailed information is given on each program. An annotated bibliography is also included. 100 pp. NATIONAL INDUSTRIAL CONFERENCE BD., INC., 845 Third Ave., New York, N.Y. 10022.

EXHIBITS SCHEDULE. An alphabetical listing of events for selection of exhibit opportunities for your products or services. Included are location and dates of exhibits. Approximately 12,000 trade and industrial shows, fairs, and expositions are listed. Annually. SUCCESSFUL MEETINGS, Directory Dept., 1422 Chestnut St., Philadelphia, Pa. 19102.

EXPORT DIRECTORY OF THE BLUE BOOK OF EUROPE. Lists over 90,000 European companies alphabetically by product, country and name, giving name, address and phone number for each. 1,850 pp. INTERNATIONAL PUBLICATIONS SERVICE, 114 E. 32nd St., New York, N.Y. 10016.

EXPORTERS DIRECTORY AND U.S. BUYING GUIDE. Lists 30,000 U.S. manufacturers, exporters, export managers, and export merchants involved in the majority of domestic products and commodities sold in world markets. Included are names, addresses, titles, and phone numbers. 800 pp. JOURNAL OF COMMERCE, 445 Marshall St., Phillipsburg, N.J. 08865.

EXTENSION FACILITIES GUIDE. Describes private degree-granting correspondence colleges in the U.S. and several countries abroad. AUREA PUBLICATIONS, Aurea House, Allenhurst, N.J. 07711.

FACT FILES. Provides key data on trends in the U.S. economy including consumer income and expenditures, population, employment, prices, retail sales, education levels, etc. Included are department store sales, fashion accessories, floor coverings, home electronics, home textiles, major appliances, beauty aids, etc. FAIRCHILD BOOKS, Dept. NFF, 7 E. 12th St., New York, N.Y. 10003.

THE FEATURE WRITER AND SYNDICATE DIRECTORY. Presents a listing of over 900 entries of free lance writers and photographers, fully indexed and cross-referenced. Includes alphabetical listings of the nation's leading free-lance writers, including mailing address and zip code. Principal subjects in which writer specializes are given. Alphabetical listing of the subject matter in which writers specialize, listing writers so occupied under each. Lists publications served by these free lance writers; special section containing detailed explanations submitted by leading magazine editors outlining type of articles they are seeking; sources of historical photographs, drawings, sketches and old prints; alphabetical listing of leading free-lance photographers; special interest listing under which the free-lance photographers are cross-referenced, and feature syndicates and their personnel, cross-referenced by subject matter. 320 pp. Annually. THE NATIONAL RESEARCH BUREAU, INC., 424 N. Third St., Burlington, Iowa 52601.

FEDERAL EDUCATION PROGRAM GUIDE. Lists more than 300 federal programs in more than eight departments and agencies. Included are complete mailing address and telephone numbers. Provides aid to securing all kinds of institutional and program assistance from the federal government. ACROPOLIS BOOKS, 2400-17th St., N.W., Washington, D.C. 20009.

FILMGOERS COMPANION, THE. An international encyclopedia of over 10,000 actors, producers, directors, writers, camera men, film-makers, art directors and composers, each entry contains a biographical note and a listing of principal credits, 1,070 pp. HILL AND WANG, INC., 19 Union Square West, New York, N.Y. 10003.

FINANCE DIRECTORY—SHOPPING CENTER WORLD. ANNUAL. An alphabetical listing of 500+ firms and organizations which finance or invest in shopping centers as follows: long term lenders, construction lenders, equity investors, mortgage brokers/bankers, etc. 8-12 pp. COMMUNICATION CHANNELS, INC., 461 8th Ave., New York, N.Y. 10001.

FINANCE-INVESTORS ISSUE. Lists alphabetically by company name the top 400 security dealers in the U.S., includes type of ownership, address, phone, teletype and telex numbers, underwriting and syndication of corporate issues in previous year by number, type and dollar volume, etc. FINANCE PUBLISHING CO., 5 E. 75th St., New York, N.Y. 10021.

FINANCIAL ANALYSTS FEDERATION—MEMBERSHIP DIRECTORY. Provides a geographical listing by constituent local or state societies of 14,000 security and financial analysts who practice investment analysis. 380 pp. FINANCIAL ANALYSTS FEDERATION, Tower Suite, 219 E. 42nd St., New York, N.Y. 10017.

FOREIGN COMMERCE HANDBOOK. Presents a grouping of listings providing sources of information for exporters and importers, giving names and addresses of sources and procedure for procurement. Published by the CHAMBER OF COMMERCE OF THE UNITED STATES, 1615 H St., N.W., Washington, D.C. 20006.

FOREIGN TRADE DEPARTMENTS AND/OR BUREAUS IN CHAMBERS OF COMMERCE THROUGHOUT THE UNITED STATES. Publication presents an alpha-geographically arranged roster of local chambers of commerce, foreign trade departments and/or bureaus in the United States which maintain foreign trade services. Gives name of director of foreign trade matters for each chamber of commerce. CHAMBER OF COMMERCE OF THE UNITED STATES, 1615 H St., N.W., Washington, D.C. 20006.

FOREST GUIDE NATIONAL. A guide to the National forest arranged geographically, including a catalog of other national recreational facilities. Maps showing the location of National Forests. 224 pp. RAND McNALLY, P.O. Box 7600, Chicago, Ill. 60680.

GROVE'S DICTIONARY OF MUSIC AND MUSICIANS. Consisting of ten volumes, this edition contains more than 12,000 entries written by over 600 expert contributors, 76 plates, thousands of musical examples, line drawings and diagrams, more than 2,000 extensive bibliographies, a calendar of operas produced between 1600 and 1959, and articles on the folk music of more than 40 countries. It defines all musical terms, describes in detail most musical instruments and lists every composition of the great composers. 8,900 pp. Published by ST. MARTIN'S PRESS, 176 Fifth Ave., New York, N.Y. 10010.

HISTORY: REFERENCE HANDBOOK. Over 700 historical publications including encyclopedias, dictionaries, abstracts, bibliographies and booklists, atlases and guides to records offices and libraries containing the political and constitutional history of the English people from the earliest times onward. 354 pp. THE SHOE STRING PRESS, INC., P.O. Box 1327, 995 Sherman Ave., Hamden, Conn. 06514.

HISTORIC AMERICA GUIDE. Listing of all 50 states including their historic shrines, monuments, battlefields, museums, and residences, covering 400 years. Includes prices, hours and how to get there. 50 full-color maps and 175 illustrations in color and black and white. 292 pp. RAND McNALLY, P.O. Box 7600, Chicago, Ill. 60680.

HISTORIC DOCUMENTS. Provides a listing of speeches, treaties, debates, proclamations, court decisions that have documented historic events. 1,050 pp. CONGRESSIONAL QUARTERLY, INC., 1414 22nd St., N.W., Washington, D.C. 20037.

HOW AND WHERE TO RAISE VENTURE CAPITAL TO FINANCE A BUSINESS. Included are 227 sources of venture capital, classified by name, address, telephone number and individual to contact. Also information as to how to approach a capital source, and many of the author's personal experiences. ENTERPRISE PUBLISHING CO., 1300 Market St., Wilmington, Dela. 19801.

INSTITUTIONAL INVESTOR—ANNUAL FINANCING. Describes alphabetically domestic and foreign firms: 85 major U.S. investment bankers and 85 abroad who handle the bulk of corporate financing during the previous year and for foreign firms, the bulk of government financing. Annually in May. INSTITUTIONAL INVESTOR SYSTEMS, INC., 488 Madison Ave., New York, N.Y. 10022.

INSTITUTIONS. Provides a listing of approximately 700 portfolio managers, analysts and traders of financial institutions in North America. Gives complete organization structures for the largest bank trust departments, mutual fund management companies, insurance group investment departments and the major investment counseling firms. Three issues per year. TECHNIMETRICS, INC., 919 Third Ave., New York, N.Y. 10022.

INSTRUMENTALIST BUYERS' GUIDE. Arranged alphabetically by category, publication provides information on several hundred instrument manufacturers, uniform manufacturers, manufacturers of musical equipment and supplies, music publishers, and other categories serving the music world. "Instrumentalist" Magazine by THE INSTRUMENTALIST CO., 1418 Lake St., Evanston, Ill. 60204.

INSTRUMENTATION REFERENCE ISSUE. Contains an alphabetical listing by product of 7,200 manufacturers and suppliers. 3-8 pp. Annually. SOUND AND VIBRATION, 27101 E. Oviatt Rd., Bay Village, Ohio 44140.

INTERNATIONAL DIRECTORY OF MUSIC EDUCATION INSTITUTIONS. Gives information on institutions offering music education training throughout the world. 115 pp. UNESCO PUBLICATIONS CENTER, P.O. Box 433, New York, N.Y. 10016.

INTERNATIONAL DIRECTORY OF SPECIALIZED CANCER RESEARCH AND TREATMENT ESTABLISHMENTS. Provides a geograhical listing of 500 cancer research and treatment institutes. Includes names of directors and department heads. Description of resarch and treatment facilities and activities. 521 pp. Every four years. INTERNATIONAL UNION AGAINST CANCER, 3 rue du Conseil-general, 1205 Geneva, Switzerland.

INTERNATIONAL FILM GUIDE. Contains reports from fifty countries, including every aspect of the cinema, including film festivals, film books, film schools, film archives, educational films, etc. 608 pp. A. S. BARNES AND COMPANY, Cranbury, N.J. 08512.

INTERNATIONAL INTERTRADE INDEX. Directory presents a descriptive listing of 1,000 foreign manufacturers' products offered to importers, with complete information on each product as to size, price and use. Gives names and addresses of manufacturers; includes a complete listing of new products released by the United States Department of Commerce and other international agencies and firms. Also lists sources of supply. Monthly. "INTERNATIONAL INTERTRADE INDEX," Box 636, Federal Square, Newark, N.J. 07101.

INTERNATIONAL REFERENCE HANDBOOK. Lists 120 nations and provides information on each, such as: publications and cultural institutions, advertising organizations, marketing research organizations, trade and investment organizations. American firms operating in the country, business directories of the country, selected bibliographical references. 600 pp. SIMON & SCHUSTER, 1 W. 39th St., New York, N.Y. 10018.

INTERNATIONAL STOCK AND COMMODITY EXCHANGE DIRECTORY. Lists more than 100 exchanges in over 50 countries, including 60 additional exchanges for which detailed data are not currently available. 350 pp. PHOENIX PUBLISHING, Canaan, N.H. 03741.

JAZZ PUBLICITY II. Provides a listing of over 200 jazz critics and jazz periodicals which are worldwide. 25 pp. REESE MARKEWICH, M.D., 39 Gramercy Park North, New York, N.Y. 10010.

JAZZ—THE LITERATURE OF. Lists and annotates books on every aspect of Jazz. Published by the AMERICAN LIBRARY ASSOCIATION, 50 E. Huron St., Chicago, Ill. 60611.

JOURNAL OF MUSIC THERAPY. Includes articles and research reports by music therapists, physicians, psychologists, psychiatrists and educators on use of music in therapy. Published quarterly by the NATIONAL ASSOCIATION FOR MUSIC THERAPY, P.O. Box 640, Lawrence, Kan. 66044.

KEMP'S MUSIC AND RECORDING INDUSTRY YEARBOOK. Contains British record companies, sound studios, sound equipment, record distributors, television and sound broadcasting companies, music publishers, music libraries, agents and managers, and other allied services and facilities. Includes selected international addresses. 150 pp. NICHOLS PUBLISHING COMPANY, 175 West 79th St., New York, N.Y. 10024.

MATERIALS REFERENCE ISSUE. An alphabetical index of 1,000 manufacturers and producers, and lists suppliers of specific types of wrought ferrous mill forms and shapes, wrought nonferrous castings and formed and shaped parts. 250 pp. Annually. PENTON PUBLISHING CO., Penton Bldg., 614 Superior Ave. West, Cleveland, Ohio 44113.

MEDIA GUIDE INTERNATIONAL: NEWSPAPER, NEWS MAGAZINE EDITION. Provides data of the 800 leading foreign newspapers and new weeklies in the world. Only those papers and magazines with national or near-national circulation and influence in their respective countries, read by top management executives, government officials and other opinion leaders. 243 pp. DIRECTORIES INTERNATIONAL, INC., 1718 Sherman Ave., Evanston, Ill. 60201.

MEDICAL DIRECTORY—U.S. Contains a listing of medical doctors, hospitals, nursing facilities, laboratories, medical information sources, poison control centers, U.S. Medical Schools and Health Care Buyers Guide. U.S. DIRECTORY SERVICE, 121 S.E. 1st Street, P.O. Box 011565-K, Miami, Fla. 33101, telephone orders (305) 371-8881.

MENTAL HEALTH AND FAMILY LIFE EDUCATION. A guide to films, recordings, pamphlets, books, programs, plays, research studies, film strips, covering all aspects of mental health and family life. 840 pp. PERENNIAL EDUCATION, INC., P.O. Box 236, 1825 Willow Rd., Northfield, Ill. 60093.

MENTAL HEALTH DIRECTORY. Listings of personnel of the National Institute of Mental Health, and its regional offices; geographical entries of state institutions and services, with varied data on each as to status and age limitations, programs and services offered, etc. United States Government Printing Office, Division of Public Document, Washington, D.C. 20402.

METALS SOURCEBOOK. Activity reports of the major world-wide producers of metal, mines, smelters and refineries. Twice monthly. McGRAW-HILL, 1221 Ave. of the Americas, New York, N.Y. 10020.

MILITARY INSTITUTIONS AND THE SOCIOLOGY OF WAR: AN ANNOTATED BIBLIOGRAPHY. Provides text and a bibliography of books and other material divided by subject area on Miliary Institutions and the Sociology of War. 338 pp. SAGE PUBLICATIONS, 275 S. Beverly Dr., Beverly Hills, Calif. 90212.

MINER: HIS JOB AND HIS ENVIRONMENT, THE. A review and bibliography of selected recent material and research on his human performance. 206 pp. NATIONAL TECHNICAL INFORMATION SERVICE, Springfield, Va. 22151.

MOTION PICTURE, TV & THEATRE DIRECTORY. Contains 7,500 entries listed alphabetically within over 130 classified headings. Listings range from Advertising Agencies through Video Tape and include Editing Services, Laboratories, Producers and others used in the fields of motion pictures, television and theatre. 152 pp. Semiannually. MOTION PICTURE ENTERPRISES PUBLICATIONS, INC., Tarrytown, N.Y. 10591.

MUSEUM GUIDE. Lists over 100 federal programs and bills in Congress which affect museums. Including the purpose of the program and eligibility requirements, type of assistance available, application tips, financial information on program budget and number of grants awarded, and who's in charge and where to write. ASSOCIATION OF SCIENCE-TECHNOLOGY CENTERS, 2100 Penn Ave. N.W., Washington, D.C. 20037.

MUSEUM MEDIA. A directory and index of publications and audio-visuals available from U.S. and Canadian museums, galleries, art institutes and similar institutions. Listed are books, monographs, catalogs of exhibits, collections, showings, pamphlets, booklets, etc. Excluded are regularly issued magazines, journals and newsletters. Includes several indexes. 456 pp. GALE RESEARCH CO., Book Tower, Detroit, Mich. 48226.

MUSIC INDEX, THE. Alphabetical entries providing a subject and author guide to material in music periodicals from all parts of the world. Published monthly and cumulated annually by INFORMATION COORDINATORS, INC., 1435-37 Randolph St., Detroit, Mich. 48226.

MUSICIAN'S GUIDE, THE. Contains data covering 1,197 colleges, conservatories, junior colleges and schools with courses and degrees offered in music, music department chairmen, and scholarships and fellowships available; over 800 music periodicals; 1,625 recent books on music; 263 competitions and awards; 634 opera companies; 814 symphony orchestras, with names of conductor, business manager and concertmaster; 572 summer camps and workshops; 412 music libraries; 5,000 music publishers; 440 newspapers and periodicals, with names of editors, critics and record reviewers; basic classical, jazz and rock record libraries; 882 music festivals. Also associations, arts councils, awards statistics, certified music teachers and registered piano tuners, many other lists. Careers chart. 1,025 pp. Published triennially by MUSIC INFORMATION SERVICE, INC., 310 Madison Ave., New York, N.Y. 10017.

NATIONAL DIRECTORY OF FREE TOURIST ATTRACTIONS. Provides a listing of free gardens, restored villages, ships, museums and other interesting presentations of history, science, folk and fine art throughout the United States. PILOT BOOKS, 347 Fifth Ave., New York, N.Y. 10016.

NATIONAL FEDERATION HANDBOOK. Presents entries of approximately 50 public high school associations, members of the Federation of State High School Associations. Biennially. NATIONAL FEDERATION OF STATE HIGH SCHOOL ASSOCIATIONS, P.O. Box 98, Elgin, Ill. 60120.

NATIONAL INDUSTRIAL RECREATION ASSOCIATION MEMBERSHIP DIRECTORY. Contains an Alpha-Geographic listing of all business, industry and military members of the National Industrial Recreation Association. Provides names and addresses of members of the association and is available at no cost to business and industry members as well as associate members. Associate members are defined as suppliers of recreation-leisure time products services. Published yearly by the NATIONAL INDUSTRIAL RECREATION ASSOCIATION, 20 N. Wacker Drive, Chicago, Ill. 60606.

NATIONAL MUSIC COUNCIL BULLETIN. Presents listings of 60 American music organizations, members of the National Music Council—membership of the 60 organizations exceeds two million persons. Entries on organization executives included. Published semi-annually by the NATIONAL MUSIC COUNCIL, 250 West 57th St., Suite 626, New York, N.Y. 10019.

NATIONAL OPERA ASSOCIATION—MEMBERSHIP DIRECTORY. Alphabetical listing within membership divisions of 750 opera companies, composers, directors, publishers, teachers, translators, and other interested persons in the National Opera Association. Annually in January. NATIONAL OPERA ASSOCIATION, c/o Mary Elaine Wallace, School of Music, Southern Illinois University, Carbondale, Ill. 62901.

NATIONAL REAL ESTATE INVESTOR DIRECTORY. An alphabetical listing of appraisers, associates, builders, contractors, developers, corporate real estate managers, economic and industrial development authorities, equity investors and investment companies, housing and urban renewal authorities, etc. 210 pp. Annual. COMMUNICATION CHANNELS, INC., 461 Eighth Ave., New York, N.Y. 10001.

NATIONAL ROSTER OF REALTORS DIRECTORY. Alpha-geographic listing of names and addresses of 110,000 members of the National Association of Realtors. Annually. STAMATS PUBLISHING CO., 427 6th Ave., S.E., Cedar Rapids, Iowa 52406.

NATIONAL SECURITY AFFAIRS. Describes key sources of information on national security affairs by subject categories. Listed are books, periodicals, research and educational organizations, libraries, etc. 400 pp. GALE RESEARCH CO., Book Tower, Detroit, Mich. 48226.

NATIONAL SOURCE AND OPPORTUNITY DIRECTORY, THE. Contains information regarding business contacts, sources, unique opportunities, financial news, mortgage and finance journal, real estate, etc. NDF, Box 703, Freeport, Ill. 61032.

NEED A LIFT. Contains source of career, scholarship and loan information for not only children of veterans, but for all children. Includes fellowships, loans and part-time jobs to help finance their education, lists information relative to state laws offering educational benefits. Serves as an excellent guide for teachers and parents in planning with students to further their education beyond high school. 132 pp. THE AMERICAN LEGION, Dept. S., P.O. Box 1055, Indianapolis, Ind. 46206.

NEW CODE NAMES DICTIONARY. A dictionary of 2,500 code names, cover words, slang terms, and nicknames. Four softbound issues. GALE RESEARCH CO., Book Tower, Detroit, Mich. 48226.

NEW YORK TIMES POLITICAL MARKETPLACE. A who's who of politics, national, state and local. Lists over 20,000 officials: U.S. Senators and Representatives, governors and all other statewide elected officials of the 50 United States. Also lists all members of every state legislature, mayors of the 10 largest cities of each state and thousands of officials of all major political parties. Also national committees, fund raising committees, etc. 800 pp. QUADRANGLE BOOKS, 3 Park Ave., New York, N.Y. 10016.

NEWS BUREAUS IN THE U.S. Contains a listing of more than 500 newspapers, magazines, business publications, wire services and syndicates. Features the addresses, phone numbers, names of editorial personnel and other information including state capital, suburban and regional news bureaus, plus Washington, D.C., and all bureaus in every state. RICHARD WEINER, INC., 888 Seventh Ave., New York, N.Y. 10019.

NEWSPAPER DIRECTORY, THE. Contains over 1,800 influential weekly newspapers, the labor press, ethnic group publications, etc. NATIONAL RESEARCH BUREAU, Burlington, Iowa, 52601. Volume 1 of five volumes.

NEWSPAPER INDEXES: A LOCATION AND SUBJECT GUIDE FOR RESEARCHERS. Identifies hundreds of newspaper indexes available in 300 locations—libraries, historical and genealogical societies, as well as indexes in the possession of individuals. Indexed into two parts, the first part is a listing of the newspapers indexed, arranged by state, county and town in which the paper was published with dates of the index coverage and a letter symbol designating the index location. Included are some listings for church publications, American foreign language newspapers, specialized subjects and other miscellaneous newspapers. 210 pp. SCARECROW PRESS, INC., P.O. Box 656, Metuchen, N.J. 08840.

NEWSPAPER PRESS DIRECTORY. Lists newspapers, periodicals, trade and technical journals, house organs and directories published in the British Isles. Also includes British Commonwealth newspapers as well as publications of other principal overseas countries. 1,062 pp. INTERNATIONAL PUBLICATIONS SERVICE, 114 E. 32nd St., New York, N.Y. 10016.

NIH FACTBOOK. A guide to programs and activities of the National Institute of Health. Including a chronological history of the growth of this powerful federal agency which accounts for nearly 40% of all expenditures for medical research in the United States. Annually. 597 pp. MARQUIS WHO'S WHO, INC., 200 East Ohio St., Chicago, Ill. 60611.

NORTH AMERICAN FILM AND VIDEO DIRECTORY: A GUIDE TO MEDIA COLLECTIONS AND SERVICES. Lists some 2,000 college, public, special museum and archival libraries and media centers with 16 mm and/or video collections and programs are listed by state and city. Also includes loan and rental policies, publications, production facilities budgets, equipment on hand, special collections, selection policies, etc. 284 pp. STECHERT MACMILLAN, INC., 866 Third Ave., New York, N.Y. 10022.

OFFICIAL BASEBALL REGISTER. Lists season-by-season records and personal data of more than 1,100 active major league players, managers, coaches, umpires, and former stars, arranged alphabetically. 528 pp. Annually. THE SPORTING NEWS, P.O. Box 56, St. Louis, Mo. 63166.

OFFICIAL NATIONAL BASKETBALL ASSOCIATION GUIDE. Guide arranged alphabetically by sports, contains a listing of all National Basketball Association records since 1946, including playoffs, championship, team and individual records. Contains a complete listing of active players and their playing statistics plus a directory of club officials. Also contains a comparison of last season team records against each other, and current season schedules. 512 pp. Annually. THE SPORTING NEWS, P.O. Box 56, St. Louis, Mo. 63166.

PACKAGING INFORMATION SOURCES. An annotated bibliography covering the literature that deals with the various aspects of the packaging industry. General subjects covered are planning and development, merchandising, management and operations, materials, adhesives, closures, retail unit packages, shipping containers, testing machinery, and special packaging problems. 225 pp. Published by GALE RESEARCH CO., Book Tower, Detroit, Mich. 48226.

PHOTOGRAPHER'S MARKET. Lists 1,616 buyers and users of free lance photography in categories such as ad agencies, PR firms, periodicals, book publishers, architectural firms, audiovisual firms, etc., as well as other firms and services of use to photographers such as galleries, clubs, technical services, competitions and foundations. Most are listed alphabetically according to category, some geographically (clubs and technical services). 432 pp. Annual. WRITER'S DIGEST, 9933 Alliance Rd., Cincinnati, Ohio 45242.

PHOTOGRAPHIC LITERATURE VOLUMES I AND II. Consists of a bibliography of approximately 12,000 basic books, journals, magazines, articles and technical papers on photography arranged under 1,200 subject headings. 335 pp. MORGAN AND MORGAN, INC., 145 Palisades St., Dobbs Ferry, N.Y. 10522.

PRICE LIST AND GUIDE TO MEDICAL PERIODICALS. An alphabetical price list and guide to 1,350 periodicals. 28 pp. Annually. Seaboard Subscription Agency, P.O. Box 1482, 44 Fulton St., Allentown, Pa. 18105.

PRINTERS BUYING GUIDE. Lists all suppliers of the printing industry located in the New York metropolitan area. Published by PRINTING INDUSTRIES OF METROPOLITAN NEW YORK INC., 461 8th Ave., New York, N.Y. 10001.

PUBLISHERS' INTERNATIONAL DIRECTORY. Names and addresses of over 30,000 active publishers in 145 countries—geographically arranged and coded to indicate the firms' specialties in 53 different publishing areas. Includes an index listing publishers by subject interests with 60,000 cross references; a guide to publishers' and booksellers' associations in 50 countries; an international bibliography of publishers' directory and index terms. Two volumes. 1,100 pp. R. R. BOWKER CO., 1180 Avenue of the Americas, New York, N.Y. 10036.

PUBLISHERS' TRADE LIST ANNUAL. Binds the trade order list of about 2,550 publishers into seven large volumes. It includes the International Standard Book Numbers. 10,000 pp. Annually. R. R. BOWKER CO., 1180 Avenue of the Americas, New York, N.Y. 10036.

RAILROADS. Contains a collection of 259 books on North American railroads, locomotives, rolling stock, stations, railroads by region, tourist and industrial streetcars and interurbans, museums and collecting. 152 pp. LIBRARIES UNLIMITED, INC. P.O. Box 263, Littleton, Colo. 80160.

REFERENCE ISSUE. Categorically describes 6,000 facilities for the deaf and hard of hearing—residential schools, public day schools and classes, denominational and private schools in the United States and Canada. Gives names of religious personnel for the deaf in the U.S., camps for the deaf and hard of hearing, organizations for the deaf in the U.S., list of homes for the aged deaf, speech and hearing centers, and information about training of the deaf. 280 pp. Annually. "AMERICAN ANNALS OF THE DEAF," 5034 Wisconsin Ave., N.W., Washington, D.C. 20014.

RESEARCH CENTERS DIRECTORY. Contains information on the existence, location, activities, and fields of interest of the nearby 5,500 university-related and independent non-profit research units. Subject index included. 1,056 pp. Published by GALE RESEARCH CO., Book Tower, Detroit, Mich. 48226.

RESEARCH AND DEVELOPMENT DIRECTORY. Provides a listing of firms involved in R&D activities, classified by type. Economic Research Bureau of the San Diego Chamber of Commerce, 233 A Street, Suite 300, San Diego, Calif. 92101.

SAFETY JOURNAL DIRECTORY. Provides entries of 2,000 American and foreign associations and trade groups in the accident and fire prevention field; includes a list of safety product manufacturers. Annually. "THE SAFETY JOURNAL," Wilmary Building, Anderson, S.C. 29621.

SAFETY MAGAZINE—ROSTER ISSUE. Contains an alphabetical listing of 1,000 members of the Metropolitan Chapter of the American Society of Safety Engineers and of the Commercial Vehicle Section of the Greater New York Safety Council; includes other members of traffic engineers and others interested in safety precautions. 20 pp. Annually. GREATER NEW YORK SAFETY COUNCIL, 302 Fifth Ave., New York, N.Y. 10016.

SAFETY MATERIALS DIRECTORY. Listed are safety aids available to the private boating industry. Arranged by categories such as: boating guides and pamphlets; courses; films; navigation; rules and regulations; safety equipment. 45 pp. THE BOATING INDUSTRY, 205 East 42nd St., New York, N.Y. 10017.

SALES AND MARKETING EXECUTIVES INTERNATIONAL—ANNUAL REPORT AND DIRECTORY. Publication contains names of approximately 800 officers, directors, national committeemen and officers of affiliated clubs of Sales and Marketing Executives International. Annual. SALES AND MARKETING EXECUTIVES INTERNATIONAL, 380 Lexington Ave., New York, N.Y. 10017.

SECURITY SYSTEMS. The market for purchased private security systems is analyzed. The structure of the industry is examined and the products-protective services, deterrent equipment, monitoring and detection systems and fire control are described. An overview of the market is presented with a list of selected companies that manufacture security equipment or provide some security service. 60 pp. PREDICASTS, INC., 200 University Center, Research Center, 11001 Cedar Ave., Cleveland, Ohio 44106.

SOCIETY OF THE PLASTICS INDUSTRY DIRECTORY AND BUYERS' GUIDE OF MEMBERS. Directory consists of an alpha-geographic listing of 1,200 plastics industry companies, giving firm name, address, key personnel, products and processes; included is a who's who of The Society of the Plastics Industry. 407 pp. Annual. SOCIETY OF THE PLASTICS INDUSTRY, INC., 355 Lexington Ave., New York, N.Y. 10017.

SOURCES OF STATISTICS. This guide provides the principal sources of statistics in the United Kingdom, the United States and various international organizations. Grouped under ten headings are those publications covering demographics, sociology, education, labor, production, trade, finance, prices, transport and tourism. 126 pp. THE SHOE STRING PRESS, INC., 995 Sherman Ave., Hamden, Conn. 06514.

STATISTICAL ABSTRACT OF THE UNITED STATES. This guide to sources list over 800 statistical publications on 50 major subjects, including population, government, health, education, agriculture, industry, construction, etc. 1,300 tables and charts are also included. 1,024 pp. Annually. Superintendent of Documents, U.S. GOVERNMENT PRINTING OFFICE, Washington, D.C. 20402.

THE TRADEMARK REGISTER OF THE UNITED STATES—1977 EDITION. Alphabetically arranged, classified entries of approximately 450,000 currently registered trademarks in the United States Patent Office since 1881, with date of registration number. 1,000 pp. Annually. THE TRADEMARK REGISTER, 422 Washington Bldg., Washington, D.C. 20005.

TRADE NAMES DICTIONARY. A guide to trade names of food, beverages, apparel, household appliances, sports equipment and other consumer products. 100,000 entries listed. Two Volumes - 666 pp. GALE RESEARCH CO., Book Tower, Detroit, Mich. 48226.

UNESCO HANDBOOK OF INTERNATIONAL EXCHANGES. A reference on international activities and exchanges in the fields of education, science, culture and mass communication. Covers the aims, programs and activities of 295 international organizations and more than 5,000 governmental and nongovernmental agencies and institutions in 130 countries and territories. 1,102 pp. Published by UNIPUB, INC., P.O. Box 433, New York, N.Y. 10016.

UNITED NATIONS LIBRARY, THE. A bibliography containing all items relating to the Library and to the documents of the United Nations Library in New York. Also a description of the historical evolution of the Library. 250 pp. AMERICAN LIBRARY ASSOCIATION, 59 E. Huron St., Chicago, Ill. 60611.

URBAN REAL ESTATE RESEARCH. Publication contains an annotated list of 951 publications and research in process related to urban land use and urban planning, including central business district, economic base, finance, housing, industry, land planning, land use, zoning, real estate, redevelopment, shopping center, taxation, transportation, and urban renewal studies. Systematic topics include bibliographies, textbooks, reference works, metropolitan area studies, regional studies, urban research, and urbanism. Entries arranged by subject, with author and geographic indexes. 90 pp. ULI-THE URBAN LAND INSTITUTE, Ring Building., 1200 18th St., N.W., Washington, D.C. 20036.

U.S. NON-PROFIT ORGANIZATIONS IN DEVELOPMENT ASSISTANCE ABROAD—1971. Lists 499 non-profit organizations and their programs in 124 countries around the world (excluding Europe). 1,038 pp. TECHNICAL ASSISTANCE INFORMATION CLEARING HOUSE OF THE AMERICAN COUNCIL OF VOLUNTARY AGENCIES FOR FOREIGN SERVICE, INC., 200 Park Ave., S., New York, N.Y. 10003.

U.S. OBSERVATORIES: A DIRECTORY AND TRAVEL GUIDE. Geographical listing of approximately 300 optical and radio observatories and planetariums, including address, description of the facility, admission charges, brief history, etc. 175 pp. VAN NOSTRAND REINHOLD CO., Division of Litton Educational Publishing, Inc., New York, N.Y. 10001.

U.S. ZIP CODE BUSINESS MARKETING MAP ATLAS. Provides over 465 U.S. cities and metropolitan markets, five digit county maps, U.S. sectional center wall map, postal region state maps, income, age and occupation information, complete zip code marketing and advertising applications, full color demographic maps, complete postal marketing data, both as numeric and alphabetic U.S. post office directory. 1,000 pp. plus. NATIONAL DEMOGRAPHIC RESEARCH, 24 East Wesley Street, South Hackensack, N.J. 07606.

U.S. ZIP CODE DIRECTORY. Lists all cities and their zip codes in the U.S. U.S. ZIP CODE SERVICE, P.O. Box 2808, Main Post Office, Washington, D.C. 20013. (Not a U.S. Government publication.)

WALLCOVERINGS—ANNUAL DIRECTORY. Directory contains a master resources list, an alphabetically arranged list of 1,000 manufacturers, wholesalers and suppliers, wallpaper mills, specialty wallcoverings, machine print lines, hand prints, scenics and murals, etc. Also included is a list of accessory and equipment manufacturers. Annually. 172 pp. WALL COVERINGS, 209 Dunn Ave., Stamford, Conn. 06905.

WHAT'S HAPPENING, WHEN. Lists all the special promotion days, weeks, months plus many important dates. Designed to assist in the coordination of advertising and marketing plans with established observances during the year. Includes names and addresses of sponsors and other pertinent data. 28 pp. Annual. NATIONAL RESEARCH BUREAU, INC., 424 N. 3rd St., Burlington, Iowa 52601.

WHO WAS WHO IN AMERICAN HISTORY—SCIENCE AND TECHNOLOGY. Listing of 10,000 scientists, engineers, and inventors of American History. Covers more than 350 years of American History. 688 pp. MARQUIS WHO'S WHO INC., 200 East Ohio St., Chicago, Ill. 60611.

WHO'S WHO IN ADVERTISING. Lists 6,500 executives in all areas of advertising in the U.S. and Canada plus professors of advertising and marketing. 764 pp. Biennially. REDFIELD PUBLISHING CO., INC., P.O. Box 556, Rye, New York 10580.

WHO'S WHO IN BOOK MANUFACTURING. A list of firms and people who produce books. Included are their suppliers, bookbinders, and the manufacturers of bookbinding equipment. Each manufacturer will have their products and specialties, their major capital equipment and back-up facilities. Their number of employees, addresses, and other company data. Published by NORTH AMERICAN PUBLISHING CO., 401 N. Broad St., Philadelphia, Pa. 19108.

WHO'S WHO IN PUBLIC RELATIONS. An alpha-geographic list of 5,000 public relation leaders in 59 countries, including full biographical sketches of each. 474 pp. Published every four or five years. PR PUBLISHING CO., INC., P.O. Box 600, Dudley House, Exeter, New Hampshire 03833.

WHO'S WHO IN PUBLISHING. An alphabetical list of over 2,000 biographical sketches for men and women throughout the world prominent and active in the world of publishing. 225 pp. Published every five years by ALEXANDER P. WALES, 18 Charing Cross, London, England.

WHO'S WHO IN RELIGION. Contains more than 18,500 sketches of outstanding men and women from America's religious community. Including church officials (both lay and clergy), religious educators, founders and directors of religious charities and other religious organizations, editors and writers for major religious publications, plus leading priests, rabbis, ministers, and other clergy. 736 pp. MARQUIS PUBLICATIONS, 200 East Ohio St., Room 5605, Chicago, Ill. 60611.

WORLD DIRECTORY OF MAP COLLECTIONS. Data on 285 map and chart collections held in national libraries, scientific and historic societies, and military departments of 46 countries. Including printed and manuscript maps, atlases, globes, relief models, aerial photographs, reference books, serials. 326 pp. UNIPUB, Box 433, Murray Hill Station, New York, N.Y. 10016.

WORLD DIRECTORY OF ORGANIZATIONS. Comprehensive guide to organizations in all parts of the world that are concerned with the pressing problems of the human environment. Describes over 3,200 organizations in nearly 200 countries. 288 pp. CENTER FOR CALIFORNIA PUBLIC AFFAIRS, P.O. Box 30, Claremont, Calif. 91711.

WORLD DIRECTORY OF RESEARCH CENTERS. Lists 4,800 American organizations and many others throughout the world engaged in research on the environment. Includes research institutes, laboratories, industrial organizations and private foundations and federal, state and local governmental organizations. Material is divided into subject categories. 330 pp. R. R. BOWKER CO., P.O. Box 1807, Ann Arbor, Mich. 48106.

WORLD GUIDE TO ABBREVIATIONS OF ASSOCIATION AND INSTITUTIONS. This two-volume edition lists 50,000 nationally and internationally accepted Roman alphabet acronyms used by more than 120 governmental, commercial, cultural, religious, and other institutions. An alphabetical index of acronyms by country is also included. 1,295 pp. R. R. BOWKER CO., 1180 Avenue of the Americas, New York, N.Y. 10036.

WORLD GUIDE TO SCIENTIFIC ASSOCIATIONS. Describes 10,000 scientific associations, organizations and academies in more than 134 countries. Covers all scientific disciplines plus medically oriented groups. Nams are arranged by countries with an index to field of endeavor. 700 pp. R. R. BOWKER CO., P.O. Box 1807, Ann Arbor, Mich. 48106.

ZIPCODER. Provides over 2,500 9-⅞" quality bond loose-leaf pages of current zip code listings with county identification and all single coded cities and over 60,000 place name listings alphabetically by state on white bond paper, etc. ZIPCO, INC., 40 Guernsey St., Stamford, Conn. 06904.

Appendix G

GUIDELINES FOR ETHICAL BUSINESS PRACTICE OF THE DIRECT MAIL / MARKETING ASSOCIATION

We hold that a responsibility of the DM/MA to its members and to all individuals and firms who use, create, produce or supply direct mail advertising is to be a constructive and useful force in business and the economy in general.

We further hold that, to discharge this responsibility, they should recognize their obligation to the public, the medium they represent, and to each other.

Finally, we believe this responsibility will best be discharged if all such individuals and firms can refer to a recognized set of guidelines.

To this end, the DM/MA recommends the following GUIDELINES FOR ETHICAL BUSINESS PRACTICE as being in the best interests of the public, all advertising, and of direct mail advertising users, creators, producers, and suppliers in particular.

These guidelines are intended to serve as a guide to the kind of business conduct which experience has shown to be wise, foresighted, and constructive.

Because we believe dishonest, misleading, immoral, salacious or offensive communications make enemies for all advertising as well as direct mail, we recommend observance of these guidelines and standards by all concerned.

OPERATING GUIDELINES FOR ETHICAL ADVERTISING PRACTICE

1. Advertisers should make their offers clear and honest. They should not misrepresent a product, service or solicitation and should not use misleading, half-true or exaggerated statements. Advertisers should operate in accordance with the Fair Practice Code of the Council of Better Business Bureaus and be cognizant of and adhere to the Postal Laws and Regulations, and all other laws governing advertising and transaction of business by mail.

2. Advertisers should not make offers which purport to require a person to return a notice that he does not wish to receive further merchandise in order to avoid liability for the purchase price, unless all the conditions are first made clear in an initial offer that is accepted by the purchaser by

means of a bona fide written order. Attention is suggested to more detailed specifications regarding negative option plans which have been formulated by the FTC.

3. Mailings should not contain vulgar, immoral, profane or offensive matter nor should advertisers use the mails to promote the sale of pornographic material or other matter not acceptable for mailing on accepted moral grounds. Advertisers should not use the mails to promote the sale of products or services by means of lottery.

4. The terms and conditions of guarantee should be clearly and specifically set forth in immediate conjunction with the guarantee offer. Guarantees should be limited to the reasonable performance capabilities and qualities of the product or service advertised.

5. Advertisers should not make exaggerated price comparisons, claims on discounts or savings; nor employ fictitious prices.

6. A product or service which is offered without cost or obligation to the recipient may be unqualifiedly described as "free." "Free" may also be used conditionally where the offer requires the recipient to purchase some other product or service, provided all terms and conditions are accurately and conspicuously disclosed in immediate conjunction with the use of the term "free" and the product or service required to be purchased is not increased in price or decreased in quality or quantity.

7. Photographs and art work implying representation of a product or service offered should be faithful reproductions of the product or service. Photographs and art work implying situations under which a product or service would be advantageous to the purchaser should be in accord with written claims.

8. If laboratory test data are used in advertising, they should be competent as to source and methodology. Advertisers should not use excerpts of laboratory test material in support of claims which distort or fail to disclose the true test results.

9. Advertisers should not use unsupported or inaccurate testimonials; or testimonials originally given for products or services other than those offered by the advertiser; or testimonials making statements or conclusions the advertiser

knows to be incorrect. If testimonials are used, they should contain no misstatement of facts or misleading implications and should reflect the current opinion of the author.

10. Advertisers who sell instruction, catalogs, mailing lists or merchandise-for-resale should not use misleading or deceptive statements with respect to the earning possibilities, lack of risk, or ease of operation.

11. Advertisers should not use promotional solicitations in the forms of bills or invoices (pro forma invoices) deceptively.

12. Advertisers should not mail unordered merchandise for which payment is demanded.

13. Advertisers should not use any list in violation of the lawful rights of the list owner; and should promptly bring to the attention of the lawful owner of any list any information they may have regarding any possible violation of his proprietary rights therein.

14. If products or services are offered on a satisfaction guaranteed or money back basis, refunds should be made promptly on request. In an unqualified offer of refund or replacement, the customer's preference shall prevail.

15. Advertisers should be prepared to make prompt delivery of orders solicited in their copy. Unforeseen contingencies should be reported to the customer promptly when delivery is unavoidably delayed. A reply device should be included, enabling the customer, if he wishes, to cancel the order and obtain a refund of any purchase price already paid.

16. Advertisers should not use misleading or deceptive methods for collecting money owed by delinquent accounts.

17. Advertisers should distribute products only in a manner that will provide reasonable safeguards against possibilities of injury to children and/or adults.

18. All advertisers including those firms who use, create, produce or supply materials and/or lists for direct mail advertising should make conscientious efforts to remove names from their mailing lists when so requested either directly or in accordance with the DM/MA Mail Preference Service.

FAIR TRADE CODE FOR ADVERTISING AND SELLING

1. Serve the public with honest values.
2. Tell the truth about what is offered.
3. Tell the truth in a forthright manner so its significance may be understood by the trusting as well as the analytical.
4. Tell customers what they want to know—what they have a right to know, and ought to know about what is offered so that they may buy wisely and obtain the maximum satisfaction from their purchase.
5. Be prepared and willing to make good as promised and without quibble on any guarantee offered.
6. Be sure that the normal use of merchandise or services offered will not be hazardous to public health or life.
7. Reveal material facts, the deceptive concealment of which might cause consumers to be misled.
8. Advertise and sell merchandise or service on its merits and refrain from attacking your competitors or reflecting unfairly upon their products, services, or methods of doing business.
9. If testimonials are used, use only those of competent witnesses who are sincere and honest in what they say about what you sell.
10. Avoid all tricky devices and schemes such as deceitful trade-in allowances, fictitious list prices, false and exaggerated comparative prices, bait advertising, misleading free offers, fake sales and similar practices which prey on human ignorance and gullibility.

(Association of Better Business Bureaus, Inc.)

PROCEDURE IN IMPLEMENTATION OF STANDARDS OF PRACTICE

DM/MA believes most violations of the STANDARDS will be inadvertent and unintentional, and can be disposed of by the DM/MA executive staff.

This will be accomplished by an informal exchange of views between the DM/MA executive staff and the member who is believed to be in violation of the STANDARDS.

An initial letter will be sent outlining the reasons why the member is believed to be in violation, requesting it be corrected, and inviting rebuttal if the member does not agree he is in violation.

If the question involved cannot be adjusted by the DM/MA executive staff, the case will be referred to the STANDARDS OF PRACTICE Committee for further action.

After the Committee has reached a determination, a formal letter will be mailed to the member, if adverse, requiring his answer as to whether he will make correction, and what steps he will take to accomplish this. If he fails to cooperate, the Committee will recommend suspension or expulsion to the Board of Directors, with subsequent action according to provision of the bylaws.

No publicity will be given on any casework until final action, and then only if no correction is accomplished, with the member either being expelled, suspended, or resigning of his own volition.

A formal report will be made and published in such cases.

The above is the procedure as it applies to DM/MA members. When a non-member is thought to be in violation of the STANDARDS, every effort will be made to apprise him of this, and he will be urged to discontinue the violation, in the interests of more effective Direct Mail.

CODE OF ETHICS

and standards of practice for the rental and exchange of mailing lists Published by the Direct Mail / Marketing Association

SECTION I

Purpose of the Code

The purpose of this Code is to standardize and improve common practices and procedures in the rental and exchange of mailing lists.

Except for the basic offer itself, lists are the most important single element in the success of any direct mail campaign. And bad list practices are the cause of more waste and more unproductive mailings than any other single phase of the direct mail operation.

When a rented mailing list fails to produce for a mailer, not only the mailer suffers, but the list owner and the list broker as well. For obviously, a mailer will not continue to use a list that fails.

But beyond these immediate financial losses, any list failure hurts the long-range interests of all mailers. The direct mail industry is completely dependent on the continued development of new and productive lists. The best way to develop such lists is to cultivate in more and more people the habit of responding to mail. That can be done *only* through successful mailings to existing lists.

Moreover, bad list practices discourage present list owners from permitting their lists to be used widely by other mailers, thus cutting down the number of good lists currently available.

The standardization and improvement of mailing list practices through the acceptance and observance of this Code will, therefore, serve the interests of all mailers by:

- *making the operations of both mailers and list owners more efficient*
- *serving as a guide for newcomers in the field*
- *reducing the risks inherent in testing new lists*
- *improving returns and so reducing order costs*
- *inducing more list owners to allow their lists to be used*

SECTION II

Obligations of the List Owner

A. *General Obligations*

A list owner is under no obligation to permit other mailers to use his list. But most owners who are themselves dependent on the use of outside lists find it to their advantage to permit such usage. And many owners have found that the responsiveness of a list is increased, rather than diminished, when such usage is permitted under properly controlled conditions.

However, when a list owner *does* permit other mailers to use his list, he must recognize that these mailers are *his customers.* If he accepts their orders, they are entitled to the same consideration, fair dealing and good service that any other type of customer has a right to expect from his suppliers.

B. *Information Furnished to Prospective Users*

Any list owner who offers a list to other mailers on a rental or exchange basis will provide those mailers with the following information, either directly or through the established list brokers:

1. *Nature and Quantity of Names Available*

a. The *name* under which a list is offered will be an accurate reflection of the nature of the list . . . buyers, subscribers, expirations, inquiries, prospects, business executives, home owners, automobile registrants, etc. These terms will be used in the meanings commonly accepted and understood by mailers.

b. The *quantity* will be an accurate statement of the names available at the time the list is offered, within a margin of 5 percent.

c. Where a list includes names of more than one type—e.g., customers *and* prospects, subscribers *and* expirations, long *and* short term expirations, paid *and* controlled subscribers, etc.—the list owner will specify as accurately as possible *the percentage of total names* available in each category, and state whether or not they can be separated.

d. As much additional information as possible will be provided to help prospective mailers evaluate the list—age, sex, economic status, business position, nature and price of product purchased, other mailers who have used the list successfully, etc.

e. If substantially the same list has previously been offered by the present or a previous owner under a different name, that information will be included in all offerings of the list.

f. If any copy of all or a portion of the list has been in the past, or is in the future, sold or otherwise turned over to any mailer on anything but a one-time rental or exchange basis, that information will be included in all offerings of the list.

g. If any substantial change occurs in the nature or size of the list, such as an addition or deletion of certain names, rearrangement, change in addressing method, etc., that information will be given promptly to all mailers who are currently using the list and to the list brokers.

2. *Source of the Names*

a. When names on a list have been obtained by more than one method, all methods used will be specified, and a reasonably accurate estimate made as to the percentage of names obtained by each method.

Examples: Prospect lists obtained by compilation from directories, from salesmen's call reports, etc. Subscribers or buyers obtained through direct mail, publication advertising, radio and television, field salesmen, etc. Inquiries obtained by direct mail, publication advertising, radio, television, etc. Compiled lists obtained from trade directories, telephone directories, news items, trade notes, convention rosters, etc.

b. When *different types* of publications have been used for space advertising, the publications mentioned as sources of the names will be an accurate reflection of the total advertising schedule. In no case shall a publication be listed as a source of names unless at least 10 percent of all the names obtained through publication advertising were obtained from that particular publication.

3. *Age of the Names*

a. When a compiled list is offered, the year of original compilation will be stated, along with the date of the latest revision. If directories were used for original compilation or revision, the date of issue of the directories used will be stated.

b. When a list is composed of buyers or inquiries, the year or years during which the purchases or inquiries were made will be specified.

c. When a list is composed of expirations, the year or years of expiration will be specified.

d. The term "current" as applied to buyers, inquiries, or expirations will be used *only* to mean less than one year old.

4. *Duplication of Names Within or Between Lists*

a. If the names of individuals or companies appear more than once at the same address within a list, the owner will estimate and state the amount of such duplication.

b. If the owner offers more than one list for rental or exchange, he will estimate and state the amount of duplication, if any, between his various lists. Duplication here shall mean the same as in paragraph "a" immediately preceding.

5. *Maintenance of List*

a. The list owner will furnish information as to how the list is maintained—on cards, on stencils and of what type, typed from original inquiries, typed to order from directories, etc.

b. The list owner will state the arrangement of the list—"geographical, alphabetical, chronological, etc." "Geographical" will mean filed by state, then by city, then alphabetically within the city, and any departure from this standard method of geographical filing will be noted. If a state breakdown is available, counts for the individual states will be given, or the availability of such counts will be noted.

c. If a list is so filed that sections can be taken from it in more than one way—e.g., by year of purchase or expiration *as well as* geographically—that information will be furnished.

d. The list owner will state how often and by what method the list is kept clean. If the list is cleaned at least once every six months by a mailing using Form 3547, then he may merely state that the list is cleaned "regularly." If not, then the date on which the list was last cleaned will be stated.

C. *Selection of Names for Tests*

1. *When List is Filed Geographically*

a. If the mailer orders specific quantities from certain test states, the list owner will provide the quantities specified. If he cannot provide the quantity called for from a certain state, he may substitute names from an immediately adjacent state. In no case, however, will he use a substitute state for more than 20 percent of the names ordered from any state without checking with the list user or the broker who placed the order.

b. If the mailer does not specify test states, but merely asks for a good cross section of the list, the list owner will select equal quantities of names from at least five different states. He will take these names from states in different geographical sections of the country—e.g., he might take Massachusetts (New England), Pennsylvania (Mid-Atlantic), Georgia (South), Illinois (Mid-West) and California (Far West). However, if his list is used frequently, he will *not* constantly use the same states, or the same cities within a state, for test orders.

c. When the mailer requests a good cross section of the list, the owner will take care to see that the test names do not all come from large cities, or all from small towns. For example, in using the test states mentioned above, he would *not* take all the names from Boston, Philadelphia, Atlanta, Chicago and Los Angeles. Instead, he would choose the names so they accurately reflected the general distribution of the list between towns and cities of various sizes.

d. If a list is regional rather than national, the list owner will select the test names so that they accurately reflect the content of the list as a whole.

2. *When List is Filed Alphabetically*

a. If the mailer specifies the sections of the list he wants, the list owner will follow these instructions.

b. If the mailer merely asks for a good cross section of the list, the owner will take one-fourth of the test names from each of the following alphabetical sections of the list:

A through D	L through R
E through K	S through Z

If the list is used frequently, the list owner will avoid constantly taking the same names from within these alphabetical groups for tests.

3. *When List is Filed Chronologically*

a. If the mailer specifies the section of the list he wants, the owner will follow these instructions.

b. If the mailer merely asks for a good cross section of the list, the owner will address 20 percent of the order from the newest names in the list, 20 percent from the oldest names, and three groups of 20 percent taken at regular intervals from the balance of the file. He will avoid using the same names constantly on test orders.

4. *When List Contains Different Types of Names*

a. If a list contains different types of names, as discussed in Paragraph 1-c of Section II-B above, or if it contains names of the same types but of varying age, the list owner will select a proportionate number of the test names from each type of name and/or from each age group.

D. *Keeping a Record of Names Used*

1. When a mailer uses part of a list, either on a test or on a continuation order, the list owner will keep an accurate record of the portion of the list used on that order. This record will be kept by the list owner's maintenance department or his lettershop, in any way that will make the information quickly and conveniently available. Such methods include notations on the purchase order or job jacket covering the addressing work, an actual imprint of the first and last addressing plate used, a schedule of completed jobs with names used on each, etc.

2. Whenever a list owner receives an order from a mailer who has previously used his list, he will consult his records and give instructions so that the names previously used will not be repeated without the mailer's knowledge. This is good practice at any time, but it is obligatory when the mailer specifically requests the omission of names used on one or more previous orders.

E. *Protection of Mailing Dates*

1. If a mailer orders a list for use on a specific date, the list owner will not accept any other order for use of the same names *within one week* of the specified date.

2. If a mailer orders a list without specifying a mailing date, the list owner will accept the order *only* if the mailer guarantees to protect mailing dates which the list owner has already assigned to other mailers. (It will usually be necessary for the list owner to *assign* a definite mailing date to users who do not request it, so that he will be able to accept orders from other mailers who *do* require such protection.)

3. To facilitate the protection of mailing dates, the list owner will maintain

an accurate schedule of all mailings to be made to this list, both by himself and by outside mailers.

F. *Addressing and Returning Mailer's Material*

1. The list owner will make every effort to return the mailer's addressed material in perfect condition, with a minimum of spoilage, and by the date requested.
2. If circumstances make it impossible to meet a requested delivery date, the list owner will notify the mailer as early as possible, either directly, or through the list broker who submitted the order.
3. Addressed material will be packed carefully in sound containers, and each container will be clearly marked on the most visible side (*not* the top) with the name of the list, the key number specified by the mailer, and the mailer's name.
4. If possible, the same quantity of addressed material will be packed in each container. Otherwise, the quantity in each container will be marked.
5. Geographical lists will be packed as nearly as possible in geographical order, to save sorting charges for the mailer.
6. If the mailer specifies the shipping method by which the material is to be returned, the owner will follow these instructions as closely as possible. If no method is specified, or if the method specified cannot be used, the list owner will return material by the best method currently available.

SECTION III
Obligations of the Mailer

A. *Restrictions on the Use of Lists*

1. *Re-using or Copying Names*

   Unless there is a specific understanding to the contrary, names obtained from a list owner on rental or exchange will be used once only. The mailer will make no copy of any names obtained by rental or exchange, nor permit any copy to be made, either for his own use or the use of any other mailer.

2. *Use Limited to Purpose Specified*

   In ordering any list, the mailer will specify the purpose for which he intends to use it and the nature of the offer to be made. The list will not be used for any other type of mailing, or for the promotion of any product or service except that specified in the list order, without notification to, and approval by, the list owner.

3. *Use of Corrected Addresses*

   a. The mailer will recognize that even though he obtains new addresses on a list by mailing using Form 3547, the names are still the property of the list owner. He may re-mail his original offer to such names at the corrected addresses, but he will make no further mailing to them without the permission of the list owner.

   b. The mailer is under no obligation to turn such corrected addresses over to the list owner unless such an arrangement has been made in advance, and suitable payment is made by the list owner.

B. *Observance of Assigned Mailing Dates*

1. When a list owner assigns a definite mailing date for the use of his list, the mailer will scrupulously observe that date. Unless at least 90 percent of the mailing to the list is put into the mails on the specified date or within 24 hours thereof, the mailer will immediately notify the list owner, directly or through the broker who handled the order.

2. If a mailer requests and is assigned a mailing date for a list, and confirms the arrangement with a definite order, and if he then fails to use that date with a resultant loss of revenue to the list owner, the mailer shall, at the list owner's discretion, be liable for a payment to the list owner of one-half the rental charge on the number of names ordered.

C. *Specifying Names for List Testing*

The mailer will recognize that it is costly for a list owner to select specified sections of a list for testing purposes, and that both the owner and the broker usually lose money on handling small test orders. He will also realize that the larger the test, the more dependable are his results. For these reasons, he will order as large quantities as are feasible for his list tests, and will keep his instructions for the selection of names as simple as possible.

D. *Placing Orders and Shipping Material*

1. Orders for the use of a list on rental or exchange will give the following information.

   a. Quantity of names desired and clear identification of the list.

   b. Date on which the list will be mailed.

   c. Rental rate.

   d. Purpose of use, with sample of proposed mailing if requested.

   e. Type of material to be addressed (envelopes, order forms, etc.) with sample.

   f. When and how material will be shipped to list owner.

   g. When, where and how addressed material is to be returned.

   h. Key number.

   i. Any special instructions, such as test specifications, omission of certain names, etc.

   j. Guarantee that names will not be copied and release dates will be honored.

2. Orders will be placed as far in advance of the proposed mailing dates as possible, to enable the list owner to schedule the addressing efficiently, and to avoid the extra expense and added chance of error involved in rush jobs.

3. Material will not be shipped for addressing until the order is accepted by the list owner or his broker. If the material cannot be shipped by the date specified in the list order, the mailer will notify the list owner or his broker promptly.

4. All containers in which material is shipped for addressing will be plainly marked, outside and inside, with the name of the mailer, the key number, and the name of the list to be used. Outside markings will be on the most visible side (*not* the top) of the container.

5. The mailer will pay the shipping charges both ways on material which he sends to a list owner for addressing.

E. *Payment for List Rentals*

Unless some other arrangement has been made with the list owner or his broker, payment for the rental of any mailing list will be made not later than 30 days after the scheduled mailing date.

SECTION IV

Obligations of the List Broker

A. *Information Furnished to Prospective Users*

1. Any broker who offers a list to prospective users will get from the list owner, and pass on to the prospective user, all the information specified under Section II-B of this code.
2. On all cards or other information sent out by a broker to prospective mailers, the broker will use *only* the name designated by the owner for that list.

B. *Selection of Lists for Recommendation*

The broker will exercise his best judgment and discrimination in sending list cards to prospective users, and will not deluge such users with cards covering lists of little or no possible use to him.

C. *Reports of Bad Service*

When mailers report bad service or other avoidable difficulties in connection with the use of any list, the broker involved in the transaction will inform the list owner of these reports, and use his influence to induce the list owner to improve his list rental practices.

D. *Education of List Owners*

The list broker will do his utmost to inform any list owner whose lists he offers as to the owner's obligations and responsibilities to users of his list and as to the ethics and standards of practice of the list rental business. He will take particular pains to convey this information to an owner who has never before rented his list, and who is induced to rent his list by the broker.

E. *Education of List Users*

The list broker will also do his best to inform mailers, and particularly inexperienced mailers, as to their obligations to list owners and as to the ethics and standards of practice of the list rental business.

SECTION V

Relations of Mailer, List Owner and Broker

A. *Choice of a Broker*

In the mailer-owner-broker relationship as presently practiced, the list owner is the seller, the broker is his special sales agent, and the mailer is the customer.

The list owner is free to choose the broker or brokers who are authorized to offer his list for rental or exchange. The broker is free to choose the list owners whom he will represent. However, in their own self-interest, list owners and mailers will usually follow such established practices as ordering a list through the first broker who recommends it, continuing to place orders on that list through the same broker as long as his service is satisfactory, etc. And as the customer, the mailer is free to deal with any broker he chooses.

B. *Commissions on List Exchanges*

When an exchange is arranged by two list owners on their own initiative, and not on that of a list broker, it will not be necessary for either owner to clear the exchange through any list broker or to pay any list broker a commission on the transaction. If one party to the exchange chooses to have the order for his names come through a list broker, he will so advise the other owner. In this case, however, the broker will bill the first owner for the usual rental commission on the use of his names, and the second list owner shall be bound neither to have the order for his names clear through the broker, nor to pay any commission on the transaction.

SECTION VI
Enforcement of the Code

A. *Voluntary Subscription*

Any mailer, list owner or broker (who is a member of the Direct Mail/Marketing Association) may subscribe to the Code by voluntarily signing a statement that he has read and understands its provisions, and that he will comply with such of those provisions as apply to his operations.

The Direct Mail/Marketing Association will maintain in its headquarters office a current list of those of its members who have subscribed to the Code, such list to be available for inspection by any member of the Association at any time.

B. *Certification of Mailing Lists*

1. Any group of 20 or more mailers who use the same type of mailing lists and who themselves subscribe to the Code may (upon written application to, and approval by, the Direct Mail/Marketing Association) nominate a List Certification Committee for their segment of the direct mail industry.
2. The Certification Committee will be composed of four mailers who are members of the industry group, one list owner, and one list broker, all of whom have subscribed to the Code.
3. Proposed members of the Committee will be selected by secret ballot, taken either at a meeting of the group or by mail. Their names will then be submitted to the Chairman of the Board of Governors of the Direct Mail/Marketing Association for his approval and formal appointment.
4. Any list owner who wishes to have a list certified as complying with this Code will sign the following statement and submit to the DM/MA Certification Committee which represents users of his type of list.

   "I hereby certify that all transactions involving the rental or exchange of the list named below will be handled in compliance with the (DM/MA) Code of Ethics and Standards of Practice for the Rental and Exchange of Mailing Lists, and I hereby apply for the Certification Committee's Seal of Compliance.

"I further certify that I have read the Code in full, that I understand its provisions, and that I exert sufficient supervision over the personnel handling this list to guarantee that the Code's provisions will be observed.

"This application is made with the full understanding that the Seal of Compliance may be withdrawn at any time by a two-thirds vote of the Certification Committee if, in their judgment, I have failed to comply with the provisions of the Code."

5. Upon receipt of such a signed statement from a list owner, the Certification Committee will assign a certification number to the list and, within 15 days, notify the list owner and all brokers handling his list that the list has been granted the Committee's Seal of Compliance.

6. After such notification by the Certification Committee, all cards or other information sent to prospective users of the list, either by the owner or by the list brokers, will clearly indicate that the list has been granted the DM/MA Seal of Compliance, and give its Certification number.

C. *Withdrawal of the Seal of Compliance*

1. Any mailer who subscribes to this Code and who has good reason to believe that a list owner has violated any of its provisions, may report the circumstances to the proper Certification Committee. The Certification Committee will investigate the circumstances and bring the complaint to the attention of the list owner. If, after investigation, the Committee concludes that the Code has been violated, and that such violations are likely to be repeated, it may withdraw the DM/MA Seal of Compliance. Such withdrawal can be made only by a two-thirds vote of all the members of the Committee.

2. Within five days after the Committee has voted to withdraw its DM/MA Seal of Compliance from any list, it will notify the list owner and all brokers handling the list of such withdrawal. The Committee may, at its discretion, also notify all the mailers whom it represents of such withdrawal.

3. After notification by the Certification Committee that the Seal of Compliance has been withdrawn from any list, the brokers will send out no more cards to prospective users of the list which would indicate that the list is still certified. Until such time as they can send out new cards without the Seal of Compliance, the list brokers will accept no rental orders or exchanges without notifying the prospective users that the Seal of Compliance has been withdrawn.

D. *Freedom to Use Uncertified Lists*

Mailers who have subscribed to this Code are free to use any mailing list, whether or not it has ever been given the Seal of Compliance of any DM/MA Certification Committee, or whether or not such Seal has ever been withdrawn. Withdrawal of the Seal merely puts the mailer on notice that the list owner, in the judgment of the Certification Committee, is no longer complying with the provisions of this Code.

Appendix H

A PRIMER ON THE POSTAL SERVICE*

By Elaine Jorpeland

IF ALL of the associations represented in ASAE were to send a first-class letter to each of their members on any given day, the total cost for postage would be $4.7 million. Staggering? Not really. It is no secret that communication is the lifeblood of every association—and that to communicate with your members, you must oftentimes rely heavily on the U.S. Postal Service to deliver your message.

The cost of postage eats up a large portion of most association budgets; thus, it is wise to make sure that you are getting the most for your postal dollar.

The place to start is to make sure that you—or someone on your staff—has a thorough understanding of postal rules and regulations, keeps up to date with changing rules, and sees that all staff members responsible for handling mailings—whether bulk or individual—follow the proper procedures.

The purpose of this article is to serve as a primer, a basic guide to the various classifications of mail that associations use most often. You should consult the *Postal Manual* for specific wording of mailing requirements. (You can order a copy of the *Domestic Postal Manual,* which contains most of the information you need, from the Superintendent of Documents, Washington, DC 20402. The cost is $17 per year; updates are sent as they become available.)

I. FIRST-CLASS MAIL

Although this is perhaps the easiest category of mail to define and understand, it is also the most expensive, and thus deserves careful scrutiny.

The *Postal Manual* describes first-class mail as follows:

1. Postal cards, which means cards that are supplied by the Postal Service with a postage stamp printed or impressed on them.

2. Post cards, which are privately printed mailing cards. These cards may be of any light color that does not affect the legibility of addresses and postmarks (brilliant colors are not allowed). In order to qualify for the first-class postage rate for post cards (13 cents, as opposed to 18 cents for regular first class), post cards must conform to these specifications:

- They must be no larger than 4¼ by 6 inches, nor smaller than 3½ by 5 inches. They must be rectangular in shape, and they should have a ratio of width (height) to length between 1 to 1.3 and 1 to 2.5.

*Courtesy of ASSOCIATION MANAGEMENT, from their July 1979 issue.

• The thickness of the card must be not less than .007 nor more than .0095 inch.

3. Matter wholly or partially in writing or typewriting, except authorized additions to second-, third- or fourth-class mail.

4. Matter closed against postal inspection.

5. Bills and statements of account. (Dues notices generally are considered as bills for postal purposes. However, solicitations and promotions are properly third-class mail.)

First-class rates of 18 cents for the first ounce or fraction and 17 cents for each additional ounce or fraction apply to all first-class mail other than post cards. Maximum weight limit for first class is 12 ounces.

First-class mail weighing more than 12 ounces is sent as priority mail, with rates charged by the weight of the package and the destination zone.

Presorting First-Class Mail

If you presort identical pieces of first-class mail, you can earn discounts of one or two cents per piece, providing that the presorting is done according to proper procedures and that you have a minimum of 500 pieces.

This is the way it works: The discount is two cents for each letter and one cent for each card that is part of a group of (1) 10 or more pieces sorted to the same five-digit Zip code; or (2) 50 or more pieces sorted to the same three-digit Zip code.

Certain other rules apply to presort. Each piece must weigh 12 ounces or less. In organizing a mailing using presort, you must be sure that all five-digit sorts in groups of 100 or more are completely exhausted before moving on to three-digit sorts in groups of 50 or more. Any mail remaining that is not presorted must be mailed at the full first-class rates.

Directions for preparing and labeling the mailing are available from your post office (or you can look them up in the *Postal Manual*). You must file a mailing statement with each mailing—Form 3602 for mailings bearing a permit imprint and Form 3602-PC for mailings bearing meter imprints or precanceled stamps. The use of presort also requires a $30 annual fee.

You can now also mail pieces of first-class metered mail that are not identical in size and weight at the presort rate, provided that all other requirements are met.

Is Presort Economical for You?

How many pieces do you need to mail in order to make presort economical for you? There are no hard and fast rules, but there is a rule of thumb, worked out by Dan Schellhorn of Swift Mailing Service, Inc., in Brentwood, Maryland. His calculations show that, on a national mailing, you need 20,000 to 30,000 pieces in order to make economical use of presort. Within a metropolitan area, that figure drops to 5,000 to 6,000. Within one state, presort may be advantageous, depending on the number of pieces you are mailing. There are exceptions, of course, particularly if you have a large concentration of recipients in one area.

Business Reply Mail

If you're planning to use business reply mail, you must file a Form 3614, Application to Distribute Business Reply Cards, and pay a $30 annual fee.

You can pay for business reply mail in one or two ways: with an advance deposit trust account at your post office, or by simply paying the person who delivers your mail for each item due. There is a big difference in the cost, however, and if you use business reply mail ex-

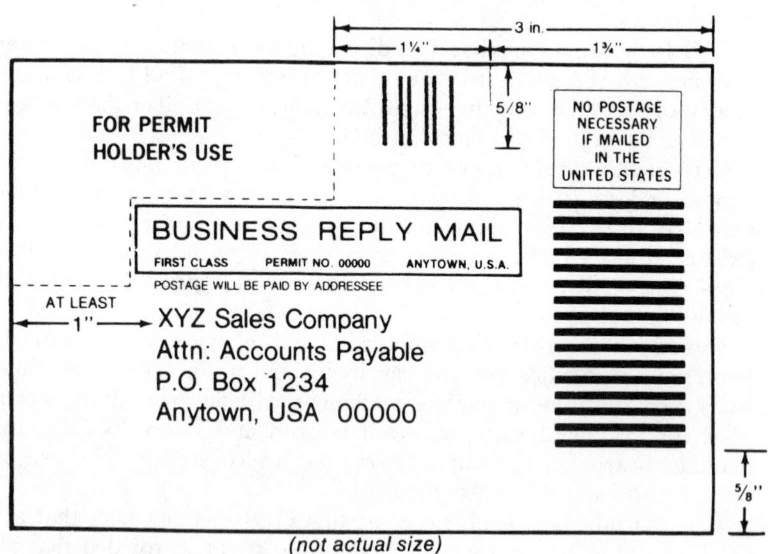

As of May 1, 1979, all business reply cards and envelopes must use this address format. The Facing Identification Mark—the vertical bar code pattern in the top right portion of this sample card — acts as an orientation mark for automatic feeding and canceling equipment.

tensively, you will definitely find the advance deposit trust account more economical.

This is how it works: You pay a $75 annual accounting fee and establish a deposit at the post office. As business reply mail is returned to you, the cost is simply deducted from your account. The cost per piece is the appropriate first-class postage plus a surcharge of 3.5 cents.

On the other hand, if you do not maintain an advance deposit trust account, the cost per piece is the appropriate first-class postage plus a surcharge of 12 cents. This must be paid when the mail is delivered to your office.

The latest news in business reply mail is the format that must be used on all envelopes and reply cards. The format requires a Facing Identification Mark, which is similar to the bar-code pattern used in electronic reading of grocery products. The illustration on page 1450 shows the new format, which went into effect May 1, 1979.

II. SECOND-CLASS MAIL

Since second-class postage is the least expensive of all classes of mail, you may want to obtain second-class privileges for any of your materials that qualify. Periodical publications would be the simplest definition of what qualifies for second class.

However, the definition of what constitutes a "periodical" has traditionally been a stumbling block. Originally, the Postal Service defined periodicals as "ordinarily containing a variety of original articles by different authors." Last year, however, a U.S. Court of Appeals ruled that the *Readers' Guide to Periodical Literature,* a compiled listing, should qualify for second-class mailing privileges.

The court said that a publication should be required to have "the feature of periodicity and be a periodical in the ordinary meaning of the term." The court also recommended that USPS develop a more complete definition of the term.

In addition to attempting to define the term "periodical," the *Postal Manual* explains in great detail what may and may not be mailed at second-class rates.

Special Editions

The manual lists the following types of extra or special editions or issues which may be mailed at second-class rates:

- Extra issues or editions issued for the purpose of communicating additional news and information received too late for insertion in the regular edition and not for advertising purposes.

• Separate editions of the issues of a second-class publication. (Exactly what constitutes a separate edition is a bit vague, and the manual does not expand on it; however, it does go on to point out that "Separate publications will not be accepted as editions.")

• Issues containing annual reports, directories, lists, and similar text as part of the contents, but the copies may not be distinguished from the regular issues by bearing designations which indicate they are annuals, directories, catalogs, yearbooks, or other types of separate publications. The regular annual subsription price must include the copies of such issues.

Thus, if one of the issues of your magazine is a membership directory issue, you can mail it second-class so long as you don't call it a directory and if you conform to the rest of the requirements. And it would have to be sent to your entire subscriber list.

Supplements

The *Postal Manual* separately defines what USPS considers to be supplements to second-class publications. Issues may include supplements, provided that they meet the following conditions:

• The supplement must be germane to the issue, and prepared in order to complete it, having been omitted for want of space, time, or greater convenience.

• Publishers must be paid at advertising rates and charges for carrying preprinted advertising supplements which are furnished to them by advertisers or others. The advertising supplements must be germane to the issue.

• Publications which are distinct from and independent of the regular issue, such as catalogs, circulars, handbills, posters, and other special advertisements are not considered to be germane to the issue and may not be inserted as supplements.

• A supplement must bear the title of the publication preceded by the words "Supplement to."

• Supplements must be folded and mailed with the regular issue.

Enclosures and Novelty Pages

Second-class publications may not include any loose enclosures, with the exception of the publisher's own subscription card or order form.

Novelty pages—or rather, what the post office considers to be novelty pages—have created more problems for publishers in recent years. The manual defines them as "printed sheets that may be used for purposes other than reading, or printed sheets with novel characteristics." Blank sheets may not be carried inside of second-class publications as pages.

The postal manual points out that only a minor portion of the total pages of the second-class publication may be novelty pages and also warns that any excessive use of novelty pages may give the publication the characteristics of a book, catalog, or other such third- or fourth-class mail.

The biggest problem has occurred in the area of what the Postal Service calls "printed coupons or printed application or order forms." However, USPS recently dropped the requirements that these pages must include the name of the publication or an authorized section and that they must be paginated or allowed for in pagination. (You should consult the *Postal Manual* for specific wording and the application of these requirements to your own publication.)

Other second-class requirements are, for the most part, precisely stated. Here are the major qualifications:

1. **Regular issuance.** The publisher must establish a statement of frequency; the frequency must be at least four times a year. Changes in frequency must be filed with the post office where your publication is entered as second-class mail.

2. **Issuance at known office.** The publication must be issued and mailed at a known office—the public office where the business of the publication is transacted during normal business hours. This is your original entry point for your second-class permit; if you wish to enter second-class mail at other entry points (for example, from the location where your magazine is printed), you must apply for additional entry points.

3. **Preparation.** The name of the publication must appear prominently on the cover or front page of the publication—something which most publishers would be likely to do anyway.

4. **Contents.** Publications must be originated and published for the purpose of disseminating information of a public character, or they must be devoted to literature, the sciences, art, or some special industry.

5. **List of subscribers.** Publications mailing at the regular second-class rates must have a "legitimate list of persons who have subscribed by paying or promising to pay at a rate above nominal." There are several exceptions to this.

Where subscriptions to the publication are paid as a part of dues or contributions to an organization, the Postal Service requires the organization to state on dues renewal notices, application forms, and billings the amount of the dues that are attributed to a subscription to the magazine. (This regulation is not a part of the *Postal Manual,* but an administrative interpretation by the Postal Service to satisfy the requirement for a paid list of subscribers.)

Second-class privileges are not accorded to publications that are

Service Standards

The Postal Service has issued these "Service Standards," which are supposed to be the maximum delivery time for any particular class of mail. If your experience shows different results, you can take it up with your local postmaster or customer service representative.

EFFECTIVE 10-11-75 — (ZIP CODED MAIL ONLY)

	OVERNIGHT	OVERNIGHT REQUIREMENTS	2nd DAY	3rd DAY	4th DAY	5th DAY	6th DAY	7th DAY	8th DAY	9th DAY	10th DAY
FIRST CLASS	LOCALLY DESIGNATED CITIES AND SCF's	UP TO AND INCLUDING 5:00 P.M. COLLECTIONS	LOCALLY DESIGNATED STATES	REMAINING OUTLYING AREAS							
AIR PRIORITY	DESIGNATED CITIES	STATED AT MAILING POST OFFICE	NATIONWIDE								
SURFACE PREF-ERENTIAL	UP TO 150 MILES	5:00 P.M. MAILINGS	300 MILES ZONE 3	600 MILES ZONE 4	1,000 MILES ZONE 5	1,400 MILES ZONE 6	1,800 MILES ZONE 7	OVER 1,800 MILES ZONE 8			
ORDINARY 2nd & 3rd CLASS	AS DEVELOPED LOCALLY	—	INTRA-SCF (FOR 5:00 P.M. CARRIER PRESORTED MAILINGS)	DESIGNATED SCF's AND NON-PRESORTED INTRA-SCF	UP TO 150 MILES ZONE 2	300 MILES ZONE 3	600 MILES ZONE 4	1,000 MILES ZONE 5	1,400 MILES ZONE 6	1,800 MILES ZONE 7	OVER 1,800 MILES ZONE 8
PARCEL POST	SEE SEPARATE STANDARDS ISSUED FOR EACH BULK MAIL CENTER.										
PLANT LOADED	DELIVERY SCHEDULES WORKED OUT BETWEEN USPS AND MAILER.										

NOTE: 2nd TO 10th DAY DELIVERY TARGETS COVER ALL OF A DAY'S MAILINGS, EXCEPT AS NOTED

distributed free or at a nominal rate. The *Postal Manual* defines "nominal rate subscriptions" as those that are sold "at a token price so low that it cannot be considered to be a material consideration," or subscriptions to publications that are sold "at a reduction to the subscriber, under a premium offer or any other arrangements, of more than 50% of the amount charged at the basic annual rate." The value of a premium is considered to be its actual cost to the publisher, the recognized retail value, or the represented value, whichever is highest.

In order to maintain regular second-class mailing privileges, no more than 10% of the circulation may be free or sample copies. And second-class publications cannot contain more than 75% advertising in more than one-half of their issues during any 12-month period.

Exceptions to Paid List Rule

There are exceptions to the requirement for a paid subscription list if the publication claims second-class privileges and is published by one of the following: (1) a benevolent or fraternal society or order organized under the lodge system and having a bona fide membership of not less than 1,000 persons, (2) a trade union; (3) a strictly professional, literary, historical or scientific society; or (4) a church or church organization. (Several other types of organizations of a non-association nature, such as institutions of higher learning, are also included in this list.)

6. Identification statement in copies. New requirements approved by the Postal Service last year call for publishers to include the following information on one of the first five pages of the magazine, preferably in the masthead, or in the masthead of the editorial page, providing that the location of the editorial page is listed in the table of contents.

- Name of publication and publication number—the publication number is six or eight digits or letters, preceded by ISSN or USPS. You must include the number within 90 days after notification from the post office. You may omit the number if it is printed on the publication's front cover or front page.
- Date of issue—may be omitted if it appears on the front page or cover.
- Statement of frequency—"Published monthly, bimonthly, quarterly, or whatever by the XYZ Association."
- Subscription price—if the publication has one.
- Issue number—every issue of each publication must be numbered consecutively. The numbering may not be broken by assigning numbers to issues unavoidably omitted.
- Name and address of known office of publication—including street address and Zip code.
- Second-class imprint—"Second-class postage paid at ....," or, if mailed at more than one office, "Second-class postage paid at ....and at additional mailing offices."
- Mailing address for change of address orders.

How to Apply for Second-Class Privileges

Application for second-class mailing privileges should be made on Form 3501 for publications that meet the basic qualifications and Form 3502 for publications published by institutions or societies where a paid list of subscribers is not required. There is no specific form for requesting additional mailing points, but application must be made in writing.

Fees required are $120 for application for original entry; $30 for

Check your mail against these templates to be sure that it meets current postal regulations. The one at right illustrates minimum letter size; below is a guide for determining proper width-to-height ratio.

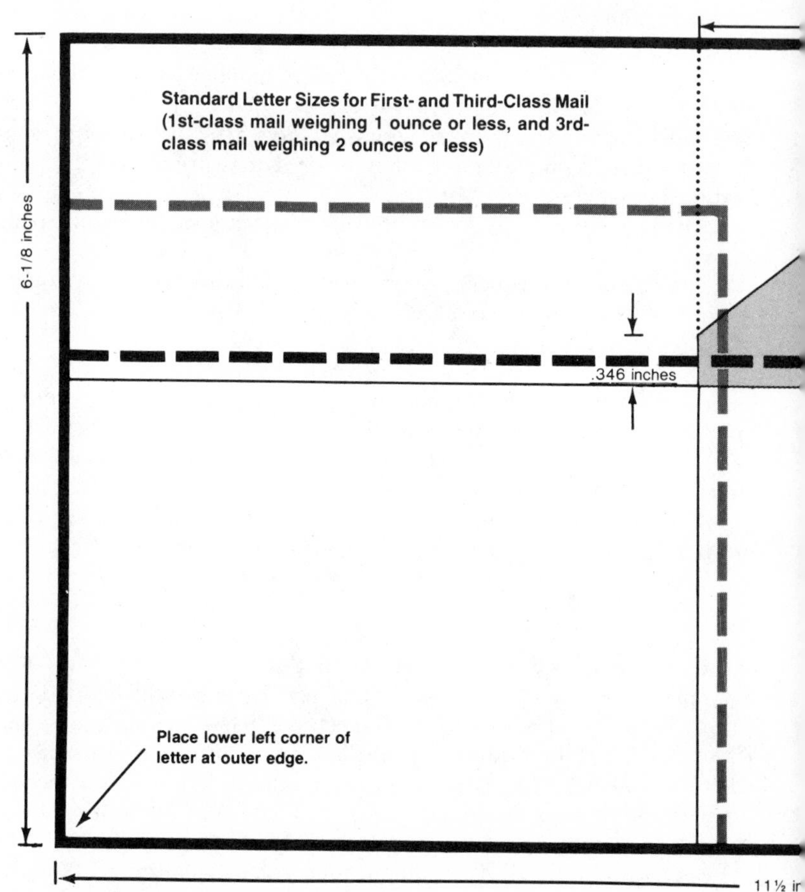

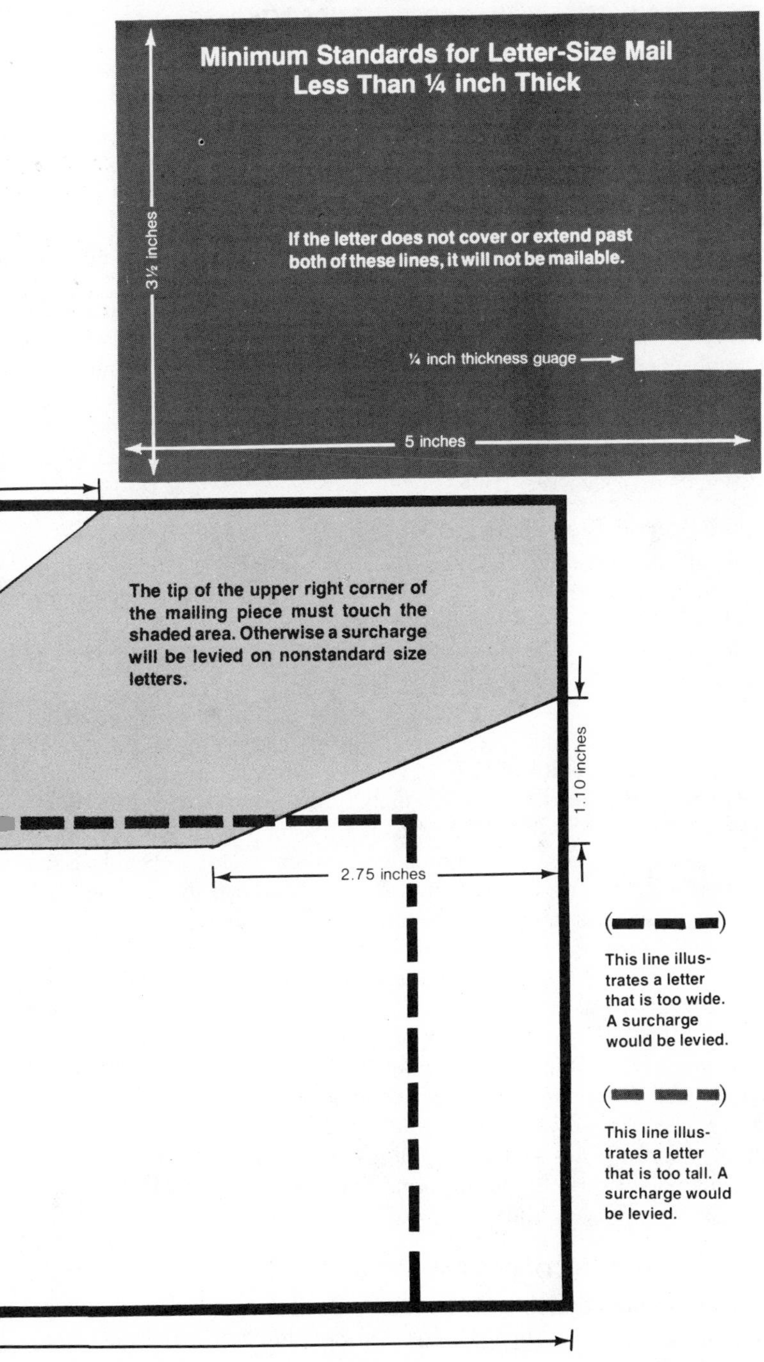
Minimum Standards for Letter-Size Mail
Less Than ¼ inch Thick
3½ inches
If the letter does not cover or extend past both of these lines, it will not be mailable.
¼ inch thickness guage
5 inches
The tip of the upper right corner of the mailing piece must touch the shaded area. Otherwise a surcharge will be levied on nonstandard size letters.
1.10 inches
2.75 inches

This line illustrates a letter that is too wide. A surcharge would be levied.

This line illustrates a letter that is too tall. A surcharge would be levied.

application for reentry because of change in title, frequency of issue, office of publication and so on; and $50 for application for additional entry. Fees cannot be refunded, even if the application is not approved.

The Director, Office of Mail Classification, Rates and Classification Department, USPS Headquarters, rules on all applications for second-class mail privileges, special rates, additional entry and reentry.

If an application is denied, the reasons for the denial must be stated. It becomes effective 15 days after receipt of the notice, unless the publisher files an appeal with the Docket Clerk, U.S. Postal Service, Washington, DC 20260, in the case of an application for original entry, or with the Assistant Postmaster General, Rates and Classification Department, in the case of applications for special rates, additional entries, or reentry.

Special Second-Class Rates

Not all organizations that qualify as nonprofit or tax-exempt organizations under the Internal Revenue Service qualify for nonprofit postal rates from the U.S. Postal Service. Congress provides a postal subsidy for second- and third-class mailings of certain types of nonprofit organizations.

Nonprofit organizations defined in the postal regulations as being eligible for the special rates are: religious; educational; scientific; philanthropic; agricultural; labor; veterans; and fraternal.

Generally, organizations which qualify for tax-exempt status under Section 501(c)3, 5, 8 or 9, can also qualify for the special nonprofit postal rates. However, it is not a controlling factor; organizations that may qualify for tax exemption under one of those categories may, for good reason, choose not to do so. Such organizations would then have to prove to the Postal Service that they qualify for the lower nonprofit rates. The *Postal Manual* defines in greater detail each of the organizations named above.

In addition, it lists the following organizations which specifically do *not* qualify for the special nonprofit rates, even though they may be organized on a nonprofit basis; automobile clubs; business leagues; chambers of commerce; citizens' and civic improvement associations; mutual insurance associations; political organizations; service clubs as Civitan, Kiwanis, Lions, Optimist, and Rotary; social and hobby clubs; and trade associations.

III. CONTROLLED CIRCULATION

Controlled circulation rates generally apply to publications that do not, for some reason, qualify for full second-class privileges. Controlled circulation publications must contain at least 24 pages, must contain 25% nonadvertising material, and must be issued at regular intervals of four or more times per year.

Publications mailed at controlled circulation rates are not required to have a paid list of subscribers. Although rates are slightly higher than regular second-class rates, they are still lower than most other rates.

Application for controlled circulation rates should be made by letter to the postmaster at the post office where mailings of qualifying publications will be made.

IV. THIRD-CLASS MAIL

Third-class mail consists of mailable matter which is:

1. Not mailed or required to be mailed as first-class mail.
2. Not entered as second-class mail.
3. Less than 16 ounces in weight.

Third-class rates apply to most printed materials that are not periodicals. In the association field, such items might include convention promotion brochures, membership or fund-raising solicitations, mass informational mailings to all members, and so on.

Single piece rates, computed by weight, apply to individual pieces of mail going out of your office.

Bulk third-class rates can apply to mailings of identical pieces separately addressed to different addresses. The mailing must be in quantities of at least 50 pounds or 200 pieces. In order to utilize third-class bulk rates, you must pay an annual bulk mailing fee of $40.

Special Nonprofit Rates

Lower nonprofit bulk mailing rates are available to organizations that qualify for them. Those qualifying for nonprofit bulk mailing rates are the same types of organizations listed under the section on second-class, special rates.

Because of the lower rates accorded under the nonprofit third-class category, those organizations qualifying for them should take care to protect the use of their permits. Postal regulations require such mailings to bear the name and address of the authorized permit holder. Cooperative mailings with organizations that do not qualify for the nonprofit rate may not be made.

Application for the special third-class rates must be made on Form 3624, Application to Mail at Special Bulk Third-Class Rates for Qualified Nonprofit Organizations or Associations. If the Application is denied, it can be appealed to Rates & Classification Department, Domestic Mail Classification Division.

V. FOURTH-CLASS MAIL

Fourth-class rates apply to mailings and packages weighing more than one pound and not sent at the priority mail rates.

Bound Printed Matter Rates

Bound printed matter rates generally apply to books and catalogs which contain advertising, but which weigh more than one pound. (A number of associations use this category for mailing directories, if the directory does not qualify under second-class because it is not part of a regular issue of the association's magazine or if it weighs more than one pound, which makes it ineligible for third class.)

In essence, the bound printed matter rate is an extension of third class to cover those items weighing more than one pound. To qualify for the bound printed matter rate, the material must be bound or securely fastened together in a permanent manner (looseleaf binders do not qualify), and at least 90% of the sheets in the publication must be printed. Bound printed matter rates are computed on weight and destination zone.

Special Fourth-Class Rates

Special fourth-class rates apply to books, sound recordings, and certain other types of educational materials. Books mailed under this rate must be bound, and they cannot contain advertising except for incidental loose announcements of other books published by the same publisher.

Presort discounts of 3.3 to 5.4 cents are available to organizations that presort mailings of 500 or more pieces or 2,000 or more pieces. If you use the fourth-class book presort rate, you must pay an annual fee of $30.

Even lower library rates are available for packages that show in the address or return address the name of a school, college, university, public library, or name of a nonprofit religious, educational, scientific, philanthropic, agricultural, labor, veterans, or fraternal organization or association. No permit is required in order to use the library rate.

Parcel Post

Parcel post rates, whch are computed on the basis of weight of the package and destination zone, apply to all other materials weighing more than one pound that do not qualify for any of the other classes of mail. This generally includes packages of merchandise or unbound printed matter.

Conclusion

This article has reviewed the major aspects of the basic classes of mail that can be sent under the U.S. Postal Service. It has highlighted those items of greatest concern to associations, but it should not serve as a substitute for checking the *Postal Manual* for specific wording of regulations in order to ensure conformity.

The U.S. Postal Service is moving into many new areas—express delivery, electronic mail, and so on—and is experimenting with new ways of handling large-volume mailings.

If you're in doubt about something, check it out with your local postmaster, either directly or through your mailer. It is better to find out in advance what can and cannot be done than to have your important materials sitting on a dock somewhere, held up because something doesn't conform to regulations.

You don't have to be an expert on everything there is to know about the Postal Service, but you do have to know when to ask questions and how to find out what is best for your organization.

With postage eating up a large portion of association budgets, your best bet is to squeeze the greatest value out of your postal dollar.

Common Sense Guidelines for Better Postal Management

You've probably heard most of them before, but it doesn't hurt to review these tips for making sure you're getting maximum service at the best cost:

- Keep mailing lists up-to-date. Print "Address Correction Requested" on envelopes. And use correct abbreviations.
- Use the proper format for addresses. (The Postal Service calls this "address hygiene.") This means a readable address, with the line just above the city, state, and Zip code giving the delivery address. (If you give both street address and P.O. box number, the line closest to the bottom line will be the one used.)
- Sort your mail to the extent possible in order to take advantage of discounts and to eliminate additional sorting steps at the post office.
- Check accuracy of mailroom equipment, particularly scales. Just a slight deviation could cause wasted time and money.
- Check paper weights before planning a major mailing. Just a slight change in size or weight—or even extra-heavy ink coverage—can put you over the one-ounce mark.

• Use lightweight packing material for large packages to reduce weight. And remember—even tape adds to the weight of a package.

• Metered mail taken to the post office in trays gets handled up to five hours faster than mail taken from bundles.

• Plan large-volume promotional mailings (such as for conventions or meetings) far enough in advance to use third-class rather than first-class mail.

• Save unused meter tapes and take them to the post office, where you can get a 90% refund.

• Mail early in the day to avoid the 5 p.m. avalanche.

• Discuss potential problem mailings with your postmaster before printing.

• Attend local Postal Customer Council meetings to find out what others are doing to handle a particular problem and to keep current on new regulations.

• Use customer service representatives to help solve knotty problems and complaints.

Keeping Up-to-Date with Postal Matters

There are a variety of publications, many of them available from the post office and many of them free, that will help you keep up-to-date with postal regulations and changes. Here are just a few of them:

• *Memo to Mailers,* monthly newsletter published by the Public and Employee Communications Department, USPS, for "customers originating significant quantities of mail." To get on the list, write to *Memo to Mailers,* P.O. Box 1600, La Plata, MD 20646. Free.

• *Mailers Guide,* handy booklet that gives pointers on the basic classes of mail, special services, and so on, in language that is less legalistic than that in the *Postal Manual.* (The guide, however, does not cover the mail classifications in as great detail.) To get a copy, write to *Mailers Guide,* USPS Consumer Affairs Department, 475 L'Enfant Plaza, Washington, DC 20260. Free.

• *Postal Bulletin,* issued every other week, is more detailed than the *Memo to Mailers.* It gives notice of changes in regulations, as well as current information relating to the Postal Service. Order from Superintendent of Documents, Government Printing Office, Washington, DC 20402. Price is $18.75 per year.

• USPS puts out numerous other booklets and bulletins, ranging from "Modern Mailroom Practices" to "A Glossary of Postal Terms." Check with your local postmaster or customer service rep.

• Your mailer can be an invaluable resource in helping you keep up-to-date. Most good mailers keep in touch with the local postmaster and can get answers to your questions.

ZIP CODE PREFIXES

The following list includes the first three digits of each assigned group of ZIP Codes and the areas associated with these numbers. The larger cities with street listings are listed in capital letters and sectional centers are listed in lower case letters. (Boston and New York are both sectional centers and large cities with street listings.) Names in boldface indicate those areas which are neither a large city with a street listing nor a sectional center.

006-009 PUERTO RICO AND VIRGIN ISLANDS
006 San Juan
007 San Juan
008 Charlotte Amalla, VI
009 SAN JUAN

010-027 MASSACHUSETTS
010 Springfield
011 SPRINGFIELD
012 Pittsfield
013 Greenfield
014 Fitchburg
015 Worcester
016 WORCESTER
017 Framingham
018 Woburn
019 Lynn
020 So. Postal Annex
021 Boston (1)
022 Boston (2)
023 Brockton
024 BROCKTON
025 Buzzards Bay
026 Hyannis
027 Providence RI (Massachusetts Offices)

028-029 RHODE ISLAND
028 Providence
029 PROVIDENCE

030-038 NEW HAMPSHIRE
030 Manchester
031 MANCHESTER
032 Concord
033 Concord
034 Keene
035 Littleton
036 Bellows Falls, VT (New Hampshire Offices)

NEW HAMPSHIRE (Cont.)
037 White River Junction, VT (New Hampshire Offices)
038 Portsmouth

039-049 MAINE
039 Portsmouth, NH (Maine Offices)
040 Portland
041 PORTLAND
042 Auburn
043 Augusta
044 Bangor
045 Bath
046 Ellsworth
047 Houlton
048 Rockland
049 Waterville

050-059 VERMONT
050 White River Junction
051 Bellows Falls
052 Bennington
053 Brattleboro
054 Burlington
056 Montpelier
057 Rutland
058 Saint Johnsbury
059 Littleton, NH (Vermont Office)

060-069 CONNECTICUT
060 Hartford
061 HARTFORD
062 Willimantic
063 New London
064 New Haven
065 NEW HAVEN
066 BRIDGEPORT
067 Waterbury
068 Stamford
069 STAMFORD

070-089 NEW JERSEY
070 Newark
071 NEWARK
072 ELIZABETH
073 JERSEY CITY
074 Paterson
075 PATERSON
076 Hackensack
077 Red Bank
078 Dover
079 Summit
080 Camden (1)
081 CAMDEN
082 Camden (2)
083 Camden (3)
084 ATLANTIC CITY
085 Trenton
086 TRENTON
087 Lakewood
088 New Brunswick
089 NEW BRUNSWICK

090-149 NEW YORK
090-098 Military
100 NEW YORK
103 STATEN ISLAND
104 BRONX
105 Westchester County
106 WHITE PLAINS
107 YONKERS
108 NEW ROCHELLE
109 Suffern
110 Long Island Terminal
111 LONG ISLAND CITY
112 BROOKLYN
113 FLUSHING
114 JAMAICA
115 Mineola
116 FAR ROCKAWAY
117 Hicksville
118 HICKSVILLE
119 Riverhead
120 Albany (A-J)
121 Albany (K-Z)

NEW YORK (Cont.)
122 ALBANY
123 SCHENECTADY
124 Kingston
125 Poughkeepsie
126 POUGHKEEPSIE
127 Monticello
128 Glens Falls
129 Plattsburgh
130 Syracuse (A-L)
131 Syracuse (M-Z)
132 SYRACUSE
133 Utica (A-L)
134 Utica (M-Z)
135 UTICA
136 Watertown
137 Binghamton (A-L)
138 Binghamton (M-Z)
139 BINGHAMTON
140 Buffalo (A-L)
141 Buffalo (M-Z)
142 BUFFALO
143 NIAGARA FALLS
144 Rochester (A-L)
145 Rochester (M-Z)
146 ROCHESTER
147 Jamestown
148 Elmira
149 ELMIRA

150-196 PENNSYLVANIA
150 Pittsburgh (1)
151 Pittsburgh (2)
152 PITTSBURGH
153 Washington
154 Uniontown
155 Somerset
156 Greensburg
157 Indiana
158 Du Bois
159 Johnstown
160 Butler
161 New Castle
162 Kittanning
163 Oil City

ZIP CODE PREFIXES

PENNSYLVANIA (Cont.)
164 Erie
165 ERIE
166 Altoona
167 Bradford
168 State College
169 Wellsboro
170 Harrisburg
171 HARRISBURG
172 Chambersburg
173 York
174 YORK
175 Lancaster
176 LANCASTER
177 Williamsport
178 Sunbury
179 Pottsville
180 Lehigh Valley
181 ALLENTOWN
182 Hazleton
183 East Stroudsburg
184 Scranton
185 SCRANTON
186 Wilkes-Barre
187 WILKES-BARRE
188 Montrose
189 Doylestown
190 Philadelphia
191 PHILADELPHIA
193 Paoli
194 Norristown
195 Reading
196 READING

197-199 DELAWARE
197 Wilmington
198 WILMINGTON
199 Dover

200-205 DISTRICT OF COLUMBIA
200 WASHINGTON
202-205 Government

206-219 MARYLAND
206 Waldorf
207 Prince Georges (A-K)
208 Prince Georges (L-Z)
209 SILVER SPRING
210 Baltimore (1)
211 Baltimore (2)
212 BALTIMORE
214 ANNAPOLIS

MARYLAND (Cont.)
215 Cumberland
216 Easton
217 Frederick
218 Salisbury
219 Wilmington, DE (Maryland Offices)

220-246 VIRGINIA
220 Northern Virginia (1)
221 Northern Virginia (2)
222 ARLINGTON
223 ALEXANDRIA
224 Fredericksburg (1)
225 Fredericksburg (2)
226 Winchester
227 Culpeper
228 Harrisonburg
229 Charlottesville
230 Richmond (1)
231 Richmond (2)
232 RICHMOND
233 Norfolk (1)
234 Norfolk (2)
235 NORFOLK
236 NEWPORT NEWS
237 PORTSMOUTH
238 Petersburg
239 Farmville
240 Roanoke (1)
241 Roanoke (2)
242 Bristol
243 Pulaski
244 Staunton
245 Lynchburg
246 Bluefield, WV (Virginia Offices)

247-268 WEST VIRGINIA
247 Bluefield (1)
248 Bluefield (2)
249 Lewisburg
250 Charleston (1)
251 Charleston (2)
252 Charleston (3)
253 CHARLESTON
254 Martinsburg
255 Huntington (1)
256 Huntington (2)

WEST VIRGINIA (Cont.)
257 HUNTINGTON
258 Beckley (1)
259 Beckley (2)
260 Wheeling
261 Parkersburg
262 Buckhannon
263 Clarksburg (1)
264 Clarksburg (2)
265 Morgantown
266 Sutton
267 Cumberland, MD (West Virginia Offices)
268 Petersburg

270-289 NORTH CAROLINA
270 Greensboro (West)
271 WINSTON-SALEM
272 Greensboro (East) (1)
273 Greensboro (East) (2)
274 GREENSBORO
275 Raleigh
276 RALEIGH
277 DURHAM
278 Rocky Mount
279 Elizabeth City
280 Charlotte (1)
281 Charlotte (2)
282 CHARLOTTE
283 Fayetteville
284 Wilmington
285 Kinston
286 Hickory
287 Asheville
288 ASHEVILLE
289 Gainsville, GA (North Carolina Offices)

290-299 SOUTH CAROLINA
290 Columbia (1)
291 Columbia (2)
292 COLUMBIA
293 Spartanburg
294 Charleston
295 Florence
296 Greenville

SOUTH CAROLINA (Cont.)
297 Charlotte, NC (South Carolina Offices)
298 Augusta, GA (South Carolina Offices)
299 Savannah, GA (South Carolina Offices)

300-319 GEORGIA
300 Atlanta (Metro)
301 Atlanta (1)
302 Atlanta (2)
303 ATLANTA
304 Swainsboro
305 Gainesville
306 Athens
307 Chattanooga, TN Georgia Offices)
308 Augusta
309 AUGUSTA
310 Macon
312 MACON
313 Savannah
314 SAVANNAH
315 Waycross
316 Valdosta
317 Albany
318 Columbus
319 COLUMBUS

320-339 FLORIDA
320 Jacksonville
322 JACKSONVILLE
323 Tallahassee
324 Panama City
325 Pensacola
326 Gainesville
327 Orlando
328 ORLANDO
329 Melbourne
330 Miami
331 MIAMI
333 FORT LAUDER-DALE
334 West Palm Beach
335 Tampa
336 TAMPA
337 SAINT PETERSBURG
338 Lakeland
339 Fort Myers

ZIP CODE PREFIXES

350-369 ALABAMA

350 Birmingham (1)
351 Birmingham (2)
352 BIRMINGHAM
354 Tuscaloosa
355 Jasper
356 Decatur
357 Huntsville
358 HUNTSVILLE
359 Gadsden
360 Montgomery
361 MONTGOMERY
362 Anniston
363 Dothan
364 Evergreen
365 Mobile
366 MOBILE
367 Selma
368 Opelika
369 Meridian, MS (Alabama Offices)

370-385 TENNESSEE

370 Nashville (A-L)
371 Nashville (M-Z)
372 NASHVILLE
373 Chattanooga
374 CHATTANOOGA
376 Johnson City
377 Knoxville (A-L)
378 Knoxville (M-Z)
379 KNOXVILLE
380 Memphis
381 MEMPHIS
382 McKenzie
383 Jackson
384 Columbia
385 Cookeville

386-397 MISSISSIPPI

386 Memphis, TN (Mississippi Offices)
387 Greenville
388 Tupelo
389 Grenada
390 Jackson (A-L)
391 Jackson (M-Z)
392 JACKSON
393 Meridian
394 Laurel
395 Gulfport
396 McComb
397 Columbus

400-427 KENTUCKY

400 Louisville (East)
401 Louisville (West)
402 LOUISVILLE
403 Lexington (North)
404 Lexington (South)
405 LEXINGTON
406 Frankfort
407 Corbin (West)
408 Corbin (East)
409 Corbin (Central)
410 Cincinnati, Ohio (Kentucky Offices)
411 Ashland (North)
412 Ashland (South)
413 Campton (South)
414 Campton (North)
415 Pikeville (East)
416 Pikeville (West)
417 Hazard (West)
418 Hazard (East)
420 Paducah
421 Bowling Green (East)
422 Bowling Green (West)
423 Owensboro
424 Evansville, IN (Kentucky Offices)
425 Somerset (North)
426 Somerset (South)
427 Elizabethtown

430-458 OHIO

430 Columbus (North)
431 Columbus (South)
432 COLUMBUS
433 Marion
434 Toledo (East)
435 Toledo (West)
436 TOLEDO
437 Zanesville (South)
438 Zanesville (North)
439 Steubenville
440 Cleveland
441 CLEVELAND
442 Akron
443 AKRON

OHIO (Cont.)

444 Youngstown
445 YOUNGSTOWN
446 Canton
447 CANTON
448 Mansfield
449 MANSFIELD
450 Cincinnati (West)
451 Cincinnati (East)
452 CINCINNATI
453 Dayton
454 DAYTON
455 SPRINGFIELD
456 Chillicothe
457 Athens
458 Lima

460-479 INDIANA

460 Indianapolis (North)
461 Indianapolis (South)
462 INDIANAPOLIS
463 Gary
464 GARY
465 South Bend
466 SOUTH BEND
467 Fort Wayne
468 FORT WAYNE
469 Kokomo
470 Cincinnati, OH (Indiana Offices)
471 Louisville, KY (Indiana Offices)
472 Columbus
473 Muncie
474 Bloomington
475 Washington
476 Evansville
477 EVANSVILLE
478 Terre Haute
479 Lafayette

480-499 MICHIGAN

480 Royal Oak
481 Detroit
482 DETROIT
484 Flint
485 FLINT
486 Saginaw (West)
487 Saginaw (East)
488 Lansing
489 LANSING

MICHIGAN (Cont.)

490 Kalamazoo (1)
491 Kalamazoo (2)
492 Jackson
493 Grand Rapids (East)
494 Grand Rapids (West)
495 GRAND RAPIDS
496 Traverse City
497 Mackinaw City
498 Iron Mountain (East)
499 Iron Mountain (West)

500-528 IOWA

500 Des Moines (A-F)
501 Des Moines (G-M)
502 Des Moines (N-Z)
503 DES MOINES
504 Mason City
505 Fort Dodge
506 Waterloo
507 WATERLOO
508 Creston
510 Sioux City
511 SIOUX CITY
512 Sheldon
513 Spencer
514 Carroll
515 Council Bluffs
516 Shenandoah
520 Dubuque
521 Decorah
522 Cedar Rapids (A-L)
523 Cedar Rapids (M-Z)
524 CEDAR RAPIDS
525 Ottumwa
526 Burlington
527 Rock Island, IL (Iowa Offices)
528 DAVENPORT

530-549 WISCONSIN

530 Milwaukee (North)
531 Milwaukee (South)
532 MILWAUKEE
534 RACINE

ZIP CODE PREFIXES

WISCONSIN (Cont.)
535 Madison
537 MADISON
538 Madison
539 Portage
540 Saint Paul, MN (Wisconsin Offices)
541 Green Bay (West)
542 Green Bay (East)
543 GREEN BAY
544 Wausau
545 Rhinelander
546 La Crosse
547 Eau Claire
548 Spooner
549 Oshkosh

550-567 MINNESOTA
550 Saint Paul
551 SAINT PAUL
553 Minneapolis
554 MINNEAPOLIS
556 Duluth (East)
557 Duluth (West)
558 DULUTH
559 Rochester
560 Mankato
561 Windom
562 Willmar
563 Saint Cloud
564 Brainerd
565 Detroit Lakes
566 Bemidji
567 Thief River Falls

570-577 SOUTH DAKOTA
570 Sioux Falls
571-SIOUX FALLS
572 Watertown
573 Mitchell
574 Aberdeen
575 Pierre
576 Mobridge
577 Rapid City

580-588 NORTH DAKOTA
580 Fargo
581 Fargo
582 Grand Forks
583 Devils Lake
584 Jamestown
585 Bismarck

NORTH DAKOTA (Cont.)
586 Dickinson
587 Minot
588 Williston

590-599 MONTANA
590 Billings
591 BILLINGS
592 Wolf Point
593 Miles City
594 Great Falls
595 Havre
596 Helena
597 Butte
598 Missoula
599 Kalispell

600-629 ILLINOIS
600 North Suburban (1)
601 North Suburban (2)
602 EVANSTON
603 OAK PARK
604 South Suburban (1)
605 South Suburban (2)
606 CHICAGO
609 Kankakee
610 Rockford
611 ROCKFORD
612 Rock Island
613 La Salle
614 Galesburg
615 Peoria
616 PEORIA
617 Bloomington
618 Champaign (North)
619 Champaign (South)
620 East St. Louis (North)
622 East St. Louis (South)
623 Quincy
624 Effingham
625 Springfield (East)
626 Springfield (West)
627 SPRINGFIELD
628 Centralia
629 Carbondale

630-658 MISSOURI
630 Saint Louis
631 SAINT LOUIS
633 Saint Charles
634 Hannibal
635 Kirksville
636 Flat River
637 Cape Girardeau
638 Sikeston
639 Poplar Bluff
640 Kansas City
641 KANSAS CITY
644 Saint Joseph
645 SAINT JOSEPH
646 Chillicothe
647 Harrisonville
648 Joplin
650 Jefferson City
651 Jefferson City
652 Columbia
653 Sedalia
654 Rolla (A-I)
655 Rolla (J-Z)
656 Springfield (A-L)
657 Springfield (M-Z)
658 SPRINGFIELD

660-679 KANSAS
660 Kansas City
661 KANSAS CITY
662 SHAWNEE MISSION
664 Topeka (A-L)
665 Topeka (M-Z)
666 TOPEKA
667 Fort Scott
668 Emporia
669 Concordia
670 Wichita (A-L)
671 Wichita (M-Z)
672 WICHITA
673 Independence
674 Salina
675 Hutchinson
676 Hays
677 Colby
678 Dodge City
679 Liberal

680-693 NEBRASKA
680 Omaha
681 OMAHA
683 Lincoln (A-L)
684 Lincoln (M-Z)

NEBRASKA (Cont.)
685 LINCOLN
686 Columbus
687 Norfolk
688 Grand Island
689 Hastings
690 McCook
691 North Platte
692 Valentine
693 Alliance

700-714 LOUISIANA
700 New Orleans
701 NEW ORLEANS
703 Thibodaux
704 Hammond
705 Lafayette
706 Lake Charles
707 Baton Rouge
708 BATON ROUGE
710 Shreveport
711 SHREVEPORT
712 Monroe
713 Alexandria (East)
714 Alexandria (West)

716-729 ARKANSAS
716 Pine Bluff
717 Camden
718 Hope
719 Hot Springs National Park
720 Little Rock (A-L)
721 Little Rock (M-Z)
722 LITTLE ROCK
723 West Memphis
724 Jonesboro
725 Batesville
726 Harrison
727 Fayetteville
728 Russellville
729 Fort Smith

730-749 OKLAHOMA
730 Oklahoma City
731 OKLAHOMA CITY
734 Ardmore
735 Lawton
736 Clinton
737 Enid
738 Woodward
739 Liberal, KS (Oklahoma Offices)

ZIP CODE PREFIXES

OKLAHOMA (Cont.)
740 Tulsa
741 TULSA
743 Vinita
744 Muskogee
745 McAlester
746 Ponca City
747 Durant
748 Shawnee
749 Poteau

750-799 TEXAS
750 Richardson
751 Mesquite
752 DALLAS
754 Greenville
755 Texarkana
756 Longview
757 Tyler
758 Palestine
759 Lufkin
760 Fort Worth
761 FORT WORTH
762 Denton
763 Wichita Falls
764 Stephenville
765 Temple
766 Waco
767 WACO
768 Brownwood
769 San Angelo
770 HOUSTON
773 Conroe
774 Bellaire
775 Pasadena
776 Beaumont
777 BEAUMONT
778 Bryan
779 Victoria
780 San Antonio (West)
781 San Antonio (East)
782 SAN ANTONIO
783 Corpus Christi
784 CORPUS CHRISTI
785 McAllen
786 Austin
787 AUSTIN
788 Uvalde
789 LaGrange
790 Amarillo
791 AMARILLO
792 Childress

TEXAS (Cont.)
793 Lubbock
794 LUBBOCK
795 Abilene
796 ABILENE
797 Midland
798 El Paso
799 EL PASO

800-816 COLORADO
800 Denver (North)
801 Denver (South)
802 DENVER
803 BOULDER
804 Golden
805 Longmont
806 Brighton
807 Fort Morgan
808 Colorado Springs
809 COLORADO SPRINGS
810 Pueblo
811 Alamosa
812 Salida
813 Durango
814 Montrose
815 Grand Junction
816 Glenwood Springs

820-831 WYOMING
820 Cheyenne
821 Rock Springs (4)
822 Wheatland
823 Rawlins
824 Worland
825 Riverton
826 Casper
827 New Castle
828 Sheridan
829 Rock Springs (1)
830 Rock Springs (2)
831 Rock Springs (3)

832-838 IDAHO
832 Pocatello
833 Twin Falls
834 Idaho Falls
835 Lewiston
836 Boise
837 BOISE
838 Spokane, WA (Idaho Offices)

840-847 UTAH
840 Salt Lake City

UTAH (Cont.)
841 SALT LAKE CITY
843 Ogden
844 OGDEN
845 Price
846 Provo (1)
847 Provo (2)

850-865 ARIZONA
850 PHOENIX
852 Phoenix (1)
853 Phoenix (2)
855 Globe
856 Tucson
857 TUCSON
859 Show Low
860 Flagstaff
863 Prescott
864 Kingman
865 Gallup, NM (Arizona Offices)

870-884 NEW MEXICO
870 Albuquerque
871 ALBUQUERQUE
873 Gallup
874 Farmington
875 Santa Fe
877 Las Vegas
878 Socorro
879 Truth or Consequences
880 Las Cruces
881 Clovis
882 Roswell
883 Carrizozo
884 Tucumcari

890-898 NEVADA
890 Las Vegas
891 LAS VEGAS
893 Ely
894 Reno
895 RENO
897 Carson City
898 Elko

900-966 CALIFORNIA
900 LOS ANGELES
902 Inglewood
903 INGLEWOOD

CALIFORNIA (Cont.)
904 SANTA MONICA
905 TORRANCE
906 Whittier
907 Long Beach
908 LONG BEACH
910 Pasadena
911 PASADENA
912 GLENDALE
913 Van Nuys
914 VAN NUYS
915 BURBANK
916 NORTH HOLLYWOOD
917 Alhambra
918 ALHAMBRA
920 San Diego
921 SAN DIEGO
922 Indio
923 San Bernardino
924 SAN BERNARDINO
925 RIVERSIDE
926 Santa Ana
927 SANTA ANA
928 ANAHEIM
930 Ventura
931 SANTA BARBARA
932 Bakersfield
933 BAKERSFIELD
934 San Luis Obispo
935 Mojave
936 Fresno
937 FRESNO
939 Salinas
940 San Francisco
941 SAN FRANCISCO
943 PALO ALTO
944 SAN MATEO
945 Oakland
946 OAKLAND
947 BERKELEY
948 RICHMOND
949 San Rafael
950 San Jose
951 SAN JOSE
952 Stockton (1)
953 Stockton (2)
954 Santa Rosa
955 Eureka
956 Sacramento (1)
957 Sacramento (2)
958 SACRAMENTO
959 Marysville

ZIP CODE PREFIXES

CALIFORNIA (Cont.)
960 Redding
961 Reno, Nevada (California Offices)
962-966 Military

967-968 HAWAII
967 Honolulu
968 HONOLULU

969 PACIFIC ISLANDS
969 Pacific Islands

970-979 OREGON
970 Portland (1)

OREGON (Cont.)
971 Portland (2)
972 PORTLAND
973 Salem
974 Eugene
975 Medford
976 Klamath Falls
977 Bend
978 Pendleton
979 Boise, Idaho (Oregon Offices)

980-994 WASHINGTON
980 Seattle

WASHINGTON (Cont.)
981 SEATTLE
982 Everett
983 Tacoma
984 TACOMA
985 Olympia
986 Portland, OR (Washington Offices)
987 Military
988 Wenatchee
989 Yakima
990 Spokane (1)

WASHINGTON (Cont.)
991 Spokane (2)
992 SPOKANE
993 Pasco
994 Lewiston, Idaho (Washington Offices)

995-999 ALASKA
995 Anchorage (1)
996 Anchorage (2)
997 Fairbanks
998 Juneau
999 Katchikan

Appendix I

QUICK REFERENCE GUIDE TO

STANDARD INDUSTRIAL CLASSIFICATIONS

TITLES AND CODE NUMBERS OF INDUSTRY "MAJOR GROUPS"

(Titles are extracted from Government S.I.C. Manual)

Industry Title	SIC Code
Agricultural services; hunting and trapping	07
Air transportation (services)	45
Amusement & recreation services (except motion pictures)	79
Apparel & other finished products made from fabrics & similar materials	23
Automobile repair, services and garages	75
Automotive dealers & service stations	55
Banking	60
Brooms and brushes	39
Chemicals and allied products	28
Clay, stone and glass products	32
Coal mining (anthracite)	11
Coal mining (bituminous & lignite)	12
Communication (services)	48
Construction, building—general contractors	15
Construction, other than building—general contractors	16
Construction—special trade contractors	17
Credit agencies (other than banks)	61
Educational services	82
Electric, gas & sanitary services	49
Farms (commercial)	01
Farms (noncommercial)	02
Federal government	91
Fisheries	09
Floor coverings, hard (linoleum, asphalt and other)	39
Food and kindred products	20
Forestry	08
Furniture and fixtures	25
Gas, natural (extraction)	13
Glass, stone and clay products	32
Hotels, motels, rooming houses, lodging places	70
Instruments—professional; scientific; controlling	38
Insurance agents, brokers and services	64
Insurance carriers	63
International government	94
Investment, holding, trust and other investment companies	67
Jewelry; silverware; plated ware	39
Leather and leather products	31
Legal services	81
Linoleum, asphalt and other hard floor coverings	39
Local government	93
Lumber and wood products (except furniture)	24
Machinery, electrical; equipment and supplies	36
Machinery (except electrical)	35
Matches	39
Medical and other health services	80
Metal—fabricated products (except ordnance, machinery and transportation equipment)	34
Metal—primary	33
Mining—anthracite coal	11
Mining—bituminous coal & lignite	12
Mining—metal	10
Mining and quarrying—non-metallic minerals (except fuels)	14
Motion pictures (production, distribution, exhibiting services)	78
Motor freight transportation; warehousing	42
Museums, art galleries, etc.	84
Musical instruments	39
Natural gas (extraction)	13
Non-classifiable establishments	99

STANDARD INDUSTRIAL CLASSIFICATIONS (cont.)

Industry Title	SIC Code
Non-metallic minerals (mining and quarrying)	14
Non-profit membership organizations	86
Optical goods	38
Ordnance and accessories	19
Paper and allied products	26
Pens, pencils and other office and artists' materials	39
Personal services	72
Petroleum, crude (extraction)	13
Petroleum refining and related industries	29
Photographic equipment	38
Pipeline transportation	46
Plastics—materials	28
Plastics—products	30
Primary metals	33
Printing, publishing and allied industries	27
Private households	88
Railroad transportation	40
Real estate	65
Real estate, insurance & law (combination firms)	66
Repair services—miscellaneous	76
Retail trade—Apparel & accessories	56
Retail trade—Building materials, hardware and farm equipment	52
Retail trade—Eating and drinking places	58
Retail trade—Food	54
Retail trade—Furniture, home furnishings and equipment	57
Retail trade—General merchandise	53
Retail trade—Miscellaneous retail stores	59
Rubber and miscellaneous plastics products	30
Security and commodity brokers, dealers, etc.	62
Services—Miscellaneous	89
Services—Miscellaneous business	73
Services—Personal	72
Signs and advertising displays	39
Special trade contractors	17
Sporting and athletic goods	39
State government	92
Stone, clay and glass products	32
Textile mill products	22
Tobacco manufacturers	21
Toys and other amusement goods	39
Transportation—Air	45
Transportation—Motor freight and warehousing	42
Transportation—Pipeline	46
Transportation—Railroads	40
Transportation—Services	47
Transportation—Transit; local, suburban & interurban systems	41
Transportation—Water	44
Transportation equipment	37
Warehousing and motor freight (transportation)	42
Watches and clocks	38
Water transportation	44
Wholesale trade	50

Appendix J

Advertising and Promotion Expenditures of Selected Major Industries (Estimated)

INDUSTRY	SIC	A&P AS Sales 1979	A&P AS Margin 1979
Agriculture production-crops	100	2.2	5.4
Agriculture produc-livestock	200	.6	1.6
Metal mining	1000	.1	.2
Copper ores	1020	.2	1.0
Lead & zinc ores	1030	.0	.1
Gold ores	1040	0.0	0.0
Coal & lignite mining	1210	.0	.1
Crude petroleum & natural gas	1310	.2	.3
Drilling oil & gas wells	1380	.2	.6
Misc nonmetallic minerals	1490	N/A	N/A
General building contractors	1520	1.1	5.1
Operative builders	1530	2.7	9.0
Construction-not bldg. constr	1600	.2	1.2
Construction-spl contractors	1700	1.5	2.0
Food & kindred products	2000	3.5	11.3
Meat products	2010	1.2	9.5
Dairy products	2020	4.1	22.2
Canned-preserved fruits-vegs	2030	2.0	8.5
Flour & other grain mill pds	2040	2.0	10.4
Bakery products	2050	1.5	3.8
Cane sugar refining	2060	2.4	5.8
Fats & oils	2070	.2	3.1
Alcoholic bev & soft drinks	2080	5.4	15.8
Food preparations NEC	2090	1.0	2.8
Cigarets	2110	6.6	15.7
Cigars	2120	2.2	4.7
Textile mill products	2200	.6	2.9
Floor covering mills	2270	2.0	4.3
Apparel & other finished pds.	2300	1.8	6.6
Lumber & wood products	2400	.8	3.4
Wood buildings-mobile homes	2450	1.0	4.9
Household furniture	2510	1.6	8.7
Office furniture	2520	.9	3.2
Paper & allied products	2600	.8	2.5
Convert paper-paperbd pd NEC	2640	2.0	5.6
Paperboard containers-boxes	2650	.4	1.2
Printing publishing & allied	2700	3.0	5.0
Newspapers publishing-print	2710	2.0	11.6
Periodicals publishing-print	2720	3.5	14.7
Books publishing & printing	2730	4.9	9.4
Commercial printing	2750	1.0	3.0
Manifold business forms	2760	.5	1.3
Greeting card publishing	2770	1.7	3.0
Service indus for print trde	2790	.0	.0
Chemicals & allied prods	2800	2.6	6.2
Indl inorganic chemicals	2810	2.2	5.4
Plastic matr & synthic resin	2820	.2	.5
Drugs	2830	5.6	11.7
Soap & detergent & cosmetics	2840	10.2	18.5
Paints-varnishes-lacquers	2850	1.7	5.3
Industrial organic chemicals	2860	.6	2.8
Agriculture chemicals	2870	1.2	2.2
Misc chemical products	2890	2.8	6.7
Petroleum refining	2910	.7	2.9
Paving & roofing materials	2950	1.3	5.1
Rubber & misc plastic prods	3000	1.1	5.0
Fabricated rubber prods nec	3060	.4	2.3
Misc plastic products	3070	3.7	4.1
Footwear except rubber	3140	2.3	7.1
Leather goods NEC	3190	1.9	4.3
Flat glass	3210	.3	1.0
Glass containers	3220	4.0	11.3
Cement hydraulic	3240	.1	.3
Structural clay products	3250	.6	1.6
Pottery products NEC	3260	1.9	5.8
Concrete gypsum & plaster	3270	.9	4.9
Abrasive asbestos & misc min	3290	.5	2.0
Blast furnaces & steel works	3310	.2	1.3
Iron & steel foundries	3320	N/A	N/A
Prim smelt-refin nonfer mtl	3330	.1	1.3
Second smelt-refin nonfer mt	3340	.2	2.8
Rolling & draw nonfer metal	3350	.5	2.4
Misc primary metal products	3390	.4	1.7
Metal cans & shipping cont	3410	2.1	8.6
Hardware NEC	3420	1.6	4.5
Heating equip & plumbing fix	3430	2.4	10.0
Misc metal work	3440	1.4	4.3
Bolts-nuts-screws-riv-washrs	3450	.5	1.4
Ordnance & accessories	3480	2.9	10.9
Valves pipe fittings ex bras	3490	.9	2.9
Engines & turbines	3510	.9	2.9
Farm-garden machinery & eqp	3520	2.2	12.3
Construction machinery & eqp	3530	.9	3.9
Metalworking machinery & eqp	3540	1.2	3.4
Special industry machinery	3550	1.6	4.2
General industrial mach & eq	3560	1.1	3.3
Office computing & acctg mch	3570	1.2	2.6
Refrig & service ind machine	3580	1.7	9.6
Elec & electr mach eq & supp	3600	1.5	6.5
Elec transmission & distr eq	3610	1.0	3.3
Industrial controls	3620	.9	2.3
Household appliances	3630	5.5	17.7
Electric lighting-wiring eqp	3640	1.7	4.2
Radio-tv receiving sets	3650	5.7	16.4
Tele & telegraph apparatus	3660	1.9	5.6
Electronic components & acce	3670	1.1	3.2
Electrical machy & eqp NEC	3690	2.9	12.0
Motor vehicles & car bodies	3710	1.3	9.3
Aircraft & parts	3720	.7	4.0
Ship-boat building repairing	3730	2.0	11.5
Railroad equipment	3740	.2	.7
Motorcycles bicycles & parts	3750	1.3	9.0
Guided missiles & space vehc	3760	.1	.5
Travel trailers & campers	3790	1.0	10.9
Engr lab & research equip	3810	1.1	2.8
Measuring & controlling inst	3820	2.0	4.2
Optical instruments & lenses	3830	2.1	4.7

(*Courtesy of Schonfeld & Associates Inc., Chicago*)

Appendix K

THE MATHEMATICS OF PLANNING PROFITABLE MAILINGS

Prepared by Virgil D. Angerman,
Sales Promotion Manager, Boise Cascade Envelope Division

One of the questions asked frequently at Direct Mail Meetings is: "How many orders per thousand can I expect?" Obviously, no one can give an accurate answer to that question for there are too many variables involved.

The response from a mailing depends upon the nature of the proposition offered; the copy used; the offer: whether cash, billed, or sold on time payments; the mailing list used; the appearance of the envelope; whether you use first or third class postage; the date of mailing; and the general economic conditions of the country at the time of mailing.

Any one of these factors, or variables, can influence the pull of a mailing. It's not a question of how many orders per thousand can I expect but How Many Orders Per Thousand MUST I GET to break even.

To determine the breakeven point, you must know the actual cost of obtaining and filling an order. We have prepared a worksheet to show you how to do it. The figures used in the Worksheet example are those experienced by several mailers of the offer.

Once you know the break-even figure, you can proceed with your tests. The illustration on the following page shows how to set up a Worksheet.

MATHEMATICS OF MAILINGS

WORKSHEET FOR PLANNING PROFITABLE MAILINGS

Date: Date

PROPOSITION 4-Vol. Set "Practical Mathematics" KEY 64

1 - Selling Price of Merchandise or Service	$25.00	
2 - Cost of Filling the Order		
a) Merchandise or Service	6.00	
b) Royalty	none	
c) Handling Expense (Drop Shipping & Order Processing)	.95	
d) Postage and Shipping Expense	.60	
e) Premium, including Handling and Postage	.30	
f) Use Tax, if any (1 x 3 %)	.75	
TOTAL COST OF FILLING THE ORDER		8.60
3 - Administrative Overhead		
a) Rent, Light, Heat, Maintenance, Credit Checking, Collections, etc. (10 % of # 1)	2.50	
TOTAL ADMINISTRATIVE COST		2.50
4 - Estimated Percentage of Returns, Refunds or Cancellations	10%	
5 - Expense in Handling Returns		
a) Return Postage and Handling (2c plus 2d)	1.55	
b) Refurbishing Returned Merchandise (10 % of # 2a)	.60	
TOTAL COST OF HANDLING RETURNS	2.15	
6 - Chargeable Cost of Returns (10 % of $2.15)		.21
7 - Estimated Bad Debt Percentage	10%	
8 - Chargeable Cost of Bad Debts (# 1 x # 7)		2.50
9 - Total Variable Costs (# 2 plus # 3, # 6, and # 8)		13.81
10 - Unit Profit after Deducting Variable Costs (# 1 less # 9)		11.19
11 - Return Factor (100% less # 4)	90%	
12 - Unit Profit Per Order (# 10 x # 11)		10.07
13 - Credit for Returned Merchandise (10 % of # 2a)		.60
14 - Net Profit Per Order (# 12 plus # 13)		10.67
15 - Cost of Mailing per 1,000	100.50	
16 - NUMBER OF ORDERS PER 1,000 NEEDED TO BREAK EVEN		9.4

For additional copies of this form, contact Marketing Services Manager, Boise Cascade Envelope Division, 313 Rohlwing Rd., Addison, IL 60101 - Tel. 312, 629-5000

Form No. 8-9

HOW TO USE THE WORKSHEET

Let's take a hypothetical mail-order proposition and go through the various steps to see what costs must be included to determine how many orders per thousand you must get to break even. First, the Worksheet should carry the date, name of proposition, and the key or code for that particular mailing. You need this for future reference.

Date: *Date*

PROPOSITION *4-Vol Set "Practical Mathematics"* KEY *64*

ITEM #1. Now, we start with Item #1, the retail selling price of the merchandise or service. In this case, let's say we are selling a 4-Volume set of books, "Practical Mathematics", for $25.00 on 10 days' free examination with a premium, a Calculating Chart, included as a "look-see" introduction. The customer keeps the chart whether he buys or returns the books. Post $25.00 in the panel opposite Item #1.

1 - Selling Price of Merchandise or Service	*$25.00*

ITEM #2. Under Item #2, we enter: 2-a, your cost of the books, including shipping carton, which is $6.00. This gives over a 4-to-1 mark-up which is an ideal selling margin.

Next consideration is Royalty, 2-b. If you are publishing a book or selling an item on which a royalty is paid to the author, manufacturer or inventor, this expense should be included as a part of the total cost of the merchandise or service. The author's royalty on books sold by mail is usually only 5% of the retail price because of the high promotional expense. Books sold through the retail trade, as a rule, carry a 10% royalty based on the retail price. Royalties to manufacturers and inventors vary from 1% to 5%, depending upon the market possibilities and the retail price of the item. In this hypothetical case there is no royalty, as the books are purchased from another publisher.

The Handling Expense (2-c) which includes the opening of the mail and processing the order for fulfillment amounts to 95¢. Postage and shipping expense (2-d) is 60¢. As we included a "look-see" premium in this offer, (Calculating Chart 2-e), we must add this item (30¢ cost) as a part of the expense of filling the order. If your State has a Use Tax (2-f), this must be added, also. Let's take 3% as an example. Multiply Item #1 by 3% and you have 75¢ tax. Adding all the expenses under #2, it costs $8.60 to fill an order.

2 - Cost of Filling the Order		
a) Merchandise or Service	*6.00*	
b) Royalty	*none*	
c) Handling Expense (Drop Shipping & Order Processing)	*.95*	
d) Postage and Shipping Expense	*.60*	
e) Premium, including Handling and Postage	*.30*	
f) Use Tax, if any (1 x *3* %)	*.75*	
TOTAL COST OF FILLING THE ORDER		*8.60*

ITEM #3. But there are other costs that must be included. How about administrative costs which include rent, light, heat, use of equipment, maintenance, expense of checking credit, collection follow-up, office supplies, etc.? Many firms make a flat charge of 10% to 20% of the Retail Price (#1) to cover these expenses. Let's use 10% of $25.00 or $2.50, and enter this under #3-a as the total administrative cost.

3 - Administrative Overhead		
a) Rent, Light, Heat, Maintenance, Credit Checking, Collections, etc. (10 % of # 1)	2.50	
TOTAL ADMINISTRATIVE COST		2.50

ITEM #4. The next question is what percentage of your customers will return the merchandise if sold on a free examination offer? Suppose we take 10% as an average and post this under Item #4.

4 - Estimated Percentage of Returns, Refunds or Cancellations	10%	

ITEM #5. How much does it cost to handle returns? It certainly costs as much as it did to ship the books. So let's charge $1.55 (2-c plus 2-d) for this item. Of course, some customers will prepay returned merchandise but let's not count on it. Some of the books may be damaged in shipping, so allow 10% of the cost of the set (10% of $6.00 (2-a) or 60¢ for refurnishing (5-b). This brings the Total Cost of Handling Returns (Item #5) to $2.15 per order.

5 - Expense in Handling Returns		
a) Return Postage and Handling (2c plus 2d)	1.55	
b) Refurbishing Returned Merchandise (10 % of # 2a)	.60	
TOTAL COST OF HANDLING RETURNS	2.15	

ITEM #6. As we are figuring that 10% of the orders will be returns, refunds or cancellations (Item #4), the Total Cost of Handling Returns will be 10% of $2.15 (Item #5), 21.5 cents per order. Let's say 21¢.

6 - Chargeable Cost of Returns (10 % of $2.15)		.21

ITEM #7. Bad debts are another expense that must be considered. This percentage will vary from about 5% to 25%, depending upon the proposition, the way the offer is presented and the list used. Let's take 10% as an average figure and enter it in Item #7.

7 - Estimated Bad Debt Percentage	10%	

ITEM #8. The Chargeable Cost of Bad Debts is 10% (Item #7) times $25.00 (Item #1). This amounts to $2.50 that must be allowed for the cost of bad debts. Enter $2.50 opposite Item #8.

8 - Chargeable Cost of Bad Debts (# 1 x # 7)		2.50

ITEM #9. The Total Variable Costs are Item #2 ($8.60) plus #3 ($2.50), #6 (.21) and #8 ($2.50) amounting to $13.81.

9 - Total Variable Costs (# 2 plus # 3, # 6, and # 8)		13.81

ITEM #10. After deducting the total variable costs (Item #9) amounting to $13.81 from the selling price (Item #1) of $25.00, this leaves a Unit Profit of $11.19.

10 - Unit Profit after Deducting Variable Costs (# 1 less # 9)		11.19

ITEM #11. But there is a return factor of 10% (Item #4) that must be accounted for. Deducting Item #4 or 10% from 100% leaves 90% of the unit profit that is left. Post 90% opposite Item #11.

11 - Return Factor (100% less # 4)	90%	

ITEM #12. Taking 90% (Item #11) times $11.19 (Item #10) leaves a unit profit of $10.07 per order. Post this amount opposite Item #12.

12 - Unit Profit Per Order (# 10 x # 11)		10.07

ITEM #13. Any merchandise that is returned after examination will be sent back to the manufacturer or put back into your inventory if you are the manufacturer. THIS REPRESENTS A CREDIT AGAINST THE ORIGINAL COST OF THE MERCHANDISE. Since we estimate the returns to be 10% (Item #4), we would have a CREDIT of 10% of our cost (Item #2-a, $6.00) or 60¢. This amount should be added to Item #12.

13 - Credit for Returned Merchandise (10% of # 2a)		.60

ITEM #14. Adding the credit per unit profit due to returned merchandise as explained above, we have a NET profit per order (Item #12 plus Item #13) of $10.67.

14 - Net Profit Per Order (# 12 plus # 13)		10.67

ITEM #15. Suppose the cost of your mailing package -- carrier envelope, letter, circular, order form, reply envelope, mailing list, lettershop labor, postage, etc., amounts to $100.00 per thousand. What about creative and production charges such as editorial preparation, art work, advertising, consultation, copy, engravings and typesetting which must be paid for?

You have the choice of charging these expenses against the test mailing or amortizing them over your projected mailing possibilities. If charged in one lump sum against the test, it will show a distorted picture. This could kill the test before you give it a chance. It's better to spread the cost over the total quantity of a projected mailing. If the charges amount to $1,000.00 and you figure you can mail 2,000,000 names if the test pulls, you could charge 50¢ per thousand against the cost of the mailing. (Item #15). If the test is a flop, you will have to absorb the expense anyway, so why not give it a reasonable chance to come through. So enter $100.50 under Item #15. ($100.00 plus 50¢).

15 - Cost of Mailing per 1,000	100.50	

ITEM #16. If you have a Net Profit Per Order of $10. 67 (#14) and the cost of mailing 1, 000 letters is $100. 50, divide $10. 67 into $100. 50 and you need 9. 4 orders, or . 94 % per thousand to break even.

16 - NUMBER OF ORDERS PER 1, 000 NEEDED TO BREAK EVEN ---------------- 9.4

Suppose your breakeven point on a test mailing is 9. 4 orders (. 94%) per thousand letters mailed. How many orders more than 9. 4 per thousand should you get to justify going ahead with a large mailing? It is generally considered safe if you get 33-1/3% (1/3) more orders. In this analysis, 1/3 more than 9. 4 would give us a total of 12. 5 orders per thousand or 3. 1 orders more than the breakeven point.

If the final mailing pulled 12. 5 orders per thousand, 3. 1 orders more than the break-even point, and the unit profit is $10. 67 per order, the net profit would be $33. 077 per thousand (3. 1 x $10. 67). On a 100, 000 mailing, the net profit would be $3, 307. 70; on 500, 000, it would be $16, 538. 50; on one million $33. 077.

A word of Caution! The time elapsing between the date of the test and the date of the final mailing may affect results. For example, a test made in January that pulls 12. 5 orders per thousand might pull only 9. 4 or less if mailed in June. So test in the poor months, if possible, and mail in the good months to eliminate unprofitable mailings.

FINAL REMARKS: Other methods are used to determine when a test mailing becomes profitable. For example, some firms figure the total dollar sales of the mailing must amount to two times the cost of the mailing. Other firms figure three times the selling price of the merchandise, plus 10%. However, the most accurate way to plan a profitable mailing is to set down all costs as outlined in this Bulletin.

Appendix L

MAIL ORDER COST ANALYSIS CHART

Balancing mailing costs, item price and rate of return in order to come out ahead of the game has always been a tricky job for the average mail order seller. Existing formulae are complicated, can easily lead to costly mistakes.

This chart—prepared for his own use by Bill Hall of Hall Brothers, Snow Shoe, Pa.,—will help any mailer determine, quickly and accurately, such vital mail order *planning* information as:

1. *How much he can spend on an item* and still break even at a known selling price, an anticipated rate-of-return, and a known mailing cost-per-thousand.
2. *What percent return he must get* to break-even at a known item cost, selling price and mailing cost-per-thousand.
3. The maximum *amount he can spend for his mailing* and still break even—at a known item cost, selling price and anticipated rate-of-return.

At first glance, the chart may seem complicated. Actually, all that is needed to use it effectively is an ability to do simple multiplication and division of decimal figures.

Practice the examples given until you understand the steps involved. From that point on, substitute your own figures to determine the facts you need for your own mail order decisions.

Naturally, you will want to double check your figures before committing yourself to final prices and costs. But, in the words of Bill Hall, this chart "gives me important information quickly and accurately when I'm planning mailings and dabbling with my costs." We hope it will do as much for you.

> *NOTE:* This chart is based on "Contribution Percentage"—i.e., the percentage of the selling price of an item which is available for advertising, overhead, profit, etc. after the item itself has been paid for. Thus, if an item sells for $4.50 and costs $1.50, each sale "contributes" $3.00 (or 66⅔%) of the selling price.

Example I: In order to break even, how much can we spend on an item which we plan to sell for $3.50, with mailing costs at $75.00 per thousand, and a 3% return anticipated?

A. Starting with the column headed "Percent Return," run your finger down the column until you come to the "3.00" line. Follow this line to the right until you intersect the "Average Purchase" column headed "3.50." The figure shown at this intersection is .0095.

B. Multiplying the mailing cost per thousand ($75.00) by this .0095 factor gives us a required "Contribution Percentage" of .7125. In other words, 71.25% of the average selling price must go toward paying for the mailing.

C. If 71.25% must go to mailing cost, only 28.75% (100% minus 71.25%) can be spent on the item. Multiplying our selling price ($3.50) by 28.75% gives us $1.01. The item cannot cost us more than $1.01 for us to break even under these circumstances.

Example II: In order to break even, what percent return is needed on an item costing $2.00, and selling for $6.00—with mailing costs at $70.00/per thousand?

A. Subtract item cost from selling price ($6.00 minus $2.00 = $4.00), and then determine the "Contribution Percentage" by dividing this result by the selling price ($4.00 ÷ $6.00 = .6666 or 66.66%).

B. Dividing this Contribution Percentage (.6666) by our mailing cost per thousand ($70.00) gives us .00952—rounded off to .0095.

C. Run your finger down the "Average Purchase" column headed "$6.00" until you come to the figure closest to ".0095." This figure appears on the sixth line. Following this line to the left we reach the figure "1.75" in the "Percent Return" column. In other words we will need a return of 1.75% on this mailing in order to break even at this item cost, selling price, and mailing cost-per-thousand.

Example III: In order to break even, what is the maximum we can spend for our mailing (mailing cost-per-thousand) on an item that costs $2.50, and which we are planning to sell for $7.00—with anticipated returns of 2% on the mailing?

A. As in Example II, above, determine the "Contribution Percentage" by (1) subtracting item cost from selling price ($7.00 minus $2.50 = $4.50) and then (2) dividing this result by the selling price ($4.50 ÷ $7.00 = .64285 rounded off to .6429).

B. Starting with the "Percent Return" line for 2% (2.00) follow the line of figures to the right until you intersect the

"Average Purchase" column headed "7.00." The figure shown at this intersection is .0071.

C. Divide the "Contribution Percentage" found in step A (.6429) by this factor of .0071. The result is 90.549—rounded off to 90.55. Thus, the maximum we can afford to spend for our mailing under these conditions is 90.55 per thousand.

MAIL ORDER COST ANALYSIS CHART

(See instruction sheet for use)

PERCENT	AVERAGE PURCHASE												
RETURN	2.00	2.50	3.00	3.50	4.00	4.50	5.00	5.50	6.00	6.50	7.00	7.50	8.00
.50	.1000	.0800	.0667	.0571	.0500	.0444	.0400	.0364	.0333	.0308	.0286	.0267	.0250
.75	.0667	.0533	.0444	.0381	.0333	.0296	.0267	.0242	.0222	.0205	.0190	.0178	.0167
1.00	.0500	.0400	.0333	.0286	.0250	.0222	.0200	.0182	.0167	.0154	.0143	.0133	.0125
1.25	.0400	.0320	.0267	.0229	.0200	.0178	.0160	.0145	.0133	.0123	.0114	.0107	.0100
1.50	.0333	.0267	.0222	.0190	.0167	.0148	.0133	.0121	.0111	.0103	.0095	.0089	.0084
1.75	.0286	.0229	.0190	.0163	.0143	.0127	.0114	.0104	.0095	.0088	.0082	.0076	.0071
2.00	.0250	.0200	.0167	.0143	.0125	.0111	.0100	.0091	.0083	.0077	.0071	.0067	.0063
2.25	.0222	.0178	.0148	.0127	.0111	.0099	.0088	.0081	.0074	.0068	.0063	.0059	.0056
2.50	.0200	.0160	.0133	.0114	.0100	.0089	.0080	.0073	.0067	.0062	.0057	.0053	.0050
2.75	.0182	.0145	.0121	.0104	.0091	.0081	.0073	.0066	.0061	.0056	.0052	.0048	.0045
3.00	.0167	.0133	.0111	.0095	.0083	.0074	.0067	.0061	.0056	.0051	.0048	.0044	.0042
3.25	.0154	.0123	.0103	.0088	.0077	.0068	.0062	.0056	.0051	.0047	.0044	.0041	.0039
3.50	.0143	.0114	.0095	.0082	.0071	.0063	.0057	.0052	.0048	.0044	.0041	.0038	.0036
3.75	.0133	.0107	.0089	.0076	.0067	.0059	.0053	.0048	.0044	.0041	.0038	.0035	.0034
4.00	.0125	.0100	.0083	.0071	.0063	.0056	.0050	.0045	.0042	.0038	.0036	.0034	.0032
4.25	.0018	.0094	.0078	.0067	.0059	.0052	.0047	.0043	.0039	.0036	.0034	.0032	.0029
4.50	.0111	.0089	.0074	.0063	.0056	.0049	.0044	.0040	.0037	.0034	.0032	.0030	.0028
4.75	.0105	.0084	.0070	.0060	.0053	.0047	.0042	.0038	.0035	.0032	.0030	.0028	.0027
5.00	.0100	.0080	.0067	.0057	.0050	.0044	.0040	.0036	.0033	.0031	.0029	.0027	.0025
5.25	.0095	.0076	.0063	.0054	.0048	.0042	.0038	.0035	.0032	.0029	.0027	.0026	.0024
5.50	.0091	.0073	.0061	.0052	.0045	.0040	.0036	.0033	.0030	.0028	.0026	.0024	.0023
5.75	.0087	.0070	.0058	.0050	.0043	.0039	.0035	.0032	.0029	.0027	.0025	.0023	.0022
6.00	.0083	.0067	.0056	.0048	.0042	.0037	.0033	.0030	.0028	.0026	.0024	.0022	.0021
6.25	.0080	.0064	.0053	.0046	.0040	.0036	.0032	.0029	.0027	.0025	.0023	.0021	.0020
6.50	.0077	.0062	.0051	.0044	.0038	.0034	.0031	.0028	.0026	.0024	.0022	.0021	.0019
6.75	.0074	.0059	.0049	.0042	.0037	.0033	.0030	.0027	.0025	.0023	.0021	.0020	.0018
7.00	.0071	.0057	.0048	.0041	.0036	.0032	.0029	.0026	.0024	.0022	.0020	.0019	.0018
7.25	.0069	.0055	.0046	.0039	.0034	.0031	.0028	.0025	.0023	.0021	.0020	.0018	.0017
7.50	.0067	.0053	.0044	.0038	.0033	.0030	.0027	.0024	.0022	.0021	.0019	.0017	.0016

Appendix M

CHECKLISTS FOR INDUSTRIAL DIRECT MAIL

Four checklists prepared by the Marketing Communications Research Center, 575 Ewing Street, Princeton, N. J. 08540, can serve as particularly helpful guides for the industrial direct mail user. These checklists were originally created for MCRC's outstanding research report, "How to Improve Results from Business Direct Mail,"[1] and are reproduced here with the permission of MCRC President, Dr. J. E. Bachelder.

The first checklist outlines the seven factors which determine results in industrial direct mail. The second checklist is a handy four-page form which can be used to guide the planning of a particular mailing. The third checklist is a companion form designed to assist industrial advertisers in conducting a systematic review and evaluation of a mailing. The fourth checklist contains questions to stimulate development of business direct mail (BDM) innovations.

In introducing the two forms included in the checklists, MCRC pointed out:

> At an early stage in the creative planning, it is wise to make a careful, analytical inspection of the mailing plan in an open-minded search for practicable improvements. This review is a long established practice in well-managed BDM operations. However, inquiry among many top-grade companies shows that the practice is hampered, as a rule, by two deficiencies:
>
> It is seldom systematic enough to cover all aspects of the projected mailing.
>
> The inspection, even when detailed, is casual in that it leaves no written record for later use in checking against actual results and in drawing conclusions for guidance in planning further mailings.
>
> The Planning and Analysis form (*Checklist No. 2*) does much to remedy these two deficiencies in the usual, or casual, inspections of the mailing plan. Using the form, the planner can systematically check his plan against the seven controlling factors and thus discover any unsuspected weaknesses that might crop up later. With the form as a guide, the planner can more readily look at his plan from the viewpoint of an objective observer.
>
> However, few persons with creative ability are at the same time well prepared to become truly objective critics of their own work. The second use of the Planning and Analysis form, therefore, is to record the thinking behind the plan, so it can be reviewed by one or more other persons—as well as by the planner himself. The review may be based upon a companion form titled "Evaluation of an Industrial Mailing" (*Checklist No. 3*).
>
> Using the seven basic factors which control mailing results, it is feasible to formulate a systematic and thorough pre-examination of any projected industrial mailing while it is still in one of the planning stages. To imple-

[1] "How to Improve Results from Business Direct Mail." Report No. 14. New Edition. © 1963, 1964, 1965 and 1973 Marketing Communications Research Center, Princeton, N. J.

ment this pre-examination the Center has prepared a four-page form titled "Planning and Analysis of an Industrial Mailing."

This form is designed to be applicable to any industrial mailing for any of the three main types of objectives. With slight modifications, it may be applied also to a series of mailings.

The three-page Evaluation form (*Checklist No. 3*) is designed to make systematic and constructive review of a projected mailing as simple and time-saving as possible. It is a companion of the Planning and Analysis form and is arranged in a parallel order of topics. Thus, it is convenient to place the two forms side-by-side and to make entries in the Evaluation form pertaining to each of the seven controlling factors as described by the planner of the mailing.

The entries are of two kinds: first, judgments on questions stated in the Evaluation form; second, suggestion of revisions and additions. The two are complementary. However, it is not implied that the evaluator is expected to make suggestions on every factor. Even where his judgments indicate that he is not wholly satisfied with the planned handling of the factor, he may not be prepared at the moment to present a constructive suggestion; if so, it may be best to leave the space blank.

Checklist No. 1

SEVEN FACTORS WHICH DETERMINE INDUSTRIAL DIRECT MAIL RESULTS

1. **Objectives** are the attainable, sharply defined goals.

2. **Theme** indicates the central thought, message, or copy idea.

3. **Treatment** is the way in which the subject matter is handled—layout, illustration, typography.

4. **Offer** is the response-stimulating mechanism.

5. **Format** includes the physical form and appearance of the combined elements of the mailing—envelope, letter, printed inserts, and other components of the mailing package.

6. **List** is the compilation of names, titles, companies and addresses to which pieces may be sent. Lists can be developed within the company, rented or purchased from a variety of sources.

7. **Conditions** encompass anything in the external situation—season of the year, current state of business, competitive activity, advertising environment, or whatever may strongly influence reactions to a mailing.

Checklist No. 2

PLANNING AND ANALYSIS OF AN INDUSTRIAL MAILING

Company or Division .... **Date** ....

By.. **Position** ....

Product, Product Line or Service Presented in This Mailing

....

Check status of proposed mailing:

- [ ] An idea under consideration, but plans not definite or completely worked out
- [ ] Mailing components planned and rough copy written
- [ ] Mailing completed on ....
- [ ] ....

Relationship of this mailing to other direct mailing activities:

- [ ] A one-shot mailing to the list addressed
- [ ] # .... in a special campaign of .... mailings addressed to the same list
- [ ] One among a series of routine mailings to the same list
- [ ] In support of other activity
- [ ] ....

What is the estimated total cost of the mailing including postage? $..............................

---

1. OBJECTIVE of This Particular Mailing

NOTE: Unless the objective is accurately defined, your handling of the other factors will be off target and the mailing cannot be expected to produce effective results.

Which **one** of the following is the main objective of the mailing?

- [ ] **1. To Motivate Direct Responsive Action**
- [ ] **2. To Exert Impact on Attitudes and/or to Increase Knowledge**
- [ ] **3. To Implement a Sales-making Drive**

If you checked #1 (Responsive Action) is your objective to draw out requests for:

- [ ] Further literature or information?
- [ ] Having a salesman call?
- [ ] Permission to make a survey of customer requirements?
- [ ] ....?

If you checked #2, are you attempting to:

- [ ] Provide a clearer concept of your company and facilities?
- [ ] Increase the knowledge about a product line?
- [ ] Gain approval of your company policies or business methods?
- [ ] ....?

If you checked #3, are you carrying on a sales-making drive in team with salesmen:

- [ ] To open up new accounts?
- [ ] To increase business with existing accounts?
- [ ] To invigorate distributor's sales activities?
- [ ] ....

Now, define the **precise** primary objective and name separately not more than two secondary objectives. ....

....

....

2. LIST to Be Addressed

What is the total number on the list or lists to be used? ....
Is this [ ] all or [ ] part of the regular customer-prospect list? If a part only, identify the segment or segments of the list to be used: ....
....
Is [ ] all or [ ] part of the list rented or purchased? If this is the case, indicate source and describe list composition: ....
.... Cost: $..................
When was the list or lists to be used last brought up to date? ....
Number of mailings to list (described above) within last 12 months: ....
Latest mailing preceded this mailing by about .... weeks.
Indicate by approximate percentage the list make-up by type of personnel:

..........% Top executives — ....% Engineers or technicians
..........% Purchasing executives — ....% Lower level personnel
..........% Production executives — ....% ....

Indicate by approximate percentages the degree of addressing to company names only ....%; company and title only ....%; company and individual name ....%; company, individual name and title ....%.

---

3. THEME of This Mailing

NOTE: Unless the mailing has a unifying theme—sometimes called the "message" or copy idea—it cannot make the right impression; (e.g. *"Analysis of your materials handling system may save you up to ....")*

State the theme here as concisely as you can: ....
....
....

Check only one of the following statements concerning the theme:

- [ ] It is plainly stated somewhere, but not emphasized.
- [ ] It dominates the copy by prominence and/or repetition.
- [ ] It underlies the copy without being stated in so many words.

---

4. TREATMENT of this Mailing

NOTE: This factor has to do with the means by which the theme is to be put across. It includes plans for copy, illustrations and the functional aspects of the various printed pieces. The physical aspects of the pieces are examined under Format.

Can a letter (and reply form) alone do the entire job of putting across the theme of this mailing and getting the desired response or effect? [ ] Yes [ ] No
If not, what are the purposes the letter is expected to serve?

- [ ] Win attention for other enclosures only
- [ ] Introduce or summarize the subject matter
- [ ] Do the main selling job
- [ ] ....

Check the enclosures planned for this mailing:

- [ ] Product booklet, brochure or catalog
- [ ] Institutional booklet or brochure
- [ ] Product or application data sheet
- [ ] ....
- [ ] Sales promotion folder or circular
- [ ] Ad reprint
- [ ] Technical or service material

Now, state briefly the main function of each of the enclosures checked above: ....
....
....
....

What is the main subject matter planned for this mailing?

- [ ] Description of user benefit
- [ ] Case history of user benefit
- [ ] Institutional appeal
- [ ] Product features
- [ ] How product works
- [ ] How product is made
- [ ] Product quality
- [ ] ....

Check below the main subject matter of the illustrations used in the principal pieces (other than catalog or manual):

- [ ] Product alone
- [ ] Cutaway view of product
- [ ] Product in use
- [ ] Product features
- [ ] Product being manufactured
- [ ] View of plant
- [ ] Graphs or charts
- [ ] ....

---

5. OFFER Presented in This Mailing

Check here [ ] if no offer of any kind is actually stated and proceed to Section 6.

Indicate the primary offer by (1), and any other offer by (2):

- [ ] To mail a printed piece
- [ ] To have a salesman call
- [ ] To supply a sample or free trial
- [ ] To make a preliminary survey
- [ ] To submit a plan or proposal
- [ ] ....

Indicate the chief means used to win acceptance of the offer by:

- [ ] Making a gift or other reward for a response
- [ ] Making the offer itself exceptionally attractive

Please explain: ....

....

Does the mailing facilitate response by supplying a reply form and envelope or a postcard?

[ ] Yes [ ] No

On the other hand, does the mailing deliberately restrict responses to persons genuinely interested by such means as requesting respondents to reply on their own letterheads?

[ ] Yes [ ] No Please explain ....

....

---

6. FORMAT of the Mailing Components

Please indicate below the format of each mailing component planned. (*Except for entering the estimated COST in each instance, it is not necessary to complete sections marked with asterisks in cases where layouts or mailing samples are available for review.)

***Letter** [ ] regular letterhead [ ] special letterhead
Paper color and stock ....
Color of ink ....
How produced ....
Cost ....

***Envelope**
Size and type ....
Paper stock and color ....
Color of ink ....
How addressed ....
Cost ....

***Self-mailer:**
Size ....
Paper stock and color ....
Color of ink ....
How addressed ....
Cost ....

***Other Enclosures:** Briefly describe physical features or appearance ....

Cost ....

Postage: ☐ first class ☐ postage meter ☐ third class ☐ hand stamp

Cost ....

Distinctive Features: Briefly point out anything unusual in physical features or appearances of the mailing: ....

---

7. CONDITIONS Expected at Time of This Mailing

Enter below any foreseeable elements which may affect the mailing results—and their probable influence:

Special interest in the product ....

Recent or current publicity or other advertising ....

Sales force activity ....

Competitive activities, including price changes ....

Technological developments ....

Economic developments ....

Seasonal elements ....

Any other conditions ....

ANTICIPATED RESULTS OF THIS MAILING

Please state (in quantitative terms if practicable) the responses, reactions or other results to be reasonably anticipated from this mailing.

....

ACTUAL RESULTS OF THIS MAILING

After the mailing is completed and has had time to exert the major part of its effect, please enter here any recorded results, indications or judgments concerning how well this mailing achieved its objective. ....

Checklist No. 3

EVALUATION OF AN INDUSTRIAL MAILING

This form is designed as an aid in evaluating the plan for an industrial mailing after the plan has been recorded on the companion *Planning and Analysis* form. Primarily it is for use by one or more persons in a position to review the plan objectively. However, the planner himself may use it to guide a critical re-examination of his own plan. The form may be used in the early planning stages, when plans are complete, or for a post-examination of a completed mailing.

1. OBJECTIVE

	POOR	FAIR	GOOD	TOPS
Is the objective so specifically and completely stated that it acts as a sure guide in handling the other factors in the mailing?				
In your opinion, is the objective realistically attainable by this mailing?				
Does the objective tie in closely with the other marketing plans for this product, product line or service?				
Over-all rating of **Objective**				

SUGGESTIONS for improving or changing the objective: ....

2. LIST

Does the list cover and concentrate on:

	POOR	FAIR	GOOD	TOPS
a. The particular markets of most importance for this mailing?				
b. The personnel (job classifications) to be influenced?				
Is the manner of addressing (i.e., title only or name and title) suited to the purpose of this mailing?				
Over-all rating of **List**				

SUGGESTIONS as to desirable improvements on the list: ....

3. THEME

	POOR	FAIR	GOOD	TOPS
Does the theme closely fit the objective of the mailing?				
Does it have a strong appeal to the list addressed?				
Is the theme put over clearly and forcefully? (a possibility even when it is not stated in so many words)				
Over-all rating of **Theme**				

SUGGESTIONS for improving the theme or its expression: ....

4. TREATMENT

	POOR	FAIR	GOOD	TOPS
Have the enclosures been well chosen to accomplish the mailing objective?				
Is the theme developed in an orderly, clear manner throughout the mailing package?				
Is the wording in the language of the reader?				
Is the copy believable throughout?				
Does the copy, including illustrations, relate to the reader's practical problems and experience?				
Have illustrations been used to best advantage in developing the theme?				
Is the over-all treatment effective in:				
a. Winning favorable attention?				
b. Building up interest and conviction?				
c. Aiming for desired response or impression?				
Over-all rating of **Treatment**				

SUGGESTIONS as to ways in which the treatment might be better handled: ....

5. OFFER

	POOR	FAIR	GOOD	TOPS
Does the offer tie in closely with the objective of this mailing?				
Is the offer especially well suited to the list addressed?				

	POOR	FAIR	GOOD	TOPS
Is the offer presented in a manner that will arouse favorable attention and (if this is desired) be easy to accept?.				
Over-all rating of **Offer**				

SUGGESTIONS as to improvements in the offer and its presentation: ....

6. FORMAT

	POOR	FAIR	GOOD	TOPS
Does the mailing as a whole attract favorable attention and promote readership?				
Are the choices of design, paper stock, color, typography, illustrations, etc. consistent with the tastes of the list addressed?				
Does the format reinforce the salient points of the treatment?				
Are the enclosures properly designed to meet the specific end uses intended?				
Over-all rating of **Format**				

SUGGESTIONS as to desirable improvements in the format: ....

7. CONDITIONS

	POOR	FAIR	GOOD	TOPS
Will the conditions noted in the **Planning and Analysis** form have a favorable over-all effect?				
Is the mailing well suited to these anticipated conditions?				
Over-all rating of **Conditions**				

SUGGESTIONS for improvements adapting mailing to fit foreseeable conditions: ....

8. ANTICIPATED RESULTS

	POOR	FAIR	GOOD	TOPS
Do the anticipated results conform closely with the objective?				
Will the anticipated results be fully satisfactory if realized?				

COMMENTS: ....

Checklist No. 4

QUESTIONS TO STIMULATE DEVELOPMENT OF BUSINESS DIRECT MAIL INNOVATIONS

Objective:

- Is the primary function of the BDM operation clearly defined? What is it? Are program objectives always consistent with that function?
- Are objectives stated in terms of the desired reactions to each mailing? Are they stated so that reactions will come from the target type of personnel?
- Are the objectives of most mailings sharply focused on selected segments of the mailing list? Should they be? Or should the appeal be to the entire list, not to a segment?
- Are the anticipated results of each mailing plainly stated? Are they attainable?
- Are the objectives always coordinated with the objectives and policies of other marketing activities?

List:

- Is the mailing list (or collection of lists) classified and otherwise qualified to provide for performance of the primary project function?
- Is it possible to pick a list for a particular mailing which precisely matches the objective of that mailing?
- Is the list so classified and maintained that the number of names in each segment is readily available for planning or for sampling?
- Is list maintenance frequent enough that the list is up-to-date?
- Are buying units (companies, divisions, onsite operations and autonomous plants) well represented by men who make or influence decisions for the products or services promoted?
- Are lists purchased or rented from outside sources adequately tested for quality?

Theme:

- Does the message of each mailing make a strong appeal to the self-interest of readers? Is the message concisely phrased in a form to command favorable attention? Does the theme lead naturally into the subject matter of the mailing?
- Should the same theme be repeated in a series of mailings? Or should each mailing in the series carry its own distinctive theme?

Conditions:

- Are conditions at the planned time of mailing foreseen (seasonal, economic, technological, etc.?)
- Are measures taken to capitalize on or counteract such conditions?

- Does each plan aim to reap all possible advantages from other concurrent marketing activities such as sales drives, advertising, etc.?
- Is adaptation to conditions an important component of every mailing?

Treatment:

- Do the pieces in this mailing package fit together to form an integrated unit?
- Is the fact that it is an integrated unit of importance to the mailing or the series?
- Is the selected theme sufficiently played up and driven home?
- Is the treatment on the right level for key people on the list? Too technical?
- What about style of copy? Is it clear? Readable? Should it be simpler and more colloquial? Would a little humor go over well or would it make a bad impression on some readers?
- Would the story get across faster if more photos or drawings were used?
- Are more charts, diagrams, engineering cross-sections needed?
- What would be the effect of putting more hard-sell into the letters? Is the mailing too dignified to be effective?

Offer:

- Does the literature contain information that is new and interesting to the list?
- Would a bigger response result by eliminating the offer to have a salesman call? Would the end result be more sales?
- When offering a bulletin or manual or other special piece, should the letter be devoted mainly to selling the value of the literature being offered?
- In a series of mailings to the same list, should the offer be different in each mailing?

Format:

- Would it pay to affix stamps to the reply forms? If so, regular or air mail?
- Would it pay to enclose more printed pieces in each mailing? Would that make the mailings appear to be overselling?
- With a big story to tell, should more brochures be issued? What about broadsides?
- Are the mailings too stodgy or dull?
- In order to reach upper level personnel, should autotyped letters be used? In such letters, should a reply form be enclosed?
- Would a colorful envelope help to attract attention? How about a "teaser" printed on the front of the envelope? Or a die-cut window so part of the content shows through?
- Would much be lost by mailing third-class? Would air-mail improve results?

Appendix N

COPYREADING MARKS

Symbols for editing copy according to the rules of style accepted for business writing. Correct editing reduces average costly alteration charges by more than half, and alterations account for from 10 to 50 percent of most jobs.

ONE WORD	If our only yard stick of business profits is dol-
BOLD FACE	lars, and we measure our every activity by the noise
APOSTROPHE	it makes on the cash register, then I say, dont join
SEMICOLON	anything. Keep out of your trade associations fight
LOWER CASE	shy of the local Service Clubs; have nothing to do
PERIOD	with executives organized on functional lines In the
COMMA	first place, with such a philosophy you probably won't
RESTORE	put much into these associations and you may be per-
RUN IN	fectly certain you won't take much out.
INSERT LETTER	It takes more then dues to make a succesful associa-
TRANSPOSE LETTER	tion. And you probably won't maek many friends, for
OMIT WORD	people haven't much use for the man who joins for
HYPHEN	business first purposes. If you are that sort of bird,
INSERT WORD	stay at your desk. Keep your head buried your papers.
ITALICS	But don't blame anyone but yourself if you and your
EXCLAMATION POINT	business soon die of hardening of the arteries
PARAGRAPH	If, however, you measure profits by the friends you
OMIT LETTER	make as well as the money your bank; if you agree with
SMALL CAPS	Theodore Roosevelt that "every man owes something to
QUOTES	his profession and are not satisfied to go through
DASH	life, taking all you can get but giving nothing in re-
TWO WORDS	turn--then join at least one of your hometown's fel-
CAPITALIZE	lowship groups. after all, you know we are only on
SPELL OUT	this earth a few years. Most of us have but 20 years
NUMERAL	at best in the harness. Why not spend one per cent of
TRANSPOSE WORDS	those remaining years doing what we to can make this
QUESTION MARK	world a better place in which to live

PROOFREADERS' MARKS COURTESY OF BOISE CASCADE

MARK	EXPLANATION	EXAMPLE
ℊ	TAKE OUT CHARACTER INDICATED.	ℊ Your prooof.
^	LEFT OUT, INSERT.	u Yor proof.
#	INSERT SPACE.	# Yourproof.
9	TURN INVERTED LETTER.	9 Your p ooof.
×	BROKEN LETTER	× Your proof.
⊥	PUSH DOWN SPACE.	⊥ Your/proof.
eq#	EVEN SPACE.	eq# A good proof.
⁀	CLOSE UP; NO SPACE.	Your pro of.
tr.	TRANSPOSE.	tr. A proof good.
wf	WRONG FONT.	wf Your proof.
lc	LOWER CASE.	lc Your Proof.
sc	SMALL CAPITALS.	Your proof. sc Your proof.
c+sc	CAPITALS AND SMALL CAPITALS.	Your proof. c+sc Your proof.
caps	CAPITALS.	Your proof. caps Your proof.
ital	ITALIC.	Your proof. ital Your proof.
rom	ROMAN.	rom Your proof.
bf	BOLD FACE.	Your proof. bf Your proof.
stet	LET IT STAND.	Your proof. stet Your proof.
out sc.	OUT, SEE COPY.	out sc. She proof.
spell out	SPELL OUT.	spell out Queen Eliz.

MARK	EXPLANATION	EXAMPLE
¶	START PARAGRAPH.	¶ read. Your
no ¶	NO PARAGRAPH; RUN IN.	no ¶ marked. Your proof.
⊔	LOWER.	⊔ Your proof.
⊓	RAISE.	⊓ Your proof.
⊏	MOVE LEFT.	⊏ Your proof.
⊐	MOVE RIGHT.	⊐ Your proof.
‖	ALIGN TYPE.	‖ Three dogs. Two horses.
═	STRAIGHTEN LINE.	═ Your proof.
⊙	INSERT PERIOD.	⊙ Your proof
,/	INSERT COMMA.	,/ Your proof
:/	INSERT COLON.	:/ Your proof
;/	INSERT SEMICOLON.	;/ Your proof
’	INSERT APOSTROPHE.	’ Your mans proof.
“ ”	INSERT QUOTATION MARKS.	“ ” Marked it proof.
=/	INSERT HYPHEN.	=/ A proofmark.
!	INSERT EXCLAMATION MARK.	! Prove it
?	INSERT QUESTION MARK.	? Is it right
ⓘ	QUERY FOR AUTHOR.	? was Your proof read by
[/]	INSERT BRACKETS.	[/] The Smith girl . .
(/)	INSERT PARENTHESES.	(/) Your proof 1
|1/n|	INSERT 1-EN DASH.	|1/n| Your proof
|1/m|	INSERT 1-EM DASH.	|1/m| Your proof
|2/m|	INSERT 2-EM DASH.	|2/m| Your proof
□	INDENT 1 EM.	□ Your proof.
□□	INDENT 2 EMS.	□□ Your proof.
□□□	INDENT 3 EMS.	□□□ Your proof.

Appendix O

PROBABILITY AS APPLIED TO DIRECT RESPONSE ADVERTISING

(Prepared by The Alan Drey Company, Inc.)

Perhaps one of the most frequently pondered questions in direct response test programs is that of deciding on how big or how small a test mailing should be. Many rules of thumb for establishing test quantities have been practiced by mailers for many years. These often follow such lines as: "I always test 10% of the list;" or "We never test more than 1,000 pieces on any test."

Often these tried and true axioms have built-in problems. For instance, if we are to test 10% of the list as a general rule, are we wise in using a test quantity of 100,000 when the list is 1,000,000 names in size? Conversely, by testing only 1,000 names will we have a reliable set of test results which can produce an accurate forecast for a larger mailing?

Testing too large a quantity forces us to spend more than is necessary to obtain reasonably reliable test results; and too small a quantity wastes money in that we cannot have much confidence in our results.

The use of probabilities can go a long way in providing us with a useful tool to decide:

1. How large a test mailing should be made. Do we test 3,000, 5,000 or 10,000 pieces?
2. What degree of confidence will we have in projecting our results? (90, 95 or 99 out of 100 times will fall within certain prescribed limits of error.)
3. What will our limits of error be in a large mailing? Suppose our test pulls 1%, can we be somewhat sure that our big mailing will fall at 1% plus or minus (±) .2 of 1%, or will our big mailing have results falling at 1% ± .5%?

Since we are talking about the use of probabilities as a tool in creating and analyzing test samples let us look at the background of statistical probability to see how it can apply to a direct mail program.

The use of statistics has as its object the arrival at general conclusions which are relatively probable based on an analysis of a number of observations. If we have as our object the desire to arrive at general conclusions through a large number of observations then how can we apply this to direct mail advertising and selling? Well, what we are really doing when we look at test mailing results is observing the response or non-response of *each piece* of mail which comprises the whole of the test. We then draw our general conclusions based on these numerous observations.

Perhaps the standard example of probabilities revolves around the simple act of tossing a coin. There are two sides to a coin and thus only two ways a coin can fall . . . heads or tails. Assuming an equally weighted coin is used, we can consider either heads or tails as equally likely to fall. Therefore, we say that the probability of obtaining a heads in a given flip is 1 out of 2. Empirically, however, we note that when a small number of flips are made heads shows up only *about* half the time . . . not *exactly* half the time. The more often a coin is tossed the closer we come to the theoretical 1 out of 2 and the smaller our error becomes.

Confusion in the use of the term "probability" comes from the idea that probability tells us something about a single particular event. When we say our coin toss has a heads probability of 1 out of 2 on any *single* toss it means nothing. What we are really saying is that if we toss the coin a sufficient number of times we will approach the ratio of 1 out of 2. The greater the number of tosses (test sample size) the smaller the limit of error from our 1 out of 2 ratio.

The mathematician has converted his observations of actual happenings into an equation which takes into account the relationship of confidence, limit of error, sample size (observations), expected response (incidence of heads) and expected non-response (tails). Since the mathematician found that there is an interrelationship between these factors we can take advantage of this information in creating and analyzing test mailings.

If we have already made a mailing of a given number of pieces (sample size) and we know the results (percentage of response) we can then predict at various levels of confidence (90, 95 or 99 out of 100 times) what degree of error (limit of error) in response we would have on a larger mailing to the *same list under identical circumstances.* With this information, we go a long way towards building into our larger mailing a degree of protection against serious loss of invested promotion dollars. Conversely, if we are about to make a test mailing we can determine how large the test should be. But first we need to know three things. What is our *anticipated* response? (What do we expect the mailing will pull?) What level of confidence do we require? (Must we be right 99 out of 100 times or can we risk being right 95 out of 100 times?) And thirdly, by how much can we miss the anticipated pull and still be within an acceptable lower response limit? (Can we live with 1% ± .2 of 1% or can we still be profitable in our mailing with a pull of 1% ± .5%?)

Because of the time required to compute a probability equation for each individual mailing made or contemplated, it is often easier to refer to a table of probability wherein the calculations have been made for various percentages of response and limits of error.

The following tables are made up of four elements; test sample size, level of confidence, expected response, and the limit of error.

At the top of each page is a notation as to the degree of confidence upon which that table is built. Running horizontally across the top of the page are the limits of error expressed in percent. The column headed "P" is the expression in percentage of the expected or anticipated response. The figures at the intersection of the coordinates of "expected response" and "limit of error" are the sample sizes.

To illustrate the use of these tables, let us take an actual example of a given mailing and determine the "limit of error" which we could expect on a larger mailing. Let us say we mailed 10,000 pieces and received a 1% response and that we want to be sure that our future will fall within this limit of error 95 out of 100 times (95%). We would first turn to the section of our tables computed upon the 95% confidence level and then read down the left hand column marked "P" until we come to the 1% response or pull. Then read horizontally until we come to the closest figure to our 10,000 piece sample size. Then reading vertically to that column's heading we find the possible "limit of error" we could expect on a larger mailing to the same list.

95% CONFIDENCE LEVEL
LIMIT OF ERROR

PULL	0.16	0.18	0.20	0.25	0.30
.1	1,499	1,184	958	614	426
.2	2,994	2,366	1,917	1,226	852
.3	4,467	3,546	2,872	1,838	1,276
.4	5,977	4,723	3,826	2,448	1,700
.5	7,464	5,897	4,777	3,057	2,123
.6	8,948	7,070	5,727	3,665	2,545
.7	10,429	8,240	6,675	4,272	2,966
.8	11,907	9,408	7,621	4,877	3,387
.9	13,382	10,573	8,564	5,481	3,806
1.0	14,854	11,736	9,506	6,084	4,225
1.1	16,322	12,897	10,446	6,686	4,643
1.2	17,788	14,055	11,385	7,286	5,060

Sample Size for Various Percentages of Expected Returns(P) and Limit of Error(E) If Factor of Confidence Is 95%

P	E 0.01	0.02	0.03	0.04	0.05	0.06	0.07	0.08	0.09	0.10	0.12	0.14
0.1	383,716	95,929	42,635	23,982	15,349	10,659	7,831	5,995	4,737	3,837	2,665	1,957
0.2	766,664	191,666	85,185	47,916	30,667	21,296	15,646	11,979	9,465	7,667	5,324	3,911
0.3	1,148,843	287,211	127,649	71,803	45,954	31,912	23,445	17,951	14,183	11,488	7,978	5,861
0.4	1,530,254	382,564	170,028	95,641	61,210	42,507	31,229	23,910	18,892	15,303	10,627	7,807
0.5	1,910,898	477,724	212,321	119,431	76,436	53,080	38,998	29,858	23,591	19,109	13,270	9,749
0.6	2,290,772	572,693	254,530	143,173	91,631	63,632	46,750	35,793	28,281	22,908	15,908	11,687
0.7	2,669,879	667,470	296,653	166,867	106,795	74,163	54,487	41,717	32,961	26,699	18,541	13,622
0.8	3,048,218	762,054	338,690	190,514	121,929	84,673	62,208	47,628	37,632	30,482	21,168	15,552
0.9	3,425,788	856,447	380,643	214,112	137,032	95,160	69,913	53,528	42,294	34,258	23,790	17,478
1.0	3,802,590	950,648	422,510	237,662	152,104	105,628	77,604	59,415	46,945	38,026	26,407	19.401
1.1	4,178,624	1,044,656	464,290	261,164	167,145	116,072	85,277	65,291	51,587	41,786	29,018	21,319
1.2	4,553.890	1,138,472	505,987	284,618	182,156	126,496	92,936	71,155	56,220	45,539	31,624	23,234
1.3	4,928,387	1,232,097	547,598	308,024	197,135	136,899	100,579	77,006	60,844	49,284	34,225	25,145
1.4	5,302,116	1,325,529	589,123	331,382	212,085	147,280	108,206	82,845	65,458	53,021	36,820	27,051
1.5	5,675,078	1,418,769	630,564	354,692	227,003	157,640	115,818	88,673	70,062	56,751	39,410	28,954
1.6	6,047,270	1,511,818	671,919	377,954	241,891	167,980	123,413	94,489	74,657	60,473	41,995	30,853
1.7	6,418,695	1,604,674	713,187	401,168	256,748	178,297	130,993	100,292	79,243	64,187	44,574	32,748
1.8	6,789,352	1,697,338	754,372	424,334	271,574	188,592	138,557	106,083	83,819	67,894	47,148	34,639
1.9	7,159,240	1,789,810	795,471	447,452	286,370	198,868	146,106	111,863	88,386	71,592	49,717	36,526
2.0	7,528,360	1,882,090	836,483	470,523	301,134	209,121	153,640	117,631	92,942	75,284	52,280	38,410
2.1	7,896,712	1,974,178	877,412	493,544	315,868	219,352	161,157	123,386	97,490	78,967	54,838	40,289
2.2	8,264,296	2,066,074	918,255	516,518	330,572	229,564	168,659	129,129	102,028	82,643	57,391	42,165
2.3	8,631,111	2,157,778	959,010	539,444	345,244	239,753	176,144	134,861	106,556	86,311	59,938	44,036
2.4	8,997,158	2,249,290	999,683	562,322	359,886	249,920	183,614	140,581	111,076	89,972	62,480	45,903
2.5	9,362,438	2,340,609	1,040,271	585,152	374,498	260,068	191,069	146,288	115,585	93,624	65,017	47,767
2.6	9,726,948	2,431,737	1,080,770	607,934	389,078	270,192	198,508	151,983	120,085	97,269	67,547	49,627
2.7		2,522,673	1,121,187	630,668	403,628	280,296	205,932	157,667	124,576	100,907	70,074	51,483
2.8		2,613,416	1,161,518	653,354	418,147	290,380	213,340	163,339	129,058	104,537	72,595	53,335
2.9		2,703,968	1,201,761	675,992	432,635	300,440	220,732	168,998	133,528	108,159	75,110	55,183
3.0		2,794,328	1,241,922	698,582	447,092	310,480	228,107	174,645	137,990	111,773	77,620	57,026
3.1		2,884,495	1,281,998	721,124	461,519	320,499	235,468	180,281	142,443	115,380	80,125	58,867
3.2		2,974,470	1,321,984	743,618	475,915	330,496	242,813	185,904	146,886	118,979	82,623	60,702
3.3		3,064,254	1,361,889	766,063	490,281	340,471	250,141	191,516	151,320	122,570	85,118	62,535
3.4		3,153,845	1,401,709	788,461	504,615	350,427	257,456	197,115	155,745	126,154	87,607	64,364
3.5		3,243,244	1,441,439	810,811	518,919	360,360	264,754	202,703	160,160	129,730	90,089	66,188
3.6		3,332,452	1,481,088	833,113	533,192	370,271	272,036	208,278	164,565	133,298	92,568	68,009
3.7		3,421,467	1,520,652	855,367	547,435	380,163	279,303	213,842	168,961	136,859	95,041	69,825
3.8		3,510,290	1,560,125	877,572	561,646	390,031	286,553	219,393	173,346	140,412	97,507	71,638
3.9		3,598,92	1,599,519	899,730	575,827	399,878	293,788	224,932	177,723	143,957	99,969	73,446
4.0		3,687,360	1,638,826	921,840	589,978	409,706	301,007	230,460	182,091	147,494	102,426	75,252

Sample Size for Various Percentages of Expected Returns(P) and Limit of Error(E) If Factor of Confidence Is 95%

P	E 0.16	0.18	0.20	0.25	0.30	0.35	0.40	0.45	0.50	0.55	0.60	0.70
0.1	1,499	1,184	959	614	426	313	240	189	153	127	106	78
0.2	2,994	2,366	1,917	1,226	852	626	479	378	307	253	213	156
0.3	4,487	3,546	2,872	1,838	1,276	938	718	567	459	379	319	234
0.4	5,977	4,723	3,826	2,448	1,700	1,249	956	756	612	506	425	312
0.5	7,464	5,897	4,777	3,057	2,123	1,560	1,194	943	764	631	530	390
0.6	8,948	7,070	5,727	3,665	2,545	1,870	1,432	1,131	916	757	636	467
0.7	10,429	8,240	6,675	4,272	2,966	2,179	1,669	1,318	1,068	882	741	545
0.8	11,907	9,408	7,621	4,877	3,387	2,488	1,905	1,505	1,219	1,007	847	622
0.9	13,382	10,573	8,564	5,481	3,806	2,796	2,141	1,692	1,370	1,132	951	699
1.0	14,854	11,736	9,506	6,084	4,225	3,104	2,376	1,877	1,521	1,257	1,056	776
1.1	16,322	12,897	10,446	6,686	4,643	3,411	2,611	2,063	1,671	1,381	1,160	853
1.2	17,788	14,055	11,385	7,286	5,060	3,717	2,846	2,249	1,821	1,505	1,265	929
1.3	19,251	15,211	12,321	7,885	5,476	4,023	3,080	2,434	1,971	1,629	1,369	1,006
1.4	20,711	16,364	13,255	8,483	5,891	4,328	3,314	2,618	2,121	1,753	1,473	1,082
1.5	22,168	17,515	14,188	9,080	6,305	4,632	3,547	2,802	2,270	1,876	1,576	1,158
1.6	23,622	18,664	15,118	9,675	6,719	4,936	3,780	2,986	2,419	1,999	1,680	1,234
1.7	25,073	19,811	16,047	10,270	7,132	5,240	4,012	3,170	2,567	2,122	1,783	1,310
1.8	26,521	20,955	16,973	10,863	7,543	5,542	4,243	3,352	2,716	2,244	1,886	1,385
1.9	27,966	22,096	17,898	11,455	7,955	5,844	4,474	3,535	2,863	2,366	1,988	1,461
2.0	29,407	23,235	18,821	12,045	8,365	6,146	4,705	3,717	3,011	2,489	2,091	1,536
2.1	30,846	24,372	19,742	12,635	8,774	6,446	4,935	3,899	3,158	2,610	2,193	1,611
2.2	32,282	25,507	20,661	13,223	9,182	6,746	5,165	4,081	3,306	2,732	2,295	1,686
2.3	33,715	26,638	21,578	13,810	9,590	7,046	5,394	4,262	3,452	2,853	2,397	1,761
2.4	35,145	27,769	22,493	14,395	9,997	7,344	5,623	4,443	3,599	2,974	2,499	1,836
2.5	36,572	28,896	23,406	14,980	10,403	7,642	5,851	4,623	3,745	3,095	2,600	1,911
2.6	37,996	30,021	24,317	15,563	10,807	7,940	6,079	4,803	3,891	3,215	2,702	1,985
2.7	39,416	31,144	25,227	16,145	11,211	8,237	6,307	4,983	4,036	3,336	2,803	2,059
2.8	40,834	32,264	26,134	16,726	11,615	8,533	6,534	5,162	4,181	3,455	2,904	2,133
2.9	42,249	33,382	27,039	17,305	12,017	8,829	6,760	5,341	4,326	3,575	3,004	2,207
3.0	43,661	34,497	27,943	17,884	12,419	9,124	6,986	5,520	4,471	3,695	3,105	2,281
3.1	45,070	35,611	28,845	18,461	12,820	9,419	7,211	5,697	4,615	3,814	3,205	2,355
3.2	46,476	36,721	29,745	19,036	13,220	9,712	7,436	5,875	4,759	3,933	3,305	2,428
3.3	47,878	37,830	30,642	19,611	13,619	10,005	7,660	6,052	4,903	4,051	3,404	2,501
3.4	49,278	38,936	31,538	20,184	14,017	10,298	7,884	6,229	5,046	4,170	3,504	2,574
3.5	50,675	40,040	32,432	20,757	14,414	10,590	8,108	6,406	5,189	4,288	3,603	2,647
3.6	52,069	41,141	33,325	21,328	14,811	10,881	8,331	6,582	5,332	4,406	3,702	2,720
3.7	53,460	42,240	34,214	21,897	15,207	11,172	8,554	6,758	5,474	4,524	3,801	2,793
3.8	54,848	43,336	35,103	22,466	15,601	11,462	8,776	6,933	5,616	4,641	3,900	2,865
3.9	56,233	44,430	35,989	23,033	15,995	11,751	8,997	7,109	5,758	4,759	3,998	2,938
4.0	57,615	45,522	36,874	23,599	16,388	12,040	9,218	7,283	5,900	4,875	4,097	3,010

Sample Size for Various Percentages of Expected Returns(P) and Limit of Error(E) If Factor of Confidence Is 95%

P	E 0.50	0.55	0.60	0.65	0.70	0.75	0.80	0.85	0.90	0.95	1.00	1.50
4.2	6,182	5,109	4,293	3,658	3,154	2,747	2,414	2,139	1,908	1,712	1,545	687
4.4	6,462	5,341	4,488	3,824	3,297	2,872	2,524	2,236	1,994	1,790	1,616	718
4.6	6,742	5,572	4,682	3,989	3,440	2,996	2,633	2,333	2,081	1,867	1,685	749
4.8	7,021	5,802	4,875	4,154	3,582	3,120	2,742	2,429	2,167	1,945	1,755	780
5.0	7,298	6,031	5,068	4,318	3,723	3,243	2,850	2,525	2,252	2,022	1,824	811
5.2	7,574	6,259	5,259	4,481	3,864	3,366	2,958	2,620	2,337	2,098	1,893	841
5.4	7,848	6,486	5,450	4,644	4,004	3,488	3,066	2,716	2,422	2,174	1,962	872
5.6	8,122	6,712	5,640	4,806	4,144	3,609	3,173	2,810	2,506	2,250	2,030	902
5.8	8,394	6,937	5,829	4,967	4,283	3,731	3,279	2,904	2,590	2,325	2,098	933
6.0	8,665	7,161	6,017	5,127	4,421	3,851	3,385	2,998	2,674	2,400	2,166	963

Sample Size for Various Percentages of Expected Returns(P) and Limit of Error(E) If Factor of Confidence Is 95%

P	E 2.00	2.50	3.00	3.50	4.00	4.50	5.00	5.50	6.00	6.50	7.00	7.50
4.2	386	247	172	126	96	76	61	51	43	36	31	27
4.4	404	258	179	132	101	80	65	53	45	38	33	28
4.6	421	270	187	138	105	83	67	56	46	40	34	30
4.8	439	281	195	143	109	86	70	58	48	41	36	31
5.0	456	292	202	149	114	90	73	60	50	43	37	32
5.2	473	303	210	154	118	93	76	62	52	45	38	33
5.4	490	314	218	160	123	97	78	65	54	46	40	35
5.6	507	325	225	166	127	100	81	67	56	48	41	36
5.8	524	336	233	171	131	103	84	69	58	50	43	37
6.0	542	346	240	177	135	107	86	71	60	51	44	38

Sample Size for Various Percentages of Expected Returns(P) and Limit of Error(E) If Factor of Confidence Is 99%

P	E 0.01	0.02	0.03	0.04	0.05	0.06	0.07	0.08	0.09	0.10	0.12	0.14
0.1	662,837	165,709	73,649	41,427	26,513	18,412	13,527	10,357	8,183	6,628	4,603	3,381
0.2	1,324,346	331,087	147,149	82,772	52,974	36,787	27,027	20,693	16,349	13,243	9,197	6,756
0.3	1,984,529	496,132	220,503	124,033	79,381	55,126	40,500	31,008	24,500	19,845	13,781	10,125
0.4	2,643,384	660,846	293,709	165,212	105,735	73,427	53,946	41,303	32,634	26,434	18,356	13,486
0.5	3,300,913	825,228	366,767	206,307	132,037	91,692	67,365	51,577	40,752	33,009	22,923	16,841
0.6	3,957,114	989,279	439,679	247,320	158,285	109,919	80,757	61,830	48,853	39,571	27,480	20,189
0.7	4,611,989	1,152,997	512,443	288,249	184,480	128,111	94,122	72,062	56,938	46,120	32,027	23,530
0.8	5,265,536	1,316,384	585,058	329,096	210,621	146,265	107,459	82,274	65,006	52,655	36,565	26,864
0.9	5,917,757	1,479,439	657,528	369,859	236,710	164,381	120,770	92,465	73,059	59,178	41,095	30,192
1.0	6,568,650	1,642,163	729,850	410,541	262,746	182,463	134,054	102,635	81,094	65,687	45,616	33,513
1.1	7,218,217	1,804,554	802,022	451,138	288,729	200,505	147,310	112,784	89,113	72,182	50,126	36,827
1.2	7,866,456	1,966,614	874,050	491,654	314,658	218,512	160,538	122,913	97,116	78,665	54,628	40,134
1.3	8,513,369	2,128,342	945,929	532,085	340,535	236,482	173,742	133,021	105,102	85,134	59,121	43,435
1.4	9,158,954	2,289,739	1,017,659	572,435	366,358	254,414	186,917	143,108	113,072	91,590	63,603	46,729
1.5	9,803,213	2,450,803	1,089,245	612,700	392,129	272,310	200,065	153,175	121,026	98,032	68,077	50,016
1.6		2,611,536	1,160,682	652,884	417,846	290,170	213,186	163,221	128,964	104,461	72,542	53,296
1.7		2,771,937	1,231,970	692,984	443,510	307,992	226,279	173,246	136,885	110,877	76,997	56,569
1.8		2,932,007	1,303,113	733,002	469,121	325,777	239,346	183,250	144,790	117,280	81,444	59,836
1.9		3,091,744	1,374,109	772,936	494,679	343,527	252,385	193,234	152,679	123,670	85,881	63,096
2.0		3,251,150	1,444,952	812,788	520,184	361,238	265,400	203,197	160,549	130,046	90,309	66,330
2.1		3,410,224	1,515,654	852,556	545,636	378,912	278,385	213,139	168,405	136,409	94,728	69,596
2.2		3,568,967	1,586,207	892,242	571,035	396,551	291,344	223,060	176,244	142,759	99,138	72,836
2.3		3,727,377	1,656,608	931,844	596,380	414,152	304,274	232,961	184,067	149,095	103,537	76,068
2.4		3,885,456	1,726,868	971,364	621,673	431,716	317,178	242,841	191,874	155,418	107,929	79,294
2.5		4,043,203	1,796,979	1,010,800	646,913	449,245	330,055	252,700	199,664	161,728	112,311	82,513
2.6		4,200,619	1,866,938	1,050,155	672,099	466,734	342,905	262,538	207,437	168,025	116,682	85,726
2.7		4,357,702	1,936,755	1,089,425	697,232	484,187	355,730	272,356	215,195	174,308	121,046	88,932
2.8		4,514,454	2,006,424	1,128,614	722,313	501,606	368,526	282,153	222,936	180,578	125,402	92,131
2.9		4,670,874	2,075,940	1,167,718	747,340	518,984	381,295	291,929	230,658	186,835	129,745	95,324
3.0		4,826,963	2,145,314	1,206,741	772,314	536,327	394,036	301,685	238,366	193,079	134,081	98,508
3.1		4,982,719	2,214,541	1,245,679	797,235	553,635	406,751	311,420	246,058	199,309	138,409	101,687
3.2		5,138,144	2,283,614	1,284,536	822,103	570,903	419,438	321,134	253,734	205,526	142,725	104,858
3.3		5,293,237	2,352,547	1,323,309	846,918	588,135	432,098	330,827	261,393	211,729	147,034	108,024
3.4		5,447,999	2,421,332	1,362,000	871,680	605,333	444,734	340,500	269,036	217,920	151,333	111,183
3.5		5,602,428	2,489,963	1,400,607	896,389	622,490	457,341	350,152	276,662	224,097	155,621	114,334
3.6		5,756,526	2,558,453	1,439,132	921,044	639,611	469,919	359,783	284,273	230,261	159,903	117,479
3.7		5,910,292	2,626,797	1,477,573	945,647	656,699	482,471	369,393	291,866	236,412	164,174	120,616
3.8		6,063,727	2,694,984	1,515,932	970,196	673,746	494,996	378,983	299,440	242,549	168,435	123,749
3.9		6,216,829	2,763,032	1,554,207	994,693	690,756	507,493	388,552	307,001	248,673	172,688	126,872
4.0		6,369,600	2,830,933	1,592,400	1,019,136	707,733	519,964	398,100	314,546	254,784	176,933	129,991

Sample Size for Various Percentages of Expected Returns(P) and Limit of Error(E) If Factor of Confidence Is 99%

P	E: 0.16	0.18	0.20	0.25	0.30	0.35	0.40	0.45	0.50	0.55	0.60	0.70
0.1	2,589	2,046	1,657	1,060	736	541	414	327	265	219	184	135
0.2	5,173	4,087	3,311	2,119	1,471	1,081	827	654	529	437	368	270
0.3	7,752	6,125	4,961	3,175	2,205	1,620	1,240	980	794	656	551	405
0.4	10,325	8,158	6,608	4,229	2,937	2,158	1,652	1,305	1,057	874	734	539
0.5	12,894	10,187	8,252	5,281	3,667	2,694	2,063	1,630	1,320	1,091	916	673
0.6	15,457	12,213	9,893	6,331	4,396	3,230	2,473	1,954	1,582	1,308	1,099	807
0.7	18,015	14,234	11,530	7,379	5,124	3,765	2,882	2,277	1,845	1,524	1,281	941
0.8	20,569	16,251	13,164	8,424	5,850	4,298	3,291	2,600	2,106	1,740	1,462	1,074
0.9	23,116	18,264	14,794	9,468	6,575	4,830	3,698	2,922	2,367	1,956	1,643	1,208
1.0	25,658	20,273	16,422	10,510	7,299	5,362	4,105	3,243	2,627	2,171	1,825	1,340
1.1	28,195	22,278	18,045	11,549	8,020	5,892	4,511	3,564	2,887	2,386	2,004	1,473
1.2	30,728	24,279	19,666	12,586	8,740	6,421	4,917	3,884	3,146	2,600	2,185	1,605
1.3	33,255	26,275	21,283	13,621	9,459	6,949	5,321	4,204	3,405	2,814	2,365	1,737
1.4	35,777	28,268	22,897	14,654	10,176	7,476	5,724	4,522	3,663	3,028	2,544	1,869
1.5	38,293	30,256	24,508	15,685	10,892	8,002	6,127	4,841	3,921	3,241	2,723	2,000
1.6	40,805	32,241	26,115	16,714	11,607	8,527	6,529	5,158	4,178	3,453	2,901	2,132
1.7	43,311	34,221	27,719	17,740	12,319	9,051	6,930	5,475	4,435	3,665	3,079	2,263
1.8	45,812	36,197	29,320	18,764	13,030	9,574	7,330	5,791	4,691	3,877	3,257	2,393
1.9	48,308	38,169	30,917	19,787	13,741	10,095	7,729	6,107	4,946	4,088	3,435	2,523
2.0	50,799	40,137	32,512	20,807	14,449	10,616	8,128	6,421	5,202	4,299	3,612	2,654
2.1	53,284	42,100	34,102	21,825	15,156	11,135	8,525	6,736	5,456	4,509	3,789	2,783
2.2	55,765	44,061	35,690	22,841	15,862	11,653	8,922	7,050	5,710	4,719	3,965	2,913
2.3	58,239	46,016	37,273	23,855	16,566	12,171	9,318	7,362	5,964	4,928	4,141	3,042
2.4	60,710	47,968	38,855	24,867	17,268	12,687	9,714	7,674	6,216	5,137	4,317	3,172
2.5	63,174	49,915	40,432	25,877	17,970	13,202	10,108	7,986	6,469	5,346	4,492	3,300
2.6	65,634	51,859	42,006	26,884	18,669	13,716	10,501	8,297	6,721	5,554	4,667	3,429
2.7	68,088	53,798	43,577	27,889	19,367	14,229	10,894	8,608	6,972	5,762	4,842	3,557
2.8	70,538	55,734	45,145	28,892	20,064	14,740	11,286	8,917	7,223	5,969	5,016	3,685
2.9	72,982	57,664	46,708	29,893	20,759	15,251	11,677	9,226	7,473	6,176	5,189	3,812
3.0	75,421	59,591	48,270	30,893	21,453	15,761	12,067	9,534	7,723	6,382	5,363	3,940
3.1	77,854	61,514	49,827	31,889	22,145	16,270	12,457	9,842	7,972	6,589	5,536	4,067
3.2	80,284	63,433	51,381	32,884	22,836	16,777	12,845	10,149	8,221	6,794	5,709	4,194
3.3	82,706	65,348	52,932	33,876	23,525	17,284	13,233	10,455	8,469	6,999	5,881	4,321
3.4	85,124	67,258	54,480	34,867	24,213	17,789	13,620	10,761	8,716	7,204	6,053	4,447
3.5	87,537	69,165	56,024	35,856	24,899	18,293	14,006	11,066	8,964	7,408	6,224	4,573
3.6	89,945	71,067	57,565	36,842	25,584	18,796	14,391	11,370	9,210	7,612	6,395	4,699
3.7	92,347	72,966	59,103	37,825	26,268	19,299	14,775	11,674	9,456	7,815	6,567	4,824
3.8	94,745	74,860	60,637	38,807	26,949	19,799	15,159	11,977	9,702	8,018	6,737	4,949
3.9	97,137	76,750	62,168	39,787	27,629	20,299	15,542	12,279	9,947	8,220	6,907	5,074
4.0	99,525	78,636	63,696	40,765	28,309	20,798	15,924	12,581	10,191	8,422	7,077	5,199

Sample Size for Various Percentages of Expected Returns (P) and Limit of Error (E) If Factor of Confidence Is 99%

P	E 0.50	0.55	0.60	0.65	0.70	0.75	0.80	0.85	0.90	0.95	1.00	1.50
4.2	10,678	8,825	7,415	6,319	5,448	4,745	4,171	3,694	3,296	2,958	2,669	1,186
4.4	11,163	9,225	7,752	6,605	5,695	4,961	4,361	3,862	3,445	3,092	2,791	1,240
4.6	11,646	9,625	8,088	6,891	5,942	5,176	4,549	4,029	3,594	3,226	2,911	1,294
4.8	12,127	10,023	8,421	7,176	6.187	5,390	4,737	4,196	3,743	3,359	3,032	1,347
5.0	12,607	10,418	8,754	7,459	6,431	5,603	4,924	4,362	3,890	3,492	3,152	1,401
5.2	13,083	10,812	9,085	7,741	6,674	5,814	5,110	4,526	4,037	3,623	3,270	1,453
5.4	13,557	11,205	9,414	8,022	6,917	6,025	5,295	4,691	4,184	3,755	3,389	1,506
5.6	14,030	11,595	9,743	8,302	7,158	6,235	5,481	4,854	4,329	3,886	3,507	1,559
5.8	14,500	11,983	10,069	8,580	7,398	6,445	5,664	5,017	4,475	4,016	3,625	1,611
6.0	14,969	12,370	10,394	8,856	7,636	6,652	5,847	5,179	4,619	4,146	3,742	1,663

Sample Size for Various Percentages of Expected Returns (P) and Limit of Error (E) If Factor of Confidence Is 99%

P	E 2.00	2.50	3.00	3.50	4.00	4.50	5.00	5.50	6.00	6.50	7.00	7.50
4.2	667	427	297	218	167	131	106	88	74	63	54	47
4.4	697	447	310	228	174	137	111	92	77	66	56	49
4.6	728	466	323	238	182	143	116	96	80	68	59	52
4.8	758	485	336	247	189	149	121	100	84	72	62	54
5.0	788	504	350	257	196	155	126	104	87	74	64	56
5.2	817	523	363	267	204	161	131	107	90	77	66	58
5.4	847	542	376	276	212	167	135	111	94	80	69	60
5.6	876	561	389	286	219	173	140	115	97	83	71	62
5.8	906	580	403	295	226	178	145	119	100	86	74	64
6.0	936	598	415	305	234	184	149	123	104	88	76	66

In like manner, suppose we want to find the number of pieces we should mail on a proposed test, if we anticipate an .8% response and cannot afford a "limit of error" greater than ± .25%, and we want to be sure that 95 out of 100 times we will stay within the .25% "limit of error." First, we read down the left hand column marked "P" until we find the .8% response figure. Then read horizontally until we locate the sample size required under the column headed by the .25% limit of error. We find that we would require a test mailing of 4,877 pieces, or for convenience, 5,000 names. This means that if when we make this test mailing and we do pull an .8% response then an identical larger mailing will produce results falling between .55% and 1.05%—95 out of 100 times.

It would perhaps be pertinent to spend some time discussing things the table cannot do. The tables are constructed on pure mathematical probabilities and can predict within certain limits of error what results could be expected from a larger mailing *exactly identical* to the test. *Only* if a good random cross-section has been used in creating the test sample can these probabilities be employed for our guidance at all. If a good random sample has not been taken the results are meaningless. No probability formula can correct for a poor cross-sectional sample. Any changes in copy, format, offer, or list will invalidate the value of the statistical study. The probability tables in no way take into account factors of seasonal variation. Therefore, if we make a test in June the tables will not apply to a December mailing. What we can do, however, is analyze our June mailings to tell us which full mailing made in December will be best. We can also establish a relationship between the two tests which will indicate in a relative way how much better one mailing will be than the other.

The tables are a very useful tool acting as guides . . . to help minimize risk . . . but only when properly applied!

Up to this point we have discussed probabilities in terms of the table of probability rather than the actual mathematical relationship of the factors which created the tables.

Theoretical mathematical probability had its beginning in the 1600's with the Frenchman, Blaise Pascal. It seems that Pascal was prodded by an acquaintance with a love for games of chance into searching for relationships to predict with a degree of probability the outcome of a given act. The relationship of confidence, error, sample size, and response has evolved into an equation stated as:

> "The 'limit of error' being equal to the confidence level expressed in terms of number of standard deviations multiplied by the square root of the quantity of expected per

centage of response times the expected percentage of non-response divided by the sample size."

Symbolically shown as:

$$D = \lesssim \sqrt{\frac{(P)\ (100 - P)}{S}}$$

A derivation of this formula which is easier to work with in mail order is:

$$S = \frac{(\lesssim^2\ (P)\ (100 - P)}{D^2}$$

S = Sample size

$\lesssim$ = Level of confidence expressed in terms of number of standard deviations

P = Expected percent of response (Pull)

D = Limit or error

Now, let's define our terms:

Sample size is the number of observations made. This correlates to the number of times we tossed a coin or the number of individual pieces of mail sent out in a test from which we will determine our percent of response and non-response.

Confidence level is the number of times out of a hundred attempts that our predictions must be correct. This degree of confidence is expressed in terms of number of standard deviations. The "number of standard deviations" refers to the area covered under a "normal curve" and for our present purposes should be accepted simply as a figure.

99% (99.74) Confidence level = 3.00 Std. Deviations

95% (95.00) Confidence level = 1.96 Std. Deviations

90% (90.10) Confidence level = 1.65 Std. Deviations

Expected percent of response is the number of times, in percentage, that our response was favorable. In terms of our coin toss, how often "heads" turned up. In terms of a mailing what was our pull. The other part of our equation called for percentage of non-response. This is simply the percentage that our response was unfavorable. In terms of our coin toss how often "tails" turned up. In terms of a mailing what percent of the people did not respond. If we had a 1% pull 99% did not respond. [e.g., (100 - P)=(100 - 1)].

Limit of error is the number of percentage points by which we are allowed to miscalculate the actual expected percent of response. In other words if we expect a 1% response by how much can we miscalculate and still be in an acceptable, or at least safe position. (e.g., 1% ± .2%)

To illustrate this equation let us take two hypothetical situations.

1. What sample size is required for a test mailing in which we anticipate a pull of 1.0% and cannot afford a margin of error greater than ± .3% at a confidence level of 95%?

Therefore, using our formula, we substitute the known facts:

Sample size	=	Unknown
Confidence level (95%)	=	1.96
Anticipated pull	=	1.00% or .01 as a decimal
Anticipated non-response	=	100.0% - 1.00% or .99 as a decimal
Limit of error	=	.3% or .003 as a decimal

Therefore:

$$\text{Sample size} = \frac{(1.96^2)\quad(.01)\quad(.99)}{(.003)^2} =$$

$$\text{Sample size} = \frac{(3.8416)\quad(.01)\quad(.99)}{.000009} = \frac{.03803184}{.000009} = 4{,}225 \text{ pcs.}$$

2. What are my limits of error if I mailed 10,000 pieces and received a 1.0% pull? I want to be within these limits 95 out of 100 times. (95% confidence level)

Therefore, using our formula we substitute the known facts.

Sample size	=	10,000 pieces
Confidence level	=	1.96
Pull	=	1.00%
Non-response	=	100.0% - 1.00% or .99 as a decimal
Limit of error	=	Unknown

Therefore:

$$10{,}000 = \frac{(1.96^2)\quad(.01)\quad(.99)}{D^2} =$$

$$10{,}000\ D^2 = (3.8416)\quad(.01)\quad(.99) =$$

$$10{,}000\ D^2 = .03803184$$

$$D = \sqrt{.00003803184}$$

$$D = .00193 \quad \text{or} \quad .19\%$$

Appendix P

USPS Study of Advertising Mail*

During 1972, the United States Postal Service conducted the first major governmental study on how the public sees advertising mail. The results provided further support to the long-held contention of direct mail advertisers that the vast majority of Americans were neither deluged with direct mail nor strongly objected to receiving it.

In presenting the results of the study at the Tenth Annual Government Affairs Conference of the Direct Mail Advertising Association, Hope S. Roman, Director of the USPS Office of Market Research, described the study and provided a summary of the results:

> There is no such thing as junk mail. There is clutter in the direct mail stream as there is clutter in newspaper inserts and in television and in radio; nevertheless, advertising remains a powerful vehicle for sales.
>
> The main thing is how the public sees advertising mail. The data I am using come from two places:
>
> First: A national probability survey based on 2,559 people who responded to questions measuring their perceptions of the amount of advertising mail they received and their attitudes toward it.
>
> Second: Actual behavioral data for 2,062 people, also selected probabilistically, each of whom kept a diary for one seven-day period during a six-week interval between June 14 and August 5, 1972. To the extent that this period of time does not reflect annual Christmas catalogs and such, it is atypical; to the extent it does reflect the normal patterns of advertising mail, it is typical.
>
> Both kinds of data have been weighed and the findings are projectable to all those 18 years of age and older, living in the 48 contiguous states.
>
> First of all, based on the behavioral data, we divided our respondents into four categories of advertising mail receivers. There were those who received no advertising mail; those who received one or two pieces (the low receivers); those who received three to five pieces (the medium receivers); and those who received six or more pieces (the high receivers).
>
> A full 25% received no 3rd class mail the week they kept the diary. This surprised us because, before doing the diary, almost every group in the population said they got an average of seven or eight pieces of 3rd class mail a week, as opposed to the three piece average recorded in the diary. The perception of 7 or 8 pieces also compares with your own estimates that the average household gets one piece of advertising mail a day. The real problem, of course, is that there is no such thing as an average household.
>
> An additional 32% of diary-keepers received one or two pieces a week although when previously asked, only 17% said they received that few. From the diary, 24% received three to five pieces a week and 19% received six or more pieces a week. This compares to 48% who said they received six or more when asked to "remember."

*The findings of the 1972 study reported here were supported by a similar USPS study in 1974.

Behaviorally, those in Eastern Region less often receive no 3rd class mail and more often receive the highest amount (six or more pieces). (By the way, when I am talking Region, I am talking Postal Region and not Nielsen or Census.) Those in Southern Region less often receive a medium or high amount and more often receive no 3rd class mail. Those in New York Region less often receive a high amount. Interestingly, there is no difference by post office class—probably because so many of us live in exurbia, today.

Those with household heads under 35 more often receive no 3rd class mail and less often receive a high amount. Those whose household heads are 35 to 54 less often receive no 3rd class mail and more often receive a high amount.

By education, the more you have the more you get. By income, them what has also gets. In fact, whether segmenting by income or by education, recipient groups follow almost the identical pattern.

Social class occupation follows the trend: nearly half of those in executive or professional occupations receive six or more pieces of advertising mail a week. A third of those in managerial positions do.

Given this, it is to be expected that those in new suburbs less often get no advertising mail and more often get lots. In single city homes built after 1950, the same is true—in spades. On the other hand, those living in city apartments more often receive no advertising mail and less often receive six or more pieces.

Men and women report receiving equal amounts of 3rd class mail; those not married (for whatever reason) more often receive few or no pieces and less often receive three or more pieces. It therefore follows that the more adults in a household, the more advertising mail is received, and vice-versa.

People do mis-remember how much advertising mail they get in a week. Nevertheless, there is some correlation—and a good one—between perception and actual behavior patterns, even though the patterns are not perceived clearly.

This is one of the few times that I can remember that both a perceptual and a behavioral study have been done at the same time, about the same thing, with the same people. From a researcher's point of view, the findings are extremely interesting. For instance, there is always the old question, that so many of you know, which goes like this: Does perception follow behavior or does behavior follow perception? Here, for the first time, in a situation where we are tracking an almost daily occurrence and an almost universal one, it is very clear that there is a relationship existing for any segment between perception and reality; moreover, there is an overall distortion existing which is biased negatively. People say they receive more advertising mail than they really do; people say they less like reading advertising mail than they really do. There are differences between the segments in real life in terms of reception and liking, and those differences follow through the segments in perceptions of reception and liking.

For example, when asked about reading patterns in the questionnaire: 37% say they read some 3rd class pieces and not others; 33% say they read all 3rd class pieces, and 30% say they don't read any. Behaviorally, 77% of the pieces received are actually read at one time or another and only 18% are not read, whether opened or not.

Interestingly, those who get less advertising and promotional mail read more of it:

—Those under 25

—Non-English speaking people

The single exception is that those living in apartments say they get less 3rd class mail (and they do) and they also read less.

Now, I'd like to tell you how your mail is received.

First of all, when asked in the questionnaire whether there were any kinds of direct mail that they particularly *liked* to receive, 40% of the people said "yes" and 51% said "no."

When they were asked about direct mail they particularly did *not* like to receive, 42% said there was some and 50% said there was none.

This is opposed to those, who in doing the diary, got two pieces or more of direct mail. 71% received all pieces favorably; and 28% received all pieces unfavorably.

Of those people who were not unfavorable toward any 3rd class mail, 85% actually welcomed it and an additional 15% said it was acceptable. Of those who were not favorable to *any* 3rd class mail, 37% did accept some such mail as necessary.

In short, most people have mixed feelings, directly correlated to the actual piece of mail.

Them what gets, likes. The higher the education, the greater the favorability. The higher the income, the same. Those with heads of household between 35 and 54 are also favorable, as are those in higher social class occupations who live in the better housing I described before.

In spite of what they say when you ask them, 77% of those receiving 6 or more pieces of advertising mail a week rate most individual pieces favorably. It's also true that 22% rate them unfavorably. There is no in-between. The same is true for those receiving 3 to 5 pieces. 72% rate most favorably; 27% rate most unfavorably.

In spite of the fact that so many people say they dislike [direct mail] so much, a lot of them buy. When the question is put to them, 55% say they have purchased after receiving a direct mail piece. This happens less in the New York and Southern regions, more by income for those earning $10,000 or more, more for professionals and managers—and, also, 63% for farmers.

It also happens more for families (with 3 or more adults), more for those between 25 and 45 and, more for those under 25 (62%).

When those who said they hadn't bought as a result of direct mail were further prodded by being asked if they had bought magazine subscriptions or items shown in a catalog, 21% said "yes," making—at a rough quesstimate—a total of about 63% of the population who say they have made a purchase as a result of direct mail solicitation.

There is an interrelationship between favorability—and, therefore, buying—the kinds of items received, and the companies they're sent from.

Actually, we derived our favorability categories like this. If the respondent received 2 or more pieces of advertising mail and if a piece was considered useful information that the respondent liked to receive, or interesting or enjoyable though not especially useful, the attitude was considered favorable. If the person considered the item neither interesting, enjoyable nor useful, or categorized it as objectionable, the piece was considered as unfavorable. In all cases where the respondent had an equal number of favorable and unfavorable pieces, we classified him as unfavorable, in order to avoid a bias in favor of 3rd class mail.

Once again, even though we did this, of those who received 2 or more pieces of direct mail, 71% received all pieces favorably and only 28% (even with ties thrown in) received all pieces unfavorably.

Of the favorables, 42% considered all pieces received as useful information that they liked to receive. Of these, 82% are opened and read, and 68% have come from a company the respondent does business with. 23% rated all pieces as interesting or enjoyable but not especially useful. Of these, 71% were opened and read.

On the negative side, 21% rated all pieces neither interesting, enjoyable nor useful and 4% considered all pieces objectionable.

As we might expect, 69% of advertising mail is not expected by the householder. (In fact, the figure seems amazingly low—I would have guessed about 90% was not expected.)

19% of direct mail *is* expected. Of that which is, 79% is opened and read immediately and another 15% set aside for later reading, for a total of 94% which is opened and read. 65% of such mail is welcome and 61% is from a company with which the respondent does business.

38% of direct mail comes in an envelope and almost all of it is addressed to a specific household member.

14% is a catalog. Three-quarters of the catalogs come from companies usually done business with and these are addressed to specific household members. Two-thirds are the kind of useful items people like to receive.

One more thing: In the questionnaire, we asked about preferred addressing of sales and promotional material.

	% Respondents		
	Prefer To Receive	Prefer Not To Receive	Net Preference
Your name/address	40	8	32
Occupant/your address	14	16	-2
Postal patron/box holder	3	18	-15
No name/no address	1	31	-30
No preference	44	49	

Clearly, there are correlations between perceptions of direct mail advertising and behavior patterns among people who receive direct mail advertising. Those perceptions tend to be negative for several reasons: It is obvious that if you buy something, you get more direct mail and the more direct mail you get the more you buy and the more you buy the more direct mail you get. In a way, this is a vicious circle because it leans to those who have money to buy and the impulse to buy and therefore get a lot of direct mail. They are also the more articulate and educated people in our society and, therefore, the most vocal. They also read newspapers. All of this conspires to contribute to the use of the words "junk mail" in a freer fashion than you would wish, or than is really true.

DATA SUMMARY

A. ADVERTISING MAIL RECEPTION

(Based on a national probability sample of 2,062 people, each keeping a diary for one 7-day period during a 6-week interval from June 14 to August 5, 1972):

Unweighted Data

23% receive no 3rd class mail in a week
17% receive one piece of 3rd class mail per week
13% receive two pieces of 3rd class mail per week

54% receive 2 or fewer

11% receive three pieces of 3rd class mail per week
8% receive four pieces of 3rd class mail per week
7% receive five pieces of 3rd class mail per week
5% receive six pieces of 3rd class mail per week
5% receive seven pieces of 3rd class mail per week

89% receive 7 or fewer

11% receive eight or more pieces, with 7 of 2,062 people receiving more than 20 pieces.

Average number of pieces received: 3.32

Of 1,229 receiving two or more pieces:

71% received all pieces favorably (interesting and enjoyable whether useful or not)

28% received all pieces unfavorably (neither interesting, useful nor enjoyable; 4% objectionable and ties for those receiving two or more pieces)

1% did not answer the question.

When specifically asked whether the piece was welcome, accepted as necessary or unwelcome:

70% said all pieces were welcome or accepted
22% said all pieces were unwelcome
8% gave us no answer

ALL FOLLOWING DATA ARE WEIGHTED.

We divided the respondents into 4 categories of advertising mail receivers.

25% received no 3rd class mail the week they kept the diary
32% received a low amount (1 or 2 pieces)
24% received a medium amount (3 to 5 pieces)
19% received a high amount (6 or more pieces)

Those in Eastern region less often received no 3rd class mail (19%) and more often received the highest amount (23%).

Those in Southern region less often received a medium (17%) or high (14%) amount, and more often received no 3rd class mail (35%).

Those in New York region less often received a high amount (14%).

Interestingly, there is no difference by post office class.

By age of head of household:

Those under 35 more often received no 3rd class mail (31%) and less often received a high amount (12%).

Those 35 to 54 less often received none (20%) and more often received a high amount (27%).

By education:

The more you have, the more you get. 27% of those with some college and 33% with college education or higher get high amounts.

By income:

Them what has also gets. (28%, 35% and 49% respectively for income groups $10-15M, $15-25M, $25M and over).

In fact, whether segmenting by income *or* by education, the recipient groups follow the identical pattern.

Social class occupation follows the trend:

43% of those in executive or professional occupations receive 6 or more pieces of advertising mail a week.

33% of those in managerial positions do.

Given this, it is to be expected that those in new suburbs less often get no advertising mail (15%) and more often get lots. (25%)

In single city homes built after 1950, the same is true—in spades. 29% of those living this way receive 6 or more pieces a week. Only 15% receive no 3rd class mail.

Those in city apartments more often receive no advertising mail (31%) and less often receive a high amount (10%).

Men and women reported receiving equal amounts of 3rd class mail; those not married (for whatever reason) more often receive few or no pieces (about 33% each) and less often receive a medium (18%) or high amount (14%).

It therefore follows that the more adults in the household (3 or more), the more advertising mail is received (27% get a high amount) and vice versa.

Nearly half (44%) of non-whites receive no advertising mail at all. And 46% of those not speaking English also receive none.

Of the total sample:

39% receive all pieces favorably
16% receive all pieces unfavorably
45% get fewer than 2 pieces or have mixed reactions

> Easterners are more often favorable (45%)
> New Yorkers are more often unfavorable (22%)
> Southerners are less often favorable (31%) and
> Southerners are less often unfavorable (11%)
>
> As in all other product areas, Southerners just accept what they get—praise it less and demand less of it.

Of those people who were not unfavorable toward any 3rd class mail:

85% said it was welcome
15% said it was acceptable

Of those people who were not favorable to any 3rd class mail:

37% did say some mail was accepted as necessary
63% said it was all unwelcome

Of those who got multiple pieces and reacted both favorably and unfavorably:

54% said some pieces were welcome
29% found other pieces acceptable
46% found some pieces unwelcome

In short, most people have mixed feelings, directly correlated to the piece of mail.

Among those who received at least two pieces of direct mail advertising, only 12% never said a piece was welcome. 30% never said a piece was unwelcome.

Them what gets, likes. The higher the education, the greater the favorability. (33% for grade-schoolers to 47% for those with college educations or more). The higher the income, the same. (31% for those with incomes of less than $5,000 to 56% of those with incomes of $25,000 or more).

Those with heads of household between 35 and 54 are also favorable (45%), as are those in higher social class occupations (46%) who live in the better housing (44%) described before.

> In spite of what they say when you ask them, 77% of those receiving 6 or more pieces of advertising mail a week rate most individual pieces favorably. 22% rate them unfavorably.
>
> There is no in-between. The same is true for those receiving 3 to 5 pieces. 72% rate most favorably and 27% rate most unfavorably.

B. THE DIRECT MAILSTREAM (ALSO FROM THE DIARY)

38% of direct mail comes in an envelope and 90% of that is addressed to a specific household member. 35% is an item not in an envelope.

14% is catalogs. 75% are from companies usually done business with. 74% are addressed to a specific household member and 64% are the kind of useful items respondents like to receive.

3% each are post cards, small packages and coupons.

47% is from a company the respondent does business with, at least occasionally. Of this, 71% is addressed to a specific household member and 72% is opened and read.

17% each are from known and unknown companies the respondent doesn't do business with. When it's from an unknown company, a disproportionate number are unfavorable toward the item.

14% is from non-profit organizations. Of this, 86% is addressed to specific household members, and 69% is opened and read.

67% is addressed to a household member (disproportionately high for those receiving 6 or more pieces) and 29% is addressed to some general address such as occupant or resident or postal patron.

63% of all pieces are opened and read (disproportionately low for those with unfavorable attitudes) and 14% is set aside for later reading.

10% is thrown away without being read (disproportionately high for those with unfavorable attitudes) and 8% is opened but not read, also disproportionately high for those who feel unfavorably.

42% of all pieces are considered useful information that the respondent likes to receive. Of these, 68% are from a company the respondent does business with, at least occasionally, and 82% are opened and read.

23% of all pieces are interesting or enjoyable, but not especially useful. 71% are opened and read.

21% are neither interesting, enjoyable, nor useful and 4% are considered objectionable.

Asked in another way, 37% of all pieces are welcome. Of these, 80% are opened and read and 17% set aside for later reading. 21% are accepted as necessary; and 16% are unwelcome.

69% of 3rd class mail is not expected. 19% is expected. Of that which is expected:

> 70% is opened and read right away and 15% is set aside for later reading for a total of 85% which is read. 65% is welcomed and 61% is from a company with which the respondent does business.

C. PERCEPTIONS

(Based on a sample of 2,502 respondents selected on a national probability basis.)

Before doing a diary, almost every group says they get an average of 7 or 8 pieces of advertising or promotional mail a week. Only 17% say they receive one or two pieces (compared to 32% who actually recorded one or two in the diary.) Only 3% say they receive none (compared to 25% who recorded none in the diary.)

—Those in Western Region say they get 9

—Those between 35 and 65 also say 9

—Those with less than high school education say 6, as do those under 25

—Those completing some college say 9 and those who have college degrees or more say 7.

While there is some correlation between perceived and actual pieces received, it is very clear that most people think they get more advertising mail than they do. At least 30% say they receive eight or more pieces compared to the 11% who actually did (from the diary.) Every group's perceptions follows actual behavior patterns, even though they do not perceive them clearly.

When asked about reading patterns before the diary,

—37% say they read some 3rd class pieces, not others
—33% say they read all
—30% say they don't read any.

Clearly, again, perceptions and behavior are different. Behaviorally, 77% are actually read at one time or another and 18% are not read, whether opened or not.

As might be expected, those who get less advertising and promotional mail read more of it.

- Those under 25 (45%)
- Non-English speaking people (41%)

The single exception is that those receiving 3rd class mail in apartments say they get less (and they do) and they also read less.

When asked whether there were any kinds of direct mail they particularly liked to receive, 40% said yes and 51% said no.

When asked about direct mail they particularly did not like to receive, 42% said there was some and 50% said there was none. (This is as opposed to 71% who, in doing their diaries, received all pieces favorably and 28% who received them unfavorably.)

In spite of the fact that so many people say they dislike so much, a lot of them buy.

When the question is put to them, 55% say they have purchased after receiving a direct mail piece.

—Less in the New York (46%) and Southern (49%) regions

—More by income (62%-67%) for those earning $10,000 or more

—More (62%) for professionals and managers

- Also, 63% for farmers—

—More for larger adult families (62%)

—More for those between 25 and 45 (63%)

—More for those under 25 (62%)

When further prodded by being asked if they haven't bought magazine subscriptions or items from a catalog, 21% of those who originally said they hadn't bought now say they have, making, at a rough guesstimate, a

Here's what people like and don't—on an open-end basis:

	Particularly Like	Particularly Don't Like	Net Liking
Sales announcements	43%	7%	36%
Store advertisements	25	5	20
Catalogs	18	1	17
Coupons	10	1	9
Merchandise offers	11	9	2
Trade information	1	1	0
Books (unspec.)	2	3	- 1
Religious mail	1	2	- 1
Political mail	1	3	- 2
Occupant-addressed mail	—	2	- 2
Loan offers	—	2	- 2
Contest offers	1	4	- 3
Magazine offers	2	6	- 4
Obscenity/pornography	—	6	- 6
Donation requests	—	7	- 7
"Junk Mail"	—	8	- 8
Land offers/deals	—	12	-12
"Everything"	—	13	-13
Insurance offers	—	23	-23

total of about 63% of the population who say they have made a purchase as a direct result of direct mail solicitation.

The claimed number of purchases is large—an average 8 pieces (this includes those who have bought subscriptions or catalog items):

—Less for those receiving mail in apartment mail boxes (4 items)

—More for those who have mail delivered through a post office box by choice (13 items)

—More for those living in small, rural towns (10 items)

—More for non-whites (10 items)

—More for those with incomes under $5,000 (10 items)

—Less for those between 55 and 64 (6 items)

D. PERCEIVED RECEIPT OF ADDRESSED SALES/PROMOTIONAL MATERIAL (also from the questionnaire)

	%
Occupant/your address	86
Your name/address	84
Postal patron/box holder	38
No name/no address	31

Rural residents (70%), those having P.O. boxes (60%) and those served by other than first class post offices (67%) are less apt to receive sales/promotional material addressed "occupant."

However, rural residents (67%), those served by second, third and fourth class post offices (73%), plus those having curb box (60%) and post office box delivery (80%) are more likely to receive promotional material addressed "postal patron/box holder."

Those having P.O. boxes are less likely to have mail addressed "occupant." (60%)

Those in higher socio-economic groups are more apt to receive sales/promotional material addressed "your name" and "occupant." (93%)

	% Respondents		
	Prefer To Receive	Prefer Not To Receive	Net Preference
Your name/address	40	8	32
Occupant/your address	14	16	- 2
Postal patron/box holder	3	18	-15
No name/no address	1	31	-30
No preference	44	49	

There is a tendency for those in higher socio-economic groups to favor material having name and address (45% to 50% range).

Respondents in New York region had highest level of "no preference" (61%) with respect to types of addressing preferred (average 44%).

**The Questions:*

Would you prefer to receive advertising and promotional material through the mail with one of these types of addresses? Which?

Would you prefer *not* to receive advertising and promotional material through the mail with one of these types of addresses? Which?

INDEX

INDEX

INDEX

INDEX

INDEX

INDEX

INDEX

INDEX

INDEX

INDEX

INDEX

INDEX

INDEX